America's Book

America's Book

The Rise and Decline of a Bible Civilization,
1794–1911

MARK A. NOLL

OXFORD
UNIVERSITY PRESS

OXFORD
UNIVERSITY PRESS

Oxford University Press is a department of the University of Oxford. It furthers
the University's objective of excellence in research, scholarship, and education
by publishing worldwide. Oxford is a registered trade mark of Oxford University
Press in the UK and certain other countries.

Published in the United States of America by Oxford University Press
198 Madison Avenue, New York, NY 10016, United States of America.

Library of Congress Control Number: 2021051250

ISBN 978–0–19–762346–6

DOI: 10.1093/oso/9780197623466.001.0001

1 3 5 7 9 8 6 4 2

Printed by LSC Communications, United States of America

To
John McGreevy, Tom Noble, Jim Turner, and Patrick Griffin
and to
Cynthia Read

Contents

Tables

Abbreviations

ABCFM	American Board of Commissioners for Foreign Missions
ABS	American Bible Society
AMA	American Missionary Association
AME	African Methodist Episcopal Church
ASSU	American Sunday School Union
ARV	American Revised Version
ATS	American Tract Society
BFBS	British and Foreign Bible Society
ERV	English Revised Version
KJV	King James Version
LOC	Library of Congress
PCUS	Presbyterian Church in the United States (southern)
PCUSA	Presbyterian Church in the United States of America (northern)
Gen	Genesis
Ex	Exodus
Lev	Leviticus
Num	Numbers
Deut	Deuteronomy
Josh	Joshua
Judg	Judges
1&2 Sam	1&2 Samuel
1&2 Chr	1&2 Chronicles
Ps/Pss	Psalms
Prov	Proverbs
Cant	Canticles (Song of Solomon)
Eccl	Ecclesiastes
Isa	Isaiah
Jer	Jeremiah
Lam	Lamentations
Ezek	Ezekiel
Dan	Daniel
Mi	Micah
Hab	Habakkuk
Mal	Malachi
Zech	Zechariah
Matt	Matthew
Mk	Mark
Lk	Luke

Jn	John
Rom	Romans
1&2 Cor	1&2 Corinthians
Gal	Galatians
Eph	Ephesians
Phil	Philippians
Col	Colossians
1&2 Thess	1&2 Thessalonians
1&2 Tim	1&2 Timothy
Phlm	Philemon
Heb	Hebrews
Jas	James
1&2 Pet	1&2 Peter
1&2&3 Jn	1&2&3 John
Rev	Revelation

Introduction

The Bible in American History

On February 1, 2003, President George W. Bush spoke to the nation in an unusual afternoon address. Earlier that day the space shuttle *Columbia* with seven astronauts aboard had disintegrated on its reentry into Earth's atmosphere. The president brought his short address to a close with "the words of the prophet Isaiah, 'Lift your eyes and look to the heavens. Who created all these? He who brings out the starry hosts one by one and calls them each by name. Because of His great power and mighty strength, not one of them is missing.'" He went on, "The same Creator who names the stars also knows the names of the seven souls we mourn today. The crew of the shuttle Columbia did not return safely to Earth; yet we can pray that all are safely home."[1]

In contrast to the consolation President Bush hoped to draw from Scripture, partisanship has often accompanied the Bible's recent appearance in American public life. As an example, President Barack Obama was the main speaker in Washington on February 2, 2012, at the sixtieth annual National Prayer Breakfast. In his address, which began with the president "giving all praise and honor to God for bringing us together here today," Obama quoted or paraphrased at least ten passages from the Bible. His scriptural repertoire included a full quotation from the New International Version of 1 John 3:17–18 (with its emphasis on love through action instead of just words) along with allusions echoing the wording of the King James Version and several modern translations to passages from Genesis, Leviticus, Proverbs, and Isaiah in the Old Testament and Matthew, Luke, and Romans in the New.[2] It was a noteworthy speech, but not only because it featured skillful biblical quotations from the nation's first African American president. Also noteworthy was the immediate response from other Bible believers who chastised the president for abusing the Scriptures. On the day after the prayer breakfast self-identified Christians associated with the Republican Party called the president's remarks "theologically threadbare" and the product of "laughable theology."[3]

A more recent example of the same partisanship occurred on Monday, June 1, 2020, as peaceful protestors against police violence on unarmed Black men filled Lafayette Square on the north side of the White House. After he had the

America's Book. Mark A. Noll, Oxford University Press. © Oxford University Press 2022.
DOI: 10.1093/oso/9780197623466.003.0001

crowd dispersed with rubber bullets and tear gas, President Donald Trump strode across the Square to St. John's Episcopal Church, "the church of the presidents," where he posed for a photo with Bible in hand but did not make a speech. Those who objected were not as reticent. Joe Biden, then the presumptive Democratic nominee for the 2020 presidential election, reportedly said, "I just wish he opened it once in a while, instead of brandishing it. If he opened it, he could have learned something."[4] The senior vice president of the American Bible Society (ABS), then in its 204th year, responded, "[W]e should be careful not to use the Bible as a political symbol, one more prop in a noisy news cycle." The ABS also announced a two-week period when it would give a bible without charge to anyone who asked.[5]

For a subject as complicated as it is immense, the Bible in American history involves much more than Scripture and the American presidents. That connection, however, is one of the important subjects of this book, which emphasizes two aspects of a story traced from the beginning of constitutional government to the early twentieth century. First is the importance of the Bible for explaining the meaning of America; second is the importance of America for explaining the history of the Bible.

America's Book concentrates on the complicated relationship between the course of American democracy and the book considered sacred by many Americans. From the nation's beginning, citizens consistently stressed the fragility of their national experiment. How could self-government survive unless Americans acted responsibly, exercised self-discipline, honored the truth, trusted the law of the land, and respected the persons and actions of other Americans? For the period treated in these pages, many influential leaders and widespread public opinion looked to the Protestant King James Bible as providing the best possible support for the qualities of character without which the republic would fail. Even when Protestant constituencies divided and as Catholic, Jewish, and nonreligious numbers grew, the conviction remained that the nation's democratic ideals somehow rested on general biblical principles.

At the same time, the nation's history strongly shaped how the Bible inherited from the colonial past would be put to use. Decisive were the emergence of factional political parties, international crises like the War of 1812, regional conflict that eventually led to the Civil War, and especially controversies over slavery and race. Those events and circumstances defined the environment in which Bible believers practiced their faith, organized themselves into new American denominations, established a plethora of voluntary religious agencies, and brought their religious convictions to bear on public life. Various ways of treating the Bible affected almost every aspect of national history even as that history affected the ways Americans appropriated Scripture.

Specific issues addressed in the pages that follow reveal much about the nation's course, but also much about the fate of the Bible itself.

Why did many Americans read the Bible's narratives as demonstrating God's special attention to the United States, while disagreeing on whether the nation had been especially blessed by God or especially condemned for falling so far short of his commands?

As a particularly pressing question, how did the same Bible that shone as a beacon of hope to many Black Americans and inspired some Americans to challenge all forms of racism also support others in preaching white supremacy?

How did the Bible open the gates of paradise to countless individuals from every social class while also serving as a marketed commodity exploited for profit in an aggressive capitalist economy?

How did Scripture both inspire extraordinary self-giving philanthropy and fuel virulent attacks on marginal, minority, or suspect populations?

How could the nation's Protestants, who enjoyed national dominance for so long, make such strong professions to follow "the Bible alone" while advocating so many contradictory messages based on Scripture?

How did other religious traditions, especially Catholic and Jewish, that also maintained great respect for Scripture, promote their beliefs in an environment where Protestant convictions exerted so much influence?

If this book were a sermon, its text would come from the well-known words of Abraham Lincoln's Second Inaugural Address, delivered by the reelected president on March 4, 1865. After describing the course of a civil war that had taken the lives of perhaps 700,000 Americans, Lincoln paused to observe, "Both [North and South] read the same Bible, and pray to the same God; and each invokes His aid against the other." After enlisting words from Genesis 3:19 to express his own judgment against slavery, he quoted another passage to plead, "[B]ut let us judge not that we be not judged." Then he added a caution for those who presumed that trusting in Scripture conveyed God-like omniscience: "The prayers of both could not be answered; that of neither has been answered fully. The Almighty has His own purposes."[6]

This book, however, is not a sermon but a historical study where the transcendent considerations that Lincoln addressed remain in the background. Yet even with that limitation, the story should be of obvious interest for those with any interest in Christianity (or Judaism) as well as for those who desire a fuller understanding of the American past. It has special pertinence for Protestants who have claimed to be guided primarily or even solely by the Bible. For those like myself who belong to that number, an account of how loyalty to Scripture significantly shaped earlier U.S. history, even as that history strongly influenced Protestant interpretations of Scripture, reveals a mixed picture. It includes incidents of remarkable integrity but also astounding self-delusion. It is full of occasions for humble gratitude alongside others requiring repentance in sackcloth and ashes. For those of other Christian faiths, other faiths, or no faith, the story may not be as immediately existential, but it still offers much to ponder concerning the place of exclusionary sacred texts in a society proclaiming freedom for all. It is relevant for understanding the interpretation of other authoritative documents like the U.S. Constitution. It explains strategies for mobilizing public opinion. And it addresses the relationship between popular practices and taken-for-granted cultural assumptions. This is a lengthy book, but it only begins to address the full range of subjects that a comprehensive history of its subject would have to include.

The Shape of This Book, and What Came Before

The book's first four parts explore the rise, fracturing, and then decline of a strongly Protestant Bible civilization that arose in the late eighteenth century and survived with considerable force to the Civil War. It was the product of energetic Protestant labors aimed at voluntarily organizing the nation's corporate existence to reflect the truths of Scripture. The last two parts treat the Bible in the much more religiously plural period from Reconstruction to the early twentieth century, when Scripture remained alive for many purposes but only as a subordinate factor in the nation's public life. This work follows my earlier study, *In the Beginning Was the Word: The Bible in American Public Life, 1492–1783*, which treated many matters affecting the nation's later history.[7] The earlier book described how the American colonies inherited Britain's strong Protestant loyalty to the King James translation of the Bible and how warfare with Catholic France intensified the colonists' attachment to Scripture as part of their attachment to British liberty. It closed with the American Revolution, during which earlier attitudes involving the Bible strengthened—except that in the eyes of American patriots a corrupt Parliament replaced Catholic France as the greatest threat to liberty, virtue, and flourishing Protestant Christianity. The colonial and Revolutionary periods set the stage for the later history of Scripture in at least four ways.

First was the culture-wide prevalence of the King James Version itself. The words as well as the cadences of this translation, published originally in 1611, had by the end of the eighteenth century become integral to the personal religious faith of countless Americans as well as a fixed resource for almost all religious occasions. It also gave the public sphere its most widely recognized source of persuasive rhetoric, with only the works of Shakespeare even distant competition.

Second was the perception of the new United States in the same frame that Protestants had once viewed Britain and its empire. Many Americans, that is, saw their new nation replicating in some meaningful sense the ancient history of God's people in the Hebrew Scriptures, or, as more commonly called among Christians, the Old Testament. Whether by analogy, a source of positive instruction, or a warning against fatal missteps, the Scriptures' record of Old Testament Israel served many in the early United States as a proleptic record of themselves.

The third legacy came from how effectively patriots enlisted Scripture to support the republican and democratic-leaning principles of their revolution. In that struggle, a republican calculus had exposed the dangers of Parliament and also provided a formula to ensure the new nation's survival. It understood social well-being to be threatened by the vice endemic in political factions and concentrations of political power. Citizens, however, could overcome the threat of tyranny if they were motived by altruistic personal virtue and if checks and balances constrained the exercise of governmental authority. For many in the new United States, classical Roman ideals defined the meaning of "virtue." Even more Americans looked to the Bible of their Protestant heritage as supplying the virtue without which republics failed. A great number effortlessly blended the classical and Christian conceptions of "virtue."

Scripture figured just as prominently in the early American commitment to democratic principles. To be sure, democracy in the modern sense was only just beginning, since the stirring phrases of the Declaration of Independence, such as "all men are created equal," applied at the time only to white men with property. Yet even that level of political empowerment made for a great change, particularly because it involved the rejection of Christendom, the formal linking of church and state. Although it took half a century for all the states to end their religious establishments, that process began with the patriots' visceral rejection of Britain's church-state regime, which they perceived as a prime source of tyrannical corruption. If in the new United States religion could not rely on the support of government, and if religion played a key role in supplying republican virtue, how would it survive? The American answer was democratic appropriation of the Bible.

Because of how effectively patriots had used Scripture to further their cause, the Bible remained the most prominent old-world feature to survive the rejection of European Christendom. Democratically read, preached, and distributed— and as the surest source of republican virtue—the Bible retained an honored place in the *novus ordo seclorum*, the American new order of the ages. A republican and democratic embrace of Scripture also meant that the traditional doctrine of *sola scriptura*, which Protestants had earlier deployed mostly to express their opposition to Roman Catholicism, would expand in the new United States in ways that stupefied Europeans.

The fourth biblical inheritance was controversy generated in the Revolutionary period over whether Scripture could sanction the American system of enslavement. Debate over the morality of slavery had begun late in the seventeenth century but did not attract much public interest before the Revolutionary era. Yet no sooner did antislavery voices condemn the institution as violating principles of civic liberty as well as biblical mandates than proslavery advocates countered with scriptural proofs to defend Black-only chattel enslavement. Contentions that began in the Revolutionary era over whether biblical revelation allowed for slavery would become the single most divisive question in the American history of the Bible.

America's Book begins with two parts exploring the remarkable national influence of Bible-centered Protestant Christianity that arose between the presidential administrations of John Adams (1797–1801) and Andrew Jackson (1829–37). It was as if Martin Luther and Thomas Jefferson had met, argued, converted each other, and then determined to work in harness. As rapidly expanding Protestant movements aligned their faith with the principles of republican liberty, Luther's belief in the Bible ("My conscience is captive to the Word of God," 1521) and Jefferson's commitment to the sovereign individual ("Whereas, Almighty God hath created the mind free," 1779) seemed to contract a marriage made in heaven.[8]

Although patriots had eagerly enlisted Scripture to support the American Revolution, not until the mid-1790s did the Bible emerge from the inherited forms of British imperial Protestantism as a distinctly American force shaping distinctly American developments. The most obvious stimulus for this sharper focus was furious controversy surrounding a two-part treatise published in 1794 and 1795 by Thomas Paine, the premier publicist of the American Revolution. The controversy sparked by Paine's denunciation of Scripture in *The Age of Reason* spurred the emergence of the nation's first political parties, stimulated plans for universal primary education, helped define the character of national public discourse, and shaped expectations for how religion should function in a democratic republic.

The book's next two sections detail the strains that fractured this Bible civilization. Debates over Scripture and slavery—and sometimes over Scripture, slavery, and race—ebbed and flowed before they intensified at the time of the Missouri Compromise of 1820, only to recede again before a series of climactic events around 1830 brought contentions to a boil. From that point, biblical controversy over the paired questions of American slavery and Africans as the sole subjects of enslavement grew increasingly intractable. At the same time, the Protestant dream of a free country voluntarily choosing to organize its public life by the Scriptures encountered more and more resistance. From the early 1830s the beginnings of mass immigration rapidly expanded the number of Catholic citizens, and eventually also Jews, who accepted the importance of Scripture but who encountered fierce Protestant resistance when they questioned Protestant programs and practices.

The very freedoms that played such a large role in the American Protestant imaginary also undercut the effort to coordinate public life around a common understanding of the Bible. If Protestant upstarts promoted novel interpretations of Scripture, if religious adepts published their own revelations from God, if Protestant women used the interpretive tools honed by Protestant men to challenge patriarchal authority, or if a small number of learned students of nature dispensed with Scripture altogether, who in a free society could stop them? During these same antebellum decades, contrasting legal developments added still more complications. Yet even as regard for Scripture faded in applications of the common law, the pioneers of systematized common schooling insisted that daily "nonsectarian" Bible readings from the King James Version provided the essential key for promoting both personal virtue and public order.

Against the background of these tumultuous decades, the Civil War witnessed an intensified turn to Scripture for spiritual nurture by many who served under arms, many of their families, and many in the communities torn apart by the fratricidal conflict. In public, however, the Bible served mostly as a partisan prop for the warring sides and a repository of lofty words for ritual thanksgiving or repentance. Lincoln's caution about claiming God's capacity to fathom events remained a rare exception to the civil religion that flourished during the conflict.

The book's final two parts begin after the Civil War, when the King James Version remained prominent in national rhetoric even as several new translations entered the lists, some with extraordinary public fanfare. During these decades, the Bible featured prominently as an evangelistic tool in the nation's rapidly growing cities, the touchstone for widely popular new theological systems, and a resource for some who worried about the effects of rapid industrialization. Although controversies over Scripture and slavery never vanished completely, public debates involving Scripture now featured advanced European approaches to scriptural criticism, questions raised by cutting-edge evolutionary science, proposals by some women for radical reinterpretations, and continued conflict over the Bible in public schools. Catholic, Jewish, and African American voices also became more assertive in advancing their own claims. The book proper comes to an end at a logical stopping point, the numerous events in 1911 that celebrated the three-hundredth anniversary of the King James Bible. The festivities marking that anniversary included notable speeches by former president Theodore Roosevelt, the presidential aspirant Woodrow Wilson, and the perennial presidential candidate William Jennings Bryan. Yet their remarks and much else in the celebrations reflected the same mixture of anodyne pieties and fervent civil religion that had prevailed in public life since the Civil War. Thereafter, as the epilogue suggests, the Bible has remained a fragmented and fragmenting force in American public life except for the years after World War II, when civil rights activists drew on a tradition of African American biblical engagement to turn the Word of God into a terrible swift sword of moral reform.

Authorities and Arguments

The principal arguments in this book rely on some archival research, but mostly my reading of published primary sources and a wealth of first-rate scholarship. Although each of the chapters draws on specialized learning for its particular subjects, a few books dealing with the Bible itself have been especially helpful. The first of these is the superlatively informative catalogue of American editions that Margaret Hills of the American Bible Society published in 1962.[9] A decade later Eugene Genovese's *Roll, Jordan, Roll: The World the Slaves Made*, which quoted Psalm 24:1 on its title page, provided an unusually effective stimulus for recovering the importance of biblical faith among enslaved Americans.[10] Further attention to the Bible as a consequential factor in American culture came in the early 1980s from independent efforts and a series of books sponsored by the Society of Biblical Literature (SBL) to mark the centennial of that organization.[11] Especially important books that broadened the purview even more came at the turn of the century from Paul Gutjahr on the physical history of Bible publication, Peter Thuesen on conflicts arising from new translations designed to replace the King James Version, and Vincent Wimbush on the neglected story of the Bible in African American history.[12] A large outpouring of innovative scholarship, which is acknowledged at appropriate places throughout the book, has followed on a wide range of related subjects. Recent collaborative volumes edited by Gutjahr and by scholars from Indiana University–Purdue University Indianapolis have provided state-of-the-art collections suggesting the breadth of current scholarly interests.[13] One of many positive effects of this scholarship has been to demonstrate how centrally beliefs about the Bible and patterns of scriptural usage have factored in so many facets of national life.

The main argument developed in the book's first chapters concerns early national history. A focus on Scripture, however, shows how unhelpful it has been to highlight an undifferentiated "Second Great Awakening" as responsible for spreading a general "evangelical" religion throughout the land. Instead, three groups of Protestants both cooperated and competed to bring about a gradual but steady Christianization of the population over a period from the 1790s and extending for more than a half-century thereafter. Those years certainly did witness memorable awakenings—on the frontier early in the century, in some settled eastern regions shortly thereafter, and with well-known evangelists like Charles Finney in later decades. But concentrating on outbursts of revival does little to illuminate developments over time or the dynamics driving those developments.

Most important for the nation's steady Christianization were the largely apolitical Methodists who relied on Scripture to preach the New Birth, train converts in holiness, and create small-group support networks as the primary expression of religious life. Methodists shared the era's standard evangelical confidence in Scripture, promotion of conversion, and concentration on the New Testament's teaching about Jesus, but they expressed that confidence with almost no interest in the political conflicts that have fascinated historians of the period. The two other Protestant groups shared these evangelical commitments but, in contrast to the Methodists, exploited the religious freedoms bequeathed by the Revolutionary era for political purposes. Baptists and other localists preached an evangelical message keyed to republican fears about abuses of concentrated authority. For them, the Bible empowered local fellowships and local leaders who best honored their Protestant heritage by wielding "the Bible alone" as militant protection for their liberty in Christ. Presbyterians, Congregationalists, and some Episcopalians were committed to a similar evangelical religion but keyed to the republican concern for the virtue required to preserve a healthy, self-governing society. For them, and also some Unitarians who had moved beyond evangelical convictions, the Scriptures inspired plans for mobilizing the entire country to voluntarily follow biblical norms in all spheres of life.

The argument is that the evangelical commitments shared by the three main groups propelled a decades-long expansion of Protestant faith—North, South, and West, Black and white, and in all economic strata. For the custodial Protestants, and eventually some Methodists, those same commitments inspired energetic efforts to Christianize the structures of society. Yet other Protestants objected strenuously; they held that loyalty to the Bible should yield maximum local freedom and minimum national coordination. As a consequence, the Bible civilization created from points of spiritual commonality struggled to incorporate the diversity that appeared first among evangelical Protestants, but then from growing numbers of Americans who were neither evangelical nor Protestant. The Bible civilization faltered especially because Bible-honoring Protestants could not agree on how Scripture should be interpreted. Controversies were particularly sharp over biblical teaching concerning slavery. These controversies, moreover, were felt almost as keenly *within* the white North as *between* the white South and the white North. In the end, trust in "the Bible alone" became an apple of discord instead of delight. Notwithstanding a common Protestant desire to convert individuals and sanctify society, and even as Scripture remained a fixture in national consciousness, the Bible civilization entered irretrievable decline.

A second argument focuses on the Bible's teachings concerning slavery and race that sparked such sharp disagreements. Scripture-inspired attacks on slavery accompanied by Scripture-inspired defenses turned the nation's ago-nized wrestling over this central American reality into a religious war. As a ne-glected contribution to that struggle, a powerful tradition of African American scriptural engagement became an integral part of the general history, but also a counterpoint strikingly at odds with scriptural usage among the nation's domi-nant white populations. Attention to Scripture's importance for considerations of race and slavery shows why national developments exerted such a powerful influence on uses of the Bible. The contention here is that only by following the course of scriptural arguments on slavery and race *before* the Civil War can the Bible's history *since that time* be understood. As influential for the later history as responses to biblical higher criticism, debates over evolutionary science, and fundamentalist-modernist controversy certainly became, even more influential remained patterns of biblical usage that fueled the standoff of civil war.

In the decades after the Civil War, the Bible by no means vanished. Yet after the inability of Bible believers to find common ground in the Book they championed as the comprehensive guide to all truth, the Scriptures retreated from public prominence. Most obviously, intense biblical debates over slavery gave way to a deafening biblical silence in the white communities that created the Jim Crow South and strengthened racial discrimination in the North. Every presidential election from 1828 to 1860 had witnessed evangelical Protestants contesting each other with bibles in hand. After the war, the King James Version con-tinued to supply political leaders with memorable rhetorical flourishes, the Bible remained important for publishing as well as in the religious marketplace, and a few citizens looked to Scripture for guidance concerning the effects of rapid ec-onomic change. But except for the campaign advocating Prohibition, which in fact lacked a strong biblical basis, religious contributions of whatever sort were most conspicuous by their absence in the political dueling over Reconstruction and its termination, as well as in controversies over tariffs, immigration, immi-grant radicalism, hard or soft money, railroad expansion, railroad corruption, and more. The King James Version did remain an honored cultural icon and a fruitful rhetorical source. Catholics and Jews also notably expanded their efforts to convince fellow citizens that they too were Peoples of the Book. But the white Protestants who had once dominated the national Bible story now turned inward to rancorous discord over questions concerning what the Bible was and how it should be understood. The argument here is that public life in the postbellum United States retained noticeable remnants of what had gone before, but that re-ligious pluralism and intra-Protestant strife had replaced the Bible civilization.

This book will succeed if its narratives convince readers of the Bible's importance, both acting and acted upon, in American history. My additional hope is that its arguments will not only highlight the simple importance of the nation's biblical heritage but will do so in a way that illuminates both positive and regrettable legacies of that heritage. If it does so, the book may teach; it will certainly reprove and correct; it may even offer hints about instruction in righteousness.

Additional Details

A comprehensive study of the Bible in American history would address many more subjects than found in this book. For several subjects worthy of fuller treatment, I economize by referring to what I have written earlier on political and social contexts for theological history, Christian interpretations of the Civil War, the religion of Lincoln, moral assessments of American economic life, and the development of biblical criticism.[14] For other important aspects of the story that are treated neither here nor in that earlier work, I can only apologize. Given the capacious nature of the Bible's history, I hope that others continue with the research required to give more attention to worthy subjects I have neglected, and perhaps in the process also correct what I offer here.

As in my earlier book on the colonial and Revolutionary periods, I have included much quoting from Scripture and specific citations of chapter and verse. At the risk of slowing the pace to a painful crawl, these quotations and citations represent a deliberate attempt to show that what has so often been taken for granted in accounts of the American past deserves full attention, reflection, and assessment in its own right.

Finally, a word is in order about how I am using relevant terms. The book's narrative features a distinction between *proprietary* (or *custodial*) Protestants, who mobilized voluntarily to shape society, and *sectarian* Protestants, who feared such mobilization as inherently corrupting. That distinction, along with the different path chosen by early American *Methodists*, receives full consideration in chapters 3 and 4. Because designating individuals simply as *evangelicals* obscures too many important distinctions, I follow the wise example of Katherine Carté's recent *Religion and the American Revolution: An Imperial History* that reserves the term *evangelical* as an adjective describing the religion that different varieties of Protestants embraced, but not as a noun for any of the Protestants themselves.[15] *Christendom* refers to the traditional European pattern where, in Hugh McLeod's apt definition, "there are close ties between leaders of the church and secular elites; where the laws purport to be based on Christian principles; where, apart from certain clearly defined outsider communities, everyone is assumed to be Christian; and where Christianity provides a common language, shared alike by the devout and the religiously lukewarm."[16]

When treating stances toward Scripture, I use the term *biblicism* for the profession to be guided by "the Bible alone" in distinction from the classical Protestant profession to follow *sola scriptura*, which could mean "the Bible as final authority over secondary authorities" as well as "the Bible as opposed to all other authorities." *Scripturalism*, *biblical*, and *scriptural* are used descriptively for undifferentiated reliance on the Bible. *Historicity* refers to issues concerning the Bible as a factual historical record, *inerrancy* to the belief that the Bible makes no mistakes, *inspiration* to the more general belief in Scripture as revelation from God. A biblical *type* is an individual, event, or circumstance (usually from the Old Testament or Hebrew Scriptures) that foreshadows its *antitype* or fulfillment at a later stage of revelation (as in the New Testament). In American history some Bible believers have viewed events in their own history as antitypes foreshadowed by types in the Bible; more commonly, the Bible (especially the Old Testament) has served as a source of illustrations from which modern commentators drew analogies to their own situations.[17]

In references to *civil religion*, I have followed Harry Stout's definition for an attitude toward the nation that neglects traditional Christian or Jewish understandings of God but practices instead "sacralized patriotism" with "a complete repository of sacred rituals and myths."[18] In discussing biblical debates concerning slavery, I simplify a complex history by using *abolition* and *antislavery* as equivalent terms, with *emancipation* used to mean a desire for an end to the institution but not to its immediate extinction.

Sources from the nineteenth century usually, but not always, capitalized *Scripture*, *Bible*, the *Word* of God, and equivalent terms. I have followed the more frequent usage except when referring to "bibles" as published products. For most of the century, when *religion* was mentioned, it meant only Christianity. Except where noted, all biblical quotations are from the King James Version.[19]

Abbreviations, including abbreviations for biblical books, are found on pages xi–xii. Short titles of frequently referenced works appear at the head of the notes, 679–80.

PART I
CREATING A BIBLE CIVILIZATION

Behold, I have taught you statutes and judgments, even as the Lord my God commanded me, that ye should do so in the land whither ye go to possess it. Keep therefore and do them; for this is your wisdom and your understanding in the sight of the nations, which shall hear all the statutes, and say, Surely this great nation is a wise and understanding people. For what nation is there so great, who hath God so nigh unto them, as the Lord our God is in all things that we call upon him for? And what nation is there so great, that hath statutes and judgments so righteous as all this law, which I set before you this day?

—Deuteronomy 4:5-8

1

The Bible after Independence and before Paine

Among the wealth of unknowns confronting the new United States after the War for Independence, the relationship of religion to public life was one of the most uncertain. The majority religious disposition remained Protestant of a narrowly British cast. Even after the banishment of Protestants who had defended loyalty to king and Parliament, however, Protestants of strongly different dispositions professed diverse beliefs as well as sharply divided opinions on public issues.

The new nation's repudiation of Christendom posed even more uncertainties than a religious terrain dominated by internally divided Protestants. The only social order Americans had ever known simply assumed the formal interweaving of religion and regime, the interweaving Europeans had long taken for granted as God's way of uniting civic order, prosperity, and the reverence due his sovereignty. But now in the new nation, governments at all levels moved to guarantee the free exercise of conscience for all beliefs and practices that did not endanger public peace. With only a little hesitation, the American states were also abandoning government sponsorship of religion, or at least the coercive establishment of only one Christian denomination as an official state church.

These innovations, reflected in the religion clauses of the Constitution's First Amendment, were anything but casual landmarks on an inevitable pathway to ever-expanding personal freedom. It had, in fact, required a singular combination of Enlightenment principles, religious convictions, and pragmatic policies to advance the new nation's commitment to "religious liberty." As historian Katherine Carté Engel has forcefully argued, that commitment marked a fundamental break with what had gone before: "The [British] empire's rupture in 1775 was not incidental to British Protestantism; it was a fracture within its heart." Britain's "dominant Protestantism" had been "a shared ideal promoted by religious leaders over decades and . . . a system of authority that encompassed most of the empire's clergy. Protestant divides did not cause the American Revolution, but the American Revolution forced a transformation of transatlantic Protestantism."[1]

When Tom Paine's *Age of Reason* broke upon the public in 1794, the intrusion redirected a nation already lurching from crisis to crisis. Specifically, reactions to this work precipitated answers to pressing questions about how

America's Book. Mark A. Noll, Oxford University Press. © Oxford University Press 2022.
DOI: 10.1093/oso/9780197623466.003.0002

religious freedom would work in the *novus ordo seclorum*, the "new order of the ages." Despite much in the new United States that fulfilled Paine's ideal of true liberty, its people also opposed much of what Paine advocated so colorfully in *The Age of Reason*. Unlike the revolutionary French, Americans exhibited very little hostility to traditional religion itself: how could they, since a robust biblical Protestantism had resolutely supported their drive for independence? Hence, the question Americans faced when Paine's tract appeared was not how to over-throw discredited remnants of the religion of Christendom but how to maintain Christianity, or even expand its reach, once the props of formal Christendom had been kicked away. To oversimplify, but only slightly, the answer was volun-tary reliance on Scripture.[2]

The Bible before Paine

Although the years between the Revolution and the second presidential admin-istration of George Washington witnessed the continuing strength of conven-tional Protestantism, Scripture faded from the prominence it had enjoyed during the war years. To be sure, biblical phrases, analogies, allusions, lessons, and quotations continued to pepper public speech. Even more, scriptural precepts, scriptural narratives, and scriptural language gave a decidedly Christian cast to crucial ideological concepts like virtue, liberty, corruption, and slavery.[3]

Yet by comparison with what had gone before, overt reliance on Scripture as a source of authoritative public wisdom receded after the struggle with Britain came to an end.[4] Solons did not cite passages from the Mosaic law to justify specific clauses of the Constitution as New England's early leaders had done in drawing up basic law for their colonies in the 1630s and 1640s. During the im-perial wars of the eighteenth century and into the Revolution, a few intrepid Quakers had argued directly from the words of Jesus to challenge the morality of warfare—and had been answered in kind by defenders who justified warfare by also expounding Scripture. In the 1760s contentious debate over Anglican plans to install a bishop in the colonies generated more print than fervent agitation over the Stamp Tax; those debates featured detailed arguments of painstaking biblical exegesis.[5] It was similar with those who enlisted Scripture to support in-dependence, or with the brave Loyalists who painstakingly explained why pa-triot interpretations of key passages sinfully abused the Bible. In the first years of the new republic, such direct, didactic appeals to Scripture largely ceased.

Of special note, no public attention to the Bible in the post-Revolutionary pe-riod came anywhere near the impact wrought by Paine's own dramatically ef-fective use of Scripture as he burst onto American consciousness. At the heart of *Common Sense*, Paine's sensational pamphlet from early 1776 that tipped the scales for revolution, stood a detailed exposition of 1 Samuel chapter 8: if the prophet Samuel and the Lord denounced Israel for requesting a king "like all the nations," surely God himself had repudiated the very principle of monarchy. Paine summarized his treatment of this passage with words written expressly for the overwhelmingly Protestant colonists: "[M]onarchy in every instance is the Popery of government." Although earnest Loyalists responded with torrents of biblical refutation, Paine's direct appeal to Scripture carried the day.[6]

With very few exceptions, nothing like such direct exegetical argument accompanied political debates during the Confederation and early constitutional years. Martin Marty's conclusion after patiently reading the 2,400 pages of Bernard Bailyn's edition of debates on the Constitution captured the situation succinctly: "God comes up often, but almost never in biblical terms."[7] Scripture survived as a public presence in those years, but mostly as a rhetorical add-on.

Typical were the ways that John Jay and Benjamin Franklin evoked the Bible as they argued for the proposed new Constitution. Jay, a dedicated evangelical Anglican who, with James Madison and Alexander Hamilton, wrote *The Federalist Papers*, also published several other pieces supporting the new instrument of government. One of them defended the new document's plan for divided government with a casual quotation of Proverbs 11:14: "It is said that 'in a multitude of counsellors there is safety,' because in the first place, there is greater security for probity." To indicate the chaos that would result if the Constitution were not approved, he quoted another passage describing Israel's disorder after the death of King Solomon: "[W]here should we be then? . . . Then 'to your tents Oh Israel!' [1 Kings 12:16] would be the word."[8]

Franklin, whose complex Deism shifted easily between near-skepticism and something closer to traditional Christianity, waxed more expansive but no less formulaic.[9] When in 1788 the irrepressible Philadelphian enlisted the Old Testament to contend against an Anti-Federalist opponent of the proposed Constitution, he may have been only jesting in his use of an elaborate Old Testament analogy. To Franklin, Anti-Federalists resembled the ancient Israelites who rejected God's plans for their government. The ancient Hebrews, he supposed, should have been eager to accept rule by those who had risked their lives to secure their liberty. "Yet there were in every one of the *thirteen Tribes* some discontented, restless Spirits, who were continually exciting them to reject the propos'd new Government." Franklin then extended his analogy with at least ten quotations from the Pentateuchal books of Exodus and Numbers, footnoted with specific reference to chapter and verse. Whatever the gamesmanship, Franklin drew a serious conclusion: "On the whole, it appears, that the Israelites were a People jealous of their newly-acquired Liberty which Jealousy was in itself no Fault; but, when they suffer'd it to be work'd upon by artful Men, pretending Public Good, with nothing really in view, but private Interest, they were led to oppose the Establishment of the *New Constitution*, whereby they brought upon themselves much Inconvenience and Misfortune." Franklin did not want anyone to believe that he thought "our General Convention was divinely inspired, when it form'd the new federal Constitution." Yet he was contending that a constitution of so much potential significance for "the Welfare of the Millions now existing, and to exist in the Posterity of a great Nation" could never have come about "without being in some degree influenc'd, guided, and governed by that omnipotent, omnipresent, and beneficent Ruler, in whom all inferior Spirits live, and move, and have their Being [quoting Acts 17:28]."[10]

Franklin's extensive, if perhaps whimsical, reference to Mosaic history illustrates the public standing of Scripture at that time. As a revered Founding Father well known for rejecting the Puritan strictures of his Boston youth, as well as for never identifying with any particular Christian denomination, he yet displayed extensive biblical knowledge and a ready willingness to employ that knowledge for a political purpose. The Bible, however, served only as an adornment for what he wanted to say.

John Dickinson, reared a Quaker, renowned for his Revolutionary pamphlets, and elected successively as governor of Delaware and Pennsylvania, also turned to Scripture for literary embellishment. In private correspondence, Dickinson called the Scriptures "the most excellent Writings in the world" because "they give a full and ample testimony to all the principal Doctrines of the Christian Faith."[11] In public, however, the Bible meant rhetoric, not doctrine. In early 1788 he closed an argument for the proposed Constitution by explaining why the activities of individuals needed to be harmonized with general public purpose. Selections from 1 Corinthians chapter 12 helped him make this point: "How beautifully and forcibly does the inspired Apostle *Saint Paul*, argue upon a sublimer subject, with a train of reasoning strictly applicable to the present? . . . If the foot shall say because I am not the hand, I am not of the body. . . . But, *now* they are *many members,* yet but *one body.*"[12]

Earlier in the same newspaper article, Dickinson quoted another passage with special resonance in this period. When he asserted that healthy societies required individuals to accept some limits on their own freedom, he described the goal as "that *perfect liberty* [echoing James 1:25] better described in the Holy Scriptures, than anywhere else, in these expressions—'When *every* man shall *sit* under his vine, and under his fig-tree, and NONE SHALL MAKE HIM AFRAID.'"[13] As it happens, George Washington also favored this phrase from Micah 4:4, which he quoted on numerous occasions. None was more memorable than in August 1790, when Washington arrived at Newport, Rhode Island, on a journey through New England to shore up support for the Union. In response to a friendly address from that city's historic Touro synagogue, Washington hoped that "the Children of the Stock of Abraham" might continue to enjoy "the good will" of other Americans, "while everyone shall sit in safety under his own vine and figtree, and there shall be none to make him afraid."[14]

As Washington, Dickinson, and others quoted the prophet Micah, they were not constructing a chain of reasoning based on the passage. Instead, they were expressing their vision for an equitable, free, and just society by using terms universally respected as divine. This distinction between arguing from Scripture and using Scripture to support an argument is crucial for any balanced assessment of the Bible's place in American history. The distinction lies between deference to the Bible as a guide and exploitation of the Bible for rhetorical effect. As the following chapters illustrate time and again, noting that distinction raises important questions about what Americans have done when they turn to the sacred book for public purposes.

The frequent citation of this one passage from an Old Testament prophet underscores the important fact that references to the Old Testament entered public life far more frequently than references to the New. As for the Puritans of early colonial history, the drama of ancient Israel—chosen by God but constantly falling into sin, repeatedly warned by divine messengers, repenting, and then restored to prosperity—continued to frame the national narrative.[15] In much the same way that William Bradford in *Of Plimoth Plantation* or John Winthrop in writing about early Massachusetts Bay melded their own histories with the history of God's covenanted people, so now many voices positioned the story of the new American republic within the story of ancient Israel.[16] Spokespersons from New England, which remained the publishing center for the entire new nation, dwelled most consistently on this Old Testament relationship, but it remained common coin throughout the realm.

The election sermons with which New England states sanctified the start of legislative sessions extended Puritan Hebraism into the national era.[17] Year after year they sustained a providential frame of reference, revived the jeremiad as an exhortation to repent (thereby saving the land), and provided a forum for exploring the intimate bonds between (Christian) virtue and social well-being.

New Hampshire legislators who assembled in June 1788 heard an unusually forceful example of the genre. Samuel Langdon took his text from Deuteronomy 4:5–8, where Moses exhorted the children of Israel as they prepared to enter the Promised Land: "Behold, I have taught you statutes and judgments . . . that ye should do in the land whither you go to possess it. . . . [F]or what nation is there so great, which hath God so nigh unto them as the Lord our God is in all things that we call upon him for?" With no attempt at nuance, Langdon titled this sermon *The Republic of the Israelites an Example to the American States*. Why, he asked his auditors, was it so pertinent to rehearse Israel's history in that hour?

"I answer—Examples are better than precepts; and history is the best instructor both in polity and morals. . . . If I am not mistaken, instead of the twelve tribes of Israel, we may substitute the thirteen states of the American union, and see this application plainly offering itself." According to Langdon, since God had given the states of the new nation "an excellent constitution of government . . . by which all that liberty is secured which a people can reasonably claim," and since God had "moreover given you his son Jesus Christ . . . and a perfect system of true religion, plainly delivered in the sacred writings," then for the nation's "true interest and happiness," it was imperative "to conform your practice in the strictest manner to the excellent principles of your government, adhere faithfully to the doctrines and commands of the gospel, and practice every public and private virtue." Langdon specified what New Hampshire needed to do if it wanted to enjoy God's blessing—in particular, promote education ("support schools in all your towns") along with the Bible ("that religion taught and commanded in the holy scriptures").[18] The combination of education and the Bible would soon emerge as a key feature of the American attempt to create a Protestant civilization.[19]

In a steady drumbeat, other election sermons consistently reiterated the same vision of the new American nation—or at least New England as a synecdoche for the nation—reprising the history of ancient Israel.[20] Against such a backdrop, it was only natural that some in New England—but not only New England— turned to Old Testament history as a template to guide American national life. Connecticut's redoubtable Roger Sherman enjoyed the unusual distinction of signing the Declaration of Independence, the Articles of Confederation, and the Constitution. This faithful member of the New Haven church pastored by Jonathan Edwards Jr. in 1784 responded to a critic of the Confederation government by rehearsing that ancient history. For Sherman, "the civil polity of the *Hebrews*, which was planned by Divine Wisdom," showed the way in many particulars: "their laws were few and simple—their judges the elders of their cities, well acquainted with the credibility of the parties and their evidences— they held their courts in the places of greater concourse, the gates of the city, and their processes were neither lengthy nor expensive."[21]

Such usage testified to the Bible's utility as a God-given endorsement of public argument. But by comparison with the Revolutionary years, explicit *reasoning* from biblical texts to contemporary problems faded during the very early national era. When citizens debated the difficulties of the Confederation, the merits of the new Constitution, or policies under the new national government, they might borrow language from the King James Version or derive inspiration from ancient Jewish history, but they did not look to Scripture for didactic instruction as they had done in debating separation from Britain or the wisdom of stationing Anglican bishops in the colonies.

Virtue and Civic Well-Being

Because the scriptural legacy of colonial Protestantism contributed so sub-stantially to the struggle for independence and because the Bible served the Revolutionary cause so powerfully, American national history began with a Protestant respect for Scripture. Yet because the patriots' political principles also drew so heavily on fears of tyrannical corruption (republicanism) and embodied such strong commitments to individual liberty (liberalism or Lockeanism), aversion to any form of top-down religious coercion advanced step by step with friendliness to religion. This combination of "religion friendly" and "coercion averse" defined the course of the new nation. As a consequence, "the central par-adox of the American approach," one historian has written, arose because "the founders realized the criticality of virtue" for republican government, yet "for all its importance, direct inculcation of virtue lay outside the purview and purpose of government."[22]

At the most abstract level, voices on every side insisted on the mutual depend-ence of personal piety, public religion, and social morality. Although variations abounded, that construction appeared absolutely everywhere—expressed in offhand utterances and detailed expositions, formulated by statesmen and min-isters, urged for primarily civic purposes or primarily religious purposes, and spelled out in legal documents as well as personal opinions. Significantly, how-ever, mechanisms for promoting the religion so necessary for republican virtue remained mostly unstated.

To herald the inauguration of Massachusetts's new state constitution in October 1780, a prominent Boston minister and patriot, Samuel Cooper, summarized certainties that had propelled the Revolution when he preached a sermon before Governor John Hancock and the incoming legislature. After citing Proverbs 14:34, "Righteousness exalteth a nation," as a truth from King Solomon, "one of the greatest politicians and wisest princes that every lived," Cooper reminded his listeners "that as piety and virtue support the honour and happiness of every community, they are peculiarly requisite in a free gov-ernment." His judgment was categorical that "virtue is the spirit of a republic." If, instead, the people "are impious, factious and selfish; if they are abandoned to idleness, dissipation, luxury, and extravagance; if they are lost to the fear of God, and the love of their country, all is lost."[23] But Cooper did not ex-plain how to fend off impiety and promote piety without the machinery of Christendom.

Similar articulation of similar sentiments, with similar vagueness, prevailed all through these years, and well beyond New England. In 1787 they guided the Confederation Congress when it established provisions for settling the area west of the Appalachians and north of the Ohio River. According to the "Northwest

Ordinance," because "Religion, Morality and knowledge [were] necessary to good government and the happiness of mankind," it was necessary to provide "Schools and the means of education" for upholding these values.[24]

If New Englanders reaffirmed these conceptual affinities most frequently, by the mid-1790s they were a national possession.[25] In 1795, when the Episcopal bishop of Virginia, James Madison, preached on a national day of Thanksgiving and Prayer, he reaffirmed the same formula with the same absence of programmatic detail. This namesake of his cousin, the political James Madison, told his hearers that if they desired to enjoy "real virtue and social happiness . . . genuine patriotism and a dignified obedience to law," and if they hoped to avoid "disorganizing anarchy," one thing only was needful: "[R]emember, that your first and last duty is 'to fear the Lord and to serve him' [Deut 10:12]; remember, that in the same proportion as irreligion advances, virtue retires."[26]

One of the Virginia Episcopalians for whom Bishop Madison provided spiritual leadership offered the era's most widely publicized statement of this vision of how virtue and liberty required religion in the deadly battle against vice and tyranny. In a document widely distributed as he prepared to leave public office for the last time, George Washington in 1796 affirmed without equivocation, "Of all the dispositions and habits which lead to political prosperity, Religion and morality are indispensable supports." These were "the great Pillars of human happiness" that established the hope for "private and public felicity." Washington went on to challenge those who asserted "that morality could be maintained without religion," before he repeated the sum of the matter: "'Tis substantially true, that virtue or morality is a necessary spring of popular government. The rule indeed extends with more or less force to every species of free Government."[27]

As the new nation took shape, so did its mental furniture. A central piece of that furniture—perhaps even *the* central piece—was the intimate bond that Washington and so many of his peers perceived between virtue and liberty and, in contrast, vice and slavery. With Washington, many who viewed this formula as a fixed law of nature looked to the Author of Nature as the surest promoter of the virtue without which liberty could not survive. As yet Americans were not focusing on the Bible as the uniquely capable engine for sustaining the divine provision of virtue.

Providence

In the new United States, a providential view of reality supported the conviction that irreligion ruined societies while virtue, particularly Christian virtue, supported liberty and well-being. During the conflict with Britain, patriots regularly invoked analogies from ancient Israel to claim God's blessings on their enterprise, as when Franklin and Jefferson proposed the image of the children of Israel miraculously crossing the Red Sea as the new country's official seal.[28] For their part, the clergy regularly preached sermons taken from Old Testament texts like Exodus 15:1 to describe God's actions on their behalf ("the Lord . . . hath triumphed gloriously; the horse and his rider hath he thrown into the sea") or like Judges 5:23 to warn slackers in the fight ("Curse ye Meroz, said the angel of the Lord, curse ye bitterly the inhabitants thereof; because they came not to the help of the lord, to the help of the Lord against the mighty"). The New Testament did not feature as prominently, though riffing on texts like Galatians 5:1 could also inspire the struggle ("Stand fast therefore in the liberty wherewith Christ hath made us free, and be not entangled again with the yoke of bondage").[29]

Washington's Farewell Address in 1796 spoke for many of his contemporaries when he gave memorable expression to this providential view: "Can it be, that Providence has not connected the permanent felicity of a Nation with its virtue?" But those words at that time only extended a theme that Washington had already expressed many times before.[30] Similar expressions during the nation's early years came in many varieties on a spectrum from the formulaic to the fervent, but, again, they appeared everywhere.[31] Into the national era, this assignment of the nation's course to God's direct oversight continued at full strength, particularly among those who supported the new Constitution.[32]

The providential overlay through which spokesmen regularly viewed the nation's founding strengthened their concern for virtue and their solicitude for the health of the nation. Actions by citizens mattered because they took place in an arena where God's actions mattered even more. Religious concerns did not by any means dominate the new American nation. Yet they were deeply embedded in the conceptual infrastructure of the most basic political commitments of the new republic. Especially for believers, but not just believers, the faith that reconciled individuals to God was a faith that could preserve the nation.

Because all religious reference to such matters, along with much from the world at large, appeared in a strongly biblical idiom, wherever providential reasoning prevailed, so also prevailed the Scriptures. Phrases from the King James Version and instructive narratives from ancient Israel supplied a common currency for public exchange. Yet Scripture remained taken for granted, a prominent element in the European Christian heritage but not itself an object of explicit attention. When, however, Paine's *Age of Reason* burst on the public, the Bible moved out of the background onto center stage.

International Contrasts

The American religious situation after the Revolution can be clarified by comparison with strikingly different developments in Britain and France. As delegates traveled to the Constitutional Convention in Philadelphia in 1787, the English Protestants who stood closest to their American confreres tried to nudge their country toward a modest separation of church and state. The Dissenting Deputies, a coalition of non-Anglican Protestants, petitioned Parliament in that year to repeal the Test and Corporation Acts, which since the Restoration of the Crown in 1660 had restricted membership in Parliament to those who received communion in the Church of England. The Deputies tried again in 1789, but the petitions came to naught as heightened tensions with France pushed the government of William Pitt the Younger to emphasize the importance of church establishment. In Britain the established churches, Anglican in England and Presbyterian in Scotland, lent their full support to the regime while the regime reciprocated by preserving these churches as the spiritual foundation of the realm.[33] Like the United States, Britain would remain comprehensively Protestant, but unlike the United States it would do so by *upholding* the *union* of church and state.

In France the opposite course prevailed, but with the same conceptual link between ecclesiastical form and religious belief. After the Revolution abolished the monarchy in 1789, successive masters of the new republic turned increasingly against the inherited dogmas of Christianity as well as the historical structures of Christendom. In July 1790 the National Constituent Assembly promulgated the Civil Constitution of the Clergy, which abolished all monastic orders and placed the Catholic Church under the control of the Assembly. In September 1792 mobs throughout France rampaged against all things Catholic, slaying three bishops and more than two hundred priests. In late 1793 the National Assembly replaced the Christian seven-day calendar with a republican ten-day week. It also replaced Christian names on streets and public structures with classical or secular names. And in June 1794 Robespierre led a great procession in Paris to proclaim a Cult of the Supreme Being aimed at replacing Catholic ritual root and branch.[34] Although anti-Catholic measures began to be rolled back after the fall of Robespierre later that same year, systematic efforts to suppress Catholic faith as well as Catholic ecclesiastical structures persisted through the Napoleonic era. Like the United States, France aggressively disestablished its historical ecclesiastical institutions, but unlike the United States it did so while also repudiating traditional Christian faith.

* * * * *

As the United States began its existence under constitutional government, citizens of widely divergent opinions worried about a common religious question: How could Protestant Christianity survive without Christendom? Many also wondered how Christianity could function as a positive civic force without Christendom. These questions lay open to any number of possible answers when Paine's *Age of Reason* arrived. In the course of events, Paine's all-out denunciation of the Christian Scriptures made voluntary, democratic appropriation of the Bible the answer to both questions.

2

The Paine Provocation

When the first part of Tom Paine's *The Age of Reason: Being an Investigation of True and Fabulous Theology* was published in early 1794, it became an immediate sensation on both sides of the Atlantic. In the United States, the work's root-and-branch attack on the Christian Scriptures turned this hero of the Revolution into a pariah. William Bentley, pastor of East Congregational Church in Salem, Massachusetts, stood out from his peers on a number of counts. In his Federalist, anti-Catholic, and still mostly Trinitarian region, Bentley supported Jefferson, counseled toleration for Catholics, and leaned toward Unitarianism. On Paine's work, by contrast, he spoke with the overwhelming American majority by calling it "a contemptible publication."[1]

The nearly universal condemnation of Paine's heresies, however, took shape in very different ways, as illustrated by the career of Francis Asbury. This itinerating dynamo who drove the rapid expansion of American Methodism took note of Paine's work on the Fourth of July, 1795. As he crossed over the Passaic River into New York City, Asbury brought along a gift from Uzal Ogden, an Episcopal rector in Newark. It was the first of Ogden's two volumes dedicated to rebutting Paine; Asbury wrote in his journal that he considered it "a most excellent compilation, taken from a great number of ancient and modern writers on the side of truth."[2] Yet although Asbury the Methodist and Ogden the Episcopalian were friends, Asbury never recorded another word on *The Age of Reason*, while Ogden continued to obsess over the work in hundreds of published pages still to come. Both the nearly universal rejection of Paine's opinions on Scripture and striking differences in how that rejection was expressed would define the American history of the Bible for more than a generation.

The *Age of Reason* at Home and Abroad

When *The Age of Reason* was published in Britain, the friends of order rose up in arms as they had during Paine's earlier titanic clash with Edmund Burke over the significance of the French Revolution—was it a harbinger of true liberty (Paine) or an assault on the foundations of civilization (Burke)? London booksellers rushed to supply demand for this latest literary thunderbolt from the era's most talented pamphleteer. After the peripatetic Paine had done his best to help the

America's Book. Mark A. Noll, Oxford University Press. © Oxford University Press 2022.
DOI: 10.1093/oso/9780197623466.003.0003

Americans win their independence, he returned from the colonies to his native Britain, only to render himself persona non grata because of how actively he championed the new order in France. Undeterred, he hastened across the Channel with the intention of advancing the cause of liberty there. But then in late 1793 he suffered an unexpected reverse when the Jacobin leaders of the new French Republic put him in prison for opposing their execution of Louis XVI and other acts of Terror. He was jailed, in fact, just as he handed off the manuscript for this latest work to the American Joel Barlow.[3]

The book responded to what Paine saw as a Revolution descending into moral chaos by announcing a better way. Even as he praised progress in France since 1789—especially an end to "compulsive systems of religion" and "the total abolition of the whole national order of priesthood"—Paine concluded that things had moved too far toward atheism. It had become imperative, he concluded, to establish proper standards "of morality, of humanity, and of the theology that is true."[4] To that end, Paine offered an enlightened religion featuring a reasonable God known primarily through nature. Yet in order to build a true theology, he found it necessary to clear away a lot of rubble.

In Britain, Paine's well-placed detractors never got past his denunciation of the rubble. They were, in fact, reading the work accurately, since it did not take superior intelligence to recognize that *The Age of Reason* continued Paine's relentless assault on the foundations of traditional European Christendom. His *Rights of Man* (1791–92) had responded to Burke's *Reflections on the Revolution in France* (1790) with an all-out attack on monarchy, aristocracy, and hereditary privilege. In *The Age of Reason* he turned to the institutional Christianity that had long supplied the moral sanction for Europe's established order. In Paine's vision, Christianity of the sort that supported Britain's constitutional union of church and state simply condemned itself. "All national institutions of churches," he asserted in an introductory "profession of faith," "appear to me no other than human inventions, set up to terrify and enslave mankind."[5] Britain's democratic radicals cheered, even as defenders of the standing order mobilized to slap him down once again. The British authors who published refutations explained in painstaking detail why the Christianity that Paine attacked was both true in itself and essential for a healthy regime. Not until another generation passed would England's political trajectory bend even partially in the direction that Paine advocated. with a slight weakening of the Anglican establishment (Catholic emancipation, 1829) and a modestly democratic reform of Parliament (the Reform Act of 1832). For Britain, *The Age of Reason* meant agitation, but not a crisis.

It was different in the new United States. Paine believed his republican protest against despotic authority and liberal assertion of individual rights would find an enthusiastic American welcome. In anticipation, he dedicated copies designated for American distribution "to my fellow-citizens of the United States of America," a dedication that many of his opponents would note with distress approaching panic.[6]

When cheap copies of Paine's book began to pour from presses in Boston, New York, Philadelphia, Albany, and elsewhere, the work became a cause célèbre with far-reaching effects. Like Paine's British opponents, Americans rushed to defend traditional Christian truths. Yet because the American reaction came primarily from figures who shared many of Paine's political principles, their defense of the Bible meant something quite different.

An Incendiary Argument

The title page of *The Age of Reason* recalled the renown Paine had won in America's own Revolution by identifying him as "Author of . . . Common Sense" (Figure 2.1). When less than two decades earlier that rousing tract convinced colonists that monarchy itself meant nothing but tyranny, Paine pushed Americans decisively toward independence. Now, in the new work from 1794, he took up what he called a logical second step: "Soon after I published the pamphlet, *Common Sense*, in America, I saw the exceeding probability that a Revolution in the System of Government, would be followed by a revolution in the system of religion."[7]

Paine advanced this second revolution boldly, with a fervent denunciation aimed at foundational principles of traditional Christianity. In particular, he attacked deference to Scripture—and as passionately as he had attacked subservience to George III. Of the Old Testament, which he had earlier enlisted to attack monarchy, Paine was utterly dismissive: "Whenever we read the obscene stories, the voluptuous debaucheries, the cruel and tortuous executions, the unrelenting vindictiveness, with which more than half the Bible is filled, it would be more consistent that we called it the word of a demon than the word of God." As for the New Testament, though Paine found much to admire in the character of Jesus, he claimed that Christian churches "have set up a system of religion very contradictory to the character of the person whose name it bears." That system featured "pomp and reverence" instead of the "humility and poverty" that Jesus himself embraced. In place of childish adherence to "the Christian mythologists," who by exalting Scripture had placed a yoke of spiritual tyranny on hapless believers, Paine announced a better way, "It is only by the exercise of reason, that man can discover God."[8]

Even more was yet to come. Paine had composed *The Age of Reason* on the run, relying on only his memory to eviscerate traditional Christianity and denounce the Scriptures. But during his stay in Paris's Luxembourg Prison, he was given several of the first published responses to his tract and had also found time to study the Bible in detail. Despite grave illness and the daily threat of the guillotine, that combination inspired him to write some more. *The Age of Reason, Part the Second* was completed in October 1795. In early November he was released from prison to the care of the American ambassador James Monroe. This second installment was published in London before the end of the year. Soon thereafter it appeared in the United States.

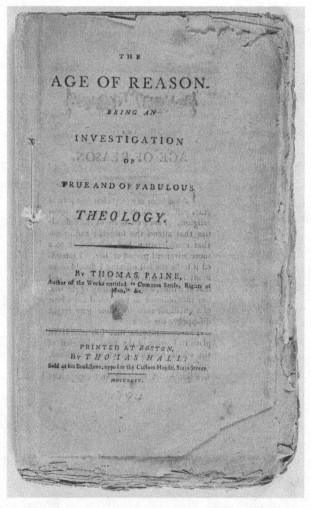

Figure 2.1 After the two parts of Tom Paine's *Age of Reason* arrived from overseas and were also reprinted in many American cities, American printers rushed to publish even more responses attacking the work.

Source: Courtesy of the American Antiquarian Society.

In *Part the Second* Paine announced that further study had convinced him that both Old and New Testaments "were much worse books than I had conceived." His book-by-book deconstruction of Scripture, stretching to almost twice the length of the original *First Part*, offered a workingman's précis of the era's advanced biblical criticism.[9] Already in the seventeenth century European savants like Baruch Spinoza, Richard Simon, and Jean Leclerc had begun to question traditional ascriptions of biblical authorship, discover numerous internal contradictions among scriptural accounts, date the Bible's prophetic passages as written *after* the events they supposedly foretold, and demythologize scriptural miracles. Paine channeled these views as they had been developed more recently by German scholars and French *philosophes*. For Paine, Scripture considered simply as literature suffered from an abundance of nonsensical errors: "Having now shewn, that every book in the Bible, from Genesis to Judges, is without authenticity, I come to the book of Ruth, an idle, bungling story, foolishly told, nobody knows by whom, about a strolling country girl creeping slily to bed to her cousin Boaz. Pretty stuff indeed to be called the word of God!"[10]

The polemic grew even hotter when Paine charged that both testaments promoted the most morally offensive views of God, the human condition, and the exercise of reason. As an example, "the wild and visionary doctrine" that Christian churches built on the supposed miracle of Jesus's Virgin Birth was "blasphemously obscene." He concluded *Part the Second* by claiming to have substantiated the "three frauds" exposed by *Part the First*: "*mystery, miracle,* and *preaching.*" Paine's vivid prose, in contrast to the stiff writing of the erudite, fairly leaped off the page. Even the most marginally literate could easily grasp what he wanted to say: the idea of verbal revelation, "the impious belief that God has spoken to man," was the prime cause for "the bloody persecutions, and tortures unto death, and religious wars, that since [biblical] times have laid Europe in blood and ashes."[11]

As in *Part the First*, Paine accompanied this elaborate denunciation of traditional Christianity with a lightly sketched account of the Deism he hoped could take its place. For Paine, moving from the fabulous to the true required "the Bible of creation." He rejected the "many wild and blasphemous conceits . . . formed of the Almighty" by Jews and Christians "setting up an invented thing called revealed religion." He would base human flourishing and a moral society on "the immutable laws of science, and the right use of reason."[12] Yet as in the original tract, Paine's deconstruction of the "fabulous" loomed much larger than his construction of the "true."

Paine's many British and American antagonists recognized immediately the tight bond he posited between religious belief and social ordering. True to his skill as a wordsmith, Paine made sure that no one could miss that integral relationship. As he spelled it out in *Part the Second*, "It has been the scheme of the

Christian church, and of all other invented systems of religion, to hold man in ignorance of the Creator, as it is of government to hold him in ignorance of his rights. The system of the one are as false as those of the other, and are calculated for mutual support."[13] Paine, in the words of Philip Foner, passionately believed that "to preserve republican political principles it was necessary to destroy the priesthood."[14] In Britain, Paine's opponents could blast away with abandon at such an absurd notion since most of them repudiated republican politics as ardently as they defended the established religion of Anglican Christendom.

Americans confronted a much more delicate challenge. Like Paine's British opponents, whose writings they gobbled up, Americans of many varieties denounced Paine's treatment of the Bible. Yet like Paine, Americans also desperately wanted republican principles to prevail. And in partial agreement with Paine they had begun to dismantle, if not fully destroy, the "priesthood" (the formal establishment of religion). Because so many Americans stood so close to Paine in his political principles, and because they so thoroughly rejected his dismissal of Christianity, their defense of the faith—and especially of the Bible—assumed great urgency.

National Contingency

To say that the United States was on edge when *The Age of Reason* reached its shores would be an exaggeration, not because things were settled but because American nationhood as a fixed possession hardly existed at all.[15] To be sure, a national government was in place with the venerated George Washington as its head. Americans also stood ideologically united in dreading concentrated authority of the sort that, as they saw it, Britain had so badly abused. Some would even have agreed with Alexander MacWhorter, a respected New Jersey Presbyterian, who waxed rhapsodic about the new Constitution on the Fourth of July in 1793: "Perhaps it is not in the reach of beings, of no more extended intelligence than man, to work up any thing nearer absolute perfection, consistent with, and creative of freedom, order and happiness, than the cardinal principles of our glorious Civil Constitution."[16] Yet for all the confidence in Washington and all the divine purpose that some claimed to see in the Constitution, American national identity remained, in the words of the historian John Murrin, "an unexpected, impromptu, artificial, and therefore extremely fragile creation of the Revolution."[17] A nation it was in name, but without strong national institutions, without a dominant urban center, without a national church, without easy transport from the coast to the interior, without national educational standards, without a common opinion on slave labor—but *with* a thin population scattered over an immense area, *with* strongly contrasting regional cultures, and *with* a national economy integrated mostly by the slave trade.

To be sure, the crises occasioned by the Articles of Confederation lay in the past. The Federalists, as proponents of the new Constitution drafted in 1787, held that its adoption had rescued their republican experiment from what James Madison called "the vices of the political system": factionalism, inflation, reckless personal ambition, runaway democracy, antagonism between debtors and creditors, and disdain for the law.[18] Opponents of the proposed Constitution, the Anti-Federalists, contended that it gave too much power to central government and too little protection for the rights of individuals and the prerogatives of individual states. State ratifying conventions witnessed intense debates in which the Federalists overcame the Anti-Federalists only by promising to amend the new constitution with a Bill of Rights. Most Anti-Federalists, and even some Federalists, regarded the explicit guarantee of these rights, including freedom of religion and the prohibition of a national state church, as the only way to secure liberties won through the blood and toil of the Revolution. With that concession, the Constitution won approval, and the new government began in early 1789 with General Washington unanimously elected as the nation's first president.

A Constitution in place did not, however, mean that a nation would inevitably emerge. Fully conscious of these circumstances, Washington undertook long and arduous journeys during his first years as president specifically to shore up what he considered the precarious state of the American union. Historian T. H. Breen has shown how creatively the new president engineered an array of theatrical displays of his presidential person to draw the far-flung American population into a common nation. The country's one universally admired hero was responding to what in July 1788 he called the pressing threats of "*Anarchy and Despotism.*"[19]

In 1793, the year that Paine penned the first part of his tract, the execution of Louis XVI and the outbreak of war between France and Britain divided Americans between those who feared the excess of Revolutionary ardor and those who saw heroic Frenchmen advancing a worldwide struggle against despotism. Despite President Washington's declaration of neutrality, national division became sharper when the flamboyant Citizen Edmond-Charles Genêt arrived in the country and urged Americans to support France's Revolutionary government. When President Washington, recently inaugurated for his second term, repudiated Genêt, it propelled a growing fissure in the body politic. Where in the recent past colonists had regarded partisan divisions within the British Parliament as a sure sign of corruption, now Americans became partisans themselves. Stalwart friends of the government who would brook no criticism of Washington, who leaned toward the British, and who favored Alexander Hamilton's plans as secretary of the treasury for a robust national financial system took the name "Federalists." Those who while respecting Washington felt free to criticize, who favored the French, and who worried about the corrupting effect of Hamilton's schemes were the "Democratic-Republicans." Already by 1793 rival newspapers in Philadelphia, the nation's temporary new capital, aggressively promoted the competing factions even as they denounced their opponents as mortal threats to the nation.

When a treaty negotiated with Britain by John Jay, the first chief justice of the Supreme Court, settled boundary and fortification issues left over from the Revolutionary War, partisanship flamed brightly. In mid-1795, while Americans were reading the second part of Paine's work, the Senate's consideration of Jay's Treaty exacerbated intensifying political antagonism: Federalists lauded the Treaty as a triumph of judicious diplomacy while Democratic-Republicans excoriated it as kowtowing to British self-interest.

If domestic factionalism was not dismaying enough, international uncertainty piled woe upon woe. As a war measure, Britain and France both preyed on American shipping, which also suffered from attacks by North African pirates in the Mediterranean. The inability of the United States to protect its commercial interests on the high seas combined with a deeply ingrained fear of standing armies or navies—along with the lurking presence of Britain in Canada, Spain to the southeast, and France in New Orleans—made national embarrassment, or even national extinction, ever-present threats.

And there was more. The admission of Kentucky as the fifteenth state (1792) and Tennessee as the sixteenth (1796) signaled the rapid westward movement of a population that had already strained the institutions of civilization to the breaking point. During 1793 an epidemic of Yellow Fever ravaged Philadelphia, the nation's commercial center, leaving at least five thousand dead and the nation's medical experts flummoxed by their inability to suppress the contagion. Just as the first American responses to Paine's tract came from the presses in mid-1794, citizens of both parties praised Gen. Anthony Wayne for destroying the Northwest Indian Confederation at the Battle of Fallen Timbers in the Ohio Territory, even as that massacre underscored the continuing threat of Native resistance in all outlying settlements.

Still more worrying than the Indian menace were protests in western Pennsylvania against a federal excise tax on whiskey that boiled over at the very same time. Those protests, which led to an armed standoff between July and October 1794, eventually dissipated, but only after a federal force of nearly thirteen thousand militiamen convinced protestors that the national government would kill in order to enforce national legislation.

Throughout the middle years of the decade, the nation's most contentious economic and social institution sparked fresh controversy. As several northern states moved to end slavery within their borders, a well-publicized slave insurrection in Santo Domingo (latter-day Haiti) that began in 1791 generated special anxiety. At the very end of 1793, a massive fire in Albany, New York, which was blamed on local slaves, resulted in the execution of three of them as the perpetrators. Americans gave their attention to Paine's assertions about the corruptions of traditional biblical Christianity as they reacted to the Albany disaster and as they learned of the decision by the French Republic under Robespierre to outlaw slavery in all French dominations, including Santo Domingo, where, notwithstanding, the killing went on.

In a word, Tom Paine's provocation in *The Age of Reason* arrived during a period of extraordinary national instability. Internally and externally—materially, ideologically, diplomatically—uncertainty abounded. Too often a thoughtless teleology dominates historical accounts of the early United States, where what existed originally led with organic inevitability to the modern nation-state. In point of fact, even after the Constitution went into effect, a nearly complete contingency marked the country's early history. Crisis followed crisis, choices required more choices, decisive actions prompted determined reactions, with no inevitability at all. Nowhere were the contingencies greater than for the relationship of religion to public life. Paine's *Age of Reason*, in other words, appeared when almost anything could have happened.

Refuting Paine

Extraordinary is the only word to describe the American response to Paine's *Age of Reason*. Extraordinary was simply the number of refutations. Extraordinary also was their near unanimity in upholding Scripture as an authentic revelation from God. Yet extraordinary as well were the striking contrasts among Paine's opponents in how they viewed the relationship between religious truth and public well-being. If these responses are viewed as coming only from "Federalists" and "conservatives," as some historians have written, it not only misconstrues what actually happened; it also obscures the way that differences in those refutations forecast the future direction of religion in America and especially the history of the Bible.[20]

Of course a single literary controversy could not by itself shape the entire history of an entire nation. In this case, it was noteworthy that Paine's attacks on traditional views of the Bible represented only the most visible example of radical religion in the early republic. Ethan Allen, a hero of the Revolutionary War, had publicized such opinions in his *Reason, the Only Oracle of Man* from 1784. With greater effect, Elihu Palmer, a former Presbyterian minister, gained notoriety from speeches that advocated a post-Christian Deism; his efforts prompted a Philadelphia mob in 1792 to threaten proprietors who let him speak at their establishments. Worried defenders of orthodox Christianity also noticed that the works of French savants, like the Comte de Volney's Deistic *Meditations on the Revolutions of Empires* (1791) and Baron d'Holbach's forthrightly atheistical *System of Nature* (1770), enjoyed at least some popularity on the new nation's few, but closely watched, college campuses.[21] Nonetheless, a focus on the furor over Paine's provocation—occurring at a precarious moment in the nation's history and against the backdrop of a broad but conventional Protestant deference to Scripture—is justified precisely because it did so much to create the American national culture.

Paine's status as a hero of the Revolution, combined with the brio of his edgy prose, guaranteed an immense readership for *The Age of Reason*. From 1794 to 1796 American printers brought out at least fifteen editions of either or both parts of the work—that is, almost as many as the twenty or so printings of *Common Sense* in 1776. The virulently Anti-Federalist grandson of Benjamin Franklin, newspaper editor Benjamin Franklin Bache, is said to have sold fifteen thousand copies from his Philadelphia bookstore alone.[22] Additional copies also circulated as imports from Britain, where printers pumped out even more editions than their American counterparts.

Yet if Paine's two-part tract was one of the most widely circulated individual titles of the decade, the response to that work became *the* publishing phenomenon of the era. One authoritative survey catalogues fifty-six different rejoinders published in Britain and the United States between only 1794 and 1798.[23] Another, with a broader time frame, speaks of at least seventy separately published refutations.[24] Newspaper coverage generated even more attention.

A geographical comparison can suggest what a full publishing history might reveal about this controversy. Thirteen of the fifteen American editions of *The Age of Reason* published between 1794 and 1796 came from the new nation's major urban centers (Boston, New York, and Philadelphia), which at that time included only a tiny fraction of the national population. The refutation of Paine most often printed in the United States came from the Anglican bishop of Landaff, Richard Watson, in a two-part answer to Paine's original two-part provocation. Of the fifteen American printings of Watson's *Apology for the Bible, in a Series of Letters Addressed to Thomas Paine,* published in 1796 and 1797, seven came from Boston, New York, and Philadelphia, but the other eight stretched much farther across the landscape: Litchfield, Connecticut; Newburgh and Albany, New York; New Brunswick, New Jersey; Lancaster and Chambersburg, Pennsylvania; New Bern, North Carolina; and Lexington, Kentucky.[25] Whether or not purchasers read Watson's *Apology* as carefully as they read Paine's tract might be questioned, since the learned bishop dispensed heavy prose in double the pages of Paine's work. Yet Watson did command an extensive market. When in 1796 the peripatetic bookseller Mason Weems checked in with his Philadelphia publisher,

Mathew Carey, he reported that the *Apology* was "much in demand" and would sell even more copies if its price could be reduced.[26] The broad geographical spread of printers willing to take a chance on Watson's *Apology* hints at the depth of Paine's challenge.

That spread has recently been underscored by Seth Perry in an article on the very first full-length publication in the far-off Mississippi Territory, which was a substantial pamphlet of about sixty pages directed against *The Age of Reason*. This 1799 work repeated many of the points made commonly, but also included a creative defense of God's providence in allowing for suffering.[27]

As suggested by this defense from the frontier, the torrent denouncing *The Age of Reason*'s treatment of Scripture rained down from many points on the theological compass. True, a majority of titles and reprinted editions were penned by elites, either British Anglicans or representatives of American proprietary denominations (Congregational, Presbyterian, Episcopal). For these authors, the threat of Paine's theological heresy and the threat of his political radicalism were two sides of the same coin. Yet rushing to join these traditionalists came also Unitarians, Universalists, Baptists, and (in the United States) one Jew and one Sandemanian. Many of these authors shared Paine's opposition to the inherited structures of establishmentarian Christendom; some worried not at all about Paine's threat to social order but only about his attack on the Bible.

Despite ranging widely in many directions, almost all who took up literary arms against Paine returned at great length to defend the Scriptures as revelation from God. Bishop Watson announced the purpose of his much-reprinted work as defending "the authenticity of the Bible," which he promised to do by demonstrating "from the Bible itself" that it was "worthy of credit."[28] Andrew Broaddus, a Virginia Baptist who shared nothing cultural, educational, or political with the English bishop, concluded his anti-Paine effort by agreeing that Scripture offered "the unerring standard of divine truth."[29]

Writers representing orthodox Christian positions repeated this judgment, but so did others who had left Christian orthodoxy behind. Elhanan Winchester, after a Congregational upbringing and serving Philadelphia's noted First Baptist Church, had renounced the traditional Christian view of eternal punishment and affirmed his belief in the salvation of all. A spellbinding orator as well as a dedicated opponent of slavery, his career as a Universalist had taken him to London and then back to the United States. To make a bad pun, Winchester's *Ten Letters Addressed to Mr. Paine* defended the Bible's truthfulness painstakingly, especially its account of the resurrection of Christ. Winchester's final verdict on Scripture? It "has done more good to mankind than all the other books that were ever written."[30]

Even more memorable was the sharp rebuff to *The Age of Reason* administered by Joseph Priestley. The renowned discoverer of oxygen, but also the object of violent opposition in England for his Unitarian theology and his pro-French politics, Priestley published against Paine almost immediately after arriving at his new home on the banks of the Susquehanna River in eastern Pennsylvania. Priestley had fled into the American wilderness after English nationalists threatened his life for defending the Revolution in France. Priestley—who shared much with Paine in castigating church-state establishments, championing the American Revolution, applauding the French Revolution, and even speaking out against American Federalists as crypto-monarchists—did not share Paine's opinions on the Bible. To counter the influence of *The Age of Reason*, Priestley ardently defended "the unspeakable value of revealed religion, and the sufficiency of its proofs."[31]

To be sure, in the face of an overwhelming majority, a bare handful of Americans did speak up for Paine. After several responses had already appeared, Elihu Palmer ventured to publish *A Defence of the Age of Reason*. Palmer acknowledged, "Europeans have in general embraced Christianity, as contained in the bible, which *they* call the word of God, as the only true and infallible system on earth, and which can only lead us to eternal happiness." Yet to Palmer, this conventional opinion only reflected the defects of "the *generality of the people*, who seldom think or inquire for themselves, but are always more or less the dupes of designing men."[32] In New York City, an anonymous citizen joined Palmer by taking on Watson's *Apology* with the sort of vigor that Paine might have approved. To this excited author, the bishop's effort only laid bare "the frantic ignorance, persevering stupidity, and unqualified malignity of the Christian fathers . . . to the present day."[33] Yet the very few who published such opinions were spitting into a gale.

By contrast, almost all American authors agreed with Elias Boudinot—friend of Washington, president of the Confederation Congress, New Jersey representative to the first Constitutional Congress, leading Federalist, guiding trustee of the College of New Jersey at Princeton, and dedicated Presbyterian layman—who in responding to Paine called the Bible simply "the most valuable book in the world."[34] Boudinot composed *The Age of Revelation*, his very long book against Paine, during the first flurry of agitation over *The Age of Reason*, but did not publish it until 1801, after he received reports about the revival of "infidelity" attending the election of Thomas Jefferson as president. Yet although Boudinot entered the lists as a well-known Federalist partisan, his defense of the Scriptures spoke for almost all the others who joined him in taking on *The Age of Reason*.

Speaking also for most of these responses was the way that Boudinot contextualized his passionate defense of the Bible. In his view, Scripture was essential for the story of redemption that believers perceived in the sacred writings. As Boudinot explained at length in introducing his response to "the age of infidelity," "the Gospel revelation is a complete system of salvation."[35] This theme—Scripture must be trusted because Scripture opens the door to reconciliation with God— sounded a chorus from an anti-Paine choir that harmonized on little else. One of the most forceful proclamations of this Scripture-salvation link came from David Levi, an English Jew, whose *Defence of the Old Testament* (Figure 2.2) against Paine was brought out by printers in New York and Philadelphia. Levi joined many others in scoring Paine's scholarship and scorning his critical handling of the Bible. Yet speaking deliberately for "our nation" (i.e., Hebrews), Levi most

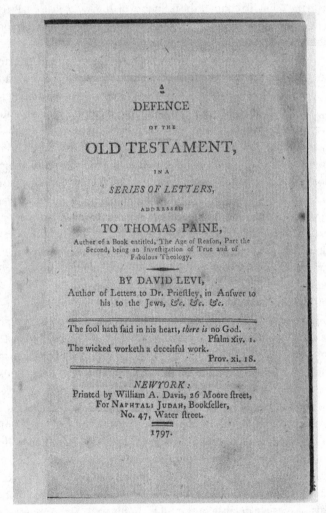

Figure 2.2 Of David Levi's many learned works in support of traditional Judaism that were published in his native England, this *Defence* against Paine was the only one reprinted in America.

Source: Courtesy of the American Antiquarian Society.

wanted to assert "the truth of Revelation" so as "to save one soul from imbibing the poison of [Paine's] pernicious tenets."[36]

Paine's opponents responded to his deprecation of Scripture with an outpouring of detailed refutation that must have been as mind-numbing for readers then as it has become now. Yet for broader historical purposes, it is crucial to note that the massive opposition to what Paine wrote about the Bible in 1794–95 contrasted sharply with the minuscule opposition that had greeted his arguments from Scripture in 1776. On that earlier occasion, Paine's Loyalist opponents responded vigorously to his reading of 1 Samuel chapter 8 as condemning monarchy *tout court*. Objectively considered, these Loyalist rebuttals presented much deeper scholarship in support of much sounder biblical interpretations.[37] The great difference was that most Americans responded enthusiastically to Paine's use of the Bible in 1776, while in the mid-1790s the vast majority passionately repudiated his treatment.

If, however, it was passionate, this later rejection of Paine did not rest on cutting-edge scholarship. Although many of his opponents caught out Paine in blatant mistakes and although some treated disputed questions more judiciously than Paine's slash-and-burn approach, none mounted particularly sophisticated rejoinders to the advanced critical reasoning of the era—like David Hume's challenge to the credibility of miracles, Gotthold Ephraim Lessing's claim that general truths could not be based on specific historical events (like the life of Jesus), the general skepticism of Voltaire, or the historical relativism of biblical critics Spinoza, Leclerc, and Simon. In particular, the authors who wrote against Paine's popular application of advanced Enlightenment thought usually themselves relied on Enlightenment notions of proof, objectivity, universal consciousness, and the innate human ability to grasp the influence of ideas on events. In the perceptive comment of James Smylie, "When the clergy attempted to turn reason against [Paine's evocation of] Reason they were on an important track. Unfortunately, in their apologetics for Christianity, they constantly appealed to rationality and reduced Christianity to mere reasonableness despite attempts to reassert the dimension of the mysterious." With Paine, his opponents also proved themselves to be "children of the eighteenth-century Enlightenment as well as heirs of the Reformation and the Evangelical Awakening."[38]

Yet even with such reservations, it does not take deep research to realize that Paine's opponents administered a comprehensive drubbing. Against Paine on the historical plausibility of Mosaic history in the Old Testament and the historical reliability of the New Testament, learned clerics like Bishop Watson and even laymen like Boudinot and Levi advanced much more evidence, much better marshaled, to defend the historicity of scriptural accounts. They did so by enlisting authorities, still widely credited in the eighteenth century, for the priority of the Pentateuch to the Greek classics, the testimony of extrabiblical sources concerning biblical events, and the extraordinary result of scriptural miracles in bringing the New Testament church into existence.[39]

Against Paine's questioning of the miraculous elements in Scripture, his opponents insisted on the credibility of the supernatural, with especially powerful defenses of the resurrection of Christ coming from the Universalist Winchester and the Unitarians Priestley and Gilbert Wakefield.[40] When in the next decade Jefferson prepared his multilingual version of the New Testament for private use, he would be one of the very few Americans to follow Paine in professing admiration for the moral character of Jesus while editing out the miracle stories of the gospels, including their account of Christ's resurrection from the dead.[41]

Against Paine's claim that trust in reason and the study of nature should replace trust in the Bible, the Baptist Broaddus spoke for most of the others when he claimed that "so far from conducing towards a forsaking the works of God in creation, the religion of the Scripture inculcates this doctrine."[42]

Most comprehensively, against Paine's claim that Deism offered a fully satisfactory replacement for Christianity—or in the case of Levi, for the faith revealed by God to the Hebrews—arose an almost universal affirmation of traditional confidence in Scripture. On this matter, the voice of Priestley, viewed by many as little different from the infidel Paine, rang out with noteworthy clarity: "[T]here are, in my opinion, no writings whatever that are at all comparable to the scriptures for their moral teaching, in giving just views of the attributes and providence of God, or in adding to the dignity of man, fitting him for the discharge of his duty in this life, and making him a proper subject of another and better state of being."[43] In a word, responses to The Age of Reason demonstrated, even as it strengthened, an overwhelming American commitment to the Bible as God's revealed word.

Religion and Society

Beyond that near unanimity, however, it was a completely different story. Even as Paine's opponents broadcast a common respect for the Bible, they differed wildly among themselves on the social implications of that respect. For understanding the effect of l'affaire Paine on the future, those differences meant just as much as the nearly universal respect for Scripture. In particular, the refutations' near unanimity in support of divine revelation collapsed on the question of how religion narrowly conceived connected to social order broadly understood.

The crux concerned the relationship between divine revelation and the function of that revelation in society. Many who wrote against Paine stressed (as in the quotation from Priestly), the payoff from true religion for personal morality or piety. Others went further and held up the morality arising from true religion as the only possible defense of the social fabric. Yet among the latter, another chasm appeared. That division separated those who viewed proper beliefs drawn from God-given Scripture as supporting traditional social hierarchies (against licentious anarchy) and those who saw a right understanding of Scripture as obliterating those hierarchies (as protection against tyranny) (see Table 2.1).

These contrasting positions anticipated much that would follow in the American history of the Bible. The first division might be called pietistic versus utilitarian. On one side stood those who turned to the Scriptures for strictly personal or narrowly ecclesiastical purposes. On the other stood those for whom the social consequences from a properly honored Bible were most important. In between came many who sometimes spoke of biblical religion as specifically spiritual and sometimes as a prop for social order.

Even deeper was the second division, for, to repeat a crucially important difference, a common commitment to the Bible could lead to radically antagonistic prescriptions for a healthy society. In decades to come, the exalted reputation of the Bible in the United States would remain remarkably secure, even as debates over what biblical religion mandated for society become remarkably intense.

"Pietistic" responses to Paine that focused exclusively on spiritual realities included the writings of the Universalist Winchester and the Jew Levi. The texts that Levi placed prominently on his title page encapsulated the entirety of his argument: "The fool hath said in his heart, there is no God" (Ps 14:1) and "The wicked worketh a deceitful work" (Prov 11:18, both quoted, as it happens, from the King James Version). In an earlier work from 1788, Winchester had used Scripture instrumentally as he applied lessons from Jewish history to the new United States in a sermon on the "Wonders" of God, based on Exodus 15:11. That celebration of the Glorious Revolution of 1688 exploited the history of Israel to claim that the new American Constitution resulted from "nothing less than a very special Providence, and divine interference." Winchester also paused in that sermon to praise the new nation's "liberty, and especially religious liberty," as a standing rebuke to Britain's oppressive church-state establishment.[44] Yet in 1794, when he took aim at *The Age of Reason*, Winchester, like Levi, said absolutely nothing about the social implications of belief or unbelief.[45]

Table 2.1 Polarities in Response to Paine's *Age of Reason*

The Purpose of the Bible	
Personal piety	Public utility

The Bible as Useful For	
Promoting public virtue	Defending against tyranny

The exactly opposite approach characterized the two-volume screed from Ogden, the Episcopal friend of Francis Asbury. From Ogden's position as an Episcopal rector in Newark, New Jersey, Paine's errors seemed primarily social-political. Ogden began his *Antidote to Deism* by countering Paine's dedication to the American people with a dedication to George Washington, "the *real* Patriot; the Father of his country; and the *sincere* Christian." He continued with an all-out attack on Paine for violating "virtue and common sense" and for "propagat[ing] his *licentious system* of infidelity." In an indictment with special resonance in this period, Ogden charged Paine with rejecting "the doctrine of the *immortality* of the soul, or a future state."[46] As historian James Hutson has shown, for the entire eighteenth century and well into the nineteenth, religious adherents of many types emphasized the vital social role performed by belief in "a future state of rewards and punishments." If citizens no longer believed in a "a future state," they would abandon God and the moral law, with devastating consequences for social order.[47]

Before he finally got around to marshaling standard proofs for Scripture, Ogden expatiated for more than one hundred pages on the social mayhem that Paine's Deism would unleash. His account was so programmatic and so much indebted to the republican calculus that dominated American ideology in this period that it deserves quotation in full:

> In *proportion* as a neglect, or contempt of religion obtains, dissoluteness of morals will prevail; and when a people, in general, become *dissolute*, probity and virtue, public spirit, and a generous concern for the interests of the nation, will be *extinguished*. Certainly then, all who wish well to civil society and the happiness of mankind, should be anxious, that *genuine Christianity*, in *principle* and *practice*, might generally prevail; and that vice and infidelity, should not predominate.[48]

In the telling contrast described by the historian Eric Schlereth, Ogden represented a growing number of Americans who hoped to secure national well-being by emphasizing the "context" of Christian faith over of its "content."[49]

Unlike Ogden, with his primary attention to society, most critics of Paine combined social-political concerns with their defense of the Bible's religious truth. Bishop Watson did ask with a shudder, "[W]hat may not society expect from those who shall imbibe the principles of [Paine's] book?"[50] But such concerns occupied only a tiny fraction of his *Apology for the Bible*. Similarly, Elias Boudinot briefly explained his reason for going into print as "an anxious desire that our country should be preserved from the dreadful evil of becoming enemies to the religion of the Gospel, which I have no doubt, but would be introductive of the dissolution of government and the bonds of civil society"—but only as a prelude to hundreds of pages of historical apologetics.[51] From a different standpoint, the Baptist Broaddus eventually took up considerations of political "corruptions" and "the shakles [sic] of tyranny"—but only after devoting almost sixty pages to "vindicate the *divine authority* of the Scriptures" as "a subject on which hangs the fates of CHRISTIANITY and DEISM—of Life and Death!"[52]

Order, Liberty, or Only Piety

As was obvious from the very different obiter dicta from Boudinot (who worried about "the dissolution of government") and Broaddus (who worried about "tyranny"), Americans who united in their defense of Scripture differed on much else. Excellent recent scholarship has documented the widespread notoriety of Deism as "infidelity" or radical religion in the early American republic. It has also documented the stiff reactions, sometimes bordering on panic, to the threat of Paine's *Age of Reason* as the epitome of the "infidel" challenge.[53] One of the few lapses of that scholarship has been an overemphasis on those who saw Paine's work undermining political order—at the cost of overlooking two other significant constituencies: those who *agreed* with Paine's politics, even as they abhorred his religion, and those who *ignored* Paine's politics in order to advance an alternative understanding of Christian faith. The contrasts can be oversimplified as a tripartite question: Did faithfully biblical Christianity support a religion of order, a religion of liberty, or a religion of disinterested piety? Representatives of all three options pitched in vigorously as they trashed *The Age of Reason*.

Ogden's blast represented an extreme version of, in Gordon Wood's summary, "the Protestant ministers and other conservatives, who had initially welcomed the French Revolution" but then "became increasingly alarmed at the threat that the upheaval in France came to pose for revealed religion."[54] Other spokesmen who respected formal learning, prized decorum, and advocated deference to ecclesiastical traditions agreed that chaos lurked behind Paine's Deism. James Muir, a Presbyterian minister in Alexandria, Virginia, published a series of ten discourses against *The Age of Reason*, eight of which concentrated on demonstrating the divine character of Scripture.[55] The last two of the ten, however, turned political. From Jesus's words in John 7:17 ("If any man will do his will, he shall know the doctrines"), Muir drew the conclusion "A Moral Life Disposeth a Man to Receive, but an Immoral to Reject the Gospel." As his last discourse, Muir published a Fast Day sermon preached in October 1793. It exploited the jeremiad form by proclaiming that "irreligion is the root of all crimes." The American crimes that Muir spotlighted included a standard array of evils defined by the canons of Christian republicanism ("idleness," "extravagance," "luxury," "folly," "vice," "degeneracy of a pestilential nature"). Yet he also paused to specify evils that did not always receive attention on such occasions, including mistreatment of slaves and ruinous frontier warfare against Native Americans. By using this jeremiad to cap his opposition to *The Age of Reason*, Muir clearly intended his final words to warn Americans against Paine's opinions: "It is very evident that national guilt draws down national calamities."[56]

Like the Episcopalian Ogden, the Presbyterian Muir spoke for many others with a stake in preserving traditional Protestant authority in the new United States, even if the coercive mechanism of Protestant Christendom no longer existed to support such authority. But their view of *The Age of Reason* as a threat to social order as well as religious orthodoxy by no means spoke for all Americans who defended Scripture against Tom Paine.

Almost as prevalent was an alternative ideal that *accepted* much of Paine's radical political critique. The very few Americans who shared Paine's Deism naturally shared his abhorrence of traditional European order. As a case in point, the anonymous author of *Strictures*, who defended Paine against Bishop Watson's *Apology*, barely mentioned the Bible; instead, his tract rejoiced that first the United States and then France had overthrown "Priestcraft" and "sacerdotal persecution"; it excoriated the bishop's Anglican establishment as "the seductive influence of a benefice"; and it blasted those who retained "blind enthusiasm of our infatuated ancestors" and "the deluded virtues of an arbitrary, sordid, oppressive system."[57] Yet as an indication of how little purchase such views gained, The *Strictures* of this New York disciple of Paine vanished without an echo.

By contrast, authors who accepted Paine's politics while denouncing his view of Scripture received a warm American welcome. One of these works came from Wakefield, who had abandoned a Cambridge fellowship when he became a Unitarian minister. He challenged Paine's dismissal of biblical supernaturalism, vigorously defended the resurrection of Christ, and argued strongly for the reality of divine revelation. Yet Wakefield's *Examination of The Age of Reason* also praised Paine for combating "the authority of venal sycophants, and the retainers of corrupt and wicked systems, whether in *politics* or *religion*." In addition, Wakefield devoted almost as much energy denouncing "the sway of *creeds* and *councils*, of *hierarchies* and *churches*, whether *Protestant* or *Popish*," as he did correcting Paine's errors concerning Scripture.[58] In other words, Wakefield's dedication to radical political reform matched his commitment to Scripture as divine. While remaining a believer in the Bible, he also remained a Dissenter on the Trinity and a virtual Paine-ite in attacking the machinery of church-state establishments. As an indication of the traction that Wakefield's arguments gained, American printers brought out five editions of his *Examination* in 1794 alone.

An even more revealing combination of convictions marked Andrew Broaddus's "animadversions" on *The Age of Reason*. This Virginia Baptist agreed with Paine's Presbyterian and Episcopalian critics concerning the reality of miracles, the Trinity, and especially the inspiration of Scripture. Yet, as he confessed, "[Although] I am disgusted with [Paine] as a *Religionist* . . . [I] admire Mr. Paine as a *Politician*." In fact, part of Broaddus's defense of Scripture was to quote portions from *Common Sense* where Paine seemed to embrace a traditional view of biblical inspiration.[59]

When he addressed political matters, Broaddus dwelled at length on his basic agreement with Paine. After summarizing *The Age of Reason*'s arguments concerning the malfeasance of traditional churches, Broaddus responded with his own denunciation: "[T]he evils spoken of are a corruption and perversion of Christianity. . . . They are not in the system of Christianity; but in the lives and transactions of those [quoting Rom 1:18] '*who hold the truth in unrighteousness.*'" With Paine, Broaddus also abominated "national establishments . . . pomp and reverence . . . popish indulgences" and all the rest of what "the Bible is an utter stranger to."[60]

In other words, Broaddus, who defended the Bible, also endorsed Paine's radical repudiation of both formal establishment structures (British Anglicanism) and informal church power (American Episcopalians, Presbyterians, and Congregationalists). His brand of Christianity, which remained orthodox on strictly doctrinal points, advocated a conception of scriptural authority that came close to a biblicism rejecting all other authorities. His animus against top-down religion was not yet as widespread as the animus of the more formal Protestants against everything that Paine stood for. But with the growing influence of Baptist churches and increasing attacks on any kind of hierarchy, the influence of those who opposed Paine as a "Religionist," while following him as a "Politician," was certain to grow.

Among Paine's opponents, this division between a proprietary repudiation of his radical politics and a sectarian endorsement was the most obvious divide. Yet in the blizzard of anti-Paine works, the most intriguing individual text fell into neither category. That work came from Daniel Humphreys, a Yale graduate and well-known New Hampshire lawyer, whose perspective on Paine exposed a prominent strand of American religion that has received too little attention. The title of Humphreys's work sounds like something a Deist friend of Paine might have written, for it challenged the much reprinted work of Bishop Watson: *The Bible Needs No Apology: or Watson's System of Religion Refuted* (Figure 2.3). Yet Humphreys was no friend of Paine's Deism or of his politics. Instead, Humphreys scored Watson's response to *The Age of Reason* for misrepresenting the character of Christian faith itself. The problem, according to the New Hampshire lawyer, lay in Watson's gratuitous understatement: "like saying, after all Paine has said against the Bible, there is a good deal to be said for it." But according to Humphreys, such a response entirely missed the point of Scripture, which was

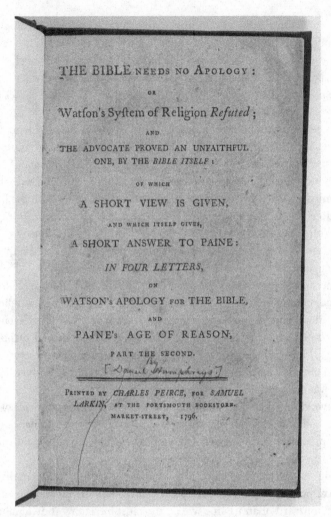

Figure 2.3 Daniel Humphreys's response to *The Age of Reason* joined a nearly unanimous chorus in denouncing Paine's treatment of the Bible. Yet Humphreys stood almost alone in attacking Bishop Watson and other Paine opponents for themselves misconstruing the essentially spiritual character of Scripture.
Source: Courtesy of the American Antiquarian Society.

to experience the glory of God. In a work jammed full of scriptural quotation, Humphreys cited Psalm 8:3 to indicate what he meant by the divine glory: "Look up, O man, and consider the Heavens, the work of God's fingers; the sun, the moon and the stars, which he has created." Watson, regrettably, had not focused on "the honor of God, and . . . his saving truth" but had merely fulfilled a task "consistent with his station and duty to society."[61]

Significantly, Humphreys's complaint against Watson's *Apology* did share the antiestablishmentarianism advocated by Paine, the Unitarian Wakefield, and the Baptist Broaddus. In his words, "[H]ow could it consist with a high dignified station in a national church, to contend for the pure doctrine of the *Kingdom of Heaven*, which condemns all national churches as anti-christian?" Yet to Humphreys, church establishments were a great evil, not because they enabled political tyranny but because they eviscerated the gospel. The contrast that meant most to Humphreys was religious; it lay between what Watson tried to do and what a real Christian should do. On the one side stood the champion of Christendom: "This learned writer, who tells us what his philosophy instructs him to believe, and how his Alma Mater, the university[,] taught him to draw consequences, steps forth as a champion armed at all points with his logic and dialectics. He is no doubt expert at . . . logomachy, a war of words among philosophers." Against him stood the true Christian: "We read of christians being called to take very different armour to fight the good fight of faith. [quoting from Eph 6:11–17] The whole armour of God, the shield of faith, the sword of the spirit, and for an helmet of the hope of salvation."[62] Although Humphreys did eventually direct his polemic against what Paine had written, his work mostly concentrated on what he considered the entirely inadequate view of Christianity represented by the bishop.

The explanation for Humphreys's unusual perspective lay in his church adherence, for he was a Sandemanian.[63] A decade or so after graduating from Yale in 1757, Humphreys shocked his friends by joining a tiny New Haven band that took its name from a Scottish Dissenter named Robert Sandeman (1718–1781).[64] Sandeman, who followed his father-in-law, John Glas (1695–1773), when the latter left his post as a Church of Scotland minister, eventually became an effective polemicist against traditional Protestant Christendom whose itinerations took him throughout Britain before he migrated to Connecticut. Glas and then Sandeman were best known for defining genuine Christianity as "bare assent" to biblical truths. They also advocated a biblicist approach to religious authority (doing only what Scripture particularly commanded) and a strongly sectarian conception of church order (absolute separation from any national, formal, or established church). As an indication of Humphreys's consistency, when President Jefferson appointed him as a U.S. district attorney in 1804, he maintained his strict sectarian convictions by leaving the courtroom whenever a minister was asked to pray at the start of a court session.

Humphreys's position versus Paine in 1796 represented two trajectories that were becoming increasingly common even as he went into print. First was a pietistic conception of Christian faith that viewed political entanglement as undermining true religion. This position came close to what Francis Asbury and his Methodist associates were promoting in their remarkably effective evangelistic efforts. Although Humphreys's Sandemanianism differed considerably from Methodism, his challenge to Bishop Watson resembled the way that Methodists of the Asbury generation stressed the personal, existential, and domestic implications of religion much more than the political.

Second was Humphreys's all-out biblicism that looked to Scripture, and only Scripture, as guidance for spiritual well-being and orientation for life in the world. Closely connected to this biblicism was also a determined primitivism that viewed the Book of Acts as a model for contemporary Christian life and that regarded the story of Christianity as a history of degeneration or even as a triumph of the Antichrist.[65] To Humphrey, the controversy surrounding *The Age of Reason* and the larger uncertainties of the mid-1790s could all be explained when a believer recognized "the scriptures are fulfilling [i.e., being fulfilled] in a manner suited to excite great interest."[66] In days to come, leaders of the Restorationist movement—including Thomas and Alexander Campbell, who had associated with Sandemanians in Scotland before immigrating to the United States—would lead many other Americans who embraced this kind of biblicism.

In summary, Paine on Scripture elicited a nearly unanimous American negative. But Paine on social and political connections to religion stimulated something else entirely.

Consequences

But why delve at such length into American reactions to *The Age of Reason*? Surely it is overkill to put such emphasis on only one literary conflict, regardless of how extensive it was. The answer is that controversy over Paine's work foreshadowed much in the later American history of the Bible. It cut channels that would direct the flow of later developments. Nothing in the new nation was certain, given, or inevitable in the wake of independence and the inauguration of national government under the Constitution. In such circumstances, the second coming of Tom Paine defined the future as powerfully as had his first coming.

Matters of cultural geography came first. Where New England dominated colonial and Revolutionary intellectual life—with its leadership in literacy, book publishing, newspaper circulation, and collegiate higher education—the responses to Paine came from all regions of the country. New Englanders would still promote American parallels with ancient Israel most actively, but on the general question of Scripture other regions stood squarely with New England. Whatever might be concluded from this controversy about attitudes toward Scripture spoke of genuinely national attitudes.

It was also telling that the most frequently reprinted refutations of Paine—Bishop Watson's *Apology* and Gilbert Wakefield's *Examination*—came from Britain.[67] The American willingness to be tutored by Englishmen suggests that the cultural estrangement caused by the political estrangement of independence had begun to moderate. Because of how eagerly Americans looked to Britain for refutations of Paine, it would soon be natural for them to look in the same direction, specifically at the British and Foreign Bible Society, to guide their own efforts in mass distribution of the Scriptures.

Eric Schlereth has insightfully specified a number of additional consequences flowing from the general excitement over "infidelity" in the 1790s.[68] In particular, the Deist challenge decisively shaped the way Americans came to relate religion and civic life in the cultural uncertainty of a post-Revolutionary world. The citizenry, having embraced the principle of religious liberty and having embarked on a course heading toward complete church disestablishment, nevertheless still contained growing numbers who hoped to maintain a Christian social presence—yet without the formal structures of European Christendom. In these circumstances, public controversies stimulated by "infidels" created the playing field on which Americans fashioned new rules for civilizing their new nation.

Those rules heightened attention to the instrumental effects of religion. Although most of the anti-Paine publications devoted most of their pages to affirming Scripture as divine revelation, authors like the Episcopalian Ogden on the right and the Unitarian Wakefield on the left—and many others in between—turned discussion away from the *truth claims* of those beliefs and toward the *effects of religious belief or nonbelief on society*. Public appeals to the utilitarian effects of religion, which became increasingly common after the age of Paine, would allow Christian activists to influence society while maintaining their commitment to religious freedom. The pathway lay open to defending the Bible not only, or even primarily, because Scripture showed humans the way to God but because it provided the resources for supporting the personal virtue without which republics must fail.

Similarly, the means used to influence others on these matters—pamphlets, locally organized societies, periodicals, and newspapers—exalted democratic argument as the prime method for shaping civic order. In the unfolding American experiment, it was no longer top-down, state-ordered coercion, but bottom-up, citizen-directed mobilization that could guide public opinion. In a public sphere defined by the free exercise of opinion, the radicals generated great excitement when they attacked Scripture as immoral and socially dangerous. But those attacks had their greatest long-term impact by provoking a popular rally around the opposite conviction—that the Bible could be trusted as the very Word of God. About the British approach to Paine, Americans could read in a work published in Philadelphia in 1797. It reprinted the speech of Thomas Erskine, Lord Kenyon, at the trial of a Londoner charged with sedition for reprinting *The Age of Reason*.[69] In Britain supporters of Paine were prosecuted; in America they were outshouted.

Controversy over *The Age of Reason* also anticipated crucial developments in education. The broad American commitment to a republican understanding of the world—which assumed that a healthy social order required self-directed virtuous citizens—almost inevitably led opponents of Deism to devise plans for educating the nation's children. Yet so long as the denominations maintained control of schooling, their competing differences in scriptural interpretation hamstrung educational cooperation. Once more, Paine came to the rescue. The overwhelming unity that Americans displayed in defending Scripture against Paine's attacks paved the way for the Protestant denominations to subordinate their conflicts over biblical interpretations when proponents of public education sought a universally respected, but nonsectarian, means of promoting morality and thereby ensuring public well-being. Their instrument would soon be obvious. It was the King James Version of the Bible.

In 1776, Thomas Paine, by convincing colonial Americans that the Bible rejected monarchy, had played a decisive role in creating an independent United States. In the mid-1790s, by convincing so many citizens that he had demeaned the Scriptures, he played an equally important role in creating an American Bible civilization. That creation depended on how enemies of *The Age of Reason* put their scriptural loyalties to work. Proprietary Protestants like Uzal Ogden and Elias Boudinot expected Scripture to shore up the republic, sectarian Protestants like Andrew Broaddus went on the warpath with Bible in hand against the schemes of proprietary Protestants, while pietists like Daniel Humphreys wanted nothing more than to preserve pure biblical religion from worldly contamination.

The next two chapters explain how much-noted contentions between proprietary and sectarian Protestants, as well as the less-noted achievements of pietistic Methodists, moved the Bible from taken-for-granted background into explicitly visible foreground. The pressing requirements for constructing a national culture acted much more like the excitements of the Revolutionary era than the steady-state environments of conventional biblical loyalty prevailing when colonists gloried in Protestant British liberty or the founders of the United States moved from Revolution to government under a Constitution. Even as the Revolution had elicited specific biblical arguments for (and, with Loyalists, against) independence, now in the fractious beginnings of American national life appeals to Scripture became more and more explicit. The conflict between Bible believers who despised Paine's politics and those who embraced those same politics (chapter 3) pushed all Protestants toward biblicism, or the reliance on

Scripture directly without the traditional mediating supports of Christendom. Pietistic devotion to Scripture, especially as exemplified by Asbury and the Methodists (chapter 4), tended in the same direction. Custodial Protestants reluctantly, but sectarians and pietists eagerly, also moved steadily away from the formal structures of Christendom toward voluntary strategies to implement their commitment to biblical authority.

When the smoke cleared from the cannonading leveled against Paine's *Age of Reason*, infidel Deism, though not entirely dead, stood decisively defeated. The next decades witnessed an extension of the fruits of victory, an extension marvelous, but also deeply ambiguous, in its triumphs.

3

Custodial Protestants versus Sectarian Protestants

The American War of Independence and the establishment of constitutional government were not so much the "foundation" of U.S. history as the "first steps" on a national path that, at many points, could have led in other directions. In the apt phrase of Sam Haselby, these founding events "posed rather than answered the question of American nationality."[1] A nation was founded, but where would it go? How would Protestants participate in the national culture? What kind of Protestantism would prevail? Could Protestants find a way of repudiating European Christendom while still advancing Christianity?

It was not a given that vigorous expressions of Bible-only Protestantism would become more prominent in the churches and exert an unprecedented cultural influence. Neither was it foreordained that Protestants would master voluntary organization as the means to build a national civilization with positive advances for many middle-order whites alongside oppressions that Alexis de Tocqueville would later describe as "the tyranny of the majority."[2] Nor, despite the ideological synergies of the Revolutionary era, was it guaranteed that Protestants would continue to embrace republican political principles and align themselves unself-consciously with free-market economic practice. It was also nowhere written in the stars that a dominant white population would strengthen the system of Black chattel slavery and advance an increasingly brutal dispossession of Native Americans while otherwise displaying a nearly manic devotion to ideals of universal human liberty.

The all but unanimous rejection of Tom Paine's opinions on Scripture showed that Americans would retain a traditional Christian respect for the Bible. The vociferous character of that rejection, arising without governmental sponsorship and coming from all sides, also anticipated the shape that scriptural influence would come to enjoy. As Americans actively embraced the Bible, so too did they embrace the ideology of the nation's founding. The history of Scripture in the United States would differ from its course in Europe as American Protestant belief merged with the principles of liberal democratic republicanism.

Into the early years of the nineteenth century, representatives of the proprietary or custodial churches continued to seek structured, corporate means for preserving the central role of Christianity in the new nation. They did embrace

America's Book. Mark A. Noll, Oxford University Press. © Oxford University Press 2022.
DOI: 10.1093/oso/9780197623466.003.0004

the Revolution's dedication to the free exercise of religion and also accepted what they considered the separation of church and state. To most Congregationalists, Presbyterians, Dutch Reformed, and Episcopalians, however, the Revolutionary changes represented *adjustments*, a bend in the road for traditional Christianity. By contrast, Baptists and other sectarian evangelicals viewed the gift of the Revolution not as a bend in the road but as a heaven-sent opportunity to reverse course and restore the Christian faith to its primitive purity. If American Protestants agreed that it was vital for the health of the new nation to preserve religion and yet do so without the coercive structures of the old world, anything but agreement existed on how Christianity might flourish without an establishmentarian Christendom.

As responses to Paine's *Age of Reason* indicate, the Bible remained a treasured object for almost all who participated in the new nation's internecine cultural battles. Yet alongside much attention to Scripture for the spiritual concerns that Methodists also stressed, the new nation's culture warriors differed passionately about the Bible's political utility.[3] Both those who struggled to refine Christendom and those who hoped to obliterate it shared a devotion to Scripture. Division came in response to a different question: Was the promotion of scriptural civilization—through all possible means short of a national religious establishment—imperative for American well-being? Or did such promotion constitute a quasi-papal, crypto-monarchical assault on American liberty?

While the work of the Methodists flowed incrementally in ever-widening circles, the clash between proprietary and sectarian evangelicals passed through three discernible phases defined by political events. When the heat from those struggles cooled, the result was a strengthening of what Methodists had carried throughout the land: deeper commitment to Scripture in general, more reliance on "the Bible only," and a turn to voluntary self-organization as the means to shape society. The bitter intra-Protestant controversies of the early national period, along with the Methodists' more irenic course, gave the American Bible civilization its distinctive shape.

The Proprietary Presumption, ca. 1776–1793

Proprietary evangelicals were Federalists at prayer.[4] They had led the way in deploying Scripture to sanctify the cause of independence. As patriots, but also fierce anti-Catholics, they fervently denounced the abuses of Christendom in Britain's Anglican establishment and the more general machinations of "popery." They had stood with the first-generation Federalists who backed the Constitution against the Anti-Federalists. To them it was axiomatic that because

Protestantism reflected divine revelation and patriotic ideology represented God's plan for political organization, "Christian republicanism," as they understood it, should guide the new nation.

By virtue of their wealth, elite status, public visibility, and active support of the Revolution, these successors of the main colonial churches regarded themselves as the new nation's natural religious guides. Congregationalists, still dominant in New England, and Presbyterians, a strong public presence from New York southward, constituted that leadership, along with Episcopalians, who were still publicly prominent despite the damage caused by Anglican associations with Britain. (The colonies' 356 Anglican churches in 1770 were reduced to 170 Episcopalian congregations in 1790.)[5]

The proprietary or custodial Protestants took for granted the comprehensive intermingling of ecclesiastical, governmental, and social interests—as well as their own leading position as intellectual and moral preceptors. While they accepted religious liberty as a hard-won principle of the Revolution, they also assumed that their respected colonial status would translate into guidance for the new nation. To them it seemed entirely natural that they would provide in the altered circumstances of the new republic what formal church establishment had once supplied for European Christians.

At the 1787 Constitutional Convention in Philadelphia, the preponderance of delegates with a religious identification came from these churches, though also with a smattering of Catholics, Lutherans, and Dutch Reformed. By that time, Methodists and Baptists had become almost as numerous as adherents of the large colonial denominations, but only two (at best) members of the Constitutional Convention were Methodists; none were Baptists.[6]

Proprietary instincts also influenced answers to the urgent question of the hour: How could the virtue without which republics failed be preserved without an established religion? State constitutions, which made more explicit room for religion than did the federal Constitution, provided part of the answer. Again, where religious affiliation can be determined for delegates to state ratifying conventions, the overwhelming majority came from the older colonial churches.[7] These instruments of government enshrined principles of religious free exercise as a foundational commitment. At the same time, the shadow of Christendom, which had seemed so threatening as Britain's church-state establishment, did not completely disappear.[8]

Virginia advanced beyond the other states by strictly separating religious institutions and beliefs from the exercises of government, first with a general statement in its Constitution from 1776 ("all men are equally entitled to the free exercise of religion, according to the dictates of conscience") and then in Thomas Jefferson's famous *Statute for Religious Freedom* from 1786 ("all men shall be free to profess, and by argument to maintain, their opinions in matters of religion,

and ... the same shall in no wise diminish, enlarge, or affect their civil capacities").[9] New York's flight from Christendom followed republican logic even more
thoroughly by stipulating that "no minister of the gospel, or priest of any denomination" could hold public office.[10]

Yet Virginia and New York long remained outliers by comparison with most
other states, which hedged absolute religious liberty in various ways. The North
Carolina Constitution of 1776 was more typical. It guaranteed religious liberty but, like New Hampshire, Vermont, New Jersey, and South Carolina, restricted office holding to Protestants and (as in Vermont and Pennsylvania as
well) to those who would affirm "the divine authority of either the Old or New
Testaments." Maryland deviated from this narrowly Protestant formula only
by restricting officeholders to those who declared "a belief in the Christian
religion."[11]

In New England—ironically, since it was the region that protested the
loudest against the tyrannical Church of England—the long tradition of tax
support for Congregational churches took several more decades to disappear.
Massachusetts's new constitution of 1780—like the new state charters for New
Hampshire (1784) and Vermont (1777), as well as Connecticut's colonial charter
of 1662 that was not replaced until 1818—strongly affirmed the rights of conscience. But to indicate how much New England regarded the health of a republic as dependent on religiously supported virtue, Massachusetts also gave the
legislature "power to authorize and require ... the several towns ... to make suitable provision, at their own expense, for the institution of the public worship of
God, and for the support and maintenance of public Protestant teachers of piety,
religion, and morality, in all cases where such provision shall not be made voluntarily."[12] Freedom of religion, yes, but also tax support for the churches.

The assumption of continuity from colonies to states extended well beyond
new state constitutions. A major publishing event in 1791, just after the federal
Constitution went into effect, illustrated that assumption.[13] It was a four-volume
collection of sermons (almost 1,600 pages) titled *The American Preacher* and edited by David Austin, a young Yale graduate who pastored a Presbyterian church
in Elizabethtown, New Jersey. Sponsorship came from the upper reaches of society: the Presbyterian governor of New Jersey, the Dutch Reformed governor
of New York, the Episcopalian president of New York City's Columbia College,
and Elias Boudinot, the Presbyterian layman who had served as president of
the Continental Congress and enjoyed the confidence of George Washington.[14]
This ambitious project gathered seventy-seven sermons from a roster of thirty-
six contributors (college graduates all), including sixteen Congregationalists
(eleven from Connecticut), fourteen Presbyterians (all but two from New York,
New Jersey, and Pennsylvania), four Episcopalians, and two Dutch Reformed
ministers.

The sermons mostly rehearsed "the great truths of the gospel" with a Protestant evangelical accent. Yet with traditional theology came also the social and political instincts of the project's elite sponsors. In particular, several expressed the hope, frequently echoed in circles of leading Congregationalists and Presbyterians, that heeding these sermons would "add no small DIGNITY and SUPPORT to the POLITICAL INTERESTS of our country," especially by ensuring "safety and protection from the encroachment of arbitrary power."[15] The book's contributors, as it happens, included Uzal Ogden of New Jersey and James Muir of Virginia, who (as we have seen) would soon frame their responses to Paine's *Age of Reason* in these utilitarian terms. By assuming that society would naturally follow the leadership of religious elites, their appraisal sustained vestiges of Christendom.

In other words, old habits died hard.[16] Even as Presbyterians, Congregationalists, and Episcopalians joined in hailing American liberties, Congregationalists insisted on tax support for their churches in New England. Episcopalians in different states maneuvered to keep at least some of the Anglican privileges of the colonial era.[17] Several Presbyterians and Episcopalians, including John Witherspoon at Princeton and Patrick Henry in Virginia, explored schemes for taxes that citizens designated to support their own churches.[18] No longer did such men seek a national state church with uniform legal interweaving of religion and government. But informal Christendom—blasphemy laws remaining in place, the Bible still acknowledged as part of the common law, provision for some tax-supported religion alongside religious free exercise, assumptions about national leadership, and (later) energetic voluntary organizations—was another matter.

Proprietary Panic, ca. 1793–1802

The Federalists who supported the Constitution and framed new state governments foresaw a republic of virtue blissfully liberated from the corrupting partisanship that had fueled British tyranny. Shock, therefore, was the reaction when bitter partisan infighting broke out as President Washington moved into his second term. At a rush the factionless republican ideal vanished in heated controversy over the French Revolution, Citizen Genêt, the Jay Treaty, and whiskey rebels in western Pennsylvania—overlaid with nervousness about Indian warfare and the threat of slave rebellions and all whipped into a frenzy by aggressive newspaper warfare.

These shocks hastened the formation of a Federalist political party out of the general Federalism that had backed the Constitution. Just as their erstwhile allies now emerging as a Democratic-Republican party championed religious freedom with no holds barred—even welcoming deistic free thought—so also did religion infuse the Federalist mobilization of the 1790s. As Jonathan Den Hartog has recently demonstrated, this new Federalism drew noteworthy Protestant laymen into strategic alliances with a number of leading clerics.[19] The former included the evangelical Episcopalian John Jay (New York), the similarly evangelical Presbyterian Elias Boudinot (New Jersey), and the more traditional Presbyterian William Paterson, a signer of the Constitution, a New Jersey senator and governor, and then, like Jay, a justice on the U.S. Supreme Court. Well-placed Federalist ministers included the president of Yale College and grandson of Jonathan Edwards, Timothy Dwight; the president of the College of New Jersey at Princeton and son-in-law of John Witherspoon, Samuel Stanhope Smith; and the new nation's leading geographer and active Congregational strategist, Jedidiah Morse of Massachusetts.

These leaders joined their political avatars, especially Washington and John Adams, in viewing themselves as virtuous, disinterested republicans menaced by upstart so-called democrats wantonly despoiling the new nation's faction-free vineyard. Instinctively, religious Federalists accepted the challenge of instructing the public as a first-order civic responsibility. In keeping with previous social-religious instincts, they also assumed that retaining a virtuous republic required some kind of structured connection between the churches and public authority. Key figures like Boudinot, Jay, and Paterson took for granted that if a healthy society were to survive, it required the political defeat of Jefferson's Democratic-Republicans.

Caleb Strong, who became governor of Massachusetts in 1800, spoke eloquently for this vision. Strong grew up in the Northampton congregation once pastored by Jonathan Edwards. After stalwart service in the Revolution, he represented Massachusetts at the Constitutional Convention and as one of the state's first two U.S. senators. As political partisanship increased, he stood foursquare against the French, chastised the Democratic-Republicans for malfeasance at home and abroad, and turned increasingly to New England's Congregational heritage for ballast to right the ship of state. Strong's antidote to national dissolution looked backward to time-tested structures linking state and church rather than ahead to voluntary mobilization. Public worship and moral instruction in the schools were crucial: "As religion is the only sure foundation of human virtue, the prosperity of the State must be essentially promoted . . . by a due observance of the Sabbath, and by meeting together of the citizens to learn the duties of moral obligation, and contemplate the wisdom and goodness with which the Almighty governs the world."[20]

Like Strong, other religious Federalists regarded the defeat of the Jeffersonians as the only way to resist infidelity and, thereby, preserve the republic. Their conceptual framework remained thoroughly scriptural—with the Bible supplying tropes, rhetoric, and analogies with ancient Israel—but they did not yet look directly to the voluntary promotion of the Bible as medicine for the ailing republic. Biblical language, but without specific prescriptions from Scripture, infused the nervous chorus that in the spring and summer of 1798 sounded a panic-stricken alarm.

In early May, Jedidiah Morse fed Congregational anxiety in Boston when he preached from 2 Kings 19:3–4 on a national fast proclaimed by President Adams ("This day is a day of trouble, and of rebuke [or reviling] and blasphemy—Wherefore lift up thy prayer for the remnant that are left"). To Morse, the threat of France, home-grown atheism, and "our astonishing increase of *irreligion*" could be overcome only by repentance, prayer, and "with one heart [cleaving] to our government." Six weeks later, on the Fourth of July, Timothy Dwight preached to the same end in New Haven from Revelation 16:15 ("Behold I come as a thief. Blessed is he that watcheth, and keepeth his garments, lest he walk naked, and they see his shame"). Dwight's prescription for curing the evils of the day featured a frankly instrumental argument: "Without religion, we may possibly retain the freedom of savages, bears, and wolves, but not the freedom of New-England. If ever religion were gone, our state of society would perish with it; and nothing would be left, which will be worth defending."[21]

In both sermons, these Congregational worthies traced the United States' grave danger to the Bavarian Illuminati. They described this pernicious European cabal as a "secret plan . . . hostile to true liberty and religion" that was spreading French infidelity throughout the world and Jeffersonian subversion at home.[22] Military action against France, if required, and electoral defeat of Democratic-Republicans, if possible, seemed the only rescue for the new nation.

Among Presbyterian Federalists in the Atlantic states, fear of the Illuminati never took complete hold, but they too worried almost as obsessively. The Presbyterian General Assembly meeting at Philadelphia in May 1798 commissioned a letter to its churches that spelled out how "formidable innovations and convulsions in Europe threaten destruction to morals and religion." What should Presbyterians do in response? The answer was pray, repent, unite with other faithful believers, and respect the nation's rulers.[23] Not yet did the Presbyterians look to the distribution of Scripture as part of the solution.

At the College of New Jersey in Princeton, the administration of Samuel Stanhope Smith along with a board of trustees led by Elias Boudinot and William Paterson reacted to the crisis in much the same way, though with a telling addition. Shortly before the trustees officially installed Smith in 1795 as John Witherspoon's successor, he preached a memorable sermon on a day of thanksgiving proclaimed by President Washington. It provided an opportunity for Smith to articulate the republican connection he would soon consider in mortal danger. While "the gospel of Christ is the most precious gift which God hath bestowed upon mankind," he asserted, it is also "the surest basis of virtue and good morals, without which free states soon cease to exist."[24]

As the Jeffersonian tide rolled in, the mood soured and Princeton trustees responded with alarm. Leading members of their circle labeled their political opponents "jacobins" and specified the Christian faith as the only sure protection against dissolution. Paterson became known as the "avenger of Federalism" as he eagerly prosecuted critics of the Adams administration for violating the Alien and Sedition Acts. Particular gloom darkened the Princeton horizon when Democratic-Republicans won the governor's chair in New Jersey, since that elected official served ex officio on the Princeton board.[25]

As darkness settled over the land, Smith also hinted at what would become a new strategy to promote godliness and redeem the nation. When in 1800 disaster struck with the election of Jefferson, Smith expressed alarm with language recalling a time when officially certified elite leaders enjoyed greater respect: could, he wondered, "the *patricians* yet . . . save the republic, when the *tribunes* have urged it to the brink of ruin?"[26] Yet already a new note was appearing when in 1799 Smith wrote to Morse, who had sent Smith documents laying out his case against the Bavarian Illuminati. Smith, while fully sharing Morse's alarm, also asked whether Congregationalists and Presbyterians might not "discern the signs of the times, & . . . awaken to some zealous & combined effort to withstand the torrent of infidelity & immorality that is overspreading our country?"[27] Smith was raising the possibility that voluntary activity rather than direct political engagement might sustain the aims of Christian Federalism.

This move toward self-generated organization, disregarding political defeats and subordinating worry about out-of-control "tribunes," was, in fact, beginning to gather momentum. The year before, in 1798, Connecticut Congregationalists had created a missionary society, funded by free-will gifts, to send ministers into the rapidly opening frontier. Shortly thereafter, in 1801, Presbyterians and Congregationalists took the step that Smith proposed, by together creating a Plan of Union. This ambitious scheme, also funded voluntarily, proposed sharing ministers, jurisdictions, publishing, and support systems in order to plant civilizing churches in the wild west of upstate New York, the Ohio Territory, and points even farther beyond.[28]

To be sure, the turn was gradual from organized political activity to voluntary mobilization. With the creation of the first local Bible societies still a few years in the future, Scripture was just coming into focus as an object valuable for more than its themes, types, and exhortations. Before then, the election campaign of 1800 marked a transition for how Protestant Federalists hoped to secure a well-ordered society. While still looking backward to structured political domination, they also began peering forward toward voluntary mobilization with Scripture as the key.

In that heated contest, Federalists called Jefferson an "infidel" while depicting their candidate, the incumbent Adams, as a paragon of Christian-republican virtue.[29] Significantly, a Dutch Reformed minister in New York City, William Linn, specified the Bible as justification for standing with Adams: "[M]y objection to his [Jefferson's] being promoted to the Presidency is founded singly upon his disbelief in the Holy Scriptures." According to Linn, Jefferson doubted the Mosaic history of Noah and the Flood; he also wanted schoolchildren to learn Greek and Roman history before even opening the Bible. Linn expatiated at length on how Jefferson's derogatory statements about African Americans, "degrad[ing] the blacks from the rank which God hath given them in the scale of being," violated Scripture's bedrock insistence on the full humanity of all persons.[30]

Some Federalists, like the worried citizens who reportedly hid bibles down wells in fear that a victorious Jefferson would issue an order of confiscation, simply panicked.[31] Linn, by contrast, painstakingly specified why he treated Jefferson's attitude toward Scripture as such a grave political threat. He was particularly infuriated by an often-quoted assertion from Jefferson's *Notes on the State of Virginia* (1788), "It does me no injury for my neighbour to say there are twenty gods, or no god. It neither picks my pocket, nor breaks my leg." To Linn, the social consequences of this opinion could not be more devastating: "[L]et my neighbour once persuade himself that there is no God, and he will soon pick my pocket, and break not only my *leg* but my *neck*." In a word, if Jefferson were elected, "the effects would be, to destroy religion, introduce immorality, and loosen all the bonds of society."[32]

In 1800 it was obvious to Federalists like Linn that attitudes toward Scripture entailed broad social consequences. If it would take a few more years for Linn and like-minded "patricians" to overcome the instincts of formal Christendom, they were in fact adjusting to new American realities. Soon it would be clear that the only way to retain influence required self-directed organization rather than licensed authorization, voluntary funding rather than tax subsidies, control of public opinion rather than control of the government. As this realization dawned, their approach to the Bible also evolved. While Scripture remained indispensable for personal religion and church order, it also became *the* tool for ensuring the well-being of a free people in a free society. Put differently, Christian Federalists needed a significant mental readjustment to catch up with other Protestants who had already grasped American liberty with both hands.

Sectarian Advance, 1776–1802

The fate of religion in the new nation did not, in fact, depend for long on what the leaders of the older denominations thought should happen. The rapidly

expanding hosts who also gloried in American liberty and who also highly honored the Bible—but who did not defer to inherited status, elite education, and
top-down organization—were already emerging from the shadows. In the new
United States, self-educated Protestants were exploiting the potential of democracy, eagerly evangelizing the rapidly filling backcountry, and trumpeting republican protests against coercion of any form. Compared to representatives of
the traditional denominations, these upstarts advocated a stronger supernat-
uralist faith, but usually without fixating on the millennium or trying to explain contemporary events as the fulfillment of biblical prophecy. Instead, they
offered a Christianity keyed almost entirely to the needs of individuals, families, and localities. Baptists and newer sectarian movements differed among
themselves in religious convictions, as well as on how actively to oppose anything like a national informal Christendom. Yet in the aggregate they offered
a forceful alternative to the proprietary Presbyterians, Congregationalists, and
Episcopalians.

As leading representatives of the older colonial churches merged their interests
with the nascent Federalist Party, took fright at the Revolution in France, rushed
to attack Paine as representing social dissolution as well as religious disaster, and
at the end of the decade panicked over the Bavarian Illuminati—so adherents
in the formerly marginal churches flocked to the Democratic-Republicans,
remained neutral concerning violence in France, joined in rebuking Paine for his
theology (but not his politics), and enlisted Scripture to combat the proprietary
Protestants. Along with the Methodists, these sectarians were also becoming
"American preachers."

A nineteenth-century German theologian, Ernst Troeltsch, gave "sectarian"
its generic meaning when he contrasted religious movements of the middle
and upper classes that wove religious concerns into efforts at directing society
("churchly") with movements of protest that sought true religion as an end in
itself with little concern for social comprehension ("sectarian").[33] Perceptive
American historians have offered roughly equivalent terms to describe those
who, fearing all top-down efforts at prescribing social conformity, instead promoted local religious self-government: *pietist* (as opposed to liturgical), *informal*
(as opposed to formal), *frontier* (as opposed to national), *democratic* and *entrepreneurial* (as opposed to deferential and proprietary).[34]

Sectarian Protestant movements had existed since the radical early
pronouncements of Martin Luther, but only as a submerged counterpoint to
the "magisterial" Protestants whose teachers (*magistri*) allied themselves with
Protestant rulers, who in turn appointed them as religious guides for their
regimes.[35] In the English-speaking world, Baptists since the seventeenth century
had led a considerable number of restive Protestants in criticizing the structures
of church-state Christendom. Sometimes these groups even allowed women a

public role, but always they insisted that coercive national organizations vitiated rather than promoted vital personal religion.[36]

Significantly, Baptists and other sectarians had always deployed the Bible as their chief weapon against the forces of formal Christendom. In these attacks, they often pushed the customary Protestant reliance on Scripture toward biblicism—the profession to follow *only* the Bible and no other authorities. Regularly they deployed straightforward, literal interpretations of biblical texts to attack inherited beliefs and practices. Usually they emphasized "the priesthood of all believers" or the intellectual democratization that long remained more Protestant theory than Protestant practice.[37] For them, the "right of private interpretation" had always been important. That "right" became even more important in the eighteenth century when strengthened by John Locke's epistemology of personal experience and republican fears of coercive elites. While not opposed to allegorical or typological interpretations of Scripture, sectarians customarily viewed local Christian assemblies, rather than the British Empire or the new United States, as the anti-type of Old Testament types.

This sectarian tradition remained a subordinate Protestant stream until it overflowed its banks in the new American nation. When in the first decade of the Reformation, peasants quoted the Bible (and Martin Luther) to support their complaints against aristocratic landowners, they drew a vicious response from Luther and violent slaughter from the landowners.[38] Roger Williams marshaled hundreds of biblical quotations in his 1644 *Bloudy Tenent of Persecution for Cause of Conscience* to protest New England's Congregational establishment. But Williams and his book were forgotten until Baptists at the time of the Revolution resurrected his memory.[39] Congregational New England dismissed the first president of Harvard College, Henry Dunster, when he concluded about the baptism of children, "All instituted gospel worship hath some express word of Scripture. . . . But paedobaptism has none."[40] In the 1750s, Quakers John Woolman and Anthony Benezet based strong attacks against slavery on the Bible—Woolman by invoking the kind of more-than-tribal love that Jesus preached in Matthew 12:48, Benezet by setting forth "the absolute Necessity of Self-Denial, renouncing the World, and true Charity for all such as sincerely Desire to be our blessed Saviour's Disciples."[41] But outside of Quaker circles, the colonists did not address questions about slavery and Scripture until the early 1770s, when Real Whig protests against "enslavement" by Parliament prompted a few Bible readers to wonder about enslavement of Africans.[42] In late colonial Virginia, Baptists who tried to organize churches according to what they considered the biblical pattern were threatened, thwarted, and sometimes assaulted by representatives of the colony's Anglican establishment.[43] During and after the Revolution, libertarian sects proliferated in the New England backcountry while beginning to appear in other regions as well. Inspired by the War of *Independence*,

Freewill Baptists, Universalists, and Shakers repudiated the establishment's Calvinistic theology even as they proselytized and formed conventicles without bothering to ask permission.[44] Yet these outcries from the frontier barely registered with the leaders busy constructing the new nation.

In those very years, however, a shift of great consequence took place. Baptist spokesmen led the way as the sectarian spirit blossomed (or, in Federalist eyes, metastasized). Isaac Backus, who was converted during the Great Awakening, later became a key organizer of Baptist fellowships in New England. During the strife with Britain, he supported the patriot cause but, encouraged by Quakers, also challenged John Adams and Sam Adams for upholding Massachusetts laws oppressing Baptists while they protested British tyranny.[45] After the war, Backus entered public life as few of his number had done before, including standing for election as a delegate to the 1788 Massachusetts convention that ratified the national Constitution. At that convention, Backus leaned on the Bible to attack religious tests for federal officeholders by contending, "[N]othing is more evident, both in reason, and in the holy scriptures, than that religion is ever a matter between God and individuals, and therefore no man or men can impose any religious test, without invading the essential prerogatives of our Lord Jesus Christ." This intervention reasserted the time-honored Dissenting principle of "the right of private judgment" for all questions of biblical interpretation and religious adherence, a principle that had earlier contributed a distinctly Christian element to the Revolutionary rejection of the Anglican state-church establishment. Now Backus turned it against the American remnants of Christendom.[46]

More remarkably, not only did Backus attempt to influence public policy through a direct appeal to Scripture, but he did so on the subject of slavery that would become the greatest challenge to the construction of a national Bible civilization. When Backus took up the concessions to slavery in the proposed federal Constitution, he moved from simply asserting the authority of "the holy scriptures" to spelling out how that authority should be heeded. In a complex argument against slavery and the slave trade, he started with the Old Testament "covenant of circumcision" that had given Abraham the right to enslave the Canaanites. But then Backus, indicating that this Abrahamic covenant had been "expressly repealed in various parts of the New Testament," launched into quotations from 1 Corinthians 6:20, 7:19, and 7:23 ("Ye are bought with a price . . . circumcision is nothing and uncircumcision is nothing . . . be not ye the servants of men"). His conclusion for the Massachusetts convention summed up what he took to be the Bible's testimony against slavery: "There the gospel sets all men upon a level."[47] Again, while not entirely new, Backus's didactic application of Scripture to a matter of public policy anticipated much more of the same to come.

The career of John Leland, who succeeded Backus as the Baptists' chief national spokesman, illustrates even more clearly the sectarian use of Scripture that gained strength in the 1790s. Leland had been converted under Baptist influence as a young man in his native Massachusetts, but then migrated to Virginia just as the War of Independence broke out. Even as he concentrated on planting Baptist churches, he soon became a political ally of James Madison because of their shared commitment to religious freedom.[48]

To Leland, the American dedication to liberty offered the most direct support imaginable for his sectarian approach to Scripture. In an early Virginia publication titled *The Bible Baptist* he energetically expanded upon Henry Dunster's claim that baptizing babies would cease if believers would "simply regard the Bible" and rely on the "plain truths of Scripture" instead of "traditions, prejudices or systematical myths."[49] In the tract's preface, Leland also explained why the temper of the times supported this way of using the Bible: "Lies have often atoned for ignorance and ill-will in the East and European worlds; but let the Sons of *America* be free. . . . Truth is in the least danger of being lost, when free examination is allowed. As our government gives us this privilege, I am determined to improve it myself, and recommend it to others."[50] Yet when Leland intervened in debates over ratification of the Constitution, he put Scripture to use only rhetorically. Addressing what seemed to him an ambiguity in the proposed document, he framed his argument with embellishment from the Book of Judges (14:18): "I Question whether a man could find out the Riddle by plowing with Samson's Heifer."[51] Not yet was the Bible for Leland a tool for shaping public opinion.

When, however, he returned to Massachusetts and in 1794 published his thoughts on the governance of that state, it was a different story. Against the continued provision of tax support for Protestant (i.e., Congregational) ministers, Leland brandished the sword of the Lord. "How much," he asked, "did John the Baptist, Jesus, Peter, James or John, ask per year?" The answer lay in a stark disjunction: "If a man preaches Jesus, he cannot take enough for it; the gold of Ophir [Job 18:26; Ps 45:9; and elsewhere] cannot equal it; if he preaches himself, it is good for nothing." To Leland, it was "harmonical" for Massachusetts to follow the New Testament, where "the Lord ordained that those that preach the gospel shall live by its institutions and precepts." In contrast, it was "discordant" when "the legislature shall require men to maintain teachers of piety, religion, and morality."[52] Leland, in short, denounced provisions in the Massachusetts Constitution designed to promote religion and morality as in fact a subversion of the Christian gospel as taught by Christ himself.

During the election of 1800, while Federalists anguished over Jefferson's abuse of Scripture, Leland enthusiastically backed James Madison's partner for protecting Baptists against the Federalists. To celebrate the Democratic-Republicans' victory, Leland collected money from Massachusetts Baptists to fashion a giant wheel of cheese he then paraded on a meandering speaking tour before presenting it to the president on January 1, 1802. The cheese, which Leland claimed came from hundreds of "republican cows," weighed in at more than half a ton; on its crust was inscribed the Jeffersonian maxim "Resistance to tyrants is obedience to God." In response, Jefferson thanked Leland and his friends with the assurance that he stood foursquare with them in supporting "the prohibition of religious tests." He also asked Leland to preach the sermon at the next Sunday worship service held, as it was for several years, at the Capitol.[53] When at that service Leland took his text from Matthew 12:42 ("a greater than Solomon is here"), apoplectic Federalists considered it sacrilege.[54] Two days earlier, on January 1, even as Jefferson acknowledged the gift of cheese from Leland, he also drafted his famous letter to the Baptists of Danbury, Connecticut. To these sectarians, who stood with their fellow Baptist Leland in supporting the president as the guardian of liberty, Jefferson wrote that he "contemplate[d] with sovereign reverence" the religion clauses of the First Amendment as "building a wall of separation between Church and State."[55]

In their opposition to religious coercion, whether experienced full-blown in the old world or only residually in the new, sectarian Protestants advanced time after time with Scripture in hand. Whenever the defenders of Christendom, and then the proprietary Protestants, augmented their own scriptural arguments with tradition, governmental authority, learned scholarship, Reason, or elitist presumptions of any kind, sectarians blasted back with the Bible alone. Backus and Leland upheld this sectarian legacy when they stepped out boldly into American public life. The difference now was that in Jefferson's "Empire of Liberty," they, rather than the hereditary elites, were setting the rules of the game.[56]

Public Advocacy Supersedes Electoral Politics, ca. 1800–1817

The framework of American religion and public life shifted decisively during the presidential administrations of Jefferson (1801–9) and his hand-picked Virginia successor James Madison (1809–17). The most visible sign of the shift was the gradual turn by Christian Federalists away from soft Christendom to informal Christendom, that is, from legal or legislative means for preserving Christian civilization to voluntary means. The most obvious development for the history of the Bible was the broader adoption of sectarian practices for putting Scripture to use. As sectarian and Methodist activity continued to expand, and as Baptists, Sandemanians, "Disciples," and "Christians" scorned the strategies of informal

Christendom (viewing it as tyrannical Christendom in a new guise), a republican Bible competed successfully against the proprietary Scriptures.

Events also transformed the Christian Federalism that custodial Protestants
had trusted to advance Christian faith and preserve the social benefits of
Christianity. When in 1800 the infidel Jefferson defeated the defender of church
establishments, Adams, the nation shuddered but did not fall. Mysteriously, the
Illuminati simply faded away. Surprisingly, peace prevailed and prosperity advanced. Population growth, almost all by natural increase, continued at 3 or 4%
per year. Leading Congregationalists and Presbyterians still lamented threats to
religion, but, as the next chapter details, Methodist expansion continued unabated. Even as the proprietary churches themselves reaped a harvest from new
seasons of revival, other Protestant movements advanced almost as rapidly as the
Methodists.

Events in the last Jefferson years and under President Madison did stimulate
New England and Federalist political zeal, though with decreasing national effect.
Jefferson's embargo of 1807—an attempt to stop British and French attacks on
American shipping and impressment of American sailors—inflamed Federalist
mercantile interests. But in the election of 1808, Madison easily triumphed
over Charles Cotesworth Pinckney of South Carolina, who represented the
Federalists' rapidly shrinking southern interests. At the next national poll, in
1812, with war declared against Great Britain and active combat around Detroit
and on the Niagara Peninsula, Federalists did better—but only by backing a
dissident Democratic-Republican, DeWitt Clinton of New York. Yet even with
Mid-Atlantic trading interests joining New England's cultural opposition to all
things Virginian, the final tally was not close: for Madison 128 electoral votes,
for Clinton 89. New England's opposition to the War of 1812, climaxed by the
ill-timed Hartford Convention of December 1814 and January 1815, delivered
the coup de grâce to national Federalism.[57] News of the convention's protests,
resistance, and even contemplation of secession had barely begun to spread before the glad tidings arrived of Andrew Jackson's demolition of a British army at
New Orleans. With this glorious national vindication added to the Federalists'
apparent disloyalty, their party was no more.

For the proprietary Protestants who had pinned their hopes for the nation
on Federalist electoral victory, additional moral and religious crises dictated a
change of course. Growing discomfort in New England with slavery—and with
southern Federalist slave owners, like Pinckney—contributed to the alteration.
Dismaying religious events closer to home meant even more.

In 1805 the appointment of a Unitarian as the Harvard theology professor exposed a theological rift among New England's establishmentarian
Protestants.[58] Even if most Massachusetts Congregationalists would together
support the state's tax provision for churches until it finally ended in 1833,

traditional Trinitarian Congregationalists embarked on a new course. Morse, who had earlier poured his energy into electoral politics, led the way. In rapid succession, he launched a new periodical to defend orthodox theology (*The Panoplist*, 1805). He overcame theological scruples about cooperating with the heirs of Jonathan Edwards's theology and with them founded a theological school, Andover Seminary, to challenge instruction at Harvard (1807). And he helped organize a new Boston church, Park Street, adjacent to Boston Common, to counter the city's drift toward Unitarianism (1809). Remaining the same for Morse and his like-minded colleagues was their expectation that broad-based institutions and organized activity were crucial for advancing Christianity and preserving the republic. New was their effort to achieve these goals through voluntary means.

In Connecticut, it took only a little longer for the state's traditional religious leaders to abandon the remnants of Christendom and adopt voluntary approaches adjusted to new American realities. As president of Yale from 1795 to 1817, Dwight stood firm for trust in the Bible, American patriotism, the Federalist Party, and Connecticut's church establishment. One of his most able students, the pastor-social activist Lyman Beecher, at first echoed his mentor's concerns. But only so long as Dwight remained alive.

When, in 1817, Connecticut's Democratic-Republicans finally defeated the Federalists and took control of state government, they moved rapidly to write a new constitution replacing the charter from colonial days. In by now standard Jeffersonian fashion, the new constitution removed references to the state's dependence on God and ended tax support for Congregational churches. Beecher, who had campaigned aggressively against the change, thought the end of Christian civilization had come. "It was," he wrote later, "as dark a day as ever I saw." But Beecher, always mercurial, recovered quickly. He reported with emphasis in his autobiography, "For several days I suffered what no tongue can tell *for the best thing that ever happened to the State of Connecticut.*" Because, as he came to see, the new constitution liberated the churches "from dependence on state support" and "threw them wholly on their own resources and on God," the defenders of Christian civilization could now "exert a deeper influence than ever." He then specified the new means: "voluntary efforts, societies, missions, and revivals."[59] Over the next four decades, Beecher exploited these means to the full—campaigning against dueling and for temperance, promoting controlled revivals while opposing revivalistic excesses, launching a substantial periodical (*Spirit of the Pilgrims*), combating Episcopal pretensions, attacking the Catholic menace, supporting collegiate and advanced theological education, and moving his own large family to Cincinnati to demonstrate his dedication to the opening West. But after his change of heart in 1817–18, he did not seek formal state support for these ventures.

A similar move from electoral politics to voluntary mobilization took place among Presbyterians and Episcopalians in the Atlantic states. At the College of New Jersey in Princeton, contrasting reactions to upsetting calamities spelled out the new course. When a fire in 1802 devastated much of the college's main building, President Smith reacted as an embattled Christian Federalist. Within a week, he wrote Jedidiah Morse that, although "direct proof" was lacking, it looked like an event caused by the conspiracy Morse had warned against: the fire, which seemed to be "communicated by design," was "one effect of those irreligious and demoralizing principles which are tearing the bands of society asunder and threatening in the end to overturn our country." Yet Smith assured Morse that the college, "the last bulwark of old principles to the South of your state," would prevail.[60]

Five years later, in late March 1807, Princeton students joined their peers elsewhere by revolting against what they considered tyrannical college authority. The trustees expelled the rioters (half of the student body) but also prescribed a new ideological remedy. Over the next several years, trustees who had grown disillusioned with President Smith's leadership filled their ranks with appointments replacing the patriotic Federalists of the Revolutionary era. The new men included Rev. Samuel Miller of New York City, who only shortly before had written an effusive letter of praise to Jefferson.[61] Most of the other new trustees did not share Miller's enthusiasm for Jefferson, but they largely abandoned overt political activity in favor of new strategies, including the creation of a theological seminary for Presbyterians in imitation of Andover in Massachusetts.[62]

Elias Boudinot, Princeton's longest-serving trustee, testified directly to this shift in direction. When classes resumed after the riot, he was chosen to address the much-reduced student body. Boudinot did echo the past when he blasted the ideologies the board held responsible for the student outrage: "the clumsy sophistry of Godwin; the pernicious subtilties of Hume, and the coarse vulgarities of Paine." But instead of a political recourse, Boudinot urged the students to an honorable pursuit of "Literature & Religion, the two main pillars of the social fabric." To which he added a plea for students to pursue "that blessed *System of Life and Immortality* [quoting 2 Tim 1:10], which has been brought to light by the divine Messenger from Heaven."[63] Already by 1807, Boudinot had also begun to admire the British and Foreign Bible Society for its efforts at voluntarily distributing the Scriptures.

Boudinot lived long enough to be joined by the offspring of some of his longtime Federalist colleagues as together they turned to promote revivals, voluntary societies, and privately funded educational ventures. Two of his younger associates, brothers William and Peter Augustus Jay, shared the Federalist convictions of their father, John Jay, but like Boudinot no longer relied on electoral politics to advance their Christian and social goals. Jonathan Den Hartog has described William Jay's public career as an exercise in "nonpolitical moral and religious reform."[64] This younger Jay maintained a strictly nonpartisan stance as a New York state judge, even as he raised money for organizations like the Bedford County Society Against Intemperance and Vice, the Westchester County Bible Society, and eventually the American Bible Society. Peter Augustus Jay took the same course. When he addressed the inaugural meeting of the American Bible Society in 1816, he lauded the spiritual good to come from widespread Bible distribution, but he also paused to envision the temporal effects: "Where do you find Knowledge & Humanity & Charity? Where does conscience flourish— where does Liberty dwell? Nowhere but in the Christian world."[65]

As Boudinot, the sons of John Jay, and other Christian Federalists put more and more of their energy into voluntary activity, they retained their earlier vision of a healthy society. Liberty, defined in both Protestant and conservative republican terms, remained the ideal. But increasingly they strove to realize that ideal by the free distribution of the Scriptures. As they made this move, they began to sound more and more like the upstart Protestants who had not required an ideological readjustment to exploit the *novus ordo seclorum*.

Sectarian Protestants surged in the new republic because of down-to-earth preaching, general earnestness, eagerness to evangelize the frontier—and aggressive reliance on the Bible alone. Accounts of Baptist expansion are riddled with Scripture deployed rhetorically, didactically, and authoritatively, as in a recent expert survey by Thomas Kidd and Barry Hankins. Baptist preachers urged crowds at frontier revivals not to "transgress all the rules of decency and order [1 Cor 14:40] established by right reason, but even by the Word of God." The New York Baptist association reported that the labors of a missionary among the Tuscarora Indians had "raised our expectations that God is about more extensively to fulfill his glorious prophecies . . . where he has said, 'I will even make a way in the wilderness, and rivers in the desert' [Isa 43:19]." In Boston, Mary Webb with thirteen other women in 1800 organized a Female Society for Missionary Purposes to distribute Bibles and other Christian literature "by missionaries in destitute places." Study of the Bible led Ann Haseltine Judson to join her missionary husband, Adoniram, in leaving the Congregationalists for the Baptists because they could find nothing in the New Testament to support infant baptism. A female slave, Letty, turned aside from thoughts of suicide because of Baptist preaching from Matthew 25:34 ("Come, ye blessed of the Father, inherit the kingdom prepared for you from the foundation of the world").[66] And more and more without let-up.

Yet even as Baptists made great strides in their biblical advocacy, new Protestants movements, either inspired directly by American liberty or flourishing in the American context, took off almost as spectacularly. In New England, Elias Smith supercharged a "Christian" movement that disdained hereditary church and social structures in favor of a gospel message preached straight from the pages of Scripture.[67] In a flurry of publications supported by energetic itinerant preaching, leading to a network of local "Christian" assemblies, Smith hammered away and hammered some more. In 1807, he defended believers' baptism by immersion as the only practice supported by "plain scriptural expressions."[68] The next year he showed how all notions of predestination "contradict[ed] the plain declaration of the scripture."[69] Then, in a bravura performance on the Fourth of July 1809, he preached a memorable sermon in Taunton, Massachusetts, under the title *The Lovingkindness of God Displayed in the Triumph of Republicanism in America*. His text was Psalm 107:43 ("Whoso is wise, and will observe these things, even they, shall understand the lovingkindness of the Lord"). As he reflected on this passage, Smith reminded listeners that the British church establishment was "tyrannical." He defended the Democratic-Republicans for guaranteeing that "no restraint or constraint is allowed by law in things respecting religion." And he defined religious liberty as above all "being wholly free to examine for ourselves, what is truth without being bound to a catechism, creed, confession of faith, discipline, or any rule excepting the scriptures." It was a liberty that included the ability to preach without molestation and to be entirely free from tax support for ministers.[70]

A similar ardent biblicism also marked the labors of Barton W. Stone and Alexander Campbell, whose "Christian" movement further to the south led to permanent networks of Christian churches, Churches of Christ, and Disciples of Christ. (It was pronounced CHRIST-i-an to stress the prominence of Christ as recorded in the biblical text.) Thomas Campbell and his son Alexander, Scots-Irish immigrants who arrived in the first decade of the century, enjoyed unusual prominence in this Restorationist movement. In the old world, the Campbells had already proclaimed their dedication to Scripture, but they had also absorbed the epistemology of John Locke (including a stress on "simple ideas"), the principles of Scottish commonsense philosophy (including commitment to inductive scientific method), and the antitraditional stance of Scottish evangelicals James and Robert Haldane (including a profession to live by the Bible as their only guide). In the new world, the Campbells' devotion to Scripture and the elaboration of their interpretive principles proved unusually attractive to Americans moving westward beyond the Appalachians. For the purpose of *restoring* the primitive, nonsectarian faith of the Book of Acts, the Campbells deliberately dispensed with the historical Christian creeds, ridiculed systems of doctrine like Calvinism as mere philosophical speculation, and denounced traditional rites like infant baptism as simply unbiblical. In a landmark "Declaration and Address" from 1809, Thomas Campbell wrote, "[I]t is high time for us not only to think, but also to act, for ourselves . . . to take all of our measures directly and immediately from the Divine Standard." Authentic Christianity should be characterized by "returning to, and holding fast by, the original standard; taking the divine word alone for our rule; the Holy Spirit for our teacher and guide, to lead us into all truth; and Christ alone, as exhibited in the word, for our salvation."[71] Alexander Campbell dedicated himself to spreading these principles, as he explained two decades later: "I have been so long disciplined in the school of free inquiry, that, if I know my own mind, there is not a man upon the earth whose authority can influence me, any farther then he comes with the authority of evidence, reason, and truth. . . . I have endeavored to read the Scriptures as though no one had read them before me."[72]

From these principles, most Restorationists interpreted Scripture as vesting all church authority in local assemblies, featuring mental assent to the Christian message as a key to redemption, viewing adult believer baptism by immersion as an ordinance required for salvation, and mandating worship without musical instruments. Alexander Campbell would become renowned for his willingness to engage in widely publicized public debates with notable opponents—including a Presbyterian over baptism and church order in 1820, the British socialist and free thinker Robert Owen in 1829, and the Catholic bishop of Cincinnati John Purcell in 1837—and then to publish transcripts of these public spectacles.[73] In person and in print, the Bible and the canons of republican freedom were Campbell's sole authorities.

Efforts by the Baptists, Elias Smith, Alexander Campbell, and other sectarians represented an ever-growing proportion of the new nation's Protestant population. Increasingly, however, proprietary Protestants also joined their sectarian peers in direct appeals to "the Bible only" as they debated contested points in the churches and tried to shape civil society. The former was illustrated by a vigorous contention between Episcopalians and Presbyterians, which reached from the last years of the Jefferson presidency well into the next decade. The leading New York defender of episcopacy, John Henry Hobart, claimed that church government by bishops "was supported by SCRIPTURE and ANTIQUITY."[74] His opponents, who included William Linn, the publicist targeting Jefferson's infidelity, and Samuel Miller, the Princeton trustee, appealed primarily to Scripture, though with supporting references to the political principles of the new nation. Linn declared, "As the . . . Presbyterial form of Church Government is the true and only one which Christ hath prescribed in his word, so it is the best adapted to the temper of the United States and the most conformable to their institutions of civil government."[75] Miller believed that "[e]very man is required to examine, to believe, and to obey the gospel for himself," a process that should lead discerning thinkers to see that Presbyterian church order was "as nearly conformable to apostolic and primitive order as any on earth."[76] A few years later, an anonymous layman wrote against Hobart for wanting copies of the Bible bound with the Book of Common Prayer, To this layman, it looked like "the early stages of Papal usurpation" for Episcopalians, "if the Scripture be the perfect rule, [to] insist on the necessity of a *digest* to accompany it."[77] Increasingly, proprietary Protestants brought the same reasoning to bear on public life, as later chapters explain in detail.

Sectarians took naturally to chapter and verse guidance for social as well as religious purposes. Their differences with Congregationalists, Presbyterians, and Episcopalians came not in loyalty to the Bible but by expressing that loyalty in ardently republican terms. To many of them, even organizations that had nothing to do with governmental coercion seemed but a pale shadow of top-down efforts to circumvent the right of private judgment, particularly concerning the interpretation of Scripture. As respected Federalist leaders like Elias Boudinot, Samuel Stanhope Smith, and the sons of John Jay moved away from electoral politics to voluntary mobilization, Baptists, Campbellites, and "Christians" barely acknowledged the difference. For them, it was not only state-sponsored top-down organization that threatened biblical Christianity, but top-down organization of any kind. So it was that even as proprietary Protestants shifted their energies from combating President Madison and trying to stop the War of 1812, sectarian Protestants began to worry about voluntary organizations like missionary societies, moral reform societies, and, not least, Bible societies.

By the early nineteenth century, American Protestants en masse had rejected even the vestiges of formal Christendom. While potent disagreements festered concerning the informal means that proprietary Protestants increasingly used to sustain Christianity without a formal Christendom, the contenders agreed that reliance on Scripture was imperative. For some, that reliance spurred heroic voluntary organization, for others, heroic resistance to these same organizations. Their approaches, though opposed, together played a large part in creating the American Bible civilization. Yet that part may not have been as crucial as the labors of Methodists who in their formative American years both ignored electoral politics and forswore polemics over how to use the Bible. Patiently, quietly, and often below the horizon of visibility, the Methodist pursuit of scriptural holiness transformed the land.

4

Francis Asbury and the Methodists

On Friday, May 29, 1789, Francis Asbury and Thomas Coke, the presiding bishops of the Methodist Episcopal Church in the United States, presented a congratulatory message from their denomination to George Washington, newly installed as the country's first president under the Constitution. Their address, which heralded the hero of the Revolution as "a friend of mankind," expressed special satisfaction that the new president had often acknowledged "the Great Governor of the universe" as "the source of every blessing, and particularly of the most excellent constitution of these states, which is at present the admiration of the world." Washington replied in kind with grateful acknowledgment of "the assistance of Divine Providence" and with a pledge that he would "always strive to prove a faithful and impartial partisan of genuine vital religion."[1]

Two days later Asbury, who had come to New York City, then the nation's capital, to convene the annual meeting of the Methodists' New York Conference, preached to this body on Isaiah 25:6, a passage describing the joy that awaited God's faithful servants: "And in this mountain shall the Lord of Hosts make unto all people a feast of fat things; a feast of wines on the lees; of fat things full of marrow; of wines on the lees well refined." Asbury regularly published his journal, which served as a tangible means for the bishop to stay in touch with his far-flung fellow itinerants and the even more widely dispersed adherents of the Methodist movement. In the account he offered the public for the last week of May 1789, Asbury made no mention of meeting President Washington but did describe how he "applied" the passage from Isaiah to the assembled Methodists.[2] That ordering of Asbury's priorities—dutifully attending to civic responsibilities but subordinating all such concerns to advance his spiritual mission—spoke volumes about the influential place of the Methodists in American religious history and especially their importance for the history of the Bible.

The rise of Methodism ranks among the most important developments in the early history of the United States. In 1780 a Delaware gentleman, observing Methodist efforts to build a chapel in his state, scoffed, "It is unnecessary to build such a house, for by the time the war is over, a corncrib will hold them all."[3] Two generations later observers knew better. When Charles Finney, who was then a Presbyterian, paused to consider the Methodists in his influential *Lectures on Revivals of Religion* from 1835, his judgment recorded an unprecedented religious transformation: "Wherever the Methodists have gone, their plain, pointed

America's Book. Mark A. Noll, Oxford University Press. © Oxford University Press 2022.
DOI: 10.1093/oso/9780197623466.003.0005

and simple, but warm and animated mode of preaching has always gathered congregations. . . . We must have exciting, powerful preaching, or the devil will have the people, except what the Methodists can save."[4]

Of course the Methodists on their own did not dominate everything and everywhere. Other religious movements and varied responses to contingent national events also wrote much of the story. These also obviously contributed substantially to the history of the Bible. Yet Methodists were the shock troops who did the most to secure the unquestioned preeminence of Scripture in post-Christendom America. To overstate things only slightly, Abraham Lincoln in his Second Inaugural Address could not have said of the Union and the Confederacy "Both read the same Bible and pray to the same God" if Asbury and his fellow itinerants had not so tirelessly preached, and had not so many heeded their appeal for, "scriptural holiness."

The Methodist Transition

American Methodism was an offshoot of an Anglican renewal movement founded by two indefatigably energetic brothers, John and Charles Wesley. At Christmas in 1784, Americans inspired by the Wesleys gathered in Baltimore to organize themselves into an ecclesiastical body separate from the Church of England—still professing to follow the lead of John Wesley on questions of church order but striking out on their own under the direction of the two "superintendents" who had been appointed by Wesley (but also elected by those who came to Baltimore). One of the superintendents, soon to be called "bishops," was Thomas Coke, an Oxford-trained doctor of civil laws who would travel regularly between England and the United States, as well as throughout the Atlantic world and beyond, on behalf of the movement. The other was Francis Asbury, already recognized as the Methodists' driving spirit on the North American mainland. Asbury had been born near Birmingham in 1745, the son of a farm laborer and gardener; as a young teen he was apprenticed to a local metal worker and also experienced an evangelical conversion. Through Methodist contacts he soon gained assurance of salvation and began to exhort as a lay preacher. In 1768 John Wesley received him into full connection as one of his authorized itinerants; three years later Wesley dispatched him to the colonies to assist the fledging bands of Methodists who had sprung up in the new world. For the next fifty-five years, apart from a brief period during the Revolutionary War when he lay low because of the Wesleys' well-publicized opposition to American independence, Asbury traveled constantly, preached the Methodist message, recruited itinerants, encouraged local societies, organized quarterly love feasts, chaired annual conferences, and in general directed what a later Baptist opponent would deride as the Methodists' "great iron wheel" of coordination and control.[5]

When the Baltimore meeting took place in late 1784, there were not quite fifteen thousand American Methodists enrolled "in society," served by eighty-three itinerant preachers—that is, a denomination with slightly fewer adherents than the tiny American Catholic church and slightly more active preachers than Catholic priests.[6] The account that follows draws on excellent scholarship from the past quarter-century that has explained how the Methodists could emerge from these humble beginnings to become within mere decades the largest and most active Protestant denomination in the predominantly Protestant United States.[7]

Shortly after the 1784 Christmas Conference, Asbury and Coke published "Minutes of . . . Conversations" that had taken place in Baltimore. As guidance for American adherents, who were giving new meaning to what "far-flung" entailed in the vast expanse of the new nation, the superintendents published their record in catechetical form: direct questions prompting pithy answers. In this short pamphlet can be glimpsed the secret not just of early American Methodism's startling numerical success but also of its enduring contribution to the history of Scripture. Three elements predominated: a specific approach to the Bible itself, a particular attitude toward religious authority, and a dedication to almost exclusively spiritual, nonpolitical goals.

Methodists, whose professions about Scripture replicated standard Protestant teaching, dedicated themselves to a singular vision of personal holiness as the central imperative of biblical religion. In the 1784 *Minutes* the first three questions and answers paid respect to the inspirational leadership of John Wesley and defined their movement as "an Episcopal church under the Direction of Superintendents, Elders, Deacons, and Helpers." Then the fourth made the Methodist distinctive explicit: "Q. 4. What may we reasonably believe to be God's Design in raising up the Preachers called *Methodists*? A. To reform the Continent, and to spread scriptural holiness over these Lands." In the fifth, a sharply pointed history lesson detailed the specific emphases they drew from Scripture:

Q. 5. What was the Rise of *Methodism*, so called?

A. In 1729, two young Men, reading the Bible, saw they could not be saved without Holiness, followed after it, and incited others so to do. In 1737, they saw Holiness comes by Faith. They saw likewise, that Men are justified, before they are sanctified: but still Holiness was their Point. God then thrust them out, utterly against their Will, to raise an holy People.[8]

The Methodist message came from "reading the Bible," but with a definite purpose in view. In the tradition of the Reformation, they would stress divine grace and justification by faith. But then they specified their alternative to traditional Calvinism; God's grace extended to *all*, and *every* believer could go on to "scriptural holiness," even to Christian perfection, in this life.[9] Throughout Britain and the United States, this twinned message of conversion by God's grace and holiness through grace-enabled exertion resonated powerfully. For many, these teachings revitalized a Protestant faith that had grown cold; it offered a Christianity especially attractive for times of dislocation, migration, and new beginnings. In America, Asbury and his colleagues spread their message with machinery developed by the Wesleys: itinerant preachers proclaiming conversion and encouraging the converted, special earnestness in taking this message into the highways and byways, lay-led local societies for strengthening believers and attracting seekers, graduated programs of quarterly and annual meetings to organize the itinerants and inspire the faithful. Historians have often highlighted the political implications or social consequences of the Methodist movement, but until well into the nineteenth century Methodists themselves devoted almost all their energy to convincing sinners they needed Christ and encouraging Christians to go on in holiness.[10]

The second distinguishing feature of the Methodist movement was an all-out reliance on Scripture as the sole determinative authority, though transparent self-deception always attended Methodist claims to be guided by the Bible alone. Methodism in fact always enjoyed a panoply of guidance for reading the Scriptures. While John and Charles Wesley enjoyed the fruits of an elite classical education and a lifetime of diligent personal study, Methodist leaders without formal education—like Asbury—devoted themselves ardently to wide reading in works of Christian devotion and surprisingly broad attention to worldly wisdom. Yet the claim to be guided preeminently by Scripture was not an empty claim. Although John Wesley published an extensive library of general reading, along with edited spiritual classics for his itinerants, by the time the American church took shape, three documents had been elevated as authoritative. In 1784 Asbury and Coke reminded the Christmas Conference that American Methodists would be guided by John Wesley's four-volume set of *Standard Sermons*, his *Notes on the New Testament*, and the minute books that recorded decisions of the English Methodists. Memorably, Wesley's famous preface to his sermons began with a ringing dedication to *sola scriptura*:

> I mean to speak, in the general, as if I had never read one author, ancient or modern (always excepting the inspired). . . . I want to know one thing, the way to heaven—how to land safe on that happy shore. God himself condescended to teach the way: for this very end he came from heaven. He hath written it down in a book. O give me that book! At any price give me the Book of God! I have it. Here is knowledge enough for me. Let me be *homo unius libri*.[11]

Whatever the irony at lapsing into Latin to introduce biblical expositions aimed at ordinary men and women, Wesley's dedication to Scripture as his absolute authority guided his American acolytes as they detailed how "the Book of God" should guide the daily lives of Methodist preachers. The 1784 *Minutes* explained "the best general Method of preaching" as "1. To convince: 2. To offer Christ: 3. To build up." These goals would be achieved if preachers in their preaching would "Chuse the plainest [biblical] Texts you can" and make a practice to "Frequently read and inlarge upon a Portion of [Wesley's] Notes [on the New Testament]."[12] To prepare privately for their public duties, itinerants were urged to rise daily at 4:00 a.m. for "Private Prayer" and to reserve an hour in the evening for the same purpose. But that prayer was always to be guided by "Searching the Scriptures." A longer quotation reveals how thoroughly biblical that searching was supposed to be:

1. Reading: *constantly*, some Part of every Day: *regularly*, all the Bible in order: *carefully*, with Mr. *Wesley's* Notes; *seriously*, with Prayer before and after: *fruitfully*, immediately practicing what you learn there.
2. Meditating: at set Times. By any Rule.
3. Hearing: Every Morning.
   Carefully. With Prayer before, at, after.
   Immediately putting in Practice.
   Have you a New Testament always about you.[13]

In a word, the message that became so compelling to so many as Asbury and his associates "spread scriptural Holiness over these Lands" could be called a Bible-only spirituality.

The third distinctive element in early American Methodism was its resolutely non- or apolitical stance. Because they could not entirely escape the public enthusiasms of their time and place, Methodists in the era of Asbury could be occasionally distracted by politics. They were, however, never really engaged.[14]

After 1784 Asbury regularly published the *Minutes* of annual conferences. These short pamphlets were mostly filled with administrative detail: the names of itinerants received on trial, admitted into "full connexion," or dismissed for cause; the results of the election for superintendents (always Asbury and Coke); the circuit assignments of preachers for the next year and the designation of elders and deacons with oversight duties. Yet in all annual reports brief memorials of deceased itinerants occupied the most space. Formulaic as they became, these death notices still communicated the movement's dedicated energy. As only one of countless examples, the *Minutes* for 1794 recorded the demise of Henry Birchett of Virginia, who had volunteered the year before to serve a vacant circuit, "notwithstanding the pain in his breast, and spitting of blood, the danger of the Indians, and prevalency of the small pox."[15]

Very occasionally, recognition of turbulence in the world broke into these laconic accounts of spiritual dedication. So it was when the *Minutes* of 1795 urged Methodists throughout the country to set aside the first Friday of March 1796 as a special day of "fasting, humiliation[,] prayer and supplication," and that also designated a thanksgiving day in October 1796 for offering "holy gratitude." These appeals appropriated the jeremiad form that had long been a regular feature of preaching in New England. The call to fast urged repentance for drunkenness, Sabbath breaking, superstition, and similar personal evils, but also for "the deep rooted vassalage" (i.e., slavery) that the nation continued to tolerate. Additionally, in an indirect but unmistakable reference to contemporary events in France, it prayed "[t]hat America may not commit abominations with other corrupt nations of the earth, and partake of their sins and their plagues." Yet the document did not explicitly mention the recent execution of Louis XVI, the de-Christianization efforts of the French revolutionaries, or the outbreak of European warfare—nor did it refer specifically to current domestic troubles: Indian warfare in the Ohio Territory, yellow fever in Philadelphia, rebellion in western Pennsylvania, bitter partisanship over the Jay Treaty with Britain, and an unprecedented wave of criticism directed against the revered George Washington. Similarly, the 1795 call for a special thanksgiving did ask Methodists to remember "the goodness and wisdom of God displayed towards America, by making it an asylum for those who are . . . oppressed with ecclesiastic and civil tyranny." But as the main cause for rejoicing, it specified "the conversion of hundreds and thousands within these two years last" and the "many drawn from the depth and sin and misery, to the heights of love and holiness among the subjects of grace."[16] The importance of this 1795 call for fast and thanksgiving days lay in its exceptional character. The rule remained determined avoidance of such temporal concerns.

The minority of Methodists who opposed Asbury's apolitical stance testify to its success. The prime case in point was James O'Kelly of Virginia, who carried into Methodism the ardent republican patriotism that had motivated his service in the Continental Army during the Revolution.[17] As the national movement consolidated, O'Kelly and a few others began to complain that Asbury overdid consolidation: too much authority in his own hands, too casually ignoring universal moral intuitions, and too much aping the despised wiles of "popery." O'Kelly and his followers troubled the movement for several years before breaking away in the mid-1790s to form their own denomination, the Republican Methodist Church. Yet Republican Methodists remained an insignificant force; only a few years after this schism the main body of Methodists experienced the explosive expansion that lasted for more than half a century.

The published journals and correspondence of Asbury offer a third indication of his almost complete indifference to political matters. Asbury of course never spoke for all Methodists, as indicated by the frequent occasions in these writings when he complained about Methodists who drifted into partisan activity.[18] Yet, overwhelmingly, Methodists either did not mind or they positively supported Asbury's course. The three-volume critical edition of Asbury's journals and letters briefly records only two of his several meetings with Washington. It contains only one sentence concerning Thomas Jefferson, from a time in 1792 when at the home of a Maryland Methodist Asbury "read in haste the most essential parts of 'Jefferson's Notes' [on the State of Virginia]." Otherwise, in 1,400 printed pages of journals and over 500 printed pages of correspondence—where thousands of Methodists and other Americans are mentioned by name and hundreds are memorialized at considerable length for their service to the Methodist cause— there is not a single reference to John Adams, Alexander Hamilton, James Madison, John Jay, and most of the other well-known movers and shakers who feature so large in standard histories of the period.[19]

Preaching, Singing, Controlled Enthusiasm

Methodists in the early United States offered a compelling message that, in David Hempton's succinct phrase, stressed "experience, assurance, and community."[20] The means they used to promote personal experience with God, help converts find assurance of salvation, and organize local lay societies to pursue "scriptural holiness" were no secret: straightforward, even simple biblical preaching, hymnody saturated with Scripture, and revivalism under control.

Asbury's regularly published *Journals* kept the ideal template for Methodist sermons constantly before the eyes of the faithful. In the fall of 1800 other Protestants were hyperventilating over the presidential contest between the Republican Jefferson and the Federalist Adams, with Presbyterians and Congregationalists in absolute panic about the prospect of a Republican triumph and many Baptists almost as eagerly looking forward to a victory by Jefferson. By contrast, Asbury could not be dissuaded from his regular course, as indicated by his record of activities in Virginia on the fourteenth of September: "I went immediately to the throng in the court house, and founded a discourse on Matthew xxii, 5. What great things the Gospel revealeth to mankind. First, The love of God. Secondly, the sufferings, and death, and merits of Christ. Thirdly, The gifts, extraordinary and ordinary, of the Holy Ghost."[21] A few years later, on December 13, 1807, just as Congress passed a controversial Embargo Act that President Jefferson hoped would punish the British for impressing American seaman, Asbury was in South Carolina: "My subject today was Matt. xxiv, 45. The *good servant*—in spiritual wisdom, in fidelity, his diligence to perform his duties. The *wicked servant*—backslidden, false, and falsely secure. His *Lord delayeth his coming*—therefore he maltreats his fellow-servants who are better than himself. He is sensual; his portion is hell."[22]

Well into the new century, Asbury's itinerants followed his lead closely. John Wigger has catalogued the 262 texts from which William Ormond preached 1,823 sermons in an itinerating career that stretched from 1791 to 1803. Ormond's favorites happened not to duplicate Asbury's exactly, but the burden of Ormond's main scriptures aligned perfectly with Asbury's main message. Ormond's favorite texts were 2 Timothy 2:11–12 ("It is a faithful saying: For if we be dead with him, we shall live with him: If we suffer, we shall also reign with him: if we deny him, he also will deny us") and the first verses of Psalm 40 ("I waited patiently for the Lord; and he inclined unto me, and heard my cry. He brought me up also out of an horrible pit, out of the miry clay, and set my feet upon a rock, and established my goings. And he hath put a new song in my mouth, even praise unto our God").[23]

By the time of Asbury's death in 1816, some Methodist ministers were venturing further afield in their sermons. Yet although many at that time paid at least somewhat more attention to social or political concerns, it meant a great deal for the history of the Bible that the Methodists' devotion to Scripture for specifically spiritual purposes remained a widespread feature of American public life.

The prominence of singing in one of Ormond's favorite preaching texts illustrates David Hempton's succinct summary of what many other researchers report: "It has long been recognized that the most distinctive, characteristic, and ubiquitous feature of the Methodist message, indeed of the entire Methodist revival, was its transmission by means of hymns and hymn singing."[24] That judgment rests on numerous contemporary testimonies. One American Congregationalist, who wanted his colleagues to move more quickly in imitating the Methodists, put it plainly: "We sacrifice too much to taste. The secret of the Methodists lies in the admirable adaptation of their music and hymns to produce effect; they strike at once at the heart, and the moment we hear their animated, thrilling choruses, we are electrified."[25]

The content of Methodist hymns, which fervent singing lodged permanently in heart and mind, featured the Bible from first to last—and the Bible, again, for narrowly spiritual purposes. From their beginnings, American Methodists published a plethora of hymnbooks. In 1800, Asbury and Coke referred to "the Select Hymns, the double collection of Hymns and Psalms . . . the Redemption-Hymns," and the "Congregational Hymn-Book." These references came in the preface to one of the great, but almost entirely unstudied, engines of American Christianization, the Methodists' *Pocket Hymn-Book Designed as a Constant*

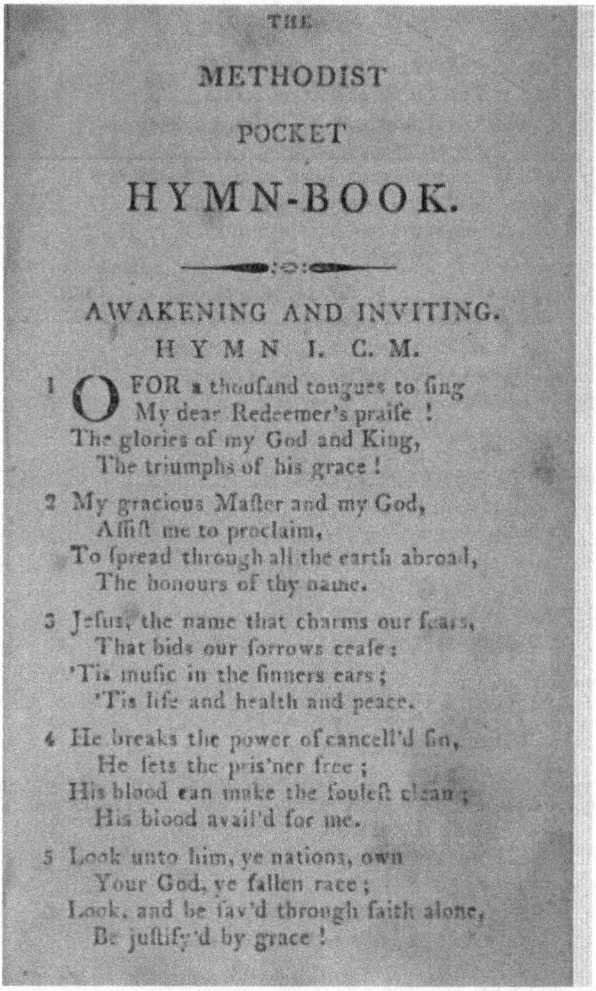

Figure 4.1 The *Pocket Hymn-Book* that Francis Asbury reissued annually for over thirty years always opened with several stanzas from a hymn that Charles Wesley titled "For the Anniversary Day of One's Conversion" but that was much better known as "O for a thousand tongues to sing."
Source: Courtesy of Princeton Theological Seminary Library.

Companion for the Pious, Collected from Various Authors (Figure 4.1). In 1800 the book was already in its twenty-third annual edition; the bishops described it as containing "all the excellencies of the former publications . . . the choicest and most precious hymns . . . in the former editions."[26] Clearly printed, expanding slightly from year to year (285 hymns in 1790, 320 in 1817), and priced to sell (fifty cents in 1800), the successive editions of this book may have touched more American homes of that era than any book except the Bible.[27]

The collection featured the signature hymns of English Wesleyanism. As they were sung in society meetings and larger Methodist gatherings, Scripture flowed into Methodist consciousness. The book opened with a selection that Charles Wesley originally titled "For the Anniversary Day of One's Conversion" but that John Wesley had abridged for his many hymnbooks. In that abridged form it appeared in America under the heading "Awakening and Inviting." It began memorably:

> O for a thousand tongues to sing [Ps 119:172],
>> My dear Redeemer's praise!
> The glories of my God and King [Ps 145:1],
>> The triumphs of his grace!

Each of the later verses carried on with Scripture in song, as the fourth:

> He breaks the power of cancell'd sin
>> He sets the pris'ner free [Isa 61:1];
> His blood can make the foulest clean [Isa 1:18],
>> His blood avail'd for me [Gal 2:20, loosely].[28]

As only one more example, the density of reference, allusion, quotation, or echo of the King James Version was exemplified in the *Pocket Hymn-Book*'s second number, a composition from around 1760 by Joseph Hart. One of its stanzas ran:

> Come, ye weary, heavy-laden,
>> Bruis'd and mangled by the fall,
> If you tarry till you're better,
>> You will never come at all;
>>> Not the righteous,
> Sinners Jesus came to call.[29]

The first two lines paraphrased the words of Jesus from Matthew 11:28 ("Come unto me, all ye that labour and are heavy laden, and I will give you rest"). "Bruis'd" in line 2 evoked the primal story of God's curse upon the serpent after Adam and Eve succumbed to temptation in the Garden of Eden (Gen 3:15, "it shall bruise thy head, and thou shalt bruise his heel"), but also the assurance of divine mercy from Isaiah 42:3 ("A bruised reed shall he not break, and the smoking flax shall he not quench"). The stanza ended again with the words of Jesus, this time even more lightly paraphrased, from Matthew 9:13 ("I am not come to call the right-eous, but sinners to repentance"). The translation of biblical prose into metrical song continued without let-up to the end of the volume.

Hart's hymn also indicated the ecumenical significance of such hymnody. Because its themes of grace, mercy, repentance, and salvation elaborated on bib-lical interpretations that almost all Protestants embraced, such hymns brought a measure of harmony to an otherwise fractious Protestant world. Hart had been converted in a Moravian church (with which the Wesleys broke in a battle royal over "stillness") after a sermon by the Calvinist George Whitefield (whose commitment to predestination the Wesleys rejected). Although Hart served a Congregational church, he urged that his hymns be sung to tunes provided by John Wesley.[30] In the new world, as in the old, a shared evangelical hymnody forged emotional bonds among doctrinally divided communities, even as it solidified the scriptural basis that, in contrast to doctrinal squabbles over biblical interpretation, united Protestants among themselves.

The care that Asbury and Coke took in annually revising the *Pocket Hymn-Book* spoke of a broader commitment to print aimed at common readers, singers, and listeners. When in 1789 the American church appointed John Dickins as its first "book steward," he immediately produced cheap editions of spiritual standards for itinerants, who thereafter functioned as colporteurs as well as preachers. With the exception of an antislavery pamphlet by John Wesley, these works (an abridgement of *The Imitation of Christ*, Richard Baxter's *The Saints' Everlasting Rest*, and a selection from William Law's *Serious Call to a Devout and Holy Life*) focused narrowly on spiritual growth in grace. Ezekiel Cooper, who succeeded Dickins in this position, expanded the publication and distribution many times over.[31]

In the new United States, Protestants, after rejecting establishmentarian Christendom, found their legs through persuasion via the popular press. In their exploitation of hymnbooks, devotional works, annual minutes, and other publications meant to be distributed widely, Methodist efforts paralleled the rapid expansion of newspapers in the political sphere. As such they also served as instruments of democratization. For the religious world, Methodists were espe-cially important for hastening a transition from religious printing dominated by New England sermons to mass publications coming from everywhere and going to everyone.

Powerful preaching and fervent hymn singing moved audiences. Revival was often the result. Intense local bursts of religious fervor had occurred irreg-ularly and in widely scattered locations since George Whitefield's great evan-gelistic campaigns of the late 1730s and 1740s. During the Revolutionary and post-Revolutionary periods local revivals continued, but mostly touching in-land sites and mostly precipitated by Baptists (General, Particular, and Free

Will) and other sectarians.[32] In the late 1790s and early nineteenth century preachers from many denominations—especially Baptists and Presbyterians, along with the Methodists—reported dramatic revivals in the frontier regions of Tennessee and Kentucky. Soon, lower-key but no less intense revivals broke out in New England and settled urban areas.[33] These local revivals could be spectacular, like the multiday festival of preaching, singing, vociferous repenting, and bodily "exercises" (barking, swooning, the jerks) that occurred at Cane Ridge, Kentucky, during the second week of August 1801.[34] Most revivals involved specially called gatherings where a preacher—or, more often, preachers—declaimed forcefully from biblical texts describing the prevalence of evil, urging sinners to turn from their wicked ways, and assuring those who did so of God's boundless mercy in Christ. These dramatic events often resulted in emotional conversions—many that stuck, many that did not. They also drew considerable criticism of runaway enthusiasm, led to some exploitation by mountebanks, and occasionally witnessed a slide from religious fervor into sexual license. In a postestablishmentarian society where no one had to go to church or pay taxes to support religious institutions, revivals became effective recruiting occasions for the churches. In an open cultural marketplace, compelling popular persuaders showed how Christianity could flourish without Christendom.

Methodists were not the first revival preachers, even though they perfected the techniques that defined American revivalism: itinerants seeking out the people where they lived, preaching carried on outdoors, sermonizing pitched to the common woman and man, promotion of memorable hymns, a welcome for emotional response, and disregard of formal learning. These last features especially troubled critics who complained loudly when women, Blacks, and uneducated men shared in the preaching that whipped up revival excitement.

The great Methodist impact on the nation came, however, not simply from participating in revivals but from the ability to regulate, control, and institutionalize revival energies. Baptists along with leaders of various "Christian" movements, as well as many Presbyterians and a few Congregationalists, preached as effectively as Methodists. But major differences surfaced as the various movements harvested the fruits of revivals. The proprietary denominations reacted slowly; they wanted properly educated ministers, fully functioning regional organizations (presbyteries or associations), and well-constructed church buildings to shepherd revival converts. Sectarians did much better at providing local fellowships for converts and others whose faith was reawakened in the revivals; they worried much less about education for ministers or regional coordination among local churches. The Methodists did the best. Their itinerants ranked among the most effective revival preachers. Their interlayered organizational system both fanned and contained revival fires. Methodist elders supervised itinerants while quarterly and annual meetings encouraged the faithful, and

Asbury benevolently, but carefully, oversaw it all. (An example of the Methodists' annually published "Discipline" is depicted in Figure 4.2.)

The movement's detailed statistics suggest something about the Methodist ability to sustain momentum. During the first six years of the nineteenth century, when many observers described powerful revivals on the frontier and in New England, the number of Methodists increased by a net of sixty-five thousand. But so also in the next six years, which have never been regarded as witnessing a

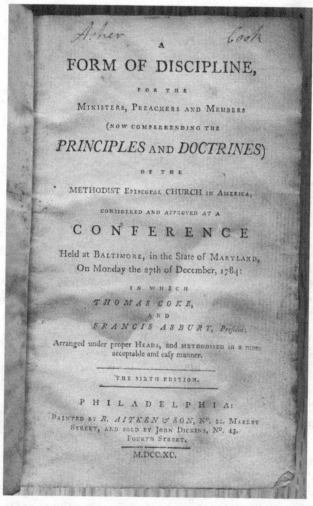

Figure 4.2 In no small part, the revival fires ignited by Francis Asbury's itinerants did not burn out of control because of their deference to the Methodist "Discipline," here shown in one of its earliest printings (1790).

Source: Courtesy of Buswell Library Special Collections, Rare Books, Wheaton College, Illinois.

"Great Awakening," another sixty-five thousand came "into society."[35] Methodist gains became even greater later in the century, when red-hot religion cooled toward respectability, though of course there was always opposition. In 1810, for example, an exasperated editor giving vent to custodial concerns could not contain his disdain: "Here all decency is outraged and the most frantic bedlamites are considered as under the influence of the Holy Spirit."[36] Yet despite such complaints, more than any other American Protestants, Methodists both enlivened and controlled the United States' most visible new way of doing religion.

For a history of the Bible, this achievement meant that a popular, spiritually focused, and largely apolitical way of internalizing Scripture remained at the center of the most dynamic religious movement in the nation's early history. In 1805, the chief Methodist publicist, Ezekiel Cooper, published a substantial book filled with reports from around the country, and into Canada, of what he called simply "the Work of God." Even granting the formulaic style of these reports, they still offer impressive documentation for how Methodists wove together deep spiritual engagement and disciplined organization. On the one side the reports brimmed over with a language of intense spirituality: "soundly converted to God . . . preached with much light and liberty . . . pleading for mercy . . . the most glorious meeting . . . sinners cut to the heart . . . peace . . . power . . . joy . . . communion . . . liberty . . . rejoicing." Step by step, on the other side, proceeded another language of energy rendered into order: "many have been awakened, converted, and added to the church . . . New-London quarterly meeting . . . the Pittsfield circuit . . . the Ganville circuit . . . the Landaff circuit."[37]

Richard Bassett of Delaware in an earlier life had been a nearly invisible delegate to the Constitutional Convention. Now as a very active Methodist elder he sent in a report from Dover, dated June 1, 1801, that encapsulated the spiritual and organizational energy of the movement:

> Last night, about eleven o'clock, we closed our annual meeting; and, glory to God, he has done wonders. About one hundred and thirteen white and black were joined in society yesterday; and from what I hear, I doubt not, but as many, if not twice the number, who went away wounded and crippled, sick and sore [a phrase from the first stanza of the Hart hymn cited earlier], will be joined in different parts of the country—all the fruits of this blessed ministry.[38]

Almost needless to say, the Scriptures, though not aggressively prominent as an object of consideration in their own right, everywhere informed these reports. From Cumberland, Tennessee, came the message that "the people felt the truth and power of the word each day." From Connecticut an elder reported that the "quarterly meetings are generally attended with the power of God, like a mighty rushing wind [quoting Acts 2:2 on the initial descent of the Holy Spirit]." From Virginia the memorial of a deceased brother contained an account of his conversion: "The next day I felt such joy and peace, yet I was not assured that the work was wrought; only one text ran greatly in my mind . . . 'Sanctify them through thy truth—they word is truth' [Jn 17:17]."[39]

Such reports underscore the Methodists' key role in making revivalism a central feature of religion in the new republic. They also show how Methodists regularized, institutionalized, and disciplined the local revivals that constantly threatened to spin out of control into enthusiasm or relapse into postrevival exhaustion. The biblical anchor in Methodist revivalism aligned perfectly with the pointed biblical injunctions in their sermons and the affective biblical content of their hymns.

Implications for the History of the Bible

Other religious movements of the period have received more attention from historians because of how eagerly they participated in the era's political, social, and economic controversies. To be sure, Methodists were by no means uncontroversial. Christine Leigh Heyrman has documented how the Methodist itinerancy—vigorous young men moving from place to place with a message that appealed especially to wives, daughters, and slaves—sharply challenged notions of honor, family integrity, and hierarchies of gender and race, especially in the South.[40] Richard Shiels has similarly shown that New England Congregationalists regarded Methodist entrance into their region as a comprehensive assault on good order.[41] Yet by comparison with the proprietary Protestants who spoke for the once-dominant colonial denominations—and also by comparison with Baptists and other sectarians who loudly denounced the civil and religious traditions that restricted their liberty—Methodists remained mostly focused on their spiritual mission.

They were, therefore, the prime agents who secured among the American people a deep, visceral, passionate, heartfelt, and all-encompassing respect for Scripture as the Book of Life. Before all else, their Bible represented peace (and struggle) with God, joy in the Holy Spirit (and despair at his absence), guidance (and rebuke) for daily life, and a bond with others who shared similar experiences. At the time, other Protestants accused the Methodists of promoting substandard or even dangerously heretical opinions on personal salvation, Christian ethics, and church order. Later historians have described how their apparently all-out piety actually supported bourgeois political agendas. Some of both contemporary and later attention has led to sharp criticism. At the least, such criticism indicates that early American Methodists should not be evaluated through rose-tinted spectacles, but rather deserve careful theological, political, and moral scrutiny.

For historical assessment, however, the focus more properly belongs on what the extraordinary Methodist success reveals about the character of national life—and, specifically for our purposes, about the place of Scripture. As many studies have shown, and the rest of this book tries to document, public appeals to the Bible—on temperance, Sunday mail, Indian removal, education, literature, and above all slavery—played a significant part in the unfolding national story. Methodist success in promoting the Bible as an indispensable foundation for private devotion and nonpolitical voluntary organization explains one of the main reasons for Scripture's public prominence. The Bible would matter for public life in substantial part because the Methodists had given it such vitality in the private lives and religious fellowships of so many Americans. Programmatic uses that highlighted how *others* should follow the Scriptures rested on a broad foundation of *personal* engagement mostly concerned with what the Bible tells *me* to be and do.

The magnitude of the Methodists' early success ensured that their way of appropriating Scripture would spill over to influence how non-Methodists also related to the Bible. When, for example, the resolute republican John Randolph (1773–1833) of Roanoke, Virginia, surprised his family and associates by becoming seriously pious in the late 1810s, he returned to active participation in the Episcopal church of his youth. His "conversion," as he called it, had come through the influence of revival-inclined Presbyterians. Yet when in September 1818 he wrote to a friend about his experience, he channeled Scripture like a Methodist: "I am at last reconciled to my God and have assurance of his pardon through faith in Christ, against which the very gates of Hell cannot prevail [quoting Matt 16:18]. Fear hath been driven out by perfect love [quoting 1 Jn 4:18]." In the same letter he even mocked those who had earlier warned him away from Methodist enthusiasm: "I am not now afraid of being 'righteous overmuch' or of 'methodistical notions.'"[42]

A memoirist writing shortly before the Civil War used the phrase "orthodoxy . . . methodized" to describe what happened to his father's Congregational church in Connecticut when the Methodists arrived early in the century. The phrase encapsulated the process by which Protestant Christianity in the United States came to feature characteristic Methodist emphases.[43] As Methodism grew, so also grew the stress on personal conversion, intense concentration on personal sanctification, and reliance on freely chosen voluntary fellowship. That process could be illustrated from many quarters, but two from the polar opposites of Protestant denominations suffice.

Few adjustments were required to shape sectarian movements in the Methodist pattern, since piety in these movements had long since foregrounded the personal emphases that also characterized Methodism. So it was with the Free Will Baptist Dolly Quimby, who in the early nineteenth century endured the agonizing loss of several children. Then, however, in Catherine Brekus's summary, "overwhelmed by grief, she turned to the Bible for answers, and eventually found peace in the life-changing experience of conversion." So grounded, Quimby embarked on a public preaching career, as did many women in her generation who had been similarly impelled to share from pulpits what God had done for them. "By identifying so closely with [Christ], as well as with biblical prophets such as Jeremiah and Deborah," Brekus summarizes, they freely breached conventions to assert "their own authority and dignity."[44] Quimby was unusual as a female preacher. She was not unusual in speaking self-confidently in public on the basis of her personal encounter with the Scriptures.

A much more famous convert-turned-preacher shared a similar experience. Charles Finney was a young lawyer in upstate New York when in the early 1820s he began to consider his eternal destiny. For instruction he turned to the local Presbyterian minister George Gale, who encouraged him to read the Bible, pray, and attend public worship. When Finney found Presbyterian Calvinism perplexing, he examined Scripture for himself, until he was convinced that "the Bible was . . . the true word of God." Then, based on what he read in the Scriptures, he "was brought face to face with the question whether [he] would accept Christ as presented in the Gospel, or pursue a worldly course of life." After further personal struggle, he recorded his conversion in Methodistical form: "Just at that point this passage of Scripture seemed to drop into my mind with a flood of light: 'Then shall ye go and pray unto me, and I will answer you. Then shall ye seek me and shall find me, when you search for me with all your heart' [Jer 29:12–13]." Made confident by this scriptural word, which he could not remember ever having heard before, Finney "cried out to Him, 'Lord, I take thee at thy Word. Now thou *knowest* that I *do* search for thee with all my heart, and that I have come here to pray to thee; and thou hast promised to hear me.' "[45] From that climactic experience, Finney went on to a spectacular preaching career in which he deftly exploited Methodist techniques, including extended nightly meetings, public speaking by women, and the anxious bench for those seeking salvation. He also followed Methodist procedures by recording his own experience in the language of the King James Version and by boldly pursuing a public career inspired by his own understanding of Scripture.

In broader perspective, confusion surrounding the notion of a "Second Great Awakening" comes from failing to recognize how pervasively over so much territory and how consistently for so much time the Methodists promoted their version of the gospel with their particular methods. The great determining factor in early national religion was not any one "awakening" or even series of "awakenings." It was the year-in, year-out success of the Methodists in building their own church and the influence they exerted on other Protestant traditions. The Methodist bequest to American religious history was Christianity defined preeminently as personal conversion, holiness understood not as social dominance but as personal growth in grace, religious renewal expected from local revivals, and popular religion spread by preaching and publication aimed at common people in ordinary life settings.

A. Gregory Schneider has pointed out that many in the early national period were just as adept at invoking biblical images as the Methodists but with applications for the political nation frequently edging aside applications to personal religious life. The difference? For Methodists "Zion" meant "the place, people, and polity where one could see and feel God working to bring the entire world under the reign of Christ." To them, "the New Israel . . . was not the American republic, but the universal church."[46] The early Methodists were a Bible people—almost a "Bible only" people—who did *not* speculate on the millennial future, who did *not* try to influence politics or education directly, who did *not* obsess about either their republican rights or their republican responsibilities. Instead, they relied on the Bible for Christian conversion, personal holiness, interpersonal encouragement, moral standards, devotional resources, and ecclesiastical identification.

Yet in so doing the Methodist surge shaped *how* the Bible would be used in public life almost as much as *that* the Bible would remain such a sacred object for so many Americans. When Asbury and his associates appealed to the "primitive church" and the "apostolic order" as their sole guide, they expressed implicit disdain for tradition, deference to inherited station, the sanction of formal learning, and the establishmentarian structures of Western Christendom. With these attitudes they aligned themselves with sectarian evangelicals who rejected the same set of once widely accepted authorities. Yet unlike the sectarians, Methodists subordinated republican complaints against centralized political power.

At the midpoint of the War of 1812, which passed with almost no Methodist comment, Asbury provided a clue for how a movement with so little interest in the public sphere could contribute so significantly to that sphere.[47] In his "Valedictory Address" composed as he saw his days drawing to a close, Asbury suggested reasons for this apparent paradox. When he noted that some critics had accused Methodism of "partak[ing] too much of the government of the nation," he paused to make an astute observation. Methodism, he claimed, did not draw its "nature" from the American pattern, "but there are some similarities of form." Specifically, in their organization, "[t]he one is civil, the other spiritual and entirely disunited." In spelling out differences, Asbury returned to his highest concern, Methodist church order: "Our government being spiritual, one election to office is sufficient during life, unless in cases of debility, a voluntary resignation of the office, corruption in principle, or immorality in practice."[48] Yes, he seemed to say, we too are democratic, but not with the democracy of the nation.

Dee Andrews has expanded insightfully on Asbury's awareness with a specific accounting of those "similarities in form." In her rendering, the larger context was crucial: although the Methodist system obviously appealed to many Americans, "there was no organic link between Methodism . . . and the United States." Instead, "both Methodism and the new emerging democratic republic were eighteenth-century products of *disassociation* from organic community, familial hierarchy, classical tradition, and the church state connection." As such, Methodist distinctives and the new nation's ideology developed on unconnected, but parallel, lines, with many individual elements assuming a similar shape: "a democratic ethos that foreswore allegiance to social or religious elites and was dedicated to the popular voice; a potent revivalism that in its most effective form equalized, even dissolved, if temporarily, the racial, gender, and social differences that republican rhetoric, in its most visionary form, lent credence to; and a sometimes blunt indifference to intellectual and academic tradition."[49]

For at least a generation, this spirit also rendered national borders and competing political ideologies irrelevant. Until long after the War of 1812 Methodists in the northern United States and their counterparts in Upper Canada (later Ontario) carried on as a seamless unit as they exchanged personnel, leadership, and organizational initiatives. Spiritual and denominational publications from the Methodist Book Concern in New York City served to unify Canadian and American Methodists for another two decades. Only when complicated political maneuvers in London and York (Toronto) raised consciousness of the U.S.-Canadian border did divisions occur between Methodists for whom the national border (and nationalism) had signified almost nothing.[50]

For their own purposes, Methodists insisted on the power of personal choice and the duties of individual responsibility. They embodied a populism with democratic orientation toward ordinary people. And they developed an organization that by combining bottom-up voluntarism with national fellowship could steer between anarchy and unchecked power. The leaders of early Methodism gave little thought to the United States as such, its possibilities, its inequities, its leadership, or its standing in the wider world. As Russell Richey observes, "Early American Methodists . . . lacked a concept of the nation. . . . [T]hey simply looked right through the nation. They did not see it."[51] Yet because of Methodist-national homologies, because so many Methodist principles aligned so closely with so much early American ideology, the Methodist attachment to Scripture and Methodist approaches to biblical interpretation decisively shaped the national attachment to Scripture and national approaches to biblical interpretation.

Methodists, Politics, and Slavery

For observers in the early twenty-first century, when the politicization of religion has become so contentious, the apolitical stance of the early Methodist leaders can appear idyllic. Simply by *not* harnessing their religious energies to political bandwagons, early Methodists can look like paragons of religious integrity. Yet with its political tabula rasa, the Methodist movement could not offer much resistance to influences from the outside once Asbury's iron discipline passed from the scene. Because they had no mechanism for connecting individual piety to systemic public responsibilities, they drifted like political chameleons after Asbury's determined apoliticism wore off. The same memoirist who described American religion as "methodized" called this reciprocal process "Methodism . . . orthodoxed."[52]

The spiritual journey of Alfred Brunson illustrates that political plasticity. In a memoir looking back over seventy years of service to the Methodist cause, Brunson opened with Psalm 66:16 on his title page: "Come and hear, all ye that fear God, and I will declare what he hath done for my soul." Brunson's account of his youth in Federalist Connecticut and his first steps toward conversion explains how Federalist-Republican political conflict intersected with his discovery of the fear of God. When Brunson first heard Methodist intinerants, their denunciations dramatized the dangers of dancing, card-playing, and other worldly amusements. Yet for Brunson it was the Methodists' "political views" that captured his attention. The entry point initially seemed paradoxical, since "the great mass, if not the entire, of the Methodist Church and her adherents were Republicans, and so were the entire infidel portion of the community, though these two classes were antipodes in all things pertaining to religion." Contending in Connecticut against both "infidels" and the Methodists stood the established Congregational (and Calvinist) churches who were fighting to retain their privileged status (and also public tax support). Brunson was offended by the fact that "Calvinism [i.e., the Congregationalists] and Federalism were yoked together, and the dominant *isms* of the State." At first he considered his rejection of Federalism (= despotism) and the Congregationalists (= Calvinism) as tantamount to rejecting Christianity entirely. But then he learned from Methodist preachers "the truth of the matter," that Calvinism was not "a Bible doctrine." Whereupon Brunson and others "dropped their opposition to the Bible, but became converted to God." Federalist-Republican division was important in the spiritual development of this Methodist convert, but only because it marked one stage that ended when he experienced "the salvation of [his] soul."[53] In Federalist Connecticut, the Methodists' alliance with the Republicans was only a marriage of convenience.

Elsewhere religious-political ties worked out differently. John Wigger has pointed out that despite Asbury's aversion to electoral competition, his teaching gave "Methodists a cultural foundation from which to move into the political realm." Asbury, that is, "taught members to be hard working and frugal, gave them confidence that as individuals they occupied a meaningful place in the world, and instilled in them the value of community involvement (as with the importance of attending class meetings) and the need for communal discipline." It did not take much to transfer "these habits . . . from the spiritual to the secular world." Yet when politicization took place, the results followed local culture, not Methodist principle. Once again Wigger: "Given Asbury's distrust of politics, it is ironic that by the early nineteenth century Methodism became a leading political force in several states, including Delaware, where Methodists were overwhelmingly Federalists, and Ohio, where they were predominantly Republicans."[54] The Richard Bassett who reported on Methodist expansion in Delaware served that state as a Federalist senator and governor; in Ohio, the Republican Methodist Edward Tiffin was that new state's first governor. Yet only much later did Methodist ministers cautiously begin to participate in partisan politics, at first drawn toward the Whigs because of that party's anti-Catholicism. Later, after the national denomination divided in 1844 over slavery, northern Methodists became strongly Whig, and then Republican. In the South they took on the coloring of the dominant political class and became reliable Democrats.[55] As had earlier happened with Canadian connections, bitter controversy over the Methodist Book Concern reinforced nationalist commitments, in this case the North-South political divide.[56]

The absence of a distinctively Methodist social policy when Methodists did enter public life explains their well-documented course with respect to slavery.[57] At the founding Christmas Conference in 1784, the new denomination boldly announced its opposition to chattel bondage: "We view it as contrary to the Golden Law of God on which hang all the Law and the Prophets, and the unalienable Rights of Mankind, as well as every Principle of the Revolution, to hold in the deepest Debasement, in a more abject Slavery than is perhaps to be found in any Part of the World except America, so many Souls that are capable of the Image of God."[58]

A potent mixture of scriptural teaching and American political ideals supported this resolute denunciation. Yet as the antislavery impetus from the American Revolution faded and as Methodists made spectacular gains in slaveholding areas, the earlier certainty that slavery contradicted "the Golden Law of God on which hang all the Law and the Prophets"—the teaching of Jesus recorded in Matthew 7:12—also lost its force. Methodist consciences certainly remained troubled. But conversions based on biblical preaching and holiness pursued along biblical guidelines could not by themselves sustain the denomination's earlier biblical protest against bondage.

In this progression, Methodists again led where other white Protestants followed. Their success in "Methodizing" American religion according to their understanding of scriptural imperatives operated on one plane. Their earlier conviction that the Bible did not allow slavery operated on another. Popularizing Methodist conceptions of biblical conversion and scriptural holiness was not the same as giving Methodist interpretations of Scripture special authority in assessing slavery or other social and political questions.

In more general terms, nearly universal Protestant agreement affirming the authority of the Bible along with significant agreement on what it meant personally to follow Christ did not translate into a common understanding of social order, common cultural attitudes, or common approaches to political decision-making. Instead, deeply ingrained assumptions about the market, personal ability, the glories of liberty, and especially race—influences not derived from biblical teaching or biblical examples—continued to exert a powerful sway. Fervent commitment to "the Bible alone" and passionate concentration on the standing of individuals before God meant that many Americans active in the public sphere often undertook that activity with Scripture in hand. Fervor and passion did not, however, guarantee anything like the spiritual commonality the Methodists did so much to create.

The relative absence of a political vision, however, did allow the Methodists to make a different sort of contribution of immeasurable significance. Like the earlier revival preaching of Whitefield in the colonial Great Awakening, the zealous Bible-only preaching of early Methodism reaped a large harvest among African Americans. That Whitefield had been a slave owner who aggressively supported the introduction of slavery into Georgia meant less to his Black auditors than the message that they too could be "born again" and enjoy all the spiritual privileges accorded to whites.[59] That the Methodists could not sustain their early antislavery testimony meant less to many African Americans in the early American republic than the message that God's grace also invited them to "scriptural holiness."

The conversionist piety that Whitefield proclaimed while maintaining a proslavery stance resembled the holiness piety that Methodists proclaimed as they backed away from abolition. Yet African Americans and African Britons won to Christ by Whitefield could read the Bible for their own purposes with respect to slavery. So too African American Methodists would translate their experience of biblical salvation into applications of Scripture that did not conform to the racist conventions that strengthened as the nineteenth century progressed.[60]

In 1816, the year of Asbury's death, African Americans made up 20% of the more than 214,000 Methodists "in society."[61] Asbury himself had retreated from

Methodist antislavery only with great reluctance. For several years he recruited a Black preacher, Henry Hosier, to accompany him on his itinerations—and frequently allowed Hosier to take the lead in addressing the public. He offered at least some support for Richard Allen when Allen organized the Philadelphia congregation that eventually formed the African Methodist Episcopal Church. In 1796 he also approved a request by Black Methodists in New York City to conduct their own worship services.[62] In addition, his own antagonism to racial barriers opened space for impressive contributions from Black theologians like Daniel Coker and indirectly paved the way for Blacks like David Walker and Nat Turner to turn Scripture aggressively against the slave system.[63]

In the colonial period, the form of Christianity that had appealed most to African Americans had least to do with Christendom. During the early history of the United States, the Methodists, who preached with almost no concern for ordering society, enjoyed a similar appeal. In both eras, a biblical message that subordinated political concerns would come back to disconcert other Americans who thought the Bible's social teachings were clear as a bell.

Over a brief span of years, the Methodists' pursuit of "scriptural holiness" secured a wide American following because of how effectively they communicated a biblical message of joyful personal liberation, disciplined personal dedication, and supportive community fellowship in a society cut loose from the recognized guideposts of the past and churned by a contentious free market. Methodists in the era of Francis Asbury deepened the entire nation's attachment to Scripture. They strengthened reliance on "the Bible alone" as a principle for interpreting the Scriptures in private—but also in public. They practiced a religion that separated common Protestant approaches to personal faith from the application of Scripture to public affairs. They also proclaimed a message with special appeal to African Americans. With sectarian and proprietary Protestants, who shared much of this religion, only more contentiously, they created the American Bible civilization.

PART II

A PROTESTANT BIBLE CIVILIZATION

Thy word is a lamp unto my feet, and a light unto my path.
—Psalm 119:105

5

The Bible Civilization in American History

The most obvious feature of religion in the new United States leaves an impression of simple continuity since Protestants of British background continued to predominate. When the Constitution took effect in 1789, there were about 4,700 places of worship in the new nation. Only sixty-five were Catholic and a bare handful Jewish. All the rest were Protestant. Between 1790 and 1830, the American population multiplied more than three times, from under 4 million to nearly 13 million. During that same period, the number of Protestant churches (or preaching stations for itinerating Methodists) grew seven- or eightfold. In the same years, the number of Catholic parishes was increasing steadily, but only at the pace of general population growth (in 1820, of over 10,000 places of worship, only 124 were Catholic).[1] The Jewish population took even longer to expand, numbering only about 15,000 as late as 1840.[2] In other words, securely Protestant colonial religion gave way to securely Protestant post-Revolutionary religion.

Yet if the overwhelmingly Protestant character of the new United States implied continuity, unprecedented disruption describes what actually took place. General theological beliefs, convictions about church organization, and the colonial fear of overreaching church authority did survive the Revolution intact. But the American *novus ordo seclorum* required a radical readjustment of the context in which doctrine, ecclesiology, and attitudes toward power had existed time out of mind. That demand, which grew spontaneously from "the causes, experience, and course of the Revolution," exposed what historian Jon Butler has called "the insecurity of Christianity's place in American society."[3]

Underlying many of the changes in the new nation's earlier years was the explosive growth of Baptists and Methodists. An insightful historian from an earlier generation, Winthrop Hudson, once offered telling comparisons to describe "the Methodist Age in America." He pointed out that by 1820, Methodist adherents and Baptists, both relatively unimportant before the 1790s, had each far surpassed all adherents of other denominations. By 1840, Methodists had outstripped Baptists by a ratio of 10 to 6. Remarkably, in that same year Methodist adherents outnumbered—also by a ratio of 10 to 6—those from *all* of the colonies' main churches *combined* (Presbyterians, Congregationalists, Episcopalians, Lutherans, and Reformed).[4] The Catholic population in 1840, though growing fast, still lagged behind. Keeping these comparisons in minds explains why the Methodists' intensely pietistic and the Baptists' strong sectarian approaches

America's Book. Mark A. Noll, Oxford University Press. © Oxford University Press 2022.
DOI: 10.1093/oso/9780197623466.003.0006

to the Bible became so important for the new nation. Their prominence also explains why the proprietary churches were willing to accept voluntary organization as *the* means for cultivating religion in a free society.

As a consequence of these developments, by 1820 and national agitation over admitting Missouri to the Union, the Bible had replaced ecclesiastical traditions as the center of American religious life. The denominations—from sectarian Baptists, "Christians," and Universalists, through proprietary Congregationalists and Presbyterians, to modernizing Unitarians and pietistic Methodists—agreed in promoting Scripture as the key to finding God. They were also united in treating the Bible as the foundation for a healthy society. Disagreements over *how* to employ the Bible, which lurked never far from the surface, did not prevent broad Protestant agreement on the supreme importance of Scripture, which approached national consensus.

The National Situation

It is only a slight exaggeration to say that until the late 1820s, the United States was no more than an unwieldly collection of primarily local economies, local cultures, and local political structures, with only minimal national cohesion.[5] National geography was emblematic. The Louisiana Purchase of 1803 doubled the national land mass, but the cautious administration of Thomas Jefferson (1801–9) deliberately minimized the federal role in the expanded nation. The Jeffersonian equation of centralized power with incipient tyranny remained a truism during the tenure of his successor, James Madison, except when hotheaded frontiersmen blundered the country into military conflict with Great Britain, a war that so disillusioned the New England states they almost broke up the Union.

In the aftermath of the War of 1812, Henry Clay, a young congressman from Kentucky who had already become Speaker of the House of Representatives, succeeded in legislating an "American System" aimed at promoting national cohesion through coordinated federal action. Its main components, however, achieved only ambiguous results. A protective tariff did encourage national manufacturing and stimulated state-to-state trade at the expense of commerce between the individual states and Britain. Yet agitation over the tariff also exacerbated tension between a South committed to free trade and a North committed to domestic manufactures. The Second National Bank, chartered in 1816, tried to mitigate distress during the depression of 1819–21, but doing so made it a symbol of overweening governmental authority to the citizens who later supported Andrew Jackson and his attacks on centralized banking. Federal assistance for interstate roads did not generate the same degree of controversy, but neither did

Congress ever appropriate enough funds for infrastructure improvements to affect more than a minority of the population. The other major achievement of the decade after the War of 1812 was the assertion by President James Monroe in 1823 that the United States would tolerate no European meddling in the Western Hemisphere. This "Doctrine," however, revealed not so much American capacities as the indifference of European nations, who took almost no notice.

From a modern perspective, it is difficult to realize the minimal heed paid to national politics before the late 1820s. The decline of the Federalist Party greatly reduced competition—and therefore also national attention (Federalists occupied fifteen of thirty-four seats in the seventh U.S. Senate, 1801–3, but rarely thereafter even as many as one-third). National vote totals for presidential elections were not recorded until 1824, when that contest only underscored the nation's political localism. John Quincy Adams secured the electoral votes of New England and New York, William H. Crawford was the favorite son of Georgia and Virginia, Henry Clay won Kentucky and neighboring Ohio, while Andrew Jackson scooped up the remaining states south and west of New York. Without a majority in the electoral college, the election for the first and only time was decided by state vote in the House of Representatives. (Each state had one vote.) Adams emerged the winner only after long and bitter contention.

The War of 1812 and debates leading to the Missouri Compromise of 1820 did galvanize national attention but only for relatively brief periods. Then, however, controversy over the 1824 election in the House, followed in 1828 by a vicious campaign between Jackson and Adams, stimulated an unprecedented national focus on national politics—which led to spiraling national controversy over slavery, followed by widespread national nervousness over South Carolina's threat to nullify tariff legislation, intense national debate over President Jackson's war on the National Bank, extensive national hand-wringing during the financial panic of 1837, intense national debate on the Mexican War—and so on to the present.

Through the same period, economic life also remained primarily local, except for trade in slaves and cotton, trade that in fact accentuated diverging regional interests as much as it tied together the fortunes of southern planters, northern bankers, and the national merchant fleet. Only with the completion of the Erie Canal in 1825 did centripetal forces begin to prevail. The finished canal, in the words of Daniel Walker Howe, "represented the first step in the transportation revolution that would turn an aggregate of local economies into a nationwide market economy."[6] The boom in railroad building that began less than a decade later accelerated the emergence of national finance, commerce, and even labor.

For cultural concerns, localism also prevailed into the 1830s. The most widely distributed periodicals in those early national years came from religious voluntary societies and the denominations. Only with the rise of the penny press in the mid-1830s and revolutions in technology, transport, and marketing that soon followed did a "secular" print culture emerge, but with religious material still providing much of its content. In Robert Gross's assessment of the nation's intellectual culture, "[t]he inhabitants of the states, loosely connected to one another by coastal vessels and rudimentary roads, still depended on the Old World and mainly Great Britain, the former mother country, for ideas and information in print. Under these circumstances, the fundamental challenge before the new nation was to gather up the diverse people of a far-flung land and enlist in a common life."[7]

A comparison can indicate the importance of voluntary Protestantism in creating a national culture. In 1816, the number of federal employees, excluding the military, stood at just over 4,600, two-thirds of that number at work for the postal service. In the same year, seven thousand Methodist class meetings dotted the land, each with a lay class leader and each connected to the national Methodist network by one of the denomination's seven hundred itinerant preachers. (Another seven hundred or so ministers were "settled" in one location and functioning as traditional ministers.)[8] In 1816 citizens were more likely to have a personal connection with Methodist circuit-riders or local Methodist assemblies than with any outreach of the federal government.

Later, when political controversy began to stimulate sustained national interest, political mobilization often followed where voluntary religious organizations had led. The first national political convention did not take place until 1831, when the Anti-Masonic Party convened such a gathering. (Previous presidential candidates had been nominated by caucuses in Congress.)[9] The convention's mix of red-hot oratory, partisan zeal, and exaggerated fears for the republic replicated what had been heard for a generation at the revival meetings to which almost all Protestants contributed, and then at the annual gatherings of national voluntary societies. When the Democrats followed suit in 1832 and the emerging Whig Party later did the same, they also testified to the ongoing importance of these religious precedents.

The Protestant organizations that mobilized to tame the new nation's expansive geography and its open cultural landscape never captivated national attention as later controversies over slavery did. Yet for a full generation they exercised as much influence over public aspirations, as much guidance over public rhetoric, and as much leadership in creating national institutions as any other political or social force. During those years, Protestant voluntarists were putting flesh on the bones of nationhood. At the center of their exertions remained always the Bible.

Thereafter, the situation changed. Conflicting uses of Scripture to defend and attack slavery intensified to the time of the Civil War and did not cease when that conflict came to an end. If the Bible was the nation's book, why could it not resolve the nation's most pressing moral problem? In addition, when the surge of immigration beginning in the 1830s brought more Roman Catholics to the country, it shook the nation's laboring system and rekindled anti-Catholicism among elites. The burgeoning Catholic presence particularly threatened instinctive deference to the Protestants' King James Bible. Agitation in 1835–36 over rechartering the Second Bank of the United States, followed immediately by economic panic and a severe depression, naturally elicited much comment from religious spokesmen (as well as a few women). But the feeble, formulaic, and fragmentary character of that commentary revealed how little serious biblical reasoning of any kind had been devoted to economic questions and spoke for a broader reticence to assess markets and their effects with Scripture in hand.[10]

Before that time, and as documented by an increasing quantity of well-researched books, articles, pamphlets, and digital archives, the centrality of Scripture was secure.[11] That scholarship has treated geography, public rhetoric, the book trade, newspapers and periodicals, the law, education, literature, reading habits, popular culture, the rapidly expanding distribution of King James bibles, and more. Hence, the challenge is Sisyphean to specify the places and occasions where the Bible appeared prominently, the individuals for whom trust in Scripture remained a mainstay, and the organizations that promoted the Bible and aspired to act on its mandates. While the chapters that follow are far from comprehensive, they suggest the scope of American Protestant efforts to replace the structures of formal Christendom with an informal Christendom relying on the Bible.

The Argument

America's Bible civilization came into existence

-- as a result of energetic Christianization by awakened Protestants of English and Scottish heritage
-- in a society shaped by its colonial and Revolutionary history
-- but largely devoid of meaningful national institutions,
-- though united around republican ideals,
-- propelled by a free market in print,
-- and manifest in the tangible organization of everyday life.

An American "imagined community" conceptualized around the centrality of Scripture was the result.[12]

An anxious appeal from a sectarian leader and a bold initiative from a recent immigrant, both in late 1790, indicate how rapidly that post-Christendom imagined community was taking shape. In September, Isaac Backus was joined by fellow New England Baptists in a petition to the new U.S. Congress. Sectarian principles lay behind Backus's long-standing dedication to religious liberty. But his appeal echoed assumptions about religion and public life that Presbyterians and Episcopalians had underscored eight years earlier, when the Continental Congress commissioned respected clergymen to monitor the first American printing of a King James Bible.[13] In the colonies there had been no printing of the "Authorized Version" because of monopolies maintained by the king's printers in Britain. Yet even with the king and royal monopolies a thing of the past, it remained second nature for these proprietary Protestants to seek official approval for a locally produced edition of the Scriptures. Now, in 1790, the New England Baptists likewise urged the nation's supreme legislature to "take such measures as the Constitution may permit, that no edition of the Bible, with its translation may be published in America, without its being carefully inspected, and certified to be free from error."[14]

Yet even as this backward-looking petition reached the Congress, an Irish immigrant recently arrived in Philadelphia was moving toward the future. On the first of December, Mathew Carey sent subscribers their copies of "the first Roman Catholic Bible and only the second edition of the Bible in English to appear in the Americas . . . [and] the first American English Bible that was not a commercial failure."[15] On his own initiative, Carey had solicited more than four hundred subscribers to subsidize the publication of a full edition of the Douay-Rheims-Challoner translation (Figure 5.1)—without asking permission and authorized only by his own willingness to enlist the supporters necessary to fund this audaciously expansive effort. Carey, a journalistic firebrand who twice fell afoul of British authorities in his native Ireland, had arrived in Philadelphia as a twenty-four-year-old only six years before. Aided by the Marquis de Lafayette, who was enjoying his first return to the United States since having joined the struggle for independence, Carey immediately set up as a printer, publisher, and bookseller.

To be sure, by 1790 the door to Bible publishing was cracking open; more than a score of New Testament editions (King James Version) had already appeared from Philadelphia, Trenton (New Jersey), Wilmington (Delaware), Boston, Elizabethtown (New Jersey), and New York.[16] But apart from the congressionally sanctioned King James Bible by Philadelphia printer Robert Aitken, who went bankrupt when trade resumed with Britain and cheaper bibles flooded the market, there had been no printing of a complete English-language Bible in the new world. Carey took advantage of an emerging Catholic infrastructure by securing a commitment for twenty copies from John Carroll, who had been named the United States' first Catholic bishop only one year earlier. He drew on international Catholic connections to sign up diplomats from Portugal and

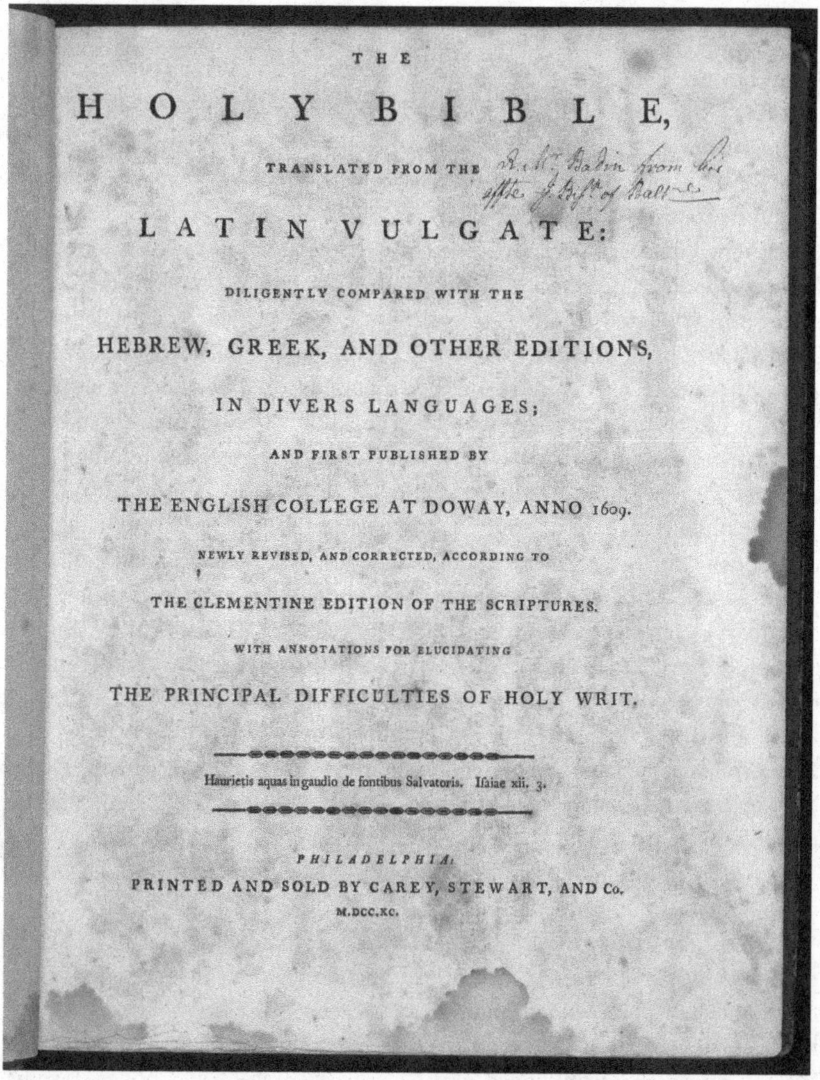

THE

HOLY BIBLE,

TRANSLATED FROM THE

LATIN VULGATE:

DILIGENTLY COMPARED WITH THE

HEBREW, GREEK, AND OTHER EDITIONS,

IN DIVERS LANGUAGES;

AND FIRST PUBLISHED BY

THE ENGLISH COLLEGE AT DOWAY, ANNO 1609.

NEWLY REVISED, AND CORRECTED, ACCORDING TO

THE CLEMENTINE EDITION OF THE SCRIPTURES.

WITH ANNOTATIONS FOR ELUCIDATING

THE PRINCIPAL DIFFICULTIES OF HOLY WRIT.

Haurietis aquas in gaudio de fontibus Salvatoris. Isaiae xii. 3.

PHILADELPHIA:
PRINTED AND SOLD BY CAREY, STEWART, AND Co.
M.DCC.XC.

Figure 5.1 In successfully marketing a full-scale edition of the Catholics' Douay-Rheims translation in a largely Protestant United States, Mathew Carey pioneered the flourishing business of Bible publication that continues to this day.

Source: Reproduced from the original held by the Department of Special Collections of the Hesburgh Libraries of the University of Notre Dame.

Spain for copies. And during an interlude of improved Catholic-Protestant relations he presold copies to Protestants Jacob Rush, a Pennsylvania jurist, and Rush's brother, Benjamin, the new nation's most famous physician.[17]

If this Douay bible helped launched Carey on his long and successful publishing career, it also spoke for the broader history of Scripture in American life. Its title page featured a Vulgate text from Isaiah 12:3, "Haurietis aquas in gaudio de fontibus Salvatoris," which reminded all who opened its pages that Carey hoped readers would "draw waters with joy out of the saviour's fountains" (Douay-Rheims). American Bible publishing has almost always reflected an explicit spiritual purpose. Yet more generally, Carey, the entrepreneurial immigrant Catholic, also showed the way that Protestants of all sorts would follow, and with a vengeance. From that time to the present, Bible publication would be undertaken by enterprising publishers, dependent only on their ability to sell copies, springing up wherever a sufficient audience existed, and waiting for no authorization except a market assessment.

Little more than a decade later, Carey received a letter in Philadelphia from his ace colporteur in the field. Behind the letter lay a revolution in print along with a prodigious labor of Protestant proselytization. In the two years after 1790 and the appearance of Carey's landmark Douay edition, other printers brought out six editions of the King James New Testament and six of the entire Bible, as well as John Wesley's three-volume *Explanatory Notes upon the New Testament*, which added commentary to the King James text.[18] In the two decades after 1790, while Carey published two more complete Douay editions and one Douay New Testament, the nation's nascent book industry produced an astonishing 139 new Bible editions, all but 10 the full King James Version or the King James New Testament. (Besides Carey's Catholic bibles, the other seven came from miscellaneous Protestant sponsorship.)

Carey himself leaped on the King James Version bandwagon in 1801 when he published his first complete "Authorized Version," a move that soon made him the nation's most prolific Bible publisher and one of its leading booksellers of any kind. The letter early in the century came from Virginia, where Mason Locke Weems, an ordained Episcopal minister, was pushing Carey's books. Weems, now famous for making up the story of George Washington and the cheery tree, at the time was best known as a demon salesman. His report: "I tell you this is the very season and age of the Bible. Bible Dictionaries, Bible tales, Bible stories—Bibles plain or paraphrased, Carey's Bibles, Collin's Bibles, Clarke's Bibles, Kimptor's Bibles, no matter what or whose, all, all, will go down—so wide is the crater of public appetite at this time."[19] The public appetite for bibles—stoked by the preaching of Methodists and other active evangelists, fueled by the energy of printers and publishers—had already become one of the most salient cultural facts in the new United States.

The Americans who purchased these bibles included not a few, like Francis Asbury and most Methodists, who desired nothing more than spiritual direction. Yet many of Asbury's peers, while of course agreeing with his spiritual goals, wanted much more from Scripture than just experimental godliness. For them, but substantially because of the number of Americans recruited by Asbury and other energetic Protestants, the Bible seemed perfectly poised to advance social, as well as strictly religious, goals.

A Lutheran sermon preached in 1817 to commemorate Martin Luther's Reformation three centuries earlier indicated how thoroughly an American frame of reference was reshaping traditional Protestant attitudes. Frederick Christian Schaeffer had won high marks for fluent preaching in both German and English at his first pastorate in Harrisburg, Pennsylvania, and then when he moved to New York City. Now, in 1817, when because of linguistic isolation and ecclesiastical stand-offishness Lutherans remained on the cultural fringe, Schaeffer nevertheless reflected a broad national consensus. In his rapturous account, when Luther promulgated the Ninety-Five Theses attacking the pope's traffic in indulgences, "a new era" of "religious light and liberty" had begun. Although Schaeffer focused on hereditary Catholic-Protestant strife, he put an American vocabulary to use in hailing Protestant victories: the "conquest of the true 'Rights of Man' over diabolical intolerance . . . the trophies of . . . Reason . . . over the blackest superstition." To sum up this glorious three-hundred-year history he wrote, "It was the triumph of the BIBLE over the combined enemies of the Cross of Christ."[20]

So pervasive had reference to Scripture become in those early national years that it could become the butt of satire. In *The Last of the Mohicans*, published in 1826, James Fenimore Cooper drew a biting contrast between the cramped Bible fixation of an itinerant singing master and the expansive nature romanticism of his hero, Hawkeye. In an effort to settle a dispute over whether God predestined events or not, David Gamut demanded that Hawkeye "name chapter and verse: in which of the holy books do you find language to support you." In response Hawkeye burst out, "Book! what have such as I, who am a warrior of the wilderness, though a man without a cross, to do with books?" Instead, Hawkeye had imbibed revealed truth by traveling "from sun to sun, through the windings of the forest." In his authorial elaboration, Cooper took a swipe at the theologians of his day who were laboring overtime to synthesize biblical teachings on the relation of human free will and divine sovereignty: Gamut had become "deeply tinctured with the subtle distinctions which, in his time, and more especially in his province [Connecticut] had been drawn around the beautiful simplicity of revelation, by endeavoring to penetrate the awful mystery of the divine nature."[21]

Much more common than Cooper's satire were the many occasions when leaders celebrated divine revelation in Scripture as the spiritual—and more than spiritual—key to American Christian advance. Robert Baird (1798–1863) stood foremost in that number. After graduation from Princeton Theological Seminary and ordination as an evangelist in the Presbyterian church, Baird labored for several years with the New Jersey Missionary Society, the American Bible Society, and the American Sunday School Union. Then from 1835 until his death, he traveled widely in Europe, often reporting back to the States about religious life in various parts of the continent. Yet his most notable publication attempted a full-scale accounting of American religion for the curious in Europe. It also became the fullest effort of its kind to date for American readers. For this extensive volume of over seven hundred pages, *Religion in the United States of America*, Baird made no apologies for focusing on, in the words of his subtitle, "the Origin, Progress, Relations to the State and Present Condition of the Evangelical Churches of the United States (with notices of the unevangelical denominations)."[22] Irony did attend the book's publication, since its upbeat picture of harmony among evangelical churches appeared in 1844, the year the Baptists and Methodists went into schism over slavery. Yet if Baird overestimated the coherence of American "evangelicalism," underestimated the dissonance created by the rising number of American Catholics, slighted the influence of the "unevangelical" groups, and neglected the nation's unchurched citizens (probably close to half the population), his narrative still conveyed a great deal about the first decades of the nineteenth century. In Baird's account, the Bible occupied center stage.

First was the crucial role played by self-directed voluntary organization, which he called "the great alternative" (286) to the inheritance of European Christendom. In fact, more than a third of the book explained the implications of what Baird termed the "grand step" that led the new nation "to abolish altogether the support of any church by the state, and place all of every name on the same footing before the law, leaving each church to support itself by its own proper exertions" (287).

Baird did pause to explain the barriers that voluntarism had to overcome: hidebound assumptions carried from Europe (69–72), thin population spread over vast spaces (72–76), the evils of slavery (76–79), and the influx of immigrants (80–84). But he insisted, "Upon *the voluntary principle alone* depends the religious instruction of the entire population, embracing the thousands of churches and ministers of the gospel, colleges, theological seminaries, sunday schools, missionary societies, and all the other instrumentalities that are employed to promote the knowledge of the gospel from one end of the country to the other" (288, emphasis added). In Baird's view, the American stage had no scenery, only actors.

He also specified why voluntary self-organization worked with unprecedented success: in a word, because of trust in an authoritative Scripture. The evangelical churches that dominated American life, as well as his book, were those "whose religion is the Bible, the whole Bible, and nothing but the Bible" (613). Although Baird as a Presbyterian exhibited strong custodial instincts, he could sound almost sectarian when he claimed that harmony among evangelical churches came from their holding "the supremacy of the scriptures as a rule of faith, and that whatever doctrine can be proved from holy scripture *without tradition* is to be received unhesitatingly, and that nothing that cannot so be proved shall be deemed an essential point of Christian belief" (658, emphasis added).[23] Although Baird cautioned against the excesses of democracy, he could likewise extoll a nearly "Bible only" stance that was more common among the nation's religious upstarts: God's "moral government . . . carries the preacher and the theologian back from the Platonic dreams and dry dogmatizing of the schools, to the Bible. It sets the theologian upon studying, and the theologian upon imitating, the freedom, simplicity, and directness, with which the apostles addressed the understandings and sensibilities of men" (663). In his telling, devotion to Scripture propelled the remarkable achievements of Methodist evangelists, guided Presbyterians and Congregationalists in founding colleges and seminaries, and fueled the sweeping efforts of the voluntary societies.

Finally, although Baird devoted most of his attention to the inner workings of churches and voluntary societies, he did not neglect the broader picture, which was a civilization organized around biblical mandates. "Good men of every name," even "statesmen, though they may not be decidedly religious," have cooperated in placing "the sacred scriptures in the hands of all who can read them." The informal bonds between religious leaders and civil leaders had molded the new nation: "The impression prevails among our statesmen that the Bible is emphatically the foundation of our hopes as a people." The time-worn republican calculus gave Baird his theory: "Nothing but the Bible can make men the willing subjects of law; they must first acquiesce with submission to the government of God before they can yield a willing obedience to the requirements of human governments." Put most directly, "It is the religion of the Bible *only* that can render the population of any country honest, industrious, peaceable, quiet, contented, and happy" (372, emphasis added).

Many of Baird's contemporaries would have agreed, and not only those who shared his proprietary instincts. Simple, sincere, and earnest biblical preaching had produced a rich harvest of converts and serious believers. It had also given the new republic a singularly biblical national character.[24]

The lithograph created by Thomas Sinclair of Philadelphia that is displayed on the cover of this book visualized Baird's main themes. It was created close to the time when Baird's book appeared. The print, titled *Christian Union*, ignored the nation's growing Catholic population, consigned Native and African Americans to the fringes, and did not acknowledge the devotion of many American women to the Bible. It did, however, communicate Baird's vision about the ability of Scripture to join otherwise contending Protestant men in the harmony represented by a lion and lamb resting peacefully side-by-side (Isa 11).[25]

Inheritance: A Translation and Belief in Providence

Well past the middle of the nineteenth century, Americans, with only a few exceptions, sustained the inherited Christian conviction that Scripture communicated the Word of God to men and women through ordinary human words. Yet for the *history* of Scripture in America, it is imperative to remember that the new nation's respect for the Bible everywhere reflected what had gone on before.

The "self-evident truths" bequeathed to the new United States by a successful Revolution had established a degree of "liberalism" unrivaled anywhere in the world, this liberalism understood in the nineteenth-century sense of heightened commitments to freedom, individual rights, and restrained democracy.[26] In a cultural landscape that continued to fear government overreach and aristocratic privilege, "liberal" appropriation of the Bible held out the promise of God-given stability. The voluntary associations that Baird praised translated liberal theory into action. Not government, not an inherited established church, not the will of aristocrats, but creative connections forged voluntarily would build American civilization. The Bible, appropriated by enterprising individuals in a liberal republic with a strongly Protestant heritage, seemed ideal for that construction.

King James Version

The new United States of course inherited the Bible, but not just any Bible. Notwithstanding challenges from the likes of Tom Paine, Bible believers across the denominational spectrum enjoyed a single textual authority of extraordinary unifying force. If they had deliberately overthrown all but one of the structures of European Christendom, the one that remained became only more significant. It was of course the King James Version (KJV) of the Bible itself.[27]

In the early republic occasional voices complained about the dominance enjoyed by the KJV. Benjamin Franklin once tried his hand at translating a passage from the book of Job because he held that "the language" from the time of the KJV was "much changed." Benjamin Rush, the famous Philadelphia physician, warned parents away from the KJV by calling it, in effect, R-rated: "[T]here are, I grant, several chapters, and many verses in the old testament, which in their present unfortunate translation, should be passed over by children." And John

Adams once told his son John Quincy that no one version of Scripture should count as a "Rule of Faith" on its own. Adams worried about "the translation by King James the first" because the monarch was "more than half a Catholick," which, when Adams wrote these words in 1816, was anything but a commendation.[28] As on many other matters, early Americans blithely disregarded this guidance from their supposed betters.

For one of the first complete American King James bibles, Isaac Collins of Trenton, New Jersey, recruited the venerable Princeton patriot John Witherspoon to write a short preface replacing the dedication to King James that had regularly been reprinted with that translation since its first appearance in 1611. According to the new preface, that earlier dedication "seems to be wholly unnecessary for the purposes of edification, and perhaps on some accounts improper to be continued in an American edition." Witherspoon followed this gentle reminder of altered political relationships with an account of "the providence of God" in the "preservation and purity" of the Bible's original Hebrew and Greek manuscripts. He then outlined a brief history of "the translations of the bible into the English language" that culminated in the learned English scholar-clerics whom James I appointed to produce a new translation. At the end of his informative preface, Witherspoon concluded that for "one hundred and eighty years," this one translation, "printed by publick authority," had been "generally approved by men of learning and piety of all denominations"—which in Witherspoon's mind proved that it had "never been superseded by any other."[29]

Witherspoon's commendation forecast a popularity for this translation that, even in the twentieth and twenty-first century, has hardly flagged.[30] For several decades American booksellers continued to reprint Witherspoon's preface. Printers also imitated Collins, who had publicized his pains in securing an accurate text by enlisting Witherspoon and several other clergymen to ensure that his KJV printing came up to the highest British standards. (Other publishers, including Carey, acknowledged the quality of Collins's work by using his edition to check the accuracy of what they printed.)[31]

Providence

Witherspoon's reference to providence in preserving the biblical text also reinforced the widespread belief that God oversaw the fate of nations as well as the fate of manuscripts. This understanding of providence was a second crucial legacy from when colonists had affirmed God's special care for Britain. Now, with king and Parliament out of the way, the earlier application of Old Testament narratives to the empire transferred that providential understanding to the new nation.[32]

The most confident declarations came during times of crisis, but only because the providential mindset did not fade during calmer periods. Political-
religious controversy during the War of 1812 illustrated both the widespread
belief in God's special attention to the nation as well as confidence in the human
ability to discern the hand of God in history. The three days of national fasting
that President Madison authorized at the request of Congress, as well as the
day of public thanksgiving he proclaimed for April 13, 1815, became occasions
for ministers to explain what God was doing. In the last presidential thanksgiving proclamation before Lincoln called for such a day during the Civil War,
Madison himself set the tone: "The Great Disposer of Events," who had blessed
the cause of independence with "multiple tokens of His benign interposition,"
had now "endowed [the states] with the resources which have enabled them to
assert their national rights and to enhance their national character in another arduous conflict, which is now so happily terminated by a peace and reconciliation
with those who have been our enemies."[33] Federalists who abhorred the war and
Democratic-Republicans who championed it filled in the details.

For Federalists, wartime suffering and the dismal record of American military
defeats represented nothing so much as divine punishment for the rash actions
that precipitated this dishonorable conflict. On Madison's Thanksgiving Day in
1815, a Federalist pastor in Falmouth, Massachusetts, made sure his congregation assigned proper credit for victory in the conflict. Specifically, it was not Gen.
Andrew Jackson's brilliance that won the Battle of New Orleans but rather divine
retribution on the British for daring to open fire on the Sabbath.[34] A southern
Federalist explained more generally, "The Supreme Governor of the Universe,
in compassion to a suffering people, hath mercifully interposed and arrested the
progress of a war, which, though not unproductive of glory to our country, has
cost rivers of precious blood unnecessarily shed."[35]

President Madison's supporters were even more self-assured. When in the
hurricane season of 1815 storms devastated the three states that had called for
the Hartford Convention, inflicted moderate damage in two other states that had
sent delegates, and completely spared New York, which had remained loyal to the
president, a Democratic editor gave God the credit.[36] The sharpest Democratic-
Republican statements came from New England, where Madisonians
represented a beleaguered minority resisting the region's Federalist majority.
From a Vermont Madisonian came first a religious analysis: beyond doubt "the
war was just and necessary, and we have abundant evidence to believe it was
a holy war, for the Lord has fought for us in battles, and given us the victories
which have been signal and marvelous on water and on land." Then followed the
political sneer: "In how much then ought we to have confidence in the political
opposers, who have declared the war unholy and unjust."[37] William Gribbin, on
whose excellent research I have drawn, sagely summarized the general effect of

the war's bipartisan providentialism: the "national messianism . . . rooted in the prewar years" was "invigorated by the crisis" and led "Americans to a still greater identification of religion with their destiny." In the outworking of a divisive war, "America's Covenant not only developed into evangelical revivalism, but was also transformed . . . into the rationale for fervid, and continuing, reform."[38]

The so-called Era of Good Feelings that followed the War of 1812 witnessed fewer attempts to discern God's design for the nation. But that interpretive legacy remained. When controversy later erupted over Andrew Jackson's regime and even more when it flared over slavery, appeals to providence were stronger than ever. The pervasive belief in the nation's providential destiny would work an especially important effect in these debates, since proslavery defenders simply knew that God brought Africans to America in order to redeem their souls, while abolitionists simply knew that God offered liberty to all he had made in his image.

For showing how scriptural materials supported providential reasoning, two substantial books from Elias Boudinot are of special interest. They were published shortly after the end of the War of 1812. Boudinot, the friend of Washington, sometime director of the Mint, and leading antislavery lay Presbyterian, was in those years playing a key role in creating the American Bible Society. The two books resulted from the twenty-five years he had spent aligning apocalyptic accounts from the Old Testament's book of Daniel and the New Testament's book of Revelation with the turmoil of contemporary Europe. In 1815 he explained that recent European events "were an exact fulfillment of the Sacred record." In particular, "that the antichrist foretold, as coming on the earth after the Man of Sin, had literally appeared in the new government of France, having Napoleon Buonaparte for her head, can scarcely be denied by any observing mind, who has become acquainted with the late history of that nation since the year 1790, and compared it with language of holy writ."[39] The second book, arising from the same immersion in Scripture, concerned Native Americans. Even as Boudinot expressed considerable remorse for how European settlement had ravaged the continent's Indian population, his interpretation of current events through a scriptural lens led him to conclude that "these unhappy children of misfortune, may yet be proved to be the descendants of Jacob and the long lost tribes of Israel."[40]

Boudinot's long life illustrated the constant flow of biblical awareness from the most sectarian enclaves to the most public arenas. As a young man he heard Witherspoon explain to a Princeton audience "the dominion of providence over the passions of men."[41] As a mature statesman he defended the Bible against Paine's threats to Christianity and to social order. As an old man he believed that God was guiding current events no less directly than he had done before. Boudinot's personal faith, his civic duties, and his evangelical voluntarism all contributed to a distinctly American story. Yet all also rested on an approach to providence and immersion in a particular biblical version inherited from the colonial past. Lifelong dedication to scriptural truth and republican virtue linked his support for American independence and his efforts to establish the American Bible Society. For Boudinot and many of his contemporaries, national destiny, awakened Protestant Christianity, and providence were bound together beyond any possible disentangling. All were anchored securely in biblical bedrock.

6

Naming, Writing, and Speaking in a Hebrew Republic

How did the Bible civilization take shape? Rhetoric throughout U.S. history has always outrun reality. Yet when Robert Baird in 1844 claimed that "the Bible is emphatically the foundation of our hopes as a people," it was hyperbole exaggerating, rather than imagining, fact. If that foundation had never provided a place to stand for all of "our . . . people," and if by the 1840s that foundation had already cracked, Baird nonetheless was not making things up.

First must come attention to rhetoric. During the century's early decades, with only a minimal federal presence, predominantly local economics, and almost no national trade, entertainment, or sport, the Bible's rhetorical salience and its Hebrew frame of reference were among the very few truly common features of American life. Apart from a set of loosely defined political ideals, they may have been the *only* common features. The unselfconscious ubiquity of scriptural reference might have done more for national cohesion than the cacophonous appeals to republican liberty that marked the years of Whig-Jeffersonian strife, controversy over the Embargo of 1807, the protests of New Englanders against "Mr. Madison's War," and bitter conflict over statehood for Missouri. Although taken-for-granted rhetoric is difficult to quantify, it literally filled the air.

In the magisterial *History of the Book in America*, Robert Gross explains how James Madison, in arguing for the Constitution, had extolled the potential of an "extended republic" with "a great variety of interests, parties, and sects" as an ideal guardian of liberty. Yet in assessing the same "extensive republic," Governor John Hancock of Massachusetts thought it would survive only if "social and private virtue" made the experiment work. As a nation so conceived took shape, "the fundamental challenge," in Gross's words, "was to gather up the diverse people of a far-flung land and enlist them in a common life." With "no center of print culture in the new republic," with national revolutions in communications, transportation, and the market still on the horizon, and in "a world of mixed media, with diverse readers and communities, moving in no single direction and sustaining a host of interests, identities, and loyalties," informal, local, and ad hoc forces filled the cultural void.[1] Alone at the forefront of those forces stood the Bible.

America's Book. Mark A. Noll, Oxford University Press. © Oxford University Press 2022.
DOI: 10.1093/oso/9780197623466.003.0007

A Hebrew Republic

Elias Smith's sectarian animus against the proprietary alliance of New England clergy and Federalist politicians knew no bounds. When this tireless itinerant, aggressive writer, and ardent Christian republican let fly, he employed every genre imaginable. As an ardent opponent of New England's church establishments, Smith took special offense when Jedidiah Morse commended New England's ordained ministry in his pioneering book on American geography. According to Morse, "The clergy . . . have hitherto preserved a kind of aristocratical balance in the very democratical government of the State; which has happily operated as a check upon the overbearing spirit of republicanism." To Smith, in sharp contrast, such "aristocratical" tendencies represented nothing less than "the Anti-Christ." As an introduction to a screed of less than fifty pages directed against Morse in 1803, Smith adorned his title page with quotations from a Psalm, the First Epistle of John, and the book of Revelation. The work itself contained a speech to be delivered at Antichrist's grave; an eight-stanza "FUNERAL SONG, to be sung after the Speech," with the Congregational establishment described as "half a murdering wolf, and half a mimic ape"; and several paragraphs refuting Morse directly. But the bulk of Smith's riposte consisted of fourteen chapters written, as the title page explained, "in Scripture stile, in Chapter and Verses" (Figure 6.1). Here is a sample from the first chapter:

> 22 Now when Anti-Christ had heard this [that Jesus was alive], he was troubled, and all his friends with him; and they adopted a federal system, which was to say one thing and do another, and to make the people think that the reason why they opposed Christ was, because they were such friends to religion and the government.
>
> 23 (Now their federal system was this, to endeavor to keep up their reputation among the people, by making them believe they were not fit to rule themselves, and that if they believed in Christ, the government would soon be in the hands of the Romans.)[2]

As historian Eran Shalev has shown, published works in this pseudo-biblical style appeared with remarkable frequency in the first generation of U.S. history.[3] In unusually creative variety, these productions underscored the deep hold of biblical form on the public imagination, but also the easy transfer of meanings from the sacred to the profane.

Biblical pastiche had first appeared in the eighteenth century, mostly from Britain but with Benjamin Franklin's "discovery" of new material on the life of Abraham an early American example.[4] It became an honored American genre

(5)

them believe that they were not fit to rule themselves, and that if they believed in Christ, the government would soon be in the hands of the Romans.)

24 Moreover Anti-Christ and his friends agreed to use all their influence to prevent the people from hearing Christ, and to bring something against him, to prove him worthy of death.

25 And Anti-Christ called together all those who possessed the spirit of Anti-Christ, and said unto them,

26 (Now the heads of them who had entered into an agreement against Christ, were the Chief Priests, the Scribes, the Pharisees, the Sadducees, the Lawyers, and the Herodians, with their disciples.)

27 Let us endeavor to prove that this Christ is an enemy to our established religion, and that he speaks against Moses and our temple :-

28 Moreover let us represent him as an enemy to the government, by saying to the people that this Christ calleth himself a king ; for whosoever maketh himself a king, speaketh against Cæsar ; for if this can be done, we shall have wherewith to prove that he ought to die.

Figure 6.1 Elias Smith was only one of many in the early Republic who used a pseudo-biblical form to satirize his enemies. Here are a few verses from his 1804 attack on New England's church-state establishment in *The Clergyman's Looking-glass.*
Source: LOC Americana, LCCN-36029087.

with the anonymous publication in 1775 of *The First Book of American Chronicles of the Times*, which began:

CHAP. I

AND behold! when the tidings came to the great city that is afar off, the city that is in the land of Britain, how the men of Boston, even the Bostonites, had arose, a great multitude, and destroyed the TEA, the abominable merchandise of the east, and cast it into the midst of the sea:

2. That the Lord the King waxed exceeding wroth.[5]

Into the early nineteenth century, political polemicists regularly deployed this style, as when in 1800 a Federalist newspaper published a "Book of the Democrats," to which a Jeffersonian paper replied in 1803 with "The First Book of the Kings."[6] Abraham Lincoln testified to the endurance of the genre when in the late 1820s he penned "The First Chronicles of Reuben" to lampoon a leading family in his Indiana neighborhood.[7] Soon, however, the Christianization achieved by Methodists and others seems to have raised suspicion about pseudo-biblicism as demeaning the unique status of Holy Writ. Whether this was the cause, the genre gave way to more conventional ways of bringing Scripture to bear on public life. But while it lasted, in Shalev's summary, "pseudobiblicism further constructed the United States as a biblical nation. The language of the King James Bible wove the Bible into American life. . . . American politics were transformed, in texts largely devoid of reference to God, into the new religion of the republic."[8]

Pseudo-biblicism represented only one indicator of a pervasive Hebraic ethos in early U.S. history. Shalev and other primarily Jewish scholars have recently highlighted the ongoing influence from the Revolutionary era when public reasoning rooted in the Old Testament decisively supported the colonial break from Britain.[9] They have joined other historians in showing that the American Revolution spread a Puritan sense of divine covenant, modeled on ancient Israel, to the whole nation.[10] At the same time, influential ministers in the generation after independence sustained a lively interest in the Hebrew language, even as mysteries of ancient Hebrew history inspired orthodox Protestants like Elias Boudinot and pioneers of new movements like Joseph Smith.[11] Everywhere the KJV's full complement of Hebraisms informed both the speech and the writing of literary adepts.[12] In their regular reference to biblical characters, custodial Federalists and sectarian Republicans alike shone light from the Old Testament on the American drama.

Examples abound to document "the Hebrew republic."[13] Early representatives included, from Connecticut, Timothy Dwight's 1785 *Conquest of Canaan: A Poem* and, from New Hampshire, Abiel Abbot's 1799 *Traits of Resemblance in the People of the United States of America and Ancient Israel*. When George Washington died the same year that Abbot's *Traits* appeared, orators throughout the new nation memorialized the nation's great hero as Moses redivivus. Even as debates over slavery and shifting theological emphases pushed the nation's public biblical consciousness from the Old Testament to the New, the identification continued.[14] In 1845 David Lee Child exploited an account from 1 Kings chapter 21 to attack the slaveholding interests responsible for the annexation of Texas; he titled his polemic *The Taking of Naboth's Vineyard*. Shortly thereafter a seminary professor in Maine and a contributor to the *Methodist Quarterly Review* published articles with nearly identical titles to explain "Republican Tendencies/y of the Bible."[15] In 1851 appeared Herman Melville's *Moby-Dick*, with its memorable opening line ("Call me Ishmael") and Captain Ahab as its central figure. In an essay published the next year, Lyman Beecher explained that "the Mosaic institute comprehends, in a high degree, all the elements and outlines of a federal national republican government, more resembling our own than any government on earth ever did, or now does."[16]

It should be obvious why a Hebrew conceptual context significantly shaped American use of the Bible. If the United States was replicating the history of ancient Israel, if the new nation stood in covenant with God as the Hebrews of the Old Testament had done, then Americans could take for granted that God superintended their history as he had once guided Israel. Political developments, like the spread of democracy or the separation of church and state, could therefore be viewed as specifically God-ordained. Conflicts over such matters were easily perceived as struggles between Righteousness and Evil—if God ordered American life as they understood it, then opponents of their understanding were not just mistaken; they were enemies of God. Circumstances at the center of American life, like the importation of bondspeople from Africa, could similarly be viewed as guided directly by God, and so sanctioned by God as well. From the opposite interpretive angle, the continuation of slavery could be read as bringing the same condemnation on the United States as Israel's sins had incurred on that nation.

Imagining the United States as a Hebrew republic raised the stakes for every dispute in the course in the nation's history. A century before, Jonathan Edwards had viewed the precedence of Israel very differently. For him the fate of any particular nation was secondary:

> That nation [Israel] was a *typical* nation. There was then literally a land, that was the dwelling place of God; which was a *type* of heaven the true dwelling place of God ... so there was an external people and family of God by carnal generation, which was a *type* of his spiritual progeny: and the covenant by which they were made a people of God was a *type* of the covenant of grace.[17]

Much more common a century later was a conception of ancient-modern connections that made biblical understanding as thoroughly American as Edwards's typology had made it thoroughly spiritual. Given that difference between a spiritual reference (Edwards) and a national reference (the early United States), it was immensely significant, as Perry Miller once wrote, that "[t]he Old Testament is truly so omnipresent in the American culture of 1800 or 1820 that historians have as much difficulty taking cognizance of it as of the air people breathed."[18]

Naming

In those early American decades the rhetorical ubiquity of biblical language, biblical quotation, and biblical style permeated almost all levels of national discourse, not least the names with which Americans designated themselves and the landscape. Scripture had long provided names for European towns as well as rivers, mountains, and other natural features. So it continued in the American colonies. Although the Bible's "toponymy," as one scholar has noted, "was the common possession of all," its names clustered most thickly where the most ardent Protestants settled.[19] The etymology for William Penn's principal city invoked an ideal, but Philadelphia, as the city of "brotherly love," also evoked the scriptural description in Revelation 3:8 of the city in Asia Minor that received a special divine commendation: "[T]hou . . . hast kept my word, and hast not denied my name." As might be expected, the settlers of New England also drew more freely on biblical nomenclature than those in the southern colonies.[20] Massachusetts is a good example: Salem ("city of peace," Gen 14:18), Sharon (Cant 2:1; Isa 65:10), Rehoboth (Gen 10:11). And Connecticut even more so: Bozrah (Isa 63:1), Mt. Carmel (1 Kings 18), Bethel (Gen 28:19), New Canaan (many biblical references). Only in eastern Pennsylvania, with the strong colonial presence of Quakers, Moravians, and other sectarians, did as many such names appear: for example, Bethlehem (Lk 2), Ephrata (Mi 5:2), Mt. Gilboa (1 Sam 31), and the like.

After independence, Americans continued to take names from the same source. To illustrate how pervasive this practice could be, travelers who today venture off the interstate highways surrounding Indianapolis find themselves motoring through Bethany, Carmel, Eden, Lebanon, Mt. Zion Corner, New Palestine, Nineveh, North Salem, Providence, Samaria, and Zionsville. Farther afield in Indiana, other names reflect the same origin: four varieties of Salem, two each of St. Mary's, Mt. Zion, Jordan, and Antioch, along with a host of others (Canaan, Gospel Grove, Bethlehem, Titus, Palestine, St. Joseph, Jericho, Goshen, Hebron, and more).[21]

Scholars who have painstakingly catalogued the *named* landscape highlight three noteworthy features of the *mental* landscape responsible for the names. First, the designation of American places with names from the Bible became especially prominent in the early nineteenth century as settlers spread westward from the settled east: for example, Zela, West Virginia (Josh 18:28), Mount Tirzah, North Carolina (Josh 12.24), Zoar, Ohio (Gen 13.10), Ruma, Illinois (2 Kings 23:36), and Promised Land, Arkansas (from Deut 9:28).[22] The regions with the densest concentration of such names are the areas settled in the first waves of nineteenth-century national expansion, especially the Ohio River Valley with its tributaries and, to a lesser degree, the sweep of settlements from the Upper South into Alabama and Mississippi.[23] New England's early biblical fixation played a particularly prominent role as settlers from that region moved westward. From the list of incorporated place-names in the 1940 U.S. census, augmented by the Post Office directory from 1958, the geographer John Leighly found many biblical names carried from New England to the twelve east north-central and west north-central states.[24] Included were forty-seven variations on Salem, eighteen each for Lebanon and Sharon, fourteen for Bethel, and fourteen more for Goshen.[25] Such names embodied the hope that crossing the Alleghenies might open a Land of Promise analogous to what Israel had experienced when it crossed over the Jordan River.

Second, in the words of another historian, settlers from regions with less visual drama "found the mountains strange, and sometimes fearsome." The names that resulted reflected "a sense of awe" referenced to Scripture.[26] Names like Mount Carmel, Mount Bethel, and even Mount Sinai could be found in the settled east. But they proliferated in the fifteen states that joined the Union between 1803 (Ohio) and 1850 (California). Five of these states contain a Mount Carmel, three a Mount Zion, and three a Mount Olive (for Mount of Olives). Mount Gilead, Ohio; Mount Horeb, Wisconsin; Mount Hermon, Mount Eden, and Mount Hebron, California; as well as Mount Salem and Mount Moriah, Missouri—all testify to the same biblical source.[27]

Third, and obviously, Bible place-names came overwhelmingly from the Old Testament. Apart from Bethlehem, Mount Olive, and a very occasional Calvary, when Americans named the landscape, they mostly echoed narratives of the Israelite chosen people rather than the story of Christian redemption. The tendency manifested, even as it reinforced, the nation's prevailing Hebraic sensibility.

Naming territory was also claiming territory, in this case not for a ruler but for a tradition. The same tradition may have exerted even more influence in the naming of children. Through midcentury, Bible names predominated among the most public Americans. In contrast to the names of postbellum presidents, for example, with only a minority from Scripture, the Bible supplied the names of a clear majority between Washington and Lincoln (ten of sixteen): four Jameses, three Johns, one Thomas, one Andrew, and one Abraham. The same shift over time marked names for the first ladies, with even a stronger majority (fourteen of seventeen) through the Civil War: two Marthas, two Abigails, two Sarahs, and one each Elizabeth, Rachel, Hannah, Anna, Priscilla, Julia, Rebecca, and Mary.[28]

One more of numberless possible examples comes from a catalogue of authors who published books in 1831. Of 276 authors whose last names began with A, L, or S, nearly half (136) had been named after biblical figures. John (at least thirty-seven authors) was most common, with Thomas, James, Samuel, and Sarah/Sara showing up frequently. The range of biblical reference mastered by an earlier generation of parents also produced authors' names like Abiel, Asa, Asahel, Eleazar, Enoch, Ichabod, Jehoiada, and Rufus.[29]

Names drawn from the Old Testament were a particularly striking feature of early U.S. history, but one to keep in perspective. Even in regions where biblical consciousness remained most pervasive, Scripture accounted for at most 2 or 3% of names for towns, cities, and counties. Physical features, borrowings from Native Americans, sites recalled from England, Spain, or France, as well as individuals of special local influence, all accounted for a greater quantity than came from Scripture. Similarly for the names of children. One study from New England shows, for example, that the majority of biblical names given in the 1780s had become a minority by the 1840s.[30] In addition, even with a ubiquitous King James Bible, consciousness of a name's scriptural origin was doubtless slight for many parents who simply named children after members of earlier generations. Still, with necessary qualifications in place, biblical names for places and with faces contributed more than a mite to the treasury of American civilization.

Writing and Speaking

It is difficult to overestimate the casual regularity with which antebellum Americans salted their day-to-day communications with the Bible. As it was for the founding generation of Washington, Franklin, Adams, Jefferson, Jay, Dickinson, and Witherspoon, so it continued. To speak in public was, time after time, to exploit biblical paraphrases, allusions, cadences, or quotations. To write for private or public purposes was to draw from the same source. Kenneth Cmiel's insightful study *Democratic Eloquence* documented clearly how basic the KJV remained for "popular speech" throughout the nineteenth century.[31] Baptist and Mormon sectarians, who sought confirmation for their particular doctrines, did publish alternatives to this translation.[32] In 1833 Noah Webster, after enjoying great success with his dictionary and even more with his school spellers, brought out a translation shorn of what he considered the KJV's unseemly barbarisms ("bowels," "pisseth," "whore").[33] A few years before, in 1826, Alexander Campbell published a translation of the New Testament for his Restorationist followers that supported his doctrinal convictions (rendering the Greek *baptizo* as "immerse" rather than "baptize"), offered euphemisms to soften the KJV, and displayed his own considerable expertise in Greek manuscript scholarship.[34] Yet none of these alternatives gained traction; their primary effect was to accentuate the secure hold on American rhetoric of the Authorized Version. In Cmiel's words, the King James Bible "was the one book read by high and low, rustics and scholars, ladies and their maids. Generation after generation memorized its words and turns of phrase."[35]

If the challenge remains to say precisely what constant reference to one source of scriptural words meant for national life, there can be no doubt about the Bible's rhetorical prominence. The snippets that follow admit of diverse interpretations—superficial? mere window dressing? spiritual? deeply rooted? But in every direction the evidence could be expanded without limit.

Scripture most obviously stood ever ready to garnish communication at almost all levels. Lincoln's use of the "house divided" metaphor from Matthew 12:25 (Mk 3:25) in his 1858 analysis of national political division remains one of the best-known instances.[36] As it happens, President Jackson had used the same phrase in 1831 to describe a bitter division in his cabinet.[37] Such usage showed up almost everywhere.

Jackson himself provides a telling example, since few in his day singled out the general and later president as renowned for piety. Yet he regularly sprinkled his correspondence and speeches with biblical language, especially evoking God's providential oversight of himself and the nation. When, for example, Jackson was urged in 1822 to run for president, he responded, "Let the people do as it seemeth good unto them," not a quotation from the KJV but an imitation of its prose.[38] The next year he assured his wife, "[T]he god of Isaac and of Jacob will protect you" (many references) and that God would surely hear her prayers since "we are told that the prayers of the righteous prevaileth much" (Jas 5:16, with "prevaileth" for "availeth").[39] A decade later he quoted Psalm 68:5 in a full paragraph of Christian consolation addressed to a daughter distressed by the death of her father: God "will be a father to the fatherless and a husband to the widow."[40] When in 1844 it became clear that fellow Democrat James K. Polk had won the presidential race, Jackson declared, "I can say in the language of Simeon of old 'Now let thy servant depart in peace'" (Lk 2:29).[41] Months later, at the very end of his life, he spoke in Christian terms of his right "to the Tree of Life" (Rev 22:2).[42] Jackson was very far from alone in the ease with which such words flowed from his pen.

An even more revealing illustration of the Bible's rhetorical ubiquity was its deeply embedded place in African American discourse. As in the colonial era, when Black writers like Jupiter Hammon, Phillis Wheatley, James Albert Ukawsaw Gronniosaw, John Marrant, David George, and Olaudah Equiano broke into print, so it continued with publishing African Americans in the national era.[43] From a population with low rates of literacy, three examples reinforce the general impression of a national discourse awash in biblical rhetoric. These examples also anticipate our later consideration of African American alternatives to dominant patterns of white biblical interpretation.

On St. John the Baptist Day, June 25, 1792, Prince Hall delivered a "charge" to Boston's African Masonic Lodge, which he had founded seventeen years before. Hall, who had been manumitted by his Boston master in 1770, when he was about thirty-five years old, had subsequently fought with the patriots at the Battle of Bunker Hill. Now, as he explained the origins and principles of Masonry, he told members of African Lodge Number One how they should comport themselves. The printed version of Hall's address, thirteen pages of relatively large print, cited chapter and verse for five Scripture quotations. More generally, Hall's prose was shot through with echoes, references, and allusions to biblical material, as in this example:

> I shall at this time endeavor to raise part of the superstructure, for howsoever good the foundation [Lk 14:29] may be, yet without this it will only prove a Babel [Gen 11]. I shall therefore endeavor to shew the duty of a Mason; and the first thing is, that he believes in one supreme Being [Ps 99:2), that he is the great Architect of the visible world, and that he governs all things here below by his almighty power,[44] and his watchful eye is over all our works. Again we must be good subjects to the laws of the land in which we dwell, giving honour to our lawful Governors and Magistrates, giving honour to whom honour is due [Rom 13:7].[45]

Readers saw more of the same five years later when Boston's African American Masons printed another "charge" from Hall, this one addressing Africa, Africans, and the evils of slavery. In these eighteen large-print pages, Hall referenced eight biblical narratives, five cited by chapter and verse, to demonstrate God's abhorrence of human bondage and explain the responsibilities of faithful Masons. When he appealed to the Bible as supreme authority, he employed a phrase with strong biblical resonance: "The Scriptures everywhere from Genesis to Revelations warns [sic] us against" the "slavish fear of men." "Slavish fear of men" was not a direct quotation, though it echoed passages like Proverbs 29:25 ("The fear of man bringeth a snare: but whoso putteth his trust in the Lord shall be safe") and also appeared regularly in the era's sermons and biblical commentaries. Hall's summary conclusion about God's condemnation of slavery quoted one more text without specifying the reference. The passage had already become a beacon of African American hope: "Thus doth Ethiopia begin to stretch forth her hand [Ps 68:31], from a sink of slavery to freedom and equality."[46]

As published works by African Americans became more frequent, the same rhetoric prevailed. In the years between 1831 and 1833, a Connecticut-born free Black woman delivered five addresses to church audiences in Boston and New York that were then published in 1835 as *Productions of Mrs. Maria W. Stewart.* Maria Stewart was, according to Benjamin Quarles, the first Black woman "to speak in public and leave extant texts of her addresses."[47] After being widowed in 1829, she was, in her own words, "as I humbly hope and trust, brought to the knowledge of the truth, as it is in Jesus, in 1830." The same autobiographical record credits "the most noble, fearless, and undaunted David Walker," author of the landmark *Appeal . . . to the Coloured Citizens of the World* (1829), with inspiring her own public advocacy.[48] As Valerie Cooper has written in an authoritative study, "rather than speak about herself, Stewart quotes the Bible again and again."[49] Stewart's scriptural attack on the degradation of African Americans is the most important feature of what she wrote. But the extraordinary extent to which the Bible infused her speech between quotations of specific passages illustrated powerfully the Scriptures' shaping rhetorical force. Illustrations of biblical diction, phrasing, and seamless scriptural quoting can be found almost at random, for instance:

> I am of a strong opinion, that the day on which we unite, heart and soul, and turn our attention to knowledge and improvement, that day the hissing [Jer 25:9] and reproach among the nations [Ezek 5:14] of the earth against us will cease. And even those who now point at us with the finger of scorn, will aid and befriend us. It is of no use, for us to sit with our hands folded [Prov 6:10], hanging our heads like bulrushes [Isa 58:5], lamenting our wretched condition: but let us make a mighty effort, and arise; and if no one will promote or respect us, let us promote and respect ourselves.[50]

An even more sophisticated use of biblical diction, quotation, and allusion appeared in 1861 with the publication of Harriet Jacobs's *Incidents in the Life of a Slave Girl*, most of which narrated the author's life of family breakup, sexual predation, steely moral resolve, and white-knuckle danger before she escaped to the North in 1842.[51] Jacobs, who published the book as "Linda Brent" and with the acknowledged editorial assistance of Lydia Maria Child, frequently brandished the Sword of the Spirit to assault the slave system.[52] The memoir from start to finish was steeped in fully scriptural rhetoric. Thus, an early passage recounted Jacobs's relationship with her father: " 'You are *my* child,' replied our father, 'and when I call you, you should come immediately, if you have to pass through fire and water' [Isa 43:2]." When Harriet heard of her father's death, "My heart rebelled against God, who had taken from me mother, father, mistress and friend" (echoing 1 Sam 12:15). But she was comforted by her grandmother: " 'Who knows the way of God?' said she [echoing Prov 20:24]."[53] As for Maria Stewart, almost all other African Americans who broke into print, and for many white authors as well, to write for the public was to enlist words, phrases, and the sacred context of the King James Bible.

Instinctive channeling of King James language, which was bred in the Protestant bone, also extended to Catholics whose leaders mandated a different translation. William Gaston, a North Carolina jurist, has been called "one of the foremost Catholics of his time, if not the greatest Catholic of the South." He had been the first student at Georgetown University in Washington, D.C., before returning to a distinguished career in his native state as a judge and legislator. At the recommendation of Supreme Court Justice and Harvard law professor Joseph Story, Gaston received an honorary Harvard LL.D., the first Catholic to be so honored. Widespread respect for Gaston's probity even survived his efforts to moderate the harsh slave legislation that North Carolina enacted after the Nat Turner rebellion in 1831. Gaston did not flaunt his religion, but its sincerity, which included an extensive knowledge of Scripture, was often manifest. During legislative debate in 1831 he once rebuked an opponent by quoting Matthew 12:34, "Out of the abundance of the *heart*, the mouth speaketh." Later, when pressed to become North Carolina's chief justice, he wrote a friend, "I know that I am to stand before the judgment seat of an all knowing and just God to render an account of the deeds done in the body [echoing Col 4:1]." As a judge he also went out of his way to deny that a slave owner enjoyed the right to kill a slave, a notion he called entirely "repugnant to the spirit of those holy statutes which 'rejoice the heart, enlighten the eye, and are true and righteous altogether'" (Ps 19:8–9).[54] It is noteworthy that in these and other citations, Gaston seems to have referenced the King James rather than the Catholics' Douay-Rheims translation.

That same knowledge also explains the frequency with which Americans drew sobriquets of honor or dishonor from Scripture. Some ascriptions became famous because of whom they described and when. In 1825, opponents of John Quincy Adams cried out "Corrupt Bargain!" when Adams named Henry Clay his secretary of state after Clay delivered his electors to Adams in that year's hotly contested presidential election. The defeated Jackson did not hold back: "[T]he Judas of the West has closed the contract and will receive the thirty pieces of silver—his end will be the same."[55] The same Judas metaphor, though now nationalized, served Orestes Brownson's purpose when, during the presidential campaign of 1840, he excoriated both Democrats and Whigs for persistent prevarication: "Think of a Judas betraying his Master. Well may he who has betrayed the truth go out and hang himself, or fall asunder and have his bowels gush out."[56] In 1850, Senator Daniel Webster's impassioned plea for the Union, even if requiring a strengthened fugitive slave law, prompted John Greenleaf Whittier to compose "Ichabod," a poem that lamented "The glory from [Webster's] grey hairs gone / Forevermore!"[57] The work took for granted universal awareness of a grisly story from 1 Samuel chapter 4 when, after Israel was defeated in battle, the high priest Eli collapsed and died from remorse, and his daughter-in-law also died after giving birth to a son whom she named Ichabod, or "the glory is departed from Israel" (1 Sam 4:21). Another New Englander, just as distraught with the Massachusetts senator, claimed that "the very Samson of New England" was now "grinding in the prison house of the Philistines."[58]

So it continued in the tumultuous decade that followed. During the debates that led to Stephen Douglas's Kansas-Nebraska Act of 1854, antislavery northern clergy exploited American history to call the senator "Benedict Arnold," but they also named him "Pontius Pilot" and "Judas Iscariot." In later campaigns he was a "sinful Jeroboam," the son of Israel's King Solomon who had betrayed his father's wise legacy. For his willingness to back Douglas, President Franklin Pierce was likened to a "latter-day Ahab, deaf to the warnings of his Elijahs, the anti-Nebraska clergy." When in 1856, South Carolina congressman Preston Brooks, inflamed by sectional loyalty and a perceived breach of honor, brutally caned Massachusetts senator Charles Sumner on the floor of the Senate, a minister in Alton, Illinois, said the attack amounted to the "same cowardly *expediency* [that] crucified the Son of God."[59] Famously, after the assassination of President Lincoln, he was mourned as "Father Abraham," especially by liberated bondsmen and -women.[60]

Implicit in these widely deployed biblical tropes was the assumption that God took special care of the American nation. It was as if an elective affinity drew together conceptions of the United States and references to Scripture, especially Old Testament narratives. The conjunction was a constant, as illustrated in the nation's early years when a Virginia Baptist bid farewell to members of his congregation who were embarking for the Kentucky frontier. Lewis Craig "extolled the bounties of the promised western lands: 'The rich and illimitable acres of a western Canaan were offered to them,' and [said that] they would go forward with faith in the same God who led the Israelites through the dessert [*sic*] as a cloud by day, and a pillar of fire by night."[61] Maj. Robert Anderson would later become famous as the Union officer who held Fort Sumter in Charleston harbor until a cannonade by Confederates began the Civil War. During earlier military duty in the Mexican War, and reflecting the biblical training of his military and land-accumulating family, he said much the same thing: "I begin to liken our position to that of some of the Armies whose exploits are recorded in the bible, and hope that our operations are blessed by God, whose instruments we may be, to effect some wise scheme of His providence."[62]

Given the great attention they received, presidential inaugurals constituted a special case of providential reasoning.[63] General references to variations on the "Almighty Being who rules over the universe" (Washington's First Inaugural, 1789) appeared in almost all the addresses, with James Monroe in 1821 the first to name that being as "Almighty God."[64] Biblical echoes or phrases were also common, as when Thomas Jefferson in 1801 spoke of the United States encompassing enough physical space for "our descendants to the thousandth and thousandth generation" (Ps 105:8) or when Martin Van Buren in 1837 declared similarly that "the stability of our institutions" would "make our land last for a thousand generations [Deut 7:9] that chosen spot where happiness springs from a perfect equality of political rights." Full quoting of biblical material was less common; John Quincy Adams was the first to do so when in 1825 he closed his address by appealing for the support of Congress, the states, the public at large, "and knowing that 'except the Lord keep the city the watchman watcheth in vain' [Ps 127:1], with fervent supplication for his favor, to His overruling providence." Lincoln's Second Inaugural, with its complex view of providence, would be the next to quote the Bible so directly.

Well before Lincoln, however, several of the presidents used biblical phrases or allusions to reinforce the idea that God sustained a special interest in the nation's fate. Many of the speeches referred to God's oversight of all things, an increasing number specifying the United States as the beneficiary of that providence. So Zachary Taylor in 1849—"the goodness of Divine Providence [that] has conducted our common country." (His address also testified to the nation's biblical commitments by being postponed until March 5, a Monday, to avoid conducting business on the Christian Sabbath.)[65] John Adams in 1797 had been the first of several to describe with direct biblical language God's special care of the United States. In his case, he invoked Psalm 2:9 to record how "under an overruling Providence" the nation's founders "broke to pieces the chains which were forging and the rod of iron that was lifted up." Jefferson's Second Inaugural in 1805 followed suit when he ended by spelling out his need for divine assistance: "I shall need, too, the favor of that Being in whose hand we are, who led our fathers, as Israel of old, from their native land and planted them in a country flowing with all the necessaries and comforts of life [Ex 3:17 and 33:3], who has covered our infancy with His providence and our riper years with His wisdom and power." Van Buren in 1837 changed the formula from declaration to petition when he ended his address by looking "to the gracious protection of the Divine Being whose strengthening support I humbly. solicit. May her ways be ways of pleasantness and peace [Prov 3:17]!"

In the longest-ever inaugural oration, Van Buren's successor, William Henry Harrison, offered the era's most specifically Christian-republican statement.[66] Although Harrison did not quote Scripture in this part of his 1841 address, its words brought together the republicanism, providentialism, and American exceptionalism that many would have instinctively heard in the phrases of Scripture:[67]

I deem the present occasion sufficiently important and solemn to justify me in expressing to my fellow-citizens a profound reverence for the Christian religion and a thorough conviction that sound morals, religious liberty, and a just sense of religious responsibility are essentially connected with all true and lasting happiness; and to that good Being who has blessed us by the gifts of civil and religious freedom, who watched over and prospered the labors of our fathers and has hitherto preserved to us institutions far exceeding in excellence those of any other people, let us unite in fervently commending every interest of our beloved country in all future time.

It is hardly a revelation to emphasize the rhetorical prominence of the King James Bible in antebellum American life.[68] To be sure, that prominence was replicated in England and Scotland during the same era, but with a crucial difference.[69] In the United Kingdom, the Bible remained central, but alongside the established churches, its ancient universities, an inherited respect for learned scholarship, and serious restraints on democratic expression—none of which cushioned reliance on Scripture in the early United States. That reliance marked a distinct chapter in the nation's rhetorical history but also underscored the strong mental linkage between the new nation and ancient Israel.

7

Publishing

As with the ubiquity of biblical rhetoric, so also did a printing landscape featuring the publication of bibles and Bible-themed literature draw new and old worlds together. Yet even with Britain's well-established leadership in Bible publishing and its development of voluntary organizations to promote Bible distribution, the United Kingdom did not witness the dominance that Scripture and Scripture-themed print achieved in the early United States.

When in 1816 a gathering of mostly Presbyterian and Congregational Federalists from New England and the Mid-Atlantic states created the American Bible Society (ABS), that landmark event immediately reshaped what had been the early republic's vigorous but highly diffuse enterprise of Bible printing. Less obviously, it also opened a new era in the more general history of American publishing—and therefore also of national culture and national self-consciousness. Though the ABS was greeted with enthusiasm in many quarters, initial publicity almost immediately alarmed some Americans, who saw coercion lurking in the projects of Protestant "voluntarism." That fear, as well as the unanticipated results that took place when the ABS eagerly participated in an economy of unrestricted market forces, has also drawn the attention of modern scholars. Such considerations—the very real achievements of the ABS and its sister organizations, the resistance to their success from republican localists and sectarian Protestants, and the critical questions raised by some historians—cut to the heart of what it meant for the United States to be a Bible civilization. The history of the ABS and, more generally, of early U.S. religious publishing, is ideal for considering the character of that civilization.

Religious Publishing before the American Bible Society

Comparisons offer the clearest means for discerning the centrality of Bible-themed publication in the early decades of the nineteenth century, with Exhibit A the popular novels and the much more widely distributed textbooks aimed at promoting basic literacy. Considering these publications alongside religious works and bibles is one way of correcting mistaken generalizations about early U.S. history, like the claim that Harper & Brothers of New York City was "the very first book [publisher] to adopt stereotyping as a regular procedure" or that "the

America's Book. Mark A. Noll, Oxford University Press. © Oxford University Press 2022.
DOI: 10.1093/oso/9780197623466.003.0008

early American novel soon became the single most popular literary genre of its day."[1] Attending to publication numbers can show, not an absolute monopoly of Bible-related materials, but far wider distribution than for any other form of print.[2]

Before the appearance of *Uncle Tom's Cabin* in 1852, the best-selling novel in the United States was *Charlotte Temple*, penned by an actress, playwright, schoolteacher, and author, Susanna Rowson, who published the book while living in England but who spent most of her life in the colonies and then the United States. Between its first American printing in 1794 and 1840, American printer-publishers brought out more editions of this work (at least seventy-three of them) than the three next most-published novels combined (Daniel Defoe's *Robinson Crusoe*, Samuel Johnson's *Rasselas*, and Samuel Richardson's *History of Pamela*).[3] Rowson's story of "sensibility and seduction" chronicled the life of a young Englishwoman who was led astray by a female French libertine, seduced by a British soldier, enticed into emigration, abandoned in her new homeland, gave birth rejected and alone, was pursued to America by a loving father, but then died just as her father arrives and pledges to take care of the baby. Even with the literary conventions of a bygone era, it remains a captivating story that has recently received serious attention from students of American popular culture, the book trade, and women's history.[4]

For a general history of American publishing, however, *Charlotte Temple* is almost a sidelight. Painstaking scholarship focused on religious works has shown that this novel's admittedly noteworthy success pales in comparison to the much greater popularity of the Bible and what David Hall has aptly called religious "steady sellers."[5] Details about publications *before* the great Protestant voluntary societies began their herculean print labors provide a telling contrast. *Before* the ABS was founded in 1816—soon followed by the American Sunday School Union (1824) and the American Tract Society (1825)—*Charlotte Temple* had already become a publishing sensation, with at least nine separate editions following Mathew Carey's inaugural American printing in 1794. Yet in the period from 1794 to 1815, the disjointed, scattered, and very local efforts of American printers issued far more copies of classic Protestant books. Richard Baxter's slim tract *A Call to the Unconverted* had been a standard among earnest Protestants since it was published in 1658 by a chaplain to Oliver Cromwell's troops. It amounted to an extended exposition of Ezekiel 33:11, the text with which Baxter opened his work: "Say unto them, As I live, saith the Lord GOD, I have no pleasure in the death of the wicked; but that the wicked turn from his way and live: turn ye, turn ye from your evil ways; for why will ye die, O house of Israel?" In the twenty years before 1815, Baxter's *Call* was published by more American printers and with a wider national distribution than enjoyed by *Charlotte Temple*. In addition, where no new British editions of *Charlotte Temple* appeared in those years, Baxter was reprinted many times by English, Scottish, and Welsh presses, many of whose copies also filtered across the Atlantic to expand the number of Americans who owned and read the book.[6]

Production of another Protestant standard reveals even more details about national book distribution in that two-decade period. As compared to the approximately ten editions of *Charlotte Temple*, American printers produced at least thirty-five editions of John Bunyan's *Pilgrim's Progress*. Many of these editions appeared from the nation's emerging publishing centers. But they also came from smaller cities, like Windsor, Vermont, and Burlington, New Jersey, as well as in a German translation from Lancaster, Pennsylvania. The American printings of Bunyan's allegorical classic, which had been published originally in 1678 and 1684, included abridgements, cheap text-only versions, and more expensive volumes bedecked with lengthy biographical introductions and elaborate woodcuts. In whatever form, all communicated the profoundly biblical frame of the work. On the first page of Bunyan's text in most of these editions, the second sentence of his narrative was footnoted with reference to Isaiah 64:6; Luke 14:33, Psalm 38:4, Hebrews 2:2, and Acts 16:31 and 2:37.[7] That anchoring of Bunyan's allegorical narrative to its biblical bedrock continued to the very last page.

Elementary instructional primers were the only publications of the time that matched the national reach of steady religious sellers or came close to the production of bibles. Jedidiah Morse, whom we have met as a panicked foe of the illusive Illuminati and the object of Elias Smith's wrath, achieved national renown with his patriotic effort to give the new nation its own geography.[8] Later editions of his *Geography Made Easy*, first published in 1784, his much more extensive *American Geography* (1789), and his gazetteer, *The American Universal Geography* (1793), eventually achieved national circulation comparable to the reach of *Pilgrim's Progress*. In 1819 nine publishers coordinated their efforts to produce a new edition of Morse's *American Universal Geography* (three in New England, three New York, and then Philadelphia, Baltimore, and Savannah) at a time when the printing of *Pilgrim's Progress* remained local and ad hoc.[9]

Noah Webster's *American Spelling Book*, first published in 1783 before being reissued in numerous later editions, and Lindley Murray's *English Reader*, with a first American publication in 1813, were even more widely used than any work by Morse.[10] Webster's "blue-back speller," so named for its characteristic binding, explained principles of pronunciation, led readers through graded lists of words (from one syllable to five syllables), and then provided sentences for practice (again moving from simple to complex). Murray's *Reader* offered substantial prose extracts for practice, as had earlier, similar books. The content of Webster's and Murray's prose selections are considered in chapter 14; here, comparative publishing numbers are in view.

Webster and Murray, as publishing phenomena, shared their prominence with religious works and especially the Bible. Webster's *American Spelling Book* in its various editions sold probably more than 3 million copies in its first thirty-five years.[11] But in the late 1820s and 1830s, even as its sales continued briskly, the number of its new editions was matched by the number for Baxter's *Call* and exceeded by those for *Pilgrim's Progress*.[12]

The "Bible Alone" (as a Publishing Marvel)

Murray's *English Reader* eventually surpassed even Webster's *Speller*. Thorough research by Charles Monaghan and E. Jennifer Monaghan has documented an astounding 925 editions of the *Reader* published before 1840. It is an incredible number, but exceeded by the 1,023 editions of the Bible (or New Testament) that American printers produced from 1801 through 1840. If, as the Monaghans conclude by aggregating sales in Britain and the America, Murray was "the largest selling *author* in the world from 1800 to 1850," production of the Bible by American printers alone made *it* the world's best-selling *book*.[13]

Whatever deserves to be said about the popularity of books like *Charlotte Temple*, *Pilgrim's Progress*, or the elementary texts of Webster and Murray, the early United States possessed only one truly national book. Another comparison underscores that fact: between 1794 and 1815, while American printers offered to the public a total of 186 *different novels*, they produced an extraordinary 246 *editions* of the New Testament or the entire Bible.[14] Questions about who in fact read, marked, and inwardly digested the Bibles that were printed are very important. Here, however, it is also important to note the characteristics of these early printings, the human stories hiding behind mere enumeration of editions, and the scale by which the availability of the Scriptures far exceeded any other material in print.

The most salient reality was the most obvious. Over 95% of the Bible editions before 1840 gave readers the King James Version. Since many of these editions were reprinted, they invariably multiplied copies of this same translation. The first American printers to use stereotyped plates were not commercial presses but the Bible Society of Philadelphia in 1812; within three years the Society's printer had run off 14,125 complete bibles and 3,250 New Testaments from this one set of plates.[15] By comparison, Carey had printed only 1,000 copies of *Charlotte Temple* in 1794, with no further copies until the next edition appeared in 1801.[16]

Already by the first decade of the century, printer-publishers were creating and meeting audience demand by packaging the King James Version in many sizes, shapes, and prices. Some bibles were cheap, like the School Edition from a Hartford printer who from 1809 sold thousands of copies for sixty cents each to local Bible societies from Rhode Island to South Carolina.[17] Others tested the market's upper limit, like the four-, five-, and six-volume editions that with the King James text offered the "original notes, practical observations, and copious marginal references" by an evangelical Anglican, Thomas Scott (Figure 7.1).[18] Still other bibles cost a great deal because of their elaborate paratextual apparatus, like the first bible printed in Vermont, which appeared in 1812. Alongside the words of Scripture it gave readers a summary of the two testaments, a chronology of biblical events, a history of the Bible, tables for proper names and measures, pages for inscribing vital family records, and "A Clergyman's Advice for Married Persons."[19]

King James bibles did not literally blanket the landscape, but in New England and the Mid-Atlantic states they came close. During the period 1794 to 1815, at least eighty-nine printer-publishers in twenty-six cities produced 235 KJV editions, including an astonishing 75 (or almost four a year) from twenty different printers in Philadelphia. Mason Weems's excited correspondence from the field to Carey spoke for the energy that some of the Philadelphia publishers devoted to selling their bibles—at a time before canals laced the land and when roads ranged from rough-hewn to nonexistent. Despite his late start, Carey quickly became the nation's leading publisher of King James bibles and New Testaments, with thirty-three editions before 1816. He was also responsible for the period's three new editions for Catholics, one replicating the quarto Douay-Rheims bible of 1791 and two a Douay-Rheims New Testament.[20] Carey's prominence illustrates the beginnings of nationalized Bible production that would be concentrated in major urban centers.

Yet commitment to printing bibles locally for local readers still remained a prominent feature of the era. Printers in Haverhill and Westfield, Massachusetts; Walpole, New Hampshire; Chambersburg and frontier Pittsburgh, Pennsylvania, could not compete with Carey in Philadelphia or other metropolitan operations that produced editions every year or two. But the outlying enterprises did respond to potential readers close at hand.

The efforts of Simeon Ide in New-Ipswich, New Hampshire, were not typical, except in getting the job done. After purchasing a small press and type that had become worn from printing an edition of Shakespeare's works, and with typesetting help from his twelve-year-old sister, he got to work. Over a period of six months Ide set twelve pages at a time of the KJV New Testament (duodecimo), the maximum his supply of type allowed, then twice a week hiked four miles with proof sheets to the home of a neighboring clergyman who had agreed to vet his work. Of the large print run of five thousand copies that Ide finished in 1815, he sold one thousand in binding to the New Hampshire Bible Society for $280 and

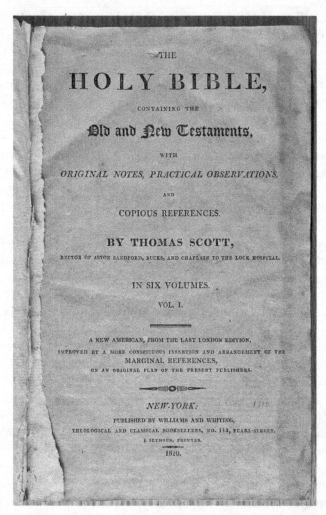

Figure 7.1 Although American Protestants became known for their loyalty to "the Bible alone," they also purchased many bibles with elaborate commentary, notes, and annotations. Especially popular was one prepared by an Evangelical Anglican, Thomas Scott. According to Margaret Hills's *ENGLISH BIBLE*, twenty-four separate editions of "Scott's Bible" were published in the United States between 1804 and 1874.

Source: Courtesy of Buswell Library Special Collections, Rare Books, Wheaton College, Illinois.

retailed the remainder for fifty cents each. (A good wage for a New England carpenter in 1815 was $1.50/day.)[21]

By the time Ide finished his work, changes that made religious printing the leading edge of a national print culture were accelerating. Alongside increased volume from larger urban firms, other signs of coordinated distribution included the beginning of Bible production by the Methodist church and by local Bible societies in Massachusetts, New York, Philadelphia, and Baltimore. Even as the War of 1812 provided a rare event capturing the interest of all Americans, these regional societies were preparing the way for a great leap forward in strengthening the nation's Bible civilization.

1816 and After

The creation of the ABS in 1816 solidified the centrality of Scripture in the emerging national culture. With its increased capacity for production, its systematic organization of philanthropy, and its aggressive schemes for national distribution, the ABS spearheaded a new phase in Protestant efforts to spread Christian faith, encourage Christian character, stabilize communities, and sanctify the nation.[22] It inspired other powerful national associations—especially the American Sunday School Union (ASSU) and the American Tract Society (ATS), but also countless regional, state, and local bodies—to disperse Scripture-based Christian literature on a hitherto unimagined scale. The ABS also modeled a program of national organization that countless others followed in pursuit of other societal goals, including temperance, peace, African colonization, hospital building, care for the deaf, prison reform, and, most significantly, abolition.[23]

Most of these well-organized voluntary societies were led by custodial Protestants eager to translate biblical mandates from the realm of personal sanctification to the sphere of national influence. If, as Daniel Walker Howe has written, "the history of the young American republic is above all a history of battles over public opinion," the directors of the ABS and similar organizations were the first to gear up for national combat.[24]

The ABS's leadership in stereotyped printing illustrated how it transformed American publishing and in so doing transformed the nation. (Figure 7.2) This new mode of production involved the preparation of metal plates allowing for reprinting books without the laborious, space-absorbing, and redundant process of setting type letter by letter for each new printing or new edition. As explained especially well by David Paul Nord, printers of Scripture were the first Americans to import stereotype plates from England and then to master the production of such plates themselves. Resources pooled by local Bible societies and then the ABS made it possible to purchase the costly plates from Britain and with these

Figure 7.2 These pages from an early (1817) New Testament from the American Bible Society illustrate the features that marked the millions of King James Bibles that followed: compact text, clean lines, division into separate verse-paragraphs, and presentation "without notes or comment" (except for headings at the top of the page).

Source: LOC Americana, LCCN-tmp96031089.

plates, soon augmented by their own, to produce great quantities of inexpensive copies. It also set an example for the ASSU, the ATS, and publishing efforts by the national denominations.[25]

Flush with bibles and other religious literature to sell or give away, the societies also pioneered methods of national book distribution. In the same way that Protestant revivalists perfected strategies for mobilizing the public copied by the nation's emerging political parties, so publishers of bibles and other religious literature pioneered procedures that commercial printer-publishers soon followed. Leadership in stereotype printing, when combined with the Protestant voluntary societies' pioneering use of steam-powered printing and machine-made paper—and with structured schemes of national distribution—made the production of Scripture and Bible-based books, pamphlets, tracts, and periodicals responsible for what Nord convincingly calls "the birth of mass media in America."[26]

Voluntary Organization

Three documents provide a particularly clear picture of how founders of the ABS and similar national initiatives strategized about the challenges of the day. They illumine, respectively, the voluntary ideal, the national scope of evangelical periodical publication, and the strategy of proprietary Protestants for advancing Christianity without Christendom.

The first was an address from August 1811 delivered by Elias Boudinot to the annual meeting of the New Jersey Bible Society, of which he was the president.[27] It exemplified the voluntary mobilization of nongovernmental Protestant energy that, like so much else in the religious life of the new United States, sprang directly from British precedents.[28] The pattern effectively began in 1699 with the founding of the Society for the Promoting Christian Knowledge. This organization provided edifying literature to Anglican outposts in the colonies, but its model of voluntary fundraising and extragovernmental direction exerted a much wider influence. Soon followed a sister Anglican organization, the Society for the Propagation of the Gospel in Foreign Parts (1701), and then a Presbyterian counterpart from North Britain, the Society in Scotland for Propagating Religious Knowledge (1709).[29] In 1750 a new London-based Society for Promoting Religious Knowledge among the Poor deliberately recruited members from Dissenting traditions as well as the state church. Its outreach also extended to the colonies, where the young Elias Boudinot and Benjamin Rush joined others who contributed annual dues in order to spread Christianity through literature, especially through the Bible offered to the indigent with no notes or commentary favoring any one denomination.[30] Although a new-world offshoot floundered because of the Revolutionary War, momentum for voluntary religious organization stumbled only briefly. In 1787 Massachusetts Congregationalists organized a Society for Propagating the Gospel among the Indians and Others in North America, and then in 1803 the Massachusetts Society for Promoting Christian Knowledge. The latter was modeled on both the older Society for the Promoting Christian Knowledge and the recently created Religious Tract Society of London (1799), which sought supporters from across the Protestant denominations. Midway in Thomas Jefferson's first term as president, Massachusetts Protestants organized the first ecumenical American organization devoted entirely to the production and distribution of religious print.

A year after this American project began, a committee of the London Religious Tract Society gathered an interdenominational circle of English Protestants to organize the British and Foreign Bible Society (BFBS).[31] Almost immediately it became an icon of evangelical cooperation, efficiency, altruism, and influence—at home as an eager adjunct to the expansion of the Second British Empire, in America as the paradigm for Protestant voluntary activity with no formal connection to government. From the start the BFBS accomplished prodigies of Bible production, distribution, and translation. Although the Society would be much imitated, it differed from later American efforts by obtaining bibles only from the three British printers authorized to publish the King James Bible (Cambridge University Press, Oxford University Press, and "the king's printer") and by strictly maintaining itself as a "non-religious" organization (because co-operation between Dissenters and the established church depended on staying as far away as possible from any official ecclesiastical sponsorship).[32] The expectation that government would naturally support such ventures came through clearly when in 1804 Britain's *Christian Observer* commended the Connecticut state legislature for circulating bibles throughout the state for use in schools and for family worship.[33] Unlike the British, Americans very soon would stop looking to governments for accomplishing their religious purposes. Instead, they adjusted the imported model of the BFBS to free-form voluntary efforts.

The first American Bible society was founded in Philadelphia in 1808 with the encouragement and a subvention from the BFBS. The Philadelphia organizers, who included Benjamin Rush, represented the vanguard of a great host. Boudinot's New Jersey society, organized the next year, would be one of the most active among the more than one hundred local Bible societies organized in the seven years before 1816.

Boudinot's address at the second annual meeting of the New Jersey society described programmatically its "object," "the means in our power," and "the importance" of their efforts. In a performance charged with millennial zeal, Boudinot praised the BFBS for having "almost performed miracles" in raising money and sending bibles throughout Europe and all the way to "India and her various casts [*sic*]." Even as he was hard at work on his own big books deciphering biblical prophecy, Boudinot channeled Scripture in a lyrical anticipation of the soon-coming End of Time:

> If the great God himself has declared, "that in the latter day he will pour out his spirit on all flesh" [Joel 2:28; Acts 2:17]; if our great Redeemer has, in his holy word, commanded his disciples "to preach the gospel to every creature in the world, and that he will be with them to the end" [Matt 28:20]; are not *we* called upon, who profess his holy religion, (and on whom the end of the world, of the present era, seems to be fast hastening) to be up and doing?—Watching and praying [Matt 26:41], with our lamps trimmed and burning, knowing by the signs of the times that the voice, proclaiming that the bridegroom is coming, is almost sounding in our ears [Matt 25:1–13]?[34]

Boudinot did not entirely neglect the social impact of Bible distribution; he was, after all, a seasoned veteran of recent Federalist battles against

Democratic-Republican anarchy. He thus spoke glowingly of how "a general diffusion of the Bible among the poor, will enable them to gain more benefit from
the sermons they hear" and so "ameliorate the manners, the tempers, and regulate the conduct of the people at large." Yet, overwhelmingly, his great concern
was the hope that increased access to Scripture would spread "the glad tidings of
salvation, through the atoning blood of the Redeemer . . . to every human creature, ignorant of the all-essential truth of the gospel of the Son of God."[35]

From his position as the head of the New Jersey Bible Society, Boudinot
orchestrated the key moves that led to the founding of the ABS.[36] Against the
distraction of war with Britain, objections from Philadelphia concerning the necessity of a *national* organization, and theological resistance from High-Church
Episcopalians who wanted bibles printed with their Book of Common Prayer, he
persevered. The 1816 meeting in New York City that established the ABS was the
result.

Boudinot's 1811 speech, with its anticipation of the Second Coming of Christ,
fueled the conviction spreading rapidly among custodial Protestants that voluntary organization to distribute the Scriptures possessed universal significance.
Yet Boudinot did not stress the national messianism to which other Federalist
veterans of the Revolutionary era clung. In his new version the United States
still enjoyed a premier role in divine Providence, but now the goal was world
evangelization.

Periodicals and the Nation

The second document, published as a public letter in the *Panoplist and
Missionary Magazine* in October 1813, reinforced Boudinot's crucial early appeal. Its content, but even more the periodical in which it appeared, revealed in
graphic detail the temper of the times. The letter was written by Samuel Mills, a
key figure in the early history of American Protestant missions.[37] Mills had been
one of five students at Williams College in Massachusetts who in 1806 participated in a "haystack prayer meeting" that precipitated the founding of American
agencies devoted to foreign missionary service. Four years later he became one of
the first volunteers of the newly created American Board of Commissioners for
Foreign Missions (ABCFM). In 1812 he and another young man were dispatched
by the Massachusetts Missionary Society on a year-long fact-finding journey to
the country's opening South and West. Most of the resulting letter detailed the
need for bibles among "the 40 or 50,000 French Catholics [in and around New
Orleans] who are destitute [of bibles]; many of whom are ready and anxious to
receive such a treasure." He also anticipated that, since "a large extent of country
will probably be opened in New Spain for the circulation of the Scriptures, in

the Spanish language," there existed additional reasons for ramping up Bible production.

To meet such needs Mills proposed "the formation of a *General Bible Society*, open for the admission of all persons, of whatever religious denomination, in the United States, who are disposed to take an active part in this good work." By pointing to the equivalent of $400,000 that consolidated benevolence had raised the previous year in "the United Kingdom of Great Britain and Ireland," he urged his fellow citizens to cooperate "for the relief of the needy" with "some general bond of union." Mills also went out of his way to highlight its ecumenical potential. A Congregational minister himself, he nonetheless proposed that local Bible societies send delegates to Philadelphia in conjunction with the Presbyterians' annual General Assembly for the purpose of establishing a national organization that could minister "to the immortal souls of [his] fellow-men, their temporal as well as their eternal felicity."

That Mills broadcast his assessment of need in a magazine like the *Panoplist* speaks more generally of the "evangelical print culture" that by 1813 was drawing together a broadening circle of like-minded Protestants into an informal but by no means insubstantial national force.[38] It was a new thing not only for the churches but for the nation as a whole. In 1787 Benjamin Rush had been, in historian Richard John's words, "the only prominent public figure" to envision the U.S. Postal Service as the key, as Rush put it, for "conveying light and heat to every individual in the federal commonwealth." Before a national culture of any kind could come into existence—before there could be a national market, national political parties, or national voluntary organizations—there needed to be, in John's succinct summary, a functioning "postal system, the stagecoach industry, and the periodical press."[39] At the forefront of the "communications revolution" that created a national culture stood Protestant magazines like the *Panoplist and Missionary Magazine*.[40] Weekly and monthly periodicals distributed for roughly the same purposes not only covered the land; they were the era's *only* public voices advancing a compelling *national* vision.

The singular authority of such magazines in New England has been well described by Mary Kupiec Cayton, arguing that "evangelical Congregationalist publications dominated all forms of magazine print culture in the region during this era [1790 to 1820]."[41] To be sure, many general, secular, and nonreligious serials also appeared during those years, but few enjoyed the reach or the staying power of the region's twenty-five evangelical periodicals. Several historians have mined to good effect the *Monthly Anthology* of Boston that for the eight years of its existence (1804 to 1811) publicized early liberal and Unitarian views. By contrast, the *Connecticut Evangelical Magazine*, which has received less attention from scholars, lasted 38 years; the serial that began life as the *Massachusetts Missionary Magazine* survived for 132. In 1805 the liberal *Monthly Anthology* reached 440 subscribers, in 1809 the evangelical *Panoplist* between 6,000 and 7,000.

New England's print culture, however influential for the nation, should never be taken as the whole story. Yet in this instance similar generalizations are justified. In later years, the nation's "penny press," with mass circulation newspapers like the *New York Herald* (founded 1835) and *New York Tribune* (1841), as well as popular magazines like *Godey's Lady's Book* (1837) and *Harper's Magazine* (1850), edged out evangelical serials as the nation's most popular. (Though it is important to remember that the latter included a great deal of religious content and that several explicitly Christian magazines, like the ATS's *American Messenger* [circulation 200,000 in the 1850s] and the Tract Society's *Children's Paper* [circulation 290,000] competed well in the broader marketplace of later decades. Similarly, when novel-reading began to take off, several of the first American best-sellers were what David Reynolds has called "Biblical fiction," stories set in New Testament times and exploiting known biblical situations.)[42]

Into the 1830s, however, evangelical efforts that shared a common vision dominated the periodical landscape. Although Morse, the main editor of the *Panoplist*, brought to his magazine a highly combative political history, the journal that published Mills's letter had mostly given up political infighting. Instead of harping on New England's objections to the War of 1812, about which nothing was said in its October 1813 numbers, the editors urged readers to make appropriate spiritual use of the bountiful harvest of grain God had recently given the region. The name of this journal, not incidentally, came from Charles Wesley's well-known hymn "Soldiers of Christ, Arise" ("And take to arm you for the fight / The panoply of God"), which the learned hymn-writer had taken from the Greek word for "full armor" (of God) that the Apostle Paul urged believers in Ephesus to put on (Eph 6:11–18). Representative of the *Panoplist*'s chief concerns in October 1813 were reviews of sermons, one on behalf of the ABCFM by Yale's president Timothy Dwight (Jn 10:16, "other sheep have I") and one for the Connecticut Society for the Promotion of Good Morals by Lyman Beecher ("a reformation of morals practicable and indispensable").[43] No one could doubt the *Panoplist*'s militancy, but at least in the eyes of its editors, it was now the battle for souls, not the ballot box, that demanded action.

And so it went with the many other periodicals associated with founders of the ABS. The delegates from local societies who in May 1816 gathered in New York City included several minister-editors along with many of the laymen who funded their magazines. Among them were Nathaniel William Taylor from New Haven, who in 1819 helped found the *Christian Spectator*; Beecher, who as a Connecticut pastor established the *Connecticut Observer* and then, after moving to Boston, the *Spirit of the Pilgrims*; and John Holt Rice from Richmond,

Virginia, who by 1820 was editing both a monthly (*Christian Observer*) and a weekly (*Family Visitor*). Another periodical, this one edited from New York by John Caldwell, who provided essential assistance to Boudinot in founding the ABS, illustrated how prominently the Scriptures loomed in these magazines. The first issue of his *Christian Herald*, published on March 30, 1816, began with Psalm 145:10–11 on its title page. Before it printed the circular letter from Boudinot calling for a national meeting of local Bible societies, Caldwell's paper gave readers an article on Sunday schools, which were "training the illiterate poor to read the Bible."[44] Before long the ABS's annual reports and its own magazine, *ABS Quarterly Extracts*, joined the throng of widely distributed periodicals.

To be sure, regional and denominational variations did differentiate the evangelical message, if only slightly. Methodists and Baptists, for instance, played only secondary roles in the ecumenical mobilizations of the era, Baptists out of commitment to principles of local autonomy, Methodists with a desire to set up their own national organizations. The latter had created an independent Book Concern in 1789 but ramped up their national print industry only when Congregationalists and Presbyterians expanded their own efforts: a Methodist Tract Society in 1817, a Sunday School Union in 1827, and a Bible Society in 1828 that cooperated with the ABS. The first issue of the monthly *Methodist Magazine* in January 1818 showed how much they considered their periodical part of the larger evangelical effort:

The few years of the present century which have already passed away, have opened the most important and auspicious events, relative to the establishment of the kingdom of Jesus Christ upon earth. The united exertions of all denominations of Christians to spread the holy scriptures—the unadulterated word of God, savours much of that catholic spirit by which the friends of Christianity should always be governed, and furnishes a pleasing prospect of the extensive triumph of evangelical truth.[45]

The same combination of friendliness to other evangelical initiatives and promotion of its own distinctives characterized the weekly Methodist *Christian Advocate*, founded in 1826. Two years later it was going out to fifteen thousand subscribers and in two more years, after merging with another Methodist magazine, to as many as thirty thousand. These stratospheric numbers meant that the *Christian Advocate* was probably the most widely circulated journal of any kind anywhere in the world. At the time, only the *American National Preacher* (also founded 1826) that month-by-month published a single sermon came close to the number of subscribers.[46] The *National Preacher*, with its sermons on an individual biblical text, alongside the *Advocate*, with scriptural injunctions, quotations, and references sprinkled liberally throughout its broadsheet, perfectly illustrated the Bible's absolute priority in the most widely circulated periodicals of the time.

The point is not just that there were so many periodicals published by evangelical Protestants. The point is that they were saying about the same thing. And the "thing" central to saying just about the same thing was the Bible.

National Christianity without an Establishment?

The third document was published by the founders of the ABS as a record of their organizing business in May 1816. It included the society's constitution, a roster of its officers, and an address to the public.[47] The pamphlet spelled out in detail the founders' vision for a society serving the nation. Proprietary Protestants articulated the vision, with a clear indication of where they hoped it would lead. They would honor the nation's commitment to religious liberty, but at the same time spread the kind of Christianity that converted individuals, sanctified families, and voluntarily promoted the personal virtue without which the republic was doomed.

The ABS's initial presentation outlined the potential benefits of a national Bible society in much the same terms Elias Boudinot and Samuel Mills had earlier used. Foremost was "the importance of spreading the knowledge of the one living and true God, as revealed in his Son, the Mediator between God and men, Christ Jesus [1 Tim 2:5]." As the best possible "single measure" for "providing 'peace on earth and good will toward man' [Lk 2:14]" and for "carry[ing] the light of instruction into the dominion of ignorance and the balm of joy to the soul of anguish," they looked to "diffusing the oracles of God."[48]

But in tone this 1816 document differed considerably from Boudinot's millennial enthusiasm and Mills's passion for "the heathen." In particular, the ABS address seemed intent on reprising recent ideological struggles. It reminded readers that the new wave of philanthropic voluntarism was rising hard on the heels of "a period of philosophy falsely so called." Without mentioning Tom Paine by name, no one doubted the reference when they wrote of schemes "under the imposing names of reason and liberality, [that] were attempting to seduce mankind." Bible distribution, they believed, was now challenging "the conspiracy of darkness, disaster, and death." The ABS's founders reprised Federalist discourse by claiming that their society had overcome "local feelings, petty prejudices, sectarian jealousies." Moreover, provision of the Scriptures would save "the prodigious territory of the United States" from "the dreadful consequences which will ensue from a people's outgrowing the knowledge of eternal life"—which, in turn would spell the ruin of "civilized society." If the ABS could do its work in sending "a Bible to a desolate family," that Bible would become "a radiating point of 'grace and truth' [Jn 1:17] to a neighbourhood of error and vice."[49]

In this first address to the public, the ABS remained clearly nonpolitical, in a narrow sense of the term. Yet it expanded beyond what Boudinot and Mills had desired, and also differed markedly from the contemporary Methodist concentration on evangelism pure and simple. Observers were not left in doubt about the virtues of national coordination ("concentrated action is powerful action"). Neither could they miss enthusiastic admiration for "The British and Foreign Bible Society" ("an example without a parallel . . . of the most unbounded benevolence and beneficence . . . embodied in a form so noble and so Catholick").[50] Yet those who wondered if the ABS was simply aristocratic Federalism reborn—if it was just another scheme of the Congregationalists and Presbyterians to recover the influence through voluntarism that they lost by the separation of church and state—found further evidence in the new society's leadership.

Fifty-nine delegates and representatives from thirty-five local Bible societies called the new organization into existence.[51] Their number included activist New England clergymen like Jedidiah Morse and Lyman Beecher, prominent Presbyterian and Dutch Reformed ministers and laymen from the Mid-Atlantic, and a few representatives from Virginia and the opening West. The delegate from Otsego, New York, was James Fenimore Cooper, whose Leatherstocking Tales, in the words of Walter McDougall, would give "the country a history free of Europe."[52] The ABS followed the BFBS by organizing with a president, a largely ceremonial body of vice presidents, and a board of managers who conducted the society's business.[53] The president, Boudinot, and the first vice president, John Jay, headed a host of other Revolutionary veterans and distinguished friends of George Washington. The twenty-three men asked to serve as vice presidents did include a smattering of Democratic-Republicans, like Governor Thomas Worthington of Ohio, a Methodist whose antislavery views aligned him with Boudinot and Jay. But the overwhelming majority of vice presidents and managers represented the flower of early national Federalism: the three Federalist candidates for president after John Adams (C. C. Pinckney, De Witt Clinton, Rufus King); Federalist governors of Vermont, Rhode Island, Massachusetts, and Connecticut; others on state courts and the national Supreme Court (John Jay, Bushrod Washington); along with distinguished Presbyterians and Dutch Reformed from New York and New Jersey, including Richard Varick, former mayor of New York, wealthy landowners (Stephen Van Rensselaer, Henry Rutgers), and prominent lawyers like Samuel Bayard of Philadelphia.

The society's first secretary for foreign correspondence was Dr. John Mitchel Mason of the Associate Reformed Church, who had cooperated with the Rev. William Linn in raising religious objections to Thomas Jefferson in the election of 1800. Mason's contribution had been a pamphlet exploiting Joel 2:1 ("Blow

the trumpet in Zion") and Exodus 32:26 ("Who is on the Lord's side?") to attack the Virginian as "an unbeliever in the scripture."[54] The eleven-member committee charged with drafting the Constitution and preparing the public address
included William Jay, who had left Federal partisanship behind, but also Beecher
and Morse, who had not. The apocalyptic notes in the address resembled much
that Morse had earlier written about the Illuminati and Beecher about the evils
arising from disestablishment in Connecticut (before he changed his mind to
consider it a boon).[55]

Given the leadership of the ABS, it is hardly surprising that some Americans
regarded the organization as a power play orchestrated by clerical New England.
Jefferson was one of them. In November 1816, John Adams mentioned in a letter
to Jefferson that "a National Bible Society" had been founded in order "to propagate King James's Bible" throughout the world. Although Adams felt it would be
much better "to purify Christendom from the Corruptions of Christianity ... than
to propagate those Corruptions" abroad, he repeated to Jefferson his positive
appreciation of the Bible as he himself read it: "The Ten Commandments and
the Sermon on the Mount contain my Religion."[56] Two years earlier Jefferson
had cheerfully subscribed the substantial sum of fifty dollars to a Virginia Bible
society since he took for granted that its efforts would be strictly domestic.
(Jefferson's "own [religion forbade] intermeddling" with other countries.) He
told his 1814 correspondent that "there never was a more pure & sublime system
of morality delivered to man than is to be found in the four evangelists." In this
opinion, he reflected the high evaluation of Jesus that Jefferson had learned from
Joseph Priestley. Shortly after writing against Paine's *Age of Reason*, Priestley had
persuaded Jefferson that honoring Jesus was far from the same as accepting traditional institutional Christianity.[57]

But in November 1816 with the ABS in view it was a different story. Only a few
months earlier Jefferson had complained to a correspondent about "the priesthood," custodial Protestants who corrupted "the purest of all moral systems,
for the purpose of deriving from it pence and power."[58] As he saw it, efforts by
the nation's aggressive evangelical philanthropists to promote the Bible worldwide only reprised a disastrous history: "These incendiaries, finding that the
days of fire and faggot are over in the Atlantic hemisphere, are now preparing
to put the torch to the Asiatic regions." To Adams he clinched his denunciation
by wondering how supporters of the ABS would react if the pope sent Jesuits to
America for the purpose of distributing mass-books and the Catholic Vulgate.
For Jefferson, scope and scale were key in opposing such efforts "to act thus nationally on us as a nation."[59]

Despite such initial opposition, the work of the ABS flourished, often by
imitating many of the features of the BFBS. In order to transcend denominational differences, it followed the BFBS and distributed bibles "without note or

comment." The ABS's managers in New York, like the BFBS's "committee" in London, handled management and production but worked through local auxiliaries to raise money, canvass for need, and distribute the books. They soon started a promotional and informative periodical, *Quarterly Extracts*, as had their English model. In principle the ABS, like the BFBS, did not give away bibles but rather made them available at discounted prices for the auxiliaries to purchase and then resell. As suggested by its 1816 address to the public, the ABS did expect positive social results from its labors, though it remained less specific about those matters than the BFBS. In the years after the Napoleonic wars (with much labor unrest) and Peterloo (the Manchester massacre of 1819 prompted by agitation for reform of Parliament), the BFBS made no secret of insisting that bibles for the poor undercut radicalism and stabilized the social order.[60]

Although it would take several decades until Bible production from the ABS reached the numbers of the BFBS, from the start it enjoyed almost uninterrupted success. In its third annual review, in May 1819, the officers reported that in the prior year they had printed over 47,000 bibles and 24,000 New Testaments, including 2,500 in Spanish. New vice presidents since its founding included Francis Scott Key and John Quincy Adams. To its auxiliaries the society was offering complete bibles in seventeen different formats and prices: eleven in English and six others in French, Gaelic, Welsh, and German. Prices ranged from sixty-four cents to three dollars (slightly higher for Welsh and German bibles); the Gospel of John was available in Mohawk for fifty cents and the epistles of John in Delaware for seven cents.[61]

After another decade of steady expansion, the Society launched an audacious plan for a "General Supply"—the provision of a Bible for every needy family in the entire country. Buoyed by the availability of new steam presses in New York, encouraged by the enthusiasm of many auxiliaries, and inspired by the "rapidly progressive march of Christian enterprise," the Society aimed high.[62] The plan was for members of the ABS's nearly seven hundred local auxiliaries to first canvass their districts in order to identify families without the Scriptures, then collect funds and order bibles from New York, where managers believed that their new presses were capable of printing 400,000 or even 500,000 books a year. If the plan worked, the estimated 800,000 American families without a copy would each possess their own.

In the event, this first General Supply fell short, but not by much. Income that had never risen so high reached over $143,000 in 1829–30 and $116,000 in 1830–31. (In 1830 the U.S. post office took in 1.85 million dollars.) In the three years from 1829 through 1831, the Society's presses printed 786,000 bibles and testaments and distributed from their depository over 638,000. (In 1830 there were about 2 million total households in the country.) In May 1831, auxiliaries reported having delivered bibles to every known family that had not previously owned a copy in Vermont, New Hampshire, New Jersey, Pennsylvania, Maryland, and thinly populated Michigan and Mississippi. A few other states came close, but results were disappointing in the South and West. It was, nonetheless, an impressive effort.[63]

Partners

Significantly, by 1830 the ABS was far from alone as a national organization passionately devoted to the distribution of Christian literature. The ASSU and the ATS, which shared many of their directors with the ABS, led a host of smaller agencies in matching the Bible Society's startling results. The ASSU originated in Philadelphia in 1817 as the Sunday and Adult School Union, with a name change in 1824 to indicate its broadened goals. By 1829, it possessed over ten thousand stereotype plates for the rapid reproduction of its teaching materials. In the four years from 1830 to 1833, the ASSU placed more than half a million books from these plates in its over seven thousand local schools. (For comparison, in 1830 there were 8,450 post offices nationwide.) For its part, from 1829 through 1831, the ATS's output—some very short pamphlets, many full-length books—amounted to five pages of published material each year for every person in the country.[64] Needless to say, the Bible featured prominently in almost everything such societies produced. As an example, a quotation from Matthew 11:5 ("The poor have the gospel preached unto them") provided the very first words of the first issue of the monthly *American Tract Magazine*, published in 1824 by the main predecessor of the ATS. The article that followed quoted several more passages in its first paragraph to encourage concentrated effort "that this mercy, obtained for us by the blood of Jesus, may, by the power of the Holy Spirit, be applied to our hearts."[65]

For a national population that in 1830 had almost reached 13 million, the evangelical voluntary societies came close to achieving nationwide coverage, at a time when, as Daniel Walker Howe points out, the Second Bank of the United States was "the only really nationwide business."[66] Titles from only the ATS and the ASSU exceeded the 1,661 editions of school textbooks published in the nation from 1816 to 1840.[67] In the twenty years from 1820 to 1839 the ATS and ASSU were responsible for far more individual titles than the 418 novels written by American authors and published by American printers.[68] The nationalization of commercial publishing did add textbooks like the *McGuffey Readers*, first published in 1835, to the earlier best-sellers of Webster and Murray Lindley. But no other type of literature came close to what Protestant printers produced.

The success of the ABS did mean that publishers like Mathew Carey, who pioneered the American printing of bibles, needed to change course. From the 1820s, Carey, the Merriam family in Massachusetts, and soon the Harper brothers in New York City mostly conceded the market in unadorned and inexpensive bibles to the ABS, while they turned to marketing more expensive books with engravings, commentary, maps, family trees, and other supplementary material. But these more elaborate bibles also gradually achieved considerable success until by the 1870s they made up more than half of new bible printings. So it was that the tidal wave of Bible publishing engulfed middle- and upper-class Americans as well as the poorer families targeted by the ABS.[69]

Christianity without Christendom?

More serious than the worries of competing printer-publishers, however, were theological or theological-political complaints that consistently dogged the ABS and other national enterprises. Theological objections from the nation's small contingent of High-Church, ritualistic Episcopalians arose even before the ABS took shape. If low-church Episcopalians like William Jay and Peter Jay eagerly joined "the evangelical united front," those who maintained High-Church convictions, like Bishop Henry Hobart of New York, insisted that faithful Christians needed more than "the Bible alone." Hobart, as a consequence, continued to support the Episcopal Bible society he had established in 1809, which distributed the KJV, but bound with the Episcopalians' Book of Common Prayer.[70]

Objections from Baptists caused more difficulty because they made up a larger segment of the national population. Although Baptists had no difficulty with the KJV that the ABS supplied in English, problems arose when translators in other regions raised the question of how to render the Greek word *baptizo*. The ABS, following the lead of the BFBS, in the early 1830s refused to fund a new translation in India that proposed rendering *baptizo* with a word meaning "immerse," which Baptists at home and on the mission field supported. In the wake of this debate, and as an indication of fragmenting evangelical labors, Baptist members resigned from the ABS in order to found a separate Baptist society of their own.[71]

The most serious resistance to the national efforts of the ABS and related philanthropies combined political with religious objections. As an instance, one of the many ways that debate over slavery dissolved national cooperation also affected the ABS. At the first annual meeting of the American Anti-Slavery Society in 1834, leading abolitionists criticized the ABS for not including enslaved families in the General Supply of 1829–31 and for letting slave owners restrict Bible distribution. When the Anti-Slavery Society founded its own organizations for getting bibles to slaves, it anticipated the momentous later crisis, when the denominations divided over competing views of the Bible and slavery.[72]

Before then, however, Thomas Jefferson and other Americans were reading professions of altruistic Christian outreach as a smokescreen for assaults on civil and religious liberty. The evolution of print from ad hoc and local to organized and national also excited the fears of sectarian Protestants who, in political lock-step with Democratic-Republicans and then Andrew Jackson, viewed such national organizations as a threat to republican freedom. Despite the enthralling prospect of intra-Protestant unity mobilized for spreading the Word of God, sectarian fears about elite influences from afar exacerbated the long-standing differences that had earlier appeared in responses to Tom Paine's *Age of Reason*.

Strife between sectarian and proprietary Protestants over national voluntary societies spoke directly to the challenge that believers inherited from the national founding: How in the absence of a state church, hierarchical learning, and automatic deference to tradition could Christianity remain a balm for the soul and a guide for society? The implicit answer that became explicit with proprietary Protestants like the leaders of the ABS was voluntary personal trust in the Bible, voluntary organization to promote the Bible, and voluntary acceptance of norms deemed biblical by tribunes of the people.

To proprietary Protestants the logic could not have been more self-evident:

Christianity was God's great gift to humanity.
The destitute often lacked the means to embrace Christianity.
The Bible supplied the means.
Christianity made citizens virtuous.
The virtue required for republican self-government required personally virtuous citizens.
Voluntary organization to provide Scripture upheld religious freedom while it sustained the republic.

To sectarian Protestants, however, it was equally self-evident that national organizations devised by proprietary Protestants threatened hard-won American traditions. In their eyes, power-mongering aristocrats were still aristocrats even if they hid behind religious verbiage and pretended to honor the American Revolution.

An 1819 petition from the managers of the ABS to the U.S. Congress exemplified proprietary logic even as it showed sectarians a power play in operation. The petition asked for exemptions from postage for mailing bibles and also from duty on imported paper used for printing the bibles. The lawyers who drew up the document informed Congress that Italian and French paper made from linen held up much better to the kind of heavy usage bibles received than domestically produced paper manufactured from cotton. They also documented similar relief provided to Bible societies in "Russia, Prussia, Saxony, Wirtemberg [*sic*], and the

Netherlands." But mostly they stressed "the national importance" of the ABS for "the national welfare."[73]

Their account drew directly on republican language ("vice," "virtue," "public morals") to explain how the Society served the nation. The ABS, as "a *National Institution*," directed its efforts "to *national objects . . .* for the *public good.*" Especially its solicitude for "the destitute and the ignorant" could lead only "to the improvement of society in knowledge and virtue." If Congress provided other subsidies for "the *bread that perisheth* [Jn 6:27], surely the claims of associations formed to supply the hungry minds of the poor and illiterate with the '*Bread of Life*' [Jn 6:35] will not be neglected or opposed by the enlightened representatives of a high-minded Christian community." The ABS closed its appeal with a classic conflation of Christian, republican, and providential reasoning:

> [Copies of the Bible] will tend to diffuse knowledge and to repress vice. They will improve public morals and increase private happiness. They will kindle and foster sentiments of piety to God, and of good will to man. And they will call down the blessings of Heaven on an enlightened and liberal government, whose highest glory it must always be, to see the people of the United States honoured and esteemed abroad virtuous and happy at home.[74]

In arguments anticipating Supreme Court litigation of recent years, the petitioners also defended the constitutionality of their request. They observed that the Constitution's prohibition "respecting religious establishments" was not meant to guard "against the *manufacture* and *circulation* of the Bible—not against the *principles* of Christianity—not surely against what its very enemies admit to be the *purest system of morals and duty* that ever was prescribed to man." Instead, the Constitution, rightly understood, prohibited "the dominant influence of any one religious sect, the union of *ecclesiastical* with *civil* power, the tyranny of *one* favoured and usurping religious denomination, and the consequent degradation and persecution of every other *dissenting* persuasion." The ABS, as "a charitable association for the *manufacture* and circulation of the Bible," could never be construed as "either in itself 'a *religious establishment*,' or . . . a tendency to create one." In fact, if taxes or tariffs diminished the number of bibles distributed, it would "violate the *spirit* of our national constitution and laws, by '*prohibiting*,' to a certain extent, '*the free exercise of religion.*' "[75]

In the event, Congress failed to act on the request for tax and tariff relief. But others who monitored the progress of national evangelical voluntarism were paying attention, Daniel Parker for one. Parker was a frontier Baptist who felt that nationally organized Christian enterprises violated the basic Protestant principle of fidelity to Scripture. As an advocate of "primitive," or Bible-only, Christianity, in 1820 he published a substantial tract against the recently formed

Baptist Board for Foreign Missions. Parker's complaints drew a theological line in the sand that others would observe in opposing the ABS, ATS, ASSU, and other national organizations. His indictment put in religious terms what some modern scholars have described in secular language: the "almost innumerable" errors of such consolidated societies "have nearly all originated amongst the wise and the learned"; they represented "the wisdom of the world, [rather] than the authority of the bible"; and they reflected "man's invention" instead of giving "the true meaning of God's word."[76]

A few years later, in 1826, a resident of upstate New York's "burned over district" extended the criticism. To Ephraim Perkins, the threat came from the inherent corruptibility of cash. The ideal of national philanthropy, with Presbyterians and Congregationalists in the lead, "is the organization of numerous societies or associations for the accomplishment of various objects . . . all of them, however, requiring to be *moved by the force of money* and sustained by large, permanent and increasing funds deposited in banking institutions or invested in the public stocks." Particularly egregious in this dangerous accumulation of capital were "about half a dozen [societies] organized upon an extended and connected plan," including "the Bible society, foreign missionary society, domestic missionary society, education society, tract society, and it is believed some others." To Perkins, the result, once again defined in traditional republican categories, endangered all of society: "pride, ambition, and haughtiness on the part of the clergy, and bigotry, ignorance and intolerance on the part of their followers."[77]

Then in 1830 appeared an all-out blast at the ABS itself, delivered anonymously by an author who claimed to be a member of the Society. With the kind of rhetoric that supporters of Andrew Jackson were then hurling at supporters of John Quincy Adams, the anonymous author blasted the Society for its "bespattering flattery" of the BFBS and for imitating the style of Britain's "arch-bishops and bishops, ministers and prime-ministers, earls, dukes, and lords." The author looked with special alarm at the ABS's plan to acquire new printing equipment, which showed that "[w]ealth and power is their grand aim." If those plans were realized, it would enable the ABS's managers "to sway that great engine, the press, to suit their own purposes of aggrandizement, without fear of being molested." Already the worried author thought that a cabal with the ABS at its center had gone too far in trying to enforce strict Sunday restrictions on trade, commerce, and the U.S. mails. Unless those leaders were "watch[ed] with utmost diligence," they would acquire increasing "influence and power." The angry author's last word recalled the Sons of Liberty two generations earlier, who worried that the accumulation of power "may enable them to subvert our present liberties by an unnatural union of clerical and secular government."[78]

Differences in perspective exemplified by the ABS and its critics revealed a fault line in aspirations for a Christian America. Proprietary Protestants exalted the spiritual benefits of Scripture but also enlisted utilitarian logic to argue for its national imperatives. In an atmosphere of religious freedom, where evangelicals of all stripes battled freethinkers and Deists, and where proprietary Protestants faced off against sectarian Protestants, it became increasingly expedient to defend the Bible for reasons that were extrinsic and social rather than intrinsic and spiritual.[79]

Organizers of the national societies also accepted without apparent hesitation the free-market practices of the nation's rapidly expanding economy. Assumptions about how business should be carried out made it easier to use standard commercial protocols for the spiritual purposes that inspired the purveyors of evangelical print. The transition that Peter Wosh called "from civil humanitarianism to corporate benevolence" was illustrated when the ABS, ASSU, and ATS turned from local voluntary auxiliaries to paid colporteurs. This "expansive complicity in the mechanization of market exchange," as R. Laurance Moore put it, "is surely the most important aspect of the particular kind of secularization" that developed throughout the nineteenth century.[80] High ideals remained in place, but they came increasingly to be carried out with instincts from the market.

If the custodial Protestants who sponsored the major publishing initiatives increasingly emphasized the social payoff from their work, and if they unhesitatingly adapted to the nation's expanding capitalist economy, how should modern historians evaluate their work? Candy Gunther Brown has judged their attempts at balancing spiritual "purity" with public "presence" as mostly commendable. While recognizing that the line between altruism and manipulation could be fine, she concludes, "Participation in the world of print did not represent an inevitable compromise as much as a proactive choice: to make the gospel more accessible by appealing to popular tastes while appropriating means of grace from extra-Christian sources."[81]

Focus on the same activities in the same cultural milieu, however, leads other scholars to opposite judgments. David Sehat has scored the elitist tendencies of the ABS and related organizations: the voluntary agencies "needed to be distinct from government to act as a watchdog. They needed to be independent of popular suffrage, because the mass of people could not be counted upon to maintain high moral standards."[82] Amanda Porterfield has viewed the moral cost of the voluntarism organized by proprietary Protestants somewhat differently, but no less harshly, suggesting that "evangelicals brought their investment in Christian reason and progress as well as their antipathy to open-ended, critical thought along with them to support, or at least not interrupt, the expansion of a national economy and political system that depended on the exploitation of blacks and consent of white women."[83]

Adjudicating such competing assessments requires patient attention to how devotion to Scripture actually played out in the religious sphere, how it related to the law, how it was experienced in a democratic milieu, and how it shaped the increasingly bitter struggle over slavery—all subjects that deserve extended attention by themselves.

8

Personal Religion

Throughout the European past, authority in church and state had descended from aristocratic hierarchies, formal establishments, and ministers set apart by their ordinations, their learning, or their family connections. Since the Reformation, the influence of lay authors, editors, and printers had moderated to some degree the Old World's top-down structures. In the new United States the diffusion of religious authority, which had expanded in colonial America, now expanded even more. As noted, Protestant writers, editors, and publisher-printers shifted successfully from overt political action to mastery of the new nation's wide-open cultural terrain. At the same time, in an environment liberated from the impediments of Christendom, dedicated Methodist circuit riders, energetic sectarians, and nervous but active custodial Protestants achieved remarkable success in Christianizing the population. Yet although church leaders and the evangelical mass media certainly played a major part in the era's remarkable spread of religion, even more important were individual commitments, individual initiatives, individual choices, and individual activities. Because personal religion in this era was so intensely scriptural, the spirituality of individuals also made a fundamental contribution to the nation's Bible civilization.

Creative research over the past generation has revealed the wide variety of religious expression in the early republic, including folk traditions, white and black magic, and beliefs about the spiritual power of material objects.[1] Yet foremost in early national religion assuredly stood the conscientious pursuit of practices inherited from the Protestant past. Among the most important were attentive listening to Scripture-based sermons, intensive personal reading of Scripture and literature infused with Scripture, and extensive use of hymn books that turned scriptural themes into verse for personal meditation and communal worship. Because these practices prevailed so widely in private, appeals to Scripture in public carried unusual weight. Here, however, it is first important to fix attention on features of ordinary American religion that are now too easily neglected— perhaps because they were once so piously invoked to support uncritical claims about a vanished "Christian America."

From one angle, much in the new United States had been anticipated in earlier Protestant history, especially the quickening of evangelical religion in the colonial era. In particular, the eighteenth-century awakenings had made inspiration from the Bible a matter of intense personal experience. Jonathan Edwards joined

America's Book. Mark A. Noll, Oxford University Press. © Oxford University Press 2022.
DOI: 10.1093/oso/9780197623466.003.0009

John Locke's epistemology of the senses with a Calvinist understanding of complete dependence on God to enliven scriptural images of the torments of hell and the delights of heaven. George Whitefield movingly portrayed a biblical drama of sinners chained in their sin and liberated by the Holy Spirit. Meditation on individual passages of Scripture had given honored spiritual exemplars like Sarah Osborne of Newport, Rhode Island, compelling experiences of forgiveness, love, and communion with God. Reliance on *sola scriptura* and the realization of an every-believer priesthood seemed to be reaching the consummation that Protestants had long devoutly wished.[2]

From another angle, however, the nineteenth-century American context mattered decisively. In the new United States, the structures of Christendom, which even in the colonial period had framed the preached, read, and hymned Word of God, were obliterated almost completely. American Protestants eagerly embraced as God's special gifts to themselves a Revolution promoting the equality of all men, a constitutional settlement rejecting church establishments as inherently tyrannical, and a republican political experiment depending on the virtue of private citizens. Protestants then energetically evangelized this culture by taking advantage of print media unleashed from prior restraints. In terms modified from Nathan Hatch, the result was Christianity Americanized.[3]

Americanization meant exchanging Calvinist insistence on God's choice of individuals for modified Calvinist or Methodist insistence on the ability of individuals to make the choice for God themselves.[4] It also meant believing that if the churches and the purveyors of Protestant print were to succeed, they needed to convince, rather than coerce, the public.

The main Protestant groups knew they faced three great challenges as the nation took shape. One was to rescue Scripture from radicals who hoped to exploit republican democracy for the triumph of freethinking; the second was to Christianize a citizenry cut loose from Christendom; the third was to shape a national culture with media adapted to democracy. Protestants united to meet the first challenge, Methodists and sectarian Protestants led in responding to the second, proprietary Protestants the third. As they met these challenges, the influence of preaching survived the loss of enforced church attendance, personal engagement with Scripture deepened even as it spread, and Americans sang the songs of Zion from the same biblical page.

Sermons

Despite their delivery by the millions and printing in the hundreds of thousands, sermons remain "curiously under-documented and under-analyzed" as a force in American history. The scholar who made that observation has also specified the reason why sermons contributed so crucially to the cultural shape of the new United States: "It is in the sacred space of preaching that the Bible has functioned most clearly as a living book with pastoral and communal significance."[5]

Like other features of national life, sermons differed in different regions and among different constituencies, even as they evolved in keeping with cultural change. The Puritan heritage meant that early national New England heard more sermons, longer sermons, and more intensely scrutinized sermons than other parts of the country. Episcopal sermons were shorter than sermons by Presbyterians. Enlightenment conceptions of the sublime influenced some urban preaching in the generation after independence. Methodist circuit riders preached with emotion and cared little about the sublime. Beginning early in the nineteenth century women appeared in pulpits with surprising frequency. Sermons heard by the enslaved could enforce bondage when delivered by white ministers, or inspire spiritual and sometimes physical liberation when delivered by Blacks. The celebrated preachers of the mid-nineteenth century, like Charles Finney and Henry Ward Beecher, deployed sentiment, anecdotes, and attention to public affairs in ways foreign to the notable preachers of a century before, like George Whitefield and Gilbert Tennent.

Yet despite immense variation, at least into the 1830s, sermons remained by far the nation's most witnessed form of public speech. In the first decades of national history, even the unchurched were likely exposed to more sermons than to public address of any other kind. And obviously, as an ever-present form of public rhetoric, sermons remained crucially dependent on the Scriptures. Ministers in colonial New England long followed the guidelines for preaching published by the stalwart Puritan William Perkins in his 1592 *Art of Prophesying:* "read the Text distinctly out of the Canonicall Scriptures . . . give the sense and understanding of it being read . . . collect a few and profitable points of doctrine out of the natural sense . . . apply . . . the doctrines rightly collected, to the life and manners of men in a simple and plaine speech."[6] The influence of this inheritance by no means vanished as the nation took shape; far beyond New England the same general approach prevailed. But even where it thinned or was unknown, sermons remained a potent vehicle for keeping Scripture central in public consciousness.

A few of countless possible examples can suggest the central role that sermons played in the lives of ordinary Americans. Gerrit Smith (1797–1874) ranked among the most visible northern reformers of the antebellum period. As an abolitionist, campaigner for temperance and women's rights, Free Soil member of Congress, presidential candidate of the Liberty Party in 1848, and benevolent owner of vast landholdings in upstate New York, Smith found much of the inspiration for his hyperactive life in the Scriptures. With his wife, Ann Fitzhugh Smith, he was converted in 1826 and soon joined the local Presbyterian church. For some time thereafter Ann read only the Bible and hymns, while, according to a recent history, "Gerrit's diary, which was lost . . . is reported to have swelled with the texts of every sermon he heard during the thirteen years following his conversion."[7]

Many Americans who lived out of the limelight that shone brightly on Smith attended to sermons—and their texts—just as conscientiously. In an unusually informative book published in 1980, Lewis Saum drew on letters and diaries written by literate but unpublished Americans to describe general habits of mind in the antebellum era. Time after time Saum found his authors referring to sermons heard, evaluated, and remembered. In 1830 Hiram Peck of New York City took in a sermon on Genesis 3:1–7 but was glad the minister had done no "medling [sic] with intricate points." In 1833 a storekeeper in the as yet unfamous Sharpsburg, Maryland, heard five sermons on a single Sunday. In 1849, Jackson Thomason embarked for California, not inspired by visons of national Manifest Destiny but heartened by a sermon from Numbers 10:29 ("We are journeying into the place of which the Lord said, I will give it to you"). Two years later, as a testimony to ministerial creativity and parishioner attention, a diary-keeper in Oswego County, New York, recorded a sermon based on the last two words of Psalm 9:16 ("Haggaion. Selah"). Saum also recorded a great deal of evidence for discriminating listening, as when Joseph Willard of Boston in 1853 heard a sermon on Isaiah 28:10 and reported, "Not much pleased."[8]

Sermonic expositions also figured prominently in antebellum literature. The fictional exposition by Herman Melville's Father Mapple in *Moby-Dick* (1851) was little read in Melville's own day but for the past century has been the object of constant critical fascination. Melville not only gave Father Mapple a memorable text from Jonah 1:17 ("And God had prepared a great fish to swallow up Jonah") that anticipated many of the novel's main themes; he also left a memorable description of the pulpit in the Seaman's Chapel as an encomium to the significance of what was preached: "Its paneled front was in the likeness of a ship's bluff bows, and the Holy Bible rested on a projecting piece of scroll work. . . . Yes, the world's a ship on its passage out, and not a voyage complete; and the pulpit is its prow."[9]

In contrast to *Moby-Dick*, *The Dairyman's Daughter* was a nonfictional narrative that achieved phenomenal popularity soon after it was published in 1810 but has been little noticed in recent decades.[10] It first appeared as a five-part serial in a magazine from the Religious Tract Society of London, but was then reprinted as a self-standing book by a number of British and American publishers in two longer and one twenty-four-page abbreviated version. Americans were responsible for the abridgement, which first appeared in 1813 and later became a featured title from the American Tract Society. In its first century the tract was reprinted 8 *million* times and translated into *forty* languages.

A genealogy of influence stretching across the centuries illustrates the cohesive force of the Christian literature that stretched across the physical terrain of Protestant America. Commitment to a common message, in other words, could function as a centripetal impulse counteracting the strong centrifugal forces of *individualized* Protestant faith. The clerical Anglican author of *The Dairyman's Daughter*, Legh Richmond, was decisively influenced by the lay Anglican William Wilberforce's *Practical View of the Prevailing Religious System of Professed Christians* (1797), a work similarly shaped by the Congregationalist Philip Doddridge's *Rise and Progress of Religion in the Soul* (1745), whose author had been converted under the influence of Richard Baxter's *Call to the Unconverted* (1657), which reflected Baxter's earlier reading of nonconformist Edmund Bunny's republication in 1584, after cutting "the popery out," of Jesuit Robert Parsons's *Booke of Christian Exercise Appertaining to Resolution* that had been first printed in 1546.[11]

Besides illustrating the attraction of a generic evangelical message, the tract testified just as profoundly to the centrality of Bible-based sermons in the Protestant imagination. The plot of this much-reprinted narrative hinged on a single text from a single sermon.

At the turn of the nineteenth century Richmond was serving as the rector of an Anglican parish on the Isle of Wight when he met Elizabeth Wallbridge and her family. After being asked to conduct the funeral for Elizabeth's sister, he heard from Elizabeth's father, the dairyman, that his surviving daughter had "some years ago . . . heard a sermon preached; and from that time she became quite an altered creature. She began to read the Bible, and became quite sober and steady." Later the Rev. Richmond learned from Elizabeth herself that the life-transforming sermon had focused on only a portion of 1 Peter 5:5, "Be ye clothed with humility." As the preacher opened this text, Elizabeth reported that she came to see him "as a messenger from heaven to open my eyes." That spark precipitated conversion and a changed life: "From that time I was led through a course of private prayer, reading, and meditation, to see my lost estate as a sinner, and the great mercy of God through Jesus Christ in raising sinful dust and ashes to a share in the glorious happiness of heaven." In her new life Elizabeth became a much-appreciated aid to her aging parents; as the alteration took place, she "read few books beside her Bible."[12]

The Dairyman's Daughter gave the world a stylized, idealized, but also affecting portrait of a self-centered sinner transformed into a believer whose "temper and conversation adorned the evangelical principles which she professed." In Richmond's account, Elizabeth displayed true religion at its best: "Her views of the divine plan in saving the sinner, were clear and scriptural. . . . She believed that the experimental acquaintance of the heart with God, principally consisted in so living upon Christ by faith, as to seek to live like him by love."[13] The narrative ended with an account of Elizabeth's wasting away, her death, and the second funeral the Rev. Richmond conducted for the dairyman's family. Throughout, the

Bible remained central—from its crucial role in Elizabeth's conversion, through a reading during her final days from 1 Corinthians 15 ("O death, where is thy sting?"), to the chapter from the book of Job that Richmond read privately to family and friends before conducting Elizabeth's public funeral.[14]

As a publishing phenomenon the tract in its three versions celebrated a Protestant ideal of a Bible-based sermon leading to a self-giving life of Bible-centered spiritual devotion, "scriptural consistency" in communicating the faith, and loving altruistic service to others.[15] When and how it was read remains mostly a mystery, but with occasional hints, as from the 1831 annual report of the American Tract Society. It passed on a letter from one reader, who wrote, "[Richmond's portrait of Elizabeth] made a deep impression on my mind. I saw my own need of the Saviour, who comforted, supported and saved the dairyman's daughter. These impressions did not leave me, till, as I hope, I found the same Saviour precious to my soul."[16]

However little sermons figure in most scholarly accounts of early U.S. history, the weekly discourses of settled ministers along with the peripatetic exhortations of Methodist circuit riders and enslaved bush preachers worked steadily on national consciousness. Because of this scriptural grounding and because, as Walter McDougall has written, "only one book had the power to bind or loose the nation," sermons played a key role in establishing the American Bible civilization.[17]

Reading

Prescriptive literature of the antebellum era frequently provided, as in the Methodist *Sunday School Magazine* from 1839, "rules for the reading of the Bible." In Candy Gunther Brown's summary of the Methodists' detailed instructions, the Bible "should be read with prayer; diligently; patiently; attentively; with faith, obedience, self-application, and fervor; daily in regular course; with commentaries; and in a manner that charges the memory."[18] The next year, the third edition of Thomas Charlton Henry's *Letters to an Anxious Inquirer* devoted an entire letter to Bible-reading that began by addressing "perplexity in reading the word of God." Henry, son of a president of the American Sunday School Union, touched on many subjects in this letter, like "mistaken apprehensions . . . failure arising from listlessness in reading . . . duty of becoming familiar with the plan of salvation." He concluded, perhaps ironically in light of the work's verbose instructions and its hundreds of biblical citations, that his correspondent, though needing "clear and full perceptions of divine truth," knew enough "to know that God demands your whole heart at once."[19] Throughout these years, the American Tract Society frequently appended its own "rules for reading" to various children's books and in its catalogues of available titles.

Everyone who saw these rules knew that the injunction "Read but few books, and those the best" meant first the Scriptures. How should the Bible and "the best" books be assimilated? "Read slowly. Read thoughtfully. Read understandingly. Review what you read. . . . Read with a view to improvement rather than amusement."[20]

Testimony to the importance of individual Bible-reading came from many sources during these years, perhaps most unexpectedly from the slave-owning white South. After the publication of David Walker's *Appeal* in 1829, with its all-out biblical condemnation of slavery, and Nat Turner's rebellion in 1831, as it became clear that Turner's Bible reading had inspired the revolt, several southern legislatures passed laws against teaching slaves to read. It went without saying that the laws were aimed at keeping the enslaved from approaching the Scriptures on their own. The prime mover of South Carolina's antiliteracy law, Whitemarsh Seabrook, who considered slaves a different "caste" of humanity, insisted that anyone who wanted slaves to read the Bible was fit only for "a room in the Lunatic Asylum." Another white South Carolinian urged a ban on slave literacy that would last "until those of our negroes who are taught to read the Bible, shall be unable to read Walker's pamphlet."[21]

Yet these hardline opponents of slave literacy were much outnumbered by slave owners whose evangelical commitment to Scripture overrode their defense of slavery. After South Carolina passed its strong antiliteracy law in 1834, petitions from several upcountry locations protested vigorously by invoking combined Christian and American principles: "We hold it to be one of the chief privileges and enjoyments of our religious profession and worship, to be permitted to search the Scriptures for ourselves, and we consider that law which robs our servants of this enjoyment to be a violation of the Constitution." The petitioners who advocated slave literacy—but never abolition—spotlighted the hypocrisy of commissioning foreign missionaries to promote the very Bible kept by the new law from the enslaved. Of paramount importance to these white southerners was the right "to teach our servants to read, with so much fluency and correctness, that they will be able to peruse the word of God and other religious books with pleasure and profit to their souls."[22]

It is important to remember a truism of modern scholarship: what readers take from their reading regularly diverges from what authors, publisher-printers, and the makers of "rules" intend.[23] Purveyors of Scripture hoped to convert individuals, advance the Kingdom of God, sanctify the nation, and make either a lot of money or enough to stay in business. But owners of bibles often paid them no heed or read them for their own purposes. Some remained simply confused, like the woman in western Virginia who showed a biography of Washington to colporteurs for the American Tract Society and told them she already owned a Bible.[24]

Evidence, however, abounds that individual Bible reading could often be as transformative as Protestant editors hoped or all-out slave defenders feared. Especially was that the case for African Americans. In chapter 6 we saw how immersion in Scripture shaped the prose that Maria Stewart and Harriet Jacobs offered to the world. The same sources also describe dynamic results arising from individual engagement with the biblical text.

When Maria Stewart published her *Meditations* in 1835, she began with a brief account of her own spiritual journey. She had "basked in the sunshine of prosperity" but also "drunk deep in the cup of sorrow," until "one year since Christ first spoke peace to my troubled soul." Immediately she desired "that I might become a humble instrument in the hands of God, of winning some poor soul to Christ." Then she explained that in giving her meditations to the world, with their witness to divine mercy in her own life and her testimony against the evils of slavery, "I have borrowed much of my language from the Bible." The reason was patent: "During the years of childhood and youth, [the Bible] was the book that I mostly studied, and now that my hands are toiling for their daily sustenance, my heart is most generally meditating upon its divine truths." She hoped that her own words in print would join many other examples to "prove to the world that there is a reality in religion, and a beauty in the fear of the Lord," without which "the cause of Christ will never be built up, Satan's kingdom will never be destroyed, the chains of slavery and ignorance will never burst, and morality and virtue will never flourish."[25]

In her memoir, Harriet Jacobs reported at length on efforts by slave owners in the wake of the Turner rebellion to pacify slaves through religious instruction. Yet after explaining why sermons from masters on texts like Ephesians 6:5 ("Servants, be obedient to them that are your masters . . . as unto Christ") left her cold, she described at even greater length a very different result when slaves encouraged each other with Scripture and hymns. In addition, when a kindhearted Episcopal minister and his wife arranged for slaves to attend worship services with sermons directly "adapted to their comprehension," Jacobs expressed heartfelt gratitude because "it was the first time they had ever been addressed as human beings."[26]

Even more extensive was her account of an old Black man "whose piety and childlike trust in God was beautiful to witness." This fifty-three-year-old gentleman begged Jacobs to teach him to read: "he thought he should know how to serve God better if he could only read the Bible." Eagerly, "as soon as he could spell in two syllables he wanted to spell out words in the Bible," because, as he told Jacobs, "when I can read dis good book, I shall be nearer to God. . . . I only wants to read dis book, dat I may know how to live; den I hab no fear 'bout dying." Within six months, he could not only read the New Testament but had mastered its content enough to "find any text in it." When Jacobs asked him how he made such rapid progress, the old man replied that he prayed for God "to help me undestan' what I spells and what I reads. And he *does* help me, chile. Bress his holy name [Ps 103:1–2]!"[27]

Jacobs then expanded her account to show how the Bible-reading that promoted sanctification easily led to reform: "There are thousands, who, like good uncle Fred, are thirsting for the water of life [Jn 4:14]; but the law forbids it, and the churches withhold it. They send the Bible to heathen abroad, and neglect the heathen at home." Such ones needed to hear that "they are answerable to God for sealing up the Fountain of Life from souls that are thirsting for it [Ps 36:8–9]."[28]

Thorough research by several scholars has demonstrated that in antebellum Black America the commitment to literacy, to personal Bible reading, and to Christian adherence represented a single phenomenon. Janet Duitsman Cornelius has described several instances when Black preachers used Noah Webster's Blue-Back Speller as the book from which they preached or as the manual for consecrating slave marriages, so closely were literacy and Scripture fused. In another account, Cornelius highlights the experience of a Kentucky slave who in the 1840s was converted, discovered a desire to preach, but fell into despair because he could not read. George Washington Dupee then chanced upon a New Testament, opened it to the Fourth Gospel, saw the letters J-O-H-N, but cried out "[T]hey don't mean anything." Nonetheless, he persevered and soon was reading the first three chapters of this gospel over and over. When he realized, as an observer noted, "that he could read the Word of God, he shouted, cried, and pressed the book to his breast in thankfulness to God for teaching him to read."[29]

In white America, individual and family Bible reading were practiced more routinely, and even more pervasively. Again keeping in mind the need not to exaggerate, solid scholarship has demonstrated the widespread extent of personal engagement with Scripture in almost all reaches of antebellum society. If it is incorrect to imagine that a majority of Americans read the Bible regularly, the substantial minority that did so still gave Scripture a uniquely prominent status.

It was no surprise that the Bible loomed large for the era's well-known evangelical leaders. Charles Finney, for one, pushed the Scriptures center stage when he wrote about his own conversion. The twenty-nine-year-old lawyer had been slowly drawn into conversations with church people and a local minister but had resisted commitment because his understanding of Scripture left him mystified: "It seemed to me that the knowledge of the Bible did not at all accord with the facts which were before my eyes." Nonetheless, "after struggling in that way for some two or three years," Finney concluded that "the Bible was . . . the true Word of God." At that point, he faced the ultimate question: "whether I will accept Christ as presented in the Gospel, or pursue a worldly course of life." But he hesitated, in part because of contradictory biblical teaching he had heard from others and in part because of the prideful disposition he found within itself. As Finney described the days immediately leading up to his conversion on October 10, 1821, he was left with only one resource: "I felt myself shut up to the Bible."[30]

Individuals of much less renown recorded the same concentrated focus. In perusing diaries by unpublished but literate Americans, Candy Gunther Brown, like Lewis Saum before her, found constant references to Bible reading, often in conjunction with reading works like *The Dairyman's Daughter*, Baxter's *Call to the Unconverted*, or periodicals produced by the tract and Bible societies.[31] Evangelicals of the period who broke into print heightened attention to the same experience. A memoir from Obadiah Echols reported on the infusion of emotion that, even as a southern white male, he did not hesitate to display when he joined the local Baptist fellowship: Echols "felt so fresh enamored with the Bible that ... I actually would hug it to my bosom, and would more willingly have done so to the God of the Bible, if I could have approached him as a man."[32]

Just as revealing were the letters and diary entries by a Philadelphia Episcopalian, Susan Allibone, that were published after her death. These writings revealed an extraordinary affection for the city's St. Andrew's Episcopal Church and its evangelical rectors, an affection that grew as, in the words of her editor, "the more deeply she studied the Divine Word, and the greater need she felt of the sustaining power of its truth in the time of suffering." The compiler of her writings, Episcopal bishop Alfred Lee, depicted a forceful, literarily active woman who, despite persistent ill health, "sought to form her views from the word of God, and when convinced of their truth she held them with firm, unrelaxing grasp." A diary entry from Sunday, May 25, 1834, is worth quoting in full to indicate the nearly ecstatic devotion that opened for Allibone when she read the Scriptures. After first recording encouragement from attending two worship services, she wrote:

What a blessing it is that the law is so strict. "Thy word is very pure, therefore Thy servant loveth it" [Ps 119:140]. I have had great delight in the Bible to-day. I wonder that my heart is not more alive to its beauties. I much enjoyed evening devotion—I could scarcely bear to go to bed. How much more happiness is to be derived from such moments, than from the vain pursuits of this world! If I live till tomorrow, I desire to be more instant in prayer, more patient in tribulation, more abundant in good words and works than I have been, and above all blessings, I desire and pray for a simple faith in the merits of my Redeemer, a grateful heart to praise Him for His Love, and a spirit of deep humility. These, and every other blessing, I ask in the name of Jesus, to whom, with the Father and the Holy Ghost, I desire grace to ascribe, with my whole heart, glory and honor for ever and ever. Amen.[33]

In addition to personal reading, many families at all social levels fulfilled the Protestant desideratum of family worship centered on Scripture. By midcentury, it was not uncommon, especially for middle-class families with regular work schedules, to read together a passage from the Old Testament in the morning and one from the New Testament in the evening. As Colleen McDannell has shown, the family Bible was "accorded special reverence," it was often displayed "prominently in the parlor," and it sometimes could be found resting on a specially embroidered cloth or specially designed display table.[34] As mothers joined fathers in daily Bible reading they fulfilled the mandate issued by Lydia Maria Child (Unitarian, ardent abolitionist, sometime Swedenborgian, and sympathetic author on world religions) in 1831: "[I]t is the first duty of a mother to make the Bible precious and delightful to her family."[35]

Although New York City was never renowned as a hotbed of piety, it too witnessed a full roster of Bible readers. In 1784 Jupiter Hammon, who a quarter-century earlier had published the first work by an American of African descent, addressed the city's African Society with a message urging his audience to advance in literacy so that they could read the Bible for themselves. A generation later, and before the city had established a school system, Mary Morgan, who attended the John Street Methodist Chapel, founded a Sunday school under Quaker auspices where she used the Bible and catechisms as aids teaching immigrant children to read.[36]

At about the same time, but at the other end of the social scale, the family of Dorothea and Henry Worrall also devoted themselves to family Bible reading. Henry, whose prosperous iron foundry supported his generosity to the Duane Street Methodist Episcopal Church, guided his family by observing the Sabbath, regularly attending the morning, afternoon, and evening services of his congregation, and gathering the family for Bible readings at the beginning and close of each day. After their marriages, two of his daughters, Sarah Lankford and Phoebe Palmer, became leaders of the city's Tuesday Meetings for the Promotion of Holiness, which eventually attracted an extraordinary range of influential participants. When in the 1850s and 1860s, Phoebe Palmer became renowned in the United States and the United Kingdom as a teacher of "holiness," or selfless consecration to God, she reflected the Worralls' early training by calling herself a "Bible Christian" and resolving "most carefully . . . to know the mind of the spirit, as recorded in the WRITTEN WORD, though it might lead to an experience unlike all the world beside."[37]

Jupiter Hammon, Mary Morgan, the Worrall family, and Phoebe Palmer represented only a portion of New York City's expanding population. Yet their personal application to Scripture did suggest a granular counterpoint to what the American Bible Society from its Nassau Street location promoted for the nation at large.

Careful recent research on practices of reading and writing between the Revolution and the Civil War has underscored their importance for women as well as men, Baptists and Methodists as well as adherents of proprietary denominations, and especially lay Americans. Throughout the nation, in Shelby Balik's words, "reading and writing opened up spiritual paths largely ungoverned by religious authorities."[38] So it was in rural New England where, as Mary Kelley has shown, "America's book trade and benevolent societies . . . produced and disseminated the books, magazines, tracts, and newspapers" that allowed this outlying region to share in calling America "to national conversion and global millennialism."[39] So also could it be for literate white women in the Blue Ridge Mountains, as documented by Beth Barton Schweiger's record of the Cooley and Speer families, whose female members read, corresponded, commented on what they read, and read and wrote some more—often in the phrases of the King James Bible, frequently attending to themes and questions from Scripture, always attuned to the flow of print into and within the South.[40]

Missionary experience reinforced American evangelical belief in the power of God's written word, even as it also revealed the ever-present fractious potential of relying on the Bible alone. In Burma, the first wave of Baptist missionaries, which included the renowned Adoniram Judson, eagerly told their American sponsors about the great achievement of translating the Bible into the language of Karen natives (1820s and 1830s). But within a few years, complications arose when Karen believers used their newly translated Bible to defend beliefs about demon possession and practices of exorcism that worried the Americans. "When pressed upon such points," one missionary wrote, "they reply by referring to the fact that such things are recognized by Scriptures, especially in connection with the miracles of Christ, e.g., in the case of the possessed of devils so frequently mentioned in the gospels."[41]

The same complication arose closer to home, among the Cherokee, whom evangelicals always approached as a "foreign" missionary challenge. Early Moravian missionaries had been heartened when Chief Yonaguska permitted missionary contact after they had translated the Gospel of Matthew for his people, but were perhaps perplexed when, after hearing the translation read, the chief said, "It seems to be a good book; strange that the white people are not better after having had it for so long." Much later, after a substantial minority of the Cherokee nation had embraced Christian faith, some of the missionaries who fiercely objected to Andrew Jackson's policy of Removal were nonetheless at least slightly concerned when Cherokee leaders used a scriptural concept of God's Kingdom to support independence from the American government and Old Testament narratives to sustain the Cherokee struggle against American tyrants.[42]

Missionary eagerness to translate the Bible, along with eagerness on the part of some of the missionized to read the Bible for themselves, exemplified both success and difficulty in trusting in Scripture alone. The success was further illustrated in the salience of biblically oriented hymnody in antebellum America; the difficulty became increasingly apparent as democratization fragmented the religious foundation of the culture. Yet even as the Bible civilization declined, Bible reading would long continue to inspire individuals and, even in retreat, often intrude into the public sphere.

Hymnody

It is scandalous in an era of flourishing social history deeply committed to retrieving the voices of previously neglected populations that historians have devoted so little attention to hymn books published, purchased, read, reread, quoted, and quoted some more. A reasonable excuse explaining this relative scholarly neglect is the daunting research challenge of comprehending, as also for Scripture, an absolutely ubiquitous phenomenon. From the first colonial publication of hymn books by the English Congregationalist Isaac Watts, with Benjamin Franklin in 1729 as one of his early American printers, to the present, hymns have constituted an integral part of the weekly and even daily lives of countless ordinary Americans.[43] Watts's innovation with hymns that did not strictly paraphrase Scripture, which had been the standard practice among English and Scottish Protestants, proved spectacularly successful. In turn, the popularity of his own hymns—along with those by his evangelical successors Philip Doddridge, Charles Wesley, John Newton, Augustus Toplady, and more— made the expansion of popular hymnody coterminous with the spread of evangelical religion.[44]

The historical challenge has been to grasp the scope of hymn books (words only) and hymnals (words plus music) published in titles and editions beyond counting; to craft appropriate prose for the essentially affective character of the singing in almost all services of Protestant worship and in some form also among Catholics, the Orthodox, and Jews; and to make sense of the extraordinary proliferation of hymn quotation, allusion, reference, and parody in the everyday language of lay women and men (as well as, of course, religious professionals). What J. R Watson has written generally about "the Bible and hymnody" applies with special force in the antebellum United States: for Protestants, "hymns supplement the readings from Holy Scripture [in worship services], or underlie points made in the sermon, and the Bible is the code in which they are written." More generally, English-language hymnody since the early eighteenth century offers "striking evidence of a circular hermeneutics, in which hymn-writers take from the Bible what they need; they come to the Bible in search of texts or passages that will supply answers to *their* problems or to *their* questions for society, and they write hymns that send singers back to the Bible."[45] In the antebellum period, hymns showed up almost everywhere, and a Protestant appropriation of the Bible infused almost all the hymns.

A parade of examples can only suggest the cultural reach of hymn texts. Bruce Hindmarsh's study of conversion in the evangelical awakenings of the mid-eighteenth century describes countless occasions when hymns reinforced biblical preaching or Bible reading at moments of conversion, but also for encouragement in life's crises or at times of particular discouragement and celebration.[46] This pattern survived for generations thereafter, and nowhere more saliently than among the marginalized. David George, in his unusually influential career, was one of the founders of the first Black Baptist church in South Carolina, then the same in Nova Scotia, and finally also in Sierra Leone. After George had been converted and was working hard at learning to read so that he could preach, words memorized from Watts's hymn paraphrase of Proverbs 8:34–35 bestowed special encouragement: "Thus saith the Wisdom of the Lord, / Blest is the man that hears my Word; / Keeps dayly Watch before my Gates, / And at my feet for Mercy waits."[47] A half-century later, Sojourner Truth inspired (and infuriated) northern audiences by the way she proclaimed her abolitionist message by quoting words from the Gospels and then singing songs and hymns, some improvised and some drawn from well-known collections.[48] In the era of troubles for the Cherokee, when native believers gathered to read the Scriptures and pray for unity in the face of President Jackson's ethnic cleansing, "it was," William McLoughlin has written, "doubly powerful when linked to the singing of hymns in the Cherokee language, which also uplifted their spirits."[49]

White Americans experienced, mutatis mutandis, almost the same. Part of the regular household instruction that Henry and Dorothea Worrall carried out in their New York City home was the gift to each child of a hymn book, which the children were expected to bring along to the family's twice-daily worship.[50] In his influential study of antebellum daily life in Rockdale, Pennsylvania, anthropologist Anthony F. C. Wallace found death rituals especially fascinating: "Those around [the dying person] helped him by singing hymns, praying, reading religious writings aloud, and asking evocative questions to keep the moribund person's mind on his final work."[51] Similarly, Heather Curtis has shown that singing or reciting hymns made up a standard feature of memoirs documenting the last hours of exemplary children.[52] More generally, for younger generations, "hymns introduced children to the principles of Protestant theology, urged them to cultivate a relationship with God through the process of repentance and conversion, and trained them to set their hearts on heaven."[53]

Hymns could also focus general concern for spreading the Christian message into active volunteering for missionary service. Robert Schneider has shown how a hymn voiced the thinking of Harriet Atwood Newell, a young woman pondering a proposal of marriage from a man headed to India as a missionary: "The *important decision* is not yet made. I am still wavering. . . . My heart aches.—I know not *what* to do!—'Guide me, O thou great Jehovah' [from a 1745 hymn by William Williams]." Then, having accepted the proposal, she adapted a missionary hymn as her personal guide: "Yes, Christian heroes go—proclaim / Salvation through Immanuel's name; / To India's clime the tiding bear, / And plant the rose of Sharon there. . . . Yes, I will go—however weak and unqualified I am, there is an all-sufficient Saviour, ready to support me."[54]

The better known the hymn, the more luxuriant could be the stories surrounding its use. In a tabulation by Stephen Marini of the most reprinted hymns in American hymnbooks and hymnals from 1737 to 1960, "All Hail the Power of Jesus' Name" came first.[55] One of the most often repeated legends that sprang up around this iconic hymn has a missionary in India, E. P. Scott, rescued from hostile indigenous peoples by playing it on his violin. Another has a dying person— variously reported as a pious lady visiting Paris for "the great exhibition," "a good man," and a once "happy Christian" who became an infidel—stammering out "bring, bring," and after some confusion finally getting auditors to realize that he was referring to lines from the hymn: "bring forth the royal diadem / And crown him Lord of all."[56]

The best-selling novels of the mid-nineteenth century testified to how immediately evocative many individual hymns had become. Susan Warner sprinkled dozens of hymn quotations in her *Wide, Wide World* (1850), the most popular work of fiction in its era alongside *Uncle Tom's Cabin* (1852). The author's sentimental but effective deployment of hymns is well illustrated in an early scene where the protagonist, Ellen Montgomery, sings to her ailing mother: "Hymn succeeded hymn, with fresh and varied pleasure; and her mother could not tire of listening. The sweet words, and the sweet airs . . . were all old friends, and brought of themselves many a lesson of wisdom and consolation, by the mere force of association." The daughter's singing led Mrs. Montgomery to feel "as if earth were left behind, and she and her child already standing within the walls of that city where sorrow and sighing shall be no more, and the tears shall be wiped from all eyes forever." But then the next hymn, this one quoted from a composition by William Cowper, "brought her back to earth again" with a divine word addressed directly to her precarious circumstances:

God in Israel sows the seeds
Of affliction, pain, and toil;
These spring up and choke the weeds

Which would else o'erspread the soil.
Trials make the promise sweet—
Trials give new life to prayer—
Trails bring me to his feet,
Lay me low, and keep me there.[57]

In *Uncle Tom's Cabin* itself, Harriet. Beecher Stowe used even more hymns even more strategically. Late in the tale, Simon Legree creeps up on the slaves' cabins "on a superb moonlight night" when he hears "a musical tenor." It is Uncle Tom singing one of Isaac Watts's most popular hymns among the enslaved: "When I can read my title clear / To mansions in the skies, / I'll bid farewell to every fear, / And wipe my weeping eyes." And then the startling response: " 'So ho!' said Legree to himself, 'he thinks so, does he? How I hate those cursed Methodist hymns!' "[58] (Figure 8.1, with Uncle Tom and Little Eva reading the Bible together)

Figure 8.1 This image of Uncle Tom and Little Eva reading the Bible together was prepared by Hammat Billings for "The Illustrated Edition" of *Uncle Tom's Cabin*, published in late 1852 by J. P. Jewett in Boston in time for Christmas. It heads chapter 22 with the title, "The grass withereth—the flower fadeth [Isa 40:8]."
Source: LOC Americana, call number-745870.

For her part, Louisa May Alcott in *Little Women* (1868–69) included as many hymn quotations as Stowe to underscore the domestic ideal that also inspired Warner's *Wide, Wide World*. Toward the end of the second part of Alcott's novel, as the Marsh family has gathered, Jo expresses the desire to "sing the good old way, for we are all together again once more." But readers are not surprised at the poignancy of the scene since they know that Beth, one of the little women, has died. Another sister, Amy, is called upon to lead from the piano, but instead of singing "in the good old way," she chose "something better than brilliancy or skill, for she sung Beth's songs. . . . The room was very still when the clear voice failed suddenly at the last line of Beth's favorite hymn. It was hard to say,— 'Earth hath no sorrow that heaven cannot heal.' "[59] The line is from "Come, Ye Disconsolate, where'er you languish," a well-known hymn by Thomas Moore, a Dublin-born solicitor, published in 1816 and reprinted in nearly half of American hymn books from 1830 to 1860.[60]

The hymns so frequently referenced by lay people outside of formal religious services supplemented the scriptural preaching dominating those formal occasions. For many Americans, however, it was the other way around: the sermons supplemented the hymns. The lines quoted in Warner's novel came from one of Cowper's contributions to *Olney Hymns*, a collection prepared by Cowper, a renowned poet, and John Newton, a former slave trader, intended primarily to provide hymns keyed to biblical texts chosen for sermons. This particular hymn was one of the few that did not follow that formula, yet it appeared under the heading "Welcome Cross," which for many readers would have personalized scriptural passages like Hebrews 12:6 ("For whom the Lord loves he chasteneth"). The hymn quoted by Stowe, Watts's "When I can read my title clear," affectively reinforced the tight bond that for enslaved believers joined literacy, Bible reading, and Christian hope.[61] For Alcott, Moore's "Come, Ye Disconsolate" represented a personal reinforcement of texts like John 14:18, where Jesus tells his disciples "I will not leave you comfortless: I will come to you." Such words in such hymns often spoke existentially to American families undergoing the strains of commercial reversals, westward movement, untimely death, and the bloodbath of civil war.

Naturally enough, it was not all of the Bible or all of the teachings possible to derive from the Bible that were personalized through hymns. Rather, it was the Bible as understood by the era's expanding Protestant networks that the hymns drove home as their memorable lyrics were sung, heard, read, and remembered. Hymns that resonated most powerfully featured the need of sinners for redemption, the refuge and healing of faith, the joy of redemption, and the hope of eternal life. Not for nothing did Simon Legree identify "When I can read my title clear" as a *Methodist* hymn.

Two notable hymns and two landmark hymn books illustrate the powerful synergy at work between this particular understanding of Scripture and the hymns that infused American religious culture. Additional research by Stephen Marini, this time in eighty-six hymn books published between 1737 and 1860, identified as the two hymns most reprinted in America: John Cennick's "Jesus, my all to heaven is gone" and Robert Robinson's "Come thou fount of every blessing."[62] Cennick, a colleague of John Wesley and George Whitefield before he became a Moravian, published his hymn in 1743 to celebrate the ascension of Christ and to express the believer's hope of joining Christ in heaven: "Jesus, my all to heaven is gone, / He whom I fix my hopes upon; / His track I see, and I'll pursue / The narrow way, till him I view." Succeeding stanzas speak of "wayfaring men to Canaan bound" and of Christ as the "blest Lamb" who becomes "a dear Saviour" showing the way to God. As explained by the liturgical scholar Lester Ruth, the images of the hymn contain a wealth of biblical material compacted into memorable verse: "The specific move was a common one in the period's hymnody in that Canaan, Jordan, the Promised Land, and other images of God's promised provision to the descendants of Abraham became ways of speaking of Christian desire for resurrection and heaven."[63]

Robinson's "Come thou fount of every blessing" similarly distilled the evangelical message of countless (and lengthy) exegetical sermons into a memorable short lyric. Robinson, whose career included service as an Independent (Congregational) minister, then a Baptist, then a Unitarian, published the hymn in 1758, when he was still closely associated with England's leading evangelicals. Partial annotation of the hymn shows how Robinson exploited one biblical narrative and a host of biblical allusions, paraphrases, echoes, and summaries to describe his conversion and the renovation of his life thereafter. The text here is from a popular English hymn book that was reprinted eight times in seven American cities during the first decade of the nineteenth century:

> Come, thou fount [**Rev 7:17, 21:6**] of every blessing [**Eph 1:3; Jas 1:17**], Tune
>   my heart to sing Thy grace:
> Streams of mercy [**1 Pet 2:10**] never ceasing, Call for songs of loudest praise:
> Teach me some melodious sonnet, Sung by flaming tongues above;
> Praise the mount—O fix me on it, Mount of God's unchanging love [**1 Jn 4:16**].
>
> Here I raise my Ebenezer, Hither by thy help I've come [**1 Sam 7:12, where
>   Israel erected a memorial called Ebenezer, meaning "Hitherto hath the
>   Lord helped us"**]:
> And I hope by thy good pleasure, Safely to arrive at home:
> Jesus sought me when a stranger [**Rom 5:8**] Wandering [**Lk 15:11–32**] from
>   the fold of God:

He to save my soul from danger Interpos'd his precious blood [**Eph 1:7;
    Col 1:14**].

O! to grace how great a debtor [**Eph 2:8–9**], Daily I'm constrained to be!
Let that grace, Lord, like a fetter, Bind my wandering heart to thee!
Prone to wander, Lord, I feel it; Prone to leave the God I love—
Here's my heart, Lord, take and seal it, Seal it [**Eph 1:13**] from thy courts
    above.[64]

Two notable hymn books, which differed in almost every other way, illustrate
the same pervasive dependence on Scripture as in these two popular hymns.
Richard Allen, founder of the African Methodist Episcopal Church, published
two editions of *A Collection of Hymns and Spiritual Songs* in 1801 as a supplement to the many hymn books personally edited by Francis Asbury. Its sixty-four
hymns appeared sans introduction, indexes, or readers' helps of any other kind.[65]
Very different was *The Sabbath Hymn Book* of 1858, edited by the nation's premier composer of church music, Lowell Mason, with the president and leading
professor at one of the nation's best-known divinity schools, Austin Phelps and
Edwards Amasa Park of Andover Seminary. Its presentation reflected the refinement and educational sophistication that were also visible in the publication of
the era's ever more elaborate family bibles—1,290 hymns plus another 24 dox-
ologies and 57 Psalms (plus the Lord's Prayer) marked for chanting, as well as a
laboriously explanatory introduction and seven indexes spread over 131 tightly
printed pages—brought to the public by a cooperative venture of seven different
publishers from five cities—and accompanied by a tune book and a hymnal
combining text and tunes.[66] One of the book's indexes, however, revealed *The
Sabbath Hymn Book*'s close kinship with Allen's much more humble book; it
was the seventeen-page "Index of Passages of the Scriptures," with thousands
of references specifying direct biblical sources for the hymns. So self-conscious
were the editors about their dependence on Scripture that they were, "at one
time, somewhat inclined to arrange the hymns of this volume according to the
Biblical sources whence they were derived."[67]

Allen offered no explanation for his selection of hymns, but his reliance on
the Bible was every bit as thorough as his Methodist mentor Asbury's or the
later sophisticates who edited *The Sabbath Hymn Book*. Allen's was decidedly a
Methodist book with hymns fully describing the wretchedness of human sin, the
threat of eternal damnation, the divine mercy displayed in the cross of Christ, the
hour of death as a trial for unbelievers but entrance into bliss for believers, and
the joy of fellowship with like-minded Christian pilgrims.

In addition, however, several features distinguished the book as compiled expressly for the sons and daughters of Africa. One hymn, "O that I had a bosom

friend," has been identified as written by an enslaved author.[68] It addressed directly an individual who sings, "O that I had a bosom friend / To tell my secrets to . . . How do I wander up and down, / And no one pities me." The hymn's response was an extended versification of John 15:13–14, "Greater love hath no man than this, that a man lay down his life for his friends. Ye are my friends, if ye do whatsoever I command you." The hymn writer admonished the friendless soul with these words: "Did Christ expire upon the cross / And is he not thy friend? . . . The Saviour is thy real friend, / Constant and true and good."[69] Other hymns with biblical references repeated standard Methodist fare, but with perhaps an eye to Allen's intended audience by including reference to the Exodus that freed Israel from bondage in Egypt and two elaborations on Jesus's story of the rich man who scorns Lazarus the beggar at his gate.[70]

Even more revealing was a hymn that Allen probably wrote himself.[71] This fourteen-stanza composition began with a standard Methodist appeal:

> See! how the nations rage together!
>   Seeking of each other's blood;
> See how the scriptures are fulfilling!
>   Sinners awake and turn to God.

Then Allen riffed on a profusion of biblical material: "the fig-tree budding" (Matt 24:32–35), "wars . . . to come before that dreadful day" (Matt 24:6), the "harvest" in danger of wasting away (Lk 10:2), "the Lord in clouds descending" (Rev 1:7). But in a fashion foreign to the strict apoliticism of Asbury, Allen's hymn also contained social references that called "the land" and "the nation" to "turn and find salvation, / While now he offers you free grace."[72]

For its part, *The Sabbath Hymn Book,* from its opening three hymns, which paraphrased the Lord's Prayer from Matthew 6:9–13 to the final section of Psalms marked for chanting, offered extended meditations on the biblical themes prominent in British evangelicalism and most American denominations. The best-represented authors provided a considerable variety of sentiment, literary skill, and metrical choices. But whether canonical hymn writers of eighteenth-century English evangelicalism (Watts, 256 hymns; Charles Wesley, 56; the Baptist Anne Steele, 48; the Independent Philip Doddridge, 41) or contemporary voices from Scotland (James Montgomery, 52; Horatius Bonar, 37) and even the United States (Ray Palmer of Albany, New York, 10), the unifying characteristic was constant, creative, and meditative engagement with Scripture. The editors hoped their collection would be used first for Sunday worship but also, in keeping with how such books had long functioned, "to aid in the more private social devotions, in the conference room, the family, and the closet."[73] Their hymns, like those of Allen's, "we have aimed to furnish a book of real life." And they succeeded.

The few scholars who have addressed the subject have made a good start in showing why hymns played such an important role in the early United States. On a first level, they bridged the spheres of private devotion and public worship. As Christopher Phillips puts it in his important study, nineteenth-century "hymnbooks moved from the private to the public, even as they continued to inhabit and shape private spaces."[74] The ones who gathered to console the dying quoted and sang hymns because the hymns had internalized the main biblical themes of public worship.

On a second level, hymns bound religious communities together, an especially important service in a United States where external bonds reinforcing religious community had mostly disappeared. Again, Phillips: "Only the most ambitious and radical new communities made the effort to produce a new translation of the Bible, but every group seems to have shared an impulse to create its own hymnbook."[75] In so doing, they illustrated the wisdom of an old German proverb: "Wer spricht mit mir ist mein Mitmensch; wer singt mit mir ist mein Bruder" (The one who speaks with me is a fellow human; the one who sings with me is my brother). When believers sang together what they had read in private or as families, cognition joined emotion to support communal life.

On a third level, the capacity of hymns to bind individuals together extended far beyond individual denominations; they linked religious communions with otherwise little time for each other. Candy Gunther Brown's account of evangelical "textual communities" has shown how hymn singing and hymn referencing drew together what race, class, gender, and theological differences sundered.[76] In particular, a common Protestant understanding of main themes read in King James language created a canon of hymnody that elaborated "a complex, meaningful pattern of significance understood by evangelical editors, compilers, and translators as interfacing the biblical narrative with experiences shared by all Christians."[77] Sojourner Truth became famous as an abolitionist in part because her audiences recognized the songs she sang to support a message of liberation grounded in Scripture. Allen's Collection was prepared for Black congregations but drew hymns from the white Calvinist Independent Watts, the white Arminian Anglican-Methodist Charles Wesley, a white Baptist John Leland (who would shift his position from antislavery to proslavery), and many more. Allen's hymn book also included at least two selections that would later appear in hymn books created for the Church of Jesus Christ of Latter-day Saints, the Mormons.[78]

Meaningful personal engagement with words—whether spoken, written, heard, read, sung, or recalled to mind—has characterized human cultures from the dawn of recorded history. In the antebellum United States, personally appropriated words, as Beth Barton Schweiger has written specifically about reading, "acquired a new sacred potential."[79] Contingent circumstances explained this new potential. At that place in those years energetic Protestant editors, preachers, organizers, printer-publishers, writers, and above all lay believers exploited expanding literacy, technical innovations in print, aggressive marketing, expectations of the millennial reign of Christ, and what they regarded as a special dispensation of the Holy Spirit. As a result, the Protestant ideal of an entire population becoming personally active in Christian faith—a true priesthood of all believers—seemed at last within reach.

9

The African American Bible

Protestantism was always a religion of the Book, or, more accurately, several religions of the Book. Each of these religions grew from devotion to the Scriptures, but with different emphases, different key passages, different interpretive strategies, different cultural assumptions, different effects on different populations, and different outcomes in different social settings. For Black and white Protestants in the antebellum years, much was shared because of their biblical foundation. Because of the differences, more diverged.[1] The place to begin when considering the Black alternatives that make up such an indispensable feature of American history is simply with the extraordinarily pervasive biblicism of so many Black Christians in the early history of the United States.[2] While this attachment to Scripture demonstrated the reach of the nation's Bible civilization, it also showed why that civilization was such a fragile construct.

The Biblical Presence in Black America

From the first publications by Africans in colonial America through the next century and beyond, to address the public as a person of color was usually to employ a biblical idiom quoting, evoking, and referring to the King James Version. There were, to be sure, exceptions. *A Narrative of the Life and Adventures of Venture, a Native of Africa*, which was first published in 1798, recorded the story of a man born in Guinea who was captured in a tribal war and sold to traders from Rhode Island; he eventually purchased his freedom, and then lived for several decades as a freedman in Connecticut. Its recital of "simple facts" made no mention of anything religious. Similarly, James Mars in 1864 published an account of life as a Connecticut slave, narrating his difficult path to personal freedom in a state that had legislated gradual emancipation. The narrative related Mars's rough handling by several clergymen but did not dwell on the author's own faith, or lack thereof.[3]

Much more common was the frequent, fluent, and unselfconscious integration of scriptural material into the flow of public discourse that we have already seen in the writings of Prince Hall, Maria Stewart, and Harriet Jacob.[4] So it had been when Black writers first appeared in print with the poems of Jupiter Hammon;

America's Book. Mark A. Noll, Oxford University Press. © Oxford University Press 2022.
DOI: 10.1093/oso/9780197623466.003.0010

the narratives of Briton Hammond, James Albert Ukawsaw Gronniosaw, John Marrant, David George, and Olaudah Equiano; and the first full-scale attack on slavery by someone who had experienced it from Quobna Cugoano.[5]

The American Bible Society made its first effort to distribute the Scriptures to African Americans within a year of its founding, when in January 1817 the African Bible Society of New York was voted into existence, recruited forty-two members, and became an official auxiliary of the ABS.[6] Because the Society depended on its auxiliaries to fund and distribute bibles, the ABS always proceeded cautiously. It was eager to see enslaved and free Blacks read the Bible but was also constrained by race prejudice, in the North as well as the South, and by the legislation in some southern states that forbade teaching slaves to read. Yet the history of African Americans and the Bible always included much more informal and unregulated access than formal or organized efforts. And well before the ABS came on the scene.

Richard Allen, founder of the African Methodist Episcopal church, began his late-life autobiography by recounting the path of assurance he experienced in 1777. Scripture and a hymn by Charles Wesley provided his language: "My sins were a heavy burden. . . . I cried to the Lord both night and day [Ps 22:2; Lk 18:7]. . . . I cried unto Him who delighteth to hear the prayers of a poor sinner [Mi 7:18], and all of a sudden my dungeon shook, my chains flew off [Wesley's "And can it be"], and, glory to God, I cried. My soul was filled. I cried, enough for me—the Saviour died."[7] Seventeen years later, Allen's preaching on a portion of Acts 8:21 ("I perceive thy heart is not right in the sight of God") triggered in Jarena Lee the spiritual struggle that led to "the power of God unto salvation to me, because I believed."[8] As Lee took up her own memorable career as a Methodist evangelist, she followed Allen with a preaching style rife with biblical images, exhortations, and imperatives.

The scriptural presence stretched from the intellectual elite to those without formal learning. An escaped slave, James W. C. Pennington, became the first Black student at Yale before serving as a minister in Congregational and Presbyterian churches and then marshaling historical, philosophical, and biblical expertise for learned attacks on slavery and race prejudice. His memoir from 1849, *The Fugitive Blacksmith*, advertised the author's extensive biblical literacy with the inscription on its title page from Isaiah 16:4: "Let mine outcasts dwell with thee, Moab; be thou a covert to them from the face of the spoiler." Similarly recondite was Pennington's account of a dramatic day filled with several narrow escapes as he fled from enslavement, ending with a feeling of peace as dusk descended: "My reflections upon the events of that day, and upon the close of it, since I became acquainted with the Bible, have frequently brought to my mind that beautiful passage in the Book of Job, 'He holdeth back the face of His throne, and spreadeth a cloud before it' [Job 26:9]."[9]

At the other end of the educational spectrum, Albert Raboteau records a story about a freedwoman in Beaufort, North Carolina. This still unlettered woman "carried a big Bible about with her through the woods and swamps"; her former mistress had helped her by turning "down the leaves at the verses she knew by heart, and often she would sit down in the woods and open the big Bible at these verses, and repeat them aloud, and find strength and consolation."[10]

It was no surprise that the Bible suffused the public speaking that sustained African American communities throughout this entire period. Philip Foner and Robert Branham's anthology of "African American oratory" does contain many examples where Scripture remained in the background, but even more where it came to the fore. The following examples from the 1830s illustrate the facility of quotation, but also a more general mastery of biblical themes, personages, and imagery. In 1833 a layman, William Whipper, eulogized William Wilberforce at a Philadelphia memorial service with what had by that time become a standard reference: "[T]hose who have not adopted for the line of their conduct toward their fellow men, the golden rule—'do unto others as you would they should do unto you'—are unfit to utter his [Wilberforce's] name." In 1836, the nineteen-year-old scion of a Philadelphia family long distinguished for its civic leadership, James Forten Jr., addressed the Ladies' Anti-Slavery Society of his city. The printed version of his oration came supplied with proof-text references: "It has often been said by anti-abolitionists that the females have no right to interfere with the question of slavery. . . . [W]hat an anti-christian spirit this bespeaks. Were not the only commands, 'Remember them that are in bonds, as bound with them,' and 'Do unto others as ye would they should do unto you,' intended for women to obey as well as man?" (footnotes to Heb 13:3 and Matt 7:12).[11]

In 1832, Sarah Douglas, a Quaker who was known for objecting when the Philadelphia Friends designated segregated "Negro pews" for men and women of color, addressed the Female Literary Society of Philadelphia:

> And now, my sisters, I would earnestly and affectionately press upon you the ne-cessity of placing your whole dependence on God. . . . Do you feel your inability to do good? Come to Him who giveth liberally and upbraideth not [Jas 1:5]. . . . What but this can uphold our fainting hearts in the swellings of Jordan. . . . In conclusion, I would respectfully recommend that our mental feast should com-mence by reading a portion of the Holy Scriptures. A pause should proceed the reading for supplication. It is my wish that the reading and conversation should be altogether directed to the subject of slavery.

Four years later, Theodore Wright, the first Black graduate of Princeton Theological Seminary and the pastor of New York City's First Colored Presbyterian Church, was given the unusual honor of addressing an integrated audience at the annual meeting of the New England Anti-Slavery Society. His evocation of biblical personages ended by giving thanks for a figure who was still very much alive: "The cause of emancipation is identified with prayer. Did you ever see an abolitionist without prayer? You have gone forth armed with prayer, in the spirit of the Prince of Peace. . . . Christianity has gone forth, though Stephen was stoned, though Paul was imprisoned and mobbed, and the city in commotion. . . . Yes, the friend of the colored man lives—blessed to God, [William Lloyd] GARRISON *lives.*"[12]

Differences

African American immersion in Scripture did not, however, mean that Black authors and speakers quoted the same texts or emphasized the same applications. To avoid mindless romanticism, it is important to recognize the same wide variation in biblical approaches that marked white America.

Frederick Douglass, the best known Black figure of the period, in 1849 vehemently opposed other African Americans who were raising funds to purchase bibles for delivery to southern slaves. Douglass's own experience under several masters had taught him, in Allen Callahan's words, "that the Bible was the highest authority of American slavery and the strongest link in the chain of oppression and violence that warranted slavery as the sacred basis for the Christian culture of what would become the Confederacy."[13] Yet the same Douglass in 1845 ended his first autobiography with an appendix explaining why his narrative's harsh comments about religion applied specifically to "the *slaveholding religion* of the land, and with no possible reference to Christianity proper." To specify this difference, Douglass quoted Jesus's lengthy denunciation of the scribes and Pharisees from Mathew chapter 23 (he quoted verses 4–7, 13–15, 23–25, 27–28), followed by a paragraph that enlisted at least four other biblical phrases in a dramatic denunciation of those who sent bibles to heathens overseas while "they despised and totally neglected the heathen at their door."[14] In his second autobiography, from 1855, Douglass filled in details about his struggle to learn to read: "The frequent hearing of my mistress reading the bible—for she often read aloud when her husband was absent—soon awakened my curiosity in respect to this *mystery* of reading, and roused in me the desire to learn. . . . Indeed, she exultingly told him [her husband] of the aptness of her pupil, of her intention to persevere in teaching me, and of the duty she felt to teach me, at least to read *the bible*." The violent response of "Master Hugh" ended his instruction: "[I]f you teach the nigger—speaking of myself—how to read the bible, there will be no keeping him . . . it would forever unfit him for the duties of a slave."[15] Douglass's arguments against sending bibles southward arose, in other words, from first-hand knowledge of its abuse, but also his own mastery of its contents.

Henry Bibb (1815–1854), whose *Narrative* from 1849 became almost as well known as Douglass's memoirs, was one of the leaders who opposed Douglass by insisting on sending bibles to slaves. As Emerson Powery and Rodney Sadler have shown, Bibb railed vigorously against white sermons to the enslaved that featured only Pauline obedience texts.[16] "This kind of preaching," as Bibb put it, "has driven thousands into infidelity." Yet for Bibb such abuse could exist only where "they have no Sabbath Schools, no one to read the bible to them; no one to preach the gospel who is competent to expound the Scriptures, except slaveholders."[17] Bibb's answer to white preaching from only parts of Scripture was Black reading of the whole Bible.

Other conflicts also illustrated the diversity of African American Bible usage, as Katherine Clay Bassard has documented for the off-and-on dispute between Jarena Lee with her Bible-centered preaching and Rebecca Cox Jackson, a Black convert to the Shakers and the celibacy they practiced. Jackson and Lee had both grown up in Richard Allen's Philadelphia Bethel Church. Both became devoted Bible readers, and for both the Old Testament story of the Exodus inspired their spiritual journey. Yet in visions that led to Jackson's choosing a celibate life and then joining the Shakers, elements of ancient African conjure also mingled with images from Scripture. Jackson recalled her conversion as a mixture of personal fright at thunder, memory of scraps of Scripture ("this day thy soul is required of thee" [Lk 12:20]), and observation of lightning coursing through her house as "the messenger of peace, joy, and consolation." In other words, as Bassard explains, the account mingled African imagery and conjure practice with a biblical "ur-narrative." Later visions that drew Jackson to the Shakers continued to feature the Bible; in one she was shown a book on a table from which she was told, "I shall be instructed from Genesis to Revelation." But the same visions divided matter and spirit by compass coordinates in the fashion of African primal religion. The conflict between Jackson and Lee indicates the centrality of Scripture for both women, but also that their approaches differed greatly.[18]

Yet neither practical debates over distributing the Bible nor contentions over how to understand Scripture alongside visionary revelation marked Black use of Scripture as much as undemonstrative referencing, quoting, evoking, and alluding. Sometimes the references came infrequently, as with the memoir that Elizabeth Keckly published in 1868 describing her service as a dressmaker for Mary Todd Lincoln and Julia Grant. Newspaper accounts had implicated Mrs. Keckly in Mrs. Lincoln's extravagant expenditures and for how the widow misspent money raised after her husband's death. Although Keckly's memoir did not feature religious concerns, the Bible remained constantly in the background.

She wrote, for example, about the fateful day of the president's assassination, April 14, 1865, which began joyfully: "The dark war-cloud was fading, and a white-robed angel seemed to hover in the sky, whispering 'Peace—peace on earth, good-will toward men!' [Lk 2:14]." But then things turned tragic: "The Moses of my people had fallen in the hour of his triumph."[19]

Often biblical references were not only more salient but crucial for creating an unusually powerful effect, as in the 1853 narrative from Solomon Northup. Early in the memoir, which served as the basis for an Oscar-winning film in 2013, Northup described the sale of Eliza, who was torn from a child that she would never see again:

Freedom—freedom for herself and her offspring, for many years had been her cloud by day, her pillar of fire by night [Ex 13:21]. In her pilgrimage through the wilderness of bondage [echoing Ex 12:2], with eyes fixed upon that hope-inspiring beacon, she had at length ascended to "the top of Pisgah" [Deut 34:1], and beheld "the land of promise" [Josh 22:4 and many others]. . . . The glorious vision of liberty faded from her sight as they led her away into captivity. Now "she weepeth sore in the night, and her tears are on her cheeks: all her friends have dealt treacherously with her; they have become her enemies" [Lam 1:2].[20]

Later, it was Northup's own experience as he fled from a brutal master who assaulted him with an axe: "A voice within whispered me to fly. To be a wanderer among the swamps, a fugitive and a vagabond on the face of the earth [Gen 4:12], was preferable to the life that I was leading." Northup's flight took him into a nearby swamp where, pursued by hounds and menaced by water moccasin snakes and alligators, he despaired:

Whither should I fly [Ps 139:7]? Oh, God! Thou who gavest me life . . . do not forsake me. . . . Such supplications, silently and unuttered, ascended from my inmost heart to Heaven. But there was no answering voice—no sweet, low tone, coming down from on high, whispering to my soul, "It is I, be not afraid" [Matt 14:27; Jn 6:20]. I was the forsaken of God, it seemed—the despised and hated of men! [Isa 53:3].

Finally, however, Northup reached a white family who knew and respected him:

When John had set the meal before me, the madam came out with a bowl of milk, and many little delicious dainties, such as rarely please the palate of a slave. I was hungry, and I was weary, but neither food nor rest afforded half the pleasure as did the blessed voices speaking kindness and consolation. It was the oil and the wine which the Good Samaritan in the "Great Pine Woods" was ready to pour into the wounded spirit of the slave, who came to him, stripped of his raiment and half-dead [Lk 10:30–47].[21]

As among white Americans, so also among enslaved and free Blacks, fixed confidence in divine revelation was not limited, as in the case of Rebecca Cox Jackson, to the canonical Scriptures. Although extrabiblical communication from God had always accompanied trust in Scripture throughout the Christian centuries, the American commitment to freedom of religion made it especially easy to heed an Emanuel Swedenborg, a Nimrod Hughes, or a Joseph Smith.[22] Direct divine communication also gave some African Americans a credibility in the United States they would not have enjoyed in Europe's settled Christendom.

As with whites, however, special revelations often simply supported scriptural revelation. Henry McNeal Turner (1834–1915), a Black political leader during Reconstruction who became a powerful bishop for the African Methodist Episcopal Church (AME), grew up free in South Carolina, but at a time when state law prohibited teaching Blacks to read. Turner recounted later in life that after several futile attempts at being taught by others, he resolved to rely on his own effort. When he was frustrated by lack of progress, he "would kneel down and pray, and ask the Lord to teach me what I was not able to understand myself." After he fell asleep, "an angelic personage would appear with open book in hand and teach me how to pronounce every word that I failed in pronouncing while awake." That "angelic teacher . . . carried me through the old Websters spelling book and thus enabled me to read the Bible and hymnbook." By age fifteen Turner had read the Bible through five times and committed long passages to a memory, for which he became renowned.[23]

For others, the voice of God was sufficient unto itself. So it was with Isabella Van Wagenen, who as Sojourner Truth (1797–1873) became renowned as an abolitionist and campaigner for women's rights. The amanuensis who recorded *The Narrative of Sojourner Truth* reported that "she talked to God as familiarly as if he had been a creature like herself." The same account included a particularly significant experience of what Isabelle Kinnard Richman has aptly styled her "mystical spirituality." While still enslaved and yet burdened with her own spiritual need, Sojourner Truth labored under great duress until "at last a friend appeared to stand between herself and an insulted Deity." Eventually, "a vision brightened into a form distinct, beaming with the beauty of holiness, and radiant with love. . . . 'Who are you?' was the cry of her heart . . . an answer came to her, saying distinctly, 'It is Jesus.' "[24] The inspiration she took from this vision was far from biblicist, yet it too resonated with the Scriptures (Ps 96:9, "the beauty of holiness").

Harriet Tubman (ca. 1822–1913) experienced something similar as she escaped from slavery and then in the 1850s led scores of bondspeople from

Maryland's Eastern Shore to safety in Canada. Thomas Garrett, who maintained one of the stations on Tubman's Underground Railroad, reported that he had "never met with any person, of any color, who had more confidence in the voice of God, as spoken direct to her soul." Yet Tubman also inhabited a world shaped by the written Scriptures. Even before the Civil War, when she received much notice in the northern press, her peers were calling her "Moses." Kristen Oertel explains the ascription succinctly: "[S]he was black and female when white and male ruled the day, but Moses determined to set her people free."[25] Alike for the learned Henry McNeal Turner and the preliterate Sojourner Truth and Harriet Tubman, divine communication did not require the Book, though they aligned their personal communications with God to what was in the Book.

The increasingly deep scholarship of the past half-century has demonstrated the Bible's central place among antebellum African Americans; in the words of Lawrence Levine, the Bible served as the only "fixed point" for the enslaved.[26] More expansive are the judgments of Allen Callahan but echoed by many others:

> African Americas are the children of slavery in America. And the Bible, as no other book, is the book of slavery's children. . . . American slaves and their descendants have taken the texts of the Bible in every sense of the word: embraced them, endured them, seized them, stolen them, caught them, and captured them. . . . African Americans embraced the Bible, a poison book, because it was so effective, in measured doses, as its own antidote.[27]

Again, as with white communities, the claim is not that all enslaved and free Blacks internalized the Bible. It is rather that a substantial minority orbited Scripture as planets revolve around the sun, which made the Bible a unique source of light for a population groping in the darkness of race prejudice and enslavement. No other source of hope, inspiration, psychological support, and guide for action came even close.

Alternative Interpretive Worlds

Because the American racial divide created such radically different cultures—reinforced by the legal machinery of slavery and even more fundamentally by assumptions about white-over-Black superiority—Bible appropriation inevitably developed differently on the two sides of the divide. "The Racism that developed from racial subordination," in Eugene Genovese's words, "influenced every aspect of American life."[28] The two cultures, though overlapping in some important particulars, were separated by history.

On one side lay more than eighteen hundred years of unbroken spiritual, pneumatic, life-orienting inspiration from Scripture, almost always accompanied by close textual analysis, Bible-referenced theological syntheses, and well-established traditions exploring Scripture's general meaning. For white America the centuries since the Reformation had bequeathed lively internalization of biblical content, but always in the context of close exegetical labor. That labor, which looked to biblical texts and themes for the ordering of church, state, and society, came naturally, since the Book that reconciled humanity to God was also obviously there to instruct humans about living in the world God providentially sustained. Thus, when contentions over enslaved Africans turned white Protestants to search the Scriptures, they did so against a backdrop of sophisticated biblical criticism of Roman Catholicism; intense intra-Protestant proof-texting on questions of church order, baptism, and the Lord's Supper; an honored tradition of systematic theology marked with several unusually influential landmarks; and, in the new United States, all sorts of biblical appeals in debates of Baptists versus Methodists versus Presbyterians versus Episcopalians versus "Christians" as well as pan-Protestant attacks on Rome (reiterated) and Mormons (new).

Forces far beyond the narrowly religious also shaped the cultural terrain in which whites bombarded each other with specific texts in their strife over slavery (chapters 10 and 11). White Americans, like all others in all circumstances, had difficulty understanding how much their own environment shaped their understanding of the Bible. That history included the expansion of Europe; colonization of what Europeans viewed as a "new world"; Africans treated as commodities for trade; personal fortunes and family security resting directly or indirectly on sugar, cotton, tobacco, or trade in these commodities; and the production of sugar, tobacco, and cotton dependent on an enslaved workforce. An equally influential intellectual history also defined the angles from which Euro-Americans came at the Scriptures: the Renaissance recovery of Greek and a scholarly ideal of returning to ancient sources (*ad fontes*); the immense prestige of natural philosophy (science) in the wake of Sir Isaac Newton; standards for knowledge proposed by John Locke, Bishop George Berkeley, Francis Hutcheson, David Hume, and Thomas Reid—and then endlessly contested; political ideals increasingly framed in terms of rights, liberty, and representation; and everywhere print emerging as *the* medium for advocating ideas of any sort and exploited as *the* vehicle for convincing the ever-expanding public sphere. The world formed by this European-colonial-American history included many conscientious, intelligent, moral, and reflective individuals. Yet even for the most devout white Americans, it was all but *unthinkable* to esteem the African as equal to themselves.

On the other side of the racial divide, it was not completely different, since an evangelical religion dependent on biblical themes of spiritual emancipation had built a bridge across the cultural chasm. Yet the chasm remained. Black Christianity emerged with almost no written reflection by African Americans, no formal theologies, no literary outlets for disputing teaching drawn from Scripture. Among white Americans, widely read books like Foxe's *Book of Martyrs* memorialized the immolation of a few early Protestants. Almost no literature recorded the Africans beyond counting who were slain in tribal warfare, who died at sea as damaged cargo, or who perished before time as slaves. Above all, the Bible had been introduced to kidnapped Africans in a completely skewed dynamic. The one overwhelming social reality that of necessity conditioned Black approaches to Scripture was disproportionate power: Europeans enslaved Africans; Africans were enslaved.

In the short time that separated the first publications by African slaves in the colonies—a poem by Jupiter Hammon and a memoir by Briton Hammon both in 1760—to the published writings of Richard Allen, Daniel Coker, Maria Stewart, Frederick Douglass, and other noteworthy authors, an extraordinary transition took place. In less than a century, determination to read, mastery of texts like the Bible and Webster's Speller, as well as increasing skill in exploiting print testified to the speed of the transformation. A significant minority of African Americans had in fact achieved fluency in the conceptual language of white America. But the disproportion, alongside assumptions about racial hierarchy, remained. In such a situation, phrases like "Scripture teaches" or "the Bible says" could never mean the same for white and Black.

Put differently, the history of biblical usage in the antebellum United States always involved questions of *hermeneutics* in a context characterized by both *traditional attitudes* toward Scripture and deep *cultural differences*. For Black Christians and almost all white Christians before the Civil War, the *traditional Christian attitude* toward the Bible prevailed, that Scripture graciously communicated God's Word to men and women through ordinary human words. For everything else, hermeneutical cultures diverged, where *hermeneutics* refers to the methods, attitudes, intellectual principles, and social-cultural instincts that govern how individuals and groups understand the Scriptures. Some are explicit, many more implicit. In that context, particular *interpretations* of Scripture always depended on hermeneutical practices—that is, on taken-for-granted assumptions in the competing white and Black cultures.

For our purposes, Vincent Wimbush has framed the challenge exactly: a genuinely historical account cannot "begin—as is typically the case . . .—in the middle, with much taken for granted about the Bible as a phenomenon, as holy book, about what is done with such a book, for whom and why, and to what end." In Wimbush's terms, the "fundamental question" is not how individuals or groups understood, discussed, preached, or applied the meaning of specific texts, but "about the whole quest for meaning (in relationship to a sacred text)." In short, historical study must begin by trying to understand the "cultural-hermeneutical template" and then proceed with "critical (= self) consciousness" about how the Bible was put to use.[29] Examination of the assumptions guiding interpretation is every bit as necessary as attention to the interpretations themselves.

The record of "contraband" African Americans during the Civil War clearly illustrates the historical complexities. Erskine Clarke's stellar account of the interwoven destinies of a white family and a Black family in tidewater Georgia provides compelling documentation. His *Dwelling Place: A Plantation Epic* features the tribe of Charles Colcock Jones, a Presbyterian clergyman renowned for carrying out the South's most extensive programs of evangelism and biblical teaching for slaves, which included the family of Lizzy Jones, the other multi-generational tribe featured in the book. By his white peers and also many of his slaves, Charles Jones was regarded as the best kind of enslaver: considerate of his charges, fair in adjudicating disputes, and before everything else deeply committed to their spiritual well-being. The revealing moment came when some local slaves heard about President Lincoln's plans for emancipation and fled to the woods, hoping eventually to find refuge as "contraband" with Union forces.

Charles Jones, his family, and their associates were staggered, uncomprehending, shocked. Jones, who had been the most solicitous of masters, now lashed out in terrified anger: the escaped slaves "are traitors who may pilot an enemy into your *bedchamber!*" A pastor friend whose most trusted servant had escaped wrote more dispassionately, but with no more comprehension: the slave's "leaving was the hardest blow which could be given. I do not remember that I ever gave him a cross word. Indeed, I never had any occasion to do it, for he was [a] most faithful and willing servant. . . . I have felt deeply hurt and mortified at Joe's leaving, more so than if the whole plantation had left."[30] Jones had devoted immense labors to prepare biblical instruction for slaves; he was himself a learned, kind, and compassionate student of Scripture. Yet he could not *imagine* why a slave who had been treated so well would want to be free.[31]

How did the Bible work? For white Protestants in antebellum America, a history stretching back through the centuries answered that question beyond doubt. For Black Americans, an equally powerful, if much shorter, history also provided a definite answer, but with a dramatic difference.

Methodism Plus

Antebellum Black religion came closest to one of the ascendant white Protestant varieties in its strongly Methodist character.[32] Time and again Black authors recorded the experience of personal redemption in much the same terms with which Francis Asbury and his associates filled their accounts. Repentant closure with Christ as the source of joy, comfort, relief, support, and hope shaped the narratives, not only of Black Methodists but of almost all African American religious writing. Significantly, Black testimony also paralleled the testimony of early Methodism by paying almost no heed to the discourse of republican freedom. The persistent clash between proprietary and sectarian white Protestants over which kind of virtue prevented which kind of corruption for which kind of social well-being was almost completely absent. As with the Methodists under Asbury, Black writers seemed indifferent to whether Federalists or Jeffersonians, and then Whigs or Democrats, prevailed.

The Methodist character of African American religion extended, however, only so far. Methodist Christianity in the era of Asbury, and in some cases beyond, remained explicitly apolitical. Black religion, by contrast, was always implicitly political. The proclamation of freedom in Christ to an enslaved, patronized population by its very nature implied this-worldly as well as eternal salvation. That message, in Dennis Dickerson's apt phrase, "sustained a dual egalitarian/evangelical thrust."[33] The difference from the politics of sectarian and proprietary Protestants lay in the nearly complete disjunction of purpose. White religious-political conflicts arose from differences over how power should shape American society; Blacks' political concerns came from the desire to exercise power over themselves. Not until many generations passed—in fact, not until the civil rights era after World War II—did the politics of Black religion intrude into the broader society as the sectarian-proprietary division had done even before the founding of the nation. Until that time, the shape of Black religion retained much of its early Methodist character as Black inhabitants of the religious "nation within a nation" put the Scriptures to use for their own purposes. Eugene Genovese explains that "the slaves, drawing on a [Bible] that was supposed to assure their compliance and docility, rejected the essence of slavery by projecting their own rights and value as human beings."[34]

Richard Allen's account of "the first African church or meeting-house that was erected in the United States of America" included a memorable statement of the Methodist affinity. Despite "much persecution from many" of Philadelphia's white Methodists, Allen resolved that his would be an African *Methodist* church. Accessibility and content explained why: "The Methodists were the first people that brought glad tidings to the colored people. I feel thankful that ever I heard a Methodist preach ... for all other denominations preached so high-flown that we were not able to comprehend their doctrines." What Allen sought, Methodism provided: "I was confident that there was no religious sect or denomination would suit the capacity of the colored people as well as the Methodist. ... [T]he reason that the Methodist is so successful in the awakening and conversion of the colored people [is] the plain doctrine and having a good discipline."[35]

A few in the swelling tide of African American converts would worship as Presbyterians or Episcopalians, and many more formed Baptist congregations. But Methodism, with its provision of connections, hymnody, structures, and especially a template for spiritual experience conjoined with community uplift, long remained paradigmatic for Black religion.

Methodist connections operated effectively both on the ground and for organization on a grander scale. In his 1855 memoir, Douglass reiterated a standard pilgrimage. First, "a white Methodist minister" awakened his "religious nature." Then came personal support along the lines of a Methodist class meeting: "a good colored man, named Charles Johnson," stood with Douglass until "I finally found that change of heart which comes by 'casting all one's care' [1 Pet 5:7] upon God, and by having faith in Jesus Christ, as the Redeemer, Friend, and Savior of those who diligently seek him." Then Douglass followed a well-worn Methodist path of self-discipline, as he taught himself to read by copying "from the bible and the Methodist hymn book, and other books which had accumulated on my hands."[36]

References to the benefits of Methodist connectionalism appear frequently in Black memoirs of the period. When Henry Williamson escaped from enslavement in Maryland to freedom in Hamilton, Ontario, his religion provided continuity: "I am a member of the Methodist church, having had good religious instruction from the Bible and catechism from my youth up."[37] Similarly, the Methodist associations that James L. Smith enjoyed when a slave in Virginia were sustained after he escaped to freedom in Ohio and as he aided a longtime friend who had become an AME bishop in conducting meetings in Springfield, "where the colored people had no church of their own at this time to worship in."[38] As we have seen, Bethel AME in Philadelphia during Allen's tenure eventually approved Jarena Lee's desire to preach, in much the same way that decades later the same church, under one of Allen's successors, prepared Amanda Berry Smith for her ministry as a globetrotting evangelist.[39]

As demonstrated by the course of Allen's career early in the century, Daniel Alexander Payne's in the middle years, and Henry McNeal Turner in postbellum decades, leadership as a bishop in the AME became a well-worn path to national recognition, respected authority in Black communities, and even some begrudging respect from white America.[40] In 1810 Daniel Coker appended to his landmark antislavery *Dialogue* a list of Black ministers and organized Black churches (most of them Methodist) in order to underscore the importance of connectional structures for Black religious community.[41]

As with the structures of white Methodism under Asbury, this machinery served a message. In the spread of African American Christianity, religion remained preeminent—nearly identical to the white variety in its spirituality, but also going beyond because of the conditions in which African Americans internalized the gospel message. The experience of evangelical redemption was of course not exclusively Methodist, but well-publicized accounts, like the conversions of Allen and Lee, established an unusually powerful template for what it meant to be saved.[42]

In this spirituality, as recorded reassuringly by James Smith from Virginia and Ohio, hymn-singing featured prominently.[43] In sometimes disturbing forms, as we will see with Nat Turner (chapter 11), it easily mixed biblical motifs with visions and dreams.[44] It was also a spirituality that, as expressed by Francis Henderson from the safety of London, Ontario, moved easily between celestial and terrestrial concerns: "[F]rom the sermons I heard, I felt that God had made all men free and equal, and that I ought not to be a slave."[45]

Extensive quotation is justified in order to underscore the character of so much Black religion as evangelical in a Methodist register. Zilpha Elaw, born free in Philadelphia, where she was nurtured by Quakers and then Methodists, was moved to become a preacher through visions and her own deep immersion in Scripture. After moving to Britain she published a memoir in 1846 that described her "regenerated constitution" as "exhibiting, as did the bride of Solomon, comeliness with blackness; and, as did the apostle Paul, riches with poverty, and power in weakness—a representation, not, indeed, of the features of my outward person . . . but of my inward man, as inscribed by the Holy Ghost, and, according to my poor ability, copied off for your edification."[46]

Mary Walker was a domestic servant in Cambridge, Massachusetts, who regularly attended Episcopal services with her household. After a serious illness, and while continuing in great distress about the enslaved children she had left behind when she escaped to freedom, she entered into serious conversation with the minister of the Old Cambridge Baptist Church. There she underwent a variation of the basic Methodist experience of forgiveness, cleansing, and new life from accepting Jesus. In the account of Sydney Mathans, taken from eyewitnesses of Mary Walker's baptism,

> [she] made use of many scriptural "expressions, and very glowing imagery seemed to float through her mind. She thanked her savior for giving her a seat in his kingdom [see Mk 10:37], for sending his spirit like a dove [Mk 1:10] and clothing her in a robe of righteousness [Isa 61:10]." Touched by a spirit like a dove, Mary Walker at last experienced the rapture felt by her mother at secret midnight prayer meetings in slavery where they had sung:

> Jesus shall break the chain
> And bear us to the throne

By & bye, by & bye.
There friends shall meet again
Who have loved, who have loved
Their union shall be sweet
At their dear Redeemer's feet,
And they meet to part no more,
Who have loved, who have loved.[47]

When preached by AME bishops, especially Daniel Alexander Payne, the quotient of formality rose, but the message remained the same. In 1852 Payne gave the opening sermon at the General Conference of the AME at which he would be elected a bishop. Its text came from 2 Corinthians 2:16, "Who is sufficient for these things?" Payne explained that those called to the ministry might be tempted to think that preaching meant "loud declamation, and vociferous talking . . . whooping, stamping, and beating the Bible or desk with their fists and in cutting as many odd capers as a wild imagination can suggest." The right way, by contrast, was to follow Jesus, "who spoke and whose wisdom is without mixture of error." A faithful preacher would "make man acquainted with his relations to his God as a sinner," but then answer "the cry of his anguished heart: 'What shall I do to be saved?,'" by responding with the Apostle Paul, "Believe in the Lord Jesus Christ, and thou shalt be saved [Acts 16:30–31]." On this basis, a godly minister would "discipline and govern the church . . . cultivate his mind by all the means in his power . . . seek the unction from above, the baptism of the Holy Ghost . . . live the life of faith and prayer, the life of unspotted holiness," and, in brief, "make Christ the model of [the minister's] own Christian and ministerial character."[48]

David Walker's *Appeal* (chapter 11) testified to the great impact of such a Methodist message—and of Methodist messengers—when he paused for an extended paean to Allen (Figure 9.1). To Walker, Allen was "a man whom God . . . raised up among his ignorant and degraded brethren, to preach Jesus Christ and him crucified to them . . . who having overcome the combined powers of devils and wicked men, has under God planted a Church among us which will be as durable as the foundation of the earth on which it stands." In short, Allen "has done more in a spiritual sense for his ignorant and wretched brethren than any other man of colour has, since the world began."[49]

Allen himself, in explaining how he understood Methodist faith, also indicated why articulation of that faith resonated so powerfully among African Americans: "Our Saviour's first and great work was that of the salvation of men's souls; yet we find that of the multitudes who came or were brought to Him laboring under sickness and disorders, He never omitted one opportunity of

Figure 9.1   Richard Allen's African Methodist Episcopal Church provided organization, networking, and discipline for the most important institutional expression of Black Christianity in nineteenth-century America.
Source: LOC, Prints & Photographs, LC-DIG-bellcm-24994.

doing good to their bodies, or sent away one that applied to Him without a perfect cure."[50]

Allen's conception of the proper business of an AME bishop justifies Dickerson's judgment that "in his devotion to spiritual fervor, social witness, and strict adherence to Methodist doctrine and discipline," Allen deserved to be known "as John Wesley's truest American heir."[51] It also explains why Allen, along with other Black notables, could, in the words of Cedric May, use "his example of leadership through Christian principles to . . . develop a social theology with which to wage an activist war against oppression that legal and ecclesiastical authorities could not ignore."[52] Yet the markedly Methodist shape of so much African American Christianity does not by itself explain the salient characteristics that predominated in African American interpretations of the Bible—and that made Black understanding of Scripture so distinctive in an environment otherwise dominated by white hermeneutical assumptions.

Orality, Narratives, Exemplars

Black religion revealed its clearest Methodist affinities in experiences of personal redemption described as immediate, urgent, liberating, empowering, often convulsive, and accomplished by God's supernatural grace. Yet if all evangelicals of the period, white and Black, emphasized the scriptural basis of this gospel proclamation and its outworking in individual lives, significant differences remained. All, to be sure, expected personal holiness before God to produce loving care for fellow humans. White Methodists sustained the intuitive antislavery implications of this conviction for only a few decades, even if longer than their white peers. For Black Christians, those implications remained irrevocably fixed.

This evangelistic-emancipationist understanding of Christian faith rested on the distinctive elements of African American biblical interpretation. Those distinctives were its *orality*, its characteristic expression in *narratives*, and the specific *exemplars* that for many African Americans simply *were* the Bible. These characteristics, always present together, paralleled the synergy for white Protestants among convinced personal religion, close exegetical study of the Scriptures, and energetic efforts to shape society.

In colonial and Revolutionary America the Bible's impression on Black consciousness came first through the spoken word.[53] The pioneering narratives of Albert Ukawsaw Gronniosaw and John Marrant (1772 and 1785) highlighted the sermons of George Whitefield and his associates as the spark that kindled their faith. Phillis Wheatley's 1770 poem on Whitefield that established her reputation likewise featured the importance of what Africans *heard* him preach. David George, who founded the first Black churches in South Carolina, Nova Scotia, and Sierra Leone, *heard* the scriptural exhortations that redirected his life and began to exhort himself from scriptural phrases he memorized—before he could read. In his widely read *Interesting Narrative* (1789) Olaudah Equiano reported that, like Gronniosaw before him, he witnessed whites speaking earnestly with Scriptures in hand and then in private grasped a bible, "talked to it, and then put my ears to it . . . in hope it would answer me." In Allen Callahan's expert account, the Bible for African Americans began as "a talking book," and so it remained.[54]

For several years late in the eighteenth century Francis Asbury traveled with Henry Hosier, an unlettered former slave, who preached effectively to Black and mixed audiences from scriptures he had learned by heart.[55] It was by no means a unique phenomenon, as a Methodist circuit rider experienced early in the next century when he ran across a well-organized cell of converts in Fishing Creek, Kentucky. The local "class" was led by Jacob, an enslaved layman, who, the circuit rider reported, "could preach a pretty good sermon" despite not being able to read.[56] The ardent desire for literacy among African Americans came from two sources: a passion to know more of the message they had already heard and because white power so frequently did everything possible to prevent Blacks from learning to read.[57]

If formal hymnody secured biblical phrases, themes, and sensibility for all audiences of the period, song for African Americans did even more. Numerous observers have expanded at great length on what Mellonee Burnim encapsulated as the "biblical inspiration" for "the African American Gift of Song": "First and foremost, Negro spirituals chronicled the word of God, as set forth in the Bible, functioning to reconstruct biblical events, condense, and distill the embedded spiritual message."[58] In the early twentieth century, James Weldon Johnson wrote from the standpoint of African American believers when he described the momentous effect brought about when "black and unknown bards" breathed life-transforming power into scriptural images:

> Heart of what slave poured out such melody
> As "Steal away to Jesus"? On its strains
> His spirit must have nightly floated free,
> Though still about his hands he felt his chains.
> Who heard great "Jordan roll"? Whose starward eye
> Saw chariot "swing low"? And who was he
> That breathed that comforting, melodic sigh,
> "Nobody knows de trouble I see"?
> . . .
> You sang far better than you knew; the songs
> That for your listeners' hungry hearts sufficed
> Still live—but more than this to you belongs:
> You sang a race from wood and stone to Christ.[59]

Without the pedigree so important for biblical exposition in the majority society, and with anonymity that was just as disconcerting, Black spirituals eventually became America's most memorable scriptural gift to the world.

Black biblical understanding rooted in the orality of exhortation and song naturally flowered in the literary form of memoir. Already in the summaries sampled in this book we have observed the importance of the narrative form when African Americans ventured into print. Examples like Maria Stewart's sermonic *Productions* only proved the rule illustrated more characteristically by the published memoirs of Gronniosaw, Marrant, David George, Equiano, Allen, Lee, Jacob, Northup, Pennington, Bibb, Douglass, and Amanda Berry Smith. In documenting historical writing by African American women, Laurie Maffly-Kipp and Kathryn Lofton explain how this kind of writing only extended what had been that most favored narrative form. For these women, denominational differences faded into the background because "biblical chronology [was] more vivid." Authors of these narratives knew that their readers had "a basic familiarity with the Bible and knowledge of the basic chronology of Christian history."[60]

Orality and narrative form were of course never monopolized by Black speakers and writers. From the time of the Puritans and Whitefield, biblical sermons of powerful preachers also moved white audiences; a reliance on familiar biblical stories was also stock-in-trade for evangelists seeking conversions and preachers using the history of Israel to explain current events. Yet proportion and context reveal sharp differences.

Standard white preaching came from a conceptual world filled with biblical commentaries, familiar with libraries, informed by learned forays into Scripture's original languages, recalling orderly family gatherings for daily Bible readings, and reinforced by a great profusion of Bible-based publications for educated and plebian readers alike. Except for the mimetic force of sacred songs and for personal dedication to the Scriptures, the conceptual world in which Blacks engaged the Bible differed entirely. Most important, whites who inwardly digested the Scriptures usually had considerable control over their own lives; African Americans most often had very little.

To be sure, significant instances of Black writing replicated standard white expositions: proof-texting, footnotes specifying biblical references, and step-by-step argumentation that synthesized biblical material for doctrinal or ethical purposes. Quobna Cugoano's 1787 polemic, *Thoughts and Sentiments on the Evil and Wicked Traffic of the Slavery and Commerce of the human Species*, contained many sections of this sort, as did Daniel Coker's 1810 *Dialogue* and later works by learned African Americans like James W. C. Pennington in his *Origin and History of the Colored People* (1841). Black female preachers like Zilpha Elaw, Jarena Lee, Julia Foote, and Amanda Berry Smith could also reason with a full arsenal of biblical texts, inferences, and implications when they defended their right to preach.[61] Frequent quotation of Psalm 68:31 ("Ethiopia shall soon stretch out her hands unto God") and the "one blood" passage from Acts 17:26 showed that African Americans had learned the rules of the white game.

Again, however, proportion explains the difference. Verse-by-verse expositions and close biblical reasoning represented only a small fraction of Black literary output compared to the great quantity of narrative memoirs. White authors also produced many autobiographies, but not nearly as many as the vast publication of text-based sermons, exegetical arguments, and detailed expositions.

Richard Allen's way of reasoning from Scripture was emblematic for an entire tradition. In a short pamphlet addressed to slave owners and their defenders, Allen appealed broadly to biblical history. In that appeal he drew special attention to key actors in the story:

I do not wish to make you angry, but excite your attention to consider how hateful slavery is in the sight of that God who hath destroyed kings and princes for their oppression of the poor slaves. Pharaoh and his princes, with the posterity of King Saul, were destroyed by the protector and avenger of slaves. Would you not suppose the Israelites to be utterly unfit for freedom and that it was impossible for them to obtain any degree of excellence? Their history shows how slavery had debased their spirits.[62]

White expositors also drew on Israel's history and its central figures, but usually, as we have repeatedly seen, for explaining contemporary national or, less frequently, ecclesiastical situations. For African American speakers and writers, biblical history especially of the ancient Hebrews spoke to personal and communal existence. The role of Moses as liberator and the Exodus as deliverance from slavery are so well known as to have become clichés—except for those whose deliverance was not simply a metaphor.[63]

The way the figure of Moses joined the figure of Jesus indicates why Black Christology—hence also Black understanding of redemption—differed from common white understandings. In Julius Lester's account, the slaves "fashioned their own kind of Christianity, which they turned to for strength in the constant times of need. In the Old Testament story of the enslavement of the Hebrews by the Egyptians, they found their own story. In the figure of Jesus Christ they found someone who had suffered as they suffered, someone who understood, someone who offered them rest from their suffering."[64] Deliverance from Egypt, the suffering of the Savior, and the final Day of the Lord concerned only incidentally the fate of the United States. Nor did they foreshadow an exclusively spiritual transaction between God and the individual. Rather, they provided the framework for a social hope and for communal aspirations in which the power of God would break in pieces the fetters of slavery *and* the bonds of sin.[65]

The importance of the Exodus as paradigmatic story and of Moses (or Moses-Christ) as paradigmatic deliverer also explains why the stories of other biblical figures loomed so large in African American biblical interpretation. As they could also for many whites, stories of suffering redeemed, sinners restored, the despised reclaimed, the forgotten remembered, and the dead brought back to life could become similes for nineteenth-century lives. Black understandings were distinguished by exemplars that functioned as direct inspiration.[66] The list was all but endless: Nimrod, a son of Cush (and therefore an African), who was "a mighty hunter before the Lord" (Gen 10: 8–10);[67] Jacob wrestling all night with the angel of the Lord;[68] Joseph sold by his brothers into slavery and protected by God in his enslavement;[69] Joshua faithfully following Moses as he led Israel into the Promised Land;[70] the Judeans taken captive into Babylon;[71] Daniel in the den of lions and his three companions in the fiery furnace;[72] the "black but comely"

Shulamite woman of the Song of Songs (Canticles 1:5–6);[73] and somewhat less often from the New Testament, Mary the mother of Jesus and Lazarus whom Jesus raised from the dead.[74]

After David Blight completed his landmark 2018 biography of Frederick Douglass, he paused to reflect on the subtitle of his book, *Prophet of Freedom*: "You cannot read Douglass and not see the Bible, especially the Hebrew prophets." Blight's conclusion specified for Douglass what in more general terms characterized so much of the African American Bible: "What Douglass found in the Old Testament was storytelling and metaphor, as well as ancient authority and power for the claims he is trying to make about the American experiment"—and, one might add, about people in general in relation to God in particular.[75] More succinctly, as Blight wrote in the biography itself, "For black Americans, Exodus is always contemporary history, history always past and present."[76]

To understand how the Exodus story functioned as the foundation for African American biblical interpretation is to understand why that hermeneutical universe coincided only casually with the hermeneutical universe of the white American majority. The interpretive divide in antebellum America also explains why, as Black devotion to Scripture grew, the Bible civilization declined. The kind of guidance required for constructing an entire civilization, even if coming from the Book regarded almost universally as life-transforming, could never be more than incidentally the same for those whom the Bible rescued from sin and those whom the Bible rescued—period.

PART III

FRACTURES

But when Paul perceived that the one part were Sadducees, and the other Pharisees, he cried out in the council, Men and brethren, I am a Pharisee, the son of a Pharisee: of the hope and resurrection of the dead I am called in question. And when he had so said, there arose a dissension between the Pharisees and the Sadducees: and the multitude was divided. For the Sadducees say that there is no resurrection, neither angel, nor spirit: but the Pharisees confess both. And there arose a great cry.

—Acts 23:5-9a

10

Slavery and the Bible before the Missouri Compromise

The rapid expansion of Bible-only reasoning in the early republic affected much more than just religion. A reliance on Scripture alone certainly did fuel the Methodists' powerful message of personal salvation and responsible personal discipline. It did make proprietary Protestants nervous about their historical confessions even as it propelled their massive efforts at publishing the Bible and distributing Bible-based reading material. It opened possibilities that sectarians of all kinds exploited with great effect. For Black Americans, the Bible alone meant something different, but no less significant. For life beyond the religious sphere, Protestant appeals to the Bible also clearly shaped national self-identity, influenced the development of public education, and kept Scripture alive in legal reasoning.

In the fuller scope of American history, however, the rise of "the Bible only" affected nothing more powerfully than public debate concerning the morality of slavery. From the first efforts in the late seventeenth century to assess the legitimacy of the institution, through the accumulation of arguments that began in the Revolutionary era, to the all-out cultural warfare that preceded (and outlasted) the shooting war, to contest slavery was to contest Scripture.[1]

In these contests Americans turned to the Bible for arguments taken from specific texts, but also for the bearing of scriptural Christianity on the institution as a whole. To complicate the arena of public debate, they also regularly enlisted other warrants as if they could be instinctively harmonized with biblical content. These warrants included notions of divine providence, perceived mandates of republican liberty, and what were taken to be the facts of American slavery.

The deployment of biblical arguments lined up neatly with discernible periods in public life. Sporadic attention to such questions in the colonial era gave way to sustained concern only when, in the words of Christopher Brown, "the colonial revolt against British rule touched off a revolution in the public conversation about human bondage."[2] The move from Revolutionary nation-creation to post-Revolutionary nation-formation also shifted biblical consideration of slavery. As proslavery influences grew because of the churches' success in converting slave owners, so also did several authors publish unusually sophisticated attacks based directly on the Bible. A sharp transition then took place when controversy

America's Book. Mark A. Noll, Oxford University Press. © Oxford University Press 2022.
DOI: 10.1093/oso/9780197623466.003.0011

surrounding the Missouri Compromise of 1819–20 coincided with reports of a major slave revolt in Charleston, South Carolina. An even sharper transition took place because of events at the turn of the next decade, particularly the 1829 publication of David Walker's incendiary *Appeal to the Coloured Citizens of the World*, the founding of William Lloyd Garrison's abolitionist newspaper, *The Liberator*, in early 1831, and the Virginia slave rebellion led by Nat Tuner later that same year.

Exploring these debates reveals a fault line growing into a fracture. The Protestant Bible civilization would eventually be threatened by the religious pluralism that arrived with an increased population of Catholics, Jews, and other non-Protestants. Before then, however, the nation's democratic commitments (chapter 12) and its fumbling toward legal clarity (chapter 13) would undermine that civilization from within. Yet nothing forecast its decline more directly than the sharp divide concerning God's revealed will for Black chattel slavery.

First Forays

Before agitation in the 1770s over Parliament's "enslavement" of the colonies prompted fresh consideration of chattel bondage, controversy over the morality of slavery, including the moral witness of Scripture, was muted. As hard as it is now to imagine that the practice of human bondage did not engender constant debate, in that era it did not. From the late Middle Ages into the early modern era, the locations from which western Europeans took their slaves did shift from eastern Europe (Slav = slave) to the Americas and Africa. While popes and other Catholics insisted on the humanity of enslaved peoples, European territorial expansion presupposed a racial hierarchy that slid easily into enslavement of the peoples encountered in that expansion.[3]

In the colonial period, most American agitation against slavery came from Quakers, who remained decidedly on the cultural margin.[4] Importantly, however, that agitation anticipated almost all later biblical arguments attacking the institution. The Golden Rule from Matthew 7:12 supported colonial protests and remained prominent wherever voices were raised against the system: "Therefore all things whatsoever ye would that men should do to you, do ye even so to them: for this is the law and the prophets" (parallel in Lk 6:31). Almost as regularly, the early abolitionists referenced the Second Commandment (after the First, loving God) that is found in Jesus's words from Mark 12:31 ("thou shalt love thy neighbour as thyself") and repeated elsewhere in the New Testament (Matt 22:39; Rom 13:9; Gal 5:14). So it was in 1688 when Quakers and Mennonites in Germantown, Pennsylvania, made the first recorded American antislavery protest: "There is a saying, that we should doe to all men, licke as we will be done ourselves: macking no difference of what generation, descent, or Colour they are."[5] The considerable roster of Quakers who opened the Bible this way—George Keith (1693), John Hepburn (1715), Ralph Sandiford (1729), Benjamin Lay (1737), John Woolman (1754), Anthony Benezet (1759)—regularly augmented arguments from the Golden Rule with appeals to liberty of conscience, humanitarian sentiment, and Enlightenment ideals.[6] The result was not proof-texting as much as biblically grounded theology, or general philosophy of life, bearing witness.

Along with such broad appeals, the early antislavery authors also argued from an array of individual texts. In 1693, the mercurial Quaker reformer George Keith enlisted the Mosaic prohibition against man-stealing (Ex 21:16, "he that stealeth a Man and selleth him, if he be found in his hand, he shall surely be put to Death"), the Mosaic mandate for protecting "the Servant which is escaped from his Master" (Deut 23:15–16), the Mosaic command "not to oppress an hired Servant that is poor and needy, whether he be of the Brethren, or of the Strangers that are in thy land" (Deut 24:14–15), and, more fancifully, a tirade from the book of Revelation against the "merchants of Babylon" (Rev 13:10, "God hath remembered her Iniquities; for he that leads into Captivity shall go into Captivity").[7] Judge Samuel Sewall, who made the one notable protest from Puritan New England in his *Selling of Joseph* from 1700, cited the Golden Rule and the Mosaic prohibition against man-stealing, even as he took time to deny that "the curse of Canaan" from Genesis 9:25 had anything to do with contemporary Africa or modern slavery.[8]

Slave owners and their defenders seem barely to have noticed. To be sure, John Saffin, a thorn in Sewall's side through many Boston disputes, replied to the judge by pointing out that Mosaic legislation allowed the Israelites to enslave non-Hebrews, including the children born to these non-Israelites. His text from Leviticus chapter 25 would long remain a pillar of proslavery arguments. But as with opponents of slavery, Saffin also festooned his argument with broader considerations; for example, if Sewall's reasoning prevailed, general application of the Golden Rule would cancel all of the social orders God had created.[9] Saffin's effort in replying to Sewall was unusual. Overwhelmingly, the untroubled acceptance of African enslavement relied much more on inertia than on argument.

Slavery and Scripture in the Time of Revolution

Hesitation about addressing the morality of slavery vanished when the colonists' agitated defense of liberty coincided with a landmark judgment in an English court. In May 1772, Lord Mansfield of the Court of King's Bench ruled that James Somerset, a slave brought by his West Indian master to England, must

be declared free because no law of Parliament had ever authorized the institution on England's soil.[10] The decision did not directly affect slavery in the
British Caribbean or British participation in the slave trade, but it marked the
beginning of concentrated opposition to the slave trade organized by Quakers,
Anglican Evangelicals, and Dissenters of all theological positions. Then, as so
often happened in the American history of the Bible, a British action precipitated
a major American reaction. In this case, a short West Indian pamphlet defending
slavery and aimed at a British audience incited contentions in America about
the Bible, slavery, and race that have, in ever new configurations, continued to
this day.

That proslavery defense, published the same year as the Somerset decision, came from Thomas Thompson, an Anglican missionary with experience
throughout the Atlantic world. Its thirty-one large print pages began by regretting
the unfortunate violence caused in Africa by the slave trade. But it then affirmed,
"[W]e must endeavor to make the best of what we have" since Parliamentary
legislation protected the trade, which could not therefore be sinful in itself.
Thompson's positive argument began with the Old Testament passage that Safin
had already cited against Judge Sewall. Leviticus chapter 25 first limited the duration of servitude by a Hebrew to another Hebrew while also mandating gentle
treatment for such fellow-Israelite "servants" (verses 39–43). Then in verses 44
through 46 came the Mosaic provision that defenders of slavery would quote
time and again in the following decades:

> 44. Both thy bondmen, and thy bondmaids, which thou shalt have, shall be
> of the heathen that are round about you; of them shall ye buy bondmen and
> bondmaids.
>
> 45. Moreover of the children of the strangers that do sojourn among you, of
> them shall ye buy, and of their families that are with you, which they begat in
> your land: and they shall be your possession.
>
> 46. And ye shall take them as an inheritance for your children after you, to
> inherit them for a possession; they shall be your bondmen for ever: but over
> your brethren the children of Israel, ye shall not rule one over another with
> rigour.

Thompson's pamphlet went on to mention the Apostle Paul's counsel for
slaves to remain in that calling (1 Cor 7:20–21) and the Apostle's return of the
slave Onesimus to his master Philemon (book of Philemon). It also considered,
though very briefly, the condition of Africans ("generally held to be a savage
people"), modern slavery as resulting from "the fortunes of war," and the actual
conditions of slave trading. But the basis for the entire argument was Thompson's
categorical assertion after he had quoted Leviticus 25:44–46: "This conclusion

may be drawn, that the buying and selling of slaves is not contrary to the law of nature."[11]

The only apologist in the last third of the century who defended slavery from the Bible without relying on the Leviticus passage was the Presbyterian William Graham, president of Liberty Hall (later Washington and Lee University) in Lexington, Virginia. As was customary for college presidents, Graham annually offered his seniors a course titled Human Nature, one of whose lectures addressed the question "[I]s it right to continue those in slavery who are found in that state?" Graham's answer rejected the Golden Rule of Matthew 7:12 as irrelevant, turning instead to 1 Corinthians 7, where the Apostle Paul urged "every man," including slaves, to "abide in the same calling wherein he was called." Then Graham cited the New Testament epistles that enjoined slaves to accept their bondage: Ephesians 6 ("Servants, be obedient to them that are your masters"), Titus 2 ("Exhort servants to be obedient to their own masters"), and 1 Timothy 6 ("Let as many servants as are under the yoke count their own masters as worthy of all honor").[12] If Graham was unusual in the 1790s for using the Bible this way, however, he anticipated how justifications from the New Testament would gain traction after another generation passed.

The era's most elaborate biblical defense came again from England in a substantial pamphlet published in London in 1788 and reprinted in Maryland two years later. Its author, "the Rev. R. Harris," was actually a Spanish Jesuit, Don Raymondo Hormaza, who had been banished from Spain, was later suspended as a priest, and at the time of the pamphlet served as the supervisor of a school for young gentlemen in Liverpool.[13] The Harris/Hormaza effort, *Scriptural Researches on the Licitness of the Slave-Trade*, presented detailed arguments that many Americans would soon echo. After beginning with a powerful affirmation of Scripture as God's infallible Word, it asserted that the only conceivable opposition to the Bible's clear teaching could come from those "who disbelieve the divine authority of those Sacred Writings." The tract included more attention to other Old and New Testament texts than simply Leviticus 25, but on that passage Harris was unequivocal. After observing that Moses had not written "you *may* buy" slaves from alien nations but "you *shall* buy" slaves (Lev 25:44), Harris made a dispositive assertion. It is worth quoting at length because of how much both its narrow conclusions and its broader implications would be repeated in later decades:

> From this most decisive, most explicit, and irrefragable authority of the Written Word of God, visibly encouraging the prosecution of the *Slave-Trade*, and declaring in the most categorical language that words can devise, that a Slave is the real, indisputable, and lawful property of the purchaser and his heirs for ever, it necessarily follows by force of consequence, that either the *Slave-Trade*

must be in its own intrinsic nature a just and an honest Trade, and by no means deserving those harsh epithets and names with which it is so frequently branded and degraded; or, that, if it does still deserve those odious names and epithets in consequence of its intrinsic turpitude and immorality, the Almighty did so far forget himself, when he made the above Law, as to patronize a manifest injustice, encourage a most criminal violation of his other laws, and give his sacred sanction to what humanity itself must for ever abhor and detest. As there can be no medium betwixt these two unavoidable inferences, and the latter is one of the most daring blasphemies that the human heart can conceive, I leave the religious Reader to judge for himself, which side of the Question is the safest to embrace.[14]

The English response to Harris's pamphlet differed considerably from how Americans would answer such arguments. For English abolitionists, the Harris controversy became one of the factors that turned them *away from* extensive use of detailed biblical arguments. In the United States it stimulated the reverse, an extensive recourse *to* Scripture.

As the English campaign against the slave trade gained momentum in the 1790s, it relied on support from a broadening coalition, including many who shared religious convictions with American Protestants. But it also included some with Paine-ite views on Scripture, as well as liberal Dissenters like the Unitarian Joseph Priestley, who in 1788 lauded the cooperation against the slave trade by groups that otherwise disagreed on how to interpret the Bible: "[I]n recommending the relief of the distressed African slaves, I can join heartily with every denomination of Christians in the country, the catholics, the members of the establishment, and dissenters of all denominations."[15] For his part, William Wilberforce devoutly believed that the New Testament condemned everything connected with slavery. But as he geared up for battle in Parliament against the slave trade, he stressed broader legal, moral, and prudential arguments, along with general warnings from providence, rather than scriptural arguments as such. Reflecting what David Brion Davis has described as "considerable moral confusion" among English abolitionists when it came Scripture, Wilberforce acknowledged that including the Bible in his Parliamentary appeals would require "explanations."[16]

In America, by contrast, opponents of slavery appealed directly to the Bible, which had the effect of ensuring that Scripture-based *defenses* of slavery also never faded. To be sure, from the early 1770s to the early 1790s, most Bible-supported attacks against enslavement remained embedded in more general political or ethical arguments. Yet not only did the Bible remain prominent in Revolutionary-era condemnations of slavery; they seemed to be winning the day.

As could be expected, Protestants who championed "the sacred cause of liberty" against British tyranny easily merged sanctions from religious precept and political principle in condemning both the slave trade and slavery itself. A follower of Jonathan Edwards, the Presbyterian Jacob Green in New Jersey typified the merger of principles when in a series of works at the height of the war he indicted slavery as a "most cruel, inhuman, unnatural sin" on four counts: it violated God's command to love one's neighbor as oneself; it unjustly placed people in bondage who had never forfeited their right to freedom; it interdicted the natural and inalienable right to freedom; and it was condemned by the Apostle Paul when he associated man-stealing with murder.[17]

The mixture of biblical and Revolutionary reasoning long continued to ground antislavery arguments. During George Washington's first term as president, the free Black astronomer Benjamin Banneker wrote (and then published) a much-noticed letter to Thomas Jefferson. Its plea for the end of slavery marshaled Acts 17:26 (God made all humankind of one flesh), with a passage from the book of Job mimicking the Golden Rule (Job 16:4, "Put your Souls in their Souls stead"), quotations from Jefferson's own Declaration of Independence, and a general appeal to those who "maintain . . . the rights of human nature, and who profess the obligations of Christianity."[18] Yet the strength of such public advocacy also defined its weakness. If Christian persuasion from Scripture could merge so smoothly with the liberating temper of the times, it could merge just as easily with the public mood when that temper cooled.

A few antislavery voices in this period did, however, stress individual texts of Scripture more or less independently of the era's ideological enthusiasms, including the Quaker Anthony Benezet and Jonathan Edwards Jr., son of the famous theologian.[19] Also in those years broad theological argument based exclusively on the Bible appeared. As noted, Isaac Backus denounced slavery with a fairly sophisticated biblical-theological argument at the Massachusetts convention to ratify the national Constitution in 1788. A few years later, David Rice also exploited a political forum to deliver this era's most extensive biblical-theological attack on the American slave system. Rice, a revival-friendly Presbyterian who helped found Hampden-Sydney College in Virginia and later Transylvania University in Kentucky, presented his argument in 1792 at the convention called to draw up Kentucky's state constitution.[20]

Because Rice's antislavery polemic, like Raymond Harris's proslavery arguments, developed most of the best biblical arguments that would reappear over the next seventy years, they are worth summarizing in some detail. Rice first claimed that *the general thrust of the New Testament* worked strongly against anything connected with chattel bondage. To prove that point, he quoted, as did so many others, the Golden Rule from Matthew chapter 7.[21]

Rice's next arguments became more complicated as he appealed to historical context, both the circumstances of biblical times and pertinent facts about the new United States. These moves anticipated what in later years would become the crucial biblical battleground. Against those contending that the Apostle Paul had given instructions to slaves as if the condition were entirely natural, he appealed to broader considerations of biblical history. According to Rice, when Paul wrote his epistles, the Christians "were under the Roman yoke, the government of the heathen" who eagerly sought excuses "to justify their bloody persecutions." That historical situation explained why "the Apostle acted with this prudent reserve."[22]

Rice also wanted his hearers to confront the differences between whatever kind of slavery could be found in Scripture and the actual operation of the American system. Although God had ordained marriage as permanent, had instructed parents to train their children in the faith, and had urged children to honor their parents, American laws allowed enslaved spouses to be sold away from each other, replaced parental authority with the slave owner's authority, and compelled children to honor masters more than parents.[23] In short, it was a different system altogether.

At greatest length Rice addressed what he called "the most formidable" objection to any emancipationist plan "taken from the sacred scriptures," specifically the Old Testament record that Abraham owned slaves and that Leviticus chapter 25 revealed Mosaic approval for enslaving non-Hebrews. In response, Rice expounded at length the argument that Backus had earlier sketched.[24] Rice stressed particularly that Scripture nowhere sanctioned bondage for the children of Israel by the children of Israel. Abraham, according to Rice, did hold slaves, but he also circumcised his slaves, which meant that they were taken into his household and so "incorporate[d] . . . into the church and the nation." As a consequence, their children counted as Israelites, who could not be enslaved.[25] As Rice moved on to other contentious issues—miscegenation, economic loss, and the practicalities of dealing with an emancipated African population—he had to his own satisfaction conclusively refuted the use of Scripture to defend the American slave system.

An outburst in one of the earliest sessions of the new national Congress showed, however, that arguments like Rice's had not carried the day. In February 1790 a Pennsylvania representative presented to the first session of the U.S. House of Representatives a petition from the Quaker Yearly Meetings of several states appealing for the end of the slave trade. The petition cited the Golden Rule, which, as the petitioners observed, was honored by "professors of faith in that ever blessed all-perfect Lawgiver, whose injunctions remain of undiminished obligation on all who profess to believe in him, 'whatsoever ye would that men should do unto you, do you even so unto them.'" It also cited Scripture to link personal morality and national morality, since "both the true temporal interests of nations, and eternal well-being of individuals, depend [quoting Mi 6:8] on doing justly, loving mercy, and walking humbly before God, the creator, preserver, and benefactor of men."[26]

When Congress took up this petition, James Madison pointed out that the question was moot because the Constitution "secures to the individual States the right of admitting, if they think proper, the importation of slaves into their own territory, for eighteen years yet unexpired." As the debate proceeded, however, it did not take long for Representative James Jackson of Georgia to match prooftexts. As he chided the Quakers for thinking they understood "the rights of mankind, and the disposition of Providence better than others," Jackson invoked defenses of slavery that would be repeated time and again: "If they were to consult that book, which claims our regard, they will find that slavery is not only allowed but commended. Their Saviour, who possessed more benevolence and commiseration than they pretend to, has allowed of it; and if they fully examine the subject, they will find that slavery has been no novel doctrine since the days of Cain."[27]

In the years when Americans threw off Parliament's yoke of tyranny, struggled with defects in government by confederation, drafted and then ratified the Constitution, flesh-and-blood enslavement emerged as a contentious public subject. Religious voices debating the subject always kept the Bible in play. Debates in political circles referenced Scripture only slightly less frequently. Remarkably, in light of the intense biblical scrutiny in the decades that followed, almost all of the specific texts, general biblical constructs, and pairings of Scripture with other considerations had already surfaced in these early years. The balance of persuasion would hinge on how white Protestants appropriated Scripture, but also on the efforts of Black Americans who also considered Scripture the Word of God.

Denominational History

In the generation after the fullest earlier statements concerning the Bible and slavery—Harris *for* (1790), Rice *against* (1792)—less dramatic but even more important developments took place. In particular, the nation's booming Protestant denominations promoted the view that Christian faith based on the Bible alone could both empower the churches and strengthen the republic. As an unintended consequence, the denominations found themselves retreating from their antislavery positions of the Revolutionary era to uneasy acceptance of slaveholding among their members. Yet during these same years some of the most thoughtful biblical arguments against the institution also appeared—and with no published rebuttals of comparable sophistication.

The story of Methodist, Presbyterian, and Baptist retreat on slaveholding is well known because of an enduringly important monograph by Donald Mathews.[28] The simple summary is that American Protestants in the Revolutionary era took strong stands against slavery as, in the words of a Baptist pastor from 1798, "contrary to the laws of God and nature."[29] But then the stance softened. Significantly, that softening occurred as Americans threw off the habits of Christendom and resolved to live by the Bible alone.

Several factors contributed to the softening: success in evangelizing increased the number of slave owners; the public continued to ignore the voices of enslaved believers; the liberationist enthusiasm of the Revolution cooled; investments in chattel grew in value after the mechanization of cotton production and then from the sale of enslaved laborers from Virginia and North Carolina to the opening cotton belts of the Southwest; reports of slave rebellions in St. Domingue (1791) and Richmond, Virginia (1800), frightened increasing numbers; and what once seemed the clear implications of the Golden Rule ("the golden law of God") no longer seemed so obvious. Mathews has summarized that for Methodists "the basic problem" was "growth and organization." Francis Asbury, who had been most responsible for Methodist growth and organization, slowly bent to the pressure. Again Mathews: "It was this small, frail prophet of lonely places and never-ending trails who had introduced opposition to slavery into the councils of the church, then caution, then compromise; and with his death [in 1816] came the final gasp of determination to oppose slavery throughout the nation."[30]

Presbyterians prided themselves on upholding a Reformed tradition reaching back to John Calvin's Geneva as well as a Puritan legacy applying all of Scripture to all of life. Yet they too followed the same course. Presbyterian demography, with churches concentrated in the Mid-Atlantic states southward into Virginia and the Carolinas, meant that proslavery voices were always more prominent than among the early Methodists. Besides the biblical arguments provided by William Graham at Liberty Hall, some Virginia Presbyterians defended slavery for pragmatic reasons and as a legitimate expression of republican patriarchy.[31] Yet for a time proslavery voices remained in the minority.

In 1787, at one of the last meetings of the Synod of New York and Philadelphia, before the Presbyterians reorganized two years later into a national General Assembly, this main denominational judicatory proceeded more cautiously than the Methodists, but in the same direction. The synod had received an overture condemning slavery because God had "made of one flesh all the children of men" [Acts 17:26] and because it violated the more general "rights of humanity." The synod responded, without reference to Scripture, by "highly approv[ing] of the general principles in favor of universal liberty that prevailed in America." It did warn that freeing slaves "without a proper education, and without previous habits of industry" would be dangerous. Yet it urged all Presbyterians to train slaves "as to prepare them for the better enjoyment of freedom." They also delivered a qualified but hopeful recommendation to "all their people" concerning the system as a whole: "to use the most prudent measures, consistent with the interest and the state of civil society, in the countries where they live, to procure eventually the final abolition of slavery in America."[32]

In the following years the same circumstances that weakened the Methodist stance also worked on the Presbyterians. Regional presbyteries and synods in the South discouraged agitation against enslavement even as antislavery sentiment continued to percolate. The 1818 national General Assembly made another comprehensive statement, this one prompted by the Bible-based abolitionist agitation of George Bourne, who had become a minister to Presbyterian congregations in Rockingham and Augusta, Virginia. Bourne's agitation had embroiled his local Lexington Presbytery since 1815. Now in 1818 the General Assembly took definitive action. It upheld the decision of the presbytery to remove Bourne from the ministry for slandering his slave-owning parishioners as vile sinners. But it also issued a decision that began by condemning the institution of slavery as a violation of both biblical teaching and natural moral law: "We consider the voluntary enslaving of one part of the human race by another, as a gross violation of the most precious and sacred rights of human nature; as utterly inconsistent with the law of God, which requires us to love our neighbour as ourselves [Matt 22:39], and as totally irreconcilable with the spirit and principles of the gospel of Christ, which enjoin that 'all things whatsoever ye would that men should do to you, do ye even so to them [Matt 7:12].'"[33] Qualifications, however, soon followed: because of the number and uneducated character of American slaves, immediate abolition was not feasible; when Presbyterians by force of circumstances could not escape slaveholding, they were not to be considered sinful; for addressing the problems of slavery, the Presbyterians recommended the programs of the American Colonization Society, which had been founded only the year before; and it confirmed the defrocking of Bourne, the denomination's best-known opponent of slavery. In James Morehead's authoritative assessment, this 1818 decision represented "a curious amalgam of urgent antislavery rhetoric and timorous conservatism. . . . It was a document poised between . . . the hope that freedom was about to break forth and fear that premature embrace of freedom would prove disastrous."[34]

For the history of the Bible, the Presbyterians in 1818 were pointing toward what would become an ever-stronger sentiment among white members of several denominations, south as well as north. As they doubled down on their commitment to follow Scripture for everything that a church and its people should do *as a church*, they increasingly cordoned off social and political questions as belonging to the sphere of civil government. The "spirituality of the church" would later become the phrase to describe this stance. Although the phrase had not yet come into widespread currency in 1818, the rising influence of the idea meant that growing numbers of Presbyterians were reversing the long-standing Reformed position and no longer expected guidance for all of the social order from the pages of Scripture.[35]

The Baptists' story differed in details because of their decentralized and congregational church governance. No national Baptist organization spoke out concerning slavery until heightened national controversy in the early 1840s forced action by the Baptist Triennial Convention, the national body that coordinated foreign missionary efforts. Yet the general movement of Baptist opinion followed closely where Methodists and Presbyterians led.

Immediately after the Revolutionary War, even as rapid Baptist expansion throughout the South took in numerous slaveholders, antislavery pronouncements came from many sides. In 1785 the General Committee of Virginia Baptists declared that "hereditary slavery [was] contrary to the word of God," a view echoed for at least a decade by regional associations in Georgia, Kentucky, Virginia, and elsewhere.[36] John Leland, a powerful preacher of sectarian and Jeffersonian convictions, made a particularly noteworthy declaration in 1791. Leland, a native New Englander who had become a respected evangelist in Virginia, thundered that he could not "endure to see one man strip and whip another, as free by nature as himself." Leland declared slavery "a violent deprivation of the rights of nature, inconsistent with republican government, destructive of every humane and benevolent passion of the soul, and subversive to that liberty absolutely necessary to ennoble the human mind."[37]

Antislavery advocacy among white Baptists did not long survive. The career of David Barrow, whose words about slavery violating "the laws of God and nature" were quoted earlier, illustrates the larger picture. In 1798 Barrow published a circular letter that categorically denounced his Baptist congregation in Southampton, Virginia, for tolerating enslavement. When Barrow retreated to Kentucky, he found some in his new home who agreed with him, but within a decade Kentucky's North District Association expelled Barrow for his reforming crusade. With messengers from nine Baptist churches, Barrow then founded a new organization, the Baptized Licking-Locust Association, Friends of Humanity, which declared its "professed abhorrence to unmerited, hereditary, perpetual, absolute unconditional slavery." But this new association did not survive Barrow's death in 1819.[38]

Even more telling was the later career of John Leland. After returning to New England and celebrating Jefferson's 1800 election with the great wheel of cheese, Leland remained silent on slavery until, decades later, he publicly reversed course. As an elder statesman he asserted in 1839 that all related questions were "*moral* and *religious*," not legislative; they could be dealt with only by "God—the master—and the slave." Drawing on his own earlier residence in the South, Leland challenged abolitionists to relocate so as to actually experience life in mixed-race communities; that firsthand experience would effectively cure their radicalism.[39]

A private letter written in 1807 by Richard Furman, a much-respected Baptist pastor in Charleston, South Carolina, and in 1814 the first president of the national Triennial Convention, illustrates the process that led other Baptists to shift their thinking. Furman conceded that slavery was "a Natural or Political Evil," but it became a "Moral Evil" only when masters treated their slaves with cruelty or slaves disobeyed. By itself, the passage from Leviticus 25 decisively proved that "God has expressly in his word also admitted of Slavery for he gave directions to the nation to whom he in an especial manner made himself known, to make slaves of those heathen who were not their particular enemies." Moreover, to follow the Golden Rule meant doing "to them as (in a change of circumstances) we would wish them to do to us." Yet providential reasoning loomed even larger for Furman than biblical reasoning. The Golden Rule, for instance, did not mean overthrowing "the order of Providence which places men in different ranks & stations." It was also inconceivable that God would have so manifestly blessed churches thronged with masters and slaves if slavery resulted from "the unrepented sin of Man Stealing" (referring to Ex 21:16 and 1 Tim 1:9–10). Furman even reluctantly concluded that the slave trade could be justified if it was "the only probable [means] of bringing them at present to an acquaintance with the Gospel."[40]

Baptists, like Presbyterians, had been warned against abolitionism by their aversion to the Methodists.[41] Furman in 1807 noted that for the most part Methodists "did not attempt to enforce their rules." But when they did, he concluded pointedly for the Baptists, they damaged the spiritual work that was their proper business.[42]

Furman's reasoning for Baptists paralleled the movement of Presbyterians toward "the spirituality of the church." In a perceptive explanation for why Baptists in the Upper South backed away from their earlier willingness to question the institution, Monica Najar pointed out the importance of American theories championing religious freedom: "[T]he boundary between church and state became of supreme importance because it allowed them to mark slavery as a 'political' and 'legislative' matter and, therefore, not their concern."[43] This same reasoning made it easier for Baptists to separate their earlier, general enthusiasm for "liberty" into an ongoing concern for spiritual freedom in Christ opposed to a political sphere now considered irrelevant to a specifically Christian life. In addition, worry about the potential of arguments over slavery dividing Baptists among themselves, which Furman clearly foresaw, dampened willingness to take up contentious issues. For Baptists in particular, political partisanship also played a role. Leland's repudiation of his earlier antislavery position occurred after he and many of his co-religionists had become enthusiasts for Jefferson and the Democratic Party—and therefore of the Democrats' solicitude for their slavery-defending constituency.[44]

The Bible remained a factor as the major evangelical denominations moved away from proclaiming serious antislavery sentiments toward justifying slavery or dismissing it as a proper church concern. As a contribution to the American history of the Bible, it is important to note that the American context played a decisive role. For at least a century, white Americans had grown confident in their ability to interpret the hand of God at work in the world. The same mentality that viewed American independence as a gift of Providence found it easy to view the slave trade as a providential means of evangelism. To Furman, trust in his ability to understand the Bible aright and trust in his ability to discern the ways of providence had become one and the same.

So also did the American separation of church and state make it easier to take for granted a sharp division between the business of the church and the workings of the world. American commitment to religious freedom did not directly create "the spirituality of the church." But it did facilitate the hands-off attitude to slavery that made political decision-making so different from what happened in the British debate over slavery. Parliament, even a "corrupt" and "factional" Parliament, was never tempted by the American notion that selectively exempted the churches from responsibility for public justice.

Landmark Antislavery Publications

In the very years when the main Bible-focused denominations moved steadily away from emancipationist positions, Protestant authors produced some of the most sophisticated Bible-based antislavery attacks in all of American history. Moreover, these full-scale scriptural arguments, encompassing both specific texts and elaborated biblical theology, came from the most energetic and most intellectual Protestant denominations: Methodists applying their gospel-intensive theology and Presbyterians sustaining some of the comprehensive instincts of the Reformation.[45]

Their arguments did not appear in a vacuum but rather countered the proslavery scriptural expositions that continued to circulate. In 1809 and 1813 Virginia Protestants published exhortations to "masters and servants" that took for granted the biblical propriety of slavery and focused on encouraging spiritual responsibilities within the system itself.[46] Bibles and catechisms published for the enslaved likewise stressed the obedience verses of the Pauline epistles and edited out anything that could be construed as emancipationist. In addition, the shock of Gabriel's Rebellion, when at the dawn of the century slaves around Richmond, Virginia, conspired to liberate themselves through violence, silenced some Methodists and Baptists who had earlier preached deliverance.[47]

Yet even as disputants repeated older arguments throughout the administrations of Presidents Jefferson and Madison, a new generation of abolitionists produced fresh arguments based more directly on Scripture and less on the Revolution's libertarian ideology. If a general assessment of the times had been drawn only from these publications, the false impression would have arisen that Gabriel's horn had blown and the Judgment Day for slavery had arrived.

The Methodist condemnations came from two leading figures who exploited the spiritual dynamic of their movement with unusual force. Freeborn Garrettson (1752–1827) authored the first in 1805.[48] Garrettson, who had been ordained at the Methodists' organizing Christmas Conference in 1784, grew up in a wealthy, slave-owning family but reported that at his conversion God told him to free his own slaves. By early in the next century, Garrettson had evangelized effectively in Nova Scotia, his native Maryland, and throughout New York state, where he married into the wealthy Livingstone clan. Although Garrettson retained conventional views about white racial superiority, he also offered wide-ranging encouragement to many African Africans, including Richard Allen in the founding of the African Methodist Episcopal Church.

The take-off point for Garrettson's pamphlet-dialogue was when "Professing-Christian" heard "several of my black people" singing hymns and praying. After he "fled to my Bible" in order to learn more about suffering endured by the godly, including his slaves, "Do-Justice" (Garrettson's alter ego) urged Professing-Christian to consider "the external evidences of religion"—that is, the "good works" that a Christian should pursue.[49] When Professing-Christian sought chapter-and-verse references, Do-Justice went into high gear, citing "a number of passages of scripture to prove, pointedly, the iniquity of the practice of slave-keeping." The more than thirty specific passages Garrettson quoted, eighteen of them crammed onto a single page, represented one of the most extensive abolitionist litanies ever published. Passages included Jeremiah 22:13 ("Wo to him that buildeth his house by unrighteousness, and his chambers by wrong; that useth his neighbor's service without wages, and giveth him not for his work"), Proverbs 22:16 ("He that oppresseth the poor, to increase his riches, shall surely come to want"), and many others that called out the strong who robbed, despoiled, abused, or cheated the weak.[50]

Impressive as such a proof-texting parade might seem, Garrettson put even more energy into rebutting the proslavery use of Leviticus 25:44–46. For Do-Justice, that passage could simply not hold up "under the gospel dispensation" once Professing-Christian understood "the intricacy of the subject" and how the Hebrews of the Old Testament were "differently circumstanced."

God commanded Israel to settle the Promised Land (not to travel "three thousand miles to capture the poor Africans, without any special command from heaven").

God authorized enslavement of Israel's enemies as an alternative to killing them outright.

But, with reference to the story of Abraham, the Israelites encouraged their slaves to believe in God and then to be circumcised.

Once circumcised, the slaves could partake of the Passover (Num 15:13–16).

And since they were now counted in God's eyes as part of Israel, they had to be freed from enslavement in the Jubilee Year (every seventh) since the Children of Israel were forbidden to enslave their fellow Hebrews.

Thus, understanding the Old Testament correctly meant understanding how its provision of slavery was only a means to extend the scope of God's mercy.[51]

For Garrettson, as a Bible-only Methodist, it was obvious that both the Scripture's individual texts and its central message of salvation ("the dispensations of God are dispensations of mercy") condemned slavery without equivocation.

The second important Methodist publication came from Daniel Coker (1780–1846), an African American who had also benefited from Garrettson's support as one of Allen's key colleagues in founding the AME (Figure 10.1).[52] Coker later became a noted missionary to Sierra Leone, where he helped establish Methodism in West Africa while also serving in several governmental positions. His compact pamphlet, published in 1810, deserves special consideration as the first full-scale abolitionist work by a Black American.[53] While also referring to a few individual texts, it mostly recapitulated Garrettson's argument in another imagined dialogue, this one between a Virginia slaveholder and an African Methodist minister.[54] Coker concentrated on Abraham's circumcision of his slaves (Gen 17:13) to show, as Garrettson had done, that slaves could be incorporated into Israel and, once incorporated, enjoyed all the benefits God bestowed on the chosen people. He reasoned that once Africans came under the hearing of the Christian gospel, they became like Israel's enslaved opponents who were invited into the company of the circumcised—and so protected against perpetual enslavement. With Garrettson, Coker also emphasized the stark differences between enslavement by the Hebrews and enslavement by Americans: "The Israelites were not sent by a divine mandate, to nations three hundred miles distant, who were neither doing, nor meditating any thing against them, and to whom they had no right whatever, in order to captivate them by fraud or force . . . and then doom the survivors and their posterity to bondage and misery forever."[55]

Significantly for what would come later in controversies over interpreting crucial texts, Coker, like Garrettson, deployed a "differently circumstanced"

Daniel Coker

Figure 10.1 In 1810 Daniel Coker published the first complete book by an African American to attack slavery with Scripture. It was also one of the best such works from any author of the period.

argument when taking up the Apostle Paul's injunctions for slaves to obey their masters. Paul issued these commands, wrote Coker, to show that early Christians supported order under a Roman government looking for any excuse to persecute the church. "In such circumstances," had "the apostle proclaimed liberty to the slaves," it would have brought violent retribution "without the prospect of freeing one single individual." "But ours," he added ironically, "is not a heathen, but is called a Christian government."[56]

For Garrettson, with his quiver full of pointed proof-texts, as for Coker, with carefully developed biblical theology, a Scripture defense of slavery failed for simply disregarding many individual verses. More important, the biblical gospel that inspired their entire lives as Methodists made the enslavement of others for whom Christ died simply unimaginable.

Although Presbyterians enjoyed a higher reputation for intellectual acumen than Methodists, the Bible arguments from Garrettson and Coker were more sophisticated than the polemics thundered by the Presbyterians' two abolitionist champions of the era. In particular, Garrettson and Coker treated the bearing of historical context on biblical interpretation more self-consciously than did the more learned Presbyterians. Where later polemics would feature history *versus* the Bible (trust *either* ancient Scripture *or* modern ethical consciousness), Garrettson and Coker insisted on addressing the question with a combination of Scripture *plus* history.

Still, in their zeal the Presbyterians gave nothing away. The works were authored by Alexander McLeod, an immigrant from Scotland who pastored in the tiny Reformed Presbyterian church, and George Bourne, who after migrating from England and a short period associating with Methodists, became a minister in the main American Presbyterian denomination. In their new homeland, both fiercely contended for an older notion of *sola scriptura* rooted specifically in the polemics of the Reformation.

McLeod (1774–1833), as a Reformed Presbyterian or Covenanter, upheld an extreme Protestant version of what Joseph Moore has aptly called "the heart of Presbyterian history," that is, "a structural concern for creating and maintaining godly societies."[57] The Covenanters took their name from the Scottish National Covenant of 1638 that memorialized Scottish opposition to King Charles I and the Solemn League and Covenant of 1643, which in the early years of the English Civil War briefly united England's Parliament and Scotland in opposing Charles I. Both covenants emphasized a bedrock commitment to Scripture for regulating all of life, state as well as church, an emphasis that Reformed Presbyterian immigrants softened but did not abandon.[58]

When in 1802 McLeod published a lengthy sermon, *Negro Slavery Unjustifiable: A Discourse*, he relied unreservedly on a commitment to *sola scriptura* coming out of the Scottish Reformation, but also on its vision of a godly society under the Christian guidance of government. While McLeod's extensive *Discourse* did range widely, at its heart lay his exposition of Exodus 21:16—"He that stealeth a man, and selleth him, or if he be found in his hand, he shall surely be put to death"—as reinforced by "the eighth precept of the decalogue" (Ex 20:15, "Thou shalt not steal") and 1 Timothy 1:9–10 ("Knowing this, that that law is not made for a righteous man, but for the lawless and disobedient—for MAN STEALERS— and if there be any other thing that is contrary to sound doctrine").[59]

McLeod had composed his *Discourse* when he discovered that the congregation to which he was called in Orange County, New York, included slave owners. At almost the same time, the Reformed Presbyterians, who were in the process of organizing their denomination went on record expelling slave owners from their churches.[60]

McLeod's *Discourse* stands as a significant landmark in the history of controversy over slavery because with other Covenanters he was, again quoting Moore, an "antislavery biblical literalist."[61] In a history of controversy when antislavery tended to focus on the Golden Rule and general teachings from Scripture while proslavery hammered at individual texts, McLeod showed that the debate did not have to break along those lines. As he catalogued numerous evils of enslavement, McLeod did move in many directions: he viewed slavery as opposed to "the natural rights of man," he contended that it paved the way for civil tyranny, and he cited the Declaration of Independence.[62] But the heart of the treatise rested on his assertion "[M]y text is in the Bible." Accordingly, he returned repeatedly to condemning American slavery as nothing but a product of unjustifiable kidnapping—while also denying the relevance of the Curse of Canaan from Genesis 9, showing that the slavery allowed by Leviticus 25:44–46 in no way resembled the American institution, and explaining the Pauline instructions to slaves in the New Testament as subordinated by "the spirit of that religion" (i.e., faith in Christ), which is "righteousness and peace."[63]

Two years after his *Discourse*, McLeod published *Messiah, Governor of the Nation*, interpreting the book of Revelation as instructing governments how they should support institutional Christianity. This work reiterated the *Discourse*'s appeal for government action. As that earlier work affirmed, "legislatures and statesmen" were responsible for "exert[ing] themselves in the cause of righteousness." About the need for governments to act against slavery there could be no doubt, because "it is inconsistent with the natural rights of man; it is condemned by the Scriptures; it is at war with your republican institutions; it ruins the minds and the morals of thousands; and it leaves you exposed to the wrath of heaven."[64]

As McLeod added natural rights and republicanism to the Bible, he brought the reasoning of Scotland's Reformation Christendom to bear on the circumstances of his new homeland. The United States may have separated the institutions of church and state, but rulers still needed to heed God's law. Scripture remained foundational and, in McLeod's view, must be followed to the letter.

If McLeod centered his shrapnel attack on the biblical prohibition against man-stealing, Bourne's *The Book and Slavery Irreconcilable* fired a massive cannon blast.[65] Bourne (1780–1845) migrated to the United States in 1804 as a Dissenter favoring republican government and a voluntary approach to religion. His Reformation stance was not McLeod's attachment to a comprehensive Christendom but the historical Protestant link between militant *sola scriptura* and militant anti-Catholicism. Historians know Bourne for his antislavery animus, but also for contributing to the anti-Catholic hysteria that grew step by step with Catholic immigration. Later in life he edited, wrote, or brought back into print a host of inflammatory publications, including a pamphlet titled *Jesuit Juggling*, an attack on the Catholics' Rheims Bible, and a convent exposé (*Lorette*) that anticipated the even more extreme *Maria Monk*.[66] For Bourne, Catholicism represented spiritual enslavement at its most malignant. He opposed the American system of Black slavery even more vigorously.

The Book and Slavery Irreconcilable arose from the conflicts that dogged Bourne's career as a Presbyterian minister. Upon his arrival in the United States, Bourne worked briefly as an editor in Baltimore, during which time he published the first American biography of John Wesley, but then moved to Virginia, where, near Harrisonburg, he organized a church for recently arrived Scots-Irish Presbyterians. After thorough examination by the Presbytery of Lexington, he was ordained to the ministry in 1812. Things began smoothly at Bourne's South River Church and as a delegate to the national General Assembly in 1813 and 1814. But trouble was brewing as Bourne pondered the Presbyterian doctrinal standards he had subscribed to as part of his ordination. The particular issue was Question 142 of the Westminster Larger Catechism, "What are the sins forbidden in the eighth commandment [Thou shalt not steal]?" The answer included "theft, robbing, man-stealing, and receiving any thing that is stolen." Bourne's emancipationist convictions fastened onto the basic question and answer, but even more on the footnote appended to "man-stealing" in the 1806 edition of the denomination's *Constitution of the Presbyterian Church in the United States of America*.

When in the early years of the English Civil War, Parliament convened an Assembly of Divines to prepare a replacement for the *Book of Common Prayer* and its *Thirty-Nine Articles of Religion*, the Assembly after intense debate over several years gave Parliament the Westminster Confession, two catechisms, and a Directory of Worship.[67] Parliament, in an early instance of the biblicism that would become endemic in the United States, requested that the Assembly provide biblical proof-texts for the assertions in all of its documents. Although Parliament never authorized the Westminster standards for England, they were adopted, with the footnoted proof-texts, by Scottish and Irish Presbyterians, and later by American Presbyterians. The first meeting in 1789 of the American General Assembly, which reorganized Presbyterians after the War for Independence, amended the Westminster Confession to eliminate the original's assignment of church oversight to government. It did not, however, eliminate the proof-texts that had been supplied for the standards, which editors over the years had adjusted in different printings.

So it was that near Harrisonburg, while the United States was engaged in warfare against Great Britain, Bourne went to war against slavery and slave owners. Omitting only the Latin of Hugo Grotius's statement against slavery and beginning with a citation of 1 Timothy 1:10, where the New Testament echoed the Old, the footnote to "man-stealing" in Answer 142 read as follows:

I Tim. i. 10 (The law is made) for whoremongers, for them that defile themselves with mankind, for men-stealers. (This crime among the Jews exposed the perpetrators of it to capital punishment; Exod. 21.16 and the apostle here classes them with sinners of the first rank. The word he uses in its original import, comprehends all who are concerned in bringing any of the human race into slavery, or in detaining them in it. . . . Stealers of men are all those who bring off slaves or freemen, and keep, sell, or buy them. To steal a freeman, says Grotius, is the highest kind of theft. In other instances we only steal human property, but when we steal or retain men in slavery, we seize those who in common with ourselves, are constituted by the original grant, lords of the earth. Gen: 1.28.)[68]

All of the fire that burned in Bourne's veins against the evils of Rome now burst forth against what Presbyterians had so clearly defined as "sinners of the first rank." He first took steps to expel slave owners from his own church. Then he overtured his presbytery and, with a few colleagues in 1815, the national General Assembly. When at this Assembly Bourne was asked why he had not himself disciplined slave owners in his Virginia church, he replied that opinion in the state was so corrupt no justice could possibly be served there. Disputes over Bourne's charges lasted until the 1818 vote, when the General Assembly agreed with the Presbytery of Lexington to defrock Bourne for harming, rather than building up, the church.

Two years before this final decision, Bourne broadcast his arguments in a 150-page cannonade that, like McLeod's *Discourse*, featured exposition of the Bible's "man-stealing" texts, Exodus 21:16 and 1 Timothy 1:10.[69] Yet compared to Bourne, McLeod had been playing games. McLeod had paused to explain that "slavery" in some forms could be justified when a lawbreaker deliberately injured an "innocent fellow creature," but Bourne made no concessions.[70] McLeod had commended the president of the College of New Jersey (Princeton), Samuel Stanhope Smith, for publishing a book explaining how skin color could change over time, while Bourne condemned Smith because in a textbook on moral philosophy Smith had excused the continuation of slavery in America despite defining it as an evil.[71] And where McLeod had begun with Exodus 21:16 but then spent most of his *Discourse* going further afield, Bourne kept outrage at man-stealing front and center throughout his entire work. To be sure, Bourne also cited the Declaration of Independence, along with libertarian assertions from several state constitutions. He added quotations from a score of authorities, like Charles James Fox, William Wilberforce, and William Paley. He also ran through an even broader array of proof-texts than Freeborn Garrettson had marshaled.

Yet throughout Bourne returned repeatedly to passionate application of the straightforward statements that almost all Americans in this era understood as coming from Moses and the Apostle Paul. On the key Exodus and 1 Timothy passages, he quoted from at least fifteen commentaries that agreed with him in viewing these texts as condemning enslavement. One of his sharpest statements came early in the book's second chapter ("The Law of God and Man") when, after quoting the key verse from Exodus and piling on additional quotations about protecting escaped slaves from Deuteronomy 24:7 and 23:15–16, 1 Samuel 30:10–16, Isaiah 16:3, and Obadiah 14–15, Bourne let fly:

> These scriptures proclaim that *slave-holding* is an abomination in the sight of God: for it justifies the slave in absconding from his Tyrant, and enjoins upon every man to facilitate his escape, and to secure his freedom. Does this injunction comport with a Christian's advertising as a fugitive criminal, a man who has merely fled from his cruel captivity, or with his aiding to trace and seize him who had thus burst from "durance vile"? It is a reiteration of the theft: yet he professes to be influenced by the Gospel! [And with this footnote:] "Well may we blush when we hear a man boasting of his rights as an American, and of his citizenship among the Saints, with a whip in one hand, a chain in the other, and before him, a Negro flayed from the head to the loins!"[72]

The Book and Slavery Irreconcilable delivered a bravura performance. Surely, if American Presbyterians honored the Scriptures, if they gave any credence at all to their own doctrinal standards, they would have to renounce slavery as a great evil and excommunicate all those who participated in the system as disobedient sinners. What could be plainer than straightforward obedience to the unambiguous words of Holy Scripture, interpreted literally? Yet, as we have seen, Bourne's denomination disagreed. Judicially, the General Assembly ruled against him on a technicality—where an earlier General Assembly had ratified the Westminster Larger Catechism, it had not specifically ratified the footnotes for Question and Answer 142.[73] Culturally, too many material interests along with the Presbyterians' deep investment in maintaining the orderly, forward movement of their denomination made it impossible to heed Bourne's appeal to scriptural literalism and their own doctrinal standards.

A near absence of recorded responses to the substantial works by Garrettson, Coker, McLeod, and Bourne suggests that they were voices crying in the wilderness. Enslaved and free Blacks in Charleston who formed an AME congregation shortly after Allen founded the denomination certainly knew about Coker, as Allen's fellow-bishop and perhaps even of his *Dialogue*.[74] William Lloyd Garrison made a life-changing discovery of Bourne's *The Book and* Slavery after it had languished for more than a decade with few convinced readers. When Garrison founded *The Liberator* in 1831, he recruited Bourne as one of the main writers for the journal.[75] Until he died in 1845 Bourne continued to publish regularly against both slavery as man-stealing and Catholicism as family-destroying.

Yet before, during, and after the War of 1812, and despite the signal efforts of the authors examined here, contention over the Scriptures' judgment on slavery remained mostly muted. The denominations drifted. The Word of God as exegeted by a notable company of dedicated abolitionists fell on stony ground. Biblical argumentation seemed to be making less and less of a difference.

Then came Missouri—and Denmark Vesey.

11

Slavery and the Bible, 1819–1833

The conjunction of controversy over admitting Missouri as a slave state (1818–20), followed shortly thereafter by news of a barely avoided slave insurrection in Charleston, South Carolina (1822), reenergized Bible-supported arguments about slavery. Then, after a decade of noisy political turmoil—but relative quiet in public agitation over slavery—a book, a periodical, and an uprising broke things loose again. In so doing, David Walker, William Lloyd Garrison, and Nat Turner sparked a flame of disputation that burned brightly for more than a generation—and that in the process consumed the American Bible civilization.

Missouri Statehood

In February 1818 residents of the Missouri Territory petitioned Congress to be admitted as a state.[1] The petition languished because of congressional uncertainty about the constitutional status of slavery in the Trans-Mississippi Louisiana Territory. Nearly a year passed before Representative James Tallmadge of New York offered an amendment to the enabling legislation. It proposed that the slaveholders already present in Missouri be allowed to retain their slaves, but with provisions for the slaves' future emancipation and a prohibition on the importation of additional slaves. The proposal unleashed a storm of congressional controversy that included lightning flashes of Christian concern. Tallmadge himself contrasted the generosity of white southerners in supporting "moral institutions for Bible and Missionary Societies" with southern states "legislating to secure the ignorance and stupidity of their slaves."[2] His fellow New York Representative, John Taylor, used a biblical analogy to suggest that if Congress missed the present opportunity to check the expansion of slavery with one simple piece of legislation, "shall we not expose ourselves to the same kind of censure which was pronounced by the Saviour of Mankind upon the Scribes and Pharisees."[3] Representative Arthur Livermore of New Hampshire used charged language to condemn "the sin of holding both the bodies and souls of our fellow men in chains."[4] And in two impassioned speeches, Senator Rufus King of New York, the Federalists' presidential candidate in 1816 and a founding manager of the American Bible Society, laid out an extensive constitutional argument against slavery in any new state. As King described evils attending the American

America's Book. Mark A. Noll, Oxford University Press. © Oxford University Press 2022.
DOI: 10.1093/oso/9780197623466.003.0012

system, like the breaking up of families, he also said he would not address moral or religious questions that "in this place, would call up feelings, the influence of which would disturb, if not defeat, the impartial [i.e., constitutional] consideration of the subject."[5] (Printed copies of King's speeches would wend their way southward to play a part in the next, more intense controversy over slavery that followed hard on the heels of agitation over Missouri.)

The Tallmadge proposal died, but the controversy did not. It boiled over once again as soon as the Sixteenth Congress convened in December 1819. The relatively noncontroversial admittance of Alabama as the eleventh slave state now balanced the eleven states that had either outlawed slavery or legislated its future demise. The extensive and heated debate that ensued included a long speech on January 26, 1820, by Senator William Smith of South Carolina, who directly attacked assertions that "slavery was forbidden by God, in his Holy Bible." To the contrary, replied the senator, who then proceeded to quote Leviticus 25:44–46 as delivering "the divine words of the Lord himself to his holy servant, Moses, as a law to his holy people." Moreover, since "Christ himself gave a sanction to slavery," there could be no doubt but that the "Scriptures teach us that slavery was universally indulged among the holy fathers." Less than a week later, Senator James Barbour of Virginia reinforced his colleague's conclusions by invoking "Providence," asserting that "the same mighty power that planted the greater and the lesser luminary in the heavens, permits on earth the bondsman and the free."[6] Missouri, in short, acted as a lever that pushed the Bible defense of slavery out of the ecclesiastical shadows and into the glare of congressional scrutiny.

Even as the Scriptures were being cited in Congress, others piled on. Especially noteworthy was a long series of articles in Virginia's leading newspaper, the *Richmond Enquirer*, that appeared just as Congress began heated debate on the Missouri question. The series included a lengthy rejoinder on December 3, 1819, to an article in the *Edinburgh Review* that had attacked slaveholding. The Virginia article was filled with references to the Curse of Canaan, Abraham as a slaveholder, the stipulations of Leviticus 25, the New Testament commands for slaves to obey their masters, and Jesus's silence on the subject—in other words, almost all the texts that had already surfaced to defend slavery and that would continue to be reiterated to the time of the Thirteenth Amendment, and beyond. The *Enquirer*'s editor, Thomas Ritchie—friend of Jefferson and ardent foe of restricting slavery anywhere—followed up in early January by giving space in his paper to two shorter but still substantial articles by "An American," asserting once again that slavery "was expressly sanctioned by the old, and recognized without censure by the new, testament," and "was sanctioned in the bible, in defiance of the precepts from the new dispensation . . . zealots." Then appeared in early February a massive two-part article, "Scriptural Researches," that began with accounts in Genesis providing "*proof positive* that the father of the faithful

[Abraham] was a slaveholder," before going on to a full exposition of all Mosaic legislation, including Leviticus 25:44–46.[7] In piecemeal fashion, the *Richmond Enquirer* had published the most comprehensive effort of its kind since the appearance three decades earlier of Raymond Harris's work.

A month after "Scriptural Researches" appeared in Richmond, Henry Clay maneuvered a compromise through Congress: Missouri would enter as a slave state; to balance Missouri, Maine was hived off from Massachusetts and became the twelfth free state; and slavery would be prohibited in the Louisiana Territory north of 36 degrees 30 minutes. With the impassioned airing of arguments that would reverberate for the next four decades, Thomas Jefferson described this debate as "a fire bell in the night." With Senator Smith's fiery address to Congress and the *Enquirer*'s provision of material to be read at leisure, the Missouri controversy also marked, in Robert Forbes's authoritative words, "a turning point in the development of the biblical defense of slavery."[8]

Denmark Vesey and Afterward

Twenty-seven months after the compromise of March 1820, during which time the American Bible Society distributed close to 110,000 bibles and testaments and other American publishers brought out at least thirty new editions of the Scriptures, news of a threatened slave insurrection in Charleston galvanized South Carolina's white citizens into a panic of investigation, judgment, retribution, and aggressive proslavery apologetics.[9] At the center of the insurrection and its far-reaching aftermath lay an open Bible.[10]

The leader of the planned uprising was Denmark Vesey, a Charleston carpenter who had lived almost a quarter-century as a freedman. The Black South Carolinians, both slave and free, who joined Vesey were inspired by what they had heard of the antislavery speeches made in Congress during the Missouri debate.[11] Some of them had also listened to the ardent sermons of a maverick Methodist, Lorenzo Dow, who over several months in 1820 and 1821 preached to Charleston's slaves without permission; his preaching elsewhere, and presumably also in Charleston, included strong attacks against slavery embellished with vivid apocalyptic imagery.[12] Some of the freed and enslaved Africans who heard Dow were also members of "the African Church," a congregation in fellowship with Richard Allen's Bethel Church in Philadelphia and the African Methodist Episcopal denomination that Allen had created with Daniel Coker and at least the passive support of Francis Asbury.[13] In the judicial proceedings that followed exposure of the plot, witnesses both Black and white identified Charleston's African Church, along with the AME's influence from Philadelphia, as fomenting sedition. Shortly after the Charleston congregation was formed, Vesey moved from a local Presbyterian church to this new body, where he became a class leader.

Vesey's use of the Bible to enlist recruits underscores the significance for all of American history of Black appropriation of Scripture—similar to the white world in devotion, strikingly different in interpretive conclusions.[14] At the inquest convened almost immediately after white authorities discovered the plot, several witnesses stressed the major role Scripture had played: "[Vesey] studies the Bible a great deal and tries to prove from it that slavery and bondage is against the Bible," and "at this meeting Vesey said . . . we ought to rise up and fight against the whites for our liberties; he was the first to rise up and speak, and he *read to us from the Bible, how the children of Israel were delivered out of Egypt from bondage.*"[15] Other witnesses testified that one of Vesey's associates read from the Apocryphal book of Tobit for the same purpose.[16] Like the Exodus story, Tobit tells of faithfulness under pressure, in this case an Israelite living in Nineveh after the Ten Tribes of Israel had been taken captive by Assyria and suffering for remaining true to Jehovah. (Since the American Bible Society did not publish English bibles with the Apocrypha, Charleston's Blacks probably used a Catholic bible for this reading or a bible published in Britain where, until the late 1820s, almost all printings included the Apocrypha.)[17] Evidence at the inquest also suggested that Vesey expounded other Old Testament texts that pronounced prophetic judgments on evil nations at the coming "day of the Lord" (Isa 19; Zech 14:1–3). With the possibility that themes from the works of Alexander McLeod or George Bourne had seeped into Charleston, he may also have quoted the denunciation of "man-stealing" from Exodus 21:16.[18]

Although some uncertainty attends the phrasing of Vesey's biblical expositions, and even the specific texts he expounded, their general character is beyond doubt. Vesey's immersion in Scripture was as deep as those who would open Scripture to denounce the insurrection. But the Grand Narrative of Liberation he took from the Bible reflected the hermeneutic that differentiated African Americans from the white mainstream.[19] The most immediate outcome of the Vesey conspiracy, however, was a sharper statement of biblical conclusions from white Americans.

The conspiracy was discovered on June 14 and 15, 1822. Vesey and five of his associates were hanged on July 2; the execution of twenty-two more Blacks followed on July 26. On September 23, the founder and sitting president of the Charleston Bible Society and two-time Federalist candidate for president, Charles Cotesworth Pinckney, dispatched a lengthy address on behalf of the Society to Governor Thomas Bennett, requesting a day of public Thanksgiving. Generous quotation from Scripture and repeated thanks for the protection of divine providence filled this address. Within months similar views were published by three other well-known Charlestonians: Richard Furman, speaking for the South Carolina Baptist Convention as its president; one of the city's leading Episcopal ministers, Frederick Dalcho; and Edwin Holland, a young lawyer who had previously edited the *Charleston Times*. Together, in the same way that the insurrectionists reflected characteristic emphases of Black Bible readers, establishment Charleston set out a full-blown proslavery biblicism that over the next four decades became increasingly influential throughout the entire nation. Three of its propositions would be crucial for bringing many northerners at least partway to white southern opinion; two spoke more directly to the South. Together their arguments sharpened what proslavery advocates had been contending since the 1770s.

The Bible sanctioned slavery, full stop. Speaking for South Carolina's Baptists, Furman began his exposition of Scripture by quoting Leviticus 25:44–46, which William Jenkins rightly labeled the biblical "rock of Gibraltar . . . used in all of the Biblical defenses from the earliest to the last."[20] To the Mosaic instructions about perpetual enslavement of non-Hebrews, the Episcopalian Rev. Dalcho added a long discussion of the Curse of Canaan from Genesis 9: "[P]erhaps we shall find that the negroes, the descendants of Ham, lost their freedom through the abominable wickedness of their progenitor."[21] On the New Testament, Dalcho's negative ("slavery is not incompatible with the principles and profession of Christianity") became the Bible Society's positive (the apostles regulated the master-slave relationship "explicitly and reinforced by eternal sanctions").[22] Reference to Abraham's ownership of slaves and to the Apostle Paul returning the slave Onesimus to Philemon completed this case. The Baptist Furman acknowledged that "the benevolent Wilberforce" had accurately pointed out the evils of the slave trade, while the Episcopalian Dalcho conceded "the evil which attends" keeping slaves. But Dalcho had no hesitation in agreeing with Furman that "the right of holding slaves is clearly established in the Holy Scriptures both by precept and example."[23]

The use of Scripture to attack slavery abused, vitiated, and perverted the Bible. So certain did the Bible's sanction appear to these apologists that they could come to only one conclusion about anyone who thought otherwise. While the Bible Society ascribed such views merely to "a misconstruction, or Perversion of the Scriptures," the lawyer Edwin Holland held nothing back: "[T]hose . . . who are acquainted with the rise and progress of that nefarious plot, know how blasphemously the word of God was tortured, in order to sanction the unholy butchery that was contemplated. . . . Religion was stripped of her pure and spotless robe, and panoplied like a fury, was made to fight under the banners of the most frightful Conspiracy that imagination can conceive."[24]

Trust in providence, reliance on Scripture as the Word of God, and the defense of slavery constituted a seamless whole. White Charlestonians moved away from proof-texting when they interpreted their rescue from the planned massacre as "a providential, gracious interposition." Like believers of all sorts, they did nothing unusual in praising God for their deliverance. Yet because that praise was combined with a biblical defense of slavery—and because they also looked so fixedly on Scripture as given "to make [Man] wise unto salvation"—their religion drew together a set of powerful convictions into a single whole.[25] God's Word, God's care, salvation in Christ, and God's provision of slavery could never be construed as separable entities, but only as one.

Furman, speaking of divine Providence, repeated the word *interposition* three times in as many paragraphs as he described the city's deliverance. The lawyer Holland also employed the word when he praised "the activity and intelligence of a wise and efficient police, strengthened and enlightened as they were by the protecting interposition of a beneficent Providence."[26] As historians know, not long thereafter the same word would express white South Carolina's defiance of a "tariff of abominations" passed by Congress and enforced by President Andrew Jackson. But the same word had already appeared in yet another context in more than half the American hymn books published in the 1790s. It came from the hymn by Robert Robinson quoted in chapter 8, "Come, thou fount of every blessing": "Jesus sought me when a stranger, / Wandering from the fold of God; / He to rescue me from danger, / *Interposed* his precious blood." Without pushing the linguistic coincidence too far, *interposition* in these three highly charged, but strikingly different, domains still testifies to the blurring of worlds that so pervasively characterized the public history of Scripture in the early United States.[27]

While a perverted Bible invited slave rebellion, the Bible properly understood encouraged model slave deportment. Robert Forbes has pointed out that the white responses to the Vesey conspiracy expressly targeted southerners who questioned the value of religious instruction for slaves.[28] As had been the case in early colonial history, once again church leaders were asserting that the Bible—rightly understood!—made slaves into better slaves. Furman and Dalcho both condemned Charleston's African Church for promoting perverse readings of Scripture; both also stressed that Blacks associated with the white churches took no part in the planned outrage. Dalcho even went out of his way to claim that Black Episcopalians never indulged in extemporaneous worship but instead kept themselves strictly to the Book of Common Prayer. The Bible Society lobbied Governor Bennett with the same message: "[O]ne of the best securities we have to the domestic Peace and Safety of the State, is to be found in the sentiments and correspondent dispositions of the religious Negroes; which they derive from the Bible."[29] Reliable exposition, in other words, made reliable servants.

Organized northern philanthropy imperiled an entire way of life by inciting Blacks to violence. A second message primarily for fellow white southerners defended their slave-based civilization. In the very years when the ABS was leading the way with bold new attempts to evangelize and reform the nation, Charleston's whites felt threatened, as the lawyer Holland fumed, "by the swarm of Missionaries, white and *black*, that are perpetually visiting us, who with the Sacred Volume of God in one hand . . . scatter, at the same time, with the other, the fire-brands of discord and destruction, and *secretly* disperse among our Negro Population, the seeds of discontent and sedition." When these incendiaries distributed "among our Negroes . . . *religious magazines, news paper paragraphs* and *insulated texts of scripture*," they threw "such a delusive light upon their condition as was calculated to bewilder and deceive, and finally, to precipitate them into ruin." Dalcho repeated the charge, but in frankly materialistic terms, when he denounced schemes to send manumitted slaves to Africa. Don't they realize, he complained in italicized type, "*our servants are our money.* . . . Manumission would produce nothing but evil."[30]

The message coming out of white Charleston in the wake of the failed Vesey insurrection spoke loudly. Backed by the Bible, rescued by Providence, and yet worried about philanthropic wolves in religious sheep's clothing, the white South would repel its enemies and survive as a blessed civilization under God.

The near conjunction of debate over Missouri and panic over Vesey hardened the trajectory of disputes on the Bible and slavery. The Revolution-inspired impetus against the institution had waned. Later events and publications only deepened the furrow dug by the simultaneous appearance of powerful antislavery works based on both literal and theological deployment of Scripture, the main denominations' retreat from earlier scriptural condemnations, and confident assertions by leading white spokesmen of scriptural sanction for the system.

Crisis

Given the centrality of Scripture in early American culture—as well as the contradictory arguments that were already firmly in place by the early 1820s—it is no surprise that agitation surrounding David Walker, William Lloyd Garrison, and Nat Turner once again pushed the Bible to national center stage. Walker's passionate 1829 *Appeal* to Blacks throughout the world and "very especially, to those of the United States of America," became an immediate sensation because of its passionate advocacy for Black militancy. The events of 1831 brought wider and deeper consternation—in January the launch of Garrison's *Liberator*, with its uncompromising demand for "immediate emancipation," followed only nine months later by the insurrection in Southampton County, Virginia, led by

Turner, that claimed some sixty white lives before being put down with the execution of many more slaves and free Blacks.

Historians are united in describing these dramatic occurrences as heating the nation's long-simmering controversies over slavery to the boiling point. They have focused particularly on Virginia's state legislators who, after the Turner revolt, debated the future of slavery in their state. By a narrow margin the solons turned away from the path of gradual emancipation to embrace instead strengthened restrictions on Blacks, both slave and free. In Daniel Walker Howe's summary, "By this fateful procrastination, Virginian statesmanship abdicated responsibility for dealing with the state's number one problem. When the Civil War came thirty years later, Virginians would still be divided; the great slavery debate of 1831 foreshadowed the bifurcation of the Old Dominion into Virginia and West Virginia. . . . A slave society could not afford to allow those in bondage to pursue a millennial vision in which the last would be first." For the nation as a whole, as Sean Wilentz has written, "Walker's and Garrison's invective, punctuated by the Southampton massacre, forced a reevaluation on all sides and led to political struggles that quickly became entangled with continuing efforts by plebian democrats to remove the remnants of patrician domination."[31]

The heightened controversies did not create a religious crisis alongside the nation's political turmoil. It was rather a single crisis in which religion keyed to the Bible took a leading part. In Virginia whites followed the strategy of white South Carolinians after Denmark Vesey. They resolved, as Charles Irons has shown, "to expand black access to evangelicalism," a religion committed to following the Bible alone, but also "to curtail autonomous black religious expression." Firm biblical support, augmented by certainty about God's providential direction of the United States, undergirded their actions. Southern whites believed "that scripture supported their position and the tangible benefits they believed they were conferring on their black brethren."[32] In thus transforming the perception of slavery from a regrettable encumbrance to a positive good, nothing was more important than confidence in the Bible as the infallible Word of God.

But the Bible was just as important to Walker, Garrison and the contributors he enlisted for *The Liberator*, and the insurrectionists who joined Turner. They, however, read or heard Scripture as condemning enslavement, the slave trade, and the entire slave system—and as doing so absolutely.

For the majority of white Americans who sided with neither the immediate abolitionists nor the principled defenders of slavery, the events of these decisive years affected their understanding of Scripture almost as decisively. Now they were forced to make a conscious decision about which biblical interpretation to follow: denouncing slavery as sin, affirming it as fully approved by God, or something in between. That "something in between" might mean believing that gradual steps would ultimately end slavery, but not for many years, or only throwing up their hands and saying "We'll figure this out as we go along." Deeper questions about the overall purpose of the Bible and the proper strategies for interpreting Scripture lay beneath the surface—and were every bit as divisive.

David Walker's *Appeal*

When Walker published his *Appeal* in September 1829, he was the proprietor in Boston of a store selling used clothing (Figure 11.1).[33] The still young man in his early thirties had been born free in Wilmington, North Carolina, before moving to live for several years in Charleston, where he almost certainly knew some of those who joined Vesey's uprising. Around 1825 Walker settled in Boston, married, joined the Prince Hall Masonic Lodge, and affiliated with the city's Black Methodists, as he had earlier fellowshipped with Methodist assemblies, including Charleston's African Church. Almost immediately he showed his commitment to Black self-assertion by helping to create the Massachusetts General Colored Association, helping the Prince Hall Masons stage "African celebrations," and acting as the main Boston agent for *Freedom's Journal*. Published in New York City by individuals closely associated with that city's Black Presbyterians and Methodists, it was the nation's first Black newspaper.

Walker's trade as a dealer in used clothing proved crucial for the impact of his pamphlet, since sailors were part of his regular clientele. After he published the *Appeal*, he enlisted his seafaring customers to smuggle the work into southern ports. On a trip to Richmond, Virginia, Walker himself distributed perhaps thirty copies. While only a very few southern Blacks, enslaved or free, ever had the chance to see the work, the mere presence of this kind of contraband was enough to frighten the entire white South. Walker himself died under mysterious circumstances—maybe poisoned, but probably of consumption—shortly after the third edition of his work appeared in July 1830.

The *Appeal* is justly famous for its biting indictment of the American slave system: "[W]e (coloured people of these United States) are the most degraded, wretched, and abject set of beings that ever lived since the world began" (1).[34] In one extended footnote, after enumerating the hundreds of thousands of enslaved in Georgia, South Carolina, and Virginia, Walker made his threat explicit: "I know that the Blacks, once they get involved in a war, had rather die than to live, they either kill or be killed" (63n). Commentators have also highlighted Walker's fierce antislavery biblicism, as has Sean Wilentz in describing Walker's determination "to unite and fight back, in accordance with the word of God," his "sermonizing thick with Biblical allusions," and the integral contribution of his "pre-millennial black Christianity" to Walker's "stunning rebuke of the United States as he knew it."[35]

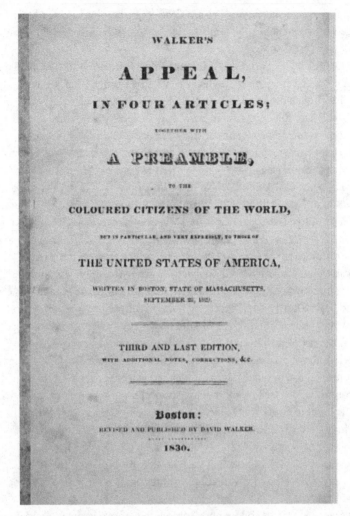

Figure 11.1 David Walker's *Appeal* put the Bible to use on almost every page, but in ways that flew in the face of conventional white hermeneutics.
Source: Courtesy of the Sheridan Libraries, Johns Hopkins University.

Walker's indictment ranged deep and wide. He quoted the Declaration of Independence's stirring paean to liberty. He described the "sufferings" endured by colonists under Great Britain as not "one hundredth part as cruel and tyrannical as you have rendered ours under you" (75). He railed against Thomas Jefferson's support for treating Africans as subhuman. His indignation flared especially against the American Colonization Society for using benevolence as a smokescreen to reinforce racial discrimination. Unlike so many of those who spoke or wrote on slavery in that era, Walker foregrounded race hatred as an even greater evil than the economic, social, or political injustices of the American system.

For our history of Scripture, it is important to document the biblicism that propelled the entire *Appeal*, especially its assertion of Black racial dignity. Walker's approach reflected, but also challenged, the standards of his day, since it was a biblicism matching in fervor, scope, and mimetic facility both the most learned proprietary divines and the most aggressive Bible-only sectarians.

Walker footnoted chapter and verse for about a dozen references to individual scriptural passages, as when he cited Matthew 18:6—Jesus's condemnation of any who "shall offend one of these little ones who believe"—to condemn enslavers who "not only beat his little ones among the Africans, but many of them they put to death or murder" (66). He quoted even more passages without specifying references. With special provocation, he weaponized the much-cited "Great Commission" of Matthew 28:19, which even then was spurring a surge in American evangelical missionary service: "You have the Bible in your hands, with this very injunction—Have you been to Africa, teaching the inhabitants thereof the words of the Lord Jesus? 'Baptizing them in the name of the Father, and of the Son and of the Holy Ghost.' Have you not on the contrary, entered among us, and learnt us the art of throat-cutting, by setting us to fight, one against another, to take each other as prisoners of war, and sell to you for small bits of calicoes, old swords, knives, &c. to make slaves for you and your children?" (42).

Surrounding Walker's many specific scriptural quotations was a text overrun with references to God ("our Maker"), the Holy Ghost, and "our Lord and Master Jesus Christ." Hardly a page flew past without invoking a biblical story:

- Slave defenders as honoring Cain who slew his brother Abel (61).
- Noah preserved in the flood that brought God's wrath upon his age's sinful society (73).
- Lot rescued from a Sodom and Gomorrah whose sins paled beside the evils of slavery (59, 73).
- Joseph as a slave ascending to become the second most powerful ruler in Egypt (7–9).
- Shadrach, Meshach, and Abednego saved miraculously in the fiery furnace of King Nebuchadnezzar (60).
- God as no "respecter of persons" sending Peter to the Roman centurion Cornelius (37).
- The sins of "Christian America" likened to the hard hearts of the scribes and Pharisees who rejected Jesus (59).
- The money changers whose booths Jesus threw over in the temple as more guilty than Americans (59).

- The same "infernal spirit" that filled the evil silversmith Demetrius, who opposed the Apostle Paul, now filling the defenders of slavery (72–73).
- Time and again, Moses's courage before the conniving pharaoh that resulted in Israel's deliverance from Egyptian captivity (10–11, 66, 73, and passim).

Only rarely did Walker pause for the kind of detailed exegesis that filled the polemical writings of white controversialists. Yet when he did, he hammered hard. Without citing the reference, a lengthy footnote obviously referred to the Leviticus permission for the Israelites to enslave enemies captured in war. To Walker, the passage proved too much, since it was vital to remember "that we are men as well as they." Therefore, "they have no more right to hold us in slavery than we have to hold them, we have just as much right, in the sight of God, to hold them and their children in slavery and wretchedness, as they have to hold us, and more" (11n). If Leviticus justified slavery, its justification was color-blind.

Repeatedly Walker also threw back in the face of white America the nation's reverence for Scripture itself. He could make the charge with a rhetorical stiletto: "It is surprising to think that the Americans, having the Bible in their hands, do not believe it" (69). But also with a bludgeon:

> Have not the Americans the Bible in their hands? Do they believe it? Surely they do not. See how they treat us in open violation of the Bible!! They no doubt will be greatly offended with me, but if God does not awaken them, it will be, because they are superior to other men, as they have represented themselves to be. Our divine Lord and Master said, "all things whatsoever ye would that men should do into you, do ye even so unto them" [Matt 7:12]. But an American minister, with the Bible in his hand, holds us and our children in the most abject slavery and wretchedness. Now I ask them, would they like us to hold them and their children in abject slavery and wretchedness? (37–38)

Walker's *Appeal* struck even the nation's few outright emancipationists as extreme. William Lloyd Garrison, for example, was living in Baltimore when it appeared and writing for Benjamin Lundy's *Genius of Universal Emancipation*. In a January 1830 article he called the work "a most injudicious publication" and "deprecated its circulation."[36] Yet once he had founded *The Liberator*, Garrison changed his tune. In the paper's second issue, on January 8, 1831, he offered a backhanded defense: "[I]t is not for the American people as a nation, to denounce [the *Appeal*] as bloody or monstrous. Mr. Walker but pays them in their own coin, but follows their own creed, adopts their own coin, but adopts their own language."[37] Over the next month his judgment softened even more as he published several letters from a reader who, while quibbling about a few matters, defended Walker for simply telling the truth.[38]

From one angle, Walker only riffed on arguments that had been developed earlier, if less confrontationally. From another, the work's passionate move from exegesis to excoriation signaled a new level of conflict. Like Martin Luther King Jr.'s *Letter from Birmingham Jail* 134 years later, the *Appeal* announced that time for hesitation had passed. Again like King's landmark outcry, publicity made a difference. Earlier antislavery publications had dropped stillborn from the press; Walker's, by contrast, was heard.

William Lloyd Garrison and *The Liberator*

So also did Garrison gain a hearing when he hoisted the banner of "immediate emancipation" in an antislavery crusade combining the new and the old.[39] New was the wholesale transport of single-minded enthusiasm from religious revival to millennial reform. Methodists had spread the demand for immediate repentance and wholehearted devotion throughout the land; in the 1820s celebrated revivalists like Charles Grandison Finney brought an urgent revivalism to the urban North and opening Midwest. For Garrison, radical religion paved the way for radical reform. Old was Garrison's reversion to a reforming spirit characteristic of the Revolutionary age. As the most outraged emancipationists in that era had combined general republican principles with some specifically biblical arguments, so Garrison and like-minded reformers enlisted romantic, democratic, humanitarian, and a few biblical arguments against what they called the national sin of slavery.

Garrison's mother, a devout Baptist, trained her son in gospel precepts from his birth at Newburyport, Massachusetts, in 1805. As still a young man his journalistic career took off with several editing jobs in New England, including a short stint with a temperance paper in Boston. Garrison broke into wider visibility with a speech to a Boston colonization meeting on July 4, 1829. It was delivered at Park Street Church adjacent to Boston Commons two years to the day before the same venue witnessed the first performance of Samuel Francis Smith's "My Country 'Tis of Thee, Sweet Land of Liberty." Garrison's encompassing denunciation of slavery as the "national sin" shocked some in his audience, especially with its indictment of New England churches. In his rhetorical floodtide Garrison paused for a general invocation of "Holy Writ"—"therefore all things whatsoever ye would that men should do to you, do you even so to them [Matt 7:12]." But his sharpest use of Scripture came as he adapted Exodus 8:1 to challenge "the ambassadors of Christ everywhere to make known this proclamation: 'Thus saith the Lord God of the Africans, Let this people go, that they may serve me.'"[40]

Immediately after delivering this address, Garrison relocated to Baltimore, where he assisted Benjamin Lundy in editing the *Genius of Universal Emancipation*, the nation's best-known antislavery periodical. In Baltimore Garrison also ran across George Bourne's *The Book and Slavery Irreconcilable*, which completed his preparation for all-out campaigning against any compromise with slaveholding, including colonialism.[41] When a Baltimore judge convicted Garrison of libel against a New Englander who had transported a cargo of slaves from Baltimore to New Orleans, he was imprisoned for debt. Arthur Tappan, a wealthy New York evangelical who had financed the American Bible Society, American Tract Society, and other such organizations, sprung him from jail by paying his fine. Garrison then determined to publish his own newspaper, first searching in vain for backers in Washington, D.C., before finding them in Boston, where he published the first issue of *The Liberator* on January 1, 1831.

In his early reforming career, Garrison never doubted that Scripture fully supported his animus against American slavery. Yet for Garrison the Bible was only one arrow in a quiver jammed full. The piety typical of revivalistic perfectionists filled *The Liberator*'s early issues. Garrison's famous opening declaration from that first issue, with its capitalized promise, "I WILL BE HEARD!," marshaled "Nature's holy laws" against "freedoms deadliest foes"; it featured the Declaration of Independence on equality and "inalienable rights"; it appealed to "Heaven . . . a God of mercy . . . a God of truth"; and it quoted the Bible once in thanking God "that he enables me to disregard 'the fear of man which bringeth a snare' [Prov 29:25]."[42] In its all-out attack on slavery laws, slave mistreatment, slave owners, economic exploitation of slaves, and colonization (also warfare, Indian removal, the theater, gambling, alcohol, and the subordination of women), the magazine did enlist the Bible, but not as often as it appealed to legal, humanitarian, and generally ethical warrants. Scripture was constantly present, but mostly on the page in each issue headed "Literature, Miscellaneous and Moral," where Bible-themed poems, meditations, and condensed homilies appeared regularly—on, for example, the glory of Christ (January 1, p. 4), the importance of public worship (January 8, p. 8), God's perception of sin (January 15, p. 12), Jonah's whale as a picture of evil swallowing up individuals (January 22, p. 16), the crucifixion and prayer (February 5, p. 24), and the importance of public baptism (February 26, p. 36). When religion did enter the polemical lists, it mostly served Garrison's demand that the nation live up to its Christian heritage.

Typical was an early article titled "Climax of Despotism" that denounced the legislators of Virginia. It reported on the narrow defeat of proposals that would have effectively expelled free Blacks and greatly restricted educational and religious gatherings for slaves. *The Liberator* was aghast that "not one of the religious

papers in Virginia published a sentence condemning this wicked effort.... Are
we in a Christian land?" (February 26, p. 31).[43] The same issue promoted "the religious instruction of the colored people," especially by "reading the Scriptures to
them, and teaching them orally" (p. 31). The one exception to a reserved use of
the Bible came in letters from African Americans. On February 19, 1831 (p. 29),
"A Man of Color" heralded the Declaration of Independence but linked "the
true spirit of the gospel" to "the golden principles of liberty." He entreated "my
brethren, to look up to Him from whence cometh their salvation; for he is able to
save to the uttermost all that will come unto him [Heb 7:25]." The very next week,
"a colored gentleman in New-York" encouraged Garrison by observing that "no
doubt . . . Pharaoh looked upon Moses, when he pleaded for the emancipation
of Israel, as meddlesome." But "Israel's God, the never changing friend of the oppressed, demonstrated clearly that however audaciously oppressors may band
themselves together, and seek to crush those who dare to oppose, He will break
their rod [echoing Ex 7:10–12]."

The same fervent but incidental recourse to Scripture marked Garrison's further mobilization for the cause. Imitating the turn in 1830 by the British Anti-
Slavery Society to a publicity campaign for immediate abolition, Garrison in
1832 spurred the organization of the New England Anti-Slavery Society. The next
year he was the driving force, again with funding from Arthur Tappan, for the
amalgamation of several local groups into the American Anti-Slavery Society.
Garrison took responsibility for drafting the new organization's *Declaration of
Sentiments*, which began by referring to Philadelphia, the founding venue, as
where "a band of patriots" founded the American "TEMPLE OF FREEDOM"
when they declared "that all men are created equal; and they are endowed by
their Creator with certain inalienable rights." In its sweeping denunciation of
the nation's "sin," Garrison reflected his tutelage from Bourne by citing with
chapter and verse, "Ex. xxi.16," the Mosaic condemnation of man-stealing. He
also upbraided Americans for "an audacious usurpation of the Divine prerog-
ative" and "a presumptuous transgression of all the holy commandments." But
this Declaration eschewed detailed biblical reasoning in favor of the general
denunciations spelled out in the Society's constitution: "Slavery is contrary to the
principles of natural justice, of our republican form of Government, and of the
Christian Religion."[44]

Neither *The Liberator* nor the early pronouncements of the antislavery societies questioned traditional trust in Scripture as supreme moral authority. Yet
some Bible-believing observers in the North, along with all such observers in the
white South, noticed unsettling causes for concern. Prominent evangelicals like
Arthur Tappan and his brother Lewis were indeed active in supporting Garrison.
But he drew just as much backing from Quakers, like his Baltimore friends James
and Lucretia Mott, who in yet another internal Quaker schism supported Elias

Hikes's emphasis on "the inner light" and the Law of Nature over Joseph John Gurney's evangelical emphasis on the inspiration of Scripture. The early leadership of the New England Anti-Slavery Society also raised eyebrows. Although Lyman Beecher, who had moved from Connecticut to take a Boston pulpit in 1826, thought Garrison was perhaps moving too fast, the Universalist-become-Freethinker Abner Kneeland and Unitarians like Bronson Alcott showed no such hesitation. In addition, Garrison promised in *The Liberator*'s first issue to seek "the assistance of all religions and of all parties" in defending "the great cause of human rights." Did this willingness to enlist all comers mean that faithfulness to Scripture did not matter?

Garrison's reforming impulse certainly shared much with the immediatism and absolutism of evangelical revival as promoted by Charles Finney. Well into his years editing *The Liberator*, deference to Scripture remained an unquestioned aspect of his labors. Yet just as clearly that deference differed sharply from how the Bible had earlier been enlisted against slavery. Not for Garrison were the Bible-based theological arguments of Freeborn Garrettson and Daniel Coker. Nor did he duel with proof-texts in the manner of Alexander McLeod and George Bourne.

But unlike the relative obscurity of those authors, Garrison's visibility clearly influenced how Scripture would be viewed in controversies to come. Defenders of slavery, along with many who simply could not conclude the Bible condemned it, relied increasingly on individual texts of Scripture. In the interpretive climate of that era—and despite acknowledged or implicit racism—those who defended slavery (or would not attack it) insisted they were following "the Bible alone." By contrast, those who like Garrison did not major in proof-texting became increasingly suspect as closet infidels. Although the opponents of slavery included many who did continue to argue with biblical proof-texts and Bible-based theological reasoning, abolitionists were increasingly associated with the type of appeal Garrison made to "the spirit" of Scripture and the instincts of humanistic moral sense. Garrison's renown exerted even more influence when, as slavery defenders predicted, his ardent emancipationism eventually led him to criticize Scripture itself as morally deficient.[45] That move would become a matter of great significance, for it profoundly affected all appeals to the Bible from whatever direction.

Nat Turner's Revolt

When Nat Turner incited a band of slaves to murder white Virginians in September 1831, white southerners and many whites in the North immediately blamed the deceased David Walker and the very-much-alive William Lloyd Garrison. To them, the Turner rebellion exposed Garrison's pacifism as a sham.

"Immediate emancipation" could only mean "immediate insurrection." The fact that Turner, like Garrison and Walker, enlisted divine revelation to serve his cause simply compounded the offense.

Like Walker and Garrison, Turner understood Scripture to condemn slavery absolutely. As with those two, Turner's fulsome reliance on Scripture exacerbated an already fraught national controversy. As the bloody outcome of Turner's revolt fueled panic in the white South and consternation among northern whites, it accelerated the Bible's transformation from a consensus object of national reverence into a contested weapon for ideological combat. Recourse to the Bible would not fade, but its capacity to unify suffered a reverse from which it has never recovered.

Turner's differences from Walker and Garrison also mattered, however much the documentary record for those differences has been contested. Doubters have long questioned the integrity of *The Confessions of Nat Turner*, which a Baltimore lawyer, Thomas Gray, published shortly after Turner was executed on November 11, 1831. *Confessions* was offered to the public as the record of a lengthy conversation between Turner and Gray less than a week before that execution. Careful historians continue to debate Turner's account of the insurrection as coming through Gray, but most agree that the document's rendering of Turner's conceptual world rings true.[46] Even a casual perusal reveals the strong biblical foundation of that world—again, however, with a difference.[47]

Turner's facility at biblical quotation was entirely typical for his era, but his elaboration of contexts less so. According to Gray, Turner first encountered Matthew 6:33 "at meetings" when others quoted, "Seek ye the kingdom of Heaven and all things shall be added unto you." But after praying "daily for light on" this passage, he heard "the spirit" speak it aloud to him "one day at my plough."[48] Typical also was his account of regular praying and fasting, but not typical the conclusion: he was himself a prophet who had received "Divine inspiration." With no apparent hesitation he told Gray, "I heard a voice," "I had a vision," "the Holy Ghost has revealed itself to me." Turner also spoke of "miracles," as when he "discovered drops of blood on the corn as though it were dew from heaven" and "on the leaves in the woods hieroglyphic characters." He also interpreted portents like a solar eclipse in February 1831 as confirmation for his call to revolt.

When Turner combined his era's common reliance on Scripture with the uncommon belief in his own prophetic vocation, the results were striking:

And on the 12th of May, 1828, I heard a loud noise in the heavens [Rev 14:7], and the Spirit was loosened, and Christ had laid down the yoke he had borne for the sins of men [Matt 11:29], and that I should take it on and fight against the Serpent [Matt 12:7], for the time was fast approaching when the first should be last and the last should be first [Matt 20:16].

For as the blood of Christ had been shed on the earth, and had ascended to heaven for the salvation of sinners, and was now returning to earth again in the form of dew—and as the leaves on the trees bore the impression of the figures I had seen in the heavens, it was plain to me that the Saviour was about to lay down the yoke he had borne for the sins of men, and the great day of judgment was at hand.

Turner's belief that God spoke to him as a specially chosen prophet was embedded in a biblicism every bit as fervent as the biblicism of Walker and the early Garrison. The difference was analogous to the difference between William Miller (a radical new biblical interpretation) and Joseph Smith (a new bible alongside the old).[49] Put in other terms, Turner represented an alternative to the Western traditions that Walker and Garrison exploited. If they transgressed standard interpretations, they maintained the Western pattern by equating divine revelation with canonical words on the page. Turner instead followed what David Holland has described as "the vibrant religious ideas of Africa, where the 'concept of revelation' between heaven and earth formed a central element of the sacred worldviews shared by various tribes and nations."[50] In this pattern, signs, portents, dreams, visions, and voices—albeit rendered in the phrases of the King James Bible—easily joined the Scriptures as compelling words from God. It was a pattern sharply transgressing the era's Protestant standard.

Yet the ease with which Turner made the Scriptures his own added a layer of complexity to the American history of the Bible, since his approach—usually absent its violent outcome—would become increasingly common. Although extrabiblical revelation aligned with the Bible enlivened Scripture for many Americans, it also rendered a single American history of the Bible impossible.

Into the Future

In the first decades of the nineteenth century Scripture became increasingly salient in many spheres of American life. In its pages people of all sorts—Black and white; female and male; North, South, and opening West; proprietary republicans and sectarian republicans—encountered a source of life, an inspiration for personal righteousness, and a rock in times of tumult. Even as trust in elites, historical precedents, and official learning continued to decline, confidence in Scripture reached new heights. But now the controversies sparked by debate over Missouri and Denmark Vesey—and then inflamed by David Walker, William Lloyd Garrison, and Nat Turner—administered a crushing blow to the ideal of an American civilization built on voluntary appropriation of the Bible. Yet even as that vision began to slip away, only a few Americans entertained doubts about the supernatural, life-giving character of Scripture itself. By far the majority—even when confronting the national entanglements of race-based slavery—continued boldly to proclaim, "Thus saith the Lord."

Nonetheless, questions that could have arisen only in a civilization fulfilling the aspirations of Protestants to live by the Bible alone now troubled that same civilization:

How could responsible citizen-believers choose between conflicting proof-texts?

How could they choose between contradictory convictions on all manner of issues expressed alike in biblical language and supported by biblical exposition?

If Scripture was God's coherent Word, how did God's revelation given in Jesus Christ (New Testament) affect interpretation of God's revelation to Israel (Old Testament)?

Could foundational loyalty to Scripture be confirmed by how individual texts were interpreted? (In other words, could a person's profession of belief in the Bible be credited if that person willfully misinterpreted scriptural passages whose meaning was transparently clear to others?)

How did assumptions about God's providential care for the United States shape interpretations of Scripture, and vice versa?

Why did biblical teachings seem to align so unselfconsciously with so many different convictions about the economy, society, politics, gender, and race?

When so many Americas debated the Bible and slavery so earnestly, who besides African Americans would be interested in biblical wisdom concerning race?

And if white and Black approaches to biblical interpretation differed, could even a common belief in the truths of Scripture ever unite such divergent interpretive traditions?

In the early decades of the nineteenth century, Scripture became America's Book. As such, discerning its meaning for the nation became ever more important, but also—as Missouri and later events pushed the questions of slavery center stage—increasingly fraught. The American history of the Bible always included much more than dilemmas concerning race and slavery, but also never less.

12

Democracy

As much as sharp divisions concerning God's will for slavery threatened the possibility of a Bible civilization, so also did the workings of American democracy. In an environment promising "liberty and justice for all," Protestant churches and voluntary societies achieved an unprecedented degree of Christianization. In that success, fervent trust in "the Bible alone" played a major part. But since reliance on the Bible rested primarily on democratic persuasion, the personal freedom inherent in democracy also undermined the possibility of freely chosen unity. While energetic white Protestants exploited "freedom to choose" with stunning effect, "freedom to choose" made cultural cohesion nearly impossible.

The contrast was sharp with Europe, where most observers believed that a Christian civilization required constraint. "Among us," wrote Alexis de Tocqueville after his American sojourn in the early 1830s, "I had seen . . . the spirit of religion and the spirit of liberty march almost always in opposite directions." For learned Europeans it was axiomatic that "religious zeal . . . must fade as liberty and enlightenment increase." To a correspondent who wrote to James Madison very shortly after Tocqueville returned to France, the chief architect of the U.S. Constitution described the past in similar terms: "[T]he prevailing opinion in Europe, England not excepted, has been, that Religion could not be preserved without the support of government, nor government be supported without an established Religion." But the two sages disagreed with Madison's correspondent, who opined that a modified version of the traditional European pattern was essential for American well-being. Tocqueville affirmed what numerous clergymen had told him, that "all attributed the peaceful dominion that religion exercises in this country principally to the complete separation of Church and State." Madison, after witnessing the "fifty years, since the legal support of Religion was withdrawn," concluded that religion was in much better shape than when it had enjoyed formal government support; in Virginia particularly "the greater purity & industry of the pastors & . . . the greater devotion of their flocks" came in substantial part from the absence of church-state ties.[1]

To put their observations in the frame of this book, freeing white men to read the Bible for themselves—and thereby inadvertently also encouraging white women, Native Americans, and Black Americans to do the same—significantly broadened and deepened active faith throughout the nation. To be sure, Native Christians and Christians of African descent were proving that religion

America's Book. Mark A. Noll, Oxford University Press. © Oxford University Press 2022.
DOI: 10.1093/oso/9780197623466.003.0013

required democracy as little as Europeans thought it required Christendom. Yet for Christianity among the white population, American democracy was working splendidly. Methodists, limited only by their own energy, were reaping an unprecedented spiritual harvest. Custodial Protestants, limited only by the creativity of their voluntary initiatives, were mobilizing the land and blanketing it with print. Baptists and Campbellite "Christians," recognizing no limits beyond the Bible and the rights of private conscience, were making sectarian forms of Protestantism increasingly meaningful for ever greater numbers.

American democracy, however, was not as favorable for Christian civilization as for Christianity itself. The broadening and deepening of personally appropriated Christian faith was the indispensable prerequisite for the rise of America's Bible civilization. It also contributed to its decline.

Historic Protestantism, enlivened by evangelical revival and adjusted to American circumstances, sustained a surprising degree of cohesion and has obviously remained a factor in national public life. Yet the unfolding American story after about 1830 pushed toward fragmentation. In the new circumstances that Tocqueville and Madison recognized, it became increasingly difficult for voluntary means to sustain Christian unity. Consensus suffered especially from sectarian opposition to licensed formal learning, rule from the center, and guidance from the Christian past. Conflict among proprietary Protestants who wanted to preserve such authorities, but who construed those authorities differently, also undercut the possibility of unified action.

External pressures of various kinds did periodically slow the fissiparous momentum of democratic religion. Warfare (1861–65) fostered at least partial regional unity on the basis of competing northern and southern civil religions. Racial difference thereafter preserved substantive cohesion for southern white Protestants. Well-publicized divisions over biblical higher criticism and the assured results of modern learning did the same for ideological blocs labeled "modernist" and "fundamentalist." In the twentieth century national mobilization against Nazism and then Soviet communism stimulated a consensus around the shared values of Protestants, Catholics, and Jews. Recent political-cultural conflicts have again created coalitions drawing diverse religions together. Yet these examples of cohesion are quite different from the broad allegiance to the principle of biblical authority that united the vast majority of active American believers in the first three decades of the nineteenth century. The influence of that principle on religion and public life owed much to effective exploitation of open American democracy. But the unfolding logic of republican democracy rendered that era unique in creating society-wide cohesion *on the basis of religion*. Thereafter, cohesion would be aided by religion, but religion in service to programs of reform, national military mobilization, racial segregation, the United States' international conflicts, and political partisanship.[2]

During the first half of the nineteenth century, pressing questions about divine revelation differed markedly between the United States and Europe. Europeans asked, *How important were the Scriptures for knowing God? Not at all* came the answer from the radical heirs of eighteenth-century French *philosophes* and the philosophically minded who followed Kant and Hegel in articulating variations of abstract theism.[3] In Britain the public debated whether sound learning and public well-being depended on the historical synthesis of divine revelation, established church, and Anglican (or Presbyterian) control of the universities. Traditionalists like the conservative Duke of Wellington in England and both sides of Presbyterian Scotland's Disruption in 1843 said *Absolutely*, while a growing collection of opponents again said *Not at all*. These naysayers included Dissenting Protestants in England, sectarian Presbyterians in Scotland, advocates for Parliamentary reform and Catholic emancipation, and the lay radicals who were developing theories of evolution that threatened orthodoxies in both science and society.[4]

Americans agitated different, but no less disruptive, questions. After the massive rebuttal of Thomas Paine, almost all of them differed from Europeans by taking the authority of divine revelation for granted. Yet the more restricted range of American questions was still divisive. If only persuasion by itself determined individual consent and if individual consent was the ground of all institutions, norms, and social structures, what would happen if growing segments of the population no longer heeded the Protestant interpretive consensus? Or if persuasive individuals used their freedom to publicize interpretations of Scripture that ignored evangelical norms? Or even exploited democratic liberty to publicize fresh revelations that superseded the Bible? In a landscape of democracy and disestablishment, creativity could not be suppressed.

Sectarian Interpretation

Sectarian movements grew faster in the United States than anywhere else in the world. They had wider impact in America, in part because they were promoted by dynamic and compelling leaders. But they also flourished because of the democratic soil in which they took root. From the perspective of European Christendom, the American progression spelled only chaos. Popular readings of the Bible proliferated that simply dispensed with time-honored biblical interpretations. Then came ever more bizarre (but also inexplicably popular) teachings drawn from Scripture. These led to claims about God speaking to individuals outside of the Bible. Finally arrived new writings offered to the public as replacing or augmenting Scripture itself. Europeans who paid attention could only gape: *Que lastima! Kaum zu glauben! O tempora, O mores!* (variations on "What in the world!").

The success of the Restorationist movement led by Alexander Campbell and Barton Stone highlighted strategies that rejected historical traditions of biblical interpretation. Restorationist missionaries to the United Kingdom attracted a handful of followers, but nothing like Restorationist success in the United States, where by midcentury churches calling themselves simply "CHRIST-i-an" (with that pronunciation) had grown from nothing into a formidable force.[5] Fifty years after Thomas Campbell issued his clarion *Address* in 1809, the new movement numbered almost 2,100 churches, or only a few less nationwide than the 2,230 Congregational parishes enumerated by the 1860 national census (Table 12.1). In several states of the Midwest and Upper South, the Christian Churches, while still far behind the Baptists and Methodists, competed on an even footing with Presbyterians and vastly exceeded the Episcopalians.

Crucially, effective promotion of "the Bible only" drove the movement. Campbell's *Address* had explained the propitious context provided by a democratic republic: the United States was "a country happily exempted from the baneful influence of a civil establishment of any peculiar [particular] from of christianity . . . and, at the same time, from any formal connexion with the devoted nations, that have given their strength and power unto the beast [i.e., Roman Catholicism]." For those who would take full advantage of this bright new day, Campbell championed a persuasive guide, declaring that "the New Testament is as perfect a constitution for the worship, discipline and government of the New Testament church" as was the Old Testament for the Jewish people. He then proclaimed what became a foundational principle for the Restorationist or "Christian" churches: "[W]here the scriptures are silent [about how to follow

Table 12.1 Churches in the Midwest, 1860

	Christian	Presbyterian	Episcopal
Illinois	148	272	67
Indiana	347	275	29
Kentucky	301	164	25
Missouri	150	127	18
Ohio	365	631	93

Source: Statistics of the United States . . . in 1860; compiled from the original returns and being the final exhibit of the Eighth Census (Washington, DC: Government Printing Office, 1866), 497–501. The census counted individual churches and "accommodations," or seating capacity. In each of these states, seating capacities showed the same relative ranking as numbers of churches.

Christ,] no human authority has power to interfere, in order to supply the supposed deficiency, by making laws for the church. . . . Nothing ought to be received into the faith or worship of the church; or be made a term of communion amongst christians, that is not as old as the New Testament."[6] Campbell's appeal to the New Testament exemplified the primitivism that would also drive the career of his son Alexander: if believers abandoned the error-filled cacophony of the centuries, they could hear the voice of God.[7]

In the public debates for which Alexander Campbell became renowned, he marshaled wide reading, mastery of the biblical languages, dedication to American ideals, and skillful casuistry to advance his father's principles. Especially when attacking what he considered false constructions of Christianity, he wielded these weapons with striking effect. Against Robert Owen in 1829 Campbell differentiated a genuine faith from "kingcraft and priestcraft . . . the creed system . . . [and] other perversions of [the] christianity" taught originally by Christ. Against the Catholic bishop of Cincinnati John Purcell, Campbell in 1837 expounded at great length on the errors of Rome, which included his charge that Catholicism was "essentially anti-American, being opposed to the genius of all free institutions, and positively subversive of them." Yet always Campbell returned to "the cardinal point," as he said early in the debate with Bishop Purcell: "Let us begin with the New Testament, which all agree, is the only authenticated standard of faith and manners—the only inspired record of the christian doctrine." Put positively, Christian people must look to the Scriptures. Put negatively, "what is not found there, wants the evident sanction of inspiration, and can never command the respect and homage of those who seek for divine authority in faith and morality."[8]

This kind of Bible-only-ism did not spur the unity of believers the Campbells expected to find when believers, freed from old-world restraints, read the Scriptures for themselves. It did, however, add significantly to the much wider circle of Protestants who made their stand on "the Bible alone." To be sure, when Barton Stone asserted in 1814, "[W]e have neither made nor adopted any party-creed, but have taken the Bible only as our standard," or when in 1845 a later leader of the Restoration asserted, "[W]e claim to be members of the Church of Christ, which had its origin in Jerusalem on the day of Pentecost," there was pushback.[9] A Methodist editor, for example, responded with exasperation when Restorationists set the Bible against the creeds. His point was that the creed of every Protestant denomination preached "the Bible as the only infallible rule of faith and practice," as "the very foundation of Protestantism."[10]

Yet the Bible-only message continued to expand. Presbyterians, as an example, never formally abandoned their allegiance to the Westminster Confession and Catechisms as guides to Scripture, but increasingly they too spoke as if reliance on the Bible alone was enough. Archibald Alexander, the first professor of the Presbyterians' first theological seminary, delivered his inaugural sermon at Princeton in August 1812 on a portion of John 5:39 ("search the scriptures"). In an address with two main purposes—"First, to ascertain that the Scriptures contain the truth of God; and, secondly, to ascertain what those truths are"— Alexander learnedly rehearsed standard Protestant teaching about the authority and life-giving character of Scripture. But he did so with an apologetic appeal to his hearers' reasoning capacity and the Bible's own internal character. In the course of his address he rejected approaches that subjected the truth of Scripture to recent philosophical ideals or to claims by individuals to be inspired channels of divine revelation. He also paused to attack Catholic reliance on oral tradition as making "the word of God of none effect, teaching for doctrines the command-ments of men [Mk 7:13]." As he attacked Catholicism, Alexander announced a primitivism worthy of Alexander Campbell: "[W]hilst we reject tradition as a rule of truth, we do not deny the utility of having recourse to the early practice of the church, for the illustration of Scripture, where there is any doubt respecting apostolic practice or institution."[11]

A telling controversy at Alexander's seminary a dozen years later underscored the spread of sectarian thinking. Princeton trustees had asked one of their number, the Rev. John Duncan of Baltimore, to deliver the opening sermon for the spring 1824 semester. Duncan, in the course of encouraging the theological student to master the Bible "as the only document . . . by which he can acquire true ministerial literature," went further, to impugn any effort not focused exclusively on Scripture. His denunciation included rejection of doctrinal systems of the sort that Princeton professors had already become famous for upholding. Duncan put his message in fully sectarian form: "To me it is of the purest astonishment to hear Christian ministers talk so untenderly about the BIBLE, and speak so affection-ately and feelingly about their own STANDARDS." In so doing, they forget "the immense difference between the word of God and the doctrines of men."[12]

Princeton's faculty thought Duncan had gone too far. In response Alexander's younger colleague Samuel Miller delivered another address to the students, this one published as *The Utility and Importance of Creeds and Confessions*. In European Protestant fashion it defended the value of written confessions of faith and also the importance of ministers subscribing to a confession as a means of enforcing discipline among a denomination's preachers.[13]

Yet even Miller's effort to sustain the Presbyterians' traditional respect for his-torical precedent was not without irony. Less than a decade later, the Princeton theologians had grown increasingly concerned about theological innovations as-sociated with Charles Finney's revivalism and the flourishing of new sectarian movements like the CHRIST-i-an churches. To stem that unwelcome tide, Miller published another substantial pamphlet, this one titled *Presbyterianism: The Truly Primitive and Apostolical Constitution of the Church of Christ*. It offered a passionate defense of traditional Presbyterianism, but the grounds on which Miller chose to argue were sectarian. In his own eyes he was following earlier English Puritans and Scottish Presbyterians in affirming that "the Scriptures[,] being the only infallible rule of faith and practice, no rite or ceremony, ought to have a place in the worship of God, which is not warranted in Scripture, either by direct precept or example, or by good and sufficient inference." On this basis he concluded that "the same mode of worship which we now believe existed in the apostolic age . . . now obtains in the Presbyterian Church in [Scotland] and in the United States."[14]

Historian Michael W. Casey has documented the knots into which Restorationists tied themselves with arguments over what Miller called "sufficient inference" from straightforward biblical teaching. He has also shown that in this period "the Presbyterians underwent theological changes and shifts that parallel the American Restorationist tradition."[15]

Sectarian Popularity

The next step seems inevitable in a milieu open to lay innovation, an economy with ready access to print, and a culture with near universal respect for Scripture. Some biblical interpretations arising as individual readers studied the ancient text strictly on their own, with all secondary authorities stripped away, were bound to become popular. And so in the American history of the Bible we come to William Miller.[16]

Miller (1782–1849), an autodidact farmer from upstate New York near the Vermont border, was converted as an adult after meritorious service in the War of 1812. As a young man he had been enamored with Ethan Allen's deism; he had also enjoyed the patronage of Matthew Lyon, a radical Jeffersonian who as a member of Congress was imprisoned for sedition during the presidency of John Adams. But after Miller experienced an evangelical conversion, it was the Bible and only the Bible. When "God by his Holy Spirit opened my eyes," Jesus was "a friend, and my only help." Thereafter, Scripture, "the *perfect rule* of duty," became "the lamp to my feet and light to my path [Ps 119:105]." In the Bible Miller discovered "everything revealed that my heart desired, and a remedy for every disease of the soul."[17] Two years of intensive study ensued during which Miller read, reread, and again read the King James Version. At the end of this period he was convinced that apparently contradictory portions of Scripture could be harmonized to specify the specific date of Jesus's return to earth, when he would establish the millennial kingdom.

Miller followed what he considered the Bible's own clear directions by understanding the "days," which featured prominently in the Old Testament book of

Daniel and the New Testament book of Revelation, as "years." (For example, Ezek 4:6, "I have appointed thee each day for a year.") He also joined a long history of interpreters by reading postbiblical events as fulfillments of biblical prophecy. One of Miller's later followers, for instance, would identify the smoke and "locusts like unto horses prepared unto battle," summoned by the fifth trumpet of the fifth angel in Revelation 9:1–12, with the Turkish Byzantine Empire's attacks on Christian Europe from July 27, 1399, to July 27, 1449.[18]

In the 1820s Miller's talks and sermons sparked a great deal of local interest, which was amplified as a growing band of followers took to the stump. This early preaching defined Miller's path for the next twenty years; it was evangelistic, urging people to repent and be born again, but with an emphasis on fleeing from the wrath to come when God would roll up time. Interest expanded when a newspaper, the Vermont *Telegraph*, began printing Miller's essays and when Miller himself put his talks into print. The first of these books appeared in 1833, *Evidences from Scripture and History of the Second Coming of Christ About the Year A.D. 1843, and of His Personal Reign of 1000 Years*. Successive editions expanded this original effort, and each edition increased the number of the convinced.

Miller's local renown became a national sensation after he met Joshua V. Himes in 1839.[19] As a young man Himes had attended Unitarian and Episcopal churches in his native Rhode Island but eventually found a spiritual home in the First Christian Church of New Bedford, Massachusetts, an assembly associated with the Christian Connection of Elias Smith. There Himes discovered, in his words, "the open Bible and liberty of thought" that inspired a career of effective preaching and aggressive reform.[20] Soon he himself became an active "Christian" preacher and eventually pastor of the Christian congregation in Boston. Above all, however, he was a reformer who, as with so many in his era, eagerly joined cause to cause: advocating for temperance and women's rights, then championing abolition as a friend of William Lloyd Garrison. In the mid-1830s he became enamored with the writings of Alexander Campbell and brought Campbell to Boston to promote his primitivist approach to the Scriptures.

When Miller's view of the apocalypse captivated Himes, a tornado of publicity followed. Himes arranged for Miller to preach in large cities. On the model perfected by the American Bible Society and other evangelical philanthropies, Himes set up spoke-and-hub networks of convinced followers to spread Millerism. He convened conferences and camp meetings. He saw to the construction of a tent seating four thousand that became a traveling venue for Miller's lectures. He raised great amounts of money with great creativity. He established several newspapers to spread Miller's conclusions about biblical teaching and—in less than half a decade—oversaw the publication of at least 5 million copies of books, hymnals, periodicals, tracts, pamphlets, and spectacularly illustrated (sometimes spectacularly large) broadsheet charts.

One of the charts that Himes mass-produced is included in the outstanding history of Millerism edited by Ronald Numbers and Jonathan Butler (Figure 12.1).[21] It is a marvel of ingenious layout and riveting graphics. Its left side depicts the image that appeared in a dream to King Nebuchadnezzar of Babylon and was interpreted by the prophet Daniel (Dan 2); it portrays, successively, Babylon, "Media and Persia," "Grecia," "Pagan Rome," and "the ten kingdoms" that succeeded the collapse of the Roman Empire—all keyed to a time line synchronized with prophetic scriptures. The middle and right side are dominated by two boldly printed enumerations of years, again keyed to biblical prophecies and world events, both culminating in 1843 as the incoming date of "GOD'S EVERLASTING KINGDOM." Interspersed are sixteen graphic images of Babylon, Pagan Rome (a seven-headed monster), Papal Rome (a beast from the sea with seven heads and ten horns), the crucifixion of Christ, fearsome "Mahometans" on horseback, several angels, and more. The "more" includes at least fourteen quotations or citations from the book of Daniel, nine from the book of Revelation, and one each from 2 Chronicles, Leviticus, Ezra, and First Maccabees. There are also a few specific explanations linking biblical prophecies to world events, such as "Death of Antiochus Epiphanes who of course stood not up against the Prince of Peace, and had been dead 164 years before the prince of princes [Jesus] was born."

The success of such captivating publicity focused mass attention on the question of when, exactly, the Second Coming would occur. Miller himself was content to forecast 1843 in somewhat general terms, but his acolytes set specific dates: for the spring equinox of 1843, March 21, and then, after recalibrating the "days" of Daniel, for October 22, 1844. As these dates approached, popular excitement grew in New England, New York, and stretching further south and west. Intense on the earlier date, it assumed a fever pitch for the later.

Millerism and especially the graphic representations that Himes produced can now seem bizarre. A similar impression can be gathered from the chorus of recriminations that swelled loudly when the Second Coming did not take place. Some voices in that chorus claimed that Millerism was directly responsible for a floodtide of suicides and committals to insane asylums, a charge that modern research does not support.[22] Yet in its day, Millerism was anything but a joke, anything but a fixation of diseased minds.

As amplified through Himes, Miller spoke a sure word that addressed perennial spiritual concerns while resonating directly with the uncertainties of contemporary life. The nation's worst depression had begun in 1837 and continued with devastating effect through the years when Himes transformed Millerism

Figure 12.1 Joshua Himes produced this extraordinary pictorial depiction of William Miller's interpretation of biblical prophecy in 1843, shortly before Miller's followers were "disappointed" when Christ did not return to earth as Miller predicted.

Source: Courtesy of James R. Nix.

into a national phenomenon. Although the secular penny press was expanding rapidly by this time, Himes's prodigies of print competed on almost equal terms. Millerism also extended its reach during the ferocious political campaign of 1840, when the Whigs' hero of Indian warfare, William Henry Harrison, triumphed over Andrew Jackson's wily successor, Martin Van Buren—and during the national disorientation that followed when Harrison's early death brought disappointment to Whigs because of how his successor, the Virginian John Tyler, tilted policies to favor the slaveholding South. In such circumstances, thousands and then tens of thousands became convinced that, in contrast to the uncertain present, Miller had seen the future definitely, truthfully, and clearly.

So it was that as many as fifty thousand Americans, after selling or giving away their possessions, assembled out of doors in many locations on October 22, 1844, to greet "The Midnight Cry" (the name of one of Himes's newspapers, taken from Matt 25:6). Many more retired that evening, wondering if it might be so. They represented only a fraction of those who had heard Miller or read Himes's publicity as a plausible word for themselves. Daniel Walker Howe has insightfully described what happened before and after the day of Disappointment: "The legend that Miller's people had donned ascension robes for the occasion was one of many humiliations heaped on Adventists over the next year by a laughing public that had not quite dared risk scorning them until *after the fact*."[23]

Miller represented a defining point in America's Bible civilization. His followers, as David Rowe has well stated, "are not fascinating because they were so different from everyone else but because they were so like their neighbors."[24] Or, in Ruth Alden Doan's explanation, "the Millerite excitement" is best understood as heightening "strains within antebellum evangelicalism," especially that culture's biblicism, revivalism, and millennialism.[25] Miller and Himes appealed because they creatively expounded common themes; only in their extremity did they begin to look foolish.

The story of Miller's biblical interpretations did not end with the Disappointment. When the End was not manifest, some Millerites returned to their previous fellowships, some grew disillusioned with evangelical religion, and still others continued to maintain Adventist beliefs in a variety of small movements. One of these, under the leadership of Ellen White (1827–1915), concluded that Christ had indeed "returned" as Miller predicted, but that the return occurred in heavenly realms when Jesus entered into the presence of the Father. Because they believed that Christian worship should take place on Saturday, White's followers became known as Seventh-day Adventists and have steadily grown, now making up the most widely distributed Protestant denomination in the world.[26]

For antebellum history, Millerism is important for sharply illustrating the ways that American values had come to inform approaches to Scripture practiced by most of the era's Protestants. Those ways can be specified. A strong sense of *democratic empowerment* sprang positively from cultural confidence in "We the people" as well as negatively from a repudiation of teaching that rested on formal authority. *Republican political principles* fostered a deep distrust of inherited or aristocratic influences, along with a conception of social well-being as dependent on the ability of ordinary citizens to cultivate personal virtue through their own study of Scripture. *American exceptionalism* took for granted the United States' special place in world history, in some versions with the assumption that God had singled out the new nation for special blessing as he had long ago singled out Old Testament Israel, and in others with the belief that the United States was called to usher the entire world to new heights of human flourishing. In turn, this buoyant expectation, when combined with the church expansion manifest on every side, encouraged *millennial thinking* that saw Christian America anticipating the End of Time. *Commonsense* philosophy encouraged the conviction that what ordinary individuals discovered by observing the operations of their own minds pointed toward truths confirmed by universal *human experience*. Finally, in an era that witnessed the founding of the Smithsonian Institute, great advances in machine tooling and manufacturing, manifold schemes for improving physical health, and the newfangled sciences of hypnosis and phrenology, the Millerite picture drawn inductively from verses throughout the Scriptures represented one more application of *science* to daily life.

Millerism faded because in an America head over heels with enthusiasm for what worked, it failed (or, for Seventh-day Adventists, seemed to fail). Yet before the Disappointment, it blazed brightly since Miller's teaching so effectively deployed the hermeneutic shared by so many Americans, and not just evangelical Americans. The techniques, assumptions, habits, expectations, and self-confidence with which he approached the Bible were American to the core.

Sectarian Prophets

Alongside increasingly popular new interpretations of Scripture, the antebellum United States also witnessed an increasing number of claims for divine revelation augmenting, or even superseding, the Bible. Not surprisingly, they emerged from the same cultural milieu in which new interpretations of Scripture flourished. If American democracy championed the ability of all men (and perhaps even women) to understand God's written revelation for themselves, it eased the way for some Americans to claim that God spoke directly to them as individuals. If the same public ethos emboldened ordinary citizens to advance the kind of comprehensive interpretations of biblical revelation once reserved for learned elites, it opened a door for convincing communicators to propose other interpretations of other channels of revelation. And if deference to written foundational documents pervaded American religious life (biblicism) as well as the political sphere (constitutionalism), the age was primed to entertain the possibility that other God-given documents might reveal other Grand Explanatory Narratives.[27]

David Holland has recently made a major contribution to early national history by documenting a surprisingly widespread debate over whether the canon of Scripture was closed or open, that is, whether no further uniquely authoritative written revelations should be expected once the Bible was complete (closed) or whether more revelations from God were still possible (open). [28] In fact, many different groups, well-known individuals, and forgotten but interesting actors busied themselves with this subject throughout the eighteenth and nineteenth centuries. For the Puritans, Jonathan Edwards, and most other religious leaders in colonial America, the traditional belief in a closed canon prevailed—though challenged by many exceptions, nuances, and subtleties.

Benjamin Franklin, for example, in July 1755 penned two documents that he circulated as newly discovered chapters in the Genesis account of the patriarch Abraham. His wickedly successful imitation of the language, phraseology, and format of published King James bibles testified to his age's universal familiarity with that version:

1. And it came to pass after these Things, that Abraham sat in the Door of his Tent, about the going down of the Sun.

2. And behold a Man, bowed with Age, came from the Way of the Wilderness, leaning on a Staff. . . .

6. And when Abraham saw that the Man blessed not God, he said unto him, Wherefore dost thou not worship the most high God, Creator of Heaven and Earth?

7. And the Man answered and said, I do not worship the God thou speakest of; neither do I call upon his Name; for I have made to myself a God, which abideth always in mine House, and provideth me with all Things.

8. And Abraham's zeal was kindled against the Man; and he arose, and fell upon him, and drove him forth with Blows into the Wilderness. . . .

11. And God said [to Abraham], Have I borne with him these hundred ninety and eight Years, and nourished him, and cloathed him, notwithstanding his Rebellion against me, and couldst not though, that art thyself a Sinner, bear with him one Night?[29]

With tongue in cheek, Franklin wanted his scriptural pastiche to advance an Enlightenment view of religious toleration. Some who read it, however, took what he had written as genuine Holy Writ. When a London newspaper printed Franklin's chapters along with an identification of their author, Franklin was disappointed that his ruse had been exposed. But he never himself considered that his handiwork was a real revelation from God.

Toward the end of the eighteenth century, the possibility of genuine revelations began to seem more plausible.[30] To be sure, claims about personal communication from God had existed throughout history, with Catholic forms augmented by Protestant varieties from the time of the Reformation. In the early years of his public career, Martin Luther had been disturbed when the Zwickau Prophets and then Thomas Muentzer claimed to receive direct messages from God. (About the latter, Luther reportedly said, "I would not believe Thomas Muentzer if he had swallowed the Holy Ghost, feathers and all.")[31] Among groups that George Huntston Williams called "radical Reformers," a spiritualist tradition that began with Muentzer and Caspar Schwenkfeld continued as a marginal presence among Protestants.[32] In England, the Quakers were renowned (and despised) for their doctrine of "the inner Light of Christ" that they believed God made available potentially to all people, women as well as men. By the eighteenth century, that Quaker emphasis had often drawn back toward a more traditional deference to the supreme authority of Scripture—as when the Pennsylvania Quakers Ralph Sandiford, Benjamin Lay, John Woolman, and Anthony Benezet deployed the Bible against slavery.[33] By that time, a Swedish Lutheran mystic, Emanuel Swedenborg (1688-1772), had convinced a public stretching across Europe into the American colonies that his book, *The Heavenly Doctrine*, represented a new, authentic Word from the Lord. Swedenborg never enjoyed an extensive following, but in the early nineteenth century Americans convinced by *The Heavenly Doctrine* were publishing newspapers and organizing churches that treated this work on a par with the Bible.[34] As the new century wore on, Protestants—like Alexander Campbell in his debate with Bishop Purcell—also grew increasingly exercised over Catholic acceptance of tradition as an authentic revelation alongside Scripture. Debating questions about the canon had moved from theological improbability to speculative possibility.

The questions intensified when Americans presented *themselves* as recipients not only of divine communication but of communications that could be recorded, printed, and distributed as scriptural. Among the best known was Nimrod Hughes of Washington County, Virginia, who in 1810 published a substantial prophetic work. It began with a reminder to his biblically literate readers: "[A]s it has happened in every age, that when the Lord commissioned any of his servants, the prophets, to bear his word to the children of men, he qualified them for their awful mission by such visions, direct revelations, and often severe trials and exercises, as convinced them that they must obey his voice or perish."[35] Hughes's title conveniently summarized what he wanted to say: *A Solemn Warning to all the Dwellers upon Earth, given forth in obedience to the express command of the LORD GOD, as communicated by him, in several*

extraordinary visions and miraculous revelations, confirmed by sundry plain but
wonderful signs, unto NIMROD HUGHES . . . Upon whom the Awful Duty of
making this Publication has been Laid and Enforced, by sundry Admonitions and
severe Chastisements of the Lord, for the space of Ten Months and Nine Days of
unjust and close confinement in the Prison of Abingdon, wherein he was shown
that the certain DESTRUCTION OF ONE THIRD OF MANKIND, as foretold in
the Scriptures must take place on the FOURTH DAY OF JUNE, 1812. The seven
printings of this work that appeared in New York, New Jersey, and Virginia (including a German translation) before June 1812 testified to its plausibility. So
also did the attention accorded by John Adams and Thomas Jefferson, who
exchanged letters on Hughes and several other contemporary prophets in the
early months of 1812.[36] As David Holland has pointed out, Hughes's book became an immediate sensation because it seemed so accurately to describe the terrible wonders that appeared soon after he published his book: the Great Comet
that illuminated the heavens from September 1811 into the new year; the massive
New Madrid earthquake of December 1811 and January 1812 that redirected the
Mississippi River and could be felt for hundreds of miles; and the heightening
tension with Great Britain that would lead to a declaration of war on June 18,
only two weeks after the doom Hughes had prophesied.[37]

When, however, June 5 succeeded June 4 without a cataclysm, interest in
Hughes vanished, and much more completely than would interest in Miller
after his followers' Great Disappointment a generation later. Yet the flash of interest that greeted Hughes's prophecy was a harbinger of things to come, especially the sustained attention that the prophetic word published by Joseph Smith
would soon receive. With Smith a new revelation took hold, in part because unlike Miller he provided no specific predictions for falsification. But like Hughes,
Mormon apologists used the same biblical warrant that the earlier prophet had
claimed: in Holland's summary, "Christ's New Testament condemnation of those
who built monuments to dead prophets while stoning heaven's living messengers
[Lk 11:47–48]."[38] If you believed the Bible, why limit belief in revelation to only
the Bible?

Sectarian Scripture

Joseph Smith and the Book of Mormon have received expert historical treatment from many scholars, some themselves members of the Church of Jesus
Christ of Latter-day Saints and many not.[39] The Book of Mormon, published
first in 1830, narrates in fifteen sections the journey to the western hemisphere
of three remnants from ancient Israel: the families of Jared and Mulek, treated
briefly, and the family of Lehi, treated at length in the rivalry between Lehi's

two sons, Nephi and Laman. Most of the Book records the course of the rivalry, with the last Lamanites evolving into the Indian tribes that Europeans encountered in the late fifteenth century. (In this one particular, concerning the origin of Native Americans, the Book of Mormon echoes Elias Boudinot's interpretation of Scripture published as he was working to establish the American Bible Society.)[40]

The Book of Mormon indicates that when two heavenly beings, Mormon and Moroni, commissioned Smith to translate this new revelation as himself a prophet, their gift was merely an abridgement of an entire library of sacred writings. The canon was definitely not closed. Mormonism from the start taught that God's people should expect ongoing authoritative divine communications—first in definitive writings from Smith, then in supplementary additions and adjustments of those writings by succeeding leaders of the movement, but also through divine perceptions in every human who read the sacred writings with an open mind. The Book of Mormon, in Terryl Givens's expert assessment, "hammers home the insistent message that revelation is the province of everyman." Givens's further explanation of this fundamental Mormon conviction suggests how thoroughly Smith's new scripture was rooted in two signal markers of his age: implicit trust in the traditional Protestant Bible and implicit belief in democratic possibilities: "Mormons assert that the rock on which the church was—and is—built is the rock of personal revelation, the process whereby truth is 'revealed' not by 'flesh and blood . . . but my Father which is in heaven' (Matthew 16:17–18). The Book of Mormon reasserts this principle while clarifying its democratic, rather than hierarchical, application."[41]

The Book of Mormon eventually succeeded as a new scripture because of how much it spoke to a culture that believed in the inherited Scriptures. Along with other scholars, Nathan Hatch has insightfully highlighted the centrality of that traditional Bible in the history behind this new scripture. Like Alexander Campbell and Barton Stone, Joseph Smith's family and his first converts wholeheartedly embraced Christianity and looked with unalloyed trust upon the Bible as the sure Word of God. Yet also like these Restorationists, the Smiths were deeply distressed by the cacophony of conflicting claims in the national religious free market. As did the Restorationists, so also did Joseph Smith's mother, Lucy Mack Smith, turn aside from the contradictory biblical interpretations of the existing denominations ("if I join some one of the different denominations, all the rest will say I was in error"). Her recourse? Discovering the truth for herself by studying the Bible on her own: "I therefore determined to examine my Bible, and taking Jesus and the disciples as my guide, to endeavor to obtain from God that which man could neither give nor take away. . . . The Bible I intended should be my guide to life and salvation."[42] Parley Pratt, an early Mormon elder, shared the same journey. His father, "an equally devout but unattached believer," in Hatch's phrase, pointed his family away from contending religious claims by pointing them to the Bible alone: "He taught us to venerate our Father in Heaven, Jesus Christ, His prophets and Apostles, as well as the Scriptures written by them . . . and was careful to preserve his children free from all prejudice in favor or against any particular denomination into which the so-called Christian world was then unhappily divided."[43]

So too it was with Joseph Smith. In 1838 he described the first heavenly vision he had received eighteen years previously that set him on a path as God's new revelator for a new age. To the fourteen-year-old appeared a pillar of light and deep darkness (reminiscent of the children of Israel coming out of Egypt [Ex 13]) accompanied by two heavenly beings, the Father and the Son. They told him that "all [of the sects] were wrong" and that "all their Creeds were an abomination." Significantly, this first revelation took place shortly after Smith had been studying "the Epistle of James, First Chapter and fifth verse which reads, 'If any lack wisdom, let him ask of God.'" About this reading Smith then spoke as a convinced evangelical of his era: "Never did any passage of scripture come with more power to the heart of man [than] this at this time to mine. . . . I reflected on it again and again . . . for the teachers of religion of the different sects understood the same passage of Scripture so differently as [to] destroy all confidence in settling the questions by an appeal to the Bible." The push (contemporary interpretive confusion) and the pull (the Epistle of James) soon led to a fateful decision: "[A]t length I came to the Conclusion that I must either remain in darkness or confusion or else I must do as James directs, that is, Ask of God."[44]

The heavenly response to this direct plea came three years later when the angel Moroni appeared to Smith with a detailed message about Golden Plates and instruments for translating the Plates, both hidden for 1,400 years near Smith's home in Palmyra, New York. Then, to reassure Smith that he spoke the truth, Moroni quoted "many other passages of Scripture," including Malachi 3:1 (about the Lord's messenger who shall prepare the way for the Lord, after which "the Lord, whom ye seek, shall suddenly come"), Isaiah 11:12 (concerning an "ensign for the nations" who would appear to gather his people "from the four corners of the earth"), Deuteronomy 18:15 (asserting "The Lord thy God will raise up unto thee a prophet," whom Moroni indicated was Christ), but also Joel 2:28 (with the promise that "my spirit" would be poured out and "your young men will see visions").[45]

There followed a seven-year period that has been the subject of intense scrutiny, debate, and contention. In it (depending on interpretive angle) Smith employed a uniquely God-given ability to translate this genuine divine revelation, plagiarized or maliciously fabricated a completely duplicitous document, or by himself created a work of enduring literary genius. Not in dispute is the outcome: publication in Palmyra of *An Account written by the Hand of Moroni, Upon*

Plates Taken from the Plates of Nephi, with "Joseph Smith, Junior" identified as "Author and Proprietor."

The book's title page explained at length that it offered "an abridgement of the Record of the People of Nephi; and also of the Lamanites. . . . Also, which is a record of the People of Jared." After a brief preliminary word explaining why the initial 116 pages of Smith's translation had been lost or stolen and would not be included in this volume, the revelation itself began "THE FIRST BOOK OF NEPHI. His reign and ministry. CHAPTER I," followed by a precis ("An account of Lehi, and his wife Sariah, and his four Sons, being called [beginning at the eldest,] Laman, Lemuel, Sam, and Nephi. . . . This is according to the account of Nephi; or, in other words, I Nephi wrote this record." (Figure 12.2) Then it began:

> I, Nephi, having been born of goodly parents, therefore I was taught somewhat in all the learning of my father; and having seen many afflictions in the course of my days—nevertheless, having been highly favored of the Lord in all my days; yea, having had a great knowledge of the goodness and the mysteries of God, therefore I make a record of my proceedings in my days; yea, I make a record in the language of my father, which consists of the learning of the Jews and the language of the Egyptians. And I know that the record which I make, to be true; and I make it with mine own hand; and I make it according to my knowledge.

So it continued for nearly six hundred tightly printed pages until the last sentences of the Book of Moroni:

> And now I bid unto all, farewell. I soon go to rest in the paradise of God, until my spirit and body shall again reunite, and I am brought forth triumphant through the air, to meet you before the pleasing bar of the Great Jehovah, the Eternal Judge of both quick and dead. Amen.[46]

In the perceptive assessment of historian Jan Shipps, a new scripture had appeared, which would mark a new stage of divine revelation beyond the New Testament in the same way that the New Testament had built upon the sacred history of the Hebrew scriptures.[47]

Taking Stock

For a history of the Christian Bible in America, the most remarkable physical feature of the Book of Mormon is how closely it resembled the bibles that at this very time were being distributed in the American Bible Society's "general supply." As Paul Gutjahr explains, "Its size and binding style strikingly resembled

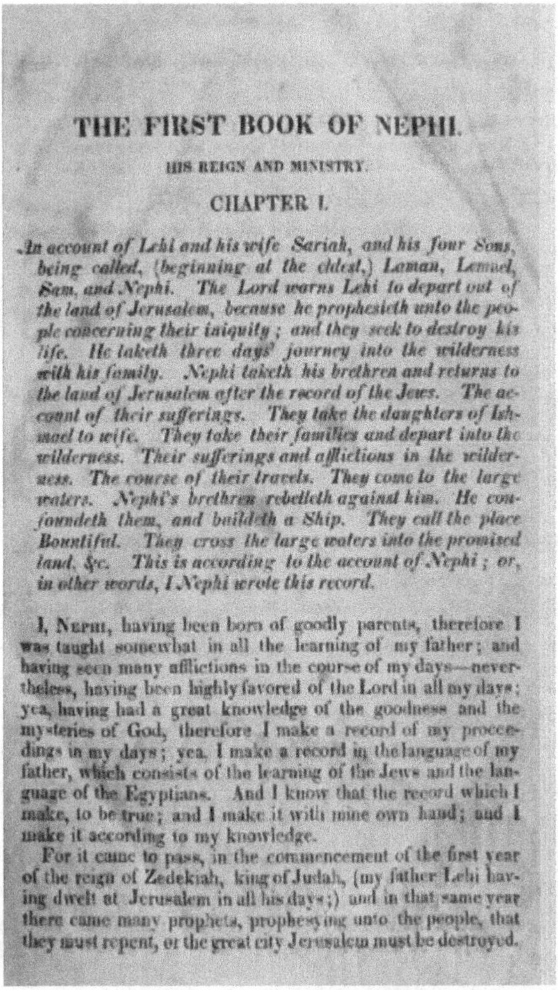

Figure 12.2 Joseph Smith's Book of Mormon imitated the typeface and layout of scriptures from the American Bible Society, except that the first edition of 1830, its opening page shown here, did not divide the text into verse units.
Source: Courtesy of the University of Pittsburgh Library System.

the most common Bible editions being passionately produced and distributed by the ABS, and its narrative was full of religious ritual and sacred commandments, and wondrous stories of divine intervention."[48] In addition, Smith's translation even more unerringly replicated the cadences, language, and phraseology of the King James Bible even more closely than had Franklin's new chapters of Genesis. Like Protestant and Catholic bibles, the Book of Mormon was itself a *biblia* (in

Greek, "the books") of individual writings that, though divergent in their form and content, presented a coherent story of God's dealing with his people. The new story also followed the Bible's overall narrative. Again Gutjahr: it "echoed the Bible in its histories of divinely favored people traveling to a promised land, the global importance of the House of Israel, the fulfillment of various sacred prophecies, and the messianic mission of Jesus Christ."[49]

To those open to its message, the Book of Mormon would appeal not as a replacement for but as an addition to the standard Protestant Bible. Throughout his subsequent career as an authoritative revelator (canonized in *The Pearl of Great Price* and the *Doctrine and Covenants*), Smith continued to quote the King James Version and reprise its style. Philip Barlow has pointed out that the Book of Mormon contains at least fifty thousand phrases of three words or more that align exactly with the KJV.[50]

Stepping back from the texts of Mormon sacred writings, it is patent that Smith's new religion, or new phase of Christianity, fit securely in the American Bible civilization. Smith and his followers flourished by exercising "the right of private judgment" that more traditional believers also exploited so successfully. Mormons illustrated powerfully the common conviction that ordinary citizens—without specialized training or license by a hierarchy—could grasp the truth, confirm it intuitively, and spread it freely through public speaking and the printed page. Mormon belief in the veracity of Smith's translated revelation likewise imitated the same literal approach to ancient texts that most of the era's Protestants followed. Above all, as Barlow has expertly stated, Smith and his movement shared fully in "the 'primitive gospel' milieu in which Mormonism initially thrived." And right down the line: "The biblicist perspective, the selectively literalist mentality, the anticreedal and antihierarchical bias, the yearning for New Testament purity in theology and polity, the millenarian expectations, and the quest for religious authority amid the conflicting biblical interpretations spawned in the young, restless, democratic America."[51]

With, however, one exception. For the Latter-day Saints it was definitely not "the Bible only" but the Bible come alive as a still authoritative but now openended signifier of God's will for humankind. God was now just as existentially present as in the days of the scriptural prophets and apostles.[52]

In the early 1840s, Philip Schaff arrived in the United States from Germany to teach at the small German Reformed seminary in Mercersburg, Pennsylvania. As a keenly interested observer of his new homeland, Schaff was immediately struck by differences from what he had experienced in his native Switzerland or in Germany, where he had trained as a theologian. Schaff at this early stage of his American career was not at all pleased. In his first major work, *The Principle of Protestantism* (1845), he explained what in his eyes had gone wrong. In America he saw "the principle of Congregationalism," which "has exercised such vast influence upon the entire conformation of [American] religion and practice," devolving into "full Atomism." Once "the separation of Church and State became general and fixed" after the American Revolution, Schaff saw nothing to restrain those regrettable "tendencies which had found no political room to unfold themselves in other lands." The resulting "evils" eviscerated the splendid inheritance of Reformation Protestantism that Schaff prized in the Lutheran, Reformed, and Anglican establishments of Europe.

In particular, Schaff highlighted the powerful, but also powerfully destructive, way that American Protestants treated the Bible: "[T]hey make their appeal collectively to the sacred volume; the Devil himself does so, when it suits his purpose." Schaff and his Mercersburg colleague John W. Nevin called the American scene characterized by this appeal "the sect system." About the work of such a system Schaff could only shake his head in bewildered distress: the American sectarian, "though thoroughly unprepared to understand a single book, is not ashamed to appeal continually to the scriptures, as having been sealed entirely, or in large part, to the understanding of eighteen centuries, and even to the view of our Reformers themselves, till now at last God has been pleased to kindle the true light in an obscure corner of the new world!"[53]

Schaff's assessment of church life in America would eventually become much more positive, as he came to view the American pattern as facilitating a depth and breadth of genuine spirituality closed to many in Europe.[54] Yet his assessment in 1845 was factually accurate, if exaggerated. Even as the Bible retained a powerful hold on American consciousness, sectarian impulses were undermining the possibility of a Bible civilization. As innovative interpretations of Scripture gained strength, claims of direct communication with God increased, and the Book of Mormon prepared the way for other new sacred texts, cohesive Protestantism could not keep up.[55] The democracy in which Protestant Christianity had flourished was now undermining the possibility of Protestant cooperation.

In southeastern Virginia little more than a year after the Book of Mormon was published, Nat Turner led his band of sixty slaves in the most violent slave revolt in American history. Turner was every bit as inspired by his own understanding of biblical prophecy as would be William Miller, every bit as convinced he had received a word from the Lord as Joseph Smith. If Smith replicated, while he transgressed, the Bible fixation of an entire culture, so too did Turner's transgressive reliance on Scripture illuminate the nemesis of slavery that imperiled the United States' Bible civilization. Together, Turner, Smith, and others who treasured the Bible—but not in terms favored by traditional white Protestantism—made a decisive difference. The Bible unleashed by American democracy could not contain American democracy.

13

The Law and a Christian Nation

Near the fiftieth anniversary of independence, well-placed Americans looked upon success in Christianizing the population and expanding the national voluntary societies as proof that Christianity could flourish without Christendom. And not just Christianity in general, but genuine Protestant Christianity following scriptural precepts, well adjusted to a free society, and sustained by trust in the Bible alone. When assumptions about the providential character of the Protestant British Empire evolved into assumptions about the new nation as a Hebrew republic, this adjustment supported the conception of the United States as a Bible civilization. The continuing (if unspecified) belief that Scripture played a crucial role in the common law tradition likewise underlay the thinking of American jurists as they plotted a legal course for the new nation. The heady prospect of a Christian civilization—not only voluntarily created, but created in fidelity to Scripture—inspired custodial Protestants to dream even bigger dreams, especially when new threats arose to the nation's hard-won gains. Perhaps, they thought, the public could be persuaded to make its implicit Christian character explicit; perhaps there was still time to preserve the Bible civilization before a tidal wave of Catholic immigration swamped the great experiment. The Bible enjoyed an even more central place among the first generation of American educational innovators. Purveyors of instructional materials hoping to promote literacy adapted for a democracy, along with the first organizers of common schools, found the King James Bible an ideal resource. Because of the translation's common currency among Protestants, they believed its "nonsectarian" character provided the moral grounding that a free society required to preserve, even in the face of mounting threats, the virtue without which republics failed.

As events unfolded, however, internal strains arising from the very liberties of a democratic republic and intractable divisions over the morality of slavery began to undermine the Bible civilization well before it was menaced by new, non-Protestant forces. So also did the development of a self-conscious American legal tradition lead to tensions between universal claims about democratic principles and the particular aspirations of dedicated Protestants. Similarly, conflicts among Protestants over slavery paralleled intra-Protestant disputing over how Christianity should be promoted in a post-Christendom society. Yet even as the Bible civilization experienced these strains in the 1830s, substantial remnants

America's Book. Mark A. Noll, Oxford University Press. © Oxford University Press 2022.
DOI: 10.1093/oso/9780197623466.003.0014

of that civilization continued their influence far into the future—and nowhere more obviously than for Scripture in "public" education. This chapter on the law and debates over a Christian America, along with the next on the development of common schooling, suggest how many roles the Bible played in a nation undergoing constant debate about its own character.

The Law

Conceptions of the law in the new nation paralleled the reflective understanding of the United States as a Hebrew republic. Into the 1830s, belief that the Protestant Bible somehow belonged at the heart of the common law remained as much an American axiom as the belief that the ancient Hebrews prefigured the new nation. Thereafter things became more complicated.

Beyond question, the War of Independence marked America's decisive rejection of Britain's Christendom, where privileges and duties of the Anglican establishment occupied a central place in jurisprudence. Yet it was also obvious that as Americans constructed legal guidelines for themselves, they maintained a general reverence for Christianity and a specific deference to Scripture. As John Witte and Joel Nichols have observed, the "publick religion" (Benjamin Franklin) or "civil religion" (Robert Bellah) of the new American nation rested foursquare on the "ethical commonplaces taught by various religious traditions at the time of the founding." First among the "icons" of this public religion—though alongside "the Declaration of Independence, the bells of liberty, and the Constitution"—was "the Bible."[1]

Yet much the same uncertainty attended law in the early United States as the question of how church and state should relate after Christendom. The precise authority of the common law, the exact shape for incorporating which entities, the relation of state law to federal law—all posed challenges requiring decisions about how much of colonial practice to retain and how much required creation *de novo*.

The dynamic tension in early American legal reasoning could not be clearer, at least in retrospect; religion would be unprecedentedly free *and* public life would be generally Christian, or specifically Protestant, or even explicitly biblical. The much-publicized contrast between the early governments in Massachusetts and Virginia illustrated the national tension as it existed in the 1780s. In Massachusetts (1780), "no subject shall be hurt, molested, or restrained . . . for worshipping God in the manner . . . most agreeable to the dictates of his own conscience." But since "the happiness of a people . . . essentially depend[s] upon piety, religion, and morality," the legislature required the state's municipalities "to make suitable provision, at their own expense, for the institution of the public worship of God."[2] Virginia (1786), because it recognized that "Almighty God hath created the mind free," famously decreed that "no man shall be compelled to frequent or support any religious worship, place, or ministry whatsoever."[3]

At a time when most Americans regarded themselves as citizens of their individual states instead of the nation, legal developments in Massachusetts and Virginia revealed the tension between the free exercise of religion and the inherited conventions of public Protestantism. Much of that tension concerning the Bible has been clarified by historians researching state histories during the years when Methodists and Baptists were evangelizing the citizenry with such great effect. On these questions, Carl Esbeck and Jonathan Den Hartog have recently demonstrated that the states proceeded with almost no attention to the First Amendment's balance of "free exercise" and "no establishment," or Thomas Jefferson's conception of a "wall of separation" between religion and government.[4] Other expert legal historians, led by Steven Green, have shown that for a history of the Bible, state judicial judgments in the 1830s and 1840s were much more important than anything in preceding decades for adjusting inherited reverence for the Protestant Scriptures to the realities of a religiously plural nation.[5]

Like so much else in the U.S. history of the Bible, English precedent loomed large for legal history. In this case, the English heritage bequeathed certainty that the common law incorporated Christianity. (American jurists understood "the common law" not as Parliamentary legislation but as the customs, principles, and usages underlying decisions of England's royal courts—which they continued to regard as authoritative long after breaking with Britain.) The much honored *Commentaries on the Laws of England* by William Blackstone provided the standard legal history. In *Blackstone*, published in 1769, generations of American lawyers saw the author treat the common law as foundational for their profession, with Christianity an accompanying presence. In a particularly conspicuous example, Blackstone cited "the belief of a future state of rewards and punishments" as critical for the oaths that ensured truth-telling in court.[6] Blackstone's explanation for why blasphemy could be rightly prosecuted by civil authorities specifically linked deference to Scripture with the Christian basis of the common law. Blasphemy, in his explanation, meant not only "contumelious reproaches of our Saviour Christ" but also "all profane scoffing at the holy scripture, or exposing it to contempt and ridicule." Such offenses were properly "punishable at common law by fine or imprisonment . . . for christianity is part of the laws of England."[7]

The state constitutions hammered out as soon as independence took effect reflected Blackstone's axiom casually. Most obvious were the new constitutions of Massachusetts and New Hampshire, along with Connecticut's continued use of its colonial charter that ensured freedom of religion while setting up tax support for Congregational churches. More typical were the state constitutions that ended tax-supported establishments but retained religious tests of various kinds, often enshrining the exclusion of Catholics carried over from British imperial warfare against Catholic France and Spain. New Jersey's constitution of 1776 decreed that "there shall be no establishment of any one religious sect in this province in preference to another," but also defined "Protestant inhabitant(s)" as those who could not be denied "the enjoyment of any civil right." The same document limited service in the legislature to "all persons professing a belief in the faith of any Protestant sect." South Carolina went further in 1778: "tolerated" persons and "religious societies" were those that acknowledged "there is one God, and a future state of rewards and punishments." Though making no provision for financial support, South Carolina also decreed that "the Christian Protestant religion shall be declared . . . the established religion of the state." Maryland in 1776 authorized something similar, though with a nod to its Catholic population, specifying "all persons professing the *Christian* religion" as entitled to "protection in their religious liberty."[8]

Several states underscored the honored heritage of Scripture by stipulating, as Delaware did in 1776, that its legislators were "required" to declare "I do profess faith in God the Father, and in the Lord Jesus Christ his only Son, and in the Holy Ghost, one God blessed for evermore; and I do acknowledge the Holy Scriptures of the Old and New Testaments to be given by divine inspiration." Delaware was joined by North Carolina (1776) and South Carolina (1778) in this requirement. Pennsylvania's similar provision in its 1776 constitution was amended only when Philadelphia's Jewish leaders protested that they too had rendered sacrificial service to the cause of independence. But the state's constitution of 1790 backed off only partially; its new requirement for legislative service specified belief in "the being of a God and a future state of rewards and punishments."[9] In a word, legislatures like Virginia's that removed all religious tests were the exception; the rule was mandated preference for Protestants and often specific recognition of the Scriptures.

These state constitutions, rather than the separation principle of the First Amendment or Virginia's type of religious freedom, long defined the American legal landscape. Although Massachusetts's effective establishment of Congregationalism was not typical, it has been much studied. That state's judicial decisions deferred to a common law that did not question the Protestant preference but rather addressed how to dispose of taxes collected to support religion. The famous "Dedham" case of 1820, *Baker v. Fales*, generated immense controversy, not by questioning the establishment principle but by ruling that the town (in this case, Unitarians) rather than the congregation (Trinitarians) could select the tax-supported minister. In 1810 Chief Justice Theophilus Parsons had denied a petition from Universalists asking to receive part of their town's religious tax assessment. He ruled that Universalists, Baptists, and the rapidly growing number of Methodists relied only on part-time ministers; they did not adequately pro-mote the social purposes of religion specified in the Massachusetts constitution as the reason for church establishment. According to the chief justice, "liberty of conscience and religious opinions and worship" were one thing (absolutely guaranteed); the "protection" of proper religious teaching (taxes for properly in-corporated churches) was something else.[10] Tax support for churches came to an end in New England only when Jeffersonians and their sectarian Protestant allies took control of legislatures from Federalists. Yet when we review the his-tory of common schooling in Massachusetts, we will see that while conflict be-tween Trinitarian and Unitarian Federalists aided the Democrats' takeover, it by no means weakened their common reliance on Scripture in public education.

Judicial decisions outside of New England revealed even more clearly a ge-neral respect for Christianity as part of the common law as well as specific rever-ence for Scripture. During these early national decades, Thomas Jefferson was an almost complete outlier when he railed against these convictions. A remarkably splenetic letter from Jefferson to John Adams in January 1814 set out his case. Besides complaining about Protestant reverence for the entirety of Scripture (rescuing the valuable parts of the New Testament from parts fabricated by "very inferior minds" was as easy as fishing out "diamonds from dunghills"), Jefferson challenged the prevailing notion that "the whole Bible and Testament are part of the Common law." That ludicrous notion, according to the Sage of Monticello, rested on frauds perpetrated under Alfred the Great and King Henry VI. Adams only partially agreed, since his interest "in what sense and to what extent the Bible is Law" came from his observation that public promotion of divergent interpretations of Scripture only further factionalized an already corrupt elec-toral process.[11]

Contradicting Jefferson, judges in state courts often referred to Christianity as part of the common law. Many jurists did not differentiate between deference to the spiritual truths of Scripture and worry about social evils if the Bible was abandoned. As an instance, early decisions protecting Sunday emphasized the religious purpose of Sabbath legislation. In 1816 a Massachusetts court ruled that Sunday was a "holy day" with legal protections designed for "the sole object" of protecting "reverence and respect for one day of the week, in order that reli-gious exercises should be performed without interruption."[12] The next year the Pennsylvania Supreme Court ruled against a Jewish merchant who had traded on Sunday. It cited the Bible as establishing the Christian Sabbath as a day in which "we should abstain from our usual labour the one-seventh part of our time, and devote the same to the worship of the Deity, and the exercise of our re-ligious duties." Yet the same decision also described profanation of Sunday prag-matically as "a crime injurious to society."[13] More than a generation later another Pennsylvania decision echoed that combination of reasons: the Christian Sunday "is an institution deeply seated in the religious affections of the community, and [it is] one of the foundations of public morals, and of our political fabric."[14]

James Kent, chief justice of the New York Supreme Court and author of the much-respected *Commentaries on American Law*, in 1811 penned the era's best-known balancing of the law's respect for religion as a spiritual force and its service for secular ends. His ruling affirmed the conviction of a man accused of blasphemy. The perpetrator had called Christ a bastard and his mother, Mary, a whore, but he also claimed that because New York had never passed an antiblasphemy law, he had committed no offense. With phrases straight out of *Blackstone*, Justice Kent simply dismissed his argument: "[C]hristianity was parcel of the law, and to cast contumelious reproaches upon it, tended to weaken the foundation of moral obligation, and the efficacy of oaths." Moreover, "[t]he people of this state, in common with the people of this country, profess the general doctrines of christianity, as the rule of their faith and practice; and to scandalize the author of these doctrines is not only, in a religious point of view, extremely impious, but, even in respect to the obligations due to society, is a gross violation of decency and good order."[15]

Thirteen years later a Pennsylvania court expanded on Kent's reasoning. Justice Thomas Duncan ruled that English precedents, Blackstone's *Commentaries*, and William Penn's early legislation for his colony made a dispositive case: "This is the Christianity of the common law, incorporated into the great law of *Pennsylvania* . . . it is irrefragably proved, that the laws and institutions of this state are built on the foundation of reverence for Christianity." Neither the Constitution nor legislation in the new states had altered "the common law doctrine of Christianity, as suited to the condition of the colony, and without which no free government can long exist." To this judge, rejecting Scripture as part of the common law led to a *reductio ad absurdum*: "The accused on his trial might argue that the book by which he was sworn, so far from being holy writ, was a pack of lies, containing as little truth as *Robinson Crusoe*. And is every jury in the box to decide as a fact whether the Scriptures are of divine origin?"[16]

In the nation's last successful judgments against blasphemy, a series of Massachusetts courts convicted and then reconvicted Abner Kneeland, "an intractable pugilist," in Steven Green's phrase, who edited a radical Boston newspaper.[17] Kneeland's well-publicized attacks on traditional Christianity, including the Bible, first landed him in court in 1833. Three years later Massachusetts's final judgment came from the chief justice of the state's supreme court, Lemuel Shaw, a conservative Unitarian (and later Herman Melville's father-in-law). Shaw cited Blackstone's definition of blasphemy while also reaffirming Blackstone's opinion about blasphemy as violating the common law. Justice Marcus Morton, not incidentally the only Jacksonian on the court, dissented strenuously. Morton claimed that disestablishment, which for Massachusetts took place in 1833, overturned the old world's judicial assumptions. Morton conceded that if blasphemers incited a public disturbance or caused direct personal harm, they could be prosecuted. But his removal of blasphemy itself from the common law, rather than Shaw's retention, anticipated later judicial rulings.

The early American rulings that took for granted the place of Christianity in the common law also invariably defended religious free exercise, so long as there was no blatant "impiety" or breach of the peace. Yet after this first legal generation, ambiguity surfaced, including in the pronouncements of Joseph Story, the most famous defender of the Christian basis of American jurisprudence. Story was a law professor at Harvard who for more than three decades (1812–45) served simultaneously as an associate justice of the U.S. Supreme Court. Like his friend Lemuel Shaw, he was a conservative Federalist Unitarian. In 1833 Story published *Commentaries on the Constitution*, the most influential treatise on its subject of the day. In 1827 Story ruled, but without elaborate commentary, that testimony from Universalists, who did not believe in a future state with punishments and rewards, could not be allowed since "the administration of an oath supposes, that a moral and religious accountability is felt to a Supreme Being, and is the sanction which the law requires upon the conscience of a person, before it admits him to testify."[18] His 1833 *Commentaries* seemed to double down on that ruling. While not questioning the right of religious private judgment or freedom of worship, he affirmed in strong terms the necessity of Christianity for American public life. His famous restatement of the custodial logic of republicanism deserves full quotation:

> The promulgation of the great doctrines of religion, the being, and attributes, and providence of one Almighty God; the responsibility to him for all our actions, founded upon moral freedom and accountability; a future state of rewards and punishments; the cultivation of all the personal, social, and benevolent virtues;—these never can be a matter of indifference in any well-ordered community. It is, indeed, difficult to conceive, how any civilized society can well exist without them. And at all events, it is impossible for those, who believe in the truth of Christianity, as a divine revelation, to doubt, that it is the especial duty of government to foster, and encourage it among all the citizens and subjects.[19]

A decade later, however, Story added a significant qualification. The case before the Supreme Court concerned a wealthy Philadelphian who had left his money to found an orphanage that would exclude religious teachers. The heirs recruited Senator Daniel Webster to contest the will. In his plea Webster cited many earlier rulings that had shown special respect for Christianity and the Bible. He framed his chief argument as a question: Could the court possibly allow something that "subverts all the excellence and the charms of social life, which tends to destroy the very foundation and frame-work of society . . . which subverts the whole decency, the whole morality, as well as the whole Christianity and government of society?"[20] Story agreed with Webster, but only up to a point. Yes, Christianity was "a part of the common law of the state," but legal actions taken on that basis must not be overly strict; so long as public order was preserved, neutrality toward religion, even non-Christian religion, must prevail.[21]

Story's caution in backing away from a rigorous application of Christian interpretation of the common law reflected a general movement of legal opinion. In 1849, a New York judge ruled that testators in court did not have to meet a religious test because "all religions are tolerated [in the United States], and none is established, each has an equal right to the protection of the law." The next year the same court ruled that religious questions were immaterial for legitimating bequests; judges could not make a judgment on what was or was not "true religion." In Steven Green's summary, the judges in these decisions "viewed the constitutional requirement of religious equality as subordinating the common-law practice that reinforced religious customs."[22]

Making Sense of Legal History

Three observations about this simplified legal history are pertinent. First, despite the definite move to limit and then remove Christianity (and Scripture) from formal jurisprudence, the removal was far from total. If legal challenges to laws enforcing a Christian Sunday began to succeed in the 1830s, many such laws long remained in force—as did the legal mandate to read the King James Bible in tax-supported public schools (the next chapter). In 1892 Associate Justice David Brewer delivered the Supreme Court's decision that exempted a New York church's call of an English pastor from labor laws restricting immigration. His lengthy opinion referenced the place of God and Scripture in several colonial charters, quoted from earlier key decisions affirming Christianity as part of the common law (*Ruggles*, 1811; *Updegraph*, 1824; *Vidal*, 1845), cited the state constitutions that still restricted public service to those who believed in a future state of rewards and punishments, and pointed to the many jurisdictions that continued to restrict Sunday activities. Brewer concluded that "these, and many other matters which might be noted, add a volume of unofficial declarations to the mass of organic utterances that this is a Christian nation."[23] Even as Brewer's opinion lost credibility, the Bible still remained in play. John Witte, for example, has shown that throughout the twentieth century in court findings concerning illegitimacy, references to Scripture that had once been considered part of the common law continued to appear (like Ex 34:7, "visiting the iniquity of the fathers upon the children, and the children's children").[24]

Complications continue to characterize recent history, as illustrated by two Supreme Court decisions issued on June 27, 2005. In *Van Orden v. Perry*, the Court ruled (5 to 4) that a monument to the Ten Commandments on the grounds of the Texas state capitol was permitted since it memorialized an aspect of the nation's history. By contrast, in *McCreary County v. American Civil Liberties Union of Kentucky*, the Court ruled (again 5 to 4) that display of the Ten Commandments in Kentucky courtrooms and schools was not legal since they had been put there with a religious purpose, that is, in order to "establish" a particular religion in violation of the First Amendment.[25] Considered as an active shaper of American law, Scripture has certainly receded from the 1830s onward, but just as obviously, effects from when the nation was a Bible civilization have never entirely vanished.

The second observation concerns the historical contingency of the belief that Scripture belonged in the common law. Especially after the repudiation of Tom Paine and the remarkable work of the Methodists, Scripture occupied a secure place in the national imagination—but neither an uncontested place nor a place immune from the flow of events. For the numerically booming and ideologically ascendant Protestants of the early republic, agreement on the value of Scripture did not mean agreement on how Scripture should influence the social order. Neither did a common deference to Scripture dictate a uniform response to national developments. In the following pages we observe strong sectarian versus proprietary disagreement over efforts to firm up the nation's voluntary Christendom, but then much greater Protestant unity on using Scripture to make public education serve the moral needs of the republic. Still later pages detail the new situation when believers in divine revelation who were *not* Protestants made up a growing part of the citizenry.

Third, legal history illustrates one of the long-term consequences from attempting to create a Bible civilization. In the Protestant imagination of those early years, little separated Scripture viewed as spiritual inspiration and considered as a social instrument. The modern notion that "religion" can be extracted from "society" or "culture" was only beginning to take hold. Gradually, however, while the spiritual function remained potent among the population, for legal and legislative purposes the two diverged. In these changes over time, Scripture remained alive, but jurists along with other public figures increasingly treated it as a utilitarian force useful primarily for serving general purposes. The more emphasis that was placed on Scripture's importance for service to the republic, the more difficulty for making a nonpartisan defense of its spiritual purposes. If the Bible became important primarily as supporting the ethics without which a republic failed, then the needs of the republic took precedence over other uses of Scripture. With partisanship in a free society inevitable when it came to guidelines for public life, the Bible easily became a casualty of partisan strife. In these terms, for those who valued Scripture for its spiritual purposes, secularization of the law would not be a tragedy. It could become an opportunity to rethink the relationship between spiritual and instrumental uses of the Bible.

A Christian Nation?

The nation's Protestant majority agreed wholeheartedly that Scripture taught believers how to live. On the question of *how* Bible-directed personal life should guide the national community, however, anything but agreement prevailed.[26] The growing number of Black Christians knew that liberty in Christ had to mean liberty per se. White believers mostly ignored that African American imperative, in part because they were so busy disagreeing among themselves. As noted, soon after the formation of the American Bible Society, sectarian Protestants worried that aggressive voluntary societies hid a lust for dominion behind ostensibly spiritual goals.

Even more aggressive efforts at civilization-building generated even more strenuous reactions. If those efforts did not represent an "evangelical united front," it was still a front constructed mostly by evangelical Protestants.[27] From the late 1820s a noteworthy series of proposals aimed to square the circle by seeking formal recognition of informal Christendom. All the proposals came from proprietary Protestants (Congregationalists, Presbyterians, Episcopalians, Dutch Reformed), but not all from New England. The proposers expressed firm commitment to the ideal of religious free exercise, but understood such freedom to mean that no individual denomination should receive official government support. The proposals reflected the strong, but also inchoate, conviction that voluntary Protestant Christianity could flourish in a polity that had rejected formal Christendom.

When viewed in the context of their times, the bearing of these proposals on a history of the Bible is evident. They appeared as the number of non-Protestant immigrants was rising sharply (chapter 15), as the railroads and the penny press established the first elements of a national culture not inspired by overt religious purpose, as disputing over slavery sharpened dramatically (chapter 11), and especially as the political landscape divided into confrontation between Jacksonian Democrats and the National Republicans who would soon form the Whig Party. Behind each of the custodial proposals lay the conviction that faithful adherence to "the book of salvation" required public expression. But the proposals also reflected an awareness that the nation's rapidly changing social order required reenergized action if the "chosen nation" was to survive.

From one angle, partisanship in the Jacksonian era seemed only to reprise the earlier Federalist-Jeffersonian conflict. Once again, political loyalty and religious adherence intertwined. An alliance between proprietary Protestants and National Republicans/Whigs proposing national solutions to national problems was squaring off against an alliance of sectarian Protestants and Jacksonian Democrats who regarded national voluntarism as tyranny under another name.

But from another angle, the diversity of pressing national challenges scrambled simple religious-political categories. Sectarian versus proprietary division mostly prevailed in debate over forcing the federal government to observe Sunday as the Christian Sabbath, as also to some degree on enforcing blasphemy laws and proclaiming official days of prayer and fasting. (Custodial Protestants said yes, Baptists and other sectarians said no.) But a coalition of sectarian Baptists and proprietary Protestants mounted the only significant protest condemning the expulsion of the Cherokee and other native tribes from Georgia and the Southeast. Heightened conflict over slavery also created a strong division within northern proprietary Protestants—some leading the abolitionist charge, others resisting stoutly, more caught in a muddling middle. The same conflict united almost all southern white evangelicals, proprietary and sectarian, against northern Protestants. Meanwhile, Protestants of almost all persuasions, including nonevangelical Unitarians, agreed on the need for Scripture to anchor the curriculum of the common school systems taking shape in many states.

In a word, even as recourse to the Bible may actually have increased during the 1830s, agreement on the public use of Scripture declined. How the Scriptures should be put to use in shaping what kind of Christian nation with which partners who were not evangelicals remained an open question.[28]

In 1828 a Presbyterian minister from Philadelphia, who happened to be a supporter of Andrew Jackson, generated nationwide attention by publicizing an idea he had been developing for many years.[29] As a conservative Calvinist, Ezra Stiles Ely worried about theological innovations promoted by Congregationalists and his fellow Presbyterians. As a dedicated patriot, he worried even more about the nation's fate if conscientious believers did not attend to the body politic. As early as 1818 Ely had published an essay bemoaning the absence of explicit Christianity in national affairs: "The religion of the Redeemer is the only steadfast basis of that morality on which republics are built."[30] But that essay fell stillborn from the press. Not so his sermon from the Fourth of July, 1827, which was reprinted in many outlets of what had become the nation's juggernaut of evangelical print, a juggernaut Ely enthusiastically supported as consumer and extended as editor. His text was Psalm 2:10–12, an admonition directed at Israel's rulers: "Be wise now therefore, O ye kings: be instructed, ye judges of the earth. Serve the Lord with fear, and rejoice with trembling." To America's "Christian freemen," Ely announced that "God . . . requires a Christian faith, a Christian profession, and a Christian practice of all our public men; and we as Christian citizens ought . . . to require the same." Acting on that truism, Ely proposed "a new sort of union, or, if you please, *a Christian party in politics.*" While realizing that the Protestant denominations differed among themselves, he hoped they could stand united against "any person whom they know or believe to sustain, at the time of his proposed election, a bad moral character." He even hoped that "thousands of moralists" who were not themselves professing Christians "might unite and cooperate with *our Christian party.*" In later printings of his relatively short sermon, Ely added a lengthy appendix seeking to "vindicate the liberty of Christians, and . . . the American Sunday School Union." Ely, himself an active supporter of several voluntary societies, addressed this addendum to the Pennsylvania legislators who, citing his sermon as a threat, had refused to incorporate the Union for fear of abetting his proposed Christian political party.[31]

The year after Ely preached his sermon, and while it was being reprinted throughout the country, Lyman Beecher published a discourse in the widely circulated *National Preacher* to spotlight one of Ely's proposals. According to Beecher, with his well-worn gift for emphatic utterance, "perhaps the most important [issue] that ever was, or ever could be, submitted for national consideration" was "the pre-eminent importance of the Christian Sabbath."[32] Beecher thus helped reopen a long-standing skirmish in the nation's culture wars. From time out of mind, English, Scottish, and then American Protestants had understood Sunday, the first day of the week on which Jesus rose from the dead, to represent a Christian fulfillment of the Jewish Sabbath (the seventh day) as spelled out in the fourth of the Ten Commandments: "Remember the Sabbath day, to keep it holy. Six days shalt thou labour, and do all thy work: But the seventh day is the Sabbath of the Lord thy God: in it thou shalt not do any work. . . . For in six days the Lord made heaven and earth, the sea, and all that in them is, and rested the seventh day: wherefore the Lord blessed the Sabbath day, and hallowed it [Ex 20:8–11]."[33]

Twenty years earlier the issue had been raised when two events occurred almost simultaneously.[34] In 1809 the Presbyterians expelled one of their members who as a postmaster had followed custom by opening his office on Sunday; in 1810 Congress legalized the custom by stipulating that the mail should be transported continuously, including Sunday, and that post offices should be open at least one hour on that day. Several years of agitation followed, with at least one hundred petitions from many religious bodies, including Unitarians, demanding repeal of the law. Its defenders ultimately prevailed with the argument that timely communication via the post was a necessity during wartime (1812–15) and then in order to ensure up-to-date intelligence for commercial purposes.

After lying dormant for a decade, the issue sprang back to life. During the intervening years the national voluntary societies and the burgeoning evangelical press had expanded like wildfire; completion of the Erie and other canals had increased the importance of timely economic information; and antagonism between National Republicans (John Quincy Adams) and Democrats (Andrew Jackson) was stimulating a new era of popular political participation. In May 1828 Beecher and Josiah Bissell Jr., an evangelical merchant who had helped found Rochester, New York, created the General Union for the Promotion of the Christian Sabbath.[35] Beecher circulated tracts; Bissell, who had already seen that a Bible was placed in every Rochester home, created a Six-Day stage coach business (that soon failed); and hundreds of petitions inundated the Congress (over nine hundred for repeal, more than two hundred to uphold the law).

On May 8, 1830, Senator Theodore Frelinghuysen of New Jersey addressed the nation's Upper House with a forceful speech demanding repeal of the 1810 law. Frelinghuysen, who began his legal career with Richard Stockton, a signer of the Declaration of Independence, had become an active Federalist when in 1829 he was sent to the Senate by a coalition of anti-Jacksonian interests. As an ecumenically minded Presbyterian, he was known as the "Christian Statesman" for his leadership in many agencies of the Evangelical United Front (Bible, foreign missions, tracts, Sunday school, colonization, temperance).[36] Frelinghuysen's 1830 address defended a Senate resolution that combined respect for scriptural authority with a classical republican view of national well-being:

> The Sabbath is justly regarded as a divine institution, closely connected with individual and national prosperity ... although the Congress ... from the peculiar and limited constitution of the General Government, cannot by law enforce its observance—yet ... they should not, by positive legislation, encroach upon the sacredness of this day, or weaken its authority in the estimation of the people—
> Therefore, it is
> *Resolved* That the committee on the Post Office and Post Roads be instructed to report a bill, repealing so much of the act on the regulation of post offices as requires the delivery of letters, packets, and papers on the Sabbath: and further, to prohibit the transportation of the mail on that day.

At considerable length Frelinghuysen stressed the necessity of heeding "the divine authority," "the commands of God," and God's "infinite benevolence." He argued from history that the colonies, the states, and the federal government had all suspended business on Sunday. He cited George Washington's memorable farewell address that called religion and morality "the only sure foundations of political prosperity." While denying any intent to "tyrannize over the consciences and rights of men," he also insisted that "a free people can preserve their liberties through moral influence alone; and that to cherish these, a Sabbath is vitally indispensable."[37]

In the event, Beecher, Bissell, Frelinghuysen, and the many petitioners who joined them failed in their objective. Sunday closing of post offices, though not restricting mail transport on Sunday, would come only later, after the telegraph had made mail delivery too slow for business. Some religious bodies rejoiced when the closure finally took place, but it occurred mostly for pragmatic reasons.

It is important for understanding the moral complexity of the times that Frelinghuysen also failed in another reform effort undertaken at the same time. In an even longer Senate speech delivered only one month before he addressed the question of Sabbath mails, Frelinghuysen orated for six hours on behalf of the Cherokee and other Natives whom the Jackson administration wanted to transport from the American Southeast to the Trans-Mississippi wilderness. This speech concentrated on the plethora of treaties, national legislation, and state laws that were being violated as the president enforced what became the Cherokee Trail of Tears. But it also invoked the providence by which "God . . . planted these tribes in the Western continent . . . before Great Britain herself had a political existence." It explained why "natural law" supported the Indians' cause, especially in the United States, where no room existed for "the tyrant's plea of expediency." He added a call upon "Heaven" to witness the nation's "sins." Frelinghuysen also explained in detail how the Cherokee had adopted Christian civilization, including "a regular constitution of civil government, republican in its principles," judicious laws, a printing press and newspaper published in English and Cherokee, flourishing schools, and "Christian temples, to the God of the Bible."[38]

The published version of Frelinghuysen's address appended several documents from firsthand witnesses in Georgia, most of them Baptist ministers, who echoed Frelinghuysen in detailing the degree to which Indians had embraced an American way of life. One of the reports explained the "very happy effects" from "the preaching of the gospel" visible among the Choctaw, who were also targeted for forced removal. This Baptist's support for the Presbyterian's speech emphasized the ideal results coming from that preaching: "The light which the Gospel has diffused, and the moral principles it has imparted to adult Choctaws, have laid a foundation for stability and permanency in their improvements."[39] But, again, Frelinghuysen's plea did not succeed—despite the extravagant praise it won from William Lloyd Garrison:

> Yet, Frelinghuysen! gratitude is due thee . . .
>   Stand boldly up, meek soldier of the Cross!
> For thee ten thousand pray'rs are heav'nward flying;
>   Thy soul is purged from earthly rust and dross:
> Patriot and Christian! ardent, self-denying—
>   How could we bear, resignedly, thy loss.[40]

Two years after Frelinghuysen's memorable orations, as cholera ravaged cities on the east coast in June 1832, the New York Synod of the Dutch Reformed

Church composed a formal appeal asking civil governments to proclaim "a day of fasting, humiliation, and prayer."[41] A Dutch Reformed supporter of Andrew Jackson forwarded this appeal to the president, but Jackson turned it down. With considerable righteous indignation, several state governments and many localities proceeded on their own to hold such days. In Congress, Senator Henry Clay of Kentucky, who admitted to his colleagues that he was not religiously observant, nonetheless introduced a resolution supporting the Synod's request. To show that he was trying to do more than simply embarrass the president and promote his own political aspirations, Clay asked Senator Frelinghuysen to offer a seconding speech in favor of the resolution. Another well-developed argument on the legal justification and moral benefits of a national prayer day followed. But this effort also failed.

The next year Jasper Adams, a respected Episcopal clergyman in Charleston, South Carolina, distributed to many high governmental officials copies of a sermon he had delivered before a local synodical convention. The discourse returned to the themes of Ezra Stiles Ely's sermon by addressing "the relation of Christianity to civil government in the United States." One of its three texts was Proverbs 14:34, "Righteousness exalteth a nation, but sin is a reproach to any people." While not as specific as Ely's scheme for a Christian party, the message was the same. Against a European union of church and state as well as against the secularization of society as witnessed during the French Revolution, Adams commended what he called "the middle course" chosen by the founding generation. The United States certainly protected "the free exercise of religion." In addition, because the founders "rightly considered their religion as the highest of all interests," they "refused to render it [in] any way or in any degree, subject to governmental interference or regulations." Adams's sermon considered ancient Hebrew history, Christianity during the time of the early church, and American history in colonial and Revolutionary times; it detailed the preference recorded for Christianity explicitly in state constitutions and implicitly in the Constitution; and it explained at great length the necessity of Christian morality for the health of the republic. In Adams's view, the nation had taken the "only course in fact warranted by Scripture, by experience and by primitive usage." The result? "Christianity is the established religion of the nation, its institutions and usages are sustained by legal sanctions, and many of them are incorporated with the fundamental law of the country." Despite receiving positive responses from Supreme Court justices John Marshall and Joseph Story, Adams's effort to formalize the nation's dependence on Christianity succeeded no more than had Frelinghuysen's appeals for the causes he championed.[42]

Ely, Adams, Frelinghuysen, their proprietary allies defending the Sabbath, the Dutch Reformed Synod, and Frelinghuysen's Baptist friends in Georgia were demanding that the nation define its heritage as republican, moral, honorable, and

Christian. Their efforts failed, not as Jack and Jill tumbling down the hill, but as Sisyphus who, despite never reaching the summit, kept on trying. (Beginning in 1845, several Protestant bodies proposed constitutional amendments that would acknowledge, as one of the proposals put it, "the Lord Jesus Christ as the governor among the Nations, and His revealed will as of supreme authority."[43] Their strongest support came from Reformed Presbyterians who, like Alexander McLeod in his attack on slavery, retained a positive memory of Scotland's established Kirk.)

Custodial Protestants saw their efforts as rising organically from the nation's earlier history and as beautifully meeting the need to promote republican virtue. Other Americans, many of them also serious Bible believers, disagreed.

Pushing Back

Except for multipartisan support for the Bible in common schools, a sectarian-proprietary stand-off prevailed on almost all other questions of national policy. The sectarian nay to the proprietary yea revived the Real Whig fears of the Revolutionary era, when every action of British authority was read as despotism just around the corner.[44] The rebuttal strengthened Baptist-style commitment to the separation of church and state. And it matched proprietary panic about the threat of moral disorder with sectarian panic about the threat of ecclesiastical tyranny. To be sure, true secularists did drive some of the opposition to the proprietary proposals. They included Thomas Cooper at the University of South Carolina, who seasoned his agnosticism with proslavery militancy; the convicted blasphemer Abner Kneeland; and Frances Wright and Robert Dale Owen, whom Christopher Grasso describes as "vocal free-thinkers."[45] But these voices were exceptions.

A more typical and much more politically influential opponent was Gen. Richard M. Johnson, a Kentuckian who had won renown during the War of 1812 for delivering the blow that killed Tecumseh at the Battle of the Thames.[46] In 1829 and 1830 Johnson authored reports for the Senate Committee on the Post Office and Post Roads that effectively killed the Save-Sunday resolution Senator Frelinghuysen supported so passionately. Johnson, a practicing Baptist, was assisted in writing at least one of these documents by Obadiah Barnes, pastor of Washington's First Baptist Church.[47] The 1829 report excoriated "the deep laid plans of Priestcraft" that inspired the Sabbatarian petitions. It explained that when governments tried to settle religious questions, the inevitable result was "religious persecutions." It recycled the classical republican fear of faction ("religious combinations, to effect a political object, are . . . always dangerous"). It also explained at considerable length why the postal question should be "regarded simply as a question of expediency, irrespective of its religious bearing."[48]

Yet Johnson also took pains to demonstrate his religious bona fides. A generation earlier James Madison had catalogued theological disagreements among Protestant bodies as a prime reason for keeping Virginia clear of anything like an established religion. Johnson did the same by pointing out that a small number of Protestants actually honored Saturday as their holy day; many more who honored Sunday had no wish to "coerce others to act upon [that] persuasion"; while still others (Frelinghuysen and the petitioners) thought the United States should imitate the Jewish "theocracy." Johnson hoped that when they came to their senses, no American would "willingly introduce a system of religious coercion into our civil institutions." He closed by commending "the professors of Christianity" who pursued their work through "deeds of benevolence—by Christian meekness"—in short, by pursuing the "moral influence" that would do "infinitely more to advance the true interests of religion, than any measures which they may call on Congress to enact."[49]

When Jackson rejected the Dutch Reformed call for a national fast day, he used even gentler language and expressed even more commitment to overriding Christian goals. The president agreed "with the Synod in the efficacy of prayer" and hoped with it "that the judgments now abroad in the earth may be sanctified to the nations." But he came down where Senator Johnson came down by concluding he could not decree a national fast day. His reasoning stressed "the limits prescribed by the constitution for the President" and his desire not "to disturb the security which religion now enjoys in this country, in its complete separation from the political concerns of the general government." Jackson added, however, that if state and local governments wished to recommend fast days, that would be the ideal way for citizens to "attest their reliance on the protecting arm of the Almighty, in times of great distress."[50]

Partisan Jacksonians were not so considerate. After Henry Clay asked the Senate to pass a resolution overriding the president's rejection of a fast day, the Jacksonian *Advertiser* of Louisville blasted away at "PRIEST CLAY" while charging that initiatives like Sabbath protection "remain for the people of the Old World, who are regarded as born with saddles on their backs for Priests and *pious Statesmen* to ride." The Louisville paper also gleefully enlisted the Scriptures to reject the scriptural appeal for Sunday protection: if the petitioners want to pray, "let it be made as the Saviour commanded, 'in secret—in the closet'—not upon the streets as the hypocrites were used to do [Matt 6:5–6]."[51]

What Did It Mean?

The proposals by custodial Protestants to recognize the United States as a Christian nation occurred just as fresh national controversy broke out over the morality of slavery (chapter 11). As much as that controversy affected the history of the Bible with its dueling interpretations of Scripture, so too did the proprietary-sectarian divide influence how the Bible would function in public life. Most obviously, mobilization to defend the Cherokee, decree a national day of prayer, and protect the Sabbath anticipated how a growing number of northern Protestants would mobilize against slavery. As revival campaigns had provided models of public assembly and apocalyptic speech for political parties to imitate at their national conventions, so did the Sabbath appeal prepare the way for immediate abolition. The hundreds of petitions defending the Sabbath in 1829–30 became, after a brief lull, the thousands of antislavery petitions that in 1836 moved southern congressional leaders to "gag," or automatically table, petitions demanding the immediate end of slavery. The desire to protect a biblical understanding of the Lord's Day showed others how to protest against a biblically defined abuse of human rights. Harnessing the power of law to protect the Sabbath came in a package with harnessing the power of law to attack slavery.

By the mid-1830s, however, the Bible's teaching concerning human rights was also contested, and contested in a divided political landscape. The political commitments of Ezra Stiles Ely track the transformations. In the election of 1828 Ely opposed John Quincy Adams, suspect in his eyes as a Unitarian, and supported Jackson, who, as Richard John observes, "was a Presbyterian [like Ely] and regular church goer who, despite his turbulent past, was widely assumed to be a deeply religious man."[52] By the middle of Jackson's second term Ely had at first reluctantly, but then zealously, transferred his allegiance from Jackson to Henry Clay and the emerging Whig Party. That new party attracted many constituencies, but chief among them were the coalitions that had formed around opposition to Cherokee removal, protection of the Sabbath, and desire for national prayer.[53] Yet those reforming actions, so clearly identified with the aspirations of proprietary Protestants, also created significant antireform reactions, just as clearly identified with the fears of sectarian Protestants.

Action and reaction in the sphere of reform translated easily onto the plane of partisan politics.[54] In so doing, those forces intensified the division taking shape between anti- and proslavery interests. With increasing clarity beginning in the mid-1830s, these entangled religious-political commitments defined the national picture. Emblematic were the later careers of Richard Johnson and Frelinghuysen. Johnson, the sectarian St. George who slew the dragon of sabbatarian tyranny, became the Democrats' vice president under Martin Van Buren (1837–41). Frelinghuysen, Garrison's "meek soldier of the cross," in 1844 became the Whigs' candidate for vice president when their presidential aspirant, Clay, wanted to advertise his bona fides with moral nationalists. In Adam Jortner's apt phrase, "political exigencies" had bred "ideological proximities"[55] (chapter 15).

An earlier generation of ethnocultural political historians carefully specified the results going forward.[56] The most reliable Whigs, and eventually Republicans, were northern custodial Protestants, whose number also included the strongest antislavery activists (Congregationalists, Unitarians, many northern Presbyterians, northern Methodists, northern Episcopalians). In sharpest contrast, the most reliable Democrats were southern sectarian Protestants, almost all of whom tolerated or defended slavery (southern Baptists, southern Methodists). Tending toward the middle were groups whose regional (slavery) commitments clashed with their sectarian-proprietary loyalties. Constituencies that leaned Whig included some northern Baptists, Campbellites in the Lower North and Upper South, and some conservative northern Presbyterians who rejected abolition. Constituencies that leaned to the Democrats included southern Presbyterians, southern Episcopalians, and Campbellites in the Deep South. A simplified chart—omitting Catholics (mostly Democrats), northern African Americans eligible to vote (mostly Whigs and then Republicans), Campbellites (divided between deep South and mid-America), and Protestants who retained European identifies (often divided internally or arrayed in opposition to regionally hegemonic Protestant bodies)—captures the most important Protestant loyalties (Table 13.1).

For the history of Scripture, the reform efforts of proprietary Protestants, sectarian reactions to those initiatives, divisions over slavery, and coalitions of the Second Party System proved decisive. Religious supporters of the competing political parties by no means abandoned their devotion to the Bible. That devotion, however, now was framed, as Richard John notes, in "organized competition

Table 13.1 Partisan Denominational Affinities, 1830 and Following

Strong Whig/ Republican	Moderate Whig/ Republican	Moderate Democrat	Strong Democrat
Custodial + northern	*Sectarian + northern*	*Custodial + southern*	*Sectarian + southern*
Unitarians	Northern Baptists	Southern Presbyterians	Southern Baptists
Congregationalists	Some northern Presbyterians	Southern Episcopalians	Southern Methodists
Most northern Presbyterians			
Northern Methodists			
Northern Episcopalians			

between the Democrats and Whigs" that completed the transformation of "the gentry-based political order of the Founding Fathers into the mass-based political order that has endured to this day."[57] In such a climate, it became inevitable that political loyalty would drive biblical interpretation and biblical loyalties increasingly to serve partisan political purposes. The rejection of northern custodial efforts to nationalize their understanding of responsible biblical citizenship by no means removed the Bible from public life. Daniel Dreisbach has summarized what Jasper Adams hoped to accomplish by spelling out "the relation of Christianity to civil government": he wanted to defend a "prudential and constitutional role of religion" at a time of "uncertainty and transition for American church-state relations."[58] Instead, the uncertainty and the transitions made prudence controversial and shook the constitutional order.

And yet. Even as the Second Party System drove Bible believers apart, the creation of American common schools, which occurred as partisanship soared, brought them together.

14

The Common School Exception

Mythology simplifies the past; actually occurring historical developments are different. On the Bible and education in the early United States, the subject's premier scholar, Steven Green, has concluded that "the story of the rise of American public schooling is complex."[1] That is an understatement.

Myths that cloud this subject abound. One holds that there exists a fixed meaning in American history or American law concerning "the separation of church and state." Another views public education as the greatest triumph of the American democratic experiment. In a more innocent age, before the cultural self-criticisms of the past half-century, a distinguished historian could define this triumph as "a school where children of all classes, faiths, temperaments, etc., mingled freely together," where such schooling neutralized "the odious distinctions of a rigidly hierarchical society" and "embrace[d] the young of the whole community in one great democratic effort."[2] A myth with considerable contemporary currency debunks triumphalism and views the promotion of common schooling as a power-engrossing plot: "The rationale for the moral establishment was internally inconsistent, claiming to support religious liberty while in fact promoting religious control."[3] Yet one more myth from still another interpretive universe postulates that an earlier America, where Protestant assumptions prevailed and Scripture was widely regarded as the keystone of public education, marked an era of singular national godliness from which the United States has grievously fallen. A variation of the latter myth holds that "Christian America" was good for Christianity.

These myths distort rather than imagine reality. Each of them incorporates an incomplete understanding of what actually took place. An effort to acknowledge their insights, while explaining fuller complexities, is appropriate for this last chapter on the nation's early Bible civilization. As with the larger story, the narrative of public education, or "common schooling" as it was then known, can be characterized in different ways: as justifiable concern for the nation's future, creative public service, dedicated Christian altruism, unprecedented expansion of democracy, callous institutional coercion, xenophobic prejudice, tangled jurisdictional conflicts, deference to a supposedly repudiated old world, shifting legal interpretations, and (not least) unintended consequences.

For the place of public education in a history of the Bible, contexts are again supremely important, as suggested by the following questions.[4]

America's Book. Mark A. Noll, Oxford University Press. © Oxford University Press 2022.
DOI: 10.1093/oso/9780197623466.003.0015

Why did tax-funded public education become the nation's chief vehicle for "the essential tasks of installing patriotism, developing civic responsibility, assimilating newcomers into the majority culture, providing occupational training, and producing the educated citizenry that is essential to a democratic society"?[5]

But also a prior question: Where did the idea of *national* moral instruction come from?

Why were Americans so impressed with innovative European plans for educating mass populations?

Finally, why did the Bible remain so central for leaders of national educational reform in the 1830s and 1840s when it was fading as an active part of the common law, when national legislators refused to formalize a Bible-based post-Christendom Protestant regime, and when contentions intensified over "plain readings" of Scripture concerning slavery and race?

A New Jersey judicial ruling from 1950 illustrates the enduring complexities. In that year the state's supreme court reaffirmed the legality of daily Bible readings in its public schools. The plaintiffs were a parent and a taxpayer who cited the First Amendment prohibition against an "establishment of religion" to challenge a New Jersey law from 1916, revised from an early 1867 provision. It stipulated the following:

At least five verses taken from that portion of the Holy Bible known as the Old Testament shall be read, or caused to be read, without comment, in each public school classroom, in the presence of the pupils therein assembled. . . . No religious service or exercise, except the reading of the Bible and the repeating of the Lord's Prayer, shall be held in any school receiving any portion of the moneys appropriated for the support of public schools.

The court's ruling expatiated at length on state and federal precedents recognizing God and the legality of military chaplains. It also cited David Brewer's statement in the U.S. Supreme Court's *Holy Trinity* ruling of 1892 that "this is a Christian nation."[6] While acknowledging that many judicatories had ended the practice, it identified the twelve states (and District of Columbia) that in 1950 "prescribe the reading of the Bible in public school classes," along with the five others that "make its use permissive." The court's unanimous (7–0) ruling upholding the law noted that the challenged school system allowed students to be excused from the Bible readings if they so requested. It also conceded the necessity of "a separation between church and state." Yet the court forthrightly defended the New Jersey statute because of its intent that "at the beginning of the day the children should pause to hear a few words from the wisdom of the ages and to bow the head in humility before the Supreme Power. No rites, no ceremony, no doctrinal teaching; just a brief moment with eternity."[7]

For early U.S. history, the pertinence of the New Jersey ruling lay in two crucial assertions. The court first clarified its understanding of the text in question: "We consider that the Old Testament, because of its antiquity, its content, and its wide acceptance, is not a sectarian book when read without comment." Then, writing in the context of the Cold War, the jurists defined the current threat to American religious and civic freedom from "organized atheistic society . . . a totalitarian power." Against such a threat they specified the purpose of the state law: "The American people are and always have been theistic. . . . The influence which that force contributed to our origins and the direction which it has given to our progress are beyond calculation. It may be of the highest importance to the nation that the people remain theistic, not that one or another sect or denomination may survive, but that belief in God shall abide."[8] A nonsectarian Bible in service to the nation's "origins, direction, and progress" was the key. Two years later the U.S. Supreme Court refused to consider an appeal of this New Jersey ruling.[9]

Early Days

The trail that led to the New Jersey court judgment in 1950 began even before there was a U.S. Constitution. A forthright early statement of the vision at work came in 1786 as a double-barreled essay addressed to the Pennsylvania state legislature from Benjamin Rush, a signer of the Declaration of Independence, a friend of Tom Paine, Thomas Jefferson, and John Adams, and the new nation's most respected physician. Like Jefferson, who in 1778 outlined a tiered, comprehensive educational program for Virginia, Rush detailed "a plan for the establishment of public schools" in Pennsylvania. But unlike Jefferson, Rush also championed regular Bible reading in his tract as he spelled out "the mode of education, proper in a republic."[10]

Rush began by listing the "advantages of education upon mankind": "it is friendly to religion," but also "it is favourable to liberty." He quickly explained how a system of primary schools set up in every community or rural district would prepare some students for county-level academies, some of those for regional colleges, and some of those for a comprehensive state university. The plan, he was sure, would promote "virtue and knowledge in the state."[11]

Then—at twice the length—Rush expanded on intimate connections among public education, the Christian faith, a healthy society, and the Bible. At stake was nothing less than the new republic's survival:

The only foundation for a useful education in a republic is to be laid in RELIGION. Without this, there can be no virtue, and without virtue there can be no liberty, and liberty is the object and life of all republican governments.... [T]he religion I mean to recommend in this place, is the religion of JESUS CHRIST.... My only business is to declare, that all its doctrines and precepts are calculated to promote the happiness of society, and the safety and well being of civil government. A Christian cannot fail of being a republican.

Rush knew that Christianity underlay true republicanism because "every precept of the Gospel inculcates those degrees of humility, self-denial, and brotherly kindness, which are directly opposed to the pride of monarchy and the pageantry of a court."[12]

In just as much detail, Rush specified why the Christian Scriptures deserved pride of place in schools. Except for two details, he articulated an entirely conventional truism for his age as well as a proposition that many embraced long after it became controversial: "[T]here is no book of its size in the whole world, that contains half so much useful knowledge for the government of states, or the direction of the affairs of individuals as the bible." One of the unusual details concerned his objection to the Bible's "division into chapters and verses . . . which render it a more difficult book to read *well.*" (This objection identified an underappreciated but influential feature of standard Bible printing.) The other was Rush's criticism of "that fashionable liberality which refuses to associate with any one sect of Christians"; he wanted teachers to "inculcate upon [students] a strict conformity to that mode of worship which is most agreeable to their consciences, or the inclinations of their parents"—though of course chosen without coercion.[13]

Rush's objection to a nondenominational, nonsectarian Bible did not, however, last long. Five years later, in a letter published as "A Defence of the Bible as a School Book," he praised the Sunday schools that had recently been established in London and Philadelphia where Scripture was the only textbook. In them he especially appreciated that the Bible's use was *not* tied to the particular tenets of any one denomination. The sectarianism that cursed churches and nations came, in his words, from factions "being more interested in catechisms, creeds, and confessions of faith, than in the scriptures."[14] With this adjustment, the theoretical importance of a nonsectarian Bible for the health of the republic, via education, was in place. In place also was a persisting ambiguity about the nature of Scripture: Was it a book of Christian salvation? A guide to republican morality? A spur for democracy? Or all wrapped together as one?

Implementation of Rush's plan was not long in coming. Quakers, in a telling repetition of colonial history, pioneered in putting educational theory into practice for those least capable of helping themselves. As earlier Quakers like Benjamin Lay, John Woolman, and Anthony Benezet had marshaled specifically Christian and broadly humanistic reasons to attack African slavery, so in the early nineteenth century Quakers became early advocates of education for poor children, specifically in New York City.[15] Thomas Eddy, whose wealth came from imports, banking, and insurance, led the way. In 1805 Eddy, who later pioneered prison reform, helped found the American Bible Society, and opposed Elias Hicks's anti-evangelical Quaker reforms, was the key figure in founding the Society for Establishing a Free School. Motivation for Eddy and his conservative Quaker associates included sympathy for the growing population of impoverished New Yorkers, concern about such populations undermining social order, and a desire to advance Christianity. Against the advice of fellow Quakers, Eddy insisted that the Free School Society operate on an interdenominational basis; six of its original thirteen trustees were Quakers, but joined by Episcopalians, Presbyterians, a Baptist, and New York City's mayor DeWitt Clinton. In a fateful move for the history of American public education, Eddy and his associates chose the monitorial program of Joseph Lancaster as the vehicle to educate the youth of New York's indigent population.[16]

Lancaster, who in 1798 started a free primary school for poor children in his native London, had already won considerable renown across the English-speaking world as an educational reformer. His innovative teaching strategy enlisted older children who, under the direction of an adult teacher, monitored the younger students. In England, Lancaster schools became immediately successful, with an ever increasing number reaching a burgeoning population of urban children. They were also controversial because of opposition from the Church of England that claimed responsibility for the nation's primary education, despite not doing terribly well at reaching children of the urban lower classes. Anglican establishmentarians worried especially about the potential for Lancasterian schools to foment democratic disruption; they also objected to the nonsectarian principles guiding monitorial religious instruction.[17]

Lancaster emphasized that his schools would inculcate "a reverence for the sacred name of God and the Scriptures of Truth," though without "the propagation of the peculiar tenets of any sect." Daily Bible readings took place in all of his schools; he also encouraged students to attend the church of their own choosing on Sundays.[18] The educational efforts of William Allen, an evangelical-leaning, antislavery Quaker and active Lancasterian, exemplified the deep commitment of these British reformers to Scripture. Allen would later team with the secular-minded Robert Owen to organize free schooling at Owen's New Lanark, a model mill town in Scotland. But very much against Owen's wishes, Allen refused his sponsorship until Owen agreed to daily Scripture readings and regular lectures explaining to workers why revealed religion was essential for their well-being.[19]

Meanwhile in New York City, Eddy enthusiastically promoted Lancaster's scheme, in part because of the democratic potential that its Anglican opponents feared. The Free Society, which opened its first schools in 1806, aimed particularly at children not enrolled in fee-paying institutions run by the city's churches. Advertising for the new venture stressed its intention to strengthen "habits of religion and morality." The charter secured by the trustees from the state legislature spelled out their goal to teach "the principles of religion and morality." All early publicity also stressed that the school would not teach the particular doctrines of any one Protestant church.[20]

The Free School Society enjoyed immediate success in attracting a growing number of students. From the start, the monitors directed twice-daily Bible readings. On Tuesday afternoons the schools provided more specific doctrinal instruction, but taught by a volunteer corps of women who allowed children to choose the particular catechism they studied. Success was so rapid that the trustees were soon appealing for funds to construct larger learning centers, appeals to which leading citizens like the Dutch Reformed Henry Rutgers responded positively. In seeking even more funding, the trustees appealed to the New York legislature, which responded with a major construction grant and the promise of a yearly subsidy for ongoing expenses. Other tax money from the state and New York City followed. When in late 1809 Mayor Clinton spoke at the opening of a new building outfitted for five hundred students, he praised Lancaster for "carefully steering clear in his institution of any peculiar creed, and his confining himself to the general truths of Christianity."[21]

A decade and a half later, after expanding to reach still more students, the Free School Society changed its name to the Public School Society. That change in 1825 accompanied a legislative decision that the state would support only the Society's kind of nonsectarian schools, and not schools run by individual denominations. Tax-supported public education in New York would continue to be Christian, with a strongly Protestant flavor, but not sectarian.

The timing of Benjamin Rush's early tract and the more extensive efforts by the New York Quakers was significant. These and the many other early educational initiatives appeared during years of relative calm between Catholics and Protestants. Moreover, Bible reading in schools did not initially look like "the establishment of religion." Instead, the focus in the nineteenth century's early decades was the importance of education for the new country's future. Controversy over the War of 1812 had underscored the nation's fragility, in that case revealing a chasm between interests in New England and the frontier Southwest. More general anxieties grew from wondering how a thin and diverse population spread over an immense area could possibly function as a single nation.

Given those uncertainties, creative educational schemes that reached the masses with a promise of self-discipline, responsible citizenship, and republican morality perfectly met the needs of the hour. Educational prescriptions keyed to what a fragile new country required took shape against the background of a Revolution viewed as the gift of providence, during decades of rapid Christianization, and as Protestant voluntary societies created effective national organizations. Along with these national societies, it seemed that tax-supported schools could aid materially in securing the nation's future. Later would come intensified Catholic-Protestant strife over mandated use of the King James Bible, heightened sensitivity about the separation of church and state, conflict among Bible believers over slavery, and wider crises that imperiled national unity. But when these appeared, the channel directing the flow of American public education had already been deeply dug. From the start, educators stressed the need for schools to promote the moral training without which the American experiment was doomed. For a very long time, most also assumed that nothing was more important for that moral training than the Scriptures.

Guidance from Europe

If an ideal for education as both widely available and addressing national needs existed from the start, progress toward the ideal advanced by fits and starts. Before the 1830s a number of institutions looked (once again) to the old world for guidance in the new. That guidance resulted from exploratory trips by educators to Britain, France, and beyond; increasingly from the impressive example of Prussian educational reform; and then as key European publications were translated into English for American audiences. Invariably the Americans came away impressed with how thoroughly religious training was integrated into Europe's advanced educational systems. Usually they also came away with heightened dedication to Scripture. The American experiment that had rejected European Christendom in order to create a new moral order once more looked for guidance from Christendom.

Thomas Gallaudet's creation of the Connecticut Asylum for the Education of Deaf and Dumb Persons exemplified the early pattern. Gallaudet, an active evangelical reformer, followed his vision of "special education" by visiting schools for the deaf in England, Scotland, and France. In Scotland he was impressed by how that country's best-publicized school for deaf children taught the students "to know who God is, and who Christ is. . . . And [the master] teaches them to love Christ, because Christ died to save sinners."[22] But for the best method of teaching sign language, Gallaudet turned to a French institute organized by Catholics, as was most of that country's education after the end of the Napoleonic era. When he returned to America to set up his own school, he hired a young Catholic assistant trained in France. The school opened in April 1817 with a worship service climaxed by a sermon on Isaiah 35:4–5 ("The eyes of the blind shall be opened, and the ears of the deaf shall be unstopped"). As instruction got under way, Gallaudet warned his young assistant not to make any extrascriptural, Catholic additions to the school's regular course of instruction but to "mention only those facts which are recorded in the bible." The nonsectarian Bible at the Connecticut Asylum illustrated how easy it was in this period for Protestants and Catholics to cooperate in anchoring education in religion.[23]

The same pattern, with slight variations, prevailed among the innovative fee-paying schools of the era. The lengthy roster included the New England Institute for the Education of the Blind, founded by Harvard-educated Unitarians who had visited Greece and Germany; the Troy Female Seminary in Troy, New York, founded by Emma Willard, who was inspired by the contemporary Greek freedom struggle; the Round Hill School in Northampton, Massachusetts, established by Unitarians eager to imitate instruction in German *Gymnasia*; an evangelical academy in New Haven, Connecticut, founded by two sons of the late Yale president Timothy Dwight; and a school in Fredericktown, Maryland, established by Jonathan Edwards Woodbridge, who was likewise inspired by the *Gymnasium* model. Uniformly these ventures stressed their intention to train students in Christianity and morality, with nonsectarian reading from Scripture the center of that training.[24]

As it happened, these schools did not long survive, with the demise of the New Haven academy especially telling. After the Dwight brothers' ill health forced them to sell their enterprise, its new owners tried, with the support of evangelical philanthropists like Arthur Tappan, to transform it into a school for young African Americans. Yet heightened controversy surrounding race and slavery, which was beginning to intensify in those years, doomed that attempt, even in reform-friendly New Haven.[25]

For educational history, these initiatives in elite education anticipated the much more influential dissemination of Prussian educational ideals that in the 1830s shaped the dream of tax-supported education stretching far beyond the privileged. The wonderfully complicated story of a singularly influential European book illustrates how reliance on Scripture remained firmly in place as cutting-edge educators moved toward creation of the common school.

In 1833 Victor Cousin, a French savant already much respected in the United States for his version of ethically inflected commonsense moral philosophy, published a report lauding the Prussian educational system, the same that American travelers had admired. The Prussians, to be sure, were not trying to promote democracy—anything but. For them better education ensured the authority of aristocratic rulers and the principality's tax-supported Catholic and Lutheran churches. Yet Prussia had expanded educational opportunities significantly by establishing new normal schools for teachers of the primary grades and by moving toward universal state-sponsored primary education. Cousin was particularly impressed with how rapidly Prussian literacy rates had grown; when he visited Prussia, already three-fourths of the population was literate, more than double the French proportion.[26]

Cousin's 1833 *Rapport sur l'État de l'Instruction Publique dans Quelques Pays de l'Allemagne, et Particulièrement en Prusse* weighed in at over four hundred tightly printed pages. Its details included the Prussians' peaceful arrangement for religious education: Catholic officials taking charge in Catholic areas, Protestant officials in Protestant areas. This *Rapport* was soon translated into English by Sarah Austin, a British Unitarian who edited (slightly) and abridged (considerably) in order to emphasize her own commitment to reforms Parliament had recently enacted to expand the franchise and remove disabilities for Catholics. Her translation, in turn, was soon published in America by John Orville Taylor, a Philadelphia teacher who had attended Princeton Theological Seminary before choosing an educational career. It was, however, still a big book. Taylor therefore in 1836 brought out a forty-seven-page abridgement of Austin's translation that distilled the report for a wider audience of American educators who in many states had begun to campaign for state-funded common schools.

Taylor's abridged and edited version of Austin's abridged and edited translation featured Cousin's appeal for state-sponsored normal schools, even as it downplayed the original report's even-handed treatment of Catholics:

> Christianity ought to be the basis of the instruction of the people.... A religious and moral education is consequently the first want of a people.... Religious and moral instruction ... produces in man a consciousness of his own weakness and, as a consequence, humility.... A more definite direction is given to religious and moral instruction by the belief in the revealed word of God in the Holy Scriptures.[27]

Taylor then expanded upon Cousin-via-Austin in a lengthy footnote of his own:

> Unless Christianity, the truths of the Bible, are made the basis of all instruction, universal education will be of little benefit. The New Testament should be introduced in all our schools: not as an easy-lesson book, as the practice now is, that the younger children may *learn to read*, but as a book of morals and duties, and as containing a complete system of ethics.[28]

The campaign for professional, systematic, and tax-supported common schools had already begun before Taylor added Cousin to the already intense American interest in European reforms. That addition only strengthened the already firmly entrenched expectation that Scripture would provide "morals and duties, and ... a complete system of ethics."

Toward the American Common School

Common school reform took different shapes in different regions. Yet whether as an extension of earlier efforts (New York), a shift of means to continue inherited ends (Massachusetts), or the establishment of something entirely new (Ohio), American educators united in their struggle to create better primary schools reaching more young Americans. Across the nation, cascading transitions in the Age of Andrew Jackson heightened the urgency of their work. As in France, industrial expansion, first in textiles and then driven by the railroads, sparked a population shift out of rural areas that continues to this day. (The nation's urban population rose from less than 8% of the whole in 1820 to more than 12% in 1840.)[29] Increased immigration added new and (some concluded) dangerous elements to the nation's urban population. The combination of a franchise extended to almost all white men and excitement generated by hard-fought Democratic-Whig electoral contests drew more and more citizens into the political process. (From 1824 to 1840 recorded votes in presidential elections multiplied sevenfold, from 366,000 to 2,411,000.)[30] Visiting Europeans commented on what they viewed as an American mania for money, and they were not making anything up; Americans were in fact working ever harder, despite a serious recession in 1819 and the shuttering depression that followed two decades later.[31]

Conscientious leaders committed to social well-being at every social level and geographical region needed to provide an American solution for American challenges. Democratic ideals demanded outreach. Republican principles required moral responsibility. Economic self-interest needed order. Immigrant newcomers required training in citizenship. Political responsibility depended on the diffusion of knowledge. To the nation's overwhelmingly Protestant population, religion responded to each of those requirements. Common schools looked like the perfect solution, although as Johann Neem has noted, "[e]fforts to encourage civic solidarity through common schools posed a challenge in an increasingly diverse society."[32] To meet this and other challenges, common school advocates took heart from the Prussian example, pored over the Cousin *Report*, and followed well-established American habits of mind.

New York

After New York City's Free School Society became the Public School Society in 1825, it soon broadened its services by absorbing other institutions, like the Infant School Society and the Manumission Society (for African Americans). As there had been from the start, regular readings from the King James Version remained a given, though unencumbered by the teachings of any specific denomination. Catholic uneasiness about required deference to a Protestant bible in tax-supported schools grew in the 1830s as the city's immigrant population swelled. But when uneasiness took shape as a petition to the state legislature asking for an end to such readings, it met a firm rebuke.[33]

Daniel Barnard, a conservative Albany Whig, firm opponent of Jackson, and later U.S. ambassador to Prussia, answered the 1838 petition with a "Report on . . . the use of the Bible, in Schools."[34] To the New York legislators he reiterated the reasoning that underlay common school reform throughout the nation. A commonplace adjusted for the times began his report: "Public education is a thing very closely connected with the healthy existence of civil society," particularly "in the form which such society has assumed with us . . . the republican mode." Then followed the republican truism restated for an expanding democracy: "that popular intelligence and popular virtue are indispensable to the existence and continuance of such a government as ours" and then that it was "the duty of every individual to be virtuous, and to possess a competent degree of intelligence." Then, as night follows day, came the prescription:

> Moral instruction is quite as important to the object had in view in popular education, as intellectual instruction. . . . But to make such instruction effective, it should be given according to the best codes of morals known to the country and the age; and that code, it is universally conceded, is contained in the Bible. Hence the Bible, as containing that code, and for the sake of teaching and illustrating that code, so far from being arbitrarily excluded from our schools, ought to be in common use in them.[35]

As in New York, where the growing Catholic population in alliance with Jacksonian Democrats challenged Protestant and Whig dominance, so in other states the shifting balance of political and religious power lay behind decisive educational developments. In 1819 legislators in New Hampshire took advantage of the state's history of support for Dartmouth College to intervene in its internal affairs.[36] Here it was an intramural conflict among Calvinist Federalists, some of whom promoted evangelical revival and others who did not. In a famous argument, the young Daniel Webster persuaded the U.S. Supreme Court to let Dartmouth break away from state control to become a private institution responsible for its own financing. For higher education, the American future pointed toward separating the private and the public. The course of primary education ran in the opposite direction.

Massachusetts

The story of common school reform in Massachusetts is well known, though the political-religious shuffle lying behind that reform has received less attention.[37]

Until the final disestablishment of Massachusetts's churches in 1833, successive revisions of the state's 1780 constitution had maintained its assertion that the state's well-being "essentially depend upon piety, religion, and morality" as inculcated by tax-supported "public Protestant teachers of piety, religion, and morality."[38] In the half-century after 1780 the right of non-Congregationalists to collect tax assessments for their churches had steadily advanced. Yet even as Jeffersonian Republicans and then Democrats chipped away at the once hegemonic Congregational Federalists, the establishment principle prevailed, with its thorough mixture of religion, schooling, and theories about communal well-being. Methodists along with Baptists, Universalists, "Christians," and other sectarians did not necessarily approve of church establishment, but once they came to share in its bounty, they muted their protests. The decisive push against the system came about when the Congregationalists split. In 1820 the state's supreme court ruled that all of a town's taxpayers, not just its church members, could vote to name a town's Congregational minister. Soon thereafter numerous towns replaced Trinitarian ministers with advocates of the newer Unitarianism (from 1820 to 1834 about one hundred such moves). The court also ruled that when ousted Trinitarians set up their own churches, the ministers of these new separatist bodies were *not* eligible for proceeds of the tax assessment. In the wake of that decision, Trinitarian Congregationalists joined the non-Congregationalists and the state's Democrats in demanding an end to establishment, which voters in 1833 ratified overwhelmingly.

Abandoning church establishment did not, however, mean abandoning the proprietary commitment to state-sponsored moral training. After 1833 Congregationalists of both types, along with the other religious groups, shrugged off the loss of tax revenues because there was still so much they could do together—promoting temperance, for instance, but even more cooperating for education. Leading citizens, who in 1834 were appalled when rioters destroyed a Catholic convent near Boston in Charleston, turned ever more eagerly to school reform as a nonsectarian means to continue what establishment had hoped to achieve. In Massachusetts, proprietary instincts ran deep.

In 1837, four years after church disestablishment, Horace Mann was appointed secretary of a new Massachusetts State Board of Education. With full support from Governor Edward Everett, Mann embarked on his famous campaign for comprehensive common school reform. With unflagging persistence he argued for teacher preparation in state-supported institutions, a legislative mandate requiring universal primary schooling, moral training liberated from the taint of sectarian particulars, and common schools as the nursery of democracy. In 1838 a leader of the American Sunday School Union asked Mann to endorse publications the Union had prepared for public schools, especially libraries of the sort that Massachusetts was funding to aid common schooling. While Mann and the Union shared a commitment to nonsectarian moral instruction, he found the Union publications, in which the way of salvation was presented in sharply evangelical terms, far too doctrinaire. His plan for moral education entailed readings from the King James Bible, without comment, and nothing more.[39]

In setting this course, the Unitarian Mann was supported by an energetic Unitarian minister, Charles Brooks, who had returned from a European trip filled with enthusiasm for Prussian education, especially its emphasis on religion. As summarized by a newspaper report of a speech in 1837, Brooks implored, "[M]ake not your schools sectarian, but make them Christian. Put the Bible into them all; and let it there be read and studied."[40] Mann famously endorsed this plan rather than the alternative proposed by the Sunday School Union that would have provided doctrinal instruction along with Bible readings. Mann's re-nowned 1849 *Twelfth Report* as superintendent of the state school board defined his ideal as the Bible only. The *Report* argued "in favor of religious education for the young upon the most broad and general grounds." After repeatedly denying that he wanted to eliminate the Scriptures, specifying at length why he opposed "a rival system of 'Parochial' or 'Sectarian Schools,'" and insisting that schools must not "inculcate . . . the peculiar and distinctive doctrines of any one religious denomination," Mann expounded at greater length on what he did support. The italicization in this defense of nonsectarian Bible reading was his own: "Our system earnestly inculcates all Christian morals; it founds it morals on the basis of religion; it welcomes the religion of the Bible; and, in receiving the Bible, it allows it to do what it is allowed to do in no other [educational] system—*to speak for itself.*"[41]

Under Mann's direction, Massachusetts's public schools clearly moved away from their Puritan roots and toward the democratic ideals of John Dewey. Yet the Bible retained an honored place.

Ohio

In Ohio, a very different narrative ended in much the same way for the Bible. More than in New York or Massachusetts, the Ohio story witnessed the challenges of the future as well as the legacy of the past. In 1800 Ohio's population of 45,000 amounted to about one-tenth of Massachusetts's; by 1840 Ohio's count of 1,519,000 more than doubled Massachusetts's. Cincinnati, a booming entrepôt on the Ohio River, fueled development in the south, the capital, Columbus, was thriving in the center, and in the north a tide of immigrants from New York and New England brought economic ambition along with their custodial cultural instincts. Methodists led in evangelizing an originally frontier population, but they were soon joined by Congregationalists in the north, Presbyterians in the south, then by Disciples, "Christians," Baptists, and other sectarian groups, and by the 1830s a rising number of Catholics, especially among Cincinnati's substantial population of German immigrants. (The Catholic diocese of Cincinnati was formed in 1821.) Soon Cincinnati would also welcome a number of Jews.

The jumble of Christian (and other) traditions, all understaffed but striving hard, led to predictable conflicts. Joshua Wilson, a conservative Old School Presbyterian in Cincinnati, took great offense at the Methodists but also worried about his more accommodating, or New School, fellow Presbyterians. Prominent among the latter was Lyman Beecher, who in 1832 had been lured from his Boston pulpit to become the president of Cincinnati's new Lane Seminary. Beecher was almost immediately hailed before the local presbytery to answer Old School charges of heresy. For his part, no sooner had Beecher scouted out the land than he published an alarmist book, A Plea for the West, that foresaw national disaster if stern measures did not check rising Catholic influence. Catholics also fueled the polemical ire of Alexander Campbell, the key editor-preacher-promoter of the Disciples or "Christian" movement. In January 1837 Campbell engaged the Catholic bishop of Cincinnati, John Baptist Purcell, in a memorable seven-day public debate in which he condemned Catholicism for its doctrinal errors, but almost as much for subverting republican liberty.[42] A smattering of Baptists, Unitarians, Episcopalians, and others contributed to the impression of chaos that Frances Trollope took back to England after her stay in Cincinnati from 1827 to 1831: "The whole people seem to be divided into an almost endless variety of religious factions. . . . The vehement expressions of insane or hypocritical zeal, such as were exhibited during 'the Revival,' can but ill atone for the want of village worship, any more than the eternal talk of the admirable and unequalled government can atone for the continual contempt of social order."[43]

In this arena of fierce religious competition, the Western Literary Institute and College of Professional Teachers provided an oasis of calm. The Institute's membership, made up almost entirely of ministers or teachers at religious institutions, nurtured the same hopes for social well-being through educational outreach that inspired reformers everywhere. With unexpected harmony, its congenial meetings drew reformers together in efforts to achieve state-sponsored normal schools, state taxation to support mandatory common schooling, and state sanction for moral education in service to society.

Religious cooperation, instead of religious strife, set the Institute's tone. In 1837, the same year as Mann's appointment in Massachusetts, Ohio's proprietary Protestants backed the appointment of a Methodist, Samuel Lewis, as the state's first superintendent of common schools. Wilson and Beecher set aside their intra-Presbyterian differences to support this Methodist superintendent. Institute gatherings listened respectfully to presentations from a Unitarian

(Benjamin Huntoon), an Episcopalian (Benjamin Aydelott), a Swedenborgian (Alexander Kinmont), the Disciples' Campbell, and many more.

Remarkably, during the 1830s the Institute enjoyed the participation of Bishop Purcell, who had assumed his post in 1833. Shortly after that appointment Purcell visited the Western Female Academy, conducted by Catherine Beecher and Harriet Beecher, who had accompanied their father when he moved west. Not only did Purcell praise the educational achievements of the academy; he also thanked the sisters for their measured attitude to his faith. Three years later, at an Institute meeting, Purcell did query a speaker who recommended Scripture as the key text for "a thorough system of universal education" and who specified "the Bible, as published in the English language, without pictorial representations, notes or comments by the British and American Bible Societies." Purcell's query about using the Protestant bible anticipated sharp disputes to come, but in October 1836 the result was only, as noted in a minute, "an interesting debate."[44]

That 1836 meeting represented the high point of ecumenical calm before an anti-Catholic storm that soon followed. After a Catholic priest in attendance asked whether using a digest of scriptural material might be a better curricular anchor than the whole Bible, Purcell agreed to serve on a committee with the Episcopalian Benjamin Aydelott to explore the possibility. When they reported at the next annual meeting, both opposed using only biblical excerpts, but Aydelott held out for "the common English version, or that effected by public authority in the reign of James the First." Purcell took care to cushion his disagreement by asserting that "the Catholic church is not opposed to the Bible"; rather he feared that using the King James Version in schools amounted to "abuse of the sacred volume." He therefore proposed not mandated readings for all but students released one or two days a week for instruction from their particular pastors. Yet even after he submitted that report, observers noted, Purcell voted in favor of the resolution passed unanimously by the Institute attendees: "Resolved, that this Convention earnestly recommend the use of the Bible in all our schools, to be read as a religious exercise, without denominational or sectarian comment, and that it is the deliberate conviction of this College, that the Bible may be so introduced in perfect consistency with religious freedom, and without offense to the peculiar [i.e., particular] tenets of any Christian sect." After the close of this 1837 meeting, participants convened for a social gathering at which they asked Purcell to offer a prayer for the whole group.[45]

Even the Campbell-Purcell debate, which had its origin in the Institute's October 1836 gathering, did not entirely destroy ecumenical goodwill. Campbell had intervened during the "interesting debate" on using the Bible as a basic textbook to make an explicitly Christian statement: "The evidence, the absolute certainty, and Divine authority of the Christian religion, of the Old and New

Testaments, ought to be taught and inculcated as an essential part of a good and a liberal and a polite education in every school in Christendom." His challenge to Purcell for a public debate grew from his conviction that the bishop's Catholicism prevented him from agreeing. At the opening of their debate in January 1837, Campbell stressed the stakes for public education, while Purcell objected to the mandated use of the Protestant bible in the schools. Yet immediately after the debate, Purcell published a letter explaining his motives: "The scope of my remarks was to banish sectarianism from the college [i.e., the Literary Institute].... I should detest myself if I believed there was a particle of illiberality in my composition."[46]

"Sectarianism" was the key. Bishop Purcell understood the sectarian threat as coming from strife between Catholics and Protestants. When the Institute's otherwise divided Protestant participants heard *nonsectarian*, for them it meant using the King James Version that all Protestants endorsed.

Calvin Stowe, who in 1836 married Harriet Beecher, took the lead in urging Ohio to follow the Prussian model—before, during, and following a European trip he undertook only months after his marriage. Repeatedly at Institute meetings and in separately published works, Stowe stressed the purpose of putting Scripture at the educational foundation: "[A]ll our laws and institutions are based on that code of morals, that is found in the bible; your committee believe that the well-being of our civil and religious institutions, depend, under Providence, chiefly on the early knowledge of the scriptures by the whole population."[47]

Along with Stowe, most of the other Ohio reformers also emphasized—more than did Mann in Massachusetts—the specifically Christian purpose of insisting on the Bible. The Episcopalian Aydelott put it like this in 1836: "If there is one point on which the public mind is entirely united, it is, that education to be useful, or even safe, must be *Christian*. . . . [A]s the Bible is the only common standard of Christianity, so it can be the only universal textbook." Christian purpose, however, always also entailed moral purpose. As Stowe and Lyman Beecher wrote in 1840, "[T]he Bible is generally recognized as the book of all others best adapted to the moral culture of the young, and scarcely any one presumes to oppose its use in the common district schools."[48]

Stowe also led the chorus in his fervent commitment to nonsectarian deployment of Scripture, a commitment he stressed in 1835 while explaining why a Bible-guided education was ideal for assimilating immigrants: "[T]he Bible, without dogmatic comment, just as it is in its own simplicity and majesty should be the textbook of religion and morals in all our institutions of education. . . . [This kind of education was ideal for instructing] the children of foreigners in the English language, the principles of republican government, and the truths of the Bible." The Swedenborgian Kinmont sang from the same page: the Bible should be studied in "the higher grade of schools, *without note or comment*."[49]

Unlike Stowe, however, Superintendent Lewis feared that Prussian-style educational reform might lead to Prussian-style aristocracy. He nonetheless agreed with the nonsectarian approach, as he wrote in his first annual report: "No creed or catechism of any sect should be introduced into our schools." Instead they should focus on the "broad, common ground, where all Christians and lovers of virtue meet" in order to "train up the rising generation in those elevated moral principles of the Bible." When Cincinnati put in place its own curricular reform, it followed through: there "the Bible or New Testament is used at certain intervals in all the schools," excluding "everything sectarian, and all that might conflict with the religious tenets of parents."[50]

Conditions that prevailed in the 1830s did not, however, last long. Catholic-Protestant ecumenicity was the first casualty. After Bishop Purcell went on a European tour in 1838 and after Catholic colleagues from elsewhere warned against further cooperation with Ohio's Protestant educators, he shifted his efforts toward establishing separate Catholic schools. As it also happened, because of local resistance to state mandates and conflicts in the state legislature, Ohio's educational reforms soon petered out. By the early 1840s what David Komline has called Ohio's "common school awakening" was over and educational reform would not gain traction for several decades.[51] When it did, a controversy that gained national attention as the "Cincinnati Bible Wars" would begin to unravel the logic that made daily Bible readings the key to the nation's public education.

Textbooks

The Bible enjoyed an unquestioned place in the first generation of American common schools in part because it enjoyed a prominent place in the textbooks schools asked students to read. The close ties that linked educational reform, textbooks, common schooling, and the Bible were especially well illustrated by the career of William Holmes McGuffey, a conservative Presbyterian minister and close collaborator with superintendent Lewis, Calvin Stowe, and the Beecher clan. During his ten years as a teacher of classics, Hebrew, and moral philosophy at Miami University in Oxford, Ohio, and then from 1836 as president of Cincinnati College, McGuffey regularly attended the meetings of the Literary Institute. His extraordinarily popular *Eclectic Readers*, the first of which appeared the year he moved to Cincinnati, have long been hailed (or condemned) for their mixture of Protestant moralism, nationalistic filiopietism, and decorous romanticism.[52] Yet as an author of schoolbooks, McGuffey only followed where others had led. Uniformly, the spellers, primers, and readers that taught the children of the early national United States sought the same ends with the same means endorsed by common school reformers.

Before he began at Miami University, McGuffey spent a year in Kentucky as an instructor of an all-grades district school. For his texts, the young teacher chose the Bible and *The New England Primer*, which until the productions of Noah Webster and Lindley Murray was the nation's most widely used schoolbook. Its editions, as one published at Philadelphia in 1813, regularly included the Westminster Shorter Catechism as an addendum. That edition, like all others, began with a table of the alphabet and then a listing of one-, two-, and three-syllable words followed by the famous abecedary:

A In Adam's fall / We sinned all.
B Thy life to mend / This book attend [an open Bible as illustration].
C The Cat doth play / And after slay.
D The Dog will bite / A thief at night.[53]

The Bible was less prominent in Webster's famous Blue Back speller and his readers than in *The New England Primer* and Murray's even more popular reader. Yet Webster left no doubt about the direction he wanted children to go. Most editions of the speller, as one published at Lexington, Kentucky, in 1823, included "A Moral Catechism" intended as "Lessons for Saturday." It prominently reiterated the era's standard dependence on divine revelation:

Q. What rule have we to direct us? A. God's word contained in the Bible has furnished all necessary rules to direct our conduct.

Q. In what part of the Bible are these rules to be found? A. In almost every part; but the most important duties between men are summed up in the beginning of Matthew, in Christ's sermon on the mount.[54]

Webster's reader included several hymns; it began with "Selected Sentences, calculated to form the Morals of Youth"; and many of its selections reflected the cadences, vocabulary, and didacticism of the King James Bible. Webster offered, however, only a few selections from Scripture itself.[55]

It was otherwise with Murray's *English Reader*. An American-born Quaker, Murray became wealthy through trade and legal work in the Revolutionary period. For reasons of health and possibly for trading with the British during the war, he migrated to the north of England in 1784, where he lived as an invalid until his death in 1826. After publishing works of edification for Quakers and several elementary textbooks intended at first for a Quaker school, he brought out the first edition of his *English Reader* in 1799. It was soon republished in

America, where Murray's policy of not seeking royalties facilitated the distribution of this and all his other books. Before noting the prominence of Scripture in Murray's *Reader*, a pause is necessary to highlight the extent of this book's distribution: 925 editions from 1801 to 1840 (compared to 221 American editions of all of Webster's books). American sales of Murray's books, of which the *Reader* was far and away the most popular, are estimated at 16 million copies in the first half of the century.[56]

Murray's preface left no doubt about his purpose: "to improve youth in the art of reading, to meliorate their language and sentiments, and to inculcate some of the most important principles of piety and virtue."[57] With the aims of common school reformers, Murry's reader aligned perfectly (Figure 14.1).

The Bible, sometimes quoted and sometimes paraphrased, made up a substantial part of what Murray offered to young readers, including those like Abraham Lincoln who studied the reader on their own.[58] The book's first prose chapter, "Select Sentences and Paragraphs," included a subsection with twenty verses taken from Psalms and Proverbs, along with quotations from other passages, like David's expression of affection for Jonathan from 2 Samuel 1:26, as well as paragraphs from Sully, Socrates, Sir Philip Sidney, Alexander the Great, and many more. The eight narratives in the book's next chapter, "Prose Pieces," included paraphrases of the encounter between Elisha and a Syrian commander (2 Kings 8) and the story of Mordecai and Ham from the book of Esther. Titles of the poems that brought the book to a close indicate its general character: "A pastoral in three parts," "The order of nature," "Confidence in divine providence," "Hymn on a review of the seasons," and "On solitude."[59]

McGuffey's *Eclectic Readers*, which followed Murray more than Webster, emerged as part of the reforming purposes that inspired his colleagues at Cincinnati's Literary Institute. A local firm, Truman and Smith, originally asked Catherine and Harriet Beecher to prepare textbook materials for Ohio's new common schools. When they were not able to comply, the firm turned to McGuffey, who produced his first four readers, a primer, and a speller in 1836 and 1837. The readers took off immediately.

In form and content, McGuffey's anthologies resembled earlier readers, though with more of his era's romanticism, more filiopietistic nationalism, more overtly Christian content, and more use of extracts directly from the King James Version. McGuffey may have encountered some resistance to his heavy use of Scripture, since his preface to an early revision of the *Fourth Reader* paused for a brief rationale: "From no source has the author drawn more copiously, in his selections, than from the sacred Scriptures. For this, he certainly apprehends no censure. In a Christian country, that man is to be pitied, who at this day, can honestly object to imbuing the minds of youth with the language and spirit of the Word of God."[60]

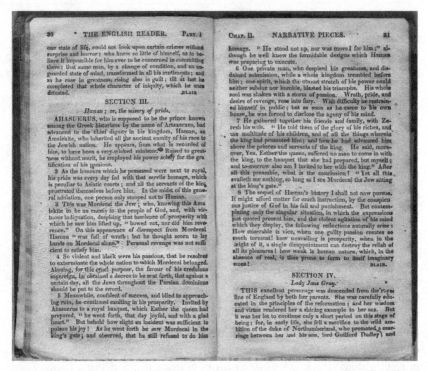

Figure 14.1 This page from an 1846 edition of Lindley Murray's reader, with its mixture of stories from the Bible and classical antiquity, illustrates the type of material that educators hoped would fulfill the goals spelled out on the book's title page: *The English Reader; or, Pieces in Prose and Verse, from the Best Writers; designed to assist young people to read with propriety and effect, improve their language and sentiments and to inculcate the most important principles of PIETY AND VIRTUE.*
Source: Courtesy of Buswell Library Special Collections, Rare Books, Wheaton College, Illinois.

McGuffey's original *Eclectic Second Reader* included eighty-five readings, each prefaced by a vocabulary list and followed by questions for discussion. Its overriding moralism was consistent ("The Little Idle Boy," "The Little Idle Boy Reformed," "The Good Boy whose parents were poor"). It included a number of readings featuring nature, often with wit ("A ship in a storm," "The bear in a stage-coach"). Theology was simple and practical ("How the World was made," "Praise to God"). Two selections told the story of George Washington; one each was devoted to Columbus and Lafayette. Biblical content came in the form of two readings on King Solomon, two on the story of Joseph, a rendering of the Lord's Prayer in verse (with one of the questions, "How can we show our gratitude to God for his constant kindness?"), and the Ten Commandments introduced in simple prose but quoted from the King James Version.[61]

The advanced selections from the *Fourth Reader* are certainly more interesting for adult readers today, as they probably were for inquiring students who advanced to that level. Besides commenting on the heavy use of Scripture, McGuffey's preface explained that he hoped common school teachers might use the questions with each selection for maximum educational effect, especially when they themselves were not entirely confident of how best to answer.[62] Selections by or featuring well-known authors like Hannah More, John Milton, Noah Webster, Washington Irving, Alexander Pope, and John Dryden appeared alongside readings from local authors like McGuffey's friend and the Ohio common school superintendent Samuel Lewis, who contributed "A Plea for Common Schools." Patriotism was the object of another series of readings, including two lessons under the heading "The Character of the Puritan Fathers of New England" and a selection titled "Happy Consequences of American Independence." A number of others underscored the importance of Christian theology, both for itself and for the social order, including "The Bible" by a member of the Literary Institute and "Religion the Only Basis of Society" by William Ellery Channing. Of the reader's eighty prose selections, six came from the King James Bible (three Old Testament, one the Gospel of John, two the book of Revelation), as did eleven of the reader's fifty-one poems (all from the Old Testament). A few of the readings referred to Scripture in decidedly evangelical fashion. A pointed comparison of "Chesterton and Paul," contributed by "Miss Beecher," ended with an evangelistic appeal that quoted 2 Timothy 4:8 concerning the "crown of righteousness, which Christ, the righteous judge shall give," a mélange of passages from Proverbs, and then Matthew 11:29 ("Take my yoke upon you, and learn of me").[63]

For a history of the Bible, the three most interesting selections featured Tom Paine, Jean-Jacques Rousseau, and an excerpt from the book of Revelation. Rousseau appeared as the author of a straightforward paean to Jesus, "The Scriptures and the Saviour," followed by such questions as "How could an infidel testify this without renouncing his infidelity?" The Paine selection came from a Scottish author who first quoted a paragraph from *The Age of Reason* and then explained at length why savants whom the author identified as forthright believers (Isaac Newton, Robert Boyle, and John Locke) so thoroughly repudiated Paine's contentions. The lengthy selection from Revelation (19:11–22:5), titled "The Celestial City," was the penultimate reading. It was followed as the book's last selection by "My country 'tis of thee," titled "America.—National Hymn." The juxtaposition of pro-Jesus, anti-Paine, and pro-America could not have been clearer. It spelled out for all who made it to the end of the book what McGuffey, with the reformers who shared his vision, hoped common schooling would achieve.[64]

In the *Fifth* and *Sixth Eclectic Reader* that McGuffey prepared with his son in the late 1840s, as well as in the revisions that others carried out later for *Readers* 1 through 4, the bond loosened between doctrinal Christianity, personal morality, and social well-being. Although the preface to the 1879 revision of the *Fourth Eclectic Reader* stated that "the aim has been . . . to preserve unimpaired all the essential characteristics of *McGuffey's Readers*," it was a substantially different book. Its ninety readings included only one from the King James Version (excerpts from Matthew 5–7, "The Sermon on the Mount"), along with a story about "Susan" illustrating the Golden Rule of Matthew 7:12 and one or two other vaguely religious selections ("Evening Hymn," "The Creation"). This new edition maintained an emphasis on personal integrity ("Emulation," "Perseverance," and two lessons on "True Manliness," which concluded that "true manliness is in harmony with gentleness, kindness, and self-control"). By comparison with McGuffey's early editions, the new one contained fewer patriotic selections and more that might be called general interest ("Popping Corn," two on "Why the Sea is Salt," and Longfellow's "Wreck of the Hesperus," where a maiden in distress on the sea prays to "Christ, who stilled the wave / On the lake of Galilee," but perishes).[65] Editors prepared these later editions, which reached even more students in ever increasing numbers of schools, for a different America than the nation that bought the originals.

McGuffey himself did not stay in Ohio for long. Cincinnati College closed its doors shortly after he became president. He then served a short stint as president of Ohio University, where locals grumbled about his plea for taxes to support his institution. He then returned to Cincinnati briefly before moving to the University of Virginia, where he served as a professor of moral philosophy until his death in 1873. Besides his teaching in Charlottesville, he preached in Presbyterian churches, joined the uphill campaign for common schooling in Virginia, and gained his colleagues' respect despite supporting the gradual emancipation of enslaved Virginians.

The Legal Exception

The appointment at Thomas Jefferson's university of this active conservative Presbyterian and iconic author of textbooks featuring the Bible marked the enduring influence of an approach to Scripture that Jefferson abhorred. It is even more noteworthy that the nation's courts continued to rule in favor of the kind of Bible-centered school instruction that Jefferson's idiosyncratic understanding of the common law would have prohibited. In fact, rulings by state courts allowing Bible readings in tax-supported schools continued long after most state courts had begun to disentangle the common law from Scripture, after courts as a whole abandoned prosecution for blasphemy, and after sectarian Protestants joined Jacksonian Democrats in frustrating efforts by custodial Protestants to formalize the nation's informal Protestant establishment. While these developments undermining the Bible civilization were in place by the 1830s, rulings questioning the Bible in public schools only began with a famous Cincinnati case from the late 1860s (chapter 22) and gained momentum only slowly thereafter. The legal exception for the Bible in public schools illustrates better than anything else the deeply ambiguous place of Scripture in the unfolding of American national culture.

Steven Green's meticulous research makes it possible to track a sinuous legal course. Catholic protests against mandated readings from the King James Version first led to court challenges in Maine and Massachusetts. But in 1853 and 1859 (respectively) the challenges were rebuffed, primarily by referring to the historic, nonsectarian character of the Protestant Bible as integral to the American project. According to the Massachusetts decision, the Bible was "the best book to teach children and youth the principles of piety, justice, and a sacred regard to truth, love of their country, humanity . . . and those other virtues which are the ornaments of human society, and the basis upon which a republican constitution is founded."[66]

And so it continued, some judiciaries agreeing and others concluding that full religious equality ruled out Christian exercises in school. Early in the next century courts in Nebraska and Illinois struck down daily Bible readings, also hymns and prayers, as prohibited sectarian infringements of religious liberty (*Freeman*, *People*). Yet only shortly before, in 1898, the Michigan Supreme Court upheld Detroit's use of a book, *Readings from the Bible*, because it excluded sectarian passages and served "merely to inculcate good morals" (*Pfeffer*). The same year a Pennsylvania court turned against the judicial tide by ruling that Bible readings were justified on both nonsectarian and religious grounds, since readings from Scripture were important precisely because they were religious (*Stevenson*).[67] These state court decisions late in the century were repeating the reasoning of Supreme Court justice David Brewer in his 1892 *Holy Trinity* opinion that the United States was "a Christian nation."[68]

As indicated by the New Jersey court decision with which this chapter began, judicial uncertainty prevailed long after the pioneers of common school reform passed from the scene. A few of the justices who upheld Bible readings cited the nation's Christian heritage or the hereditary place of Christianity in the common law. Most stressed Scripture's importance for the moral development of citizens. The same rulings invariably emphasized that because the readings were nonsectarian, they did not violate the universally accepted principle of nonestablishment. Jurists who ruled against the readings repudiated such reasoning.

For clarifying the history behind this judicial muddle, debates in Cincinnati's Literary Institute during the 1830s offer special insight. The Catholic bishop Purcell sought peace with his nonsectarian plan for released-time religious instruction. Ohio's Protestant reformers brushed that proposal aside because of an educational vision resting on truth claims deeply embedded in the nation's history:

> A democratic republic required a virtuous citizenry.
> Divine providence had brought this republic into existence.
> Because churches must be free to promote their particular interests, common schools were the best vehicle for society-wide moral training.
> Therefore, the fate of the nation depended on state-supported common schools for all.
> The Bible provided the ideal basis for moral instruction.
> *The Bible* meant the King James Version, whose prose had shaped the national culture.
> In the schools, the King James Version met the nonsectarian test that avoided the dreaded establishment of religion.

The educational, moral, political, civic, and religious complexities of common school reform exemplify much of the general history of Scripture in the early United States. That history—from Tom Paine and Francis Asbury to Horace Mann and William Holmes McGuffey, but also including Nat Turner, Robert Baird, Richard Furman, Theodore Frelinghuysen, and Richard Johnson—constituted a distinct period unto itself. Protestants dominated the early republic and dictated the formula for preserving it. The Bible played a central but uncontroversial role in that early history. When the nation evolved toward greater religious pluralism and intensified intra-Protestant strife, the Bible was no longer uncontroversial, though it remained central. Whether that centrality was good for the country and whether it was good for the Bible itself are the main questions posed by this book: Does a republic require citizens with a self-directed moral compass? Does reading the King James Version in common schools provide that compass? If the Bible civilization was already fading when common school reform took shape, the relevance of at least the first of those questions has never gone away.

PART IV

THE ECLIPSE OF *SOLA SCRIPTURA*

In those days there was no king in Israel: every man did that which was right in his own eyes.

—Judges 21:21

And the brethren immediately sent away Paul and Silas by night unto Berea: who coming thither went into the synagogue of the Jews. These were more noble than those in Thessalonica, in that they received the word with all readiness of mind, and searched the scriptures daily, whether these things were so.

—Acts 17:10-11

15

1844

During the month of May 1844, the Bible occupied as much space in American public life as it ever had. Yet even as the Bible civilization seemed to roll on from strength to strength, the possibility that Scripture-centered conflict could rend the nation moved from distant threat to looming reality. Throughout the entire year, as Holy Writ figured prominently in an unusual array of public events, those events both reinforced and mocked the message that Robert Baird delivered to Europeans that same year in his landmark book, *Religion in America*. He claimed that almost all American Protestants were united on "vital and essential" matters of religion because they "take the Bible as their inspired and sole authoritative guide."[1] Instead, the events of 1844 indicate how much the nation was divided, how much American public life had shifted in the thirteen years since William Lloyd Garrison launched *The Liberator* and Nat Turner led slaves in revolt. Although the King James Version remained fixed in American consciousness, the ability of "the Bible alone" to direct the nation was coming to an end.

In 1844 the Bible civilization seemed most alive in the publishing realm, where the American Bible Society reported record revenues from record Bible production. For-profit Bible publishers also reached an expanding public that during the year welcomed a spectacular new addition to its selection of scriptural wares. Publishing, however, also testified to the era's multiplying tensions. The literary combat on the Bible and slavery/race that had raged since early in the previous decade did calm, though still with significant additions addressing that ongoing tension. By contrast, the battle of words between Protestants and Catholics, which always spotlighted the Bible, heated up intensely. And beyond the glare of publicity, the nation's marketplace of ideas also heard from other voices that advanced new but conflicting appeals to scriptural authority.

In the flesh, as opposed to merely on the page, Scripture fueled literal flames. In Philadelphia fake news concerning the Bible sparked rioting that left death and massive destruction in its wake; that the same did not happen in New York City was due only to on-the-spot mobilization orchestrated by a militant Catholic bishop.

In the sphere of national politics, the Bible played a prominent role during a bitterly contested presidential campaign. In religious politics, Methodists and Baptists, the nation's two largest denominations, went into schism as a result of conflict between the southern biblical proslavery position and a

America's Book. Mark A. Noll, Oxford University Press. © Oxford University Press 2022.
DOI: 10.1093/oso/9780197623466.003.0016

northern combination of biblical abolitionism and more cautious biblical emancipationism. As if that was not enough, Americans attuned to tidings from Rome—whether for guidance or in trepidation—learned of a new encyclical from Pope Gregory XVI that stridently condemned voluntary efforts to distribute the Bible of the sort that American Protestants had perfected. The year, in short, was full of achievement, innovation, and a great deal of conflict.

Bible Publishing Expands and Diversifies

In mid-May, the annual meeting of the ABS heard encouraging reports about financial support received during the previous year, and also about new levels of Bible production and distribution. The economic challenges created by the Panic of 1837 and the ensuing depression seemed to have lifted. The ABS's receipts, which totaled $153,678.05, exceeded by $10,000 the previous funding high from the General Supply of 1829–30. With increased printing efficiency in New York City and increased dedication from colporteurs in the field, the ABS leveraged this 7% rise in financing into a 32% increase in production (more than 314,000 bibles and New Testaments). If this solid result was not keeping up with the nation's rapid population growth, which increased by 52% from 1830 to 1844 to well over 19 million, it was a sign of better things to come. Each year over the next decade and a half the ABS would report record revenues. Only the next Panic, in 1857, and the start of the Civil War checked the funding surge. Still, Bible production was soaring. The ABS's report for 1846–47 saw the number of Bibles and New Testaments exceed half a million (627,764) for the first time. For the reporting year 1861–62, and despite reduced funding, the push to supply New Testaments to Union troops moved the total to more than a million (1,093,842) for the first time.[2]

By the 1840s the ABS's philanthropic business plan and its industry-leading efficiency made it the dominant purveyor of affordable scriptures, still in every format and at every price point published "without note or comment." Yet far from monopolizing the Bible market, the ABS's herculean labors still left plenty of room for others. In 1844 enterprising publishers were supplying an American appetite for bibles that seemed limitless.

Production figures are staggering in themselves but also tell a tale—in fact, several tales. During that one year American printers brought out fifty-three editions of the Bible in English, forty-nine in the King James Version and four for Catholics in the Douay-Rheims.[3] (Led by the ABS, American presses in 1844 also printed three editions of the Bible or New Testament in German, two in Chippewa, and one each in Tamil and Modern Greek, which represented a typical annual total for non-English editions during that era.)[4] By comparison, the first best-selling novel in the United States, *The Wide, Wide, Wide World* by Susan Bogart Warner, appeared in something like 20 U.S. editions during its first three years, 1850–52. If more buyers of the novel read it straight through than was the case for those who bought or received a Bible, the contrast in sheer quantity of published volumes nonetheless indicates a pervasive scriptural presence.

Of the King James bibles in 1844, nineteen different publishers in nine different cities brought out a total of twenty-seven editions offering only the text of this honored translation. A further twenty-two editions with commentaries, notes, illustrations, polyglot parallels, or other paratextual material were published by nineteen different printers in six cities. (A few of the publishers provided both plain and augmented versions.) Together the roughly thirty firms that issued bibles in 1844 demonstrated how, despite the nation's rapidly growing population spread over an increasingly large area, the Scriptures remained available almost everywhere to almost everyone. To consider that the American Tract Society, the American Sunday School Union, and similar agencies annually produced more individual works than publishers offered bibles—if fewer total pages—underscores the extraordinary dimensions of Bible-centered print circulating throughout the nation.[5]

Yet the Bible that joined so many Americans together was also pushing Americans apart. The two Catholic New Testaments and complete Douay-Rheims Bibles, published with an engraving of New York's St. Patrick's Cathedral, "From the Last London and Dublin Editions . . . with the Approbation of the Most Reverend John Hughes, Archbishop of New York," represented the most Catholic editions yet printed in the United States during a single year. It indicated a rising tide: where Catholic bibles had represented barely 1% of editions published in the 1810s, by the 1830s the rate was now over 4%, and by the 1850s to over 18%. When on December 12, 1847, Archbishop Hughes delivered a sermon in the U.S. House of Representatives, he read his text from the Douay version.[6] It was an act of unmistakable symbolism in an era when controversy over the King James Bible in tax-supported schools sparked sharp Protestant-Catholic controversy.

The configuration of the Protestant bibles revealed even more, if less explosive, divisions. Seven of the forty-nine King James Versions were produced under denominational auspices, all by groups that for different reasons had chosen not to work with the ABS. The two Baptist editions came from the American and Foreign Bible Society, which had originated when Baptists on the ABS board resigned in protest over missionary translations.[7] The three editions sponsored by Episcopalians represented their continued uneasiness with "the Bible alone" when not accompanied by the Book of Common Prayer. Editions by a Philadelphia Quaker group and the Methodist Publishing House were not protests so much as indications of a desire to preserve denominational distinctives.

Bible publishing in 1844 reflected not only denominational diversity but also sharper cultural divides. Before the year was out, a mob would murder Joseph Smith in a Carthage, Illinois, jail, even as his go-it-alone Book of Mormon continued to attract a growing number of readers. In October the Americans convinced by William Miller and his go-it-alone interpretations of Scripture suffered the Great Disappointment. Much more popular were King James bibles marketed for the rising middle classes.

The nine publishers of the year's twenty-two enhanced bibles were obviously aiming at up-scale buyers who aspired to at least some level of intellectual sophistication. The same well-placed buyers also indicated their sophistication by letting well-credentialed experts help them interpret what they read. Specifically, eight of the scriptures published in 1844 came with extensive explanatory commentary from English authors. An astounding nine editions reproduced at least parts of Samuel Bagster's Polyglot Bible. "Bagster" included commentary *plus* the Bible in other languages. This ambitious text had been first published by a London bookseller in 1816, but in that era before copyright protection, American printers ripped it off with abandon. (At least one hundred American printings of some version of Bagster appeared between 1825 and 1944.)[8] Not for the common man or common woman confident in their own interpretive ability was the Polyglot Bible, as its title page made clear: "The Old and New Testaments, having a rich and comprehensive assemblage of half a million parallel and illustrative passages, from these esteemed authors Canne, Browne, Blayne, and Scott, and with those from the Latin Vulgate, the French, and German Bibles, the whole arranged in scripture order and presenting in a portable pocket volume, a complete library of divinity."[9]

Publishers of the Polyglot and other augmented bibles tried to keep them affordable, but they invariably cost more than bibles from the ABS. For those who had means, Harper and Brothers in New York City made Bible-printing history in 1844 by releasing folios of a new edition advertised from the year before.[10] The title page of Harper's *Illuminated Bible* spelled out what consumers were getting from a print run of fifty thousand for each of fifty-four separate sections marketed over three years at twenty-five cents each (with a higher price for printing in a two-color format): "The Illuminated Bible . . . With Marginal Readings, References, and Chronological Tables . . . Apocrypha . . . Embellished with Sixteen Hundred Historical Engravings by J. A. Adams, more than Fourteen Hundred of Which are from Original Designs by J. B. Chapman." (Figure 15.1) The investment that many buyers made in expensive bindings showed how much they valued the Adams-Chapman illustrations featuring scenes from the Holy Land, including many depicting the female characters of Scripture. Illustrated

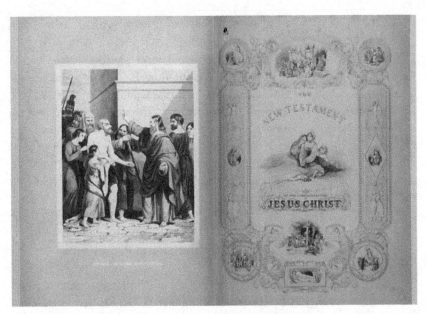

Figure 15.1 The *Illuminated Bible* that Harper & Brothers brought out in fifty-four separate fascicles from 1843 to 1846 set a high standard for the elaborate family bibles that proliferated during the rest of the century.
Source: Courtesy of Boston University, School of Theology Library.

family-size bibles had appeared before, but never on the scale achieved by James Harper and his brothers with *The Illuminated Bible*. In Paul Gutjahr's authoritative assessment, "The volume's popularity had much to do with the rising religious importance of a home's domestic space and the growing concern with the authenticity and trustworthiness of the biblical text."[11] Gutjahr adds a discerning question about the particularly effective way the Harpers integrated the volume's pleasing illustrations with words on the page: Could this and the many large-scale illustrated family bibles that followed have "created a text that made readers concentrate more on the bible's illustrations than on the bible's words"?[12] It is a question that would only become more pertinent as more cultural filtering of Scripture took place in Bible-based novels, plays, and eventually radio, cinema, television, and the internet.

Bibles published with extensive commentary highlighted the ironies of a Bible-only civilization eager for interpretive guidance from old-world authorities. The bibles interweaving text and images also revealed the multidimensional role of Scripture in the nation's culture by showing how different printings of a common King James Version could reinforce the nation's growing economic and cultural divisions. Still further dimensions were illustrated by the geography of

Bible printing in 1844 as well as a much-noticed speech at the ABS's mid-May convention.

That geography testified to increasingly important regional differentiation. Of the fifty-three editions from 1844, all came from Philadelphia and cities to the north except for one Douay-Rheims New Testament published in Baltimore. If Bible *distribution* disregarded the Mason-Dixon line, the northern monopoly of Bible *publishing* spoke of the growing divide between states where slavery remained legal and where it was gone or on the way out. It also gave more grounds for southerners to worry, as Charleston's Edwin Holland had expressed it in 1822, about "the swarm of Missionaries . . . perpetually visiting us, who with the Sacred Volume of God . . . scatter . . . discontent and sedition."[13]

A Contentious Month: Catholics and Protestants

The speech at the ABS's convention that gained so much attention requires a fuller narrative. It was delivered by Theodore Frelinghuysen, "the Christian statesman," a member of the ABS board and former president of the ASSU and ATS who two years later would be elected the ABS's president. When he addressed the ABS in 1844, however, Frelinghuysen represented political partisanship as much as evangelical philanthropy. Only a fortnight before his ABS speech, the quadrennial convention of the Whig Party had chosen him as its vice-presidential running mate for Henry Clay of Kentucky.

Four years earlier the combination of an enthusiastic campaign for Gen. William Henry Harrison ("Tippecanoe and Tyler Too!") and lingering effects from the Panic of 1837 had propelled the Whigs to victory over Martin Van Buren, "the Little Magician" who had created a formidable Democratic machine in New York while serving as Andrew Jackson's secretary of state and then vice president before his own term in the White House (1837–41). Harrison began his term splendidly, with an inaugural address that for the first time made biblical quotations key to his presentation.[14] But he died only a month later, and northern Whigs became bitterly disappointed with John Tyler, a Virginian who blocked all attempts to check the slave states' power. Now in 1844 with Clay, widely heralded as the most capable political leader of his generation, Whigs were confident they would cruise to victory. Their selection of Frelinghuysen to run with Clay would be crucial.[15]

In his speech to the ABS, Frelinghuysen repeated what had been said by many American leaders many times before; it was the message about the character of the United States that Baird was delivering that year to Europeans: "[O]ur free institutions," orated Frelinghuysen, "are based on the oracles of the Living God."[16] But when Frelinghuysen went on to rebuke efforts aimed at eliminating the King James Bible from New York's tax-supported schools, he served up this bromide with acid. Even as he spoke, ashes had not yet cooled from what was already being called Philadelphia's "Bible War."

On Wednesday, May 8, less than a week after Frelinghuysen was chosen as the Whigs' vice-presidential candidate, mobs of nativists torched Philadelphia's St. Augustine's and Saint Michael's Catholic churches.[17] The death of at least twenty Philadelphians and massive destruction of property followed as the rioting spread. (Figure 15.2) As an instant exculpatory literature explained, the rioters were simply reacting to Catholic bishop Francis Patrick Kenrick's demand that Bible reading stop in the city's common schools. In later scholarly accounts, the May riots, and more rioting two months later, have been viewed as the climax of a two-year period of agitation over this subject, but as only one ingredient in a witches' brew of long-simmering ethnic, economic, and racial tension.

After Pennsylvania joined the national push for common school reform, the state's legislators in 1838 mandated required daily readings from the King James Bible. As in Massachusetts, Ohio, and elsewhere, the solons' repeated a common rationale: "The Old and New Testaments, containing the best extant code of morality, in simple, beautiful and pure language, shall be used as a school book for Reading, without comment by the Teacher, but not as a textbook for religious discussion."[18]

In New York City, Bishop Hughes vigorously protested similar legislation with the result that by the early 1840s many of that city's schools no longer required these daily readings from the Protestant Bible. In Philadelphia, Bishop Kenrick heeded Hughes's example but was slow off the mark; not until 1842 did he petition the Philadelphia school board to allow Catholic children to substitute readings from the Douay-Rheims version in the required daily exercises. The school board responded positively to the bishop's request, but with language reflecting deeply ingrained American habits of mind. Catholic students would be excused from reading the King James Version and could substitute any text they wished so long as it was a Bible "without note or comment."[19] Whether or not board members knew that American printings of the Douay-Rheims included paratextual commentary, the effect was a solution without a resolution.

Controversy over the bishop's request and the board's decision only embittered an already poisonous environment. For nearly two decades mobs had repeatedly given the lie to Philadelphia's name as a city of "brotherly love." In 1828 aggrieved old-stock Protestants rioted against Irish workers. In 1834, 1835, 1838, and 1842 mobs attacked abolitionists and African Americans. Conflict between earlier Protestant immigrants from Ulster and later arrivals from Ireland's Catholic South, alongside deep racial antagonism, had made Philadelphia a powder keg primed for a match.

Figure 15.2 This pamphlet, reflecting a nativist viewpoint, was rushed into print soon after the Philadelphia riots that in May 1844 left death and the destruction of Catholic churches in its wake.
Source: LOC, LCCN-01010559.

In broader perspective the Philadelphia conflagration was a response to new patterns of immigration that seemed to be creating a new nation.[20] In 1832 the number of newcomers exceeded fifty thousand for the first time in the nation's history. From the middle of the decade, a sharp spike in numbers from Ireland—mostly impoverished, overwhelmingly Roman Catholic—created particular consternation among guardians of what had hitherto been the nation's default political, economic, and religious character. In 1842 the immigrant total from Ireland by itself rose to 51,342, or almost half of the newcomers who arrived from abroad in the first year with a total of more than 100,000. Philadelphia reflected the national pattern.

If the incoming tide was tiny when compared to the great swells of later decades, it nonetheless convinced some custodial Protestants that *their* nation faced a deadly threat. One of these frightened leaders was Lyman Beecher, who had followed his own advice by embarking for a new position as head of Lane Seminary in Cincinnati. Beecher's *Plea for the West* from 1835 called upon "native" Americans to first acknowledge, then teach, and by teaching, discipline the Catholic newcomers. Otherwise, Beecher feared, they would overwhelm the opening frontier and turn American freedom into papal tyranny.[21]

Even more worried was Samuel F. B. Morse, the son of Jedidiah Morse, who inherited his father's energy as well as his penchant for sniffing out conspiracies. In the son's case, rough treatment from a papal guard during a visit to Rome in 1830 combined with reports about new American initiatives by the Catholics' Leopoldine Foundation turned him as vigorously against the pope as his father had turned against the Bavarian Illuminati. As Irish immigration picked up, Morse countered with newspaper essays turned into books. Their titles conveyed their content unambiguously: *Foreign Conspiracy Against the Liberties of the United States* (1835), *Imminent Dangers to the Free Institutions of the United States through Foreign Immigration and the Present State of the Naturalization Laws* (1835), *The Proscribed German Student . . . Edited by S. F. B. Morse . . . To which is added a Treatise on the Jesuits* (1836), and *Confessions of a French Catholic Priest, To Which are Added Warnings to the Americans* (1838). These works by Beecher and Morse, along with the era's burgeoning literature of lurid anti-Catholicism like *The Awful Disclosures of Maria Monk* (1836) and several anti-Catholic screeds from abolitionist George Bourne, always included references to Scripture. If they rarely featured close biblical exegesis or careful theological reasoning, the Bible's prominence as a threatened marker of identity nevertheless suggested the Book's revered symbolic status.[22]

Proprietary-minded civic leaders in New York City and Philadelphia, where many of the immigrants settled, soon mobilized to meet this "Catholic aggression." In New York, a new American Republican Party gave voice to nativists who wanted to defend threatened "American" values. In the fall of 1844 the new party drained support from the Whigs' candidate for mayor to elect its own standard-bearer. That successful candidate happened to be James Harper, who served out his one-year term before returning to help his Methodist brothers finish publication of *The Illuminated Bible*. The American Republican Party later changed its name to the Native American Party and joined with other nativists to form the American, or Know Nothing, Party.

In Philadelphia a clergy-led group of citizens organized to pursue similar aims. About its governing principles this American Protestant Association left no doubts. Its founding document began with praise for "the privileges and blessings which have resulted to mankind from the glorious Reformation of the 16th century." It then immediately explained its opposition to "the untiring efforts, covert and open, which are constantly making [i.e., being made] to delude Protestants with the vain idea, that the character and tendencies of the great Apostacy, which for many centuries had blinded and oppressed a large portion of mankind, have been essentially changed." Having identified the papacy as the threat bearing down on Philadelphia, the document specified the new association's first duty as "maintain[ing] an open Bible." It was organizing, in short, as a vehicle for stimulating "true Protestants" to protect "freedom of religious opinion and . . . the cause of truth and godliness."[23]

The sixty-four clergymen who sponsored the new association did not themselves join the mobs in May 1844. However much the rioters may have been encouraged by rhetoric from their betters, they came from lower orders and acted out of economic uncertainty, political competition, and ethnic antagonism as well as simple religious panic.[24]

About half of the American Protestant Association's organizers were Presbyterians who, despite a schism several years earlier between "New School" and "Old School" factions, found common cause in defending a Protestant America. Episcopalians contributed far fewer organizers but joined the Presbyterians as the Association's elected leaders. A handful of Baptist pastors and at least ten Methodists signed on as well. These recruits indicated broader support for proprietary anti-Catholicism from Baptists, who on political matters usually sided with the Democrats and their Catholic supporters. It was also noteworthy that Methodists, who had earlier avoided political involvement, joined this Protestant crusade.[25]

To all and sundry it was therefore obvious that, when Frelinghuysen addressed the ABS in May, the nation's earlier era of good feelings between Protestants and Catholics had passed. No longer did the spirit prevail that barely a decade earlier allowed Bishop Purcell to join amicably with Cincinnati's Protestant clerical establishment as a dissenting but welcomed member of the city's Literary Institute.[26] In addition, a new generation of bishops were on the scene who had trained in Rome, where a revival of Catholic devotional practice had begun.

Before many weeks passed, news from Europe convinced alert Protestants that their alarums were well grounded. In an uncanny coincidence, Pope Gregory XVI had published an encyclical, *Inter Praecipuas* (later subtitled in English *On Biblical Societies*) on May 8, the very day that the Philadelphia mob destroyed Catholic churches in anger over Bishop Kenrick's objections to the King James Bible. Americans who followed papal pronouncements knew that Gregory was no friend of republican liberty. The first encyclical of his pontificate, *Mirari Vos* from 1832, had already taken pains to condemn "liberty of conscience," "the never sufficiently denounced freedom to publish any writings whatever," and "the torches of treason" that undermined "the trust and submission due to princes."[27]

In the new encyclical Gregory repeated his fears concerning "indifference to religion propagated . . . under the name of religious liberty," which only alienated "the populace from fidelity and obedience to their leaders." But this time he singled out "biblical societies" as particularly dangerous disseminators of these poisonous principles. Their sins exemplified the catalogue of evils that Catholics had seen in Protestantism since the Reformation. The unregulated distribution of the Bible replaced responsible teachers with "babbling old women and crazy old men and verbose sophists." The Bible societies encouraged the reader in "judging for himself." Their "many translations" propagated "serious errors . . . either through ignorance or deception." They repudiated "the very authority of the Church" and "slander[ed] the Church and this Chair of Peter." They "deceive[d] the faithful with perverse explanations of the sacred books." And more.[28]

Adherents to the American Republican Party would have noticed that the pope devoted much of his encyclical to attacking "a number of men of various sects [who] met in the city of New York last year on June 12 and founded a new society called Christian League" with the "common purpose . . . to spread religious liberty, or rather the insane desire for indifference concerning religion among Romans and Italians." The encyclical claimed that this organization intended to corrupt Italian immigrants in the United States, though to that time there had been very few. The corruption? Despite professing other goals, the League was bent on "inciting sedition" as "they advocate allowing every man of the masses to interpret the Bible as he likes."[29]

By August, when New York City's main Catholic newspaper, the *Freeman's Journal*, took aim at Frelinghuysen and his ABS speech, its editor may well have read this encyclical. Even if he had not, his stern denunciation treated the mob in Philadelphia and the speech in New York as coordinated parts of the same whole: "While people in a neighboring city were committing murders and burning churches in the name of the Bible, and some others were ready here in New York to begin the same horrors, it was no time to be making speeches in crowded meetings about our resolve, [now quoting Frelinghuysen] 'Mr. Chairman,' 'to live by the Bible and TO DIE FOR THE BIBLE.'"[30]

Unlike Philadelphia, in New York City conflict over "an open Bible, and freedom of religious opinion" did not result in fatalities. It was, however, a near-run thing. Even as mobs gathered in Philadelphia on Tuesday, May 7, nativists in New York City rallied to propose a similar response to the same threat. At that meeting another gathering was announced for Central Park on Thursday, May 9, when a delegation from Philadelphia would display what they advertised as an American flag desecrated by Catholics. Two years earlier an angry mob had trashed Bishop Hughes's residence to protest his protest against mandatory King

James readings in the city's common schools. The bishop's resolution then and in the face of other outrages had earned him the nickname "Dagger John." Living up to his moniker, Hughes acted with dispatch in May 1844. He first conferred with city officials to ask if state law provided payments to churches destroyed by mobs. No was the answer. The bishop then took matters into his own hands. He rushed a special edition of the *Freeman's Journal* into print with instructions for Catholics to remain calm if at all possible—but also to courageously defend church property if necessary. He then recruited an instant militia estimated at more than one thousand men, procured rifles for his recruits, and stationed them around the city's Catholic churches. City authorities, fully abreast of Philadelphia's death and destruction on the eighth, prohibited the Central Park rally called for the ninth. On Sunday the twelfth, parishioners gathered for mass under armed guard. Peacefully. The next week Frelinghuysen addressed the ABS. Events in the first half of May 1844 illuminated the American history of the Bible with unusual clarity. The light was bright for the ABS, for Harper & Brothers, for the Protestant voluntary societies that continued to expand the reach of their Bible-themed publications, and for the major Protestant denominations. Later that month, also in New York City, the quadrennial Methodist General Conference reported an active membership of almost 1.2 million served by 4,282 itinerant and 8,087 settled ministers, each total more than double from only eight years before.[31] The light from the evangelical Bible was indeed burning brightly.

Flames from churches ablaze also burned brightly in the same month of May. The panicked anti-Catholicism of the 1830s that sparked the violence in 1844 and midwifed the nativist American Party reprised old-world conflicts between Protestants and Catholics. They also echoed the panicked Federalist attacks against Thomas Jefferson from earlier U.S. history. These reactions came from proprietary fears for civilization, supported by sectarian defense of "the Bible only" principle. Except in the prominence of Scripture, anti-Catholicism in the antebellum period differed considerably from clashes over slavery that featured detailed arguments based on the text of Scripture. It was the difference between Scripture as a passive honored icon and Scripture as an active interpreting authority.

The Bible as the path to personal salvation, moral responsibility, and the safety of the republic was the Bible leading to religious conflict, mob violence, and a sharply divided citizenry. It was also the book poised to fracture the Methodists and imperil the Union.

A Contentious Month: The Bible and Slavery

The Whigs' selection of Frelinghuysen as Clay's running mate seemed at first a shrewd political move. By 1844 the bond between Whig and proprietary

Protestant values had solidified. In Daniel Walker Howe's classic formulation, the alliance grew from a wealth of formal and substantial shared commitments: self-realization linked to care for community, personal liberty coordinated with self-discipline, "moral responsibility" alongside "moral conditioning"—in a word, "the balancing of freedom and control."[32] They shared as well a care for the entire nation, expressed through voluntary societies in the religious sphere and by Whig support for a national bank, internal improvements, and a tariff to assist American industry. To many Whigs, in Richard Carwardine's apt phrase, "[b]ank-burners were of the same ethical stripe as infidels and Bible-burners."[33]

Frelinghuysen's New Jersey origins and his responsibilities in 1839 as chancellor of New York University added eastern appeal to Clay's supposed strength in the South. His earlier advocacy for Sabbath observance and against Cherokee removal offered special reassurance for those who worried about Clay's well-known fondness for gambling, his many duels, and the absence of a regular church connection. Joining together the era's master, if secular, politician and its most respected Protestant statesman seemed a ticket made in heaven.

Slavery made it a disaster. Frelinghuysen's antislavery stance was almost as well-known as his sabbatarianism, but like Clay, he expressed his opposition in two commitments that spelled trouble for the election. First, they united to oppose the admission of the Republic of Texas as a state. In the Senate, Clay had derailed a treaty that would have accomplished this purpose, mostly because he feared adding to the disproportionate influence that the slave states already exercised over national policy. Martin Van Buren, who remained a force among Democrats despite losing to Harrison in 1840, had also gone on record against admitting Texas.

By the end of May, the Whigs' stance on Texas was doing serious damage. The Democrats' nominating convention, meeting in Baltimore, was dominated by forces either actively proslavery or passively noncommittal. Because of Van Buren's well-publicized opposition to Texas statehood, the Democrats rebuffed his bid for another term and chose instead the first "dark horse" to come out of nowhere and receive a major party's presidential nomination. The dark horse was James Knox Polk, a Tennessee protégé of Andrew Jackson with an expansionist vision, including the immediate admission of Texas. The Democrats concerned about religion could point to Polk's Presbyterian family, reports of his Methodist-style conversion, and the conspicuous piety of his Presbyterian wife, Sarah Childress Polk, who would later banish card-playing and dancing from the White House.[34] Strategically, the Democrats' all-out support for Texas undercut Clay's appeal in the slaveholding South and turned an election conceded to the Whigs into a horse race.

(As it happened, the Democrats' convention in late May also figures in the history of American technology. On May 24 Samuel Morse successfully sent the first message from his electromagnetic telegraph apparatus; it was a quotation from Numbers 22:23 ["What Hath God Wrought!"]. In the days that followed, Democrats in Washington crowded around the new machine to receive frequent updates from the delegates gathered in Baltimore. When Morse and his associates succeeded in marketing their invention, its speedy transmission of economic information deflated whatever energy remained in the campaign of proprietary Protestants to legislate a day of rest for the postal service. Yet as Daniel Walker Howe has explained, the invention struck many as providential. In the words of a Methodist women's magazine, "This noble invention is to be the means of extending civilization, republicanism, and Christianity over the earth.")[35]

The second difficulty for Clay and Frelinghuysen returned the Bible to center stage. For both, opposing slavery meant supporting the American Colonization Society and its plan for transporting enslaved and free Black Americans to Africa. One of Frelinghuysen's early teachers had been Robert Finley, the leading founder of the Society; from its early days Clay had been among the Society's most prominent supporters. Colonization troubled relatively few Whigs, but by the 1840s it had become anathema to the nation's most active abolitionists. They bristled particularly at the offense to Americans of African ascent who could never "return" to Africa because they had never been there in the first place. Among the convinced antislavery campaigners who abominated colonization were many who based their abolitionism on the Bible.

In 1840 two differences of opinion had divided the American Anti-Slavery Society that William Lloyd Garrison helped organize. When the Garrisonian faction insisted on adding equality for women to the Society's mandate, a more conservative faction led by the wealthy New York merchants Arthur and Lewis Tappan broke away to found the American and Foreign Anti-Slavery Society. The second dispute concerned political strategy: given the Democrats' determination to assist slave owners and the Whigs' vacillation, was it time for a new political party that would make opposition to slavery its raison d'être? A small number of abolitionists concluded that, indeed, the time had come. Acting on that conclusion, they formed the Liberty Party. In the 1840 presidential election, their candidate, James G. Birney, barely registered with far less than 1% of the nation's votes.

In 1844 it was a different story. Additional supporters had joined the Liberty Party, including the wealthy Gerritt Smith from upstate New York, the merchant Lewis Tappan, and an impressive young orator who had begun canvassing for the American Anti-Slavery Society named Frederick Douglass. This time the party succeeded in drawing off a modest number of northern Whigs who heeded the insistent message of Birney.

Birney's abolitionist credentials had been hard won.[36] After growing up in a Kentucky slaveholding family, he experienced doubts about the system that were planted by professors at Kentucky's Transylvania College and the College of New Jersey. These doubts were reinforced by the white Quakers and Black businessmen he met while studying for the bar in Philadelphia. Yet when Birney returned to Kentucky and then moved to Alabama, he continued to own slaves. His gradual conversion to reform coincided with an evangelical conversion that led him to join a Presbyterian church and support Bible, Tract, and Sunday school societies. In 1832 he began canvassing for the American Colonization Society, a duty that introduced him to abolitionists who soon convinced him that colonization was a morally bankrupt idea. After returning to Kentucky, Birney associated with even more militant abolitionists, including a convert of Charles Finney, Theodore Dwight Weld, who disrupted Lyman Beecher's Lane Seminary with his ardent attack on slavery. Soon Birney came out as an abolitionist foursquare.

The first full-scale publication of Birney's new views featured an impassioned rebuttal of the biblical proslavery position. It appeared in a public letter sent in 1834 to the leaders of Kentucky Presbyterianism. The letter included a catalogue of slavery's evils and an appeal for "immediate abolition." But more than half of this lengthy epistle described the errors of slave owners who denied "the sin of holding slaves." Birney began with a general condemnation of a system "marked by a violence that is utterly at variance with the mild spirit of the gospel," but then he addressed four proslavery arguments in considerable detail. First, Abraham held slaves. No, said Birney, they were only "bondsmen." Second, the Hebrews enslaved their neighbors. Yes, but that was only the exception that proved the Bible's more basic rule to love the stranger. Third, Jesus never condemned slavery. Of course, because he was preaching to the Jews, who held no slaves, and not the Romans, who did. And fourth, Peter and Paul sanctioned the system in their counsel for slaves to obey their masters. Yes, but (at considerable length) they were accommodating the Christian message to the brutal political realities of their own time. Birney summarized his rebuttal with a biblical quotation and a reductio ad absurdum. As had many before him he quoted the Golden Rule from Matthew chapter 7 ("Thou shalt do unto others as ye would that they should do to you"). Then, in rare attention to the racism underlying American slavery, he suggested that if the Bible sanctioned slavery, it sanctioned the enslavement of all races, whites by Blacks as well as Blacks by whites.[37]

Six years later, as Birney prepared for his first presidential campaign, he delivered a blast aimed directly at the nation's religious institutions. In *The American Churches, the Bulwarks of American Slavery*, which he published in London while attending the World Anti-Slavery Convention, Birney first outlined the nature and extent of American slaveholding and then quoted copiously from Methodist, Baptist, Presbyterian, and Episcopal statements either defending the institution or describing it as a civil matter beyond the jurisdiction of the churches.[38] For his own countrymen, Garrison's *Liberator* reprinted the work in 1842 and 1843, just in time for the next presidential election.

At the end of the 1844 campaign, which witnessed an unprecedented level of partisan vilification, Birney and the Liberty Party increased their vote nearly tenfold to over sixty-two thousand—still a paltry number compared to the nearly 2.7 million total. Yet Birney's support in the twelve northern states where he appeared on the ballot probably tipped the election to Polk. In New York, the big prize, Birney's votes totaled 15,812; Clay lost to Polk by 5,106. A not incidental factor in New York was the nearly unanimous support of the state's growing Catholic population for Polk, a vote that was locked up tight because of Frelinghuysen's notoriously aggressive Protestantism. If Clay and the Whigs had carried New York, their 170–105 defeat in the electoral college would have become a 141–134 victory.[39]

Frelinghuysen, the "Christian statesman," did not possess enough Christianity to convince Birney and his supporters that the Whigs were serious about opposing slavery. For Birney and many of those who voted for him, that lack of seriousness came from disregarding the Bible's antislavery imperatives. So it was that the clash of biblical interpretation contributed to the fateful result of this decisive election. The ardently abolitionist Birney helped defeat the moderately antislavery Whigs, which led directly to the admission of Texas and the Mexican War and less directly to heightened conflict over slavery in the territories, the collapse of the Whig Party, the rise of the exclusively northern Republican Party, and then the Civil War.[40]

A Contentious Month: Methodists

Such hypotheticals can be only speculation. Far more concrete was the factual record of what led to the Methodist schism when delegates from the Annual Conferences gathered in New York City for their quadrennial General Conference that fateful month of May 1844. About this schism there was no question concerning the divisive effect of contradictory readings of Scripture.[41] Six months later slavery would also divide the nation's Baptists. It is significant, however, that because Methodist and Baptist histories differed, so too did the Bible's role in the conflict over slavery develop along different lines.

Many observers have seen in these schisms of 1844 and later years the first substantive divisions leading to civil war.[42] In simple demographic terms, these denominational controversies fractured the nation's most widely distributed constituencies of any kind. In addition, the contrasting Methodist and Baptist paths to division showed how disputing over slavery drew together substantially different religious histories into a common, politically driven narrative. For some

Baptists, national politics strengthened strongly local and sectarian traditions; others it drew toward proprietary viewpoints.

For Methodists, the division of 1844 saw politics edging aside the movement's earlier pietistic apoliticism. Richard Carwardine, the premier scholar of the subject, has shown that Francis Asbury's single-minded devotion to evangelism and spiritual nurture never faded completely among later generations of Methodists.[43] As just one example, a young itinerant in Illinois confessed late in 1860 that he had compromised himself in recent public contentions and had "indulged in talking politics too freely, also in speaking of the faults of others rather than of their excellencies."[44] Yet over time, a number of other concerns gradually qualified and then substantially eclipsed Asbury's vision. The Methodists' successful outreach eventually won over increasing numbers who did not abandon political interests when they converted. Increasing wealth and cultural sophistication led many Methodist leaders to feel a responsibility for the nation's civilization as well as its spiritual life. When Asbury died in 1816, there were no Methodist colleges and only a minimal presence in print; a generation later the Methodists were sponsoring a full handful of colleges, a flourishing publishing house, a learned quarterly, and more than a dozen weekly or monthly periodicals. The circulation of these periodicals dwarfed the output from all other sources except the voluntary Protestant philanthropies. By midcentury, to adapt Carwardine's summary, "Methodists had widely absorbed a [proprietary Protestant] understanding of political responsibilities, viewing the state as a moral being and believing that Christians as active citizens had to take responsibility for ensuring that the highest standards of virtue flourished in civic life."[45] A few years later, Ulysses S. Grant could joke about the nation's three great political parties: Democrats, Republicans, and the Methodist Church.[46]

In this denominational history, the connectional system that Asbury and his associates perfected gradually expanded its purview from the spiritual to the political. That expansion, though, did not happen in a rush. In 1842–43 a small group of northern Methodists, thoroughly disillusioned by the unwillingness of the national church to take a stand against enslavement, broke away to form the Wesleyan Methodist Church. Their move represented an ecclesiastical parallel to the formation of the Liberty Party. In fact, Birney anticipated the Wesleyans' disillusionment in his 1840 book, *The American Churches, the Bulwarks of American Slavery*, when he quoted extensively from denominational leaders who at the 1840 General Conference had refused to take a stand on whether Black Methodists could testify in disciplinary cases.[47] As the General Conference debate in 1840 indicated, the inherited desire to preserve Methodist unity in order to protect Methodist spirituality died hard.

Methodists had also been reluctant to let Bible-only reasoning translate into adversarial politics. Early in the century, they had leaned politically toward

Jefferson, especially in New England, where Methodists suffered at the hands of the Federalist-Congregational establishment—but with almost no direct application of Scripture to political concerns. By the 1830s change was under way; more Methodists were enlisting for temperance reform or joining with nativists who feared the influx of Catholic immigrants. Even more were drawn into public debates concerning the morality of slavery. In step with many other Americans, Methodists entered these debates with the Bible in hand. An early intervention came from a New Englander, La Roy Sunderland, who in 1834 helped organize the first Methodist antislavery society. A series of his periodical publications climaxed the next year in a thorough 180-page examination of all Scripture passages that he had encountered in defense of the institution. A title page announcing "the testimony of God against slavery" and including a text from Jeremiah chapter 2 about malefactors in whose "*skirts is found THE BLOOD OF THE SOULS OF THE POOR INNOCENTS*" led to a predictable thesis: enslavers would never abandon the practice "till they feel it to be a sin against God," a conviction that has not yet prevailed because "they have not examined it in light of God's word."[48]

Just as predictably came the response, as from William Capers, editor of the *Southern Christian Advocate,* which had been established by the General Conference to give southern Methodists a voice. In a lengthy exchange with *Zion's Herald*, the newspaper of the New England Annual Conference, Capers concluded that abolitionists "follow not the word of God, and walk not as the Apostles did." Instead, they heeded "Philosophy falsely so called [1 Tim 6:20]," which betrayed them into offending "against Moses and the prophets, Christ and the Apostles, and confessors, and martyrs, and all who have suffered slavery to exist without uprooting society and overthrowing government for its removal."[49]

Such biblical argumentation contributed directly to the 1844 schism, but the division, characteristically for the Methodists, hinged on an ecclesial question. At the New York City gathering, the issue that could not be avoided concerned the Methodists' only southern bishop, James Andrew of Georgia, who had inherited slaves from two different bequests. Andrew, himself an irenic leader known for his solicitude to local enslaved populations, became the occasion for stalemate. Northern and western "Moderates," who in 1840 had refused to take a definite stand, were obviously stung by the Wesleyan seceders. Now they resolutely refused to countenance a slaveholding bishop. Debate on the issue dragged on from before the Democrats convened their convention in Baltimore and lasted until after Polk was nominated. Finally on June 1 the Conference voted 110 to 70 that Bishop Andrew must step aside from his episcopal office "so long as this impediment remains."[50]

The minority, overwhelmingly from the South, could not abide this decision. They had argued that if the General Conference deposed Andrew, the church's authority in slave states would be destroyed. Acting on that (accurate) prediction, the General Conference appointed a committee to work out a "plan of separation," which did its work in time for approval by southern Annual Conferences and the first meeting of the Methodist Episcopal Church, South, in May 1845. For a brief period, it looked like a peaceful no-fault divorce might be possible. Reality, instead, led to squabbling, lawsuits, and some physical violence, most concerning assets of the Methodist publishing machine. Fifteen hypercontentious years followed before Fort Sumter cut off debate, which then picked up again after Appomattox.

For Methodists, the King James Bible remained central—the source of their evangelical piety, the template for their public speech, the one substantial continent in their oceans of print. Yet by 1840 many Methodists in the South were reading the Bible through a lens provided by John C. Calhoun; biblical proof-texting now served the conviction that providence had smiled on the provision of slavery and that the institution was a "positive good." Many northern Methodists had become dedicated Whigs; for them deference to Scripture could only mean active anti-Catholicism, active anti-Mormonism, and some degree of opposition to slavery. Methodist abolitionists accused bishops of violating the Bible's Golden Rule when they throttled discussion of slavery; their southern counterparts responded by appealing to Romans 13 and the Christian obligation to obey "the powers that be," which soon came to include state legislators as well as conference bishops. Ripple effects from the 1844 General Conference demonstrated how important Methodists had become for the nation's future. They also aligned Methodist religion with, instead of against, the dividing currents of the American mainstream.

A Contentious Year: Baptists

The Baptist schism of 1844 paralleled the Methodists', but after a Baptist fashion. In contrast to the national Methodist "connection," Baptists organized by regional "associations" that facilitated fellowship but also preserved the autonomy of local congregations. The sectarian fear of authority from on high remained a cardinal principle. In 1814 this localism gave way slightly when a desire to enhance fundraising for missionaries led to the creation of a new body known as the Triennial Convention (because it assembled every three years).[51] A Home Mission Society followed in 1832 with a similar purpose of promoting evangelism in frontier America. Although these agencies were limited to approving missionary candidates proposed by local associations and coordinating financial support, even that degree of centralization proved too much for a significant Baptist minority. The wariness of these "anti-mission" or "primitive" Baptists went beyond opting out of their own mission societies to also rejecting the national Protestant philanthropies like the ABS. Concerning slavery, the Baptists' piecemeal abolitionism of the Revolutionary era soon faded. Thereafter, mission society Baptists joined the anti-mission Baptists in avoiding contention by treating enslavement as a matter for individual decision or as a concern beyond the churches' proper business.[52]

Beginning in the early 1830s, however, events made it increasingly difficult to keep controversy at bay. Nat Turner's rebellion in 1831 brought special consternation because of both his Baptist connections and his reliance on Scripture. When two years later the British Parliament legislated the final abolition of slavery in the empire, English Baptists wrote expectantly to their fellows across the Atlantic with the hope that they would join in celebrating the end of this blot on Christendom. Instead, their communication only heightened American controversy.

The Triennial Convention of 1841 responded to ever more heated intra-Baptist debate by trying to maintain neutrality. In the effort to sidestep controversy, it took one much-noticed measure: replacing a vice president who had founded the American Baptist Anti-Slavery Society the year before with a respected South Carolinian, Richard Fuller, who defended the hands-off policy. At its meeting in early 1844, the Home Mission Society maintained neutrality, but only after much bitter debate. But in November, at the Triennial Convention, neutrality collapsed. To force a decision, the Alabama Baptist Convention demanded to know if the Convention would appoint missionaries who owned slaves. When the question came to a vote, slaveholders were disappointed, but not surprised, by two decisions. The Convention appeared to follow northern radicals by asserting, "[W]e can never be party to any arrangement which would imply approbation of slavery." Almost as telling was its declaration that the Convention, and not local associations, enjoyed the authority to appoint Baptist missionaries.[53] At a stroke, the Convention seemed to abandon the Baptist principle of localism and its tradition of impartiality. As with the Methodists, these actions prompted a southern reaction. Six months later a convention in Augusta, Georgia, created a regionally separate body, the Southern Baptist Convention. Perhaps ironically, it turned out to exercise more centralized authority than the Triennial Convention had ever allowed.

In the same way that Methodists were bending their distinctive traditions to the United States' central political drama, so too did the Baptists. Both the Convention's 1844 decision and the southern reaction showed how controversy over slavery altered the trajectory of their history. An unusually clear demonstration of this alteration came from a literary exchange that followed hard on the heels of the 1844 Triennial Convention. When Richard Fuller, the Convention vice president, addressed a short defense of slaveholding to a Massachusetts

Baptist newspaper, Francis Wayland, the president of the nation's leading institution of Baptist higher education, Brown University, responded at great length. Eventually the epistolary exchange made its way into a book that highlighted Baptist reliance on the Scriptures. Before Fuller briskly reviewed what he considered especially New Testament evidence for the institution, his initial letter begin with what had become the standard proslavery challenge: "In affirming what you do [against enslavement], ought it not to give a pious mind pause, that you are brought into direct conflict with the Bible?"[54] Wayland, himself a gradual emancipationist rather than an unambiguous abolitionist, went out of his way to address Fuller with all possible charity. Yet his conclusion, though requiring a longer explanation, was just as definite. It addressed directly Fuller's claim that, though Jesus had condemned polygamy and divorce, which the Old Testament had approved, Jesus said nothing about slavery—which must mean that it was not disallowed. Wayland's appeal to the New Testament suggested that God often taught by "principle" as well as "precept." His reply to Fuller's proof-texting deserves extended quotation to illustrate the larger point about how this dispute was redirecting Baptist tradition:

> I suppose the Most High to deal with us, as with beings endowed with an intelligent and moral nature; and, therefore, that he frequently makes known to us his will by teaching us the relations in which we stand, and the obligations thence resulting, without specifying to us the particular acts which he intends thereby to forbid. Whatever our reason clearly perceives to be contradictory to a relation which he has established, is thus forbidden. In this manner I suppose God to have made known his will concerning slavery. Again, on the other hand, I find in the Bible the precepts concerning masters and slaves which we have both quoted. I receive both of these as a revelation from God; and I hence conclude that it is consistent with the attributes of God to teach us in this manner.[55]

The dispute that led to the 1844 schism affected different Baptist constituencies differently. Among white slaveholders, it intensified traditional sectarianism by strengthening the practices Fuller emphasized in his debate with Wayland: the Bible-only principle and interpretation based on text-only literalism. By contrast, Black Baptists and increasing numbers of whites in the North moved in the direction of proprietary Protestantism. As illustrated by Wayland's arguments, scriptural authority remained prominent but cushioned in alignment with reason, self-conscious moral sentiment, and changing historical conditions. As this internal conflict climaxed, southern Baptists gained new respect in their region for forthright defense of slavery (and "the Bible alone"), while Baptists in the North came closer in their use of Scripture to national proprietary movements they once had feared.

Still More

It would leave a false impression to suggest that the Bible engaged Americans in 1844 only when it contributed to political or ecclesiastical controversy. Much evidence shows, by contrast, how much Scripture still served spiritual purposes. Or if not spiritual, then at least a concern for family reputation, a desire to point the rising generation toward respectability or some other politically neutral end. So it was with the many bibles that Americas secured that year from the ABS, Harper & Brothers, and other publishers. So also it was for those who read the American Sunday School Union's new edition of Joseph Alleine's *Alarm for the Unconverted*, the American Tract Society's new printing of Richard Baxter's *Saints Everlasting Rest*, or the five new editions of John Bunyan's *Pilgrim's Progress* brought to the public by American publishers that year.[56]

In New York City throughout 1844 a growing number of visitors came to participate in the Tuesday Meetings for the Promotion of Holiness that were conducted by sisters who had grown up in the Bible-intense Worrall family.[57] Sarah Lankford and Phoebe Palmer were advocates of what Palmer had described the year before in a book called *The Way of Holiness*. Some years earlier, the devastating loss of three young children in a house fire and her own spiritual disquiet had led Palmer to a special experience of the Holy Spirit, which she was now sharing with the world. The title page of her book indicated its apolitical appeal by quoting from the book itself: "I will . . . seek only to be fully conformed to the will of God, as recorded in his written WORD. My chief endeavors shall be centered in the aim to be a humble *Bible Christian*."[58]

Without forgetting quotidian Bible reading by persons and families, the wealth of Bible-centered literature pouring from both nonprofit and for-profit publishers, as well as pulpit expositions of Scripture everywhere in the country on Sundays and often at midweek services, the degree of Scripture-centered controversy is still striking. In February the young Frederick Douglass began his career as an orator with two addresses in Concord, New Hampshire, delivered in the courthouse because the local churches rejected his request for a platform. In his lecture "Southern Slavery and Northern Religion," he concentrated on "your religion . . . which sanctifies the system under which I suffer [as a fugitive slave]."[59] Everyone present knew that Douglass was referring to biblical arguments for slavery, which he would later denounce explicitly.

Meanwhile, across the entire year, the era's other great controversy over the Scriptures—between Protestants and Catholics—received a full airing in a learned debate that had begun in 1841 and was not concluded until four years later. It started when James Henley Thornwell, a Presbyterian professor at South Carolina College, published a short article on the apocryphal books regarded by Catholics, but not most Protestants, as Scripture. In Thornwell's blunt assessment, that claim rested on "the intolerable arrogance of the Church of Rome . . . in the authority she . . . pretends to exercise, of dispensing the Holy Ghost not merely to men themselves, but also to their writings." The response came from an Irish-born priest, Patrick Lynch, in contributions to the *United States Catholic Miscellany* from Charleston, which Bishop John England had earlier established as the nation's first Catholic periodical. The 417-page book that Thornwell brought out in 1845, along with the Rev. Lynch's replies that stretched to a comparable length, treated what Orestes Brownson, the best known Catholic convert of the period, called "nearly the whole ground of controversy between Catholics and Protestants."[60] Almost needless to say, contrasting approaches to Scripture constituted the heart of this dispute from first to last.

Yet to indicate how the era's other great controversy over biblical interpretation could trump even the deep divide between Protestants and Catholics, within half a generation Thornwell, now a professor of theology at the Presbyterians' Columbia Theological Seminary in Georgia, and Lynch, who in 1857 became the bishop of Charleston, South Carolina, would serve the Confederacy as, respectively, their most prominent Protestant and Catholic advocates.[61]

In 1844 biblical argumentation over slavery percolated steadily in the nation's periodical press, though the most widely noticed volumes on the subject had been published earlier or came out later. Still, the beat went on. To indicate why Bible believers outside the South worried about abolition, that year's most extensive *proslavery* scriptural exposition came from Ohio, a free state. Its author was William Graham, a minister in the New School Presbyterian Church that scholars have treated as leaning slightly more toward antislavery than its conservative Old School counterpart.[62] Graham was especially concerned that because of public opinion running wild, "the power and purity of the Church are impaired." He hoped "to recal [sic] the attention of Christians to the only effective means of reform—the word of God." In a work divided about equally between exposition of the Old Testament, exposition of the New, and warnings about the dangers of radical abolitionism, Graham explained the Leviticus 25 permission for Hebrews to enslave "the nations" as a demonstration of benevolence (the alternative to killing captured warriors). His conclusion, as had become routine, elided confidence in his own exposition and insinuations of infidelity against those who differed: "The question whether the relation of master and slave, be in itself sinful, has now been abundantly answered: at least to all who believe the Bible, and accord to its author the privilege of explaining his own law."[63]

A much longer, but also more unusual, work by Robert Benjamin Lewis provided the most substantial work of biblical antislavery in 1844. Lewis, a resident in Maine most of his life, was the son of a Native American father and an African mother who in 1836 had published a fascinating compendium of biblical and historical material to demonstrate the foundation of all human history in "the

Colored and Indian Race." In 1844 his book was reprinted by "a committee of Colored Gentlemen" in Boston. Beginning with fifty packed pages of biblical argument starting with the first chapter of Genesis, Lewis claimed to show that all humanity had been dark-hued until at the Tower of Babel (Gen 11) God divided the nations and so inaugurated a light-skinned branch of humanity. Moses had been "colored," Egyptians were Ethiopians, and Native Americans were descended (as Elias Boudinot and the Book of Mormon had also suggested) from the children of Israel. Hundreds of pages of historical and anthropological detail filled out the story of the human race that Lewis brought to a close with contemporary "Guiana" and "Hayti." A short poem on the work's title page indicated Lewis's belief in the work's biblical foundation: "Search this work with care and candor; / Every line and page you read / Will brighten all the truths of Scripture, / Proved by history—plain indeed."[64] Apart from a common profession to honor the Scriptures, Lewis's universe differed entirely from the universe of the Rev. Graham.

In 1844 that common profession still exerted a measure of cohesive force. Yet as animosity flared between Protestants and Catholics, as the Methodists and Baptists fractured, and as religiously fueled controversy over slavery intensified, the ideal of a Protestant civilization based on a plain reading of the Bible was fading fast.

16

Whose Bible? (Catholics)

National publicity in 1844 highlighted Catholic-Protestant tensions as well as an array of antagonists contending over slavery. Largely ignored by the white public were African American voices like Frederick Douglass's that attacked both slavery and racial prejudice (chapter 9). Although long-standing contentions among proprietary Protestants, sectarian Protestants, and Methodists still simmered, they too were overshadowed by the more dramatic controversies. For representatives of all such groups, whether at the center of national attention or completely ignored, it remained second nature to approach the public with Bible in hand.

For the *history* of the Bible, however, it is also significant that more constituencies were making ever stronger claims to their scriptural right to be heard in an increasingly jumbled public square. The small but rapidly growing number of Mormons remained distinctive in setting Joseph Smith's revelations alongside the Bible. More representative of more Americans were Catholic spokesmen, leaders of the still tiny Jewish population, Germans whose Protestantism differed from Anglo varieties, and women Bible readers from many denominations, all of whom appealed to the Scriptures but challenged the conventions of white Anglo-American men. To make a complicated picture even more complex, the antebellum decades also witnessed a resurgence of opinion from those who had no use for the Bible, or at least the Bible revered as the authoritative Word of God. This chapter and the next two show that by midcentury *the* Bible had come to mean many different things to many different Americans.

Perennial Outsiders

In American religious history, no once-outside group has received more attention than adherents to the Church of Rome.[1] Even as national history ebbed and flowed, the challenge for Catholics remained fixed. Two hurdles posed a seemingly impossible task. How could Catholics convince other Americans that they honored the Scriptures, despite believing that only their church possessed the authority to say what the Bible meant? The second was like unto the first: How could this view of church authority ever refute the charge of despotism that,

America's Book. Mark A. Noll, Oxford University Press. © Oxford University Press 2022.
DOI: 10.1093/oso/9780197623466.003.0017

having been bred in the bone of British imperial Protestantism, continued with full force in the new American republic?

The general Protestant objection had been first articulated by Martin Luther and then repeated wherever Protestantism appeared. It held that Catholicism's supposed reverence for Scripture was a sham. Proof could be found in the very first decrees from the Council of Trent, the church's response to the Protestant rebellion. In 1546 the Council had begun its formal definition of the authentic faith with a common Christian affirmation: "Following the example of the orthodox fathers, the council accepts and venerates with a like feeling of piety and reverence all the books of both the Old and New Testament, since the one God is the author of both"—then came the stinger—"as well as the traditions concerning both faith and conduct, as either directly spoken by Christ or dictated by the Holy Spirit, which have been preserved in unbroken sequence in the Catholic Church." A further assertion would be especially galling for American Protestants: "[N]o one, relying on his personal judgment . . . shall dare to interpret the Sacred Scriptures . . . by twisting its text to his intended meaning in opposition to that which has been and is held by Holy Mother Church."[2] For Protestantism, which began with Luther declaring "[M]y conscience is captive to the Word of God," Catholicism's "traditions" and its claim to sole interpretive authority simply eviscerated the "Sacred Scriptures" it claimed to honor.

The specifically American Protestant objection expanded from dogmatic theology to civic certainty.[3] It had been expressed repeatedly during the colonial era, but never more forcefully than when John Adams turned the British Protestant inheritance against Britain itself. Adams penned his *Dissertation on the Canon and Feudal Law* in 1765 to denounce Parliament's despotism in imposing the Stamp Tax without colonial representation. His indictment charged Parliament with the very crimes that for a century Parliament had laid at the feet of Catholic France. According to Adams, the Catholic church and the medieval civilization it inspired were "the two greatest systems of tyranny" in all of Christian history. More particularly, the canon law, which was "framed by the Romish clergy for the aggrandizement of their own order," institutionalized "the desire of dominion" with all restraints removed. The result had been "an encroaching, grasping, restless, and ungovernable power"—in fact, "the most refined, sublime, extensive, and astonishing constitution of policy that ever was conceived by the mind of man."[4] For Adams and many who joined him in the break from Britain, Catholicism represented the very worst of the old world the United States wanted to leave beyond.

The American history of Protestant-Catholic conflict can appear entirely uniform—from Adams's *Dissertation*, through the antebellum polemics of George Bourne, Lyman Beecher, and Samuel F. B. Morse, the Blaine Amendment of 1876 (chapter 22), Protestant panic in 1928 at the prospect of electing the Catholic Al

Smith as president, to similar fears expressed thirty-two years later by both the liberal *Christian Century* and the evangelist Billy Graham when John F. Kennedy ran for that high office.[5] Yet probing a little deeper reveals that the actual unfolding of events contained surprising twists and turns. Almost all concerned the Protestant (and then secular) certainty that when Catholics claimed to revere the Bible and honor America, they really could not mean it.

Calm before Storm

The first surprising revelation is that in the immediate wake of independence, Protestants and Catholics got along fairly well. Inherited suspicions did not exactly vanish, but the general mood was restrained. Experiences during the war certainly helped, especially after New Englanders in the army that invaded Quebec in 1775–76 found much to admire in the Catholic Québécois, when Gen. George Washington banned Pope's Day, which commemorated the Catholic Gunpowder Plot of 1605, and then as Catholic France lent its navy in the fight against Britain.[6] Immediately after the conflict ended, the College of New Jersey at Princeton and some other Protestant institutions made a point of extending a welcome to Catholic young men.[7] Well into the nineteenth century, Protestant communities in Pennsylvania, in the South, and on the frontier regularly contributed to the construction of Catholic churches once a sufficient Catholic population had arrived.[8]

Traditional Protestant nervousness did show up in an 1811 pamphlet from Maryland Presbyterians on the subject of religious education. When the Presbyterians addressed parents about the need to catechize their children, they paused to denounce a Latin-language catechism used at St. Mary's College, recently established by Baltimore Catholics under the Rev. Louis DuBourg. As opposed to Protestant instructional manuals "founded on the Word of God; the *only infallible rule* of faith and practice," this Catholic version was "very insidious and imposing . . . in principle and practice." Yet even this attack did not deliver the kind of all-out denunciation that had characterized panicked Protestant sermons during the French and Indian War or that would appear in the sensationalistic literature of the 1830s. The Presbyterians devoted twice as many pages in their pamphlet to chastising "wicked and ungodly parents" who did nothing for their children, as in warning against Catholicism. They admitted that the catechism in question, which had been prepared by Abbé Claude Fleury, contained a great deal of basic Christian truth. Parts of this catechism had in fact been translated into English by John Wesley for the use of his itinerants. And unlike later Protestant anti-Catholicism, the Presbyterians remained focused on doctrinal differences (transubstantiation, prayer to saints and angels, the church's claim to infallibility). Consigned to only a footnote were concerns about Catholic violations of civil and religious liberty. Moreover, when President DuBourg responded with a lengthy apology for his college, the catechism, and Catholicism, his repost featured a mild *tour d'horizon* rather than harsh polemics. It emphasized the beauties of Catholic worship, the worldwide appeal of the church, the immaturity of Protestant education, and Catholicism's support for government, including republican governments.[9] It certainly was a skirmish, but not all-out warfare—and the Bible played a subordinate role.

The same relative restraint had marked the first and most important early American defense of Catholicism. It was published by John Carroll in 1784, five years before he was installed as the nation's first Catholic bishop. Carroll and Charles Henry Wharton were American-born Catholics who studied at Catholic institutions in Europe before joining the Jesuits. When that order was dissolved by Pope Clement XIV in 1773, Carroll returned to Maryland, and Wharton took up duties as a Catholic chaplain in Worcester, England. While working at that post, Wharton converted to the Church of England. Then in early 1784 he published a letter-memoir addressed to the Catholics of Worcester that was soon republished in Philadelphia. Wharton's account of "the Motives which induced him to relinquish their Communion, and become a Member of the Protestant Church," prompted Carroll's reply, *The Address to the Roman Catholics of the United States of America, By a Catholic Clergyman*. For readers expecting Catholic-Protestant polemics to feature Protestant flame-throwing (Lyman Beecher, Samuel F. B. Morse) or uncompromising Catholic rebuttals (Bishop "Dagger John" Hughes), the Wharton-Carroll exchange makes for surprising reading.

Wharton explained his spiritual pilgrimage as disillusionment with "the dead weight of authority" and a resolve "to acquiesce ultimately in the authority of revelation, the light of reason, and the dictates of conscience." Almost completely absent were the complaints about Catholic tyranny that would become staples of later American polemics. For a history of the Bible, it is noteworthy that Wharton did not bring the Scriptures into play until the second half of his memoir, at which time he explained, but fairly briefly, why passages used by Catholics to support the church's infallibility (especially Matt 16:18 and Matt 28:19–20) did no such thing.[10]

Again of interest for a history of the Bible, Carroll's reply relied on much more extensive scriptural argumentation than had Wharton, as Carroll examined Jesus's conveying of authority to Peter (Matt 16) and to the apostles in general (Matt 28). He also expanded at some length on John 14:15–16, a promise from Jesus to the disciples that the Holy Spirit would lead them into all truth. In good Catholic fashion, Carroll did quote liberally from church fathers and church authorities; he admitted that Catholics had sometimes persecuted Protestants (but also noted the reverse while hoping that such times of "fanaticism and frenzy" had passed); he made the time-worn point that, although the Bible was God's Word, it required the church to ascertain which writings should be treated as Scripture; he defended transubstantiation as an ancient teaching; and with a quotation from Deuteronomy 23:21 about breaking oaths made to God, he chided "the chaplain" for abandoning his vow of celibacy to marry. Yet remarkably, in light of later controversies, Carroll's biblical quotations came mostly from the King James Bible.[11] Perhaps he wanted to avoid offending the Protestant readers he hoped to reach, for when he opened his tract with Paul's exhortation to the elders at Ephesus from Acts 20:28, he quoted the KJV's "overseers" instead of the Douay-Rheims's "bishops."[12]

Almost as significant as Carroll's religious apology was the care he took to speak as an enlightened republican to a nation of enlightened republicans. Throughout, Carroll matched what had been Wharton's calm tone of voice; like Wharton he made his case with very little of the name-calling that would later attend such disputes. For American patriots who had defended breaking from Britain with Real Whig arguments, he used the language of those arguments in urging families to train children in "virtue" and to flee from "vice." At the end of the work, Carroll praised at considerable length "the harmony now subsisting in all Christians in this country, so blessed with civil and religious liberty," as well as the "general and equal toleration" that all Americans now enjoyed.[13] His experience as a young Jesuit whose life had been drastically redirected when Catholic monarchs pressured the pope to shut down the Jesuit order was probably a factor in his warm embrace of American freedoms.[14] In any event, for those with eyes to see, this first major statement of Catholic principles in U.S. history made an audacious claim, as summarized aptly by Catherine O'Donnell: "A religion that could thrive in the Republic did not have to be a republican religion."[15]

Relatively peaceful relations continued during the decades when Catholic numbers grew slowly and the nation's ideological temper cooled. That situation applied also to Scripture, with the early history of the American Bible Society a prime case in point. At its 1816 organizing meeting in New York City the founders nominated one Catholic, the respected North Carolina jurist William Gaston, to serve as a vice president.[16] They also responded positively when Quaker participants asked the new organization to solicit the participation of local Catholics. Within the ABS's first year of operation, it announced plans to produce Catholic-authorized translations of the Bible in French, Gaelic, and German. For their part, church officials in Catholic-majority Louisiana responded positively to one of the early Protestant proposals for distributing bibles in their region, as did other officials in Catholic-minority New York City during the first decade and more of the ABS's existence. The ABS routinely included the Apocrypha in its Spanish-language editions until 1828, at which time it stopped, not so much because of American objections but out of deference to the British and Foreign Bible Society that, after an intense Scottish-English dispute, had taken that step.[17] Only in the early 1830s, when ancient Protestant-Catholic antagonisms sprang back to life, did the ABS's distribution of Scripture "without note or comment" began to look like deliberate Protestant provocation.

The early American career of Bishop John England featured another signal moment of relative calm.[18] In 1820 England had been ordained in his native Ireland as the first bishop of Charleston, South Carolina. Very soon after he arrived to take up that post, and despite the minuscule Catholic population in a diocese that took in all of South Carolina and Georgia, he founded his church's first American periodical, the *United States Catholic Miscellany*. It would later win renown (or obloquy) for vigorously defending the church against detractors, but in its early years the paper's effective journalism won Bishop England more general respect than angry opposition. The prime expression of that respect came on January 8, 1826, when the bishop was asked to preach the Sunday sermon at the weekly worship service held in the hall of the U.S. House of Representatives. From the time when the capital moved from New York to Washington and these services began, this duty had fallen exclusively to Protestant ministers.

When published, England's sermon became a "discourse," which more accurately described a lengthy lecture during which some in attendance may have dozed off.[19] England took pains to disclaim any intent "to wound the feelings of those from whom I differ," while also expressing thanks for kindnesses shown to him in his American career. Still, the two parts of his discourse did attempt a comprehensive apology to show "that we are not those vile beings that have been painted to [the American] imagination." The first part dealt directly with the Bible. Catholics, he explained, relied on evidence to ascertain facts, including the fact of revelation from God. But in considering that revelation, "the essential difference between the Roman Catholic Church and every other" lay in believing that God gave to Peter, the other Apostles, and then their successors the authority to decide which written documents constituted that revelation. Consequently, for any later religious question, "the mode originally used will procure for us evidence of truth"; that mode, moreover, had always been exercised by "the great majority of the bishops united with their head, the Bishop of Rome, who succeeds to Peter."[20] The discourse's second part took up the Catholics' civic challenge. In England's account, the popes enjoyed authority only on religious matters; Catholicism was not "despotic . . . in its principles." Moreover, many great Catholics (William Tell, Charles Carroll [who signed the Declaration of Independence], Bishop John Carroll, Simón Bolívar) had been exemplary republicans. England also explained that incidents of Catholic persecution were anomalies arising from mistakes, the different conditions of the Middle Ages, or singular historical circumstances.[21]

This address from 1826 drew brighter dividing lines than did a Catholic who wrote to the Methodists' *Christian Advocate* at about the same time. This reader expressed appreciation for the paper by observing, "[A]s a Roman Catholic . . . I look upon all good men as brethren . . . whether they acknowledge the spiritual supremacy of 'His Holiness' or the more republican system of the 'Wesleys.'"[22] Yet England, who quoted only two scriptures in his entire discourse, and those only in its last paragraphs, used these texts to raise a white flag of peace: the Second Commandment ("Thou shalt love they neighbor as thyself for the sake of God") and an apostolic injunction to love the "neighbor."[23] It was an irenic conclusion to a forthright explanation of why Catholics approached Scripture so differently from Protestants, but also of his claim that Catholics posed no threat to the republic.

Contention

If the relatively peaceful atmosphere nurtured by Bishop Carroll, the early directors of the ABS, and Bishop England before Congress has received inadequate historical attention, a wealth of excellent scholarship has treated the perfect storm of contention that followed.[24] For a history of the Bible, the militancy that flared in the 1830s—and that has not yet entirely died away—entailed a significant change. Early polemics (as between Carroll and Wharton), public statements (as the first part of Bishop England's discourse), and a few later polemics (as between Bishop James Lynch and James Henry Thornwell) enlisted Scripture to establish specific points of doctrine or defend specific theories of revelation. The new polemical era, by contrast, followed the second part of England's discourse by concentrating on the compatibility of Catholicism with American principles.

Increased immigration from Catholic Europe was largely responsible, but not by itself. General public extremism intensified when political leaders imitated the apocalyptic zeal of revivalists by treating ideological conflict with life-or-death urgency. Intense loyalty to Andrew Jackson met by intense anti-Jacksonianism sparked the heightened ideological excitement of the Second Party era. The relative absence of effective policing encouraged rioting as a favored means of expressing ethnic, class, or racial discontent. The Panic of 1837 and the depression that followed added economic strain to an already overheated public sphere. As a constant backdrop, escalating conflict over slavery intensified every other national dispute.

Nativism, with its sharp edge of anti-Catholicism, was the political result. The mobilization of the early 1840s that took shape in Philadelphia's American Protestant Association and New York's American Republican Party metastasized into the Order of the Star Spangled Banner and then the militantly anti-Catholic American (or Know Nothing) Party. As the Whigs splintered beyond repair over the Fugitive Slave Act of 1850 and the Kansas-Nebraska Act of 1854, Know Nothings won impressive local victories in Massachusetts, Pennsylvania, Indiana, and elsewhere; they elected almost a fourth of the U.S. House of Representatives in the midterm election of 1854; in the 1856 presidential race they garnered more than 21% of the national vote for Millard Fillmore, the former Whig who had served as president from 1850 to 1853 when the last successful Whig candidate, Zachary Taylor, died in office.

Yet because intense anti-Catholicism lay at the root of organized nativism, it meant that beginning in the 1830s, whenever Catholics spoke publicly about the Bible, they had to defend its compatibility with American freedom. The difficulty came from nativists who weaponized Scripture as a totem for American liberty even as they repeated age-old attacks on Catholic doctrine and practice.

The challenge flared with particular brightness when zealous abolitionists mingled slavery and "Romanism"—and just as Protestants grew increasingly nervous about Catholic immigration.[25] Specifically, the burning of the Ursuline convent by a Massachusetts mob (1834) and the appearance of Lyman Beecher's *Plea for the West* (1835) coincided with anti-Catholic screeds that Elijah Lovejoy published in his St. Louis newspaper only shortly before this ardent abolitionist was killed by a proslavery mob. George Bourne's career as an elderly reformer is emblematic. Even as he continued to publish antislavery articles in William Lloyd Garrison's *Liberator*, he also penned a searing tract titled *Controversy Between Protestants and Romanists* (1835), and he brought out *Lorette* (1834), a tale of Catholic licentiousness that paved the way for the even more salacious *Awful Disclosures of Maria Monk* (1836). The genre of semi-pornographic memoir-fictions almost always highlighted Catholic disregard for the Bible, even as its stoked Protestant fears of Catholic sexual license that paralleled white American panic about abolitionism leading to Black-white "amalgamation."[26] Angelina Grimké exemplified the frequent conjunctions of the period when in 1836 she pled with southern Christian women to renounce slavery: "The Catholics are universally condemned, for denying the Bible to the common people, but, slaveholders must not blame them, for *they* are doing the very same thing, and for the very same reason, neither of these systems can bear the light which bursts from the pages of that Holy Book."[27]

The Bishops Speak

Attention to the church's leading antebellum prelates reveals vigorous responses to such challenges, even as it shows them fully engaged in attending to the pressing demands of a burgeoning Christian population. Scripture was never far away in those efforts.

The battling Bishop John Hughes has served as the prime example of antebellum Catholic militancy, especially because of his vigorous campaign against mandated readings from the Protestant Bible in New York City's public schools. From the start of his career as a young priest in Philadelphia, Hughes had demonstrated a special eagerness to defend the faith of his fathers. Beginning in 1830, a years-long dispute with a learned young Presbyterian, John Breckinridge, became one of the nation's first of many extensive Protestant-Catholic duels. It eventually led to a weighty published volume in which Hughes attacked head-on Protestantism's guiding principle: "The Bible alone, cannot be our rule of faith, because we are bound as Christians to believe that the Bible is an *authentic* and *inspired* book; and this I defy any one to prove *from the Bible alone*."[28] A second volume between the same disputants, on whether Catholics or Presbyterians were stronger champions of "civil or religious liberty," nearly doubled the more than three hundred pages of Round 1.[29] Hughes never wavered in expressing the opinion that, as he put it in 1843, "Catholics have but little respect for King James' translation of the Bible."[30] Nor did he hesitate in many speeches, letters, and formal treatises to repeat the gist of his second argument with Breckinridge, as in a later tract from 1844, "Catholicism Compatible with Republican Government."[31]

The bishop, however, was also capable of nuance. As an example, his comment on Catholics and the KJV appeared in a short essay responding to a report about a priest in upstate New York who in the heat of conflict with a local school authority had publicly burned a copy of that translation. New York's *Freeman's Journal*, supposedly the bishop's house organ, crowed, "To burn or otherwise destroy a spurious or corrupt copy of the Bible, whose circulation would tend to disseminate erroneous principles of faith or morals, we hold to be an act not only justifiable, but praiseworthy."[32] Hughes hastened to reject that militancy in a letter sent under his own name to the New York *Evening Post*. If the report was true, he wrote:

> I condemn, with the same emphasis, the burning of Protestant Bibles, as I would the burning of a Catholic convent; and, as I hold that it would be unjust to condemn the Protestant ministers, and the Protestant people of the United States, for the burning of a convent at Boston, so I maintain it would be equally unjust to hold the Catholic people, or the Catholic priesthood, accountable for the burning of a Protestant translation of the Scriptures, in the town of Champlain, Clinton County, New-York.[33]

When Hughes preached before Congress in December 1847, he went even further.[34] Unlike Bishop England's "Discourse" two decades earlier, Hughes "took a text" that he then exposited for a mostly didactic purpose. The text was Matthew 20:20–28, the story of Jesus's rebuke to two disciples who asked for preferential treatment in the coming Kingdom: "whosoever will be the greater among you, let him be your minister. And he that will be first among you shall be your servant. Even as the Son of Man is not come to be ministered unto, but to minister, and give His life a redemption for many" (Douay). Hughes, who addressed his audience as "Christian brethren," interpreted the passage to declare that "the object of [Christ's] mission on earth was of a higher and holier character than the mere settlement of human government"—but also that the "indirect consequences" of that spiritual mission "seem to constitute the only true ground of hope and happiness, even in the affairs of this world." The sermon itself did include one or two apologetic asides, as when Hughes claimed that "it was necessary, beloved brethren, that man should be taught by authority." But most of the sermon simply explained the great benefit through time past of "the hallowed influence of the religion of peace and love." Hughes's penultimate words could just as easily have been spoken by an American Protestant: "[W]hatever of political liberty is enjoyed by men—whatever increase of popular freedom is discoverable—whatever progress of equality is manifest, must all be traced to the influence of Christ."[35] Likewise with his ultimate words that contrasted the beneficence of Washington with the destructive genius of Napoleon. At least for this occasion, Hughes set aside his well-earned polemical reputation for sentiments to which his Protestant listeners could have responded with "Amen."

Bishop England in a Vise

Considerable irony and genuine poignancy marked the Catholics' antebellum balancing act of defending against outsiders while nurturing insiders. An example of irony was the last scene in Bishop England's life, when his death cut short another extensive literary duel. During the presidential campaign of 1840, the Democratic secretary of state campaigned throughout the South for the incumbent Martin Van Buren. In a reversal of the usual ethnocultural loyalties, Secretary John Forsyth tried to link southern Catholics to William Henry Harrison and the Whigs. He did so by claiming that Pope Gregory XVI had come out as an outright abolitionist, which proved that southern Catholics represented a Whig fifth column since everyone knew that the Whigs tolerated abolitionists as Democrats did not.

The charge illustrated the tangled international meanings of descriptors like "conservative," "liberal," "moderate," and "modern." Many of the pope's best-known statements, like *Mirari Vos*, defended rock-solid European traditionalism.

Yet in December 1839 he issued an apostolic letter, *In Supremo Apostolatus*, that so harshly condemned the slave trade that many observers in Europe and North America considered it a denunciation of slavery itself.[36]

The pope's unlikely expression of "modern" moral sensitivities posed a dilemma for Charleston's Bishop England, who, even with his vigorous apologetics for the church, was viewed as a "moderate" Catholic voice. To Congress—and despite the official papal position—he had repeated Bishop Carroll's praise for the American polity: "[Y]our constitution wisely kept [church and state] distinct and separate."[37] Now, however, the "moderate" bishop chose to explain away the "conservative" pope's "liberal" directive. He did so by distinguishing the slave trade (condemned by the pope) from slavery itself (supposedly still allowed). The series of substantial letters he addressed in response to Forsyth began with a characteristically Catholic appeal to natural law. But then, and most significant, England turned to defend the propriety of slavery with the scriptural arguments of American anti-abolitionists. That move, important as it was in the context of the 1840 presidential campaign, meant even more as a forecast of later American Catholic history.

In his apostolic letter, Pope Gregory mostly relied on church precedent: Gregory of Nyssa's account of liberating slaves at Easter and the decrees of various popes that had ameliorated treatment of slaves. Yet he also referred in general to "the law of the Gospel" as enjoining "a sincere charity toward all" and specifically cited "Our Lord Jesus Christ" who "had declared that He considered as done or refused to Himself everything kind and merciful done or refused to the small and needy" (paraphrasing Matt 25:40).[38] England, by contrast, took the Bible along the well-worn path of slavery defense. The third of his letters responding to Secretary Forsyth rehearsed standard Old Testament references, including from Leviticus 25:44–46, the permission to permanently enslave aliens. He even turned Exodus 21:16, with its sentence of death for "man-stealers," into evidence justifying slavery: "[W]here slavery did not exist, there would not be the crime which is made capital in Exodus xxi.16." In his fourth letter England repeated standard defenses from the New Testament, including a by then commonplace proslavery reading of Galatians 3:28 ("there is neither bond nor free"). According to England, the Apostle designated "not a civil, but a religious right."[39]

England's proslavery defense played at least a small role in the election of 1840, but it was even more important for indicating the future for American Catholics on slavery. As national controversies became more intense, Catholics would join those, both north and south, who interpreted the Bible as allowing slavery, even as they would align themselves ever more strongly with the Democrats in defending the interests of slaveholders. "No one in the Catholic camp," Michael Hochgeschwender has summarized, "opposed England. . . . The emotions of

the political campaign, the recent economic crisis, the growing radicalism of
evangelicals and immediate abolitionists, [and] worry about nativism . . . all
came together to push Rome and the American episcopate to a clear stopping
point."[40] This stopping point meant, as phrased succinctly by John McGreevy,
"no one prominent American Catholic urged immediate abolitionism before the
Civil War."[41] Politically considered, the Forsyth-England exchange marked one
of the last attempts to enlist proslavery southerners for the Whig Party, as well as
an impetus cementing the Catholic-Democratic alliance that would be almost
complete by the next national election in 1844. Religiously considered, the irony
lay in England's use of the Bible to both neutralize the pope's appeal to Scripture
and set Catholic interpretations allowing for enslavement in stone.

Bishop Kenrick as a Catholic Translator

Poignancy rather than irony attended the efforts of Bishop Francis Patrick
Kenrick to give American Catholics a better English version of the Scriptures.[42]
The one note of irony in his story comes from the fact that the bishop whom
Philadelphia Protestants denounced for trashing the Bible spent the bulk of his
scholarly life devoted to scriptural studies. The Irish-born Kenrick had studied
in Rome for several years as a young man, then taught at St. Thomas's Seminary
in Bardstown, Kentucky, before serving as a theological advisor at the American
Catholic Bishops' first Provincial Council in 1829. Kenrick began work as a translator in 1830 during his years as coadjutor and then full bishop of Philadelphia.
His time as bishop of Philadelphia came to an end in 1851, when he was promoted to the see of Baltimore, where he served as the nation's leading prelate
until his death in 1863.

Provincial meetings of the bishops repeatedly extolled the Scriptures, as at
that first gathering in 1829. "[O]ne of the most precious legacies bequeathed to
us by the Apostles and Evangelists is the sacred volume of Holy Scriptures"; besides its value to pastors, it was also profitable, "when used with due care, and
an humble and docile spirit, for the edification and instruction of the faithful."
The same council, however, also repeated standard Catholic restrictions: "We
therefore earnestly caution you against the indiscriminate use of unauthorised
versions. . . . The Douay translation from the Vulgate of the Old Testament with
the Remish translation of the New Testament, are our best English versions."[43]
Kenrick set himself a threefold challenge: remain faithful to the Vulgate, prepare
a corrected edition of the Douay-Rheims translation, and in the process improve
the readability of the Bible for American Catholics.

As detailed by Gerald Fogarty, S.J., *moderate* was exactly the right word to
describe Kenrick as a biblical scholar and translator. While he knew more of

advanced European scholarship than most of his Protestant peers, he remained skeptical about theories that diminished the Bible's supernaturalism or questioned its historical reliability. As a scholar, Kenrick showed unusual independence of mind—for example, by daring to translate the Greek word *metanoeo* with Protestants as "repent" instead of the Douay's "do penance" and to render *baptizo* with the Baptists' "immerse" instead of the Douay's and King James's "baptize."[44] Kenrick also aligned himself with Orestes Brownson and a small number of other Catholics who did not hide their admiration for the KJV, or at least its prose. As Brownson would suggest in a review of Kenrick's revised English Bible, "What we propose is, not that we adopt the Protestant version bodily, but simply that it be made the basis of an amended version, and departed from only for some reason,—doctrinal, philological, scientific, or critical reason of some sort."[45] Kenrick did not agree entirely with Brownson, but when he published his revision of the Pentateuch in 1860, he paid the KJV the high compliment of having "deferred to its usage, although of Protestant origin, feeling that, in things indifferent, conformity is desirable, and that every approach to uniformity in the rendering of the inspired word, without sacrifice of principle, or violation of disciplinary rules, is a gain to the common cause of Christianity."[46] Still, Kenrick took pains to maintain the distinctly Catholic character of his work, as when he added a note in this same edition to Genesis 3:15 and its prophetic words about "the seed of the woman" that would ultimately defeat the serpent: "The woman is not Eve only, or principally, although she no doubt detested the tempter, the occasion of her fall; but Mary, the mother of Him who came to repair the ruin."

As it happened, and despite diligent labor extending over two decades, Kenrick's edited version of the Douay bible never caught on.[47] A plan fell through to cooperate with John Henry Newman for a common edition serving Catholics on both sides of the Atlantic. Some of his fellow bishops thought his translation took too much from the KJV or heeded too closely scholarly *eurekas* from the continent. Kenrick's moderation was also growing increasingly out of step with the conservatism of Pope Pius IX, who succeeded Gregory XVI in 1846. In addition, Kenrick's desire that more lay Catholics engage more directly with the Bible worked against the era's "Catholic devotional revival," which placed greater emphasis on older practices not directly drawn from Scripture.[48] The escalating conflicts between Catholics and Protestants over schools, in which Kenrick had been such a visible figure, pushed many in the church toward Bishop Hughes's militancy rather than Kenrick's moderation. Not until a century passed, with developments after World War II and especially the Second Vatican Council, would Kenrick's irenic engagement with critical scholarship and willingness to learn with Protestants finally win the day among American Catholics.

Building Pressure

Once the nation's episodic violence surrounding the perpetuation of slavery broke into open warfare, the national cataclysm affected Protestant-Catholic relations as it did nearly everything else. In the runup to open conflict and during the Civil War itself, Catholics targeted Protestant biblicism as *the* cause of the Civil War. That polemic rebutted, if it did not halt, the fervent anti-Catholicism that grew over the decade of the 1850s, often focusing on Catholic disdain for Scripture.

A new weapon in the Protestant arsenal came with speeches and publications from former Catholic priests who explained to American audiences how old-world Catholicism continued to throttle alike both Scripture and liberty. In 1853, public lectures by Alessandro Gavazzi sensationalized the disabilities he had suffered as an Italian monk who supported Italian Revolutionary parties in the late 1840s. One of his lectures in New York, with an account of how authorities in Rome prosecuted a lay couple for attending a Bible study, singled out Bishop Hughes for disseminating lies on the subject. He closed the same New York City lecture with ominous words: "Take heed of your Bible, watch it well; remember that America will [be] lost when she loses her Bible."[49] After protests disrupted his appearances in America, irate Francophone Catholics mobbed his meetings in Quebec City and Montreal, resulting in multiple fatalities. Another former priest, also with a Canadian connection, featured prominently in articles in the *Chicago Tribune* in 1857 and 1858. Father Charles Chiniquy had been dispatched to serve a settlement of expat Québécois in Illinois, but then he broke with his Canadian bishop and became a Presbyterian. Always an eager communicator, Chiniquy began to publicize the abuses he suffered for, as the *Tribune* reported, "possessing this spirit of religious independence."[50]

For Protestants the preservation of the King James Bible in public schools continued to stimulate strong anti-Catholic animus. In 1852, an aggrieved Bostonian published an article in the journal founded by Horace Mann to complain about "ignorant immigrants" calling for the end to readings from the KJV. The article pled with the newcomers to realize that common schools "owe their origin to religious principles." The author concluded, "[I]t should be a condition of citizenship, that their children shall be educated in our free schools with our own children, and under the influence of our free school system, which we trust will never repudiate the Scriptures."[51] In December of the next year Cincinnati Protestants protested the arrival of Archbishop Gaetano Bedini, whom Gavazzi had earlier called "the Butcher of Bologna" for overseeing the execution of republican participants in the European Revolution of 1848. The protests prompted yet another round of agitation about the place of Scripture in Cincinnati's tax-supported schools.[52] The very next year, George Cheever in upstate New York used nearly identical language to defend both abolition and Bible reading in public schools: "At the South, the slave-holders and slave laws forbid the teaching of the Bible; at the North [so do] the Romanists and Romish laws."[53]

Violence sometimes accented the Protestant drumbeat on the school question. In 1854 a Jesuit who had been on the losing side of a Catholic-Protestant civil war in his native Switzerland found himself under fire in Ellsworth, Maine. When the local school authority denied John Bapst's request to exempt Catholic children from reading the KJV, he opened a new school for those students. The local bishop transferred Bapst to another Maine town to shield him from possible violence, but on a return visit to the village in October, he was discovered, threatened (some in the crowd called for burning him alive), and then tarred and feathered.[54] Although much of New England denounced that outrage, tensions remained high. In Boston the so-called Eliot School Rebellion of 1859 was sparked when an assistant to the principal at a public school used a rattan stick to bloody the hands of a ten-year-old boy, Thomas Whall, when Whall refused to recite the Ten Commandments from the KJV. Whall's priest and his parents did not object to reciting the Ten Commandments, but they did object to the mandatory use of the Protestants' KJV for the recitation.[55]

Coming out of Boston was also one of the era's major antipapal statements. Edward Beecher published it in 1855, three years after the appearance of *Uncle Tom's Cabin* from his more famous sister Harriet. It is hard to imagine a more energetic marshaling of "Reason, History, and Scripture" against Rome. Beecher's father, Lyman, had earlier edited a periodical called *The Spirit of the Pilgrims*. Now the son began his polemic by evoking "the Pilgrim Fathers," who had established their society on the basis of "civil and religious liberty," located as far as possible from "the corruptions and pollutions of Rome in doctrine, organization, and morals." To Beecher the secret of the Pilgrims' success was as obvious as the malevolence of Rome: "Their foundation was the Bible, and the Bible alone—not the Bible neutralized or rendered poisonous by the traditions of man; the Bible in the hands of the churches and of the people, and not in the hands of a hierarchy falsely calling herself *the church*."[56]

Guardians and Pastors

In a national climate still defined in considerable part by a mix of Christian hope, republican virtue, and the King James Version, Catholics made their way through aggressive civic self-defense, individualized pastoral counsel, ongoing theological argument, and instruction of the faithful. Bishop Hughes, for example, published an angry rebuttal when American Protestants jumped on the reports from Italy about the lay Italian couple prosecuted for attending a local

Bible study.[57] In order to open channels for asserting Catholic responsibility with whoever was in power, Hughes took pains to cultivate good relations with Whigs like New York's governor William Seward as well as leading Democrats. From first to last the bishop energetically maintained the message that Bishop Carroll had delivered for the first time in 1784: Catholics were both genuine Christians and trustworthy Americans.

Leaders like Bishop Hughes were always quick to declare their loyalty to America as they countered aspersions against Catholics for undermining "civil and religious liberty." Many also continued to defend Catholicism specifically as a religion. After his conversion in 1844, Orestes Brownson regularly published lengthy articles responding to Protestant complaints about Catholic abuse of Scripture—in 1846 against statements about the authority of the Bible in the Presbyterians' Westminster Confession, in 1847 on the impossibility of "the Bible alone" to achieve Christian unity, and in 1860 when defending Catholic approaches to the Scriptures.[58] Other Catholics joined with Brownson in such apologetics, sometimes even more aggressively. Between 1848 and 1859, Boston publishers brought out at least four editions of an Australian priest's challenge to Protestant claims about Scripture. Beginning on his title page with pointed Douay texts from Psalm 129:2 ("many a time have they afflicted me") and 2 Timothy 3:9 ("their folly shall be made manifest unto men"), the Rev. Lawrence Sheil turned to the Bible itself to expose Protestant error. His treatise specified twenty-nine doctrines and practices where Protestants were not "conformable to the express word of God."[59]

Although much of American Catholic attention to Scripture by necessity had to be defensive, priests, bishops, and some among the laity also labored to assist the faithful. One case sometime in the 1850s involved Archbishop Kenrick when a priest asked him to adjudicate a crisis of conscience involving a young Catholic laywoman. She was employed in a public school where, following local guidelines, she read the Bible to her students daily—but the Douay-Rheims version. When one of the school commissioners found out, he demanded that she use the KJV or be dismissed. Now the teacher, whose family depended on her salary, asked her priest if it was permissible to read to the students from the Psalms in the Protestant Bible. He did not think so, but informed Kenrick that another priest had earlier allowed something similar when the young woman was only substituting. Kenrick's reply is not recorded, but it was obvious that he and the local priest were caught in a dilemma—trying to be faithful to the church, but also sympathetic to the young woman.[60]

Polemics were also not uppermost when other Catholics addressed the public, including a landmark reference work published in 1859. In that year John Gilmary Shea, the first layman to carry out extensive research in American Catholic history, brought to the public a bibliography of Catholic bibles printed in the United States. His preface briefly rehearsed a history that began with persecution by early English Protestants, then the relaxed atmosphere after the Stuart Rebellion of 1745 that gave Richard Challoner the freedom to publish his revision of the Douay-Rheims translation, and finally the "comparative freedom and seeming equality" brought to American Catholics by the War of Independence. Most of the pamphlet's forty-five pages, however, was devoted to a detailed list of the fifty-three Bibles, New Testaments, or portions that had been published, from Mathew Carey's 1790 Douay-Rheims Bible in 1790 to Archbishop Kenrick's translation of Job and the Prophets in 1859. It is noteworthy that his list included five Catholic editions published by the New York and American Bible societies, three in Spanish, one each in French and Portuguese. Shea inserted a few polemical notes in describing the various editions, but the spirit of the work mostly reflected the calm words of his preface: "For reverential perusal and devout meditation, a comparatively small number of [Bibles] suffices."[61] Although such Catholic works aiming at information and edification, rather than argumentation, increased rapidly after the Civil War, a number had already appeared to guide, and not just defend, Catholics in their own use of the Scriptures.

Assessment

The history of Catholics and the Bible from Bishop Carroll to Archbishop Kenrick can be assessed from several directions. Historical research by itself cannot adjudicate rival theological claims about proper or improper use of Scripture. Yet it can illuminate contexts for what in the twenty-first century can look simply like inflamed Protestant bigotry met by ad hoc Catholic reaction.

Protestants who worried about Catholics were not making things up, or at least not entirely. The irate priest in upstate New York really had incinerated a copy of the King James Bible. Roman authorities really did prosecute an Italian couple arraigned for private Bible study, though they contended it was for sedition rather than anything specifically religious. Priests and bishops did warn the faithful against unauthorized attention to Scripture that could easily sound like warnings against reading the Bible at all. Sensational Protestant revelations about abuses of the confessional—in American Protestant eyes an antibiblical practice of there ever was one!—rested on at least occasional matters of fact.[62]

Above all, Americans who heeded news from Europe saw in papal pronouncements proof positive of deep-seated opposition to much that Americans held dear. Whatever Gregory XVI might have said about slavery, his programmatic encyclicals trumpeted the official Catholic rejection of church-state separation, common schooling, press freedom, and voluntary religious organization. The coalition of moderate and liberal cardinals that in 1846 elected Pius IX as Gregory's successor evidently wanted a change. But when Rome's republican revolution in 1848 led to violence that forced the pope into exile, he returned to the arch conservativism of his predecessor. It lay a few years into the future, but Pius IX's *Syllabus of Errors* from 1864 only confirmed what observers already knew about his convictions. It was wrong, according to the pope, that "civil liberty" should be given to "every form of worship" and that the pope himself should "come to terms with progress, liberalism, and modern civilization."[63] To more than a few Americans, such statements proved that when leading Catholics claimed to endorse American freedoms, they were lying through their teeth.

A comparison may be helpful. In the generation before the Civil War anxious anti-Catholics like Edward Beecher spoke against the Catholic threat in ways reminiscent of "the Sons of Liberty," who in the Revolutionary generation described Parliament as a tyranny poised to spring. The comparison is of course not exact, since papal pronouncements did not have the force of law like Parliament's tax legislation, and the quartering of British troops bespoke a kind of power different from Catholic immigrants voting for Democrats. Yet a common mental framework linked the two situations. The ability to discern a parliamentary conspiracy and then a Catholic conspiracy depended on an ideology that transformed any restriction on any free action into threats against all free action. For the purposes of this book, the two situations were also connected by a strong biblical presence. Stories from the Old Testament about the Lord rescuing Israel from oppression and apostolic injunctions from the New Testament about "standing fast in the liberty wherewith Christ hath made us free" nerved the political struggle against British tyranny. Defense of the Bible as the key to personal virtue, and therefore the survival of the republic, excited similar passion against Catholics in antebellum decades. It also reprised on a small scale the violence that on a large scale had won national independence.

Such conspiratorial thinking had received a check when in the generation of Jedidiah Morse the Bavarian Illuminati faded into thin air. It roared back in the generation of Morse's son, Samuel, in response to the surge in Catholic immigration. Even more indisputable evidence about the ability of "the slave power" to dictate the nation's future increased fears about all conspiracies against freedom. The success of Protestant denominations and Protestant voluntary organizations in promoting "the Bible alone" also heightened anxiety about every Catholic advance.

In 1821, almost sixty years after John Adams published his dissertation on the canon and feudal law, he repeated the thesis of that work to Thomas

Jefferson: "I have long been decided in opinion that a free government and the Roman Catholick religion can never exist together in any nation or Country."[64] Another generation on, a Maine attorney who decried the violence directed at John Bapst nonetheless expressed the same concern that Catholicism violated the "freedom of thought, and personal responsibility, necessary to the support of republican institutions."[65] In these concerns Adams and the Maine lawyer spoke for many other Americans, a few eager to riot against anything Roman, more simply uneasy to varying degrees about the swelling Catholic presence.

Were they in any sense justified in their worries? If American well-being really did depend on free institutions organized to ensure self-directed inner virtue, then the answer is "perhaps." Catholics also wanted personal virtue to flourish, but Catholic virtue could mean patient endurance of unjust suffering rather than active reform of present evils.[66] Catholic "freedom" thus came closer to Puritan "freedom"—liberty from outside pressure in order to pursue the proper course— more than the nineteenth-century liberal American notion of *choosing* which course to pursue. The antebellum Catholic presence may not have created the barrier to freedom and well-being that many Protestants perceived. But it did not align clearly with what many Americans, especially custodial Protestants, simply knew was the essential foundation for personal liberty and communal flourishing.

Because the Bible was an indispensable part of that foundation, antebellum Catholics faced an ongoing challenge to show the faithful and convince outsiders that their church did in fact honor the Scriptures, though not in the fashion of American Protestants. In the early United States, that combination made simply no sense at all. Could a Catholic approach to Scripture ever hope to gain credibility when the language of the King James Bible sanctified the nation's self-definition as a republic? That translation had figured centrally in the British imperial heritage when Roman Catholicism loomed as an ever-present threat. Once adjusted for new American circumstances, that heritage made it all too easy to express economic, ethnic, cultural, or political fears in the venerable Protestant idiom of opposition to Rome. The channel of biblical anti-Catholicism dug deeply in British and colonial history lay open and close to hand. It instinctively substantiated all such fears, especially if they could be confirmed by words from the Roman pontiff himself.

Whatever the justice in Protestant worries about Catholic contributions to a free republic, those worries also contributed to what might be termed "the Protestant crisis of Scripture" in antebellum America. A fraught question defined this crisis: Could Protestants ever see any difference between their loyalty to the Bible and their loyalty to the republic? Even as contentions over slavery called into question basic Protestant assertions about the life-giving clarity of Scripture, Catholic-Protestant disputes threatened to turn the Bible into merely a symbol of American liberty. That transformation, in turn, meant that biblical loyalty to America could be as dangerous for the integrity of Scripture as anything done by Catholics.

17

Whose Bible? (Lutherans, Jews, Naysayers, Natives)

The swelling tide of immigration that brought lower-class Irish Catholics to America—and consternation to many Protestants—carried almost as many German speakers. The approximately fifty thousand German speakers who arrived from 1826 to 1835 quadrupled during the next decade and then quintupled in the years from 1846 to 1855 to nearly a million.[1] Jewish arrivals, also usually from German-speaking lands, created a rising population curve from less than 15,000 in 1840 to at least 150,000 twenty years later.[2] Where the surge of Irish immigrants created conflict with Protestants focused on Scripture, the result of the German surge was not conflict, but isolation. The slower increase in Jewish numbers added further complications, especially with the beginning of efforts to protect the Hebrew Scriptures from Christian absorption while providing an American Bible from Jews for Jews.

As immigrants streamed in, earlier trajectories carried on, though now with variations. When on January 7, 1827, one year minus one day after Bishop John England offered the first Sunday sermon by a Catholic in the hall of the U.S. House of Representatives, Harriet Livermore became the first woman to perform that duty. In time-honored fashion, Livermore took her text from the King James Version, this time King David's closing exhortation to Israel: "He that ruleth over men must be just, ruling in the fear of God. And he shall be as the light of the morning when the sun riseth, even a morning without clouds: as the tender grass springing out of the earth by clear shining after rain [2 Sam 23:3–4]." A newspaper reported that, though out of deference to convention Livermore called her address a "testimony" rather than a "sermon," it lasted for more than an hour; it was "not only bold, but felicitous and eloquent"; and she kept her audience entirely attentive, including President John Quincy Adams, who because of the crush of interested listeners found himself seated on the steps leading to the podium. As had many men who had preached on such texts, she too emphasized that a just ruler would mean great good for the people. Yet it was entirely novel for a woman to expound the Scriptures this way for that audience.[3]

Similarly, when in the 1840s and 1850s a rising school of American ethnology broadcast its opinions on the question of human diversity, its members advanced their claims with the same respect for empirical evidence and commonsense

America's Book. Mark A. Noll, Oxford University Press. © Oxford University Press 2022.
DOI: 10.1093/oso/9780197623466.003.0018

moral certainties that biblical defenders had been putting to use for nearly two centuries. Yet they did so to attack, rather than confirm, traditional deference to Scripture.

German American Lutherans, new American Jews, "scientists" dismissing the Scriptures, and Native Americans (this chapter) as well as women preachers and writers (the next chapter) were only some of the Americans who joined the ever-expanding chorus of voices claiming to speak for, from, or about the Scriptures. In every case they shared at least some convictions or habits of mind with the white Protestant men who had labored so diligently to build a Bible civilization. But in every case the differences were as important as the similarities.

Germans, Lutherans, *Die Heilige Schrift*, and the Augsburg Confession

German America was never uniformly Lutheran, nor were American Lutherans ever isolated from the English-speaking majority.[4] But until the backwash of Europe's failed 1848 revolutions spilled significant numbers of German immigrants into the Midwest, "the majority of German speakers in North America," in Gregg Roeber's authoritative summary, "remained steadfastly tied to Christianity."[5] Beginning in the early 1830s, German-speaking Catholics were well represented in this immigrant demographic. The 1844 Bible Riots in Philadelphia revealed something about how they were viewed since the mobs that torched the churches of Irish American Catholics did not disturb the Catholic churches of recent German arrivals. In Cincinnati, where by the 1840s over one-fourth of the local printers brought out their wares in German *Fraktur*, Bishop John Purcell launched *Der Wahrheitsfreund (The Friend of Truth)* in 1837, the nation's first German Catholic newspaper and long one of its most influential.[6]

Yet duly noting the presence of unchurched multitudes and a growing Catholic population, it was still the case that the Lutheran heritage long exerted inordinate influence on the consciousness of German Americans. Martin Luther's land-mark translation of the Bible, *Die Heilige Schrift*, remained a treasured inherit-ance for Lutherans, but also for the German Reformed, Moravians, Mennonites, Dunkers (Church of the Brethren), and smaller groups. (Figure 17.1) Luther's *Small Catechism* enjoyed almost as wide circulation, as did his hymns and later German hymnody. The distinctive conservatism of confessional Lutheranism also shaped more in this immigrant stream than just the Lutherans.

From the earliest waves of German migration during the first half of the eighteenth century, colonial German printers-publishers-booksellers supplied a vast quantity of imported and locally produced reading material for these

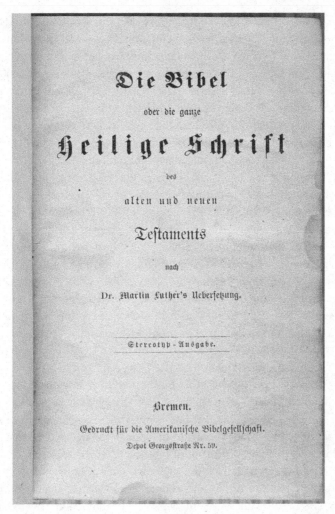

Figure 17.1 The American Bible Society regularly cooperated with European publishers, in this case from the independent German city-state of Bremen, in printing bibles for newcomers to the United States.

Source: Courtesy of Buswell Library Special Collections, Rare Books, Wheaton College, Illinois.

new Americans. For decades the Christopher Saur family of Philadelphia (Germantown) led the way. Christopher Sr. began by importing bibles, hymn books, and catechisms from the pietist Francke Foundation in Halle (Prussia). Early on the imports also included *Fraktur* type with which Saur began his own printing ventures. Soon thereafter, in 1743, Saur produced the first European-language Bible in North America.[7] Its print run of 1,200 copies used a Halle edition of Luther's translation, but with enough mistakes and variations introduced by Saur himself that the colonies' leading Lutheran, Henry Melchior Muhlenberg, joined pastors of German Reformed churches in warning against this edition. Nonetheless, the Saur family persevered, with a second edition of 2,000 copies in 1763, this one managed by Christopher's son. Just as hostilities broke out between the colonies and Britain in 1776, Christopher II published yet a third edition. When the printer, who sided with the Loyalists, later petitioned Parliament to compensate for books destroyed by the patriots, he detailed a lost stock of 2,900 full bibles along with almost fifteen thousand hymnals, catechisms, and psalters.[8] When Mathew Carey and his generation began to publish full English Bibles, they trailed the Saurs' German editions by a full half-century.

The Revolutionary War and the slow pace of immigration thereafter meant that some German-language American publishing began to drift toward English. Yet as Hermann Wellenreuther has documented, the desire for reading material in German spread as German speakers migrated west and south. Much of that material came from printers on the way to becoming publishers, but bookshops that produced one- and two-sheet broadsides added significantly to the total. Wellenreuther has identified 288 such bookshops or printers that produced broadsides in the century before 1830, about three-quarters of them from thirty-one different locations in Pennsylvania. Many of the 1,682 separate broadsides he found in this dispersed publishing enterprise came out in multiple editions. For our purposes, it is significant that Bible passages or Bible-based devotional material (hymns, funeral sermons, liturgies, folk spirituality) made up 45% of the total.[9] In the new nation's first half-century German-language printers or printers serving populations shifting from German to English produced besides these broadsides a vast outpouring of bibles, psalters, catechisms, and hymn books. Only almanacs and, from the 1820s, manuals of homeopathic medicine came anywhere close to the steady production of German Bibles and biblical byproducts.[10] This was, moreover, not a passing phenomenon. During the sixty years between 1860 and 1920 American publishers brought out at least one hundred new German-language editions of the complete Bible.[11]

Prime readers of this material were always the Lutherans. Their confessional tradition held about the same place among German Americans as did Episcopal and Presbyterian confessions in the Anglo-American population. Against Catholic opponents, these traditions echoed the sectarian Protestants; they stood forthrightly on *scriptura sola*, "the Bible alone." At the same time, formal statements of faith that had been officially mandated in Europe checked moves toward the democratic biblicism that flourished in the early United States. For Lutherans in German lands as well as Scandinavia, the Augsburg Confession of 1530 functioned like the Thirty-Nine Articles for Anglicans/Episcopalians and the Westminster Standards for Scottish Presbyterians. In the face of the democratic individualism encouraged by the American Revolution, confessional traditions battled back. In the very early years of the United States, one of the first American Episcopal bishops, Samuel Seabury, even asked Presbyterians and Congregationalists to leave their "errors" and their ill-founded church governments in order to unite around the Thirty-Nine Articles/Book of Common Prayer.[12] Later, John Henry Hobart's unwillingness to join the American Bible Society because its texts were not published with the Book of Common Prayer (chapter 3, 72), and George Bourne's insistence that Presbyterians follow the Westminster Larger Catechism to the letter (chapter 10, 220) illustrated similar respect for European confessional traditions.

Among the new nation's German-speaking population, a Philadelphia pastor, Justus Henry Christian Helmuth, followed a parallel course. While Helmuth welcomed the Revolution and the new nation's religious freedom, he also worked diligently to preserve a distinctive Lutheranism, along with an array of institutions aimed at keeping the German language alive (a newspaper, books, hymn books, schools). In the same way that Muhlenberg protested against Saur for printing a Luther Bible with variations approved by no one but himself, Helmuth tried to keep Lutheran allegiance to the Bible within the framework of the Augsburg Confession. But by the 1790s, Helmuth was worrying about free-form, catch-as-catch-can deployment of Scripture, which he called "altogether harmful when someone reads his whims and fantasies into this holy book." Such usage, in Helmuth's eyes, turned the Bible into "a weathervane" blowing in "every direction of the imagination." It made the Bible "a dark chaos."[13]

In the first decades of the nineteenth century, and despite Helmuth's hope that the Augsburg Confession would continue to guide biblical understanding, Lutherans tracked with the other confessional traditions in gradually paying less heed to their old-world inheritance. For Lutherans, this movement coincided with the increasing use of English for worship and religious instruction. As Presbyterians challenged by Bourne's strict confessionalism chose peace over strict adherence to the Westminster Larger Catechism and Episcopalians like William Jay became increasingly committed to the evangelical united front of voluntary agencies, so also Lutherans began to Americanize. In 1830, when Lutherans celebrated the Augsburg Confession's three-hundredth anniversary, a few worried about the American claim to follow "no creed but the Bible." But concern at that stage represented only a hand-size cloud on the horizon.[14]

The career of Samuel Simon Schmucker illustrates the Lutheran evolution that eventually did generate a significant backlash.[15] From his respected position as the leading theologian at the Lutherans' leading theological seminary (Gettysburg in Pennsylvania), Schmucker walked a fine line. His commitment to historic Lutheranism constrained, but did not entirely overcome, the pull of American Protestant conventions. A major textbook that Schmucker published in 1834 indicated his course. This hefty volume announced itself as setting forth "Popular Theology" according to "the Doctrines of the Reformation, as Avowed before the Diet of Augsburg." When Schmucker took up the question of Bible translations, he first recorded the objection of all Protestants to "the Roman Catholic church, which maintains, that the scriptures do not teach all the necessary features of true Christianity." He then recommended the King James translation as "a very correct and able version," but also opined that in comparisons to Luther's Bible, it was "too rigidly literal to be entirely perspicuous [clear]." For Schmucker, *Die Heilige Schrift* remained the standard: "The language of Luther's version is remarkably pure and elegant, has justly been ranked with the German classics, and is at the present day entirely intelligible to the popular reader."[16]

Yet even as Schmucker's "Popular Theology" mostly presented standard Lutheran teaching, it drifted closer to the views of American Presbyterians and Congregationalists. Although the articles of the Augsburg Confession structured this work, Schmucker also explained that only the Confession's "fundamental doctrines," and not necessarily all its details, should guide American Lutherans. Schmucker did not spell out those fundamentals, but he did explain in detail why Lutherans should celebrate the principles of the American Revolution.[17] Things became clearer when in 1855 Schmucker with associates proposed a "Definite Platform" to guide American Lutheranism as a whole. It began with the Augsburg Confession, but then specified what the authors considered errors in that document. All of Schmucker's improvements bent toward common American convictions. Augsburg, that is, had mistakenly *not* mandated careful observance of the Christian Sabbath, but it had *mistakenly affirmed* baptismal regeneration, Christ's real presence in the Lord's Supper, the need for private confession, and the continuity of ceremonial taken over from the Catholic mass.[18] Shortly before, Schmucker had defined these traditional doctrines as "minor or non-fundamental points." He had also claimed that Luther and his associates had not been "rigid symbolists"—that is, strict adherents to the confessional "symbols."[19]

By the 1850s, many of Schmucker's fellow Lutherans could not have disagreed more. In a decade when the number of Lutheran churches grew from 1,217 to 2,128, opposition to such modifications became intense.[20] It came from some Lutherans who had begun to use English, more who, though living in the United States for some time, still worshiped and wrote in German, but most from among the newer hosts of German immigrants. (Between 1840 and 1860, Lutherans established thirty-three new regional associations, or synods, some reorganizing what had been there before, but most serving the incoming flood.)[21] The most prominent leader of the opposition was Carl Ferdinand Wilhelm Walther, who migrated from Saxony to the St. Louis area in 1838. To his new homeland Walther brought the long-standing Lutheran abhorrence of Roman Catholicism and stiff opposition to eighteenth-century Enlightenment rationalism. He also opposed the 1817 merger of Lutherans and Reformed churches that Frederick III of Prussia had decreed for his regime and that rapidly became a template for other German lands. Walther, a dynamo with exhaustless drive, almost immediately founded a newspaper, *Der Lutheraner*, which, as stated succinctly in a helpful chronology of his life, called "scattered Lutherans to unite around Scripture and the Confessions."[22] Its masthead long carried the slogan "Gottes Wort und Luthers Lehr' vergehen nie und nimmermehr" (God's Word and Luther's teaching will never, ever pass away).

In 1855, at the height of debate over Schmucker's proposals for modifying the Augsburg Confession, Walther inaugurated a monthly journal pitched to ministers and educated laymen. Its title, *Lehre und Wehre* (*Teaching and Defense*), came from Luther's famous Reformation hymn "Ein fest Burg ist unser Gott, / Ein gute Wehr und Waffen" (A strong fortress is our God, a good defense and weapon). Its opening article, "Teaching About the Holy Office of Pastor," insisted that a minister's preaching must follow "Schrift und Symbolen" (the Bible and the Confessions).[23] The article, which warned against allowing any Catholic or modernizing pathogens to infect Lutheranism, set the tone for every issue thereafter. In June of that year a similar article asked, "How will truly Lutheran congregations be established and built up?"[24] The answer again was Scripture and the historical Confessions. Three years later Walther himself underscored this commitment in "Why Should Our Pastors, Teachers, and Professors Subscribe Unconditionally the Symbolical Writings of Our Church?" His answer: because "without any exception the doctrinal contents of our church are in complete agreement with the Holy Scriptures and are not in conflict with the same in any point, whether a major or secondary point."[25]

Walther's Lutheran Church–Missouri Synod and smaller confessional bodies made up only one part of American Lutheranism. But a significant number of like-minded and often influential leaders agreed with him that to follow the Reformation's most distinctive banner, *sola scriptura*, meant to read Scripture as, and only as, it was understood in the Lutheran confessions. This insistence paralleled for Lutherans what some American Episcopalians absorbed from England's Oxford Movement of the 1830s and 1840s, a determination to embrace a "Catholic" or "high church" understanding of the Anglican tradition. But for Lutherans, already partially isolated by the German language as well as a hymn tradition quite different from Anglo-American hymnody, the confessional emphasis exerted much greater influence. Presbyterian confessionalism centered on the Westminster Standards also paralleled the Lutheran commitment to Augsburg. In their case, however, intense American debates over slavery and then the Civil War caused Presbyterians to sit more lightly toward their historical confession. The closest parallel to the Lutheran story would come later in the century, when increasing numbers of Dutch immigrants pulled the American

Dutch Reformed churches back toward the use of the mother European tongue and a confessionally Protestant, but not American Protestant, use of Scripture.[26]

The membrane separating even strongly confessional American Lutherans from other Protestants was always semi-permeable. In the run-up to the Civil War, as an instance, Walther's Missouri Synod and smaller Norwegian synods agreed with northern conservative Protestants in not condemning slavery as such. They were determined to follow only the Scriptures; with so many of their white peers they did not understand the Bible to condemn the system.[27]

Yet for the American history of Scripture, the confessional Lutheran stance made a real difference. To the present day, conservative American Lutherans, like so many other Protestants, adhere to an "inspired" and even "inerrant" Scripture, but unlike most other Protestants, they insist that Scripture be understood within the Lutheran confessional tradition.[28] Lutherans who did not follow the Walther path nonetheless remained quasi-detached from the main American trends, partly because of the confessional Lutheran influence but even more because of the European immigrant stream that continued through the 1920s. Only during the past half-century have these groups, like the contemporary Evangelical Lutheran Church in America, marched in step with the modern-day descendants of nineteenth-century proprietary Protestants.[29]

In broader perspective, the Lutheran presence added more diversity to a narrative that by the mid-nineteenth century had already become diverse. The Lutheran steadfast stand for the Bible did reinforce selected aspects of the nation's Bible civilization, but because of their forthright adherence to old-world traditions, that stand also made agreement on the meaning of the Bible more elusive.[30]

Another People of the Book

In the antebellum United States no single "Jewish America" existed any more than a single "German America" or "Lutheran America." Yet especially on the Bible, ambiguity remained constant. In the Revolutionary period, Pennsylvania Jews petitioned the state to remove the discrimination entailed by the requirement that members of the general assembly acknowledge "the Scriptures of the Old and New Testament" as divinely inspired. The very next year, however, Rabbi Hendla Jochanan van Oettingen composed a prayer that sounded almost Protestant in the way it enlisted ancient Jewish history to bless the new United States: "As Thou didst give of Thy glory to David, son of Jesse, and to Solomon his son Thou didst give wisdom greater than all of men, so mayst Thou grant intelligence, wisdom, and knowledge to our lords, the rulers of these thirteen states."[31]

As for all communities with a small legacy population rapidly swelled by immigration, Jews committed to their religious tradition strove to preserve, strengthen, and practice it. Still, as with Catholics and Lutherans, the common goal of meaningful survival resulted in a variety of defensive and offensive strategies.[32]

For defense, it was no surprise as numbers grew that Jews joined Catholics in complaining about mandatory readings from the KJV in tax-supported common schools. Such readings, beyond their civil and religious imposition, also threatened Jewish loyalty to the *Tanakh*, the collection that Christians called "the Old Testament" but for Jews designated simply the Scriptures. Isaac Leeser, who in 1824 arrived in Richmond, Virginia, as a teenage immigrant from Westphalia, soon moved to Philadelphia, where he became the new world's leading advocate of Jewish "regeneration."[33] Leeser complained that making Jewish children read the KJV in common schools amounted to forcing them to attend church or receive baptism.[34]

To be sure, at least a few leaders in the antebellum period were able to make somewhat light of that issue. Isaac Mayer Wise followed Leeser to America by about two decades, in his case from Bohemia, as one of the first officially ordained rabbis in America. (Leeser served Philadelphia's Congregation Mikveh Israel as a *hazan*, or cantor, prayer leader, speaker, and community coordinator.)[35] Wise's influential career in Cincinnati made him the leader of Reform Judaism, which resembled the Protestant groups that took to American ways with enthusiasm. Like many Protestants, he also claimed, as in a book from 1854, *History of the Israelitish Nation*, that the United States' democratic republicanism rested on truths from the Hebrew Scriptures. Yet during one of his city's early, interminable debates over Bible reading in the schools, Wise expressed forceful opposition. He also suggested, however, that if the practice was deemed necessary for the health of the republic, the best solution was the most thoroughly neutral solution, which to Wise meant readings made without comment in Hebrew and Greek![36] Wise's solution was ingenious, but it also illustrated the weight of the mainstream Protestant Bible, since he apparently overlooked the fact that for Cincinnati's Catholics the Vulgate's Latin also functioned as an authoritative scriptural language. Later, opposition to Protestant Bible reading in tax-supported schools increased in direct proportion to the scale of Jewish immigration.

Decades earlier, however, Isaac Leeser had already turned to offensive action aimed at overcoming Jewish apathy as much as staving off Protestant assimilation. As the energetic equal of peers like Bishop Francis Patrick Kenrick or Lutherans Schmucker and Walther, Leeser organized and published at a ferocious pace—the first printed volume of sermons by a Jewish America, the first translation of Sephardic and Ashkenazi prayer books, the first Hebrew grammar for students, the first Jewish magazine, the first Jewish publication society, the first theological seminary, and more.[37]

Leeser's most significant achievement combined the defensive and the offensive. In 1838, about the same time and in the same city where Bishop Kenrick was also translating, he began work on an English-language version of the Hebrew Scriptures. The first fruits followed seven years later with a translation of the Five Books of Moses and a bilingual Hebrew-English text of Genesis, the latter intended for public worship in the growing number of American synagogues. Successive volumes followed until the publication of a complete English translation in 1853.[38]

For this work Leeser did not simply dismiss the KJV translators, "who may have been as honest as men writing for their sect are ever likely to be." That version itself he called "an eminently clever work, considering the state of knowledge then available."[39] Guarded admiration also led to cautious imitation since much of his English echoed, when it did not copy, the KJV. For instance, the title page of his 1853 translation quoted Deuteronomy 31:21, "For it shall not be forgotten out of the mouth of his seed," which almost replicated the KJV's "For it shall not be forgotten out of the mouths of their seed." Leeser's rendering of the Twenty-third Psalm provided a clearer alternative. (Table 17.1)

Much more obvious than any debt to the KJV was Leeser's search for an emphatically Jewish alternative. In the preface to his 1845 bilingual edition of Genesis, he wrote, "I love my religion as the heir-loom of Israel, which I, as one of the people, have inherited from my fathers." At the same time, he repudiated any "falsehood" in his work, which he "endeavoured to make as strictly literal as possible, and even the order of the words . . . wherever this was practicable."[40] In successive publications, Leeser spelled out his defensive purposes more

Table 17.1 The KJV and Isaac Leeser's Translation

Psalm 23	
KJV	Leeser
A psalm of David 1. The Lord *is my* shepherd; I shall not want.	1. A PSALM of David. The Lord is my shepherd, I shall not want.
2. He maketh me to lie down in green pastures: he leadeth me beside the still waters.	2. In pastures of tender grass he causeth me to lie down: beside still waters he leadeth me.
3. He restoreth my soul: he leadeth me in the paths of righteousness for his name's sake.	3. My soul he refresheth: he guideth me in the tracks of righteousness for the sake of his name.

clearly. Occasionally his complaints sounded academic by noting that even loyal Protestants complained about errors in the KJV and that the KJV's "perfectly arbitrary" verse divisions "disfigured" the originals' narrative flow.[41] But mostly he objected to the Protestant overlay of the KJV and the duplicity of groups like the American Bible Society that advertised their texts as "without note or comment." Although it had mostly sunk below Protestant consciousness, Leeser could not forget that almost all KJV Old Testaments included Christianized chapter and section headings, many editions appended distinctly Christian notes, and all perpetuated what he considered mistranslations. The very first page of his advertisement for the English edition of *Twenty-Four Books* specified as an egregious example the KJV's "a virgin shall conceive" from Isaiah 7:14 and other messianic translations from the Hebrew Scriptures/Old Testament. Even before explaining his intentions for his own translation, he made a point to correct these errors (in this case by rendering the offending phrase "a young woman shall conceive"). Only then did he call out groups like the American Bible Society who deceived Jewish readers, along with everyone else, by claiming to publish their texts "without note or comment." Given the heavy Christological overlay the Society gave to the Old Testament, such claims could be regarded only as "feigned liberality."[42] How, he wondered, could innocent, uneducated Jews realize that when they read marginal comments like "the Prediction of Christ" for Psalm 110, "A Description of Christ" for the Song of Solomon, and "Christ's Birth and Kingdom" for Isaiah 9, they were being manipulated into accepting errors masquerading as inoffensive marginal aids? Jonathan Sarna has exactly captured the standpoint from which Leeser embarked on his work: "These theologically charged translations do not . . . capture the literal meaning of the biblical idiom. Instead, they distort the text, reduce the sanctity and significance of the Hebrew Bible, and engender interreligious hostility."[43]

In at least one particular, however, Leeser's herculean labors did replicate a pattern experienced by other groups that began as marginal and suspect. Leeser in Philadelphia, Wise in Cincinnati, and a rapidly growing Jewish intelligentsia clearly resembled proprietary Protestants in their desire to bestow dignity, order, respectability, and recognized standing on Jewish communities. Leeser, for example, was surprised but also pleased at the reception of his 1853 complete English translation that, though overwhelmingly based on Jewish scholarship, also made some use of Luther's Bible, the KJV, and occasional insights from Protestant authorities like Matthew Henry and Samuel Bagster.[44] The author of a short notice in Charles Hodge's *Biblical Repertory and Princeton Review*, the nation's premier journal of conservative Presbyterian theology, ignored Leeser's obvious alternatives to Christological readings in order to praise his affirmation of the "authenticity of prophecies and their ultimate biblical fulfillment." The result was an "excellent" work in which the reader "will find much to instruct and interest him."[45] A similar recognition of Jewish respectability came on the eve of the Civil War. When an editor in New York City published a collection of sermons on the impending crisis, Rabbi Morris Raphall of New York's Congregation B'Nai Jeshurun was asked to join the ten Presbyterians, Unitarians, and Episcopalians who made up the rest of the book.[46] The substance of Rabbi Raphall's sermon, which offered a qualified judgment on slavery as a biblically justified system, resembled the conclusion of many northern Protestant conservatives.[47] His inclusion in this collection also recognized the conspicuous wealth of his New York congregation and the high standing of some of its members. The same recognition arrived shortly thereafter when, on February 1, 1860, Raphall became the first Jew asked to open a session of Congress with prayer.

In the sweep of American history, respect for Leeser, Raphall, and Congregation B'Nai Jeshurun indicated how a civilization shaped by its biblical fixation could provide opportunities for another People of the (nearly same) Book. But as Jonathan Sarna has again commented, Leeser, then Wise, then Raphall, then many more "also complicated the Protestant theological principle of *sola scriptura* . . . by demonstrating that, in some cases, the Jewish understanding differed markedly from traditional Protestant teachings."[48]

Criticism and "Science"

During the antebellum decades, Americans with traditional respect for the Bible experienced their most serious intellectual challenge since Tom Paine's *Age of Reason*. The challenge had almost nothing to do with the European higher criticism of Scripture and only a little more with European notions of human evolution, matters that did exert great influence after the Civil War. Instead, the crucial antebellum challenge concerned the unity of the human species. For some Americans, race in conjunction with science undercut the intellectual authority of the Bible before they grappled with Darwin and the higher criticism of Scripture. As this book has already suggested, the generation *before* the Civil War witnessed the crucial turning point for the Bible in American history. In those decades the Bible civilization splintered beyond repair, however much Scripture remained significant for many spheres of national life. Among powerful agents of fragmentation—hermeneutics, ecclesiology, and race—the most powerful was race.

Broader considerations explain why modern biblical criticism gained only marginal traction in the antebellum era. When the 1686 publication of Jean Leclerc's *Bibliothèque universelle et historique* inaugurated what James Turner has called "modern historical criticism of the Bible," Britons and their colonial offspring barely noticed.[49] During the first half of the eighteenth century, as British traditionalists mobilized against the Deism that exploited work like Leclerc's, Americans in the colonies showed little interest in specific questions of biblical criticism or in the non-Western religions that fascinated English Deists. Later in the century, as the momentum of European biblical criticism accelerated, British interest flagged and American interest never got off the ground. The small number of scholars who could read German, communications with the continent severed by the French Revolution and Napoleon, the pressing practical needs of the new American nation, and what Turner calls "the ahistorical American approach" indebted to the principles of Common Sense philosophy"—all explain why "the earthquakes that transformed biblical and classical philology in Germany barely stirred the English-speaking world until well into the nineteenth century."[50]

In the generation after the Revolution, the crushing response to Tom Paine's *Age of Reason* also stifled interest in European biblical scholarship. To be sure, as the nation's new centers of formal learning gathered strength, many of their sharpest minds realized that intellectual self-respect required attending to European, especially German, learning. Beginning in the 1810s figures prominent among Boston Unitarians (Joseph Stevens Buckminster), at Harvard (Edward Everett, Andrews Norton), Andover Theological Seminary (Moses Stuart, Edward Robinson), and Princeton Theological Seminary (Charles Hodge, Joseph Addison Alexander) either traveled for study on the continent or immersed themselves in up-to-date German scholarship. The result was a rapid escalation in the technical competence of the United States' first generation of university-conversant biblical scholars. Yet as Turner also notes, "the most competent British and American scholars devoured German philological expertise but choked on any serious revision of inherited biblical orthodoxy."[51]

The example of George Noyes, a learned Massachusetts Unitarian who eventually became Hancock Professor of Hebrew and Dexter Professor of Sacred Literature at Harvard, illustrated the difficulty in transplanting German cuttings in American soil. In 1834, Noyes concluded his review of a book advocating a traditional view of Scripture by contending, "The commonly received doctrine of the inspiration of all the writings included in the Bible, is a millstone hung around its neck, sufficient to sink it."[52] Twelve years later, after he had become a Harvard professor, Noyes announced a principle that would be repeated in a much-noticed book, *Essays and Reviews*, published by English scholars in 1860: "[I]t is idle to pretend that we have a right to study the Old Testament critically, unless we have a right to judge of its contents according to the laws of critical and historical investigation."[53] Yet unlike the tidal wave of opposition that greeted this English provocation in their country, barely a ripple registered in the United States to the critical position that Noyes and a few others espoused. As succinctly summarized by Jerry Wayne Brown, "The strangest feature of American critical biblical studies in this early period is the fact that they vanished so quickly and made so little impact on the development of American religion."[54]

American circumstances explain this "strange feature." Part of the reason lay in the United States' approach to intellectual authority. Unlike Germany, where universities were adopting the principle of *Lehrfreiheit* (academic freedom) that would inspire the postbellum American university, leaders of antebellum intellectual life either taught at theological seminaries that upheld traditional views or mostly deferred to them on anything involving technical European learning. American critical acumen also came into play. As Turner summarizes the scholarship of Andrews Norton, a Massachusetts Unitarian who in the 1830s and 1840s published a three-volume work titled *The Evidences of the Genuineness of the Gospels*, Norton "and other American biblical critics hit the target in griping about how often philosophy drove German philology to its conclusions."[55] American intellectuals, secure in the grip of common-sense philosophy, had no interest in European scholarship beholden to Kantian or Hegelian idealism. Put differently, the gap between learned elites and lay readers was much narrower in the antebellum United States than in Germany.

Although American culture in the 1830s and 1840s was not as chaotic as fifty years earlier, it remained manifestly fragile. Scripture—open to all without academic distinction, interpreted commonsensically, and functioning as an all-purpose authority—remained the essential moral guide for a civilization in constant motion. For Lyman Beecher, only the biblical religion of the Pilgrims could save the United States from the aggressive minions of the pope. For abolitionists, the Bible pointed the way to overcoming the evil stranglehold of "the slave power." For slave owners, the Bible shone a spotlight on the perfidy of those who would subvert a God-ordained institution. For educational reformers, the "nonsectarian" KJV provided a stable moral basis for universal public education. For southern and western Baptists, others in the backcountry, and many members of the Democratic Party, the right of private interpretation of Scripture held at bay the aggressions of meddling Yankees. For Yankee reformers, northern urban dwellers, and many members of the Whig Party, biblical righteousness inspired prodigies of voluntary national organization. For the tens of thousands who heeded William Miller, the Bible spelled out how and when the world would end. For Joseph Smith, imitating the King James Bible with a new Scripture represented the highest form of flattery. The Bible civilization may have been under strain, but not due to the higher criticism of Scripture. Attachment to a precritical Bible remained so widespread, united so many levels of society, inspired so many necessary purposes, and retained such intuitive cultural authority that little space existed for those who brought European scholarship to America.

By contrast, a great deal of space existed for those who exploited deeply in-grained American certainties about race in order to challenge traditional views of Scripture. No antebellum American publication championing modern bib-lical criticism, for instance, received anywhere near the attention generated by an eight-hundred-page volume published in 1854 by Josiah Clark Nott, a surgeon-anthropologist from Alabama, and George Gliddon, a peripatetic Egyptologist.[56] Their *Types of Mankind: or, Ethnological Researches based upon . . . Crania of Races, and upon their Natural, Geographical, Philological, and Biblical History* synthesized several intellectual enterprises: the craniological research of a late Philadelphia physician, Samuel George Morton; the theories of Harvard zool-ogist Louis Agassiz about the geographical distribution of different human spe-cies; Gliddon's on-the-ground investigations of ancient Egyptian skeletons; and Nott's reading of books on ancient history and natural science. Of special note for a history of the Bible was the authors' disdain for orthodox theologians (*skunks* was their word) who tried to harmonize the era's modern ethnology with biblical accounts of a single human origin.[57]

The book's prolific quotations from contemporary researchers, its many maps, and its even more numerous sketches of skulls and faces demonstrated, according to the book's preface, that "the diversity of races must be accepted by Science as a *fact*, independently of theology." As they had done in earlier works, Nott and Gliddon vigorously rebutted standard American accounts that had har-monized contemporary scientific research with biblical teaching. Gliddon, for example, held that "commentaries of the genuine English evangelical school" on the Table of Nations found in Genesis chapter 10 were "of trivial value in them-selves" and carried even "less weight in science." Not incidentally, the authors made no excuses about their passionate defense of the American slave system. As an instance, the book took special care to show that even when Africans were brought to the United States as slaves, they remained physically and intellectually distinct from Caucasians, except where Black-white "illegitimate consequences" had "deteriorated the white elements in direct proportion that they are said to have *improved* the blacks."[58]

This much-noticed volume, published in at least five Philadelphia and London editions before 1860, immediately became the signature statement of the American School of ethnology. Its stance was crystal clear: cutting-edge sci-ence demonstrated the fact of polygenesis, or the division of humankind into separate species. From this premise came an equally indubitable conclusion: the different species ranked themselves from inferior (Black) to superior (white). Scripture, moreover, was either irrelevant or flat-out harmful to serious ethno-logical research.

As might be expected, *Types of Mankind* generated immense controversy.[59] It particularly offended the Rev. John Bachman, a Lutheran clergyman from

Charleston, South Carolina, who had earlier written against Morton and Nott in order to defend both scriptural accounts of human origins and the unity of the human race (monogenesis). Yet Bachman, whose family owned slaves, supplemented his ardent biblical monogenism with a comparably ardent defense of the American slave system.[60] Europeans also followed the controversy over Nott and Gliddon's book, but with concerns that differed substantially from the Americans'. Charles Darwin in England, who appreciated Bachman's efforts to defend monogenesis, utterly rejected his defense of slavery.[61] In France, Pierre Paul Broca appreciated Nott and Gliddon's arguments for polygenism, but along with Darwin considered their defense of Black chattel slavery reprehensible.[62]

A particularly intriguing effort to advance Nott and Gliddon's conclusions illustrates how thoroughly race, science, and Scripture had become entangled in the decades before the Civil War. Shortly after *Types of Mankind* appeared, Nott arranged for Henry Hotze, a recent Swiss immigrant living in Mobile, Alabama, to translate a weighty tome recently published by a French diplomat, the Comte de Gobineau, *Essai sur L'inégalité des Races Humaines*. Gobineau's massive study publicized his long-germinating belief that the human race had entered irrevocable decline. In his opinion, ethnological science held the key to two world-historical conclusions: first, the Black, yellow, and white races originated separately; second, civilization declined wherever the races mingled.[63] Hotze, who seems to have been already captivated by his own reading of the American ethnologists, readily agreed.

This new arrow in the American ethnological quiver appeared in 1856 with a lengthy introduction by Hotze, his translation of the first volume of Gobineau's work, and an appendix from Nott on the question of polygenesis versus monogenesis. Their title for the American translation, *The Moral and Intellectual Diversity of Races*, emphasized the message they wanted Americans to learn from Gobineau.

For a history of the Bible, the translation shows how the Americans' racist motives maneuvered Gobineau's work to promote not Gobineau's but the Americans' purposes—purposes that included displacing traditional reliance on Scripture with trust in ethnological research. Hotze's lengthy editor's preface innocently claimed that he did not intend "to re-agitate the question of unity or plurality of the human species."[64] That was a question "which the majority of [his American] readers considered satisfactorily and forever settled by the words of Holy Writ." Instead, Gobineau's history would support the science so profusely exhibited in Nott and Gliddon's *Types of Mankind* in order to further demonstrate that within the human family the various races differed "not only in degree, but in kind."[65] Yet Hotze, though claiming to avoid theological conflict, also explained that Gobineau had shown the permanent "diversities among the various branches of the human family"—that is, polygenesis. Hotze clinched his case with a biblical word, though changing Jeremiah 13:23 from a question to a statement and transforming the prophet's observation about Israel's moral intractability into a proof-text for racial differentiation: "The Ethiopian cannot change his skin."[66]

Where Hotze in his introduction finessed the debate between unity or plurality of human species, Gobineau addressed it directly. The French savant concluded that although scientific evidence pointed to the plurality of human species, he was held back from that conclusion by "another argument which, I confess, appears to me of greater moment: Scripture is said to declare against difference of origin. If the text is clear, preemptory, and indisputable, we must submit."[67] Quite different was Nott in the appendix he added to the translation. Nott boldly asserted that "the Bible should not be regarded as a text-book of natural history." In his view, "none of the writers of the Old or New Testament give[s] the slightest evidence of knowledge in any department of science beyond that of their profane contemporaries." As a result, Nott articulated a position that would later be argued at great length by John William Draper and Andrew Dickson White about an ineradicable conflict between science and theology: study of "the natural history of man is a department of science" that should be liberated from a history long "stifled by bigotry and error."[68]

In a letter from the translator to the author, Hotze tried to explain why Gobineau's "argumentative subject" needed to be treated differently in the United States than in France. Since Americans, he reminded Gobineau, were "proverbially the busiest, most hurried, nation of the world," things had to be spelled out for them clearly. That circumstance, in turn, required "certain alterations" in the original. As Hotze informed the Count in the same letter, bloodshed over slavery had already occurred "in a newly formed territory" (Kansas); this contention was "the rock upon which the vessel of state will wreck one day, perhaps ere long." Hotze knew that the Count would certainly understand "the intimate connection of the questions you agitate and those which make this so-called Union anything but what its name implies." In Hotze's America, race meant slavery and slavery meant race.

Behind their translating effort, Nott and Hotze hoped that Gobineau's prestige would advance what scholars have called "scientific racism" as a replacement for a biblical anthropology. That biblical view of humankind, even with the prevailing white view of Black racial inferiority, insisted on the unity of humankind (monogenesis).[69] Hotze may have been thinking of William Archer Cocke when he explained to Gobineau that "the united Protestant Churches, but especially the Presbyterian, are bitterly opposed to the slightest intimation of original diversity." Cocke, in harshly attacking Nott and Gliddon's Types of Mankind, had stated his case unequivocally: "If there are distinct species of Man, then the Bible is untrue; if there are other races than the descendents of Adam, they are free from the penalty 'of man's first disobedience' and the tragic scene of Calvary but a mockery and a delusion."[70] Hotze told Gobineau he was trying to preserve the Frenchman from "the slightest suspicion of what is called infidelity" because in the United States "we are a very religious people, and the pulpit, in some form or other, exerts a much more potent influence than it does in Europe."

Whatever Hotze and Nott hoped to accomplish, American readers had to be confused when they dipped into Gobineau's translated book. On the one hand, Gobineau rejected out of hand a scriptural interpretation deeply ingrained in the American imagination; in his view, the "curse of Ham" from Genesis chapter 9 had nothing to do with dark-skinned people, for "the pretended black color of the patriarch Ham rests upon no other basis than an arbitrary interpretation." On the other hand, and with a claim that strongly supported the racial differences upheld by defenders of slavery, Gobineau also asserted that "the Bible speaks of Adam as the progenitor of the white race."[71] That is, of only the white race. Although Gobineau claimed to accept biblical teaching on the unity of the human species, his reading of early Genesis placed him among the advocates of "polygenetic co-adamitism," those who postulated that other species of humanity existed alongside the biblical Adam. For Nott and Hotze, although Gobineau's rejection of the "curse of Ham" undercut their own defense of slavery, his interpretation of Adam directly supported their "scientific racism."[72]

Gobineau had written his book to explain why human civilization had entered into terminal decline. In his view, North America illustrated that decline since by the 1850s the mixing of ethnic streams had become a pronounced feature of the United States. For Gobineau, the mingling of Celtic, Gallic, Anglo-Saxon, and Germanic strains predicted the civilized degeneration just as much as Black-white amalgamation. Nott, with Hotze, did not particularly care what Gobineau had in mind. It was enough that his *Essai* defended the racial differences that for them legitimated slavery. Hotze, as he told Gobineau, had needed to "consult ... the spirit of the nation for whom I was writing." But beyond "consulting," the American ethnologists also hoped to change "the spirit of the nation" from the traditional belief that, even if Blacks were inferior, they were still part of humanity. To accomplish that purpose, they needed science to push the Scriptures aside.

The antebellum challenge of American Ethnology spotlighted a considerable irony. Racial prejudice was fully, integrally, and comprehensively part of the American Bible civilization. Yet within that Bible civilization, belief in the unity of humanity prevailed, however constrained by that prejudice. When after the Civil War—and in substantial part because of the Civil War—the Bible lost intellectual credibility, scientific racism became much more acceptable.[73] Postbellum American scientists would question the details of Nott and Gliddon's *Types of Mankind* and mostly dismiss the Gobineau argument publicized by Hotze's translation. Yet when science replaced the Bible as the nation's prime authority on race, the American racial regime after emancipation *intensified* the inequalities that existed before. As Nott and Gliddon, along with Gobineau through Hotze, hammered the wedge between science and Scripture, they mounted the nation's first successful challenge to the intellectual authority of the Bible.

And Still More

The array of antebellum voices claiming public space for their appropriation of Scripture ranged well beyond Catholics, Lutherans, Jews, and the American ethnologists. Chief among others were the Native American Christian communities that dated from the evangelizing efforts of Jesuits, Moravians, and a few Congregationalists in the colonial period. The character of that colonial experience prefigured much of what developed in later U.S. history. The Bible in evangelical Protestant terms became a mainstay for a modest but still significant number of Indian converts. Such believers, however, regularly encountered opposition from other Natives who rejected accommodation with white society. Even greater difficulty came from forces in that society—religious as well as economic and political—that could not deal with self-guided Native Christianity or that actively subverted Native attempts to fashion their own versions of Christian civilization.

The history of scriptural engagement began with an early effort by the Puritan minister John Eliot to translate the Bible into Wôpanâak, a dialect of the Algonquian language family. Eliot has long been celebrated for his dedicated labors in completing what became the first full printing of a Bible in the western hemisphere, eleven hundred copies of a twelve-hundred-page translation run off by a Cambridge, Massachusetts, printing press in 1663. Recent scholarship has documented how much Eliot's Native collaborators contributed to producing the translation and then how seriously, but also with independent minds, they read this text. In Linford Fisher's summary, this first printed American Bible was "a thoroughly indigenized creation in which Natives greatly aided in the translation, typesetting, and printing and, to some degree, adopted it as their own in Indian communities in southeastern New England." Yet within a generation, the outbreak of violent warfare stymied Native efforts to chart a course guided by the new translation. Indians under King Philip (Metacom) singled out Christian Natives for special attack, while Puritan Massachusetts decimated the fledgling Christian settlements into which Eliot had gathered converts.[74]

The life of Samson Occom, the best known Indian convert of the eighteenth-century Great Awakening, followed a similar pattern. For several years Occom was celebrated as a preacher, missionary to the Montauk, Oneida, Mohegan,

Nantic, and other Indian communities, and fundraiser for Eleazer Wheelock's scheme to create an Indian school of higher learning. During the years of his cooperation with Wheelock, Occom published the first full work by a North American Native. It was an evangelistic execution sermon based on Romans 6:23 ("For the wages of sin is death, but the gift of God is eternal life, through Jesus Christ our Lord") that followed the pattern for such sermons earlier perfected by John and Charles Wesley in England.[75] Some of the many later editions of the sermon included details about Occom's successful fundraising and preaching in Britain during the mid-1760s, along with other information drawn from white-Indian contact. By the time these later editions circulated, however, Wheelock had alienated Occom by abandoning his original plan for Indian higher education. Conflict with Massachusetts and Connecticut authorities over Indian lands, exacerbated by animosity generated because of warfare with Native groups, also undercut Occom's reputation. In the end, Occom's skill at expounding the Christian Scriptures, which made him well received in Britain, could not overcome the paternalism and land-hunger that so strongly shaped white relations with Native populations on this side of the Atlantic.[76]

The Bible became even more prominent for more Native Christians in the nineteenth century, even as the pressure from standing between two contrasting visions of civilization intensified. Three examples illustrate the intractability of this liminal tension. They roughly parallel the paths taken by proprietary Protestants, Methodist Protestants, and sectarian Protestants in the wider society.

After he had taken the name Elias Boudinot to honor the founder of the American Bible Society, Buck (or Galagina) Watie became the leading advocate for implanting the norms of white civilization among the Cherokee.[77] As a student in a Moravian mission school in Georgia, he excelled in his studies, as he then did at a Connecticut academy run by the American Board of Commissioners for Foreign Missions (ABCFM) from which he graduated in 1820. Boudinot's marriage six years later to Harriet Gold, a white woman he had met in Connecticut, incensed the school's sponsors, who in reaction shut it down. Boudinot, however, remained undaunted in seeking to nurture among the Cherokee the religious and political ideals he had learned at the mission schools. In a landmark address to Philadelphia philanthropists in 1826 he began by citing the "one-blood" passage from Acts 17:26 that had already become an anchor for African Americans. In recounting "the rise of these people in their movement toward civilization," Boudinot then told his audience about the significant minority of the Cherokee who had already responded positively to "the word of God" that was "regularly preached and explained, both by missionaries and natives." He detailed the concrete steps that would "certainly place the Cherokee Nation in a fair light, and act as a powerful argument in favor of Indian improvement":

First. The invention of letters.

Second. The translation of the New Testament into Cherokee. (Figure 17.2)
And third. The organization of a Government.

In Boudinot's telling, a quotation from Hebrews 8:11 ("for all shall know him
from the greatest to the least") outlined what could happen when "persons of

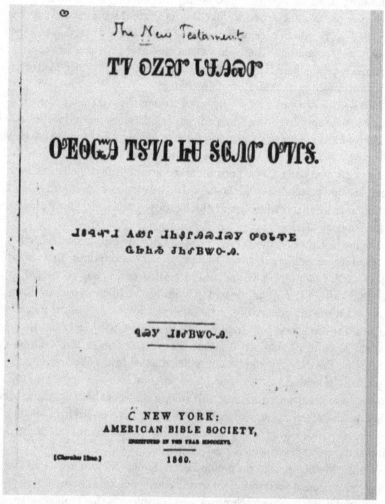

Figure 17.2 Although Sequoyah, creator of the Cherokee syllabary, thought
that publishing a Bible in Cherokee would undermine the independence of his
nation, the syllabary he invented was used from the start for bibles provided by the
American Bible Society.

Source: Courtesy of Harvard University Libraries.

all ages and classes . . . read the precepts of the Almighty in their own language." Another quotation, from Isaiah 35:1 ("the desert shall blossom like a rose"), expressed his hope that as the Cherokee "rise in information and refinement" and "arrive at that state of advancement," they would be "admitted into all the privileges of the American family."[78]

While explaining the system of writing recently perfected by George Guest (or Sequoyah), Boudinot did not add that Sequoyah himself warned against Bible translating, which he regarded as hastening the onset of annihilation. Two years later, after overcoming resistance like Sequoyah's and securing assistance from the ABCFM, Boudinot became the editor of *The Phoenix*, a biweekly that in both English and Sequoyah's Cherokee syllabic alphabet provided his community with timely news, offered Christian encouragement, and provided instruction in civil ideals keyed to the American Constitution.

As is well known, however, the fledgling structures of Cherokee Christian civilization came crashing down when officials in Georgia conspired with President Andrew Jackson to break treaties and forcibly remove the Cherokee, along with other tribal groups, from land coveted by white settlers. Against the wishes of many of his own people, Boudinot chose to join the Trail of Tears that took the Cherokee into present-day Oklahoma. In this new land he was murdered in 1839 by unknown assailants who blamed him for the physical and cultural devastation of the removal.

The life of Kahgegagahbowh (or George Copway) represented a Methodist-oriented career different from the proprietary aspirations that Boudinot represented.[79] Copway, a Canadian-born Mississauga, was converted in the late 1820s after listening to preaching from Native Methodist evangelists and hearing a white missionary discourse on Revelation 6:17 ("For the great day of his wrath is come, and who shall be able to stand").[80] In the 1830s, he helped a white American Methodist translate the New Testament into Ojibwa, then studied for the ministry and was himself ordained in the Wesleyan Methodist Canadian Conference. As he rose to higher levels of authority among the Ojibwa, Copway also itinerated as an evangelist among Natives in both the United States and Canada. When a charge of embezzlement abruptly ended his Canadian career, he rebounded swiftly to become a Nine Days Wonder in America as a lecturer and the author of a widely read memoir from 1847.

With its Methodist tone, the memoir echoed much African American writing. The work included accounts of dramatic conversions and many references to hymns and hymn signing (including Charles Wesley's "O for a thousand tongues to sing" presented in English and an Ojibwa translation).[81] It also offered an upbeat account of how Indian acceptance of Christianity dramatically transformed the morals, family lives, and work discipline of converted Indians.

The memoir ended, however, with an appeal that went beyond narrowly spiritual concerns to focus on the wrongs "that my poor people have suffered at the hands of the white man." According to Copway, whites had scorned the peaceful example "of the great philanthropist, William Penn." Instead, they practiced the same hypocrisy David Walker had also attacked: "You have sent your missionaries to Burmah, China, the Sandwich Islands, and to almost every part of the world; and shall the Indians *perish at your own door?*" A litany of biblical quotations brought the work to a close, including an appeal for love, mercy, and justice echoing the words of Micah 6:8 and again a reference to the divine creation "of one blood all the nations of the earth [Acts 17:26]." In passing, Copway also cited the text from Matthew 18:17, concerning "if offences must come," that Abraham Lincoln would later quote in his Second Inaugural Address.[82]

For a brief period Copway flourished in his new career. But then, in what Brend Peyer has described as Copway's rapid transition from itinerating missionary among the Indians to popular speaker for white audiences, those audiences soon tired of his account of white-Native relations and "abruptly let him fall into oblivion."[83]

For William Apess, the son of a Pequot mother and a Caucasian father, the Scriptures became as important for personal self-definition and for addressing white society as they were for his contemporaries Boudinot and Copway. Apess differed, however, in how clearly his enlistment of Scripture echoed themes prominent among African Americans, particularly the impetus for a life-changing conversion combined with biblical fuel for a searing critique.[84]

In his memoir from 1829, *A Son of the Forest,* Apess recounted how he had emerged from an extended period of doubt and despair when he "became very fond of attending the word of God."[85] Like Richard Allen and many Black Americans, Apess found Methodist emphases and organization ideal for his spiritual development—in his case, ordination in the Protestant Methodist Church, a republican breakaway from the main Methodist body. Again like Allen, who had defended Philadelphia's African American community after it was slandered for its actions during the Yellow Fever outbreak of 1793, Apess enlisted Scripture when Native Americans came under fire. In his case, he assisted the Indians of Mashpee, Massachusetts, in trying to redress the seizure of land by the state and Harvard College. But then charges flew, calling Apess the fomenter of rebellious anarchy. In reply, he described the resistance of their tiny band by quoting Deuteronomy 32:30 ("One shall chase a thousand, and two shall put ten thousand to flight").[86]

In January 1836 Apess delivered a stirring oration that did for Natives what David Walker had recently done for Blacks and Frederick Douglass would later repeat. He inverted New England's filiopietism by praising Metacom, the Native leader in the destructive King Philip's War of 1675–76, as "the greatest man that ever was in America." With Walker and Douglass, Apess's denunciation of the dominant culture drew liberally on the Scriptures, in this instance contrasting the spirit of forgiveness exhibited by Jesus in Luke 23:34 and Stephen in Acts 7:60 with the violent vindictiveness of New England's clergy during that colonial war.[87] Close to the time he delivered this speech, lawsuits from creditors stripped Apess of his property and seemed to intensify his struggle against alcoholism, a struggle that he lost only shortly thereafter in 1839.

With Elias Boudinot and George Copway, William Apess exemplified Native intellectual achievement, even as he also became a casualty of cultural warfare. In different ways, each of these figures was caught in a vise. They did appreciate some positive gifts from white society; as Copway put it, "What else could I do but love and esteem the American people? I love their Bible and their institutions." But each also knew brutal devastation; again from Copway: "The white men have been like the greedy lion, pouncing upon and devouring its prey. They have driven us from our nation, our homes, and possessions."[88] In their contributions to the nation's history, these Native Americans, like their Black contemporaries, found the Bible of the American mainstream something to grasp as they were swept away by that mainstream.

18

Whose Bible? (Women)

Since time immemorial, women had left a public record as biblical interpreters, but nowhere on the scale of the nineteenth-century Western world, especially in the United States.[1] In significant contrast to male Catholics, Lutherans, Jews, and Native Americans, most of the women who spoke publicly on the Scriptures shared intellectual and political conventions of the period. In contrast to the school of American Ethnology, articulate women in the antebellum era almost all retained belief in Scripture as the Word of God. Participation in the broader culture meant they approached biblical interpretation in much the same way as the nation's Anglo-American Protestant men. Although these approaches sometimes led to the same conclusions that men drew, just as often similar approaches produced different results. Whether or not the results resembled what was heard from men, they marked a new era in the history of the Bible simply because they came from women. Significantly, because debates surrounding scriptural interpretations by women paralleled debates over the Bible and slavery, controversies over women's roles in society and over the legitimacy of slavery reinforced each other with effects that have extended to the present.

An offhand comment by the reviewer of Harriet Livermore's sermon before Congress in January 1827 spoke to the new American reality: "Miss Livermore seems to unite the Quaker and the Methodist; and conducts herself in such a manner as to please both sects."[2] Livermore's call to preach came from something close to the Friends' inner testimony; she also found most opportunities to fulfill that calling among Freewill Baptists and churches of the "Christian Connection" associated with Elias Smith, sectarian movements that called no man *father*. But Livermore's conversion as a young adult and the consistent stress in her preaching on conversion, repentance, and salvation also built a bridge to the Methodists, who occasionally allowed her to speak at their assemblies. She was, moreover, a self-described biblical "literalist." She also became deeply interested in millennial calculations similar to speculations about the Ten Lost Tribes of Israel that Elias Boudinot explored, even as the same calculations led her down the Millerite path of trying to specify a date for the return of Christ. She testified to a stubborn conservatism when she refused to label her "testimonies" as "sermons"; she showed no interest in administering the sacraments or seeking ordination; and she remained indifferent to advancing women's political goals.[3]

America's Book. Mark A. Noll, Oxford University Press. © Oxford University Press 2022.
DOI: 10.1093/oso/9780197623466.003.0019

In short, Harriet Livermore was an altogether typical sectarian evangelical of the era—except for speaking publicly as a woman.

In that role she joined a chorus swelling beyond the imagination of any earlier period. In the mid-eighteenth century John Wesley had distressed his brother Charles and the English religious establishment by allowing a handful of lay-women to exhort at Methodist class meetings.[4] Less than a century later the handful had grown considerably. Besides the more than one hundred exhorters, testifiers, and preachers that Catherine Brekus has identified, a new day was also dawning for women in print.[5] During the colonial era, alongside occasional contributions to newspapers and then periodicals, women published only a very few titles, and then almost always mediated to the public by men: a book of poems by Anne Bradstreet; the captivity narrative of Mary Rowlandson; the spiritual narrative of Sarah Osborn, a Rhode Island participant in the eighteenth-century revivals; and a book of poems by an enslaved Bostonian, Phillis Wheatley—that is about all.[6] Along with much else, the Revolution changed this picture almost immediately.

Conforming and Subverting

From Boston, as an example, Mercy Otis Warren showed the way by publishing poetry, political commentary, and eventually a full-scale history of the War of Independence.[7] At about the same time, a pioneering work by a founder of the Universalist movement opened the floodgate for consequential works of se-rious biblical engagement. In 1782, Judith Sargent Murray first acknowledged the need for an apology "when a female steps outside the line which custom hath circumscribed." Hers spelled out an intention to provide "sacred attention to those interests that are crowned with immortality." The "interests" were chil-dren for whom Murray published a catechism after "methodizing the evangelical views of sacred texts."[8]

The prolific Hannah Adams of Brookline, Massachusetts, began her pub-lishing career in 1784 with a dictionary of world religions, notable for its disinter-ested impartiality on a subject that Western Christians had almost always treated polemically.[9] Despite Adams's serious Congregational commitments, which leaned toward Unitarianism, early editions of the dictionary played down her personal religious standpoint. Yet driving her work from the start was the first of seven resolutions she penned as a young adult: "I resolve to read the Bible more attentively; and diligently, and to be constant and fervent in prayer for divine illumination and direction."[10] Throughout her life she seems to have retained that purpose. In the fourth edition of her well-received dictionary from 1817, Adams paused in an appendix to explain why "the diversity of sentiment among

Christians" should not be considered "an argument against divine revelation." Instead, a mass of evidence demonstrated that Scripture spoke truly, including the New Testament miracles, fulfillment of prophecies, the spread of Christianity despite opposition, and Scripture's "agreement with the moral attributes and perfections of the Deity; and their benevolent tendency to promote the good of society, and advance our present and future happiness."[11]

By the time Adams brought out this fourth edition, she had used her command of Greek and access to the libraries of John Adams (a distant cousin) and the Harvard faculty to author a two-volume history of the Jews based on her understanding of the Hebrew Scriptures. It too was a remarkably impartial work, though Christian enough to be reprinted in Britain by a society for evangelizing the Jewish people. A few years later, in 1824, she published *Letters on the Gospels*, with the hope that that book would illuminate Scripture by explaining the historical contexts of Jesus's life. In particular, she wanted young people to "read the New Testament with more pleasure and advantage, and that they may be induced to make the sacred Scriptures the object of their daily study, the rule of their life, and their guide to everlasting happiness."[12]

Much the same purpose led to Sarah Hall's *Conversations on the Bible*, a narrative retelling that imaginatively filled silences in the biblical record.[13] Published first in 1818 and then in several later editions, Hall hoped the stories would also advance the equality of the sexes. To the didactic intentions of Judith Sargent Murray and Hannah Adams, she added the aesthetic: "The Bible is the inexhaustible source from which rhetoric and poetry have delighted mankind in every age."[14] The full life of this Philadelphia-based Presbyterian included mastery of Greek and Hebrew as well as giving birth to eleven children.

The works by Murray, Adams, Hall, and several others displayed far-reaching expertise in Scripture that extended to many genres: catechisms and narratives, but also memoirs, novels, practical theology, hymns, and ethical argument. For their place in national history, it is important to underscore that the great majority of antebellum women Bible interpreters fully shared the era's central Protestant convictions as well as the conventional ways of understanding the Bible—even when they transgressed what Murray called "the line which custom has circumscribed." They came as close to practicing a "Bible only" faith as most of the men who championed that principle. Although most women who opened the Scriptures to the public came out of sectarian or Methodist traditions, such voices were not unknown among proprietary Protestants.

Regardless of denominational background and despite the absence of formal education, women could be as thoroughly steeped in Scripture as the most Bible-centered men. The deep biblical immersion we have already seen in Maria Stewart, Harriet Jacob, and Harriet Beecher Stowe extended to many more. Virginia Lieson Brereton's study of female conversion narratives has shown that women "often alluded to biblical events, places, and characters, comparing their own circumstances to those of scriptural personages." Even when not quoting directly, "they tended to echo biblical usage anyway," extending to biblical pronouns ("thou," "thy"), verbs in the King James pattern ("shalt," "builded," "availeth"), inverted prose ("it withstands not the arrests of death"), and common biblical prepositions ("unto," "believed on," "accepted of").[15]

Entirely typical was Livermore's recital of her turn to God: "I sat in the corner of my room, trying to meditate upon my situation, when a sudden impulse moved me to give myself away to Jesus. I dropped quick upon the floor, crying, 'Jesus, thou Son of David, have mercy on me [Lk 18:38].'"[16] Similar expressions appeared just as naturally in the memoir of Nancy Towle, a New Hampshire participant, like Livermore, in Freewill Baptist and Christian Connection assemblies. About her call to preach, she wrote that she began to feel "*the Word of the Lord as fire shut up in my bones* [Jer 20:9]." After describing the years of her itinerant ministry, she summed up her life by saying, "[T]hese hands of mine have often ministered to the necessities of those that were with me; and to others [Acts 20:34]."[17] When, as happened fairly regularly, women authors recorded visions, voices, or special promptings of the Holy Spirit, these too were expressed in scriptural terms. Black evangelist Zilpha Elaw, who grew up among Quakers and Methodists in the greater Philadelphia area, preached in the United States and Britain during the quarter-century after 1825. As she wrote about God's communion with her, the external word and the internal word became one: "When I had been contemplating the wonderful works of creation, or revelation of the mind and truth of God to man, by the inspiration of his prophets, I have been lost in astonishment at the perception of a voice, which either externally or internally, has spoken to me, and revealed to my understanding many surprising and precious truths."[18]

Much scholarship has queried the extent to which antebellum female religion emphasized "feeling" in contrast to stereotypical male reliance on "reason." That the distinction was never absolute is suggested by the work of Phoebe Palmer. Her much-noticed *Way of Holiness*, the first of many editions in 1843, explained the postconversion gift of the Holy Spirit in purely rational terms: read the Bible, believe the Scriptures, pray to experience what has been set out in divine revelation, testify immediately that you have received that gift.[19] Yet women themselves often stressed that their faith exemplified, as in phrases from the Anglican Hannah More, "honest warmth," "genuine feeling," "a warm, tender, disinterested, and enthusiastic spirit."[20] When Harriet Beecher Stowe upbraided her husband, Calvin, for losing sight of his faith's Living Foundation because of obsessing over academic superstructures, she did so with biblical phrases: "If you studied Christ with half the energy you have studied Luther . . . If you were drawn toward him & loved him as much as you loved your study & your books, then would he be formed in you [Gal 4:19], the hope of glory [Col 1:27]."[21]

An apt metaphor from Elizabeth Elkin Grammer well summarizes the character of much that antebellum women wrote; it deserves extended quotation:

> Biblical typology is so embedded in these narratives that they resemble a palimpsest. . . . In effect, these autobiographies are written over—both in the sense of writing on top of and in the sense of revising or updating—the Bible. Several of these women . . . preface their works with passages from the Bible that call attention to the history of women's prophesying and leadership. But these autobiographies also quote the Bible on almost every page, often without quotation marks or citations, so much so that many readers might not recognize how often these women write what was for them an everlasting, ever-living *Word*—the "word made flesh" (John 1:14).[22]

The rub came when public women—imbued with the Bible; preaching, testifying, or writing from the Bible; guided by the Bible; committed to "the Bible alone"—concluded that they enjoyed the same right to speak out as men. When critics demanded silence by citing tradition, denominational regulations, or biblical passages thought to enjoin female subservience, these Scripture-saturated women were ready. Even as they conformed to nineteenth-century usage, they subverted much that had previously been taken for granted. Unlike some kinds of later feminism, their subversion arose from within the biblical framework rather than in rebellion against it.[23]

Female Interpreters and Their Interpretations

It was no surprise that female interpreters devoted considerable attention to texts that had traditionally enforced the divide between male and public versus female and private, men as preachers and pastors versus women as hearers and doers. Yet as contentions over female public speaking grew, women again followed men in *how* they put the Bible to use. Significantly, most (but not quite all) of the antebellum women who spoke out on such subjects continued to affirm the Bible's full inspiration. Without exception, they also scoured the Scriptures as diligently as Protestant men had done since the days of Luther and Calvin.

Opinions about women's place in public life could regularly be read in memoirs, narratives like Sarah Hale's *Conversations*, or even novels like Harriet Beecher Stowe's *Uncle Tom's Cabin* and *The Minister's Wooing*.[24] But entire works also took up the question of women speaking publicly or exercising any kind of authority in, as the contemporary phrase put it, "promiscuous" audiences of men and women. These works came from several points on the ecclesiastical compass, including the sectarian Harriet Livermore's *Scriptural Evidence in Favour of Female Testimony* (1824) and the upper-class Methodist Phoebe Palmer's *Promise of the Father* (1859). Sarah Moore Grimké also based her *Letters on the Equality of the Sexes* from 1837–38 "solely on the Bible."[25] (Grimké's tortuous personal pilgrimage began with Episcopalian baptism in a slaveholding Charleston family and continued with evangelical conversion under Presbyterian influence, removal to Philadelphia, and affiliation with the Society of Friends, before she broke with the Quakers because of their unwillingness to embrace immediate abolition.) A young Oberlin graduate, Antoinette Brown, in 1849 contributed a scholarly challenge addressed specifically to traditional interpretations of the two injunctions from the Apostle Paul that seemed most categorically to rule out public speaking by women. (Brown was a Congregationalist in the Charles Finney revivalistic mold who, as Antoinette Brown Blackwell, would later be the first American woman to receive formal ordination. It took place in the South Butler, New York, Congregational Church in 1853 with the ordination sermon preached by Luther Lee, an active Methodist abolitionist.)[26]

Together, these separate publications, along with significant sections in the works of other women, represented at once a conservative replication of standard hermeneutical practices and a forthright proclamation of revolutionary results. They first called attention to biblical incidents, and even more to biblical individuals, who had earlier been slighted. Time after time, antebellum women spoke of the general encouragement they received from biblical women whom the sacred writers commended for their faithfulness.[27] In the same way that ministers at times of national peril had readily found direct, indirect, or typical inspiration from often obscure corners of Scripture, speaking and publishing women did the same for their particular interests. From the Old Testament: Abigail (1 Sam 25), Abishag (1 Kings 1–2), Bathsheba (1 Kings 1–2), Dinah (Gen 34), Jael (Judg 4–5), Rachel (Gen 29–35), Rahab (Josh 2 and 6), and Rebekah (Gen 22–28). From the New Testament, Julia (Rom 16:15), Joanna (Lk 8:3, 24:10), Mary and Martha (Jn 11; Lk 10), the other Marys mentioned in the Gospels (Matt 27:56; Jn 19:25), Narcissus (Rom 16:11), Persis (Rom 16:12), Salome (Mk 15:40, 16:1), Susanna (Lk 8:3), Tryphosa and Tryphena (Rom 16:7).

More particularly, they rejoiced in the full record of biblical women who had spoken publicly or exercised public authority. From the Old Testament: the prophet Deborah (Judg 7); the prophet Huldah (2 Kings 22:14); Miriam the sister of Moses, who chanted a victory psalm after Israel triumphed in battle (Ex 25:20–21); Hannah, who offered a prayer of thanksgiving after her son Samuel was born (1 Sam 1:26–2:10); and Esther, who ventured her life to address her husband, King Ahasuerus, and so saved Israel (Esther 5–8). But they found just as many examples in the New Testament: the Virgin Mary, who amplified Hannah's song to pray the *Magnificat* (Lk 1:38–55); her cousin Elizabeth, who hailed Mary and the prenatal Messiah "with a loud voice" (Lk 1:42–45); aged Anna, who "spoke of him [the infant Jesus] to all them that looked for redemption in Jerusalem" (Lk 2:38); Mary Magdalene, whom Jesus commissioned to tell his disciples that he was raised from the dead; Lydia, who organized the Christian church in Thyatira (Acts 16:14); Priscilla, who with her husband Aquilla "expounded unto him [a new convert, Apollos] the way of God more profitably" (Acts 18:14); the four daughters of Philip the evangelist "which did prophesy" (Acts 21:19); and Junia, whom the Apostle Paul designated "of note among the apostles" (Rom 16:7). As it had always been for their male counterparts, women were richly rewarded when they followed the biblical injunction "seek, and ye shall find" (Matt 7:7). They drew on biblical precedents, usually with a plain-sense hermeneutic.

Second, antebellum authors also reversed judgments about biblical women who had been regarded negatively. The early Universalist Judith Sargent Murray, Sarah Hale (the editor of *Godey's Ladies Book*), Harriet Livermore, and Sarah Grimké were among those who specifically rejected the poet John Milton's depiction of Eve as the great malefactor precipitating the Fall of humanity. In their reading of early Genesis, verse 27 of the first chapter provided the interpretive key: "God created man in his own image, in the image of God created he him; male and female created he them." From that basis of primal equality, they read the story of Eve and the serpent as indicting Adam equally with Eve; if she gave into temptation, so also did Adam when he disobeyed God's command to protect Eve. Hale also suggested that because Eve came last in the sequence of creation, her task, as an inherently more spiritual being, included the elevation of men.[28]

Female interpreters, third, regularly provided what they considered more accurate translations of passages in the KJV that marginalized women. After Sarah Grimké began her *Letters on the Equality of the Sexes* by announcing an intention to follow Scripture "solely," she expanded on a common complaint: standard teachings on the sexes had substantially arisen as "the result of a misconception of the simple truths revealed in the Scriptures, in consequence of the false translation of many passages of Holy Writ. My mind is entirely delivered from the superstitious reverence which is attached to the English version of the Bible. King James's translators certainly were not inspired. I therefore claim the original as my standard, *believing that to have been inspired*."[29] (Figure 18.1) A primary example was wording from Romans 16:1, where the Apostle Paul commended "our sister Phoebe" as, in the King James, "a *servant* of the church which is at Cenchrea." But, as many of these writers pointed out, everywhere else in the New Testament, the crucial word *diakonon* was translated as "deacon" or "minister."[30]

The most important use of conventional practices to promote unconventional conclusions, however, came when these women found the King James wording

Sarah M. Grimké

Figure 18.1 Sarah Moore Grimké, who joined her sister Angelina in publishing strong attacks on slavery based on Scripture, used the same source to contend, again with Angelina, for the rights of women.
Source: LOC, Prints & Photographs, LC-USZ61-1608.

acceptable, but not what had been made of its words. Of examples the cupboard was full.

> When God created Eve as "an help meet" for Adam (Gen 2:20), it meant, in Sarah Grimké's reading, not a subordinate creature but "a companion *in all respects* his equal."[31]
> Standard interpretations of the curse that God pronounced on Adam and Eve after the Fall in Genesis 3:16 ("Unto the woman [God] said . . . thy desire shall be to thy husband, and he shall rule over thee") supported conventional treatments of gender roles. Against those treatments, some women claimed that God in this passage was *predicting*, not *prescribing*.[32]
> Even more explained that when biblical women "prophesyed," it did not mean an extraordinary prediction of the future but an ordinary message from God spoken in ordinary circumstances—and of the sort that prophetesses in both testaments modeled.[33]

Another reinterpretation concerned women described as the "weaker vessel" in 1 Peter 3:7, which could only refer to physical strength and nothing else.[34]

Reinterpretations predictably concentrated on New Testament texts that traditionally confined women as subordinate, sidelined, or silent. They included *Haustafel*, or house code, passages like Ephesians 5:24 ("as the church is subject unto Christ, so let the wives be to their own husbands in everything").[35] But above all stood the two Pauline injunctions that made efforts by women to address "promiscuous" audiences seem so heterodox. First, 1 Corinthians 14:34–35 ("Let your women keep silence in the churches: for it is not permitted unto them to speak. . . . And if they will learn any thing, let them ask their husbands at home: for it is a shame for women to speak in the church"). And 1 Timothy 2:11–12 ("Let the woman learn in silence with all subjections. But I suffer not a woman to teach, nor to usurp authority over the man, but to be in silence. For Adam was not deceived, but the woman being deceived was in the transgression. Notwithstanding she shall be saved in childbearing, if they continue in faith and charity and holiness with sobriety").

On these passages Antoinette Brown, the Oberlin graduate, returned to questioning the accuracy of the King James translation. Most extensively she queried the meaning of the Greek verb *lalein*, which in 1 Corinthians 14:34 the KJV rendered "to speak." Brown canvassed other New Testament uses of the verb to argue that it could be translated variously; it was, she claimed, a generic term with a general meaning of "to give utterance" that could be translated accurately only by attending to specific circumstances. She then pointed out, as many others did, that the Apostle in 1 Corinthians 11:4 provided instructions for "every women that prayeth or prophesieth"—that is, guidance for when, as Paul took for granted, women would be speaking in church assemblies. Brown's conclusion? Whatever the prohibitions of 1 Corinthians 14 and 1 Timothy 2 entailed, these passages could not mean that women could never speak or teach in all circumstances. Hence, from the range of possible translations for *lalein* in 1 Corinthians 14:34, Brown suggested that "prattle" would be much more accurate than "speak."[36]

She undertook a less extensive examination of *didaskein* (to teach) from 1 Timothy 2. Yet her comparison of the word's usage in other New Testament passages led to a similar conclusion, that this verb could connote either proper teaching or damaging teaching. To her it was obvious this passage had the latter in view instead of a blanket prohibition.[37]

With others, Brown stressed that the Apostle's words also needed to be understood contextually, against the background of what was known about the church in Corinth and about the situation that Paul's assistant, Timothy, faced in his leadership of the church in Ephesus. The authors appealed for readings sensitive to what Brown called "attendant circumstances" and Palmer referred to as "explanatory connections and contradictory passages."[38] To these interpreters, it was obvious that Paul addressed the often-cited prohibitions to situations where recently converted women were either taking over the meetings or simply babbling nonsense.[39] After citing 1 Corinthians 11 and several other passages where the Scriptures described women speaking publicly, Sarah Grimké defined the interpretive decision in the same terms that others echoed: "[W]e must be compelled to adopt one of two conclusions." Either "the apostle grossly contradicts himself" or "the directions given to women, not to speak, or to teach in the congregations, had reference to some local and peculiar customs, which were then common in religious assemblies, and which the apostle thought inconsistent with the purpose for which they were met together." Because she spoke as one who believed the Apostle wrote by divine inspiration to readers sharing that belief, Grimké concluded, "No one, I suppose, will hesitate which of these two conclusions to adopt."[40] Livermore, who regularly expressed her affection for "our beloved brother Paul," would have agreed wholeheartedly.[41]

Sarah Grimké spoke out more forcefully than most on house code texts requiring that women "be subject" to their husbands. Some women preachers, like Harriet Livermore and Zilpha Elaw, expressly approved the traditional asymmetry of domestic authority.[42] Others, like Jarena Lee and Julia Foote, sidestepped the traditional interpretation by appealing to other texts providing exceptions for women called by the Holy Spirit to public ministry.[43] Grimké's reading was more radical, though still a reinterpretation of an authoritative biblical word rather than a claim to see an error. In her interpretation, passages commanding men to love their wives meant that Paul was enjoining the mutual submission of spouses to each other. More daringly, she suggested that if the passages should still be understood traditionally, it meant that the Apostle "designed to recommend to wives . . . to carry out the holy principle laid down by Jesus Christ, 'Resist not evil [Matt 5:39].'"[44]

Reductio ad absurdum also served these interpreters as they reinterpreted the key passages. Antoinette Brown on 1 Timothy and Phoebe Palmer on 1 Corinthians 14 said almost the same thing: if the Apostle's injunction were a universal command, it would mean that Episcopal women could not articulate liturgical responses, no women could say the Lord's Prayer in church, they could not sing, and it would be wrong for any woman to teach in Sabbath schools or open her mouth in what Brown called any "social circle."[45] Sarah Grimké again went further to challenge standard interpretations of what it meant in the 1 Timothy 2 passage for women not to "usurp authority." If, she wrote, "God ordained man the governor of woman he must be able to save her, and to answer in her stead for all those sins which she commits to her destruction." But that conclusion flew in the face of firm Protestant doctrine pertaining to all people, women as well as men—that Christ was the only mediator of salvation.[46]

The "analogy of Scripture," or in modern terms, "intertextuality," was another time-honored technique that regularly appeared in these writings—that is, the practice of letting clear biblical statements illuminate the obscure. The women innovated only by taking what men had deemed obscure (or secondary) as clear (or primary) and then prioritizing what they now considered clear to contextualize what they now regarded as secondary. Several writers agreed that all questions regarding gender roles should begin with Galatians 3:28 ("There is neither Jew nor Greek, there is neither bond nor fee, there is neither male nor female: for ye are all one in Christ Jesus").[47] Even more authors appealed to a prophecy in Joel 2:28–29 and its fulfillment on the day of Pentecost (Acts 2:16–18) as proof positive about the freedom given in Christ to all believers in the Age of the Spirit. From the prophet: "And it shall come to pass afterward, that I will pour our my spirit upon all flesh; and your sons and your daughters shall prophesy. . . . And also upon the servants and upon the handmaids will I pour out my spirit." And from Peter at Pentecost: "But this is that which was spoken by the prophet Joel: And it shall come to pass in the last days, saith God, I will pour out of my Spirit upon all flesh: and your sons and your daughters shall prophesy. . . . And on my servants and on my handmaidens I will pour out in those days of my Spirit; and they shall prophesy." The title page of Palmer's *Promise of the Father* quoted these two texts, separated by a passage from the Gospel of Luke from which she took her title: "And, behold, I send the promise of my Father upon you: but tarry ye in the city of Jerusalem, until ye be endued with power from on high [Lk 24:49]." To Palmer and others who thrilled to such passages, the "power from on high" had arrived.[48]

It is important to stress once again that well into the 1840s interpretations advanced to justify female public speaking—and sometimes even ordination— came uniformly from women who affirmed traditional biblical authority in order to advance traditional Protestant goals. Above all, most devoted all energies to a Methodist-style concentration on the path of salvation.[49] Harriet Livermore's vocation and the purpose of that vocation were as one: "I believe . . . that some female disciples are called and qualified by their living head, to visit churches, with messages from God, and to warn the wicked to flee from the wrath to come [Matt 3:7]." She rejoiced that she lived "in a day when a number of my sex are essaying to blow the silver trumpet, and publish salvation to a dying world."[50] Antoinette Brown deployed all of her technical learning for the purpose of giving women the privilege "to stand up in the name of her Redeemer, administering the cup of salvation to the lips of dying immortals."[51] Phoebe Palmer dared to abandon tradition because, as she quoted the Apostle, she longed to speak "unto men . . . edification, exhortation, and comfort [1 Cor 14:3]."[52] Most of these early preachers also rejected association with those like the Grimké sisters who added social reform to their evangelistic concerns.[53] They were as strictly "gospel women" as the early Methodists.

To be sure, Sarah Grimké was an exception with the connections she drew between gospel proclamation and social reform. Yet she too spoke with the Methodists when she expressed her supreme desire that women with men would recognize "the signs of the times" that shone light on manifest evil and so "come to the rescue of a ruined world, and to be found co-workers with Jesus Christ."[54]

In her wider social concerns, Grimké with the others practiced a sectarian commitment to "the Bible alone." Harriet Livermore claimed no more for her defense of women speaking publicly than the desire that "scripture be permitted to speak for itself." She added, "I love pure Gospel liberty."[55] Grimké followed her profession to follow the Bible "solely" by claiming "to justify for myself what is the meaning of the inspired writers, because I believe it to be the solemn duty of every individual to search the Scriptures for themselves, with the aid of the Holy Spirit, and not to be governed by the views of any man or set of men."[56] The sectarian character continued into the 1840s, when several women preachers, convinced by William Miller's apocalyptic reckoning, committed themselves to his cause.[57]

To even casual observers who sampled the writings of these women, it was as obvious as it is to us today that debates over the Bible and women did not stand alone. They were overwhelmingly evangelical and sectarian as these characteristics had been shaped by American experience. They traded in the common interpretive coinage of their era— finding new inspiration in neglected corners of the sacred text, worrying about the accuracy of the KJV, carrying opponents' arguments to absurd conclusions, invoking context, pursuing meaning intertextually with the analogy of Scripture, while always insisting on "the Bible alone." Significantly—for the nation and the history of the Bible—the parallel between debates over Scripture and women, and over Scripture and slavery, were also clear as a bell.

Hermeneutics, Natural Rights, Moral Sense—and Slavery

Observers at the time recognized that the most comprehensive defense of female activity in public life came from Sarah Grimké's 1838 *Letters on the Equality of the Sexes*. They also knew that this most prominent advocate for the equality of the sexes was one of the two most prominent female advocates for immediate abolition. Two years earlier, Grimké's ardently antislavery *Epistle to the Clergy of the Southern States* had been joined by an equally passionate abolitionist tract, *Appeal to the Christian Women of the South*, from her sister, Angelina Emily

Grimké. (Angelina, thirteen years younger than Sarah, had followed her sister to Philadelphia and affiliation with the Society of Friends. When in September 1835 William Lloyd Garrison published her letter of support in *The Liberator* and Philadelphia Quakers cautioned her about such open advocacy, Angelina instead published her *Appeal* with Garrison's American Anti-Slavery Society.)[58]

It did not take a subtle intellect to discern connections between the pamphlets from 1836 demanding an end to slavery and the pamphlet from 1838 demanding equal rights for women.[59] Observers then and since have concluded that the turn to Scripture in support of women's rights strengthened lines of division that hardened as men—along with a few women—searched the Scriptures for a word from God concerning the American slave system.

Along with advocacy for women's rights, antebellum efforts would spur later mobilization for temperance, settlement houses, women's suffrage, and eventually modern feminism—though with much of the original biblical basis fading away. During the antebellum decades, the perception of links between the Grimké sisters' two great causes had an immediate impact. That perception decisively affected not just what Americans thought the Bible *said*, but what they thought the Bible *was*. The most-noticed literature on the rights of women appeared in the very years when intensified biblical consideration of slavery deepened national fissures pointing toward fracture. As clearly as scriptural expositions on slavery, the women's biblical expositions revealed why there could be no ongoing American Bible civilization.

As many historians have demonstrated, campaigns against slavery and for women's rights arose from the same revivalistic energy spread first by the Methodists and sectarians like Elias Smith, then routinized under popular evangelists like Charles Finney.[60] With that common origin, no one could be surprised that obiter dicta attacking slavery seasoned Sarah Grimké's ardently evangelical and massively biblical *Letters on the Equality of the Sexes*. When she paused, for example, to denounce violence against women, she included the plight of enslaved women who often had to "satisfy the brutal lust of those who bear the name of Christ." She also linked the Pauline prescription of female sub-servience with the Apostle's instructions for slaves to obey their masters: both provided opportunities to "Resist not evil"; they could not be sanctions relevant in the nineteenth century as they had been in biblical times. In her peroration concerning "the signs of the times," which she hoped would motivate women to become "co-workers with Jesus Christ," she included "the fearful ravages of slavery."[61]

The same affinity was just as evident in Angelina Grimké's 1836 *Appeal to Christian Women of the South*. Evangelical sentiment clearly motivated the work ("it is then, because I *do feel* and *do pray* for you, that I address you thus"), which she grounded explicitly on Scripture ("the Bible is my ultimate appeal in all matters of faith and practice, and it is to *this test* I am anxious to bring the subject at issue between us").[62] But even as she unleashed the standard biblical arguments against slavery, she regularly paused for generic assertions like those found in Sarah's *Letters* on the sexes—for instance, "this doctrine of equality is based on the Bible." In urging southern women to stand and be counted, even in the face of personal danger, she also enlisted a list of heroic biblical women similar to what Harriet Livermore, Phoebe Palmer, her sister Sarah, and others evoked in support of women's rights.[63]

Parallels in the biblical arguments on gender and slavery are especially noteworthy. In neither case did questions about the authority, reliability, historicity, inspiration, or even inerrancy of Scripture arise until debates on these subjects had been under way for decades. The women who advocated gender reform did not enlist conclusions from advanced biblical scholars in Europe that might have advanced their cause—especially the conclusion that Ephesians and 1 Timothy, with their restrictions on women, were pseudonymous epistles not really written by the Apostle Paul.[64] It was the same for opinions about the evolution of religious consciousness that a few antislavery men began to entertain before the Civil War and that gained much more popularity during the last third of the nineteenth century.[65] Into the 1840s, and for many well beyond, these women reformers paid little heed to the modern proposals that would later be used to justify antislavery principles and expanded rights for women.

The decisive moves on women's questions were not critical, but hermeneutical. How should the inspired Bible be read? What interpretive strategies allowed readers of the sacred text to find the way of salvation, the path to God-honoring daily life, and proper directions for society? How should the Bible's universal and eternal truths be applied in nineteenth-century America? The crucial historical point is that the era's hermeneutical strategies and conclusions drawn from Scripture lay deeply embedded in American circumstances. Because that embedding was so often unselfconscious, confusion often resulted from claims to speak definitively from Scripture. Far into the nation's future, the polarizations from this era's ideological contentions and intellectual confusion would strongly affect popular uses of the Bible.

From a modern perspective, at least four hermeneutical strategies can be distinguished, however much expositors in the era elided them in appealing to the Bible alone. Two were entirely noncontroversial, even if they could lead to controversial conclusions. Both had been sanctioned by Protestant usage time out of mind and by much Christian tradition well beyond Protestantism. First was reliance on specific biblical verses—proof-texting. When Phoebe Palmer quoted Joel 2:28 and Acts 2:16–18 on "maidservants" receiving the Holy Spirit, or when others quoted Romans 16:7 with its reference to Junia as "of note among the apostles," they treated the citations as conclusive demonstration that God allowed women to speak publicly and to exercise ecclesiastical authority.

The second convention involved bringing together passages from different parts of Scripture to make a theological claim with practical implications. The structures of Protestant life—doctrine, church order, personal piety, social advocacy—were always presented as the result of careful construction of scriptural stone upon scriptural stone, as was the case in other Christian traditions to a lesser degree. Writers on gender only repeated standard procedures when, for example, they joined Genesis 1:28 ("male and female created he them") with Lydia organizing the church at Thyatira (Acts 16) to justify a public role for women in antebellum America. Many contemporaries objected strenuously to that justification, but not to the procedure by which it was formed—since the objectors uniformly followed the same procedure in deriving their own conclusions about biblical teaching.

The third convention might seem to follow naturally from the appeal to proof-texts and synthetic biblical construction. The logic appears noncontroversial: if a better grasp of what individual verses meant is sought or a clearer judgment about whether material drawn from different parts of Scripture actually belonged together, then surely exploring the *contexts* of biblical utterances should become singularly useful. How might knowledge of Hebrew and Greek clarify the meaning of words in the KJV? How did more information about the times and places of the biblical writers shed more light on what they wrote? What were the common practices for describing events, composing poetry, penning epistles, or articulating theology in whatever form when biblical authors did their work? The appeal to context, as routine as it now seems, in fact excited great controversy.

Few had objected when Hannah Adams drew on ancient history, travel narratives, and similar sources to compose her impartial accounts of world religions or to fill in background information on the four Gospels. This kind of work seemed only to be following a well-worn path. John Lightfoot, a leading member of the seventeenth-century Westminster Assembly, had won lasting renown for how his expertise in rabbinic scholarship aided his Christian interpretation of the Old Testament.[66] Similarly, from the eighteenth century onward, Americans afforded an unusually warm welcome to educated Jews who were willing to instruct eager Protestants in the Hebrew language.[67] By the 1830s, the popularity of polyglot bibles like Bagster's and elaborate family bibles jam-packed with information about the Holy Land revealed an intuitive sense that more was always better when it came to "Bible backgrounds."

Yet for new interpretations concerning Eve, the Fall, prophetesses, or Pauline mandates, it was a different story—and for several reasons. Most obviously,

Americans knew that the European scholars who led the way in championing study of the Bible's language, history, and especially Middle Eastern settings were also the champions of theological neologisms—new views that challenged traditional convictions about the Bible's unique status as divine revelation. It was one thing for Hannah Adams to use seventh-century Arabian history to illuminate Mohammed's life; it was quite another to contextualize what the Apostle Paul said about husbands and their wives by referring to his personal biography, Jewish traditions, or the conventions of Mediterranean life in that era.

A turn to contextual analysis also exposed persistent ambiguities in traditional Christian understanding of biblical inspiration. When the Second Epistle to Timothy said "all scripture is given by inspiration of God" (3:16), what exactly did it mean? Regular Protestant evoking of "what the Bible says" or "the Bible alone" pushed toward conceptualizing the words of Scripture as dictated immediately by God. Yet another set of routine Protestant references to what Moses, David, the Gospel writers, or Paul "wrote" suggested a more complicated understanding. Thoughtful efforts to parse the relation of the human and the divine in Scripture turned away from dictation, as in John Calvin's famous suggestion that God "accommodated" to human understanding when revealing himself and his purposes.[68] Yet in the nineteenth century, Americans again knew that European scholars who stressed "accommodation" did so for much more radical purposes than Calvin ever imagined. Only a few Americans were prepared to follow these scholars who claimed to be treating the authorship of Scripture as they would the authorship of any other ancient text.

So it was that when Harriet Livermore, Sarah Grimké, or Phoebe Palmer asked Bible believers to rethink interpretations about female public speaking or equal rights for women, the problem was not primarily the appeal to context. Instead, guilt by association became the pressing concern. It did not take a prejudiced mind to ask whether an appeal to context should be taken at face value or was a smoke screen hiding denigration of Scripture as the true word of God.

The fourth hermeneutical convention complicated interpretation and heightened confusion even more. Confusion reflected the perennial problem of Protestant biblical interpretation. As clearly as *sola scriptura* sounded a tocsin for battle against Roman Catholics, its note had always wavered in guiding Protestants toward unified belief or practice. Protestants, in point of fact, regularly looked to other sources of authority alongside their reliance on Scripture. Sometimes those other authorities had edged into consciousness. Often they did not.[69]

Most antebellum Americans who believed implicitly in Scripture as inspired revelation also believed implicitly in other intellectual, political, or ethical principles that they often took for granted as coordinate with their trust in Scripture. The list of such other implicit beliefs varied by constituency and time but was extensive. In earlier Protestant history, implicit convictions guiding biblical interpretation included the assumption that monarchs should secure the Christianity of a nation, that Jews were inherently dangerous, and that specialized learning clarified the meaning of Scripture. In nineteenth-century America other assumptions shaded biblical interpretation: that divine providence had uniquely blessed the United States, that top-down regulation of religious life violated true liberty, that specialized learning was not required to understand Scripture, that "all men [for some purposes] were created equal," that only republican government could protect the liberty of citizens and forestall the vices of tyranny, that free markets were the only equitable way of organizing an economy, that people of European descent constituted a higher stratum of civilization than Africans or Native Americans, that men exercised their proper responsibilities in the public sphere and women in the domestic sphere, and that God's intention for human life could be ascertained by assembling "verses" from throughout the Bible into fundamental theological truths or imperative ethical guidelines. For all of these implicit convictions, except perhaps the last about "verses," believers could rally credible arguments from Scripture if they were challenged. But when such challenges appeared, confusion also reigned because of how seamlessly belief in divine revelation and whichever other conviction had been amalgamated. To challenge any of the amalgamated beliefs could seem to challenge them all.

In the early nineteenth century, the idea that women should speak publicly to "promiscuous" audiences or exercise authority in ecclesiastical life would have seemed preposterous anywhere in the Christian world. And not only strange. More important, it seemed a distinctly antibiblical move because of deviating so drastically from traditional behavior long considered a simple mandate of divine revelation.

In the American context, that new idea posed an even sharper problem. Not only did it contradict practices assumed to rest on scriptural teaching. It also hijacked honored national principles for alien purposes. Because of how often Scripture had been cited to support the Revolution and interpret the course of the young republic, many Americans again viewed these national principles and traditional uses of Scripture as parts of one whole. When in 1792 Judith Sargent Murray explained to parents that "nature" taught the benevolence of God in terms favored by Universalists, almost no one noticed.[70] Hannah Adams also did not raise concern when she used "natural" categories to explain the world religions or when she enlisted ideals of benevolence to commend the religion of Jesus. But by the 1840s and Antoinette Brown's appeal to "the nature of things" and "the united testimony of history and human nature" to support expanded women's rights, it was a different story.[71]

Among other sparks, the pamphlets by Angelina and Sarah Grimké burned most brightly. Angelina might claim, "[T]he Bible is my ultimate appeal in all matters of faith and practice," but before she put those words on the page she had already written that abolitionism sprang from "moral . . . light," that "to suppose a man can be legally born a slave under our *free republican government*" was absurd, and that it was "self evident . . . that all men every where and of every color are born equal, and have an *inalienable right to liberty*."[72] The conjunction of claims was disturbing, precisely because moral instinct, republican ideals, self-evidence, and inalienable rights belonged to the American nation that the God of Scripture, traditionally interpreted, had established.

Sarah Grimké might begin her tract on female equality by asserting that "this doctrine of [female] dependence upon man is at variance with the doctrine of the Bible." But her *Letters on the Equality of the Sexes* deviated even further from ideological and religious orthodoxy. Her outrageous claims not only transgressed long-honored biblical interpretations. She also hurled the building blocks of American nationhood, which other long-honored biblical interpretations had sanctified, against social constructs resting on these very interpretations. Granted, Sarah did clearly deploy prime features of the American civil religion as she made her case for gender equality—specifically, that men who upheld contemporary coverture should remember that "taxation without representation" brought on "our Revolutionary war," that the Ten Commandments illustrated a general moral law of equality between the sexes, that "all rights spring out of the moral nature" of humans, and that when women "become better acquainted with their rights as moral beings, and with their responsibilities growing out of these rights, they will regard themselves as they really are, FREE AGENTS."[73] To a tiny minority in Jacksonian America, Grimké's arguments based on Revolutionary precedent, the innate constitution of human nature, freedom, rights—and not least the Word of God—sounded completely convincing. Many more reacted in disbelief.

Such appeals were again suspect because of the company they kept. Before the Grimkés burst onto the scene, the most active campaigner for women's equality and against slavery had been Frances (Fanny) Wright.[74] This Scottish-born firebrand grew up in a household that honored Tom Paine. Early first-hand encounters with urban destitution in London and later experience in slaveholding Tennessee made her a passionate champion of the downtrodden. By the late 1820s she had become notorious for the farm she established near Memphis that imitated the utopianism of Robert Owen in its scheme to dismantle slavery—and also for apparently winking at sex outside of marriage and sex between whites and Blacks. By that time she had also become the first widely recognized American woman to address the public in "promiscuous" assemblies. Her themes? The evils of slavery, the folly of capital punishment, the necessity of full human rights for females—and the disaster of organized religion. In the early 1830s, she set up the Paine-ite Hall of Science in New York City, campaigned for the anticapitalist Workingman's Party, and expanded her advocacy for women's rights to include public discussion of birth control. For the many who thought of Wright ("The Great Red Whore of Infidelity") when they read Sarah Grimké, the credibility of Grimké's national and biblical bona fides vanished like dew in the sun.

Neither did developments after the Grimkés addressed the public help their cause, especially their association with Lucretia Coffin Mott.[75] Observers knew that Mott, like the Grimkés, was a Philadelphia Quaker and, with her husband, James Mott, a passionate abolitionist. They also knew she enjoyed the rare distinction of being designated an official minister in the Society of Friends and that she had sided with the more progressive Hicksite faction when it broke with the more evangelical Gurneyites. Mott's theological trajectory confirmed the fears that many harbored when they read the works of Angela and Sarah Grimké or heard them speak on behalf of the American Anti-Slavery Society. The Grimkés presented themselves as defenders of the Bible, as Lucretia Mott had once also done. But wasn't it obvious that their loyalty to radical reform went deeper than their loyalty to Scripture? Such fears grew when in 1849 Mott preached a memorable sermon at the Cherry Street Meeting in Philadelphia. Its explanation of "abuses and uses of the Bible" justified those who worried about the trajectory of egalitarian and abolitionist reforms. Mott preached without reserve: "The great error of Christendom is that the Bible is called the word, that it is taken as a whole, as a volume of plenary inspiration and in this way has proved one of the strongest pillars to uphold ecclesiastical power and hireling priesthood." Instead of servile deference to a supposedly infallible Scripture, Mott pointed to "one source which is higher." It was "faith . . . in accordance with reason and the intelligent dictates of the pure Spirit of God." On the basis of such faith, Mott disparaged the trappings of traditional Christianity like observation of the Sabbath, the rite of baptism, and the authority of ministers—even as she advocated freedom for the enslaved and equality for women. She closed this forthright discourse by adapting for herself the words that Jesus was recorded as speaking at the outset of his public ministry: "The Spirit of the highest is upon me; the Spirit of the Lord is upon me, because he hath anointed me to preach the gospel, because he hath anointed me to bind up the broken-hearted, to preach deliverance to the captive, the opening of the prison to them that are bound, and so preach the acceptable year of the Lord [Lk 4:18]."[76]

In Protestant lands, reluctance long prevailed about acknowledging other authorities crowding out supreme loyalty to Scripture. Nowhere was that reluctance stronger than in the early United States, where so many voices proclaimed their allegiance to the Bible alone. But here stood Mott openly broadcasting her allegiance to an extrabiblical authority (her own spiritual consciousness). Especially to those who did not or could not acknowledge the influence of other authorities on their own interpretation of Scripture, she represented a clear and present danger. Again there was guilt by association. Whatever anyone claimed who championed Mott's causes, wasn't it transparent that they (like her) really exalted the causes and their own moral sentiments over scriptural truth? Which had to mean they actually despised the Bible they claimed to follow.

Resistance to claims that the Bible demanded more rights for women, or even gender equality, ran deep. The claims upset well-established traditional interpretations. They seemed to slide into a denial of Scripture's final authority. They threatened long-standing centers of religious and social power—male ministers, male-run denominations, the male monopoly on public speech. They undercut the ability of churches to ensure social stability—within the family, within the churches, in the public at large.

Perhaps most important, they threatened general confidence in convictions long considered basic to Protestant Christianity and, in more recent history, to the well-being of the United States. Innovative uses of Scripture that challenged those convictions, which rested so solidly on traditional biblical interpretations, could easily shake confidence in Scripture itself. For millions of Americans, however, that general confidence bestowed meaning on existence now and for eternity, wisdom necessary for daily life, security for children and grandchildren, and the ability to face death unafraid. In the United States the same general beliefs sustained their hopes for the nation's future. An adjustment to one of the truths integrally grounding those most basic human concerns, like the Bible's teaching on gender, might seem like a secondary concern. Implications of such an adjustment in the American context were anything but.

In American religion from the 1790s, energetic preachers, writers, orators, and organizers exploited the national commitment to religious free exercise with remarkable results for the spread of Christianity in heretofore unimagined variety, as well as for an unprecedented flowering of alternatives extending well beyond Christianity. The constant reiteration of ideological principles like liberty, equality, democracy, and individual rights accompanied the expanding influence of these Protestant and Protestant-like movements. The biblicism that flourished as the Protestant heritage evolved in this free environment reached far and wide.

For women not to share in the driving forces of the era would have been unthinkable. Even in the heyday of European Christendom, no single authority had ever succeeded in commanding a uniform interpretation of Scripture's diverse collection of history, myth, law, poetry, epistles, theology, and more. Now in the American setting, was it any surprise that radically new questions about gender produced radically new answers from such a fecund source? Religion driven by the Protestant Bible could not be confined within limits taken for granted throughout earlier Protestant history. The biblical religion that stabilized American civilization destabilized it as well.

19

The War before the War

From the early 1830s contentions over the Bible's teaching concerning race and slavery multiplied exponentially. The rivulets of dispute generated by Quakers in the colonial period became, after 1776, rivers fed by springs of Revolutionary and evangelical principle flowing toward abolition. But those streams subsided and new channels were cut by storms over Denmark Vesey and the admission of Missouri. Torrents associated with David Walker, Nat Turner, and William Lloyd Garrison began the swelling of currents that over the next generation flooded the national landscape with massive destruction. In that flood the Bible was washed away as a decisive influence on national development.

The deployment of Scripture by different communities with different conclusions about slavery and race made this antebellum history unusually complex. Least complicated was the situation in the white South. As in the Revolutionary period, when patriots enlisted Scripture for republican principles and national independence, southern whites mostly enlisted biblical interpretation to justify their slave-owning society. In the North an array of contrasts created interpretive uncertainty. Those who read the Bible as an abolitionist text favored different approaches. Some continued to rely on literal exegesis featuring proof-texts, while others enlisted historical study of biblical contexts to make their case. Still others aligned biblical teaching alongside of, or even subordinate to, moral intuitions. But more numerous than all northerners who attacked slavery were those who held that Scripture in at least some sense allowed for, or actually approved, slavery. Differences also differentiated these figures, with some contending that while slavery was not a sin as such, the Bible did lean toward gradual emancipation. Others came closer to southern white apologists who depicted slavery as a positive good. Meanwhile, a smaller array of biblical arguments from Black Americans gained almost no traction among the white population.

Antebellum biblical arguments—of which there were many more on slavery than on slavery *and* race—have been expertly treated by a number of historians.[1] Yet given the extent of controversy and the deep commitment to the ideal of biblical authority, a full-scale study would require a more comprehensive effort than anyone has yet attempted, or can be attempted here. This chapter offers instead only a simplified history of biblical proslavery and biblical abolitionism from the time of David Walker and Nat Turner through the Civil War. An explanation for

America's Book. Mark A. Noll, Oxford University Press. © Oxford University Press 2022.
DOI: 10.1093/oso/9780197623466.003.0020

why the proslavery arguments appeared to be so strong along with an assessment of the controversy's long-term effects are reserved for the following chapter.

For these antebellum arguments it is important to remember that the same hermeneutical strategies prevailed that women Bible expositors and their opponents put to use. Because the general reliance on Scripture was so pervasive, confusion resulted from the indiscriminate mingling of those strategies: proof-texting, synthesizing passages from different parts of Scripture, invoking the historical contexts of especially controversial passages, and reasoning from Scripture shaped by other authorities. This last hermeneutical practice generated especially visceral conflict since so many different authorities influenced biblical interpretation and since those authorities so often remained unselfconscious. Common assumptions about the role of providence in founding the United States or in creating the American slave system operated with particularly inflammatory effect.

To see that common interpretive patterns led as often to conflict as to agreement, to observe the powerful sway of conventions that remained beneath the level of consciousness, and to grasp the place of Scripture in the sweep of American history more generally is to prepare for the conclusions spelled out in the next chapter. In this national drama, the more conflicted biblical interpretations became on race and slavery, the less Scripture influenced national development, but the more determinative those conflicts became for the later use of the Bible itself.

Biblical Proslavery Arguments

Although considerable variation characterized proslavery biblical arguments in the generation after 1830, their commonality, as had been the case before 1830, remained much more obvious than their differences.[2] At the outset it is important to realize that these arguments appeared in all parts of the country—the white North as well as the white South—from representatives of almost all denominations, from an obviously diverse range of intellectual abilities, and with the accumulating force of consistency. Whatever a neutral tribunal might have concluded about the credibility of these arguments—assuming that such a tribunal were ever possible—the repetition of similar arguments in similar form made them unusually effective.

A short but much noticed work by a Virginia Baptist from 1841 became a *locus classicus* when it sparked immediate controversy, was reprinted, then expanded, and in 1860 was included in E. N. Eliot's landmark defense of white southern ideology, *Cotton Is King*.[3] Thornton Stringfellow of Locust Grove, Culpeper County, Virginia, began his *Brief Examination of Scripture Testimony on the Institution of*

Slavery with theses others constantly repeated: "Slavery is a political institution, and ought to be discussed on political grounds alone. Christ and his apostles did not stop to enter into a discussion of its evils. How much better would it be if all his professed disciples would be equally wise." Stringfellow's straightforward argument matched his succinct title: "Slavery has received . . . the sanction of the Almighty in the Patriarchal age . . . it was incorporated into the only national constitution which ever emanated from God . . . its legality was recognized, and its relative duties regulated by Jesus Christ in his kingdom; and . . . it is full of mercy."[4]

In twenty-three pages of modest-size print, Stringfellow marshaled the texts that in his view demonstrated God's approval of slavery for Abraham and the patriarchs (Gen 9, 12, 16, 20, 24, 26, 47; Ex 12, 20; Job 3, 7, 31), the divine sanction of the institution in the Law of Moses (Lev 25; Jer 34; Ex 21), and the universal acceptance of slavery in the New Testament (the silence of Jesus plus Rom 13; 1 Cor 7; Eph 6; Col 3; Titus 1, 2, 3; 1 Tim 6; 1 Pet 2). In the course of his "brief examination" and an added thirteen pages responding to a northerner who had challenged his biblical citations, Stringfellow leaned most heavily on the permission allowing Hebrews to enslave "the heathen that are round about you" from Leviticus 25:44–46 (cited at least seven times) and the Pauline mandate, "let . . . servants . . . count their masters worthy of all honour," from 1 Timothy 6:1 (three times). He closed with a short section of ten assertions, each beginning "I have shown," followed by a pithy recapitulation of how a particular bit of biblical evidence required the conclusion that God allowed, indeed ordained and sanctioned "Slavery" (which Stringfellow capitalized throughout the work). Stringfellow and the many who agreed with his interpretations were blind to much that in the twenty-first century seems obvious, not because they were stupid but because they lived with a different universe of assumptions.

Proslavery Variations

Beyond general agreement among proslavery advocates with Stringfellow's reasoning, some variety can still be glimpsed. Differences usually came from the way biblical reasoning was aligned with other forms of authority rather in the interpretation of individual passages—with one important exception. Whether the much disputed "curse of Canaan" from Genesis 9:25 supported the American slave system remained a point of disagreement. Although Stringfellow's 1841 *Brief Examination* referred only obliquely to the fate of Africans as perpetual slaves, others placed heavy stress on the Noahic curse as justification for African enslavement. In the fast-day sermon from January 1861 that brought unusual recognition to New York City's Jewish community, Rabbi Morris Raphall

expatiated at length on "the doom of Ham's descendants, the African race, pronounced upwards of 4000 years ago" in Genesis chapter 9. Josiah Priest, a maverick but popular writer from Albany, New York, based most of a lengthy book
first published in 1843 on the same curse. Yet in sharpest disagreement stood
the Virginia Presbyterian Robert Dabney, who after the war became one of the
most ardent defenders of the Confederacy's Lost Cause. In 1856 Dabney classed
"the argument that African slavery is righteous because Noah foretold it of the
descendants of Ham" with "absurdities" distracting Bible readers from genuine
evidence.[5]

Worry about the disruptive effects of agitation over slavery became more pronounced after the church schisms of 1844–45, then as the Fugitive Slave Act of
1850 legislated much harsher penalties for assisting escaped slaves, and when
the Kansas-Nebraska Act of 1854 substituted "popular sovereignty" for the earlier prohibition against the institution in territories from the Louisiana Territory
north of 36 degrees 30 minutes. Controversy reached the breaking point in
1857 when the Supreme Court's *Dred Scott* decision ruled that the Missouri
Compromise was unconstitutional and declared that African Americans
could never be "citizens." When Henry Bascom, a leading southern Methodist,
published on the subject in 1845, his worry about things falling apart reflected
the effort that had recently failed to keep his denomination together. Bascom,
who had earlier served as a chaplain to the U.S. House of Representatives, was the
president of Transylvania University in Kentucky when he published his analysis
Methodism and Slavery. Although he took many pages to repeat the standard
biblical arguments, he devoted even more to the practical consequences for a
church that had now divided North and South.[6]

A similar concern for the practical effects of controversy informed Nathaniel
Wheaton's discourse on the New Testament's Epistle to Philemon that he
published in 1851. Wheaton, a Yale graduate, Episcopal minister, and former
president of Trinity College in Connecticut, used his sermon to defend the
Fugitive Slave Act that was part of the Compromise of 1850. Wheaton explained
Paul's return of the slave Onesimus to his master Philemon as a justification for
slavery, but ended with his eye on current events: "No desirable change can be
wrought by violence; by denunciation; by withholding from any citizen [viz., the
slave owner] the rights secured to him by law; by any resistance, secret or open,
to the execution of law."[7]

Efforts to ensure that southern enslavers followed biblical precepts in treating
their slaves appeared with some frequency, but rarely with as much stress as from
James Henley Thornwell, one of the South's most respected Presbyterians and
author of iconic apologies for the institution. In 1847 he urged slave owners to
provide baptism for converted slaves. Three years later he devoted a sermon to
spelling out biblical requirements for slave owners. His text was Colossians 4:1,

"Masters, give unto your servants that which is just and equal; knowing that ye also have a Master in heaven." From it he concluded, "[T]he Negro is of one blood with ourselves ... he has sinned as we have sinned, and ... he has an equal interest with us in the great redemption. . . . We are not ashamed to call him our *brother*." Consequently, masters must honor "the moral agency of slaves" and (with the Apostle Paul) "treat . . . them as possessed of conscience, reason, and will." A later sermon from 1854 expanded on what Thornwell called "Duties of Masters." Because of a shared humanity and the biblical consideration of slaves in parallel with instructions for the family, Thornwell concluded, "it is the duty of masters, by all proper and lawful means, to seek to promote the welfare of this class of our fellow-beings, and to secure to them the greatest amount of happiness their condition will admit." On that basis, he urged slave owners to instruct their "servants" in reading, to protect their marriages, to provide substantial Christian instruction, and to allow some Blacks a leadership role in slave worship.[8] Only implicitly did he censure masters who sexually assaulted their female slaves.

Direct attention to racial theory did not surface frequently, but when it did, disunity also prevailed. In sharp contrast to Thornwell's defense of the full humanity of enslaved African Americans, the later works of Stringfellow increasingly emphasized the "inferiority of the black race," a subject emphasized in a compendious work he published on the eve of secession.[9] In even sharper contrast to Thornwell, Josiah Priest—the freelance author, antiquarian, publicist, and popular writer from Albany—concentrated on African inferiority in his *Bible Defence of Slavery*, which was republished ten times under various titles between 1843 and 1876. The claims of this work came very close to the polygenesis that George Gliddon and Josiah Nott espoused in secular terms. As Priest did often in his popular writing, he seems here to have borrowed without attribution, in this case the eighteenth-century ethnological speculation of Scotland's Henry Homes, Lord Kames. Priest concluded that the physical disruption resulting from Noah's flood led God "to produce two *new* races of men, who were adapted ... to this *new* state of things." Priest's profoundly racist tome maintained that white, Black, and red strains of humanity had always been separated; with the Comte de Gobineau, he likewise contended that "amalgamation" always led to disastrous consequences for civilization.[10] If the degree of Priest's racism was unusual, it probably expressed a more common sentiment in the white South (and with some, like Priest, in the North) than did Thornwell's.

A noticeable difference among proslavery advocates surfaced in the works of northerners who, along with Thornwell and increasing numbers of southern theological conservatives, condemned prohibitions restricting religious education for slaves, failures to honor slave marriages, and treatment of slaves as chattel. Many of these authors hoped for a speedy end to the system but would not condemn it as such. Especially in their use of Scripture, modern historians are correct in classifying these northern emancipationists as "proslavery" because when they differentiated between abuses and the institution, they invariably justified their stance with the standard proslavery texts from both testaments. The most prominent representatives were well-known theological stalwarts like Moses Stuart of Andover Seminary and Charles Hodge of Princeton Seminary, but they were joined by a significant number of other well-respected figures that included, as only a few examples, George Washington Blagdon, pastor of Boston's Old South Church and a member of the Harvard Board of Overseers; John Chase Lord, a well-known Presbyterian pastor in Buffalo, New York; and a respected father and son in the Dutch Reformed Church, Samuel Blanchard How and Henry K. How.[11] These individuals complained about the evils attending American slavery even as they regularly emphasized, with Thornwell, that the African origin of American slaves abrogated none of their basic dignity as human beings made in the image of God. Yet they also strengthened the credibility of proslavery Bible argumentation by refusing to call the institution sinful and by expending as much energy criticizing abolitionists as cautioning defenders of the institution.

A painstakingly erudite (and lengthy) book by John Henry Hopkins, the Episcopal bishop of Vermont, demonstrated the staying power of this mostly northern variety of proslavery argumentation. In his treatise from 1864 (!), Hopkins declared that when considering "the institution of slavery," all of his "prejudices of education, habit, and social position stand entirely opposed to it." Yet he also held that "as a Christian, I am solemnly warned not to be 'wise in my own conceit [Prov 26:12],' and not to 'lean to my own understanding [Prov 3:5].'" He was rather "compelled to submit my weak and erring intellect to the authority of the Almighty." The question could "only be settled by the Bible," which, beginning with a reference to the curse of Canaan from Genesis 9, Hopkins interpreted as never condemning the institution.[12]

Significant as was this northern biblical proslavery variant, the greatest variety in proslavery publications came from the differing degrees to which authors supplemented biblical arguments with other authorities. Simon Clough, a minister of the Christian Society in Fall River, Massachusetts, in 1834 issued a "candid appeal" against abolitionists that resembled Stringfellow's *Brief Examination* from a few years later. Clough's populist tract, like Stringfellow's direct parade of quotations, offered a recitation of texts defending the institution, and almost nothing else.[13] George Patterson, a Massachusetts-born Episcopalian who served churches in North Carolina, did the same in 1850 by packing more than fifty texts into a pamphlet of only ten pages.[14] More common, however, were the authors who added contemporary observations, the burden of history, or other certainties to support their reliance on biblical texts.

In the early 1830s, Joseph Tracy was editing the main periodical for Vermont Congregationalists when he preached a sermon in support of the American

Colonization Society. Tracy would later become renowned as the author of a major history that named the eighteenth-century colonial revivals "The Great Awakening." In this earlier sermon, however, he did not rely so much on historical research as on nature and "common sense" to support a Bible-based defense of slavery and of colonization as the ideal means to end controversy over the institution.[15] Later apologists followed a similar course, sometimes with only offhand *obiter dicta*. As one example, the fiery Methodist editor William Brownlow of Tennessee began a sermon based on 1 Timothy 6:1 ("Let as many servants as are under the yoke count their own masters worthy of all honor") not with careful exegesis of his text but by appealing rapidly to "the nature of man," "[n]ature's great system," and "a known principle of our nature."[16]

Much more careful, learned, and historically informed was the major American Catholic treatment of the antebellum era. Besides his active service as bishop of Philadelphia and diligent translator of Scripture, Francis Patrick Kenrick authored a three-volume moral theology, which remained the Catholics' most important textbook for more than a generation. In its lengthy section on slavery, Kenrick regretted that slaves in southern states lived with "laws prohibiting their education and in some places greatly restricting their exercise of religion." Yet his extensive consideration of "the law of nature," "the law of nations," and a wealth of official church pronouncements over the centuries confirmed "the rules" left by the Apostles allowing for the institution. According to Kenrick, to break those rules would "overturn the entire established order" and "in most cases but aggravate the condition of the slaves."[17]

A similar proportion—respect for Scripture, briefly considered, but also extensive treatment of supporting factors—marked a learned work from 1861 by Samuel Seabury, the grandson of a founding bishop of the American Episcopal Church and the minister of a prestigious Episcopal parish in New York City. Seabury took 250 pages to show why "the law of nature" justified American slavery, before treating the "argument from Scripture" briefly. He insisted that while the progress of Christianity brightened the whole world, "the light which Christ imparts is the knowledge of salvation." He meant a spiritual salvation with none of the social implications taken for granted by African American Bible readers. To Seabury, it was absurd that "the light of the gospel, which teaches masters to be mild and gentle and servants to be diligent and faithful, can indirectly, and in process of time, abolish a relation which it directly now and always, cements."[18]

Awareness of diversity within proslavery apologies shows that the biblical defense of slavery extended deeply into national consciousness. Scripture anchored arguments from both the North and the South, both learned and plebian, both long-winded and abrupt, both measured and bombastic, both overtly racist and solicitous for the welfare of slaves, both respectful of refined scholarship and dismissive of all refinements. Most important—and in sharp contrast to those who attacked slavery—almost all apologists shared common racial assumptions, favored the same hermeneutic, and drew the same conclusions about anyone claiming that the Bible condemned the institution.

Proslavery Arguments in Step

First and most indelibly, an American cultural convention fixed racial difference as a fundamental axiom of proslavery biblical interpretation. Proslavery advocates uniformly—yet along with most white antislavery voices as well—simply assumed that "slavery" had to mean Black-only slavery (or, in a few instances, also Native American). With a bare handful of exceptions, they reasoned that if Scripture allowed, regulated, or even sanctioned "slavery," then God allowed the racially specific slave system of the United States.[19] As a prominent example, the list of topics taken up in Stringfellow's lengthy *Slavery: Its Origin, Nature and History* from 1860 proceeded with no sense of disjunction: "What slavery is—what freedom is . . .—slavery as necessary—why the white race is invested with political freedom at 21—Why it is withheld from the black race for life—Slavery is just."[20]

Despite protests from Black authors and a very few whites, the identification remained, as in Seabury's metaphor, set in cement. A collection of sermons published in early 1861 that addressed "the state of the country" illustrated the dispositive certainty of this conviction. It was no surprise that James Henley Thornwell slid in the same paragraph from discussing "our duty to our slaves" to describing "the Africans." Or when Benjamin Palmer, a well-known Presbyterian pastor from New Orleans, likewise moved without apparent awareness from describing southern whites as "the constituted guardians of the slaves" to decrying opponents whom he called "the worst foes of the black race." Yet the same taken-for-granted identification extended far beyond the South. The sermon contributed by Henry Van Dyke, an Old School Presbyterian from Brooklyn, decried "the character and influence of abolitionism"; one of his paragraphs began by referring to "the condition of the African race" but soon transitioned to affirming "that slavery is permitted and regulated by Divine Law, under both the Jewish and Christian dispensations." The pastor of a New Light Presbyterian church in New York City, William Adams, wondered how "this great embarrassment" brought on by agitation over slavery "could be solved without detriment to either race, our own or the Africans."[21] For individuals who as justifiers of slavery invariably claimed to follow the teachings of Scripture, it might have given pause that no biblical precept or example limited "slavery" to Africans. But it did not.

Those who defended slavery from Scripture also united in affirming the sovereign authority of the Word—often its exclusively sovereign authority. In this affirmation, however, they only resembled most abolitionists through the 1830s, and many thereafter. Still, as those who attacked slavery began to explain, expand, or qualify what they meant by deference to scriptural authority, their opponents kept things simple. Almost all echoed Stringfellow's statement of intentions from 1841: "What I have written was designed for those who reverence the Bible as their counseller—who take it for rules of conduct, and devotional sentiments." Or as Charles Hodge put it in a work of much greater sophistication, with much more condemnation of slaveholding abuses, but while refusing to label slaveholding as sinful: "[W]e recognize no authoritative rule of truth and duty but the word of God."[22]

The repetition of this unequivocal profession often accompanied the programmatic distinction between church and world that had been strengthening since early in the century. That distinction separated the sphere of Christian activity, governed in detail by Scripture, from the sphere of civil activity, regulated apart from Scripture by law, nature, or "politics." To Clough, the sectarian Christian Connection minister in Massachusetts, Jesus's command "Render unto Caesar the things which are Caesar's, and unto God the things that are God's" (Matt 22:21) could mean only one thing: "[T]he question of slavery, as it exists in this country, is a political and not a religious question, and that it must be settled upon the floor of Congress, and in the halls of legislation, and not in pulpits and ecclesiastical councils."[23]

This notion came to its clearest expression as southern defenders of the slave system—whether sectarian, Methodist, or proprietary—developed a full-blown doctrine of "the spirituality of the church." The Tennessee Methodist William Brownlow adopted this stance by emphasizing Jesus's answer to Pontius Pilate from John 18:36 ("my kingdom is not of this world"). From this passage, Brownlow concluded that "the Church of Christ, when originally constituted, claimed no right, *as an ecclesiastical organization*, to interfere with the secular government. This was the principle upon which the Church was founded, as announced by its immortal Head." Presbyterians, who had once read Scripture as providing general guidelines for every area of life, eventually became the most articulate defenders of the "spirituality" concept. At the first General Assembly of the Presbyterian Church in the Confederate States of America (December 1861), Thornwell was commissioned to prepare an address "to all the Churches of Jesus Christ throughout the earth." As its crux, Thornwell explained the "spirituality" doctrine as an organic outgrowth of his new denomination's determination to follow the Bible alone. In asking whether slaveholding was a sin, Thornwell averred that for the church "the only rule of judgment is the written Word of God." It then followed that "she has a positive Constitution in the Holy

Scriptures, and has no right to utter a single syllable upon any subject, except as the Lord puts words in her mouth."[24]

Brownlow's invocation of this principle in a sermon vindicating the southern Methodists' position upholding slavery and Thornwell's in an apology for the Confederacy might have been viewed as self-contradictory. To reason that, if the Bible did not explicitly condemn slavery, then the Confederate Presbyterian Church dare not, could look like a biblical interpretation applied to adjudicate a problem in the world. A quite different approach to "spirituality" was found among the nation's Mennonite and Amish communities. Their almost total public silence on the divisive issues of the day, except to defend the principle of nonresistance, illustrated a more consistent, if German-inflected determination to separate scriptural faithfulness from political activity.[25]

For the history of the Bible, the common proslavery approach meant even more than the specific shape of arguments. In almost all anti-abolitionist polemics, the key interpretive strategy was concentration on individual texts interpreted literally. If Abraham, the father of the faithful, owned slaves, then Christian believers, as the spiritual descendants of Abraham, may own slaves. If Moses allowed the ancient Hebrews to enslave the "heathen" and their children perpetually, then so may Christians who honor Moses as the great lawgiver. If the teaching of Jesus could be applied to *how* masters treated their slaves but not *that* masters enslaved Africans, then to follow Jesus meant to make the same distinction. If the Apostle Paul sent the escaped slave Onesimus back to his owner, Philemon, then apostolic testimony sanctioned the acceptability of slavery itself. If the Apostles admitted slave owners to Christian fellowship, then so may nineteenth-century American churches.

Proslavery biblical advocates often spoke as if only two steps were necessary to secure their position: first, set out the key texts taking slavery for granted or giving it positive sanction; second, refute the proof-texts that abolitionists cited to support their campaign. This strategy gained credibility when it won a clear victory over one of the most prominent abolitionist arguments. Leading abolitionists like Theodore Dwight Weld in his *The Bible against Slavery* (1837) and Albert Barnes in *An Inquiry into the Scriptural View of Slavery* (1846) rested much of their case on a specific issue of translation. They noted that proslavery advocates routinely took the King James Version's *servant* to mean *slave*; but they then asked: What did the Hebrew and Greek terms so translated really mean? Barnes, for instance, contended that the Greek word *doulos* might not apply to a person "in any way regarded as a slave" because it could designate several different kinds of labor: "servant, slave, waiter, [or] hired man." Similarly, because the Hebrew word *ebedh* included "all the relations of servitude," it was only conjecture that treated Abraham's "servants" and Mosaic regulations as justification for American slavery.[26] Although proslavery advocates did allow for some flexibility in these terms, they also contended persuasively that whatever else the key words designated, they certainly denoted inheritable and lifelong permanent servitude. Their conclusion? No one should doubt that when the King James Version spoke of "servants," the Scriptures for American purposes meant "slaves." Works like Stringfellow's *Brief Examination* made this rebuttal crudely, but it appeared with extensive references to older and newer critical scholarship from learned authorities like Stuart, Hodge, and others both North and South.[27]

Other exegetical battles seemed to be won with equal ease. From the first efforts by Quakers like Anthony Benezet and John Woolman to enlist the Bible against slavery, abolitionists returned time and again to the Golden Rule, either Jesus's command to do unto others as you would be done unto (Matt 7) or that the followers of God should love their neighbors as themselves (Matt 22). Yet also from the first, proslavery advocates scorned abolitionist understanding of these texts as risible. Simple attention to the wider context of biblical revelation sufficed to expose abolitionist error. The Golden Rule should of course govern the Christian's conduct, but it could not possibly mean the destruction of social relations that Scripture everywhere prescribed. Proof for the anti-abolitionists came from the Pauline instruction that slaves obey their masters as unto the Lord (Eph chapter 6 and Col chapter 4). Alongside these instructions to slaves, Paul also gave instructions for husbands and wives, for parents and children, and (from elsewhere) for rulers and citizens. In each case the instructions pertained to how individuals should act in what Albert Taylor Bledsoe, an aggressive apologist who taught mathematics at the University of Virginia, called the "relations of life." The lengthy work of scholarship by Samuel Seabury, the New York City Episcopalian, put it like this: "I am to love my neighbor ... with the same *sincerity* that I love myself; and I am to do to others, not all that I might selfishly and lawlessly wish, but all that I could reasonably desire them, consistently with duty, to do to me, were I in their place and they in mine."[28] This last phrase about the "places" that God had appointed seemed such an obvious qualification of the Golden Rule that proslavery spokesmen laughed away its use by abolitionists: if you mean that children should exercise authority over their parents, wives over their husbands, and citizens over rulers, then, and only then, might you suggest that slaves should change positions with their masters.[29]

Although anti-abolitionists devoted much less attention to Galatians 3:28, they dispatched abolitionist appeals to that text with equal ease. When the Apostle proclaimed that there was no longer "Jew nor Greek ... bond nor free ... male nor female," he was obviously speaking of spiritual realities. Stuart Robinson, a passionate defender of the "spirituality" view, had fled from his Presbyterian pulpit in Louisville, Kentucky, during the Civil War when Union troops interpreted his ecclesiology as thinly veiled support for the Confederacy. In a learned proslavery tome published from Toronto in 1865, Robinson quickly handled the passage by quoting an Anglican authority, Henry Alford, who read it as addressing strictly spiritual, not temporal, freedom.[30]

Abolitionist reliance on the "man-stealing" prohibitions from Exodus 21:16 and 1 Timothy 1:10 posed a more serious problem. True to his title, Stringfellow's *Brief Examination* of 1841 dismissed this prohibition briefly. By claiming that the prohibition itself took for granted what abolitionists denied, he hoped to turn the tables: "Unless slavery exists, there would be no motive to steal a man."[31]

Other proslavery advocates recognized that this abolitionist claim required a more serious response. Such a response came from Frederick Ross, a New School Presbyterian pastor in Huntsville, Alabama. Ross apparently enjoyed the polemical life, as witnessed by the titanic battle (Presbyterian versus Methodist) he had earlier waged with William Brownlow. But now the Presbyterian stood shoulder to should with the Methodist against the abolitionists. Ross's learned work from 1857, *Slavery Ordained of God*, began as a response to Harriet Beecher Stowe's *Uncle Tom's Cabin* but soon broadened to take on other abusers of Scripture. Against Albert Barnes, who had doubled down on George Bourne's abolitionist exposition of Exodus 21:16, Ross devoted twenty pages of careful exegesis and painstaking casuistry. His crucial argument emphasized the difference between what had happened in Africa generations before and the current situation in the United States: "*The master does NOT assume the same relation which the original man-stealer or buyer held to the African.* The master's relation to God and to his slave is now *wholly changed* from that of the man-stealer." As Ross explained the difference he took from Scripture, however, he drifted in another direction by appealing to circumstances and to providence. The master, "with no taint of personal concern in the African trade," now found himself "holding control over his black fellow-man, who is so unlike himself in complexion, in form, in other peculiarities, and so unequal to himself in attributes of body and mind, that it is *impossible in every sense* to place him on a level with himself in the community." Moreover, "God has placed the master under law entirely different from his command to the slave-trader." The predictable conclusions followed: the slave was "to know the facts in his case as they are in the Bible, and have ever been, and ever will be in Providence:—that he is not the white man's equal."[32] Unlike interpretations of the Golden Rule and Galatians 3:28, Ross's proslavery interpretation of biblical prohibitions against man-stealing relied as much on modern ethnology and his reading of providence as on exegesis.

As Ross indicated, recourse to providence frequently accompanied exposition of Scripture. In fact, a common view of providence played a huge part in biblical proslavery arguments. Advocates partook completely of the assumption, shared as widely in the North as in the South, that God had providentially directed the history of the United States in ways that believers could see clearly. They also took for granted—again, with substantial numbers in the white North—that the same divine hand charted the course of American slavery.

The fast-day sermons published in early 1861 again illustrate the nation-wide extent of this providential reasoning. From the South, James Henley Thornwell recited the achievements of American civilization that "national sins" now imperiled: "It was ours to redeem this continent to spread freedom, civilization and religion through the whole land. . . . We were a city set upon a hill [Matt 5:14], whose light was intended to shine upon every people and upon every land." From the North, the minister of New York City's Trinity Episcopal Church, Francis Vinton, said virtually the same thing. Himself unwilling to condemn slavery as sinful, Vinton appealed to the Golden Rule (by which he meant masters treating slaves justly) as the means to overcome "the extremes of abolitionism and [proslavery] propagandism." But Vinton rested this assessment of the present on a view of American history that he summarized by tracing Old Testament history from Noah through the prophet Samuel to the prophet Isaiah. He then concluded with this rhetorical question: "In this short history is not the portrait of our country sketched?"[33]

More specifically, Henry Van Dyke from his New York pulpit explained why American slavery was justified "as an important and necessary process in their ['the African race's'] transition from heathenism to Christianity—a wheel in the great machinery of Providence, by which the final redemption is to be accomplished."[34] Van Dyke, in other words, held that slavery was God's way of evangelizing Africans. The southern Presbyterian Benjamin Palmer did not differ, except in expanding upon the same sentiment. His defense of "slavery as a divine trust" was full of references to "the dispensations of Providence," "a universal and ruling Providence," and the like. In his view, African Americans "providentially [owed] me service, which, providentially, I am bound to exert." Once Palmer defined slavery as a providential necessity, so also was established in his mind "our present trust to preserve and transmit our existing system of domestic servitude, with the right, unchanged by man, to go and root itself wherever Providence and nature may carry it."[35]

Finally, because proslavery advocates believed so firmly in the biblical righteousness of their cause, they invariably impugned the orthodoxy and integrity of those who claimed Scripture supported abolition. In his well-known *Brief Examination*, Thornton Stringfellow specifically chastised those who augmented biblical augments by appealing to the Declaration of Independence's statement that "all men are created equal." Everyone knew that Thomas Jefferson had authored that proposition, and everyone also knew about Jefferson's religion. Abolitionists were obviously "throw[ing] away the Bible as Mr. Jefferson did." Frederick Ross also found abolitionists guilty by association: "Tom Paine rejected the Bible" because it did not align with "*his* sensibilities, *his* great law of humanity, *his* intuitional and eternal sense of right"; abolitionists like Albert Barnes did just the same in rejecting "all the word of God." Stuart Robinson in 1865 waxed apoplectic when he described the abolitionist desecration of Scripture as simply what the Devil had been doing time out of mind, "counterfeiting the philanthropist, and seeking to destroy the faith of mankind in so popular a doctrine of the gospel [i.e., the scriptural approval of slavery], by urging upon them a garish, flashy, mob-delighting philanthropy, and especially so cheap a philanthropy as one that demands no sacrifice of one's own property and comfort, as the gospel philanthropy does, but only a noisy clamor against the property and comfort of other people." Among those who repeated the indictment, Albert Taylor Bledsoe stood out for the relish he took, as a southerner with Methodist associations, to quote from what respected northern Presbyterians at Princeton had written: "The history of interpretation furnishes no examples of more willful and violent perversions of the sacred text than are to be found in the writings of the abolitionists. They seem to consider themselves above the Scriptures; and when they put themselves above the law of God, it is not wonderful that they should disregard the laws of men."[36]

Black authors and many white abolitionists at the time, along with a host of commenters in the recent past, have objected strenuously to the conclusions drawn from Scripture by proslavery advocates. Their counterarguments deserve the most serious consideration by anyone hoping to understand the course of American history, concerned about the nature of Scripture, or eager to see how culture shapes the interpretation of sacred texts. In antebellum America, however, the arguments of Stringfellow and Thornwell, of Seabury and Hodge, and of the many others who enlisted Scripture to defend slavery carried great conviction.

Biblical Abolition

In the heated polemics of the antebellum decades, abolitionist appeals to Scripture could not match the popular influence of proslavery advocates. Yet their persistence came close to proslavery persistence, the scholarship was often just as deep, and their rhetorical acumen often superior. Again, if an unbiased court could be imagined, abolitionists would have to be judged at least as persuasive as proslavery advocates in using the Bible to support their cause, even under the prevailing intellectual conventions of the era.[37]

Reputable observers at the time and since do not concur with that judgment. Leonard Bacon, a Connecticut Congregationalist deeply opposed to American slavery, nevertheless expressed a reluctant conclusion in 1846 after a thorough perusal of the relevant literature. According to Bacon, it was necessary to "torture the Scriptures" in order to affirm "that which the anti-slavery theory requires them to say."[38] Four years later, the nation's most respected advocate of technical biblical scholarship agreed. Moses Stuart of Andover Seminary was no friend of American slavery. On many occasions in many ways he had explained why he considered slavery wrong and how he thought it could be eventually eliminated. Yet harsh criticism of his friend Senator Daniel Webster for supporting the Fugitive Slave Law as part of the Compromise of 1850 drove Stuart into a frenzy of scholarship. As he once again distinguished slavery as regrettable from slavery as an evil in itself, he gave full vent to his irritation. Abolitionists, according to Stuart, faced only one choice: they "must give up the New Testament authority, or abandon the fiery course which they are pursuing."[39] The magisterial scholarship of Elizabeth Fox-Genovese and Eugene Genovese echoes that judgment: "Southern evangelicals, having cited chapter and verse, successfully enlisted the Bible to unify the overwhelming majority of slaveholders and nonslaveholders in defense of slavery as ordained by God." For a large part of the North as well, abolitionists, in the Genoveses' conclusion, could not show "how any of the alternatives could ground antislavery Christian doctrine in Scripture."[40]

Contexts help explain why Bacon, Stuart, the Genoveses, and many others have drawn this conclusion. The violent rhetoric of David Walker's 1829 *Appeal* and the actual violence of Nat Turner's 1831 rebellion made it easy to associate biblical antislavery with bloodshed and disorder. More generally, radical denunciations read in William Lloyd Garrison's *Liberator* or heard from platforms of the American Anti-Slavery Society worked at cross purposes. When in the last major work of biblical antislavery before the war George Cheever attacked opponents with terms like "treason . . . synagogue of Satan . . . horrible corruption . . . abomination . . . iniquity and madness," it did little to win over even the North's moderate emancipationists for whom slavery had become, if regrettably, a part of American life.[41] For the biblical case itself, however, the chief abolitionist difficulty lay in the multiplicity of arguments relying on a welter of hermeneutical procedures.

J. Albert Harrill has perceptively distinguished among those main hermeneutical strategies.[42] Some matched proof-text for proof-text as they relied on the Bible's "plain sense." Others reasoned from Scripture's "immutable principles" or a biblical "seed" developing over time into manifest antislavery. Still others drew on "moral intuition" to clarify what the Scriptures should mean.

As George Bourne, Alexander McLeod, and Freeborn Garrettson had done in the early years of the nineteenth century, and La Roy Sunderland followed when Methodists took up this explosive issue, abolitionists appealed to many specific passages in many different ways. An extensive book from 1847 by a Baptist minister who had been born a slave owner in South Carolina but then renounced the institution illustrated the extent of efforts to destroy slavery with the Holy Book. William Henry Brisbane's *Slaveholding Examined in the Light of the Holy Bible* cited ninety-seven texts from twenty-eight Old Testament books and sixty-eight from twenty-two New Testament books to make his case.[43]

The great variety of passages that Brisbane and other Christian abolitionists cited did convince a significant minority of Americans. To differentiate those uses is to comprehend the fulsome resources at hand for those who both loved Scripture and hated slavery. It is also to understand why the multiplicity caused such serious problems. Because different hermeneutical procedures invariably mingled within individual works, it added a degree of complexity to almost all abolitionist attempts that opposing works lacked. That mingling also made it easy for proslavery advocates to unravel biblical abolition by pulling at isolated threads of argument. Proslavery drew a straight line from proof-texts to a single destination; abolition came from all over the biblical map.

Abolitionist Proof-Texting

From the first public debates, defenders of slavery regularly accused antislavery advocates of abandoning the plain meanings of God's Word for eurekas from mere human ingenuity. In point of fact, abolitionists never abandoned straightforward proof-texting and a reliance on literal meaning, even if only one weapon in an overfull arsenal.

Proof-texts directly applied. An elderly George Bourne himself reentered the lists in 1845 with *A Condensed Anti-Slavery Bible Argument.* As if the intervening decades since the 1816 publication of *The Book and Slavery Irreconcilable* had changed nothing, his new title page called readers " 'to the law and to the testimony,' etc. Isa. viii.20," as an announcement of his intention to exploit "plain sense" interpretation. Although, as in his earlier abolitionist works, Bourne cited many passages, he began with another appeal to Moses's sentence of death for "man-stealers" from Exodus 21:16 and the New Testament repetition of that prohibition from 1 Timothy 1:10. Plain-sense interpretation sufficed for Bourne to make the Bible's case against slavery as "compounded of the crimes of kidnapping, assault and battery, and false imprisonment."[44] Many abolitionists held that these texts supplied a stronger literal condemnation of the American slave system than the support proslavers found in Leviticus 25:44–46 or 1 Timothy 6:1–10. To be sure, it required one tiny intellectual step to secure the force of these man-stealing passages. But was it not transparent that anyone who "owned" a slave had become an accessory after the fact to man-stealing? (Bourne and others made a comparable argument about the Mosaic condemnation in this same verse of "he that . . . selleth [a man].")

Proof-texts supplying principles or precedents. As we have seen, biblical abolitionists appealed constantly to the Golden Rule. In their eyes, this single command from Jesus enunciated a principle that, if taken seriously, would end slavery in an instant. Despite equally constant proslavery insistence that Jesus never intended the Rule to revolutionize the social order, antislavery advocates steadfastly read it as a command to rescue human dignity from the unique degradations of enslavement. In his 1860 tome that applied extreme language to his opponents, George Cheever concluded that a right understanding of biblical Hebrew and Greek, the Mosaic law, and biblical history undergirded the imperative of not only the Golden Rule but many similar texts:

> [A]ll converge in the great lesson of universal charity taught by the gospel. Whatsoever ye would that men should do to you, do ye even so to them [Matt 7:12], and, Thou shalt love they neighbor as thyself [Matt 22:39]. . . . God hath made of one blood all the races of men that dwell upon the face of the earth [Acts 17:26] . . . every wall of caste, color, national peculiarity and prejudice, is broken down in Christ, and that in him, in the church, there is neither Jew nor Greek, circumcision nor uncircumcision, Barbarian nor Scythian, bond nor free [Gal 3:28].[45]

Much in the full library of biblical antislavery moved easily from texts considered as grounding abolitionist principles to assaulting enslavement with those principles and then to citing additional evidence. Sometimes observers described these moves as appealing to the Bible's "spirit" instead of its "letter." John Greenleaf Whittier used this language to describe the commitments of Lydia Maria Child, a formidable New England reformer, editor, and author. According to Whittier, Child "held to the spirit of the Scripture rather than its letter" because "she lived in a time when the Bible was cited in defense of slavery."[46] Child herself had also appealed to standard antislavery texts, but with characteristic pithiness did stress the distinction between "spirit" and "letter." As she wrote in 1833, "Among other apologies for slavery, it has been asserted that the Bible does not forbid it. Neither does it forbid the counterfeiting of a bankbill. It is the *spirit* of the Holy Word, not its particular *expressions*, which must be a rule for our conduct."[47]

In contrast to Child's clear distinction between "spirit" and "letter," abolitionists more often mingled them with abandon. In October 1845, Jonathan Blanchard engaged in a multiday debate over slavery in Cincinnati with a proslavery Presbyterian minister. (Figure 19.1) Blanchard, a fellow Presbyterian

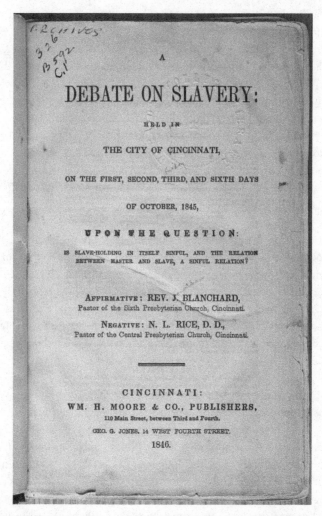

Figure 19.1 The 1845 "Debate on Slavery" between two Cincinnati Presbyterian ministers, Jonathan Blanchard (against) and Nathan Rice (for), wrestled with the same texts that by that time featured in almost all contentions over the subject.
Source: Courtesy of Buswell Library Special Collections, Rare Books, Wheaton College, Illinois.

who would become a proto-fundamentalist after the Civil War, gathered up principles, texts, and auxiliary authorities into a rhetorical whirlwind. In his view, "abolitionists take their stand upon the New Testament doctrine of the natural equity of man. The one-bloodism of human kind [Acts 17:26]:—and upon those great principles of human rights, drawn from the New Testament, and announced in the American Declaration of Independence, declaring that all men have natural and *inalienable* rights to person, property, and the pursuit of happiness."[48] The celebrated Henry Ward Beecher provided a more dramatic example of how texts propelled principles in the sermon from January 1861 that he contributed to the anonymously edited *Fast Day Sermons*. As was characteristic of his oratory, Beecher ranged widely: he repented for national sins against Native Americans and against Mexico; he praised "this Puritan land, this free Government"; and he sloganeered with abandon ("the Spirit of God is the spirit of liberty"). But he also paused to challenge proslavery biblical reasoning with a forceful rhetorical toggle between the words of Jesus (Lk 4:18; Jn 8:12) and an assault on enslavement:

> "I come to open the prison-doors," said Christ; and that is the text on which men justify shutting them and locking them. "I come to loose those that are bound"; and that is the text out of which men spin cords to bind men, women, and children. "I come to carry light to them that are in darkness, and deliverance to the oppressed"; and that is the Book from out of which they argue, with amazing ingenuity, all the infernal meshes and snares by which to keep men in bondage. It is pitiful.[49]

African Americans characteristically voiced a variation by emphasizing that Christian principles sprang from biblical precedents as well as from biblical commands, an emphasis aligned with Black approaches to treating Scripture more as a narrative than as a guidebook. The sermon that Absalom Jones preached in 1808 to celebrate the legal end of the African slave trade expounded his text, Exodus 3:7–8 ("I have surely seen the affliction of my people"), as establishing such a principle. For Jones, this verse was not a "seed" that needed to grow into an antislavery plant: "The God of heaven and earth *is the same, yesterday, and to-day, and for ever* [Heb 13:8]." Thirteen times Jones repeated, "He has seen": Africans "thrust into the holds of . . . ships"; slaves experiencing "the pangs of separation between members of the same family . . . the neglect with which their masters have treated their immortal souls . . . all the different modes of torture"; and more.[50] What God did then, Jones proclaimed, he could do now. Frederick Douglass and other Black leaders followed in the same pattern, sometimes with a specific text, sometimes not, as they took their stand on principles based on the actions of the Bible's God.[51]

Typology as "American" proof-texting. Similar in some regards were antislavery arguments based on Old Testament texts but put to use typologically. A remarkable manuscript that was not published until 2018 illustrated how orthodox Bible believers could rely on this way of using individual texts to excoriate enslavement. Eli Washington Caruthers had served a leading Presbyterian church in Greensboro, North Carolina, for forty years until in 1861 he was dismissed because of a prayer for soldiers from his congregation serving with Confederate forces, that they "be blessed of the Lord and returned in safety, though engaged in a lost cause." Immediately after being turned out for that indiscretion, Caruthers penned a lengthy treatise that took up many antislavery texts and arguments, but all based on his reading of Exodus 10:3 ("Let my people go that they may serve me").[52] Jack Davidson, who is responsible for the recent publication of Caruthers's work, has documented thirty other instances from 1836 to 1865 where ministers and laity, in published works and private communications, cited the same text as a divine command addressed to American slaveholders.[53]

By leaning on a verse from a narrative part of the Old Testament, Caruthers departed from a plain-text reading, strictly considered. Yet he was also following well-established American hermeneutical practice. As honed throughout the colonial period and then perfected during the Revolutionary crisis, typological interpretations featuring the analogy of ancient Israel and contemporary America came close to dominating public expositions of Holy Writ. James Patterson, pastor of a Philadelphia Presbyterian church, anticipated Caruthers's usage with a thanksgiving sermon on July 4, 1825. His text, also from the story of Israel's liberation, expounded Moses's command to Pharaoh from Exodus 4:23 ("Let my son [i.e., Israel] go, that he may serve me, and if thou refuse to let him go, Behold I will slay the son"). While not literal exegesis, the "plain sense" in American usage could not be mistaken: Israel enslaved in Egypt was a type for Africans enslaved in America; the command of God to Pharaoh should be heard as a command of the Lord to the United States.[54]

Proof-texts versus proof-texts. Abolitionists also practiced the negative art of deconstructing proslavery proof-texts with antislavery proof-texts. Moreover, these defensive moves usually relied on textual, contextual, or historical facts rather than (or along with) appeals to moral consciousness. While serving as the pastor of a Black Congregational church in Hartford, Connecticut, James Pennington provided a notable example of such deconstruction in a "textbook" explaining the history of African peoples. Although most of this work summarized general historical authorities (Herodotus, Josephus, later authors), it began by showing that Black people were not descended from Cain and by thoroughly dismantling "the curse of Canaan" from Genesis 9:25 as a defense of modern American slavery. Pennington's reading of that passage, which he supported with careful cross references, traced the genealogy of Africans through Ham's brother Cush and Cush's son Nimrod ("a mighty hunter before the Lord," Gen 10:9).[55] His explanation of Genesis chapter 9, though aimed at a Black audience and therefore almost entirely neglected by everyone else, replicated the conclusion of learned pastors like Robert Dabney. As he ended his treatment of the descendants of Noah, Pennington made another typical abolitionist move by augmenting close-grained exegesis with a general appropriation of Scripture.

Even if, he asked rhetorically, Noah had intended to curse his offspring, did "the sudden effusions of man's anger control the administrations of the great God?"[56]

Proof-texts rightly understood. Despite conclusive interpretative efforts like Pennington's on the curse of Canaan, the main effort to refute proslavery proof-texts encountered special difficulties. Although the scholarly consensus confirmed that the word appearing in the King James Version as *servant* often did mean a chattel slave, abolitionists resisted. Proslavery advocates, as they trumpeted this conclusion, directed most of their fire against the major works by Theodore Dwight Weld (1837) and Albert Barnes (1846). The success of those arguments can be illustrated by the December 1860 sermon from the respected New York Presbyterian Henry Van Dyke. At the very beginning of his discourse based on 1 Timothy 6:1 ("let as many servants as are under the yoke count their own masters worthy of all honor"), Van Dyke cited five respected commentators to refute Barnes's reading of "servants under the yoke" as anything but slavery.[57]

Still, abolitionists kept trying. George Bourne in 1845 argued that Leviticus 25:44–46 counted only as an explanation for why the Hebrew nation, considered collectively, was allowed to "hire" non-Hebrews until they too were incorporated into the nation by circumcision. As he reprised his earlier antislavery arguments, Bourne also reprised his lifelong anti-Catholic animus to blame "the Catholic priests who first forged these perversions, falsely dressed upon in their English version of this statute, so as to resemble the modern Christian practice of negro slavery as nearly as possible."[58] Two years later, William Brisbane based his entire biblical case on the same contentions: "I unhesitatingly say, that neither *ebedh*, *doulos*, nor *servant* ever means *slave*." In addition, when the word *master* or an equivalent appeared in Scripture, it never meant *slave owner*.[59] In other words, opponents of proslavery proof-texting never gave up.

Pastor George Cheever of the tall-steeple Church of the Puritans in New York City published the last full-scale biblical argument before the war, from which we have already quoted. The Fugitive Slave Act of 1850 had ignited Cheever's antislavery animus, which became all-out abolitionism in response to the *Dred Scott* decision of 1857. By that time this principled opponent of the Mexican War, ardent anti-Catholic, passionate Sabbatarian, and dedicated temperance advocate had become one of the North's most respected preachers. Though claiming to make "the argument plain and simple to the English reader," Cheever gave the public a massively learned discussion "demonstrated from the Hebrew and Greek Scriptures." His tome eventually advanced many different arguments, but it began with what he considered literal, plain-sense readings of crucial passages from both testaments: "There is no word in the Hebrew language for slave. . . . [D]oulos . . . is used for the varieties of service. . . . [Philemon proves] the utter repudiation of slavery."[60] In his mind, abolitionists had no need to leave the "letter" of Scripture for its "spirit": "If the letter of Christianity is not against slavery, then its spirit is not. If the spirit of Christianity is bound to abolish slavery, it is because the law of Christianity reprobates and forbids it. . . . The Bible, from Genesis to Revelation, is a continuous line of living fire against this iniquity."[61]

By 1860, however, Cheever's was an increasingly lonely voice. While he campaigned on many fronts and far afield, his base camp remained what he took to be the Bible's literal plain sense. Unfortunately for his cause, Cheever's insistence that biblical authors never approved "slavery" made for a threefold problem. First, his reading of Old Testament passages convinced very few that the crucial Hebrew word *ebedh* did not mean lifelong, inheritable servitude. That failure, second, made it all the more difficult to argue that the crucial New Testament word *doulos* did not mean the same. Third, because hard evidence seemed to bring down this linguistic argument, many in the South and not a few in the North concluded that Cheever was "eisegeting" rather than "exegeting," that is, in bad faith reading his private, predetermined opinions into the Bible instead of simply accepting Scripture as a revelation from God.

"History"

While the likes of Weld, Barnes, and Cheever relied on linguistic science to clarify biblical interpretation, others invoked history.[62] That invocation, however, entailed even deeper complications. In the first instance, all such efforts required a willingness to respect specialized learning, for example, by explaining how the ways that servitude among the Hebrews did or did not resemble servitude among other ancient peoples. In addition, the appeal to history demanded an ability to follow a chain of reasoning, for example, to understand why the Apostle Paul's request that Philemon treat the returned slave Onesimus as a brother changed the nature of Onesimus's servitude after he returned. In a democratic society where populist voices dominated the public sphere, specialized learning and connected reasoning proceeded at a disadvantage.

"History" was also ambiguous. If it meant only enlisting the results of research into ancient times for the purpose of better understanding biblical passages or demanding more attention to the contexts of biblical revelation, those approaches should have been recognized as completely orthodox efforts. On these terms, "history" did no more than clarify the "real sense" that contemporary assumptions about the "plain sense" may have misunderstood.

But if history meant reinterpreting biblical truths because of the progressive development of humankind's moral sensibilities, then more difficult questions emerged. When considering "development," how was it possible to differentiate between moral trajectories growing organically out of scriptural revelation and moral standards derived only from contemporary sensibilities and then imposed on the Scriptures? The distinction between historical resources and historical development often remained implicit. The distinction between moral sensibility developing organically out of Scripture and moral sensibility imposed on Scripture always remained contested. Two things happened as a consequence when abolitionists appealed to history. First, confusion. In addition, proslavery advocates disregarded conceptual distinctions in order to condemn all appeals to history as the illegitimate imposition of fallible modern consciousness on the infallible Word of God.

Historical context: Israel/Rome. Tayler Lewis, a professor at Union College in Schenectady, New York, made one of the era's strongest antislavery presentations in an essay contributed to the 1861 book of fast-day sermons. Prominent among Lewis's many arguments were claims about "the vastly changed condition of the world" since Bible times. In particular, he explained at length why slavery in both the Hebrew and Roman worlds was fundamentally different from slavery in the modern United States. The principle underlying his entire effort was the conviction that, "whilst truth is fixed, eternal, immutable as God himself, its application to distant ages, and differing circumstances, is so varying continually that a wrong direction given to the more truthful exegesis may convert it into the more malignant falsehood, making it, in fact, 'the letter that killeth instead of the spirit that giveth life [2 Cor 3:6].'" Putting this principle to work, he argued that since Hebrew slavery did not permit a slave trade (the Old Testament spoke of the Jews buying slaves, but never selling them) and that Roman slavery denoted absolute governance rather than absolute ownership of the slave, the biblical permissions of slavery did not address the American situation at all. He was, in other words, asserting that valid applications of Scripture had to assess the historical cultures of biblical times and the historical circumstances of the contemporary United States. With those assessments in place, it was clear to Lewis that the proper question was not "Does the Bible allow slavery?" but "Does the Bible's allowance of slavery in ancient times sanction the American slave system?" He answered no unequivocally.[63]

Lewis only elaborated on arguments that had been aired many times before. In a much-noticed address from 1835, William Ellery Channing contended that slavery in the New Testament was completely different from the American system. In his view, the Pauline instructions to slaves no more indicated Paul's approval of slavery than his command in Romans chapter 13 that believers honor "the powers that be" sanctioned despotism as a political ideal.[64] In the wake of the North-South schism of the Baptist Foreign Mission Society, we have already seen how Francis Wayland of Brown University engaged Richard Fuller, a South Carolina minister, in one of the era's most extensive debates. Wayland, although never an abolitionist, supported his emancipationist position by noting that the Old Testament slaves of Abraham were circumcised and so incorporated into

Israel as the people of God. Conclusion: that kind of slavery differed completely from the American system.[65] When Albert Barnes published his major biblical study in 1846, he differentiated ancient from American slavery by emphasizing that "Hebrew servitude in the time of the prophets" knew nothing about "foreign traffic in slaves" and by noting that the prophets repeatedly criticized "the injustice of slavery."[66] James Pendleton of Kentucky, a feisty biblical inerrantist, would later launch the sectarian Landmark movement that claimed a straight line of descent from the Apostles to self-governing Baptist churches. In 1849 he challenged majority white opinion in his home state with a scathing attack on American slavery as something completely different from biblical forms. According to Pendleton, proslavery advocates argued that "the slavery which sacredly regards the marriage union, cherishes the relation between parents and children, and provides for the instruction of the slave is not sinful. Therefore the system of slavery in Kentucky, *which does none of these things*, is not sinful." Pendleton's conclusion: "Is it not . . . a burlesque on logic?"[67]

Historical context: race. Abolitionist consideration of race sharpened the importance of historical context for contemporary applications of Scripture. For the relatively few who raised this issue, the fact that the American system enslaved only Africans demonstrated its categorical difference from whatever "slavery" meant in the ancient world. William Ellery Channing was one of the authors who noted, but only in passing, that when the Apostle Paul referred to enslavement, it was "not so much of blacks as of white men."[68] Others made much more of that inconvenient fact. To his Kentucky peers, James Pendleton reduced the proslavery position to a *reductio ad absurdum*: "If then it could be established that slavery promotes the holiness and happiness of slaves, it would follow that as it does not promote the holiness and happiness of the white population it would be well for white people to be enslaved in order to their holiness and happiness."[69] Pendleton's fellow-Kentuckian, John Fee, drove home the same point even more vigorously. What, Fee asked, was the color of all the peoples enslaved by Rome after its military triumphs in Germany, Gaul, Spain, Greece, and Egypt? If "the apostles' teaching and practice sanctioned slavery, it sanctioned *the slavery of the age*—the slavery amongst which the apostles moved. N.B. THIS SLAVERY WAS WHITE SLAVERY."[70] For Lewis, writing in 1861, the restriction of American slavery to one "caste" confirmed its absolute difference from biblical forms.[71] When Daniel Goodwin, the Episcopal provost of the University of Pennsylvania, responded to the proslavery work of Episcopal bishop John Henry Hopkins, he stressed the same reality. If Hopkins believed that "Christ and his apostles approved and sanctioned such slavery" as existed in the New Testament world, that meant they sanctioned "a slavery of *whites*." He then mocked Hopkins for commending the owners of American slaves for "having restricted this large Christian liberty of theirs within such narrow bounds as to content themselves with having for their slaves only the still more degraded and vastly inferior race of the blacks."[72]

The historical point that whites found so difficult to grasp Blacks found impossible to ignore. In 1861 Frederick Douglass once more underscored a fact that other African Americans had highlighted many times before: "[N]obody at the North, we think, would defend Slavery, even from the Bible, but for this color distinction. . . . Color makes all the difference in the application of our American Christianity."[73]

Historical development from seed or principle. Quite different from history as a source of evidence were antislavery appeals to history as a way of affirming moral progress through the centuries. Yet as with so many abolitionist arguments, this criterion of moral progress could be applied in different ways.

Tayler Lewis tethered his understanding of such progress quite closely to what he considered the original biblical message. In his view, proslavery references to providence were especially egregious when they willfully ignored how biblical revelation moved outward in ever-widening circles of benevolence. In particular, he singled out those who claimed that the institution had been a providential means for bringing Christianity to Africans. Lewis's withering response affirmed a principle of progressive revelation: "What a commentary . . . on the world's ethical progress, that the enslaving of those called heathen should be justified by going back to this old Jewish 'statute' [Lev 25:44–46], and perverting it to an end historically so remote from anything intended by the ancient law-giver."[74] Even if enslavement now resembled ancient slavery in some particulars, it could not justify the modern system. In Lewis's perspective, the moral development witnessed within the Bible itself—especially in Jesus's refinement of the Mosaic law—indicated that such development was meant to continue as Christianity spread throughout the world. The spread outward from all that the New Testament revealed justified contemporary condemnation of slavery in whatever form.

For other antislavery voices, modern conscience played a more independent role. Cortlandt Van Rensselaer, a prominent Old School Presbyterian with close ties to Princeton Seminary and his denomination's bureaucracy in Philadelphia, relied on such consciousness, along with his reading of providence, to articulate a more expansive understanding of history. With his conservative Presbyterian associates, like Charles Hodge, Van Rensselaer agreed that the Bible's teaching applied to all areas of life. But going well beyond Hodge, he also argued that when applying its "spirit and principles," Bible believers should not rely on a wooden literalism—in his phrase, "not limited to the mere word of its letter, nor to any general or universal formula of expression." Instead, proper biblical exposition "requires enlargement of scriptural statement, and application implies a regard to providential developments and to the varying circumstances of social and public life."[75]

Precisely that form of reasoning troubled many in the North, as of course also in the South, who saw it bypassing the rock of scriptural authority for the shifting sands of contemporary "developments" or "circumstances." Critics conceded that ethical progress could be glimpsed within the pages of Scripture itself—for example, as the Old Testament acceptance of polygamy gave way to the New Testament standard of monogamy. But, they contended, the Bible itself authorized that clarification of moral standards; the moral sensitivities of the Enlightenment were a different matter altogether.

Additional Authorities

The charge of negating scriptural authority intensified when abolitionists added their interpretations of providence and their evocations of sacred American truths to their reliance on the Bible—and even more when they made overt, direct appeals to moral consciousness. Yet for all but a small number of antislavery voices, it seemed entirely unproblematic to align truths of Scripture with truths from other sources. So it was when David Barrow had published an abolitionist pamphlet for his fellow Kentucky Baptists early in the century. For Barrow "the Principles of Nature, Reason, Justice, Policy, and Scripture" flowed together into one powerful tide.[76] Half a century later Albert Barnes decried the great influence wielded by editors who dared defend slavery against what Barnes obviously considered a harmony of authorities: "the teachings of the Bible and the principles of religion, liberty, and morals."[77] Even George Cheever, who put such weight on the antislavery message of the Bible's "plain sense," reached much further when in 1860 he claimed that the defense of slavery required a stand "against conscience, against benevolence, against law, natural and divine, against history, against both the letter and spirit of the Scriptures, against the Old and New Testament theology, against the gospel, against God."[78]

For polemical purposes, abolitionists who appealed to "conscience," "benevolence," and "history" could have pointed out that proslavery advocates also liberally salted their biblical arguments with authorities not drawn from the Bible's "plain sense." The authorities enlisted for proslavery included self-confident assertions about the hand of providence bringing Africans to Christianity through slavery, unquestioned reliance on a commonsense hermeneutic focused on the "literal" meaning of individual Bible "verses," and especially the completely unbiblical idea that Black people were the only ones deserving to be slaves. Yet in the tumult of the times, most disputants—except African Americans—criticized the use of extrabiblical authorities to support abolition much more strenuously than they condemned such usages to defend slavery.

In the use of such authorities, contrasting views of providence and contrasting appeals to sacred national truths mostly canceled each other out. If the defenders of slavery claimed God's special providence had brought Africans to America so that they might receive the Gospel message, slavery's opponents asserted that God's special providence had created the United States as a beacon of universal liberty for the whole world. Similarly, against abolitionists who quoted the Declaration of Independence's "all men are created equal," opponents countered with sacred American principles summoned for the defense of slavery. (The Confederate Constitution of early 1861 offered a striking instance. It did piously expand the form of words it took from the U.S. Constitution ["secure the blessings of liberty to ourselves and our posterity invoking the favor and guidance of almighty God"], and it did refer specifically to "slaves" and protection of slave owners' "property." But by aping most other particulars of the U.S. Constitution, Confederates staked their claim that *they* were maintaining the founding ideals threated by the election of Abraham Lincoln.)

Arguments against slavery that appealed to moral consciousness were different. When antislavery authors reached beyond the Bible to counter the Bible-based claims of proslavery, it contributed to what Ronald Walters has described as the "broad antebellum process through which moral authority . . . ceased to be a monopoly of clergymen and gentlemen" and thus "subverted much of the religious base from which antislavery originally drew inspiration."[79] That process marked a new era in the nation's moral history. In the century's early decades, the most important question about religion and public life had been *how* the great truths of Scripture could align with the nation's founding ideals. To be sure, a small minority of advanced thinkers had with Thomas Jefferson protested against a self-consciously Protestant moral order, and the Methodist-inclined mostly kept to their spiritual tasks. Yet the combined efforts of Methodists, custodial Protestants, and sectarian Protestants had made the Bible central to the emerging national civilization, even as proprietary aspirations and sectarian fears continued to clash. From the early 1830s, immigration, religious diversification, and renewed political competition worried Protestants of all sorts but did not shake the belief that a healthy society must be a biblical society.

Again, abolitionist arguments that appealed to moral consciousness were different. Mitchell Snay is only one of several historians to recognize that "the debate over the scriptural view of slavery inevitably raised the issue of the moral authority of the Bible" itself.[80] It did so because of what seemed to be a natural progression, from appealing to moral intuition alongside the Scriptures to treating those institutions as superseding the Scriptures. Although most antislavery advocates who made such an appeal did not think they were negating Scripture, their opponents uniformly made the charge. If only a minority of abolitionists did eventually conclude that conscience should supersede the Bible, they nonetheless gave proslavery polemicists a real advantage.

Conflict among the nation's Protestants over the role of moral intuitions for biblical interpretation broke out with special fervor when Massachusetts Unitarians came out of the closet against Trinitarian Congregationalists. William Ellery Channing's landmark sermon of 1819 that defined the "distinguishing doctrines" of Unitarianism became an object of endless scrutiny. Part of Channing's discourse explained why interpretation of Scripture should resemble how Americans interpreted their Constitution, "fix[ing] the precise import of its parts by inquiring into its general spirit, into the intentions of its authors, and into the prevalent feelings, impressions, and circumstances of the time when it was framed."[81] This conservative appeal to original intent became controversial, however, when Channing specified the factors that should guide biblical interpretation. For that purpose, he went beyond mere consideration of historical contexts, and even the Bible's "general spirit." As his basis for rejecting the Trinitarian interpretation of key texts, Channing explained that "we must limit all these passages by the known attributes of God, of Jesus Christ, and of human nature" and also "by the circumstances under which they were written." Moreover, "God never contradicts . . . in revelation, what he teaches in his works and providence." Consequently, Unitarians rejected "every interpretation which, with deliberate attention, seems repugnant to any established truth."[82]

Calvinists were not the only ones who howled in protest. Whence cometh Channing's certainty about "providence," "God's work," and "established truth"? The answer, they charged, was out of his own presumptuous, idiosyncratic, and self-congratulatory head.

Later in 1835 Channing began his famous essay on slavery by saying that "great truths, inalienable rights, [and] everlasting duties" would form "the chief subjects" of his treatment.[83] In response, hardcore proslavery southerners howled again. They were joined by many moderate northern emancipationists who feared, despite Channing's thorough attention to contested scriptures and his opposition to immediate manumission, that he made his own conscience the final arbiter of truths, rights, and duties. Did not the Unitarian path lead directly away from the trust in supreme biblical authority that had miraculously evangelized the nation and given its fragmented and disorganized citizenry coherent moral stability?

Those who worried about undermining the Bible's unique authority might have been slightly less worried if appeals to conscience, like Tayler Lewis's appeal to history, had claimed only to expand moral principles rooted directly in Scripture. But they did not. When the Rev. Goodwin wrote against Bishop Hopkins, he did argue that abolition came from "the general principles of Christianity" as expressed in the Golden Rule. But he went much further to specify that abolition emerged as those biblical principles were "modified and determined in their application by the mental and moral condition of those who are to apply them, by their views of rights and notions of happiness ... [w]hat they claim for themselves as rights, what they regard as constituting happiness."[84]

By 1863, when Goodwin conflated the authority of contemporary "rights" and notions of "happiness" with the Golden Rule, southern whites along with many in the North had long since condemned such reasoning as fatal. A few had watched Massachusetts closely enough to see a parallel between Channing on slavery and his fellow-Unitarian Horace Mann on education. Both still claimed to value the Scripture, but both eagerly compromised its unique authority whenever the obvious meaning of important biblical passages stood in the way of what they had independently concluded were "great truths, inalienable rights, [and] everlasting duties."

Many more had observed with schadenfreude as William Lloyd Garrison and friends of *The Liberator* raced from loud affirmations of trust in Scripture to betraying their true colors. In point of fact, the fascinated attention on these radical abolitionists greatly oversimplified a more complicated history. The ardently evangelical abolitionists of the early 1830s had embraced revival, personal redemption, social reform, and longing for the millennium as a seamless whole. Within a decade, however, these abolitionists were heading in different directions.[85] Some, like James Birney and promoters of the Liberty Party, turned aside from revivalistic moralism and biblical argumentation to political mobilization. (They would diverge even more when they joined the Free Soil movement, despite its negative stance toward free Blacks.)

Many others, however, maintained their earlier revivalistic commitments, including trust in the Bible interpreted according to standard American usage. Arthur and Lewis Tappan, for example, broke with the Garrisonian radicals when in 1840 the American Anti-Slavery Society added equal rights for women to its brief against slavery. The Tappans' new American and Foreign Anti-Slavery Society kept its focus on the antislavery cause; most of its supporters also maintained their support for Bible-based voluntarism as the best strategy for national redemption. A few early abolitionists, like Angelina Grimké Weld, followed a commitment to the Bible's "plain sense," disdain for ecclesiastical hierarchy, and their own millennial hopes into the Millerite camp.[86] More biblical conservatives, like George Cheever, fought on, trying to defend a strict biblical literalism showing that "servants" were never "slaves." African Americans like James Pennington maintained their text-based loyalty to Scripture. Frederick Douglass represented Black activists who steadfastly insisted on principles they took from the biblical record of God's acts of deliverance. (Behind Douglass's break with Garrison in the mid-1840s lay his continued loyalty to the Constitution as well as the Bible, both of which Garrison increasingly described as impediments to the cause.)[87] In a word, what the Tappans, Grimké Weld, Cheever, Pennington, Douglass, and many others took from the Scriptures should have made proslavery advocates pause, since it came from the same divine authority they revered—and interpreted with the same hermeneutical conventions they followed.

Proslavery, however, depicted all Bible-based antislavery as either dangerously liberal or outright heretical. Abolitionists like Albert Barnes and Daniel Goodwin insisted that they too honored the Scriptures. But when they drew on intuited truths from the moral sense to shape biblical interpretation, they seemed to their opponents to be doing self-consciously only what all abolitionists did unwittingly—that is, abandoning the secure Word of God for heretical flights of egotistical presumption.

Radical Garrisonians gave the proslavery position even more credibility when they turned self-intuited truths against the Scriptures. Yes, some abolitionists may still cling to the Bible, but look how their stance leads inevitably to those like Barnes and Goodwin who welcome alien gods into the temple—and then to the Garrisonian crowd that dismantles the temple entirely. The broad highway leading to that destination began with what later seemed only pretense. Garrison may have once published a poem lauding the Bible: "O Book of books! . . . / The Oracles are holy and divine, / Of free salvation, through a SAVIOUR, telling: / All Truth, all Excellence, dost thou enshrine— / The mists of Sin and Ignorance dispelling!"[88] He may have continued in that vein for several years, as in 1836: "Slavery at a single blow annihilates THE WHOLE DECALOGUE."[89] Other Garrisonians may have concurred, like Elizur Wright Jr. in 1833: "The doctrine of the immediate abolition of slavery asks no better authority than offered by Scripture. It is in perfect harmony with God's word."[90] But it did not take long for the pretense to fade, as it did as early as 1837, when Garrison showed his true colors by claiming, "A slavish devotion to Scripture is morally no less abominable than the whip or manacle."[91] The inevitable soon followed, as in Garrison's notorious statement made in 1845 when he reviewed a new edition of Paine's *Age of Reason*: "To say that everything contained within the lids of the Bible is divinely inspired, and to insist upon the dogma as fundamentally important, is to give utterance to a bold fiction, and to require the suspension of the reasoning facilities." As Garrison crashed onward, he made a mockery of even the spirit-letter distinction: "It is the province of reason to 'search the scriptures,' and determine what in them is true, and what fabulous—what is compatible with the happiness of mankind, and what ought to be rejected as an example or rule of action—what is the letter that killeth, and what the spirit that maketh alive."[92]

In this review and much writing that followed, Garrison actually discriminated more than his critics and later scholars have indicated. After the statements just quoted, he went on to chastise Paine-ites for failing to "select . . . the wheat from the chaff" of Scripture and for not adhering to "those portions of the Bible which inculcate the most stringent morality, the noblest sentiments, the most expansive benevolence, the purest life."[93] Few critics, however, paused for nuance. And few doubted that Henry C. Wright spoke for Garrison and his ilk when shortly thereafter he asserted in *The Liberator*, "The Bible if opposed to self-evident truth, is self-evident falsehood."[94]

Less radical abolitionists certainly regretted that the Garrisonians endangered their efforts by seeming to link abolition with scorn for Scripture. Albert Barnes certainly recognized the peril when in 1857 he published *The Church and Slavery*. In this substantial work, which, however, no longer denied that the King James Version's *servant* meant *slave*, Barnes did sound nearly Garrisonian: "[I]f a book professing to be a revelation from God by any fair interpretation defended slavery . . . such a book neither ought to be, nor could be, received by mankind as a divine revelation." But after alarmed criticism from friends, he rushed a second edition into print with the offending statement moderated: "[A]ll attempts to show that the Bible does thus authorize and sanction slavery, contribute . . . to sustain and diffuse infidelity in the world."[95] To the extent, however, that readers associated Barnes's abolitionism with the Bible-denying abolitionism of *The Liberator*, the damage had been done.

Most advocates of biblical antislavery were not as liberal as Barnes; very few stood with Garrison. Yet the radicals had given at least some credibility to the identification between belief in abolition and disbelief in Scripture that many contemporaries constantly stressed—including, as we have seen, Thomas Stringfellow, Frederick Ross, Stuart Robinson, Albert Taylor Bledsoe, the *Princeton Review*, Leonard Bacon, and Moses Stuart. Antebellum Americans who could not get beyond that identification also found it difficult to credit the sincerity of abolitionists like Albert Barnes, who thought *they* stood on firm scriptural ground. Barnes's earlier major work from 1846 had directly addressed the issue that held back so many moderate emancipationists from embracing abolition—and that gave passionate defenders of slavery an advantage whenever they ventured into print. That issue was the apparent biblical approval for "slavery in the abstract," the permission for enslavement seen in the Mosaic legislation and its routine acceptance in the New Testament's apostolic teaching. To Barnes that issue was a distraction, "a question . . . that has usually given rise only to perplexing logomachies." It was simply "not necessary to agitate the inquiry whether slavery is a *malum in se*." Instead, Barnes wanted contemporaries to back away only a half-step from proof-texts and move only a half-step toward a synthetic understanding of divine revelation:

> If it shall appear . . . that slavery is an institution which God has never originated by positive enactment; that his legislation has tended from the beginning

to mitigate its evils; that he has asserted great principles in his word, which cannot be carried out without destroying the system; that he has enjoined on man, in the various relations of life, certain duties, of which slavery prevents the performance; that slavery engenders inevitably certain bad passions, which are wholly contrary to religion; and that *it is the tendency and the design of the Christian religion, when fairly applied, to abolish the system*, it will be apparent that slavery is a moral wrong.[96]

In the phantom court of objectivity, his case many not have been airtight, but it was pretty good.

20

Scriptural Arguments in Context

The first casualty of the exegetical war before the shooting war was the exegeted object itself, the Scriptures. The antebellum interpretive controversies over slavery and race affected the American history of the Bible more decisively than any other development or set of circumstances before or since. For public discourse, literature, publishing, and many levels of education, Scripture would of course remain important in American history long after the Union armies subjugated the breakaway slave republic that so many white Bible believers had so ardently supported. As a source of individual and communal spiritual inspiration, encouragement, and guidance, the Bible also never faded away. Yet in E. Brooks Holifield's definitive assessment, "the theological impasse [over the Bible and slavery] meant that theology could no longer articulate the moral vision that held the culture together."[1] As earlier chapters have detailed, the ideal of a Bible-centered national moral vision had already come under irreversible pressure from internal Protestant disagreements and the rapidly increasing population of non-Protestants. Creative religious movements exploiting the possibilities of democratic freedom and the separation of church and state were likewise undercutting the ideal of Bible-based national moral unity. Yet the division over racial slavery was different because it featured not claims about alternative religious authorities but conflict among those who professed to believe the same truths from the same Book interpreted in the same way.

In broader perspective, it is of course too simple to think that contentions over biblical interpretation dominated the great national divide that led to the Civil War. In much recent historiography, slavery appears as an economic-cultural juggernaut driving every national development of any significance whatsoever.[2] A more generally humanistic mobilization for abolition that relied only incidentally on Scripture had also existed since early in the republic.[3] The Bible played only a supporting role as elite white intellectual life diverged North and South.[4] Some Black Americans, like Robert Alexander Young in his *Ethiopian Manifesto* from 1829, stressed Afro-centered natural rights more than explicit biblical mandates.[5] When the Republican Party finally emerged, broad moral, economic, and political interests defined its efforts against "the slave power" rather than anything specifically biblical.[6] Still, the inability of biblical antislavery arguments to convince the nation's white population, among whom the Protestant Scriptures

America's Book. Mark A. Noll, Oxford University Press. © Oxford University Press 2022.
DOI: 10.1093/oso/9780197623466.003.0021

enjoyed unmatched respect and where the Bible had played such a large part in creating the national civilization, contributed significantly to the national story.

Just as important, but from another angle of assessment, antebellum biblical arguments over slavery decisively influenced the history of the Bible after the war. For a clearer sense of complex historical developments, a pause for reflection on two related questions is appropriate: Why were biblical proslavery arguments so persuasive in the antebellum United States, but only the United States? And how did the relative success of those arguments affect the history of Scripture long after the Civil War was over?

Persuasive Proslavery Arguments

Exceedingly able scholars have, as noted, concluded that in the antebellum decades the biblical proslavery position triumphed over biblical abolition. Although I once agreed, further reading in the works of antebellum abolitionists, and not disregarding the confusion caused by the great diversity of antislavery appeals to Scripture, I no longer agree.[7] In fact, the Bible in antebellum America, and understood in traditional terms, offered wider, deeper, and more thorough support for abolition than for slavery.[8] Contingent historical circumstances, rather than the intrinsic credibility of the arguments, created the opposite impression.

The Bible's defense of slavery seemed simple. It rested on proof-texts from the Old Testament that authorized the ancient People of God to enslave non-Hebrews, proof-texts from the New Testament that took slavery for granted, and an inference from Jesus's silence on the subject that the Son of God did not object to enslavement as such. The fact, however, that the United States of America was the only place in the Protestant world—and just about the only place in the entire Christian world—where the Bible defense was persuasive indicates that it was not simple at all.[9]

To borrow a phrase popularized by Max Weber to describe the relationship between early modern Calvinism and the spirit of early modern capitalism, a complicated web of *elective affinities* linked American national history and biblical proslavery arguments.[10] The American appropriation of a primal Protestant profession came first.

From the early sixteenth century, the tocsin of *sola scriptura* had led to spiritual liberation for great numbers of Europeans who suffered from what they experienced as the soul-destroying effects of state-church Christendom. They complained first and continually about Roman Catholic Christendom even as some Protestants also took up the cry against Protestant regimes with monolithic establishments. For those Protestants—depending on point of view, the more engaged or faithful or obsessive or deluded—the spiritual liberation of *sola scriptura* demanded broader reforming efforts guided by the same authority, but now more a battle cry than a simple tocsin.

Yet not until the appearance of an American nation that deliberately repudiated Christendom and looked to "the people" for the construction of a national civilization did *sola scriptura* emerge in its full constructive potential, but also as a delusive impossibility. The extraordinary story of apolitical Methodist evangelization, which reached even enslaved Americans, best exemplified the constructive potential. But *sola scriptura* also drove the sectarians who—rejecting all but local, self-selected leaders—created self-governing churches and self-disciplining memberships in every corner of the land. The same ideal inspired the noteworthy achievements of voluntary societies organized by proprietary Protestants who strove for a dynamic Christianity without Christendom. Just as much, however, American history shone a bright light on the self-delusion that had always lurked in Protestant conceptions of *sola scriptura*. The American republican experiment gave a redeemed population an opportunity to be guided by nothing except the Bible; American experience showed that for the pursuit of common social, economic, political, and social goals, *sola scriptura* simply did not work.[11]

American experience pushed *sola scriptura* toward hard biblicism. Most European Protestants had understood that, after critiquing Roman Catholicism on the basis of *sola scriptura*, God-fearing churches and godly societies needed the direction of magistrates, guidance from pastors and scholars with specialized learning, and the structures of tax-supported church establishments. Americans who dispensed with the secondary authorities of Protestant Christendom moved closer to thinking about *sola scriptura* in terms that Alexander Campbell employed when in 1839 he founded Bethany College: "[W]e make the Bible, the whole Bible, and nothing but the Bible our creed, our standard of religion and of all moral science."[12]

As specific American values led to the strengthening of biblicism, so also did they strengthen proslavery biblical interpretation. When Thornton Stringfellow assembled his proof-texts to defend slavery, they carried persuasive weight because of their obvious reliance on *sola scriptura*. They also benefited from distinctly American commitments to democracy, republican political principles, national exceptionalism, and the superiority of commonsense reasoning. Stringfellow's biblical interpretations did not rely on the sanction of specially trained scholars; they implied distrust of complex or learned arguments that deflected the "plain sense" of God's word; they assumed a wide audience of literate readers who could judge moral truth for themselves; they took for granted that special providence had originated the American slave system; and they relied especially on powerful commonsense intuitions about Africans as especially fit for enslavement.

Even when proslavery reasoning departed from *sola scriptura*, American experience made it very difficult to recognize that departure. A special paradox was at work when proslavery advocates stressed that slavery was the God-given means by which Africans could be evangelized. Although nothing in Scripture promised believers certain, God-like knowledge concerning general historical developments, in America such providential reasoning looked simply like another demonstration of loyalty to the Bible.

Black authors, especially David Walker and Frederick Douglass, responded with outraged derision when white authors described enslavement as a missionary strategy. Yet abolitionists found it difficult to challenge proslavery certainty about the ways of Providence, because similar self-confidence had been secured through generations of European and American public discourse. Assumptions about the divinely directed course of American history were so commonly expressed that it became almost impossible to disentangle conclusions about Providence from interpretations of Scripture—especially because biblical language, biblical typology, biblical analogy, biblical exegesis, and the perception of American history as reprising the Old Testament had reinforced both a providential understanding of America and great self-confidence in the human ability to chart Providence. As a consequence, to question the proslavery interpretation of providence seemed to question both the reality of God's control over the world and the truth of God's Word.[13]

Deeply ingrained American assumptions about the inferiority of African-descended people also strengthened proslavery Bible arguments, and strengthened them beyond measure. Unlike reasoning about providence, these assumptions were self-conscious. Yet they almost never registered as a contradiction to either proof-texting biblicism or more sophisticated interpretations. The unthinking equation of biblical justifications for slavery with a slave system restricted to Africans colored almost all arguments by proslavery advocates—as also most advocates for gradual emancipation and some campaigners for immediate abolition. If Americans claimed to follow the Bible alone, or even the Bible as the chief witness alongside other authorities, and Scripture contained almost no examples of African slaves—and no credible directives that only Africans should be enslaved—the proslavery arguments should not have enjoyed the impact they so obviously did enjoy.

Despite the unmistakable character of American slavery as Black only and the difference in fact between American racial slavery and the ancient world's all-race slavery, most white abolitionists did not stress what could have been the strongest weapon in their arsenal. Molly Oshatz has described the situation bluntly for the northern moderate emancipationists who decried the evils of American slavery but refused to call it a sin. These Protestants, she shows, viewed "slavery as a moral issue between slaveholders and abolitionists, not between

Christians and black slaves." Consequently, "in the debate over sin and slavery, black slaves tended to disappear." This disappearance meant that "racism was largely to blame for the failure of the antebellum antislavery debates to provide a cogent and sustained attack on the antibiblical racist nature of Southern slavery." In her reading, when debaters focused on the general "theological and moral question of slavery's sinfulness in itself [*malum in se*]," that focus "deflated every moderate antislavery attempt to demonstrate what should have been obvious, that the Bible did not sanction slavery as it existed in the Southern states."[14] Failure to acknowledge this black-and-white fact hollowed out much of the scriptural debate over slavery, which had the effect of trivializing the Bible and so short-circuiting the possibility of speaking biblical truth to American power.

Conventions of Discourse

Oshatz and Bruce Mullin have explained clearly why the *malum in se* argument kept most northern Protestant intellectuals from embracing abolition.[15] These savants had invested great energy in conveying the results of cutting-edge European scholarship to their American peers. If the world's most technically proficient scholars had concluded that *ebedh* in the Old Testament and *doulos* in the New Testament meant lifelong, inheritable enslavement—and since slave owners remained in good standing among the people of God in both testaments—then slavery as such could not be condemned as a sin. Despite the logical force of this reasoning, its implications could be challenged. As many biblical abolitionists asked, what did "slavery in the abstract" have to do with "slavery in America"? Why should the dictionary meaning of a word carry more weight than differences in real life on the ground? Was not root-and-branch condemnation of the American slave system justified because contemporary American slavery systematically violated so many straightforward biblical commands? Did not biblical precedents as well as biblical commands amount to a powerful indictment as well? Yet Moses Stuart, Charles Hodge, Charles Blagdon, and other northern moderates were not convinced, in part because they reacted so strongly when abolitionists called them despicable sinners for worrying so much about slavery as a *malum in se*.

Other intellectual conventions of the era also warned northern moderates away from abolition, in particular reliance on commonsense moral intuitions and a Baconian model for scholarly inquiry.[16] Moses Stuart illustrated the former when his 1835 commentary on the book of Romans took up the question of imputation (the doctrine that saw God imputing to all subsequent humans the effects of Adam's sin in the Garden of Eden, and likewise imputing to all believers divine grace won through Christ's death and resurrection). According to Stuart, traditional theology had distorted "the simple facts as stated by the Apostle Paul." Yet as Stuart described those facts, he based his interpretation of the Pauline assertions by elaborating on modern intellectual instincts: "immutable principles of our moral nature," "an immutable law of moral sense," and "self evident principles."[17]

Fifteen years later, while denouncing much about the slave system, Stuart relied on similar reasoning to defend the rights of southern enslavers to recover fugitive slaves. Common sense along with treasured American convictions led him to consider the states to be analogous to the tribes of Old Testament Israel. This assumption meant that the federal union created a more important bond than the bond of unity in Christ. To Stuart's intuition, escaped slaves—considered as either Christians or potential Christians—did not have the claim on fellow believers that southern slaveholders did as fellow Americans. Analogical Israel meant more than Spiritual Israel.[18] In the era's prevailing moral philosophy, an individual's definite moral intuitions could lead to universal truth. Using such reasoning to expound the relevance of scriptural teaching for the Fugitive Slave Law, however, entailed an anomaly: specifically, why common sense viewed the rights of fellow citizens as more important than duties to fellow believers, when nothing in Scripture supported that view.

The Baconian ideal that inspired so many American intellectuals in the first two-thirds of the century extended beyond confidence in moral intuitions (facts of consciousness) to confidence as well in empirical investigation (facts from observation). The intellectual methods championed by Francis Bacon in the early seventeenth century established ideal procedures for the genuine *Wissenschaftler* (systematizer of knowledge).[19] The tasks before the trustworthy ethicist (moral philosopher), faithful scientist (natural philosopher), and conscientious student of Scripture appeared formally identical: gather facts, organize those facts by strict induction, draw conclusions that count as "laws" unless modified by other facts inductively presented. Moses Stuart's reasoning about the Fugitive Slave Law illustrated Baconianism as moral philosophy. Charles Hodge's definition of theological method exemplified Baconianism for "the queen of the sciences." By the early 1870s, when Hodge introduced his three-volume *Systematic Theology* with a reiteration of principles he had learned more than fifty years earlier as a student at the College of New Jersey and Princeton Theological Seminary, Baconian approaches had come under sharp criticism. Hodge nonetheless repeated what had once been conventional wisdom. "The theologian," he wrote, is "to be guided by the same rules as the Man of Science. . . . The duty of the Christian theologian is to ascertain, collect, and combine all the facts which God has revealed concerning himself and our relation to Him. These facts are all in the Bible."[20]

This methodological Baconianism played an important part in determining what Americans thought Scripture said about slavery. In the same way that Baconian moral philosophy reinforced the intuitive racism that skewed American conclusions about scriptural teaching, Baconian empiricism tilted the interpretive scales toward biblicism. In turn, biblicism strengthened proslavery by making biblical proof-texts the default path for understanding divine revelation.

Beginning with sixteenth-century European printers who were the first to divide the Bible into verses (often setting each verse as the beginning of a new paragraph), the tendency had strengthened to treat verses as separable building blocks from which the careful biblical student could construct impregnable theological redoubts.[21] In the Baconian perspective adopted by learned and unlearned alike, verses became the empirical facts of theology. The appeal of William Miller's apocalypticism showed how compelling a layman's ingenious, well-publicized arrangement of biblical verse-facts could be.

The Restorationist movement likewise became noteworthy for taking its stand on "no creed but the Bible," operationalized as "no Christian beliefs or practices except as demonstrated by specific prooftexts." In 1832, Elder John Smith, who had been drawn to the movement by Alexander Campbell's teaching, underscored this Baconian standard: "[T]he Gospel is a system of facts, commands and promises, and no deduction or inference from them, however logical or true, forms any part of the Gospel of Christ." The same year Campbell himself defended the organic tie he saw between water baptism and the forgiveness of sins simply by quoting Acts 2:38, where the Apostle Peter had preached, "Repent, and be baptized every one of you in the name of Jesus Christ for the remission of sins."[22] Restorationists stood out, however, only because they insisted so forcefully on the often-repeated profession of so many other American Protestants to follow the Bible alone.

The versification of Scripture, even if only a comparatively recent innovation, became a literal godsend for a Protestant public eager to heed biblical truths, discern biblical guidelines for personal and corporate life, ponder difficulties of biblical interpretation, and dispute the misguided conclusions others drew from Scripture. Especially in a largely Protestant land where the expansion of literacy coincided with democratic access to print, citation of chapter and verse assisted all manner of communicators to verify divine sanction for all manner of communications. In debates over slavery, the relevant biblical "facts" were often simply "verses," specified numerically (e.g., "Leviticus 25:44–46" when cited to defend slavery or "Exodus 21:16" when cited for an attack). Debates on many other contested ideas or practices followed the same practice. Sometimes a reference would appear after the quotation of an individual verse. Just as often, citations

appeared only in parentheses or footnotes. In either case, verse references reinforced the author's claim to divine approval for the point under consideration.

If the division of Scripture into verse units did in fact facilitate a hitherto unprecedented level of Bible accessibility, that assistance came at a stiff cost. The cost
was the idea that individual verses (proof-texts) taken by themselves, or assembled as discrete facts from throughout the Scriptures, simply equaled biblical
revelation. In David Norton's authoritative judgment, where the early English
bibles of William Tyndale "stressed the importance of context," beginning with
the Geneva Bible of 1560, "the change to verses set like paragraphs atomizes the
text."[23] Given that atomization, other approaches not based on proof-texting
could appear suspect or be easily disregarded. The abolitionist appeal to broad
principles was *automatically* disadvantaged by the verse-fact numbered layout of
the biblical text. To be sure, although African Americans internalized Scripture
primarily as narratives of redemption, it did not stop figures like Richard Allen or
James W. C. Pennington from proof-texting. But it did mean that proof-texting
played a less important role for them than in circles where discerning God's will
simply meant following chapter and verse.

Exceptions to the general pattern were especially interesting. Alexander
Campbell, despite his strict Baconianism, published his own New Testament
translation without verses. Although this translation is better known because it
rendered the Greek *baptizo* as "immerse," for a cultural history of the Bible it was
more important that Campbell was trying to differentiate his version from the
versified texts provided so prolifically by the American Bible Society. By publishing without paratextual extras, Campbell also differentiated his work from the
bibles liberally festooned with readers' "helps" provided by for-profit publishers.
According to Paul Gutjahr, Campbell "felt that the traditional verse and chapter
markings destroyed the Bible's narrative . . . and that annotations encouraged
a piecemeal approach to reading and interpretation." Gutjahr has also pointed
out that Joseph Smith published early editions of the Book of Mormon without
verses, perhaps in order to emphasize the new horizon of divine revelation
opened by the Book's narrative accounts.[24] Similarly, biblical material in the
school readers edited by Noah Webster, William Holmes McGuffey, and Lindley
Murray also appeared without verses and usually without chapter designations.
School authorities who hoped that exposure to Scripture would promote virtuous character, deliberately defined as "nonsectarian," knew very well how regularly spokesmen (and much more rarely spokeswomen) weaponized chapter
and verse citations to battle for their individual denominations or theological
positions. School readers put the Bible to use for a unifying purpose.

Exceptions in this instance proved a rule: biblical usage in antebellum America
took absolutely for granted the propriety of referring to scriptural passages
by numbered verses. Charles Hodge did not want to promote either racism or

anti-intellectualism by explaining theology as a collection of facts. But in a literate society that had deliberately rejected the traditional intellectual guides of European Christendom, the honor accorded to Baconian procedure bestowed unusual authority on anyone who could organize discrete verses of Scripture to demonstrate God's will. That authority worked equally well for those without formal learning as those with such learning. As a consequence, verse-emphasizing Baconianism significantly strengthened proslavery credibility. To be sure, biblical abolitionists could also quote chapter and verse, but because their scriptural appeals were not as simply Baconian and because abolitionists appealed in so many other ways to Scripture, they suffered by comparison.

Polemical Advantage

In the end, however, nothing strengthened the biblical proslavery position more than the radical antislavery position. A civilization that had wed honor for national ideals to respect for Scripture could only react in shock when radicals announced a divorce. If by the late 1840s William Lloyd Garrison's deliberately provocative assertions about biblical authority alienated erstwhile allies like Lewis Tappan and Frederick Douglass, they were a godsend to proslavery advocates. As that beat went on, so did "I told you so" echo and re-echo from the white South and many in the North. The once ardently evangelical Gerritt Smith only added fuel to the anti-abolitionist fire when in 1861 he repeated the Garrisonian conclusion: the pressing question was not "What does the Church or the Bible think of slavery?" but "What think *you* of it—*you yourself*?" Slavery "is not to be tried by the Bible, but the Bible by freedom."[25] To the apologists for slavery, Smith, Garrison, and the like showed the way not to "freedom" but to moral, social, and national disaster.

Proslavery voices also made equally quick work of abolitionists who interpreted Scripture through modern moral consciousness. When Frederick Ross identified Albert Barnes with Tom Paine, when Stuart Robinson denounced "counterfeit philanthropists," and when Albert Taylor Bledsoe quoted the *Princeton Review* on abolitionists who "put themselves above the law of God," they spread doubt among those who might otherwise have been persuaded by antislavery biblical arguments. Obviously, the polemicists concluded, all such appeals *were* in fact only covert assaults on Scripture.

Whatever the rhetorical success from sowing such doubts, biblical abolitionism deserved better. Many of its advocates followed the same, or nearly the same, conventional hermeneutical procedures as defenders of slavery. George Bourne and others who hammered on the "man-stealing" texts were as Baconian in their proof-texting as Thornton Stringfellow. Tayler Lewis, John Fee, and the Black authors who contended that ancient slavery was dramatically different from the American variety also proceeded inductively, this time by using extrabiblical facts to clarify how verse-facts should be understood. Their appeal to history for the purpose of illuminating the context of biblical material in fact resembled the scholarship that northern moderates so greatly respected in their rejection of abolition. Many abolitionists also followed an unexceptionable practice by insisting on the contemporary application of overarching Christian principles drawn from biblical commands or biblical precepts. Unexceptionable, that is, except when slavery created an exception.

Even when abolitionist appeals to "history" became more ideological than factual, most antislavery advocates remained basically conservative. Their emphases on benefits from the spread of Christianity reflected the standard perspective of almost all proprietary Protestants. Only after the Civil War did appeals to "history" align with liberal or modernist attitudes to Scripture. Despite the claims of Stringfellow, Thornwell, Palmer, Bledsoe, Ross, and company, biblical abolitionism was never uniformly or even primarily radical. While a spectrum could be discerned among abolitionists as moving from the right (conservative proof-texting and "history" oriented to facts) to the left (liberal moral sensibility and "history" oriented to progressive instincts), that spectrum was not a slippery slope leading abolitionists to abandon traditional orthodox Protestantism.

In a telling comparison, the proslavery stance also benefited from American resistance to the path of British antislavery arguments. That path has been described by several careful students of Granville Sharp, Thomas Clarkson, William Wilberforce, and the other Evangelicals who mobilized against the slave trade and then slavery itself.[26] The significant Quaker contribution to British abolition followed the pattern of Anthony Benezet, John Woolman, and other American Quakers who read broad scriptural principles as a definitive repudiation of enslavement. British Evangelicals, with their special respect for the verbal inspiration of Scripture, differed slightly. In the phrase of John Barclay, Granville Sharp early on insisted that the slave had "to be categorized on biblical grounds as a *brother*." This move deferred to modern moral consciousness only incidentally. It did not feature creative exegesis or innovative hermeneutical practices. Instead, according to Barclay, "what changed was the classification of the slave, and therefore, on that basis, the applicability of the biblical text." Crucially, the change entailed "a refusal to let slaves remain locked within the texts that speak about slaves." As in the language of the famous Wedgwood emblem depicting an unchained African, "slaves were reframed, redescribed, and re-presented as 'brothers' and 'men.'" As a result, the most relevant texts became not those specifically referring to enslavement but the Golden Rule, the parable of the Good Samaritan, and the many other biblical passages addressing humanity at large or the "brotherhood" of the redeemed.[27]

The difficulty for American abolitionism was not the absence of similar arguments. Isaac Backus and David Rice had set out a similar case in the Revolutionary period; Daniel Coker, Freeborn Garretson, and David Barrow repeated variations in the early national period. Frederick Douglass and James W. C. Pennington were prominent among African Americans who emphasized the scriptural references to "brother" in their denunciation of a system that treated Africans as "heathen," "strangers," or aliens." Even James Henley Thornwell claimed to view Christian slaves as "brethren" in Christ.[28]

In early 1861 Tayler Lewis elaborated on a similar reframing in his contention that believing in doctrinal development did not compromise biblical orthodoxy. While agreeing that ethical guidance from individual texts should not be discounted, he stressed that Christian ethics should be rooted in the biblical story as a whole. For Lewis, Christology loomed as most prominent in that story. The brutalization of Africans that Lewis held slavery to entail "reaches the deep spot where we are all one in Adam, and hope to be one in Christ. May we not say with all reverence, He feels it too, that Ineffable One who took our sin-degraded nature and now bears it in the highest heavens?" Proper contemplation of the Incarnation, of "Christ's taking our one common, universal humanity," demonstrated "how unchristianlike when worldliness and selfishness lead us to degrade ourselves by casting out of the bound of human brotherhood any whose nature Christ assumed, and for whose salvation He gave his own human life." Lewis's exegesis of the crucial Leviticus passage focused on the Hebrew permission to purchase "heathen" slaves. But, he argued, "Israel, with all its imperfections, was the type of the better humanity to come." Specifically, what Leviticus called "the nations that are round about you" must now be viewed differently because "God has given them to Christ." Lewis then carried this theological principle into his reading of the much-contested book of Philemon, where he concluded that the Christian slave owner "could rule [his slaves, but] he could no longer own them, because they were his kind, Adamically and Christianly."[29]

The difference for the American context was that biblical reframing of Africans as "brethren" could not convince a critical mass of the white Bible-believing population. Southern apologists like James Henley Thornwell could not even contemplate such a reframing; northern moderates like Moses Stuart rejected the reframing with extensive arguments.[30] Although African Americans constantly promoted this reframing, for a majority of white Americans, it remained unthinkable.

Much else shaped the American context in which learned exegetes and populist preachers enlisted the Bible for and against enslavement. The loyalty of sectarian Protestants (and Catholics) to the Democratic Party inhibited Baptists, Restorationists, southern white Protestants of all varieties, and (for different reasons) Catholics from challenging the Democrats' proslavery stance. For white custodial Protestants, especially in the South, "the spirituality of the church" justified the perpetuation of the status quo. Yet before the Civil War the biblical proslavery interpretation won the day mostly because of how easily it fit the broader contours of American culture. Proslavery proof-texting persuaded because it seemed to honor the foundational Protestant commitment of *sola scriptura*. It benefited from the belief that American history had been uniquely blessed by God. It comported well with antebellum conventions of common-sense moral reasoning and Baconian empirical science. Above all, the inability to conceive of Africans as "brothers" made it all too easy for the biblical proslavery position to brand *all* abolitionism as inherently heterodox or worse.

The Future

The relative success of proslavery biblicism and the divided strategies of biblical abolitionists also exerted a decisive influence on later developments. In Protestant history, unadulterated biblicism, except when attacking the Roman Catholics, had been rare. Proof-texting had usually been augmented by other approaches to Scripture, like those to which abolitionists appealed. Yet now in America to downplay proof-texting and biblicism had enormous consequences when proslavery apologists insisted that loyalty to Scripture demanded nothing but proof-texting biblicism. Northern emancipationists who attacked the evils of slavery, but not enslavement itself, strengthened the impression that honoring Scripture meant endorsing the hermeneutical procedures most useful for proslavery arguments. As a result of this contentious history, a significant part of the nation's white population came to believe that standing on the authority of Scripture meant relying primarily, even exclusively, on proof-texts.

The changes set in motion during the full antebellum generation of all-out biblical strife over slavery took place well before Americans learned of Charles Darwin and also before most paid serious attention to biblical higher criticism from Europe. Debate over evolution did eventually affect general attitudes toward Scripture, but not with a decisive impact until well into the twentieth century. The higher criticism of Scripture had an earlier and deeper effect. "History" meaning an expansion of knowledge about the ancient biblical world also contributed to the influence of the new biblical criticism. But "history" understood as the evolving worldviews of biblical authors and progress in contemporary moral understanding contributed even more. Controversy over Scripture and "history" (in all senses) fractured Protestantism in the postbellum decades, and also to a limited extent Catholicism and religious Judaism. Yet that fracture began not in debates over the Mosaic authorship of the Pentateuch or the interpretation of New Testament miracles but over the Bible's teaching on enslavement. In the history of hermeneutics, later Protestant modernists were the direct heirs of those who insisted most strenuously that intuitive moral consciousness condemned slavery; later fundamentalists were the direct heirs of those who contested that judgment. In between stood great numbers of Protestants who became neither modernists nor fundamentalists, but who combined loyalty to traditional scriptural authority with some acceptance of modern moral consciousness.[31]

One final but exceedingly important word must be added in an assessment of antebellum biblical controversies. Among African Americans, a strikingly different history unfolded. Black abolitionists who spoke with Scripture in hand did appeal to overarching moral principles, but these principles were anchored in the Bible's Exodus narrative and the redemptive proclamations of Jesus, as well as in universal application of American founding truths. African Americans also characteristically maintained what would later be called fundamentalist devotion to an authoritative Bible understood as a record of God's supernatural actions. In the unfolding of the nation's history after the Civil War, this particular combination of commitments, which partly matched several different strands in white America but none with that combination, remained mostly out of sight—until it burst on the nation's consciousness with revolutionary force in the generation after the Second World War.

21

The Civil War

During the relatively short duration of the American Civil War, the nation's citizens read, pondered, preached, distributed, internalized, exploited, and abused the Bible with unprecedented fervor. George Rable concluded his magisterial religious history of the Civil War with a summary based on unusually deep research: the conflict was "the 'holiest' war in American history. Never before and likely never again would so many ministers, churches, and ordinary people turn not only to their Bibles but to their own faith to explain everything from the meaning of individual deaths, to the results of battles, to the outcome of the war."[1] Evidence for Rable's judgment lies thick on the ground. Two years before he would be nominated as the second Republican candidate for president, Abraham Lincoln's quotation from Matthew chapter 12 about a "house divided" propelled him into the national spotlight.[2] Toward the end of his life, on March 4, 1865, Lincoln once again addressed the public with words from Scripture; much of the incomparable gravity of his Second Inaugural Address came from its four strategic biblical quotations.[3] Many of the period's landmark expressions were similarly infused with biblical allusions or quotations, including the most popular song of the war, Julia Ward Howe's "Mine Eyes Have Seen the Glory of the Coming of the Lord":

> Mine eyes have seen the glory of the coming of the Lord [Matt 24:30; Mal 4:5];
> He is trampling out the vintage where the grapes of wrath are stored [Rev 6:17];
> He has loosed the fateful lightning of His terrible swift sword [Rev 8:5; Ezek 32:12][4]

Unsurprisingly, the same Scriptures that advanced a political career, informed a profound meditation, and supplied apocalyptic images served many other purposes. Some were comically trivial. After Lincoln's reelection, for a celebratory parade in Middletown, Connecticut, a minister constructed an illuminated transparency emblazoned with a quotation from Genesis 22:15, "And the angel of the Lord called unto Abraham out of heaven a second time."[5] Others bordered on delusion, like an essay published in the Confederate *Army and Navy Messenger* two weeks after Lincoln's Second Inaugural, as the Confederacy hung by a thread. "The Southern people," it read, "have the grandest privilege and

America's Book. Mark A. Noll, Oxford University Press. © Oxford University Press 2022.
DOI: 10.1093/oso/9780197623466.003.0022

opportunity ever providentially afforded a nation: of defending truth. . . . Above all, the providence of God has made it their special privilege to defend with their lives the right of freedom of conscience, the essential issue of the war; the right to interpret the bible for themselves."[6]

As an episode in the history of the Bible, the Civil War strengthened several features of earlier development. Among combatants and their families on the home front it sparked a resurgence of Methodist-style spirituality looking to the Bible for apolitical spiritual nurture. At the same time it strengthened the instrumental use of Scripture as the servant of Union and Confederate civil religion through typology, political preaching, and creative quotation. The war years extended the trajectory of previous decades that had witnessed more non-Protestants making more aggressive claims for *their* rights to the Scriptures. The eye of the war's religious hurricane—the domain where Scripture remained mostly silent—was the application of biblical reasoning to foundational questions of political principle, social order, economic justice, and race. For a nation in turmoil, the Bible spoke loudly. For the future, its silence became increasingly significant.[7]

In the Field

Among the more than 3 million men who served under arms in the opposing forces, Bible reading was never as widespread as religious propagandists for both sides made out, but it was present from the start and almost certainly became more prevalent as the war went on. Soldiers used the Bible to demonize the other side and crow about their own righteousness. Sometimes Bible-based sermons fueled patriotic ardor as they geared combatants for battle. Lay soldiers were almost as adept as their chaplains at enlivening rhetoric on all imaginable subjects by injecting well-chosen biblical phrases for merely rhetorical effect. Quite often, however, the soldiers opened the Bible with the kind of focused spiritual attention characteristic of early Methodism—not for doctrinal or denominational distinctives, not to secure rights or energize campaigns, but to sustain the soul. For soldiers experiencing interminable boredom punctuated by spasms of horrific carnage, the republican anxieties of sectarian Protestants and the national ambitions of proprietary Protestants were irrelevant. Well-documented accounts of revivals that swept southern encampments with increasing intensity from late 1862 have sometimes left the impression that southern soldiers became more pious and more devoted to Scripture than their northern counterparts. This notion, encouraged in the vigorous tradition of Lost Cause historiography, substantially underestimates the piety found in northern camps, where attention to Scripture was almost as serious as in the South.[8]

Several agencies made extraordinary efforts to distribute Bibles to the troops, at least as much out of basic spiritual concern as for self-serving patriotism. During the conflict's first year the American Bible Society employed sixteen power presses at its New York headquarters to print approximately 400,000 Bibles (or New Testaments) for Union troops. Most were the King James Version, but the Society also produced Bibles in several other languages for soldiers whose native tongue was not English. From the start the Society was joined in its effort by other churches and agencies, especially the American Tract Society and the United States Christian Commission, a pan-Protestant voluntary association that paralleled the work of the Union's Sanitary Commission. (Some of the much appreciated stationery the Commission provided to troops was headed with 1 Timothy 4:9, "This is a faithful saying, and worthy of all acceptation, that Christ Jesus came into the world to save sinners, of whom I am chief.")[9]

For Union troops, the annual production of Bibles, testaments, and portions reached over a million copies each year.[10] The more than 200,000 Catholic soldiers who served under arms heard or read the Douay-Rheims translation, including Scripture selections in the *Manual of the Christian Soldier*, the most popular religious book supplied to Catholic soldiers during the war.[11] By the end, the North had supplied more than two such copies for each of its more than 2 million combatants. It was also common for local churches to supply Bibles to troops marching off from their localities, including in the little town of Ashby, Massachusetts, where each volunteer was given a revolver, a bowie knife, and a Bible.[12]

Confederate soldiers had greater difficulties obtaining Bibles since most southern states lacked extensive book-printing capacity. Although it was technically against the law, the Bible Society and other northern publishers managed to pass something like 300,000 Bibles to southern troops during the war. The Rev. Moses Hoge of Richmond won considerable renown for braving the Union blockade to smuggle 10,000 Bibles, 50,000 New Testaments, and 250,000 portions of Psalms and Gospels from England to the South. Yet even with intensive effort, there was probably no more than one Scripture provided for every four or five southern soldiers.[13]

Copies of the *Soldier's Bible* or the *Soldier's Pocket Bible*, a thin pamphlet of selected verses first produced by the Presbyterian Edward Calamy for use by Oliver Cromwell's troops in the English Civil War, appeared among troops both North and South (Figure 21.1). As with this selection of biblical texts, amplitude mattered. More soldiers carried New Testaments than complete Bibles because of the necessity to travel light. The prevalence of the New Testament in the field may explain why analogies between Israel and either the Union or the Confederacy appeared much more frequently in sermons far from the front lines. For the Union so many different organizations provided so many bibles

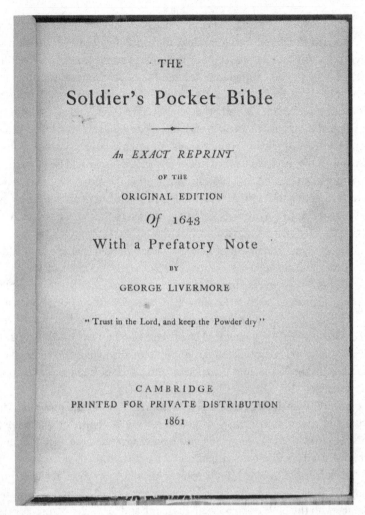

Figure 21.1 The sixteen pages of *The Soldier's Pocket Bible*, reprinted from a work prepared for the army of Oliver Cromwell, included many passages from the Psalms and a long extract from a battle recounted in Judges chapter 20, but only ten verses from the New Testament.

Source: Courtesy of Buswell Library Special Collections, Rare Books, Wheaton College, Illinois.

that troops sometimes threw them away or begged to receive clean socks or warm food instead.[14]

Many reports circulated of the Bible as talisman, some of them actually well documented. Sortilege—the random opening of Scripture to find guidance from a verse selected at random—was not unknown, as when the Confederate general John Bell Hood expressed confidence he would survive the war because he had opened the Scriptures at random to read Psalm 118:17 ("I shall not die but live").[15] Many more stories told of miraculous protection from the Bible as a physical object. One Confederate soldier, Philip Stephenson, reported that a lieutenant in his regiment at the 1863 battle of Ringgold Gap "was struck square in the heart by a bullet! Or rather, he would have been, had not a little testament stopped it." Unlike General Hood, this lieutenant was later killed in a subsequent action.[16] A private from Georgia, Evan Lawrence, reported that as he marched with his regiment toward Kennesaw Mountain he had been meditating on a passage from Isaiah 52:7, "How beautiful upon the mountains are the feet of him that bringeth good tidings, that publisheth peace"; in the battle he, or rather his Bible, was stuck by a minié ball that penetrated to that very passage. A Tract Society volunteer relayed a macabre variation on this common story; when he sent home the New Testament of a fallen solider, he said that the fatal ball had first torn the testament at Revelation 22:20 ("Surely I come quickly") before killing the lad.[17] Observers learned that when heading into battle, card players sometimes substituted a New Testament for a deck in their breast pocket. But there were also a few recorded occasions when a deck of card stopped a bullet. Confederate soldier David Holt told of a friend who had received a new deck of cards as a gift from his mother, an upright Episcopalian, and who claimed never to gamble with the cards; he was struck in battle, but the ball penetrated only to the ace of spades.[18]

The Rev. William Taylor represented the Christian Commission in providing spiritual and material assistance to Union troops. A report on his battlefield experiences from early January 1864 may have exaggerated the intimate connection between bibles carried and biblical messages accepted, yet reflected what many in the conflict saw as the Scriptures' primary purpose. Taylor reported hearing of a "poor rebel dying, stretched out upon one of the battle-fields of the Peninsula, with the Bible open beneath his hand, and his skeleton fingers pressed upon the words, 'Yea, though I walk through the valley of the shadow of death, I will fear no evil, for Thou art with me; Thy rod and thy staff, they comfort me [Ps 23:4].'" He explained to the Commission that many fatally wounded soldiers had been identified "in no other way than by the Testaments in their pockets, saturated with their patriot blood." Another story from Taylor concerned a New England woman whose husband had died at the front. When the army returned her husband's effects, "[t]here was no letter there to tell the story; but there was the Bible! When it was opened, there were found, heavily underscored, simply these words: 'Woman, why weepest thou? [Jn 20:13]' and 'Why should it be thought an incredible thing with you that God could raise the dead? [Acts 26:8].'"[19] The redoubtable South Carolina diarist Mary Chesnut was in the minority who found such stories reprehensible: "How *dare* men mix up the Bible so with their own *bad* passions."[20]

Soldiers had many occasions to hear sermons from chaplains and visiting missionaries; some were shrugged off when the preacher seemed insincere or spoke too long, but many accounts suggest that the soldiers appreciated pointed, direct, and succinct sermons from preachers whom they respected. They also confirm that sermons in the camps spent much less time on themes of national righteousness, analogies with ancient Israel, inspiration for heroic action, and even courage under fire than the sermons preached at home. After the war J. William Jones published influential accounts of the southern revivals, which were based in part on his experience as a Baptist chaplain in Robert E. Lee's Army of Northern Virginia.[21] Although his diary from the conflict usually upheld his reputation as the enthusiastic "Fighting Parson," it also recorded instances of more immediate spiritual concern. After preaching twice to troops in East Tennessee on July 6, 1862, he spoke privately with an earnest youth who "wished to know if one who had been converted fell into sin might hope for pardon and heaven." Jones "offered him the precious promises of God's word for his encouragement" and "had reason to hope the word spoken to-day has been as seed sown in good ground [Matt 13:23]."[22] Such instances seem to have been frequent.

Texts chosen by chaplains often had a Methodistic flavor, like the sermon on Amos 4:12 ("prepare to meet thy God") preached with effect in late October 1864 by the chaplain for a New York regiment.[23] Similar was the experience of Lt. Chesley Mosman of Illinois, who was with Union troops in North Carolina on Sunday, April 16, 1865, shortly after word arrived of Lincoln's assassination. He attended a sermon preached by a Union sergeant on the text "I am not ashamed of the gospel of Christ [Rom 1:16]." Two weeks later, on April 30, 1865, Alfred Fielder (with Joseph E. Johnstone, the last southern general to surrender) heard a sermon on Hebrews 13:14 ("For here we have no continuing city, but we seek one to come"); he responded, "I felt that my abiding home would be in heaven."[24] Preaching during the revivals in southern military camps did not usually feature nationalistic texts but passages like "Except ye repent, ye shall all likewise perish [Lk 13:3]," "What must I do to be saved? [Acts 16:30]," and "The wages of sin is death, but the gift of God is eternal life through Jesus Christ our Lord [Rom 6:23]."[25]

More even than the most appreciated sermons, the soldiers' letters and diaries indicate how often many read, marked, and inwardly digested biblical passages for their spiritual content as opposed to anything overtly political, military, or adversarial. Usually personal initiative lay behind that inspiration. George Rable believes "the nightly prayer meetings, along with Sunday schools and Bible studies became the real centers of religious devotion."[26] From countless such examples, several in connection with one major battle are representative.[27]

In March or very early April 1862, when Sgt. William Edmund was marching toward Shiloh with Ulysses S. Grant, he paused to write, "I for one am ready for the fray and having put my faith and confidence in Him who knows and directs all things for the best, in Him who has said I will never leave or forsake [Heb 13:5] those that come unto me in faith and sincerity."[28] After the first day of bloody fighting at that landing on the Tennessee River, a Confederate soldier, Alfred Fiedlers, when asked to read Scripture by his fellows, chose Psalm 71, which begins, "In thee, O Lord, do I put my trust: let me never be put to confusion. Deliver me in thy righteousness, and cause me to escape: incline thine ear unto me, and save me."[29] Another firsthand account recorded immediately after the same battle illustrates how often hymns based on scriptural themes functioned like the Bible itself. A Union captain wounded during the fight and left overnight on the battlefield struggled to reach a pool of water. As he gazed at the night sky, he "began to think of that great God who had given his Son to die a death of agony for me . . . and that I was going home to meet him and praise him there." He then began to sing the Isaac Watts hymn that meant so much to African Americans, "When I can read my title clear." Soon other wounded soldiers picked it up and "made the field of battle ring with the hymns of praise to god." The officer died of his wounds.[30]

Historians who have mastered the primary sources left by ordinary troops do not picture entire armies fixated on Scripture. Neither do they paper over the drunkenness, malingering, resort to prostitutes, endless card playing, desertion, and fractious quarrelling that so often characterized life in the camps. They do, however, note the religious seriousness of a sizable minority of soldiers. Steven Woodworth reports multiple examples recorded in diaries or letters home: "read the scriptures"; "I finished reading the book of John"; "I read the testament"; "I have read five chapters in the Testament today"; "I must now read some in the Testament"; "I shall endeavor to obey your wishes in reading my Bible every night." He also found that quite a few Bible readers wrestled more seriously with moral dilemmas than accounts at the time or later recognized. What, for example, did it mean to follow the Prince of Peace while shooting to kill the enemy? For at least a few southern soldiers, concern for spiritual freedom moved them to query the many restrictions on slaves' religious freedom.[31] George Rable also notes that, before going into battle, some "soldiers opened their pocket bibles to comforting passages from the Psalms, the Gospels, or Paul's Epistles; they sought refuge in the promises of strength in the day of adversity. As the troops moved into formation, a few men would quietly read from the scriptures and perhaps offer one final, silent prayer."[32]

Religion in the Civil War years moved in several different directions. Combatants also experienced tension between Protestants and Catholics, defended or attacked slavery on religious grounds, witnessed occasional doctrinal disputes among Protestants, included small but growing numbers giving up on traditional belief, and were very occasionally inspired by sermons encouraging holy war. Yet much more than on the home fronts, religion for men under arms meant awareness of standing before God as responsible agents. Catholic chaplains, as Robert Miller summarizes, added "[s]acramental administration" to the duties they shared with their Protestant counterparts: "They visited hospitals, followed soldiers into battle, provided comfort to the sick and dying, helped instruct people on various religious points, offered counsel to the condemned and dying, and became 'jacks of all trades' to help the soldiers they worked for." But they also heard confessions, sometimes for hours on end, and at strategic movements offered masses of "general absolution"—as Father William Corby, CSC, did so memorably on the second day of Gettysburg, including to quite a few non-Catholics who assembled with the Irish Brigade.[33]

For the much larger proportion of troops associated with the nation's Protestant traditions, personal engagement with Scripture took on something like a sacramental significance. That engagement strengthened personal faith; it reduced the importance of secondary concerns; it pushed to the background Scripture's utilitarian support for republican principles, American exceptionalism, and individual rights. Biblical religion in the camps was not Methodist in a narrow sense, but it did feature characteristics similar to what Methodists had brought to the nation in the early decades of the century: a serious renewal of personal faith, but also uncertainty about how that faith affected politics, economics, and society.

At Home

Beyond the camps, use of Scripture mostly flowed in channels that had been cut before the war began. As with the men and the few women under arms, ministers and laity regularly turned to the Bible for personal and family support, comfort, or encouragement. Yet along with this surge, exploitation of the Bible for nationalistic, political, or self-justifying purposes surged even more.

After cataloguing over thirty-four thousand biblical passages from over two thousand period sources, James Byrd's list of most-cited texts tells a revealing story.[34] Of the ten passages appearing most frequently from white southerners, only three can be considered political; Psalm 46:7 ("the God of Jacob is our refuge"), Genesis 13:9 (Abraham's agreement with Lot to divide the land), and Romans 8:31 ("If God be for us, who can be against us?"). The others offered consolation, exemplified by the passage Byrd found most frequently, Job 1:21 ("Naked came I out of my mother's womb, and naked shall I return thither: the Lord gave, and the Lord hath taken away; blessed be the name of the Lord").

Others reflected on the meaning of death (Matt 25:21, "well done, thou good and faithful servant") or offered general encouragement (Ps 46:1, "God is our refuge and strength").

By contrast, the most frequently referenced passages in the North tilted heavily toward the war itself. At the top of the list by a considerable margin stood Acts 17:26 ("he hath made of one blood all nations of men"), which indicates that Abraham Lincoln's decision for Emancipation resonated powerfully—despite early northern reluctance to view the war as an abolitionist crusade. The only two passages without direct bearing on conflict were two from Matthew 25, including verse 21, which southerners also favored. The others either echoed emancipationist themes (the Golden Rule from Matthew 7:12 and a verse from Isaiah 58:6 about letting the oppressed go free) or commented directly on the conflict, like Matthew 12:25 (house divided), Jeremiah 8:11 ("Peace, peace, when there is no peace"), or Romans 13:1 ("the powers that be are ordained by God"). The North's favorite passages thus came much closer to the favored texts that Byrd, in an earlier study, documented for the Revolutionary era. In that conflict *all* of the most cited passages, except reference to the Sermon on the Mount (Matt 5), bore directly on political or military themes.[35]

As with the troops, however, citizens on both sides did turn more directly to Scripture for personal comfort and spiritual support than was the case during the Revolutionary era. That change reflected the broadly democratic Christianization of the population that active Protestants, with Methodists in the lead, had accomplished from the first years of the century. As an instance, the book of Job, where Yahweh's servant bemoans the tragedies of his existence yet continues to believe, sustained many readers both North and South.[36] Others took hope in times of great distress for families from passages like Philippians 1:6 ("Being confident of this very thing, that he which hath begun a good work in you will perform it until the day of Jesus Christ").[37]

Yet on the whole, overt political uses predominated, even in the South, where texts of personal encouragement enjoyed more currency. As a Methodist editor in Nashville wrote with specific reference to favored biblical passages, "We must study Joshua and Ezra and Nehemiah [books of military mobilization], as well as Job and St. John." Significantly, that editor's comments reflected a much deeper political involvement by Methodists both north and south than in the Asbury era. The Nashville editor put it like this: "[I]t is the part of a religious paper that is not a fossil . . . to treat of these duties in their season."[38] The Illinois itinerant Peter Cartwright, who on occasion had sparred with a young Lincoln, blasted seceding clergymen with echoes of Revelation 14:6 and Isaiah 34:4: "Rivers of blood will flow, but this Union must stand though the heavens fall."[39] With equal conviction, a southern counterpart, J. W. Tucker, told southern Methodists in May 1862, "Your cause is the cause of God, the cause of Christ, of humanity. It is a conflict of truth with error—of the Bible with Northern infidelity—of pure Christianity with Northern fanaticism."[40] War turned even sectarian Protestants toward custodial concerns.

Like the bishop of Vermont, John Henry Hopkins, and his Episcopalian antagonist, Daniel Goodwin, a few ministers continued to argue about whether Scripture allowed for slavery.[41] Mostly, however, the conflict confirmed southern whites in their equating of abolition with infidelity, while leading increasing numbers in the North to emphasize biblical motives for ending slavery.

African Americans during the war continued to read the Bible as a book of liberation with little distinction between the spiritual and the political. Favored scriptures included a text from Galatians 5:1 that patriots in the Revolution had also enlisted ("Stand fast therefore in the liberty wherewith Christ hath made us free") and the hope found in Ethiopia "stretching out her hands to God" (Ps 68:31). Others ranged further afield, as when Frederick Douglass likened the American conflict to the "war in heaven" of Revelation chapter 12 between the Archangel Michael and the Dragon, or when a North Carolina slave hailed emancipation with words from Isaiah 66:8, "These are the times foretold by the Prophets, 'When a Nation shall be born in a day.' "[42]

Many others joined this slave as they discerned the ways of providence through a scriptural lens. Occasionally that discerning could be sophisticated, as when the northern Episcopal bishop Charles Petit McIlvaine affirmed God's mysterious control of events while specifying northern sins that deserved chastisement.[43] More common were blithely confident pronouncements about how and why God was directing the course of the war. A southern Methodist defended the practice by saying that to deny God's specific direction of all things was "to close the book of Revelation and plunge ourselves into inextricable difficulties." It was illustrated when a Cincinnati paper wrote about Gen. George Pickett's failed charge at Gettysburg that "the voice of the Lord" had sounded above the din of battle to proclaim "Hitherto shalt thou come, but no further [Job 38:11]."[44]

Along with all other deployments of Scripture, ministers and laypeople repeatedly exploited individual texts for extended commentary on the war or, even more commonly, drew partisan analogies between biblical narratives and the course of American events. Imagination offered the only constraint in these exercises that revived patterns witnessed in earlier American crises from the French and Indian Wars through the Revolution and the War of 1812, though not so often during the War with Mexico of the mid-1840s.[45]

On rare occasions a text with mostly religious implications could be used by both sides, as when 1 Samuel 17:47 ("the battle is the Lord's") served preachers north and south on Thanksgiving Day 1863. Partisanship much more commonly ruled the day, even when preachers knew better. In late 1864, after Sherman's destructive march through Georgia, one northern minister took note of Proverbs 24:17 ("Rejoice not when thine enemy falleth"), but concluded that if Solomon had known about Jefferson Davis's perfidy, he would have dropped the "not." Earlier a Georgia Baptist editor had reasoned similarly about Matthew 5:44, Jesus's command to pray for enemies; maybe so, he wrote, but nothing should prevent Confederates from slaying Yankees with "fire and sword."[46]

The application of Scripture could be straightforward. A northern Unitarian tried to bolster morale after the disastrous First Battle of Bull Run with 1 Timothy 6:12 ("fight the good fight of faith").[47] Two years later, after Union victories at Gettysburg and Vicksburg, southern appeals to Romans 8:31 hid a note of panic ("if God be for us, who can be against us").[48] Use of the Scriptures could also be *exultant* (after early southern victories, the rabidly proslavery Episcopalian Stephen Elliott expatiated on Exodus 15:1, "I will sing unto the Lord, for he has triumphed gloriously");[49] *vindictive* (David's "perfect hatred" of God's enemies, Psalm 139:22, justified the call to arms for a northern Republican);[50] *sanguinary* (a Pennsylvania editor rallied the Union with Jeremiah 49:10, "cursed is he that keepeth back his sword from blood");[51] or *apocalyptic* (Matt 16:18, "the gates of hell" could not stop the northern effort to destroy slavery; and an impending northern victory allowed one Connecticut Congregationalist to glimpse "the vials of Jehovah's wrath pouring their dread contents upon the guilty land," Rev 16:1).[52]

Women who knew their bibles lacked nothing in playing this game. Nancy Mitchell of Ohio defended her pastor for peaching against the Confederates from Malachi 3:9 ("Ye are cursed with a curse; for ye have robbed me, even with this whole nation"). To Mitchell, regardless of what southerners claimed about the spirituality of the church, her minister had "found it [his message] in the Bible." Mary Robinson of Princeville, Illinois, matched her male Bible adepts by targeting Democratic Copperheads who dared challenge President Lincoln with 2 Timothy 4:14, the Apostle Paul's denunciation of "Alexander the coppersmith."[53]

In a reprise of the War for Independence, ministers and not a few of the laity once again turned the Bible into a cornucopia of exemplars.[54] Not incidentally, two enterprising northern editors published collections of sermons from that earlier era aiming to promote both piety and northern resolve.[55] Time after time Bible-savvy writers and speakers found, usually in the Hebrew Scriptures or Old Testament, what they considered the exact biblical type for a contemporary anti-type. Biblical fluency marched step for step with partisan ardor.[56]

For African Americans, President Lincoln was obviously Moses—or Jesus, or a combination of Moses and Jesus—and Emancipation was the Exodus. But the story of Israel's deliverance from Egypt also illustrated the plasticity of the American Bible imagination. As for Blacks, many northern white Protestants

THE CIVIL WAR 455

and a few Jews also viewed Lincoln as Moses; he had been hidden away until required for the crisis hour, and despite intrepid leadership he had to endure much murmuring from Israel. Moreover, if Lincoln was Moses, Jeff Davis was Pharaoh and General Grant was Aaron. For a very brief period after the war, a few northerners hailed Andrew Johnson as Joshua.[57] For the same story read from the South, the North was obviously Egypt and Lincoln obviously Pharaoh, yet to an Iowa congressman early in the war, Lincoln was Pharaoh for moving so slowly to emancipate the slaves. A southern woman, Eliza Fain, responded to Union typology by claiming that a northern victory, though touted as "Exodus," would actually reduce former slaves to "a bondage more cruel, more exacting than the Egyptian." After his death, Stonewall Jackson became Moses, who, despite heroic service, would not live to see the Promised Land.

The later history of Israel proved almost as fruitful as the Exodus story. At the end of the war, Henry Ward Beecher explained that the Union had been forced to dwell long in the wilderness before it could cross the Jordan River. Southerners saw themselves as God's servant David going forth to battle the haughty giant Goliath. After the First Battle of Bull Run, they depicted the Union army as the Assyrians, Midianites, and Philistines scattered by the arm of the Lord. Both sides made the most of the division that took place after the death of King Solomon between the ten tribes of Israel, led by the rebel king Jeroboam, and Judah, where the throne descended to Solomon's heir, Rehoboam. The ascriptions were as creative as they were contradictory: the South was justified in following Jeroboam's example; the South was condemned for following Jeroboam's example; northern ministers criticized Lincoln for laying on heavy burdens like those that had driven Jeroboam to secede, praised Lincoln for not laying on those heavy burdens, and then praised him again for waging war like Rehoboam on the rebel Jeroboam. From the Jonah story, northern preachers applied to the Union Jonah's threat of punishment against Nineveh, but also suggested that the only remedy for slavery was to pitch it overboard as the sailors had thrown Jonah to the great fish.

New Testament references appeared much less frequently, though to a few in the North the Confederacy predictably became Judas. Otherwise, apocalyptic imagery prevailed. If Gettysburg meant that the war's end was nigh, it must have been the Battle of Armageddon. When it seemed that Robert E. Lee's invasion of Pennsylvania might end in Philadelphia or Washington, southern preachers hailed the impending fall of Babylon the Great (Rev 17). Or maybe, perceived from the North, the Confederacy itself was Babylon of the End Times. The one Old Testament reference most often exploited for the same purpose came from Daniel chapter 11, with its account of warfare between "a king of the south" and "a king of the north."

Also predictably, the torrent of political preaching generated a counterswell of preaching against political preaching. Yet from a modern perspective, that

groundswell sounds strange since it came mostly from defenders of "the spirituality of the church" who opposed church meddling in politics on principle. Very
few observers, if any, addressed the ludicrous lengths to which expositors went
in bending scriptural passage away from anything even close to their original
intentions. Constitutional originalism (though not under that term) enjoyed a
healthy life in the era's debates over the *Dred Scott* decision and the Republican
Party's intention to curb slavery expansion. By contrast, users of Scripture in
their partisanship systematically ignored what the biblical authors' original
intentions might have been.

While white southerners continued to complain about the North's politicization of Scripture, northerners debated among themselves how biblical texts
should be applied. A militant Cincinnati Methodist, Granville Moody, who later
traded his clerical garb for an officer's uniform, dared to interpret John 18:36 as
a spur to combat. Most preachers worried about the pacifist implications of the
text, "My kingdom is not of this world: if my kingdom were of this world, then
would my servants fight." Moody instead reasoned that Jesus's followers in their
dual capacity as also citizens *of this world* should be eager for the fight against
slavery. His opponents countered with Matthew 26:52 ("all they that take the
sword shall perish with the sword")—and the hope that Moody would be first in
line among the perishing.[58] Church bodies opposed to political preaching cited
1 Thessalonians 5:22 ("abstain from all appearance of evil") or stipulated that
preachers, like the Apostle Paul, limit themselves to themes directly expounding
"Christ and him crucified" (1 Cor 2:2).[59] One northern Presbyterian, R. B.
Thurston, responded learnedly: race, slavery, and loyalty to one's nation did not
involve politics "in a degraded sense" but questions of morality in the highest
sense: "Hence to unfold in due proportion those oracles of God which should
govern rulers is a part of the minister's official work, divinely appointed." It was
"in a genuine and high sense . . . a scriptural science."[60]

In the face of considerable pressure, the historical peace churches mostly
maintained their nonresistant stance, as when a Mennonite bishop, John
Brenneman, published an entire tract with nothing but pacifist texts. They included Christ's command to love your enemies and his warning about those
who live by the sword.[61] Such arguments, however, encountered stiff resistance.
Immediately after the First Battle of Bull Run, one northern minister renounced
what had been his pacifist principles in a sermon expositing Luke 22:36 ("he that
hath no sword, let him sell his garment, and buy one").[62]

As almost all of such examples show, deep familiarity with Scripture combined with deep political commitments to trivialize the Holy Book. The religious press, in George Rable's authoritative summary, "became increasingly
secular." Almost all papers offered unqualified support to either the Union or the
Confederacy, with the result that "editorials often became indistinguishable from

those in regular newspapers, and their main points seldom rested on biblical or theological arguments." In a similar judgment, Rable concludes that sermons preached on the three fast days called by Abraham Lincoln and the ten decreed by Jefferson Davis did offer "some prodding, comfort, and a bit of guidance to people beset by doubts, anxieties, and fears." But he also describes these efforts as "an often perplexing mix of sectional chauvinism, sterile dogma, and doubtful theology sprinkled with occasional insight."[63]

The last sections of this book chart the public presence of Scripture in post-bellum American life, a presence often characterized by fragmentation, ethnocentrism, indecision, and nationalism. Much else affected the history of the Bible during the Gilded Age and Progressive Era. But for the Protestants who had played such a dominant part in all aspects of the earlier history, the war years confirmed the insight of William Ralph Inge's oft-cited aphorism, "[W]hoever marries the spirit of this age will find himself a widow in the next."

Catholics Censure "the Unctuous Advocates of an 'Open Bible'"

By the Civil War years, however, other significant constituencies now competed vigorously with those Protestants for public recognition, including claims for how best to treat the Bible. None was as active as the nation's Roman Catholics, whose growing numbers supported a growing host of publications eager to assign responsibility for the nation's crisis.[64]

Compared to lengthy and learned publications by foreign Catholics on the Civil War, the United States' twelve or so English-language weekly papers along with a handful of foreign-language weeklies covered the conflict with short news items laced with editorial comment.[65] These periodicals differed among themselves in several important ways. Some were sponsored by bishops, others by lay associations; some treated events in their home countries (Ireland, Germany, France) more extensively than events in the United States; some rebutted anti-Catholic attacks vigorously, others with moderation. Politically, the weeklies reflected the loyalties of their respective regions, with northerners strong for the Union, southerners after early 1861 committed to the Confederacy, and border-state Catholics defending states' rights while lending reluctant allegiance to the federal government. Yet despite regional, personal, organizational, and ecclesiastical differences, they united with one voice in assessing the most important question of the hour: beyond doubt, American Protestants bore primary responsibility for the Civil War.

In typical fashion the Boston *Pilot*, under its Irish nationalist editor, Patrick Donahoe, repeated that denunciation like a drumbeat.[66] On one occasion, shortly before the First Battle of Bull Run, Donahoe mocked Anglo-American boasting about their "[f]reedom and enlightenment in thought"; in reality these Protestants displayed only a "violent, vulgar Saxonism," especially by maliciously claiming that popery and slavery were of a piece. In contrast, "[i]t is Anglo-Saxon Protestantism itself that is incompatible with freedom and civilization. What has it done in Ireland?"[67]

In their bill of particulars, Donahoe and other public Catholics insisted that Protestant claims about the Bible and practices of biblical interpretation were particularly destructive. Although this charge reprised an age-old Catholic complaint, it resonated powerfully in an American setting. Donahoe, for example, once mocked a phrase made famous by the Bible societies when he charged that "Joe Smith," by reading "the Bible 'without note or comment,'" had created Mormonism, "this most loathsome offshoot of Protestantism."[68]

Catholic communities that retained strong ties to Europe were quick to give tried and true old-world polemic a new-world twist. *Der Wahrheits-Freund* served German-speaking Catholics in Cincinnati as one of the papers overseen by Bishop John Baptist Purcell, who during the war continued his efforts to strengthen the city's Catholic school system. One of its issues in July 1861 publicized what a leading German Lutheran had reported about his own flock: "The Bible was not understood where it is read, and not read where it can be understood." What baffled the German Lutheran was no mystery to the Cincinnati Catholics: "In order to understand the Bible truly, one must have before one's eyes not only the sense of the words themselves, but also an ongoing commentary accompanying the text in order to clarify all of the phrases that would not be understood by non-theologians without an explanation."[69]

As these critiques indicate, the most common Catholic charge centered on Protestants who championed the private interpretation of Scripture. That charge at that time spotlighted how the nation's individualistic democracy had, in Catholic eyes, made bad Protestantism even worse. At the start of the war the *New York Freeman's Journal* called Protestants "the unctuous advocates of an 'open Bible' who trampled on the honored traditions of antiquity." Such advocacy demonstrated that "[t]here is no middle ground between unbelief and the Catholic faith. The soul of man must either bow itself before the Word of God, and the consecrated traditions of the past, or its must cast its creed in a mould of its own devising."[70] Shortly after the war came to an end, *The Catholic* from Pittsburgh summed up what many other Catholics had said in many other ways: Protestants "claim to go by the Bible. But that volume of sacred writings, when judged and interpreted by each one for himself, has been demonstrated to be the very parent of uncertainty, and is no sure and infallible guide of faith."[71]

Again, when reporting on specific events, Catholics singled out Protestant Bible usage as the prime culprit threatening the nation. Shortly after the *Dred*

Scott decision in 1857 the *New York Tablet* explained why internal Protestant differences were so perilous: "Is not 'the Bible' the prime subject and cause of the disputes between Baptist, Presbyterian, and Methodist persuasions North and South? Instead of being a bond of brotherhood, is it not a torch of discord, and an apple of enmity?" Multiplied examples, in fact, demonstrated that "American Protestantism is logically doomed to knock its brains out on 'the Bible' or to add hypocrisy to its failings and to hold 'the Bible' aloft as the Aegis of the Union while secretly believing that it is only useful in the sense of a sunshade."[72] As the war began, the *New York Freeman's Journal* charged, "The country is chiefly indebted for the present war to the religious societies or sects which have within the last fifty years interpolated politics tests into their religious creeds, subordinating the church of Christ to party platforms. . . . The Christian Bible teaches no such dogma."[73] At the war's end, the *New York Tablet* canvassed a number of Protestant periodicals in order to illustrate how the various journals emphasized many different (and contradictory) aspects of Christian belief and practice. That cacophony first explained how Protestant use of Scripture intensified anti-Catholicism: "Of the five millions [i.e., anti-Roman Catholics in the United States] who would harm us if they could, there are fifty separate organizations, the fruit of three centuries of free inquiry into the meaning of the Open Bible without note or comment." But according to this article, the effects extended much further; in fact, "the Luther leaven" was the prime source of rebellion, secession, revolt, insurrection, sedition, and mutiny.[74]

Even as they advanced this polemic concerning the Civil War, these same Catholics expended increased effort to promote their own understanding of Scripture and how it should be read. With their foes, they certainly agreed that religious well-being required the Scriptures, but against Protestants they insisted that a proper use of Scripture required a proper authority. An alternative approach to the Bible, in other words, accompanied the denunciation of Protestant error.

Some of that promotion rode the back of critique, as in a book from an Australian bishop published in 1859 by Patrick Donahoe of the Boston *Pilot*. It's title, *The Bible against Protestantism, and for Catholicity*, advertised its intention explicitly, but the volume devoted as much effort to showing how Scripture functioned appropriately in the stable context of Roman authority as it did attacking Protestants for abusing the Bible.[75] Donahoe later contrasted what he considered a proper understanding of Scripture with the ravings of abolitionists: "[T]he divines who now occupy pulpits in the North are leading their flocks in pursuit of false gods . . . by worshiping the negro instead of the God of the Bible."[76] The 1859 bibliography of American Catholic bibles published by John Gilmary Shea took pains to explain a proper Catholic approach to Scripture.[77] Similar was the extensive material on the Bible in a two-volume history of the Reformation from Bishop Martin John Spalding of Louisville, published just as the nation fell apart. His account excoriated Protestant beliefs and practices, but for the larger purpose of demonstrating a proper use of Scripture.[78] Much the same double purpose—fending off Protestant error, explaining proper Catholic practice—lay behind the papers' reporting on other events during the war years: protests against required readings from the King James Version in New York's common schools, explanations for reported Bible burnings by European Catholics, and general refutations of the common Protestant charge that Catholics were prohibited from reading the Scriptures.[79]

Even more directly positive were nonpolemical initiatives, like Donahoe's promotion of a new "Bible History" as a text for use in Catholic schools.[80] Catholic editors did not spend as much time as their Protestant peers defining correct approaches to Scripture. It was, however, still notable that the American Catholic press included substantial treatment of books demonstrating the factual historicity of the Old Testament and also joined in condemning the South African Anglican bishop John Colenso when he questioned traditional interpretations of the Pentateuch.[81]

The Civil War prompted several Catholics to repeat Alexis de Tocqueville's prophecy that "our descendants will tend more and more to divide into only two parts, some leaving Christianity entirely, others going into the Roman Church."[82] In early 1860, the *Catholic Mirror* of Baltimore observed that, with American Protestantism degenerating into "Unitarians, Humanitarians, Spiritualists," there could "be but one result. The great mass of the people of this country must become, within a few years, Catholics or infidel; and as no nation can remain infidel, the true problem for us is, Catholicity or destruction; Catholicity or a deluge of crime and immorality; Catholicity or social and political annihilation."[83]

Predictions about a simple division of the population between Catholicism and infidelity did not of course come to pass. Yet they did accurately foresee the future by predicting a loss of influence for the main engines of antebellum American Protestantism. In addition, if predictions about a new era of Catholic dominance did not pan out, they nonetheless testified to a new situation. It was not only that American Catholic numbers were expanding; it was also that the anti-Protestant polemic of the war years revealed new self-confidence. Thus, editors and a few other public voices made bold claims:

> Given that a well-ordered Christian society needed a sound foundation, the United States required a principle by which disputes over the interpretation of Scripture could be peacefully adjudicated.
> Since it was in fact necessary for a well-ordered civilization to rely on the Bible, Catholic approaches to Scripture offered much more for the stability, health, and well-being of society than did Protestant approaches.

Even if the public at large was not convinced of those arguments, Catholics could demonstrate—at least to themselves, if not yet to a watching world—that they were capable of promoting the right kind of biblical use for the right kind of religious and social purposes.

The self-confidence reflected in such testimonies translated into heightened religious competition after the war. If that increased competition eventually led to a more pluralist, or even secular outcome than Catholic leaders desired, it nonetheless did mark a new stage in the internal maturity of American Catholic communities—and in the public history of the Bible.

Abraham Lincoln and the Jews

Abraham Lincoln and the Bible is a time-worn subject about which caution is required. It is well established by the best disciplined scholarship that Lincoln's unusually retentive memory gave him a gift for apt biblical quotation and that over the course of his career those quotations moved gradually from the humorous and the political to the contemplative and the nonpartisan. Beyond that, efforts have not held up to depict the sixteenth president as a convinced evangelical, a doubter who retained the Paine-ite skepticism of his young adulthood, or an amoral pragmatist using every means, including Scripture, for immediate political ends.[84] More recent scholarship, however, has illuminated a domain where Lincoln's scriptural awareness made a difference in broadening the scope of the nation's Bible history. As with Catholics, the Civil War years pushed that history beyond previous Protestant boundaries. After Lincoln, that history made room for an authentically Jewish element.

By comparison with his contemporaries, Lincoln stood out for how he put the Bible to use rather than for how he internalized Scripture himself. Dedicated scholars have examined the sixteen copies of the King James Version that Lincoln owned or can be documented to have read.[85] They have examined the hymns, Bible reading, and preaching of his youth.[86] They have gone well beyond the explicit references in the nine-volume *Collected Works of Abraham Lincoln* to demonstrate the pervasive presence in his speaking and writing of quotation, allusion, and parallels to the King James Bible.[87] They know he had at least some awareness of Protestant apologetics for the truth of Scripture.[88] They have highlighted the very few times when, at least for public notice, he seemed to speak more personally. The most notable of such occasions was when he thanked a contingent of Black Baltimore ministers who in September 1864 presented him with a pulpit Bible bound in violet-tinged velvet, furnished in gold, and with a raised design depicting an emancipated slave. "In regard to this Great Book,"

Lincoln responded, "I have but to say it is the best gift God has given to man." Then, in an almost unique reference to Jesus—"All the good the Saviour gave to the world was communicated through this book."[89]

Above all, the public has joined careful scholars in parsing time and again Lincoln's observation in his Second Inaugural Address, "Both read the same Bible, and pray to the same God; and each invokes His aid against the other."[90] Yet more striking than that mere statement of fact were indications in this speech of how Lincoln read the Bible. Unlike most public evocations of Scripture in the war years, Lincoln spoke with a degree of tentativeness: "It may seem strange that any men should dare ask a just God's assistance in wringing their bread from the sweat of other men's faces [Gen 3:19]." He downplayed partisanship: "but let us judge not that we be not judged [Matt 7:1]." Most importantly, with only a very few others, Lincoln used Scripture to define divine providence as inexplicable. He knew the Bible, and yet he did not use it to claim special understanding of God's judgment: "The Almighty has His own purposes. 'Woe unto the world because of offences! for it must needs be that offences come; but woe to that man by whom the offence cometh [Matt 18:7].'" Most memorably he recognized that God's sovereignty overruled all human control of events: "If God wills that [the scourge of war] continue, until all the wealth piled by the bond-man's two hundred and fifty years of unrequited toil shall be sunk, and until every drop of blood drawn with the lash, shall be paid by another drawn with the sword, as was said three thousand years ago, so still it must be said 'the judgments of the Lord, are true and righteous altogether [Ps 19:9].'"

About Lincoln and the Jews there is less complexity but more significance touching the general history of the Bible.[91] During Lincoln's lifetime the number of Jews in the United States increased dramatically, from less than 5,000 in 1809 to as many as 200,000 in 1865, but still at that latter date less than 1% of the nation's population. In most ways their participation in the war paralleled Christian patterns, as in disagreements concerning Scripture and slavery. Against Rabbi Morris Raphall's proslavery sermon of early 1861, Rabbi David Einhorn responded with a discourse on Exodus 17:16 ("God's is the war with Amalek from generation to generation"). Einhorn, calling himself a representative of Radical Reform Judaism, did not campaign aggressively for abolition, but he did identify slave owners with "Amalek . . . the arch foe of Israel, for he inflicted upon them the most unheard of cruelties." From that text, Einhorn defended "the necessity . . . of a war against the *Enslavement of Race*, which has brought the Republic to the verge of destruction."[92] During the war, Jews served in both armies; among prominent officials, Judah Benjamin became one of Jefferson Davis's most capable cabinet members. Jewish scripturalism made possible a particularly vehement expression of southern patriotism by Phoebe Yates Pember, a Richmond widow. At a gathering with Christian women, she rejoiced "at being born of a nation and a religion that did not enjoin forgiveness on its enemies, that enjoyed the blessed privilege of praying for an eye for an eye [Ex 21:24]." She therefore felt no qualms about setting aside "forgiveness and peace and good will" in order to trust wholeheartedly in "the sword of the Lord and Gideon [Judg 7:20]."[93]

Lincoln's relevance for American Jewish history came from his unusual rich connections with Jewish communities in Illinois and throughout the nation—according to Jonathan Sarna and Benjamin Shapell, at least 171 direct personal contacts. Over the course of his adult years the first of these occurred on February 22, 1843, when Lincoln heard a Washington's Birthday address in Springfield by Abraham Jonas, an English-born retailer, lawyer, Mason, ardent Whig (later Republican), and one of the founders of Congregation B'nai Abraham in Quincy, Illinois. The last came late on the evening of April 14, 1865, when Dr. Charles H. Liebermann, a Russian-born eye doctor and in that year president of the District of Columbia Medical Society, administered brandy as a stimulant to the unconscious president and joined other attending physicians in diagnosing his wound as mortal.[94]

Lincoln's friendship with Jonas extended until the latter's death in 1864. Less intimate but considerably more mysterious was his relationship with Issachar (or Isachar) Zacharie, an English-born chiropodist who tended to the president's corns and bunions in the White House but also served him as a private diplomat. In late 1862, Lincoln speedily reversed an order by General Ulysses S. Grant that banned all Jews from the Military Department of Tennessee for purported illegal speculation and smuggling. When a delegation including Rabbi Isaac Mayer Wise thanked Lincoln in person for this reversal, Wise quoted the president as saying that he knew "of no distinction between Jew and Gentile" and that he would not allow any citizen to be "wronged on account of his place of birth or religious confession."[95] In addition, Lincoln went out of his way to appoint Jews to military and civilian jobs. In an era when casual, but no less dismissive, anti-Semitism peppered the rhetoric of editors, generals, cabinet officers, and many members of the general public, the absence of such language in the obsessively documented record of Lincoln's spoken and written words testifies almost as loudly as the many records of his positive actions. In Jonathan Sarna's summary, "Lincoln dramatically improved the status of Jews in the United States."[96]

American Jews responded to Lincoln's friendship with a respect, gratitude, and emotional depth bordering on hagiography. Public expressions of affection began only hours after Lincoln died. The designated Sabbath reading for some Jewish communities on April 15, 1865, came from Ezekiel's vision of the Valley of the Dry Bones, which those who received the news of Lincoln's death turned into a lament for the fallen president. Lamentation continued through the week that followed, when, in a representative statement, a Republican activist

Lewis Naphtali Dembitz proclaimed to his Beth Israel Synagogue in Louisville that "of all the Israelites throughout the United States, there was none who more thoroughly filled the ideal of what a true descendant of Abraham ought to be than Abraham Lincoln." Writing soon after the national day of mourning on April 19, 1865, Isaac Wise noted that ministers on that occasion "all resorted to Old Testament texts, or compared Lincoln to Old Testament heroes like Moses, Joshua, Samuel and others."[97] An unnamed New Jersey Jew did protest when praises for Lincoln as a modern Abraham or even Moses resounded in synagogues: "Is there a Jew in this whole land, educated in the history and traditions of his people . . . who in a moment of calm reflection can find any comparison between the late President and their great law-giver 'whom the Lord knew face to face [Deut 34:10]'?" This complaint was noteworthy because it was so rare.[98]

It can only be speculation, but Lincoln's Jewish connections may have contributed to his own expression of a deeper theism and also his greater caution about evoking an explicitly Christian understanding of American civilization. Near the close of his first inaugural address on March 4, 1861, Lincoln repeated conventional themes about the divinely chosen, Christian character of the United States: "Intelligence, patriotism, Christianity, and a firm reliance on Him, who has never yet forsaken this favored land, are still competent to adjust, in the best way, all our present difficulty."[99] But by December 1861, as he was commending plans by the recently founded Christian Commission to distribute Bibles and promote Christian observance in the army, Lincoln also supported Jewish efforts to change the requirement for military chaplains from "Christian denomination" to "a religious denomination." A year later, in December 1862, when Lincoln issued an executive order urging military commanders to let troops whenever possible observe the Christian Sabbath (Sunday), Jewish editors like Isaac Leeser complained about the absence of an equivalent provision for those who honored the Hebrew Sabbath (Saturday). Although there is no record of Lincoln's response to these complaints, he may well have taken them to heart. In Jonathan Sarna's words, "One suspects . . . that the Jewish community's complaints reached Lincoln's ears. Significantly, he never again, in his official correspondence, referred to Americans as a 'Christian people.' "[100]

It is also noteworthy that Lincoln discouraged efforts by the National Reform Association to amend the Constitution with an acknowledgment of the nation's dependence on Jesus. Moreover, in the memorable words of the Gettysburg Address from November 1863 and the Second Inaugural Address of 1865, Lincoln movingly invoked "God" and "the Lord," but without direct reference to anything distinctly Christian. As it happens, the memorable opening of the Gettysburg Address, "Four score and seven years ago," repeated a phrase that Rabbi Sabato Morais of Mikveh Israel congregation in Philadelphia had used four months earlier in a sermon on the Fourth of July.[101] Whether Lincoln read and remembered Morais's published sermon or both drew independently from the phraseology of Psalm 90:10 ("the days of our years are three score years and ten"), the president's speech reflected a consciousness steeped in the Hebrew Scriptures.

Fairly reliable documentation attests that in March 1863 Lincoln told a visiting Jewish visionary, Henry Wentworth Monk, "I myself have a regard for the Jews."[102] If that "regard" extended beyond the political to the personal, it supports the suggestion that Lincoln's direct contact with Jews played a part in making him more seriously religious, but not exclusively Christian.

In more general terms, Lincoln's unusually close relationship with Jews of various kinds took place at a time of national crisis when public references to the Hebrew Scriptures multiplied. The increasing visibility of Jewish editors, publicists, and spokesmen who joined other Americans as they interpreted the conflict in religious terms contributed significantly to that surge. The relevant point is that the Hebrew Scriptures served as a well-traveled bridge between Lincoln and his Jewish friends and acquaintances. In turn, because that bridge was so public, a Hebrew frame of reference—drawn from the Old Testament and applied to the United States, its history, its woes, and its prospects—became more prominent. As it did so, the Jews also gained credibility as more obviously "American," and yet devoted to a Scripture that was not the King James Version.

From Biblical Monogenesis to Scientific Polygenesis

The Civil War further redirected the history of Scripture by how it opened space for alternative conceptions of race and the unity of humankind. Traditional regard for the Bible's authority had tied antebellum disputes on these subjects into knots. All but the most radical abolitionists and a few American ethnologists like Josiah Nott and George Gliddon consistently affirmed their trust in the Bible. But as we have seen, maintaining that loyalty entailed a constant struggle between the Bible's clear affirmation of monogenesis (all humanity was one) and Scripture's toleration of slavery. In the colonial context, racism had entered the picture when, in Colin Kidd's words, "colour [became] the central justification of the American slavery system."[103] Biblical proslavery interpretations in the antebellum era maintained monogenesis; anti-abolitionists appealed to Scripture even as they took for granted the (nonscriptural) racial inferiority of Africans. As we have seen, this proslavery position had weaknesses that are much more obvious now than they were then—specifically, reliance on "the curse of Canaan" from Genesis chapter 9 and (extrabiblical) interpretations of providence as justification for treating Africans as the only ones fit for enslavement. Proslavery racism was kept partially at bay, however, by the commitment to biblical monogenism. Antebellum biblical abolition also affirmed monogenesis. But because most white abolitionists held back from affirming full racial equality and because they also relied confidently on their own interpretations of providence, they only occasionally attacked the racism upholding slavery. Most of their biblical argumentation relied instead on alternative proof-texts, like the prohibitions against man-stealing, or appealed to broader scriptural teachings like the Golden Rule that did not address race directly. The resultant standoff endured throughout the Civil War years and beyond.

Because that standoff dominated the field of biblical reflections on slavery and race—and because it seemed to exhaust what Scripture might teach about these subjects—alternative accounts took advantage of the opening. In particular, as Kidd explains, "the intellectual respectability of racism in the nineteenth and twentieth century depended crucially upon the gradual withdrawal of scriptural claims to police the legitimacy of philosophical and scientific ideas, a process inaugurated during the Enlightenment."[104] In the United States fierce antebellum controversy strengthened that process significantly.

In later decades, enhanced confidence in "science" led to two developments important for the history of the Bible. Later chapters will examine these complications: first, a rising belief in evolution that challenged traditional biblical interpretations; second, a backlash against modern science and learned biblical scholarship that strengthened racism when some populists resuscitated "the curse of Canaan." For these postbellum intellectual disputes, the Civil War years were important for advancing the theories of polygenism and racial hierarchy earlier publicized by the Comte de Gobineau and the American ethnologists.

For that advance the Swiss-born translator of Gobineau's work, Henry Hotze, again played a key role. After his translation effort, Hotze continued to move in elite southern circles until the Confederate secretary of war dispatched him to purchase arms and fund southern agents in Europe. Based on that experience, Hotze convinced Confederate officials to appoint him as the South's "commercial agent" in Britain and then to assist him in publishing a weekly newspaper aimed at influencing European opinion and securing British recognition of the Confederacy. While Hotze's London paper, the *Index*, which lasted from May 1862 to August 1865, did generate some sympathy for the South, its pages also revealed a shift with respect to Scripture. That shift has been well described by Robert Bonner: "Both Hotze's private dispatches and his public statements indicate a conscious move from an earlier emphasis on the white South's Christian piety and martial heroism to a consideration of how its defining system of slavery exemplified the scientific principles of racial anthropology."[105]

In mid-1863 Hotze was still emphasizing Christian piety when he published a major statement of southern propaganda, "Address to Christians throughout the World by the Clergy of the Confederate States of America."[106] Proprietary Protestants, mostly Presbyterians, predominated among the ninety-seven ministers who subscribed to the document, but with a substantial minority of twenty-four Baptists and several Methodists. Much of the "Address" focused on current events, for example, by denouncing the Emancipation Proclamation. The statement's positive argument rested on the claim that "the relation of master and slave among us, however we may deplore abuses in this, as in other relations of mankind, is not incompatible with our holy Christianity." Although the "Address" spoke mostly about providence in creating American slavery, it also dwelled on one passage from the white South's well-filled storehouse of apposite scriptures, 1 Timothy 6:1–5 ("Let as many servants as are under the yoke count their own masters worthy of all honour").

In keeping with his stated policy of editorial balance, Hotze also published a rejoinder by one thousand Scottish ministers to the Confederate "Address." Its authors had nothing but scorn for the document, denouncing the "apologists for slavery, attempting to shelter themselves and it under the authority of God's word and the Gospel of Jesus Christ."[107] In the same issue, however, Hotze offered his own rejoinder to this rejoinder. His apology for the southerners' "Address" acknowledged that "abuses" marred the American slave system. But he still turned to Scripture with the claim that Confederates would "deem [it] a fearful sacrilege of God's Word to justify such crimes." Yet even as he made this biblical reference, Hotze also insisted that Africans—as "a whole race, instead of individuals only"—were fit subjects for this lifelong "tutelage."[108] To the Scottish Christians he spoke as a Confederate Christian so that by this means he might win over at least some to the principle of permanent racial differentiation.

By the end of the same year, however, Hotze had shifted his defense of racial hierarchy from Christianity to science. The publication of a lecture titled "The Negro's Place in Nature" by the physician James Hunt marked this transition.[109] Hunt was the leading figure in London's Anthropological Society and editor of its journal, the *Anthropological Review*, both founded only after the promulgation of Lincoln's Emancipation Proclamation. This new organization arose out of a schism in the Ethnological Society of London, which itself had been created in the 1840s as an offshoot of the Aborigines Protection Society, a body founded by Quakers and Anglican Evangelicals to mobilize concern for the natives of India and Africa who suffered under the British imperial juggernaut.[110] Although some members of the Ethnological Society promoted polygenesis, most were monogenists who explained human difference as a result of climate, education, or what would later be called culture. Charles Darwin, a prominent member of the Ethnological Society, was distinguished from most of his fellow members by explaining monogenesis as a result of natural evolutionary processes instead of direct divine creation. Hunt's new society, in opposition, became the era's leading champion of polygenesis.

As Hotze explained in a communication to the Confederate secretary of state, "a new scientific society . . . had been formed in London" with the express intention of "exposing the heresies that have gained currency in science and politics, of the equality of the races of men." According to Hotze, Hunt recruited him for the new society with an explicit reference to racial hierarchy; quoting Hunt: "for in us [the Ethnological Society] is your only hope that the negro's place in nature will ever be scientifically ascertained, and fearlessly explained."[111] Although Hotze did not entirely give up appealing to religion when he joined Hunt's new society, from that time he relied ever more consistently on an adamantine deep structure of scientific racism. According to Hotze, scientific ethnologists were presenting "truly philosophic" arguments that could not "fail to command the critical attention of the scientific world." Their "earnest, single desire to discover the truth" demonstrated that the same "marvelous progress of physical science since the days of Bacon" would now be replicated "with respect to moral and social science." Grounded firmly on that scientific basis, Hotze's conclusions proceeded categorically:

"[T]he brain of the negro is of smaller capacity."
"[T]he negro has no history,"
"[T]he negro is indubitably inferior in intellect."
And with Africa in view, "it is utterly impossible to exaggerate the savage barbarity and the utter degradation of the negro at home."

Hotze, the paid propagandist, then put science to work by asserting that "the best condition of life in which the negro has until now been placed is that in which he is found in the Confederate States." But also, as an intimation for what his stance would become once the military tide turned, he conceded that "perpetual slavery" might not be the only destiny for "the negro," but "surely . . . the guidance and the intellect and the will of the white man are indispensable to him."[112]

Throughout his editorship of the *Index*, Hotze defended ineradicable racial difference with many arguments, including religious arguments. Yet after the collapse of the southern war effort, Hotze could only bewail the misguided actions of individuals motivated by religion. In the *Index*'s next-to-last issue, he heaped scorn on "philanthropic . . . apostles of freedom and equality, who in the presence of Federal officers preach to the negroes in churches and schools that they are the superior race, that God created man black, but that Cain, his face blanched by fear and his hair straightened by his rapid flight from the wrath of the Almighty, is the father of the white man."[113] Although a few references to

Providence remained in Hotze's correspondence, appeals to Scripture faded almost completely away in the last years of the *Index*.

Henry Hotze's career as a Confederate publicist indicated how the American stalemate on the Bible and slavery eased the way for the promotion of scientific polygenism. When translating Gobineau's *Essai*, Hotze had taken care not to disparage the Bible. Although that strategy continued during the first part of his London career, when scientific racism became available, the science almost immediately replaced the Scriptures. Hotze, who never returned to the United States after the Confederate defeat, was only a minor player in the great events of his day. But on questions concerning race, his move from worrying about the Bible to deferring to science became a straw in the wind.

During the years of the Civil War the engine of Anglo-Scottish-American Protestantism that had made Scripture so central to American public life ran out of steam. By no means did it vanish; by no means did it entirely lose its capacity to influence later developments. But after the early 1860s the history of the Bible became a much more contested and a much more genuinely pluralistic story. The war witnessed a deeper turn to Scripture for personal devotion *and* more instrumental subservience to partisan interests *and* a retreat from serious biblical attention to pressing social problems. For the kind of Protestants who had dominated the story to that point, erosion of the informal establishment of the King James Version posed numerous difficult challenges. Non-Protestants who favored other scriptures, who practiced other ways of honoring Scripture, or who wanted nothing to do with Scripture encouraged that erosion, but with very different proposals for an alternative. The Bible civilization that Protestants in the early republic had striven to create was no more, though attempts to revive it have never stopped. Questions about what might replace Scripture as a moral compass for the sprawling democratic republic have likewise never gone away.

PART V

AFTER THE BIBLE CIVILIZATION

Attended church and did not listen much to the sermon. The feeling is growing upon me that preaching of the ordinary sort is rapidly losing its power over the minds of men. . . . [T]he religion of Jesus like all religions is divided into three parts: its worship; its aspirations; and its theology. In its aspirations to take hold of the sentiments and the everlasting principles of morality and wickedness it is eternal and unchangeable, but in its form of worship and its intellectual doctrines and theology, it is perishable and must pass away. It is clear to my mind, that the theological and formal part of Christianity has in great measure lost its power over the minds of men. But the life and Christianity of Christ are to me as precious and perfect as ever.

—*The Diary of James A. Garfield*, ed. Harry James Brown
and Frederick D. Williams, vol. 2 (1872–1874)
(East Lansing: Michigan State University Press, 1967),
248, Sunday, November 3, 1873.

These attributes surely described the [evangelical] sermon that Dr. T. W. Henderson delivered at the 1896 North Georgia Annual [AME] Conference at Cedartown. . . . Henderson announced his text, Psalm 34:8, "Taste and see that the Lord is good." During this "happy hour," according to the conference scribe, "the sermon came red-hot from the speaker's heart, rich in illustrations and seasoned with scriptural promises for the heart of man. He came sinner-hunting, and before he closed thirty-two fell at the altar begging for mercy. Each of them enrolled their names with a promise to meet us on high when the general roll is called."

—Dennis C. Dickerson, *African Methodism
and Its Wesleyan Heritage: Reflections on AME Church History*
(Nashville, TN: By the author, 2009), 116.

22

1865–1875

As recently as 1994, a distinguished historian concluded about the Reconstruction era, "There were no really significant developments in American religion."[1] John Hope Franklin made a great contribution to reinterpreting American history, but not with this inadequate statement. In fact, when considering the Civil War and Reconstruction as a single historical era, it would be more accurate to say that between the firing on Fort Sumter in April 1861 and the inauguration of President Rutherford B. Hayes in March 1877, almost everything about religion changed.[2] For the Bible, the war and North-South controversy signaled the end of a civilization premised on white Protestant scriptural agreement. If the decline of the nation's Bible civilization was not the same as the decline of the Bible in America, it did occasion a host of new relationships involving Scripture and the nation's cities, citizens, industries, learning, racial divides, laws, political configurations, and expressions of civil religion.

These shifting relationships precipitated a second restructuring of American Protestant history. The first had come with the Revolutionary era's rejection of Christendom, the announcement of religious liberty, the separation of church and state, the reliance on voluntarism, and the successful Christianization of the population through democratic means. Unlike that first transition, from colonial Christendom to republican post-Christendom, the second exerted less of an impact on the nation as a whole. With the expansion of Catholic, Jewish, Mormon, and other non-Protestant populations, Protestant developments no longer dominated as they once had done. Moreover, the ongoing effect of antebellum disputes and then the ecclesiastical fallout of the Civil War irrevocably divided a white Protestantism already prone to sharp internal disagreements. If the Bible retained a considerable public presence through generations after 1865, the displacement of Protestant Scripture from its once central position had well and truly begun.

For the nation, the decline of the Protestants' Bible civilization opened welcome space for other religious groups, and for the nonreligious, to take full advantage of the promise of *liberty* and *justice for all*. Protestants not of British origin, Roman Catholics, Jews, Eastern Orthodox, freethinking secularists, the religiously indifferent, and a host of smaller religious bodies all came to enjoy more practical freedom. The complicated maneuvers by which the Mormons abandoned their earlier practice of plural marriage as the price for the liberty to

America's Book. Mark A. Noll, Oxford University Press. © Oxford University Press 2022.
DOI: 10.1093/oso/9780197623466.003.0023

sustain a Latter-day Saints regime in Utah was only one illustration of the space that non-Protestants could win.[3]

Diversity, however, came at a cost. *Liberty for all* raised one set of questions, *justice for all* something else quite different. The multiform but powerful shared conviction that the Bible revealed God's absolute moral standards for personal faith, corporate religious organization, and proper social order lay shattered amid the intellectual debris of debates over slavery and the material rubble created by two great armies both convinced that God was on their side. In Allen Guelzo's apt phrases, "For every Northern divine claiming God's favor for the Union, and every Southern one claiming God's favor for the Confederacy, there were far more who could not make up their minds what to say about slavery. . . . Taken together, they created a popular perception that religion had nothing reliable or coherent to say about the greatest American issue of the nineteenth century." Whether a reliable and coherent religious authority could have made a difference must remain speculative. As the nation's history actually unfolded, the widespread reverence for Scripture that did remain was now fragmented by new fractures as well as the older divisions among denominations, over conflicting interpretations, and between sectarian and proprietary factions. In such a situation the simple fact of loyalty to the Bible by itself provided little to address the nation's most pressing postbellum challenges. No comprehensive biblical authority engaged the terrorism propelling the retreat from Reconstruction, the indifference in almost all white communities to the rise of Jim Crow, or the plight of workers in the American Industrial Revolution that motivated only a few. Guelzo explains the result: "In exposing the shortcomings of religious absolutism, the Civil War made it impossible for religious absolutism to address problems in American life—especially economic and racial ones—where religious absolutism would in fact have done a very large measure of good."[4]

This chapter and the next describe some of the important developments in the nation's postwar history where Scripture remained central and more where its influence declined. The three chapters that follow concentrate on the nation's major religious communities among whom questions concerning divine revelation generated tremendous interest but almost no consensus. Going forward, the Bible that millions of individuals, countless families, and many religious organizations still regarded as a life-giving center of their world would not shape the nation decisively or guide it in any one particular direction. Gone were the days when Bible belief had structured the Puritan colonies of New England or flickered as a beacon in early U.S. history. The challenge is to explain how and why the Bible remained an important part of American life even as the Bible civilization faded away.

Reconstruction

For the Bible as for general religious history, the impact of Reconstruction differed dramatically depending on location.[5] Physical location divided northern and southern white Protestants; denominational location differentiated Protestants among themselves and from Catholics; social location separated Blacks and whites. Antebellum biblical themes remained foundational for African Americans, even as the emergence of strong self-directed churches allowed for new platforms to proclaim those themes and new sophistication in biblical learning. Southern white Protestants clung to the Bible as to pieces of wreckage after a disaster at sea. Northern white Protestants suffered from internal fissures and a degree of moral exhaustion as they sought to exploit the fruits of victory. Because armies rather than biblical arguments had preserved the Union and ended slavery, Scripture could not do much to bind up the wounds of war.

For many Americans, providential reasoning embedded in scriptural consciousness did remain instinctive. Yet as Edward Blum has shown, Emancipation and Reconstruction disoriented widespread antebellum certainties "about God's designs for the nation." The traumas of war "shattered the old America," even as it left many citizens still convinced that God cared especially for the United States. After 1865, as "all types of Americans recast their faiths," ambiguity, flexibility, disappointment, celebration, disillusionment, novel prophetic interventions, reinterpretations of Scripture, and doubts about Scripture led to a much more diverse understanding of Providence.[6] That fragmentation explains why one interpretation of God's dealing shaped southern white resistance to Republican Reconstruction, another led northern white abolitionists to prioritize national reconciliation over Black liberation, still another caused Black Americans to anticipate the promised fruits of liberty, and yet one more turned some biblical premillennialists away from social activism to passive preoccupation with the future.

Behind both public uses of Scripture and efforts to discern the ways of Providence lay postbellum political realities. Southern white Protestants became even more uniformly Democratic. Africans Americans were as uniformly Republican. As the allegiance of northern white Protestants strengthened for the Republican Party, so did the allegiance of Catholics throughout the country strengthen for the Democrats. These sharp political divides guaranteed that the religious nation would divide against itself after every national election as believers offered contradictory assessments of how God was dealing with the United States of America.

Black Americans

The most obvious religious change of Reconstruction was the spectacular growth of self-guided African American churches.[7] Before the Civil War, Black church adherents in the North were found in the larger white-guided denominations as well as in Black ecclesiastical bodies, with Richard Allen's African Methodist Episcopal Church (AME) the most widely spread. Other Methodist groups like the African Methodist Episcopal Zion Church (AMEZ) had also emerged, along with still smaller Black Presbyterian and Black Baptist organizations. In the antebellum South informal Christianity had often flourished under enslaved and free leaders, but with only a few exceptions, like "the African Church" in Charleston, South Carolina, formal church adherence meant participation in local white churches and white denominations.

After Emancipation, southern African Americans, aided by missionaries from Black and white northern denominations, recast their ecclesiastical allegiance. Almost immediately, Baptists organized new regional associations for themselves, like the Zion Baptist Association that in July 1865 drew together twenty-six churches from South Carolina, Georgia, and Florida.[8] Similar state and regional associations soon enrolled most of the swelling numbers that made Baptist churches the most prevalent choice for freed people. Methodist expansion, which began even before the war ended, took a little longer to sort out. Daniel Stowell has shown that the Methodist Episcopal Church South retained some Black members into the early 1870s. But by the end of Reconstruction in 1877, that number shrank close to zero while the number of African Americans in other Methodist denominations rose dramatically. In Georgia, for example, the thirty thousand or so Black members of the Methodist Episcopal Church South in 1860 had become by 1872 about eighty thousand Methodists, but almost all in other denominations—about half in the AME and the other half divided among the AMEZ, the new Colored Methodist Church that remained closer to the Methodist Episcopal Church South, and newly formed congregations of the northern Methodist Episcopal Church.[9] When in 1864 the Rev. James Walker Hood left his AMEZ pulpit in Connecticut to follow the victorious Union armies into North Carolina, he was the state's only member of his denomination. Less than a decade later the AMEZ numbered some twenty thousand members in 366 local congregations.[10]

For Reconstruction, ecclesiastical history played a crucial role. In the words of Leon Litwack, "the black church" became "the central and unifying institution in the postwar black community." In the judgment of Eric Foner, "the creation of an independent black religious life" was "a momentous and irreversible consequence of emancipation."[11] Other scholars have shown in much greater detail how the AME of Reconstruction promoted both bourgeois respectability and self-assertive Black pride, but also how the new flourishing of Black churches allowed more space for African survivals, new contacts with African church bodies, and increased interest in Black nationalism.[12] In the Mississippi delta, a thick network of church connections—augmented by participation in fraternal orders, commercial associations, and creative arrangements with the railroads—helped blunt the force of white racism.[13] In New Orleans the Catholic Church's unusual triracialism (Blacks, whites, Creoles) flourished during Reconstruction and even held off the imposition of biracial segregation for several decades until in the 1890s Catholics gave way to the Jim Crow discrimination that had over-taken the city's Protestants years earlier.[14] Throughout the South and into the North, the explosion of self-guided church life created a diversity of African American expressions that foreshadowed twentieth-century developments while giving the lie to notions about a single "Black church."[15]

Postbellum Black engagement with Scripture grew organically from what had gone before. The Bible remained a golden treasury of narratives detailing the mi-raculous unfolding of God's egalitarian redemptive purposes. Michael Harper has listed the stories that "mattered" as Flood, Jubilee, Exodus, Exile, Crucifixion, Resurrection, Pentecost. In continuing the hermeneutical practices of the ante-bellum years, "African American believers saw these stories as ongoing, living stories likely to be replayed in nineteenth-century America."[16]

White America paid attention to the African American Bible, but only when it was sung. Although authorship, development, and distribution of "Negro spirituals" lay beyond historical recovery, by midcentury they had become an an-chor of African American religion.[17] Where the Christianization of the nation's white communities had led to intensified Bible study, Christianization for the enslaved meant singing about Adam, Eve, and the Fall, about "wrestlin' Jacob" who "would not let [God] go," about Moses and the Exodus from Egypt, about Daniel in the lions' den, about Jonah in the belly of the fish, about the birth of Jesus and his death and future return. White soldiers and relief workers with Union armies began serious collecting of these songs after they heard them on the South Carolina Sea Islands and then in other southern locations. When the first major collection appeared in 1867 under the title *Slave Songs of the United States*, the book's editors stated the obvious: "The words are, of course, in a large measure taken from Scripture, and from the hymns heard at church."[18] Not as obvious was the alternative that the spirituals' offered to the biblicism of white America.

Although the 136 selections in the 1867 *Slave Songs* included a few with themes of work or romance, the overwhelming majority reflected a biblical frame of reference. The first song in the collection, "Roll, Jordan, Roll," set the tone. A procession of rich scriptural evocation followed:

(2) "Jehovah, Hallelujah, de Lord is perwide" ("will provide," quoting Gen 22:14)

(3) "Hear from Heaven Today" ("my sin is forgiven and my soul set free")

(4) "Blow Your Trumpet Gabriel" (second verse: "Paul and Silas bound in jail / Sing God's praises both night and day")

(6) "Wrestle on, Jacob"

(7) "The Lonesome Valley" ("Go down in de lonesome valley; / To meet my Jesus dere")

(10) "The Trouble of the World" ("I cast my sins in de middle of der sea")

As in the sermons and publications of Alexander Campbell, William Miller, and Elias Smith, the songs came from consciousness fixated on "the Bible alone." But connotations and context made a great difference, as Lydia Maria Child discovered after interviewing a freed slave in the mid-1830s. This informant, Charity Bowery, told about her life in bondage, including the praying and singing that continued even after the Nat Turner rebellion frightened white owners into banning all such exercises. When Child asked to hear one of the songs, Bowery recited:

> A few more beatings of the wind and rain,
> Ere the winter will be over—
> Glory, Hallelujah!
> Some friends has gone before me,—
> I must try to go and meet them—
> Glory, Hallelujah!
> A few more risings and settings of the sun,
> Ere the winter will be over—
> Glory, Hallelujah!
> There's a better day a coming—
> There's a better day a coming—
> Oh, Glory, Hallelujah!

But then she reported, "They wouldn't let us sing that. They thought we was going to rise, because we sung 'better days are coming.'"[19]

More than just a troubled conscience led white slave owners to take that step. While the spirituals did feature the kind of intense personal piety that Richard Allen found so appealing in Methodism, the resonance when *slaves* sang about freedom in Christ carried an unmistakable political undertone. One of the songs that the Fisk Jubilee Singers of Nashville's Fisk University added to their repertoire in the early 1870s carried the same implication. "The Gospel Train (Get on

Board)" included the lines "Behold your station there / Jesus has paid your fare / Let's all engage in prayer."[20] The song did unmistakably call for listeners to pray, but just as unmistakably audiences could imagine that some of the singers or their parents or older friends had once boarded an underground train headed out of bondage.[21]

The ensemble of talented musicians from Fisk University, along with the Hampton Singers of Hampton Normal and Agricultural Institute in Virginia, had been encouraged in their efforts by the American Missionary Association (AMA), the agency that established both schools after the war.[22] James W. C. Pennington and other Black ministers had founded the AMA as an abolitionist alternative to the American Board of Commissioners for Foreign Missions, though the association soon came to be controlled by Lewis Tappan and other white philanthropists who wanted to preserve the combination of antislavery and evangelistic emphases that the ABCFM from the right and Garrisonian radicals on the left did not sustain. When white music teachers at Fisk and Hampton recruited gifted Black students to sing, arrange the music, and accompany the singers, the AMA supported their tours as a way of raising funds for the institutions, but also to advance its core evangelistic goals. Concerts by both groups drew rapturous audiences in the northern United States and for the Jubilee Singers also in the United Kingdom. Well-known figures like the evangelistic team of D. L. Moody and Ira Sankey, the renowned Baptist preacher Charles Haddon Spurgeon in London, and many others joined a chorus of grateful thanksgiving for the singers' work. The successful tours came to an end in the late 1870s due to internal conflicts as well as the nation's declining seriousness about enforcing the Fourteenth (equal protection for all) and Fifteenth (franchise for all male citizens) Amendments.

As these popular singing groups stopped touring and study of the spirituals was left to only a handful of Black researchers, few in the majority culture paused to consider the spirituals' challenge to conventional hermeneutics. By drawing so single-mindedly on Scripture, the spirituals fit securely within central American traditions that understood the Bible as unique divine revelation. But they departed from those traditions when they answered the question: How do humans grasp divine revelation and then act? As a homegrown exercise in precritical biblical interpretation, the spirituals exemplified approaches much closer to Jesuit mimesis or modern Pentecostalism than any nineteenth-century Protestant alternative.[23] The spirituals, that is, proceeded story-by-story instead of verse-by-verse. They featured not exegesis but imagination, not commonsense Baconianism or progressive "history" but internalization and enactment. They did not embrace politics directly or shun it piously but remained cryptically political. They prized not critical objectivity but existential immediacy. They did look to Scripture for guidance, but even more for liberation. Again, these powerful but little-noted alternatives to standard approaches did not generate much attention, but they did survive as a crucial part of the Bible nation.[24]

In the Nation

For reasons concerning the trauma of conflict, rapid postwar social change, and proliferating competition from more secular media, public recourse to Scripture noticeably faded after the war. Lewis Saum's study of the nation's postbellum "popular mood" found less ready quotation of the Bible than his earlier volume found from before.[25] In this period the names that Americans gave their cities, organizations, and children were also not as likely to be taken from the Bible. The main denominations' inability to agree on biblical teaching regarding slavery before the war seems to have warned their adherents away from trying to find specific biblical teaching for most public issues after the war. That tendency was supported by even stronger adherence to "the spirituality of the church," which became official doctrine among the South's white churches and unofficial practice in much of the North.[26] To be sure, Scripture remained central to internal church affairs, and it was never absent in a variety of activities reaching out beyond church doors. Yet those interventions generally relied less explicitly on scriptural argument than earlier disputes about the legitimacy of slavery.

Biblically themed preaching did continue to sustain the era's evangelistic efforts. Such preaching could also spark revival in many places both North and South. The increasingly popular urban evangelism of D. L. Moody, supported by his popular song leader Ira Sankey, also exploited biblical themes, but oriented mostly toward personal peace with God (see chapter 25).

Organized philanthropic activity did continue to elevate the Scriptures. Beth Barton Schweiger has shown that as comprehensive efforts for public education stalled in Virginia, white ministers took the lead in promoting Sunday schools for white children as their "longest-lived project of postwar educational charity." These schools featured the Bible, often with standard lessons provided by the American Sunday School Union, but in the context of broader instruction in reading, writing, and other skills of basic literacy.[27] Other educational efforts in Reconstruction also included Bible reading as a key component. Among the many Black and white northerners who hoped to educate freed slaves was Mrs. Samantha J. Neil, who soon after the end of the war set up a school under an oak tree for newly liberated African Americans in Amelia Court House, Virginia.[28] A few white southerners also joined in similar efforts, like Samuel C. Alexander and Willis L. Miller, who in 1867 founded a college for freed people in Charlotte, North Carolina, that would be known as the Biddle Institute and then Johnson

C. Smith University. (Alexander and Willis began their ministries as pastors in the southern Presbyterian church but transferred their membership to the northern church about the time they began this work.)[29] Frances E. W. Harper, a Black poet, active member of the American Anti-Slavery Society, and later a key organizer for the Colored Section of the Pennsylvania Women's Christian Temperance Movement, memorialized such efforts in her poem "Learning to Read":

> Very soon the Yankee teachers
> Came down and set up school;
> But, oh! how the Rebs did hate it,—it was agin' their rule. . . .
> And I longed to read my Bible, For precious words it said;
> But when I begun to learn it,
> Folks just shook their heads. . . .
> So I got a pair of glasses, And straight to work I went,
> And never stopped till I could read
> The hymns and Testament.[30]

With one exception, white Protestant uses of Scripture mostly followed earlier patterns. The Bible most obviously remained an open treasure of sanctified terms and pointed exemplars to illuminate public events. As an instance, when Henry Ward Beecher shifted his public advocacy from African American liberation to reconciliation between the white North and the white South, he was called "Judas Iscariot" by a writer from Washington, D.C., who had kept the abolitionist faith.[31] From a very different angle, a contributor to the *Southern Review* in 1876 could find no description for the plans of Radical Republicans except to recall Lucifer's revolt in heaven against God.[32]

Ministers also found it nearly as easy as before to discover in otherwise obscure texts a word for the times from the Lord. The Rev. T. E. Bliss, pastor of a Memphis church serving newcomers from the North, followed this ancient pattern on Sunday, May 6, 1866. The week before, rioters, alarmed by the continuing presence of Black Union troops, had murdered several African Americans and destroyed much Black-owned property. Bliss preached on Jeremiah 5:29, "Shall I not visit for these things? saith the Lord: shall not my soul be avenged on such a nation as this?" In his sermon Bliss pledged that efforts to educate the freed people would not be deterred.[33]

A biblical mentality certainly continued to inform readings of providence, though with even less connection than before between specific biblical reasoning and God's-eye efforts at explaining current history. In the summer of 1865 Horace Bushnell, a respected minister in Hartford, Connecticut, told the graduating class of Yale College that the national unity restored by victorious Union armies "will no more be thought of as a mere human compact . . . but it will be that bond of common life which God has touched with blood; a sacredly heroic, Providentially tragic unity, where God's cherubim stand guard over grudges and hates and remembered jealousies, and the sense of nationality becomes even a kind of religion."[34] From his pulpit in New Orleans, one of the South's leading Presbyterians, Benjamin Morgan Palmer, naturally read providential direction very differently. Instead of Bushnell's celebration, Palmer developed an elaborate philosophy of history in which centuries were sometimes necessary to discern the true character of individual developments. Even if it took many years, "a sublime Providence raises up the advocates" of the God-given instinct for justice, and they will set the record straight. Where now "an impudent partisanship manipulates the facts," in "the solemn decision of that great Tribunal [of final adjudication], the good and the brave will find an honest vindication."[35] Where for Bushnell the present state of American affairs revealed God's judgment, Palmer believed that it would take a very long time before God's approval of the South's "good and brave" was recognized.

A Disturbing Interpretive Innovation

For white Protestants, the one innovation in biblical interpretation during the immediate postbellum years reflected the racist heritage represented by the American ethnologists Josiah Nott, George Gliddon, and Henry Hotze. After southern whites suffered the trauma of defeat and with the Thirteenth Amendment overthrowing their entire way of life, the long-standing fear of Black-on-white sex metastasized. (Passing over the longer-standing reality of white-on-Black sex underscored the primal insanity of this postbellum white fear.) That fear, however, not only propelled the lawlessness of lynching, described by Donald Mathews as "the white terror [that] ravaged the American South between 1865 and 1940."[36] It also occasioned creative intellectual justifications for strict racial difference, permanent subjugation of Blacks, and absolute ethnic purity.

The creative innovation in interpretation was *biblical polygenesis*, or the contention that Scripture itself regarded Black-skinned people as a species separate from the white-skinned. This innovation showed how flexibly anti-Black racism could operate as a foundation for different readings from the Bible as well as for reasoning dispensing with Scripture. It represented an effort to jam the conclusions of the ethnologists into a biblical frame.[37]

A bold new interpretation of early Genesis by a Nashville minister became in 1867 the cause célèbre propelling the new reading. "Ariel," the pen name of Buckner H. Payne, answered the question of his title *The Negro: What Is His*

Ethnological Status? by claiming that Blacks were created with the other "beasts" before the creation of Adam and Eve (he was affirming *pre-Adamic* polygenesis). In addition, Ariel held that the major disasters recorded in the Old Testament arose from miscegenation, the union of white humans with black beasts.

The next year a Georgia minister, D. G. Philips, added novel exegetical support for Ariel's general picture. With supreme self-confidence, Philips corrected the generations that in his view had misread the biblical record. First, when it is recorded in Genesis 1:26–27 that God created "man in our/his own image," the English "man" translated the Hebrew "Adam," which "means a red man, or as we now use the color—a *white man.*" Consequently, all of Noah's offspring were white, and none ever served as slaves. Third, *nachash*, the word usually translated as "the serpent" in Genesis 3, should properly be rendered as "negro," which means that God's "curse on the serpent" entailed the "low, crouching, menial, abject slavery of the negro.... The Bible teaches it; facts teach it; all history teaches it."[38] The same year, 1868, an anonymous author, "M.S.," published in New York City a study that reclaimed Blacks as humans but repeated Ariel's assertion that God made Black-skinned people in a separate pre-Adamic act of creation.[39] A few years later the Philadelphia firm of J. B. Lippincott, a major publisher of family bibles, brought out a book by A. Hoyle Lester that reaffirmed polygenesis, but this time with five separate creations (Blacks the lowest, then Malays, American Indians, Chinese, and finally Caucasians as highest). The wrinkles Lester added to the creation story included the claim that "the serpent" was really a Mongolian and that Eve's original sin was sexual intercourse with this "serpent."[40] Variations on these arguments continued to be published into the twentieth century, as in two works by Professor Charles Carroll, who described himself as "an enthusiastic believer in, and ardent student of the Bible" and whose works advanced a paired thesis: "the Bible is the Word of God" and "the negro is an ape."[41]

The parade of works from Ariel to Carroll resembled the earlier ethnology of the Comte de Gobineau. They postured a deference to Scripture while dwelling mostly on geographical, anthropological, cranial, and cultural "proofs" for Black inferiority drawn from the surging school of scientific racism. "The basic thrust of the scheme," in David Livingstone's conclusion, could not be misunderstood: "to bestialize the African and to provide warrant for a fixation with blood purity."[42]

The broader context for works in the Ariel vein is important from two contrasting perspectives. On the one hand, it shows the increasing credibility of the scientific racism that Colin Kidd, George Fredrickson, and others have documented as gaining scholarly traction in the latter decades of the nineteenth century.[43] Such racism also took other forms besides the polygenesis that regarded Blacks as subhuman. It reinforced German anti-Semitism as well as American attitudes toward Indians and eastern European immigrants as genetically inferior. Evolutionary eugenics was different in positing a unified human species, but similar in treating non-Caucasians as representing lower stages of evolutionary development.[44] Those who defended biblical polygenesis, including a view of Blacks as a separate species created before Adam and Eve, were obviously bending to the increasing prestige of these purportedly scientific views. Just as obviously, ethnologists were developing their "science" without much concern for biblical revelation.

In the American context advocates of biblical polygenesis also exerted an ironic influence on those who still did honor biblical teaching. Before the war fewer and fewer respectable biblical expositors were enlisting "the curse of Canaan" from Genesis 9:25–27 as a justification for Black slavery. We have seen that Robert Lewis Dabney, as one learned example, dismissed the relevance of that passage even as he penned a robust defense of Black-only enslavement.[45] Yet after the war, the culture of interpretation shifted. As orthodox southern Protestants saw the rise of scientific racism that cared not at all about the Bible and polygenesists who, in their view, abused the Bible, they redoubled their defense of monogenesis (all humans coming from a single act of divine creation). Any treatment of Blacks as subhuman made a mockery of their efforts at Christianizing the slave system or their understanding of providence as bringing Africans to America where they could hear the gospel message. In response to these postwar challenges, opponents of polygenesis revived "the curse of Canaan" as an explanation for how a single humanity could be divided into permanent racial divisions.[46] A biblical interpretation that had been fading sprang quickly back to life. For some leaders, like Benjamin Morgan Palmer, the story of Noah and his sons took on added importance for explaining not only the inferiority of Blacks but also the superiority of white-skinned peoples as the descendants of Noah's son Shem.

Other southern apologists offered a creative new account of racial difference with an interpretation of the biblical history that followed Noah, the Flood, Ham, and Canaan. It was the Babel story from Genesis 11, when early humans planned to build "a tower, whose top may reach unto heaven" (Gen 11:4). In this interpretation, when God divided humans into various language groups, he condemned the indiscriminate mixing of people speaking a common tongue (or miscegenation) as well as the overweening power of centralized government. In a word, to meet the threat of nonbiblical polygenesis, southern white interpreters strengthened the link between general faithfulness to Scripture and specific biblical interpretations reinforcing racial difference (and opposing a strong federal government).

In these same postbellum years, as Luke Harlow has shown, southern white Protestants were also recapitulating the biblical defenses of slavery that had been heard so often in earlier decades.[47] Presbyterians in formal documents, prominent Methodist newspapers, and influential Baptist spokesmen acknowledged that the outcome of the war and the passage of the postwar constitutional amendments necessitated practical changes. But significant numbers continued to defend the case that Palmer made in 1870 as the author of an official explanation of "distinctive principles" from the southern Presbyterian church: those who condemned slavery as "always contrary to the Divine will" were "completely contradicted by the plainest facts and teachings of the Old Testament and New." Moreover, to assert the sinfulness of slaveholding was "a pernicious heresy, embracing a principle not only infidel and fanatical, but subversive of every relation of life, and every civil government of earth."[48]

Bizarre proposals advocating pre-Adamite polygenesis, responses by Bible believers to those proposals that heightened racial difference, and continued insistence on the Bible's justification of slavery exercised a decisive effect on the general history of the Bible. In particular, these postbellum developments strengthened the perceived link between traditional loyalty to Scripture and efforts to preserve strict racial separation. Robert Lewis Dabney's career exemplified that link. The war had turned this relatively flexible thinker, who had embraced secession only reluctantly, into a cantankerous theological naysayer and an ardent defender of the southern Lost Cause.[49] In his long postwar career at Union Seminary in Virginia and then at the University of Texas, Dabney repeatedly insisted on the strictest application of biblical inerrancy as his reason for opposing evolution, women's suffrage, new translations of the Bible, and public education. Preeminent in his concerns was always the overarching purpose of keeping African Americans in their place. Of many expressions of that purpose, one of the sharpest appeared in 1876, when he spoke out against proposals for state-funded schooling in Virginia that included Black children. If "negro schools" were successful, they would "only prepare the way for that abhorred fate, *amalgamation*." Virginians, therefore, should mobilize to prevent "the gradual but sure approach of this final disaster." The proponents of the plan, "the satanic artificers of our subjugation," had only one goal in mind: "to mingle that blood which flowed in the veins of our Washingtons, Lees, and Jacksons, and which consecrated the battle fields of the Confederacy, with this sordid alien taint."[50]

Careers like Dabney's reinforced affinities that had begun to take shape before the war. On one side stood allegiance to Scripture strictly followed, accompanied by tendencies toward the use of Scripture to support racism, but also toward literalism and biblicism in general.[51] The latter tendencies prepared for the popularity of a new theology, premillennial dispensationalism, based on innovative readings of the prophecies in the biblical books of Daniel and Revelation. On the other side stood a number of positions questioning traditional views of Scripture and exploring various ways of adjusting traditional biblical interpretations to more up-to-date sensibilities. These tendencies prepared the way for theological revisions that would look kindly on biblical higher criticism and the recasting of previous doctrinal certainties (see chapter 24).

Old Arguments, Renewed Reforms

The first postbellum decade also witnessed a notable standoff on the perennial question of Bible reading in public schools as well as a new era of reform advanced by proprietary Protestants. Both new sophistication in revising the old arguments and new zeal in proposing social reforms testified to the shifting contexts in which Scripture addressed the public.

Cincinnati (1869–1870)

The much-publicized "Cincinnati Bible War" of 1869–1870 focused national attention on the practice of daily readings from the King James Version that remained customary in many American schools.[52] After Bishop John Baptist Purcell's initial cooperation with Protestant educational reformers in the 1830s, he had turned to develop a robust alternative in Catholic parochial schools. By 1869 these schools were educating almost as many students as the city's tax-supported system. Heated debate on several proposals advanced during that summer and fall complicated an already contentious situation. One of the proposals suggested folding parochial schools into the public system. Bishop Purcell advanced a different plan to allow Catholic schools equal access to taxes collected for education. The prominence of Catholics in these discussions sparked renewed Protestant fears. It also led to a proposal before the city's school board to neutralize the religion question by ending Bible readings and other religious exercises. Outrage from some of the city's Protestants was led by a school board member who happened to be a conservative Unitarian, Amory D. Mayo. When on November 1 the board nonetheless passed a resolution banning the exercises (with all eleven Catholic members voting in favor), an ad hoc group of Protestants filed suit to block the resolution's implementation. Proceeding with remarkable dispatch, the Superior Court of Cincinnati held four days of arguments at the end of November to consider the suit. The three-judge panel included an Episcopalian, a Methodist, and a Unitarian, Alphonso Taft, father of the future president. Three distinguished attorneys spoke for the plaintiffs to overthrow the resolution, three for the Board to uphold it. A book of four hundred pages brought their arguments, as well as the court's decision, to the public soon after that decision was announced on February 1, 1870.

Lawyers for the plaintiffs stayed on well-worn paths. They cited the provision in the Northwest Ordinance of 1787 that provided for "schools and the means of education" to support the "Religion, Morality and knowledge" that was required for "good government and the happiness of mankind." They recalled the many state court decisions that upheld similar practices as well as the goals articulated by pioneers of the common schooling movement like Ohio's Calvin Stowe and Horace Mann in Massachusetts. Most of all they hammered on the school board's error in disregarding a key paragraph in Ohio's revised constitution of 1852 that echoed the Northwest Ordinance: "Religion, morality and knowledge . . . being essential to good government, it shall be the duty of the General Assembly to pass suitable laws, to protect every denomination in the peaceable enjoyment of its own mode of public worship and to *encourage schools and the means of instruction.*" To the plaintiff's attorneys, the civil purpose of this provision dominated their concerns: "Compliance with the teachings and requirements of the Christian religion is all that is necessary to make a perfect citizen. . . . The recognition of religion and God necessarily implies the recognition of the Holy Bible." Occasionally, the plaintiffs' attorneys also hinted at malevolent motives lying behind the board's action: "Infidelity always fights under a mask."[53]

Attorneys for the board mostly responded predictably. From the Ohio constitution, they stressed the "peaceable enjoyment" phrase. Many of their arguments followed the emerging trend of American jurisprudence in appealing to Thomas Jefferson, stipulating a constitutional standard of "no religious test," questioning the importance of Christianity for the common law ("I deny . . . that our modern European and American civilization can in any just sense be called Christian"), and labeling readings from the King James Bible manifestly sectarian, especially in a city where so many Catholics used a different translation.[54] One of the attorneys, a Unitarian, summed up the board's case by concluding that a "total absence of interference" offered the only safe course.[55]

Yet far and away the most interesting arguments came from another of the board's attorneys, Stanley Matthews. As a young adult he had practiced a vague Unitarian faith, but after several of his children died from scarlet fever, he was converted and joined an Old School Presbyterian church.[56] With unprecedented clarity Matthews's extensive brief disentangled questions concerning the nature of the Bible, its intrinsic religious purposes, and its extrinsic civic functions that had rarely been separated with such precision.

Speaking as a friend of traditional Christianity, Matthews began his brief by affirming that the Bible "contains the very words of God." Repeatedly, he returned to his own religious stance: "I am a Calvinist Protestant. I believe in the doctrines of election and predestination. . . . [The Bible is] a sacred book in the highest sense of the terms."[57] But then Matthews reversed the customary logic. Precisely *because* he valued Christian truth so highly, he did not want its transmission handed over to "the civil power." In an echo of arguments made by Roger Williams in early colonial history and some sectarians in his own day, Matthews contended that "wherever religion organized in any church has sought or consented to receive any alliance with the civil power, it has corrupted her purity and shorn her of her strength, and it will be so to the end of time."[58] An image from the Old Testament underscored his reasoning: "Let no unholy hands be laid upon the sacred ark." The religious education that children most needed was not ethics for citizenship, "not merely . . . the learning of abstract morals." Instead, "the duties of a religious life" could be found only "in the Gospel of God our Savior, and the scheme of redemption for a lost and sinful race as revealed in the person and work of the God-Man, Christ Jesus, and held forth in the instructions, and services, and means of grace, and living oracles, committed to the keeping of the church of the living God, as his kingdom on the earth."[59] The responsibility for *that* religious training belonged to parents and the churches. In his concern for religion, Matthews stressed doctrinal content rather than civic utility.

His second clarification concerned the civil sphere. While Matthews repeated several arguments advanced by the board's other attorneys, he also asserted that orthodox Protestant theology mandated strict neutrality in serving all members of the community. Cincinnati's Protestants should realize that when they insisted on readings from the KJV, they were not promoting "religious education" but asserting "denominational supremacy." To be true to the principles of their own religion, Protestants had to defend the rights of Catholics, Jews, and all others. To show his sincerity in making these points, Matthews quoted the Westminster Confession as revised by American Presbyterians after the Revolutionary War: "[C]ivil magistrates may not . . . in the least, interfere in matters of faith." In sum, "it is not orthodox Presbyterianism in this country, to deny to an infidel the same civil rights that belong to a saint."[60]

The Methodist and Episcopal judges were not persuaded. In light of the long history of adjudication on these issues, their lead opinion began strangely, by asserting that "the difficulties . . . in this case do not seem very great."[61] To these jurists it was obvious that the board had violated the Ohio provision that linked "religion, morality and knowledge" with "schools and the means of instruction." Therefore, the board's resolution must be vacated and readings from the KJV reinstated.

Justice Taft in an important dissent begged to differ. For him it was the Ohio constitution's clause about "protect[ing] every denomination" that should prevail. In his own lengthy opinion Taft went beyond questions of simple fairness to make a broader claim. In Steven Green's summary, Taft articulated "that government patronage of Christianity generally, and religious exercises in the public schools . . . were inconsistent with separation of church and state. . . . Taft also identified government neutrality toward religion as a constitutional principle."[62] Taft agreed with the plaintiff's lawyers, including Matthews, in appealing to a foundational principle of the constitution. He did not comment on Matthews's argument that a mandate from orthodox theology also supported the board's resolution.

In the event, when the Cincinnati school board appealed the superior court's decision, the Ohio Supreme Court reversed the lower court and reinstated the board's prohibition of religious exercises. Their reversal emphasized the authority of local school boards over their own policies, though one of the judges in *obiter dicta* repeated what Matthews had said about the danger *to Christianity* if its advocates insisted on maintaining Bible readings in common schools.[63] The questions raised by this case would remain alive in many places for a very long time.

For the history of the Bible, the Cincinnati controversy marked an important stage of legal development, but also much more. With the plaintiff's arguments and Justice Taft's dissent, the principle of prioritizing general constitutional guarantees over the nation's specific Protestant heritage gained traction (negative liberty as simply the opportunity to choose instead of positive liberty as the opportunity to choose the correct path). The controversy also seemed to put Catholics on the side of opposing religion in tax-supported schools even though Bishop Purcell had argued for public funds supporting a variety of religious practices in a variety of schools. Additionally, in an era with increased awareness of how powerful corporations like the railroads could corrupt national and state legislatures and with southern "redeemers" demonstrating how might could triumph over right, worries about the fate of democratic republican government were not fantasies. If the idea almost universally accepted in the early days of the United States no longer prevailed—that the personal morality without which republics sank into factionalism, corruption, and tyranny required religion— what if anything would take its place? Or was it even necessary for a healthy republic that citizens possess an inner moral compass? Finally, could American Protestants of British background work through the tensions created by exalting the Scriptures as the herald of salvation, championing the KJV as a necessity for American public life, and insisting that they too upheld liberty and justice for all? For many Americans it was unthinkable that these situations could be addressed or these questions answered without some recourse to the Bible.

Cleveland (1874)

The notion that society should be left to its own devices without guidance from God remained just as unthinkable to many Protestants in postbellum America.

The shift in predisposition that took place after the war concerned the specific reforms to be pursued, not for most Protestants the reform imperative itself. Much reduced were activities aimed at rectifying the structures of society, as the antebellum abolitionist crusade had attempted. As John McKivigan and Mitchell Snay have written, "Expediency rather than antislavery principles produced decisive action against slavery by the church leaders. Because of these fragile origins, the churches' commitment to the welfare of blacks proved no better able to weather the storms of Reconstruction than that of other northern institutions."[64]

By contrast, much increased were reforms aimed at protecting the family, preventing sexual exploitation, and, above all, attacking abuse of alcohol. These efforts were led by northern proprietary Protestants and Methodists linked to the Republican Party, but they also drew support from Baptists and other sectarians allied with the Democrats as well as from the Black churches. Mobilization against alcohol abuse, Mormon polygamy, and obscenity appealed to the enhanced authority exercised by the federal government during the war. The reformers, according to Gaines Foster, sought "to expand the moral powers of the federal government and to establish the religious authority of the state," but with a focus on the sphere of personal morality.[65] The federal legislation that resulted included the Comstock Law to suppress obscene literature (including information on birth control and abortion) and later the Mann Act against interstate sex trafficking, various restrictions on narcotics, and alcohol reform, leading with the Eighteenth Amendment (1919) to Prohibition. Such federal legislation can now appear oppressively Victorian, but as with debates in the Cincinnati Bible War, it reflected deep and overlapping concerns for personal religion, public well-being, and the fate of the nation. For the energetic women who championed temperance reform, biblical resources proved particularly important.

Alcohol abuse had earlier been one of the most prominent targets of organized Protestant voluntarism, spurred by such widely noticed works as Lyman Beecher's 1827 *Six Sermons on the Nature, Occasion, Signs, Evils, and Remedy of Intemperance*.[66] Promoters of the Bible civilization had regularly shuffled stints as agents for temperance societies with their work on behalf of Sunday schools, revivals, dietary reform, and abolition.[67] The Washington Societies and other total abstinence groups established organizational parallels to the American Tract Society and similar agencies. In 1869 a small group of northern proprietary Protestants, seemingly satisfied that the war against slavery was won, established the Prohibition Party to fight what they considered the nation's greatest evil. Beginning in 1872 and continuing to the present, the party has nominated candidates for president and vice president for each general election, their greatest success coming in 1888 and 1892, when they won over 2% of the national vote. (In 1924 the Prohibitionists became the first national party to nominate a woman for vice president.)

The postbellum temperance campaigns are important for the history of the Bible in at least two ways.[68] Methodists, first, supplied much of the energy, leadership, and organizational modeling for the movement. As such, temperance campaigning brought Methodists closer to the active reforms traditionally associated with proprietary Protestants and their efforts to create a Bible civilization. But, second, some proprietary Protestants, especially Presbyterians and Episcopalians, did not sign on to this campaign. They certainly agreed that the Bible condemned drunkenness and related evils, but that conclusion led them to support temperance defined as moderation. Temperance understood as teetotalism or prohibition was another matter. Ritual use of wine throughout the Old Testament, not to speak of Jesus's miracle of turning water into wine (Jn 2), convinced them that prohibition could never be a biblical mandate.

These differences among Protestants who in common honored the Scriptures echoed the internal Protestant division over Scripture and slavery, though with less far-ranging consequences. The similarity lay in the popularity of biblical interpretations that lacked strong scholarly support. In the debates between proslavery and abolition, reformers like T. D. Weld and Albert Barnes had argued in vain that the relevant Greek and Hebrew words more often meant indentured servants rather than chattel property. An interpretation that arose at about the same time made a parallel argument that the Greek *oinos* and comparable Old Testament terms really designated both a nearly alcohol-free beverage and a highly intoxicating alternative. In a thorough discussion of this "two-wine" theory, John Merrill has shown how eagerly early temperance reformers sought a specific biblical mandate for their cause.[69] Then, however, when the "two-wine" theory could not stand up to critical scrutiny, temperance reformers concentrated mostly on the perceived evils of drink. A few even went so far as the convinced abolitionists who were ready to give up on Scripture if it was shown to tolerate enslavement. According to one campaigner, "If intoxicating wine is the only kind of wine spoken of in the Bible, and we are recommended to use it temperately by our biblical guides, on scriptural grounds, then I must say . . . I ABHOR IT!"[70] As an indication of how much had changed from before the war, such occasional professions did not undermine the main temperance effort or curtail the reformers' constant reference to Scripture.

So it was that when the Women's Christian Temperance Union (WCTU) emerged as the most effective force for alcohol reform, and eventually for much wider advocacy on behalf of women and children, the Bible occupied an unmistakably central place. The WCTU was founded at a convention in Cleveland, Ohio, in November 1874. Four years later the WCTU's first president, Annie Wittenmyer, published a compendious history of what she called "the women's temperance crusade." Frances Willard, the organization's corresponding secretary and like Wittenmyer an active Methodist, supplied the book's introduction.

The two made a formidable team.[71] Wittenmyer had won her spurs as an effective voluntarist by organizing assistance for wounded Union soldiers and convincing the federal government to professionalize kitchens at military hospitals. As an author, she published well-received books like *Woman's Work for Jesus* (1873) and *The Women of the Reformation* (1888). Willard, who at various times assisted D. L. Moody in setting up women's ministries in connection with his evangelistic campaigns, came to the WCTU after experience as a teacher in Evanston, Illinois. In a fracture resembling the history of the American Anti-Slavery Society, Wittenmyer and Willard parted ways in 1879 over whether women's suffrage should be supported as an extension of temperance reform. Willard convinced the WCTU to take that step, after which she became the movement's globe-trotting president; Wittenmyer demurred with the hope of preserving an undivided focus on personal moral reform. Before that break, however, the two spoke with one voice in portraying the movement as a tree with firm biblical roots.

The subtitle of Wittenmyer's *History of the Women's Temperance Crusade* spelled out her sense of its distinctly religious character: *A Complete Official History of the Wonderful Uprising of the Christian Women of the United States against the Liquor Traffic, which Culminated in the Gospel Temperance Movement.* She opened the volume with a preface that could be mistaken for biblical pastiche:

> The women who walked with God in the fiery furnace [Dan 3] of the Crusade have been allowed as far as possible to tell of their work in their own words. . . .
> In this record there are glimpses of home life, "like apples of gold in pitchers of silver" [Prov 25:11], for these women are true homemakers. . . . [T]here are scenes in the streets, where bands of pure, true women, surrounded by a howling mob, kneel in the snow, and with the light of the excellent glory on their faces, pray as did their Master for just such another blaspheming, mocking mob: "Father, forgive them, they know not what they do" [Lk 23:34].[72]

In her introduction Willard featured vignettes with a similar tone. One concerned "a sweet-voiced Quaker woman" who led a group of women into her town's main saloon and then, when challenged by the proprietor, "laid her Bible down" and told the saloon-keeper about her five sons and twenty grandsons who had been destroyed by drink from that establishment: "[C]an't thee let his mother lay her Bible on the counter whence her boy took up the glass and read thee what God says: 'woe unto him that puts the bottle to his neighbor's lips [Hab 2:15]'?" Willard then described another incident when an Episcopal woman knelt to pray the Lord's Prayer in front of a saloon with women from Methodist, Congregational, Baptist, and Presbyterian churches, but also Unitarians, Swedenborgians, Universalists, and Quakers—as well as "Bridget with her beads and her Ave Marie." According to Willard, because the women were united in the Spirit, they could "join hands with any who had the Bible and the temperance pledge for the two articles in their 'Confession of Faith'—who rallied to the tune of 'Rock of Ages cleft for me,' or had for their watchword: 'Not willing that any should perish [2 Pet 3:9].'"[73]

Wittenmyer began the history proper by describing the crusade's beginning as a day of Pentecost akin to what happened in the second chapter of the Book of Acts: "Suddenly the world was startled by a flash of heavenly light. Hands of faith touched the hem of power, and a mighty spiritual swirl came down upon the people. Christian women, many of whom had never spoken or prayed in their own churches, under this Pentecostal baptism went into the streets and saloons preaching the gospel of Christ." She traced the spark igniting the movement to late December 1873, when a woman in Hillsboro, Ohio, despairing over the toll of alcohol abuse in her community, urged her mother to take action. The urging came from Psalm 146: "Put not your trust in princes. . . . The Lord God executeth judgment for the oppressed; the Lord looseth the prisoners . . . the Lord raiseth them that are bowed down." Thus encouraged, the mother gathered like-minded women, boldly entered a saloon, and after reading "a selection in the Bible" convinced the owner to abandon what he admitted was a "bad business."[74] From Hillsboro similar actions spread like wildfire until less than a year later the flames came together in Cleveland as the WCTU.

Wittenmyer, Willard, and the hundreds of women whose stories filled the pages of *History of the Women's Temperance Crusade* entertained no doubts about the biblical righteousness of temperance. In a much-repeated pattern, zeal for the cause transcended denominational boundaries, drew common inspiration from a liberationist understanding of biblical revelation, and hoped to redeem the nation by saving individuals. Their reliance on Scripture was not exegetical, as had been the case for those who attacked and defended enslavement, nor did they worry about hermeneutical matters. Instead, they were motivated by an ardent desire to save lives wasted and homes destroyed by drink. Close, detailed, or doctrinal attention to the Bible receded; few looked to Scripture for direction concerning the market economy that made brewing and distilling so profitable; other evils of the times, like the steady imposition of Jim Crow, faded into the background, yet much of the traditional proprietary zeal for nationwide biblical reform remained.

The Presses Keep Rolling

Meanwhile, religious publishing, with the Bible always prominent, proceeded from strength to strength. Yet in a communications landscape marked by greater ethnic and religious diversity, competing with more newspapers and periodicals, serving a population growing rapidly in absolute numbers, expanding rapidly westward, and riven by sharper economic divisions, the national preeminence that English-language Protestant publishing once enjoyed had become a thing of the past.[75]

The sheer quantity of religious publication remained impressive. In the decade from 1866 through 1875, the American Bible Society raised almost seven million dollars, which enabled it to publish more than eleven and a half million bibles and New Testaments. (The national population had climbed to over 45 million by 1875.) Until the Depression of 1873 the ABS nearly matched the prodigious output of the late war years, when its annual production exceeded one and a half million copies. All of its English-language bibles were the KJV.[76]

While the ABS retained a near monopoly on inexpensive bibles, commercial firms published a growing quantity of family, illustrated, and annotated bibles for the middle and upper classes. Of the 119 new Bible editions produced in the decade 1866 to 1875, two Philadelphia firms, J. B. Lippincott and A. J. Holman, were each responsible for almost one new edition each year. As an example of the genre, A. J. Holman published its first of many bibles in 1872, with supplemental features specified on the title page: "Frontspiece, Order of Books, and Improved Comprehensive Helps to the Study of the Bible (by Nevin, Rawson, & Horne)... With Apocrypha... Family Record. Maps of Jerusalem, Concordance, and Metrical Psalms . . . Illustrated."[77] Publishers also continued to provide a steady supply of well-known older works. In that decade, twenty-three different firms in six cities brought out twenty-six editions of *The Pilgrim's Progress*.[78] The 550 religious periodicals that were available in 1880 also suggested the strength of denominational and interdenominational networks.[79]

Impressive as these publishing regimes were, however, religious publishing also reflected the cultural fragmentation that accompanied religious diversification, the spreading population, and economic inequalities. Newspapers bulked much larger for the reading public. Although some still carried substantial religious content, daily and weekly papers just as often competed against religious interests. By the 1870s they were pervasively present: over eight hundred in

New York, over five hundred in Illinois and Pennsylvania, over two hundred in California, Indiana, Iowa, Massachusetts, Michigan, and Missouri.[80]

Religious diversification also reduced the general influence of the antebellum Bible, Tract, and Sunday School societies. While their work remained impressive, denominational presses and publishers serving new transdenominational networks steadily gained ground. The prime illustration of the latter was Fleming H. Revell, D. L. Moody's brother-in-law, who in 1870 started a publishing career that would later make him a prime resource for fundamentalist circles.[81] By the 1870s, Catholic publishing was also advancing steadily. Where in the period 1820 to 1852 Catholics accounted for less than 6% of the nation's religious periodicals, by 1880 the figure had risen to over 14%. In 1865 the *Catholic World*, edited by a celebrity convert, Isaac Hecker, joined *Brownson's Quarterly Review* as a notable but reader-friendly magazine reaching out to non-Catholics as well as Catholics. When Hecker the following year began the Catholic Publication Society, he inaugurated a venture that provided a wide variety of tracts and full-length books for the nation's growing Catholic constituency.[82] Catholic Bible publishers were also expanding their efforts by contributing eleven editions of the Douay-Rheims translation during the decade. The ratio of KJV bibles to the Douay-Rheims translation was still high (more than 8:1) but had noticeably declined from the situation in the 1810s (70:1) and even the 1840s (14:1).

While the KJV remained the unquestioned leader in Bible publication, the appearance of several translations serving specific communities reflected growing Protestant diversity—ten for Baptists and Restorationists, five with Unitarian sponsorship. The decade also saw the appearance of *The Holy Scriptures, Translated and corrected by the Spirit of Revelation, by Joseph Smith, Jr., the Seer.* It offered an edited version of the KJV that Smith had prepared in the early 1830s, now brought to the public by the Reorganized Church of Jesus Christ of Latter Day Saints (in Independence, Missouri) that had broken from the Utah Mormons under Brigham Young.[83]

As with national publishing as a whole, religious presses and the production of bibles experienced sharper geographical and class divides. For publishing of all kinds, the war left the most obvious divide: flourishing in the North and West, moribund in the South. None of the new editions of *The Pilgrim's Progress* came from below the Mason-Dixon line; of the 119 new Bible editions during the decade, only four came from southern publishers (two from Louisville, one each from Nashville and New Orleans). Foremost continued the Northeast, with ninety-five of the editions from New York and Philadelphia, another fourteen from other northeastern cities, and fifteen more from Chicago, Cincinnati, St. Louis, Pittsburgh, and Plano, Illinois.

In a word, the Civil War did not slow the provision of Bible and Bible-related publications. That provision, however, now reflected the economic effects of the war even as more constituencies in more northern and western regions sponsored a more diverse array of publications. The South remained dependent on Yankee publishers even as its white citizens won a war of words interpreting the shooting war they had lost. For the nation as a whole, print without religious sponsorship continued to expand. The Bible was by no means fading away, but diversity, competitors, innovations, and fragmentation made it harder and harder to specify any one message as national.

23

The Centennial Divide: 1876 and After

In 1876 the United States celebrated its centennial with a grand exposition spread over 450 acres of Philadelphia real estate, featuring exhibits in more than two hundred buildings, and visited during its run of six months by more than 8 million curious, gawking, sometimes cynical or exhausted, but mostly enthralled Americans.[1] When the International Exhibition of Arts, Manufactures, and Products of the Soil and Mine opened in May, the U.S. Congress was considering an amendment to the Constitution proposed by James G. Blaine of Maine that would have prohibited the use of public funds for any sectarian educational institution or purpose.[2] When the exposition closed in November, the nation faced a constitutional crisis because of a disputed presidential election.[3]

The Centennial Exhibition, the Blaine Amendment, and the election indicate clearly why the year 1876 marked a transition for the history of the Bible. The trajectory of Scripture as a force in the nation's public life and its trajectory as a guide for personal and community religion were clearly diverging. In sharp contrast to the Bible's central role in the nation's antebellum controversies over slavery and its prominence in the civil religion of the war years, Scripture almost disappeared at the Philadelphia Exhibition and during the year's presidential election. For debate on the Blaine Amendment it remained, but as a function of political partisanship with only an incidental connection to anything distinctly religious.

In the same year, however, almost every important sphere of national religious life witnessed significant developments keyed to the Scriptures. For Protestants of all sorts, for Catholics and Jews, men and women, Blacks and whites, and a growing cohort of freethinkers, these developments ushered in what Robert Handy once called "decades of expansion and tension" when "long familiar views and practices, accepted by many, became increasingly problematic for others."[4]

Although writing about an absence poses a challenge, this chapter begins by describing the near absence of Scripture in the headlining public events of the centennial year. It then examines the year's special meaning for the Bible among American women, followed by attention to how succeeding decades witnessed an ever-expanding range of female engagements with Scripture. The story of women and the Bible bridges to succeeding chapters that feature other events from 1876 that also proved pivotal for the history of the Bible.

America's Book. Mark A. Noll, Oxford University Press. © Oxford University Press 2022.
DOI: 10.1093/oso/9780197623466.003.0024

The centennial year, with the Bible's near irrelevance in politics alongside its ongoing vigor in the nation's religious communities, prompts obvious questions. Since the Bible's importance in the various religious traditions still affected public life to some degree, how should those ongoing connections be assessed? Some Protestants, both Black and white, never stopped promoting Scripture as a substantive guide for the nation. Jews, smaller Christian communities, and other religious and nonreligious minorities struggled with ever greater success to escape the culture's inherited Protestant restraints. More Catholics argued that their version of Christianity provided what the country needed. Literary efforts at every level of sophistication and then the cinema regularly exploited scriptural narratives, themes, and vocabulary. Scripture (and contentions over Scripture) remained prominent in the nation's schools, colleges, and universities. To put the question differently, although the earlier Bible civilization had passed away, what part did the remembered, reenacted, or reconfigured remnants of that civilization play in the nation's ongoing history?

Finally, what did the history unfolding over the last decades of the century and into the new century mean for those who treasured Scripture as first a spiritual authority? This question asks what the Bible itself gained and lost as the Book that believers considered universally valid and eternally true wound its way through this particular nation in those particular years?

The Blaine Amendment

As the centennial year dawned, the former Speaker of the U.S. House of Representatives and future secretary of state James G. Blaine was maneuvering to win the Republicans' presidential nomination and the right to succeed Ulysses S. Grant, now at the end of his second term. Blaine's party was in trouble. Collusion between distillers and collectors of excise taxes on liquor in addition to payoffs to congressmen by railroad entrepreneurs had besmirched the sterling reputation Grant brought from the battlefield into the White House. Resentment in the white South had grown steadily against the federal troops charged with enforcing Reconstruction. In the North more and more citizens, whether Republican or Democrat, increasingly questioned the federal effort required to create civic space for freed slaves. A depression that began in 1873 shook the Republicans' hold on power; in its wake the congressional elections of the next year saw Democrats win control of the House of Representatives for the first time since before the war (and so oust Blaine from his post as Speaker).

Blaine, who has hoping to divert attention from Republican corruption and resentment at Reconstruction, fastened on immigration, religion, and partisanship as his winning issues. At the Republican National Convention held in Cincinnati in June, Blaine was put in nomination by a rising midwestern orator-attorney, Robert Ingersoll, already known for his heterodox religious views, but even more for his spellbinding oratory. Ingersoll's riveting speech described Blaine as "a plumed knight" who had "thrust his shining lance full and fair against the defamers of his country."[5] As he gave Blaine a nickname that stuck, Ingersoll also "waved the bloody shirt" that impugned Democrats as traitors responsible for the carnage of the Civil War. By implication, he also impugned the constituencies strongest for the Democrats, including the nation's Catholics.

Blaine's proposed amendment took dead aim at that constituency. Its introduction for congressional consideration followed a well-publicized speech by President Grant from the previous September. In his own effort at distracting the electorate, Grant invoked grand American principles defending freedom of religion and guaranteeing the separation of church and state. For preserving these hallowed principles, Grant exhorted an audience of Union veterans to "encourage free schools," prevent money appropriated for "free schools" from supporting "sectarian schools," deny forever any public funding for "institutions of learning . . . [that teach] sectarian, pagan, or atheistical dogmas," leave religion entirely in the control of "family altar, the Church, and the private school," and "keep the Church and State forever separate." The Blaine Amendment, which came before Congress in December 1875, followed Grant's proposals by prohibiting any tax money raised "for the support of the public schools" to be used "under the control of any religious sect."[6]

One more issue was in play for Grant, Blaine, and some of their Republican supporters. They wanted the new constitutional amendment to guarantee free public education for all children throughout the entire country. Transparently, this move would force the southern states to aid the children of freed slaves who, with their parents, constituted the Republicans' key southern constituency.

It did not require clairvoyance to grasp the Republicans' main goal. The tides of immigration flowing strongly since the 1830s had brought an unprecedented number of Roman Catholics into the country. Increasingly, as Catholics— and then smaller numbers of Jews and freethinkers—sent their children to the nation's public schools, they were deeply offended at how Protestant those schools felt. The main manifestation of that Protestantism was the common practice of daily readings from the King James Version.

When in the summer of 1876 the Senate took up the Blaine Amendment, it added a clause reflecting the Republican-Protestant consensus about a nonsectarian Bible. The Senate's final version stipulated that nothing it contained "shall be construed to prohibit the reading of the Bible in any school or institution."[7] This amendment to the amendment directly rebutted the Catholic parents who complained that tax-supported imposition of the King James Bible violated their religious liberty. In some regions with growing Catholic populations, appeals could be heard for tax money to support schools where the Catholic Douay-Rheims translation could be read—in other words, not freedom *from* Bible reading but freedom *for* individually chosen Bible readings. For the most part, Catholics agreed with Bishop Purcell of Cincinnati, who held that religious instruction did indeed support the virtue without which republics failed. They insisted, however, that they should not have to pay for instruction in public schools that forced Catholic children to read the Protestants' Bible.

As it happened, the Blaine Amendment passed the House with more than the two-thirds majority required for sending it on to the states. But in the version approved by the House, the amendment did not include the Senate's protection of nonsectarian Bible reading. It did contain a provision inserted at the behest of House Democrats, that the Amendment as a whole not "vest, enlarge, or diminish legislative power in the Congress" of the United States.[8] In the Senate, the Amendment, with the protection of Bible reading but without the House's clause against enlarging federal power, gained a majority, but not a sufficient majority to send it for consideration to the states. So died the Blaine Amendment of 1876.

A messy tangle of political-religious interests had prepared the way for this legislative history. Politically, northern Republicans supported Blaine as a distraction from their own troubles and in order to disadvantage Catholics and southern Democrats. Southern Democrats opposed the Amendment because if a federal mandate existed for free public education, it would have been necessary to create schools for African Americans. Catholics, almost unanimously Democrats, opposed the Amendment because they saw it (accurately) as undermining their arguments for a share in tax money for schools where the Douay-Rheims Bible could be read. Jews and secularists, of which there were still not very many, favored the Amendment without the Bible provision because they believed in truly secular public education. Most Protestants supported the Amendment, especially with the Senate addition protecting nonsectarian Bible reading, because it would have kept tax money from going to Catholic schools while preserving the time-honored practice of reading the KJV. But when the Amendment failed, its life as a Republican lifesaver was over. In the aftermath, Blaine, its sponsor, did not win the Republican Party's nomination for president, which went instead to Rutherford B. Hayes, who only shortly before had been elected governor of Ohio on a strongly anti-Catholic Republican platform.

What was the result of this debate for the Bible? As in the Cincinnati Bible War, assumptions were being shaken that had once been taken for granted. Was nonsectarian Bible reading in fact the best means for promoting republican virtue while preserving the separation of church and state? Put differently, should the United States still be considered a nonsectarian Christian country, yet one where generic Protestant convictions, habits, instincts, and agendas remained essential for the survival of American liberty? Was nonsectarian neutrality possible only when Protestant presuppositions about the Bible's ultimate authority prevailed?

Beyond the nation, what about the Bible itself? What did it mean when Scripture's proponents focused almost entirely on its utilitarian service to the nation? In terms articulated by Stanley Matthews before the Cincinnati Superior Court, was a strong emphasis on the pragmatic public functions of a nonsectarian Bible undermining the spiritual value of the Bible for individuals, families, and communities?

A footnote concerns the prominence won by Robert Ingersoll at the Republicans' national convention. Although Ingersoll's speech-making before he nominated Blaine had already revealed his admiration for Tom Paine, his disdain for religious censorship of science, and his frank anti-supernaturalism, the rapturous response to his Cincinnati oratory made him a national celebrity. Ingersoll's publication in 1879 of *Some Mistakes of Moses*, which gathered speeches dismissing the credibility of the Pentateuch, indicated how much the nation had moved on since the publication of Paine's *The Age of Reason* eighty-plus years earlier. Ingersoll's advocacy of what Eric Brandt and Timothy Larsen have called "the dethroning of biblical authority" did generate considerable opposition, but nothing like the intellectual stone wall Paine confronted when he disparaged the Old Testament.[9] Instead of causing his social ostracization, Ingersoll's book mainly enhanced his reputation as an orator who simply had to be heard.

The Centennial and the Election

At the Philadelphia Exposition of 1876, Christianity of a Protestant hue contributed a ritual presence but little else. At the ceremonies opening the Exhibition on May 10, the throng assembled between the Main Building and Memorial Hall heard performances of Handel's "Hallelujah Chorus" and a vaguely theistic hymn penned by John Greenleaf Whittier ("Our fathers God! from out whose hand / The centuries fall like grains of sand, / We meet to-day, united, free, / And loyal to our land and Thee").[10] The prayer that preceded Whittier's hymn was offered by Methodist bishop Matthew Simpson, a respected educator, editor, and strong supporter of the Union who had consulted with Abraham Lincoln during the war and gave one of the speeches when the assassinated president was laid to rest in Springfield, Illinois. Now he provided the expected paean to American exceptionalism by thanking God for giving "our fathers, a land veiled from the ages . . . but revealed in the fullness of time to Thy chosen people." The prayer closed with petitions underscoring the Exposition's international aspirations: that "our beloved Republic may be strengthened in every element of true greatness until her mission is accomplished by presenting to the world an illustration of the happiness of a free people, with a free church, in a free State.... And may the coming centuries be filled with the glory of our Christian civilization."[11] While the press acknowledged Whittier and Simpson with respect, their contributions could not compete with the day's main attractions. A "Centennial March" composed for the occasion by Richard Wagner drew thunderous applause. The crowd strained to hear a short speech by President Grant in which he acknowledged that, while the nation's first century had been "burdened by . . . great primal works of necessity," the Exhibition would show "older and more advanced nations" what the country had already accomplished in "law, medicine, and theology, in science, literature, philosophy, and the fine arts."[12] The highlight of the day, however, came when Grant and other dignitaries processed to Machinery Hall where the president and the emperor of Brazil depressed levers that set in motion the gigantic Corliss steam engine. This industrial marvel provided the energy that ran the eight thousand other machines in the hall's capacious thirteen acres, "combing wool, spinning cotton, tearing hemp, printing newspapers, lithographing wallpaper, sewing cloth, manufacturing envelopes, sawing logs, shaping wood, making shoes, pumping water."[13] Its continuous operation until the fair closed on November 10 dazzled visitors and always featured prominently in written reports on fair.

The Bible at the Centennial Exhibition was tucked away in corners. A quotation from Proverbs 31:31 was inscribed above the entrance to the Women's Pavilion ("Her words do praise her in the gates").[14] In a modest building erected by the Pennsylvania Bible Society, its parent organization, the American Bible Society, sold bibles at cost in a hundred different languages and gave away a pamphlet with John 3:16 printed in 164 languages.[15] Among the commercial exhibitors, the A. J. Holman Company of Philadelphia put up a slightly larger structure with copies of its elaborate family bibles showcased in five floor-to-ceiling display windows. Beneath each of the windows was an inscription, in the center the Holman trademark ("let there be light, 1776–1876") and the other four with appropriate Bible verses.[16] On September 27, the Exhibition bestowed the Centennial Award Medal on the Holman Company to honor its family Bible, first published in 1872 and expanded in an edition from 1874 that along with 1,300 illustrations by Gustave Doré included even more supplementary material.[17] Otherwise, neither of these exhibits seemed to have attracted particular attention.

One of the most notable events of the Centennial celebrations indicated how times had changed for the Bible's place in national consciousness. It took place on July 4, Centennial Day, when the Exposition joined with Philadelphia to sponsor a huge celebration on Independence Square in the heart of the city.[18] A massive crowd approaching 200,000 could glimpse Gen. Philip Sheridan, Gen. William Tecumseh Sherman, assorted governors, and a host of foreign dignitaries in the platform party; they heard at least snatches of an Independence Day hymn composed by Oliver Wendell Holmes; and they witnessed a gesture toward North-South reconciliation as Richard Henry Lee of Virginia was called to the podium to recite the Declaration of Independence. Immediately after he was finished, five women strode purposefully to the platform and shouldered aside the master of ceremonies. Their leader, Susan B. Anthony, made a short statement announcing that the National Woman's Suffrage Association had prepared a "Declaration of Rights of the Women of the United States" especially for the occasion. Anthony and her associates then descended from the platform and distributed copies of their Declaration as they strode across the Square to the musicians' platform, where they proceeded to declaim the entirety of their lengthy statement. After a Philadelphia poet tried to get on with the announced program by reading his Centennial ode, the presider quieted the restless crowd by asking it to join in reciting the 100th Psalm ("Make a joyful noise unto the Lord, all ye lands").

So it was that Scripture edged into the Centennial celebration. (At the Exhibition's closing ceremony on November 10 there would be a planned singing of the well-known hymn based on the same Psalm, the "Old Hundredth.")[19] More than the ritual recitation of a well-known Psalm, the women's Declaration spoke to how the nation's religious climate had changed over the preceding generation.

Organized efforts to advance the rights of American women first came to wide public attention because of a conference held in July 1848 at Seneca Falls, New York. The Quaker "recognized Minister" Lucretia Mott had met Elizabeth Cady Stanton in 1840 at the World Antislavery Convention in London, where no woman had been allowed to speak. Their efforts to change that situation, which was supported by the Garrisonian faction of the American Anti-Slavery Association, led to the 1848 conference that convened in a Wesleyan Methodist church near Stanton's home. The call to arms promulgated by the 1848 convention followed closely the nation's Declaration of Independence ("we hold these truths to be self-evident; that all men and women are created equal"), including references to "the laws of nature and of nature's God" and "their Creator." As one of sixteen specified "repeated injuries and usurpations on the part of man toward woman," the Declaration of Sentiments and Grievances included a specifically religious complaint: man "allows [woman] in Church as well as State, but a subordinate position, claiming Apostolic authority for her exclusion from the ministry, and with some exceptions, from any public participation in the affairs of the Church." As an addendum to this complaint, one of the Convention's resolutions became even more specific: "*Resolved*, That woman has too long rested satisfied in the circumscribed limits which corrupt customs and a perverted application of the Scriptures have marked out for her, and that it is time she should move in the enlarged sphere which her great Creator has assigned her."[20]

In the comparable document prepared for the Centennial in 1876, theistic, Christian, and biblical references all but disappeared. The argument instead rested on "the broad principles of human rights" that exposed "the degradation of disfranchisement" borne by the nation's female citizens. The religious motives of some reformers did receive a brief mention in the "article of impeachment" that concerned "taxation without representation." Women were described as "believers in temperance" who were nonetheless required to pay taxes that supported "the Liquor Traffic." In that campaign, "mothers were arrested, fined, imprisoned, for even praying and singing in the streets, while men blockade the sidewalks with impunity, even on Sunday, with their military parades and political processions."[21] Otherwise the document reflected the trajectory of Anthony and Stanton's reforming efforts. Their movement had begun in association with antebellum revivals and an undifferentiated zeal for both personal holiness and social reform. For Anthony and Stanton, though not for all others who supported their social goals, reform had become a secular crusade that viewed the churches' traditional reverence for Scripture as a prime impediment to the empowerment of female citizens.

Like the voices of women reformers heard in Philadelphia on the hundredth anniversary of Independence Day, the presidential election campaign of 1876 and its contested aftermath testified to a striking religious change from what had gone before. Throughout the campaign season and the crisis that followed, the Bible remained all but invisible. In sharp contrast to the nation's political sphere from Andrew Jackson through Abraham Lincoln, when appeals to Scripture appeared regularly, it is difficult to find examples of any prominent Protestant, whether clerical or lay, who turned to Scripture for evaluating the times— whether the election, the constitutional crisis, the fate of Reconstruction, or the "redemption" of the white South.[22]

In the disputed contest, the Republican Rutherford B. Hayes of Ohio gained the White House, despite receiving 3% fewer popular votes than his Democratic opponent, Governor Samuel J. Tilden of New York. Tilden, who stood for a pull-back of federal authority in all areas of national life, gained some support in the North while sweeping the southern states that had returned to white control. But in three former Confederate states where significant numbers of Blacks still voted and significant numbers of ex-Confederates were still kept from the polls, and for one of Oregon's three electoral votes, the popular totals were too close to declare a winner. Rancorous contention followed because Congress, which had ultimate authority over ratifying electoral votes, was divided between the Democratic House elected in 1874 and the Republican Senate. In the controversies after election day, November 7, the crisis was even more dire than the nation faced 124 years later in the contested election between Al Gore and George W. Bush. In the modern case, both sides in effect agreed to abide by findings of the U.S. Supreme Court. In the earlier situation, charges and countercharges flew back and forth so fervently and for such a long time that some observers believed open sectional conflict would reignite the Civil War. In the event, but only hours before Inauguration Day on March 5 (a Monday, to avoid dishonoring Sunday), both sides finally agreed to accept the decision of a federal commission that ignored both the violent intimidation keeping Blacks from the polls throughout the Democratic South and what probably were narrow victories for Tilden in the disputed states. It tallied the electoral count as 185 for Hayes and 184 for Tilden. In return, the Republicans agreed to end congressionally mandated Reconstruction, which led immediately to the stand-down of federal troops in the former Confederacy. Tacitly, the agreement returned state governments in Louisiana, Florida, and South Carolina into the hands of ex-Confederate white leaders. In the two years preceding 1876, Democrats in Mississippi had shown what the return of white rule would mean, as systematic terror against African Americans and their Republican allies began the process of fastening Jim Crow on the public life of the state.[23]

In the congressional melee, Scripture was invoked, but only for rhetorical garnishment. After the election commission reported its pro-Hayes findings, a New York congressman who supported Tilden tried to read out Psalm 94:20: "Shall the throne of iniquity have fellowship with thee, which frameth mischief by a law?" When a Hayes supporter objected, the first congressman retorted that Republicans had sunk so low they no longer honored the Bible. Later, after Congress issued its final decision for Hayes late in the evening of Friday, March 2, Kentucky congressman Joseph Blackburn, a former colonel in the Confederate army, drew an extended analogy: "Today is Friday. Upon that day the savior of the world suffered crucifixion between two thieves. On this Friday constitutional government, justice, honesty, fair dealing, manhood, and decency suffer crucifixion amid a number of thieves." A quick-witted Wisconsin Republican fired back—no, Friday was rather "hangman's day" that has finally brought an end to the Democrats' "bogus, pretentious brat of political reform," now "gibbetted higher than Haman" (a reference to the fate of the Persian official who plotted the destruction of the Jews as recorded in the book of Esther).[24]

Julia Smith's Translation

The course of biblically inspired campaigns against slavery and for women's rights made for a strange echo of congressional trivialization of Scripture. Sarah

Grimké, Angelina Grimké Weld, and Theodore Dwight Weld began their public careers in the 1830s by wielding a scriptural Sword of the Lord against injustice suffered by both women and slaves. Well before the Civil War, however, they stopped campaigning. After the war they maintained their concern for Black Americans, but not their commitment to activism or their confidence in the evangelical approach to Scripture. For her part, Elizabeth Cady Stanton undertook a more definite journey away from the stern biblical religion of her youth to an active denunciation of the Bible as irredeemably patriarchal. As David Hempton has aptly summarized the life course of these reformers, "Evangelicalism's sacred text did not emerge unscathed from the early history of the women's movement, nor did the evangelical faith of some of its most famous leaders."[25]

Connections between the Bible and women's concerns over the last third of the century, however, involved more than disenchantment (the Grimkés) or denunciation (Stanton). The campaign for women's rights that drew national attention to Centennial Day in Philadelphia witnessed other developments in that same year with a much more prominent place for the Christian Scriptures. In turn, those developments led to further reforming efforts and expanded women's engagement with the Bible, some related only incidentally to reform. In the decades after 1876, the history of Scripture and American women illustrated a national situation greatly altered from antebellum fixations, but a history that still revealed much about the fate of the Bible and the course of the nation.

In May 1876, two months before Susan B. Anthony read aloud the "Declaration of Rights of the Women of the United States" on the Fourth of July in Philadelphia, the National Women's Suffrage Association gathered in New York City to finalize plans for the Centennial Exhibition. At this New York meeting, Anthony, Lucretia Mott, Amelia Jenks Bloomer, who had invented a "sensible costume for females," and other well-known suffragists paused to honor two octogenarian sisters from Glastonbury, Connecticut.[26] The younger, Abby Smith, had become the center of a news storm in late 1873 when she refused to pay property taxes to the town; her refusal rested on a canonical American principle, "No taxation without representation." If she and her sisters who owned their farmstead could not vote, the demand to pay taxes constituted a grave injustice. Public interest grew when local officials sold off the sisters' cows and some of their land, while Smith spoke boldly for expanded suffrage in the town, throughout Connecticut, and via nationwide media coverage.

A noteworthy byproduct of this local dispute was the decision by Abby's older sister, Julia Smith, to publish her own translation of the Bible. When it appeared in 1876, *The Holy Bible: Containing the Old and New Testaments; Translated Literally from the Original Tongues* represented the product of intense study for more than half a century. It was also a classic demonstration of American sectarian biblicism. In a letter from mid-1875, Julia explained the connection between her family's dispute with Glastonbury and this first complete translation by a woman. "If," she wrote, "it be wrong to take a man's property without his consent, [it] must be equally wrong to take a woman's property without her consent; and the men, therefore, must take it from her on the ground that her intellect is not as strong as theirs." Yet "no learning . . . is so much respected by the whole world . . . as the knowledge of the most ancient languages, in which the Bible was written." If, however, women did possess intellect just as much as men, they deserved just as much protection against "robbery." The proof of that claim? "And here is a woman, with no motive but the love of doing it, and no instructions since her school days, has gone further alone, in translating these languages, than any man has ever gone, and without any of his help." Yet despite this demonstration of equal intellectual capacity, "*no law of the land gives her any protection*."[27] (Figure 23.1)

The National Women's Suffrage Association leaped to honor the Smith sisters for making such bold demonstrations in support of women's enfranchisement. Julia Smith's translation certainly did serve that purpose. Even more, however, it testified to the enduring strength of the peculiarly American tradition of honoring the Bible with idiosyncratic zeal in harness with antiestablishmentarian fervor.

Julia Smith, born in 1792, grew up in a family where her father, Zephaniah, and mother, Hannah Hickok, encouraged the educational endeavors of their five daughters. Through short stints of formal schooling, patient parental assistance, and intense autodidactic effort, Julia mastered Latin and Greek while still a teenager. For more than two decades as a young adult she kept a daily diary in French. Her father, a Yale graduate, had served as a Congregational minister for a few years before turning to the law and an active public life. He left the ministry for reasons that shaped his family's entire future course. Like Daniel Humphreys, the New Hampshire jurist who had blasted Paine's *Age of Reason* but also New England's established churches, Zephaniah Smith fell under the influence of Sandemanian teaching. The Sandemanians' intense biblicism and ardent opposition to formal ecclesiastical authority led in the Smiths' case to a family wary of formal church membership but totally immersed in Scripture. (Between her eighteenth and thirty-third year, Julia's diary records that she read through the Old Testament forty times and the New ninety-six times!)[28] In the early 1840s the family also became intrigued by William Miller's predictions concerning the End of Time. After the Millerite Great Disappointment of 1844, Julia remained intrigued but now determined to see for herself by learning Hebrew so that she could test the conclusions Miller and others drew from Scripture.

This determination led to decades devoted to translating the Bible literally, assigning one English word to each Hebrew or Greek word. (After her translation appeared, several learned Americans commended its sense for Hebrew, though

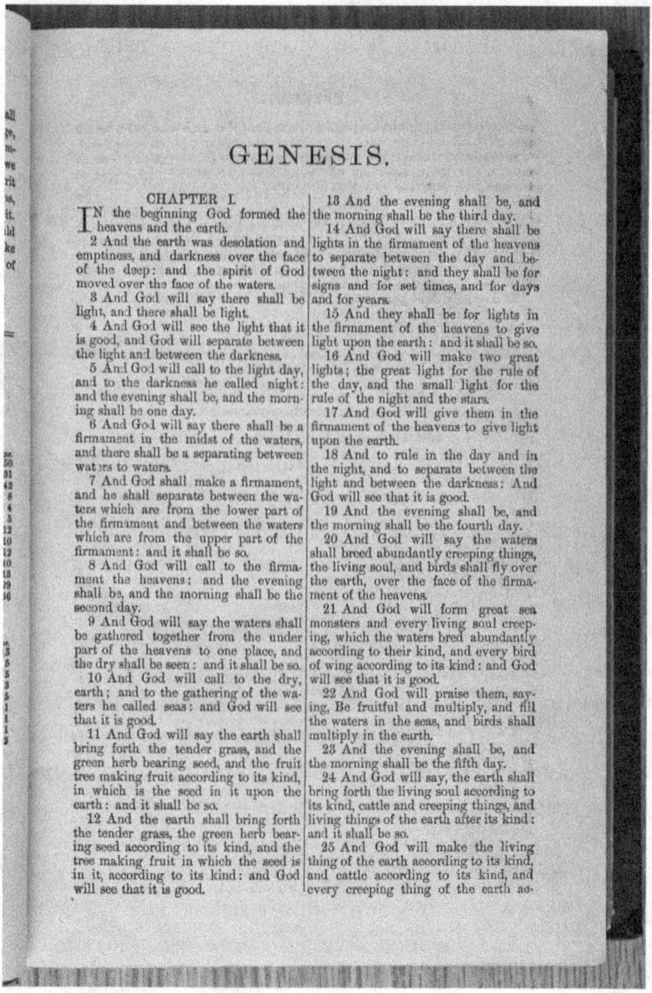

GENESIS.

CHAPTER I.

IN the beginning God formed the heavens and the earth.

2 And the earth was desolation and emptiness, and darkness over the face of the deep: and the spirit of God moved over the face of the waters.

3 And God will say there shall be light, and there shall be light.

4 And God will see the light that it is good, and God will separate between the light and between the darkness.

5 And God will call to the light day, and to the darkness he called night: and the evening shall be, and the morning shall be one day.

6 And God will say there shall be a firmament in the midst of the waters, and there shall be a separating between waters to waters.

7 And God shall make a firmament, and he shall separate between the waters which are from the lower part of the firmament and between the waters which are from the upper part of the firmament: and it shall be so.

8 And God will call to the firmament the heavens; and the evening shall be, and the morning shall be the second day.

9 And God will say the waters shall be gathered together from the under part of the heavens to one place, and the dry shall be seen: and it shall be so.

10 And God will call to the dry, earth; and to the gathering of the waters he called seas: and God will see that it is good.

11 And God will say the earth shall bring forth the tender grass, and the green herb bearing seed, and the fruit tree making fruit according to its kind, in which is the seed in it upon the earth: and it shall be so.

12 And the earth shall bring forth the tender grass, the green herb bearing seed according to its kind, and the tree making fruit in which the seed is in it, according to its kind: and God will see that it is good.

13 And the evening shall be, and the morning shall be the third day.

14 And God will say there shall be lights in the firmament of the heavens to separate between the day and between the night: and they shall be for signs and for set times, and for days and for years.

15 And they shall be for lights in the firmament of the heavens to give light upon the earth: and it shall be so.

16 And God will make two great lights; the great light for the rule of the day, and the small light for the rule of the night and the stars.

17 And God will give them in the firmament of the heavens to give light upon the earth.

18 And to rule in the day and in the night, and to separate between the light and between the darkness: And God will see that it is good.

19 And the evening shall be, and the morning shall be the fourth day.

20 And God will say the waters shall breed abundantly creeping things, the living soul, and birds shall fly over the earth, over the face of the firmament of the heavens.

21 And God will form great sea monsters and every living soul creeping, which the waters bred abundantly according to their kind, and every bird of wing according to its kind: and God will see that it is good.

22 And God will praise them, saying, Be fruitful and multiply, and fill the waters in the seas, and birds shall multiply in the earth.

23 And the evening shall be, and the morning shall be the fifth day.

24 And God will say, the earth shall bring forth the living soul according to its kind, cattle and creeping things, and living things of the earth after its kind: and it shall be so.

25 And God will make the living thing of the earth according to its kind, and cattle according to its kind, and every creeping thing of the earth ac-

Figure 23.1 Julia Smith published her 1876 translation with typographical features common to almost all the bibles of her era, but it was very much her own work.
Source: Courtesy of Buswell Library Special Collections, Rare Books, Wheaton College, Illinois.

not its fluency in English.) Smith's intense labor eventually produced five different manuscript versions—two of the Hebrew Old Testament, two from Greek for the entire Bible (including the Old Testament Septuagint), and one from the Latin Vulgate. The manuscripts remained private until the sisters' clash with Glastonbury officials spurred Julia to redact the five into one publishable English version.

The translation won immediate attention as a phenomenon, but it did not catch on in either the $2.50 cloth edition or the $3.00 text bound in sheepskin.[29] Julia's work did, however, testify to the enduring resilience of sectarian biblicism as well as her own linguistic persistence. If her self-confidence was breathtakingly naïve, it was also quintessentially American. As she wrote in the translation's preface:

> It may seem presumptuous for an ordinary woman with no particular advantages of education to translate and publish alone the most wonderful book that has ever appeared in the world, and thought to be the most difficult to translate. . . . It may be thought by the public in general, that I have great confidence in myself in not conferring with the learned in so grand a work, but as there is but one book in the Hebrew tongue, and I have defined it word for word, I do not see how anybody can know more about it than I do.[30]

Her translation ordered the books in the Jewish manner, with the "law and the prophets" preceding the "writings" that include Psalms, Ruth, and Esther; she followed Alexander Campbell in translating *baptize* as "immerse"; she eliminated all of the words the KJV had supplied as italicized clarifications for its text; it was, as the samples in Table 23.1 suggest, a truly distinctive effort.

Nearly two decades later, Elizabeth Cady Stanton's *Woman's Bible* singled out Smith for special recognition. Although this publication mostly relied on the KJV when citing the Scriptures, an appendix to the first of its two parts hailed Smith's translation as "the only one ever made by a woman, and the only one, it appears, ever made by man or woman without help."[31]

The twenty years lying between Smith's *Holy Bible* and Stanton's *Woman's Bible* reveal a great deal about the place of Scripture in the public life of that era. If a crisis over suffrage led to Smith's translation, it was not a distinctively feminist work. By contrast, Stanton's *Woman's Bible,* though not a translation, was feminist from first to last. The *Holy Bible* was an object of curiosity, *The Woman's Bible* a site of conflict. Both demonstrate the ongoing presence of Scripture in the national narrative, but Smith's work was a cultural sideshow while *The Woman's Bible* conveyed ambiguity about Scripture's public authority. Although great numbers of women continued to revere the Bible, that reverence in private, in families, and in religious organizations carried only mixed messages into public life. How to regard and interpret the Scriptures did remain pressing questions for women committed to suffrage, temperance, or more general feminism. Yet if the Bible was almost always front and center in temperance movements, it played an ambiguous role among suffragists, while the era's most aggressive feminists worked hard to undercut its authority. Compared to the great host of antebellum writing with biblical arguments on slavery and race, far fewer publications, among them the WCTU's pamphlet *The Bible for Woman Suffrage*, appeared in the century's last decades.[32] Scripture sustained many in the WCTU for their campaign, but it did not figure prominently in how they set forth their case.

Table 23.1 The KJV and Julia Smith's Translation

Genesis 3:20–21

Smith's Translation	KJV
20 And Adam will call his wife's name Life, for she was the mother of all living.	20 And Adam called his wife's name Eve; because she was the mother of all living.
21 And Jehovah God will make to Adam and to his wife, coats of skin, and will clothe them.	21 Unto Adam and also to his wife did the Lord God make coats of skin, and clothed them.

Psalm 23:1–2

Chanting of David. Jehovah my shepherd, and I shall not want.	A Psalm of David The Lord *is* my shepherd; I shall not want.
2 He will cause me to lie down in pastures of tender grass: he will lead me to the water of rest.	2 He maketh me to lie down in green pastures: he leadeth me beside the still waters.

1 Timothy 2:11–12

11 Let the woman, in freedom from care, learn in all subjection.	11 Let the woman learn in silence with all subjection.
12 And I trust not the woman to teach, neither to exercise authority over the man, but to be in freedom from care.	12 But I suffer not a woman to teach, not to usurp authority over the man, but to be in silence.

The Woman's Bible

Elizabeth Cady Stanton's *Woman's Bible* marked a rapidly changing landscape.[33] At its publication in 1895 and 1898, great numbers of American women still regarded Scripture in more or less traditional terms, but with striking variations in where and how the Bible touched their lives. For a significant minority of articulate white women, traditional deference to Scripture was gone, but again with great variety in how they turned to other sources of authority.

In early adulthood Stanton had been briefly influenced by Protestant revivalism in the person of Charles Finney, but that phase soon gave way to her lifelong reforming passions. Those passions had originally included temperance and abolition as well as women's suffrage. But then Stanton's heterodox religious opinions alienated her from mainstream temperance advocates. After bitterness over the Fifteenth Amendment that granted the vote to Black men but not to women, she concentrated on women's suffrage while also developing increasingly racist views of African Americans, male and female. In the last period of her life even the suffrage cause was partially eclipsed by her obsessive effort to show that contemporary science discredited the forces she held most responsible for demeaning women: traditional Christianity, its use of the Bible, and even the Bible itself. In her mind, modern science unfettered by dogmatic constraints showed the way to full human dignity.[34]

Stanton's *Woman's Bible* provided commentary on scriptural passages about women that she hoped would disenthrall the deluded Americans, especially educated white women, who still considered Scripture divine revelation. With much effort beginning in the mid-1880s, Stanton recruited an advisory Revising Committee of twenty-five and eight others to assist her as editor. Four of these co-laborers were ordained ministers; only one was identified as a "Mrs." (Mrs. Robert G. Ingersoll). Many of them had begun life in Baptist, Presbyterian, Congregational, or Quaker families but then turned as adults to Free Thought and its reverence for science, to varieties of New Thought like the Theosophy of Madame Helena Blavatsky, or to liberal Protestantism (Unitarianism, Universalism).[35] A few, like Eva Ingersoll, were known to share her husband's very public agnosticism. Opinions in the book that resulted, however, ranged well beyond Stanton's own convictions.

Her introduction to the project's first volume sounded the kind of militancy that those who knew her expected. It complained especially about women who continued to accept Scripture as "the Word of God" even when clergy quoted it to preserve "their civil and political degradation" and "their unequal position in the church." She wrote with disappointment about the number of women who declined her invitation to contribute, including "Hebrew and Greek scholars" nervous about their academic reputations and others of "evangelical faith" worried about "affiliating with those of more liberal views, who do not regard the Bible as the 'Word of God,' but like any other book, to be judged by its merits."[36] Many of the commentaries that followed, however, reinterpreted rather than repudiated the texts under consideration. When, for example, Stanton herself commented on Genesis 1:26–28 and the creation of humanity ("let us make man in our image"), she opined that "there was consultation in the Godhead, and that the masculine and feminine elements were equally represented." As a result, "we have in these texts a plain declaration of the existence of the feminine element in the Godhead, equal in power and glory with the masculine."[37]

So it continued in Part II. Stanton's preface responded angrily to women who had criticized the first volume despite her effort to show that "this idea of woman's subordination is reiterated times without number, from Genesis to Revelation." In her mind, the contrast could not have been clearer between the "Revising Committee . . . in denying divine inspiration for such demoralizing ideas" and the general run of American women who would not abandon tradition: "We have made a fetich [sic] of the Bible long enough."[38] Again, however, much of the commentary did not so much deny divine interpretation as seek its reinterpretation. Lucinda B. Chandlar, a prominent official in the WCTU and an author of widely read works on moral purity in marriage, commented on the controversial passage from 1 Timothy chapter 2 enjoining "women [to] learn in silence with all subjection." About this text she suggested that if the Apostle Paul had known of the work accomplished by Florence Nightingale, Clara Barton, other exemplary nineteenth-century females, and the women who labored so faithfully as teachers in "the public school system of this Republic," he "might have hesitated to utter so tyrannical an edict."[39]

A lengthy appendix to the second volume of The Woman's Bible revealed even more clearly the multiplicity of female views on Scripture. It contained responses to two questions Stanton posed to a number of suffragists: "(1) Have the teachings of the Bible advanced or retarded the emancipation of women? (2) Have they dignified or degraded the Mothers of the Race?"[40] Stanton asked for these responses, many of which disagreed with her, because she wanted to show women uniting in discussion on the subject. She also hoped that a debate with conflicting opinions would increase sales while also reaffirming her lifelong belief in the female capacity for careful thought.[41]

As it happened, only a few of those who responded shared Stanton's point of view. Eva Ingersoll was one. She wrote, "I regard the Bible as I do the other so-called sacred books of the world. They are all produced in savage times, and, of course, contain many things that shock our sense of justice." A large majority, however, illustrated an observation once made by Aileen Kraditor: "Most suffragists found all they sought in the pages of the Old and New Testaments."[42] Alice Stone Blackwell, editor of the Woman's Journal, did offer a criticism, but in the context of approval: "the general principles of righteousness and justice laid down in the Bible" had elevated the human race, "the mothers included." But, she added, "the specific texts of Saint Paul enjoining subjection upon women have undoubtedly been a hindrance." Several respondents, including Mary Livermore, a veteran campaigner for abolition, temperance, and women's suffrage, forthrightly defended the Apostle Paul: "[T]he advice, or the commands, to women given by Paul in the Epistles, against which there has been so much railing, when studied in the light of the higher criticism, with the aid of contemporary history and Greek scholarship, show Paul to have been in advance of the religious teachers of his time."[43]

Frances Willard offered the sharpest, but also the gentlest, riposte. Willard, then at the height of her influence, had become particularly valuable for the suffragist campaign by convincing many in the WCTU to join Anthony and Stanton in their efforts. When Willard replied, she defended not just Scripture but also its relevance for the causes pursued by suffragists. "No such woman," she wrote, "as Mrs. Elizabeth Cady Stanton, with her heart aflame against all forms of injustice and of cruelty . . . has ever been produced in a country where the Bible was not incorporated into the thoughts and the affections of the people and had not been so during many generations." Willard did agree that the Scriptures had often been used to demean women, but she also affirmed forthrightly, "I believe that the Bible comes to us from God, and that it is a sufficient rule of faith and of practice." In her eyes, the Bible had made possible "a hallowed motherhood . . . because it raises woman up, and with her lifts toward heaven the world. . . . [I]t has produced the finest characters which I have ever known; by it I propose to live; and holding to the truth which it brings to us, I expect to pass from this world to one even more full of beauty and of hope."[44]

In the end, as Kathi Kern has demonstrated, *The Woman's Bible* weakened Stanton's desire to undercut biblical authority. All-out denunciations from many men did less to frustrate her project than discord among women. As a result of that discord even the National American Woman Suffrage Association, which Stanton had served as its first president, resolved by a vote of 53 to 41 to distance itself: "[T]his Association is non-sectarian, being composed of persons of all shades of religious opinion, and that it has no official connection with the so-called 'Woman's Bible,' or any theological publication."[45] (It was, however, characteristic of Stanton's respect for debate that she included this rebuke in the appendix to Part II of *The Woman's Bible*.)

All Over the Map

The mixed responses to Stanton's *Woman's Bible* illustrate a more general picture. Among women who were committed to suffrage as well as among American women as a whole, outright repudiation of Scripture remained rare. But the number of reinterpretations, repositionings, reworkings, and retranslations was increasing rapidly. Because these numerous efforts operated on different tracks, only occasionally did interests overlap among suffragists, members of the

WCTU, authors writing for proprietary Protestant audiences, and members of sectarian movements going their own way. The resulting chorus contained many strong voices, but very little harmony.[46]

Susan B. Anthony's stance showed how some reforming women cared for Scripture only as it helped or hindered their cause. From the time she met Stanton in 1851 to her death more than fifty years later, Anthony labored indefatigably, first as an agent for the Women's New York State Temperance Society, then all out and all the time for women's suffrage.[47] Unlike Stanton's antagonism to Scripture or the respect found among temperance campaigners, Anthony was religiously indifferent; above all, she wanted nothing to impede suffrage reform. At a meeting in 1888 of the International Council of Woman, an organization with many who opposed traditional deference to Scripture, Anthony showed how that prioritization worked. On the conference's last day, which happened to be Easter Sunday, several speakers referred dismissively to Scripture. Spontaneously Anthony as the chair called on Frances Willard for an unscripted response. Willard said exactly what Anthony hoped she would say: "[It would betray my] inmost heart . . . if I didn't, above all the teachings and all the voices, reverence the voice that calls to me from the pages of the Bible; if I didn't, above all things and always, in my mentality and spirituality, translate God into the term of Jesus Christ. I can not rest except there."[48] For Anthony, Willard saved the day, not because she spoke highly of Scripture but because her comments reassured others with evangelical convictions that it was safe to support the suffrage cause.

Anthony acted with similar purpose in responding to *The Woman's Bible*. After Part II appeared, she complained to Stanton that her obsession with overturning the Bible's authority damaged their campaign for the vote, while also wickedly reinforcing the oppression of African Americans. To her old friend she spoke freely: "Now this barbarism [mistreatment of Blacks and women] does not grow out of ancient Jewish Bibles—but out of our own sordid meanness!! And the like of you ought to stop hitting poor old St. Paul—and give your heaviest raps on the head of every Nabob—man or woman—who does injustice to a human being—for the crime! of color or sex!!"[49]

Attitudes toward Scripture within the woman's suffrage movement reflected attitudes in the nation's female population at large. Anthony's kind of pragmatism competed with passionate commitment, passionate rejection, and much that was simply taken for granted. In categories provided by Carolyn Osiek, a few "rejectionists" did want to escape traditional biblical authority.[50] Alongside Stanton and Eva Ingersoll stood, for example, the well-known author and lecturer Helen Hamilton Gardener. As an indication of their shared convictions, Gardener dedicated her book *Men, Women, and God* (1885) to Eva Ingersoll. After an introduction by Ingersoll's husband Robert, Gardener explained why facts and good sense disproved the notion that "without the Bible and the

Church the status of woman in Christian countries would be lower and her lot harder."[51]

Other women were "sublimationists" who found some biblical symbols useful for their overriding commitments to New Thought, Theosophy, or Spiritualism. "Liberationists" accepted Scripture but only after radical reinterpretation undertaken in service to universal standards of justice.

By far the majority of American women, however, appeared as "revisionists," accepting Scripture after appropriate adjustments, or "loyalists" who continued to uphold traditional views, though sometimes with modest reinterpretations of what remained for them an infallible authority. Foremost among the loyalists of her era was Frances Willard.[52] Although she came to appreciate some aspects of non-Christian religions as the WCTU expanded its international presence, Willard's own path led straight from conversion before the Civil War and an experience of the Second Blessing after the war to her reforming career. Under Willard's direction the Bible remained central for the WCTU, most of whose local meetings began with Scripture, prayer, and a hymn. Nor did Willard hesitate to enlist specific texts, like Ephesians 5:18 ("be not drunk with wine, wherein is excess"), in service to her cause.

In her northern Methodist church, conservatives did view her as a radical, as when they objected to her appearance as a "fraternal delegate" at the church's General Conference in 1880 and then in 1888 to her presence as an officially elected delegate. ("No women need apply" remained the denomination's position until its General Conferences in 1922.) Willard's own convictions, however, always remained close to the center. Her 1888 book, *Woman in the Pulpit*, mostly repeated arguments of antebellum Methodist authors like Phoebe Palmer. To Willard it made no sense to take the Apostle Paul literally in 1 Corinthians 14:34 ("let your women keep silence in the church"), and not when he instructed the Corinthians against going to court or preferring singleness over matrimony. In her judgment, as with many of her male peers, biblical interpretation needed to keep pace with the progress of Christian ethics: "[A]s the world becomes more deeply permeated by the principles of Christ's Gospel, methods of exegesis are revised. The old texts stand there, just as before, but we interpret them less narrowly." Her examples featured firsthand American experience: in the same way that "Onesimus and Canaan are no longer quoted as the slave-holder's mainstay," she was glad that now "theologians, not a few, find in the Bible no warrant whatever for the subjection of women in anything." To bring exegesis and interpretation where they should be, Willard hoped for the day when women would "share equally in the translating of the sacred text."[53] Certainly she leaned toward revision, but from a steady platform of Protestant loyalty.

Further toward the pole of revision stood the most popular female authors of Bible literature for custodial Protestants. Their concerns overlapped with those of suffragists and also sometimes with those of temperance reformers, but were by no means identical. Lucy Rider Meyer, who revived the order of deaconesses among Methodists, in 1888 published a book justifying that revival. *Deaconesses* followed Phoebe Palmer and other antebellum reformers who argued against restricting women to exclusively private spheres. The institutions that Meyer and her husband, Josiah Shelley Myer, founded—the Chicago Training School (1885) and the Chicago Deaconess House (1887)—featured much scriptural study but aimed at preparing women for active service as deaconesses or missionaries at home and abroad.[54]

Elizabeth Stuart Phelps's father, Austin Phelps, the president of Andover Seminary as well as an editor of *The Sabbath Hymnbook*, read the Bible as op- posing women's public activity. She, however, followed the course of her mother, Mary Gray Phelps, who had written a number of popular novels, including *The Angel over the Right Shoulder* (1852). In the immediate wake of the Civil War, Elizabeth published her own novels, some that became widely read, like *The Gates Ajar* (1868), which seasoned traditional Christian themes with spiritualist accounts of life beyond the grave for soldiers killed in the war. A generation later her *Story of Jesus Christ: An Interpretation* deliberately turned away from close textual or exegetical presentation to what she labeled "narrative." One scholar has called this book "a uniquely feminine portrait of Jesus; he is the ideal friend of women but displays many conventionally 'womanly' virtues himself; he is humble, nurturing, craving love and loyalty, and uniquely sensitive to the needs of others, particularly those of women."[55]

Louise Seymour Houghton enjoyed an unusually thorough education, which prepared her for, among other duties, translating books from French and German for American audiences. After working in a shelter home in France for several years, she returned to the States as a supporter of the Shelter House movement and advocate of the Social Gospel. Her own books reflected moderate use of European higher criticism, but also a firm commitment to what she considered scriptural values. In particular, she wanted contemporaries to view the Pentateuch as a guide for present-day needs, especially in protecting young women from sexual preda- tion, believing "the Mosaic code is in advance of any system of laws now in force so far as consideration for women is concerned, as the struggle good women are making in many states of our Union today, to get the 'age of consent' raised above sixteen years, fourteen, even ten years, will suffice to indicate."[56] Revision, adjust- ment, and reinterpretation marked the biblical engagement of widely read authors like Meyer, Phelps, and Houghton. Yet they still stood with religious women for whom the Bible provided encouragement, support, and even guidance.

Meanwhile, women in pietist, Holiness, strongly sectarian, proto-funda- mentalist, and (after the turn of the century) Pentecostal circles interacted only occasionally with suffragists. They did offer more support to the temperance movement, but only rarely engaged the works of Phelps, Houghton, and the like. Although uniformly loyalist in doctrine, these women could also be strikingly revisionist in practice. While the Methodist, Holiness, and then Pentecostal churches welcomed some women to some positions of public responsibility, spokesmen in churches moving toward fundamentalism often reaffirmed a separate domestic sphere for women and warned them off from public ministry.[57] In even these churches, however, practicality often trumped ideology.

On the traditionalist side of such loyalism, some women from custodial as well as sectarian churches rallied *against* the suffrage movement. As an example, in 1871 "Mrs. General Sherman" headlined a petition from "One Thousand Ladies" to the U.S. Senate opposing the vote for women. Their reason? "Holy Scripture inculcates a different, and for us higher, sphere apart from public life."[58] Such sentiments would continue among women who agreed with the male leaders who regarded any expansion of women's ministry as violating Scripture and decorum.

Far on the other side of the loyalist spectrum labored the era's women evangelists for whom Scripture remained meat and drink but who pursued all-out public ministry. Among these women, Black Holiness preachers like Julia A. J. Foote stood out. She was born in 1823 as the daughter of former slaves in New York.[59] At age fifteen Foote was converted through a sermon on Revelation 14:3 at a quarterly meeting of the AMEZ church. ("And they sung as it were a new song before the throne, and before the four beasts and the elders, and no man could learn that song but the hundred and forty and four thousand which were redeemed from the earth.") She later tried to convince church officials that she had been sanctified by reciting passages like Ezekiel 36:25–26 ("Then I will sprinkle clean water upon you, and ye shall be clean; from all your filthiness and from all your idols will I cleanse you; a new heart also will I give you, and a new spirit will I put within you, and I will take away the stony heart out of your flesh, and I will give you a heart of flesh. And I will put my spirit within you, and cause you to walk in my statutes, and ye shall keep my judgments, and do them"). With the Bible supplying much of the prose, her autobiography recounted travels, preaching, setbacks, joys, and sorrows, as on the sad day when her husband left for a long sea voyage: "While under this apparent cloud, I took the Bible to my closet, asking Divine aid. As I opened the book, my eyes fell on these words: 'For they Maker is thine husband.' I then read the fifty-fourth chapter of Isaiah over and over again. It seemed to me that I had never seen it before. I went forth glorifying God." After an angel called her to preach in the cadences of the KJV ("You have I chosen to go in my name and warn the people of their sin"), she itinerated for more than fifty years in Canada, the northern states, and the border South.[60] Late in life, in 1894, she became the first recognized deaconess in the AMEZ church.[61]

Few women biblical loyalists in white sectarian, Holiness, and Pentecostal movements gained the renown of Julia Foote. Yet a similar scriptural urgency carried many of them into surprisingly active ministry. To employ a typology proposed for such women by John Stackhouse, these groups often did include a "speechless majority" that accepted principles restricting women to a separate, private sphere.[62] Yet in many of the same movements, a variety of contextual factors opened doors wide to the world.

First was the surge in American missionary activity that after the Civil War inspired the imagination of more Protestant women than men. Female organizations for fundraising were one of the results in many denominations. So also was a steady stream of volunteers for the field. The China Inland Mission (CIM), founded in Britain in 1865 as a nondenominational "faith mission," pioneered in recruiting men and women with ordinary life and educational backgrounds. In Stackhouse's typology, the "missionary exception" of the CIM and other agencies provided many opportunities for teaching, organizing, doctoring, and even preaching often denied to women at home. Lottie Moon, a Southern Baptist missionary in China from 1873 to her death in 1912, inspired the creation of her denomination's Woman's Missionary Union, one of the largest and most active female associations of any kind in the United States.[63]

"Para-church autonomy" and "activity under authority" are categories describing the activities of many women who attended the surging number of Bible schools founded in the latter part of the century. As the nation's older colleges gradually moved away from their religious foundations, pedagogical entrepreneurs loyal to older traditions created a host of new institutions. They served young men, but also young women, eager for training oriented toward public service. Schools like the Moody Bible Institute in Chicago prepared both men and women to serve as Sunday school superintendents, religious education teachers, and even preachers or ministers in rural districts and small towns. For such graduates, gender distinctions based on careful exegesis gave way to local exigencies where welcome awaited any man or woman who volunteered.[64]

Stackhouse's final category, "equal partners in ministry," describes at least some Wesleyan groups, the Church of the Nazarene that organized in 1895, Black and white Holiness churches, and the earliest Pentecostal bodies that emerged after the Azusa Street revival of 1906. Male-female hierarchies never entirely disappeared in these movements, but to a far greater degree than in the custodial denominations and many sectarian bodies, women shared almost equally in the tasks of ministry.[65]

In summary, American religious movements known for their strict loyalty to Scripture, even for their biblicism, only sometimes translated convictions about the indispensability of the Bible into formulaic restrictions on women's public activity. For them, as with many suffragists, women active in the WCTU, and women who published on Scripture, the Bible remained a mainstay. But because reliance on Scripture had come to mean so many different things to so many different women, that diversity spread out the impact of the Bible on the nation as a whole.

The publication of Julia Smith's complete Bible translation was far from the only important contribution of 1876 to the history of Scripture. The Smith translation alongside these other events made the Centennial year as noteworthy for the Bible as it was for conflict between Native Americans and the federal government (Custer's "last stand"), American literature (the publication of *Tom Sawyer*), American popular culture (the circus of P. T. Barnum at the height of its popularity), American banditry (Jesse James running wild), American sacrilege (a failed attempt to disinter Abraham Lincoln's remains), and American learning (the founding of the American Library Association).[66]

As in other spheres of national life, Bible-connected events drew on what had gone before while also opening pathways to the future. The chapters that follow return frequently to breakthrough developments of the Centennial year before showing how, as with women and the Bible, the afterlife of those breakthroughs contributed significantly to the history of Scripture, but also to the increasingly fragmented presence of the Bible in national life.

24

Protestant Wounds of War

The Women's Christian Temperance Union showed that custodial Protestants employing traditional efforts to guide the nation could still make a difference, especially when joined by Methodists and some in sectarian churches willing to address the body politic on issues of personal moral reform. At the same time, as indicated by the campaign for women's suffrage, secular forces were also gaining ground. In all spheres of American life, the once pervasive influence of the Protestant traditions encountered heightened competition.

Yet quite apart from the growing multitudes who opposed or ignored traditional Protestant voices, fundamental changes among Protestants themselves played a large part in fragmenting the Bible civilization. While the original distinctions among Methodist, custodial, and sectarian traditions did not go away, the passage of time added new differences. Chief among them were fault lines created by the antebellum disputes over slavery, the visceral traumas of the war, divergent reactions to postbellum national developments, and new ideas from Europe. The overarching questions for the fragmenting Protestant world were how views of the Bible were changing and how those changes affected Protestants' place in the nation.

In response to such questions, disaggregation characterized the historically dominant Protestant movements. This chapter begins with the obvious: denominational divisions keyed to the Civil War that scrambled patterns dating from the early republic. It continues with a less obvious story: how divisions arising from antebellum controversies over slavery transformed Protestant intellectual life from intellectual cohesion to competition. The next chapter takes up other challenges that flared with particular intensity from the Centennial year onward.

In the nation's early decades, sectarian Protestants, Methodists, and proprietary Protestants had argued among themselves about how to create a God-honoring social order. If sectarians criticized the custodial Protestants for hanging on to vestiges of Christendom, they nonetheless shared the conviction that Methodists also emphasized, that Scripture was a rock-solid foundation for the practicalities of life and for all important intellectual questions. Beginning with the intractable controversies over Scripture and slavery, followed by the convulsions of civil war, and then full American attention to intellectual currents from Europe, the rock-solid foundation split and split again.[1]

America's Book. Mark A. Noll, Oxford University Press. © Oxford University Press 2022.
DOI: 10.1093/oso/9780197623466.003.0025

Denominational Upheaval: The South

The change from earlier patterns was most dramatic in the former Confederacy and the slave states that had remained in the Union (West Virginia, Kentucky, and Missouri).[2] Traditional differences of doctrine and church order never faded away completely among white Presbyterians, Methodists, Baptists, "Christians," and Disciples. But the trauma of defeat followed by white "Redemption" and Jim Crow segregation created a tribal unity that overrode previous distinctions. The white churches' support for this tribal unity exerted great influence in the former slave states since adherents to these churches dominated the religiously affiliated population, in some cases almost absolutely. Baptists, for instance, accounted for over half the churched population in Virginia, Georgia, and Mississippi. Baptists plus Methodists, Presbyterians, and the Restorationist churches enrolled more than 95% of the religiously affiliated in four states (Georgia, Mississippi, Alabama, and Arkansas) and over 80% in seven more.[3] Since Blacks included in those denominational numbers exercised negligible political power, the white tribal loyalty that enforced segregation and voted Democratic soon became the generic definition of "southern Protestant."

From one angle, all of these churches, including the Presbyterians and Methodists, became sectarian. As they embraced "the spirituality of the church" and defined social-political involvement as beyond the remit of corporate Christian concern, they looked like the Baptists of old. (As an abstract theological proposition, restricting church action to only what was spelled out explicitly in Scripture offered an intriguing alternative to both European Christendom and the informal American mingling of ecclesiastical and social influence. But when the South's custodial Protestants embraced this notion as they defended slavery and then Jim Crow segregation, they came much closer to sectarian but internally inconsistent biblicism. A principle denouncing social engagement became a silence enforcing social policy.)

From another angle, however, whites in these same churches displayed proprietary instincts by supporting segregation and lining up in lockstep behind the Democratic Party. With the strong support of the white churches and the exclusion of most Black voters, from 1880 to 1924 the Democratic candidate was victorious in the states of the former Confederacy in 131 out of 132 presidential ballots. It was a new kind of state-church establishment. (This dominance wavered only in 1928, when Protestant anti-Catholicism overrode Protestant anti-Republicanism and five states of the former Confederacy voted for the Quaker Herbert Hoover over the Catholic Al Smith. The earlier pattern then prevailed until the voting rights legislation of the 1960s.)[4]

Transformations in southern church life involved what from the outside looked like contradictions. Despite upholding the "spirituality" ideal that had developed in response to antislavery agitation, many southern white Protestants actively supported the temperance crusade of the late nineteenth century. By reinterpreting drunkenness as a "crime" instead of a "sin," laws limiting or banning alcohol came to be viewed as public goals that citizens (even if they were active church members) could support.[5] Similarly, the Southern Baptist Convention, though functioning increasingly as a custodial denomination, maintained historical principles of congregational autonomy and hands-off disengagement from politics. In many cities, small towns, and rural areas Southern Baptist churches attracted leading citizens who exerted a powerful cultural influence over their entire communities. The multiplication of such local situations came close to making the Convention, in Bill Leonard's apt phrase, "the Established church of the South."[6] Earlier distinctions between "custodial" and "sectarian" were transformed into new alignments for the white South.

During the century's final decades, Scripture certainly remained important for personal and family devotions, Sunday-by-Sunday sermons, revival preaching, and formal doctrinal teaching. Biblical language also served other purposes. As white Democrats in the South maneuvered to regain control of state governments, their choice of the Christian term "Redemption" for this violent process was no accident. It was only one of the ways, as Paul Harvey has written, that "white Southern Redemptionists . . . cast their political language in Kingdom language, making the struggle against 'Black Republicans' a religious duty."[7]

In addressing the world at large, the Bible remained highly visible. Temperance campaigns frequently resembled revivals with Scripture playing a secondary, but still important, part of arguments focused on the well-being of families, wives, and children. Sabbath observance and social purity, rather than race or poverty, received consistent attention. Voices from the fringes also advanced scriptural prescriptions for society. Authors who promoted polygenesis shoehorned the Bible into their arguments for Black racial inferiority. From the other ideological pole, the thin corps of southern ministers who supported the Social Gospel appealed to biblical teaching about the Kingdom of God in what Paul Harvey has called their "active but isolated and frustrated" efforts.[8]

In 1881 Atticus G. Haygood, a minister in the Methodist Episcopal Church, South, who was serving as president of Emory College near Atlanta, published one of the rare full appeals for fair treatment of African Americans.[9] His book, *Our Brother in Black*, did not argue directly from Scripture for Black equality or against the biblical proslavery interpretation; nor did he refer to the British precedent that called Black Americans "brothers." Instead, he used the Bible in a typically American way by describing the enslavement and emancipation of Africans as guided directly by providence. In an interesting reprise, he quoted the text John Witherspoon had used in justifying the American Revolution to explain why the evils of slavery did not frustrate God's beneficent purposes: God regularly "makes the wrath of men to praise him" (Ps 76:10). By appealing repeatedly to "facts" about the cultural deprivations of slavery, the capacity of Blacks for educational attainment, the demonstrated contributions of Black churches, and many forms of discrimination, Haygood was inspired by the words of Jesus to believe that "the truth makes free." In time-honored fashion, he also wove biblical quotations and precedents into the presentation of his case—for example, by likening the challenge of Black education to the difficulties faced by Nehemiah in the rebuilding of Jerusalem. In the book's one section of extended exegesis, he cited many of the passages used by Freeborn Garrettson and other abolitionists channeling the prophets who commanded Israel to "not defraud thy neighbor, neither rob him."[10] Yet despite the biblically infused tone of the book, when white periodicals took notice, it was for the purpose of denunciation: "the term [brother in black] . . . is full of error and sentimental nonsense, calculated to deceive."[11]

By the beginning of the new century, upstart Holiness and Pentecostal churches had revived forms of pietism that replicated certain sectarian emphases. As they did so, these newer movements partially followed the Landmark, antimission, Hardshell, and independent Baptists who had never abandoned their opposition to denominational mission agencies and their republican loyalty to strict local independence. In general terms, a sharp distinction prevailed between white denominations in the South and white denominations in the North. For the former, postbellum changes pushed all groups toward a new landscape dominated by sectarian biblicism; for the latter, the changes, while just as extensive, were more evolutionary than revolutionary.

Denominational Upheaval: Methodists

One of the many turning points in 1876 revealed the ongoing impact of earlier disruptions on Methodist history. In August of that centennial year the Methodist Episcopal Church and the Methodist Episcopal Church, South, concluded a series of discussions at a special meeting in Cape May, New Jersey. The meeting announced an agreement hammered out by fraternal delegates from the two denominations, that each would regard the other as "an evangelical Church, reared on Scriptural foundations."[12] Although the Southern Methodists had never renounced their biblical defense of slavery (some, indeed, continued to make that defense), the northern church was willing to move on.

Unlike their southern former colleagues, northern white Methodists wanted to leave the crises of civil war behind. As their expansion continued after the war (though at a slower pace), northern Methodists seemed to illustrate another instance of Max Weber's "routinization of charisma," with increased numbers spread over increased territory calling for increased bureaucracy and less simple fervor. Yet more was at work than merely structural formalization of institutional procedures over time. That "more" entailed Methodists using Scripture in ways they had earlier avoided by concentrating on the Bible for evangelization and personal sanctification. Engagement with Scripture on arguments concerning the Bible and slavery had opened the door for that change. Further participation in national public life moved some Methodists toward a sectarian Bible-only hermeneutic; many more adopted broader custodial concerns. In the process, the singularly gospel-centered character of early Methodism weakened.[13]

Early American Methodists had emphasized evangelism, godly living, entire sanctification, and the work of the Holy Spirit—and they did so while remaining somewhat detached from the political turmoil of the day. As Methodists established colleges and seminaries, expanded their bureaucracies, and ramped up all manner of publishing enterprises, they looked increasingly like the custodial Protestants who had organized the antebellum united front of voluntary agencies. In the centennial year, some Methodists called like Asbury for spiritual dedication, but more joined the chorus that hymned the nation. Orations at state and regional conferences sometimes even took up the rhetoric of national filiopietism—for example, that divine providence had not been more manifest in Israel "than in the history of this nation since the fourth day of July, 1776." One 1876 address titled "Our Bible and Our Liberties" lauded the Scriptures but devoted more attention to the American "development of liberty, as something practical, as a mighty destiny-shaping force in the world."[14] When Methodists took an interest in the Philadelphia Exhibition itself, they joined the other proprietary Protestants who petitioned the Centennial directors to close the Exhibition on Sunday.

A second worry about the Centennial reflected an additional proprietary interest. Methodists, who by 1876 had taken the national lead in temperance reform, opposed the sale of beer and other alcoholic beverages at the Exhibition. To many Methodists, it was only fitting for a concern about physical holiness to flow from intense concentration on spiritual holiness and then out to passionate mobilizing for social holiness. Methodists followed that logic by taking the lead at all levels of the temperance and later prohibition campaigns—from Frances Willard leading Methodist women to support the Women's Christian Temperance Union, significant Methodist involvement in the Anti-Saloon League (established in 1893), forceful lobbying for the Eighteenth Amendment, and commitment to enforcing this Prohibition Amendment after it became law in 1920.[15] For this reform, southern Methodists abandoned the "spirituality of the church" to link arms with their northern fellows, as did most of the other older Protestant denominations (except Episcopalians and Lutherans)—and regardless of internal theological differences.[16]

In the process of Methodist maturity, the Bible of course remained central, even as emphases shifted.[17] In Asbury's generation, Scripture's importance for society was incidental to its importance for the repentant person and the cell group gathered to promote holiness. By the time the serious Methodist William McKinley became president in 1897, social, public, and political inferences from Scripture were no longer incidental.[18]

The Methodist Publishing company's *Sunday School Journal for Teachers* of October 27, 1889, illustrated the redirection. The week's assigned Scripture was the story of King David's sin (adultery and murder) from 2 Samuel chapter 11. The lesson plan outlined "practical teachings," "questions for young scholars," "words with little people," and further scriptures in "hints for home study." This Bible study breathed the spirit of Asbury. ("Who came to show [David] his sin when he had yielded? **The Holy Spirit**. Who can forgive sin? **God alone**.") The same issue, however, ran a lengthy article urging study of the Bible "as a text book in our literary institutions." For its main points, the article quoted former Secretary of State William Seward, "President [Timothy] Dwight of Yale," and these words from Senator Daniel Webster: "If we abide by the principles taught in the Bible, our country will go on prospering and to prosper. But if we neglect its instructions, no man can tell how sudden a calamity may overwhelm us."[19] Asbury's single-minded focus had passed.

Given the expansion of American Methodism into so many levels of society, its course of development was almost inevitable. When, however, the emphasis shifted from redeeming individuals to redeeming society, that transition made a difference. As so often in American history, it proved difficult to attempt both at the same time.

The earlier Methodist spirituality, including the earlier wariness about political distractions, continued to flourish, but in smaller breakaway denominations like the Free Methodists and the Wesleyan Methodists. By the turn of the century, Holiness advocates, who established new denominations like the Church of the Nazarene, and a variety of Pentecostal movements also replicated much of the early Methodist stance over against "the world." The nondenominational Keswick movement, which promoted its own variation of Holiness teachings among proprietary and sectarian Protestants, also spread emphases similar to traditional Methodist spirituality.[20]

In short, important aspects of Asbury's religion, especially his dedication to internalizing the Scriptures in direct, personal address, lingered in the large Methodist denominations, inspired personal faith and spiritual community in a number of newer denominations, and bled out to influence other Protestants without direct Methodist connections. But now these earlier elements lacked a unifying organizational structure. They were receding in the large Methodist denominations in favor of custodial concerns. Where those emphases continued, they looked more simply sectarian in their all-out preoccupation with the Bible and personal holiness (or the Bible, the Holy Spirit, and personal holiness). In this later Methodist and post-Methodist history, forces behind the North-South schism of 1844 played a large part, especially differences on what it meant to follow the Scriptures that arguments on slavery and race had made impossible to ignore.

Denominational Upheaval: Northern Presbyterians

Postbellum northern Presbyterian history moved in the opposite direction, not exactly toward all-out sectarianism but with a definite curbing of earlier custodial concerns.[21] The Presbyterians who had been the national leaders in articulating abolitionism (Albert Barnes), cautious emancipationism (Charles Hodge), and the proslavery argument (James Henley Thornwell) became the Presbyterians fixated on questions of church reunion, biblical criticism, and the historical Presbyterian confessions. While the northern Presbyterian Church in the United States of America (PCUSA) never embraced "the spirituality of the church" as did the southern Presbyterian Church in the United States (PCUS), it struggled with cultural shifts taking place among the better educated, wealthier, and self-reliant white middle classes that had always been its prime constituency. Presbyterians remained more prominent in national life than their numbers might have indicated, as suggested by the Presbyterianism practiced in different ways by President William Henry Harrison (1889–93), President Woodrow Wilson (1913–21), and the populist three-time Democratic presidential candidate William Jennings Bryan. Yet as a denomination the PCUSA mostly shied away from addressing the sharpest challenges caused by the Civil War.[22]

Presbyterians had contributed fully to creating these daunting challenges. Heated debates over whether Scripture permitted slavery, which remained in play even after Lee surrendered, presented first-order questions about biblical interpretation. After Appomattox, the inability of the Thirteenth, Fourteenth, and Fifteenth Amendments to secure basic civil rights for African Americans kept questions alive about racial difference. Such questions became even more pressing as sporadic discrimination gave way to systematic Jim Crow regimes and extralegal lynchings. The impetus given by wartime mobilization to breakneck postbellum industrialization brought further challenges for Christian reasoning about wealth, poverty, social alienation, and the economy—especially for the Presbyterian churches where leaders of the new industry worshiped.

Northern Presbyterians remained every bit as earnest about Scripture after the war as they had been before, As a prime example, extensive debates over interpreting Scripture and applying the Westminster Confession's distillation of biblical doctrine preceded the 1869 merger of New School and Old School factions that had divided in 1836–37. Just as often, however, ideological commitments from the war edged aside concern for direct biblical teaching. The northern Old School's decision at its 1864 General Assembly to call slavery an unmitigated evil (and so overcoming earlier worries about whether it was a *malum in se*) brought its ethical stance closer to the New School and so paved the way for reunion. That decision, however, worked in the opposite direction for other Presbyterians. In combination with the northern Old School's demand in 1865–66 that southern and border-state ministers pass a loyalty test and publicly repent if they had supported the Confederacy, several Kentucky and Missouri presbyteries left their former confreres in the North for the southern church (the PCUS). Animosities remaining from the war also aborted attempts to explore reunion between the PCUS and the PCUSA.[23]

While Presbyterians North and South strengthened their commitment to a learned ministry, continued to publish serious theology in books and their many periodicals (popular weeklies, serious monthlies, weighty quarterlies), and expanded their churches' bureaucracies, the scope of their interests shrank. Ecclesiology became a major concern with the postwar formation of the PCUS and the PCUSA fixing the denominational order that would last for more than a century, until the reunion of these large bodies in 1983. For the PCUSA, the other signal events in the century's last decades were the removal from the Presbyterian ministry of David Swing in Chicago (1874), who was charged with departing from the Westminster Confession; learned controversies over biblical criticism (treated in the next chapter); and sharp contentions over whether to revise the Westminster Confession. (Proposed changes failed in 1893 after much discussion; ten years later the PCUSA added new chapters on the Holy Spirit and "the Gospel and the Love of God and Missions" along with a Declaratory Statement disavowing God's reprobation of the damned before they were born and affirming the salvation of those who died in infancy.)[24]

Concentration on these disputes reflected choices on how to maintain the integrity of the Bible that had been tested by interpretive strife over slavery. The main Presbyterian answer affirmed that taking the measure of higher criticism took priority over determining how Scripture might address race discrimination, burgeoning economic expansion, and the conditions propelling industrial strife.

Decisions about what mattered can be illustrated from the pages of the *Presbyterian and Reformed Review*, a new journal with high intellectual standards that began publishing in 1890 under the editorship of theological leaders from the PCUSA and representatives from German Reformed, Dutch Reformed, and Canadian Presbyterian churches. The journal's first six years of publication, from 1890 to 1895, coincided with the peak years of lynching outrages and the final implementation in the South of Jim Crow laws. They were also the years of severe economic downturn and sharp labor conflict, with the Homestead Strike in 1892, the Panic of 1893, the Pullman Strike of 1894, and the march of Coxey's Army of unemployed on Washington in 1894 pushing issues of the American economy to the forefront. During these years the *Presbyterian and Reformed Review* published many high-level studies on theological and church historical topics, including at least forty-two separate articles on questions relating to biblical criticism, many monographic in length and quality, as well as a separate four-part series on the composition of Genesis. Yet in the same years there were no major articles on race, Jim Crow, or the general treatment of African Americans. Eight articles touched on issues of society in some sense. One directly addressed the reasons Presbyterians were losing touch with "the working poor." Its author, the Rev. R. V. Hunter from Terre Haute, Indiana, quoted a Boston minister on why "the masses" where leaving the churches: "the effect of the recent Civil War, speculation and wealth, the Sunday newspapers, weakening in Sabbath observances, lower standards of proper worldly pleasures, rented pews." But Hunter disagreed, pointing instead to problems of preaching and confidence in Scripture.[25]

American Presbyterians did hear a visitor explain how traditional confessions could be relevant to an industrial age when Abraham Kuyper came from the Netherlands to Princeton Seminary in 1898 for much-noticed lectures on Calvinism.[26] The lectures did not provide much assistance for how traditional Reformed theology might counteract the race prejudice prevailing in the United States or—closer to Kuyper's own interests—in the Dutch colonies of South Africa. But they tried to show how confessional Calvinists could respond to the theological problems of rapid industrialization as well as challenges from new accumulations of wealth and new pluralization of social interests.

If Presbyterians devoted only minimum attention to such problems and challenges, some proprietary instincts did survive, though usually directed toward issues originating from before the war. A few members of the PCUSA joined forces with leaders of the Reformed Presbyterian Church who spearheaded the National Reform Association and its goal to amend the Constitution in order to acknowledge "Almighty God as the source of all authority and power in civil government, the Lord Jesus Christ as the Governor among the nations, and His revealed will as of supreme authority."[27] Other Presbyterians took up the fight to keep Bible reading in the public schools.[28] Still others continued an old Protestant tradition of attacking Catholics as harmful to the republic or took up a new cause in warning about Mormons as a similar threat.[29]

In sum, the PCUSA's commitments to learning and its middle-class constituency did sustain custodial interests. Yet the denomination's main focus in these postbellum years remained fixed on internal doctrinal questions. For most Presbyterians most of the time, it was never "the Bible only," even as the denomination pulled back significantly from the national leadership it had exercised for the half-century before the Civil War.

Common Sense

Earlier conflicts shaped the postbellum intellectual history of the main Protestant bodies as much as their denominational histories. Unlike those histories, which reflected the overt divisions of the war, postbellum intellectual history represented a less obvious, delayed response to the complex issues raised by antebellum disputing over slavery. Molly Oshatz borrowed a strong metaphor from Grant Wacker in her persuasive account of how conflicts that flared among Protestants in the last third of the century arose from sparks already burning more than a generation before: "The dynamite that blew apart biblical civilization was not . . . the issue of evolution or of historical criticism. Rather, it was the development of historical consciousness."[30] By "historical consciousness" Oshatz means the second broad sense of "history" that antebellum abolitionists often invoked in their debates over the Bible and slavery, not merely more information about more details of ancient civilizations but the progressive development of humankind's moral sensibilities. As noted, most of the biblical abolitionists believed that the Bible itself testified to such development in its own pages, which they were simply extrapolating into their own day. To them, universal moral consciousness—humanity's "common sense"—left no doubts.

"Common sense," however, had meant something different during the antebellum decades as taught at the colleges and seminaries organized first by proprietary Protestants, then by the Methodists, and eventually by Baptists and Campbellites as well. Sectarian spokesmen who looked askance at these institutions nonetheless embraced nearly the same set of intellectual commitments. All treated Scripture and the deliverances of conscience as essentially compatible. Common sense understood conceptually as the universal testimony of conscience matched common sense as the best way of grasping the "plain meaning" of scripture. What conscience revealed to individual minds confirmed, supported, and applied what the Bible revealed from God.[31]

In the postbellum decades "common sense" became anything but common. In particular, although those who appealed to "historical consciousness" made up a widely varying constituency, almost all were indebted in some way to the twinned meanings of "historicism" coming from Germany. First, as Grant Wacker explains, historical consciousness at its most extreme meant "the belief that culture is the product of its own history . . . ideas, values, and institutions of every sort are *wholly* conditioned by the historical setting in which they exist . . . the meaning of events is given not from outside history, not anterior to and independent of the process, but forged *wholly* within the process."[32] In other words, grasping the meaning of human existence required a move from transcendence to immanence. The second component, as defined by Gary Dorrien in his definitive history of American theological liberalism, followed the lead of Friedrich Schleiermacher from the early nineteenth century, who taught that "the proper subject of theology is religious consciousness." As a consequence, theology worthy of the name must appeal to "the authority of critical rationality and religious experience."[33] In other words, understanding the secrets of the universe required a move from external to internal revelation.

But how, in American circumstances, did "historical consciousness" become so important? Oshatz agrees that Darwinian evolution and biblical higher criticism played important parts after the war, but she also shows that deference to historical consciousness began with antebellum arguments over slavery. In particular, when some abolitionists felt it necessary to cede Scripture's "plain sense" to slavery proponents, they turned to the belief that "God's revelation unfolded progressively through human history, moral action had to be considered in its historical and social context, and the ultimate source of Protestant truth was the shared experience of believers rather than the letter of the biblical text."[34]

The genealogy of these convictions extended back to the early Unitarian movement, for example, when William Ellery Channing in 1820 wrote "The Moral Argument against Calvinism." Calvinism, he asserted, owed its longevity "to the influence of fear in palsying the moral nature." Yet reliance on "the great moral principles of human nature, and . . . the general strain of the Scriptures" would be enough to "free Christianity from the reproach of that system."[35] Channing, though, continued to believe in a normative Bible and the credibility of scriptural miracles, even as he expressed his opposition to slavery (as an emancipationist rather than an abolitionist). When Garrisonian radicals declared their willingness to give up Scripture if it did defend slavery, Channing—like Moses Stuart, Albert Barnes, Francis Wayland, and other northern moderates—disagreed because they held that developing ethical principles rooted in Scripture supported the testimony of conscience against enslavement. Yet even as these relatively traditional figures walked the tightrope between the forthright biblical proslavery position and radical postbiblical abolitionism, they changed the logic of the argument. They contended, again in Oshatz's careful phrases, that "God had educated humankind through the gradual unfolding of principles." This view represented a significant shift from "the early national apologetic, which held that scripture and the universal moral sense agreed and made their clearly discernible truths available to every reasonable person."[36]

After the war, effects from that change in logic precipitated further Protestant fragmentation. Some Protestants reaffirmed the early national consensus that had mobilized to repudiate Tom Paine (trust in conscience as delivering permanently fixed truths about the world and trust in the Bible *as* the Word of God). Others moved slowly or rapidly to the new views (trust in conscience meaning the progressive development of moral truths and trust in the Bible as *containing* the Word of God.) The important historical point is that this parting of the ways was hastened first by the antebellum biblical debates and then by the outcome of the war itself.

Many leaders of liberalizing Protestant theology explicitly traced their reliance on progressive common sense to earlier dissatisfaction with traditional biblical views. In 1872 Samuel Harris, professor of theology at the Yale Divinity School, published articles indicating his belief that the abolition of slavery showed how revelation developed over time: "The Organic and Visible Manifestation of Christ's Kingdom, and the Human Agency in Its Advancement" and "The Progress of Christ's Kingdom in Its Relation to Civilization."[37] According to Harris, if Jesus had spoken out against slavery, he would never have been able to complete his mission, but now the recent abolition of slavery demonstrated that God had actively guided the progressive clarification of Christian morality.[38]

Newman Smyth was a "New Theologian" who had studied in Germany with the conservative historicist F. G. A. Tholuck and the moderate historicist Isaak August Dorner while becoming thoroughly committed to Schleiermacher's approach to religion. He was serving a Presbyterian church in Quincy, Illinois, when in 1879 he used slavery as his main illustration to explain how Scripture initiated a progressive revelation of God's will for humanity. To Smyth, "the fact that arguments in defense of slavery used to be drawn from the Bible, shows the need of popular instruction with regard to the development of revelation, and the guiding spirit of the Bible." Carrying out such instruction would lead to the realization that "revelation, in the end has succeeded in developing the idea of the individual and his rights, which was wanting in an early day, and which could be firmly secured only by a patient work of God in human history." Without a doubt, the Mosaic record was the "fountain-head" of what followed, which meant that "historically, the abolition of slavery is due to the Bible, and the religion of the Bible." Yet there had been "faults of the Old Testament," like the permission of enslavement, which Smyth described as "the necessary incidents in a course of moral education . . . the unavoidable limitations of a patient and progressive revelation." A proper understanding of Scripture would take these faults in stride because "the Bible is not an abstract of useful doctrines to be understood by rule; it is rather like nature, full of mystery, and full of life."[39] Smyth, who soon became the pastor of New Haven's First (Central) Congregational Church, was not giving up on the Bible, but for him it had become crucial to read Scripture as supporting "the individual and his rights."

In battling the conservatives in his Presbyterian denomination, Charles Briggs's leadership in promoting a moderate view of biblical higher criticism is examined in the next chapter. Here his thinking on the New Testament and slavery is relevant. Briggs knew very well that "polygamy and slavery have been defended from the New Testament because Jesus and His apostles did not declare against them." Yet in the same way that these biblical figures simply accepted their era's precritical views concerning the authorship of Old Testament writings, so on slavery they simply reflected "the views of men of the time of Christ." For Briggs and those who agreed with him, the mistake lay in thinking of Scripture as, in Oshatz's words, "a blueprint for human life and a closed, complete container of truth" rather than as "an inspired record of the living communion of God with humankind."[40] "History" as a principle of development over time and a belief in contemporary sensibility about right and wrong were the keys.

And so this beat went on. A generation later, Charles Jefferson of New York City's Broadway Tabernacle Church, which Charles Finney had served as its first pastor, weaponized the biblical defense of slavery for a new purpose. In attacking individuals who would not support a League of Nations because the Scriptures said nothing about such a body, Jefferson called that approach to the Bible "a millstone around the neck of the Christian church." True, Scripture has "furnished proof texts for Mormonism, and it bolstered up the cause of the slaveholder, and it has often fed the flames of war," but those abuses merely turned the Bible into "one of the most dangerous books in all the world." A right understanding of "the spirit of Jesus" showed that he condemned "war just as he condemns slavery, and all other institutions which work havoc with the hearts and homes of men." More generally, "whoever preaches the doctrine of the Fatherhood of God and the brotherhood of man, is striking heavy blows at polygamy and slavery and war."[41]

Memoirs of leading liberal Protestants made the antebellum-postbellum connection even more explicit.[42] Lyman Abbott served as the collegiate pastor with Henry Ward Beecher and was longtime editor of the *Outlook*, an influential periodical that treated all manner of religious and general subjects with a roster of well-known authors that included Theodore Roosevelt. Abbott titled the chapter of his autobiography related to slavery "A Religious Revolution." In his youth (1840s and 1850s), Abbot held a conventional view of Scripture as dictated verbal revelation. Soon, however, "the moral problems which this [older] view of the Bible involves puzzled me increasingly." In particular he wondered, "What answers should I make to the Biblical arguments for slavery and polygamy?" Abbott first concluded that Jesus had said nothing about such matters as "a statesman's concession to the passions and prejudices of a primitive people."

But then Abbot went beyond "history," meaning new information about first-century Palestine, to "history" as progressive moral conscience. The real issue, he reasoned, "was not one between theories of inspiration, Trinity, atonement, miracles, or any other, but between materialism and the life of the spirit." By the Centennial year Abbott had reached the settled conclusion that prevailed for the rest of his life: "[T]he foundation of spiritual faith is neither in Christ nor in the Bible, but in the spiritual consciousness of man. . . . The Bible is not a book, fallible or infallible, *about* religion; it is a literature full *of* religion."[43]

The liberalizing theologies represented by Harris, Smyth, Briggs, Jefferson, and Abbott paralleled the course of proof-texting biblicism in one significant particular. In the same way that antebellum proslavery arguments tightened the affinity between traditional trust in Scripture and treatment of the Bible as a collection of verse-facts, so antebellum antislavery arguments tightened the affinity between willingness to rethink the authority of Scripture and treatment of the Bible as confirming the progressive development of moral consciousness.

Complicating Common Sense and a Spectrum of Views on Scripture

Viewed within the larger framework of nineteenth-century intellectual developments, the path from Channing in 1820 to Abbott nearly a century later can be viewed as changing the meaning of foundational terms while continuing to rely on those same terms. The opponents of Tom Paine in the 1790s as well as the evangelical Protestants featured in Robert Baird's 1844 history trusted just as much in what Channing called "conscience and reason" as did the Unitarians.[44] The earlier era's standard teaching of moral philosophy appealed to conscience as revealing universal human belief in a creating First Cause and universal human trust in shared moral norms. The college presidents who regularly taught seniors in their capstone moral philosophy classes moved easily from these theistic conclusions to affirming traditional Protestant Christianity, including traditional views of the Bible. Similar confidence in the fixity of facts understood in Baconian terms testified to an equally strong reliance on "reason" and what would soon be called "science." The great change prompted first by antebellum slavery arguments and then the Civil War, followed by the introduction of Darwinism and higher criticism, left confidence in "conscience and reason" intact. But now conscience was thought to reveal a progressive moral sensibility. Similarly, reason and science remained supreme intellectual guides, but as they revealed a world of organic natural development. Appeal to the same intellectual standards by constituencies that defined key terms differently fueled much of the late nineteenth-century conflict between Protestant liberals and Protestant conservatives, and then between modernists and fundamentalists in the early twentieth century.[45]

Disagreements among postbellum Protestants resulted, however, in anything but clear-cut lines between the older theology and newer perspectives. On questions concerning Scripture, an entire spectrum emerged with differences keyed, first, to degrees of accepting the progressive understanding of "history," but also to whether that new understanding replaced or only augmented earlier traditional Protestant theology. Because of their long-standing commitments to formal education and learned publication, divisions among proprietary Protestants are easiest to identify.

A spectrum can be traced from left to right, beginning with *post-Christian skeptical pragmatists*. As Louis Menand and others have shown, the apparently mindless devastation of the Civil War led savants like Oliver Wendell Holmes Jr. and William Dean Howells to abandon traditional belief in God, revelation, and providence. Along with a handful of thoughtful bourgeoisie, they turned instead to life guides from science, law, literature, business, or government.[46]

More complicated were the ranks of *evangelical liberals* or *liberal evangelicals*, the custodial Protestants who embraced the new common sense but who also retained some, or even many, aspects of orthodox Protestantism. Liberals in the late nineteenth century agreed on the need to move beyond biblical inerrancy and the reliance on proof-texting that often accompanied such belief. But they differed on how much to demythologize the Bible's miracle stories, how much hope for salvation could be found in historical progress, and how far to understand the Bible as simply a marker of human moral development. Unitarians like Thomas Wentworth Higginson represented liberalism at its most thorough. In 1871 he opined that Christianity offered "Inner Light," but only as the clearest representation of that which "lighteth every man that cometh into the world [quoting Jn 1:9]."[47] Somewhat more traditional faith remained with Crawford Toy, who became a professor of Hebrew at the Harvard Divinity School after an earlier career at Southern Baptist Seminary. In 1890 Toy published a major work that explained Christianity arising from Judaism "as a product of human thought," but also depicting Jesus, who "made the essence of the new law to be the purity of the individual soul," as the omega point to which all world religions pointed.[48] William Rainey Harper, Hebrew professor at Yale before becoming the founding president of the University of Chicago, defended biblical higher criticism by writing in 1894 that religion should be "moved by the spirit of our time" and that study of Scripture should be "influenced by the methods of investigation prevalent in other fields of study." Yet Harper also remained a lifelong friend of the popular evangelist D. L. Moody, who invited Harper to speak at his summer conferences in Massachusetts and who shortly before his death in 1899 received an invitation from Harper to address students at the University of Chicago.[49]

Charles Briggs remained even more rooted in traditional belief, as evident by his negative reaction in the early twentieth century when younger colleagues at Union Seminary questioned the historicity of Jesus's birth narratives in Luke and Matthew, the general historicity of all biblical narratives, and traditional belief in Christ as fully divine and fully human.[50] Liberalism for nineteenth-century American theologians was, as always, a relative term that covered many degrees of reliance on the new "history."

Even more complicated were the *progressive conservatives* who whole-heartedly embraced a modern sense of organic development, but who also maintained traditional Bible-centered convictions. These figures embraced "historicism" as understood by Germany's "Mediating Theology," an approach that included a conservative form taught to many Americans by F. G. A. Tholuck at Halle and a moderate form that Isaak Dorner in Berlin bequeathed to a comparable number of Americans.[51] Only in the twentieth century did the liberal historicism of Albrecht Ritschl, which stressed Christianity's social-ethical character taking shape wholly within culture, exert a decisive influence on American theologians.[52] Henry Boynton Smith, who taught at Union Seminary until his death in 1877, advocated a kind of American mediating theology that affirmed the importance of religious experience *and* the development of Christianity through history *and* the historicity of scriptural narratives, including miracles.[53] The ecumenical polymath Philip Schaff continued a moderate version of this tradition in his work as church historian, ecumenist, and Bible translator. More traditional Protestants criticized Schaff's historical works for viewing the Reformation as growing out of, instead of repudiating, medieval Catholicism, and for using recently discovered biblical manuscripts to correct mistakes in the King James Version. But Schaff's commitment to progress in history coexisted with a traditional respect for biblical revelation.[54]

Still more complicated were what might be called the *patchwork conservatives*, like Augustus H. Strong, the main theologian of the Northern Baptist Seminary in Rochester, New York, and E. Y. Mullins, president of Louisville's Southern Baptist Theological Seminary from 1899 to 1927. Without advocating the "historicism" communicated from Germany, these figures nonetheless, in Grant Wacker's phrases, "patch[ed] together—the historical processes revealed by the modern world and the timeless certitude of an earlier era."[55] Although Strong and Mullins retained the confidence of most of their fellow Baptist traditionalists, Strong tried to show how insights from evolution and theistic personalism could enhance rather than subvert Protestant orthodoxy. Mullins did something similar by speaking of personal religious experience as an enrichment of traditional Christianity in terms almost like those used by Friedrich Schleiermacher.[56]

A final constituency among educated custodial elites, the *confessional conservatives*, spoke out strongly against any concession to modern historical conscience. Charles Hodge at Princeton Theological Seminary represented other northern Presbyterians, as well as some Congregationalists and Episcopalians, when he claimed, only semi-facetiously, "that a new idea never originated in the seminary."[57] As a traditional custodial Protestant, Hodge nonetheless came close to "the Bible only" position when he took a stand against abolition because it could not be supported by explicit scriptural teaching. Only during the Civil War did Hodge reluctantly allow a measure of influence from contemporary moral conscience to influence his thinking on that contentious subject.[58] Benjamin Breckinridge Warfield, Hodge's successor as the main theologian at Princeton, raised a conservative standard in an 1881 article with Hodge's son (Archibald Alexander Hodge) that updated the doctrine of biblical inerrancy, though with more care than from some of the doctrine's later advocates. Warfield also opposed amending the Westminster Confession's statements on divine providence and predestination, which other Presbyterians proposed in order to adjust them to modern moral sensibility.[59]

Yet even for such forthright conservatives nuance is required. Confessional conservatives did eventually form an alliance of convenience with Bible-only sectarians, who enlisted the Warfield-Hodge statement on inerrancy in order to oppose liberal theology. Nonetheless, the conservatives never became fundamentalists. Warfield, for instance, expressed more opposition to Jim Crow segregation than many of his era's more liberal theologians.[60] He remained opposed to the premillennialism of his era, and he criticized sectarians when they purported to define Christian doctrines by simply collecting Bible verses from throughout the Scriptures and organizing them without context by themes or subjects.[61] Geerhardus Vos, who began teaching at Princeton Seminary in 1892, even advanced a view of progress within the scope of biblical revelation that brought him somewhat closer to the progressive conservatives of the late nineteenth century.[62]

Before paying attention in the next chapter to the sectarians who were allied to the most conservative thinkers in custodial Protestant traditions, it is important to note the wider effects of intra-Protestant differences concerning "history." Northern proprietary Protestants united in trying to align the truths of Scripture with common sense. But when arguments over Scripture and slavery exposed conflicting opinions about what common sense revealed, American Protestant theology began to divide, as it remains divided to this day. Still, if "history" did blow apart what once had been the shared intellectual universe of these Protestants, representatives of the contending approaches to Scripture continued to express concern for the welfare of the nation. Yet because that concern now came from so many different directions, disputes over "history" and Scripture made it much more difficult for distinctly Protestant theology to exert any kind of concentrated influence.

For the history of the Bible, the Civil War did not end in 1865. Ecclesiastical separations among white Protestants long outlasted the military victory that brought rebelling states back into the Union. Racial divisions between Black and white churches survived the Thirteenth, Fourteenth, and Fifteenth Amendments almost entirely intact. White Protestant reliance on Scripture never regained the cohesion that first unraveled in antebellum disagreements over what God's Word revealed about slavery. Events in the Centennial year, to which we now return, signaled an array of new challenges that produced new levels of stress and strain.

25

Protestant Realignments

For white Protestants, the history of the Bible after the Civil War featured a series of divisions of what had earlier been joined together. Events from 1876 once again showed where those divisions were headed.

For Dwight L. Moody, the Centennial year began in the Centennial city. Moody and his song-leader Ira Sankey had returned to the United States from Britain the previous summer after two years of unexpected success in conducting urban revivals. News of that success once again illustrated American cultural dependence on Britain by how it generated multiple requests for similar campaigns at home. After considerable deliberation, Moody and Sankey agreed to a short series of meetings in Brooklyn followed by a longer stay in Philadelphia, where Moody greeted the new year by preaching to three different crowds of twelve thousand people each. They assembled in a freight depot that the entrepreneur John Wanamaker was planning to remodel as a shopping emporium. With his warm, colloquial manner, Moody's message of personal consecration clearly moved his largely middle-class audience, though without much apparent effect on the working people he also hoped to reach.[1] Only a few weeks later Washington Gladden, a young Congregational minister in Springfield, Massachusetts, startled his congregation by turning Sunday evening sermons into lectures focused on the laboring classes. Soon the lectures became a book, *Working People and Their Employers*. Like Moody, Gladden had a message for the time, but that message went beyond the personal to address social conditions directly. Because Gladden believed that "the lawfulness of doing good on the Lord's Day is not an open question," he found Sunday evenings perfect for bringing "the truth of the New Testament to bear directly upon the matters now in dispute between labor and capital." Such questions had become urgent, Gladden declared, "now that slavery is out of the way."[2]

Slavery, however, was not "out of the way" for some who had fought the good fight before and during the war. The *Christian Cynosure* was published in Wheaton, Illinois, by Jonathan Blanchard, an early supporter of Charles Finney's revivals, one-time traveling agent for the American Anti-Slavery Society, and longtime friend of the Beecher clan. In 1876 Blanchard's magazine included several obituaries of comrades remembered with honor primarily because of their antislavery stance, as in one memorial: "He was a bitter opponent of slavery, and an old-time abolitionist."[3] A small group of Presbyterian and Baptist ministers

America's Book. Mark A. Noll, Oxford University Press. © Oxford University Press 2022.
DOI: 10.1093/oso/9780197623466.003.0026

who otherwise shared much in common with Blanchard were, however, looking forward rather than back when they gathered that summer at Swampscott, Massachusetts, 110 miles east of Gladden's Springfield on the coast north of Boston. Some who attended this annual gathering of the Believers Meeting for Bible Study had once been ardent abolitionists, but now a new approach to some of Scripture's most recondite apocalyptic passages fueled their excitement. Their deliberations led to publications and further meetings promoting a way of reading the Bible that detailed what would happen in the future, perhaps very soon. It became known as dispensational premillennialism.[4]

From a completely different intellectual universe, on September 21 a young, German-trained Bible scholar, Charles A. Briggs, delivered his inaugural address as the Davenport Professor of Hebrew and Cognate Languages at Union Theological Seminary in New York City. To Briggs, a responsible grasp of Scripture required serious study of the ancient world, but also careful attention to the ethical norms of his era's most learned intellectuals.[5] Asa Gray, a renowned Harvard botanist, also hoped that a book he published in 1876 would encourage a sounder grasp of Scripture. To that end, the collection of essays and reviews he called *Darwiniana* spelled out repeatedly why he found no difficulty in affirming both a traditional Christian belief in the Bible and the evolutionary science of Charles Darwin.[6]

With the history of Scripture in view, Moody, Gladden, Blanchard, the Swampscott gathering, Briggs, and Gray were moving in different directions. As the century wore on, the differences became only more pronounced.

Society

The "evangelical united front" of the early nineteenth century had been led by custodial churchmen, with some help from Methodists, but always regarded warily by Baptists and other sectarians even when they occasionally joined in. White Protestants had pursued social reform optimistically, with the expectation that converted individuals would be convinced from Scripture to clean up their own lives and then guide society to gospel norms. At the beginning all seemed a matter of simply following transparent biblical guidelines. The transformation of individual consciences, with perhaps subordinate attention to social structures, would then transform public life. Jonathan Blanchard even foresaw that such reform could lead to what in 1839 he called a "perfect state of society," where sin was exterminated and "the law of God is the law of the land."[7] As late as 1845, Blanchard had explained to a debate audience in Cincinnati that if Christian slave owners truly understood "the one-bloodism of human kind [Acts 17:26]," they would emancipate their chattel, acknowledge the human dignity of the formerly enslaved, and come closer to the Kingdom of God built upon "those great principles of human rights, drawn from the New Testament, and announced in the Declaration of Independence."[8] In the past, Gladden, Moody, and some of the Swampscott Bible students had expressed similar expectations. By 1876 the similarities had vanished.

Washington Gladden still remained buoyantly hopeful that the Golden Rule applied to conflict between capital and labor could repeat the great work it had so recently accomplished: "[W]hen Christ appeared, declaring that the law and the prophets were all summed up in the rule which bids us do to others as we would have others do to us, the doom of [slavery] was sealed." As with earlier reformers, Gladden also stressed the importance of self-discipline, especially by warning "the working-men" away from "strong drink" as their worst enemy. To the individual capitalist he promised "instant peace" if the business owner "would measure his profits, and the working-man his wages, by the Golden Rule." Gladden, however, did make one significant adjustment to the pattern of antebellum reform by reversing priorities, that is, by subordinating individual conversions to a social application of "the power that came into the world when Christ was born." In his 1876 lectures, Gladden proclaimed that this "power" could overcome the nation's intensifying industrial strife. He did not think it would lead to socialism or disruptive union action by the working classes, but to "industrial co-operation" whereby industry was governed by "the virtue Paul indicates when he wrote the Romans, 'Be kindly affectioned one toward another with brotherly love, in honor preferring one another [Rom 12:10].' "[9] As many historians have pointed out, the path to this kind of social program ran straight from antebellum abolition, the only bend in the road Gladden's concentration on social structure instead of personal conversion.

For the Swampscott Bible students that path diverged sharply. Although they still held that personal conversion necessitated personal discipline, they no longer believed that converting individuals would lead to a better society. Instead, their new premillennial beliefs indicated that the world would continue to deteriorate until the Second Coming of Christ. Where earlier active programs of social renewal accompanied premillennial beliefs, as they had for Cotton Mather in colonial New England, the dispensational premillennialists turned almost completely aside from trying to reform social structures.[10]

The divergence from antebellum patterns was not as complete for Moody and Blanchard, since they still held that genuine Christianity would bring about a better social order, though not in Gladden's terms. For Moody, society would be renewed when individuals made rootless by mass industrialization were converted and then practiced the virtues that had once dignified life in rural and small-town America. Especially after firsthand experience with urban squalor in Britain, Moody devoted considerable energy to raising money for orphans, schooling for the poor, and relief for the indigent. Despite his spectacular success as an urban evangelist, from about 1880 he gave increasing attention to schools founded in his Massachusetts hometown and in Chicago, where he hoped to train Christian workers who could effectively reach all levels of society. Yet during his era's well-publicized clashes between labor and capital, Moody remained silent because of his overarching commitment to personal redemption as the key to well-being in this life as well as the world to come.[11]

A comparison shows how times had changed. Charles Grandison Finney, like Moody the leading evangelist of his age, had concentrated his own energies on preaching, and then theological exposition, but he also blessed Theodore Dwight Weld and other converts when they launched their crusade against slavery. Moody throughout his career was always pleased with opportunities to address Black audience. Yet when in 1876 he conducted a preaching campaign in Augusta, Georgia, and local white leaders insisted upon segregating the audience, Moody reluctantly gave in to their wishes.[12] Only late in his life did he finally end the segregation of his meetings.[13] Revival and reform had gone their separate ways.

The history of the Wesleyan Methodist Connection followed a similar path. It was founded in 1843 by proponents of "perfectionism" who complained that the main Methodist body had exchanged John Wesley's doctrine of "perfect love" for a reprehensible accommodation to slavery.[14] Within its first decade of existence, many Wesleyans helped slaves escape through the Underground Railroad; one of its churches supplied the venue for the famous women's rights convention at Seneca Falls, New York, in 1848; one of its ministers preached the sermon when Antoinette Brown was ordained to the Christian ministry in 1853; and several of its leading spokesmen stood with William Lloyd Garrison in renouncing warfare (though they objected to how he attacked the churches and relativized biblical authority). By 1876 the first generation of the Wesleyans' leaders had either died, embraced spiritualism rather than the Holy Spirit, or begun to emphasize personal holiness *instead of* social reform. Some had replaced opposition against the slave power with opposition to the Masons and other secret societies; they opposed the Ku Klux Klan because of its secret oath-taking more than for its violence against Blacks and Catholics.

Blanchard, who in 1860 helped reorganize Wheaton College, which had been founded by Wesleyan Methodists, shared Moody's belief in the primacy of the personal, but continued as an aggressive social campaigner. Yet Blanchard's antebellum optimism about social change turned to pessimism because the Civil War, though ending slavery, did not permanently Christianize the nation. He still hoped for social betterment but continued to think that it would come strictly from personal moral transformation. Ever the activist, he not only devoted his energies to promoting temperance and supporting the Prohibition

Party; he also mounted a ferocious campaign against the Masons, especially the secrecy of their organization, which he excoriated as wielding the same kind of malevolent influence that "the slave power" had exercised before the war. In the shrewd assessment of Richard Taylor, Blanchard and other Protestants dismayed by the postbellum state of the nation remained "under the influence of a social philosophy rooted in Jacksonian America." All-or-nothing concentration on individual conversion and individual social responsibility left them unequipped to understand the systemic assaults on Black citizens and with "little appreciation for moral issues at stake in the development of industrial capitalism."[15] The Bible spoke with unabated authority to the new premillennialists, Moody, and Blanchard. But its meaning for society could hardly be further removed from how it spoke to Washington Gladden.

Gladden emerged as a pioneer of a Social Gospel movement that has been well studied by numerous scholars.[16] It would culminate in the work of Walter Rauschenbusch, whose widely regarded writings from the first years of the next century included *Christianity and the Social Crisis* (1907) and *Christianity and the Social Order* (1910). More than pioneers of the Social Gospel like Gladden, Rauschenbusch grounded his assessments in a biblical exaltation of Jesus and an expansion of scriptural themes on the Kingdom of God.[17]

Yet as other historians have recently shown, laboring men and women not usually recognized as part of the formal Social Gospel movement or sharing the custodial instincts of that movement had been applying Scripture to the structures of American economic life from the beginnings of industrialization. This tradition represented a sectarian alternative that depended on bottom-up appropriation of the Bible rather than deference to seminary-sanctioned voices. In the 1830s some urban activists insisted that they were only following the principles of Jesus in organizing working people.[18] After the Civil War, as documented by Heath Carter and others, the Bible was a constant resource for opposing economic extravagance and supporting labor reform.[19]

Andrew Cameron, a Scottish immigrant who was familiar with labor-organized Chartist churches in his native land, began publishing the *Workingman's Advocate* shortly after the Civil War. The editorial stance of his newspaper as well as his advocacy for Chicago's General Trades Assembly illustrated the way labor organizers could rely on the Scriptures. During the course of his career, Cameron supported campaigns for the eight-hour day, complained about the captivity of wealthy urban churches to the lords of trade, and differentiated between responsible unionism and radical socialism. As a teetotaler and a believer in traditional Christian doctrines like the reality of hell, Cameron also embraced standard attitudes about the relation of Christian teaching and the fate of the nation; as he wrote in 1867, "[U]pon the spread of the gospel depends the perpetuation of the American republic." Biblical references peppered the pages of his paper, as when he echoed the Psalmist's lament on behalf of laboring people ("How long O Lord! How long!") or when he quoted Luke 10:7, a passage much beloved by union organizers ("the laborer is worthy of his hire"). Cameron had been employing such arguments for nearly a decade before 1876 and the appearance of Gladden's *Working People and Their Employers*, a book that Cameron in fact took to task. Against Gladden's appeal to the Golden Rule, Cameron drew on his experience in arguing for the eight-hour day to conclude, "Employers have rebelled against Christ's teachings too often and too persistently to hope for a solution of the trouble in this way." As an elderly man in 1888, Cameron sustained his indictment against ministers who genuflected to industrial titans: "Instead of the gospel of Christ, their audiences are regaled with tirades against labor, about which they know as little as they do about the Master whom they claim to serve. They have become the apologists of the oppressor instead of the advocates of the oppressed."[20]

Although Cameron was unusual in the consistency of his biblicism, he did not stand alone. Especially after major flare-ups in this era of labor-industrialist strife, scriptural language and images supplied fulsome resources for the friends of labor. During the famous strike of 1877, the first attempt to apply national pressure on railroad barons, many Chicago ministers appealed for harsh treatment of the strikers. But a few, like Simon McChesney at Park Avenue Methodist Church, once again quoted Luke 10:7 in order to preach, "[T]he bible, as I read it, is the friend of the workingman."[21] In the wake of the Haymarket bomb that killed seven policemen on May 4, 1886, one of the individuals sentenced to death for the outrage defended active opposition to the capitalist class by channeling the Gospel of Matthew; he compared "the Jerusalem Board of Trade" that crucified Jesus to Chicago's industrialists who "drummed up" charges in their rush to judgment against him.[22] In 1894 a bitter strike against the Pullman Palace Car Company led to a federal injunction, a call-out of federal troops by President Grover Cleveland, and heated commentary from all sides. Again, many of Chicago's clergymen lauded the aggressive action against the strikers, but ministers in a few churches (Methodist, Danish Lutheran, Baptist, Christian Reformed) who read Scripture as supporting the strike or criticizing the owners witnessed an influx of working people into their churches.[23]

Similar appeals from similarly positioned workers to similar biblical warrants continued into the twentieth century. As Rauschenbusch's *Christianity and the Social Crisis* from 1907 was being hailed as a landmark theological breakthrough, laboring men and women continued a use of Scripture that some had plied for decades. As reported by the *Chicago Tribune*, teamsters petitioned their employers with biblical quotations like the Commandment "Six days shalt thou labor and do all thy work" and words of Jesus about honoring the Sabbath (May 24, 1906); "The bible as an aid to unionism has been discovered by the waitresses' union" (January 15, 1907); and "Bible as a Strike Weapon . . . Story of Esau Recalled and Telegraphers Urged Not to Sell Birthright for Mess of Potage" (September 29, 1907).[24]

This deployment of Scripture on behalf of labor paralleled some aspects of the earlier debate on slavery. In particular, a few elite ministers spoke out against labor by appealing to God's division of humanity into fixed classes. During early agitation for the eight-hour day, for instance, the minister of Chicago's leading First Congregational Church attacked agitators who caused "mechanics and laboring men," in his words, "to be dissatisfied and discontented with the position to which the Supreme Ruler of all has assigned them in this world." Against such appeals, labor activists responded, as did another of those who would be hanged after the Haymarket bomb, by citing Jesus's attack on the Temple moneychangers and by quoting Luke 10:7 as well as Matthew 6:24 ("ye cannot serve God and mammon").[25]

If American Protestants had once held roughly compatible positions on the responsibilities of workers and employers in supporting the common good, agreement now lay far in the past. The Bible turned some Protestants away from the present to contemplate the End of the Age. It served others as a guide to how personal reform could still improve society. It gave yet others practical directions for asserting the rights of working people. And it helped still more to fashion a formal Social Gospel. For imagining a healthy social order, the Bible remained central, but now speaking in confusion from a once cohesive Protestant world.

Biblical Higher Criticism

A similar story of disaggregation characterized formal study of Scripture. Beginning in the mid-1870s, the newer biblical criticism steadily gained traction among northern white Protestants, propelled especially by several well-publicized controversies. In 1875 learned Americans closely watched the conservative Free Church of Scotland tying itself in knots when its rising academic star, William Robertson Smith, published "The Bible" article in a new edition of the *Encyclopedia Britannica*. Concerned Americans paid special attention to how the Scot boldly appropriated German critical theories while trying to hold them together with some elements of traditional Reformed theology.[26] As they followed the whirlwind of controversy arising in the wake of his article, some were eager to join the fray. In 1878 the geologist Alexander Winchell was dismissed from Vanderbilt University for claiming that an intellectually responsible interpretation of the early chapters of Genesis required harmonization with modern theories of evolution.[27] The next year Crawford Toy lost his post as an Old Testament professor at Louisville's Southern Baptist Seminary for promoting his version of German higher criticism.[28] The change in critical climate was signaled most clearly, however, by the address that Charles Briggs delivered at Union Seminary on September 21 of the Centennial year.

The thirty-five-year old Briggs had enjoyed an excellent education at the University of Virginia, Union Seminary, and the University of Berlin before serving briefly as a Presbyterian pastor and then returning to Union as a professor.[29] During his time in Virginia, Briggs had been twice converted—first to the empiricism of Baconian common-sense philosophy and then, in the movement known elsewhere as the Businessmen's Revival, to Christ. At Union, two professors, Edward Robinson and Henry B. Smith, had made a deep impression—Robinson by combining archaeological expertise with theological allegiance to the Westminster Confession, Smith by communicating an American version of Continental "mediating theology." As noted, Smith held that Christian revelation, including the Bible, should be understood as participating fully in history, but he remained traditional with the conviction that Scripture communicated factually about whatever it reported, including supernatural events. It was "historicism" in a precritical sense of the term.[30]

In Berlin under Isaak August Dorner, Briggs deepened his commitment to disciplined study, which the Germans called *Wissenschaft*, of everything connected to the Bible. Encouraged by cutting-edge German scholarship, Briggs also exchanged the static epistemology of Scottish common sense for an organic conception of ancient history that viewed the Bible as subject to what Dorner described as ordinary historical development. Again, this sense of "historicism" was moving toward the view that revelation meant human conceptions of God within history rather than reception of communication from a transcendent God.[31] Briggs nonetheless remained broadly evangelical, with enduring belief in God's supernatural activity in converting sinners and sustaining personal growth in grace. He was, however, definitely an evangelical liberal who interpreted both God's direction of Israel and his saving work in the present as occurring within ordinary historical processes. Briggs's "historicism" wavered between the precritical and the modern.

Union Seminary had been founded in 1836 as an institution for advanced theological study serving New School Presbyterians. In contrast to the denomination's Old School faction represented by Princeton Seminary, the New School was more attentive to American circumstances and less narrowly devoted to upholding strict Calvinist standards. But with their Old School colleagues, New School Presbyterians remained strongly committed to the ideal of a learned ministry and so upheld high intellectual standards for their theological faculties. In 1876 Union's contingent of 150 students made it one of the nation's largest centers of advanced higher education. When Briggs delivered his address, that kind of training was still in its infancy; the first American Ph.D. had been granted at Yale only fifteen years before, and the number of doctorates earned in the United States before 1876 totaled fewer than two hundred.[32]

If Briggs's September oration would not have been considered radical in Europe, it startled Americans. Early in his address, he noted accurately what was at stake for groups that had relied on the Bible's integrity: "[T]he whole of theology depends upon the exegesis of the Scriptures, and unless this department be thoroughly wrought out and established, the whole structure of theological truth will be weak and frail."[33]

Then, however, Briggs suggested that those who claimed to stand by the Bible should be carrying out the necessary research to grasp accurately how the Scriptures had been composed. At this point, Briggs acknowledged the influence of his German professors and announced his intention to set aside long-cherished convictions: "These questions [e.g., the authorship of biblical books] must be settled partly by *external historical* evidence, but chiefly by *internal* evidence, such as the language, style of composition, archaeological and historical traces, the conception of the author respecting the various subjects of human thought, and the like."[34] "Subjects of human thought" was the key phrase because it implied that true biblical science (*Wissenschaft*) required not only sharpened awareness of facts from the ancient world but also closer attention to the evolution of human consciousness.

To make sure his audience understood the implications of his remarks, Briggs explained exactly what the new scholarship rejected: "[W]e have nothing to do with traditional views or dogmatic opinions." Then he laid out what the new scholarship required: "Whatever may have been the prevailing views of the church with reference to the Pentateuch, Psalter, or any other book of Scripture, they will not deter the conscientious exegete an instant from accepting and teaching the results of a historical and critical study of the writings themselves." In passing he took a dig at the conservative traditions that had dominated American attitudes toward Scripture: "It is just here that Christian theologians have greatly injured the cause of the truth and the Bible by dogmatizing in a department where it is least of all appropriate, and, indeed, to the highest degree improper, as if our faith depended at all upon these human opinions respecting the word of God."[35] In other words, the Bible could indeed remain relevant as "the word of God" in the modern scholarly world, but only if Bible readers did not back themselves into obscurantism and anti-intellectualism as they approached the Scriptures.

After the *Presbyterian Quarterly and Princeton Review* published Briggs's address in January 1877, the next issue contained a response by the traditionalist William Henry Green of Princeton Seminary, who chastised those who "attacked" the "perpetual authority of the Old Testament" from "within" the Protestant churches, supposedly "in the interests of Christianity itself."[36] (Figure 25.1)

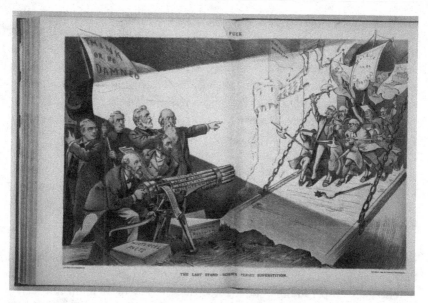

Figure 25.1 This cartoon from the English satirical magazine *Puck* depicts Charles A. Briggs (top row, second from right) joining a crew of distinguished savants firing away at a horde of benighted clergy with "history, archeology, evolution, enlightenment, geology, scientific facts, historical facts, and rational religion."
Source: LOC, Prints & Photographs, LC-DIG-ppmsca-28614.

Modest as this rejoinder seemed, it became the opening wave in a tsunami of argument about the character of Scripture. Within a half-decade of Briggs's inaugural address, controversy over biblical criticism engulfed the leading academic periodicals of the Presbyterians, who were widely perceived as the intellectual leaders of American Protestantism. Within two decades Briggs had been censured by the Presbyterians for teaching unacceptable views and was forced out of the Presbyterian ministry. In response, Union Seminary chose to support its most famous professor and followed Briggs out of the Presbyterian church to become an independent theological school. By the time that step took place, the Congregationalists, Episcopalians, Methodists, and even some Baptists, the least inclined to the innovations of biblical higher criticism, were embroiled in internal debates on the character of Scripture, the appropriateness of using modern biblical criticism, and the effects on ordinary Bible readers of the new critical views.

The history of scholarly journals in this period demonstrates the rapid segmentation of American views. The first extensive debates on the new criticism occurred where such debates had always been carried out, in the weighty quarterly reviews sponsored by denominations or theological seminaries, in this case the *Presbyterian Review*.[37] In an exchange that took place between 1881 and 1883 in that journal, Briggs and two other seminary professors contended for a moderate use of the new criticism. They were willing to question whether the Pentateuch was written by Moses or put together by later editors and whether the Apostle Paul actually wrote all of the epistles traditionally ascribed to him. Most important, they adopted the conviction now dominant in German universities that the biblical writings reflected a progressive development of human religious consciousness, with anthropocentric primitivism evolving toward the purest human expression in Jesus. The Bible was thoroughly *in* history. Five conservative authors, mostly from Princeton Seminary, begged to differ. They held that the newer criticism compromised what the inspiration of Scripture had always meant and should continue to mean. They believed objective research confirmed traditional views of authorship, but they objected most strenuously to the evolutionary idea that religious consciousness developed over the centuries. Instead, they insisted that truth meant the same thing for Moses, the Old Testament prophets, the gospel authors, and the Apostle Paul as it meant in the nineteenth century. Archibald Alexander Hodge of Princeton Seminary and Benjamin Breckinridge Warfield of Western Seminary put their position most forcefully in 1881: "[T]he Scriptures not only contain, but ARE, THE WORD OF GOD, and hence . . . all their elements and all their affirmations are absolutely errorless and binding the faith and obedience of men."[38]

Within a half-generation the most advanced biblical scholarship moved from denominational journals to publications of the professional societies. The journal of the Society of Biblical Literature, founded in 1880, became the chief venue. Into the early twentieth century authors upholding traditional views published in both the society's *Journal of Biblical Literature* and the denominational periodicals. Within another half generation, traditionalists contributed only rarely to the *Journal of Biblical Literature*. In it and in publications sponsored by the nation's most liberal denominations, the newer views dominated the field.[39]

The division over higher criticism was not without ironies, especially concerning pioneers like Briggs. When he died in 1913, a representative of the prevailing academic consensus opined that the Union professor had been so cautious in affirming higher criticism that the only figure with whom he could properly be compared was the conservative Warfield from Princeton![40] Obviously, the Protestant consensus about the Bible itself, the consensus on which the Bible civilization of the early republic had been built, was no more.

To simplify a complex picture, before roughly 1876 American Protestants certainly knew about many of the new ideas questioning a traditional understanding of Scripture, but those ideas had been marginalized intellectually and quarantined institutionally. But now, unlike the brief flurry of controversy over Tom Paine and the aborted antebellum consideration of European criticism, debates over the character of the Bible divided constituencies that had once stood relatively close together. Before the latter decades of the nineteenth century, for most Protestants most of the time, the overwhelmingly dominant concern had been how to put the Bible's message to work. From this point forward, that earlier concern did not vanish, but it was forced to compete with other concerns. Thereafter among many Protestants for much of the time, controversy over what the Bible was and how it should be read absorbed an immense amount of the energy that had previously been focused on what the Bible said and how it should be followed.

The Bible Alone

The interests of those who convened the Swampscott Bible Conference stood diametrically opposed to the preoccupations of Charles Briggs and other advocates of Continental biblical criticism. A few years later their annual conference relocated to the Queen's Royal Hotel at Niagara-on-the-Lake in southern Ontario, where it continued as the Niagara Bible Conference into the early twentieth century. In 1878 leaders of the Swampscott meeting organized a gathering for the public in New York City, the American Bible and Prophetic Conference, that publicized their convictions in annual rallies over the next twenty years (and was revived on the eve of World War I).

Two years after the 1876 meeting, the Niagara Conference issued a fourteen-point Creed detailing basic beliefs. Most of the points were standard fare for conservative and revivalistic Protestants. The fourteenth point, however, spelled out the distinctive conclusions arising from a new, concentrated focus on scriptural prophecy. Supported by references to seven New Testament texts, this fourteenth point challenged progressive Protestantism root and branch:

> We believe that the world will not be converted during the present dispensation, but is fast ripening for judgment, while there will be a fearful apostasy in the professing Christian body; and hence that the Lord Jesus will come in person to introduce the millennial age, when Israel shall be restored to their own land, and the earth shall be full of the knowledge of the Lord; and that this personal and premillennial advent is the blessed hope set before us in the Gospel for which we should be constantly looking.[41]

The Niagara Bible students were promoting a dispensational and premillennial interpretation of Scripture. A full history of these terms would require investigations back to the time of St. Augustine. It would also require detailed attention to the nineteenth-century history of Irish Anglican dissatisfaction with the course of British ecclesiastical life that led to the formation of the "Plymouth Brethren" and the worldwide influence of John Nelson Darby, the era's most influential dispensationist teacher.[42] But for the American story, things can be simplified considerably.[43]

Conveners of the Niagara Conference wanted to keep the Bible alive as a balm for individual souls, they hoped to see scriptural Christianity give purpose to pointless lives, and they worried that the nation's rapid social changes were turning multitudes away from the Scriptures.[44] Because these purposes depended on Scripture understood as an uncontaminated word from God, they reacted against the increasing emphasis by elite scholars on the Bible's human character. With particular fervor they objected when the new critics employed categories of myth and primitive social organization to separate Scripture's spiritual message from its literal expression. Instead, they insisted on treating the Bible as a factual historical record of God's supernatural provision for needy sinners. Concerning the Bible itself and the use of Scripture to address present needs, they "developed solutions," in Brendan Pietsch's apt account, "that were the mirror opposite of historicist thinking."[45] Against the new critics' emphasis on the progressive and evolutionary development of advanced Western societies, the Niagara organizers affirmed just the opposite. In their view, civilizations throughout the world were descending into chaotic darkness.

For a rapidly growing number of preachers, publishers, editors, and serious lay Bible students, scriptural prophecy held the key to the crises of the day. They were *dispensationalists* because they believed the Bible prophesied distinct epochs or dispensations (usually seven of them) through which humankind must pass before God brought about the end of the world. They were *premillennialists* because they believed that Christ would return to earth—visibly, literally, bodily—before he set up the thousand-year (millennial) Kingdom of Peace described in the twentieth chapter of the Book of Revelation.

The leaders who expressed these concerns were mostly proprietary Protestants who in classic American fashion mobilized by founding periodicals, publishing books aimed at educated lay readers, and creating national voluntary organizations (though "national" in these postbellum years often bypassed the South). James H. Brookes, the main organizer of the Swampscott and Niagara meetings, had attended Princeton Theological Seminary before holding forth in St. Louis at the well-regarded Walnut Street Presbyterian Church. He found a wide audience through his monthly periodical, *The Truth; or Testimony for Christ*, but even more from his many evangelistic, expository, and polemical works, of which *Present Truth* (1877) was best known. That book defended and illustrated the approach to Scripture favored by the Niagara participants.

Brookes's short introduction set out principles of biblical interpretation that simplified long-standing democratic and Baconian habits of mind. They began with an assertion that "the Bible is a plain book addressed to plain people, and easy to be understood with the aid of the Holy Spirit." The second principle stressed that "because the Bible is a plain book," it was imperative to believe that "it means what it says." In explaining this principle, Brookes specified the errors of those who either spiritualized what to him seemed transparent statements about Christ's return or who, with modern critics, described such accounts as only primitive mythic expressions. Other principles emphasized spiritual realities at stake, as the fifth: "All Scripture is written for our personal instruction and profit." There followed three commendations by figures associated with both the Brethren Movement in Britain and D. L. Moody in the states. The book proper was made up of what Brookes called "Bible readings" on three topics: the Second Coming, the deity of Christ, and the personality of the Holy Spirit. These "readings" consisted of consecutive printing without further comment of passages from the King James Version. The first part of the first reading demonstrated the prominence of the Return of Christ throughout the New Testament—fifty-six passages presented without commentary and ranging in length from a single verse to extended selections from the four Gospels, Acts, the Epistles, and the Book of Revelation. The next section on "the literal and personal coming of our Lord" offered twenty more New Testament passages identified, as for all of the book's quotations, only by chapter and verse(s).[46]

"Bible readings" had come to the United States in the 1860s, mostly as an outgrowth of practices among the early Plymouth Brethren that were spread by John Nelson Darby's itinerations. The use of verse-facts in the typical Baconian fashion admirably served the devotional purposes of the readings. Their advocates included layman like the Englishman Henry Moorhouse, who had been turned from a life of dissipation by attending such a reading. (Moorhouse was one of the commenders for Brookes's *Present Truth*.)[47] The American Businessmen's Revival of 1857–58, with its nondenominational, lay-led weekday meetings of simple scriptural messages, had prepared the way for the similar practices of the Bible readings. When D. L. Moody and the annual Keswick meetings for Holiness in England promoted the format, it spread even further and faster. Needless to say, for those who found the readings spiritually nourishing, concerns of the higher critics hardly registered.[48]

For popularizing the techniques, mindset, and spiritual purposes exemplified in Bible readings, no one was more important than Cyrus Ingerson Scofield.[49] After serving as a Confederate soldier and drifting aimlessly as a young adult, Scofield had been converted at Brookes's St. Louis church in 1879. Even as he almost immediately entered the ministry as a Congregational pastor, Scofield began the diligent biblical study he would continue through a succession of pulpits, including several years at Moody's Trinity Congregational Church in East Northfield, Massachusetts. By carefully systematizing the perspective he learned first from Brookes, Scofield became the most effective publicist of the new premillennial teaching. His 1888 book, *Rightly Dividing the Word of Truth*, brought him to the attention of a wider public.

The text from 2 Timothy 2:15 that gave Scofield his title is "Study to shew thyself approved unto God, a workman that needeth not to be ashamed, righty dividing the word of truth." According to Scofield, this passage taught that because Scripture "has right divisions . . . *any study* of that Word which ignores these divisions must be in large measure profitless and confusing."[50] The first of the ten divisions Scofield laid out in his short book of eighty-nine pages explained a categorical difference between Old Testament Israel and the New Testament church. Further differentiations included "The Seven Dispensations," "The Two Advents," "The Two Resurrections," and "The Five Judgments." Although this study included more authorial commentary than in Brookes's *Present Truth*, it featured the same rapid move from quoting individual verses to immediate statements of their meaning in connection with other scriptural verses.

After two more decades of intense personal study, Scofield published one of the most comprehensive reference bibles to appear since the Geneva Bible of 1560. Its title page advertised its extensive scope: "a new system of connected topical references to all the greater themes of Scripture, with annotations, revised marginal readings, summaries, definitions, and index. To which are added helps at hard places, explanations of seeming discrepancies, and a new system of paragraphs." In a brief introduction Scofield explained that "modern study of the Prophets" had recovered "not only a clear and coherent harmony of predictive portions, but also great treasures of ethical truth," which he would point out in "expository notes." He defended his emphasis on prophetic passages because "this portion of the Bible, nearly one-fourth of the whole, has been closed to the average reader by fanciful and allegorical schemes of interpretation."[51] The book that followed often included more words in notes, cross references, short explanatory footnotes, and long theological footnotes than in its scriptural text from the King James Version. A note after Genesis 1:27 was typical of the "helps" Scofield provided: "The First Dispensation: Innocency (Gen. 1.29–2.13). The First or Edenic Covenant: conditioned the life of unfallen man. (Add Gen. 2.8–17)." The extensive footnotes to Genesis chapter 3 took up two-thirds of the page, one describing the first of Scofield's seven dispensations where God promised Adam and Eve eternal life if they did not eat from the Tree of the Knowledge of Good and Evil, the other providing "a chain of references" linking God's judgment in Genesis 3:15 to the coming of Christ. (Figure 25.2)

The Scofield Reference Bible caught on immediately with those already familiar with dispensational teaching: among the wide circle inspired by Moody,

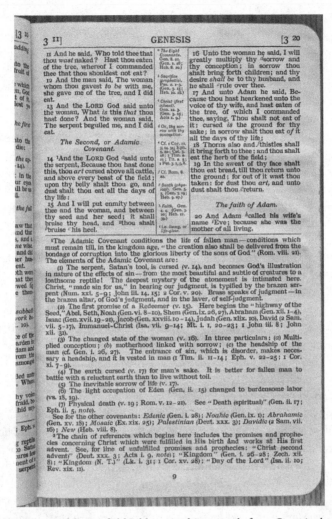

Figure 25.2 Pages of the Scofield Bible, as in this example from Genesis chapter 3, often included as much paratextual material as text.

Source: Courtesy of Buswell Library Special Collections, Rare Books, Wheaton College, Illinois.

who had died a decade earlier; at the Bible schools training lay believers, which were proliferating in this era; for those who attended prophecy conferences or read the works of conference headliners; wherever the influence of the Keswick conferences had spread; for white and Black members of the newer Holiness denominations and the even newer Pentecostal bodies; and with many in the more traditional denominations as well. The cachet of publication by Oxford University Press only added to the appeal. Under its publisher Henry Frowde, the press in Britain had greatly improved its standing with religious audiences by exploiting lighter but durable Oxford India paper to offer a much-expanded line of Bible offerings. Frowde, himself a lifelong member of the Plymouth Brethren, was drawn to Scofield's theology but even more to the sales potential of his book. When Frowde decided to make this bible the first major venture of the press's recently established branch in New York City, it paid off in a publishing bonanza that continues to this day.[52]

The "consulting editors" Scofield listed on his title page showed his savvy in bringing together democratic populism and certified expertise. It included the president of the Toronto Bible College and the dean of Chicago's Moody Bible Institute, but also the president of Crozer Theological Seminary (Baptist) and a professor at the United Presbyterians' Xenia Seminary in Pennsylvania. (United Presbyterians were a conservative denomination with Scottish roots that joined the northern PCUSA only in 1958.) The others were William Jacob Erdman, a Union war veteran and irenic northern Presbyterian minister with strong connections to Keswick in England; Arno Gaebelein, who had separated from the northern Methodist church in order to found a mission to Jews strongly influenced by his understanding of biblical prophecy; and the Presbyterian Arthur T. Pierson, whose commitment to missionary outreach and his editing of the *Missionary Review of the World* made him one of the most world-aware Americans of his era.[53]

In the firmament of American Scripture, the Niagara Prophecy Conference, the Scofield Reference Bible, and the wider spread of dispensational premillennialism represented something old and something new. George Marsden has well described how much they drew on the theological themes of an older American revivalism: "These teachers held that the Bible was absolutely reliable and precise in matters of fact, that its meanings were plain, and that whenever possible it should be taken literally." But he has also shown the novelty of the new perspectives as its teachers turned aside from the buoyant expectations of the earlier revivalism: "Christ's kingdom, far from being realized in this age or in the natural development of humanity, lay wholly in the future, was totally supernatural in origin, and discontinuous with the history of his era."[54]

In earlier decades, advocates of revivalism who appropriated the Bible in mostly literal terms similar to the Niagara organizers and Scofield had seen revival, along with the reform of society entailed by revival, as gradually moving American society toward the Kingdom of God. (Theirs was a postmillennial stance looking to steady moral improvement before the dawn of the millennium.) By contrast, the newer fixation on the supernatural reality of biblical prophecy moved its adherents *away from* contemporary social involvement. Charles Finney's *Lectures on Revival* from 1835 and the Niagara Creed of 1878 both described the Bible as authoritative in all particulars. Unlike Finney and that earlier generation, dispensational premillennialists were pushing the Bible to the sidelines of American history.

Brendan Pietsch has provided a particularly shrewd account of how up-to-date this revival tradition actually was. In his depiction, the popularity of magazines like James Brookes's *The Truth*, various denominational publications, and the *Sunday School Times* out of Philadelphia, which by the mid-1890s enjoyed a circulation of over 150,000, anticipated the techniques perfected by Scofield in his bible. In different ways they were adapting their message to an era fixated on *taxonomy*, the belief that carefully parsing tasks into their component parts would bring understanding, promote efficiency, and advance civilization. It was the era when the railroads succeeded in dividing the country into four uniform time zones, when primary schools instructed their charges in how to diagram sentences grammatically, when time management became the rage in industry, and when zoos tried to acquire two of every known animal. Yet to reap its richest rewards, taxonomy also required *expertise*. In the years when American universities began doctoral studies, when scientific organizations continued the transition from amateur to professional and newspapers paid healthy sums to recruit recognized experts for their pages, Bible students moved in the same direction. For some, like Charles Briggs, taxonomy meant dividing the strands of Old Testament narratives and expertise required study at German universities. For others, like C. I. Scofield, expertise did not require formal linguistic or historical training if his mastery of taxonomy could convince readers. In Pietsch's terms, Scofield used "classification, quantification, cross-referencing, and typological comparison" to further his "relentless pursuit of division, organization, and classification."[55]

Dispensational premillennialists did rely on historical Protestant teachings like "the priesthood of all believers" to justify the standing of those like Scofield who lacked formal higher education. They of course also leaned heavily on traditions of *sola scriptura*. But if the result was a resurgence of biblicism, it was biblicism in a modern form—not the *republican biblicism* of an earlier America inspired by the triumph of liberty over Christendom but *prophetic biblicism* responding to the decline of civilization and the threat of biblical higher criticism.

The rise of dispensationalism contributed substantially to further Protestant realignment. Its popularity transformed some custodial Protestants and a few Methodists into sectarians who disdained university-certified learning as they deepened their belief in the ability of plain people to grasp the Bible's plain meaning. In earlier decades, sectarian biblicism had grown stronger among white Protestants because of debates over race and slavery. A mentality relying on proof-texting from the King James Version did help keep alive scriptural defenses of racism like the curse of Ham from Genesis 9. It also undergirded opposition to new translations that relied on modern scholarship and later fueled the turn of Protestant conservatives against evolution. But approaches to Scripture that relied on the simple organization of verse-facts exerted their longest lasting impact as they eased the way for the spread of dispensational premillennialism.

In many ways the new teaching reprised William Miller's fascination with the apocalypse. Like Miller, the teachers of dispensationalism diagrammed the future in elaborate charts, and like Miller they assembled verses from throughout the Scriptures to form law-like conclusions about the present age, the Second Coming of Christ, and the end of the world. Yet unlike Millerism, dispensationalism could expand its influence over time because, while it gave lay people mastery of scriptural content, it avoided the specific date-setting that discredited Millerism. Dispensationalism also flourished because some of its best-known teachers encouraged Christian godliness even more effectively than the dispensational hermeneutic.

As with other developments of the era, the new dispensational premillennialism scrambled long-prevailing patterns. With their concentrated focus on *sola scriptura*, Bible readings certainly shared some characteristics with earlier Methodist class meetings. They differed, however, by exhibiting a much greater concern for understanding the future than for the single-minded concentration on personal sanctification. In addition, although the new teachers opened yet another chapter in the history of sectarian biblicism, their obvious reverence for biblical inspiration led to a marriage of convenience with confessional conservatives.[56] Representatives of traditional custodial interests, like the Presbyterians of Princeton Seminary, rejected premillennialism; they also strongly criticized the hermeneutics of the Bible readings and Scofield's assembling of verse-facts into his dispensational scheme. Yet because the dispensationalists appreciated the conservatives' defense of biblical inerrancy and celebrated their opposition to higher criticism, these points of commonality gradually overcame the once great gulf between the conservatives' proprietary interests and the sectarian character of the new teaching.[57]

As with many other American populist movements, irony also attended the rise of Bible-only dispensationalism. In particular, an approach to the Bible promoted as an antidote to the destructive higher criticism of learned elites ended up with an elite corps of teachers guiding others step by step in reading the Bible "on their own." For counteracting modernist elites, the Scofield Reference Bible installed a note-writing elitist in its place. Like the massively annotated "Self-interpreting Bible" of the Scottish minister John Brown, which had been reprinted many times since its first American publication in 1792, Scofield's bible guided readers by proclaiming their freedom from guidance.[58]

In broader perspective, and whatever the ironies, the new dispensational approach added to the disruption of once dominant Protestant traditions.

Dispensationalism would bestow new confidence in Scripture for a wide cohort of Protestants that continued to grow throughout the twentieth century, but this Protestantism differed considerably from any of the main traditions of earlier American history.

Evolution

In the United States' centennial year, Washington Gladden's proposal for Christian economic reform, Charles Briggs's inaugural lecture, and the Swampscott meeting of dispensational premillennialists revealed significant fissures among Protestants that widened steadily as the years advanced. By contrast, the publication of Asa Gray's *Darwiniana*, a collection of articles and reviews on Darwin's theory of natural selection, sought to preserve an older unity, in this case scientific learning in harmony with traditional trust in Scripture. To Harvard's Gray, the nation's most respected botanist, evolution posed a strictly scientific question with no determinative implications for theology. Gray's view, although shared by the nation's leading geologist, James Dwight Dana at Yale, and others, was admittedly contested. Gray held that Darwin's research justified *revising* traditional interpretations of Scripture; he did not view it as creating a *conflict* between religion and science. Evolution as a construct applied to human history and the development of moral consciousness was, however, another matter. In this second sense, evolution did join the other challenges fragmenting the Protestant world.[59]

A guest whom Gray entertained on a visit to Harvard in 1876 represented the conflict view that Gray rejected. Thomas Henry Huxley had traveled across the Atlantic to deliver the keynote address at the opening of Johns Hopkins University in Baltimore. Two years earlier, when the president of the British Association for the Advancement of Science, John Tyndall, had delivered a rousing attack on theologians who impeded the course of scientific advance, Huxley blasted the clergymen who attacked Tyndall as "pygmies in intellect."[60] Although Huxley was on record advocating the required reading of the King James Version in England's primary schools, he made it clear that this advocacy supported culture, not religion.[61] Huxley had earned the nickname "Darwin's Bulldog" not only for his aggressive promotion of natural selection but also for his dismissive attitude toward religious traditions that in any way hindered free scientific inquiry. In his person Huxley exemplified the champion for science in what an English-born American chemist, John William Draper, had only just described in a polemic entitled *The History of the Conflict Between Religion and Science* (1875).

Asa Gray defended a different conceptual universe. In his own botanical research and as an adjudicator of contemporary scientific proposals, he too had become a dedicated Darwinian, in fact the chief American proponent of Darwin's theory. Yet far from sensing a disconnect between this new science and older religious convictions, Gray remained, as he wrote in the introduction to *Darwiniana*, "one who is scientifically, and in his own fashion, a Darwinian, philosophically a convinced theist, and religiously an acceptor of the 'creed commonly called the Nicene' as the exponent of the Christian faith."[62]

Gray's importance for his era lies in recognizing how much respect he earned for defending evolution while also rebutting those who viewed Darwin's theory as overturning traditional Christianity. Already by the publication of *Darwiniana* he had answered the arguments of several leading North American scientists, including his Harvard colleague Louis Agassiz and the distinguished Canadian geologist John William Dawson. Agassiz, a philosophical idealist, believed God had created different species directly (including different human species); Dawson rejected natural selection for traducing traditional Presbyterian theology and the standards of Baconian empiricism.

Gray was also holding his own against Huxley and other proponents of the conflict thesis. In the judgment of Gray's biographer, A. Hunter Dupree, "Gray's arguments for the compatibility of evolution with theism were full of life in 1874" and for many years thereafter.[63] Most notably, Gray engaged Darwin in a long, mutually respectful correspondence in which the American urged the English researcher to see that his theory did not undercut conclusions about design, purpose, and teleology in nature.[64] In *Darwiniana* Gray spelled out this perspective by reprinting his review of an 1873 work by Charles Hodge titled *What Is Darwinism?*[65] Hodge had answered his own question carefully: although he personally did not see how the early chapters of Genesis could accommodate evolution, and although the notion of natural selection acting incrementally over a vast span of years violated common sense, Hodge recognized that these were secondary concerns that did not trouble other traditional believers. Instead, because he read *The Origin of Species* (1859) and Darwin's later *Descent of Man* (1871) as denying purpose or design in the evolutionary process, he concluded that Darwinism meant "atheism." In his review, Gray conceded that Hodge had read Darwin almost correctly, but with one crucial mistake that Hodge shared with Darwin. Both the theologian and the scientist believed (using words from Hodge that Gray highlighted) that "the efficiency of physical causes" operated without reference to "mind-force, or . . . the efficiency of the First Cause." Gray believed that Hodge, like Darwin, made a category mistake. Gray supported Darwin's conclusions about "physical causes," but he claimed that those who denied a directing purpose, "the First Cause," imposed a philosophical judgment not required by the physical evidence. In his own view, which he stated in several different ways, "the difference between the theologian and the naturalist is not fundamental, and evolution may be as profoundly and as particularly theistic as it is increasingly probable. The taint of atheism which, in Dr. Hodge's view, leavens the whole lump is not inherent in the original grain of Darwinism . . . but has somehow been introduced in the subsequent treatment."[66]

Concerning evolution as a strictly empirical question with no necessary "taint of atheism," Gray's conclusions survived for decades, though not without growing opposition. At Princeton Seminary itself, Hodge's successors as the school's principal theologians, his son Archibald Alexander and then B. B. Warfield, agreed with Gray.[67] So long as evolution was not presumed to mean *purposeless* development, it could be held by traditional Bible believers, especially the custodial Protestants whose view of inspiration made room for specialized historical study and considerations of context in biblical interpretation. Warfield even coined a term, "mediate creation," to describe the God-given capacity of natural selection to produce the full range of plant and animal species.[68]

Although Gray's position had lost some ground by the 1910s among both scientists and traditional believers, it could still be found in *The Fundamentals*, the series of tracts that publicized a militant stance against modern biblical criticism and modernist theology. For the series, George Frederick Wright, who as an enthusiastic supporter of Gray had helped him prepare *Darwiniana* for the press, explained why he had lost that earlier enthusiasm.[69] But another contributor, James Orr, professor of theology at the United Free College in Scotland, held that the development of species by natural selection was fully compatible with traditional orthodox Christianity. Orr even offered an explanation echoing Warfield's "mediate creation": " 'Evolution,' in short, is coming to be recognized as but a new name for 'creation,' only that the creative power now works from *within*, instead of, as in the old conception, in an *external* fashion."[70] Wright, rather than Orr, anticipated the stance that would soon become dominant, but that dominance was secured only in the 1920s rather than earlier.[71]

Gray maintained his position on evolution as science until his death in 1888. Yet he also spoke out consistently against evolution as a paradigm for social or moral development. As A. Hunter Dupree has shown, Gray repudiated the materialism that Huxley claimed to find in evolution, a view of history illustrating evolutionary progress held by the American philosopher-historian John Fiske and especially the "social Darwinism" promoted by Herbert Spencer. Against such metaphorical applications of Darwin's scientific conclusions, Gray, in Dupree's summary, "was refusing to give his assent to all extensions of evolutionary theory into the sphere of social and political development."[72]

Similar "extensions," however, made evolution a much earlier contributor to the history of the Bible. The autobiography of Lyman Abbott, the influential New York City minister and editor, illustrated that contribution. Though without any experience of his own in scientific research, Abbott nonetheless became a vocal proponent of Darwin's views. His reading of *The Origin of Species* and *The*

Descent of Man gave Abbott the perspective from which to bemoan the attacks on Briggs and other practitioners of the new biblical criticism. For Abbott, Darwin's evolution proved "fatal to the theological doctrine of the fall and involving, not only the origin of the race and the scientific accuracy of the Bible, but the origin, reality, and nature of sin and its cure."[73] For Abbott and others who joined him in modernizing Christian theology, Darwin's evolutionary biology became hugely important, but much more for adding credibility to the notion of progressive human development than for conclusions about occurrences in nature.

By the 1870s doubts had begun to undercut the earlier certainty among American Protestants that "God's two books," nature and the Bible, told the same story. But evolutionary *science* did not lead to deep fissures in the population at large and among Protestants until a later generation. By contrast, evolution as a comprehensive *metaphor* did exert a significant influence much earlier.

After the Civil War the history of the Bible became even less a narrative exclusively for white Protestants. Yet because of the considerable presence they maintained, the internal Protestant story remained important for the nation. Into the immediate prewar years, Protestants enjoyed a mostly unified framework for understanding themselves and their place in the world—or "unified" at least compared to what came later. The earlier framework included only strategic differences for conceptualizing personal redemption and social reform along with a great deal of agreement about the relation of the human mind to what lay outside the mind and about the human person in relation to the natural world. For these and other purposes, Scripture, theologies of self and society, moral philosophy (the study of conscience), and natural philosophy (the study of nature) reinforced each other mutually. As illustrated by the events of 1876, and with consideration of evolutionary science only a partial exception, that mutual reinforcement was long gone.

26

Marginal No More (Jews and Catholics)

As the nation experienced an accelerating pace of change between the Civil War and the First World War, the Bible remained important, but with new configurations for a substantially new America. As the nation's population swelled from 31.5 million in 1860 to 106.5 million in 1920, immigrants and their children made up an increasing share of the total. (The number of an-nual arrivals topped 500,000 for the first time in 1881, and then 1 million in 1905.)[1] Increasingly these new Americans came not as before, from Britain and northern Europe, but from central and eastern Europe—from, that is, regions without strong Protestant traditions but with many Catholics, Jews, and Eastern Orthodox Christians. As only one striking instance, the numbers of Jews in New York City alone increased from around 80,000 in the mid-1880s to more than 1.4 million by 1915.[2] A relocation of the population also accompanied the surge in immigration. By 1920, over half of the nation lived in urban areas of 2,500 or more, which represented a great increase from the 20% figure of only a single lifetime (sixty years). Chicago, with only slightly more than 100,000 residents in 1860, had become by 1890 the nation's transportation hub with a population, despite the devasting fire of 1871, of more than 1.1 million.

In this emerging America, English-speaking white Protestants no longer controlled public space. In particular, Protestant moral standards had become largely irrelevant for an economy producing opportunities for unprecedented wealth but also creating conditions of unprecedented urban destitution. The de-mography of religious adherence, as indicated by Table 26.1, also reflected that receding dominance.

The reordering of public space affected the history of the Bible just as much as the reordering taking place among Protestants that was examined in the previous two chapters. In a rapidly expanding America, more religious groups followed the path opened earlier by Campbellites, Mormons, and Millerites by advancing their own scriptures or their distinctive approaches to the King James Version (treated in chapter 27). More Americans also went public with their disdain for traditional scriptures of any sort (also chapter 27). African Americans of several kinds intensified their engagement with the Bible but, as before, mostly unrecog-nized by the wider society (chapter 30).

Of all previously marginalized groups, however, American Catholics and American Jews advanced the most obvious alternatives to prominent Protestant

America's Book. Mark A. Noll, Oxford University Press. © Oxford University Press 2022.
DOI: 10.1093/oso/9780197623466.003.0027

Table 26.1 Proportion of Religious Adherents: 1800, 1860, 1920

	1800 (%)	1860 (%)	1920 (%)
White Protestants, British origin	83	69	43
Reformed, Lutherans	10	3	7
Catholics	4	21	30
African American adherents	2	2	11
Jews	—	1	6

Notes: For 1800, Stephen A. Marini, "The Government of God, Religion and Revolution in America, 1764–1792" (unpublished manuscript, ca. 1997): Edwin Scott Gaustad, *Historical Atlas of Religion in America*, rev. ed. (New York: Harper & Row, 1976), 43; personal communication from Stephen Marini. For 1860 and 1920, Roger Finke and Rodney Stark, "Turning Pews into People: Estimating Nineteenth-Century Church Membership," *Journal for the Scientific Study of Religion* 25 (1986): 180–92; Gaustad, *Historical Atlas*; Arthur A. Goren, "Jews," in *Harvard Encyclopedia of American Ethnic Groups*, ed. Stephen Thernstrom (Cambridge, MA: Harvard University Press, 1980); U.S. census reports for 1890, 1906, 1916, and 1926.

patterns. As they Americanized, both groups did adapt by expressing the time-honored conviction that a democratic republic required religious institutions that promoted personal morality and civic virtue. But both also challenged the Protestant formulation of this conviction.

The struggle over these issues sometimes resembled tribal conflict more than principled debate, in large part because a number of worried Protestants framed the situation in those terms. One much-noticed example was published in 1885 by Josiah Strong, the general secretary of the Evangelical Alliance for the United States. Austin Phelps, the president of Andover Theological Seminary and one of the co-editors of the biblically rich *Sabbath Hymnbook*, provided an introduction for Strong's *Our Country: The Possible Future and Its Present Crisis* that emphasized the "crisis" of the book's subtitle. Phelps, that is, hailed the book for spotlighting "the crisis in the destiny of the country, and through it the destiny of the world." In his mind no doubts remained about the question framing the crisis: "how the original stock of American society could bear the interfusion of elements alien to our history and to the faith of our country." Strong followed with chapters identifying "the perils" confronting the nation. His ranking began with "Immigration and Romanism," followed by "Mormonism," "Intemperance," "Socialism," "Wealth," and "The City." Neither Phelps in his introduction nor Strong in the text enlisted much scriptural teaching, except for very occasional rhetorical flourishes; instead, it was a call to arms appealing to "the Anglo-Saxon" and "our" endangered land.[3]

Catholic and Jewish communities created their own institutions to overcome this Protestant tribalism, whether exemplified by Strong and Phelps, organized in the appeals of the strongly anti-Catholic American Protective Association (founded in 1887), shared to some extent by Protestant-dominated organizations like the Woman's Christian Temperance Union, or expressed as anti-Semitism (a new term for Americans) in imitation of Russian pogroms and European scientific racism.[4] As it happened, events in and around the Centennial year anticipated the specific course that both communities would take with respect to the Bible. Yet as they rose to the challenge of explaining how a paired commitment to Scripture and the well-being of America did not require the Protestant Bible, Catholics and Jews found themselves fighting an older battle concerning the central role of that Protestant Bible in the nation's tax-supported public schools.

The School Question

For Jews, readings from the KJV in public schools, and particularly readings from the New Testament, provoked continuing complaint.[5] Objections had been clearly stated even before the massive immigrations of the 1880s. In the famous Cincinnati Bible War of 1869–70, the two Jews on the Cincinnati school board divided over the board's decision to exclude Bible readings. But Isaac Mayer Wise, the moving spirit of American Reform Judaism, was joined by another of Cincinnati's prominent Reform rabbis, Max Lilienthal, to support the board's effort at eliminating daily readings from the KJV. As Wise put his position: "We are opposed to Bible reading in the schools. We want secular schools and nothing else. . . . Having no religion [the state] cannot impose any religious instruction on the citizen."[6]

Jewish sensitivity to the way Bible reading in public schools imposed civil and religious burdens increased substantially as new immigrants arrived from eastern Europe. In 1906 the Central Conference of American Rabbis published a pamphlet setting out its reasons why, as the title had it, "the Bible should not be read in public schools." The next year the Union of Orthodox Jewish Congregations succeeded in having the New York City Board of Education end teaching of religion in the city's public schools.[7] For several years near the start of the First World War *The American Jewish Yearbook* catalogued instances where courts or legislators addressed Bible reading in the schools. In its listings— alongside notices concerning legal action on general religious education in public schools, the observance of Sunday as a holy day, and provision for Jewish religious observances—the *Yearbook* listed twenty-six Bible rulings in thirteen states over just three years. Some states eliminated the practice, others upheld it.[8]

Readings from the KJV in public schools joined other Bible-related offenses (like rampant anti-Semitism in popular biblical fiction) and the continuing efforts of several Protestant groups to define the United States as a Christian nation (as when the American Protective Association attacked non-Protestants or the National Reform Association sought to amend the Constitution in order to recognize the rule of Christ over the nation).[9] Opposition generated by such concerns spurred an array of countermeasures. Separate, privately financed Jewish schools, in which study in Hebrew of Scripture and rabbinic commentaries figured prominently, expanded on Isaac Leeser's earlier campaigns to become a favored means for exploiting American religious freedom while strengthening Jewish identity.[10] Navigating through controversy also sharpened the sense of what American Jews desired from the Bible.

For Catholics "the school question" remained every bit as challenging after the Civil War as it had been before. Prominent custodial Protestant voices continued to insist that republican morality needed the public schools to foreground the Bible as the key to imparting that morality. To be sure, a few Protestants did follow the logic of Stanley Matthews, the Cincinnati lawyer who opposed Bible readings because of damage to the Bible. In the wake of public debate generated by the failed Blaine Amendment, a prominent Brooklyn Presbyterian, Samuel Spear, used the pages of the *Princeton Review* to argue that "masterly inactivity, in the sense of leaving the administration and propagation of the Christian religion, exclusively to the *voluntary* principle, is . . . the best policy, alike for the state and for religion."[11]

The most frequent position, however, remained the answer given by a Universalist written, as was Spear's essay, in 1877. It answered the question "[S]hall we retain the Bible in our common schools[?]" unequivocally: "The founders of the Constitution deliberately intended that the government should be based in the practical morality of unsectarian Christianity. . . . To once admit the principle of Secularism, by which to exclude the Bible from the school-room, is to incur a train of evils compared with which all that are even imagined of the present policy are mere bagatelles."[12]

One of Jonathan Blanchard's daughters, who became the president of the Chicago Woman's Education Union, stood firm by this logic when in 1898 she published *The Nation's Bible in the Nation's Schools*. Elizabeth Blanchard Cook also stated her opinion without ambiguity: "The Bible has been to our educational officers[,] teachers and pupils like the decision of an infallible supreme court, always on the side of reason, justice and victory. . . . It is the supreme classic in knowledge of every sort and the foundation of National prosperity, morality and religion." To support her claim, Cook enlisted the testimonies of over thirty distinguished leaders, including the French historian Francois Guizot, the Harvard law professor and Christian apologist Simon Greenleaf, Horace Mann,

Philip Schaff, Calvin Stowe, Frances Willard—and the nation's leading Catholic prelate, Cardinal James Gibbons of Baltimore.[13]

Cook's disingenuous inclusion of Cardinal Gibbons, however, underscored the complexity of Catholic-Protestant contentions. Catholics usually agreed about the need to train young citizens in Christian morality, but they strongly objected to providing that teaching in a Protestant framework and with required readings from the Protestant Bible. As more Catholics participated more actively in public life, they pursued different strategies to overcome what had been the prevailing American practice.

Long-standing Catholic complaints continued wherever rising Catholic populations met entrenched educational traditions. Again, many Catholics had no objection to religious instruction, but not from a translation condemned by the hierarchy. A well-publicized court case in Wisconsin illustrated how that Catholic opposition could be expressed.

In 1886 Catholic parents in Edgerton, Wisconsin, petitioned their local school board to stop the customary practice. The board replied that reading the KJV without comment gave all children the right to interpret the Bible for themselves. To read the Bible without comment was nonsectarian; to stop reading it because it offended Roman Catholics was sectarian. This reasoning infuriated Humphrey Desmond, for fifty years the editor of the *Catholic Citizen*, who galvanized support to save the parents and their children "from the sectarian inquisition presently established in the tax-payers' public school." To suggest the absurdity of the mainstream position, he wrote in February 1887, "Where in the whole land is the Catholic Bible read in the public school each morning; where is the Ave Maria compulsorily recited by Protestant pupils. . . ? On the other hand, we have public Normal Schools in this state run as part of the Methodist Book Concern; public school establishments turned into Protestant ecclesiastical machines . . . and proselytism at the expense of Catholics whose children are being proselytized." A local judge ruled against the parents, stating that the KJV's "very presence, as a believed book, has rendered the nations having it, a chosen race; and then too, in exact proportion as it is more or less generally known and studied." According to this judge, the Bible was "beyond compare the most perfect instrument of humanity." But the Wisconsin Supreme Court reversed that ruling in favor of the parents and forbade local boards to mandate readings from the KJV.[14]

In the postbellum decades other Catholics moved from defense to offense. A few leading Catholics expanded the earlier proposals of Cincinnati's Bishop Purcell by calling for parent-directed schools where tax money could be used to support the kind of schools *parents* desired.[15] Zachariah Montgomery, descended from a Maryland family with deep roots in colonial Catholicism, became a leading advocate of this stance after he migrated to California and joined the Democratic Party in order to combat the anti-Catholic Know Nothings. In an active career as a lawyer and in several public offices, Montgomery some-times turned to the Bible to demonstrate the responsibility for parents to take charge of their children's education, as he did in 1864 by citing Ecclesiasticus (Sirach) 3:2 from the Douay-Rheims version, "Children, hear the judgments of your father, and so do that you may be saved." Montgomery insisted that "the command does not read 'Children, hear ye the Judgments of the President,' nor 'the Judgments of the Legislature,' nor even 'the Judgments of the San Francisco Board of Education,' but the injunction is '*Children, hear the Judgments of your father.*'"[16] Montgomery's advocacy for parental rights extended broadly, even to defending the rights of Jewish parents to set up publicly funded schools that taught their children in accord with Jewish precepts. As the years passed, those who agreed with Montgomery tried to convince American school boards to follow the example of Canada, Britain, and continental Europe, where national education programs supported denominational schools in various ways.

The main response of the American bishops moved in a different direction.[17] In effect they abandoned Montgomery's reasoning as hopeless. Instead, at the bishops' Third Plenary Council held at Baltimore in 1884, they amended ear-lier episcopal *recommendations* for parish parochial schools to *require* each church to set one up within two years. The Council also *mandated* that Catholic parents enroll their children in these schools. Their main item of debate con-cerned how severe the penalties should be for parents who did not follow this directive. As Philip Gleason has explained this logic, "the basic reason the fathers regarded the subject as so important was their conviction that differing views as to the meaning and purpose of life entailed different approaches to educa-tion."[18] Behind their reasoning, however, lay not only the traditional worry about Protestants but a growing conviction that the United States was moving rapidly in the direction advocated by European secularists, socialists, and communists. In a similar way that some Protestants reacted with alarm to continental ideas about biblical criticism and humankind's progressive evolutionary develop-ment, the Catholic bishops viewed the general threat of European secularism, illustrated in conflicts like the Prussian *Kirchenkampf* between Chancellor Otto Bismarck and the church, as a foretaste of the American future.

As Jews joined Catholics in resisting the Protestant defaults of American public education, court challenges, counterstrategies, and alternative proposals stressed what in their eyes seemed an obvious contradiction: How could the United States promote genuine civil liberty and still bestow special privileges on the Protestant Bible? Yet having made this point well enough for at least some recognition in court and among the public at large, it remained for scriptural religions like Judaism and Catholicism to define the positive steps that in the American en-vironment could promote a proper use of Scripture. Once more, events in the Centennial year pointed the way—for Jews to a translation by American Jews for

American Jews, and for Catholics to demonstrations that their religion did much more for the nation than anything Protestants had ever done.

"Jewish America"

By the mid-1870s, the arrival of more Jewish immigrants from central and eastern Europe, where traditional forms of Jewish culture prevailed, collided with important developments in the Jewish communities that had grown slowly from the colonial period. Depending on point of view, those developments represented either positive accommodation to American ways or a cataclysmic threat to Judaism in its entirety. As Jonathan Sarna has described the "two worlds of American Judaism," the dynamics of these years stimulated the energy, but also created the tensions, that have characterized American Jewish life ever since.[19]

Isaac Mayer Wise represented the path of accommodation by taking advantage of the rising Jewish population and the consolidation of sentiment behind Reform Judaism to advance an ambitious agenda. It led to the establishment in 1873 of the Union of American Hebrew Congregations and two years later the opening of Hebrew Union College in Cincinnati. These institutions and their related publications would, in Wise's vision, stabilize Jewish identity, provide well-trained, English-speaking rabbis for Jews who were beginning to feel more at home in the United States, and align Judaism with the movement of modernity.

The scattered congregations of recent immigrants and the swell of Yiddish-speaking newcomers viewed these moves with alarm. A focal point of their concern was Felix Adler, the son of a rabbi who had excelled at his own studies for the rabbinate in both the United States and Germany, but who in the Centennial year left Reform Judaism to found the Ethical Culture Society. With its advocacy of a universal moral code based on world religions in general and its rejection of specifically Judaic practices, Ethical Culture was to traditional forms of Judaism something like Transcendentalism had been to traditional forms of Christianity. When Adler announced "Judaism is dying" and when one of Wise's daughters eloped to marry a Presbyterian, some asked whether, as Sarna puts it, "the effort to modernize Judaism [had] gone too far."[20]

A revival of Orthodoxy soon followed, sparked by a new organization, Keyam Dishmaya, founded in 1879 to honor the traditional Jewish Sabbath in traditional Jewish ways. The American Jewish Historical Society (1885) and the Jewish Publication Society (1889) accompanied a revival of Isaac Leeser's hopes that Judaism could take advantage of American liberties, but in order to strengthen traditional Judaism. Other Jews went even further to define American liberties themselves as a modern instantiation of historical Hebrew principles. Oscar

Straus, who led the American Jewish Historical Society, made such a claim in *The Origin of Republican Form of Government in the United States*, published the same year as the Historical Society's founding. According to Straus, "The children of Israel on the banks of the Jordan, who had just emerged from centuries of bondage, not only recognized the guiding principles of civic and religious liberty that 'all men are created equal,' that God and the law are the only kings, but also established a free commonwealth, a pure democratic-republic under a written constitution."[21]

Celebrations of Abraham Lincoln in these years reinforced the conviction that the course of Judaism and the course of America flowed together in a common stream. Emil Hirsch, the respected rabbi of Chicago's Sinai congregation (Reform), lauded the Great Emancipator in highly biblical-nationalist terms at a birthday remembrance on February 12, 1892. His peroration, which relied on a passage from Isaiah chapter 9, expressed a biblical nationalism worthy of the most exuberant Protestant:

> America, land of freedom, washed by the blood of martyred presidents, America, hope of humanity, star of the morning, sing thy song, "Today a child was born unto us, a son was given unto us. Upon him was the dominion, his name was great counsellor, mighty in deed, witness of the great Father in heaven; Prince of Peace [Isa 9:6]!" For in this old biblical description of Israel's ideal ruler, America, thou mayest well breathe thine appreciation of thine own son, immortal Abraham Lincoln.[22]

Such sentiments set a pattern, illustrated again in 1954 when a New York City rabbi celebrated the three-hundredth anniversary of the arrival of Jews in colonial America: "The principles for which we stand are inscribed upon the Liberty Bell and the Statue of Liberty.... The influence of Judaism and of our Bible stands out clearly in the annals of American history."[23]

This reference to "our Bible" carries us back to the turbulence of the last quarter of the nineteenth century that resulted in the push for an English-language translation of the Bible undertaken especially for Jewish America. An array of motives propelled that effort: to express appreciation for biblical aspects in American culture, to escape subversion from the Christian and often distinctly Protestant character of the KJV, and to preserve a strong religious element in Jewish ethnic identity. It might also show other Americans why a new version of the Hebrew Scriptures comported well with long-standing Christian use of the Old Testament that viewed the United States as an object of special divine concern.

The remarkable career of Solomon Schechter illustrated the tension between Jewish identity and American identity, but also the importance of Scripture in working through that tension.[24] The fifty-three-year-old Schechter came to the

United States in 1902 as the most respected English-speaking Jewish scholar in the world. His unusual breadth of experience began with his birth and early years in Romania and continued with his education in Poland, Austria, and Germany, teaching assignments at Cambridge and the University of London, and greatly esteemed discoveries of ancient Hebrew texts in Egypt. As a youth in Foscani, Romania, Schechter received a positive impression of the United States when he read Lincoln's Second Inaugural Address, probably in a Yiddish translation. In a 1909 speech on the centennial of Lincoln's birth, Schechter reported that when he contemplated the theistic expressions of this address, he could "scarcely believe that they formed a part of a message addressed in the nineteenth century to an assembly composed largely of men of affairs." Schechter imagined himself "transported into a camp of contrite sinners determined to leave the world and its vanities behind him, possessed of no other thought but that of reconciliation with their God, and addressed by their leader when about to set out on a course of penance."[25]

Earlier in 1903, when he dedicated a new building at New York's Jewish Theological Seminary, Schechter expressed a more general opinion about scriptural influences on American national development: "This country is, as everybody knows, a creation of the Bible . . . and the Bible is still holding its own, exercising enormous influence as a real spiritual power, in spite of all the destructive tendencies."[26] Remarkably, Schechter spoke these words as he was actively supporting Jewish efforts to end Christian Bible readings in New York public schools, when he was working to establish an independent network of private Jewish day schools, and as he had begun to serve as head of the Jewish Publication Society's work on its own Bible translation. (Figure 26.1)

Before outlining the course of that project, Schechter's reasoning deserves attention as he navigated between respect for the nation's religious heritage and commitment to the uniqueness of Judaism.[27] He first suggested that it was "particularly the Old Testament" that gave the United States its biblical character. But then he expanded on problems he saw when Americans took such a conviction too literally—including an "excess of zeal," a spate of "caricature revelations," and the presence of "quacks" who "create new Tabernacles here, with new Zions and Jerusalems." Schechter used a Hebrew vocabulary, but observers knew that these excesses, and more, had characterized much American Christian zeal. Although Schechter highlighted problems in the Bible-centered character of American history, he wanted even more to defend that character. Specifically, he was pleased that trust in the Bible was holding up against what he called "all the destructive tendencies, mostly of foreign make." He was convinced that, despite genuine difficulties, "the large bulk of the American people have, in matters of religion, retained their sobriety and loyal adherence to the Scriptures, as their Puritan forefathers did."

Figure 26.1 Solomon Schechter is shown (second from the left) in this photograph of distinguished American Jewish scholars from the early twentieth century.
Source: LOC, Prints & Photographs, LC-B2-2920-15.

Schechter's final point in praising the biblical character of the United States came back, however, to the Bible rather than to America. He wanted to stress to his New York Jewish audience in 1903 that they were celebrating a *Jewish* theological seminary. His explanation included ways that ancient Jewish teaching could profitably adapt to the American context—by, for example, respecting American democratic traditions and so downplaying aristocratic, centralizing, or autocratic tendencies brought from Europe to the new world. Yet in the end, Judaism was more important than America: "Any attempt to confine its activity to the borders of a single country, even be it as large as America, will only make its teachings provincial, narrow and unprofitable." Rather, the point of a *Jewish* theological seminary must be "to teach the doctrines and the literature of the religion which is as old as history itself and as wide as the world." An American setting for studying Judaism could have special significance precisely because of how much the Bible had contributed to shaping the United States. But because the study of Judaism took in all of history and implicated the whole world, it, rather than the United States, had to remain the highest concern.

Schechter advanced that programmatic assessment at a time when progress on the translation project had slowed. In 1892 the Jewish Publication Society of America appointed a committee charged with achieving this objective, but by

1903 only the Psalms had been published. At that point, however, the committee was reorganized to function as an advisory board for Max Margolis, an accomplished scholar who was charged with preparing a complete draft for the entire Hebrew Bible.[28]

As this work went on, Jewish leaders underscored the high stakes. In 1913, Schechter, who would die shortly before the full translation appeared, looked forward expectantly to the finished product, "which the Jew of the future will use habitually, sometimes crying over a Psalm in it, or deriving comfort from a chapter of Isaiah, or reading a story to his children—his own Bible, not one mortgaged by the King James Version." The new translation would be "a Jewish translation, instinct with Jewish tradition and Jewish sentiment." Yet for Schechter a translation was not enough. He also hoped to see "the publication of a commentary to the Bible" because "our people should know the Bible from the Jewish point of view." It was necessary to "be a Jew and have a Jewish soul to understand the passage fully." How could Judaism "be made intensive if there are no Jewish Bible commentaries? If sentiment is borrowed from others? . . . All efforts through synagogue extension, Chautauqua classes, or Talmud Torahs will be futile so long as the very life of Judaism is not written for Jews and by Jews."[29]

When *The Holy Scriptures According to the Masoretic Text* finally appeared in 1917, the surviving members of the editorial committee carried Schechter's argument further. To them it was clear that the times demanded a translation of the Bible fulfilling Schechter's vision. The editors could have mentioned, but did not, that since the end of the nineteenth century, a Christian Zionism based on dispensationalist readings of the Old Testament had been rapidly gaining adherents among populist and conservative Protestants.[30] The dispensationalist interpretation seemed pro-Jewish, but because its themes grew directly out of historical Protestantism, it brought scant comfort to Jews wary of being co-opted by the KJV.

If the particular challenge of dispensationalism was not uppermost in the mind of the committee, the more general situation for American Jews certainly was. The committee thought "the English language . . . unless all signs fail" would soon "become the current speech of the majority of the children of Israel." Their new version, regarded strictly by itself, "gives to the Jewish world a translation of the Scriptures done by men imbued with the Jewish consciousness." But regarded in competitive biblical context, the work meant even more. The committee went out of its way to praise the KJV and the English Revised Version of 1881/1885, but added the telling reservation "[T]hey are not ours." It also defined clearly what was at stake for minorities like the Jews in a culture dominated by a strong Protestant tradition:

> The repeated efforts by Jews in the field of biblical translation show their sentiment toward translations prepared by other denominations. The dominant feature of this sentiment, apart from the thought that the christological

interpretations in non-Jewish translations are out of place in a Jewish Bible, is and was that the Jew cannot afford to have his Bible translation prepared for him by others.... If a new country and a new language metamorphose him into a new man, the duty of this new man is to prepare a new garb and a new method of expression for what is most sacred and most dear to him.[31]

Not the least of the new translation's virtues in Jewish eyes was its rescue of Scripture from the phraseology of the KJV. In the 1917 translation of Isaiah 7:14, for example, "the young woman shall conceive" replaced the KJV's "and a virgin shall conceive." The translators also left no doubt about their intention to avoid inferences from the string of titles in Isaiah 9:5–6 that Christians routinely applied to Jesus:

> For a child is born unto us,
> A son is given unto us;
> And the government is upon his shoulder;
> And his name is called
> Pele-joez-el-gibbor-
> Abi-ad-sar-shalom.[32]

In a nation so strongly influenced by the Protestant bible, this 1917 translation and its many reprintings announced that Jews no longer occupied the margins of national culture.

Schechter's interpretation of American history along with the successful completion of this translation offer much for general reflection. To those who downplay the importance of scriptural grounding for the American experiment, these Jewish scholars offered a more positive assessment. To those who have focused only on excesses of Christian imperialism, these Jews would claim—as Jews—that the American Christian heritage provided a commodious home for Judaism to thrive. But to those from a far different perspective who have equated the Protestant bible with America, this Jewish testimony has issued a sharp warning: because Scripture embraces all of history and all of the world, it must be able to assess, evaluate, and even judge the United States rather than the reverse.

Catholics Make Their Own Way

American Catholics faced challenges different from those confronted by Jewish Americans. Age-old Catholic-Protestant antagonism had never been absent since the beginning of European exploration in the new world. As was the case before the Civil War, the steady state of simmering contention regularly boiled over in response to specific events at home or in Rome. Still, the nature of Protestant-Catholic contention did evolve. On the Catholic side, the steady increase in numbers expanded the church's physical presence, while an increasingly adept corps of bishops succeeded in gaining a new measure of cultural respect.

The nature of Protestant opposition also evolved. Anti-Catholic fantasies, like the claim by the former priest Charles Chiniquy that Abraham Lincoln had been assassinated by Jesuits, enjoyed some currency, but far less than the tales of convent debauchery in the 1830s.[33] After its founding in 1887 the American Protective Association mobilized with some effect, particularly in the Midwest, but with considerably less national influence than the antebellum American Party (Know Nothings) in the 1850s. As John McGreevy has pointed out, many sources of friction remained, but with the antebellum mixture of doctrinal complaint and worry about Catholic anti-Americanism tilting strongly in the direction of the latter.[34] The Syllabus of Errors from Pope Pius IX in 1864 and the declaration of papal infallibility at the First Vatican Council in 1870 caused alarm because of what American Protestants read as signs of political despotism and intellectual obscurantism. John William Draper's *History of the Conflict between Science and Religion* (1874) focused intently on Catholics in making its polemical case. As Catholic support for the Democratic Party became even stronger, Republicans sharpened their criticism of the church's encouragement of corruption and tolerance of dissipation. In 1876, James Garfield, an Ohio congressman, Union veteran, and committed member of the Disciples of Christ, wrote in a private letter that Democrats owed their rising strength to the "combined power of rebellion, Catholicism, and whiskey."[35] Eight years later when a New York supporter of the Republican presidential candidate James G. Blaine publicly called Democrats the party of Rum, Romanism, and Rebellion, it tipped the New York vote against him and gave the election to the Democrats' Grover Cleveland.

For the history of the Bible, these circumstances defined an arena in which, as before, Catholics made defensive moves, but also in which bold positive initiatives took place. Defense was well represented by two controversies from 1871. A New York priest, James V. McNamara, responded to the claim of a Baptist author that the Scriptures definitively refuted almost everything Catholic. According to McNamara, *au contraire*, "you would never have heard of the Bible" without the church. (Ironically, McNamara would later agree with the charge of his antagonist when he left Rome to found the Independent Irish Catholic Church.)[36] An author in the *Catholic World* made a similar point in refuting the notion that the church kept Scripture from the faithful: "Does the Catholic Church condemn the Bible and forbid her people to circulate and read it? We answer: NO! On the contrary, the Catholic Church believes the Bible to be the inspired word of God himself, and constantly incites her people to its diligent perusal."[37]

Alongside arguments that reprised long-standing Catholic critique of Protestant claims about the Bible, more church leaders provided new programs encouraging appropriately Catholic use of Scripture. One came from John Joseph Keane, bishop of Richmond, Virginia, who in 1880 produced "A Sodality Manual for the Use of the Servants of the Holy Ghost," which many Catholics in his diocese and elsewhere used for several years thereafter. When the complete office was recited at monthly gatherings, or when parts of it were used in private devotions, Catholics read many portions of Scripture from the Douay version (forty-one different passages in the complete office), and read them, moreover, in the context of historical Catholic spirituality. Similar efforts with the Bible, like Thomas F. Hopkins's "Novena of Sermons on the Holy Ghost" (published 1901), which featured the Virgin Mary in its exegesis of various biblical texts, again showed Catholics how they could use the Bible for their own edifying purposes.[38]

Such devotional ventures rested on the restatement of official teaching about Scripture that the bishops at their Third Plenary Conference provided. Its compendious guide, usually called "Baltimore Catechism No. Three," repeated doctrines expressed first in the Council of Trent in the mid-sixteenth century, but without anathematizing Protestants as Trent had done. Its positive teaching clearly spelled out Catholic exceptions to common American and Protestant convictions, beginning with the importance of church tradition alongside the written word: "The Church finds the revealed truths it is bound to teach in the Holy Scripture and revealed traditions." Believers could trust the Bible because "the Church has prepared us to teach what sacred writings are Holy Scripture." Individual Catholics, moreover, did not need to work out the Bible's meaning for themselves since "God has appointed the Church to be our guide to salvation and we must accept its teaching as our infallible rule of faith." It also explained in some detail why "the Holy Scriptures alone could not be our guide to salvation and infallible rule of faith." The reasons included that although not everyone can read, "all can listen to the teaching of the Church," that the message of salvation in Christ was proclaimed before the New Testament appeared, and since only confusion resulted from treating the Bible alone ("those who take the Scripture alone for their rule of faith are constantly disputing about its meaning and what they are to believe").[39]

Most consequential in making a positive Catholic statement, however, were not such publications for the faithful but a book appearing just at the end of the Centennial year that addressed the public at large. For American Catholic history, as well as the general history of the Bible, it was a landmark.

James Gibbons's *Faith of Our Fathers*

When James Gibbons, bishop of Richmond and administrator apostolic of North Carolina, published *The Faith of Our Fathers* in December 1876, he stated the book's purpose forthrightly in its subtitle: *Being a Plain Exposition and Vindication of the Church Founded by Our Lord Jesus Christ.* If this relatively short book has remained a much-read apology for Catholicism to this day, its publication in the Centennial year also marked a new historical era with its three large claims: first, the Bible belonged to Catholics every bit as much to Protestants; second, Catholicism should be regarded as the normative expression of Christian faith because, among other important reasons, its handling of Scripture was sanctioned by God; third, Catholicism deserved to be considered a fully American religion.[40]

Gibbons of course was not the first Catholic attempting to demonstrate the compatibility of Catholicism with both Sacred Scripture and American values. The record of such efforts extended back nearly a century to John Carroll's notable defense of Catholicism in the new United States and had been replayed with variations by Bishop John England, Bishop John Purcell, Father Patrick Lynch of Charleston, and many others. In fact, only shortly before Gibbons published his book, a member of the recently founded Paulist order, Augustine F. Hewitt, produced a work with similar intent for a similar audience. Hewitt, the son of a New England Congregational minister, had once counted himself among "the stricter form of what is called Evangelical Protestants." His 1874 apologetic, *The King's Highway*, which explained why he had converted, was written "expressly for the benefit of that class of Protestants among whom [he] was born and brought up," by which he meant those "who still believe in the Bible and the divinity of Christ," though separated from "the true church" by "the sins of their ancestors."[41]

Yet Hewitt's work had an edge that undercut its effectiveness. The climax of his discussion of the church and Scripture provided this less-than-gentle application of John 14:16–17, where Christ promises the Holy Spirit:

The pretence of sectarians to the illumination of the Holy Spirit and the possession of the truth, and all the illusions of false mysticism, of private, interior light, of private judgment on the Scripture, of immediate union with Christ apart from the communion of the true church—the whole baseless, shadowy fabric of Luther and Calvin is swept away by these declarations of Scripture when correctly explained and understood according to the ancient tradition and doctrine of Catholic antiquity.[42]

Unlike Gibbons, Hewitt quoted Scripture from the KJV rather than the Douay-Rheims. But also unlike Gibbons's work, Hewitt's apology generated little attention.[43]

The Faith of Our Fathers came in the early years of Gibbons's distinguished career. In 1869–70 he had been the second youngest bishop at the First Vatican Council. Shortly after the book's publication, he was named archbishop of Baltimore, where he would serve for over four decades, be named only the second American cardinal, and become the recognized leader of American Catholicism. His responsibilities as a young bishop resident first in Wilmington, North Carolina, and then Richmond, Virginia, were difficult because of both regions' overwhelmingly Protestant character. When Gibbons in 1868 began his service as the missionary vicar apostolic of North Carolina, there were more *congregations* of both Methodists and Baptists in that state than individual Catholics. Virginia enjoyed a larger Catholic presence, but when in 1872 he added the see of Richmond to his North Carolina charge, Catholics made up at most 2% of the state's population.[44] In such an environment, Gibbons found that the talks he prepared for "mixed audiences" and "especially on the occasion of a mission in the rural districts" multiplied the need for "books or tracts . . . which could be read and pondered at leisure."[45] After having his own manuscript checked by a convert whose Protestant upbringing gave him special appreciation for "the non-Catholic American mind" and a Jesuit professor at Woodstock College, he delivered it to John Murphy in Baltimore. Murphy was so impressed that he printed an unusually large run of ten thousand copies and in April 1877 added another ten thousand to meet immediate demand.[46] Catholic reviewers naturally praised the book, especially its relatively moderate tone in contrast to standard Protestant polemics. Protestants reacted with predictable dismissals, though over time even some Protestant authors praised at least the style with which Gibbons took up his task.[47]

The book's initial popularity has been sustained. When in 1917 Gibbons, by then the long-serving cardinal archbishop of Baltimore, wrote a short preface for its "83rd edition" (i.e., "reprinting"), he reported that "up to the present time, fourteen hundred thousand copies [i.e., 1.4 million] have been published, and the circulation of the book is constantly increasing" (x). That total compares favorably with the approximately 1 million copies of Lew Wallace's *Ben-Hur: A Tale of the Christ* sold between its publication in 1880 and 1912, which pushed *Ben-Hur* past *Uncle Tom's Cabin* as the nation's bestselling novel.[48] The appeal of Gibbons's book continues, with at least nine editions advertised on Amazon.com in October 2020, including an audio version and a translation in French.

One of the Catholic reviewers highlighted the book's feature that made it so historically important. It specified that the bishop's "chief aim" was to stress "those [Catholic] truths to persons who accept the Holy Scriptures as divinely inspired."[49] Gibbons himself wrote that since his "chief aim has been to bring home the truths of the Catholic Faith to our separated brethren, who generally accept the Scripture as the only source of authority in religious matters, he has endeavored to fortify his statements by abundant reference to the sacred text" (ix). Gibbons knew his audience. His treatise would not simply explain Catholicism, but explain it as *the* genuine "religion of the Book."

The book's opening paragraphs set the tone. Gentle confrontation, biblical allusions, forthright assertion, identification with readers, a voice of reason—all combined to make an apologetic informed by audience receptivity as well as apologetical intent.

> MY DEAR READER—Perhaps this is the first time in your life that you have handled a book in which the doctrines of the Catholic Church are expounded by one of her own sons. You have, no doubt, heard and read many things regarding our Church; but has not your information come from teachers justly liable to suspicion? You asked for bread, and they gave you a stone [Matt 7:9; Lk 11:11]. You asked for fish, and they reached you a serpent [Matt 7:10; Lk 11:11]. Instead of the bread of truth [1 Cor 5:8], they extended to you the serpent of falsehood [Gen 3:1]. Hence, without intending to be unjust, is not your mind biased against us because you listened to false witnesses [Matt 26:60; Acts 6:13; 1 Cor 15:15]? This, at least, is the case with thousands of my countrymen whom I have met in the brief course of my missionary career. (xiii)

The introduction also drew readers toward the bishop's goal, expressed in the same scriptural register. He promised an ideal outcome if readers would become Catholics:

> You give up none of those revealed [i.e., biblical] truths which you may possess already. . . . You gain everything that is worth having. You acquire a full and connected knowledge of God's revelation. You get possession of the whole truth as it is in Jesus [Jn 14:6]. . . . You exchange opinion for certainty. You are no longer "tossed about by every wind of doctrine" [Eph 4:14], but you are firmly grounded on the rock of truth [Lk 6:48].[50]

Although Gibbons's temperate style marked a change from much confrontational literature, polemic did not disappear. His first provocation was the title. The day when an abridged version of Frederick Faber's 1849 hymn—"Father of our fathers, living still . . . Faith of our fathers, holy faith! / We will be true to thee till death"—would be found in nearly half of all Protestant hymnals was still a generation into the future.[51] But already by the mid-1870s, several hymnal editors had begun to include this text, which was destined to become a much-loved Protestant standard. Gibbons, however, knew that Faber was a Catholic convert from an evangelical Protestant background, that he had written "Faith of Our Fathers" to memorialize Catholic martyrs in Protestant England, and that Faber's original included a polemical evocation of the Virgin Mary:

> Faith of our fathers, Mary's prayers
> Shall win our country back to Thee;
> And through the truth that comes from God,
> England shall then indeed be free.

Gibbons's polemics also rehearsed many well-worn themes in traditional Protestant-Catholic debates over Scripture: there would never have been a Bible if early Catholic councils had not defined the canon and the church preserved copies of the sacred text; Jesus proved his divinity by testimony more than by Scripture; the church's teaching authority was required to clarify difficult passages, instruct the illiterate, and restrain irresponsible interpretations; the diversity of Protestant opinions from the very start of the Reformation showed "conclusively . . . the utter folly of interpreting the Scriptures by private judgment" (75). Again, knowing his audience, Gibbons deployed at least twenty-one biblical quotations and several biblical allusions to demonstrate that the church preserved the Bible, was its only proper interpreter, and desired faithful Catholics to read it under proper guidance. At least a few quotations on these points read exactly the same in the Douay-Rheims and King James translations; in one instance he interpolated a word from the KJV in order to clarify a Douay-Rheims quotation (68).

The themes of Gibbons's book contained no surprises: standard Christian doctrines, the church and its organization under the papacy, Catholic teaching concerning the invocation of saints, the Virgin Mary (added in a very early revision), sacred images, purgatory, Catholic sacramentalism, and the church's seven sacraments. Significantly, two full chapters addressed issues of civil and religious liberty. The TAN Books edition of 360 pages includes almost four hundred scriptural quotations that Gibbons identified (with only about a dozen from the Apocrypha, which most Protestant readers would not have considered canonical) along with at least 250 other references or allusions to scriptural material. The quotations were all from the Douay-Rheims translation, while the allusions and references often employed phrases shared by the Douay-Rheims and the KJV.

Gibbons's scriptural usage was most intense for those doctrines that Protestants most decried. The longest chapter in later editions of the book dealt with the Virgin Mary, a chapter added in an early revision in response to a vigorous Protestant attack. In its twenty-nine pages Gibbons supported Catholic doctrine on the Virgin Mary with over fifty biblical quotations and at least another twenty-five to thirty scriptural allusions or references. In describing Mary's perpetual virginity (145–47), he employed fourteen quotations or references and more than a dozen each for the propriety of venerating Mary along with Jesus (159–62) and invoking Mary's prayers (162–66). One of the few Marian doctrines not so extensively supported with scriptural citations (only three of them) was the claim that Mary should be imitated, with which few Protestants disagreed (166–69). For the Catholic teaching on the Virgin's immaculate conception (147–50) there were likewise only three biblical citations, but with this explanation: "Although the Immaculate Conception was not formulated into a dogma of faith until 1854, it is at least implied in Holy Scripture [and] . . . is in strict harmony with the place which Mary holds in the economy of Redemption" (148).

To drive home his message about Scripture, the young bishop described the central place the Bible occupied in his clerical training and continued to occupy in his daily devotional life. He explained that Catholic restrictions on lay reading of Scripture arose only in response to Protestants' abuse of the Bible. He also addressed the perennial Protestant charge that the church kept Scripture from lay men and women: "What is good for the clergy must be good, also, for the laity. Be assured that if you become a Catholic you will never be forbidden to read the Bible. It is our earnest wish that every word of the Gospel may be imprinted on your memory and on your heart" (81).

As prominently as Gibbons stressed his fidelity to Scripture, so extensively did he describe Catholicism as a perfect faith for the United States. Twice, for example, he likened the church's rule in guiding biblical interpretation to the functioning of American law: "Our civil government is not run by private judgment, but by constitutional authorities. . . . Why not apply the same principle to the interpretation of the Bible and the government of the Church?" (76).

The emphasis on Catholic-American compatibility took over completely in the chapters on religious and civil liberty. Rather than addressing American concerns about the Syllabus of Errors or papal infallibility, he cited examples of Catholic tolerance and offered explanations for episodes of apparent Catholic intolerance. His goal remained unambiguous: "[T]he proposition, which I hope to confirm by historical evidence, [is] that the Catholic Church has always been the zealous promoter of religious and civil liberty" (195). About his own commitments, he was just as bold: "Thank God, we live in a country where liberty of conscience is respected, and where the civil constitution holds over us the aegis of her protections, without intermeddling with ecclesiastical affairs. From my heart, I say: America, with all thy faults, I love thee still." To demonstrate that love, Gibbons went on to affirm that he much preferred the American pattern of voluntary church support to "the system which obtains in some Catholic countries in Europe, where the church is supported by the government" (212).

An alternative reading of American history expanded his case—for instance, that Catholics were legislating religious freedom in Maryland in 1649 while Puritans in New England were executing Quakers. The Catholic Mary Tudor reigned over England for only five years, with one spasm of violence against Protestants, while her Protestant half-sister Elizabeth reigned for forty-four years and with a consistent policy of persecution that executed more Catholics than Mary had Protestants. In a particularly sensitive comparison for a prelate whose parents were born in Ireland and who had lived there as a youth during the Famine of the 1840s, Gibbons offered one of the book's few passages of extended italicization: "*How is it that Catholics are persistently reproached for the persecution under Mary's reign, while scarcely a voice is raised in condemnation of the legalized fines, confiscations and deaths inflicted on the Catholics of Great Britain and Ireland for three hundred years—from the establishment of the church of England, in 1534, to the time of the Catholic emancipation?*" (225–26).

The reception history of *The Faith of Our Fathers* included an exceedingly dense exchange prompted by Edwin J. Stearns, a Maryland Episcopalian whose skill in quoting Scripture had earlier been displayed in a biblical defense of slavery contained in an attack on Harriet Beecher Stowe's *Uncle Tom's Cabin*.[52] Yet such controversy pales into insignificance when compared to the extraordinary popularity of Gibbons's book. To be sure, its unusual success by no means ended Protestant (and then secular) worries about Catholicism as a dangerous foe of American liberty. Yet what Steven Green has written about the politics of 1876 applies just as well, mutatis mutandis, to Gibbons's book of that year: "The [Blaine] amendment . . . took on the much larger question of how to perpetuate American values and institutions in light of the pressures imposed by immigration, race, Reconstruction, urbanization, and industrialization."[53] For his part, Gibbons asserted that a Bible other than the KJV and a form of Christianity other than evangelical Protestantism supported general American values better than any Protestant alternative and that they met the deepest personal needs of Americans as individuals as well as the nation as a whole. This case has rarely been argued so well.

"Americanism" and "Modernism"

After Gibbons became a cardinal, he figured prominently in a complicated series of events that would exercise a different kind of long-term impact on Catholics and the Bible. The "Americanist Controversy" developed out of concern by traditional European Catholics that their American counterparts had accommodated too much and too fast to Americans' love of liberty, conventions of democracy, and rejection of church-state ties.[54] An 1895 encyclical by Pope Leo

XIII, *Longinque Oceani*, praised the American church for its rapid advances but also cautioned against making American distinctives into principled norms for Catholicism as a whole. Then in 1898 Europeans reacted with alarm when they read the French translation of a biography of the American founder of the Paulist order, Isaac Hecker. Hecker, who became a Catholic after passing through Methodism, Unitarianism, and Transcendentalism, had pioneered vigorous evangelism among non-Catholic Americans. As a Catholic, however, he retained some of the reforming perfectionism and democratic instincts of his pre-Catholic life—precisely the features that European conservatives viewed as fatally dangerous.[55] These Europeans also knew that a few American bishops, like John Ireland of St. Paul, Minnesota, had won a reputation for celebrating distinctly American institutions, as an example in Ireland's cause, the potential of public education to helpfully complement Catholic parochial schools.[56] In response to the specific concerns raised by the Hecker biography alongside uneasiness about general American looseness, Leo XIII in 1899 directed a papal letter, *Testem benevolentiae*, to Cardinal Gibbons. Leo instructed the cardinal that, if American Catholics were tolerating individual interpretations of church doctrine or embracing American ways as entirely in keeping with the church's teaching, they must abandon such notions immediately. Gibbons responded shrewdly that, if such errors were alive in the United States, he would snuff them out—but he did not really believe they had taken hold among the faithful.

"Americanism" became important for the history of the Bible when church officials in Rome viewed American susceptibility to democracy, individualism, and the separation of church and state as part of the general threat of "modernism."[57] By this threat, Catholic officials meant the progressive ethics and biblical higher criticism that in various degrees had influenced American Protestants. Although very few American Catholics embraced the latter ideas, conservative Europeans and their allies in the American church (German, Polish, and conservative Irish bishops) perceived a clear connection with what Leo had condemned as "Americanism." The upshot was an encyclical from Pope Pius X in 1907, *Pascendi Dominici gregis*, that prohibited any Catholic acceptance of the kind of progressive or liberal opinions undergirding higher biblical criticism.[58]

The result turned out to give some American Catholics another reason for criticizing their Protestant fellow citizens. Some years after church officials had enforced the strictures of this encyclical, Hugh Pope, O.P., drew on American history to defend traditional Catholic views and criticize Protestant capitulation to dangerous intellectual fashion: "[I]t is not the Bible that is condemned [by the hierarchy], nor the use of it, but the abuse of it." He then offered a back-handed complement to Protestant sectarians, like those who promoted premillennial dispensationalism, by noting, "Ironically enough, it is the Catholic Church which (outside a comparatively small body of men who still base themselves on an exact literal interpretation of the English translation made three hundred years ago) is, in the modern world, the defender of Scriptural authority."[59] So it was that the American hierarchy during Cardinal Gibbons's lifetime, and taking care to avoid raising suspicions about anything too distinctly "American," came to strictly enforce traditional approaches to Scripture (and Catholic teaching in general) until 1943 and an encyclical from Pope Pius XII, *Divino Afflante Spiritu*, opened the door to the Catholic practice of moderate biblical criticism.

Well before the end of the nineteenth century, Jews and Catholics had made signal contributions to the American history of the Bible. Yet with new force, the four decades between James Gibbons's *Faith of Our Fathers* and the Jewish Publication Society's fresh English translation of the Hebrew Scriptures enlivened, enriched, expanded, but also complicated that history. Both communities contributed significantly to the vitality of Scripture among the population, which in turn sustained the Bible as a prominent cultural object. Yet by further contesting traditional Protestant assumptions about the Bible, the movement of Catholics and Jews from the margins only intensified already pressing questions about how or whether religious convictions should influence the public sphere and shape the nation's course into the future.

PART VI

TOWARD THE PRESENT

Gift .

All our righteousnesses are as filthy rags;
and we all do fade as a leaf—Isaiah 64:6

After my mother's father died,
she gave me his morocco Bible.
I took it from her hand, and saw
the gold was worn away, the binding
scuffed and ragged, split below the spine,
and inside, smudges where her father's
right hand gripped the bottom corner
page by page, an old man waiting, not quite
reading the words he had known by heart
for sixty years: our parents in the garden,
naked, free from shame; the bitterness of labor;
blood in the ground, still calling for God's
curse. His thumbprints faded after the flood,
to darken again where God bids Moses smite
the rock, and then again in Psalms, in Matthew
every page. And where Paul speaks of things
God hath prepared, things promised them who wait,
things not yet entered into the loving heart,
below the margin of the verse, the paper
is translucent with the oil and dark
still with the dirt of his right hand.

—From *They Lift Their Wings to Cry* by Brooks Haxton,
copyright (c) 2008 by Brooks Haxton. Used by Permission of
Alfred A. Knopf, an imprint of the Knopf Doubleday Publishing Group,
a division of Penguin Random House LLC. All rights reserved.

27

Still a Bible Nation

In the early decades of its second century, the United States remained a Bible nation, but not as the civilization envisioned by antebellum custodial Protestants and not by fulfilling the hopes for mass conversion entertained by almost all English-language Protestant bodies in that earlier period. "The Bible's enduring ubiquity in American culture . . . as a commercial product, as a cultural icon, and as a material object" did continue, as William Trollinger has explained in a perceptive account of Protestant publishing in the latter era. It remained the chief guide of spiritual life for countless individuals and families, supplied liturgical content for numerous worshiping communities, and received week-by-week exposition in countless sermons and even more attention in gatherings organized informally.[1] Commercial, nonprofit, and a small number of scholarly publishers supplied reams of Bible-based literature for every possible interest. Newspapers contained a steady stream of biblical quotation, with upsurges in the 1870s, 1890s, and 1910s.[2] The King James Version remained a bottomless resource for seasoning public speech. And the same KJV was still read daily in probably more than half of the nation's public schools.

But what did that ubiquitous presence *mean*? How could ubiquity translate into a coherent public influence when no mass movement enjoyed the scriptural benediction received by the American Revolution or that supported the southern and northern sides in the Civil War? How important was the Bible, really, when the nation's breakneck economic expansion and accompanying economic conflicts generated only occasional biblical attention, and when white believers mostly ignored the potential of Scripture to bridge the expanding cultural divide separating them from Black believers? What happened when American missionaries, who moved around the globe desiring to spread biblical Christianity, sometimes adjusted that message to their new host cultures, but often presented loyalty to Scripture as loyalty to American ways? How could Scripture function as a national guide when most of the eleven new states that filled out the continent between 1876 (Colorado) and 1912 (New Mexico and Arizona) had not been shaped by the Protestant Scriptures, as had many of the earlier thirty-seven? In an environment where "the production, distribution, and consumption of print was so pervasive a part of daily live in the United States that it became the habitual arena for the achievement of all sorts of purposes," how could religious purposes keyed to the Bible compete with purposes keyed

America's Book. Mark A. Noll, Oxford University Press. © Oxford University Press 2022.
DOI: 10.1093/oso/9780197623466.003.0028

to business, leisure, news of the world, and the interests of many new organizations?[3] And how could "*the* Bible" remain meaningful when its most ardent Protestant proponents differed so much among themselves, when Catholics, Jews, and many others honored their own bibles, and when influential sectors of the population had left behind the notion of an authoritative Scripture?

The logic that had once made the Bible central may not have been airtight, but it had inspired much in the nation's early life.

1. Bible-based Protestantism revealed God's pathway of salvation for individuals, families, and perhaps even communities.
2. Salvation liberated its recipients as nothing else imaginable could free them.
3. The character traits that Protestants believed salvation nurtured (self-restraint, honesty, loving one's neighbor as oneself, respect for others as made in the image of God) were exactly the character traits without which the free American republic would lapse back into the tyrannical corruptions of old Europe.
4. Therefore, as a unique herald of salvation, an icon of purest liberty, and a guide for social well-being, Scripture should be honored by the entire society in every way possible within a polity that had rejected European Christendom as inherently corrupting.

By the 1870s and 1880s dismembered fragments of this conceptual unity were still very much alive, but incoherently. Various Protestants still proclaimed compelling spiritual messages drawn from Scripture, but the Protestant canopy, which itself had torn, no long covered an ever-growing proportion of the population. Liberty under God remained a national mantra, but often an ideal meaning "freedom from" rather than "freedom for." (H. W. Brands relates that John D. Rockefeller once took on a business partner who "didn't drink or swear, and he took his Protestant religion as seriously as Rockefeller did—which was to say, he read his Bible religiously but kept his ledger books in a different drawer.")[4] The Bible could also still feature prominently on public occasions—in fact, more prominently than at events of the Centennial year. Public voices, however, regularly stressed Scripture's utility for civic virtue with scant mention of its role in personal conversion or for sanctified living. In reaction, a few believers thought that treating Scripture like this, as socially useful while downplaying its spiritual function, betrayed Christianity itself. For many more citizens, the Bible had meaning only for its social utility. Still others continued to stress the older connection between personal faith and public well-being but without explaining why this distinctly Protestant conception could fairly serve an increasingly pluralistic nation.

The book's epilogue attempts an assessment of the questions raised by the continued salience of Scripture in a nation that had moved beyond the aspirational Bible civilization of its early decades. Before making that attempt, however, it is important to observe the many features that continued to mark the United States as a Bible nation in the decades between the Centennial and the First World War, which is the subject of this chapter and the next. A later chapter then describes the central role of Scripture in the outbursts of national civil religion after the assassinations of two presidents (1881, 1901) and at the widespread celebration of the three-hundredth anniversary of the King James Bible (1911). The book's final chapter returns to the Bible's importance for African American communities that, at least in that period, still received little attention from the general public.

The Bible Business

Scripture in American history has always been more than a merchandised commodity, but also never less. If by the late nineteenth century, the enterprises involved in Bible production were ceding their cultural dominance, they nonetheless remained large in scale, energetic in execution, creative in conception, and impressive in outcomes.

The publishing numbers again reveal a meaningful, if admittedly partial, reality. Because the industry had become more concentrated, fewer editions of the Bible were being produced, but with more copies because of larger print runs. New York and Philadelphia still dominated the business; meaningful production also occurred in Boston but not too many other places. For a few major efforts joint publication could be arranged, as for the five-volume *Illustrated Bible Commentary on the New Testament, for family use and reference, and for the great body of Christian workers of all denominations* that the New York City editor Lyman Abbott brought out from the mid-1870s to the late 1880s.[5] Although more translations were entering the market, the KJV and its revisions remained dominant, and by far. Of the 312 separate new editions carefully recorded by Margaret Hills for the years 1881 to 1920, 52% were of the KJV and another 25% revisions of that translation. Catholic editions (all but two the Douay-Rheims) accounted for 8.5%, and other translations, mostly from Protestants, another 13.5%. Two editions of the 1917 *Tanakh* from the Jewish Publication Society and two other Jewish editions filled out the total.[6]

The English Revised Version and American Standard Version

Publication of the English Revised Version (ERV)—the New Testament in 1881 and the entire Bible in 1885—illustrated the national excitement a Bible event could generate, but also revealed complexities in the American allegiance to Scripture.[7] This project began as an initiative of England's still-established Anglican church. A committee of scholars, mostly from Oxford and Cambridge and mostly Anglican with only a few Dissenters, had been charged in 1870 with preparing a revision of the KJV. The charge specified the use of more reliable Greek and Hebrew manuscripts than had been available in 1611 and asked the revisers to update the language where changes in English had made KJV readings deceptive (as an example, in the older version "meat" meant food of any kind). To make a version useful for all speakers of English, a committee of American scholars was formed to consult with their English counterparts.

After sometimes acrimonious debate within the British committee and not much cooperation across the Atlantic, the New Testament was released to the British public on Tuesday, May 17, 1881, and to Americans on Friday the 20th. The United States, with a population of just over 51 million, was responsible for more than 1 million pre-orders.[8] By 3:00 p.m. on the day of publication in New York City, Thomas Nelson, the firm authorized by Cambridge University Press and Oxford University Press as the copyright holders, had retailed 250,000 copies in more than twenty different formats with prices ranging from twenty-five cents to sixteen dollars. Two days later the Sunday edition of the *Chicago Tribune* drove the price lower: for a nickel, Chicagoans and readers in the six states served by the *Trib* received a full copy of the new version as part of their Sunday paper. Over the next four days, an additional 107,000 midwesterners, besides the approximately 50,000 Sunday subscribers, had purchased the sixteen-page supplement that included the revisers' introduction plus the New Testament itself.[9] To bring off this coup, the Chicago paper had arranged to receive the ERV by telegraph from New York, after which ninety-two compositors worked for twelve hours to make it ready for distribution very early Sunday morning.[10]

Interest and enthusiasm were at first stratospheric. From May through December, the *New York Times* ran eight editorials and seventeen news stories on the revision. (In 1885 it hailed the appearance of the entire Bible with five editorials and seven stories.)[11] Most periodicals and religious church leaders praised the new version for providing a more accurate translation in less archaic language.

Publishers scrambled to share in the bonanza.[12] Margaret Hills's admittedly incomplete catalogue lists forty-three separate editions from thirty-three different publishers for 1881. Several firms brought out substantial books that documented every change.[13] Of the forty-three editions, only nine printed the

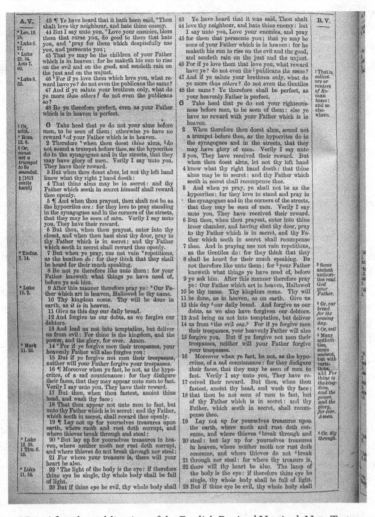

Figure 27.1 After the publication of the English Revised Version's New Testament in 1881, many American firms brought out editions with side-by-side comparisons with the King James Version. This page from Matthew chapter 6 shows the ERV's relegation to the margin of the Protestants' traditional ending of the Lord's Prayer.

Source: Courtesy of Buswell Library Special Collections, Rare Books, Wheaton College, Illinois.

English text of the ERV by itself. Fourteen included the alternative wording proposed by the American committee, ten ran the ERV and the KJV in parallel columns, fifteen offered histories of Bible translation with the text, and at least three supplied engravings or maps. (Figure 27.1) By the end of the year, in less than seven months, American sales topped 3 million. As a comparison to gauge this scale of production and distribution, it took five years for Lew Wallace's *Ben-Hur*, which was published in 1880, to be selling fifteen thousand copies annually; this runaway bestseller did not reach a million total sales until the twentieth century, a publishing number that nonetheless made it the nation's best-selling novel before *Gone with the Wind*.[14]

Despite this extraordinary launch, the ERV fell far short as a replacement for the KJV. Even after the American committee issued its own revision as an entire Bible in 1901 (the American Standard Version, ASV), the ERV and the ASV together attracted only a small minority of Bible users. In contrast to its coverage of the ERV, the *New York Times* gave the ASV only one short review.[15] During the first two decades after the ASV's publication, American publishers produced more than four times as many editions of the KJV; that ratio only grew as the new century wore on.[16]

David Daniell has explained the failure of the ERV in Britain categorically: "The chief and uncontrovertible reason for the British public not accepting the Revision Version was that it was not very good."[17] By focusing on the revisers' goals, Kenneth Cmiel offered a more analytical explanation for the ERV's similar failure in America. The revisers, he notes, sought a more accurate rendering of the best "Greek and Hebrew texts," but while also trying to preserve "Elizabethan diction" and writing "idiomatic English."[18] The first problem came in subordinating the pursuit of "idiomatic English" to the goal of preserving "Elizabethan diction." On too many occasions academic pedantry replaced the music that had made the KJV (often only following Tyndale) so beloved (see Table 27.1).[19]

Beyond stilted diction, several other factors checked the use of this or any other alternative to the KJV. Readers of the new version immediately confronted two challenges. First, could innovations be accepted even if they clearly made for a more understandable Bible? By the nineteenth century, "charity" had become

Table 27.1 The ERV and the KJV

Matthew 6:10	
ERV	KJV
Thy will be done, as in heaven, so on earth.	Thy will be done in earth, as it is in heaven.

Galatians 5:1	
ERV	KJV
With freedom did Christ set us free: stand fast therefore.	Stand fast therefore in the liberty wherewith Christ hath made us free.

a prime case in point. It now meant gratuitous gifts to the needy, which made the well-known verse 1 Corinthians 13:3 nonsensical: "And though I bestow all my goods to feed the poor . . . and have not charity, it profiteth me nothing." The ERV, employing what Philip Schaff, chair of the American revising committee, called "a strong Saxon monosyllable," provided wording that did make sense.[20] Instead of reading at the end of this famous chapter, "now abideth faith, hope, and charity, these three, but the greatest of these is charity," readers found that monosyllable: "now abideth faith, hope, love, these three: and the greatest of these is love." But this rendition left many readers feeling as if something fundamental had been lost.

A similar reaction greeted the formatting of the ERV, which, while retaining verse numbers, printed them as small superscripts within complete paragraphs. With this change, the translation looked a little bit more like the unnumbered Greek and Hebrew originals, but for many it was disconcerting.

More serious difficulties came when readers discovered that the ERV omitted several much-loved passages that had been sacrificed to carefully verified advances in scholarship.[21] Earlier in the century explorations in the Near East had uncovered older manuscripts than the King James translators possessed. At the same time the Vatican allowed scholars to study old manuscripts it had long kept from view. From the so-called Vaticanus and Sinaiticus codexes, scholars, led by B. F. Westcott and F. J. A. Hort at Cambridge, were preparing a new critical edition of the Greek New Testament that the revisers put to use. In an important distinction for that period when several kinds of "critics" proposed new approaches to Scripture, the Cambridge scholars practiced "lower criticism," a commitment to ascertain the most accurate possible texts of the first-century documents. Westcott in particular denounced efforts to interpret Scripture with contemporary questioning of the supernatural and contemporary certainties about the evolution of ethical consciousness in "history."

Yet even that kind of cautious criticism created consternation when the revision reached the public. Where was the salutation to Mary from Luke 1:28 ("Blessed art thou among women")? Why was the one New Testament text with unequivocal proof for the Trinity missing (1 Jn 5:7, "For there are three that bear record in heaven, the Father, the Word, and the Holy Ghost: and these three are one")? Most egregiously, what happened to the ending of the Lord's Prayer that Protestants had been reciting for hundreds of years (Matt 6:13, "For thine is the kingdom, and the power, and the glory, for ever. Amen")? For portions that still remained, why did brackets surround the story of Jesus and the woman caught in adultery (Jn 7:53–8:11) with a note about its not appearing in "most of the ancient authorities"? And the same for the ending of the Book of Mark, chapter 16, where a footnote read, "The two oldest Greek manuscripts, and some other authorities, omit from ver. 9 to the end."

In every case the omissions and cautionary notes reflected the considered judgment that, though these passages had entered the bloodstream of English-language biblical culture, they were extraneous intrusions. They did not appear in the manuscripts that came closest to what the original biblical authors had written. Significantly, these alterations did not bother the conservative scholars at Princeton Seminary, including William Henry Green, who helped revise the Old Testament, and B. B. Warfield, who in 1881 co-authored the definitive statement on the Bible's inerrancy.[22]

These changes, however, certainly bothered many others. As one prominent example of a mixed reception, the KJV text in C. I. Scofield's reference Bible included the material deleted in the ERV, but with notes indicating that the disputed texts were not found in the oldest manuscripts.[23] In both Britain and the United States, purported facts from the credentialed scholars also confronted stiff resistance. A generation earlier, the American Bible Society had sponsored a large-scale research effort to correct the twenty-four thousand discrepancies that had crept into contemporary KJV texts when compared to the first edition of 1611, owing to editorial mistakes, printers' fiddling, and errors from multiple reprintings. Although none of these discrepancies affected the sense of any significant passage, and although the effort aimed only at securing a "purified" text of the KJV, the uproar from local Bible society committees, the public press, and one or two angry ministers doomed the effort. "The Common Version," in Kenneth Cmiel's summary, "was untouchable."[24]

The outcry resounded many times more loudly in 1881. It was led by Dr. J. W. Burgon, the dean of Chichester Cathedral in England who had earlier complained vociferously when a Unitarian was asked to join the Old Testament revision committee.[25] Now Burgon blasted away by defending the "textus receptus" that had been used for the KJV in 1611 as superior to the new Greek and Hebrew manuscripts employed for the revision. Burgon also hinted that recourse to manuscripts secreted away for centuries in the Vatican automatically destroyed the creditability of textual work by Westcott and Hort. Later American defenders of the KJV regularly expanded on this anti-Catholic criticism.[26]

Some American critics played the anti-elitist card that has appeared so frequently throughout the nation's history. When one of the American revisers on the New Testament committee complained about "old grannies and croakers" who mindlessly opposed their work, T. DeWitt Talmage of the Brooklyn Tabernacle fired back by attacking ecclesiastical "bossism." To Talmage the credentials of the revisers represented anything but a commendation: "D.D. and Ph.D. and LL.D. are often only the heavy baggage of a very slow train." Peter Thuesen, using expressions from a contemporary review, made the shrewd observation that "in spite of all the scholarly clamor for King Truth, most people still preferred King James."[27]

Marketing

The very success of the KJV as both a spiritual and a commercial object loomed even larger than specific criticisms of the revision. By blanketing the land with their product, voluntary societies and commercial presses had come close to creating an equivalence between "the Bible" and the KJV. What Margaret Hills once wrote about Bible printing in general applies especially to this particular translation. She conceded that it was doubtless the world's "most unread book," but also observed that "a good proportion of the copies printed, somewhere, sometime, [met] a heartfelt need of some man, woman, or child."[28] Where such men, women, and children clung to the KJV, they testified to the enduring legacy of a translation that shaped an entire civilization and had given transcendent purpose to lives from the highest ranks to the most despised.

It is obviously impossible to disentangle the KJV's place in the history of American religion, considered as the sphere of spirituality, from its history as an object of social organization and a marketed commodity. In 1853 the ABS moved its New York City headquarters into an impressive new building on Astor Place near the Cooper Union, where seven years later Abraham Lincoln made the speech against the expansion of slavery that won the support of many eastern Republicans. The move to this upscale neighborhood signaled the ABS's acceptance of the nation's growing class divisions. Its trajectory of professionalization meant, as Peter Wosh has written, the Society "had narrowed its mission from Christianizing the world to producing the Scriptures and coordinating their distribution." Increasingly, "it appeared to be a purely corporate task, measurable by purely corporate standards."[29]

In the second half of the century Methodists, themselves rising in wealth and status, replaced Presbyterians and Congregationalists as the Society's most active supporters. For its fourth "general supply" of the years 1882 to 1890, the ABS's managers devoted more attention to supplying bibles to Native Americans, the incoming tide of European immigrants, and even the Chinese population increasing on the West Coast. Along with ongoing religious concerns, service to the nation was becoming increasingly important, as indicated by words from the Society's 1882 annual report: "Patriotism demands [the Bible] for the preservation of our liberty, union, and government of this republic, which owes its existence to the open Bible and tolerant Christianity."[30]

Commercial publishers responded to different needs, but almost as energetically. The massive family bibles that had become a mainstay by midcentury cost a lot, but marked their owners as responsible Christian citizens.[31] Illustrators returned often to images of the family gathered for readings from such weighty tomes, though it is hard to imagine how readers of ordinary muscle power could handle, say, the book provided by Baird and Dillon of New York in 1883: "The

Holy Bible . . . with Complete Concordance . . . 100,000 Marginal References and Readings, and . . . Smith's Standard Bible Dictionary, A Complete History of the Books of the Bible . . . A History of All Religious Denominations. Apocrypha and Psalms in Meter . . . With Revised New Testament . . . over 2500 Scripture Illustrations on Steel, Wood, and in Colors."[32] By this time, Catholics were also keeping pace, as in a Bible published in 1875 by John E. Potter of Philadelphia with comparable paratextual material graced by the imprimatur.[33]

Whether from nonprofits like the ABS or commercial firms marketing elaborate family bibles, the provision of God's Word participated unreservedly in the very human world of market exchange. About that association, R. Laurence Moore's *Selling God* phrased a perennially pertinent question: "Was there any way for religious leaders to avoid a market mentality—the imperative to expand, the association of growth with innovation, the reliance upon aggressive publicity, the assumed importance of building networks that linked the local to the nation, the habit of thinking in tangible exchange terms that allowed a quick calculation of returns (converted souls or its measurable equivalent, moral behavior) for expended effort?" In Moore's opinion, "religion's systematic and expansive complicity in mechanisms of market exchange is surely the most important aspect of the particular kind of secularization that has characterized the nineteenth and twentieth centuries."[34] The American history of the Bible cannot be explained in its entirety by that well-considered judgment, but with the commercial expansion of the latter decades of the nineteenth century it now factored as a larger element of the story.

Anything but a Single "*The* Bible"

In the two generations after the Civil War the KJV remained the Bible that most Americans recognized, quoted, and often purchased, even non-Protestants and Americans whose first language was not English. As indicated by the words most often referenced by skeptics, novelists, and poets, in the law, and in popular books about Jesus, it was not an entirely misplaced instinct to think of this supremely visible translation as "the nation's Bible." Yet as the history of Catholic and Jewish scriptures as well as the ERV and ASV suggests, there has always been a fuller story that, explored even briefly, greatly complicates any effort to speak of a single "*the* Bible" in American history.

Not in English

As an instance, during this period when immigrants arrived in great numbers, the printing of bibles not in English became increasingly important. For a telling comparison, Margaret Hills's indispensable catalogue lists 584 new English-language editions for the years 1860 to 1925, but during the same period American publishers brought out more than half that many (at least 316) separate editions of bibles not in English.[35] Most appeared in the major European languages of the largest immigrant groups or in Hebrew (thirty-seven editions of the latter). But several served Native Americans (ten editions in Dakota, two in Kalispel, as well as one each in Arikara, Cheyenne, Choctaw, Hidatsa, Navaho, and Winnebago) and language communities with missionary connections (eight editions in Hawaiian, four in Zulu, two in Kussaie, one each in Burmese, Marshall, and Sheetswa).

Although several different religious groups and a number of individuals produced new or reprinted non-KJV English-language versions during these years, considerably more common were editions in the European languages of the immigrants. Lutherans, while turning to the KJV when congregations moved to English, were responsible for a majority of the non-English bibles. Until the restrictive immigration legislation of the mid-1920s, striking numbers continued to appear. Most of the *one hundred* (!) German-language Bibles published between 1860 and 1925 served this constituency, including editions from Muscatine, Iowa; Erie, Pennsylvania; Ravenna, Ohio; Joliet, Illinois; and Nashville, Tennessee; as well as from the major publishing centers. The same constituency was largely responsible for twenty-two Swedish-language bibles (including editions published in Rockford and Rock Island, Illinois, and Worcester, Massachusetts), ten Danish editions, seven Norwegian editions, and four Finnish editions.[36]

When English finally became unavoidable, Lutherans still did not produce their own translation, as did Catholics and Jews. Rather, their path of Americanization lay in siding with one of the alternative Protestant approaches. The result was the appearance of Lutheran variations on Protestant liberalism, as with Charles Michael Jacobs (1875–1938) of Mt. Airy Theological Seminary in Philadelphia, or on Protestant fundamentalism, as with Michael Reu (1869–1943) of Wartburg Theological Seminary in Dubuque, Iowa.[37] It can only be speculation, but one of the reasons for the amorphous influence of Lutherans in the United States may have something to do with a tradition suspended between Luther's German translation (or its Scandinavian equivalents) and the competing approaches to the Bible among the mainstream Protestant traditions. The absence of their own English translation of the Bible may help explain why American Lutherans, despite large numbers and exemplary individuals, have rarely succeeded in communicating a sense of Lutheran distinctives to the culture at large.

Alternative Translations

English-language translations from the nineteenth and early twentieth centuries provided a different kind of alternative to the KJV.[38] "Immersionist" translations of the New Testament, which rendered the Greek *baptizo* to support Baptist and Restorationist (Disciples of Christ, Church of Christ) practice appeared frequently, especially before the turn of the century. The American Baptist Union, which had earlier split off from the ABS over this issue, brought out at least eleven editions of their New Testament between 1861 and 1881. Alexander Campbell's New Testament was reprinted four times between 1860 and 1914, during which five other Disciples of Christ ministers were responsible for nineteen editions of their translations. Several other translators produced versions for their denominations, but none of the bibles or testaments produced by Unitarians, Universalists, Congregationalists, Anglicans, or Episcopalians enjoyed anything like the success of the immersionist texts—and those served only a restricted audience.

The Holiness tradition that arose out of nineteenth-century Methodism illustrates the dynamics that led to such targeted translations.[39] The leaders who left the main Methodist denominations regarded themselves as outcasts providentially commissioned to preach the Bible's doctrine of entire sanctification. As they did so they developed what Stephen Lennox has called "the holiness hermeneutic," which stressed subjective appropriation of entire sanctification as the central theme of the Bible. The struggle for a Holiness identity soon became a two-front battle, where Holiness preachers defended their interpretation against the traditional mainstream, which rejected their notion of sanctification, and the new Pentecostal movement, which carried Holiness emphases to unacceptable conclusions about Holy Spirit baptism. Given the stress on understanding the Bible correctly, it is not surprising that one of the leading Holiness evangelists, W. B. Godbey, after years of preaching entire sanctification from the Greek text of Scripture, in 1902 published his own translation of the New Testament "dedicated to the Holiness people in all lands."[40] Although Godbey's Testament did not differ substantially from the KJV, it showed how religious self-definition could lead to a distinctive translation. Like the others prepared for narrow constituencies, it never caught on.

Versions that can only be described as oddities fared just as poorly. They included the spiritualist Leonard Thorn's *New Testament . . . As Revised and Corrected by the Spirits* (1861) and a second edition of *De Nu Testament ov or Lord and Savyor Jezus Krist . . . In Fonetic Spelin* (1865). Frederick Grant, a learned member of the Plymouth Brethren, thought he had discovered "a law of numbers" in his study of the Scriptures; the result was *The Numerical Bible* (published in parts from 1891 to 1931). After diligent study of the Westcott and

Hort edition of the Greek New Testament, Ivan Panin, a Russian-born Harvard graduate, in 1914 published a translation that he also based on "Bible Numerics." Unlike Grant's work, Panin's translation was later reprinted several times by Oxford University Press and the Book Society of Canada.[41]

The translation of the entire Bible that Julia Smith published in 1876 remained the sole example by a female scholar until in the early 1920s the American Baptist Publication Society commissioned Helen Barrett Montgomery to carry out a translation of the New Testament based on the best Greek manuscripts. Montgomery, who had been licensed to preach in 1892, three decades later became the president of the Northern Baptist Convention, the first woman to serve in such a position for any American denomination. Her translation, published in 1924, presented the text as paragraphs in a single column, with verse markers in the margin. It would be reprinted frequently.[42]

A new era in the American history of translation began in 1899, when Frank Schell Ballentine, a renegade Episcopalian who later drifted toward Christian Science, published a New Testament "in modern American form and phrase." Translators like Ballentine who broke completely from the language of the KJV, while also basing their work on the best scholarly manuscripts, soon included well-positioned authorities from major universities. In 1904 Charles Foster Kent, the Woolsey Professor of Biblical Literature at Yale, began publishing *The Student's Old Testament Logically and Chronologically Arranged*. Its modern language text not only arranged the biblical books in the order they were written (as determined by recent critical study); it also presented the text in paragraph form. James Moffatt, Yates Professor of Greek at Oxford, gained more popularity for his translation, a New Testament in contemporary language that he published in 1917. (He had earlier prepared a fresh translation but rendered in Elizabethan English.) George H. Doran in New York partnered with Hodder and Stoughton in England as the publisher of Moffatt's translation, which was well received by the scholarly community and still remains in print. Edgar Goodspeed, professor of biblical and Patristic Greek at the University of Chicago, soon followed with a translation that received more American attention than any such venture since the ERV in 1881. This New Testament in "simple, straight-forward English of the everyday experience" was later joined by the Old Testament, translated by a team of scholars, to make *An American Translation*. It is available today from Goodspeed's original publisher, the University of Chicago Press.[43]

Before the wave of modern-language translations that began in the 1950s, Moffatt and Goodspeed dominated this particular corner of the biblical world. Scholars and some preachers who found the versions helpful for sermon preparation appreciated their up-to-date scholarship and were reassured by their publication from reputable presses. In larger perspective, however, they and all other

Table 27.2 KJV, Moffatt, and Goodspeed

John 1:14

KJV	Moffatt	Goodspeed
And the word was made flesh, and dwelt among us, (and we beheld his glory, the glory as of the only begotten of the Father,) full of grace and truth.	So the Logos became flesh and tarried among us; we have seen his glory—glory as an only son enjoys from his father—seen it to be full of grace and reality.	So the Word became flesh and blood and lived for a while among us, abounding in blessing and truth, and we saw the honor God had given him, such honor as an only son receives from his father.

alternatives to the KJV remained important primarily as a contribution to the history of Bible translation. For scriptural phrases circulating in public, evoked on ceremonial occasions, and secured in the memories of Americans of high estate and low, "the" Bible remained the KJV (see Table 27.2 for a comparison).

Alongside Other Scriptures

A telling indication of the Bible's centrality, usually as the KJV, was its respected status among Christian groups that also honored other sacred writings. During the latter part of the nineteenth century—in fact, to the present—these groups have often deferred to the KJV as each honored an additional source of special revelation for defining its own identity.

In southeastern Iowa, the Amana Society was unusual in its allegiance to the Bible in German. This church-as-community remained mostly undisturbed by its more conventionally religious neighbors for most of the period between its arrival from New York in 1855 to its dissolution during the Great Depression. The Community of True Inspiration, a pietist offshoot that had been established in Germany and then guided in America by *Werkzeuge* (leaders who received prophetic revelations from God) and that practiced a religious communism far outside the usual American conventions, nonetheless regularly stressed the conformity of its faith with the traditional Christian Scriptures. At the start of the twentieth century, one of the first full histories of the Amana Society noted that in the Society's literature, "the phraseology of the [German] Bible is frequently used or imitated" and that the record of divine communications through the *Werkzeuge* was always "in common with the written word of the prophets and apostles." In addition, the Society wanted outsiders to realize that it had never "acknowledged any basis of faith other than the literal word of

God as contained in the Scriptures and in *Bezeugungen* [the revelations from *Werkzeuge*]."[44]

Seventh-day Adventists and followers of Christian Science were much more visible than the Amana Society, but their use of Scripture resembled the way the Inspirationists also proceeded. Two weeks after the "Great Disappointment" of October 22, 1844, when Christ did not return as the calculations of William Miller had led many to believe, seventeen-year-old Ellen Gould Harmon (later Ellen White) received her first vision, which explained why Adventists should not abandon hope.[45] Like Joseph Smith and the Mormons, White and her later followers also believed in the possibility of ongoing revelation. For White, later messages from God—recorded as "I saw," "I was shown," or "I looked and saw"— became for her growing number of followers genuine prophetic utterances worthy of standing alongside the received Scripture. But the question remained *how* they stood alongside. White produced a steady stream of authoritative works, among them *The Great Controversy between Christ and His Angels and Satan and His Angels*, first released in 1870 and expanded and republished several times before a last edition in 1911. (She died in 1915.) Interpretations of the Christian Scriptures always remained prominent in such utterances. Some ambiguity in White's own words, as well as considerable debate among her followers and former followers, left the exact character of her authority a matter for debate—"a live, functioning, albeit noncanonical prophet," in Nicholas Miller's words.[46]

Against the background of controversies about the character of Scripture in the wider Protestant world, a few Adventists in White's lifetime and afterward debated whether her utterances were verbally inerrant or inspired as to their thoughts. In his comprehensive study of the question, Denis Kaiser has characterized White's own expressions as depicting a "dynamic and diverse" understanding of inspiration.[47] In the century since White's death, some Adventists have treated her interpretations of the Bible as uniquely authoritative, while others have assigned them a lesser degree. Significantly, throughout the decades of her own teaching, White insisted that the Christian Scriptures provided "definite, unmistakable instructions," that the Bible must be accepted as "an authentic, infallible revelation of [God's] will," that her followers dare not think that Scripture should be mistaken, and that unlike herself "God alone is infallible."[48] In other words, a consistent feature of Seventh-day Adventist history has been reliance on the Bible, usually understood in traditional Protestant terms, even as honor is paid to White's writings. For Adventists it remains important to parse carefully the relationship between those two sources of authority. In wider perspective the Adventists have testified to the central importance of the common Scripture, even as they developed their own understanding of White's prophetic gift.

Like the Amana communists, who used a German translation of the Bible from the early eighteenth century as their Scripture, Christian Scientists also eventually produced their own alternative to the KJV. This metaphysical movement, founded in 1875 by Mary Baker Eddy, drew on liberal strands of New England Calvinism, Swedenborgianism, Theosophy, and contemporary spiritualism to advance a faith translating the healing work of Christ into a modern form of mind-cure.[49] As indicated by the title of its foundational text, Eddy's *Science and Health with Key to the Scriptures*, the movement provided yet another American instance of a unique scriptural interpretation arising from conventional reliance on the Bible. A translation specifically for Christian Sciences was published in 1925 by Arthur E. Overbury, who set it forth as interpreting "the New Covenant . . . from a Spiritual or Meta-Physical Standpoint, and [that] Recognizes Healing as well as Teaching as a Component Part of True Christianity." Overbury wanted this version to be "unhampered by So-Called Ecclesiastical Authority," but also to be "based on the premise of 'Scientific Statement of Being' as given in 'Science and Health,' by Mary Baker Eddy."[50] Yet Overbury's translation does not seem to have been nearly as important as efforts among Christian Scientists to show the compatibility between Eddy's writings and the Bible. In the 1906 edition of *Science and Health with Key to the Scriptures*, Christian Scientists were committed, "as adherents of Truth," to the "inspired Word of the Bible as our sufficient guide to eternal Life." The argument prefacing the book's "glossary," moreover, was a historically American one—if only people understood the Bible correctly, they would have all the religion they needed: "In Christian Science we learn that the substitution of the spiritual for the material definition of a Scriptural word often elucidates the meaning of the inspired writer. . . . [This chapter] contains the metaphysical interpretation of Bible terms, giving their spiritual sense, which is also their original sense."[51] Revelations to Mary Baker Eddy had led to the formation of Christian Science as a new religious tradition. But the desire to honor those revelations led most of her followers to align her teaching with the KJV rather than to prepare a new translation as Arthur Overbury tried to do.

As we have seen, the Church of Jesus Christ of Latter-day Saints (LDS) has combined respect for the KJV similar to attitudes of conservative Protestants with its belief in an open biblical canon and steadfast reliance on revelations to Joseph Smith and later Mormon leaders. As explained clearly in Philip Barlow's *Mormons and the Bible*, both Smith and Brigham Young reverenced the traditional Protestant Bible, used the language of the KJV in their own sermons (and revelations), and set Mormons on a course of faithful biblical engagement that continues to this day. Yet almost from the start a spectrum of attitudes prevailed.

Young felt free to adjust, expand, or revise the Bible as occasion demanded, but his contemporary Orson Pratt, whose authority came close to Young's, treated Scripture as an absolute standard. Later Mormon generations witnessed a variety of approaches. By the early twentieth century, as LDS scholars participated in wider academic discussions, Joseph Fielding Smith adopted a strict biblical literalism that resembled in principle, though not necessarily in content, Protestant fundamentalism. B. H. Roberts practiced a mediating Mormonism by showing how the Bible and the Book of Mormon could be reconciled to some modern ideas, such as evolution (if not taken as a total life philosophy). William H. Chamberlin came closer to Protestant modernists as he approached Mormon sacred writings as modern higher critics treated the Bible.[52]

Mormon scripturalism has been complicated by the fact that Joseph Smith himself revised the KJV through selective abridgment and emendation, while also offering this qualification: "We believe the Bible to be the word of God as far as it is translated correctly."[53] Further complication resulted when one of his sons brought out an edition of the KJV in 1867 with his father's editing and editions incorporated, but after the son had broken with the Utah Mormons to establish the Reorganized Church of Jesus Christ of Latter Day Saints.[54] This sponsorship meant that the Bible published by the younger Smith has been regarded ambiguously by the main LDS body.[55] After generations of discussion, the church authorities in 1979 authorized an official LDS edition of the KJV, published by Cambridge University Press, that included an elaborate set of notes keyed to the Book of Mormon and other LDS sacred texts.[56] Then in 1992 the church's First Presidency declared, "While other Bible versions may be easier to read than the King James Version, in doctrinal matters latter-day revelation supports the King James Version in preference to other English translations." The statement continued by saying that all of the church's presidents, beginning "with the Prophet Joseph Smith," have relied on this translation. As a consequence, the KJV "is the English language bible used by the Church of Jesus Christ of Latter-day Saints."[57]

The main takeaways for an American history of the Bible is that Mormonism flourished as a distinct religion with its own written revelation, but also that while never replicating conservative Protestant attitudes toward Scripture, Mormon leaders moved ever closer to embracing the KJV. The Book of Mormon and subsequent revelations gave Latter-day Saints their distinct identity, but that identity continued to be shaped by widely shared Protestant biblical attitudes, especially reliance on the King James Version.

The Bible, it was obvious, remained nearly everywhere in the United States as the old century gave way to the new. Publishers, traditional Protestant adherents of the KJV, Jews and Catholics with their own bibles, Christian Scientists, Adventists, and Mormons kept the Bible alive for various publics even as it continued its course as a mainstay for individuals and in local religious communities. Yet if this ubiquity kept Scripture alive as a resource to be exploited for public purpose, it also made it increasingly difficult for any one approach to exert a coherent effect on that public life.

28

An Enduring Cultural Landmark

By the early twentieth century it had become impossible to explain the American attachment to Scripture in simple terms. Although not as visible as in earlier decades, the Bible continued to appear at all manner of public occasions. Yet indifference or opposition to Scripture was also on the rise, and public references to Scripture often led in contradictory directions. This was the period, in other words, when the religiously diverse, competitive, and media-fragmented culture of our twenty-first century first came into view.

The near-frenzied greeting for the English Revised Version was far from the only indication of the Bible's enduring cultural salience. In 1893, at the Chicago Columbian Exhibition, the Southern Methodist Publishing House gained considerable publicity for trying to demonstrate that a southern publisher could compete with the major houses of the North. It won the Medal for Specific Merit when it exhibited a complete copy of the Scriptures with pages fashioned from sheepskin and the printing executed in pure gold.[1] In 1917, as American forces prepared to embark for Europe, the American Bible Society staged another much-noticed event. To mark the release of the first 100,000 New Testaments prepared for the troops, it sponsored a rally in New York City with "martial music, patriotic anthems, abundant speeches," the display of many American flags, and the presentation of initial copies to representatives of the army, the navy, and the YMCA, which would staff an extensive network of relief stations near combat zones.[2] Before the troops returned, the ABS by itself would supply almost 5 million copies of various "Army and Navy Editions" of the Bible and the New Testament to service personnel.[3]

Casual, unremarked, or subliminal biblical usage testified even more clearly to the Bible's pervasive presence. The day-in, day-out industry of the ABS might be called Exhibit A. By the time in 1922 when the Society decided to outsource its printing, thus closing the plant set up in 1853, it had produced in the preceding seventy years 76,051,112 copies of Scripture in sixty-eight languages and six kinds of embossed printing for the blind.[4] During the height of the immigration tide, the ABS and its New York subsidiary distributed hundreds of thousands of scriptures, eventually in fifty-three languages, first at Castle Garden and then Ellis Island. After the Immigration Act of 1917 required a literacy test for incoming residents, cards were made up for that purpose; most of the cards testing English literacy carried Bible verses from the KJV.[5] Although Americans

America's Book. Mark A. Noll, Oxford University Press. © Oxford University Press 2022.
DOI: 10.1093/oso/9780197623466.003.0029

drew on Scripture less frequently for place names, parents, however unselfconsciously, sustained a biblical frame of reference. From 1880 to 1920, John was the name most often chosen for sons, Mary the most popular for daughters. Joseph also remained very popular, as did Anna, Ruth, and Elizabeth.[6] Except on festive public occasions, biblical rhetoric may have been falling off, though many instances sustained the older pattern. After the Chicago Fire of 1871, Chicago booster William Bross came east to woo young people to the rebuilding city. His message: "You will never again have such a chance to make money. . . . [N]ever was there such a field for employment since God said 'let there be light [Gen 1:3]!'" The Washington, D.C., editor of a Black newspaper recycled a familiar trope when he learned that Booker T. Washington had been asked to speak at the Atlanta Exhibition of 1895: "Every colored woman, man, and child who can possibly get there ought to go, if for no other reason than to hold up the hands of Prof. Washington, as the children of Israel held up the arms of Moses while he fought the battles of the Lord."[7]

In complete obscurity a chance meeting on September 14, 1898, began a Bible distribution scheme that continues throughout the world to this day. On that night two traveling salesmen, John Nicholson and Samuel E. Hill, were staying at the Central Hotel in Boscobel, Wisconsin, which was hosting a convention of raucous lumberjacks. The salesmen, discovering a common love of the Scriptures, soon did the American thing by forming a voluntary society, the Christian Commercial Travelers Association. After changing its name to the Gideons in honor of the Hebrew judge who led a tiny force into battle armed only with torches and water jugs, and after the commitment of support from a convention meeting in Cedar Rapids, Iowa, the Gideons made their first order for twenty-five copies of the Bible, which they placed in the Superior Hotel in Iron Mountain, Montana. Since then, this entirely lay-run association has put the Bible, translated into at least a hundred languages, into hotels, motels, schools, military installations, prisons, rescue missions, hospitals (in large print), airplanes, ships, and trains. In 2017 the Gideons' membership of 171,000 (with 96,000 more in women's auxiliaries) distributed over 87 million Bibles and Bible portions (26 million in Latin America), with total placements to that time numbering more than 2.5 billion.[8] Exemplary of national characteristics as the Gideons were, they represented only one of the many ways that the Bible remained a presence in the nation's history.

Unbelief

Where bibles abounded, however, so also did scorn for the Bible. To be sure, open derision did not usually characterize leaders of the new universities that were moving American higher education in a more secular direction. The wider public did notice when the agnostic Thomas Huxley was invited to open Johns Hopkins University in 1876, when Harvard ended compulsory chapel a decade later, and when Andrew Dickson White vowed that the institution he was building with Ezra Cornell's money would "afford an asylum for Science—where truth shall be sought for truth's sake, where it shall not be the main purpose of the Faculty to stretch or cut sciences exactly to fit 'Revealed Religion.'"[9] But a great deal of traditional religion remained on college and university campuses even after assumptions about truth as realistic, static, and absolute (with reverence for Scripture taken for granted) gave way to idealistic, developmental, and historicist conventions (usually bypassing the Bible).[10]

Derision, though, was the stock in trade of Robert G. Ingersoll, "the evangelist of unbelief," and the growing number of other public voices who joined him in broadcasting their disdain for the Bible. The ever-quotable Ingersoll had grown up the son of a Presbyterian and Congregational minister who served as Charles Finney's assistant during the evangelist's tenure as a pastor in New York City. For the son, however, the father's heritage was only an incubus: his father "had one misfortune and that was his religion. He believed the Bible, and in the shadow of that frightful book he passed his life. . . . My father was infinitely better than the God he worshiped, infinitely better than the religion he preached."[11] During the 1880s Ingersoll engaged in several literary duels with conventional believers that received considerable publicity, though not the level of interest generated by the multiday antebellum debates over slavery or Catholic-Protestant differences. One of his opponents was the popular pastor of the Brooklyn Tabernacle, Thomas DeWitt Talmage, also the editorial force behind the *Christian Herald* and its extensive efforts at providing disaster relief around the world.[12] Another was the British prime minister William Gladstone, who ventured into print against Ingersoll in the *North American Review*. In his response to Gladstone, Ingersoll conceded that "the good, the self-denying, the virtuous and the loving" had honored the Bible. But they had done so "in spite of all its cruelties and crimes." Against Gladstone, Ingersoll especially stressed how Scripture had supported the defense of slavery. Bible believers clung to the book despite the fact that "it has been upheld by countless tyrants—by the dealers in human flesh—by the destroyers of nations—by the enemies of intelligence—by the stealers of babes and the whippers of women."[13]

Advertisements in the endpapers of the volume printing the Gladstone-Ingersoll exchange showed how wide the audience for skeptical literature had become. The publisher C. P. Farrell, who happened to be Ingersoll's brother-in-law, offered the public ready access to twenty-eight works by Ingersoll, many other titles like *Self-Contradictions of the Bible*, *Thomas Paine's Complete Works*, George Eliot's translation of David Friedrich Strauss's radical *Life of Jesus*

Critically Examined, the celebratory life of Paine by Moncure Daniel Conway, and eight publications by Helen Gardener, the most outspoken anti-Scripture author recruited by Elizabeth Cady Stanton for her *Woman's Bible*.

When Ingersoll died in July 1899, obituaries in the *Chicago Tribune*, the *New York Times*, and other national papers mingled respect for his ability to captivate audiences with cautious rebuke for what he had communicated.[14] That combination showed once again that by the time Ingersoll passed away, the American history of the Bible included much more room for unbelief than had been the case a century before.

Bestsellers

Unbelief, however, produced only a fraction of the era's most popular books drawing on scriptural material, though Ingersoll did play a role in creating the best-selling novel of his generation. According to Lew Wallace, Ingersoll once defended his skepticism about all things Christian in a long conversation with the General that took place in 1876. The conversation spurred Wallace to study the matter in time-honored American fashion. He resolved to "read the Bible and the four Gospels, and rely on myself."[15] Wallace's autodidacticism led him to a firm belief in traditional Christianity. It also prompted him to expand a short story he had recently written into the book that became *Ben-Hur: A Tale of the Christ*, published by Harper & Brothers in November 1880. Judah Ben-Hur, the well-born Jewish protagonist of this romantic tale, falls out with his childhood friend Messala, who grows up to be a powerful Roman soldier and Ben-Hur's sworn enemy. In a tale filled with battles, intrigue, betrayals, reunion with long-lost family, and a thrilling chariot race, Ben-Hur eventually becomes a follower of Jesus and a witness to the events of the Passion. As a character, Jesus appears only briefly, his dialogue taken from the KJV. The popularity of this work demonstrated the enduring American fascination with biblical narratives, even as its approach to scriptural material indicated a decisive shift from the formal apologetics that had been directed against Tom Paine and the style of evoking Scripture practiced by Harriet Beecher Stowe.

The initial response to *Ben-Hur* was mixed. The *Baptist Review* was typical in seasoning its praise ("In the words ascribed to Christ there is scarcely any departure from the sacred text") with concern ("the description of the awful scene of Christ's last days is so minute as to be exceedingly painful, without being any more effective than the simple narration of the Gospels").[16] A few reviews, as from the Episcopalians' *American Church Review*, found nothing to praise: "[Wallace] has ventured to weave the simple and sacred narrative of the Gospel into a poor tissue of religious fancies and sentimentality.... The best we can bring ourselves to wish for the General's venture is that a copy may never be sold."[17] The offended Episcopalians notwithstanding, Harper & Brothers enjoyed steady sales, which took off spectacularly when it was learned that President James A. Garfield stayed up late reading the novel and wrote a letter of thanks to the General (and also named him to a diplomatic post in Turkey).[18] After this commendation and swelling popular interest, Harper & Brothers rushed multiple formats into print, including an illustrated "Garfield Edition" that included a facsimile of the president's letter and over one thousand "drawings . . . representing the characters of the book, the natural scenery, architecture, manners and customs, art and antiquities in general of Palestine, Egypt, Rome, and the Orient, as the story shifts from one point to another."[19]

Even before *Ben-Hur* was transformed into a wildly successful touring play (Figure 28.1), and then into films for succeeding generations (1907, 1925, 1958, 1989 [animated], 2010), the book illustrated the singularly American capacity for profiting from religiously inspired cultural artifacts. By the end of the century an entrepreneur in Detroit was marketing Ben-Hur cigars; other retailers tested demand with Ben-Hur flour (Fort Collins, Colorado), Ben-Hur bicycles (Indianapolis and Philadelphia), a Ben-Hur bicycle wrench (Chicago), Ben-Hur tomatoes (Janesville, Wisconsin), and paddlewheelers named *Ben-Hur* (Wheeling, West Virginia, and Austin, Texas).[20] Also American was Wallace's own religious stance. As Hilton Obenzinger has noted, he remained firmly Christian but with no denominational affiliation, without attending a particular church, and having "learned to believe in the Bible's truth through the force of imagination as he wrote *Ben-Hur*."[21]

Wallace's bestseller followed in the path of "Bible fiction" that had begun with William Ware's *Julian: Or Scenes in Judea* from 1841.[22] When Henryk Sienkiewicz's *Quo Vadis: A Narrative of the Time of Nero* appeared in English shortly after its initial Polish publication in 1896, it too attracted many readers with a narrative interweaving fictional Romans with the Apostles Peter and Paul. To indicate the esteem that such books could enjoy, Sienkiewicz in 1905 received the Nobel Prize in Literature, largely on the strength of *Quo Vadis*.

Authors who mined the New Testament, with a special focus on Jesus, produced several other noteworthy publications. With one exception, however, they did not come close to the popularity of *Ben-Hur*. Henry Ward Beecher's 1871 *The Life of Jesus, the Christ* imitated a thriving genre of European and British books by filling out the gospel narratives with a combination of Palestinian detail and imaginative reconstruction. Beecher's fame secured simultaneous publication of his book in Edinburgh, London, and Toronto, as well as New York, but it enjoyed only modest sales.[23]

More common and also more controversial were books that pictured Christ as responding to the era's economic inequalities, vicious business cycles, and

Figure 28.1 Before Lew Wallace's *Ben-Hur* moved from the page to the silver screen, it was brought to the stage, where it was received with great public enthusiasm.
Source: LOC, Prints & Photographs, LC-POS-TH-1901.B45, no. 1.

urban squalor.[24] Elizabeth Stuart Phelps's novel *A Singular Life* and Archibald McCowan's admonitory *Christ the Socialist* both appeared in 1894; their themes resonated with the social Christianity promoted by some labor activists and that was taking shape in a formal Social Gospel. Neither, however, won the readership of another book published in the same year with the same general purpose. W. T. Stead's *If Christ Came to Chicago* drew on the author's firsthand experience as a visitor to Chicago's 1893 Columbian Exposition. While at the fair, Stead, already a noted journalist in Britain, wandered away to explore Chicago's railyards, slums, saloons, brothels, stockyards, city government, and other dens of iniquity. The result was a message conveyed by the book's subtitle, *A Plea for the Union of All who Love in the Service of All who Suffer*, and by a frontispiece that quoted Matthew 21:13 ("ye have made it a den of thieves") underneath a lithograph depicting Jesus driving out moneychangers from the Jerusalem Temple.[25]

Stead's exposé, along with knockoffs like Edward Everett Hale's *If Christ Came to Boston* (1895), generated considerable interest, but nothing like the runaway popularity of Charles Sheldon's *In His Steps*, which appeared in 1897. This tale took shape, as had Washington Gladden's *Working People and Their Employers*, in weekly sermons that Sheldon delivered from his pulpit at the Central Congregational Church in Topeka, Kansas. As parishioners at the fictional Rev. Henry Maxwell's church took to heart his challenge to ask "What would Jesus do?" when confronted by the practical demands of daily living, the city of Raymond is transformed. Social barriers yield to altruistic service and economic disparities fade in response to practices inspired by the Christian socialism that Sheldon advocated. Because of a defective copyright, multiple publishers brought out multiple cheap editions totaling millions of copies, with "What would Jesus do?" echoing to the present.[26]

The subjects treated in Bible-themed books reached much further than novels set in the first century and the enlistment of Jesus for the Social Gospel. Publishers continued to reprint bestsellers from the past, though not the stiffer Puritan classics like Richard Baxter's *Call to the Unconverted* or Joseph Alleine's *Alarm to the Unconverted*. John Bunyan's *Pilgrim's Progress* headed the list of perennial favorites, with at least twenty-three new American editions in the decade 1881–90, including one Swedish translation, a newspaper reprinting in East Las Vegas, New Mexico, and a New York publisher's edition "in words of one syllable."[27]

From a very different corner of the landscape, Harold Frederic's *The Damnation of Theron Ware* presented a memorable fictional protagonist unlike anything imagined by Lew Wallace or Charles Sheldon.[28] Theron Ware is a young Methodist minister who plans to write a book on an Old Testament subject in order to display his intellectual prowess and advance his social aspirations. Frederic's depiction of the small-town pieties that his protagonist wants to escape anticipates the treatment later found in the novels of Sinclair Lewis. But Frederic's sensitive rendering of Ware's introduction to biblical higher criticism, his disillusionment with the pastoral calling, and his final descent into self-destructive delusion proceeds with an empathy foreign to the characters in Lewis's *Mainstreet* (1920), *Babbitt* (1922), or *Elmer Gantry* (1927). An indication of a reading public attuned to the dilemmas Frederic portrayed was the success of his book, one of the nation's best-selling novels in 1896.[29]

A Move to the New Testament

John Bunyan's comprehensively biblical allegory and Harold Frederic's narrative with a major role for Old Testament higher criticism represented exceptions to the most popular biblical referencing of the period. Much more common were books like Sheldon's *In His Steps* and Stead's *If Christ Came to Chicago* that drew from Jesus's denunciations in the synoptic gospels (Matthew, Mark, Luke) of economic exploitation and the struggle between serving God and serving money. These and similar popular books did not offer detailed biblical exposition or develop broad themes linking the Old Testament with the Gospels, as Walter Rauschenbusch would later attempt. The popularity of their works did, however, speak for a broad movement in American culture, which intensified as the century wore on. Specifically, attention to the Old Testament inherited from colonial, Puritan, and early American emphases was shifting to the New Testament. Perceptive studies of this "Jesus movement" by Stephen Prothero, Richard Wightman Fox, and Stephen J. Nichols have shown that, except for the nation's rising Jewish population and in civil religion on public occasions, fewer Americans turned to the Hebrew Scriptures/Old Testament for rhetoric, narratives, and exemplars to explicate the present.[30]

Lincoln Mullen has provided impressive support for that conclusion from innovative digital exploration of biblical quotations in American newspapers.[31] Using the techniques of machine learning, Mullen examined the nearly 11 million newspaper pages digitized in the Library of Congress's online collection *Chronicling America*. For the period from the 1840s to the 1920s, Mullen found over 866,000 biblical quotations or specific allusions (keyed to the KJV). A few instances illustrated the perennial American ability to mine the sacred volume for a quirky word addressing current events. In 1876, a supporter of the Democratic presidential candidate Governor Samuel Tilden of New York found such a passage in 1 Samuel 3:4 ("the Lord called Samuel"). A few years later the *Pascagoula (Mississippi) Democrat-Star* reported on a sign posted by a minister in an East Tennessee region infamous for its local stills; it riffed on Matthew 7:1, "Jug not that ye be not jugged."

A much broader picture is revealed, however, by the New Testament texts that provided by far the most citations. Throughout the ninety years Mullen examined, newspapers quoted most frequently a verse popularized by the American Sunday School Union, Luke 18:16 ("Jesus called them unto him, and said, Suffer little children to come unto me, and forbid them not: for of such is the kingdom of God"). Almost as popular was Matthew 25:21 ("His lord said unto Him, Well done, thou good and faithful servant . . . enter thou into the joy of thy lord"), a verse much favored in obituaries of that time, and since. Mullen's listing of the ten most popular citations decade by decade underscores the dominant presence of material from the synoptic gospels in these popular outlets.[32] Luke 18:16 and Matthew 25:21 ranked among the two or three most often-quoted in every decade. A few of these most popular texts did reflect preoccupations of the day, as during the 1840s, 1850s, and 1860s when Golden Rule verses (Matt 7:12; Lk 6:31) were quoted frequently along with the assertion much favored by abolitionists from Acts 17:26, that God "made of one blood all nations of men." Late in the century, heightened awareness of economic strife led to one of the few verses from the Old Testament appearing among the most often-quoted texts (Ex 25:16, "Thou shalt not steal") as well as what could be called Social Gospel verses, including Acts 20:35 ("ye ought to support the weak, and so remember the words of the Lord Jesus, how he said, It is more blessed to give than to receive"). Also toward the end of the century, as D. L. Moody and other evangelists expanded their efforts into the nation's rapidly growing cities, evangelistic texts appeared for the first time among the most popular, including John 3:16 ("For God so loved the world, that he gave his only begotten Son, that whosoever believeth in him should not perish, but have everlasting life").[33]

Yet, as might be expected given Mullen's sources, ethical injunctions, often from the Sermon on the Mount (Matt 5–7), predominated. Of the ninety verses making up the ten most popular from each decade, more than half (fifty-two) came from the gospels of Matthew and Luke (Table 28.1).

After the verse from Luke 18, Jesus welcoming the children, and the commendation from Matthew 25 for the faithful deceased, the other texts appearing most frequently were, in order of popularity: Matthew 7:20 ("by their fruits ye shall know them"), Matthew 6:11 ("Give us this day our daily bread"), and Exodus 20:15 (quoted earlier).[34]

Scriptural references seasoning the nation's expanding supply of newspapers testified to the Bible's ongoing familiarity but indicated little about what that familiarity meant. Whether meaningless ornaments of conventional rhetoric, meaningful reminders of life's seriousness, or more likely a mixture, depended on readers more than on the intentions of writers and their editors.

The popular new hymns of the nineteenth century's second half also illustrate a heightened focus on Jesus. As with the meaning of biblical quotations

Table 28.1 Source of the Most Popular Texts in American Newspapers, 1840–1930

Matthew	34	Pauline Epistles	11
Luke	18	Revelation	1
John	5	Old Testament	16
Acts	5		

in newspapers, hymnody poses difficult questions of interpretation. Yet as with newspaper reading, hymn singing and hymn reading were activities that engaged a much wider portion of the citizenry than any of the period's activities with more accessible records. Stephen Marini's list of the hymns that in these years entered the canon of most-reprinted texts includes a few referring traditionally to God (Jeremiah Rankin, "God be with you till we meet again"), generating religious enthusiasm (Sabine Baring-Gould, "Onward, Christian soldiers"), or promoting patriotism (Katharine Lee Bates, "O beautiful for spacious skies").[35] Most that became widely popular, however, featured Jesus as a comforting presence, perhaps with the Civil War's carnage fresh in popular consciousness: "He leadeth me, O blessed thought" (Joseph Gilmore); "Asleep in Jesus blessed sleep" (W. P. Mackay); "I love to tell the story / of Jesus and his love" (Katherine Hankey); "What a friend we have in Jesus" (Joseph Scriven); "Take my life and let it be" (Frances Ridley Havergal).

The prominence of women among the authors of these Jesus-centered hymns underscores the recognition gained by an ever-expanding circle of biblical expositors, as earlier with Hannah Adams, Phoebe Palmer, and the Grimké sisters. Especially significant among that number was the blind author Fanny Crosby, some of whose hymns became especially well known when Ira Sankey included them in songbooks prepared for D. L. Moody's preaching campaigns. That number included "Pass me not, O gentle Savior"; "Blessed assurance, Jesus is mine"; and "Rescue the perishing, care for the dying / . . . Jesus is merciful, Jesus will save."[36]

The rescue motif that Crosby often deployed appeared as well in other popular new hymns of the era, often featuring nautical motifs, including Edward Hopper's "Jesus, Savior, pilot me"; Priscilla Owens's "Will your anchor hold in the storms of life"; Edward Ufford's "Throw out the lifeline"; and a hymn by Philip Bliss, who often cooperated with the Moody-Sankey team, "Let the lower lights be burning." In an age of rapid dislocations, "for many nineteenth-century white Protestants," as Richard Mouw has noted, "rescue . . . was a dominant motif . . . as they attempted to spell out their conception of the Christian mission in the world."[37] The centrality of Jesus in many of these rescue songs reinforces the awareness that the Bible remained a capacious resource. Especially in the American setting, its pages were open to all, its message eminently adaptable to new circumstances.

Art and Photography

From the beginning of European settlement, biblical themes have been a staple of American popular art, including many early expressions in German broadsheets.

While most examples remained of only local interest, the paintings of Elias Hicks, a Quaker recorded minister, were a prominent exception. Especially after his death in 1849, Hicks's many renditions of *The Peaceable Kingdom* became prized for their artless exploitation of images from Isaiah 11:6–8 ("The wolf also shall dwell with the lamb, and the leopard shall lie down with the kid"), sometimes conflated with historical references (especially William Penn in peaceful conversation with Native Americans). Other folk painters continued to employ this theme along with many depictions of other stories, like Adam and Eve in the Garden of Eden, Noah's Ark, and occasional scenes from the life of Christ.[38] Artists with higher aspirations also exploited dramatic biblical scenes, including Washington Allston. His *Belshazzar's Feast*, with the Prophet Daniel appearing as a Moses-clone pointing dramatically to the miraculously appearing words that condemned the Babylonian kingdom, drew some interest during the artist's lifetime. (Allston died in 1843.) It received even more attention when William Ware, author of the pioneering biblical novel *Julian: Or, Scenes in Judea*, devoted his last years to promoting Allston and this particular painting.[39] When a Scottish painter, David Roberts, produced a series of lithographs from impressions drawn from a trip to the Middle East, they were well-received by the well-to-do in Britain and American who were able to afford the individual prints or the three-volume published work titled *The Holy Land*.[40]

At the end of the century a French artist, Jacques Joseph Tissot, executed a lengthy series of Bible-based gouache paintings (opaque watercolor) that, as with popular books of his era, dealt imaginatively with Jesus's life. After being exhibited in Paris and London, Tissot's 365 paintings arrived in New York City to great acclaim. Especially after publishers in London, Toronto, and New York brought out large, attractive books with reproductions of these works, the response in hundreds of articles from scores of newspapers was rapturous, as from the *New York Tribune* in April 1898: "M. Tissot is a master of picturesque effect . . . gained not only through the choice of subject, but through management of line and light and shade."[41]

Erastus Salisbury Field of Sunderland, Massachusetts, a master of the architectonic grandiose, was something of a throwback with his reliance on narratives from the Old Testament. Field is best known for *The Historical Monument of the American Republic*, a vast canvas of 150 square feet that was originally prepared for the 1876 Centennial. It depicts American history from Jamestown to the Centennial in a series of panels featuring massive Babel-like towers with intricate inscribed figures and a great deal of text. The extensive prose at the base of the painting begins, "The BIBLE is a brief recital of all that is past, and a certain prediction of all that is to come." In reflecting Field's own conservative Congregational faith, the painting is both a celebration of American achievement and a jeremiad denouncing the nation's often violent course. Field also executed a series depicting with similar romantic grandeur key moments in Israel's deliverance from Egypt. These paintings, including *Death of the First Born* and *Israelites Crossing the Red Sea*, are now located in the National Gallery of Art in Washington, the Metropolitan Museum in New York, and other major museums, though they are rarely exhibited.[42]

The notable painter Henry Ossawa Tanner was the son of Benjamin T. Tanner, an African Methodist Episcopal bishop who argued that biblical religion anticipated Black Christian expressions more than white.[43] Bishop Tanner's 1895 book, *The Color of Solomon—What?*, backed up that argument with detailed ethnological research. The bishop's son began his artistic life with a camera, including photographing the 1888 AME General Conference. After study with Thomas Eakins in Philadelphia, Tanner's paintings depicted everyday scenes of Black American life with Eakins's sensitive realism. (*The Banjo Lesson*, 1893, would become his most celebrated image.) In order to escape the discrimination he encountered even in the North, Tanner moved to Paris, where, after a spiritual struggle deepened his Christian commitment, he painted mostly biblical scenes. *Daniel in the Lion's Den* and *The Resurrection of Lazarus* (both 1896) won him a secure place in the French artistic world. His riveting depiction of *The Annunciation* (1898), in which the Angel Gabriel is represented by a shaft of light and the Virgin Mary is dressed in ordinary Middle Eastern garb and without a halo, became the first painting by a Black American purchased by a major American gallery, the Philadelphia Museum of Art.[44]

A popular photographic image from the early 1870s illustrated how easily biblical motifs could reinforce a national story. The pioneering photographer William H. Jackson accompanied Ferdinand Hayden when this surveyor explored regions in the Rocky Mountains where a mystic cross had been rumored to be visible at the right time of year. The photo Jackson secured of "The Mount of the Holy Cross" memorialized the moment when perpendicular crevices on a mountain face preserved the winter snowfall after the surrounding snow had melted. For "Americans of a mystical bent," H. W. Brands has written, the image let them "see the hand of God in the work of the explorers."[45] One generation on, some of the paintings of George Bellows took a more skeptical stance by satirizing the frenetic preaching of evangelist Billy Sunday in images like *The Sawdust Trail* (1915).[46] As with many artists before his time, though, Bellows could still count on a viewing public thoroughly steeped in the Bible stories that Sunday expounded after his distinctive fashion.

Poetry

Like novelists and artists, poets throughout American history have often drawn on scriptural resources. Even limited to canonical voices and excluding the reams of verse corresponding to folk art, the quantity of such work is impressive. So it was near the beginning of European colonization when Anne Bradstreet meditated at length on the Book of Ecclesiastes in her poem "The Vanity of All Worldly Things." So it continued into the twentieth century, as when Edgar Lee Masters retold the story of Jesus turning water into wine from John chapter 2 in a twenty-stanza poem of rhymed quatrains, "The Wedding Feast."[47]

Poems that expanded imaginatively upon the original biblical narratives have always been popular. When Joel Barlow was asked in 1785 to prepare the works of Isaac Watts for American publication, he filled out the Psalms that Watt had not paraphrased with his own compositions, including a work based on Psalm 137 ("Along the banks where Babel's current flows") that re-created the sentiments of "captive bands in deep despondence."[48] James Greenleaf Whittier and Henry Wadsworth Longfellow, whom contemporaries at home and abroad regarded as America's finest poets of the mid-nineteenth century, regularly composed such works, for example, an entire collection of lyrics based on the life of Christ, *The Divine Tragedy*, published by Longfellow in 1871. Although Longfellow was a Unitarian and Whittier a Quaker who leaned in a Unitarian direction, their poems did not shy away from the Bible's miracle stories, as in Whittier's "Blind Bartimaeaus" ("Go in peace, / Thy faith from blindness gives re-lease") or Longfellow's "The Three Kings" ("The star was so beautiful, large, and clear . . . by this they knew that the coming was near / Of the Prince foretold in prophecy").[49] Whittier's "Ezekiel" even imitated at great length what Isaac Watts often achieved in miniature by turning reflections on an Old Testament theme into a Christian statement:

> With bonds, and scorn, and evil will,
> The world requites its prophets still.
> So was it when the Holy One
> The garments of the flesh put on![50]

Poems with a biblical a reference became popular hymns (or Christmas carols), but along different paths. The pathway for Phillips Brooks, the minister of Philadelphia's Episcopal Church of the Holy Trinity, and his "O Little Town of Bethlehem" was conventional. Three years after visiting Bethlehem in the Holy Land on Christmas Day in 1865, Brooks wrote a poem that he asked his choir director to set to music. Very soon after his own congregation sang "The hopes and fears of all the years are met in thee tonight," publishers included it in hymnals, where it has been a fixture to this day.[51] By contrast, Longfellow penned "I heard the bells on Christmas day" as a cri de coeur in 1863 as the Civil War raged, as his son lay desperately ill from a battlefield wound, and as the bells of Cambridge, Massachusetts, pealed out on December 25. Although keyed to Luke 2:14 ("peace on earth, good-will to men") and although ending with the affirmation "God is not dead, nor doth He sleep; / The Wrong shall fail, / The Right prevail," the poem also commented despairingly on current events:

> Then from each black, accursed mouth
> The cannon thundered in the South . . .
> It was as if an earthquake rent
> The hearth-stone of a continent,
>   And made forlorn
>   The households born
> Of peace on earth, good-will to men.

It took several years for this poem to find a musical setting and have its battle image stripped away. It did not become a Christmas standard in hymnals and the wider public until Bing Crosby made a popular recording of a sanitized version in 1956.[52]

Poets proved as adept as preachers, political pundits, and ordinary Americans in bending biblical material into commentary on current events. In perhaps his most powerful poem, Whittier's "Ichabod!" evoked the tragic story from the fourth chapter of 1 Samuel, where the daughter-in-law of the prophet Eli died giving birth to a son after her husband perished in battle against the Philistines, who also took captive the Ark of the Covenant. To express his profound disappointment that Senator Daniel Webster approved the harsh Fugitive Slave Law of 1850, Whittier bestowed upon the senator the name of that newborn, meaning "the glory has departed from Israel": "So fallen! so lost! the light withdrawn / Which once he wore! / The glory from his gray hairs gone / Forevermore."[53] In the early twentieth century Vachel Lindsay also mastered that way of using the Bible. When Theodore Roosevelt left the White House in 1913, the poet memorialized the president with a short poem reprinted when Roosevelt died five years later. "In Which Roosevelt Is Compared to Saul" honored TR as "Judge and monarch, merged in one," but did so with ambiguity by writing more about the incoming King David than the out-going King Saul. With its mimicry of language from the eighth chapter of the Book of Revelation, Lindsay's exuberant "General William Booth Enters into Heaven" offered a less ambiguous encomium for the founder of the Salvation Army:

(Bass drum beaten loudly)
Booth led boldly with his big bass drum—
(Are you washed in the blood of the Lamb?)
The Saints smiled gravely and they said: "He's come."
(Are you washed in the blood of the Lamb?)
Walking lepers followed, rank on rank,
Lurching bravos from the ditches dank,
Drabs from the alleyways and drug fiends pale—
Minds still passion-ridden, soul-powers frail:—
Vermin-eaten saints with moldy breath,
Unwashed legions with the ways of Death—
(Are you washed in the blood of the Lamb?)[54]

Scripture also offered poets much raw material for general social commentary. John Greenleaf Whittier's "King Solomon and the Ant" exemplified the genre with its tale of the Hebrew king being unwilling to tread on an ant hill as he made a general point about good governance to the visiting queen of Sheba: "Happy must be the state / Whose rulers heedeth more / The murmurs of the poor / Than the flatteries of the great."[55] Included in such verse were poems criticizing what the poet considered short-sighted reverence for Scripture. Edgar Lee Masters, whose fame was secured as the author of *Spoon River Anthology* (1915), included many such poems in *Starved Rock* (1919) and *The Open Sea* (1921). One of them, "Oh ye Sabbatarians," matched H. L. Mencken in its acerbic denunciation of "methodists and puritans; / You bigots, devotees, and ranters . . . Eyes blind to color, ears deaf to sound," who were shown up, in another reference to John chapter 2, by "the free spirits . . . / Drinkers of the wine made by Jesus."[56]

Very different from the pieties of Whittier or the peevishness of Masters were the poems of Emily Dickinson, which remain in a class by themselves for subtle, creative, and emotionally compelling engagement with the Bible. In the considered judgment of literary scholar-theologian Roger Lundin, the biblical references, allusions, and quotations that Dickinson drew from at least thirty-eight separate biblical books constituted, "without question, her richest poetic lexicon."[57] In a writing life that extended from before the Civil War to the first administration of President Grover Cleveland, Dickinson frequently reimagined biblical narratives, for example, Jacob wrestling with the angel from Genesis 32 or Jesus's attention to the repentant thief on the cross.[58] More often her gimlet eye fastened on features of biblical stories that prompted objections. The objections could be whimsical when she thought it "a wrong" for Moses not to be allowed to enter the Promised Land. They could bite, as when she queried God's command that Abraham sacrifice his son, Isaac. Sometimes they seemed more academic, such as when she queried the Apostle Paul's assertion in 1 Corinthians 15 that the dead are "sown in dishonor."[59] At other times Dickinson considered the Bible a helpful teacher, as when she used the story of the little David and the giant Goliath to write with deprecation about her own ambition.[60] Scripture also prompted reflections on general truths of human nature: from Genesis 2 on the escalating awareness of loss, from John 1:14 ("and the word was made flesh") on the potential of language, or from Acts 16 (the miraculous rescue of Paul and Silas from prison) on the impossibility of keeping humans from thinking freely.[61]

The many Dickinson poems in which Jesus features prominently combined all of these elements. He was for her the "Tender Pioneer" and "docile Gentleman" who could perplex and alienate but also inspire and guide.[62] Robert Atwan and Laurance Wieder fittingly chose her meditation on the Bible as "an antique Volume" to open their two-volume collection of poems based on biblical passages. Its brief evocations of gospel stories ("Bethlehem . . . Judas—the Great Defaulter") appear in a lengthy compilation of similar cryptic references. The poem ends by comparing these narratives to "Orpheus' Sermon" that did not "condemn" but only "captivated." It is a signal example of what Roger Lundin has called Dickinson's use of parody, but parody in the medieval sense that calls forth laughter, but rueful laughter with respect.[63] If Jonathan Edwards was the most penetrating public expounder of Scripture in colonial America and Reinhold Niebuhr the twentieth-century theologian who most effectively assessed public life with insights from the Bible, the mostly private Emily Dickinson peered more deeply than any other recognized voice from her century into the transcendent yet very human character of the Bible.

The Law

The Bible did not exactly vanish from legal reasoning during this period, but the effacement that had been evident since midcentury did continue. When in 1905 Supreme Court Justice David J. Brewer lectured at Haverford College on "the United States a Christian nation," he quoted his own opinion from the 1892 *Church of the Holy Trinity* decision that had affirmed "this is a Christian nation." He went on to say specifically of the Bible, "No other book has so wide a circulation, or is so universally found in the households of the land. . . . [O]ur laws and customs are based upon the laws of Moses and the teachings of Christ."[64]

Although some jurists may in fact have agreed with Brewer, in the adjudication of important cases reference to Scripture almost disappeared.[65] One who may have agreed was Justice John Harlan of Kentucky. During his time on the

Court, Harlan organized a men's Bible class at Washington's New York Avenue Presbyterian Church that he taught personally from 1896 until his death in 1911. His famous dissents on the *Civil Rights Cases* in 1883 and *Plessy v. Ferguson* in 1893 opposed the Court's decisions that sanctioned state-permitted segregation. Yet these dissents remained strictly legal, as his bold words in *Plessy v. Ferguson*: "There is no caste here. Our constitution is color-blind."[66]

Oliver Wendell Holmes Jr., who joined the Supreme Court as an associate justice in 1902 and who did not agree with Justice Brewer, articulated an increasingly influential approach to the law that stressed contingencies of modern life more than fixed, eternal principles. His renowned book on the common law from 1881 rejected the importance of "syllogism," deductive "logic," or "axioms and corollaries." Instead, jurists should be guided by "the felt necessities of the time, the prevalent moral and political theories, intuitions of public policy . . . even the prejudices which judges share with their fellow-men." This view, which held that "the law embodies the story of a nation's development through many centuries," comported well with the expansive sense of "history" embraced by higher critics of Scripture.[67] Adjudicating by these principles, Holmes did not object to legally enforced segregation or eugenics, but he did dissent against the *Lochner* decision of 1905, where the majority held that the Fourteenth Amendment's guarantee of due process could not supersede individual contracts.[68] That dissent would undergird much later legislation aimed at curbing the unfettered power of corporations. Whether guided by Harlan, a Christian, or Holmes, a skeptic, the ongoing course of American jurisprudence would witness scant reference to the once common understanding of Scripture as integral to the common law.

That direction had already been anticipated in 1879, when for the first time the Supreme Court answered the question about federal authority in relation to the First Amendment's guarantee of religious liberty. The case, *Reynolds v. the United States*, ruled that the Mormon practice of polygamy violated federal law; it could not be justified by appealing to the First Amendment.[69]

In the immediate background to adjudicating this case, an effort had been made to settle this question by direct appeal to Scripture. In 1870 the chaplain of the U.S. Senate, J. P. Newman, traveled to Salt Lake City to engage the Mormon elder Orson Pratt in three days of public debate on the question "Does the Bible sanction polygamy?" In much the same way that antebellum slavery defenders had exploited quotation of Old Testament texts and the example of honored Hebrew patriarchs, Pratt tied his opponent into knots, and Newman was left flailing away with vague references to general New Testament teaching and forced readings of a few Old Testament passages.[70] But unlike the earlier controversy over slavery that went on and on, the defeat of Newman's arguments hardly mattered. In a contemporary account from the *New York Times*, "the tournament of quotations now in progress at Salt Lake" could have no possible effect except on "weak-minded people" who failed to heed "the plainest dictum of common sense in the nineteenth century."[71]

Rather than concerning itself with such appeals to Scripture, the Supreme Court rendered its decision against a backdrop of general national sentiment treating plural marriage as the same kind of personal tyranny over wives and children that had only recently been outlawed in the abolition of slavery. To be sure, the Bible was not entirely out of the picture. Only a few years earlier a Michigan jurist, Thomas Cooley, had published a celebrated book concluding that on questions concerning marriage and the family, Christianity and the common law spoke with one voice.[72] In arguments before the Supreme Court on *Reynolds*, the Mormons' attorney did not object to that conclusion, but rather tried to use it to his advantage. He pointed out that the Old Testament Decalogue did not prohibit the practice and added that, while the New Testament might seem to teach strict monogamy, that interpretation was a theological conclusion rather than a legal judgment.[73]

These arguments failed to sway the Court. Significantly, the decision written by Chief Justice Morrison Remick Waite chose not to address biblical arguments pro or con. Instead it concentrated on questions of federal power over the territories and other matters of constitutional applicability. After reviewing a history of religious freedom featuring Thomas Jefferson, James Madison, and the Virginia Statute for Religious Liberty, Waite wrote that "from that day to this we think it may safely be said that there has never been a time in any State of the Union where polygamy has not been an offence against society." He therefore concluded that "it is impossible to believe that the constitutional guaranty of religious freedom was intended to prohibit legislation in respect to this most important feature of social life."[74]

Sarah Barringer Gordon has well described the upshot: "The Court upheld the criminal punishment of participants in a marital system that was perceived by the majority of the nation as a fundamental violation of humanitarian precepts, a sexual analogy to slavery."[75] The decision highlighted how the nation had moved on from the time when what the Bible had to say about slavery mattered in every venue of the land.

If, however, American law witnessed decreasing attention, the Bible's place as an enduring cultural landmark remained secure. Despite the increasing variety of scriptural usage, which reflected the nation's increasing religious pluralism, there could be no doubting that the Bible was still a significant presence in many domains for many purposes.

29

Civil Religion

The speech-making attending the deaths of American presidents, especially when those deaths prompted extraordinary outpourings of national grief, highlighted one of the Bible's main public services in the decades before the First World War. At those traumatic moments, a large proportion of the commemorative speeches were sermons, which were often published as separate works or reported in detail by the press. So it was when James A. Garfield was shot by the disgruntled office seeker Charles Guiteau on July 2, 1881, and died ten weeks later on September 19; and again when William McKinley was shot by the anarchist Leon Czolgosz on September 6, 1901, and died eight days later. In providing ministers with texts for their memorial addresses, the Bible was serving the public much as it had in the outpouring of emotion that followed the death of George Washington on December 14, 1799, and the assassination of Abraham Lincoln on April 14, 1865.

On each of these occasions clergy became spokesmen for the nation as they led congregations in mourning, eulogized the fallen leader, and explained how the presidential death spoke to the nation's political, social, and religious health. A Brooklyn Episcopalian described those functions eloquently after Lincoln's death: "It is made the duty of the pulpit, beyond any other organ of public sentiment, to deal with the overwhelming sorrow of the hour, to guide and temper the nation's grief, to teach it how and for what to weep, to interpret the sober philosophy of the grave, and to press home upon the softened, pain-stricken sensitivities of the people those gifts, privileges, and destinies which the world can neither give nor take away."[1]

For a history of the Bible, these moments are particularly telling. As ministers turned to Scripture for sermons they often prepared in a great rush, their instinctive usage revealed characteristic habits of thought, fundamental convictions, and common conventions of interpretation. That instinctive use sheds particular light on the nation's civil religion, whether described by Harry Stout as "sacralized patriotism" with "a complete repository of sacred rituals and myths," or in the famous definition by Robert Bellah as an "apprehension of universal and transcendent religious reality as seen in or . . . as revealed through the experience of the American people."[2]

As a guide to the evolution of civil religion over the course of the nineteenth century, the record of scriptural usage at those traumatic occasions shows both

America's Book. Mark A. Noll, Oxford University Press. © Oxford University Press 2022.
DOI: 10.1093/oso/9780197623466.003.0030

considerable continuity and significant change. In order to specify that continuity and change, the first part of this chapter identifies the texts most often enlisted and shows how some of them were put to use. The Bible's role in national self-understanding came even more clearly into focus in 1911, when an extraordinary range of public events celebrated the three-hundredth anniversary of the King James Bible. These celebrations, which are the subject of the chapter's next section, testify to the obvious fact that the nation remained deeply attached to the Christian Scriptures. But they also raise an important interpretive question: Was the Bible in any sense shaping public life, or had it become entirely subservient to national ideals treated as ultimate? This examination of civil religion at the turn of the century for the nation's majority-white population prepares the way for the book's final chapter, which returns to biblical usage in the nation's Black communities, where a different form of civil religion prevailed with a different set of key biblical texts.

Presidential Deaths: 1799, 1865, 1881, 1901

Scriptural usage for roughly comparable public events occurring at different moments in the nation's history provides one gauge for change over time in a complex cultural landscape. To be sure, national circumstances differed considerably in 1799, 1865, 1881, and 1901, as did perceptions of the deceased presidents. The publishing media for transmitting memorial sermons also underwent far-reaching change over the course of the century. Sermons that were printed or otherwise reported of course did not necessarily represent all the preached addresses.[3] Yet broad patterns in scriptural usage are nonetheless revealing.

Table 29.1 summarizes where ministers found their texts for a selection of sermons on those four occasions. The tabulation comes from 111 sermons preached as memorial addresses for Washington (which drew on 120 separate texts); 77 sermons preached either on the Sunday after Lincoln was shot, which happened to be Easter Sunday, or on June 1, 1865, the day designated by President Andrew Johnson for national mourning and humiliation (84 separate texts); 150 sermons after the death of Garfield (158 separate texts), and 200 sermons to commemorate McKinley (219 separate texts).[4]

The most obvious feature of the Washington funeral addresses is what Evan Shalev has called their "Old Testamentism" or "political Hebraism."[5] Of the 47 different texts chosen for those addresses, 41 came from the Hebrew Scriptures. In addition, of the 6 passages chosen from the New Testament, 4 referred to Old Testament personages. For 23 of the 111 Washington sermons, ministers spoke from 2 Samuel 3:38, a passage recording the lament of King David after his troops had slain Abner, the resourceful general of King Saul. To David, Abner was "a

Table 29.1 Texts for Presidential Memorial Sermons

	From Old Testament	From Old Testament, from Pss.	From New Testament	Total
Washington[1]	113 (94%)	16 (13%)	7	120
Lincoln[2]	60 (71%)	14 (17%)	24	84
Garfield[3]	101 (64%)	35 (22%)	57	158
McKinley	106 (51%)	22 (5%)	113	219

Notes: [1]Old Testament totals include one sermon from the Apocrypha, Wisdom of Sirach, chapter 8, used to praise Washington for his sagacity and trust in Providence; Bishop John Carroll, *A Discourse on General Washington; Delivered in the Catholic Church of St. Peter, in Baltimore-Feb 22d 1800* (Baltimore, MD: Warner & Hanna, 1800).

[2]For his book, *"No Sorrow like Our Sorrow": Northern Protestant Ministers and the Assassination of Lincoln* (Kent, OH: Kent State University Press, 1994), David B. Cheseborough examined 340 sermons from northern Protestants where, as in my sample, "Old Testament texts outnumbered New Testament texts by almost a three-to-one ratio" (xvii), and 2 Samuel 2:38 was the text most often selected.

[3]Old Testament totals include one sermon from 2 Maccabees 6:31 ("And this man died, leaving his death for an example of noble courage, and a memorial of virtue") and one from Sirach 38:16 ("My son, let tears fall down over the dead, and begin to lament").

prince and great man in Israel." Eighteen more ministers chose verses about Moses, and other ministers selected texts that drew parallels to Abel, Cyrus, Daniel, David, Hezekiah, Jacob, Jehoiada, Jephthah's daughter, Joshua, Josiah, Mordecai, Othniel, and Samuel. In contrast, the Washington memorials made use of only one New Testament exemplar, the early martyr Stephen.

For the Lincoln sermons, it is noteworthy that funeral preachers turned to the Old Testament almost as instinctively as their predecessors two generations before, even though Lincoln was shot on Good Friday and much northern sentiment viewed him as the Savior of the Union.[6] The same text from 2 Samuel chapter 3 appeared as the most frequently chosen verse, as it would be as well for the Garfield and McKinley sermons. Lincoln was also eulogized as a modern Moses, but with a much shorter roster of other Old Testament worthies.[7]

For Garfield, Old Testament usage appeared less often, with an even greater turn in the McKinley sermons to the New Testament. Some of that shift probably involved particular circumstances. The upsurge in Psalm texts for Garfield suggests strong bewilderment occasioned by anguish reopened from the relatively recent observances for Lincoln. Several sermons referenced Psalm 97, which begins "The Lord reigneth," because of an incident from Garfield's life. As widely reported in the memorial addresses, Garfield had been in New York City on April 15, 1865, when Lincoln's death was announced. As a mob threatened an

outbreak of violence, it is said that Garfield stilled their rage with a bold proclamation from this Psalm: "God reigns, and the government at Washington still
lives."[8]

For McKinley, the second most popular text after 2 Samuel 3:38 was Luke
23:34 ("Father, forgive them, for they know not what they do"). Its presence can
be explained by the fact that immediately after Leon Czolgosz fired on McKinley,
the wounded president is reported to have spoken words ("Be easy with him,
boys") that kept the assassin from being immediately pummeled to death. Yet
even with such particulars noted, the general drift of Bible usage cannot be mistaken: in a strong difference from 1800 and significant difference from 1865 and
even 1881, the nation's public Bible in 1901 had become the New Testament.

This turn to the New Testament supports the conclusion of scholars who have
described the figure of Jesus becoming more prominent as the nineteenth century wore on.[9] The trajectory from a dominant Old Testament to an increasingly
popular New Testament becomes even clearer by examining how Scripture was
put to use in individual sermons—for this comparison, two memorials preached
from the most popular text, 2 Samuel 3:38, in each of 1799, 1865, 1881, and 1901.

The sermonic treatments of King David's lament at the death of Abner show
that some things did not change in the public use of Scripture.[10] Together,
sermons revealed a deep national immersion in Scripture and an ongoing desire
to bolster, encourage, comfort, and discipline personal spiritual life. Especially at
crisis moments, the Bible remained an anchor for a public unnerved by tumult
and uncertainty.

The ministers who spoke from this text at different times all found biblical
warrant for making partisan comments about the crises of the hour. One of the
Washington sermons in 1799 drew on the Old Testament narrative describing
the God-ordained succession of the prophet Elijah by the prophet Elisha to warn
the nation against replacing John Adams (the Elisha to Washington's Elijah) with
any Democratic-Republican.[11] After Lincoln's assassination William Hague
of Boston hailed the destruction of the slave power as "accelerat[ing] the progress of the republic upon its new career of a free, Christian civilization."[12] After
Garfield's assassination, P. G. Blight in Jersey City joined a mighty chorus in
denouncing the spoils system that drove a disappointed office seeker to shoot
the president.[13] In similar fashion, E. P. Ingersoll, a Brooklyn Congregationalist,
used the assassination of McKinley by an anarchist to call for immigration laws
that would keep out "moral lepers, the depraved and offscouring of many nations" who have "stealthily crept in upon us to degenerate our nation."[14]

As consistently as preachers made partisan political comments, so uniformly did they continue the long-standing habit of making more general use
of biblical quotations or Bible-like rhetoric. In 1799 Thomas Baldwin, pastor
of Boston's Second Baptist Church, cited a text that many others used on these

occasions when he praised Washington for the religious content of his Farewell Address by quoting Hebrews 11:4—the late president, though "being dead, yet he speaketh."[15] The same kind of rhetoric marked the sermon of a Grand Army of the Republic chaplain, T. K. Noble, when in San Francisco he preached a Garfield memorial sermon before a GAR contingent. As Noble described the sad occurrence that drew them together, he joined an allusion to the woman who anointed the feet of Jesus from Luke 7:37, with a direct quotation of the Apostle Paul's valediction from 2 Timothy 4:7: we "have come together to break the alabaster box of our honest affection over our dead comrade, and to anoint him for his burial. 'He has fought the good fight, he has finished his course, he has kept the faith.'"[16]

From only this small selection of sermons, however, it is also apparent that uses of Scripture were evolving, the most important shift from perceiving the nation as a Hebrew civilization to describing it in broadly Christian terms.[17] At the death of Washington, Thomas Baldwin from New England (but a Baptist) and John Armstrong from Pennsylvania (not New England) filled their sermons with quotations from the Old Testament in the style New England Congregationalists had perfected. These preachers may not have been quite as explicit in detailing the Israel-America link as had Ezra Stiles of Yale, who in 1788 referred to the Lord's "american [sic] Israel" that was now exalted "*high above all nations which he hath made, in numbers, and in praise, and in name, and in honor!*"[18] Yet Baldwin and Armstrong in 1799 did incorporate the American story into the Old Testament narrative they so highly honored. Baldwin even came close to Stiles when he declared, "You cannot help . . . observing a coincidence of character and circumstances, between the Jewish Lawgiver [Moses] and the American President."[19]

By 1865, this Israel-America typology had faded. Episcopalian A. N. Littlejohn on Long Island did affirm that as a result of Lincoln's life, slavery now bore "the mark of Cain . . . upon it."[20] Otherwise, the Lincoln sermons described the American character without referring to ancient Israel. One called Lincoln the "angel of deliverance" able to "work out for us that 'great salvation' which has just now become the most amazing and hopeful of the nineteenth century in the sight of the whole wide world." The same minister asserted that God had made events to become "vocal with prophecies of our glorious future, as sure to us as any that ever came from Isaiah's lips."[21] One of the Garfield sermons even abridged the text from 2 Samuel 3 by omitting the phrase "in Israel."[22] At McKinley's death, the Brooklyn Congregationalist E. P. Ingersoll praised press coverage of the assassination in high biblical terms, but Christian rather than Hebraic: "[S]o penetrated have the leaders of thought become with Christian ideals and principles that, almost to a man, when disaster or troubles 'come in like a flood [Isa 59:19]' they rise to the thought and plea of the gospel minister."[23]

The difference between a rhetoric keyed to Old Testament accounts of God's sovereignty and rhetoric dominated by New Testament phrases describing the nation's Christian character shaped the lessons ministers drew from national tragedy. For Washington, the jeremiad still prevailed: since the American people had been visited with affliction, it was now imperative that the entire community repent of its sin and turn to God for sustaining mercy. Or, in the phrases of the Rev. Armstrong from Pottstown, Pennsylvania, "if we continue to provoke him, he can inflict judgments upon us much more severe" than witnessed in Israel's history; so "let us with one consent, strive to walk in the fear of God."[24]

Lessons driven home in the later sermons still expressed full confidence in God's providential direction of the nation's destiny, but they no longer repeated the jeremiad's call for repentance.[25] The final lesson that William Hague of Boston took from Lincoln's death concerned the United States' new global prominence: we have, he said, proved to the world "that our republican government had enough of coherent strength to withstand the shocks of a great rebellion."[26] Sixteen years later Chaplain T. K. Noble took from Garfield's murder a civics lesson concerning "the inherent excellence of the American ideals and institutions which made possible the character and career of James A. Garfield" and a reminder to his listeners of how "a genuinely unselfish and consecrated life" could display "ever-increasing usefulness and . . . ever-widening influence."[27] At McKinley's death, ministers focused on how all could be inspired by the late president's "exalted and pure faith, his sublime devotion—home and national," and with the hope that such virtues could "pass like particles of iron into the blood of our higher life."[28] As indicated by these sermons, which all began with the text from 2 Samuel 3, the narrative of Israel's triumphs and failures had given way to Christian-themed accounts of the nation's present condition and future possibilities.

The shifting use of Scripture probably had something to do with the presidents being memorialized. In contrast to Washington (Episcopalian, but very reserved) and Lincoln (theistic, but even more reserved about anything explicitly Christian), the later presidents were well known as active churchmen. Garfield's military service in the Civil War featured more prominently, but he also enjoyed the distinction of being the only ordained minister (Disciples of Christ) to become president.[29] McKinley's active Methodist membership also recommended him to a significant portion of the populace. As an example of a public statement quite different from what Washington or Lincoln ever made, McKinley a year before his death welcomed the delegates to the 1900 Ecumenical Missionary Conference in New York City, the largest gathering of its kind to that date. Before this group, the president praised Protestant missionaries for teaching "the race of men . . . the truth of the common fatherhood of God and the brotherhood of man" and for "wielding the Sword of the Spirit" in their battle against "ignorance and prejudice."[30]

(An ironic indication of heightened Christian salience in the latter period was a book published by Charles Guiteau only two years before he shot Garfield. It defended Scripture against skeptics like Robert Ingersoll by emphasizing the biblical sayings of Jesus showing, according to Guiteau, that such unbelievers "belong ... to the devil's seed.")[31]

From the memorial sermons as a whole it is apparent that the United States in 1800 was demographically Protestant but scripturally Hebraic. By 1900 the nation had become much more religiously pluralistic, even if on public occasions spokesmen could sound more Christian as they favored texts from the New Testament. The uncertainties addressed in these sermons also changed. In 1800 anxiety focused on questions of character: Would personal virtue be strong enough to realize the potential of the republican government that a beneficent providence had bestowed upon the new nation? In the second half of the century, anxiety came more from external enemies: Would the slave power, political corruption, or unregulated immigration undermine what providence had given to a nation rapidly rising as a beacon for the world?

Consistent use of Scripture accompanied consistently strong convictions that God providentially oversaw the national destiny and that attentive observers could chart the course of that providential guidance. For assessing the health of the nation, those convictions meant that preachers treated Scripture as a moral standard, though the shift from an Old Testament and Hebraic context to the New Testament and Christian emphases made a difference. With the decline of the jeremiad, the focus on personal sinfulness also declined, while confidence grew in the heaven-sanctioned goodness of American ideals and institutions. A surprising number of preachers expressed that confidence with the assurance of a New York Unitarian, Henry Bellows, who addressed his congregation on the Easter Sunday immediately after Lincoln died: "Heaven rejoices this Easter morning in the resurrection of our lost leader, honored in the day of his death; dying on the anniversary of our Lord's great sacrifice, a mighty sacrifice himself for the sins of a whole people."[32] Whether in the form of a jeremiad or the Christian language of the New Testament, hubris remained a temptation for those who believed that they possessed the ability to discern how God was dealing with the nation.

Throughout the century, the civil religion of the sermons preached after the noteworthy presidential deaths remained characteristically Protestant after the American pattern. Ministers did not hesitate in moving directly from their personal apprehension of crisis to finding a biblical text supporting their apprehension to preaching a word from God about the crisis. They did not wait for approval from higher ecclesiastical authorities or pause to explain the interpretive assumptions with which they worked. Neither did they doubt the special relationship the United States enjoyed with the divine. As these sermons were Protestant, they were of course Christian—but often only vaguely so. It was not, in fact, always clear whether the ministers regarded the Scriptures as a book for all nations or only for their own. The same ambiguity marked even more strongly the 1911 celebrations of "the authorized version."

The King James Version at Three Hundred

At the four-hundredth anniversary of the King James Bible in 2011, well-publicized events and numerous publications made for a noteworthy celebration. In the lead, Queen Elizabeth II devoted part of her 2010 Christmas Broadcast to praising the KJV "as a masterpiece of English prose" and as providing "the most widely recognised and beautiful description of the birth of Jesus Christ."[33] An op-ed in the *New York Times* echoed the first part of the queen's commendation: this Bible "captures and preserves the unavoidable rhythms of good English."[34] Yet for the most part, celebrations of the KJV in 2011 seem to have been left to academics and aficionados. It was far otherwise a century earlier.[35]

In 1911, the collective leadership of the English-speaking world stood at attention to salute this notable translation. The president, the king, the prime minister, and other statesmen of the first rank led a grand chorus of praise for the literary, political, ethical, and religious virtues of what their contemporaries were hailing as "the greatest book in the English language," the most vital book in the world," and "the chief classic of our English language and literature."[36]

In the first decade of the twentieth century, the Bible remained secure as a cultural icon, but also increasingly insecure against rapid shifts in society, culture, and national intellectual life. Diverging purposes among the nation's Protestants, whose patronage had made this translation so important, illustrated the uncertainty. In 1911 Oxford University Press released a special tercentenary edition of the Scofield Reference Bible that had appeared for the first time only two years before. Also in 1911, Francis Grimké, a theologically conservative Black Presbyterian minister in Washington, D.C., addressed the nation's racial situation as he had been doing for decades. One of his orations that year addressed "the paramount importance of character," almost half of quoted Scripture in order to define "the true standard by which to estimate individuals and races."[37] Walter Rauschenbusch in 1911 was struggling to complete a book that would be published the following year as *Christianizing the Social Order*. His time was constrained because of demands resulting from the 1907 publication of *Christianity and the Social Crisis*. In both books extensive quotation from especially the Old Testament provided Rauschenbusch with the substance of his Social Gospel.[38] Also in 1911, the pamphlet series titled *The Fundamentals: A Testimony to the Truth* entered its second year. Of the twenty-five articles that made up the first four numbers of this series, fifteen were devoted to defending traditional Protestant attitudes toward Scripture.[39]

In 1911 Protestants united in honoring the Bible but divided over what they thought the Bible said. The Scofield Bible promoted a conservative biblicism focused on an apocalyptic future. Francis Grimké was almost as conservative, but much more socially engaged. Walter Rauschenbusch was also deeply committed to social engagement, but from a modern approach to Scripture. The authors who contributed to *The Fundamentals* matched a conservative biblicism with almost no social engagement.

Obvious as these differences now seem, celebrants at the time hardly noticed. The three main events took place in London, New York, and Chicago, but they were joined by a host of less elaborate observances and a wealth of publications from both religious and secular sources.[40] The first event, which took place in London at the Royal Albert Hall on Wednesday, March 29, featured representatives from many churches, addresses by the British prime minister Herbert Asquith and the American ambassador Whitelaw Reid, and a reading of letters from President William Howard Taft and King George V. The one discordant note was an intervention by suffragettes who, imitating their American sisters from the Philadelphia Centennial in 1876, unfurled a banner urging "justice for women" when the prime minister rose to speak.[41] The rest of the ceremony rode a wave of exaltation, as illustrated by Ambassador Reid's contention that the Bible "has furnished, and furnishes, the strongest and most indestructible bond for the present practical unity in aims and aspirations of the great English-speaking family of nations which, as has been so often said, occupies over one-fourth of the inhabitable surface of the globe, and governs nearly one-third of its inhabitants. (Cheers)."[42]

The exultant mood continued at a mass meeting in New York's Carnegie Hall on Tuesday, April 25. The assembled throng joined in singing "How Firm a Foundation, ye saints of the Lord / Is laid for your faith in His excellent Word." Secretary of State John W. Foster read the same letter from President Taft that was presented in London. The British ambassador, James Bryce, read King George's earlier response to Taft's letter and then spoke himself about the cultural bonds between the United States and Britain that had been sustained by common use of the KJV.[43]

The next week in Chicago, five days of celebration began on Sunday, April 30, when more than one thousand churches held individual or union services; they concluded with a mass rally at Orchestra Hall on Thursday, May 4. The Sunday gatherings were addressed by luminaries, including the Oak Park

Congregationalist minister W. E. Barton, who would later write a popular book describing Abraham Lincoln as a convinced Christian, and the University of Chicago theologian Shailer Mathews, renowned as one of the nation's leading modernist theologians. Elsewhere in Chicago tributes rained down, including one from the rabbi of the city's Israel Temple.[44] The Thursday climax of Chicago-area celebrations featured choruses from Haydn's "Creation," Mendelssohn's "Elijah," and Handel's "Messiah"; a reading from a 1611 King James Bible normally held "under lock and key" at the Newberry Library; and a series of speeches ending with an address by William Jennings Bryan.[45]

The letters from President Taft and King George V underscored the themes that others would develop in the American celebrations. Taft declared that the KJV was "the Bible of our American forefathers. Its classic English has given shape to American literature. Its spirit has influenced American ideals in life and laws and government." The monarch observed that "the version which bears King James's name is so clearly interwoven in the history of British and American life that it is right we should thank God for it together."[46] The day after these statements were read at the Carnegie Hall celebration, the *New York Times* commented editorially that, while it probably was time to move on to newer, more reliable translations of Scripture, nonetheless the three-hundred-year old version still deserved to be considered "the bud of the herb of civilization, the spring of a new day, the trumpet of a prophecy."[47] The encomia that echoed from near and far repeated these themes, as in one typical account that heralded the KJV as "the foundation of our civilisation and our religion" while claiming that "if we were to take the Bible out of the world we would destroy music, art, and literature."[48]

As had been the case since the early nineteenth century, much tercentenary comment also hymned the KJV for its beneficent effects on leading figures in Anglo-American intellectual life. The catalogue of authors, scientists, politicians, and religious figures specified as decisively influenced by this Bible included, as only a partial list, John Bunyan, Thomas Carlyle, James Clark-Maxwell, Samuel Taylor Coleridge, Charles Dickens, Michael Faraday, W. E. Gladstone, Thomas Ken, Abraham Lincoln, John Locke, Thomas Babington Macaulay, the geologist Hugh Miller, John Milton, Isaac Newton, John Ruskin, Walter Scott, the Earl of Shaftesbury, Alfred Tennyson, Walt Whitman, and William Wilberforce.[49]

As had become customary well before 1911, pundits especially lauded the KJV for its contribution to the language: it was "the noblest monument of the English language in the time of its greatest perfection and vigor" and "the most noble, beautiful, and wonderful book which the world holds to-day." Others praised "its vast simplicity and moving eloquence" or concluded, "The Bible has . . . been an untold formative power to mold the English language itself into that 'incommunicable simplicity' which is its strength and beauty." In short, when considering the language and literature, "[t]here is but one sun in the firmament, though there may be a moon (or moons) and galaxies of stars."[50]

Very occasionally authors paused for nuance in this floodtide of praise. One commentator singled out William Tyndale and his bibles from the 1520s, instead of the 1611 translators, for "the peculiar genius . . . the mingled tenderness and majesty, the Saxon simplicity—the preternatural grandeur" of the KJV.[51] But mostly it was an unending recital of literary and linguistic virtues. Not surprisingly, some got carried away, as when one report on the Albert Hall celebration stated that separate languages would certainly have developed on the two sides of the Atlantic were it not for "the fact that until within recent years during all those three centuries every child in England and America heard the King James translation of the Bible read aloud daily."[52]

Description of the KJV's role in uniting the English-speaking people flowed naturally into describing the translation's role in promoting political ideals. A Methodist, now fully comfortable in a custodial role, provided one of the clearest statements: "For the English-speaking peoples [the KJV] is the fountain-head and perpetual spring of our common laws and free institutions. Tyranny, oppression and class privilege cannot survive where the principles of the Bible are imbibed; and not a little of the history of liberty among English-speaking peoples is directly due to the fact that the inspiring sentences of this book have been familiar to the ears and understanding of the common people."[53] Several American commentators made special reference to Abraham Lincoln's adept use of the KJV; one exaggerated by applying the epithet of John Wesley, that Lincoln "was essentially a man of one book—the Bible."[54]

With such a chorus of praise, but also with the awareness that the celebrations were honoring a text now three hundred years old, it is not surprising that some observers reflected on the possibility of a newer version. A particularly interesting article by Edgar J. Goodspeed, who later produced his own memorable translation of the New Testament, noted the KJV's inferior Greek text, its difficulties in rendering tenses and proper names, and some outright errors. Yet Goodspeed was also highly appreciative: "Not only is it an English classic, but it has served well the religious needs of ten generations of readers and hearers."[55]

Only a few brave souls stood up to this torrent of praise. An occasional voice reminded readers of the inadequate Greek and Hebrew texts upon which the KJV was based.[56] An Oregon editor, perhaps was remembering "Fifty-Four Forty or Fight!" the slogan that in the nineteenth century contested British claims for what became the American northwest. He objected mildly by suggesting that political institutions of the English-speaking world actually owed more to ancient German and Saxon traditions than to the KJV.[57] But with the exception of opinion from one specific community, reservations about KJV in 1911 were hard to find.

The Catholic Minority View

As the exception, Roman Catholics considered the hoopla a misreading of history and an offense to true Christianity. Some of this wounded opinion may have been responding to what Protestant commentors said about their church when they lauded the KJV. Several, for example, quoted the comments of Frederick Faber, the convert to Catholicism best known for the hymn "Faith of Our Fathers." Faber had once written at length about "the uncommon beauty and marvelous English of the Protestant Bible" while contending that "in the length and breadth of the land there is not a Protestant with one spark of religiousness about him whose spiritual biography is not in his Saxon Bible." Only a few, however, went on with the rest of Faber's commentary, which held that this translation was "one of the greatest strongholds of heresy in this country [England]. . . . It is part of the national mind, and the anchor of the national seriousness. Nay, it is worshipped with a positive idolatry, in extenuation of whose fanaticism its intrinsic beauty pleads availingly with the scholar."[58]

Although a few Protestants who commended the KJV paused for charitable words about the Catholic translations published before it, most expressed nothing but disdain.[59] One typical comment criticized the prefaces and notes of Catholic bibles that merely "propagated the dogmas of Popery" and offered "a mass of bigotry, sophistry and unfairness."[60]

American Catholics responded in kind, often by relying on English sources for their criticism. One borrowed essay included the prediction that, since Protestant higher critics were eviscerating the supernatural realities of Scripture, the Bible might "survive, indeed, for the non-Catholic, but only as Homer survives, a classic collection of beautiful myths and legends, with little appeal to the spirit and no authority over heart and intellect."[61]

The Jesuit periodical *America* provided one of the fullest critiques when it summarized a blast from the Liverpool *Catholic Times*: William Tyndale's Bible not only unleashed "anarchy and communism preached by the Lollards" but was an English "corruption from a badly translated German one." Tyndale, moreover, filled his margins "with most abusive and inflammatory notes assailing all the sacred teachings and the worship of the Catholic Faith." This summary of early Protestant versions inverted the hagiography coming from Protestants: "Tyndale was not burnt at the stake for anything to do with religion, but for fomenting by his writings . . . political turmoil and fanaticism against the authorities of Church and State." The same critic did concede that although Protestant translators had incited "revolutionary horrors," nonetheless the KJV "certainly deserved the eulogiums bestowed upon it as to its pure and elegant English language and style." But of course, those superior qualities resulted from heavy dependence upon the Catholics' Rheims translation. In sum, to the Catholic church "alone we owe the bible-today, and from her pulpit all who attend, both Catholic and Protestant will hear to their great spiritual profit the doctrines of the bible and the preaching of Christ crucified."[62]

The reprise of ancient Catholic-Protestant disputation added a discordant note to the sympathy of praise that otherwise marked American celebrations. Yet as historically informed and factually accurate as many of the anniversary pronouncements were, only a few commentators paused to consider broader questions about what they were celebrating.

Latent in the effusive commentary was a conundrum that resulted from the dual role played by the KJV as a mainstay of Protestant tradition and a central element in the American imagination. Because Protestant traditions had flourished in the American environment and because Protestants had done so much to shape that environment, biblical vocabulary, biblical images, and biblical literary styles became coin of the realm. Considered from one angle, the KJV near-monopoly served American Christians splendidly for spiritual liberation, personal moral discipline, and ethical guidance. It prompted many believers, grounded in that biblical frame, to carry out self-sacrificing good works undertaken as an expression of their faith. Considered from another angle, the near-monopoly of this particular version in this particular nation facilitated a civil religion that subordinated God to Caesar, provided the language for a self-deceiving reliance on "the Bible alone," and could stoke an anti-intellectual populism that substituted biblicism for thought. The Christian book and the Christian book appropriated for specific American circumstances were the same—for better and for worse.

Roosevelt, Wilson, Bryan

The major addresses that Theodore Roosevelt, Woodrow Wilson, and William Jennings Bryan delivered to commemorate the KJV underscored the esteem in which the translation was held, but also some of the problems related to that esteem. The speeches of Roosevelt and Wilson were classics of American civil religion; Bryan's address offered a striking instance of populist Christian biblicism.

Roosevelt delivered the first of these speeches on March 26 as the centerpiece of a lecture series at Pacific Theological Seminary in Berkeley, California. As famed leader of the Rough Riders during the Spanish-American War, governor of New York, and then U.S. president from 1901 to 1909, Roosevelt in 1911 was the nation's most celebrated public figure. For him, the KJV meant simply public virtue. It was "the book to which our people owe infinitely the greater part of their store of ethics, infinitely the greater part of their knowledge of how to apply that store to the needs of our every-day life." As a good historian, the former president conceded that the KJV used earlier translations, but he was also characteristically dramatic in what he wanted to say about this one version: "No other book of any kind ever written in English—perhaps no other book ever written in any other tongue—has ever so affected the whole life of a people as this authorized version of the Scriptures has affected the life of the English-speaking peoples." Roosevelt based his conclusion less on specific Christian reasoning than on broad humanitarian appeal. As he stressed the KJV's excellence, he urged his auditors to study the Bible, not necessarily "as an inspired book" but as an essential volume for every person "who seeks after a high and useful life."[63]

What could readers derive from reading the KJV? To answer, Roosevelt quoted from "the great scientist Huxley," who had called the KJV "the Magna Charta of the poor and the oppressed . . . the most democratic book in the world." To Roosevelt, the democracy that Bible reading encouraged was a robustly moral enterprise: "I ask you men and women to treat the Bible in the only way in which it can be treated if benefit is to be obtained from it, and that is, as a guide to conduct." Roosevelt readily conceded that the Bible's content was important for dogma and that its language was important aesthetically. But, for him, all other purposes fell far short of the ethical:

> If you read it without thought of following its ethical teachings, then you are apt to do but little good to your fellow-men. . . . Our success in striving to help our fellow-men, and therefore to help ourselves, depends largely upon our success as we strive, with whatever shortcomings, with whatever failures, to lead our lives in accordance with the great ethical principles laid down in the life of Christ, and in the New Testament writing which seek to expound and apply his teachings.[64]

Six weeks later, on May 7, the sitting governor of New Jersey gave a comparable address in Denver before an attentive crowd of twelve thousand. Wilson, who served as president of Princeton University from 1902 to 1910, had already gained a nationwide reputation for his efforts as a progressive reformer. His Denver speech, part of a nationwide tour to explore the possibilities of a presidential run, was just as this-worldly as Roosevelt's address to the Berkeley seminarians. Wilson summarized matters to a correspondent immediately afterward: "I spoke on the Bible and Progress, and the great audience moved me deeply. The Bible (with its individual value of the human soul[)] is undoubtedly the book that has made democracy and been the source of all progress."[65]

To Wilson, as to Roosevelt, the KJV inculcated a particular political outlook—it had revealed "men unto themselves, not as creatures in bondage" but as "distinct moral agent[s]." And so he could argue that "not a little of the history of liberty lies in the circumstance that the moving sentences of this book were made familiar to the ears and the understanding of those peoples who have led mankind in exhibiting the forms of government and the impulses of reform which have made for freedom and for self-government among mankind."[66]

What Wilson called "the people's book of revelation" not only originated American democracy but also guided it. Roosevelt had claimed that the nation's greatness lay not in its wealth but in its ideals.[67] Wilson exalted the Bible in similar terms: "America is not ahead of the other nations of the world because she is rich. Nothing makes America great except her thoughts, except her ideals, except her acceptance of those standards of judgment which are written large upon these pages of revelation." At the end of his address, Wilson, like Roosevelt, conflated what he wanted to say about the Bible as a general guide for American civilization and his own stance as a Christian reader of the Scriptures:

> America was born a Christian nation. America was born to exemplify that devotion to the elements of righteousness which are derived from the revelations of Holy Scripture.
>
> Ladies and gentlemen, I have a very simple thing to ask of you. I ask of every man and woman in this audience that from this night on they will realize that part of the destiny of America lies in their daily perusal of this great book of revelations—that if they would see America free and pure they will make their own spirits free and pure by this baptism of the Holy Scripture.[68]

With Roosevelt, Wilson made bold claims about the influence of the KJV on American life. What remained after the Bible's service to democracy and American ideals, what it might mean for Scripture to challenge democracy or American ideals, were subjects they did not address.

Three days before Wilson's speech in Denver, Bryan, the three-time presidential candidate of the Democratic Party (1896, 1900, 1908), spoke as the capstone orator for Chicago's day-long celebration.[69] Unlike Roosevelt and Wilson, Bryan spoke much about the Bible's character as a primarily spiritual book. In his best stump-speaking style, he began by asserting that "atheists and materialists have assailed the Bible at every point," including its "facts . . . prophesies . . . account which it gives of creation . . . miracles." In response, Bryan reminded his listeners of Elijah's challenge to the priests of Baal and then proposed "a Bible test." There could be, he averred, no better time for such a contest than when "we are celebrating" the three-hundredth anniversary of the King James translation. Then Bryan posed the question that structured his speech: "Is the Bible the work of man or is it an inspired book?"[70]

He began by acknowledging that Scripture came from only "a single race," the Hebrews who inhabited only a tiny plot of land and knew only antiquated technologies—no "printing presses" or "the learning of the schools." Yet from such an obscure location arose the Bible, whose "characters grapple with every problem that confronts mankind, from the creation of the world to eternal life beyond the tomb." From this same unpropitious place, moreover, came also "the foundation of our statute law" (the Ten Commandments), "the rules for spiritual growth" (the Sermon on the Mount), the world's best "code of morality," and—above all—"the story of him who is the growing figure of all time, whom the world is accepting as Saviour and as the perfect example." Bryan expanded his case by arguing that humankind had advanced in every domain of life "except in the line of character-building." In that one vital area, however, "wherever the moral standard is being lifted up . . . the improvement is traceable to the Bible and to the influence of the God and Christ of whom the Bible tells."

Up to a point Bryan sounded like Wilson and Roosevelt in praising Scripture for its utilitarian value: "back of the progress of the present day is the code of morals that Christ proclaimed." But he went further to make an explicit theological claim the others did not make: "and back of that code of morals is the divine character of him who is both Son of God and Saviour of Mankind." Bryan closed his address by contrasting the stance of the Bible-believing Christian with beliefs held by a small but rapidly growing number of his fellow Americans: "the followers of Buddha . . . the followers of the Arab prophet . . . the followers of Confucius . . . the materialist . . . the atheist." Against these alternatives, Bryan responded boldly, "To the doubts and 'I don't knows' of the agnostic, the Christian, Bible in hand, answers: 'I believe.' "

While Bryan echoed some of the ethical injunctions of Roosevelt and some of the political emphases of Wilson, his main points were not only more directly religious but also more explicitly Christian. They were also more characteristically populist. While neither Wilson nor Roosevelt delivered an academic address, both took time to sketch a little history and elaborate nuances of their arguments. Bryan did not.

For positioning the KJV in that memorial year, it is helpful to remember how skillfully the orators had used Scripture in their public lives. For Bryan, memorable evocation of a biblical image had made him a political celebrity. The image came at the conclusion of his speech to the Democratic National Convention in 1896, which featured an ardent appeal for the free coinage of silver as means to overcome a national economic crisis. He ended with these memorable words: "Having behind us the producing masses of this nation and the world, supported by the commercial interests, the laboring interests, and the toilers everywhere, we will answer their demand for a gold standard by saying to them: You shall not press down upon the brow of labor this crown of thorns, you shall not crucify mankind upon a cross of gold."[71]

Roosevelt was similarly adept. His memorable speech accepting the Progressive Party's nomination for president in 1912 addressed a standard array of the day's economic and political problems. But its peroration climaxed with a powerful biblical image:

> Our cause is based on the eternal principles of righteousness; and even though we who now lead may for the time fail, in the end the cause itself shall triumph. . . . To you men who . . . have come together to spend and be spent in the endless crusade against wrong . . . to you who gird yourselves for the great new fight in the never-ending warfare for the good of humankind, I say in closing . . . We stand at Armageddon, and we battle for the Lord.[72]

For his part, Wilson employed a biblical notion of "covenant" as his central theme for taking the United States into the First World War and even more directly in announcing his goals for a League of Nations.[73] In keeping with the resonance of that biblical idea, Wilson promoted the League with a prophet's disregard for anything standing in his way—even when a more accommodating course might have overcome the opposition that ultimately kept the United States from joining the League. With Roosevelt and Bryan, Wilson knew the Bible and knew how to put it to use.

Civil Religion at Work

As national leaders, Roosevelt, Bryan, and Wilson promoted policies in keeping with the principles they outlined in their speeches from 1911.[74] Those policies fleshed out their commitment to "righteousness" as well as their confidence in the ideals of democratic liberty. For all three, an active national government seemed the proper agent for reforming the social order along lines they envisioned, at least partially, in biblical terms.

All, for example, were foes of corruption. All tried to use government to protect at least some of those most in need of protection. In their era, progressive support for an active government came mostly from Roosevelt's wing of the Republican Party, which provided his avenue for reforming the civil service and the police during his years in New York. As president, Roosevelt worked energetically to clean up the civil service, protect the public against monopolies, and preserve western land for public use. When Wilson became president in 1913, he justified many of his appeals for progressive legislation by the imperative to help people in actual need. With this motivation, he backed restrictions on corporate trusts, created the Federal Reserve for ensuring stability in banking, secured an eight-hour day for railroad workers, and established the first national standards protecting child labor.

Although Bryan's populism was constrained by the Democratic Party's need to placate the segregationist policies of its southern wing, he remained a lifelong champion of women, children, and the working poor. An especially poignant episode at the end of his life testified to the reputation Bryan won by advocating for the powerless. When in 1925 he was enlisted by the state of Tennessee to help prosecute John Scopes for teaching evolution in a high school classroom, the organization funding Scopes's defense had second thoughts. It was the American Civil Liberties Union, several of whose leaders were great admirers of Bryan for his efforts on behalf of the defenseless, to which the ACLU was also committed.[75]

A similar effort to promote what could be described as biblical ideals inspired the international efforts of these three men. In Cara Lea Burnidge's phrase, Wilson "made the social gospel a matter of U.S. foreign relations."[76] With Wilson, Roosevelt won renown for using the United States' rising power to promote peace among nations and liberty for oppressed peoples—in particular, his success in brokering the end of a war between Japan and Russia, for which he was awarded the Nobel Peace Prize. Wilson was even more admired for the idealism of his Fourteen Points, the plan at the end of World War I to create an international peacekeeping order that would make destructive warfare impossible. For his part, Bryan as Wilson's secretary of state was so dedicated to peaceful resolution of international disputes that in 1916 he resigned when he concluded that Wilson's actions toward Germany violated the principle of noncombative neutrality. In short, the record of these three notable Americans included many efforts to act morally at home and abroad. In considerable measure they practiced as politicians what they preached about the KJV in the spring of 1911.

Yet the limits of their policies, as well as their uses of Scripture, have become increasingly evident with the passage of time. Roosevelt (throughout his life) and Wilson (after he became president) championed variations of the Social Gospel that came near to equating the biblical "Kingdom of God" with a set of American political axioms. As fundamentalist critics at the time and advocates of Neo-orthodox theology later pointed out, such reliance on ethics reformulated historical Christian teaching to bring it into line with the spirit of their age. They practiced a Christianity guided by the norms that right-thinking, scientifically informed, and politically energized progressives hoped would reform the world through their own efforts.

As the two presidents enlisted biblical themes and language for their efforts, their civil religion left behind much of what traditional Christianity had emphasized. For a sense of sin as an ever-present reality threatening even the best efforts of the most noble political actors, they substituted a nearly utopian confidence in what disciplined human effort could accomplish. Instead of viewing humanity as united alike before God's law and the offer of salvation, they followed the era's theories on race, eugenics, and Social Darwinism to view "Anglo-Saxons" or "Teutonic peoples" as qualitatively superior. This thinking, in turn, affected their attitudes toward race. Although Roosevelt broke custom by welcoming the Black leader Booker T. Washington to the White House, neither president saw African Americans, Native Americans, or Asian Americans as deserving the same consideration as whites. For the Bible's words of warning and reassurance for all nations, they substituted supreme confidence in the United States as uniquely qualified to lead the world through sheer moral effort to a new day of universal peace.

Wilson's stance seems particularly incongruous. Shortly after his election in 1912, Francis Grimké, the Black Presbyterian minister, sent him a congratulatory letter, not so much for his electoral triumph as for having recently published an article in *The Expositor* on the importance of studying the Bible in Sunday Schools. Grimké, speaking as "a colored man," believed Wilson knew that "the triumph of the Democratic Party has always been attended, more or less, with a sense of uneasiness on the part of the colored people for fear lest their rights might be interfered with." But Grimké's mind was "greatly relieved" when he read Wilson's article. The reason? "I said to myself, No American citizen, white or black, need have any reasonable grounds of fear from the Administration of a man who feels as he does, who believes as he does in the word of God, and who accepts as he does, without any reservation, the great, eternal, and immutable principles of righteousness for which that Word stands."[77]

Yet it was not to be. Wilson soon resegregated the nation's civil service, which prompted another letter from Grimké that upbraided the president for an action that was "undemocratic . . . un-American . . . un-Christian [and] is needlessly to offend the self-respect of the loyal black citizens of the Republic."[78]

Wilson also gave in to the spirit of his age during the next major American celebration of Scripture. In 1916, the president responded positively when invited to participate in a one-hundredth anniversary celebration for the American Bible Society scheduled for the Daughters of the American Revolution building in Washington. Yet before the event could take place there was, in the words of a Society official, "one difficult corner to turn—the color question." This official explained to the staunchly segregationist president that, as a national organization, "having an Agency among colored people with a colored minister at its head, we have certain obligations which we cannot avoid."[79] Despite this obligation, it came to pass on May 7, 1916, that, because of unrecorded backstage maneuvering, the president addressed the Society with no Blacks on the platform. On that occasion, the same Wilson who in 1911 had praised the KJV—"How these pages teem with the masses of mankind! . . . These are the annals of the people— of "the common run of men"—now spoke loftily of how "the Word of God" was "weaving the spirits of men together" throughout the whole world."[80]

Bryan on this score had a somewhat different perspective. Perhaps because of the many defeats he suffered in his political life, perhaps because of his cooperation with conservative forces in his Presbyterian denomination, perhaps because his approach to Scripture made more room for a theological appreciation of Jesus, Bryan was less convinced that progressive effort would succeed by itself in reforming the world. By comparison he seemed somewhat more alert to an existential sense of sin as an ever-present reality threatening even the best political efforts. He was less prone to racism than the strongly segregationist Wilson. His later campaigns against Darwinism were aimed directly at the Anglo-Saxon Social Darwinism that Roosevelt accepted. His resignation as secretary of state indicated that he could see how the biblical story might conflict with American political ideals as well as support them.

But if Bryan's attachment to the Bible allowed him to keep some distance from the civil religion of Roosevelt and Wilson, it did not protect him from the anti-intellectual excesses of his populism. If Bryan retained a sense of the Bible's ability to challenge as well as define America, he rarely acknowledged the increasing pluralism about Scripture within Christian communities or the more general religious pluralism in the nation. During the years when he earned much of his income as a public speaker, one of his most frequently repeated lectures described Christ as "The Prince of Peace."[81] In his later years, as is well known, Bryan became a leader in the crusade against Darwinism. Both "The Prince of Peace" speech and his anti-Darwinism activities distinguished him from many of the era's progressive leaders.[82] Yet they did not explain how Bryan's more explicitly Christian biblical faith could reconcile principles of democratic liberty with his personal evangelical convictions. Not for him was the effort to explain how his biblical Christian faith could be foundational for public life committed also to democratic liberty. Not for him was an effort to articulate an alternative to the ideological Americanism of Wilson and Roosevelt or the biblicist demagoguery some of his own oratory promoted.

The speeches of these three leading statesmen were highlights in the KJV commemorations of 1911. From one angle, they testified to the durability, force, and moral depth of the Bible in American public life. From another, they showed how easily the Bible could become simply the servant of civil religion or a vehicle for unchecked populism.

Given deeply rooted American traditions, it was all but inevitable that sermons memorializing deceased presidents, as well as national celebrations of the KJV, would stress the uniqueness of the nation as much as the universal authority of Scripture. Wilson, Roosevelt, and Bryan were men of their age, which makes their failures as moral leaders all the more poignant; with only a few exceptions, they acted as American leaders have always acted. Most communities of religious minorities shared their civil religion of American exceptionalism to one degree or another. But objections in these communities to the predominantly white and Protestant-inflected articulation of that exceptionalism contribute just as much to an American history of the Bible—and nowhere more obviously than among African Americans who shared trust in Scripture but read it as challenging the dominant culture.

30

Still under a Bushel

In January 1922 Ida B. Wells-Barnett found herself in Little Rock, Arkansas. It was the first time she had returned south of the Mason-Dixon line since she had been driven out of Memphis thirty years earlier for publicizing the lynching of three respected members of the city's African American community. Wells-Barnett had traveled to Little Rock against the backdrop of bickering among local and national civil rights organizations. The infighting arose from debate over who should take the lead in advocating for a dozen Black farmers who had been sentenced to death after a murderous race riot sparked by their refusal to sell their cotton below market prices. Before the organizations could settle their differences, Wells-Barnett acted with characteristic dispatch, writing in the Chicago *Defender* about the scores of Blacks killed in the original riot and sending expedited letters to President Warren G. Harding, various legislators, and the Arkansas governor. Spurred by her appeals, the governor convened a special panel, which included an AME bishop and the president of the largest Black Baptist denomination, that convinced him to order a new trial for the twelve men.

On her arrival in Little Rock, Wells-Barnett joined a group of the prisoners' wives and others who had come to the penitentiary to visit their loved ones. From the prisoners she learned that after the original riot they "were beaten, given electric shocks, and in every possible way terrorized" to make them confess that their farmers' organization existed for the purpose of killing white people and stealing their property. After the prisoners passed on this information, the men and their visitors broke into song, and with such winning effect that the warden brought along a number of his white guests to listen. For two hours the singing, mingled with prayers, continued. Wells-Barnett then gained the attention of the prisoners. She told them she had heard them praying and singing "about dying, and forgiving your enemies, and of feeling sure that you are going to be received in the New Jerusalem because your God knows that you are innocent of the offense for which you expect to be electrocuted."

But then she challenged them. Shortly before, Wells-Barnett had finished a ten-year stint as the teacher of a men's Bible class in one of Chicago's Black Presbyterian churches. She described it as "one of the most delightful periods of my life in Chicago" as "every Sunday we discussed the Bible lessons in a plain common-sense way and tried to make application of their truths to our daily

America's Book. Mark A. Noll, Oxford University Press. © Oxford University Press 2022.
DOI: 10.1093/oso/9780197623466.003.0031

lives." Now to the Little Rock prisoners she put her Bible knowledge to work. "Why," she asked, don't you pray to live and to be freed? The God you serve is the God of Paul and Silas who opened their prison gates [Acts 16], and if you have all the faith you say you have, you ought to believe that he will open your prison doors too." To Wells-Barnett it was time for the prisoners to "quit talking about dying; if you believe your God is all powerful, believe he is powerful enough to open these prison doors, and say so."[1] At their second trial, the accused were acquitted. Years later in Chicago one of the men met Wells-Barnett and thanked her for the peaceful life he had been able to fashion for himself after moving north.

Wells-Barnett's words in Little Rock sustained themes in the Black history of the Bible that had been established long before. The Scriptures certainly inspired confidence that God offered eternal life to all people, including the most despised. But the Bible was also read with the conviction that "the sacred and the secular were not discrete elements in the lives and experiences of black Americans."[2] Although African Americans differed among themselves on scriptural interpretations (though not as much as white Americans did), the understanding that the Bible proclaimed an undivided message of both eternal salvation and temporal redemption remained a prominent interpretive stance. Well into the twentieth century, however, the American public at large paid little or no heed.

An Enduring Presence

For the vast majority of African Americans who throughout the nation's history have turned in any way to the Scriptures, the King James Bible supplied a conceptual frame of reference as well as words of singular power. Innovative scholarship of recent years, especially as showcased in a compendium edited by Vincent Wimbush in 2000, has documented the pervasive biblical presence in the speaking, thinking, singing, and writing of generations of Black Americans stretching from the late eighteenth century to the present.[3] Most obvious has been the biblical imprint on musical expression, from the spirituals first recorded at the time of the Civil War, through the celebrated tours soon thereafter of singers from Fisk University and Hampton Institute and the proliferation of hymnals for the Black denominations that emerged in the half-century after the war, to twentieth-century "gospel" and the surprising presence of Scripture in contemporary rap. What James Abbington has written about that earliest expression is almost as true for later genres: "There is probably no other vocal repertoire in the western world with such imagination and creativity in bringing the Scriptures to life like the Negro spiritual."[4]

In many southern settings as well as in the northern cities to which Blacks streamed in the Great Migration of the early twentieth century, Black churches anchored Black culture. And for the churches, a capacious biblical awareness was always bedrock. What one researcher has written about Black Primitive Baptists in the North Carolina Piedmont obtained widely: "So central a role has the church played in the lives of these families that even people who have never sat down to read the Bible on their own nevertheless have internalized large portions of it."[5]

Decade after decade, writing from and about the nation's Black population testified to that internalization. The themes resonant in the spirituals were the themes expanded, altered, deepened, and sometimes disputed by a full roster of Black voices, many of them already cited in this book. Four examples illustrate adjustments, but also continuity, that extended into the twentieth century.

Examples

Frederick Douglass's engagement with the Bible illustrated how themes of scriptural deliverance that he had first articulated with such force in the 1840s carried on to the end of his life a half-century later. In late 1887, after returning from an overseas trip to Britain and the Continent that had taken him also to Egypt, Douglass described what affected him most. As reported by David Blight in his award-winning biography, Douglass experienced his "greatest thrill of satisfaction" from visiting the sites in Egypt associated with the Old Testament story of Joseph, betrayed by his brothers, sold into Egypt as a slave, and miraculously raised to prominence as the pharaoh's righthand man, which led to Israel's long captivity in Egypt and then their deliverance under Moses. In Blight's rendering, Douglass "had seen the landscape that had given the world the Exodus story. He had seen the ancient roots of his own story."[6] Shortly before embarking on that journey, Douglass had delivered an address in Washington, D.C., at an anniversary celebration of the Emancipation Proclamation that chastised the federal government for abandoning the nation's Black population to the violence of resurgent white nationalism. In a speech that included a reference to the "the blood of Abel" that "cries from the Ground" (Gen 4:10) he repeated a prominent theme from his entire orating life: the divine deliverance of Israel from Egyptian bondage originated the history that African Americans were reliving in their own day.[7] Only weeks before his death in February 1895, Douglass mesmerized the young Black Presbyterian minister Francis Grimké as they sang hymns together. "In the singing," reported Grimké, Douglass "took the leading part," especially a hymn based on Psalm 32:7 by their white contemporary, Fanny Crosby, "Hide thou me."

> In the sight of Jordan's billow,
> Let Thy bosom be my pillow;
> Hide me, O Thou Rock of Ages,
> Safe in Thee.[8]

Much had changed for Douglass since as a young slave he connived to learn to read, but not the centrality of Scripture's prophetic witness in his own remarkable career.

Other spheres of Black life illustrated a similar scripturalism. From the very beginning of Black self-organization, notable leaders joined their white counterparts in speaking out against the abuse of alcohol. Even before Richard Allen founded the Philadelphia church that became the headquarters of the AME, he and Absalom Jones had organized the Free African Society that excluded the "drunkard or disorderly person" from membership.[9] The temperance testimony strengthened considerably during the boom of Black church formation that followed the Civil War, transformed in that era into a campaign for total abstinence. In Atlanta the temperance reforms advocated by the AME connectional system and local Baptist churches played a major role as that city's African American population sought the active citizenship promised by the Civil War's constitutional amendments. Their advocacy in the 1870s and 1880s exploited several strands of argument, including a desire for respectability and a concern for economic self-sufficiency. AME leaders also mirrored the move toward custodial instincts among white Methodists by linking Christian temperance to republican concerns for a virtuous citizenry. But for both Black Methodists and Black Baptists, the Bible remained a fixture. In H. Paul Thompson's well-documented account, "over half the temperance reports cited Scriptural authority by direct quote, summary, or reference, to assert the personal sinfulness of intemperance." As among white reformers, African Americans drew from the same wellspring of passages, which could be applied directly, like Proverbs 20:1 ("Wine is a mocker and strong drink is raging, and whoever is deceived thereby is not wise"), or that served as indirect motivation, like Hebrews 12:1 ("Lay aside very weight and the sin that doth so easily beset us").[10]

On temperance, Black and white church-goers heard a similar message that pictured God enabling the liberation of bodies as well as the redemption of souls. Beyond this one reform, however, much of the white Protestant world was beginning to think in terms of *either* eternal salvation *or* social reform, a distinction resisted among the nation's Black believers.

The life and times of Ida B. Wells (Wells-Barnett after she married Ferdinand Barnett in 1895) showed how that resistance took shape in the nation's most determined opponent of white nationalist terrorism.[11] In 1897 a white minister who had studied at the Southern Baptist seminary in Louisville published "a vindication of the Afro-American race" that documented in great detail the struggles, but also the achievements, of Black Americans. In a work that began by quoting Matthew 23:8 ("For one is your master, even Christ, and all ye are brethren") and Acts 17:26 (God making all nations from "one blood") and that claimed "there are more professing Christians (Protestants) among [African Americans] in proportion to numbers than of any body of people in the world," it was not surprising that Scripture served the author when he wrote about Wells. For her campaign against lynching, which had begun five years earlier and was still going strong, Norman Wood called Wells "a modern Deborah" in memory of the Hebrew judge who led a campaign to free the Israelites (Judg chapters 4–5). With reference to lynchings carried out by immolation, he declared that she had portrayed these outrages with "a flame of righteousness" that "by God's grace will never be extinguished until a Negro's life is as safe in Mississippi and Tennessee as in Massachusetts or Rhode Island."[12]

Ida Wells, who was born in 1862 as a slave in a small northern Mississippi town, was sent to a missionary-conducted school with her siblings shortly after the end of the Civil War. Her mother, Lizzie, attended with her children until she too learned to read the Bible, after which time she and her husband, James, made Scripture a center of their family's life. On Sundays no reading was permitted except the Scriptures, which meant that Wells read the Bible several times through while still very young. (Figure 30.1)

For Wells, the Bible remained a steady resource in a writing career that began with columns in a magazine from the National Baptist Convention and continued as she worshiped in AME churches and then with the Chicago Presbyterians. In her reforming activity, as in her challenge to the Arkansas farmers, Wells used Scripture mostly to support her campaigns for universal justice and Black communal resilience. Although she did not channel the Bible like David Walker or her contemporary Amanda Berry Smith, she did not forget the sacred volume she had read so diligently in her youth.

Wells's approach in the antilynching articles, books, and speeches that followed the Memphis outrage of 1892 was intensely empirical. As a self-described "student of American sociology," she urged all whom she could convince simply to "tell the world the facts."[13] In the torrent of works where she followed that plan—*Southern Horrors: Lynch Law in All Its Phases* (1892), *The Reason Why the Colored American Is Not in the World's Columbia Exposition* (with Frederick Douglass, 1893), *A Red Record: Tabulated Statistics and Alleged Causes of Lynchings in the United States 1892–1893–1894* (1895), *Lynch Law in Georgia* (1899)—the Bible sometimes supplied examples, metaphors, and charged language. In an interview for a British periodical, for example, she defended her claim that "the dark race ... is the most practically Christian known to history" with a catena of texts: "Who has ever shown himself 'meek in spirit [Matt 5:5; 1 Cor 4:21]' if not

Figure 30.1 For Ida B. Wells the Bible remained a stable part of the worldview from which she campaigned against lynching in the 1880s and 1890s, and then later on behalf of Black self-improvement and women's suffrage.

the negro? Who, if not he, has for centuries answered not again, turned the left cheek when smitten on the right [Matt 5:39], blessed them that persecuted him, prayed for those that despitefully used him [Matt 5:44]?"[14]

Yet with her older friend Douglass, Wells devoted more energy arguing for how a Bible-based religion should function than in quoting chapter and verse. In 1894 she told a British audience, "[O]ur American Christians are too busy saving the souls of white Christians from burning in hell-fire to save the lives of black ones from present burning in fires kindled by white Christians."[15] During that same trip she described a sermon on Hebrews 10:31 ("it is a fearful thing to fall into the hands of the Almighty God") as "the most wonderful . . . I have ever heard in my life." But that judgment was influenced by the fact that the preacher, Charles Frederic Aked, who hosted Wells during this British trip, helped her "to uproot my natural distrust and suspicion" of whites.[16] The Bible, though not always front and center in her advocacy was nonetheless never far away.

Early in the motion-picture era other African Americans turned more directly to Scripture as they addressed the public. The great success of D. W. Griffith's

Birth of a Nation, which was released in 1915 as a cinematic version of the Rev. Thomas Dixon's novel *The Clansman*, posed a sharp challenge to African Americans and a small number of whites who were together appalled by the film's egregious racism. Several times in *The Birth of a Nation* Griffith deployed biblical words or images to emphasize the degeneracy of African Americans and the nobility of the Ku Klux Klan in triumphing over Reconstruction's despicable regimes. Most dramatic were the movie's closing scenes that mixed visions of civilized whites triumphing over bestial Blacks with apocalyptic images of Jesus coming to establish a millennial reign of joyful peace.[17]

Leaders of a relatively new organization, the National Association for the Advancement of Colored People, tried, but in vain, to block showings of the movie.[18] They also developed plans with other interested parties to mount a cinematic counterattack. From this effort eventually came a 1919 movie directed by John W. Noble and entitled *The Birth of a Race*. While neither an artistic nor a commercial success, the film did publicize a completely different understand of scriptural teaching.[19]

Like the Griffith epic, *The Birth of a Race* made a series of grand statements about well-known American heroes and patriotic events that, as the film put it, created for the first time "a government of the people, for the people and by the people." Seventy of the film's ninety minutes, however, featured four biblical episodes—the creation of Adam and Eve, Noah and the flood, Moses and the Exodus from Egypt, and the life and passion of Jesus—all set forth as defining a charter of "Equality" for all humanity. The film depicted the family of Noah not as the contentious clan producing the so-called curse of Canaan but as a unit living together in harmony. Moses received the movie's most extensive treatment as the one who called for "the liberation of his people." Then, as head shots from Africa, the Far East, and Europe flashed on the screen, Jesus appeared as a teacher of "all races," with the declaration "Christ made no distinction between them—His teachings were for all." The biblical portion of the film ended with the crucifixion, depicted as Roman retribution for Jesus's effort to teach "equality instead of slavery."

The film's final twenty minutes, with a rapid jumble of Christopher Columbus, Paul Revere, signers of the Declaration of Independence, Abraham Lincoln, and racially integrated troops marching off to World War I, sustained the same message. With perhaps dubious theology but a definite word for the times, it described Lincoln's assassination as kindling "the torch of freedom—which today is the Light of the World." The Bible in this film echoed much of the standard civil religion of white Americans. It differed significantly from *The Birth of a Nation*, however, by insisting that the race singled out for special divine consideration in Scripture was the human race.

The Bible did not function identically for the elderly Frederick Douglass, the Atlanta temperance advocates, Ida B. Wells, and the sponsors of *The Birth of a Race*. Yet in different ways all spoke from a hermeneutic that allowed the Bible to proclaim hope for this life as well as the life to come.

Intellectual Maturity

During the half-century after the Civil War, African American communities reaped mature intellectual fruit from roots that had been firmly established before the conflict. About this intellectual maturation two matters are especially noteworthy. First, it took place while terrorists violently resisted the economic, educational, and social promises held out by emancipation; while the nation's white powerbrokers, including its white church leaders, ignored or even supported that terrorism; while scientific racism gained a secure foothold in leading academic circles as a new rationale for segregation; while conservative white Protestants, in pushing back against scientific racism, revived "the curse of Canaan" to justify the American caste system; and while most white reformers turned aside from civil rights to champion temperance as their primary concern. In other words, African American intellectual life deepened despite active resistance or studied national indifference.

Second, the internalization of Scripture in Black churches played a prominent part in driving these intellectual efforts. Historians are aware of how contrasting religious emphases informed the standoff over means and ends between Booker T. Washington and W. E. B. Du Bois. Washington's recommendation of regular church attendance and daily Bible reading fit well with his belief that Black responsibility in industrial vocations could overcome the challenges of Jim Crow. Du Bois acknowledged the importance of Black churches for promoting education and providing organizational infrastructure, but he looked to aggressive mobilization of a Black "talented tenth" for achieving civic and political equality.[20] Going beyond that important division, however, allows for a fuller picture of Black intellectual life. As churches strengthened organizationally, the Bible was taken for granted. For a growing number of solid theological expressions, it remained foundational. It also featured prominently in sophisticated efforts to reinterpret Black history alongside aggressive efforts to link African Americans with Africa.

In *The Soul of Black Folks* (1903), Du Bois heralded the AME church as "the greatest Negro organization in the world."[21] Although African American adherence to Baptist churches grew faster, the connectional system of the AME fostered a remarkable advance of outreach, education, uplift, and cohesion.[22]

Efforts by the AME Zion and the Colored Methodist church were not far beyond, as they also channeled energy through the authority bestowed upon bishops and in regional circuits, annual state meetings, and the "general conferences" held at four-year intervals. The system that had done so much to Christianize the nation under Francis Asbury now gave unusual strength to Black churches and their communities.

For the AME, the episcopal career of Daniel Alexander Payne, which stretched from his ordination in 1852 to his death in 1893, illustrated the dynamics at work.[23] (Figure 30.2) Even as many in his denomination resisted Payne's efforts to impose biblical order in the Wesleyan mode, his leadership left an enduring mark. Payne was born in Charleston, South Carolina, less than a decade before the Denmark Vesey conspiracy, from which, however, his family carefully distanced itself. As a studious young man benefiting from some formal training but mostly independent reading, Payne established a successful school

Figure 30.2 Throughout his decades of service to the African Methodist Episcopal church, Bishop Daniel Alexander Payne combined a traditional Methodist dependence on Scripture with practical programs to enhance Black education, respectability, and family stability.

Source: LOC, Prints & Photographs, LC-DIG-bellcm-02865.

for young Blacks that was shut down when South Carolina outlawed the education of slaves. He then left the South, graduated from the Lutherans' Gettysburg
Theological Seminary, and served briefly as a Lutheran minister before joining
the much more congenial AME. From the start Payne campaigned to raise the
educational standards of the Black pastorate, a goal he furthered by purchasing
Ohio's Wilberforce University in 1863 and making it, with its theological school,
the lodestar of AME educational efforts. Payne's campaign for advanced ministerial training and decorum in public worship dismayed some in the AME
who favored direct reliance on the Spirit, refused to retire the spirituals that
Payne disparaged, and cultivated the passionate emotions that had sustained
religion under slavery. Against such pressure, Payne maintained that only the
scripturalism of Richard Allen's founding vision could enable Black Christianity
to build a culture even as it redeemed a people.

The energies Payne poured into Wilberforce, considerable travel, and his
episcopal duties sustained much of the vision that John and Charles Wesley had
communicated to inspire Francis Asbury and Richard Allen. That vision shone
clearly when, at an advanced age and as the AME's senior bishop, Payne was asked
to speak twice at its General Conference of 1888. For the assembly's featured
sermon, he preached from a catena of passages that described the Christian ministry as fulfilling the lofty ideals of the Old Testament priesthood. The sermon
expounded Malachi 3 ("Behold, I will send my messenger, and he shall prepare
the way before me") and Deuteronomy 23 (on the tribe of Levi commissioned
as Israel's priests) to inform his account of the Apostle Paul's charge to Christian
leaders from 1 Timothy 3 and 4 ("A bishop must be blameless"). When he was
asked to preach the ordination sermon for four new bishops, Payne turned to
what Christians of the era routinely understood as the messianic promises of
Isaiah chapter 11. For Payne, "the spirit of wisdom and understanding" (verse
2) that he viewed as perfectly revealed in Jesus was the spirit into which ministers
were called: "I beg you to follow this example, and struggle with Christ until you
are conformed to him."[24]

Payne's vision of an educated Black ministry promoting the highest standards
of propriety and decorum never dominated the AME, but the ideals he
championed certainly paid off. Dennis Dickerson has documented how successful AME preachers became in displaying levels of biblical expertise long
characteristic of the white pastorate. With Georgia as an example (an AME
membership by 1900 of 140,000 in at least one thousand churches) he shows
that Black ministers were delivering high-quality exegetical and ecclesiological
sermons alongside more traditional evangelistic efforts. Breadth of learning now
accompanied traditional depth of zeal. In 1896, Dr. T. W. Henderson preached
a sermon to the North Georgia Annual Conference on Psalm 34:8 ("O taste and
see that the Lord is good: blessed is the man that trusteth in him"). An observer

reported that "he came sinner-hunting, and before he closed thirty-two fell at the altar begging for mercy." A few years later the Rev. S. D. Roseborough addressed the Southwest Georgia Annual Conference on John 10:11 ("The good shepherd gives his life for his sheep"). With citations from Ezekiel 34 and Zechariah 11 that described shepherds who failed in their duties, Roseborough drew a contrasting portrait of the good minister-shepherds who "attend flocks, leading them to the folds, pastures, and waters." Dr. W. G. Alexander, the dean of Turner Theological Seminary, followed soon thereafter at the Georgia Annual Conference with an ordination sermon on Psalm 32:8 ("I will instruct thee and counsel thee in the way which thou shalt go)." From it he developed four points: "God, the Greatest Instructor, The Way We Should Go, God, the Great Counselor, God Will Execute His Promises."[25] The Bible whose narratives continued to inspire was becoming the Bible taught with exegetical skill.

In the century's latter decades, the noteworthy public oratory that had graced Black communities from the time of Henry Hosier and Richard Allen followed white precedent by finding its way into print. As a noteworthy example, volumes of sermons published by Alexander Crummell in 1882 and 1891 revealed this sui generis Episcopalian Africanist as a pulpit master. Crummell, whom Du Bois ranked with Bishop Payne as the greatest leaders of nineteenth-century Black America, lived anything but a complacent life.[26] Born in New York City in 1819, he was denied entrance into the Episcopalians' General Theological Seminary because of his race but gained a thorough education nonetheless through short stints at several American institutions, including Yale College, and eventually at Queen's College, Cambridge, where he was awarded a bachelor's degree in 1853. Despite the initial rebuff, he was ordained to the Episcopalian ministry in 1844. After he completed his time at Cambridge, the American Episcopalians commissioned Crummell as a missionary to Liberia, where he served for two decades as church organizer, editor, educator, and promoter of African civil society. Upon his return to the United States in 1873 he became the rector of St. Luke's Episcopal in Washington, D.C., and then a professor at Howard University.

Crummell's sermons were strong on the necessity of reason, in which he had been tutored at Cambridge, as well as on the need for purposeful moral action, an imperative he drew from experience in both America and Liberia. His sermons featured these themes in the context of traditional Protestant orthodoxy. Jesus, for example, was revealed by the Scriptures, which offered "the grandest ideas and principles which ever entered the mind of man . . . and which could only be of divine origin," as announcing the purest truth. But he was also revealed in the gospels as purest love, the one who "receiveth sinners and eateth with them." The story of Joseph told in the book of Genesis gave needy humans the finest pre-Christian illustration of "the tone and value of virtue," which in turn allowed Crummell to emphasize that "all virtue is evangelical; it comes from God." An ability to riff off of Old Testament texts that he shared with his most adept white peers was on display in the passionate memorial he preached in 1882 for his life-long friend, the Presbyterian minister Hugh Henry Garnet. With a text from Zechariah 11:2 ("Howl figtree; for the cedar is fallen") Crummell expatiated masterfully on Garnet's life as a preacher, militant abolitionist, temperance advocate, Liberty Party stalwart, proponent of African colonization organized by African Americans, and U.S. minister to Liberia.[27]

Opportunities for more and better education paved the way not only for the publishing of memorable sermons but also for substantial Bible-based theology. Methodists, like the Rev. T. G. Steward, D.D., led the way. Born free in 1843 in New Jersey, Steward graduated from the Episcopal Divinity School in Philadelphia. After the Civil War he served as an AME missionary establishing churches in South Carolina and Georgia. Later he carried out missionary work in Haiti, served as a chaplain to Black U.S. soldiers in the Philippines, and ended as a teacher of French and logic at Wilberforce University.[28]

The nuanced discussion of human origins in Steward's *Genesis Re-Read* from 1885 marked new depth in African American biblical exposition. To Steward, it was important to stress that while Scripture "sheds an unborrowed light upon the moral and spiritual phases of life . . . it also receives light from the facts of nature discovered by the industry and attention of man." From this interpretive standpoint, Steward affirmed the Mosaic authorship of Genesis and defended the truthfulness of the Genesis record, since if that book was "overthrown . . . the entire basis of the evangelical system of faith would be removed, and much of the Epistles would be rendered meaningless. Christian theology would be impossible." In his discussion considering various theories of origins, he quoted James McCosh, president of Princeton, to defend the unity of humankind. Yet as Steward accepted the positive contributions of contemporary scientists, he did "not regard the evidences of evolution as in any way affecting the credibility of the Bible."[29] With this book Steward gave his African American readership a combination of traditional theology and accommodation to evolution that paralleled the conclusions of other theologians like Benjamin B. Warfield and scientists like Asa Gray.

A few years after Steward's study of Genesis appeared, another AME minister, James Embry, published the denomination's first systematic theology, a work that would long be studied by candidates for the ministry. Embry, who later became a bishop, was managing the denomination's Book Concern when in 1890 he published his *Digest of Christian Theology, Designed for the Use of Beginner*. While Embry kept his target audience of "beginners" in view, he also wanted them to know that he had thoroughly studied the works of John Wesley, consulted several English-language Bible translations along with the Greek New Testament and the Latin Vulgate, and "many other books . . . too numerous to mention."

His *Digest*, which stressed the integrity and reliability of Scripture, took a more conservative position than Steward on the creation of Adam and Eve—"No evolution here, from the lower forms of life." Yet like Steward, he took pains to rebut the theories of polygenesis that respected scientific voices of the era promoted. With nine separate scriptures beyond Genesis 1–3, Embry reached a categorical conclusion: "Every attempt to disprove the common origin and unity of man is the instigation of human pride whose aim is to degrade and dishonor some less fortunate variety . . . of the human family."[30]

Beyond Methodist circles, a similar process of formalization was at work. The same year that Embry's *Digest* appeared, an Alabama Baptist, Charles Octavius Boothe, published a manual entitled *Plain Theology for Plain People*. Boothe, born enslaved 1845, had served with the Freedman's Bureau, filled leadership positions at Selma University and with the Colored Baptist Missionary Convention, and for several years edited a periodical for Alabama's Black Baptists. His theological primer arose from passionate commitment to literacy and racial uplift. The *Digest*, which resembled the Bible readings published by white dispensationalists, did not circulate as widely as the books for connectional Methodists. Yet its careful arrangement of texts (two affirming God's creation of the world, five explaining the universal scope of providence, sixteen on the authority of Scripture) provided a regular account of biblical teaching that for Baptists who, like their Methodist peers, sought a more systematic grasp of the faith.[31]

In the development of more sophisticated general theology, millennial and apocalyptic themes that supported a growing African consciousness received particular emphasis. In the immediate wake of the Civil War, Black preachers and periodicals turned increasingly to Acts 17:26 (God "hath made of one blood all nations of men") as they promoted the goal of full American citizenship. As the years rolled by, the same text bolstered opposition to scientific racism and drew attention to Africa.[32] Shortly after publishing *Genesis Re-Read*, T. G. Steward brought out a full-scale interpretation of End Times filled with careful references to the work of recognized biblical scholars from throughout the Protestant world. Like many others in his day, he described "the visions of Nebuchadnezzar and Daniel in the Old Testament, and in the wonderful vision of St. John in the New" as foretelling the successive rise and fall of worldly powers. Yet his conventional interpretive procedures supported an unconventional reading keyed not to the dispensations specified by C. I. Scofield but to the racism of his era. The Day of the Lord would come, Steward concluded, but in coming it would overcome "Saxon domination . . . these bloody knife-men" who always upheld "clan" over "civil liberty" and who were promoting nothing "but the old pro-slavery doctrine revamped."[33]

At the end of the century, J. W. Hood, the AME Zion pastor whose church-planting in North Carolina was noted in an earlier chapter, published a detailed commentary on the Book of Revelation, which for half a century he had been studying along with a wide range of academic literature. Hood's active life included labor with the Freedman's Bureau, several positions in North Carolina's Reconstruction government devoted especially to improving Black schools, founding and leading Livingstone College in Salisbury, North Carolina, and many services for the Republican Party. Although his commentary was less overtly political than the expositions by Handy or Steward, Hood's scholarly treatment testified to a remarkable depth of learning by the representatives of yet another Black Methodist tradition.[34]

A natural affinity linked such apocalyptic expositions and the Pan-Africanism that became stronger as the promise of Reconstruction faded. Black schemes for African settlement varied almost as much as found in the white-dominated American Colonization Society, but they differed by drawing more consistently on the sacred text. Alexander Crummell's published sermons reflected his leadership in promoting cultural and Christian advance in Africa. In an 1863 sermon from his time in Libera titled "Emigration: An Aid to the Evangelization of Africa," Crummell peached on Deuteronomy 26:1–11, a passage describing God's protection of Israel as he brought them out of Egyptian bondage into the Promised Land. To Crummell this text spoke just as clearly about what God could accomplish if African Americans would move en masse to Africa. He ended by quoting Psalm 68:31, as so many others had done: "[T]he tide of salvation, sweeping along, in one broad, mighty current, shall bear along the masses of thy people to salvation and to glory; and then 'Ethiopia,' from the Mediterranean to the Cape, from the Atlantic Ocean to the Indian, 'shall soon stretch forth her hands unto God.'" Two years later, during a visit to the United States, Crummell preached before the Pennsylvania Colonization Society on the Great Commission of Matthew 28:19 ("Go ye therefore, and teach all nations") in a sermon titled "The Regeneration of Africa." That exposition spotlighted missionary and indigenous African exertion as heralding that regeneration.[35]

After resettling permanently in America, Crummell delivered a particularly powerful sermon based on a short section of Isaiah 61:7 ("For your shame ye shall have double, and for confusion they shall rejoice in their portion"). God, according to Crummell, dealt in two ways with nations: either to destroy them or to refine them through trials. As he had done with Israel, so Crummell proclaimed, he was now doing with the Black population of his day: "We have seen . . . the great truth that when God does not destroy a people, but, on the contrary, trains and disciplines it, it is an indication that He intends to make something of them and to do something for them." Not quite on the level of Israel, "but parallel, in a lower degree," Crummell held that "the Negro" should believe that "God presides, with sovereign care, over such a people; and will surely preserve, educate, and build them up."[36]

A speech by Crummell promoting an African vision for Black Americans particularly inspired Henry McNeal Turner, whom we earlier saw learning to read with the help of angels. In the generation after the collapse of Reconstruction, Turner, now an AME bishop, became the most widely recognized pan-Africanist. As a bishop Turner would be the key figure in establishing a branch of the AME in South Africa. The Bible for Turner contributed only one part of an Africanist ideology that, as James Campbell summarized, "was a curious amalgam of racial chauvinism, evangelical Protestantism, and Social Darwinism."[37] In 1895 Turner became notorious, and later celebrated, for declaring as a guest speaker at the first assembly of the National Baptist Convention, "I believe God is a Negro. Negroes should worship a God who is a Negro." For the National Baptists, Henry Lyman Morehouse responded with alarm. Turner's claim was "blasphemous" because "God is not a God of any nationality or any race, but of the whole human family; and as to color—*God is a Spirit* to be worshipped by renewed spirits in whatever colored bodies for a time they tabernacle on earth." When Turner mounted a defense three years later in his own journal, the *Voice of Missions*, he explained why his particular claim carried a universal message. "We have as much right biblically and otherwise," he wrote, "to believe that God is a Negro, as you . . . white people have to believe that God is a fine looking symmetrical and ornamental man." Against the notion that "God is a white-skinned, blue-eyed, straight-haired, projecting-nosed compressed-lipped and finely-robed white gentleman," Turner declared there was no "hope for a race of people who do not believe that they look like God." This logic fueled Turner's promotion of Black emigration to Africa, writing, "[A]s long as we remain among whites, the Negro will believe that the devil is black and that the Negro favors the devil and that God is white and the Negro bears no resemblance to Him."[38] Although Turner did not feature proof-texting in his appeal, the Scriptures that had spoken to him when he first learned to read remained part of the message he hoped other Black Americans would heed.

In the final decades of the nineteenth century, increasingly sophisticated ethnographies paralleled the rise of increasingly passionate Pan-Africanism. James W. C. Pennington's *Textbook of the Origin and History &etc. of the Colored People* from 1841 had pioneered such studies, a form that William Wells Brown extended with a book from 1874, *The Rising Sun; or, the Antecedents and Advancement of the Colored Race*. Four decades earlier Brown had escaped from Kentucky and the slavery into which he had been born. As an abolitionist on the British circuit in the early 1850s he published the first novel by an African American, *Clotel;*

or, The President's Daughter, a work in which reverence for the Bible played an important part.[39] Brown's ethnography from 1874 displayed the same reverence by beginning with an extensive discussion of "the Ethiopians and the Egyptians." In detailing that ancient history, Brown enlisted Homer, Josephus, and other ancient sources, but with Scripture prominent, to follow Pennington's refutation of the "curse of Canaan" (Gen 9) and the "curse of Cain" (Gen 4). Brown brought to a close this discussion, which grounded the entire work, with an ethnographic conclusion followed immediately by a biblical warrant. First ethnography: "Although the descendants of Cush were black, it does not follow all the offspring of Ham were dark-skinned; but only those who settled in a climate that altered their color." Then the Bible: "The word of God by his servant Paul has settled forever the question of the equal origin of the human race, and it will stand good against all scientific research. 'God hath made of one blood all the nations of men for to dwell on all the face of the earth [Acts 17:26].' "[40]

The same year that Brown published *Rising Sun*, George Washington Williams became the first Black student to graduate from the white Northern Baptists' Newton Theologian Seminary.[41] Williams had earlier served as a Union soldier. Later he became the pastor of Boston's Twelfth Baptist Church, but he would also work as a lawyer and a journalist and be elected the first African American to serve in the Ohio legislature. In 1882 this multitalented Baptist minister extended the work of Pennington and Brown by publishing a comprehensive history of "the Negro Race in America," from the 1619 arrival of the first indentured Blacks to his own day. Williams began this work of well over a thousand pages with the chapter "The Unity of Mankind," which directly challenged the earlier American ethnologists as well as his contemporaries, such as the "Ariel" authors. To rebut assertions that denied the full humanity of Africans, Williams expounded upon the creation accounts of Genesis chapters 1 and 2, highlighted an assertion from the Babel story (Gen 11:6, "Behold, the people is one and they all have one language"), and again quoted the Apostle Paul from Acts 17:26 (God "hath made of one blood all nations of men"). His further biblical argument included detailed references from the Apostle Paul concerning the unity of all humanity in Adam; he explained that the Simon conscripted to carry Jesus's cross (Lk 23:26) was an African from Cyrene; and he cited copious material from Scripture and ancient histories to discredit the "curse of Canaan" from Genesis chapter 9. As Williams ended this opening chapter of his massive work, he set its conceptual framework by concluding that "the human race is *one*, and . . . Noah's curse was not a divine prophecy."[42]

Hardly more than a century after the first African Americans broke into print, a small but growing company of well-read Black preachers and preacher-scholars were making their intellectual mark. They were moving fast, but not leaving the Bible behind.

Francis J. Grimké

The career of Francis Grimké exemplified the highest level of Black scripturalism. It also provides a compelling example of the characteristic holism with which many African Americans continued to approach the Scriptures.[43] (Figure 30.3) In his long service at Washington's Fifteenth Street Presbyterian Church that lasted, with one brief interruption, from the late 1870s into the 1930s, Grimké preached a thoroughly traditional theology and was just as thoroughly committed to the pursuit of racial justice. Near the end of his life, he penned a brief profession of faith that underscored the principal themes of his lifelong ministry: abiding trust in divine revelation, belief in the unity of humankind, commitment to the hope of Christian redemption, and facility in evoking the Scriptures: "I accept and accept without reservation, the Scriptures of the Old and New Testaments as God's Word, sent to Adam's sinful race and pointing out the only way by which it can be

Figure 30.3 From his pulpit in Washington, D.C.'s Fifteenth Avenue Presbyterian Church, the Rev. Francis Grimké preached sermons grounded in Scripture, supported a wide range of Black reform movements, and campaigned tirelessly for African American civil rights.

Source: New York Public Library, Schomburg Center for Research in Black Culture, Photographs and Prints Division.

saved. [W]ithout the Holy Scriptures and what they reveal, there is no hope for humanity. To build on anything else is to build on sand [Matt 7:24–26]."[44] This Presbyterian pastor, who befriended the elderly Douglass and who did not hesitate to commend and chastise the president of the United States, was one of the great, if still unheralded, figures of his age.[45]

Grimké's father, Henry, was the brother of Sarah and Angelina. For many years the sisters did not know that Henry had fathered three sons, their nephews, with Nancy Weston, a slave taken as a common-law wife after the sisters' mother died. Francis Grimké, born in 1850, enjoyed his father's protection during his first years, but after Henry passed away he was himself enslaved during the Civil War. After Emancipation and through the efforts of a northern teacher employed by a segregated Charleston school, Francis made his way to Lincoln University in Pennsylvania. He then pursued legal studies at Howard University, but decided during that time to train for the ministry at Princeton Theological Seminary. During his three years at that institution (1875–78), he won the respect of the elderly Charles Hodge ("equal to the ablest of his students"), Hodge's son and successor, A. A. Hodge ("a very able man, highly educated, and of high character), and James McCosh, president of Princeton College ("I have heard him preach and I feel as if I could listen to such preaching with profit from Sabbath to Sabbath").[46] The year he graduated and was called to the Washington church, he married Charlotte Forten, the daughter of a notable family of Philadelphia reformers. The day after her death in 1914 he began a journal of "thoughts and meditations" that he continued until shortly before his own death in 1937. Besides its frequent expression of love for his departed wife, this revealing record's 640 printed pages was filled with reflections on Scripture, meditations on the saving work of Christ, reiteration of the necessity for Christianity to be an actively lived religion, and expressions urging racial justice. The burdens of his advancing years mirrored the emphases of his life.

Grimké was never a doctrinaire believer, as indicated by his appreciation for the AME's Payne and the Episcopalian Crummell.[47] Carter Woodson recorded that Grimké did maintain high doctrinal standards when he listened to other preachers, especially on guard for "any tendency toward modernism." Yet although "there was not a scintilla of such thought in his preaching," Grimké could celebrate individuals like William Lloyd Garrison, John Greenleaf Whittier, and Theodore Roosevelt even if they did not share the particulars of his piety.[48]

Grimké was also numbered among the few Protestants of his era who sustained the range of voluntary causes pursued by antebellum reformers. Typical was his strong support for traditional family life, strict moral guidance to young people, and especially his advocacy for temperance. Grimké's sermons on that subject, including one titled "Temperance and the Negro Race" that he preached many times around the turn of the century, acknowledged the debilities under which African Americans lived. But he did not hesitate to say that "after we have made every allowance for prejudice and injustice," the record of Black intemperance was "still alarmingly large" and a problem to be addressed by Blacks themselves.[49]

He was not, however, typical in keeping his passion for racial justice uppermost alongside other reforms. In 1897 Grimké joined Alexander Crummell and W. E. B. Du Bois in establishing the American Negro Academy, an organization to encourage Black academic achievement that he served for two decades as treasurer. He also supported the Niagara movement of 1905, led by Du Bois, and in 1909 helped establish the National Association of the Advancement of Colored People.

Grimké's comments on Du Bois from a later period shone light on how he assessed his own priorities. First was the commendation that when "men, like DuBois . . . speak on economics, or on the civil and political rights of the Negro as an American citizen," they could be "safely followed." But he worried, because "when it comes to religion and morality . . . they are far, far out of the way as tested by the Word of God and the ideals and principles of Jesus Christ." He specified his ideal in a comment on a speech by Du Bois at Howard that "attempted to scoff at religion and to ridicule prayer": "What the race needs, more than anything else, are moral and spiritual leaders—men who fear God and are committed to the great ideals an principles set forth in the Scriptures of the Old and New Testament, and in the character and life of Jesus Christ."[50] In Grimké's eyes, Frederick Douglass had been such a one.[51]

Grimké's commitment to gospel proclamation, traditional morality, and the development of African American character could make him sound on some occasions like an advocate of "the spirituality of the church." Since, according to those who followed James Henley Thornwell's memorable definition, God had "ordained [the Church] for spiritual purposes," involvement in political life, with "its changes and caprices," should remain outside "the province of the Church."[52] As an example, in 1892, at the very time the violent imposition of Jim Crow was overtaking much of the South, Grimké proclaimed that African American "character" was the key factor for "race elevation."[53] In an 1919 address reviewing Reconstruction, he stressed almost exclusively "the spiritual needs of men" that were and were not met in Reconstruction efforts.[54] When he later defined "Christ's Program for the Saving of the World," he sounded more like an early apolitical Methodist than a proponent of the Social Gospel. Christianity, he affirmed, was primarily defined by "the publication of God's plan for the saving of sinners—namely, repentance and faith in Jesus Christ."[55]

Yet unlike many white religious leaders, Grimké did not follow the bifurcation common in his day. The same preacher who could expound so eloquently on the spiritual imperatives of Christian faith also spoke constantly about the

imperative for believers to *live out* their faith, especially the imperative to oppose race prejudice with all their might. In a preaching career full of explicitly
Christian appeals for racial justice, a series of four lecture-sermons from late
1898 or early 1899 were especially memorable. He delivered them on the heels of
the violent coup by white terrorists that ousted the elected Black and Republican
officials of Wilmington, North Carolina.[56]

For all four sermons his text came from Psalm 27:14, "Wait on the
Lord; be of good courage, and He shall strengthen thine heart." The first,
"Discouragements: Hostility of the Press, Silence and Cowardice of the Pulpit,"
detailed the realities confronting the nation's Black communities (violence in the
South, white indifference, silence from the churches) but urged his congregation
to remember how God had strengthened Elijah and Moses when they despaired.
The second pointed to "the general government" and "political parties" as
"sources from which no help may be expected." It provided a primer in American
history in order to praise the examples of the most ardent earlier abolitionists,
especially Frederick Douglass but also John Brown. The third found reasons for
hope: "Signs of a Brighter Future." Those signs included more wealth and education for Blacks, along with a growing number of white allies. But foremost
Grimké dared to hope "because I have faith in the power of the religion of the
Lord Jesus Christ to conquer all prejudices, to break down all walls of separation,
and to weld together men of all races in one great brotherhood."[57]

The fourth, "God and Prayer as Factors in the Struggle," returned to primarily
scriptural exposition. It began with references to Abraham, Isaac, and Jacob and
the confident word of Moses when Israel was caught between the Red Sea and
the advancing Egyptian army: "Stand still and see the salvation of the Lord [Ex
14:13]." He told of a discouraged Frederick Douglass who once in a speech "was
going on in this dismal strain when he was interrupted by Sojourner Truth, who
said, 'Is God dead, Frederick?'" Then in a parade of biblical exhortations Grimké
included this admonition: "[I]n praying we must not stop with self, we must not
forget to pray also for those who are oppressing us, who have their heels upon
our neck, and whose cry is 'this is a white man's government.' Jesus himself says,
'Pray for them which despitefully use and persecute you [Matt 5:44].'"[58]

The torrent of Grimké's spoken and written words—sermons, addresses,
pamphlets, articles, letters—returned consistently to the themes of these
sermons. Some brought lessons of history, others analyzed current events, many
chastised white indifference, a great number criticized the failings of African
Americans, but all drew explicitly or implicitly on a biblical understanding of
Christian truth.

Grimké's career as a Presbyterian revealed with particular clarity the stark
challenges of his day. This part of his life was especially poignant as it reprised
the earlier denominational retreat on racial issues we have noted from the late

eighteenth century into the 1830s. When he enrolled at Princeton Seminary, Grimké not only won the respect of his professors; he also experienced a promising social situation as the seminary's handful of Blacks joined the other students to live in the seminary's dormitory. One of these fellow students, Matthew Anderson, reported favorably on the absence of prejudice he had experienced at the seminary and also on the help that President McCosh of Princeton College provided in counteracting the race prejudice of white students at the college. Anderson, who maintained his friendship with Grimké, would go on to pastor Philadelphia's Berean Presbyterian Church and become a forceful advocate for Black civil rights.[59]

As Jim Crow advanced, however, Princeton Seminary gave way. In 1914, a young Black student informed Grimké that he was "pleased with the Seminary" but angered that its housing was now segregated. Four years later Grimké wrote to the organizers of his fortieth class reunion to protest against the institution's retreat. When they would meet after death "around the throne," Grimké reminded his classmates, "the color of a man's skin or his race identity, will count for nothing there, and ought not to count for anything here, certainly among people calling themselves Christians."[60]

Grimké's combination of strongly spiritual commitments and strong opposition to discrimination also guided his denominational activities. On May 27, 1904, a memorable intervention on the floor of the northern church's General Assembly (PCUSA) allowed him to state his position. At issue was the proposed reunion of the largely southern Cumberland Presbyterian Church with his northern church. It was a reunion facilitated by the PCUSA's recent additions to the Westminster Confession, but also a reunion that the Cumberlands would not consider unless the PCUSA racially segregated its regional units, the presbyteries.[61] Grimké's appeal directly challenged the opinion that "public sentiment" should supersede "the organic law of the church." His words hit hard: "If the Bible is true, if Jesus Christ meant what he said in the Sermon on the Mount and in his other utterances, and if we are to follow His example, and to be influenced by His Spirit, in a word, if Christianity is not a miserable farce, there can be no doubt . . . the duty is to seek to mould public opinion in accordance with Christian principles, and not to be moulded by it."[62] Before the General Assembly, he ended by invoking Martin Luther's words before the Holy Roman emperor in 1521: "Union? Yes; but never at the sacrifice of a great principle; never by the sanctioning of the spirit of caste, or by putting the stamp of inferiority upon any class or race within the Church. Here is where I stand; and here is where the church ought to stand; where it will stand; if it is true to Jesus Christ."[63] The protest failed to sway the General Assembly.

A sobering comparison came from statements by Benjamin B. Warfield on the proposed reunion of Princeton Seminary. Warfield's comments on this occasion are especially telling in light of his rare willingness as a white Presbyterian to publish criticisms of the nation's enduring race prejudice. Yet when Warfield went on record opposing reunion, his opposition stressed only theological issues, with no mention of segregated presbyteries.[64]

Even more discouraging was the result when Grimké spoke out against the General Assembly's decision in his own Washington presbytery. In 1880 he had been elected that presbytery's first Black moderator, but now it voted to segregate itself. On that occasion Grimké's appeal failed despite an impassioned speech of support from the lay elder Justice John Harlan of the U.S. Supreme Court. In his speech Harlan asserted that Christianity "has nothing to do with race, but only with men." It followed reasoning he had expressed in 1896 when he registered a dissent to the Court's authorization of "separate but equal" in its landmark *Plessy v. Ferguson* case: "Our Constitution is color-blind, and neither knows nor tolerates classes among citizens."[65]

As a respected minister, forceful communicator, passionate believer, and dedicated reformer, the Black Presbyterian Grimké stood above his peers in his dedication to the "emancipationist ethos" that in Dennis Dickerson's phrase also remained definitive for the AME. For Grimké, one and the same biblical message opened the door to eternal life and could renew the body politic.[66]

Francis Grimké—like Ida B. Wells, Alexander Crummell, Theophilus Steward, and the producers of *Birth of a Race*—did not speak for all African Americans in the period of Reconstruction, Jim Crow, and the early twentieth century. Yet in the fuller picture of that era, the singular character of Black reliance on Scripture stands out, especially when set against developments in the white world. Few African Americans were caught up in the battles over higher criticism that tied white Protestants in knots. Some entertained visions of a coming millennium, but not as described by C. I. Scofield and premillennial dispensationalists. Many saw Scripture outlining a course for social change but were not theological modernists. Most remained committed biblical supernaturalists but did not follow the path of social disengagement taken by most fundamentalists. Not too many Americans were paying attention, but their day would come.

Epilogue

The central question this book poses for the history of the United States should be obvious: How does a nation created to secure what the Declaration of Independence called the "unalienable right" of liberty protect that liberty while maintaining public order? For the great majority of citizens who addressed this question from the early nineteenth century through the time of the Civil War, there was only one answer. In a republic that had repudiated the authoritative constraints of European Christendom, citizens must cultivate personal virtue through voluntary means or the corruption endemic in old-world tyrannies would destroy republican liberty. Many in that great majority believed the Protestant Bible provided the best means to encourage the personal virtue without which republics were doomed.

In the last decades of the nineteenth century, more and more citizens rejected that conviction about the Protestant Bible. Some may have continued to believe in the importance of sacred scriptures for communal well-being but objected to the imposition of the King James Version (or any Protestant bible) as discriminating against themselves. Large numbers also turned away entirely from religious guides in favor of secular authorities or complete preoccupation with life in this world. Beyond a much more pluralistic religious environment, opinions about the relationship between personal virtue and the health of the nation also evolved. These trends have continued. As the role of government has increased in response to the military and economic crises of the twentieth century, public concern for national well-being has increasingly focused on how its actions (or failures to act) affect the liberty of citizens and the general good. Yet however much the specific history of the Bible from the age of Tom Paine to the era of Woodrow Wilson may now seem a matter of only historical interest, the larger question has not gone away. How does a democracy organized around a set of principles—without a powerful monarchy, a formal aristocracy, a dictator, or an all-powerful party, with only an informal class system and civic authority as a function of wealth, charisma, and inherited privilege—preserve both personal liberty and social order?

A second question should be almost as obvious for this and any other history of the Bible in a particular nation:[1] How may Scripture be deployed to support the health of the body politic in a specific place without being reduced to a utilitarian tool of this-worldly interests and so lose its potential as a spiritual guide

America's Book. Mark A. Noll, Oxford University Press. © Oxford University Press 2022.
DOI: 10.1093/oso/9780197623466.003.0032

for all times and all places? Although only a few Americans addressed this question, while many others were advancing proposals for strengthening the republic with Scripture, the question has been raised from the beginning. In the mid-twentieth century the British literary critic and lay theologian C. S. Lewis put the issue in more general terms: "Foolish preachers, by always telling you how much Christianity will help you and how good it is for society, have actually led you to forget that Christianity is not a patent medicine." He urged that, "[i]f Christianity is untrue," then it should be rejected, "however helpful it may be." By contrast, if it is true, it deserves belief, "even if gives . . . no help at all."[2]

A book treating the question of the Bible and national well-being alongside the question of the Bible's own integrity must attempt final words on several levels. Where the two questions have been so intimately conjoined, as in the history of the United States, it is especially important to avoid simplistic answers.

The Question of the Bible

In the early 2010s a team of scholars organized by the Center for the Study of Religion and Culture at Indiana University–Purdue University Indianapolis (IUPUI) carried out the most extensive survey ever attempted to gauge the public's engagement with sacred writings, including the Bible.[3] Some of the results from two extensive national surveys were predictable—for example, that reading sacred texts correlated with age, gender, region, and education (older, female, and southern Americans reported more personal engagement, less for those with higher levels of education). Given scholarship from earlier research, other results were also not unexpected. Almost exactly half (50.2%) of the respondents reported they had read "the Bible, Torah, Koran, or other religious scriptures" sometime in the previous year (of that number, 78% at least monthly, 54% at least weekly).

At that point, however, things became more interesting. Of those who had read sacred writings, 95% specified the Bible. In addition, regard for the Christian Scriptures seemed to extend well beyond regular church participants:

- Two-thirds of Americans who did *not* read the Bible within the year said they nonetheless regarded it as either "the inerrant Word of God" or the "divinely inspired Word of God."
- The percentage of respondents who read the Bible regularly was greater in the population with no religious affiliation than in several of the groups who told researchers they went to church regularly.

For the purposes of this book, the survey makes clear that, if deference to Scripture no longer dominates public life, the Bible still occupies a remarkably large space in the cultural landscape. In addition, although there is no denying the increased religious pluralism of the contemporary United States, for an overwhelming proportion of the population, "sacred scriptures" still means the Bible. Questions about how to assess these realities, which the events of the nineteenth century brought so clearly to the surface, remain very much alive.

Other important findings of the IUPUI researchers bore even more directly on matters central to this book:

- Although Protestants reported reading the Bible more than Catholics, the margin of difference has become quite small.
- Despite the increasing popularity of many new English-language translations since World War II and despite sales of the KJV now having been exceeded for many years by sales of the New International Version, 55% of Bible readers reported that the KJV remained their reading Bible of choice; of churches surveyed, 40% still used the same translation.[4]
- "The strongest correlation with Bible reading is race," the researchers concluded. "Specifically, black people read the Bible at a higher rate than people of other races, and by a considerable margin. . . . 70% of all blacks said they read the Bible outside of worship at least once in the past year, compared to 44% for whites [and] 46% for Hispanics."[5]
- Regarding motives for Bible reading, the research team concluded that respondents were three times more likely to read the Bible for personal prayer and devotion than for anything having to do with culture war issues like abortion, homosexuality, war, or income inequality.

From such findings it is clear that the era of Bible history defined by Harriet Beecher Stowe, James Pennington, Charles Grandison Finney, Maria Stewart, Abraham Lincoln, Orestes Brownson, Sarah Grimké, and William Jennings Bryan has both passed and goes on. The Bible no longer divides Protestants and Catholics as it once did so decisively, even violently. Especially since the directives from the Second Vatican Council (1962–65) encouraging lay Bible reading, the heirs of Bishop Carroll and Cardinal Gibbons now share practices, fellowship, and sometimes even the same translations with the heirs of Alexander Campbell and George Bourne. But alongside that seismic change is the continued popularity of the KJV. For the great numbers for whom "the Bible" is still the KJV, as well as others who heard this version as youths but then migrated to other translations or away from the Bible altogether, the language of the KJV remains a spiritual mother tongue. (It also means that despite the profusion of modern translations, biblical references in public rhetoric come predominantly from this same source.)

The survey's findings concerning contemporary scriptural usage among African Americans and for reasons people read the Bible can be linked. They reflect the importance of what might be called Methodist or African Methodist traditions. When Francis Asbury directed early Methodists to the Scriptures, he was not motivated by a custodial interest in managing society or a sectarian worry about overreaching centralized power. He had in mind the healing of the nations, not the political health of this nation. Richard Allen's Methodism involved more this-worldly opposition to the bonds of American racism, but without losing the early Methodist fixation on the Scriptures as balm for the sin-sick soul.

As this book has shown, a significant number of other Americans joined in considering the Bible basically (Allen) or only (Asbury) a book of personal redemption that needed protection against extraneous exploitation. This number included the Sandemanian Daniel Humphreys, who worried that attacks on Tom Paine's *Age of Reason* missed the point by defending the Bible as a prop for traditional church structures instead of as an elixir for sinners.[6] From a different angle, it included the anonymous Jewish correspondent who, after the assassination of Lincoln and an outpouring of grief from American Jewry, declared that things had gone too far in likening Lincoln to the uniquely inspired biblical Moses.[7] Stanley Matthews, the lawyer who defended the Cincinnati school board in the famous "Bible War," spelled out a similar danger. Although he was a theologically conservative Presbyterian elder, he wanted to stop mandatory readings from the KJV in the city's schools for fear of trivializing the book's message of salvation as a civics lesson.[8]

The most charitable Catholic commentary on celebration of the KJV in 1911, but also the most discerning, made almost the same point. The American Jesuit A. J. Maas found a great deal to praise in the KJV, especially "its marvelous felicity of style . . . chaste, dignified, and impressive, and of a rhythm which is always melodious and grateful to the ear." Yet as he observed the adulatory Protestant celebrations, he worried that "the Authorised Version is to a certain extent substituted for the Bible itself or for the Christian truths it conveys." In particular, he questioned King George V's speaking of the KJV's "inexhaustible springs of wisdom, courage, and joy." Surely, the priest responded, those are qualities belonging to the scriptural message: "The Authorised Version is at best the faucet through which Biblical truth is communicated."[9]

The concerns raised by Humphrey, the anonymous Jewish correspondent, Matthews, and Father Maas underscore a complexity at the heart of the American history of the Bible. The KJV gained its secure hold in large part because readers found in its pages a source of spiritual liberation—or because those who only *heard* its words took the same message to heart even more passionately. But because that popularity extended so widely, the Bible became a useful tool for all manner of projects, some growing organically from that spiritual message, others tangentially related, if at all.

Events in our nation's very recent past have highlighted the two-sidedness of this history. When the Bible now shows up in the political sphere, it is usually as a weapon—frequently from the Right to advocate for policies defending traditional sexual mores, protecting traditional marriage, and speaking for unborn children, but also from the Left for advocating policies defending the poor, protecting abused women, and speaking for disadvantaged children at risk. Yet as shown by the IUPUI survey, the day-to-day and week-by-week engagement with Scripture by most Americans mostly involves prayer, worship, and personal devotion, with partisan political purposes only secondary.

A Protestant who celebrated the tercentenary of the KJV described this disjunction inadvertently. After dwelling at length on the KJV's spiritual importance for believers, he affirmed that "its secondary service to society" was "even more important" for "helping to realize the exalted ideals and beneficent tendencies of those social institutions which at the last have grown up, if not wholly yet chiefly, under the inspiration and sanction of the Gospel itself."[10] Yet observers aware of the history recorded in these pages could never simply equate spiritual benefits enjoyed by believers with a rosy view of the "ideals" and "tendencies" of Bible-influenced "social institutions." The actual history has been much more involved.

Christian and Jewish adherents of scriptural religion have not been wrong to think that democratic self-government requires virtues of the kind encouraged by biblical teaching. In times long before the United States existed and in societies far removed from North America, believers have held that the Bible, properly understood, does nurture discipline, promote personal integrity, and strengthen the family bonds undergirding a healthy social order. The same believers, however, have also understood that the Bible teaches humility, self-criticism, honesty, and a constant need for repentance. Bible religion, in other words, has been understood to empower but also restrain.

The circumstances of American history have encouraged more empowerment than restraint. The new United States possessed a Protestant Bible inherited from the British colonial past, but modified, enlarged, and energized by fusion with the principles of American democracy. For the reasons spelled out in these pages, the Bible civilization created by the early republic's Protestants did not last long, yet the Bible in ever more numerous configurations remained a fixture. As a fixture, Scripture naturally became the tool of choice for many different citizens to promote all sorts of civic purposes—protecting property, advancing political ideologies, stabilizing family life, promoting literacy and moral education, and especially organizing voluntary societies to address perceived public needs. As a consequence, the story of the Bible in America expanded well beyond the goals that dominated the thinking of Francis Asbury and the early Methodists.

The crux for evaluating the fate of Scripture itself in American history lies in what to make of that expansion. As a standard for such an assessment, nothing could be more appropriate than the Golden Rule as found in the words of Jesus from Matthew 7:12: "Therefore all things whatsoever ye would that men should do to you, do ye even so to them: for this is the law and the prophets." A great deal of the Bible's history in America has witnessed an altruistic focus on the "them." As believers have taken advantage of America religious liberty, they have been empowered by the Scriptures to feed the hungry, tend the sick, educate the unlettered, protect the unprotected, and hammer at the chains of physical bondage.

Yet as this book has shown in detail, empowerment has also led to confident applications of Scripture that *forged* the chains of physical bondage. The same confidence has neglected the reciprocal challenge of the Golden Rule in order to sanction possessions, partisanship, privilege, and racial difference. The Bible has been used with particular precision to highlight the evil of others but less often to acknowledge evils within.

In assessing the history of Scripture among Black Americans, Allen Callahan penned the most profound statement I have read in over four decades of studying this history. It is worth repeating: "Ultimately African Americans embraced the Bible, a poison book, because it was so effective, in measured doses, as its own antidote."[11] The Bible never exists as an unmoved mover in any culture where it has appeared. The difference is never *whether* local cultures shape the understanding and use of Scripture but *how*. Because the history of the Bible in America has been so thoroughly the history of America, and because the driving forces of American history have always done as much to empower as to restrain, American Bible believers have indeed been able to proclaim tidings of great joy to all people, but the proclamation has only sometimes been unmuffled, pure, and clear.

The Bible and the Nation

In the early history of the United States, active white Protestants failed in their effort to create a Bible civilization. The attempt to structure the nation voluntarily by the precepts of the King James Bible proved simply impossible when Protestants could not agree among themselves on how those precepts should be followed and when most of those Protestants agreed that *liberty for all* needed in some sense to include non-Protestants, non-Christians, and even nonbelievers. As more and more of those non-Protestants, non-Christians, and nonbelievers also took advantage of democratic liberties, the earlier effort encountered still further resistance. As a result, it became increasingly difficult to take seriously what the custodial denominations and the voluntary societies tried to pull off.

Yet when stepping back to consider the fractious character of national public life that has continued to the present, the early attempt to ground the American experiment in common respect for a biblical higher law might not appear so pointlessly arbitrary or destructively coercive. In the century since the First World War insistent public voices have time and again evoked justice, equality, well-being, security, and liberty as ideals to guide the nation. Yet only rarely has a substantial majority of the citizenry agreed about what these ideals meant or how they should be balanced one against the other. In addition, when leaders have achieved a measure of consensus, they have often done so by retrieving language from the age of the Bible civilization. As a prominent example, during the Second World War, Franklin Roosevelt and Winston Churchill rallied the Western Alliance against the Axis Powers by appealing, if vaguely, to the values of "Christian civilization."[12] Significantly, citizens in the Alliance who condemned the internment of Japanese Americans, the saturation bombing of noncombatants, and the use of the atomic bomb against Japan also invoked Higher Law reasoning, sometimes backed by an appeal to Scripture.

As has been extensively documented, the civil rights movement of the 1950s and 1960s represented the most effective reprisal of the nineteenth century's aspirational Bible civilization. Among the many forces at work in achieving the victories of that movement, even if they were only partial victories, effective use of scriptural resources played a well-recognized part. This retrieval of warrants, which had seemed outdated, occurred at several levels.

One genealogy featured sophisticated theological argument. It stretched from Daniel Coker's *Dialogue between a Virginian and an African Minister* (1810) through James W. C. Pennington's *Origin and History of the Colored People* (1841) and Henry McNeal Turner's "God Is a Negro" (1898) to James Cone's *Black Theology and Black Power* (1969). In the mid-twentieth century the handling of biblical texts and pointed applications of biblical reasoning found in such works at last reached white audiences that had before paid them little heed.

A more popular strand began with Maria Stewart and Harriet Jacobs and then expanded with the many former slaves who passionately clamored for schooling in the postbellum South. During the perilous summers of civil rights mobilization, this legacy became visible in the names of the local Black churches where freedom marchers were fed, housed, and sheltered (Antioch, Bethel, Bibleway, Ebenezer, Liberty, Mount Carmel, Mount Zion, New Hope, St. John, Tabernacle, Zion).[13] Fannie Lou Hamer embodied this tradition when as a leader of Mississippi's Freedom Democratic Party she was jailed and beaten in the summer of 1964. Hamer related the following conversation with a jailer's wife and daughter who brought water and ice to the imprisoned marchers:

And I told them, "Y'all is nice. You must be Christian people." The jailer's wife told me she tried to live a Christian life. And I told her I would like her to read two scriptures in the Bible, and I tol' her to read the 26th Chapter of Proverbs and the 26th Verse ["Whose hatred is covered by deceit, his wickedness shall be shewed before the whole congregation"]. She taken it down on a paper. And then I told her to read the [17th] Chapter of Acts and the 26th Verse ["Hath made of one blood all nations of men for to dwell on all the face of the earth"]. And she taken that down. And she never did come back after then.[14]

Meaningful public action was once again being guided, not by formal theology but by visceral internalization of a biblical message.

Leaders of the civil rights movement also inherited the biblical forms of public address that had once been put to use by many Americans for many purposes but that remained especially vibrant in the Black churches. Those forms had been perfected by the first generations of Black preachers in the nineteenth century and then passed on to a dedicated corps of twentieth-century ministers, motivators, and teachers. Theological convictions varied widely among college presidents like Mordecai Johnson and Richard McKinney, scholar-teachers like Benjamin Mays and George Kelsey, independent thinkers like Howard Thurman, and many local Methodist and Baptist ministers. Some were traditionally conservative, others took their cues from Protestant liberalism, still others added principles of nonviolent resistance from the example of Mahatma Gandhi. All, however, drew on Scripture in keeping with Black hermeneutical traditions. For them the Book taught personal salvation and social reconstruction simultaneously. Documenting the importance of these exemplars for later leaders like the Rev. Martin Luther King Jr. has been a signal contribution made by Dennis Dickerson and other scholars.[15]

Leaders of the movement skillfully put to use several of the ways the Bible had earlier been commonly present, and did so with startling effect.[16] They were masters first of *rhetoric,* where words gained power by echoing the phrases, cadences, and tones of the King James Bible. King's memorable speech at the March on Washington for Jobs and Freedom on August 28, 1963, was filled with such language: "[T]he Negro . . . finds himself in exile in his own land. . . . [N]ow is the time to rise from the dark and desolate valley of segregation to the sunlit path of racial justice. . . . Let us not seek to satisfy our thirst for freedom by drinking from the cup of bitterness and hatred. . . . Let us not wallow in the valley of despair."[17]

The same speech illustrated an *evocative* use of Scripture when King put actual Bible phrases to use, but as fragments jerked out of their original context, in order to drive home his appeal. A quotation from Amos 5:24 performed that function: "[W]e will not be satisfied until justice rolls down like waters and righteousness like a mighty stream."

In spelling out his dream for the nation, King went beyond rhetoric and evocation to use the Bible for *persuasion*. Toward the end of his address, he quoted Isaiah 40:4 to enlist a divine sanction for the vision of a society free of racial discrimination: "I have a dream that one day every valley shall be exalted, every hill and mountain shall be made low, the rough places shall be made plain, the crooked places shall be made straight and the glory of the Lord will be revealed and all flesh shall see it together." That this Old Testament passage also described Jesus at the beginning of his public ministry (Lk 3:5) only heightened the moral significance of what King foresaw as the possibility of a racially healed society.

Earlier in the nation's history, persuasive deployment of Scripture had often been more effective—and more dangerous—than the merely rhetorical or evocative. The risk was obvious in the many instances this book has recorded when the scriptural baptism of a particular political position inspired confidence that the stance reflected God's will absolutely. When the language of the KJV everywhere informed common speech, it was easy to bestow a sacred aura on public discourse. In turn, the sacralization of public rhetoric easily encouraged the absolutization of public principle, and the absolutization of principle easily led to the demonization of opponents, which inspired crusading with no quarter for anyone standing in the way. Whether it was loyalists to Great Britain in 1776 attacked as servants of Satan, Federalists depicting Democratic-Republicans as conspiring anarchists, Protestants in arms against Catholics as minions of the papal Antichrist, or southerners (and northerners) in the era of the Civil War excoriated as raving infidels for their arguments in favor of (and against) slavery, persuasive use of Scripture more than occasionally overwhelmed deliberative democracy.

Such attempts at biblically inspired persuasion could also be simply disregarded as impractical, untimely, or quixotic. Abraham Lincoln's paraphrase from Matthew 7:1 ("Let us judge not that we be not judged") in his Second Inaugural Address illustrates this more prosaic danger. Lincoln hoped with this biblical word to distribute the assignment of blame for the continuation of slavery. But despite his scriptural appeal for charity to all, judgment from all sides of all sides has never ceased in interpretations of the Civil War.

Yet sometimes the use of Scripture did convince the wider public that a particular goal enjoyed the stamp of divine approval, as when after World War II it reassured many Americans that civil rights reform really did express a divine imperative. As historian David L. Chappell and others have argued, it is hard to imagine that the admittedly partial achievements of the civil rights movement could have been possible without widespread, however reluctant acceptance of that imperative.[18]

If they are correct, then the biblical language that helped persuade the public was also making a *theological* claim about God and the working of providence in the world. Admittedly, theological deployment of Scripture has had a check-ered American history. Apologists for slavery claimed biblical support for the view that God ordained permanent structures in society, including enslavement (but without biblical support for the idea that only Africans, or Indians, could be enslaved). In his Second Inaugural Address Abraham Lincoln claimed that no human community could ever infallibly discern the working of God in his-tory. That assertion, however, did not check the deeply ingrained American habit of emphatic declarations about what God was doing in the world or who was standing on the right side of history.

Yet when the civil rights movement repeated assertions that had gained only a partial hearing from abolitionists before the Civil War and that were repeated by postbellum opponents of systematic segregation, they stuck. King and other leaders effectively blended axioms of the American civil faith into their speech, but in support of basically theological claims: God is not a respecter of persons; all individuals are made in the image of God; dignity is God's gift to all humanity. The result was nationwide recognition—sometimes celebrated, sometimes begrudged—that civil and biblical mandates together opposed segregation, ra-cial discrimination, and formal definition of some Americans as second-class citizens.

The decades since have shown that the victories of the civil rights movement represented stages in transition, more like surviving the winter at Valley Forge than achieving the decisive triumph at Yorktown. Especially in the twenty-first century, an ever widening array of appeals to contrasting interpretations of American history and competing interpretations of American ideals has roiled the public square—as it had been roiled many times before (at the Revolution and during the War of 1812; in response to Andrew Jackson; before, during, and after the Civil War; in the heyday of lynch law; amid controversy over the New Deal; during Freedom Summer). Contemporary public life has been frac-tured by appeals for radical reform confronting appeals to uphold once-honored traditions, by violence springing from urban decay and ideological extremism, by rancorous disputing over judicial philosophies, and by a public square riven into partisan camps. Although Scripture has not been nearly as prominent in these contemporary fractures as in the antebellum era, Bible believers have con-tributed their share to stoking the flames of national discord. These are the flames menacing a much more secular America.

Yet as an indication of a present still connected to the past, the Bible continues to appear in public with the stated intention to unify and heal. One such occasion occurred in the funeral address that President Barack Obama delivered for the Rev. Clementa Pinckney on June 26, 2015, nine days after the pastor and eight members of his congregation were murdered by a white supremacist as they gathered for a Bible study at the Mother Emanuel AME church in Charleston,

South Carolina.[19] History, in a saying attributed to Mark Twain, does not repeat itself, but this address—with its rhetorical, evocative, persuasive, and even theological appeal to Scripture—certainly rhymed with much from the nation's past.

The president began by "[g]iving all praise and honor to God." He then declared, "The Bible calls us to hope. To persevere, and have faith in things not seen [quoting Heb 11:1 from the KJV]." He read Hebrews 11:13 from the New International Version: "They were still living by faith when they died. . . . They did not receive the things promised; they only saw them and welcomed them from a distance, admitting that they were foreigners and strangers on Earth."

The address eulogized Rev. Pinckney in a frame of reference taken from generations of African American preaching. The hermeneutics at work allowed the president to speak of personal religion and social outreach as a unit. "Our Christian faith," he asserted, "demands deeds and not words." It requires that "the 'sweet hour of prayer' actually last . . . the whole week long . . . that to put our faith in action is more than individual salvation, it's about our collective salvation." In the president's words, "to feed the hungry and clothe the naked and house the homeless is not just a call for isolated charity but the imperative of a just society."

Most unusually, Obama then made a specific theological claim. He said that the murderer had been "blinded by hatred"; he had not comprehended "what Reverend Pinckney so well understood—the power of God's grace." Obama explained what he meant by this theological concept: "According to the Christian tradition, grace is not earned. Grace is not merited. It's not something we deserve. Rather, grace is the free and benevolent favor of God . . . as manifested in the salvation of sinners and the bestowal of blessings." As a consequence, only grace could empower the wronged to forgive those who did great evil, even the murder of loved ones. Only grace could acknowledge the full wrong of slavery and its evil legacy. Only grace could turn aside the tide of murderous violence and tap what the president called the "reservoir of goodness." He ended by leading the congregation in singing the hymn of the one-time slave trader John Newton, "Amazing grace, how sweet the sound / That saved a wretch like me."

Events since 2015 suggest that only a few Americans have agreed that a right understanding of divine grace could bring public healing, overcome partisan strife, and calm the body politic. Events in fact have moved in the opposite direction. Yet this speech from 2015 showed that the biblical resources once so prominent in the nation's history could still be brought back to life.

In 1989 Bruce Metzger, a venerable biblical scholar at Princeton Theological Seminary, supplied the preface for the New Revised Standard Version, a modernization of the revision of an earlier revision of the King James Bible. In this preface Metzger described the Scriptures much as Solomon Schechter had done when Schechter opened New York's Jewish Theological Seminary in 1903. According to Metzger:

In traditional Judaism and Christianity, the Bible has been more than a historical document to be preserved or a classic of literature to be cherished and admired; it is recognized as the unique record of God's dealing with people over the ages.... The Bible carries its full message, not to those who regard it simply as a noble literary heritage of the past or who wish to use it to enhance political purposes and advance otherwise desirable goals, but to all persons and communities who read it so that they may discern and understand what God is saying to them.[20]

Much in American history speaks against what Metzger wrote, especially the many instances when Bible believers have forgotten the universal reach of Scripture in order to enhance their own personal goals. But if Metzger, along with Schechter, was correct in describing the Bible as fundamentally a universal book, it follows that Scripture can never be the possession of any one denomination, a single interpretive tradition, only one nation, or one faction within a particular nation. Still more, if much in the Bible can be put to use for civic or political purposes, whether wisely or disruptively, those purposes can never exhaust or circumscribe what it says "to *all* persons and communities who read it so that they may discern and understand what God is saying to them."

From Christopher Columbus to the present day, the appropriation of universal scriptural values in American history has mingled constantly with its use for particular purposes, sometimes in keeping with those values, sometimes violating them with abandon. That mixed record must temper anything triumphalist Bible believers might say in its favor. Yet an honest assessment of the nation's history, and at no time more than the present, should also recognize that a democratic republic needs something like the Bible more than Bible believers need a democratic republic.

Acknowledgments

Many of the individuals thanked in the acknowledgements for *In the Beginning Was the Word: The Bible in American Public Life, 1492–1783* once again provided much appreciated assistance, direct or indirect, in the preparation of this book. Here I would like to express special gratitude to the Ph.D. students with whom it was so enjoyable to work during my years at the University of Notre Dame. For insights particularly relevant to this book, I am pleased to recognize Raully Donahue, Ashley Foster, Andrew Hansen, Nicholas Miller, Laura Rominger Porter, Jonathan Riddle, Ben Wetzel, and especially, for reasons obvious from chapters 14 and 25, David Komline and Heath Carter. I am also thankful for the Notre Dame administrators who provided so much support for faculty scholarship while maintaining their commitment to the university's Catholic mission— particularly Dean of Arts and Letters John McGreevy, Provost Tom Burish, and President Father John Jenkins. To Notre Dame librarians Jean McManus and Rachel Bohlmann, I owe a special debt for securing resources that proved crucial for several of the book's chapters. I am also grateful that Notre Dame's Hesburgh Library extends borrowing privileges and online access to emeritus faculty.

Writers of books are made in large part by books they have read. Although I have tried in the notes to give full credit to the scholarship I have used, I want to specially acknowledge several authors whose works materially changed the way I viewed the subjects of this book: Edward Blum, Catherine Brekus, Candy Gunther Brown, Allen Callahan, Richard Carwardine, Dennis Dickerson, Gary Dorrien, Gerald Fogarty, S. J., Eugene Genovese and Elizabeth Fox-Genovese, Steven Green, Paul Gutjahr, Luke Harlow, Brooks Holifield, Liana Lupus, George Marsden, Lincoln Mullen, Brendan Pietsch, Linda Przybyszewski, George Rable, Albert Raboteau, Jonathan Sarna, Beth Barton Schweiger, Eran Shalev, Marion Ann Taylor, Peter Thuesen, James Turner, John Wigger, and Vincent Wimbush. Of preeminent importance throughout have been Nathan Hatch's *The Democratization of American Christianity*, Daniel Walker Howe's *What Hath God Wrought: The Transformation of America, 1815–1848*, and Margaret Hills's *The English Bible in America*.

I once said semi-facetiously that Grant Wacker was a formidable whacker of conceptual nonsense and verbal infelicities. After his careful reading of this entire manuscript, nothing in the least facetious remains in my admiration for Grant's learning, wisdom, wit, clarity of thought, and mastery of the English language. For a wealth of exceedingly helpful corrections and suggestions for the entire book, I am also grateful to Peter Thuesen and an anonymous scholar who read the manuscript for Oxford University Press. Criticism for portions of the book from Luke Harlow, John McGreevy, Nicholas Miller, and David Noll was also deeply appreciated. To Bruce Kuklick I am indebted not only for illuminating conversation but also for showing me how to benefit from older and supposedly dated historical scholarship while attending to the latest and most fashionable. I thank Steve Marini for once again sharing his unrivaled grasp of early American ecclesiastical demography. I'm also glad to thank Bill and Cindy Koechling for much-appreciated assistance in preparing the book's images.

Editors at Oxford have helped with admirable professionalism at every stage, including Cynthia Read, Theo Calderara, Drew Anderla, Rachel Gilman, Sean Decker, Hinduja Dhanasegaran, and Judith Hoover.

Proverbs 31 may have become suspect in an age rightly worried about patronizing patriarchy, but this iconic scriptural passage nonetheless expresses my abiding love for Maggie Noll, a diligent reader for me of many books (old and new), the mother and grandmother of those who are the dearest in this world to me, and my fellow traveler on the twisting road to the celestial city. Strength and honor are her clothing.

The book is dedicated with special gratitude to the History Department chairs who made the decade I was at Notre Dame so enriching in so many ways, and to the editor who has done as much as anyone to make the study of the nation's religious past such a dynamic historical enterprise.

Short Titles for Notes

Notes include full citations except for subsequent references in a chapter and for the following frequently cited works.

ANB. John A. Garraty and Mark C. Carnes, general eds., *American National Biography* (New York: Oxford University Press, 1999); *American National Biography Online,* https://www.anb.org.

Brown, *WORD IN THE WORLD.* Candy Gunther Brown, *The Word in the World: Evangelical Writing, Publishing, and Reading in America, 1789-1880* (Chapel Hill: University of North Carolina Press, 2004).

Dreisbach and Hall, *SACRED RIGHTS.* Daniel L. Dreisbach and Mark David Hall, eds., *The Sacred Rights of Conscience: Selected Readings on Religious Liberty and Church-State Relations on the American Founding* (Indianapolis, IN: Liberty Fund, 2009).

Gutjahr, *AMERICAN BIBLE.* Paul C. Gutjahr, *An American Bible: A History of the Good Book in the United States, 1777-1880* (Stanford, CA: Stanford University Press, 1999).

Gutjahr, *OXFORD HANDBOOK.* Paul C. Gutjahr, ed., *The Oxford Handbook to the Bible in America* (New York: Oxford University Press, 2017).

Hatch, *DEMOCRATIZATION.* Nathan O. Hatch, *The Democratization of American Christianity* (New Haven, CT: Yale University Press, 1989).

Hatch and Noll, *BIBLE IN AMERICA.* Nathan O. Hatch and Mark A. Noll, eds., *The Bible in America: Essays in Cultural History* (New York: Oxford University Press, 1982).

Hills, *ENGLISH BIBLE.* Margaret T. Hills, *The English Bible in America: A Bibliography of the Bible and the New Testament Published in America, 1777-1957* (New York: American Bible Society and New York Public Library, 1962).

HISTORICAL STATISTICS. U.S. Bureau of the Census, *Historical Statistics of the United States, Colonial Times to 1957* (Washington, DC: Government Printing Office, 1960).

HISTORY OF THE BOOK. David D. Hall, general ed., *A History of the Book in America,* vol. 1, *The Colonial Book in the Atlantic World,* ed. Hugh Amory and David D. Hall; vol. 2, *An Extensive Republic: Print, Culture, and Society in the New Nation, 1790–1840,* ed. Robert A. Gross and Mary Kelly; vol. 3, *The Industrial Book, 1840–1880,* ed. Scott E. Casper, Jeffrey D. Groves, Stephen W. Nissenbaum, and Michael Winship; vol. 4, *Print in Motion: The Expansion of Publishing and Reading in the United States, 1880–1940,* ed. Carl F. Kaestle and Janice A. Radway (Chapel Hill: University of North Carolina Press, 2007–10).

Holifield, *THEOLOGY IN AMERICA.* E. Brooks Holifield, *Theology in America: Christian Thought from the Age of the Puritans to the Civil War* (New Haven, CT: Yale University Press, 2003).

Howe, *WHAT HATH GOD WROUGHT.* Daniel Walker Howe, *What Hath God Wrought: The Transformation of America, 1815–1848* (New York: Oxford University Press, 2007).

Lincoln, *COLLECTED WORKS.* Roy P. Basler, ed., *The Collected Works of Abraham Lincoln,* 9 vols. (New Brunswick, NJ: Rutgers University Press, 1953–55).

Noll, *AMERICA'S GOD.* Mark A. Noll, *America's God: From Jonathan Edwards to Abraham Lincoln* (New York: Oxford University Press, 2002).

Noll, *CIVIL WAR.* Mark A. Noll, *The Civil War as a Theological Crisis* (Chapel Hill: University of North Carolina Press, 2006).

Noll, *IN THE BEGINNING.* Mark A. Noll, *In the Beginning Was the Word: The Bible in American Public Life, 1492–1783* (New York: Oxford University Press, 2016).

PRESIDENTIAL ELECTIONS. Presidential Elections, 1789–2000 (Washington, DC: CQ Press, 2002).

WORLDCAT. WorldCat.org.

Notes

Introduction

1. NASA, "President Addresses Nation on Space Shuttle Columbia Tragedy," accessed July 16, 2020, https://history.nasa.gov/columbia/Troxell/Columbia%20Web%20Site/Documents/Executive%20Branch/President%20Bush/president1.html. The president quoted Isaiah 40:26 from the New International Version.

2. White House, "Remarks by the President at the National Prayer Breakfast," February 2, 2012, https://obamawhitehouse.archives.gov/the-press-office/2012/02/02/remarks-president-national-prayer-breakfast.

3. Ralph Reed, quoted in David Nakamura and Michelle Boorstein, "At Prayer Breakfast and with Birth-Control Decision, Obama Riles Religious Conservatives," *Washington Post*, February 3, 2012, https://www.washingtonpost.com/local/at-prayer-breakfast-and-with-birth-control-decision-obama-riles-religious-conservatives/2012/02/02/gIQAgy1blQ_story.html ; Peter Wehner, *Commentary Magazine* online, in email to Mark Noll, February 3, 2012.

4. "Bishop, Joe Biden Angered by Trump's Use of Washington Church for Photo Op," CBC, June 2, 2020, https://www.cbc.ca/news/world/washington-diocese-trump-criticism-1.5594552.

5. Whitney T. Kunkholm, quoted in "American Bible Society Responds to Trump's Photo Op: 'Scripture Is More Than a Symbol,'" *Christianity Today*, June 3, 2020, https://www.christianitytoday.com/news/2020/june/american-bible-society-responds-president-trump-photo-op-sy.html.

6. The quotation is from Matthew 7:1; "Second Inaugural Address," Lincoln, *COLLECTED WORKS*, 8:333.

7. Noll, *IN THE BEGINNING*.

8. Martin Luther, "Luther at the Diet of Worms, 1521," trans. Roger A. Hornsby, in *Luther's Works*, vol. 32, *Career of the Reformer*, ed. George W. Forell (Philadelphia: Fortress, 1958), 112; "A Bill for Establishing Religious Freedom, Virginia," in Dreisbach and Hall, *SACRED RIGHTS*, 250.

9. Hills, *ENGLISH BIBLE*.

10. "The earth is the Lord and the fulness thereof; the world and they that dwell therein." Eugene D. Genovese, *Roll, Jordan, Roll: The World the Slaves Made* (New York: Random House, 1972).

11. Hatch and Noll, *BIBLE IN AMERICA*; David Paul Nord, "The Evangelical Origins of Mass Media in America," *Journalism Monographs* 88 (May 1984): 5–39, with insights later expanded in Nord, *Faith in Reading: Religious Publishing and the Birth of the Mass Media in America* (New York: Oxford University Press, 2004). General editors for the SBL series were Edwin S. Gaustad and Walter Harrelson; Fortress Press and Scholars Press published the books. They included David Barr and Nicholas Piediscalzi, eds.,

The Bible in American Education (1982); Ernest R. Sandeen, ed., *The Bible and Social Reform* (1982); Giles Gunn, ed., *The Bible and American Arts and Letters* (1983); James T. Johnson, ed., *The Bible in American Law, Politics, and Rhetoric* (1985); Allene S. Phy, ed., *The Bible and Popular Culture in America* (1985); and Ernest S. Frerichs, ed., *The Bible and Bibles in America* (1988).

12. Gutjahr, *AMERICAN BIBLE*; Peter J. Thuesen, *In Discordance with the Scriptures: American Protestant Battles over Translating the Bible* (New York: Oxford University Press, 1999); Vincent Wimbush, ed., *African Americans and the Bible: Sacred Texts and Social Textures* (New York: Continuum, 2000).

13. Gutjahr, *OXFORD HANDBOOK*, with Gutjahr's introduction (xix–xxxvii) particularly helpful on the historical study of the Bible in America; Philip Goff, Arthur E. Farnsley II, and Peter J. Thuesen, eds., *The Bible in American Life* (New York: Oxford University Press, 2017). The earlier SBL series has also been helpfully updated in Claudia Setzer and David A. Shefferrman, eds., *The Bible in the American Experience* (Atlanta, GA: SBL Press, 2020). An insightful report examining the near-present is Kenneth A. Briggs, *The Invisible Best Seller: Searching for the Bible in America* (Grand Rapids, MI: Eerdmans, 2016).

14. Noll, *AMERICA'S GOD*; Noll, *CIVIL WAR*; "'Both Pray to the Same God': The Singularity of Lincoln's Faith in the Era of the Civil War," *Journal of the Abraham Lincoln Association* 18 (Winter 1997): 1–26; as editor, *God and Mammon: Protestants, Money, and the Market, 1790–1860* (New York: Oxford University Press, 2002); and *Between Faith and Criticism: Evangelicals, Scholarship, and the Bible in America*, 3rd ed. (Vancouver: Regent College, 2004).

15. Katherine Carté, *Religion and the American Revolution: An Imperial History* (Chapel Hill: University of North Carolina Press, 2021). For fuller historical treatment of ambiguities in the terms *evangelicals* and *evangelicalism*, see Mark A. Noll, David W. Bebbington, and George M. Marsden, eds., *Evangelicals: Who They Have Been, Are Now, and Could Be* (Grand Rapids, MI: Eerdmans, 2019).

16. Hugh McLeod, *The Religious Crisis of the 1960s* (New York: Oxford University Press, 2007), 18.

17. For the difference between *typology* and *analogy*, see the careful distinctions explained by Holifield, *THEOLOGY IN AMERICA*, 77.

18. Harry S. Stout, *Upon the Altar of the Nation: A Moral History of the Civil War* (New York: Viking, 2006), xviii.

19. For checking the quotations, I have depended on the Oxford World's Classics edition, Robert Carroll and Stephen Prickett, eds., *The Bible: Authorized King James Version with Apocrypha* (New York: Oxford University Press, 1997).

Chapter 1

1. Katherine Carté Engel, "Connecting Protestants in Britain's Eighteenth-Century Protestant Empire," *William and Mary Quarterly* 75 (January 2018): 70. For a

persuasive expansion of this argument, see Katherine Carté, *Religion and the American Revolution: An Imperial History* (Chapel Hill: University of North Carolina Press, 2021).

2. Students of this period are very well served by an unusual array of carefully edited source collections, especially Charles S. Hyneman and Donald S. Lutz, eds., *American Political Writing during the Founding Era, 1760–1805*, 2 vols. (Indianapolis, IN: Liberty Press, 1983); Ellis Sandoz, ed., *Political Sermons of the American Founding Era, 1730–1805* (Indianapolis, IN: Liberty Press, 1991); Bernard Bailyn, ed., *The Debate on the Constitution*, 2 vols. (New York: Library of America, 1993); and Dreisbach and Hall, *SACRED RIGHTS*.

3. The best account of that Christian cast is now Daniel L. Dreisbach, *Reading the Bible with the Founding Fathers* (New York: Oxford University Press, 2016).

4. On the Revolutionary-era uses of Scripture for direct, didactic teaching that are mentioned in this paragraph, see Noll, *IN THE BEGINNING*, chap. 11, "Revolutionary Argument," 289–324.

5. For that comparison, see Patricia P. Bonomi, *Under the Cope of Heaven: Religion, Society, and Politics in Colonial America*, 2nd ed. (New York: Oxford University Press, 2003), 199. On the contribution of this controversy to how Americans after the war "articulate[d] a new language of American religious nationalism," see Katherine Carté Engel, "Revisiting the Bishop Controversy," in *The American Revolution Reborn*, ed. Patrick Spero and Michael Zuckerman (Philadelphia: University of Pennsylvania Press, 2016), 132–49.

6. *Common Sense*, in Tom Paine, *Selected Writings of Tom Pain*, ed. Ian Shapiro and Jane E. Calvert (New Haven, CT: Yale University Press, 2014), 16 (see 13–16 for Paine's exposition of 1 Samuel 8). Loyalists who challenged Paine's reading with extensive biblical exposition of their own included Anglicans William Smith of Philadelphia and Charles Inglis of New York; see Noll, *IN THE BEGINNING*, 307–15. On the influence of Paine's appeal to Scripture, see especially Eric Nelson, "Hebraism and the Republican Turn of 1776: A Contemporary Account of the Debate over *Common Sense*," *William & Mary Quarterly* 70 (October 2013): 781–812.

7. Martin E. Marty, "Religion and the Constitution: The Triumph of Practical Politics" (reviewing Bailyn, *Debate on the Constitution*), *Christian Century*, March 1994, 316.

8. John Jay, *An Address to the People of New York, on the Subject of the Constitution, Agreed upon at Philadelphia* (New York: Samuel and John Loudon, [1788]), 9, 16.

9. On the difficulties in defining Franklin's religious stance with modern categories, see Thomas S. Kidd, *Benjamin Franklin: The Religious Life of a Founding Father* (New Haven, CT: Yale University Press, 2017); and D. G. Hart, *Benjamin Franklin: Cultural Protestant* (New York: Oxford University Press, 2021).

10. Benjamin Franklin, "The Antifederalists Compared with the Ancient Jews as Rejectors of Divine Constitutions" (from the *Federal Gazette*), in Bailyn, *Debate on the Constitution*, 2:404–5.

11. John Dickinson, "Religious Instruction for Youth" (undated), in *The Founders on Religion: A Book of Quotations*, ed. James H. Hutson (Princeton, NJ: Princeton University Press, 2005), 24. An up-to-date treatment is Jane E. Calvert, "Introduction,"

in *Complete Writings and Selected Correspondences of John Dickinson*, vol. 1 (Newark: University of Delaware Press, 2020).

12. Fabius [John Dickinson], "Observations on the Constitution Proposed by the Federal Convention" (April 1788), in Bailyn, *Debate on the Constitution*, 2:412.

13. Fabius [Dickinson], "Observations," 410.

14. Mark A. Mastromarino, ed., *The Papers of George Washington: Presidential Series*, vol. 6: *July–November 1790* (Charlottesville: University Press of Virginia, 1996), 286. On the address at Touro, see T. H. Breen, *George Washington's Journey: The President Forges a New Nation* (New York: Simon & Schuster, 2016), 203–6. For fifteen different occasions when Washington quoted this passage, see Peter A. Lillback and Jerry Newcombe, *George Washington's Sacred Fire* (Bryn Mawr, PA: Providence Forum, 2006), 316–18. Lillback and Newcombe's chapter, "George Washington and the Bible," 305–33, and their "Appendix 2: Representative Biblical Quotations and Allusions Used by George Washington," 739–60, provide useful compilations. See also in Dreisbach, *Reading the Bible*, chap. 10, "Under Our Own Vine and Fig Tree: Creating an American Metaphor for Liberty in the New Nation."

15. See especially Eran Shalev's documentation of the wide use of the "American Zion" trope in *American Zion: The Old Testament as a Political Text from the Revolution to the Civil War* (New Haven, CT: Yale University Press, 2013).

16. For the difference between Bradford's and Winthrop's concern for a universal Protestant church and later use of their writing in service to American nationalism, see Abram Van Engen, *City on a Hill: A History of American Exceptionalism* (New Haven, CT: Yale University Press, 2020).

17. On the election sermon as a potent genre, see Harry S. Stout, *The New England Soul: Preaching and Religious Culture in Colonial New England*, new ed. (New York: Oxford University Press, 2011), 29–30, 167–74 and Mark A. Noll, "The Election Sermon: Situating Religion and the Constitution in the Eighteenth Century," *DePaul Law Review* 59 (Summer 2010): 1223–48.

18. Samuel Langdon, *The Republic of the Israelites an Example to the American States: A Sermon, Preached at Concord, in the State of New-Hampshire* (1788), in Sandoz, *Political Sermons*, 945 (text), 943 (title page), 957 (answer), 960 (education), 961 (holy scriptures).

19. In 1775 Langdon had preached a remarkably parallel sermon, this one on Isaiah 1:26 ("afterward thou shalt be called, The city of righteousness, the faithful city") in which he claimed, "The Jewish government, according to the original constitution which was divinely established, if considered merely in a civil view, was a perfect Republic." Samuel Langdon, *Government Corrupted by Vice, and Recovered by Righteousness: A Sermon Preached before the Honorable Congress of the Colony of the Massachusetts-Bay* (Watertown, MA: Benjamin Edes, 1775), 11

20. As only two of many possible examples, see Jonathan Edwards Jr. in Connecticut in 1793 on Psalm 144:15 ("happy is that people, whose God is the Lord"), *The Necessity of the Belief of Christianity by the Citizens of the State, in order to our political Prosperity*, in Sandoz, *Political Sermons*, 1187–216; David Osgood in Massachusetts also in

1793 on Psalm 114:4 ("He has made his wonderful works to be remembered"), *The Wonderful Works of God are to be remembered*, in Sandoz, *Political Sermons*, 1219–34.

21. A Connecticut Farmer [Roger Sherman], *Remarks on a Pamphlet, Entituled "A Dissertation on the Political Union and Constitution of the Thirteen States of North-America"* (N.p.: n.p., 1784), 25–26; and for context, Mark David Hall, *Roger Sherman and the Creation of the American Republic* (New York: Oxford University Press, 2013), 73–77. It is worth recording that one of the grandchildren of Roger Sherman, who helped bring the nation into existence, was William Tecumseh Sherman, who helped put it back together.

22. Derek H. Davis, *Religion and the Continental Congress, 1774–1789: Contributions to Original Intent* (New York: Oxford University Press, 2000), 196. Or see Eric R. Schlereth, *An Age of Infidels: The Politics of Religious Controversy in the Early United States* (Philadelphia: University of Pennsylvania Press, 2013), 19: "public religious expressions became problematic in new ways."

23. Samuel Cooper, *A Sermon . . . Being the Day of the commencement of the Constitution and Inauguration of the new Government* (1780), in Sandoz, *Political Sermons*, 647–48.

24. "Northwest Ordinance," in Dreisbach and Hall, *SACRED RIGHTS*, 238.

25. A notable example from a notable day was Samuel Miller, *A Sermon, Preached in New-York, July 4th, 1793, Being the Anniversary of the Independence of America* (1793), in Sandoz, *Political Sermons*, 1156–58.

26. James Madison, *Manifestation of the Beneficence of Divine Providence towards America: A Discourse* (1795), in Sandoz, *Political Sermons*, 1320.

27. "Farewell Address" (September 19, 1796), in George Washington, *Writings*, ed. John Rhodehamel (New York: Library of America, 1997), 971.

28. For more examples, see Noll, *IN THE BEGINNING*, chap. 10, "Revolutionary Rhetoric," 271–88.

29. On the favored texts of the Revolutionary era, see James P. Byrd, *Sacred Scripture, Sacred War: The Bible and the American Revolution* (New York: Oxford University Press, 2013).

30. See George Washington, "Circular to the States" (1783), in Dreisbach and Hall, *SACRED RIGHTS*, 296 (independence resulted from "the glorious events which Heaven has been pleased to produce in our favour"); George Washington, "First Inaugural Address" (1789), in Dreisbach and Hall, *SACRED RIGHTS*, 447 (every step by which the United States advanced to independence "seems to have been distinguished by some token of providential agency"); George Washington, "Proclamation of a Thanksgiving day, October 1789," in *Papers of George Washington, Presidential Series*, vol. 4: *Sept. 1789–Jan. 1790*, ed. Dorothy Twohig (Charlottesville: University Press of Virginia, 1993), 131–32 (the United States had the greatest reason for acknowledging "the favorable interpositions of his Providence which was experienced in the course and conclusion of the late war").

31. See two examples from 1782: John Witherspoon, "Sermon Delivered at a Public Thanksgiving after Peace" (1782), on the text Psalm 3:8 ("Salvation belongeth to the

Lord"), in Dreisbach and Hall, *SACRED RIGHTS*, 281; Zabdiel Adams, *Mr. Adams' Election Sermon, May 29, 1782* (Boston: T. & J. Fleet and J. Gill, 1782), 46–47.

32. See in the sermon quoted earlier by Bishop James Madison, *Manifestation of Divine Providence*, in Sandoz, *Political Sermons*, 1320 ("thy glorious providence . . . hath hitherto nurtured, protected, and conducted [these happy republics] to this day of praise and thanksgiving"). The same judgment about God's role in bringing about the Constitution appears in Federalist 37 from the political James Madison ("It is impossible for the man of pious reflection not to perceive in it a finger of that Almighty hand which has been so frequently and signally extended to our relief in the critical stages of the revolution").

33. Stephen Botein, "Religious Dimensions of the Early American State," in *Beyond Confederation: Origins of the Constitution and American National Identity*, ed. Richard Beeman, Stephen Botein, and Edward C. Carter II (Chapel Hill: University of North Carolina Press, 1987), 318; Michael R. Watts, *The Dissenters*, vol. 2: *The Expansion of Evangelical Nonconformity* (Oxford: Clarendon Press, 1995), 349.

34. John McManners, *The French Revolution and the Church* (London: SPCK, 1969); Dale K. Van Kley, "Christianity as Casualty and Chrysalis of Modernity: The Problem of Dechristianization in the French Revolution," *American Historical Review* 108 (2003): 1081–104.

Chapter 2

1. William Bentley, *The Diary of William Bentley, D.D.*, ed. Joseph G. Walters, Marguerite Dalrymple, and Alice G. Walters, 4 vols. (Salem, MA: Essex Institute, 1907), 2:107, September 28, 1794.

2. Francis Asbury, *The Journal and Letters of Francis Asbury*, ed. Elmer T. Clark, 3 vols. (Nashville, TN: Abingdon, 1958), 2:54–55.

3. For expert positioning of Paine and this book, see the texts and essays in Thomas Paine, *Selected Writings of Thomas Paine*, ed. Ian Shapiro and Jane E. Calvert (New Haven, CT: Yale University Press, 2014), especially J. C. D. Clark, "Thomas Paine: The English Dimension," 579–601; as well as Edward H. Davidson and William J. Scheick, *Paine, Scripture, and Authority: The Age of Reason as Religious and Political Idea* (Bethlehem, PA: Lehigh University Press, 1994); J. C. D. Clark, *Thomas Paine: Britain, America, and France in the Age of Enlightenment and Revolution* (New York: Oxford University Press, 2018), 331–55.

4. *The Age of Reason*, in Paine, *Selected Writings of Paine*, 372–73.

5. *The Age of Reason*, in Paine, *Selected Writings of Paine*, 373.

6. For the dedication written for distribution in the United States, see *The Age of Reason*, in Thomas Paine, *The Life and Major Writings of Thomas Paine*, ed. Philip S. Foner (New York: Citadel, 1945), 463.

7. *The Age of Reason*, in Paine, *Selected Writings of Paine*, 372, 373.

8. *The Age of Reason*, in Paine, *Selected Writings of Paine*, 382, 387, 391.

9. For an overview of that critical history, see Jonathan Sheehan, *The Enlightenment Bible: Translation, Scholarship, Culture* (Princeton, NJ: Princeton University Press, 2005).

10. *The Age of Reason, Part the Second*, in Paine, *Selected Writings of Paine*, 421, 438.

11. *The Age of Reason*, in Paine, *Selected Writings of Paine*, 470, 493 (emphasis Paine's), 494.

12. *The Age of Reason*, in Paine, *Selected Writings of Paine*, 501.

13. *The Age of Reason*, in Paine, *Selected Writings of Paine*, 499.

14. Foner, "Introduction," in Paine, *Life and Writings of Paine*, xxxvii

15. I am following Gordon S. Wood, *Empire of Liberty: A History of the Early Republic, 1789–1815* (New York: Oxford University Press, 2009); Walter A. McDougall, *Freedom Just around the Corner: A New American History, 1585–1828* (New York: Harper, 2004); Sean Wilentz, *The Rise of American Democracy: Jefferson to Lincoln* (New York: Norton, 2005).

16. Alexander MacWhorter, *A Festival Discourse, Occasioned by the Celebration of the Seventeenth Anninersary* [sic] *of American Independence* (Newark, NJ: John Woods, 1793), 11–12.

17. John M. Murrin, "A Roof without Walls: The Dilemma of American National Identity," in *Beyond Confederation: Origins of the Constitution and American National Identity*, ed. Richard Beeman, Stephen Botein, and Edward C. Carter II (Chapel Hill: University of North Carolina Press, 1987), 344.

18. James Madison, "Vices of the Political System of the United States, April 1787," in *The Mind of the Founder: Sources of the Political Thought of James Madison*, ed. Marvin Meyers (Hanover, NH: New England University Press, 1981), 58.

19. T. H. Breen, *George Washington's Journey: The President Forges a New Nation* (New York: Simon & Schuster, 2016), 88.

20. For this oversimplification, see Richard D. Brown, "The Revolution's Legacy for the History of the Book," in *HISTORY OF THE BOOK*, 2:68. Especially insightful on the American impact of *The Age of Reason* are Vernon Stauffer, *New England and the Bavarian Illuminati* (New York: Columbia University Press, 1918), 72–76; James H. Smylie, "Clerical Perspectives on Deism: Paine's *The Age of Reason* in Virginia," *Eighteenth-Century Studies* 6 (Winter 1972–73): 203–20; Davidson and Scheick, *Paine, Scripture, and Authority*; Eric R. Schlereth, *An Age of Infidels: The Politics of Religious Controversy in the Early United States* (Philadelphia: University of Pennsylvania Press, 2013), 49–65; Christopher Grasso, *Skepticism and American Faith: From the Revolution to the Civil War* (New York: Oxford University Press, 2018), 114 and passim.

21. For a good survey, see the introduction and selections in Kerry S. Walters, ed., *The American Deists: Voices of Reason and Dissent in the Early Republic* (Lawrence: University Press of Kansas, 1992).

22. Wood, *Empire of Liberty*, 199–200, which counts seventeen separate editions from 1794 to 1796. My count of fifteen in 1794–96 comes from *Early American Imprints, 1639–1800: a Readex Microprint of the Works Listed in Evan's American Bibliography, Evans Numbers 1–39162* (Worcester, MA: American Antiquarian Society, Readex

Microprint, nd.). According to Stauffer, Bache received the fifteen thousand copies directly from Paine in a cheap edition printed in Paris expressly for the American market (Stauffer, *Bavarian Illuminati*, 73n2).

23. Davidson and Scheick, *Paine, Scripture, and Authority*, 108–16, "Appendix 2 . . . Contemporary Responses to *The Age of Reason* (1794–98)."

24. Patrick W. Hughes, "Irreligion Made Easy: The Reaction to Thomas Paine's *The Age of Reason*," in *New Directions in Thomas Paine Studies*, ed. Scott Cleary, Ivy Linton Stabell, and Quinlan Short (New York: Palgrave Macmillan, 2016), 110. J. C. D. Clark cites other authorities who have identified up to 110 individual published responses; *Thomas Paine*, 347n75.

25. *Early American Imprints.*

26. Paul Leicester Ford, *Mason Locke Weems: His Works and Ways*, 3 vols. (New York: Plimpton, 1928–29), 2:36, Weems to Carey, September 16, 1796.

27. Seth Perry, "*Paine Detected* in Mississippi: Slavery, Print Culture, and the Threat of Deism in the Early Republic," *William and Mary Quarterly* 78 (April 2021): 313–38.

28. Richard Watson, who was identified on his title page as "D.D. F.R.S., Lord Bishop of Landaff, and Regius Professor of Divinity in the University of Cambridge," *An Apology for the Bible in a Series of Letters, Addressed to Thomas Paine* (Boston: Manning & Loring, 1796), 8.

29. Andrew Broaddus, *The Age of Reason & Revelation; or Animadversion on Mr. Thomas Paine's Late Piece, Intitled "The Age of Reason, &c." containing a vindication of the Sacred Scriptures* (Richmond, VA: John Dixon, 1795), 68.

30. Elhahan Winchester, *Ten Letters Addressed to Mr. Paine, in Answer to his Pamphlet, Entitled the Age of Reason: Containing Some clear and satisfying Evidences of the Truth of Divine Revelation; and especially of the Resurrection and Ascension of Jesus* (Boston: John W. Folsom, 1794), 17.

31. Joseph Priestley, *An Answer to Mr. Paine's Age of Reason: Being a Continuation of the Letters to the Philosophers and Politicians of France, on the Subject of Religion . . . in Answer to Mr. Paine's Age of Reason* (Northumberland-Town, PA: Andrew Kennedy, 1794), v.

32. Elihu Palmer, *The Examiners Examined: Being a Defence of the Age of Reason* (New York: L. Wayland and J. Fellows, 1794), 5–6.

33. A Citizen of New York, *Strictures on Bishop Watson's "Apology for the Bible"* (New York: John Fellows, 1796), 2–3.

34. Elias Boudinot, *The Age of Revelation. Or the Age of Reason Shewn to be an Age of Infidelity* (Philadelphia, PA: Asbury Dickins, 1801), xv.

35. Boudinot, *Age of Revelation*, xvi.

36. David Levi, *Defence of the Old Testament, in a Series of Letters Addressed to Thomas Paine* (New York: William A. Davis, 1797), 7.

37. For example, Charles Inglis [writing as "An American"], *The True Interest of America Impartially Stated, in Certain Strictures on a Pamphlet Intitled COMMON SENSE* (Philadelphia, PA: James Humphreys, 1776); William Smith, "To the People of Pennsylvania," *Pennsylvania Ledger*, March 30 and April 13, 1776.

38. Smylie, "Perspectives on Deism," 218. On the intellectual problems created by this use of Enlightenment reasoning in favor of traditional doctrine, see Henry F. May, "The Didactic Enlightenment," in *The Enlightenment in America* (New York: Oxford University Press, 1976), 307–57; Noll, *AMERICA'S GOD*, 93–113, chap. 6, "Theistic Common Sense."

39. For examples, see Boudinot, *Age of Revelation*, 306–19.

40. Winchester, *Ten Letters*, 17–23: Priestley, *Answer to Mr. Paine*, 57–59; Gilbert Wakefield, *Examination of The Age of Reason, or an Investigation of True and Fabulous Theology, By Thomas Paine* (New York: B. Forman, 1794), 21–32. Defense of the resurrection by the more orthodox was even more strenuous.

41. For Jefferson's two edited versions of the gospels, along with expert commentary, see Thomas, Jefferson, *Jefferson's Extracts from the Gospels*, ed. Dickinson W. Adams and Ruth W. Lester, in *The Papers of Thomas Jefferson, Second Series* (Princeton, NJ: Princeton University Press, 1983). An account tracing the attention given to these versions is Peter Menseau, *The Jefferson Bible: A Biography* (Princeton, NJ: Princeton University Press, 2020).

42. Broaddus, *Age of Revelation*, 58.

43. Priestley, *Answer to Mr. Paine*, 98.

44. Elhanan Winchester, *A Century Sermon on the Glorious Revolution* (London, 1788), in Ellis Sandoz, ed., *Political Sermons of the American Founding Era, 1730–1805* (Indianapolis: Liberty Press, 1991), 997–99.

45. Along with Levi, Winchester, and a few others, a Boston Congregationalist and pioneer American historian, Jeremy Belknap, likewise responded to Paine in entirely religious, nonpolitical terms, in *Dissertations on the Character, Death & Resurrection of Jesus Christ, and the Evidence of His Gospel; with remarks on some sentiments advanced in a book intitled "The Age of Reason"* (Boston: Joseph Belknap, 1795).

46. Uzal Ogden, *Antidote to Deism: The Deist Unmasked; or an ample Refutation of all the Objections of Thomas Paine, Against the Christian Religion*, 2 vols. (Newark, NJ: John Woods, 1795), 1:v, ix (last two quotations).

47. James Hutson, "'A Future State of Rewards and Punishment': The Founders' Formula for the Social and Political Utility of Religion," in *Forgotten Features of the Founding: The Recovery of Religious Themes in the Early American Republic* (Lanham, MD: Lexington, 2003), 1–44. For one of countless other examples of this reasoning directed at Paine, see Watson, *Apology for the Bible*, 4.

48. Ogden, *Antidote to Deism*, 1:17–18.

49. Schlereth, *Age of Infidels*, 17.

50. Watson, *Apology for the Bible*, 4.

51. Boudinot, *Age of Revelation*, xxii.

52. Broaddus, *Age of Reason and Revelation*, 68–69, 10.

53. Schlereth, *Age of Infidels*; Christopher Grasso, "Deist Common Sense in the Wake of the American Revolution," *Journal of American History* 95 (June 2008): 43–68; Amanda Porterfield, *Conceived in Doubt: Religion and Politics in the New American Nation* (Chicago: University of Chicago Press, 2012); Christopher Grasso, *Skepticism and American Faith: From the Revolution to the Civil War* (New York: Oxford

University Press, 2018). These works follow a trail blazed by Stauffer, *Bavarian Illuminati*.

54. Wood, *Empire of Liberty*, 199.

55. As an example, the second, which exegeted 2 Timothy 3:16 ("All scripture is given by inspiration of God"), enlisted traditional biblical evidence to support a high doctrine of inspiration. James Muir, *An Examination of the Principles contained in The Age of Reason: In Ten Discourses* (Baltimore, MD: S. & J. Adams, 1795), 19.

56. Muir, *Examination*, 124 (John 7), 145–48 (American crimes), 149–51 (Native Americans), 161 (national guilt). Muir's combination of detailed historical apologetics and a conservative social diagnosis also marked a blockbuster volume assembled by Moses Hoge, a Presbyterian minister who later became president of Hampden-Sydney College in Virginia: *Christian Panoply* (Shepherd's-Town, VA: P. Rootes & C. Blagrove, 1797).

57. A Citizen of New York, *Strictures*, 3–5.

58. Wakefield, *Examination of The Age of Reason*, 5, 7.

59. Broaddus, *Age of Reason and Revelation*, 6, 7–8n.

60. Broaddus, *Age of Reason and Revelation*, 57–58.

61. Daniel Humphreys, *The Bible Needs No Apology: or Watson's System of Religion Refuted; and the advocate proved an unfaithful one, by the Bible itself; of which a short view is given, and which itself gives, a short answer to Paine* (Portsmouth, NH: Charles Peirce, 1796), 13 ("like saying"), 6 (all other quotations).

62. Humphreys, *Bible Needs No Apology*, 7 (national churches), 11–12.

63. For details on Humphreys's career, see F. B. Dexter, *Biographical Sketches of the Graduates of Yale College*, vol. 2: *May, 1745–May, 1763* (New York: Henry Holt, 1896), 471–73.

64. On the Sandemanians, see D. B. Murray, "Sandeman, Robert," in *Dictionary of Scottish Church History and Theology*, ed. Nigel M. deS. Cameron (Downers Grove, IL: InterVarsity, 1993), 744.

65. In 1801 Humphreys published a Sandemanian tract whose long title referred to "the falling state of the Antichristian Kingdom," by which he meant Catholicism specifically but also Christendom more generally: *The Inquirer: Being an Examination of the Question, lately agitated, reflecting the legitimate Powers of Government; whether they extend to the Care of Religion . . . . with a Supplement On the Prevalence of Infidelity— The falling State of the Antichristian Kingdom—and the Revival of Christianity* (Boston: Printing Office, Union Street, 1801).

66. Humphreys, *Bible Needs No Apology*, 96.

67. Another English work, by the evangelical Anglican Thomas Scott, was reprinted twice in the United States, *A Vindication of the Divine Inspiration of the Holy Scriptures, and of the Doctrines Contained in Them: Being an Answer to the Two Parts of Mr. T. Paine's Age of Reason* (New York: G. Forman, 1797), and as part of *The Force of Truth* (Carlisle, PA: George Kline, 1810).

68. Schlereth, *Age of Infidels*.

69. *Christianity vindicated, in the admirable speech of the Hon. Tho. Erskine, in the trail of [T.] Williams, for publishing Paine's "Age of Reason"* (Philadelphia, PA: J. Carey, 1797).

Chapter 3

1. Sam Haselby, *The Origins of American Religious Nationalism* (New York: Oxford University Press, 2015), 1.
2. Alexis de Tocqueville, *Democracy in America*, 4 vols., vol. 2, part 2, ed. Eduardo Nolla, trans. James T. Schleifer (Indianapolis, IN: Liberty Fund, 2010), 2:410–16.
3. The intense controversy between custodial and sectarian evangelicals has received superb historical treatment, including signal works by Vernon Stauffer, *New England and the Bavarian Illuminati* (New York: Columbia University Press, 1918); William G. McLoughlin, *New England Dissent, 1630–1833: The Baptists and the Separation of Church and State*, 2 vols. (Cambridge, MA: Harvard University Press, 1971), 2:915–1284; Nathan O. Hatch, "*Sola Scriptura* and *Novus Ordo Seclorum*," in Hatch and Noll, BIBLE IN AMERICA, 59–78; Hatch, DEMOCRATIZATION; Chris Beneke, *Beyond Toleration: The Religious Origins of American Pluralism* (New York: Oxford University Press, 2006); Amanda Porterfield, *Conceived in Doubt: Religion and Politics in the New Nation* (Chicago: University of Chicago Press, 2012); Haselby, *Origins of American Religious Nationalism*; Christopher Grasso, *Skepticism and American Faith: From the Revolution to the Civil War* (New York: Oxford University Press, 2018).
4. For the periodization of this early history as well as my treatment of Federalist Protestants, I am following Jonathan Den Hartog's impressive *Patriotism and Piety: Federalist Politics and Religious Struggle in the New American Nation* (Charlottesville: University of Virginia Press, 2015). Den Hartog's account of Federalist religious evolution parallels the record of their political evolution in David Hacket Fischer's *The Revolution of American Conservatism: The Federalist Party in the Era of Jeffersonian Democracy* (New York: Harper & Row, 1965).
5. For numbers of churches, see Edwin Scott Gaustad, *Historical Atlas of Religion in America*, rev. ed. (New York: Harper & Row, 1976), 43; Stephen A. Marini, "The Government of God: Religion and Revolution in America, 1764–1792" (unpublished manuscript).
6. Stephen A. Marini, "Religion, Politics, and Ratification," in *Religion in a Revolutionary Age*, ed. Ronald Hoffman and Peter J. Albert (Charlottesville: University Press of Virginia, 1994), 184–217; Marini, "Government of God."
7. Marini," Religion, Politics, and Ratification."
8. On the importance of these state constitutions, see John K. Wilson, "Religion under the State Constitutions, 1776–1800," *Journal of Church and State* 32 (Autumn 1990): 753–73; Vincent Phillip Munoz, "Church and State in the Founding-Era State Constitutions," *American Political Thought* 4, no. 1 (Winter 2015): 1–38; and especially Carl H. Esbeck and Jonathan J. Den Hartog, eds., *Disestablishment and Religious Dissent: Church-State Relations in the New American States, 1776–1833* (Columbia: University of Missouri Press, 2020). For an outstanding survey of the various state situations, see Thomas J. Curry, *The First Freedoms: Church and State in America to the Passage of the First Amendment* (New York: Oxford University Press, 1986).

9. Virginian Constitution (1776) and A Bill for Establishing Religious Freedom (1786), in Dreisbach and Hall, *SACRED RIGHTS,* 241, 251.

10. Constitution of New York, in Dreisbach and Hall, *SACRED RIGHTS,* 259.

11. Constitution of North Carolina (1776), Maryland State Constitution (1776), in Dreisbach and Hall, *SACRED RIGHTS,* both 257.

12. Massachusetts Constitution (1780), in Dreisbach and Hall, *SACRED RIGHTS,* 246. For an insightful interpretation, see John Witte Jr., "'A Most Mild and Equitable Establishment of Religion': John Adams and the Massachusetts Experiment," in *Religion and the New Republic: Faith in the Founding of America,* ed. James H. Hutson (Lanham, MD: Rowman and Littlefield, 2000), 1–40.

13. On the significance of this publication, see Beneke, *Beyond Toleration,* 206.

14. Gov. William Livingstone, Gov. George Clinton, William Samuel Johnson, and Elias Boudinot, *Proposals for Printing by Subscription, the American Preacher* (N.p.: n.p., ca. 1789).

15. David Austin, "Preface," in *The American Preacher; or a Collection of Sermons from some of the Most Eminent Preachers Now Living in the United States, of Different Denominations in the Christian Church,* 4 vols. (Elizabeth-town, NJ: Shepard Kollock and Abel Morse, 1791), 1:vi.

16. For recent works interpreting the carryover of those old habits as oppressive, see David Sehat, *The Myth of American Religious Freedom* (New York: Oxford University Press, 2011); Steven K. Green, *Inventing Christian America: The Myth of the Religious Founding* (New York: Oxford University Press, 2015).

17. Beneke, *Beyond Toleration,* 188.

18. John Witherspoon, *An Annotated Edition of Lectures on Moral Philosophy by John Witherspoon,* ed. Jack Scott (Newark: University of Delaware Press, 1982), 52–53, 61n173 (on the printed edition of Witherspoon's lectures, compiled from student notes from 1772, 1774, and 1795); 160–61 ("what the magistrate can do" to promote religion while defending "the rights of conscience," even for Catholics, included the possibility that "the magistrate ought to make public provision for the worship of God, in such manner as is agreeable to the great body of the society; though at the same time all who dissent from it are fully tolerated"). Thomas S. Kidd, *Patrick Henry: First among Patriots* (New York: Basic, 2011), 168–73.

19. Den Hartog, *Patriotism and Piety,* 1–12. Also perceptive on the religion of the Federalists is Harry S. Stout, "Rhetoric and Religion in the Early Republic: The Case of the Federalist Clergy," in *Religion and American Politics: From the Colonial Period to the Present,* ed. Mark A. Noll and Luke E. Harlow, 2nd ed. (New York: Oxford University Press, 2007), 65–78.

20. Strong, quoted in Den Hartog, *Patriotism and Piety,* 81.

21. Jedidiah Morse, *A Sermon . . . [in Boston] . . . May 9th, 1798, Being the Day Recommended by John Adams, President of the United States of America for Solemn Humiliation, Fasting and Prayer* (Boston: Samuel Hill, 1798), 17, 27; Timothy Dwight, *The Duty of Americans at the Present Crisis, illustrated in a discourse preached on the fourth of July, 1798* (New Haven, CT: Thomas and Samuel Green, 1798), 18.

22. Morse, *A Sermon,* 20.

23. *Acts and Proceedings of the General Assembly of the Presbyterian Church in the United States of America, May 11, 1798* (Philadelphia, PA: Samuel H. Smith, 1798), 11–15 (quotation 12).

24. Samuel Stanhope Smith, *The Divine Goodness to the United States of America: A Discourse on the Subjects of National Gratitude . . . a Day of General Thanksgiving and Prayer* (Philadelphia, PA: William Young, 1795), 29, 31.

25. For these and many more such indications of Federalist angst, see Mark A. Noll, *Princeton and the Republic, 1768–1822* (Princeton, NJ: Princeton University Press, 1989), 140–49.

26. Smith to Jonathan Dayton, December 22, 1801, Samuel Stanhope Smith Collection, Manuscript Division, Firestone Library, Princeton University.

27. Smith to Jedidiah Morse, February 24, 1799, Samuel Stanhope Smith Collection.

28. See James R. Rohrer, *Keepers of the Covenant: Frontier Missions and the Decline of Congregationalism, 1774–1818* (New York: Oxford University Press, 1995).

29. On religion and this election, see Den Hartog, *Patriotism and Piety*, passim; Edward J. Larson, *A Magnificent Catastrophe: The Tumultuous Election of 1800, America's First Presidential Campaign* (New York: Free Press, 2007); John Ferling, *Adams vs. Jefferson: The Tumultuous Election of 1800* (New York: Oxford University Press, 2004), 153–55; Mark A. Noll, *One Nation under God? Christian Faith and Political Action in America* (San Francisco: Harper & Row, 1988), 75–89 ("The Campaign of 1800: Fire without Light").

30. William Linn, *Serious Considerations on the Election of a President: Addressed to the Citizens of the United States* (New York: John Furman, 1800), 4 (disbelief), 6–8 (Mosaic history), 14–15 (schoolchildren), 13 (Blacks). The pamphlet was also printed in Trenton, New Jersey.

31. Frank Luther Mott, *A History of American Magazines, 1741–1850* (New York: Appleton, 1930), 132.

32. Linn, *Serious Considerations*, 17 (quotation), 19 (my neck), 24 (conclusion).

33. Ernst Troeltsch, *The Social Teachings of the Christian Churches* (1912), many English translations.

34. Respectively, Robert P. Swierenga, "Ethnoreligious Political Behavior in the Mid-Nineteenth Century: Voting, Values, Cultures," in *American Religion and Politics*, ed. Noll and Harlow, 145–68; Curtis D. Johnson, *Redeeming America: Evangelicals and the Road to the Civil War* (Chicago: Ivan Dee, 1993); Haselby, *Origins of American Religious Nationalism*; Hatch, *DEMOCRATIZATION*.

35. See Carlos M. N. Eire, *Reformations: The Early Modern World, 1450–1650* (New Haven, CT: Yale University Press, 2016), chap. 11, "The Radical Reformation"; Brad S. Gregory, *The Unintended Reformation: How a Religious Revolution Secularized Society* (Cambridge, MA: Harvard University Press, 2012), 89–93.

36. For an up-to-date account, see Michael A. G. Haykin, "Separatists and Baptists," in *The Oxford History of Protestant Dissenting Traditions*, vol. 1: *The Post-Reformation Era, c. 1559–1689*, ed. John Coffey (Oxford: Oxford University Press, 2020), 113–38.

37. On the difference between theory and practice, see W. R. Ward, "Pastoral Office and the General Priesthood in the Great Awakening," in *Studies in Church*

History, vol. 26: *The Ministry, Clerical and Lay*, ed. W. J. Shiels and Diana Wood (Cambridge: Cambridge University Press, 1989), 303–27, now available online.

38. For details, see Noll, *IN THE BEGINNING*, 42–44.

39. For details, see Noll, *IN THE BEGINNING*, 134–36.

40. Thomas S. Kidd and Barry Hankins, *Baptists in America: A History* (New York: Oxford University Press, 2015), 14.

41. John Woolman, *Some Considerations on the Keeping of Negroes* (Philadelphia, PA: James Chattin, 1754), ii ("And he stretched forth his Hands toward his Disciples, and said, Behold my Mother and my Brethren: For Whosoever shall do the will of my Father which is in Heaven [arrives at the more noble Part of true Relationship] the same is my Brother, and sister, and Mother, Matt. xii.48"); Anthony Benezet, *Observations on the Inslaving, Importing and Purchasing of Negroes* (Germantown, PA: Christopher Sower, 1759), quotation from title page.

42. For details, see chapter 10.

43. A classic account is Rhys Isaac, "Evangelical Revolt: The Nature of the Baptists' Challenge to the Traditional Order in Virginia, 1765–1775," *William and Mary Quarterly* 31 (July 1974): 345–68.

44. Stephen A. Marini, *Radical Sects in Revolutionary New England* (Cambridge, MA: Harvard University Press, 1982).

45. McLoughlin, *New England Dissent*, 1:559–64.

46. Isaac Backus, "Isaac Backus on Religion and the State, Slavery, and Nobility," in *The Debate on the Constitution*, ed. Bernard Bailyn, 2 vols. (New York: Library of America, 1993), 1:931. For the considerable American influence of the Dissenters' appeal to "the right of private judgment," see Nicholas P. Miller, *The Religious Roots of the First Amendment: Dissenting Protestants and the Separation of Church and State* (New York: Oxford University Press, 2012).

47. Backus, "Isaac Backus on Religion and the State," 1:932–33.

48. See Jon Butler, "James Ireland, John Leland, and John 'Swearing Jack' Waller, and the Baptist Campaign for Religious Freedom in Revolutionary Virginia," in *Revolutionary Founders: Rebels, Radicals, and Reformers in the Making of the Nation*, ed. Alfred F. Young, Gary B. Nash, and Ray Raphael (New York: Knopf, 2011), 169–84.

49. John Leland, *The Bible Baptist* (Baltimore, MD: Wm. Goddard, 1789), 23, 24.

50. Leland, *Bible Baptist*, 4.

51. "Joseph Spencer to James Madison, Enclosing John Leland's Objections," in Bailyn, *Debate on the Constitution*, 2:269.

52. John Leland, *Jack Nips: The Yankee Spy* (1794), in *American Political Writing during the Founding Era*, ed. Charles S. Hyneman and Donald S. Lutz, 2 vols. (Indianapolis, IN: Liberty Press, 1983), 2:981–82.

53. L. H. Butterfield, "Elder John Leland, Jeffersonian Itinerant," *Proceedings of the American Antiquarian Society* 62 (October 1952): 155–242 (on the cheese, 219–27; Jefferson's response, 225). On Leland's significance, see Hatch, *DEMOCRATIZATION*, 95–101.

54. Butterfield, "Elder John Leland," 226.

55. Dreisbach and Hall, *SACRED RIGHTS*, 528, with supplementary documents, 525–31.

56. This phrase from Jefferson is the title of Gordon S. Wood's illuminating *Empire of Liberty: A History of the Early Republic, 1789–1815* (New York: Oxford University Press, 2009).

57. See James M. Banner, *To the Hartford Convention: The Federalists and the Origin of Party Politics in Massachusetts, 1789–1815* (New York: Knopf, 1970).

58. Holifield, *THEOLOGY IN AMERICA,* 199–203.

59. Lyman Beecher, *Autobiography, Correspondence, etc.*, ed. Charles Beecher, 2 vols. (New York: Harper & Bros., 1864), 1:344.

60. Smith to Morse, March 10, 1802, Samuel Stanhope Smith Collection.

61. On Miller's friendship with Jefferson and his later repudiation of "everything that I ever said or wore in his favor," see Samuel Miller, Jr., *The Life of Samuel Miller,* 2 vols. (Philadelphia, PA: Claxton, Remsen, and Haffelfinger, 1869), 1:129–32. The spate of college rioting in this era is described in Steven J. Novak, *The Rights of Youth: American Colleges and Student Revolts* (Cambridge, MA: Harvard University Press, 1977).

62. Noll, *Princeton and the Republic,* 239–43.

63. Noll, *Princeton and the* Republic, 236.

64. Peter Augustus Jay, quoted in Den Hartog, *Patriotism and* Piety, 186, with 186–200 on William Jay.

65. Quoted in Den Hartog, *Patriotism and* Piety, 181.

66. Kidd and Hankins, *Baptists in America,* 89, 93–94, 104.

67. On Smith, see Hatch, *DEMOCRATIZATION,* 68–80; and especially on Smith's appeal to "the plain sense of Scripture," see Michael G. Kenney, *The Perfect Law of Liberty: Elias Smith and the Providential History of America* (Washington, DC: Smithsonian Institution Press, 1994), 20, 26, 61–62, and *passim.*

68. Elias Smith, *A Sermon on New Testament Baptism, in Distinction from All Others,* 2nd ed. (Exeter, NH: Norris & Sawyer, 1807), 11.

69. Elias Smith, *Three Sermons on Election* (Exeter, NH: Norris & Sawyer, 1808), 4.

70. Elias Smith, *The Lovingkindness of God Displayed in the Triumph of Republicanism in America, being a Discourse . . . at the Celebration of American Independence* (N.p.: n.p., 1809), 4, 6, 18, 27.

71. Thomas Campbell, *Address of the Christian Association of Washington* (Washington, PA: Brown and Sample, 1809), 4, 5.

72. Alexander Campbell, "Reply" (to an Episcopal bishop who had reproved Campbell for breaking with Christian traditions), *Christian Baptist* 3 (April 3, 1826): 204.

73. Beth Barton Schweiger, "Alexander Campbell's Passion for Print: Protestant Sectarians and the Press in the Trans-Allegheny West," *Proceedings of the American Antiquarian Society* 118, part 1 (2009): 117–54. On the popularity of such debates, see E. Brooks Holifield, "Theology as Entertainment: Oral Debate in American Religion," *Church History* 67 (September 1998): 499–521.

74. John Henry Hobart, *An Apology for Apostolic Order and Its Advocates* (New York: T. & J. Swords, 1807), 219.

75. William Linn, *A Collection of Essays on the Subject of Episcopacy* (New York: T. & J. Swords, 1806), 1.

76. Samuel Miller, *Letters Concerning the Constitution and Order of the Christian Ministry as Deduced from Scripture and Primitive Usage* (New York: Hopkins & Seymour, 1807), 3, 7.

77. Anon., *Strictures on a Pastoral Letter to the Laity of the Protestant Episcopal Church, on the Subject of Bible and Common Prayer Book Society by John Henry Hobart ... by a Layman* (New York: Van Winkle and Wiley, 1815), 9–10.

Chapter 4

1. Francis Asbury, "To the President of the United States" and "Answer of George Washington to Asbury and Coke," in *The Journal and Letters of Francis Asbury*, 3 vols., ed. Elmer T. Clark (Nashville, TN: Abingdon, 1958), 3:70–71, 71–72. For helpful context, see John Wigger, *American Saint: Francis Asbury and the Methodists* (New York: Oxford University Press, 2009), 180–81.

2. Asbury, *Journal*, 1:598, May 28 and May 31, 1789.

3. Quoted in John H. Wigger, *Taking Heaven by Storm: Methodism and the Rise of Popular Christianity in America* (New York: Oxford University Press, 1998), 180.

4. Charles G. Finney, *Lectures on Revivals of Religion* (1835), ed. William G. McLoughlin (Cambridge, MA: Harvard University Press, 1960), 273.

5. James Robinson Graves, *The Great Iron Wheel: or, Republicanism Backwards and Christianity Reversed* (Nashville, TN: Graves and Marks, 1855).

6. A year-by-year record of Methodist members and preachers is found in *Minutes of the Annual Conferences of the Methodist Episcopal Church for the Years 1773–1828*, 2 vols. (New York: T. Mason and G. Lane, 1840).

7. A pioneering work that inserted Methodists into the national story was Donald G. Mathews, *Slavery and Methodism: A Chapter in American Morality, 1780–1845* (Princeton, NJ: Princeton University Press, 1965). Outstanding recent examples include Thomas C. Oden, *Doctrinal Standards in the Wesleyan Tradition* (Grand Rapids, MI: Zondervan, 1988); Hatch, *DEMOCRATIZATION*; Russell E. Richey, *Early American Methodism* (Bloomington: Indiana University Press, 1991); Russell E. Richey, Kenneth E. Rowe, and Jean Miller Schmidt, eds., *Perspectives on American Methodism: Interpretive Essays* (Nashville, TN: Kingswood, 1993); A. Gregory Schneider, *The Way of the Cross Leads Home: The Domestication of American Methodism* (Bloomington: Indiana University Press, 1993); Christine Leigh Heyrman, *Southern Cross: The Beginnings of the Bible Belt* (New York: Knopf, 1997); Cynthia Lynn Lyerly, *Methodism and the Southern Mind, 1770–1810* (New York: Oxford University Press, 1998); Wigger, *Taking Heaven by Storm*; Dee E. Andrews, *The Methodists and Revolutionary America, 1760–1800: The Shaping of an Evangelical Culture* (Princeton, NJ: Princeton University Press, 2000); Lester Ruth, *A Little Heaven Below: Worship at Early Methodist Quarterly Meetings* (Nashville, TN: Kingswood, 2000); Nathan O. Hatch and John H. Wigger, eds., *Methodism and the Shaping of American Culture* (Nashville, TN: Kingswood, 2001); David Hempton, *Methodism: Empire of the*

Spirit (New Haven, CT: Yale University Press, 2005); Russell E. Richey, *Methodist Connectionalism: Historical Perspectives* (Nashville, TN: United Methodist Church, 2009); Wigger, *American Saint*.

8. *Minutes Of Several Conversations between The Rev. Thomas Coke, LL.D., The Rev. Francis Asbury, and others, at a Conference, begun in Baltimore ... the 27th of December, in the Year 1784: Composing a Form of Discipline for the Ministers, Preachers, and other Members of the Methodist Episcopal Church in America* (Philadelphia, PA: Charles Cist, 1785), 3–4.

9. For the milieu in which English Methodism emerged, see D. Bruce Hindmarsh, *The Spirit of Early Evangelicalism: True Religion in a Modern World* (New York: Oxford University Press, 2018).

10. Treatments of British Methodism for its political and social implications include a landmark study by E. P. Thompson, *The Making of the English Working Class* (New York: Pantheon, 1964), as well as significant ripostes, especially David Hempton, *Methodism and Politics in British Society, 1750–1850* (Stanford, CA: Stanford University Press, 1984) and David Hempton and John Walsh, "E. P. Thompson and Methodism," in *God and Mammon: Protestants, Money, and the Market, 1790–1860*, ed. Mark A. Noll (New York: Oxford University Press, 2002), 99–120. For the United States, the most extensive attempts in a similar direction have been made by Hatch, *DEMOCRATIZATION* and Heyrman, *Southern Cross*.

11. John Wesley, "Preface," in *Sermons on Several Occasions* (1746), in *The Works of John Wesley*, vol. 1: *Sermons I, 1–33*, ed. Albert C. Outler (Nashville, TN: Abingdon, 1984), 104–5.

12. *Minutes Of Several Conversations* (1784), 20–21.

13. *Minutes Of Several Conversations* (1784), 25. The *Minutes* appear with question marks instead of periods since the answers are framed as questions asking whether itinerants followed these instructions.

14. For fuller treatment of early Methodist apoliticism, see Noll, *AMERICA'S GOD*, 338–41.

15. *Minutes of the Methodist Conferences, Annually held in America from 1773 to 1813* (New York: Hitt and Ware, 1813), 138.

16. *Minutes of the Methodist Conferences* (1773–1813), 162–64.

17. For fuller treatment of O'Kelly, including bibliography, see Wigger, *American Saint*, 189–215; Hatch, *DEMOCRATIZATION*, 69–70, 82.

18. On such complaints, but also the ability of Asbury to keep Methodism "at its core a Wesleyan movement: a part of, but as often as not in conflict with, the main currents in American history," see Andrews, *Methodists and Revolutionary America*, 220.

19. Asbury, *Journal*, 1:732 (on Jefferson). A few references to the political names are found in the indexes, but those mentions occur in the critical apparatus, which sometimes tracks Asbury's career by reference to a sitting president.

20. Hempton, *Methodism: Empire*, 67.

21. Asbury, *Journal*, 2:250.

22. Asbury, *Journal*, 2:560.

23. John Wigger, "Fighting Bees: Methodist Itinerants and the Dynamics of Methodist Growth, 1770–1845," in Hatch and Wigger, *Methodism*, 127. Asbury seems to have preached twice on the text from 2 Timothy but never from Psalm 40; Asbury, *Journal*, "Index of Sermon Texts," 2:818, 823.

24. Hempton, *Methodism: Empire*, 68,

25. Quoted in Leland Howard Scott, "Methodist Theology in America in the Nineteenth Century" (Ph.D. diss., Yale University, 1954), 132n81.

26. *Pocket Hymn-Book, Designed as a Constant Companion for the Pious, Collected from Various Authors*, 23rd ed. (Philadelphia, PA: Ezekiel Cooper, 1800), i–ii.

27. Inexplicably, there is scant treatment of hymn collections and none of the Methodists' *Pocket Hymn-Book* in the splendid *HISTORY OF THE BOOK*. Lack of scholarly attention to such publications probably comes from the fact that most hymns concentrated intensely on relations between God and humans rather than on human interactions. For exceptions, where hymns became vehicles for intense political expressions, see Hatch, *DEMOCRATIZATION*, "Appendix: A Sampling of Anticlerical and Anti-Calvinist Christian Verse," 227–43. For careful treatment of Methodist publishing in cross-border contexts, including hymnbooks, see Scott McLaren, *Pulpit, Press, and Politics: Methodists and the Market for Books in Upper Canada* (Toronto: University of Toronto Press, 2019).

28. *Pocket Hymn-Book*, 5. For this hymn and its scriptural content, see Frank Baker, ed., *Representative Verse of Charles Wesley* (Nashville, TN: Abingdon, 1962), 24–26

29. *Pocket Hymn-Book*, 6.

30. John S. Andrews, "Hart, Joseph," in *The Blackwell Dictionary of Evangelical Biography*, ed. Donald M. Lewis, 2 vols. (Cambridge, MA: Blackwell, 1995), 1:526.

31. On these early enterprises, see Wigger, *Taking Heaven by Storm*, 179.

32. See the later sections of Thomas S. Kidd, *The Great Awakening: The Roots of Evangelical Christianity in Colonial America* (New Haven, CT: Yale University Press, 2009). Especially for the last third of the eighteenth century, see Steven A. Marini, *Radical Sects of Revolutionary New England* (Cambridge, MA: Harvard University Press, 1982).

33. David William Kling, *A Field of Divine Wonders: The New Divinity and Village Revivals in Northwestern Connecticut, 1792–1822* (University Park: Pennsylvania State University Press, 1993); Richard D. Shiels, "The Second Great Awakening in Connecticut: Critique of the Traditional Interpretation," *Church History* 49 (1980): 401–15.

34. Paul Keith Conkin, *Cane Ridge, America's Pentecost* (Madison: University of Wisconsin Press, 1990).

35. *Minutes* (1773–1828). 1800: 65,000 in society with 287 itinerants; 1806: 130,500 in society with 452 itinerants; 1812: 195,000 in society with 688 itinerants.

36. Frank Luther Mott, *A History of American Magazines, 1741–1850* (New York: Appleton, 1930), 133.

37. Anon., *Extracts of Letters, Containing some Account of the Work of God* (New York: Ezekiel Cooper, 1805), 3–19.

38. Anon., *Extracts of Letters*, 19.

39. Anon., *Extracts of Letters*, 4, 17, 22.

40. Heyrman, *Southern Cross*, 117–205.

41. Richard D. Shiels, "The Methodist Invasion of Congregational New England," in Hatch and Wigger, *Methodism*, 257–80, esp. 266–69.

42. William Cabell Bruce, *John Randolph of Roanoke, 1733–1833*, 2 vols. (New York: G. P. Putnam's Sons, 1922), 2: 653, 655–56, "Conversion" from a letter of September 25, 1818; other quotations from Randolph to Francis Scott Key, September 7, 1818. And for context, Henry F. May, *The Enlightenment in America* (New York: Oxford University Press, 1976), 329–31.

43. Samuel Goodrich, *Recollections of a Lifetime, or Men and Things I Have Seen: In a Series of Letters to a Friend* (New York: Miller, Orton, and Mulligan, 1856), 1:217.

44. Catherine A. Brekus, *Strangers and Pilgrims: Female Preaching in America, 1740–1845* (Chapel Hill: University of North Carolina Press, 1998), 176, 193.

45. Charles G. Finney, *The Memoirs of Charles G. Finney: The Complete Restored Text*, ed. Garth M. Rosell and Richard A. G. Dupuis (Grand Rapids, MI: Academie/Zondervan, 1989), 14, 20.

46. Schneider, *Way of the Cross*, 18. Methodist history as described by Schneider parallels the situation for colonial American Puritans: when John Winthrop invoked the scriptural [Matt 5:14] "a city on the hill," he was referring to an international Reformed Puritan movement defined by its spiritual character; by the time of the American Revolution the "city" had become localized as a description of colonial America's providential destiny under God. See Abram Van Engen, "Origins and Last Farewells: Bible Wars, Textual Form, and the Making of American History," *New England Quarterly* 86 (December 2013): 543–92.

47. I am not aware of any focused scholarly treatment of the Methodists and the War of 1812.

48. Asbury, *Journal*, 3:491.

49. Andrews, *Methodists and Revolutionary America*, 239.

50. See especially McLaren, *Pulpit, Press, and Politics*.

51. Richey, *Early American Methodism*, 33.

52. Goodrich, *Recollections*, 1:217.

53. Alfred Brunson, *A Western Pioneer* (1872; New York: Arno, 1975), 42–43, 48.

54. Wigger, *American Saint*, 182.

55. On the political allegiances of the Methodists and other denominations, see Robert P. Swierenga, "Ethnoreligious Political Behavior in the Mid-Nineteenth Century: Voting, Values, Culture," in *Religion and American Politics: From the Colonial Period to the Present*, ed. Mark A. Noll and Luke E. Harlow, 2nd ed. (New York: Oxford University Press, 2007), 156.

56. See especially Richard J. Carwardine, "Methodist Ministers and the Second Party System," in Richey, Rowe, and Schmidt, *Perspectives on American Methodism*, 159–77; Richard J. Carwardine, *Evangelicals and Politics in Antebellum America* (New Haven, CT: Yale University Press, 1993), 165–66, 190–91; Richard J. Carwardine, "Trauma in Methodism: Property, Church Schism, and Sectional Polarization in Antebellum America," in Noll, *God and Mammon*, 195–216.

57. The superb scholarship on this subject includes Mathews, *Slavery and Methodism*; Andrews, *Methodists and Revolutionary America*; Lyerly, *Methodism and the Southern Mind*.

58. *Minutes Of Several Conversations* (1784), 15.

59. For a full account of Whitefield and colonial slavery, see Peter Y. Choi, *George Whitefield: Evangelist for God and Empire* (Grand Rapids, MI: Eerdmans, 2018). For his appeal to the enslaved, see Phyllis Wheatley, "An Elegiac Poem, On . . . Whitefield," in *Phyllis Wheatley: Complete Works*, ed. Vincent Carretta (New York: Penguin, 2001), 15–16.

60. On the embrace of Scripture by African Americans and African Britons in the colonial era, see Noll, *IN THE BEGINNING*, 209–32.

61. *Minutes* (1773–1828).

62. Wigger, *Taking Heaven by Storm*, 130 (Hosier); Dennis C. Dickerson, The *African Methodist Episcopal Church: A History* (New York: Cambridge University Press, 2020), 29–30 (Allen); Kyle T. Bulthuis, *Four Steeples over the City Streets: Religion and Society in New York's Early Republic Congregations* (New York: New York University Press, 2014), 70–71 (New York City).

63. These figures are treated in chapter 9.

Chapter 5

1. Edwin Scott Gaustad, *Historical Atlas of Religion in* America, rev. ed. (New York: Harper & Row, 1976), 43; Stephen A. Marini, "The Government of God: Religion and Revolution in America, 1764–1792" (unpublished manuscript); Andrew Reed, *American* Churches (1834), in *The Voluntary Church: American Religious Life, 1740–1860, Seen through the Eyes of European* Visitors, ed. Milton B. Powell (New York: Macmillan, 1967), 103–4.

2. Jonathan D. Sarna, *American Judaism: A History* (New Haven, CT: Yale University Press, 2004), 63.

3. Jon Butler, *Awash in a Sea of Faith: Christianizing the American Faith* (Cambridge, MA: Harvard University Press, 1990), 193.

4. Winthrop S. Hudson, "The Methodist Age in America," *Methodist History* 4 (April 1974): 3–15 (numbers, 11). Even twenty years later, the U.S. census found 5,854 more Methodist churches (19,883) than Presbyterian, Congregationalist, Episcopalian, Lutheran, and Reformed combined (14,029). *Statistics of the United States . . . in 1860; compiled from . . . the Eighth Census* (Washington, DC: Government Printing Office, 1866), 497–501.

5. The simplified account that follows has benefited from Robert H. Wiebe, *Opening of American Society: From the Adoption of the Constitution to the Eve of Disunion* (New York: Knopf, 1984); Walter A. McDougal, *Freedom Just around the Corner: A New American History: 1585–1828* (New York: HarperCollins, 2004), 280–513; Sean Wilentz, *The Rise of American Democracy: Jefferson to Lincoln* (New York: Norton,

2005); *HISTORY OF THE BOOK*, vol. 2; Bruce Kuklick, *A Political History of the USA: One Nation under God* (London: Red Globe, 2020), 73–102; and especially Howe, *WHAT HATH GOD WROUGHT*.

6. Howe, *WHAT HATH GOD WROUGHT*, 118.

7. Robert A. Gross, "Introduction: An Extensive Republic," in *HISTORY OF THE BOOK*, 2:3.

8. *HISTORICAL STATISTICS*, 710; *Minutes of the Annual Conferences of the Methodist Episcopal Church for the Years, 1773–1828* (New York: T. Mason and G. Lane, 1840).

9. Howe, *WHAT HATH GOD WROUGHT*, 269.

10. For the relatively meager assessment of the business cycle from religious perspectives, see Mark A. Noll, ed., *God and Mammon: Protestants, Money, and the Market, 1790–1860* (New York: Oxford University Press, 2002) and Stewart Davenport, *Friends of the Unrighteous Mammon: Northern Christians and Market Capitalism, 1815–1860* (Chicago: University of Chicago Press, 2008).

11. Besides the works cited in the introduction, see Seth Perry, *Bible Culture and Authority in the Early United States* (Princeton, NJ: Princeton University Press, 2018).

12. Benedict Anderson, *Imagined Communities: Reflections on the Origin and Spread of Nationalism* (London: Verso, 1983).

13. Facsimile of the *Congressional Journal*, September 12, 1782, in Dreisbach and Hall, *SACRED RIGHTS*, 232–33; for fuller context, Noll, *IN THE BEGINNING*, 332–33. The KJV was often called "the authorized version," though it had never been so designated by Britain's Parliament.

14. Isaac Backus, *The Diary of Isaac Backus*, ed. William G. McLoughlin (Providence, RI: Brown University Press, 1979), 1295–96.

15. Michael S. Carter, "Mathew Carey, the Douai Bible, and Catholic Print Culture, 1789–1791," *Journal of the Early Republic* 27 (Fall 2007): 437–69 (quotation, 437). For the specific date of publication, see Hills, *ENGLISH BIBLE*, 4–5.

16. Hills, *ENGLISH BIBLE*, 1–4.

17. "Subscribers Names," in *The Holy Bible, translated from the Latin Vulgate; Diligently compared with the Hebrew, Greek, and other editions, in divers languages; And first published by the English College at Doway, Anno 1609, Newly revised, and corrected, according to the Clementine edition of the Scriptures, With Annotations for elucidating the principal difficulties of Holy Writ* (Philadelphia, PA: Carey, Stewart, 1790), [v–viii]. Particularly helpful on the reduced Catholic-Protestant strife in this period is Margaret Abruzzo, "Apologetics of Harmony: Mathew Carey and the Rhetoric of Religious Liberty," *Pennsylvania Magazine of History and Biography* 134 (January 2010): 5–30.

18. Hills, *ENGLISH BIBLE*, 4–8.

19. Quoted in Garry Wills, "Mason Weems, Bibliopolism," *American Heritage*, February–March 1981, 68. Full treatment of the Weems-Carey partnership is found in Gutjahr, *AMERICAN BIBLE*, 23–29.

20. Frederick Christian Schaeffer, *The Blessed Reformation: A Sermon . . . on occasion of the Solemnization of the Third Centurial Jubilee in commemoration of the Reformation*

commenced by Dr. Martin Luther on the 31st of October, 1517 (New York: Kirk & Mercein, 1817), 6.

21. James Fenimore Cooper, *The Last of the Mohicans: A Narrative of 1757*, 2 vols. (Philadelphia, PA: H. C. Carey & I. Lea, 1826), 1:177–78. I thank Tyler Gardner for this reference. For the complex theological disputes of the 1820s, see Holifield, *THEOLOGY IN AMERICA*, 341–94; Noll, *AMERICA'S GOD*, 253–327.

22. Quotations that follow, with indicated page numbers, are from *Religion in the United States of America: The Origin, Progress, Relations to the State and Present Condition of the Evangelical Churches of the United States (with notices of the unevangelical denominations)* (Glasgow: Blackie and Sons, 1844). On the wide acceptance of Baird's book, at home and abroad, see Howe, *WHAT HATH GOD WROUGHT*, 193–94.

23. Baird here echoed the words much quoted in Protestant circles from William Chillingworth (1637): "[T]he BIBLE, I say, THE BIBLE only is the Religion of Protestants." For the context and ironies of Chillingworth's assertion, see Noll, *IN THE BEGINNING*, 93–94; Alec Ryrie, *Unbelievers: A History of the Abolition of God* (Cambridge, MA: Harvard University Press, 2019), 65–69.

24. As testimony to Baird's claim about American evangelical ecumenicity, the domestic publisher for this Presbyterian's book was the firm of the Methodist Harper brothers. Examples of the positive domestic response include two lengthy reviews by Presbyterians who, even if they stood more firmly for distinctly Reformed convictions than did Baird, still lauded his efforts in lofty terms: "Baird's Religion in America," *Biblical Repertory and Princeton Review* 17 (January 1845): 18–43; expanded edition of "Baird's Religion in America," *Biblical Repertory and Princeton Review* 28 (October 1856): 642–54.

25. LOC: Prints and Photographs, 98505150. On Sinclair, see Library Company of Philadelphia, "Sinclair, Thomas," accessed November 11, 2021, https://digital.library company.org/islandora/object/digitool%3A79775.

26. For the bearing of this liberalism on American religious history, see Noll, *AMERICA'S GOD*, 210–12, 448–49. For a most instructive cross-border comparison, see Michel Ducharme, *The Idea of Liberty in Canada during the Age of Atlantic Revolutions, 1776–1838* (Kingston: McGill-Queen's University Press, 2014).

27. Outstanding accounts of this translation include, among a multitude, David Norton, *A History of the Bible as Literature*, 2 vols. (New York: Cambridge University Press, 1992); David Daniell, *The Bible in English* (New Haven, CT: Yale University Press, 2003), 427–98; Gordon Campbell, *Bible, 1611–2011: The Story of the King James Version* (New York: Oxford University Press, 2010); Hannibal Hamlin and Norman W. Jones, eds., *The King James Bible after 400 Years* (New York: Cambridge University Press, 2010); David Lyle Jeffrey, ed., *The King James Bible and the World It Made* (Waco, TX: Baylor University Press, 2011); David Norton, *The King James Bible: A Short History from Tyndale to Today* (New York: Cambridge University Press, 2011). The next paragraphs summarize Noll, *IN THE BEGINNING*, 62–69.

28. James H. Hutson, ed., *The Founders on Religion: A Book of Quotations* (Princeton, NJ: Princeton University Press, 2005), 36, 25, 26.

29. John Witherspoon, *The Holy Bible* (Trenton, NJ: Isaac Collins, 1791), preface.

30. On that continued popularity, see the epilogue.

31. Hills, *ENGLISH BIBLE*, 7 (#31).

32. Excellent on the British background for American trust in providence is Nicholas Guyatt, *Providence and the Invention of the United States, 1607–1876* (New York: Cambridge University Press, 2007); and on the long-term effects of that American disposition, Walter A. McDougall, *The Tragedy of U.S. Foreign Policy: How America's Civil Religion Betrayed the National Interest* (New Haven, CT: Yale University Press, 2016).

33. James Madison, "Proclamation 20—Recommending a Day of Public Thanksgiving for Peace," March 4, 1815, Founders Online, https://founders.archives.gov/docume nts/Madison/03-09-02-0066.

34. William Miltimore, *A Discourse, delivered at Falmouth, March 1, 1815, on the ratification of peace between American and Great Britain*, in William Gribbin, *The Churches Militant: The War of 1812 and American Religion* (New Haven, CT: Yale University Press, 1973), 132.

35. *Charleston (SC) Courier*, March 2, 1815, in Gribbin, *Churches Militant*, 131–32.

36. *Columbian Phoenix* (RI), October 14, 1815, in Gribbin, *Churches Militant*, 134.

37. *Rutland (VT) Herald*, August 23, 1815, in Gribbin, *Churches Militant*, 134.

38. Gribbin, *Churches Militant*, 130; William Gribbin, "The Covenant Transformed: The Jeremiad Tradition and the War of 1812," *Church History* 40 (September 1971): 305.

39. Elias Boudinot, *The Second Advent; or, Coming of the Messiah in Glory, Shown to be a Scripture Doctrine, and Taught by Divine Revelation from the Beginning of the World* (Trenton, NJ: D. Fenton and S. Hutchinson, 1815), iii–iv.

40. Elias Boudinot, *A Star in the West: A Humble Attempt to Discover the Long Lost Ten Tribes of Israel, Preparatory to their Return to their Beloved City, Jerusalem* (Trenton, NJ: D. Fenton, S. Hutchinson, and J. Dunham, 1816), iii.

41. John Witherspoon, *The Dominion of Providence over the Passions of Men, A Sermon Preached at Princeton, on the 17th of May, 1776* (Philadelphia, PA: R. Aitken, 1776).

Chapter 6

1. Robert A. Gross, "Introduction: An Extensive Republic," in *HISTORY OF THE BOOK*, 2:1–50 (quotations in this paragraph, 2, 3, 5, 13).

2. Elias Smith, *The Clergyman's Looking Glass; Being a History of the Birth, Life, and Death of Anti-Christ, In three books . . . Written in Scripture stile, in Chapter and Verses* (Portsmouth, NH: N. S. and W. Peirce, 1803), 45 (quoting Morse), 43 (song quotation), 4–5 (verses 22 and 23). Especially helpful on Smith are Michael G. Kenny, *The Perfect Law of Liberty: Elias Smith and the Providential History of America* (Washington, DC: Smithsonian Institution, 1994) and Hatch, *DEMOCRATIZATION*, 68–81, 134–38, and passim.

3. Eran Shalev, *American Zion: The Old Testament as a Political Text from the Revolution to the Civil War* (New Haven, CT: Yale University Press, 2013); Eran Shalev, "'Written

in the Style of Antiquity': Pseudo-Biblicism and the Early American Republic, 1770–1830," *Church History* 79 (December 2010): 800–826. This section has also benefited from Shalev's "Beyond the Republican Synthesis: Biblical Republicanism and the American Revolution," in *The Liberal Republican Quandary in Israel, Europe, and the United States: Early Modern Thought Meets Contemporary Affairs*, ed. Thomas Maissen and Fania Oz-Salzberger (Brookline, MA: Academic Studies Press, 2012), 87–114 and his "Evil Counselors, Corrupt Traitors, and Bad Kings: The Hebrew Bible and Political Critique in Revolutionary America and Beyond," in *Resistance to Tyrants, Obedience to God: Reason, Religion, and Republicanism at the American Founding*, ed. Dustin Gish and Daniel P. Klinghard (Lanham, MD: Lexington, 2015), 105–24.

4. See chapter 12, 255–56.

5. Identification of the author as John Leacock and of publication in Boston by John Baylem in 1775 has been made by Carla Mulford, ed., *The First Book of American Chronicles of the Times, 1774–1775* (Newark: University of Delaware Press, 1987).

6. Shalev, *American Zion*, 210n13.

7. Richard Carwardine, *Lincoln's Sense of Humor* (Carbondale: Southern Illinois University Press, 2017), 10.

8. Shalev, *American Zion*, 94.

9. See especially Eric Nelson, *The Hebrew Republic: Jewish Sources and the Transformation of European Political Thought* (Cambridge, MA: Harvard University Press, 2010); Eric Nelson, "Hebraism and the Republican Turn of 1776: A Contemporary Account of the Debate over *Common Sense*," *William and Mary Quarterly* 70 (October 2013): 781–812; and for additional references, Noll, *IN THE BEGINNING*, 308, 378nn76–70.

10. Daniel J. Elazar, ed., *Kinship and Consent: The Jewish Political Tradition and Its Contemporary Manifestations* (Lanham, MD: University Press of America and Center for Jewish Community Studies, 1983); George McKenna, *The Puritan Origins of American Nationality* (New Haven, CT: Yale University Press, 2009).

11. Shalom Goldman, *God's Sacred Tongue: Hebrew and the American Imagination* (Chapel Hill: University of North Carolina Press, 2004); Eran Shalev, "Tribes Lost and Found: Israelites in Nineteenth-Century America," in *American Zion*, 118–50; on Boudinot, see chapter 5, 113; on Smith, see chapter 12, 257–60.

12. William Rosenau, *Hebraisms in the Authorized Version of the Bible* (Baltimore, MD: Friedenwald, 1903); Robert Alter, *Pen of Iron: American Prose and the King James Bible* (Princeton, NJ: Princeton University Press, 2010).

13. Shalev, *American Zion*, 50–83, "'The United Tribes, or States of Israel': The Hebrew Republic as a Political Model before the Civil War."

14. For more on these memorials, see chapter 29, 622–27; for the turn to the New Testament, see chapter 29, 624–27.

15. Eran Shalev, *American Zion*, 74, citing Enoch Pound, "Republican Tendencies of the Bible," *Biblical Repertory and Classical Review*, 3rd ser., 4 (1848); and J. V. Moore, "Republican Tendency of the Bible," *Methodist Quarterly Review*, new ser. 6 (1846).

16. Lyman Beecher, "The Republican Elements of the Old Testament," in *Lectures in Political Atheism and Kindred Subjects* (1853), quoted in Shalev, *American Zion*, 71.

17. Jonathan Edwards, *A Humble Inquiry into the Rules of the Word of God, Concerning the Qualifications Requisite to . . . Full Communion in the Visible Christian Church* (1749), in *Works of Jonathan Edwards*, vol. 12: *Ecclesiastical Writings*, ed. David D. Hall (New Haven, CT: Yale University Press, 1994), 271 (my emphases on *typical* and *type*).

18. Perry Miller, "The Garden of Eden and the Deacon's Meadow," *American Heritage*, December 1955, 54.

19. John Leighly, "The Town Names of Colonial New England in the West," *Annals of the Association of American Geographers* 68 (June 1978): 242. Besides the other sources mentioned in the following notes, much relevant information can be found in George R. Stewart, *American Place-Names: A Concise and Selective Dictionary for the Continental United States of America* (New York: Oxford University Press, 1970); Edwin Scott Gaustad and Philip L. Barlow, "Place Names," in *New Historical Atlas of Religion in America* (New York: Oxford University Press, 2000), 335–40.

20. The rest of this paragraph draws on Moshe Davis, *America and the Holy Land, with Eyes toward Zion—IV* (Westport, CT: Praeger, 1995), 12–15 and 135–46, chap. 7, "Biblical Place-Names in America"; Abraham I. Katsh, *The Biblical Heritage of American Democracy* (New York: Ktav, 1977), 169–72, Appendix B, "Place Names of Biblical or Hebrew Origin."

21. "City and County Names," Indiana, http://www.in.gov/core/city_county_facts.html; http://www.whateveristrue.com/heritage/biblenames.htm, accessed July 31, 2014; "List of Biblical Place Names in North America," Wikipedia, https://en.wikipedia.org/wiki/List_of_biblical_place_names_in_North_America, accessed November 3, 2021.

22. John Leighly, "Biblical Place-Names in the United States," *Names* 27 (March 1979): 56.

23. Stanley D. Brunn and James O. Wheeler, "Notes on the Geography of Religious Town Names in the U.S.," *Names* 14 (December 1966): 197–202. A third cluster appears in places named for biblical and Catholic saints extending from Florida westward to California in regions of early Spanish and French settlement.

24. Ohio, Indiana, Michigan, Illinois, Wisconsin, Iowa, Minnesota, Missouri, Kansas, Nebraska, South Dakota, and North Dakota.

25. Leighly, "Town Names," 241.

26. George R. Stewart, *Names on the Land: A Historical Account of Place-Naming in the United States*, rev. ed. (Boston: Houghton Mifflin, 1958), 132.

27. For state-by-state tabulations, see Davis, *America and the Holy Land*, 135–46; and Katsh, *Biblical Heritage*, 169–72.

28. Martha Washington, Abigail Adams, Martha Jefferson Randolph (Jefferson's daughter), Elizabeth Monroe, Rachel Jackson (deceased before Jackson took office), Sarah Yorke Jackson (wife of Jackson's adopted son), Hannah Van Buren, Priscilla Tyler, Julia Tyler (whom the president married in the White House after his first wife died), Sarah Polk, Abigail Fillmore, Harriet Rebecca Lane Johnston (niece of the bachelor Buchanan), and Mary Todd Lincoln.

29. Scott Bruntjen and Carol Bruntjen, compilers, *A Checklist of American Imprints for 1831* (Metuchen, NJ: Scarecrow, 1975).

30. David W. Dumas, "The Naming of Children in New England, 1780–1850," *New England Historical and Genealogical Record* 132 (July 1978): 196–210. Dumas found that 76% of the boys and 55% of the girls received biblical names in the 1780s, but in the 1840s only 25% of the boys and 31% of the girls.

31. Kenneth Cmiel, *Democratic Eloquence: The Fight over Popular Speech in Nineteenth-Century America* (Berkeley: University of California Press, 1990).

32. See for Baptists, chapter 7, 149; see for Mormons, chapter 27, 600–1.

33. Webster also replaced "spilled it on the ground" with "frustrated his purpose" in Genesis 38:9 for Onan's act of coitus interruptus. C. Dowdell, "Correcting the Grammar of God: Noah Webster's 1833 Bible," CHASS, University of Toronto, 2006, http://homes.chass.utoronto.ca/~cpercy/courses/6362-dowdell.htm.

34. Hill, *ENGLISH BIBLE*, 88–89 (#567). Campbell's translation is discussed perceptively in Gutjahr, *AMERICAN BIBLE*, 101–5.

35. Cmiel, *Democratic Eloquence*, 96.

36. "'A House Divided': Speech at Springfield, Illinois (June 16, 1858)," in Lincoln, *COLLECTED WORKS*, 2:461.

37. Walter A. McDougall, *Throes of Democracy: The American Civil War Era, 1829–1877* (New York: HarperCollins, 2008), 61.

38. Robert Pierce Forbes, *The Missouri Compromise and Its Aftermath: Slavery and the Meaning of America* (Chapel Hill: University of North Carolina Press, 2007), 212.

39. Andrew Jackson, *The Papers of Andrew Jackson*, vol. 5: *1821–1824*, ed. Harold D. Moser et al. (Knoxville: University of Tennessee Press, 1996), 330–31, Jackson to Rachel Jackson, December 21, 1828.

40. Andrew Jackson, *Correspondence of Andrew Jackson*, 7 vols., ed. John Spencer Bassett (Washington, DC: Carnegie Institute, 1926–35), 5:158, Jackson to Mary Coffee, August 15, 1833.

41. Howe, *WHAT HATH GOD WROUGHT*, 689.

42. "'Old Hannah's Narrative' of Jackson's Last Days," in Jackson, *Correspondence of Andrew Jackson*, 6: 415.

43. The biblical usage of those earlier writers is examined in Noll, *IN THE BEGINNING*, 211–30.

44. Here the source is Isaac Watts's 1715 hymn, "I sing the almighty power of God."

45. Prince Hall, *A Charge Delivered to the Brethren of the African Lodge on the 25th of June, 1792* (Boston: T. & J. Fleet, 1792), 3. Helpful positioning of Hall's use of Scripture is provided by Joanna Brooks, *American Lazarus: Religion and the Rise of African-American and Native American Literatures* (New York: Oxford University Press, 2003), 48–49, 115–17, 136–46.

46. Prince Hall, *A Charge Delivered to the African Lodge, June 24, 1797, at Menotomy* (Boston: Benjamin Edes, 1797), 15, 12.

47. Benjamin Quarles, *Black Abolitionists* (New York: Oxford University Press, 1969), 7.

48. Maria W. Stewart, *Productions of Mrs. Maria W. Stewart, Presented to the First African Baptist Church and Society* (Boston: Friends of Freedom and Virtue, 1835), 4–5, as found in *Spiritual Narratives*, introduction by Sue E. Hutchins (New York: Oxford University Press, 1988).

49. Valerie C. Cooper, *Maria Stewart, the Bible and the Rights of African Americans* (Charlottesville: University of Virginia Press, 2011), 2.

50. Stewart, *Productions*, 15.

51. Harriet Jacobs, *Incidents in the Life of a Slave Girl: Written by Herself*, ed. L. Maria Child (Boston: For the Author, 1861). I have used the edition prepared by R. J. Ellis, which contains a full introduction, a careful chronology, and helpful annotations that identify Jacobs's biblical references (Oxford World's Classics, New York: Oxford University Press, 2015).

52. The title page, for instance, printed a text from Isaiah 32:9 ("Rise up, ye women that are at ease! Hear my voice, ye careless daughters! Give ear to my speech"). Among many others she also quoted (*Incidents*, 45) the much-used antislavery text from Acts 17:26 (defenders of slavery "seem to satisfy their consciences with the doctrine that God created the Africans to be slaves. What a libel upon the heavenly Father, who 'made of one blood all nations of men!' ").

53. Jacobs, *Incidents*, 13.

54. The judgment of "foremost Catholic" is from J. Herman Schauinger, *William Gaston: Carolinian* (Milwaukee, WI: Bruce, 1949), 299, with the quotations from this same source: 134, 161, 168–69. I thank Keiler Pulling for introducing me to William Gaston.

55. Andrew Jackson, *The Papers of Andrew Jackson*, vol. 6: *1825–1828*, ed. Harold D. Moser et al. (Knoxville: University of Tennessee Press, 2002), 29–30, Jackson to William Berkeley Lewis, February 14, 1825.

56. Orestes Brownson, "A Discourse on Lying," *Boston Quarterly Review*, April 1840, 419. Brownson's essay began by quoting Revelation 21:8 ("But—all liars shall have their part in the lake that burneth with fire and brimstone") (409). As context for Brownson's outburst, see McDougall, *Throes of Democracy*, 592.

57. John Greenleaf Whittier, "Ichabod!," in *Songs of Labor and Other Poems* (Boston: Ticknor, Reed, and Fields, 1850), 93–94.

58. Quotation from Richard J. Carwardine, *Evangelicals and Politics in Antebellum America* (New Haven, CT: Yale University Press, 1993), 177.

59. Quotations from Carwardine, *Evangelicals and Politics*, 239 and 302 (Douglas), 239 (Pierce), 244 (crucifixion).

60. That ascription is noted throughout David S. Reynolds, *Abe: Abraham Lincoln in His Times* (New York: Penguin, 2020).

61. Thomas S. Kidd and Barry Hankins, *Baptists in America: A History* (New York: Oxford University Press, 2015), 68.

62. Harry S. Stout, *American Aristocrats: A Family, a Fortune, and the Making of American Capitalism* (New York: Basic, 2017), 223. On the family's immersion in Scripture, see 176, 181, 218.

63. All quotations in the following are from *Inaugural Addresses of the Presidents of the United States from George Washington 1789 to Harry S. Truman 1949* (Washington, DC: Government Printing Office, 1952).

64. Other examples include "Invisible Hand" and "benign parent of the Human Race" (Washington, 1789); "that Being who is supreme over all, the Patron of Order, the

Fountain of Justice, and the Protector in all ages of the world of virtuous liberty" (John Adams, 1797); "Divine Author" (Monroe, 1817); "Almighty Ruler" (Polk, 1845); "kind Providence" (Buchanan, 1857).

65. See also Jackson's Second Inaugural in 1833, when he spoke of "that Almighty Being . . . who has kept us in His hands from the infancy of our Republic to the present day."

66. According to Adam Jortner, the key paragraph was written by Harrison's secretary of state Daniel Webster. It was ironic in coming from Harrison, whose personal faith, though committed to the providential destiny of the nation, ran close to the religion promoted by Paine and other deists. Adam Jortner, *The Gods of Prophetstown: The Battle of Tippecanoe and the Holy War for the American Frontier* (New York: Oxford University Press, 2012), 5–16, 48, 179 (Harrison's religion), 226 (Webster's authorship).

67. Earlier in the speech he had added another rare, specifically Christian reference by likening tendencies toward monarchy and aristocracy, or toward "the spirit of faction" that undercut "the spirit of freedom" to "the false Christs whose coming was foretold by the Savior" (Matt 24:24).

68. For a general account that begins in this era before addressing more contemporary patterns, see Gregory J. Books, "The Two-Edged Sword: The Bible in American Public Discourse" (Ph.D. diss., Pennsylvania State University, 1996); and for a superlative treatment of the KJV and American canonical literature, Alter, *Pen of Iron*.

69. Timothy Larsen, *A People of One Book: The Bible and the Victorians* (New York: Oxford University Press, 2011).

Chapter 7

1. Eugene Exman, *The House of Harper: The Making of a Modern Publisher* (1967; New York: Harper Perennial, 2010), 10; Cathy N. Davidson, *Revolution and the Word: The Rise of the Novel in America*, 2nd ed. (New York: Oxford University Press, 2004), 4.

2. All information about number of editions in this chapter, except where noted, comes from *WORLDCAT*. Information on printing of individual bibles is from Hills, *ENGLISH BIBLE*. It is important to remember that *WORLDCAT*, as well as Hills, *ENGLISH BIBLE*, record *editions* and not *printings*. Because a single edition of a book could have multiple printings, it limits the value of simply comparing number of editions, yet such comparisons remain the most readily available indices to sales and readership. Further reference to Hills's information on individual Bibles specifies her pages and the number she assigned for each Bible edition.

3. Elizabeth Barnes, "Novels," in *HISTORY OF THE BOOK*, 2:443.

4. Barnes, "Novels," 2:448 ("seduction and sympathy"). For recent interest in Rowson and her novel, see Cathy N. Davidson, "The Life and Times of *Charlotte Temple*: The Biography of a Book," in *Reading in America: Literature and Society History*, ed. Cathy

N. Davidson (Baltimore, MD: Johns Hopkins University Press, 1989), 157–79; Steven Epley, *Susanna Rowson: Sentimental Prophet of Early American Literature* (Evanston, IL: Northwestern University Press, 2016).

5. David D. Hall, "Readers and Writers in Early New England," in *HISTORY OF THE BOOK*, 1:126. As leading examples of that scholarship, see Gutjahr, *AMERICAN BIBLE*; David Paul Nord, *Faith in Reading: Religious Publishing and the Birth of Mass Media in America* (New York: Oxford University Press, 2004); Brown, *WORD IN THE WORLD*; Beth Barton Schweiger, *A Literate South: Reading before Emancipation* (New Haven, CT: Yale University Press, 2019).

6. The nine identifiable editions of *Charlotte Temple* in those years all, with the exception of Carey's 1794 printing (which he did reissue several times), came from New York and New England. The thirteen identifiable editions of Baxter's *Call* represented a more national distribution: five from New England, four Philadelphia, two New Jersey, one New York, and one Paris, Kentucky.

7. The sentence: "I dreamed; and behold, I saw a man clothed with rags standing in a certain place, with his face from his own house, a book in his hand, and a great burden upon his back."

8. On the patriotic intentions of Morse's work, see David N. Livingstone, *The Geographical Tradition: Episodes in the History of a Contested Enterprise* (Oxford: Blackwell, 1992), 146.

9. In 1819 individual printers published new editions of *Pilgrim's Progress* in Montpelier, Vermont; Exeter, New Hampshire; Hartford, Connecticut; and Newark, New Jersey.

10. Charles Monaghan and E. Jennifer Monaghan, "Schoolbooks," in *HISTORY OF THE BOOK*, 2:304–12.

11. Monaghan and Monaghan, "Schoolbooks," 308.

12. For the years 1825 to 1834, *WORLDCAT* shows eleven new editions of *The American Speller*, at least ten of Baxter's *Call*, and of *Pilgrim's Progress* twenty-six editions from twenty-one printers in nine cities, including two editions of a German translation from Harrisburg and (as indicating the emergence of national Protestant enterprises) two each from the American Tract Society and the American Sunday School Union and one from the Sunday School Union of the Methodist church.

13. Monaghan and Monaghan, "Schoolbooks," 309, emphasis added; Hills, *ENGLISH BIBLE*, 14 (#76), 164 (#1099).

14. Barnes, "Novels," 442; Hills, *ENGLISH BIBLE*, 10–47. A few of the editions recorded by Hills were of only the gospels or the Pauline epistles. It is worth remembering that all of the enumerations that follow are approximations for "printing" and "publishing" since these trades were not yet clearly separated.

15. The plates for this 1812 Bible were imported from England; Hills, *English Bible*, 37 (#213). The first New Testament printed with American-manufactured plates appeared the next year (Hills, *English Bible*, 41 [#249]), the same year that Isaac Collins in New York City used stereotype plates for a large edition of Murray's *Reader* (Monaghan and Monaghan, "Schoolbooks," 309).

16. Barnes, "Novels," 448.

17. Hills, *ENGLISH BIBLE*, 29–30 (#168).

18. For the first American edition of Scott's Bible, Hills, *ENGLISH BIBLE*, 20–21 (#113). Between the first publication of Scott's Bible in 1804 and 1815, American printers brought out ten editions of this one extensive set, or more editions than they published of *Charlotte Temple*.

19. Hills, *ENGLISH BIBLE*, 36 (#209). On the importance of such paratextual material, see especially Seth Perry, *Bible Culture and Authority in the Early United States* (Princeton, NJ: Princeton University Press, 2018), 41–55.

20. The other non-KJV versions of the period included three editions of the four gospels rendered from Greek by George Campbell, a Scottish Presbyterian; a New Testament translation by a Church of Ireland archbishop, William Newcome; a translation of the New Testament epistles by another Scottish Presbyterian, James Macknight; and most remarkably a complete Bible translated from Greek (including the first ever English translation of the Greek Septuagint, or Hebrew Scriptures) by Charles Thomson, former secretary of the U.S. Congress, printed in Philadelphia by Jane Aitken, daughter of Robert Aitken, who in 1781 printed the first KJV in the new United States. On the last, see Hills, *ENGLISH BIBLE*, 27 (#153) and J. Edwin Hendricks, *Charles Thomson and the Making of a New Nation, 1729–1824* (Rutherford, NJ: Fairleigh Dickinson University Press, 1979), 168–83 ("Greek and Biblical Scholar").

21. *The New Testament . . . Carefully examined and corrected, by the Rev. S. Payson* (New-Ipswich, NH: Simeon Ide, 1815); Hills *ENGLISH BIBLE*, 47 (#286); Anon., "Wages of Early Building-Trades Workers: Nineteenth Century," *Monthly Labor Review* (U.S. Bureau of Labor Statistics) 30 (January 1930): 13–14.

22. The ABS has been well served by its historians, including Nord, *Faith in Reading*; Gutjahr, *AMERICAN BIBLE*; Henry Otis Dwight, *The Centennial History of the American Bible Society*, 2 vols. (New York: Macmillan, 1916); Peter J. Wosh, *Spreading the Word: The Bible Business in Nineteenth-Century America* (Ithaca, NY: Cornell University Press, 1994); and John Fea, *The Bible Cause: A History of the American Bible Society* (New York: Oxford University Press, 2016).

23. On these societies, see Charles I. Foster, *An Errand of Mercy: The Evangelical United Front, 1790–1837* (Chapel Hill: University of North Carolina Press, 1960); Clifford S. Griffin, *Their Brothers' Keepers: Moral Stewardship in the United States* (New Brunswick, NJ: Rutgers University Press, 1960); Nord, *Faith in Reading*.

24. Howe, *WHAT HATH GOD WROUGHT*, 6.

25. Outstanding on the importance of stereotyping are David Paul Nord, "The Evangelical Origins of Mass Media in America," *Journalism Monographs* 88 (1984): 8–10; Nord, *Faith in Reading*, 46–51, 67–68; and David Paul Nord, "Benevolent Books: Printing, Religion, and Reform," in *HISTORY OF THE BOOK*, 2:227–29.

26. Nord, the subtitle of *Faith in Reading: Religious Publishing and the Birth of Mass Media in America*.

27. Elias Boudinot, *An Address Delivered before the New-Jersey Bible Society, at their Annual Meeting . . . At the Request of the Board of Managers, By the President of Said Board* (Burlington, NJ: Allinson, 1811).

28. A recent two-part article by Frederick V. Mills Sr. provides an up-to-date genealogy of transatlantic voluntarism from the late seventeenth century to the early

nineteenth: "Samuel Davies, George Whitefield, John Rogers, and the Legacy of the Society for Promoting Religious Knowledge among the Poor in North America, 1750–1816," *Anglican and Episcopal* History 87 (March 2018): 34–68 and 87 (June 2018): 129–58.

29. The Society in Scotland for Propagating Religious Knowledge was the organization that funded Jonathan Edwards's work among the Mohican Indians of western Massachusetts after he was dismissed by his Northampton congregation in 1750. George M. Marsden, *Jonathan Edwards: A Life* (New Haven, CT: Yale University Press, 2003), 375–413.

30. Mills, "Samuel Davies," 132 (Boudinot) and 133 (Rush). Mills observes that the 1750 London society did not use the phrase "without note or comment" that became canonical with the BFBS, but did distribute bibles in accordance with that principle (40–41).

31. On the founding and early history of the BFBS, see Leslie Howsom, *Cheap Bibles: Nineteenth-Century Publishing and the British and Foreign Bible Society* (New York: Cambridge University Press, 1991), 1–34.

32. Howsom, *Cheap Bibles*, 6–7 (the BFBS as *not* a religious organization), 118 (on the millions of bibles produced for the BFBS by the three printers, 1837–47).

33. Emma Macleod, "British Evangelicals and America, 1775–1820," in *Pathways and Patterns in History: Essays on Baptists, Evangelicals, and the Modern World, in Honour of David Bebbington*, ed. Anthony Corss, Peter J. Morden, and Ian M. Randall (London: Spurgeon's College and the Baptist Historical Society, 2015), 308,.

34. Boudinot, *Address*, 2, 5, 7. On Boudinot's books interpreting prophecy, see chapter 5, 113.

35. Boudinot, *Address*, 12, 7.

36. Fea, *Bible Cause*, 8–18.

37. M. [Samuel Mills], "Plan of a General Bible Society," *Panoplist and Missionary Magazine* 6, part 1 (October 2013): 356–58. Quotations that follow are from this source. On Mills, the letter, and its importance, see Nord, *Faith in Reading*, 3–5; Fea, *Bible Cause*, 12–13; Dwight, *Centennial History*, 1:11–15.

38. The phrase is from Brown, *WORD IN THE WORLD*, 1. For the general significance in these early national decades of evangelical periodical publishing, see Brown, *WORD IN THE WORLD*, passim; Nord, *Faith in Reading, 37–40*; Nord, "Benevolent Books," 2:242–46; Hatch, *DEMOCRATIZATION*, 141–46 ("Creating a Mass Religious Culture in Print"); Frank Luther Mott, *A History of American Magazines, 1741–1850* (New York: D. Appleton, 1930), 131–39 and passim.

39. Richard R. John, "Expanding the Realm of Communications," in *HISTORY OF THE BOOK*, 2:212–13, 211.

40. Among many others who have described this revolution, see especially Howe, *WHAT HATH GOD WROUGHT*, 5–7; Richard R. John, *Spreading the News: The American Postal System from Franklin to Morse* (Cambridge, MA: Harvard University Press, 1995).

41. Information in this paragraph is from Mary Kupiec Cayton, "Harriet Newell's Story: Women, the Evangelical Press, and the Foreign Mission Movement," in *HISTORY OF THE BOOK*, 2:408–16 (quotation 410).

42. David S. Reynolds, *Faith in Fiction: The Emergence of Religious Literature in America* (Cambridge, MA: Harvard University Press, 1981), 123–44. Circulation figures are from Brown, *WORD IN THE WORLD*, 155, 265n23.

43. Jedidiah Morse, "An Address to the Christian Public on the Subject of Missions to the Heathen and Translations of the Scriptures," *Panoplist* 6, part 1 (October 1813): 315–28 (quotation 315); reviews of sermons by Dwight and Beecher, *Panoplist* 6, part 2 (October 1813): 360–68, 368–71.

44. "Sunday Schools," *Christian Herald*, March 30, 1816, 6. Psalm 145:10–11 reads, "All thy works shall praise thee, O Lord; and they saints shall bless thee. They shall speak of the glory of thy kingdom, and talk of thy power."

45. "Address," *Methodist Magazine*, January 1818, 2.

46. Hatch, *DEMOCRATIZATION*, 141, relying on Gaylord P. Albaugh, "The Role of the Religious Press in the Development of American Christianity" (unpublished manuscript, 1984). Sermons in *The American National Preacher* were mostly from Congregationalists and Presbyterians.

47. American Bible Society, *Constitution of the American Bible Society, Formed by a Convention of Delegates, held in the city of New-York, May 1816, Together with their Address to the People of the United States; a Notice of their Proceedings; and a list of their Officers* (New York: G. F. Hopkins, 1816).

48. American Bible Society, *Constitution*, 13, 15.

49. American Bible Society, *Constitution*, 13, 14, 16, 17, 19.

50. American Bible Society, *Constitution*, 16, 14 (emphasis on BFBS in original).

51. American Bible Society, *Constitution*, 3–5.

52. Walter A. McDougall, *Freedom Just around the Corner: A New American History, 1585–1828* (New York: HarperCollins, 2004), 500.

53. For a full list of officers, American Bible Society, *Constitution*, 3–6;

54. John Mitchell Mason, *The Voice of Warning, to Christians, on the Ensuing Election of a President of the United States* (New York: G. F. Hopkins, 1800), title page (text), 6 (Jefferson on Scripture). His denomination was a Presbyterian splinter from the Scottish Kirk.

55. For members of the drafting committee, American Bible Society, *Constitution*, 5.

56. Lester J. Cappon, ed., *The Adams-Jefferson Letters*, 2nd ed., 2 vols. in 1 (Chapel Hill: University of North Carolina Press, 1987), 494, Adams to Jefferson, November 4, 1816.

57. Thomas Jefferson, *The Papers of Thomas Jefferson: Retirement Series*, vol. 7, ed. J. Jefferson Looney (Princeton, NJ: Princeton University Press, 2010), 178, Jefferson to Samuel Greenhow, January 31, 1814. On the impact of Priestley's *An History of the Corruptions of Christianity* (1793) in changing Jefferson's mind about Jesus, see Thomas Jefferson, *Jefferson's Extracts from the Gospels*, Papers of Thomas Jefferson, second series, ed. Dickinson W. Adams (Princeton, NJ: Princeton University Press, 1983), 14–16, 327–29, 347–49, and passim.

58. Jefferson, *Jefferson's Extracts from the Gospels*, 376, Jefferson to Margaret Bayard Smith, August 6, 1816.

59. Cappon, *Adams-Jefferson Letters*, 496, Jefferson to Adams, November 25, 1816.

60. Howsom, *Cheap Bibles*, 49–50, 58.

61. *Third Report of the American Bible Society, Presented May 13, 1819* (New York: D. Fanshaw, 1819).

62. Quotation in Fea, *Bible Cause*, 41.

63. Figures for Bible production from Gutjahr, *AMERICAN BIBLE*, 187, which differ slightly from Dwight, *Centennial History*, 2:576–77. On Post Office income and national population, *HISTORICAL STATISTICS*, 497, 16. On details about the General Supply, Fea, *Bible Cause*, 48–49.

64. Figures on the ATS and ASSU are from Nord, "Benevolent Books," 235, 238; for the number of post offices, *HISTORICAL STATISTICS*, 497.

65. *American Tract Messenger* 1, no. 1 (June 1824): 1.

66. Howe, *WHAT HATH GOD WROUGHT*, 374.

67. Monaghan and Monaghan, "Schoolbooks," 307.

68. Barnes, "Novels," 442; in the same period, American printers brought out 281 novels from authors not from the United States.

69. For early complaints by printers about the ABS, but then the turn of commercial presses to more elaborate bibles, see Gutjahr, *AMERICAN BIBLE*, 35–37.

70. On Hobart and his objections, see Fea, *Bible Cause*, 17 and more generally Robert Bruce Mullin, *Episcopal Vision / American Reality: High Church Theology and Social Thought in Evangelical America* (New Haven, CT: Yale University Press, 1986). On low-church Episcopalian cooperation with other evangelicals, see Diana Hochstedt Butler, "The Church and American Destiny: Evangelical Episcopalians and Voluntary Societies in Antebellum America," *Religion in American Culture* 4 (Summer 1994): 193–219.

71. Fea, *Bible Cause*, 65–66; Wosh, *Spreading the Word*, 48; Gutjahr, *AMERICAN BIBLE*, 106–7. On the BFBS's stance, see Howsom, *Cheap Bibles*, 16.

72. Wosh, *Spreading the Word*, 48; Fea, *Bible Cause*, 73–75.

73. *Memorial of the Board of Managers of the American Bible Society, soliciting from Congress an exemption from the charge of postage, and from duty on paper for printing bibles: accompanied with reasons in support of the memorial* (New York: Daniel Fanshaw, 1819), 5, 3.

74. *Memorial*, 6–8, 13. An appendix (14–15), quoted George Washington on the necessity of religion to support personal virtue and the public morality without which republics would sink into vice and tyranny.

75. *Memorial*, 10.

76. Daniel Parker, *Pubic Address to the Baptist Society, and Friends of Religion in General, on the Principle and Practice of the Baptist Board of Foreign Missions for the United States of America* (Vincennes, IN: Stout and Osborn, 1820), 5. For context, see Thomas S. Kidd and Barry Hankins, *Baptists in America: A History* (New York: Oxford University Press, 2015), 110–11.

77. Ephraim Perkins, *A "Bunker Hill" Contest, A.D. 1826* (1826), quoted in James D. Bratt, ed., *Antirevivalism in Antebellum America: A Collection of Religious Voices* (New Brunswick, NJ: Rutgers University Press, 2006), 57–59.

78. *An Expose of the Rise and Proceedings of the American Bible Society, during the Thirteen Years of its Existence. By a Member*, 2nd ed. (New York: N.p., 1830), 14, 15, 28–29, 31.

79. Again, on the move from advocating "content" to heeding "context," see Eric Schlereth, *An Age of Infidels: The Politics of Religious Controversy in the Early United States* (Philadelphia: University of Pennsylvania Press, 2013), 17 and passim.

80. Wosh, *Spreading the* Word, 35–61; R. Laurence Moore, *Selling God: American Religion in the Marketplace of Culture* (New York: Oxford University Press, 1994), 91.

81. Brown, *WORD IN THE WORLD*, 14. For further refinement of this argument, see also 6, 33, 113.

82. David Sehat, *The Myth of American Religious Freedom* (New York: Oxford University Press, 2011), 58.

83. Amanda Porterfield, *Conceived in Doubt: Religion and Politics in the New American Nation* (Chicago: University of Chicago Press, 2012), 76.

Chapter 8

1. Prominent examples of that scholarship include David D. Hall, *Worlds of Wonder, Days of Judgment: Popular Religious Belief in Early New England* (New York: Knopf, 1989); Jon Butler, *Awash in a Sea of Faith: Christianizing the American People* (Cambridge, MA: Harvard University Press, 1990); Laurie F. Maffly-Kipp, Leigh E. Schmidt, and Mark Valeri, eds., *Practicing Protestants: Histories of Christian Life in America, 1630–1965* (Baltimore, MD: Johns Hopkins University Press, 2006).

2. For details, see Noll, *IN THE BEGINNING*, 177–205.

3. Hatch, *DEMOCRATIZATION*.

4. For details, see Holifield, *THEOLOGY IN AMERICA*, 341–69 ("Calvinism Revised").

5. Dawn Coleman, "The Bible and the Sermonic Tradition," in Gutjahr, *OXFORD HANDBOOK*, 242.

6. Perkins quoted in Michael Warner, ed., *American Sermons: The Pilgrims to Martin Luther King Jr.* (New York: Library of America, 1999), 889. On the enduring national influence of New England sermonic traditions, see Harry S. Stout, *The New England Soul: Preaching and Religious Culture in Colonial New England*, 2nd ed. (New York: Oxford University Press, 2011).

7. Hadley Kruczek-Aaron, *Everyday Religion: An Archeology of Protestant Belief and Practice in the Nineteenth Century* (Gainesville: University Press of Florida, 2015), 65.

8. Lewis O. Saum, *The Popular Mood of Pre-Civil War America* (Westport, CT: Greenwood, 1980), 38, 34, 8, again 34, 39; and for more examples, 35, 37, 39, 48, 89, 147.

9. Herman Melville, *Moby-Dick* (1851), ed. G. Thomas Tanselle (New York: Library of America, 1983), 836. A sophisticated example of criticism on this sermon is Dawn

Coleman, *Preaching and the Rise of the American Novel* (Columbus: Ohio State University Press, 2013), 140–53, 241–43.

10. An excellent work of retrieval is Kyle B. Roberts, "Locating Popular Religion in the Evangelical Tract: The Roots and Routes of *The Dairyman's Daughter*," *Early American Studies* 4 (Spring 2006): 233–70. Information that follows on the tract's production and reception is from this article.

11. For this spiritual genealogy, see Brown, *WORD IN THE WORLD*, 79.

12. Quotations are from what was probably the first American printing: Legh Richmond, *The Dairyman's Daughter* (Boston: Lincoln and Edmands, 1813), 3, 12, 13, 8. Besides the Bible, Elizabeth read the steady sellers that the tract societies were already publishing in ever-increasing numbers, including works by Philip Doddridge, John Bunyan, Henry Alleine, and Richard Baxter.

13. Richmond, *Dairyman's Daughter*, 7.

14. Richmond, *Dairyman's Daughter*, 19 (1 Cor), 22 (Job).

15. Richmond, *Dairyman's Daughter*, 10.

16. Quoted in Roberts, "Locating Popular Religion," 233.

17. Walter A. McDougall, *Freedom Just around the Corner: A New American History, 1585–1828* (New York: Harper Collins, 2004), 379.

18. Brown, *WORD IN THE WORLD*, 121.

19. T. Charlton Henry, *Letters to an Anxious Inquirer, Designed to Relieve the Difficulties of a Friend under Serious Impressions*, 3rd ed. (Philadelphia, PA: Presbyterian Board of Publication, 1840), 195–212 (letter VIII), 212 (last quotation).

20. Quoted in Brown, *WORD IN THE WORLD*, 121. Brown's entire book is unusually helpful on the importance of religious reading throughout the nineteenth century.

21. Quoted in Janet Duitsman Cornelius, *When I Can Read My Title Clear: Literacy, Slavery, and Religion in the Antebellum South* (Columbia: University of South Carolina Press, 1991), 41, 33.

22. Quoted in Cornelius, *When I Can Read My Title Clear*, 56. David Walker had already broadcast that same indictment; see chapter 11, 234.

23. For the relevance of this truism for Bible reading, see the unusually clear explanation in David Paul Nord, *Faith in Reading: Religious Publishing and the Birth of Mass Media in America* (New York: Oxford University Press, 2004), 132–35.

24. Nord, *Faith in Reading*, 138.

25. *Productions of Maria W. Stewart, Presented to the First African Baptist Church and Society, of the City of Boston* (Boston: By Friends of Freedom and Virtue, 1835), in *Spiritual Narratives*, ed. Sue E. Houchins (New York: Oxford University Press, 1988), 23–24

26. Harriet Jacobs, *Incidents in the Life of a Slave Girl* (1861), ed. R. J. Ellis (New York: Oxford University Press, 2015), 67, 70.

27. Jacobs, *Incidents*, 71–72.

28. Jacobs, *Incidents*, 72.

29. Cornelius, *When I Can Read My Title Clear*, 93, 94.

30. Charles G. Finney, *The Memoirs of Charles G. Finney: The Complete Restored Text*, ed. Garth M. Rosell and Richard A. G. Dupuis (Grand Rapids, MI: Academie/

Zondervan, 1989), 13–14, 17 ("shut up"). The edited version of the memoirs was first published in 1876.

31. Brown, *WORD IN THE WORLD*, 126–30.

32. Quoted in Christine Leigh Heyrman, *Southern Cross: The Beginnings of the Bible Belt* (New York: Knopf, 1997), 211–12.

33. Alfred Lee, *A Life Hid with Christ in God, being a Memoir of Susan Allibone, Chiefly Compiled from her Diary and Letters* (Philadelphia, PA: J. B. Lippincott, 1856), 34–35, 97.

34. Colleen McDannell, *The Christian Home in Victorian America, 1840–1900* (Bloomington: Indiana University Press, 1986), 77–85. Many helpful illustrations are found in Colleen McDannell, *Material Christianity: Religion and Popular Christianity in America* (New Haven, CT: Yale University Press, 1995), 67–102 and Liana Lupus, *The Book of Life: Family Bibles in America* (New York: Mobia, 2011).

35. McDannell, *Christian Home*, 82

36. Kyle T. Bulthuis, *Four Steeples over the City Streets: Religion and Society in New York's Early Republic Congregations* (New York: New York University Press, 2014), 69 (Hammon), 83 (Morgan). The biblical character of Hammon's 1760 "An Evening Thought: Salvation by Christ, with Penitential Cries," is treated in Noll, *IN THE BEGINNING*, 212–14.

37. Kyle B. Roberts, *Evangelical Gotham: Religion and the Making of New York City, 1783–1860* (Chicago: University of Chicago Press, 2016), 183–84 (the Worralls' household), 190 (quoting Phoebe Palmer).

38. Shelby M. Balik, "'Scattered as Christians Are in This Part of Our Country': Layfolk's Reading, Writing, and Religious Community in New England's Northern Frontier, 1780–1830," *New England Quarterly* 83 (December 1810): 639.

39. Mary Kelley, "'Pen and Ink Communion': Evangelical Reading and Writing in Antebellum America," *New England Quarterly* 84 (December 2011): 557.

40. Beth Barton Schweiger, *A Literate South: Reading before Emancipation* (New Haven, CT: Yale University Press, 2019).

41. Quoted in Jay Riley Case, *An Unpredictable Gospel: American Evangelicals and World Christianity, 1812–1920* (New York: Oxford University Press, 2012), 44.

42. William G. McLoughlin, *Cherokees and Missionaries, 1789–1839* (New Haven, CT: Yale University Press, 1984), 36, 345–50 (on the merger of biblical and ancestral Cherokee perspectives).

43. Isaac Watts, *The Psalms of David, imitated in the language of the New Testament, and apply'd to the Christian state and worship* (Philadelphia, PA: Benjamin Franklin and Hugh Meredith, 1729). Indispensable for the history of hymnody are John Julian, *A Dictionary of Hymnology* (New York: Charles Scribner's Sons, 1892); Stephen A. Marini, "Hymnody as History: Early Evangelical Hymns and the Recovery of American Popular Religion," *Church History* 71 (June 2002): 273–306; Christopher D. Phillips, *The Hymnal: A Reading History* (Baltimore, MD: Johns Hopkins University Press, 2018). Much that follows draws on the chapters published in Edith L. Blumhofer and Mark A. Noll, eds., *Singing the Lord's Song in a Strange Land: Hymnody in the History of North American Protestantism* (Tuscaloosa: University of Alabama

Press, 2004); Mark A. Noll and Edith L. Blumhofer, eds., *Sing Them Over Again to Me: Hymns and Hymnbooks in America* (Tuscaloosa: University of Alabama Press, 2006); Richard J. Mouw and Mark A. Noll, eds., *Wonderful Words of Life: Hymns in American Protestant History and Theology* (Grand Rapids, MI: Eerdmans, 2004). .

44. Watts remained the most popular "American" hymn writer into the early twentieth century. For the early part of the story, see Esther Rothenbusch Crookshank, "'We're Marching to Zion': Isaac Watts in Early America," in Mouw and Noll, *Wonderful Words of Life*, 17–41.

45. J. R. Watson, "The Bible and Hymnody," in *The New Cambridge History of the Bible: The Bible from 1750 to the Present*, ed. John Riches (New York: Cambridge University Press, 2015), 725.

46. D. Bruce Hindmarsh, *The Evangelical Conversion Narrative: Spiritual Autobiography in Early Modern England* (Oxford: Oxford University Press, 2005), 14–15, 63–66, 107, 152–53, 179–80, 290–91, 209, 332, 344.

47. Grant Gordon, *From Slavery to Freedom: The Life of David George, Pioneer Black Minister* (Hantsport, Nova Scotia: Lancelot Press, 1992), 29.

48. Bulthuis, *Four Steeples*, 185.

49. McLoughlin, *Cherokees and Missionaries*, 348.

50. Roberts, *Evangelical Gotham*, 183.

51. Anthony F. C. Wallace, *Rockdale: The Growth of an American Industrial Village in the Early Industrial Revolution* (1972; New York: Norton, 1980), 431.

52. Heather D. Curtis, "Children of the Heavenly King: Hymns in the Religious and Social Experience of Children, 1780–1850," in Noll and Blumhofer, *Sing Them Over Again to Me*, 227–28.

53. Curtis, "Children of the Heavenly King," 215.

54. Quoted in Robert A. Schneider, "Jesus Shall Reign: Hymns and Foreign Missions, 1800–1870," in Mouw and Noll, *Wonderful Words of Life*, 70. The 1805 hymn by Bourne H. Draper, an English Baptist, read as published, "Ye Christian herald, go proclaim / salvation through Emmanuel's name / to distant climes the tidings bear; / and plant the Rose of Sharon there." From the Hymnary website, accessed May 13, 2019, https://hymnary.org/text/ye_christian_heralds_go_proclaim.

55. Stephen A. Marini, "Appendix I: American Protestant Hymn Project: A Ranked List of Most Frequently Reprinted Hymns," in Mouw and Noll, *Wonderful Words of Life*, 253.

56. For documentation and further stories about this one hymn, see Mark A. Noll, "'All Hail the Power of Jesus' Name': Significant Variations on a Significant Theme," in Noll and Blumhofer, *Sing Them Over Again to Me*, 53.

57. Quoted from a German edition to indicate the novel's international popularity: Elizabeth Wetherell (pseudonym for Susan Warner), *The Wide, Wide World: Author's Edition* (Leipzig: Bernhard Tauchnitz, 1854), 46. A full discussion of hymns in this novel is found in Phillips, *The Hymnal*, 24–32 ("The Wide, Wide World of Hymns").

58. Harriet Beecher Stowe, *Uncle Tom's Cabin; or, Life among the Lowly* (1852; New York: Library of America, 1982), 458.

59. Louisa May Alcott, *Little Women: or Meg, Jo, Beth, and Amy; Part Second* (Boston: Roberts Brothers, 1869), 307.

60. Thomas Moore, "Come, ye disconsolate, where'er ye languish," Hymnary, accessed May 15, 2019, https://hymnary.org/text/come_ye_disconsolate_whereer_ye_languish.

61. See Cornelius, *When I Can Read My Title Clear*.

62. Stephen Marini, "From Classical to Modern Hymnody and the Development of American Evangelicalism, 1737–1970," in Blumhofer and Noll, *Singing the Lord's Song*, 11.

63. Lester Ruth, "The Most Republished Evangelical Hymn and Multiple Senses of Scripture: Text with Commentary," *Liturgy* 28, no. 2 (2013): 48–49. For the text and further commentary, see John Cennick, "Jesus, my all, to heaven is gone," Hymnary, accessed May 16, 2019, https://hymnary.org/text/jesus_my_all_to_heaven_is_gone.

64. John Rippon, *A Selection of Hymns from the Best Authors intended to be an Appendix to Dr. Watts's Psalms and Hymns* (Burlington, NJ: S. C. Ustick, 1801), 509–10. On Robinson and the hymn, Emily R. Brink and Bert Polman, eds., *Psalter Hymnal Handbook* (Grand Rapids, MI: CRC, 1998), 654–55 (hymn #486); Bruce Hindmarsh, "Was He Too Prone to Wander? Robert Robinson (1735–1790)," *Gospel Coalition*, June 16, 2019, https://www.desiringgod.org/articles/was-he-too-prone-to-wander. On American publication of Rippon's *Selection*, see *WORLD CAT*.

65. Richard Allen, *A Collection of Hymns and Spiritual Songs, from Various Authors*, 2nd ed. (Philadelphia, PA: T. L. Plowman, 1801). Excellent on this book are Dennis C. Dickerson, "Heritage and Hymnody: Richard Allen and the Making of African Methodism," in Noll and Blumhofer, *Sing Them Over Again to Me*, 175–93 and Eileen Southern, "Hymns of the Black Church," *Journal of the Interdenominational Theological Center* 14 (1986–87): 127–40.

66. Edwards A. Park, Austin Phelps, and Lowell Mason, eds., *The Sabbath Hymn Book: For the Service of Song in the House of the Lord* (New York: various publishers, 1858). On this hymn book, see Phillips, *Hymnal*, 194–95. I acknowledge with thanks the gift of this hymn book many years ago from Charlie Philips. The quotations that follow are from the Mason Brothers printing (New York).

67. Park, Phelps, and Mason, *Sabbath Hymn Book*, v.

68. Peter Randolph ("an Emancipated slave"), *Sketches of Slave Life: or, Illustrations of the "Peculiar Institution"* (Boston: by the author, 1855), 69.

69. Allen, *Collection of Hymns*, 13–14.

70. Allen, *Collection of Hymns*, #41 with the stanza "The pillar went before them, / And Moses with his rod. / No doubt we shall win the day, / If we but trust in God"; #7 with a casual reference; #25 with a full paraphrase of the entire parable.

71. On the identification of Allen as the author, see Dickerson, "Heritage and Hymnody," 189 and John Michael Spencer, "The Hymnody of the African Methodist Episcopal Church," *American Music* 8 (Fall 1990): 275.

72. Allen, *Collection of Hymns*, 78–80.

73. Park, Phelps, and Mason, *Sabbath Hymn Book*, ix.

74. Phillips, *The Hymnal*, 34.

75. Phillips, *The Hymnal*, 34.

76. Brown, *WORD IN THE WORLD*, 1, 9–10, and passim.

77. Brown, *WORD IN THE WORLD*, 231, and more generally on hymnody, 190–241; also Candy Gunther Brown, "Singing Pilgrim: Hymn Narratives of a Pilgrim Community's Progress from This World to That Which Is to Come, 1830–1890," in Noll and Blumhofer, *Sing Them Over Again to Me*, 194–213.

78. Allen, *Collection*, #50 ("From Regions of Love"), 66–67; #5 ("The glorious day is drawing nigh"), 8–9.

79. Beth Barton Schweiger, "The Literate South: Reading before Emancipation," *Journal of the Civil War Era* 3 (2013): 338.

Chapter 9

1. Exemplary works on both the harmony and the divergence include Eugene D. Genovese, *Roll, Jordan, Roll: The World the Slaves Made* (New York: Random House, 1972), esp. 159–324; Mechal Sobel, *Trabelin' On: Black and White Values in Eighteenth-Century Virginia* (Princeton, NJ: Princeton University Press, 1987); Erskine Clarke, *Dwelling Place: A Plantation Epic* (New Haven, CT: Yale University Press, 2005); Charles F. Irons, *The Origins of Proslavery Christianity: White and Black Evangelicals in Colonial and Antebellum Virginia* (Chapel Hill: University of North Carolina Press, 2008).

2. The notes to this chapter can only hint at the immense quantity of first-rate scholarship that now exists for questions about the Bible in African American history. The works that have most guided my thinking are Genovese, *Roll, Jordan, Roll*; Albert Raboteau, *Slave Religion: The "Invisible Institution" in the Antebellum South*, 2nd ed. (1978; New York: Oxford University Press, 2004); Vincent L. Wimbush, ed., *African Americans and the Bible: Sacred Texts and Social Textures* (New York: Continuum, 2000); Allen Dwight Callahan, *The Talking Book: African Americans and the Bible* (New Haven, CT: Yale University Press, 2006).

3. *A Narrative of the Life and Adventures of Venture a Native of Africa, But resident above sixty years in the United States of America, Related by Himself* (1798; Middletown, CT: J. S. Stewart, 1897), 3; *Life of James Mars, a Slave Born and Sold in Connecticut, Written by Himself* (Hartford, CT: Case, Lockwood, 1864), both in *Five Black Lives*, introduction by Arna Bontemps (Middletown, CT: Wesleyan University Press, 1971). Mars, though, became an active deacon in James W. C. Pennington's Black Presbyterian church in Hartford. Christopher L. Webber, *American to the Backbone: The Life of James W. C. Pennington* (New York: Pegasus, 2011), 136, 139, *passim*.

4. See chapter 6, 123–25. The extraordinary biblical presence in Maria Stewart's work has been documented by Katherine Clay Bassard in "Appendix: Scriptural References in the Prayers of Maria W. Stewart," in *Transforming Scriptures: African American Women Writers and the Bible* (Athens: University of Georgia Press, 2010), 107–31.

5. On these figures, with references to a rapidly growing literature, see Noll, *IN THE BEGINNING*, 211–30 ("The Biblical Black Atlantic") and, with an especially apt title, Joanna Brooks, *American Lazarus: Religion and the Rise of African-American and Native American Literatures* (New York: Oxford University Press, 2003).

6. Liana Lupas, *Reaching Out: American Bible Society and the African American Community* (New York: MOBIA, 2013), 11.

7. Richard Allen, *The Life, Experience, and Gospel Labors of the Rt. Rev. Richard Allen* (1833; Philadelphia, PA: F. Ford and M. A. Ripley, 1880), 5.

8. Jarena Lee, *Religious Experience and Journal of Jarena Lee, giving an account of her call to preach the gospel* (Philadelphia, PA: By the author, 1849), in *Spiritual Narratives*, ed. Sue E. Houchins (New York: Oxford University Press, 1988), 5–8 ("power of God," 8).

9. James W. C. Pennington, *The Fugitive Blacksmith: or, Events in the History of James W. C. Pennington*, 3rd ed. (London: Charles Gilpin, 1850), title page, 29.

10. Raboteau, *Slave Religion*, 240.

11. William Whipper, "Eulogy on William Wilberforce" and James Forten Jr., "Put on the Armour of Righteousness," in *Lift Every Voice: African American Oratory, 1787–1900*, ed. Philip Foner and Robert Branham (Tuscaloosa: University of Alabama Press, 1998), 144, 161.

12. Sarah M. Douglass, "The Cause of the Slave Became My Own" and Theodore S. Wright, "The Slave Has a Friend in Heaven, Though He May Have None Here," in Foner and Branham, *Lift Every Voice*, 123, 164–65.

13. On Douglass's dispute with Henry Highland Garnet, a learned Presbyterian pastor, see Callahan, *The Talking Book*, 21–23 (quotation, 23), and for his argument with Henry Bibb, Bassard, *Transforming Scriptures*, 38–40.

14. Frederick Douglass, *Narrative of the Life of Frederick Douglass, an American Slave. Written by Himself* (1845; Boston: Anti-Slavery Office, 1846), 118–22—"strain at a gnat and swallow a camel" (Matt 23:24), "man-stealing" (1 Tim 1:10), "neglect the weightier matters of the law" (Matt 23:23), "professing to love God whom they have not seen" (1 Jn 4:20).

15. Frederick Douglass, *My Bondage and My Freedom* (1855), ed. David W. Blight (New Haven, CT: Yale University Press, 2014), 117–18.

16. Emerson B. Powery and Rodney S. Sadler Jr., *The Genesis of Liberation: Biblical Interpretation in the Antebellum Narratives of the Enslaved* (Louisville, KY: Westminster John Knox, 2016), 35, 45–46, 55, 117, 158–59, and passim.

17. Henry Bibb, *Narrative of the Life and Adventures of Henry Bibb, An American Slave, Written by Himself* (1849; New York: By the author, 1859), 23–24.

18. Katherine Clay Bassard, *Spiritual Interrogations: Culture, Gender, and Community in Early African American Women's Writing* (Princeton, NJ: Princeton University Press, 1999), 108–26 ("Rituals of Desire: Spirit, Culture, and Sexuality in the Writings of Rebecca Cox Jackson"), 119, 125 (quotations).

19. Elizabeth Keckly, *Behind the Scenes: or, Thirty Years a Slave, and Four Years in the White House* (1868), ed. William L. Andrews (New York: Penguin, 2005), 81, 84.

20. Solomon Northup, *Twelve Years a Slave: Narrative of Solomon Northup, a Citizen of New-York, Kidnapped in Washington City in 1841, and Rescued in 1853 from a Cotton Plantation near the Red River in Louisiana* (London: Sampson, Low, 1853), 135–36.

21. Northup, *Twelve Years a Slave*, 144–45.

22. On these figures, see chapter 12, 256, 260.

23. William J. Simmons, *Men of Mark: Eminent, Progressive, and Rising* (Cleveland, OH: George M. Rewell, 1887), 807; for a fuller account, Andre E. Johnson, *The Forgotten Prophet: Bishop Henry McNeal Turner and the African American Prophetic Tradition* (Lanham, MD: Lexington, 2012), 17–19.

24. Sojourner Truth, *Narrative of Sojourner Truth, A Bondswoman of Olden Time* (Battle Creek, MI: For the Author, 1878), 61, 66–67; Isabelle Kinnard Richman, *Sojourner Truth: Prophet of Social Justice* (New York: Routledge, 2016), 17.

25. Kristen T. Oertel, *Harriet Tubman: Slavery, the Civil War, and Civil Religion in the Nineteenth Century* (New York: Routledge, 2016), 42, 5.

26. Lawrence W. Levine, *Black Culture and Black Consciousness* (New York: Oxford University Press, 1977), 32.

27. Callahan, *Talking Book*, xi, xi, 39 For only a few of many similar judgments, see Genovese, *Roll, Jordan, Roll*, 209–54; Grey Gundaker, "The Bible *as* and *at* a Threshold: Reading, Performance, and Blessed Space," in Wimbush, *African Americans and the Bible*, 754; Laurie F. Maffly-Kipp, *Setting Down the Sacred Past: African-American Race Histories* (Cambridge, MA: Harvard University Press, 2010), 27, 32; Laurie F. Maffly-Kipp and Kathryn Lofton, eds., *Women's Work: An Anthology of African-American Women's Historical Writings from Antebellum America to the Harlem Renaissance* (New York: Oxford University Press, 2010), 11; Powery and Sadler, *The Genesis of Liberation*, 25.

28. Genovese, *Roll, Jordan, Roll*, 3. On the interpretive questions addressed in this section, I have been helped especially by Vincent L. Wimbush, "Introduction: Reading Darkness, Reading Scripture," in Wimbush, *African Americans and the Bible*, 1–43; John Saillant, "Origins of American Biblical Hermeneutics in Eighteenth-Century Black Opposition to the Slave Trade and Slavery," in Wimbush, *African Americans and the Bible*, 236–50; Bassard, *Transforming Scriptures*, chap. 2, "Private Interpretations: The Bible Defense of Slavery and Nineteenth-Century Racial Hermeneutics," 25–46; Lisa M. Bowens, *Sacred Matters: African American Readings of Paul—Reception, Resistance, and Transformation* (Grand Rapids, MI: Eerdmans, 2020).

29. Wimbush, "Introduction," 9 (omitting Wimbush's italicization and brackets around "sacred").

30. Erskine Clarke, *Dwelling Place: A Plantation Epic* (New Haven, CT: Yale University Press, 2005), 415–16.

31. An immense literature exists in the wake of Charles Taylor's discussion of "social imaginaries" in his book *A Secular Age* (Cambridge, MA: Harvard University Press, 2007).

32. An imperative starting point is Dennis C. Dickerson, *The African Methodist Episcopal Church: A History* (New York: Cambridge University Press, 2020).

33. Dennis C. Dickerson, *African Methodism and Its Wesleyan Heritage: Reflections on AME Church History* (Nashville, TN: By the author, 2009), 26.

34. Genovese, *Roll, Jordan, Roll,* xv ("nation"), 7 (I have substituted "Bible" where Genovese wrote "religion").

35. Allen, *Life, Experience, and Gospel Labors,* 17–19. For a good explanation of that Methodist attraction, see Richard S. Newman, *Freedom's Prophet: Bishop Richard Allen, the AME Church, and the Black Founding Fathers* (New York: New York University Press, 2008), 41–43, 47–49, 177–79 and Dickerson, *African Methodist Episcopal Church,* 21–55.

36. Douglass, *My Bondage and My Freedom,* 134, 139.

37. "Henry Williamson," in *Refugees from Slavery: Autobiographies of Fugitive Slaves in Canada,* ed. Benjamin Drew (1969; Mineola, NY: Dover, 2004), 94.

38. *Autobiography of James L. Smith* (1881), in *Five Black Lives,* 162, 184.

39. On the importance of Bethel for Smith, see Jualynne E. Dodson, "Introduction," in Amanda Smith, *An Autobiography: The Story of the Lord's Dealing with Mrs. Amanda Smith the Colored Evangelist* (1893; New York: Oxford University Press, 1988), xviii–xix.

40. Newman, *Freedom's Prophet*; on Payne, Dickerson, *African Methodism,* 64–73; Stephen Ward Angell, *Bishop Henry McNeal Turner and African-American Religion in the South* (Knoxville: University of Tennessee Press, 1992). On the organization of Black Methodism more generally, see J. Gordon Melton, *A Will to Choose: The Origins of African American Methodism* (Lanham, MD: Rowman and Littlefield, 2007).

41. Daniel Coker, *A Dialogue between a Virginian and an African Minister* (Baltimore, MD: Benjamin Edes, 1810), 40–42; on the significance of that listing, Will Gravely, "'. . . many of the poor Africans are obedient to the faith': Reassessing the African American Presence in Early Methodism in the United States, 1769–1809," in *Methodism and the Shaping of American Culture,* ed. Nathan O. Hatch and John H. Wigger (Nashville, TN: Abingdon, 2001), 193–94. See, for discussion of Coker's *Dialogue,* chapter 10, 216–17.

42. On that Methodist pattern, see chapter 4 . Excellent on the synergy of Methodist evangelicalism and Methodist machinery is Rita Roberts, *Evangelicalism and the Politics of Reform in Northern Black Thought, 1776–1863* (Baton Rouge: Louisiana State University Press, 2010), esp. 36, 107–8.

43. Smith, in *Five Black Lives,* 167, 179.

44. Patrick H. Breen, *The Land Shall Be Deluged in Blood: A New History of the Nat Turner Revolt* (New York: Oxford University Press, 2015), 20.

45. "Francis Henderson," in Drew, *Refugees from Slavery,* 111.

46. Zilpha Elaw, *Memoirs of the Life, Religious Experience, Ministerial Travels and Labours of Mrs. Zilpha Elaw, An American Female of Colour . . . (written by herself)* (London: by the author, 1846). Especially helpful on Elaw are Bassard, *Transforming* Scriptures, 21–22 and Elizabeth Elkin Grammer, *Some Wild Visions: Autobiographies of Female Itinerant Evangelists in Nineteenth-Century America* (New York: Oxford University Press, 2003), passim.

47. Sydney Nathans, *To Free a Family: The Journey of Mary Walker* (Cambridge, MA: Harvard University Press, 2012), 131–32.

48. Daniel Alexander Payne, "Who Is Sufficient for These Things?" (1852), in *The Faithful Preacher: Recapturing the Vision of Three Pioneering African-American Pastors*, ed. Thabiti M. Anyabwile (Wheaton, IL: Crossway, 2007), 85–89.

49. David Walker, *Appeal to the Coloured Citizens of the World* (1829), ed. Sean Wilentz (New York: Hill & Wang, 1995), 58–59.

50. Allen, *Life, Experience, and Gospel Labors*, 57.

51. Dickerson, *African Methodism*, 27.

52. Cedric May, *Evangelism and Resistance in the Black Atlantic, 1760–1865* (Athens: University of Georgia Press, 2008), 114.

53. For details on these figures and their books, see Noll, *IN THE BEGINNING*, 211–30.

54. Equiano quoted in Callahan, *The Talking Book*, 14; also illuminating on "the talking book" metaphor is Katherine Clay Bassard, "The King James Bible and African American Literature," in *The King James Bible after 400 Years*, ed. Hannibal Hamlin and Norman W. Jones (New York: Cambridge University Press, 2010), 298.

55. John Wigger, *American Saint: Francis Asbury and the Methodists* (New York: Oxford University Press, 2009), 114–15.

56. Gravely, ". . . many of the poor Africans," 190.

57. See on the desire to read, chapter 8, 162. On orality as imperative because of legal strictures against reading, see Callahan, *The Talking Book*, 10, 13, 18.

58. Mellonee Burnim, "Biblical Inspiration, Cultural Affirmation: The African American Gift of Song," in Wimbush, *African Americans and the Bible*, 606.

59. James Weldon Johnson, "O Black and Unknown Bards," in *Fifty Years and Other Poems* (Boston: Cornhill, 1917), 6–8. On Johnson's claim that "all in all, the King James Version is the greatest book in the world," see Manfred Siebald, "James Weldon Johnson's Biblical Tuning of *God's Trombones*," in *Religion in African-American Culture*, ed. Winfried Herget and Alfred Hornung (Heidelberg: Universitätsverlag, 2006), 78n13, and the entire article (76–90) on Johnson's complicated relation to religion.

60. Maffly-Kipp and Lofton, *Women's Work*, 11.

61. Excellent treatment of the biblical reasoning of these Black, as well as white, women preachers is found in Catherine A. Brekus, *Strangers and Pilgrims: Female Preaching in America, 1740–1845* (Chapel Hill: University of North Carolina Press, 1998); Grammer, *Some Wild Visions*.

62. Allen, *Life, Experience, and Gospel Labors*, 52.

63. See especially Eddie S. Glaude Jr., *Exodus! Religion, Race, and Nation in Early Nineteenth-Century Black America* (Chicago: University of Chicago Press, 2000); John Coffey, *Exodus and Liberation: Deliverance Politics from John Calvin to Martin Luther King, Jr.* (New York: Oxford University Press, 2013); Albert J. Raboteau, "African-Americans, Exodus, and the American Israel," in *African American Christianity*, ed. Paul E. Johnson (Berkeley: University of California Press, 1994), 1–12.

64. Julius Lester, *To Be a Slave* (New York: Scholastic, 1968), 79. Particularly insightful on the Moses-Jesus fusion are Genovese, *Roll, Jordan, Roll*, 252–55; and Raboteau, *Slave Religion*, 312.

65. The last sentences are adapted from Mark A. Noll, "The Image of the United States as a Biblical Nation, 1776–1865," in Hatch and Noll, *BIBLE IN AMERICA*, 50.

66. For many biblical figures prominent in Black consciousness, see Genovese, *Roll, Jordan, Roll*, 213, 244, 249, 252–54.

67. Anthony B. Pinn and Allen Dwight Callahan, eds., *African American Religious Life and the Story of Nimrod* (New York: Palgrave Macmillan, 2008).

68. Erskine Clarke, *Wrestlin' Jacob: A Portrait of Religion in the Old South* (Atlanta, GA: John Knox, 1979).

69. Philip Richards, "The 'Joseph Story' as Slave Narrative," in Wimbush, *African Americans and the Bible*, 221–35.

70. Benjamin Mays, *The Negro's God as Reflected in His Literature* (1938; New York: Athenaeum, 1973), 21.

71. Maffly-Kipp, *Setting Down the Sacred Past*, 75.

72. Mays, *Negro's God*, 26.

73. Bassard, *Transforming Scriptures*, 19–21.

74. On Mary, Levine, *Black Culture*, 37; Brooks, *American Lazarus*.

75. Ian Shapiro and David Blight, "A Conversation about Frederick Douglass," *Bulletin of the American Academy of Arts & Sciences* 77 (Summer 2019): 17–18.

76. David W. Blight, *Frederick Douglass: Prophet of Freedom* (New York: Simon and Schuster, 2018), 238. Douglass's memorable speech in Rochester, New York, to commemorate the Fourth of July, 1852 ("What, to the American slave, is your 4th of July?") illustrated the depth of his biblical immersion. Besides evoking the ancient history of Israel and employing many biblical phrases, it quoted eleven different passages, including Psalm 68:31 ("Ethiopia") and Acts 17:26 ("one blood"). Frederick Douglass, *Oration, Delivered in Corinthian Hall, Rochester, July 5th, 1852* (Rochester, NY: Lee, Mann, 1852), 15 (Isa 35:6), 15–16 (Ps 137:1–6), 27 (Matt 5:23), 29 (Jas 1:27), 29 (Jas 3:17), 29–30 (Isa 1:13–17), 34 (Acts 17:26), 34 (Jn 13:34), 37 (Isa 59:1), 38 (Gen 1:3), and 39 (Ps 68:31).

Chapter 10

1. Particularly pertinent for this chapter and the next is Larry R. Morrison, "The Religious Defense of American Slavery before 1830," *Journal of Religious Thought* 37 (Winter 1980): 16–29. Several books that shed even more light on the decades after 1830 are also essential for earlier periods: William S. Jenkins, *Pro-Slavery Thought in the Old South* (Chapel Hill: University of North Carolina Press, 1935); H. Shelton Smith, *In His Image, But: Racism in Southern Religion, 1780–1910* (Durham, NC: Duke University Press, 1972); Larry E. Tise, *Proslavery: A History of the Defense of Slavery in America, 1701–1840* (Athens: University of Georgia Press, 1988); John R.

McKivigan and Mitchell Snay, eds., *Religion and the Antebellum Debate over Slavery* (Athens: University of Georgia Press, 1998).

2. Christopher Leslie Brown, *Moral Capital: The Foundations of British Abolitionism* (Chapel Hill: University of North Carolina Press, 2006), 105.

3. Elizabeth Fox-Genovese and Eugene D. Genovese, *The Mind of the Master Class: History and Faith in the Southern Slaveholders' Worldview* (New York: Cambridge University Press, 2005), 2: "Today, almost everyone views slavery as an enormity and abolition as a moral and political imperative. Yet as recently as two or three hundred years ago, the overwhelming majority of civilized, decent people would not have agreed: Indeed, they would have found such notions surprising." David Brion Davis, *The Problem of Slavery in Western Culture* (Ithaca, NY: Cornell University Press, 1966), remains a landmark assessment. For a recent summary focused on early modern Christendom, see Katharine Gerbner, *Christian Slavery: Conversion and Race in the Protestant Atlantic World* (Philadelphia: University of Pennsylvania Press, 2018), 13–48. Fuller discussion of biblical argumentation on slavery in the colonial period is found in Noll, *IN THE BEGINNING*, 211–32, 315–21.

4. For illuminating discussion of those Quakers, see Davis, *Slavery in Western Culture*, 291–332, 486–93.

5. James G. Basker, ed., "Gerret Hendricks, Derick op de Graeff, Francis Daniell Pastorius, and Abraham op den Graef," in *American Antislavery Writings: Colonial Beginnings to Emancipation* (New York: Library of America, 2012), 1.

6. George Keith, "An Exhortation & Caution to Friends concerning Buying or Keeping Negroes," in Basker, *American Antislavery Writings*, 4–8; John Hepburn, "The American Defence of the Christian Golden Rule, or an Essay to Prove the Unlawfulness of Making Slaves of Men," in Basker, *American Antislavery Writings*, 15–19; Ralph Sandiford, *Brief Examination of the Practice of the times* (Philadelphia, PA: Benjamin Franklin, 1729); Benjamin Lay, *All slave-keepers that keep the innocent in bondage . . . it is a notorious sin* (Philadelphia, PA: Benjamin Franklin, 1737); John Woolman, *Some Considerations on the Keeping of Negroes: Recommended to the Professors of Christianity of Every Denomination* (Philadelphia, PA: James Chattin, 1754); Anthony Benezet, *Observations on the Enslaving, Importing and Purchasing of Negroes* (Germantown, PA: Christopher Sower, 1759).

7. Keith, "Exhortation," 4–8.

8. Samuel Sewall, *The Selling of Joseph: A Memorial* (Boston: Bartholomew Green and John Allen, 1700).

9. On Saffin and his response, see Davis, *Slavery in Western Culture*, 345–46.

10. On Lord Mansfield's own religious position as a traditional Anglican who practiced toleration according to the precepts of John Locke, see Norman S. Poser, "Lord Mansfield: The Reasonableness of Religion," in *Great Christian Jurists in English History*, ed. Mark Hill and R. H. Helmhoz (New York: Cambridge University Press, 2017), 186–211 (190–92 on the decision).

11. Thomas Thompson, *The African slave trade for Negro slaves, shewn to be consistent with principles of humanity, and with the laws of revealed religion* (Canterbury: Simmons and Kirkby, [1772]), 11, 24, 25, 15.

12. For an introduction and the text of Graham's lecture, see David W. Robson, "'An Important Question Answered': William Graham's Defense of Slavery in Post-Revolutionary Virginia," *William and Mary Quarterly* 37 (October 1980): 644–52 (quotations, 649–52).

13. Excellent on Harris/Hormaza, his pamphlet, and the English conflict it sparked is David Brion Davis, *The Problem of Slavery in the Age of Revolution, 1770–1823*, new ed. (New York: Oxford University Press, 1999), 542–51.

14. R. Harris, *Scriptural Researches on the Licitness of the Slave-Trade, shewing its conformity with the principles of Natural and Revealed Religion, Delineated in the Sacred Writings of the Word of God* (Fredericktown, MD: John Witner, 1790), vii, 42–43.

15. Joseph Priestley, *Sermon on the Subject of the Slave Trade* (1788), 33, quoted in G. M. Ditchfield, "Abolitionism and the Social Conscience," in *The Oxford History of Protestant Dissenting Traditions*, vol. 2: *The Long Eighteenth Century, c. 1689–c. 1828*, ed. Andrew C. Thompson (Oxford: Oxford University Press, 2018), 294. Ditchfield's entire chapter (285–301) is particularly helpful for American comparisons, as is Leland J. Bellot, "Evangelicals and the Defense of Slavery in Britain's Old Colonial Empire," *Journal of Southern History* 37 (February 1971): 19–40.

16. Davis, *Slavery in the Age of Revolution*, 547 ("moral confusion"), 549 (Wilberforce on "explanations"), and 547–64 for a superb general account of American-British differences on the use of Scripture. On the British antislavery appeal to providence, see John Coffey, "'Tremble Britannia': Fear, Providence, and the Abolition of the Slave Trade," *English Historical Review* 127 (2012): 844–81. A helpful website with information on British antislavery publications reveals the relatively subordinate place of Scripture in those works: Recovered Histories, accessed July 22, 2019, http://www.recoveredhistories.org/search.php.

17. Jacob Green, *A Sermon Delivered at Hanover, New-Jersey . . . Being the Day of public fasting and prayer* (Chatham, NJ: Shepard Kollock, 1779), 14. For the context, Mark A. Noll, "Observations on the Reconciliation of Politics and Religion in Revolutionary New Jersey: The Case of Jacob Green," *Journal of Presbyterian History* 54 (Summer 1976): 217–37.

18. "To Thomas Jefferson from Benjamin Banneker, 19 August 1791," Founders Online, https://founders.archives.gov/documents/Jefferson/01-22-02-0049.   Noteworthy clerics making similar arguments included the anti-revivalist James Dana, *The African Slave Trade: A Discourse Delivered in the City of New-Haven, September 9, 1790, before the Connecticut Society for the Promotion of Freedom* (New Haven, CT: Thomas and Samuel Green, 1791) and the pro-revivalist Samuel Hopkins, *A Discourse upon the Slave-Trade and the Slavery of the Africans* (Providence, RI: J. Carter, 1793).

19. Anthony Benezet, *Serious Considerations on Several Important Subjects; viz., On War and Its Inconsistency with the Gospel. Observations on Slavery* (Philadelphia, PA: Joseph Crukshank, 1778), 31–32 (citing Jer 34:8–17, where the prophet chastised Judah for promising to free its slaves but then retreating from the promise); Jonathan Edwards Jr., *The Injustice and Impolity of the Slave-Trade, and of the Slavery of the Africans . . . illustrated in a sermon preached . . . September 15, 1791* (Providence, RI: John Carter, [1792]). This sermon inaugurated the Connecticut Society for the

Promotion of Freedom and Relief of Persons Unlawfully Holden in Bondage; it engaged in considerable hand-to-hand exegetical combat on "the curse of Canaan" from Genesis 9:25 (14), the slaves of Abraham (16), prohibitions against man-stealing (26), and the contested passages from Leviticus 25:44–47 (16).

20. Rice's wide-ranging speech also included numerous arguments based on currently popular ideologies, especially the conventional republican calculus concerning social well-being: "Slavery naturally tends to sap the foundations of moral, and consequently of political virtue; and virtue is absolutely necessary for the happiness and prosperity of a free people." David Rice, *Slavery Inconsistent with Justice and Good Policy* (1792), in *American Political Writing during the Founding Era, 1760–1805*, 2 vols, ed. Charles S. Hyneman and Donald S. Lutz (Indianapolis, IN: Liberty Press, 1983), 2:858–83.

21. Rice, *Slavery Inconsistent*, 878.

22. Rice, *Slavery Inconsistent*, 877–78.

23. Rice, *Slavery Inconsistent*, 863–64.

24. See chapter 3, 63 on a variation of the same argument to be made later by Freeborn Garrettson and Daniel Coker.

25. Rice, *Slavery Inconsistent*, 875–77 (quotation 876).

26. Joseph Gales, *The Debates and Proceedings of the Congress of the United States,* vol. 1 . . . *from March 3, 1789, to March 3, 1791* (Washington, DC: Gales and Seaton, 1834), 1224–25. For context, see David Brion Davis, *Inhuman Bondage: The Rise and Fall of Slavery in the New World* (New York: Oxford University Press, 2006), 155.

27. *Debates of the Congress*, 1226 (Madison, with reference to Article I, section ix, which prohibited Congress from outlawing the slave trade until 1808), 1229 (Jackson).

28. Donald G. Mathews, *Slavery and Methodism: A Chapter in American Morality* (Princeton, NJ: Princeton University Press, 1965); and for a general account, Davis, *Slavery in the Age of Revolution*, 203–12. Excellent later treatments for Methodists include John H. Wigger, *Taking Heaven by Storm: Methodism and the Rise of Popular Christianity in America* (New York: Oxford University Press, 1998), 125–50; Cynthia Lynn Lyerly, *Methodism and the Southern Mind, 1770–1810* (New York: Oxford University Press, 1998), 119–45; Douglas Ambrose, "Of Stations and Relations: Proslavery Christianity in Early National Virginia," in McKivigan and Snay, *Religion and the Antebellum Debate over Slavery*, 35–67; Dee E. Andrews, *The Methodists and Revolutionary America, 1760–1800* (Princeton, NJ: Princeton University Press, 2000), 122–39; Charles H. Irons, *The Origins of Proslavery Christianity: White and Black Evangelicals in Colonial and Antebellum* Virginia (Chapel Hill: University of North Carolina Press, 2008), 74–76; John H. Wigger, *American Saint: Francis Asbury and the Methodists* (New York: Oxford University Press, 2009), 122–25 and passim.

29. Carlos R. Allen Jr., "David Barrow's Circular Letter of 1798," *William and Mary Quarterly* 20 (July 1963): 445.

30. Mathews, *Slavery and Methodism*, 28.

31. Jewel L. Spangler, "Proslavery Presbyterians: Virginia's Conservative Dissenters in the Age of Revolution," *Journal of Presbyterian History* 78 (Summer 2000): 111–24.

32. *Records of the Presbyterian Church in the United States of America[,] Embracing the Minutes of the General Presbytery and General Synod, 1706–1788* (Philadelphia, PA: Presbyterian Board of Publication, 1904), 539–40.

33. Quoted in James H. Morehead, "Between Hope and Fear: Presbyterians and the 1818 Statement on Slavery," *Journal of Presbyterian History* 96 (Fall/Winter 2018), 49; this entire article (48–61) provides excellent context for these actions in 1818.

34. Morehead, "Between Hope and Fear," 49.

35. For the historical stance, see the early chapters of D. G. Hart, *Calvinism: A History* (New Haven, CT: Yale University Press, 2013). A clear statement of the emerging Presbyterian position, though without naming it "the spiritual of the church," is found in Jenkins, *Pro-Slavery Thought*, 207–18. For proponents of this concept, see E. T. Thompson, *Presbyterians in the South*, vol. 1: *1607–1861* (Richmond, VA: John Knox, 1963), 339–48, 529–31.

36. The 1785 quotation is from Jon Butler, "James Ireland, John Leland, John 'Swearing Jack' Walker, and the Baptist Campaign for Religion Freedom in Revolutionary Virginia," in *Revolutionary Founders: Rebels, Radicals, and Reformers in the Making of the Nation*, ed. Alfred Y. Young, Gary B. Nash, and Ray Raphael (New York: Knopf, 2011), 183. For similar statements elsewhere, see Thomas S. Kidd and Barry Hankins, *Baptists in America: A History* (New York: Oxford University Press, 2015), 100; and Irons, *Origins of Proslavery Christianity*, 68–72.

37. Quoted in Bruce Gourley, "John Leland: Evolving Views of Slavery, 1789–1839," *Baptist History and Heritage* 40 (Winter 2005): 107.

38. Allen, "David Barrow's Circular Letter," 440–51; Kidd and Hankins, *Baptists in America*, 102.

39. Gourley, "John Leland," 110.

40. Anne C. Loveland, "Richard Furman's 'Questions on Slavery,'" *Baptist History and Heritage* 10 (July 1975): 177–181 (quotations, 178, 178, 180).

41. For that influence in Virginia, see Frederika Teute Schmidt and Barbara Ripel Wilhelm, "Early Proslavery Petitions in Virginia," *William and Mary Quarterly* 30 (January 1973): 134, 141, 143.

42. Loveland, "Richard Furman's 'Questions,'" 180.

43. Monica Najar, "'Meddling with Emancipation': Baptists, Authority, and the Rift over Slavery in the Upper South," *Journal of the Early Republic* 25 (Summer 2005); 157–86 (quotation, 182).

44. Excellent on reasons for this Baptist disposition is Gourley, "John Leland," 111–13.

45. Writing about the four works detailed in this section has made me wish once again that Eugene Genovese and Elizabeth Fox-Genovese were still alive so that they could rethink the conclusion they drew—that antislavery arguments could not be grounded in a traditional, orthodox understanding of Scripture—in *The Mind of the Master Class*, 526–27.

46. See Irons, *Origins of Proslavery Christianity*, 90, for discussion of William Gray, ed. of Samuel Davies's earlier *The Duty of Masters to Their Servants* (1809); and Thomas Bacon, *Sermons Addressed to Masters and Servants*, ed. William Meade (1753; 1813).

47. On the impact of Gabriel's Rebellion on the churches, see Davis, *Slavery in the Age of Revolution*, 210; Davis, *Inhuman* Bondage, 222–25; Mathews, *Slavery and Methodism*, 31, which points out that Gabriel's conspirators planned to exempt Methodists from their attacks because of the denomination's antislavery stance. My thanks to Helene Fisher, whose script on the Bible among America's enslaved was prepared as background for the abridged "Slaves' Bible" (London, 1807) that belongs to Fisk University and was on display during 2019 at the Museum of the Bible in Washington, DC.

48. See Ian B. Straker, "Black and White and Gray All Over: Freeborn Garrettson and African Methodists," *Methodist History* 37 (October 1998): 18–27; George A. Rawlyk, "Garretson, Freeborn," in *Dictionary of Canadian Biography*, vol. 6, University of Toronto/Université Laval, 2003–, http://www.biographi.ca/en/bio/garrettson_freeborn_6E.html.

49. Freeborn Garrettson, *Dialogue between Do-Justice and Professing-Christian, Dedicated to the . . . Abolition Societies, and to all other Benevolent, Humane Philanthropists, in America* (Wilmington, DE: Peter Brynberg, [1805]), 5–7. The pamphlet is dated 1805 by Straker, "Black and White," and other authorities on Garrettson.

50. Garrettson, *Dialogue*, 25 (prove pointedly), 29 (eighteen on this page).

51. Garrettson, *Dialogue*, 11–14.

52. Will B. Gravely, "African Methodism and the Rise of Black Denominationalism," in *Perspectives on American Methodism: Interpretive Essays*, ed. Russel E. Richey et al. (Nashville, TN: Kingswood, 1993), 109; H. T. Maclin, "Coker, Daniel," in *Biographical Dictionary of Christian Missions*, ed. Gerald H. Anderson (Grand Rapids, MI: Eerdmans, 1998), 143; Richard S. Newman, "Prince Hall, Richard Allen, and Daniel Coker: Revolutionary Black Founders, Revolutionary Black Communities," in Young, Nash, and Raphael, *Revolutionary Founders*, 317–18.

53. See chapter 9, 175, on the first such work: Quobna Ottobah Cugoano, *Thoughts and Sentiments on the Evil of Slavery: Or, the nature of servitude as admitted by the law of God, compared to the modern slavery of the Africans in the West-Indies* (London: By the author, 1791).

54. There is fuller treatment of Coker's pamphlet in Noll, *CIVIL WAR*, 65–71.

55. Daniel Coker (who is identified on the title page as "a descendent of Africa" and "Minister of the African Methodist Episcopal Church in Baltimore"), *A Dialogue between a Virginian and an African Minister* (Baltimore, MD: Benjamin Edes, 1810), 22.

56. Coker, *Dialogue*, 23.

57. Joseph Moore, "Epilogue," in *Faith and Slavery in the Presbyterian Diaspora*, ed. W. H. Taylor and P. C. Messer (Bethlehem, PA: Lehigh University Press, 2016), 252.

58. On the biblicism of this Scottish heritage, Noll, *IN THE BEGINNING*, 92–93. I am grateful to Ashley Foster for much pertinent information on Scottish covenants.

59. Alexander McLeod, *Negro Slavery Unjustifiable: A Discourse*, 11th ed. (1802; New York: Alexander McLeod, 1863), 6.

60. For the occasion of this work, see the "Advertisement" prefacing the 1863 ed. of the *Discourse*, [iv] and Joseph S. Moore, *Founding Sins: How a Group of Antislavery Radicals Fought to Put Christ in the Constitution* (New York: Oxford University Press, 2016), 93–100. On Covenanter antislavery, mostly before McLeod, see Joseph S.

Moore, "Covenanters and Antislavery in the Atlantic World," *Slavery and Abolition* 34 (December 2013): 539–61. In the generation before and during the Civil War, Reformed Presbyterians also led an effort to add acknowledgment of Christ's lordship to the Constitution: Daniel Ritchie, "Radical Orthodoxy: Irish Covenanters and American Slavery, circa 1830–1865," *Church History* 82 (December 2013): 812–47.

61. Moore, *Founding Sins*, 93.

62. McLeod, *Negro Slavery Unjustifiable*, 8, 18, 21.

63. McLeod *Negro Slavery Unjustifiable*, 40 (Bible), 6, 11–13, 37–37, 40 (man-stealing), 27–29 (curse), 32–33 (Leviticus), 37 (Paul).

64. McLeod, *Negro Slavery Unjustifiable*, 41–42. Government support for the churches was the part of the original Westminster Confession (XXIII.3) edited out by the American Presbyterians in 1789.

65. On Bourne, see especially John W. Christie and Dwight L. Dumond, *George Bourne and* The Book and Slavery Irreconcilable (Philadelphia, PA: Presbyterian Historical Society, 1969), with a monographic introduction and a complete reprinting of *The Book and Slavery*; Ryan C. McIlhenny, *To Preach Deliverance to Captives: Freedom and Slavery in the Protestant Mind of George Bourne (1780–1845)* (Baton Rouge: Louisiana State University Press, 2020), 5: "Bourne's approach to reform harked back to the doctrinal and ecclesiastical revolution of the sixteenth-century Reformation."

66. On Bourne's anti-Catholic exertions, see Cassandra L. Yacovazzi, *Escaped Nuns: True Womanhood and the Campaign against Convents in Antebellum America* (New York: Oxford University Press, 2018), 24 (on the possibility that Bourne was the real author of *Maria Monk*) and 51–55.

67. For the centrality of Scripture at Westminster, see Noll, *IN THE BEGINNING*, 83–89.

68. *The Constitution of the Presbyterian Church in the United States of America, Containing the Confession of Faith, the Catechisms, and the Director of Worship of God, Together with the Plan of Government and Discipline as Amended and Ratified by the General Assembly at Their Sessions in May, 1805* (Philadelphia, PA: Jane Aitken, 1806), 277–78.

69. George Bourne, *The Book and Slavery Irreconcilable, with Animadversions upon Dr. Smith's Philosophy* (Philadelphia, PA: J. M. Sanderson, 1816). On the title page, Bourne printed a combined quotation from Peter (Acts 3:17) and Paul (Acts 17:30): "I wot that through ignorance ye did it, as did also your rulers; and the times of this ignorance GOD winked at; but now commandeth all men, every where to repent." The "winking" passage had also been used by Jonathan Edwards Jr. to excuse his father and others of the father's generation for owning slaves. Kenneth P. Minkema and Harry S. Stout, "The Edwardsean Tradition and the Antislavery Debate, 1740–1865," *Journal of American History* 92 (June 2005): 57–58.

70. McLeod, *Negro Slavery Unjustifiable*, 7.

71. McLeod, *Negro Slavery Unjustifiable*, 26; Bourne, *Book and Slavery*, 143–54. On these works of Smith, see Mark A. Noll, *Princeton and the Republic, 1768–1822* (Princeton, NJ: Princeton University Press, 1989), 115–24, 186–87.

72. Bourne, *Book and Slavery*, 27.

73. Christie and Dumond, *George Bourne*, 18, 26, 52.

74. For references to Coker in connection with Denmark Vesey, see Douglas R. Egerton and Robert L. Paquette, eds., *The Denmark Vesey Affair: A Documentary History* (Gainesville: University Press of Florida, 2017), 19, 702.

75. On the Bourne-Garrison connections, see Christie and Dumond, *George Bourne*, vi, 83–98; McIlhenny, *To Preach Deliverance*, 105–8, 113–16, and passim.

Chapter 11

1. Superb background for this section is found in Robert Pierce Forbes, *The Missouri Compromise and Its Aftermath* (Chapel Hill: University of North Carolina Press, 2007); and Robert Pierce Forbes, "Slavery and the Evangelical Enlightenment," in *Religion and the Antebellum Debate over Slavery*, ed. John R. McKivigan and Mitchell Snay (Athens: University of Georgia Press, 1998), 68–106.

2. *Papers Relative to the Restrictions on Slavery: Speeches of Mr. King in the Senate and of Messers. Taylor and Talmadge* [sic] *in the House of Representatives* (Philadelphia, PA: Hall and Atkinson, 1819), 28.

3. *Annals of Congress, 15th Congress—Second Session* (November 1818–February 1819) (Washington, DC: Gales and Seaton, 1855), 1174.

4. *Annals of Congress*, 1191.

5. Rufus King, *Substance of Two Speeches delivered in the Senate of the United States on the Subject of the Missouri Bill* (Philadelphia, PA: Clark and Raser, 1819), 5.

6. *Annals of Congress, 16th Congress—First Session* (December 1819–May 1820) (Washington, DC: Gales and Seaton, 1855), 269–70 (Smith, January 26); 335 (Barbour, February 1).

7. *Richmond Enquirer*, December 3, 1819, p. 2; January 1, 1820, p. 3; January 8, 1820, p. 3; February 10, 1820, p. 3; February 12, 1820, p. 3. On Thomas Ritchie's deep investment in national debates, see Sean Wilentz, *The Rise of American Democracy: Jefferson to Lincoln* (New York: Norton, 2005), 200, 233, and passim.

8. Forbes, *Missouri Compromise*, 100 (Jefferson), 149.

9. Henry Otis Dwight, *The Centennial History of the American Bible Society*, 2 vols. (New York: Macmillan, 1916), 2:577; Hills, *ENGLISH BIBLE*, 63–71.

10. I follow Douglas R. Egerton and Robert L. Paquette and their extraordinarily comprehensive edition of primary source documents in treating "the Vesey plot [as] one of the most sophisticated acts of collective slave resistance in the history of the United States": *The Denmark Vesey Affair: A Documentary History* (Gainesville: University Press of Florida, 2017), xv. For extended controversy over whether an insurrection had actually been planned, see Michael P. Johnson, "Denmark Vesey and His Conspiracy," *William and Mary Quarterly* 58 (2001): 915–76; and responses, *William and Mary Quarterly* 59 (2002): 135–202.

11. Egerton and Paquette, *Denmark Vesey*, 37, 214n4, 221, 450, 491.

12. Egerton and Paquette, *Denmark Vesey*, 18–19. On Dow's distinctive preaching, see Hatch, *DEMOCRATIZATION*, 102, 185–86.

13. Egerton and Paquette, *Denmark Vesey*, 21–25.

14. See chapter 9.

15. Egerton and Paquette, *Denmark Vesey*, 181, 166, also 295 for another testimony about Vesey's reference to the Exodus.

16. Egerton and Paquette, *Denmark Vesey*, 212, 286.

17. The ABS printed Spanish-language bibles with the Apocrypha for distribution in Catholic Latin America until the BFBS's controversy over the Apocrypha moved the ABS to end even those printings (Dwight, *Centennial History*, 100–101).

18. On these specific texts, see Egerton and Paquette, *Denmark Vesey*, 323.

19. For Vesey's place in the history of such a Grand Narrative, see John Coffey, *Exodus and Liberation: Deliverance Politics from John Calvin to Martin Luther King, Jr.* (New York: Oxford University Press, 2014), 162, 167, 219.

20. Richard Furman, *Rev. Dr. Richard Furman's Exposition of the Views of the Baptists, Relative to the Colored Population of the United States, in a Communication to the Governor of South-Carolina* (Charleston: A. E. Miller, 1823), 8; William S. Jenkins, *Pro-Slavery Thought in the Old South* (Chapel Hill: University of North Carolina Press, 1935), 202.

21. A South Carolinian [Frederick Dalcho], *Practical Considerations founded on the Scriptures, Relative to the Slave Population of South-Carolina* (Charleston, SC: A. E. Miller, 1823), 8. Dalcho expatiated at length on Ham and Canaan as the progenitors of Africans (8–20) because he felt Furman had slighted the passage for the Baptists.

22. Dalcho, *Practical Considerations*, 20; "The Charleston Bible Society Asks Governor Bennett for a Day of Thanksgiving," in Egerton and Paquette, *Denmark Vesey*, 674.

23. Furman, *Views of the Baptists*, 7, 11; Dalcho, *Practical Considerations*, 6.

24. "Charleston Bible Society," 674; [Edwin Holland], *A Refutation of the Calumnies Circulated against the Southern & Western States, respecting the institution and exist- ence of Slavery among them* (Charleston, SC: A. E. Miller, 1822), 12.

25. Furman, *Views of the Baptists*, 4; "Charleston Bible Society," 674 (quoting 2 Tim 3:15).

26. Furman, *Views of the Baptists*, 4–5; Holland, *Refutation*, 13.

27. Robert Robinson, "Come, thou Fount of every blessing," Hymnary, accessed August 9, 2019, https://hymnary.org/text/come_thou_fount_of_every_blessing. On the "blurring of worlds" in this era, see Hatch, *DEMOCRATIZATION*, 34.

28. Forbes, *Missouri Compromise*, 149–51.

29. Furman, *Views of the Baptists*, 17; Dalcho, *Practical Considerations*, 33–35; "Charleston Bible Society," 675.

30. Holland, *Refutation*, 11–12; Dalcho, *Practical Considerations*, 6.

31. Howe, *WHAT HATH GOD WROUGHT*, 326–37; Sean Wilentz, *The Rise of American Democracy: Jefferson to Lincoln* (New York: Norton, 2005), 341. Walter A. McDougall, *Throes of Democracy: The American Civil War Era, 1829–1877* (New York: Harper, 2008), 65 is even pithier: the Virginia assembly "judged an inquiry [into the root causes of Turner's rebellion] 'inexpedient' . . . and instead passed laws to hasten the removal of free blacks and outlaw unsupervised worship among slaves. . . . [T]he 're- public of words' moved on, and many southern women learned how to handle a gun."

32. Charles F. Irons, *The Origins of Proslavery Christianity: White and Black Evangelicals in Colonial and Antebellum Virginia* (Chapel Hill: University of North Carolina Press, 2008), 12–14.

33. Good biographical material on Walker's somewhat mysterious life is found in Sean Wilentz, "Introduction," in *David Walker's Appeal To the Coloured Citizens of the World, but in Particular, and Very Expressly, to those of The United States of America* (New York: Hill and Wang, 1995), vii–xxiii; Peter P. Hinks, "Walker, David," in *ANB*; Wilentz, *Rise of American Democracy*, 332–34.

34. Page references in the text are to Wilentz's edition of Walker's *Appeal*.

35. Wilentz, "Introduction," xvi, xix.

36. Quoted in John L. Thomas, *The Liberator: William Lloyd Garrison, a Biography* (Boston: Little, Brown, 1963), 135–36.

37. William Lloyd Garrison, "Walker's Appeal," *Liberator*, January 8, 1831, 6, http://fair-use.org/the-liberator/.

38. A Colored Bostonian, "Death of Walker," *Liberator*, January 22, 1831, 14; J. I. W., "The Appeal," *Liberator*, February 5, 1831, 22.

39. For Garrison, I have relied on Thomas, *The Liberator*; Bertram Wyatt Brown, *Lewis Tappan and the Evangelical War against* Slavery (Cleveland, OH: Press of Case Western Reserve University, 1969); Ronald G. Walters, *The Antislavery Appeal: American Abolitionism after 1830* (Baltimore, MD: Johns Hopkins University Press, 1976); James Brewer Stewart, "Abolitionists, the Bible, and the Challenge of Slavery," in *The Bible and Social Reform*, ed. Ernest R. Sandeen (Philadelphia, PA: Fortress, 1982), 31–58; James Brewer Stewart, "Garrison, William Lloyd," in *ANB*.

40. "Garrison's First Anti-Slavery Address in Boston," in *Old South Leaflets*, vol. 8, no. 180 (Boston: Old South Meeting House, 1890), 6 ("Holy Writ"), 10. He continued in the same vein by imploring ministers (10) "to 'proclaim liberty to the captives and the opening of the prison to them that are bound [Isa 61:1; Lk 4:18]," "to light a flame of philanthropy that shall burn till all Africa be redeemed from the night of moral death and the song of deliverance [from Ex 15] be heard throughout her borders."

41. John W. Christie and Dwight L. Dumond, *George Bourne and The Book and Slavery Irreconcilable* (Wilmington: Historical Society of Delaware, 1969), 78–80; Ryan C. McIlhenny, *To Preach Deliverance to the Captives: Freedom and Slavery in the Protestant Mind of George Bourne, 1780–1845* (Baton Rouge: Louisiana State University Press, 2020), 1–2.

42. Quotations that follow are from that first issue, available at the Fair Use Repository, accessed November 11, 2019, http://fair-use.org/the-liberator/.

43. This Virginia debate preceded the legislators' even more contentious arguments after the Turner uprising. See in this chapter, 231.

44. *Declaration of Sentiments of the American Anti-Slavery Society, Adopted at the Formation of said Society, in Philadelphia, on the 4th day of December, 1833,* Penny Tracts, Number 1 (New York: American Anti-Slavery Society, 1833), 2–3.

45. On the rising force of humanitarian instinct, see Margaret Abruzzo, *Polemical Pain: Slavery, Cruelty, and the Rise of Humanitarianism* (Baltimore, MD: Johns Hopkins University Press, 2011); Molly Oshatz, *Slavery and Sin: The Fight against*

Slavery and the Rise of Liberal Protestantism (New York: Oxford University Press, 2012). Insightful on how Garrison's views affected the course of both pro- and antislavery stances is Kathryn Gin Lum, *Damned Nation: Hell in America from the Revolution to Reconstruction* (New York: Oxford University Press, 2014), 187–91.

46. For a convincing defenses of *Confessions* as basically trustworthy, see Patrick H. Breen, *The Land Shall Be Deluged in Blood: A New History of the Nat Turner Revolt* (New York: Oxford University Press, 2015), 15–16, 169–79; and Christopher Tomlins, *In the Matter of Nat Turner: A Speculative History* (Princeton, NJ: Princeton University Press, 2020). Tomlin's book is particularly persuasive on Turner's deep immersion in the Scriptures (27–82).

47. Quotations in the following are from *The Confessions of Nat Turner, Leader of the Late Insurrection in Southampton, Va. as fully and voluntarily made to Thomas R. Gray . . .* (Baltimore, MD: By the author, 1831), 2–7.

48. Turner quoted Luke 12:47 similarly (5). He told Gray that after an earlier episode, when he had run away and hid in the woods for a month, "the Spirit appeared to me" and spoke this passage about the servant knowing his master's will, which induced him to return to his own master.

49. See chapter 12.

50. David F. Holland, *Sacred Borders: Continuing Revelation and Canonical Restraint in Early* America (New York: Oxford University Press, 2011), 123.

Chapter 12

1. Alexis de Tocqueville, *Democracy in* America, ed. Eduardo Nolla, trans. James T. Schleifer, 4 vols. (Indianapolis: Liberty Fund, 2010), 2:479–80; National Archives, Founders Online, James Madison to Jaspar Adams, September 1833, https://founders.archives.gov/documents/Madison/99-02-02-2830.

2. For a stimulating expansion of this conclusion, see Walter A. MacDougall, *The Tragedy of U.S. Foreign Policy: How America's Civil Religion Betrayed the National Interest* (New Haven, CT: Yale University Press, 2016).

3. Excellent, among many other treatments, are Michael G. Legaspi, *The Death of Scripture and the Rise of Biblical Studies* (New York: Oxford University Press, 2010) and James Turner, *Philology: The Forgotten Origins of the Modern Humanities* (Princeton, NJ: Princeton University Press, 2014), 210–29.

4. On the traditionalists, see especially J. C. D. Clark, *English Society, 1660–1832*, 2nd ed. (New York: Cambridge University Press, 2000); on the conflict of tradition and reform in Scotland, see Stewart J. Brown, *Thomas Chalmers and the Godly Commonwealth in Scotland* (New York: Oxford University Press, 1982); on Protestant opposition to the Protestant establishment, see Timothy Larsen and Michael Ledger-Lomas, eds., *The Oxford History of Protestant Dissenting Traditions*, vol. 3: *The Nineteenth Century* (Oxford: Oxford University Press, 2017); and on the social disruption of evolutionary

theory, see Adrian Desmond and James Moore, *Darwin: The Life of a Tormented Evolutionist* (New York: Time Warner, 1992).

5. On the marginal nineteenth-century place of Campbellites in Britain, see Tim Grass, "Restorationists and New Movements," in Larsen and Ledger-Lomas, *The Oxford History of Protestant Dissenting Traditions*, 150–74 (esp. 154–56). Helpful general accounts for the United States include Richard T. Hughes, *Reviving the Ancient Faith: The Story of Churches of Christ in America* (Grand Rapids, MI: Eerdmans, 1996); David Edwin Harrell Jr., *Quest for Christian America, 1800–1865: A Social History of the Disciples of Christ* (Tuscaloosa: University of Alabama Press, 2003).

6. [Thomas Campbell], *Address of the Christian Association of Washington* (Washington, PA: Brown and Sample, 1809), 7–8, 16–17.

7. For expert treatment of that emphasis, see Richard T. Hughes and C. Leonard Allen, *Illusions of Innocence: Protestant Primitivism in America, 1630–1875* (Chicago: University of Chicago Press, 1988); Richard T. Hughes, ed., *The American Quest for the Primitive Church* (Urbana: University of Illinois Press, 1988).

8. *The Evidences of Christianity: A Debate between Robert Owen . . . and Alexander Campbell . . . Held in the City of Cincinnati, Ohio, in April 1829* (1829; St. Louis, MO: Christian Pub., 1906), 13, 14, 370; *A Debate on the Roman Catholic Religion. Held in the Sycamore-Street Meeting House, Cincinnati, from the 13th to the 21st of January, 1837, Between Alexander Campbell, of Bethany, Virginia, and the Rt. Rev. John B. Purcell, Bishop of Cincinnati* (Cincinnati, OH: J. A. James, 1837), viii, 13. For more on the contexts of these debates, see Noll, AMERICA'S GOD, 242–44; Herbert Dean Miller, "Enacting Theology, Americanism, and Friendship: The 1837 Debate on Roman Catholicism between Alexander Campbell and Bishop John Purcell" (Ph.D. diss., University of Dayton, 2015).

9. Hughes and Allen, *Illusions of Innocence*, 126, 131.

10. Hughes and Allen, *Illusions of Innocence*, 127 (from 1829 or 1830).

11. *The Sermon Delivered at the Inauguration of the Rev. Archibald Alexander, D.D., as Professor of Didactic and Polemic Theology, in the Theological Seminary of the Presbyterian Church, in the United States of America* (New York: J. Seymour, 1812), 58, 62, 74, 75. The same reasoning appeared when John Holt Rice was inaugurated as the first professor of the Presbyterians' Union Seminary in Hampden Sydney, Virginia; John H. Rice, *An Inaugural Address, Delivered on the First of January, 1824* (Richmond, VA: Nathan Pollard, 1824), esp. 5, 7, 9, 21.

12. John M. Duncan, *A Plea for Ministerial Liberty* (1824), quoted in Allen Stanton, "Samuel Miller: The Forgotten Founder and Shaper of Old Princeton," *Journal of Presbyterian History* 91 (Spring–Summer 2013): 15.

13. For discussion, see Stanton, "Samuel Miller," 15.

14. Samuel Miller, *Presbyterianism, the Truly Primitive and Apostolical Constitution of the Church of Christ* (Philadelphia, PA: Presbyterian Board of Education, 1835), 65.

15. Michael W. Casey, *The Battle over Hermeneutics in the Stone-Campbell Movement, 1800–1870* (Lewiston, ME: Edwin Mellen, 1998), 146.

16. Miller and Millerism have been very well served by historians, including Ruth Alden Doan, *The Miller Heresy, Millennialism, and American Culture* (Philadelphia,

PA: Temple University Press, 1987); Ronald L. Numbers and Jonathan M. Butler, eds., *The Disappointed: Millerism and Millenarianism in the Nineteenth Century* (Bloomington: University of Indiana Press, 1987); David L. Rowe, *God's Strange Work: William Miller and the End of the World* (Grand Rapids, MI: Eerdmans, 2008).

17. Rowe, *God's Strange Work*, 67 (quoting one of Miller's later memoirs).

18. Eric Anderson, "The Millerite Use of Prophecy," in Numbers and Butler, *The Disappointed*, 80.

19. David T. Arthur, "Joshua V. Himes and the Cause of Adventism," in Numbers and Butler, *The Disappointed*, 36–58, is a superb essay.

20. Arthur, "Joshua V. Himes," 37.

21. J. V. Himes, *A Chronological Chart of the Visions of Daniel and John* (Boston: B. W. Thayer,[ca. 1842]).

22. Ronald L. Numbers and Janet S. Numbers, "Millerism and Madness: A Study of 'Religious Insanity' in Nineteenth-Century America," in Numbers and Butler, *The Disappointed*, 92–118.

23. Howe, *WHAT HATH GOD WROUGHT*, 291 (emphasis added).

24. David L. Rowe, "Millerites: A Shadow Portrait," in Numbers and Butler, *The Disappointed*, 15.

25. Ruth Alden Doan, "Millerism and Evangelical Culture," in Numbers and Butler, *The Disappointed*, 118.

26. See Nicholas Miller, ed., *The Oxford Handbook of Seventh-day Adventism* (New York: Oxford University Press, 2022).

27. Perceptive on the wider connections between fidelity to divine revelation and loyalty to the Constitution is Jaroslav Pelikan, *Interpreting the Bible and the Constitution* (New Haven, CT: Yale University Press, 2004); and for later in the nineteenth century, Sarah Barringer Gordon, *The Mormon Question: Polygamy and Constitutional Conflict in Nineteenth-Century America* (Chapel Hill: University of North Carolina Press, 2002).

28. David F. Holland, *Sacred Borders: Continuing Revelation and Canonical Restraint in Early America* (New York: Oxford University Press, 2011). On the important parallels that Holland has identified between biblicist and constitutional thinking, see 44–46, 75–76.

29. Benjamin Franklin, "Chap. XXVII," in *The Papers of Benjamin Franklin: Digital Edition*, vol. 6 (July 1755), http://franklinpapers.org/framedNames.jsp. See Holland, *Sacred Borders*, 69–76.

30. See especially Susan Juster, *Doomsayers: Anglo-American Prophecy in the Age of Revolution* (Philadelphia: University of Pennsylvania Press, 2003).

31. Roland Bainton, *Here I Stand: A Life of Martin Luther* (New York: Abingdon, 1950), 203.

32. George Huntston Williams, *The Radical Reformation*, 3rd ed. (Kirksville, MO: Truman State University Press, 1992).

33. See chapter 10, 203.

34. On Swedenborgians in the new United States, see Holland, *Sacred Borders*, 98–104.

35. Nimrod Hughes, *A Solemn Warning* (New York: Largin and Thompson, 1812), 4.

36. Lester J. Capon, ed., *The Adams-Jefferson Letters* (Chapel Hill: University of North Carolina Press, 1959), Adams to Jefferson, February 10, 1812; Jefferson to Adams, April 20, 1812; Adams to Jefferson, May 1, 1812; Adams to Jefferson, May 3, 1812, 296–304.

37. Holland, *Sacred Borders*, 92–98.

38. Holland, *Sacred Borders*, 151.

39. On Joseph Smith, I have benefited especially from Richard Lyman Bushman, *Joseph Smith, Rough Stone Rolling: A Cultural Biography of Mormon's Founder* (New York: Knopf, 2005). On the Book of Mormon, from Terryl L. Givens, *By the Hand of Mormon: The American Scripture that Launched a New World Religion* (New York: Oxford University Press, 2002); Terryl L. Givens, *The Book of Mormon: A Very Short Introduction* (New York: Oxford University Press, 2009); Paul C. Gutjahr, *The Book of Mormon: A Biography* (Princeton, NJ: Princeton University Press, 2012). And for broader contexts, Jan Shipps, *Mormonism: The Story of a New Religious Tradition* (Urbana: University of Illinois Press, 1985); Hatch, *DEMOCRATIZATION*; Philip L. Barlow, *Mormons and the Bible: The Place of the Latter-day Saints in American Religion* (New York: Oxford University Press, 1991); Holland, *Sacred Borders*.

40. See chapter 5, 113.

41. Givens, *By the Hand of Mormon*, 221, 225.

42. Lucy Smith, in *Biographical Sketches of Joseph Smith, the Prophet* (1853), 37, 46–49, quoted in Hatch, *DEMOCRATIZATION*, 43.

43. Hatch, *DEMOCRATIZATION*, 256–57n101, quoting *The Autobiography of Parley Pratt* (1874), 17.

44. Steven J. Harper, *Joseph Smith's First Vision: A Guide to the Historical Accounts* (Salt Lake City, UT: Desert, 2012), 47–49.

45. Givens, *By the Hand of Mormon*, 12–13.

46. *An Account Written by the Hand of Mormon, Upon Plates Taken from the Plates of Nephi . . . By Joseph Smith, Junior* (Palmyra, NY: E. B. Grandin, 1830), title page, 5, 588.

47. Shipps, *Mormonism*.

48. Gutjahr, *Book of Mormon*, 5.

49. Gutjahr, *Book of Mormon*, 34.

50. Barlow, *Mormons and the Bible*, 27.

51. Barlow, *Mormons and the Bible*, 95.

52. Barlow, *Mormons and the Bible*, 101.

53. Philip Schaf [he later changed the spelling to Schaff], *The Principle of Protestantism as Related to the Present State of the Church*, trans. John W. Nevin (Chambersburg, PA: German Reformed Churchy, 1845), 115–16.

54. For a more positive assessment, see Philip Schaff, *America: A Sketch of the Political, Social, and Religious Character of the United States* (New York: Charles Scribner, 1855).

55. David Holland views Transcendentalism and the kind of romantic theology promoted by Horace Bushnell in his 1858 *Nature and the Supernatural* as reflecting the growing presence of spiritual self-reliance over traditional trust in the Bible (*Sacred Borders*, 184–92, 201–13).

Chapter 13

1. John Witte Jr., and Joel A. Nichols, *Religion and the American Constitutional Experiment*, 4th ed. (New York: Oxford University Press, 2016), 37–38.

2. "Massachusetts Constitution (1780)," in Dreisbach and Hall, *SACRED RIGHTS*, 246; with expert exposition in John Witte Jr., "'A Most Mild and Equitable Establishment of Religion': John Adams and the Massachusetts Experiment," in *Religion and the New Republic: Faith in the Founding of America*, ed. James H. Hutson (Lanham, MD: Rowman and Littlefield, 2000), 1–40.

3. "A Bill for Establishing Religious Freedom, Virginia (1779 and 1786)," in Dreisbach and Hall, *SACRED RIGHTS*, 250–51. This important bill is nicely contrasted with the legal situation in the other states by Thomas J. Curry, *The First Freedoms: Church and State in America to the Passage of the First Amendment* (New York: Oxford University Press, 1986).

4. For a lucid summary, see the section on "key findings" in Carl H. Esbeck and Jonathan J. Den Hartog, "Introduction," in *Disestablishment and Religious Dissent: Church-State Relations in the New American States, 1776–1833* (Columbia: University of Missouri Press, 2019), 8–17. A parallel assessment is offered by Philip Vincent Muñoz, "Church and State in the Founding-Era State Constitutions," *American Political Thought* 4 (Winter 2015): 1–38.

5. Steven K. Green, *The Second Disestablishment: Church and State in Nineteenth-Century America* (New York: Oxford University Press, 2010). Where Green stresses how belief in the Christian character of the common law "impeded the secularization of the law and the movement toward greater disestablishment" (150), Stuart Banner finds changes in that belief crucial for "the shift from a common law *discovered* by judges to a common law *made* by judges": "When Christianity Was Part of the Common Law," *Law and History Review* 16 (Spring 1998): 29. For a helpful survey of recent scholarship, see Daniel L. Dreisbach, "The Bible in American Law," in Gutjahr, *OXFORD HANDBOOK*, 276–88.

6. Blackstone, "Commentaries on the Laws of England," in Dreisbach and Hall, *SACRED RIGHTS*, 65. On the enduring importance in American history of this principle, see James Hutson, *Forgotten Features of the Founding: The Recovery of Religious Themes in the Early American Republic* (Lanham, MD: Lexington, 2003), 1–44.

7. Blackstone, "Commentaries on the Laws of England," 72.

8. Dreisbach and Hall, *SACRED RIGHTS*, 257–58 (New Jersey), 244 (South Carolina), 257 (Maryland, my emphasis).

9. Dreisbach and Hall, *SACRED RIGHTS*, 257 (Delaware), 257 (North Carolina), 244 (South Carolina), 242–43 (Pennsylvania). On Jewish interventions in Pennsylvania, see Jonathan D. Sarna and David G. Dalin, eds., *Religion and State in the American Jewish Experience* (Notre Dame, IN: University of Notre Dame Press, 1997), 72–73.

10. *Barnes v. First Parish in Falmouth*, quoted in Green, *Second Disestablishment*, 138.

11. Lester J. Cappon, ed., *The Adams-Jefferson Letters* (Chapel Hill: University of North Carolina Press, 1959), Jefferson to Adams, January 14, 1814; Adams to Jefferson, March 3, 1814, 421–24, 427.

12. *Pearce v. Atwood* (1816), quoted in Green, *Second Disestablishment*, 184.

13. *Commonwealth v. Wolf* (1817), quoted in Green, *Second Disestablishment*, 185.

14. *Omit v. Commonwealth* (1853), quoted in Green, *Second Disestablishment*, 185.

15. James Kent, in *People v. Ruggles* (1811), in *The Founders' Constitution,* ed. Philip B. Kurland and Ralph Lerner, vol. 5, *Amendment I (Religion),* document 62, http://press-pubs.uchicago.edu/founders/documents/amendI_religions62.html.

16. *Updegraph v. Commonwealth* (1824), in Kurland and Lerner, *The Founders' Constitution,* vol. 5, *Amendment I (Speech and Press),* document 30, http://press-pubs.uchicago.edu/founders/documents/amendI_speechs30.html.

17. Green, *Second Disestablishment,* 174 (174–78 for the judicial history). Also outstanding on Kneeland and his blasphemy trials is Christopher Grasso, *Skepticism and American Faith: From the Revolution to the Civil War* (New York: Oxford University Press, 2018), 337–46.

18. *Wakefield v. Ross* (1827), quoted in Green, *Second Disestablishment,* 196.

19. Story, *Commentaries on the Constitution,* in Kurland and Lerner, *The Founders' Constitution,* vol. 5, *Amendment I (Religion),* document 69; http://press-pubs.uchicago.edu/founders/documents/amendI_religions69.html.

20. Webster, quoted in Green, *Second Disestablishment,* 200.

21. *Vidal v. Girard's Executors* (1845), quoted in Green, *Second Disestablishment,* 199–202 (quotation, 201).

22. *Avery v. the Methodist Church* (1849) and *Andrew v. New York Bible and Prayer Book Society* (1850), in Green, *Second Disestablishment,* 219.

23. *Church of the Holy Trinity v. United States* 143 U.S. 457 (1892), quotation 471.

24. John Witte Jr., *The Sins of the Fathers: The Law and Theology of Illegitimacy Reconsidered* (New York: Cambridge University Press, 2009), esp. 155–57.

25. *Van Orden v. Perry,* 545 U.S. 677 (2005); *McCreary County v. ACLU,* 545 U.S. 844 (2005).

26. An excellent account of the mostly northern custodial Protestants who sought a stronger recognition of Christianity is found in Gillis J. Harp, *Protestants and American Conservatism: A Short History* (New York: Oxford University Press, 2019), 71–98 ("The Antebellum Era and the Civil War").

27. Solid older studies that often referred to proprietary Protestants simply as evangelicals include John R. Bodo, *The Protestant Clergy and Popular Issues, 1812–1848* (Princeton, NJ: Princeton University Press, 1954); Clifford S. Griffin, *Their Brothers' Keepers: Moral Stewardship in the United States, 1800–1865* (New Brunswick, NJ: Rutgers University Press, 1960); Charles I. Foster, *An Errand of Mercy: The Evangelical United Front, 1790–1837* (Chapel Hill: University of North Carolina Press, 1960).

28. Important recent works have debated whether the matters treated in this chapter constituted an abusive attempt at conformist coercion or a mostly benign adjustment of legitimate concerns to a post-Christendom America. The case for abuse has been made by David Sehat, *The Myth of American Religious Freedom* (New York: Oxford University Press, 2011) and Steven K. Green, *Inventing a Christian America: The Myth of the Religious Founding* (New York: Oxford University Press,

2015); it is countered in Chris Beneke, *Beyond Toleration: The Origins of American Pluralism* (New York: Oxford University Press, 2006), 203–25 ("'Mingle with Us as Americans': Religious Pluralism after the Founding") and Chris Beneke, "The Myth of American Religious Coercion," *Common-Place* 15, no. 3 (Spring 2015), www.common-place.org. Especially useful for adjudicating this belief are Eric R. Schlereth, *An Age of Infidels: The Politics of Religious Controversy in the Early United States* (Philadelphia: University of Pennsylvania Press, 2013) and Sam Haselby, *The Origins of American Religious Nationalism* (New York: Oxford University Press, 2015).

29. Excellent on Ely is Grasso, *Skepticism*, 194–215.

30. Ezra Stiles Ely, "Gov. William Findlay of Pennsylvania, Inaugural Address," *Quarterly Theological* Review 1 (January 1818), quoted in Grasso, *Skepticism*, 209.

31. Ely Stiles Ely, *The Duty of Christian Freemen to Elect Christian Rulers . . . With an Appendix, designed to vindicate the liberty of Christians, and of the American Sunday School Union* (Philadelphia, PA: William F. Geddes, 1828), 6, 8–9, 15–32 (tightly printed appendix).

32. Lyman Beecher, "Pre-eminent Importance of the Christian Sabbath," *National Preacher* 3 (March 1829): 156, quoted in Richard R. John, "Taking Sabbatarianism Seriously: The Postal System, the Sabbath, and the Transformation of American Political Culture," *Journal of the Early Republic* 10 (Winter 1990): 517. John's article (517–67) is essential reading.

33. That this was the *third* of the Ten Commandments for Catholics and Lutherans remained an irrelevant distraction so long as Catholics and Lutherans remained silent minorities.

34. For an excellent summary, see Isaac Kramnick and R. Laurence Moore, *The Godless Constitution: A Moral Defense of the Secular State* (New York: Norton, 1996), 131–49 ("Sunday Mail and the Christian Amendment").

35. See Jim DeVinny, "Josiah Bissell, Jr.," *Corn Hill Neighbors*, accessed November 5, 2021, https://cornhill.org/josiah-bissell-jr.

36. Herman K. Platt, "Frelinghuysen, Theodore," *ANB*.

37. *Speech of Mr. Frelinghuysen on his Resolution Concerning Sabbath Mails* (Washington, DC: Rothwell and Ustick, 1830), 5, 10, 12, 10, 14, 6.

38. *Speech of Mr. Frelinghuysen of New Jersey, delivered in the Senate of the United States, April 6, 1830, on the bill for an exchange of lands with the Indians residing in any of the states or territories, and for their removal west of the Mississippi* (Washington, DC: National Journal, 1830), 7 (providence and natural law), 26 (sins and Bible).

39. Rev. Cyrus Kingsbury, contribution to "Appendix," in *Frelinghuysen Speech . . . Indians*, 40.

40. William Lloyd Garrison, "To the Hon. Theodore Frelinghuysen, On Reading his Eloquent Speech in Defense of Indian Rights," in *Sonnets and Other Poem* (Boston: Oliver Johnson, 1843), 71.

41. On the importance of this episode, see Adam Jortner, "Cholera, Christ, and Jackson: The Epidemic of 1832 and the Origins of Christian Politics in Antebellum America," *Journal of the Early Republic* 27 (Summer 2007): 233–64.

42. For Adams's sermon, letters from Marshall and Story (and also Madison who, while disagreeing with Adams's argument, commended its presentation), and learned consideration of the sermon's historical context and contemporary relevance, see Daniel L. Driesbach, ed., *Religion and Politics in the Early Republic: Jasper Adams and the Church-State Debate* (Lexington: University Press of Kentucky, 1996), 48–49 (quotations from sermon).

43. From an 1863 proposal by the National Association for the Amendment of the Constitution, quoted in Kramnick and Moore, *Godless Constitution*, 146. A full history of these efforts is found in Gaines M. Foster, *Moral Reconstruction: Christian Lobbyists and the Federal Legislation of Morality, 1865–1920* (Chapel Hill: University of North Carolina Press, 2002).

44. See Noll, *IN THE BEGINNING*, 271–88.

45. Grasso, *Skepticism*, 212.

46. Adam Jortner, *The Gods of Prophetstown: The Battle of Tippecanoe and the Holy War for the American Frontier* (New York: Oxford University Press, 2012), 216, 229.

47. Kramick and Moore, *Godless Constitution*, 139.

48. *Transportation of the Mail on the Sabbath, In the Senate of the United States, January 19, 1829 . . . Mr. Johnson of Kentucky Made the Following Report* (Frankfort, KY: N.p., 1829), https://www.loc.gov/resource/rbpe.02106400/?st=text.

49. *Transportation of the Mail.*

50. Andrew Jackson, *The Papers of Andrew Jackson*, vol. 10: *1832*, ed. Daniel Feller et al. (Knoxville: University of Tennessee Press, 2016), Jackson to the Synod, June 12, 1832, 302.

51. Louisville (KY) *Advertiser*, quoted in Jortner, "Cholera, Christ, and Jackson," 258–59.

52. John, "Taking Sabbatarianism Seriously," 565.

53. John, "Taking Sabbatarianism Seriously" and Jortner, "Cholera, Christ, and Jackson" are superb on the political reforms they examine; also insightful on the same developments is Grasso, *Skepticism*, 213–15.

54. The nonpareil account of those divisions remains Richard J. Carwardine, *Evangelicals and Politics in Antebellum America* (New Haven, CT: Yale University Press, 1993).

55. Jortner, "Cholera, Christ, and Jackson," 235.

56. That research is well summarized in Robert P. Swierenga, "Ethnoreligious Political Behavior in the Mid-Nineteenth Century: Voting, Values, Cultures," in *Religion and American Politics: From the Colonial Period to the Present*, ed. Mark A. Noll and Luke E. Harlow (New York: Oxford University Press, 2007), 145–168; Swierenga's table (156) is much simplified later in this chapter.

57. John, "Taking Sabbatarianism Seriously," 567.

58. Dreisbach, *Religion and Politics*, 151.

Chapter 14

1. Steven K. Green, *The Bible, the School, and the Constitution: The Clash That Shaped Modern Church-State Doctrine* (New York: Oxford University Press, 2012), 11.

This chapter has benefited from this book, but even more from Green's *The Second Disestablishment: Church and State in Nineteenth-Century America* (New York: Oxford University Press, 2010). For general orientation and its specific outline, however, the chapter is most indebted to David Komline, *The Common School Awakening: Religion and the Transatlantic Roots of American Public Schools* (New York: Oxford University Press, 2020) and Komline's longer dissertation that preceded the book, "The Common School Awakening: Education and Religion, 1800–1848" (Ph.D. diss., University of Notre Dame, 2015).

2. Lawrence A. Cremin, *The American Common School: An Historic Conception* (New York: Teachers College, Columbia University, 1951), 56.

3. David Sehat, *The Myth of American Religious Freedom* (New York: Oxford University Press, 2011), 155.

4. Besides the works mentioned in note 1, the scholarship on this general subject is unusually rich. Other particularly helpful works include Donald E. Boles, *The Bible, Religion, and the Public Schools* (Ames: Iowa State University Press, 1965); John H. Westerhoff III, "The Struggle for a Common Culture: Biblical Images in Nineteenth-Century Schoolbooks," in *The Bible in American Education*, ed. David L. Barr and Nicholas Piediscalzi (Philadelphia, PA: Fortress, 1983), 25–40; Tracy Fessenden, "The Nineteenth-Century Bible Wars and the Separation of Church and State," *Church History* 74 (September 2005): 1–28; Suzanne Rosenblith and Patrick Womac, "The Bible in American Public Schools," in Gutjahr, *OXFORD HANDBOOK*, 263–75. Important works for wider educational contexts include Timothy L. Smith, "Protestant Schooling and American Nationality, 1800–1850," *Journal of American History* 53 (March 1967): 679–95; Carl F. Kaestle, *Pillars of the Republic: Common Schools and American Society, 1780–1860* (New York: Hill & Wang, 1983), esp. 44–50; Joan DelFattore, *The Fourth R: Conflicts over Religion in America's Public Schools* (New Haven, CT: Yale University Press, 2004), 32–51; Daniel Walker Howe, "Religion and Education in the Young Republic," in *Figures in the Carpet: Finding the Human Person in the American Past*, ed. Wilfred M. McClay (Grand Rapids, MI: Eerdmans, 2007), 373–404; Johann N. Neem, *Democracy's Schools: The Rise of Public Education in America* (Baltimore, MD: Johns Hopkins University Press, 2017), esp. 46–48.

5. Westerhoff, "Struggle for a Common Culture," 25.

6. *Church of the Holy Trinity v. United States*, 143 US (226) 1892, 471.

7. *Doremus v. Board of Education of Hawthorne*, 5 NJ 435 (1950), 75 A.2d 880 (quotations, 437, 446, 451).

8. *Doremus*, 448, 451–52.

9. *Doremus v. Board of Education*, 342 U.S. 429 (1952).

10. Benjamin Rush, *A Plan for the Establishment of Public Schools and the Diffusion of Knowledge in Pennsylvania: To which are Added Thoughts upon the Mode of Education, Proper in a Republic, Addressed to the Legislature and the Citizens of the State* (Philadelphia, PA: Thomas Dobson, 1786).

11. Rush, *Plan*, 3, 8.

12. Rush, *Plan*, 15–16.

13. Rush, *Plan*, 18–19.

14. Benjamin Rush, "A Defence of the Use of the Bible as a School Book, Addressed to the Rev. Jeremy Belknap, of Boston" (March 10, 1791), in John Eyten, *Our Lord Jesus Christ's Sermon on the Mount . . . Intended Chiefly for the Instruction of Young People*, 2nd ed. (Baltimore, MD: B. W. Sower, 1810), 57.

15. See chapter 10, 203, on those earlier efforts.

16. On Eddy, see H. Larry Engle, *ANB*. For an emphasis on Eddy's concern for social control, see Kaestle, *Pillars*, 32–34; on his Christian concerns, see Komline, *Common School Awakening*, 29–30.

17. On Lancaster, see Neem, *Democracy's Schools*, 105–6; Komline, *Common School Awakening*, 12–37.

18. Komline, *Common School Awakening*, 16.

19. David Brion Davis, *The Problem of Slavery in the Age of Revolution, 1770–1823*, new ed. (New York: Oxford University Press, 1999), 249.

20. Komline, *Common School Awakening*, 30.

21. Komline, *Common School Awakening*, 31.

22. Komline, "Common School Awakening," 114.

23. Komline, *Common School Awakening*, 54, 57.

24. Komline, *Common School Awakening*, 61–82.

25. Bertram Wyatt-Brown, *Lewis Tappan and the Evangelical War against Slavery* (Cleveland, OH: Press of Case Western Reserve University, 1969), 87–89.

26. For the multinational influence of Cousin's *Rapport*, see Komline, *Common School Awakening*, 102–38.

27. J. Orville Taylor, *A Digest of M. Victor Cousin's Report on the State of Public Instruction in Prussia* (Albany, NY: Packard and Van Benthuysen, 1836), 38–40,

28. Taylor, *Digest*, 40–41n.

29. *HISTORICAL STATISTICS*, 14.

30. *PRESIDENTIAL ELECTIONS*, 112–16.

31. Many such opinions are recorded in Milton B. Powell, ed., *The Voluntary Church: American Religious Life, 1740–1860: Seen through the Eyes of European Visitors* (New York: Macmillan, 1967).

32. Neem, *Democracy's Schools*, 141.

33. Kaestle, *Pillars*, 58–59; Komline, *Common School Awakening*, 215–16.

34. On Barnard, see Sherry H. Penney in *ANB*.

35. Daniel D. Barnard, "Report on the Subject of Religious Exercises, and the use of the Bible, in Schools—Jan. 23, 1838," in *Speeches and Reports of the Assembly of New York* (Albany: Oliver Steele, 1838), 56, 57, 59,

36. For a clear precis of the Dartmouth case and its larger ramifications, see Howe, "Religion and Education," 384–89.

37. Excellent on Massachusetts disestablishment is Green, *Second Disestablishment*, 131–45.

38. Dreisbach and Hall, *SACRED RIGHTS*, 246.

39. Komline, *Common School Awakening*, 156–57.

40. Komline, *Common School Awakening*, 149.

41. Horace Mann, *Twelfth Annual Report of the Board of Education, Together with the Twelfth Annual Report of the Secretary of the Board* (Boston: Dutton and Wentworth, 1849), 102, 104, 116, 117 ("to speak for itself," repeated on 131). Mann's argument for nonsectarian Bible reading, which defended it as continuing the best of what "the Pilgrim Fathers" (141) had tried to do, extended for more than forty tightly printed pages.

42. See chapter 3, 71.

43. Mrs. Trollope, *Domestic Manners of the Americans*, 2 vols., 4th ed. (London: Whitaker, Treacher, 1832), 1:148, 150.

44. Komline, *Common School Awakening*, 202.

45. Komline, *Common School Awakening*, 207.

46. Komline, *Common School Awakening*, 203, 205.

47. Komline, *Common School Awakening*, 178.

48. Komline, *Common School Awakening*, 203, 192.

49. Komline, *Common School Awakening*, 197; Komline, "Common School Awakening," 471.

50. Komline, *Common School Awakening*, 186, 209.

51. Komline, *Common School Awakening*.

52. Westerhoff, "Struggle for a Common Culture"; John Hardin Best, "McGuffey, William Holmes," in *ANB*.

53. *The New England Primer, Improved: For the more easy attaining the True Reading of English: to which is added The Assembly's Shorter Catechism . . .* (Philadelphia, PA: J. Pounder, 1813), 26 (the abecedary).

54. Noah Webster, *The American Spelling Book, Containing the Rudiments of the English Language, for the Use of Schools in the United States* (Lexington, KY: W. W. Worsley, 1832), 156.

55. Noah Webster, *An American Selection of Lessons in Reading and Speaking: calculated to improve the minds and refine the taste of youth: to which are prefixed, rules in elocution, and directions for expressing the principal passions of the mind* (Salem, MA: Joshua Cushing, 1805).

56. On Murray and his school texts, see Hugh Barbour, "Murray, Lindley," in *ANB*. Publishing figures are from Charles Monaghan and E. Jennifer Monaghan, "Schoolbooks," in *HISTORY OF THE BOOK*, 2: 308–9.

57. Lindley Murray, *The English Reader, Pieces in Prose and Poetry, selected from the Best writers, Designed to assist Young Persons . . . with a few preliminary observations on the Principles of Good Reading* (Yellow Falls, VT: James I. Cutler, 1835), v.

58. On Lincoln's intense engagement with Murray's *English Reader*, see Louis A. Warren, *Lincoln's Youth: Indiana Years, 1816–1830* (Indianapolis: Indiana Historical Society, 1991), 103–6, which cites William Hendon's record of Lincoln calling it the best schoolbook for American students (239n16).

59. Murray, *English Reader*, 38–39 (Psalms and Proverbs), 37 (David and Jonathan), 290–300 (final poems).

60. William H. McGuffey, *The Eclectic Fourth Reader: Containing elegant extracts in prose and poetry, from the best American and English writers, With copious rules for reading,*

and directions for avoiding common errors (Cincinnati, OH: Truman and Smith, 1838), vii (the title page calls this the sixth edition; McGuffey's preface, dated 1837, calls it the second edition).

61. W. H. McGuffey, *The Eclectic Second Reader: Consisting of progressive lessons in reading and spelling: for the younger classes in schools, with engravings* (Cincinnati, OH: Truman and Smith, 1836).

62. McGuffey, *Fourth Reader*, v–vi.

63. McGuffey, *Fourth Reader*, 209.

64. The inclusion of selections refuting Paine and enlisting Rousseau for orthodoxy may have been McGuffey's response to the upsurge in Free Thought in some of the nation's urban areas when he published his first *Eclectic Readers*; see Eric R. Schlereth, *An Age of Infidels: The Politics of Religious Controversy in the Early United States* (Philadelphia: University of Pennsylvania Press, 2013), 190–201; Christopher Grasso, *Skepticism and American Faith: From the Revolution to the Civil War* (New York: Oxford University Press, 2018), 333–46.

65. *McGuffey's Fourth Eclectic Reader*, revision of 1879 (New York: American Book Company, 1896), 54 (manliness), 192 (Longfellow).

66. *Commonwealth v. Cooke* (Massachusetts), quoted in Green, *Second Disestablishment*, 274; *Donahue v. Richards* (Maine), in Green, *Second Disestablishment*, 271–47.

67. These cases are thoroughly discussed in Green, *Second Disestablishment*, 319–21 (*Freeman*), 321–22 (*People*), 318–20 (*Pfeffer*), and 313 (*Stevenson*).

68. For more on Brewer, see chapter 28.

Chapter 15

1. Robert Baird, *Religion in the United States of America* (Glasgow: Blackie and Sons, 1844), 635. On Baird's book, see 108–10.

2. All ABS figures for revenue and production are from Henry Otis Dwight, *The Centennial History of the American Bible Society*, 2 vols. (New York: Macmillan, 1916), 2:576–77.

3. All information on editions from 1844 is from Hills, *ENGLISH BIBLE*, 176–83 (#1193–#1245).

4. *The National Union Catalogue, Pre-1956 Imprints*, vols. 53, 55, and 56 (Chicago: American Library Association, 1980). In the decade of the 1840s, American publishers produced at least seventy-one Bible or New Testament editions in at least seventeen non-English languages. Six of the languages represented books for immigrant communities (twenty-nine German editions, six French, three Spanish, one each Danish, Dutch, and Modern Greek); two of the languages served the scholarly inclined (ten biblical Greek, three Latin); four provided Bibles for Native Americans (three Cherokee, three Chippewa, two Choctaw, one Ottawa); and five represented service for missionaries (four Hawaiian, one each Syriac, Urdu, Tamil, and Oriya).

5. A helpful summary of the extraordinary publishing numbers generated by Protestant agencies in the 1850s is found in Brown, *WORD IN THE WORLD*, 51.

6. Hughes's sermon text began with Matthew 20:20 in Douay-Rheims, "Then came to him the mother of the sons of Zebedee, adoring and asking something of him" (KJV is similar, but with "worshipping" and "desiring"). John Hughes, *Complete Works of the Most Rev. John Hughes, D.D., Archbishop of New York*, 2 vols., ed. Lawrence Kehoe (New York: Lawrence Kehoe, 1866), 1:558.

7. On the resignation, see 149 and Peter J. Wosh, *Spreading the Word: The Bible Business in Nineteenth-Century America* (Ithaca, NY: Cornell University Press, 1994), 143–44.

8. Hills, *ENGLISH BIBLE*, 470.

9. Hills, *ENGLISH BIBLE*, 83 (#534), quoted here from the first American edition of 1825; later editions often abbreviated the title-page description.

10. On this Harper initiative, a superb account is found in Gutjahr, *AMERICAN BIBLE*, 70–76.

11. Gutjahr, *AMERICAN BIBLE*, 71. On the importance of these family bibles, see also Brown, *WORD IN THE WORLD* and Coleen McDannel, *The Christian Home in Victorian America, 1840–1900* (Bloomington: Indiana University Press, 1986).

12. Gutjahr, *AMERICAN BIBLE*, 76.

13. See 230.

14. See 128–29.

15. Excellent treatment of the contest is found in Robert V. Remini, *Henry Clay: Statesman for the Union* (New York: Norton, 1991), 642–67; Howe, *WHAT HATH GOD WROUGHT*, 658–700.

16. Frelinghuysen in *New York Evangelist*, May 16, 1844, quoted in Richard J. Carwardine, *Evangelicals and Politics in Antebellum America* (New Haven, CT: Yale University Press, 1993), 85.

17. The extensive scholarship on the riot has been insightfully surveyed by Amanda Beyer-Purvis, "The Philadelphia Bible Riots of 1844: Contest over the Rights of Citizens," *Pennsylvania History* 83 (Summer 2016): 366–93; superb on details is Zachary M. Schrag, *The Fires of Philadelphia: Citizen-Soldiers, Nativists, and the 1844 Riots Over the Soul of a Nation* (New York: Pegasus, 2021). For useful introductions, see Ray Allen Billington, *The Protestant Crusade: A Study of the Origins of Nativism* (1938; Chicago: Quadrangle, 1964), 220–37; Villanova University, "Chaos in the Streets: The Philadelphia Riots of 1844," accessed March 3, 2020, https://exhibits.libr ary.villanova.edu/chaos-in-the-streets-the-philadelphia-riots-of-1844.

18. *Twenty-Fourth Annual Report of the Controllers of Public Schools* (1842), 5, quoted in Beyer-Purvis, "Philadelphia Bible Riots," 376.

19. The board's response quoted from Villanova University, "The Bible Controversy in Philadelphia," accessed March 10, 2020, https://exhibits.library.villanova.edu/chaos-in-the-streets-the-philadelphia-riots-of-1844/bible-controversy.

20. Immigration figures are from *HISTORICAL STATISTICS*, 57.

21. Lyman Beecher, *A Plea for the West* (Cincinnati, OH: Truman and Smith, 1835).

22. On Morse, see Billington, *Protestant Crusade*, 122–38.

23. *Address of the Board of Managers of the American Protestant Association; with the Constitution and Organization of the Association* (Philadelphia, PA: American Protestant Association, 1843), 5.

24. Much of the tension in Philadelphia came from clashing interests between Ulster Protestants who had arrived earlier and later appearing Catholic Irish. The rioters ignored Philadelphia's German Catholic churches; on this ethnic dimension, see Carwardine, *Evangelicals and Politics*, 82–83.

25. For the roster of clergy who called and signed on to the organization, see *Address*, 5–6.

26. On that earlier relative calm, see 298.

27. Pope Gregory XVI, *Mirari Vos: On Liberalism and Religious Indifferentism*, 1832, Papal Encyclicals Online, accessed March 4, 2020, https://www.papalencyclicals.net/greg16/g16mirar.htm.

28. Pope Gregory XVI, *Inter Praecipuas: On Biblical Societies*, 1844, Papal Encyclicals Online, accessed March 4, 2020, https://www.papalencyclicals.net/greg16/g16inter.htm.

29. *Inter Praecipuas*.

30. *New York Freeman's Journal*, August 24, 1844, quoted in Carwardine, *Evangelicals and Politics*, 83.

31. *Minutes of the Annual Conferences of the Methodist Episcopal Church for the Years 1829–1839*, vol. 2 (New York: T. Mason and G. Lane, 1840); *Minutes of the Annual Conferences of the Methodist Episcopal Church for the Years 1839–1845*, vol. 3 (New York: T. Mason and G. Lane, 1840 [*sic*]).

32. Daniel Walker Howe, *The Political Culture of the American Whigs* (Chicago: University of Chicago Press, 1979), 158–61. Also excellent on this affinity, usually described as "evangelical" and Whig, are Carwardine, *Evangelicals and Politics*; Daniel Walker Howe, *Making the American Self: Jonathan Edwards to Abraham Lincoln* (Cambridge, MA: Harvard University Press, 1997); Allen C. Guelzo, *Abraham Lincoln: Redeemer President* (Grand Rapids, MI: Eerdmans, 1999); Stewart Winger, *Lincoln, Religion, and Romantic Cultural Politics* (Dekalb: Northern Illinois University Press, 2003); Howe, *WHAT HATH GOD WROUGHT*.

33. Carwardine, *Evangelicals and Politics*, 78, with 71–89 excellent on salient religious factors in the presidential campaign of 1844.

34. Carwardine, *Evangelicals and Politics*, 75.

35. Howe, *WHAT HATH GOD WROUGHT*, 2–3.

36. Betty Fladeland, *James Gillespie Birney: Slaveholder to Abolitionist* (Ithaca, NY: Cornell University Press, 1955).

37. James G. Birney, *Letter to Ministers and Elders, on the Sin of Holding Slaves, and the Duty of Immediate Emancipation* (New York: S. W. Benedict, 1834), 1, 4 (Golden Rule).

38. An American [Birney], *The American Churches, the Bulwarks of American Slavery* (London: Johnston and Barrett, 1840).

39. *PRESIDENTIAL ELECTIONS*, 117, 188.

40. In these hypothetical counterfactuals, I am following Howe, *WHAT HATH GOD WROUGHT*, 689–90, which quotes Horace Greeley's later conclusion that if Clay had been elected, "great and lasting public calamities would thereby have been averted."

41. Of many sources on this General Conference, a detailed account that highlights the resulting controversies over Methodist publishing is found in James Penn Pilkington, *The Methodist Publishing House: A History*, vol. 1, *Beginnings to 1870* (Nashville, TN: Abingdon, 1963), 294–321.

42. See especially Clarence C. Goen, *Broken Churches, Broken Nation: Denominational Schisms and the Coming of the American Civil War* (Macon, GA: Mercer University Press, 1985).

43. Alongside full treatment of the Methodists in his *Evangelicals and Politics*, see the following, all by Richard Carwardine: "Methodist Ministers and the Second Party System," in *Perspectives on American Methodism: Interpretive Essays*, ed. Russell E. Richey, Kenneth E. Rowe, and Jean Miller Schmidt (Nashville, TN: Kingswood, 1993), 159–77; "Trauma in Methodism: Property, Church Schism, and Sectional Polarization in Antebellum America," in *God and Mammon: Protestants, Money, and the Market, 1790–1860*, ed. Mark A. Noll (New York: Oxford University Press, 2002), 195–216; and "Methodists, Politics, and the Coming of the American Civil War," in *Religion and American Politics: From the Colonial Period to the Present*, ed. Mark A. Noll and Luke D. Harlow (New York: Oxford University Press, 2007), 169–200.

44. Diary of Leonard Smith, Illinois State Historical Society, Springfield, quoted in Carwardine, "Methodists, Politics, and the Coming of the Civil War," 314.

45. Carwardine, "Trauma in Methodism," 172 (the quotation specified "Calvinist," which I have changed to "proprietary").

46. Carwardine, "Methodists, Politics, and the Coming of the Civil War," 309.

47. In seventeen pages of proslavery quotations from Methodists in Birney's *The American Churches* (14–30), almost all were taken from debates at the 1840 General Conference (23–30).

48. La Roy Sunderland, *The Testimony of God against Slavery: A Collection of Passages from the Bible, which show the Sin of Holding and Treating the Human Species as Property, With Notes, To which is added the testimony of the civilized world against slavery*, 2nd ed. (1835; New York: R. G. Williams for the American Anti-Slavery Society, 1836), iii (the text on the title page was Jer 2:34).

49. William A. Capers, *Southern Christian Advocate* 2 (August 10, 1838): 30, quoted in Harmon L. Smith, "William Capers and William A. Smith: Neglected Aspects of the Pro-Slavery Moral Argument," *Methodist History* 3 (October 1964): 26–27 (entire article, 23–32).

50. Pilkington, *Methodist Publishing House*, 299.

51. The official name was the General Missionary Convention of the Baptist Denomination in the United States for Foreign Missions.

52. For excellent succinct treatments of the anti-mission impetus and of the path leading to schism, see Thomas S. Kidd and Barry Hankins, *Baptists in America: A History* (New York: Oxford University Press, 2015), 110–14, 123–29.

53. Kidd and Hankins, *Baptists*, 128.

54. Richard Fuller (with Francis Wayland), *Domestic Slavery Considered as a Scriptural Institution* (New York: Lewis Colby, 1845), 3.

55. Wayland, *Domestic Slavery*, 248.

56. *WORLDCAT*.

57. See 165.

58. Phoebe Palmer, *The Way of Holiness, with Notes by the Way; being a Narrative of Experience resulting from a determination to be a Bible Christian* (New York: Piercey and Reed, 1843).

59. Frederick Douglass, "Southern Slavery and Northern Religion: Two Addresses delivered in Concord, New Hampshire, on February 11, 1844," in *The Frederick Douglass Papers*, vol. 1, ser. 1: *Speeches, Debates, and Interviews, 1841–1846*, ed. John W. Blassingame (New Haven, CT: Yale University Press, 1979), 24.

60. Orestes Brownson, "Thornwell's Answer to Doctor Lynch," *Brownson's Quarterly Review*, new ser. 2 (April 1848): 199 (entire article, 198–222), a review of James Henley Thornwell, *The Arguments of Romanists from the Infallibility of the Church and the Testimony of the Fathers in Behalf of the Apocrypha* (New York: Leavitt, Trow, 1845). Thornwell is quoted here from James Henley Thornwell, *Collected Writings of James Henley Thornwell*, vol. 3: *Theological and Controversial*, ed. John B. Adger and John L. Girardeau (Richmond, VA: Presbyterian Committee of Publication, 1873), 745. For a full account, see Adam Tate, "Catholics and Southern Honor: Rev. Patrick Lynch's Paper War with Rev. James Henley Thrownell," *Catholic Historical Review* 99 (July 2013): 455–79.

61. See James Oscar Farmer Jr., *The Metaphysical Confederacy: James Henley Thornwell and the Synthesis of Southern Values* (Macon, GA: Mercer University Press, 1986), 278–82; David C. R. Heisser, "Bishop Lynch's Civil War Pamphlet on Slavery," *Catholic Historical Review* 84 (October 1998): 681–96.

62. George M. Marsden, *The Evangelical Mind and the New School Experience* (New Haven, CT: Yale University Press, 1970), 88–103.

63. William Graham, *The Contrast, or the Bible and Abolitionism: An Exegetical Argument* (Cincinnati, OH: Daily Cincinnati Atlas, 1844), 3, 21.

64. Robert Benjamin Lewis [described on the title page as "A Colored Man"], *Light and Truth; Collected from the Bible and Ancient and Modern History, containing the Universal History of the Colored and the Indian Race, from the creation of the world to the present time* (Boston: Benjamin F. Roberts, 1844). A helpful summary of this work is found in Rita Roberts, *Evangelicalism and the Politics of Reform in Northern Black Thought, 1776–1863* (Baton Rouge: Louisiana University Press, 2010), 153.

Chapter 16

1. Of many outstanding general accounts, I have found most useful James Hennesey, S. J., *American Catholics: A History of the Roman Catholic Community in the United States* (New York: Oxford University Press, 1981); Philip Gleason, *Keeping the Faith: American Catholicism Past and Present* (Notre Dame, IN: University of Notre Dame Press, 1989); Jay P. Dolan, *In Search of an American Catholicism: A History of Religion and Culture in Tension* (New York: Oxford University Press, 2002); John

T. McGreevy, *Catholicism and American Freedom: A History* (New York: Norton, 2003); Leslie Woodcock Tentler, *American Catholics: A History* (New Haven, CT: Yale University Press, 2020).

2. Council of Trent, "First Decree . . . Second Decree" (April 8, 1546), in *Creeds and Confessions of Faith in the Christian Tradition*, vol. 2: *Reformation Era*, ed. Jaroslav Pelikan and Valerie Hotchkiss (New Haven, CT: Yale University Press, 2003), 822–23.

3. On the colonial history in which fidelity to the Bible was intrinsic to British imperial and anti-Catholic identity, see, with references to an extensive literature, Noll, *IN THE BEGINNING*, 150–76.

4. John Adams, *Dissertation on the Canon and Feudal Law*, Online Library of Liberty, accessed March 18, 2020, https://oll.libertyfund.org/titles/adams-revolutionary-writings#lfAdams_label_023.

5. For only one of many useful books treating this history, see Robert N. Bellah and Frederick E. Greenspahn, eds., *Uncivil Religion: Interreligious Hostility in America* (New York: Crossroad, 1987).

6. Charles P. Hanson, *Necessary Virtue: The Pragmatic Origins of Religious Liberty in New England* (Charlottesville: University of Virginia Press, 1998); Francis D. Cogliano, *No King, No Popery: Anti-Catholicism in Revolutionary New England* (New York: Praeger, 1996).

7. Mark A. Noll, *Princeton and the Republic, 1768–1822* (Princeton, NJ: Princeton University Press, 1989), 91.

8. Steven M. Nolt, *Foreigners in Their Own Land: Pennsylvania Germans in the Early Republic* (University Park: Pennsylvania State University Press, 2002), 110–13; John R. Dichtl, *Bringing Catholicism to the West in the Early Republic* (Lexington: University Press of Kentucky, 2008); Andrew Stern, *Southern Crucifix, Southern Cross: Catholic-Protestant Relations in the Old South* (Tuscaloosa: University of Alabama Press, 2012).

9. Excellent on this exchange is Michael T. DeStefano, "DuBourg's Defense of St. Mary's College: Apologetics and the Creation of a Catholic Identity in the Early American Republic," *Church History* 85 (March 2016): 65–96. Quotations are from *A Pastoral Letter from the Ministers, or Bishops, and Ruling Elders of the Presbytery of Baltimore, to all under their charges: on various duties, but, especially, on the religious education of their Youth* (Baltimore, MD: Warner and Hanna, 1811), 15, 18 (footnote). See John Wesley and Claude Fleury, *The Manners of the Antient Christians: Extracted from a French Author* (many editions from 1749).

10. [Charles Henry Wharton], *A Letter to the Roman Catholics of the City of Worcester, from the Late Chaplain of that Society, Stating the Motives which induced him to relinquish their Communion, and become a Member of the Protestant Church* (Philadelphia, PA: Robert Aitken, 1784), 14 ("acquiesce"), 19–29 on biblical texts (the American edition contained a typo, with "Math. 19.20" where Wharton intended "Math. 28:19.20")

11. [John Carroll], *An Address to the Roman Catholics of the United States of America, By a Catholic Clergyman* (Annapolis, MD: Frederick Green, 1784), 29–46 (biblical exegesis), 22 ("fanaticism"), 44 (church authority for the canon), 67 (transubstantiation), 115 (vow of celibacy). To make the Douay-Rheims version available in the United States, however, Carroll offered unflagging support to Mathew Carey, including

technical help on translating the Vulgate's Latin, when Carey published his path-breaking 1790 edition (see 104–6); Thomas O'Brien Henley, *The John Carroll Papers*, vol. 1: *1755–1791* (Notre Dame, IN: University of Notre Dame Press, 1976), 380–81, 425, and passim.

12. Carroll, *Address*, 3 (citation from Acts in KJV).

13. Carroll, *Address*, 9 ("virtue . . . vice"), 114 (closing comments).

14. On this possibility, see Raymond A. Schroth, "Death and Resurrection: The Suppression of the Jesuits in North America," *American Catholic Studies* 128 (Spring 2017): 51–66. I am grateful to JohnJo Shanley for further enlightenment on how Carroll's European experience prepared him to embrace American republicanism.

15. Catherine O'Donnell, "John Carroll and the Origins of an American Catholic Church, 1783–1815," *William and Mary Quarterly* 68 (January 2011): 121. O'Donnell's whole article (101–26) is unusually helpful, as is Nicholas Pellegrino, "John Carroll, American Catholics, and the Making of a Christian Nation," *American Catholic Studies* 126 (Summer 2015): 47–68.

16. *Constitution of the American Bible* Society (New York: ABS-G. F. Hopkins, 1816), 7; and for other details, Peter J. Wosh, *Spreading the Word: The Bible Business in Nineteenth-Century America* (Ithaca, NY: Cornell University Press, 1994), 105–7. On the relative calm of this period, see the last sections of Maura Jane Farrelly, *Anti-Catholicism in America, 1620–1860* (New York: Cambridge University Press, 2018).

17. Leslie Howsom, *Cheap Bibles: Nineteenth-Century Publishing and the British and Foreign Bible Society* (Cambridge: Cambridge University Press, 1991), 13–15.

18. On England, see John Gilmary Shea, *The Defenders of Our Faith: Their Devotion to the Church, Biographies and Portraits of our Cardinals, Archbishops, and Bishops, Setting Forth their Zeal in the Development of Faith and Morals* (New York: Office of Catholics Publications, 1892), 197–200; Patrick W. Carey, in *ANB*.

19. John England, "The Substance of a Discourse, Preached in the Hall of the House of Representatives . . . on Sunday, January 8, 1826," in *The Works of the Right Rev. John England, First Bishop of Charleston*, 5 vols., ed. Ignatius Aloysius Reynolds (Baltimore, MD: John Murphy, 1849), 4:172–90. England indicated that this published version represented a reconstruction he made several days after it was delivered (173), which may mean the spoken version was not as long-winded as appears by the printed text.

20. England, "Discourse," 180–83.

21. England, "Discourse," 185 ("despotic").

22. Communication to the *Christian Advocate*, February 24, 1827, quoted in James Penn Pilkinton, *The Methodist Publishing House*, vol. 1 (Nashville: Abingdon, 1968), 203.

23. England, "Discourse," 190, with the Second Commandment (Matt 22:39) and the apostolic injunction from 1 John 4:20.

24. Among the most useful accounts are Ray Allen Billington, *The Protestant Crusade, 1800–1860: A Study of the Origins of American Nativism* (1938; Chicago: Quadrangle, 1964); Jenny Franchot, *Roads to Rome: The Antebellum Protestant Encounter with Catholicism* (Berkeley: University of California Press, 1994); McGreevy, *Catholicism and American Freedom*; and for important international comparisons, John Wolffe, *The Protestant Crusade in Great Britain, 1829–1860* (Oxford: Clarendon, 1991). For

the best brief statement of the 1830s as a pivotal period of transition in national religious history, see James D. Bratt, "The Reorientation of American Protestantism, 1835–1845," *Church History* 67 (March 1998): 52–82.

25. On that mingling, see McGreevy, *Catholicism and American Freedom*, 57–59 and Brian C. McIlhenny, *To Preach Deliverance to the Captives: Freedom and Slavery in the Protestant Mind of George Bourne, 1780–1845* (Baton Rouge: Louisiana State University Press, 2020), 150–73.

26. See especially Cassandra L. Yacovazzi, "'Are You Allowed to Read the Bible in a Convent?' Protestant Perspectives on the Catholic Approach to Scripture in Convent Narratives, 1830–1860," *U.S. Catholic Historian* 31 (Summer 2013): 23–46.

27. Angelina Grimké, *Appeal to the Christian Women of the South* (New York: American Anti-Slavery Society, 1836), 18.

28. *Controversy Between the Rev. John Hughes, of the Roman Catholic Church, and the Rev. John Breckinridge, of the Presbyterian Church, Relative to the Existing differences in the Catholic and Protestant Religions* (Philadelphia, PA: Joseph Whetham, 1833), 3.

29. John Hughes and John Breckinridge, *A Discussion of the Question, Is the Roman Catholic Religion . . . Inimical to Civil or Religious Liberty? And of the Question, Is the Presbyterian Religion . . . Inimical to Civil or Religious Liberty?* (Philadelphia, PA: Carey, Lea, and Blanchard, 1836).

30. John Hughes, "Alleged Burning of Bibles" (January 1, 1843), in *Complete Works of the Most Rev. John Hughes, D.D., Archbishop of New York*, 2 vols., ed. Lawrence Kehoe (New York: Lawrence Kehoe, 1866), 1:502.

31. On the literary exchange leading to that work, see W. Jason Wallace, *Catholic Slaveholders and the Dilemma of American Evangelicalism, 1835–1860* (Notre Dame, IN: University of Notre Dame Press, 2010), 141–43.

32. Quoted in Billington, *Protestant Crusade*, 158.

33. Hughes, "Alleged Burning," 501–2.

34. John Hughes, "Christianity, the Only Source of Moral, Social, and Political Regeneration: A Sermon Preached in the Hall of Representatives . . . Sunday, December 12, 1847," in *Works*, 1:558–73. It shows something about the fluid ethnoreligious politics of the late 1840s that the twenty senators and thirty-three representatives who signed the invitation to Hughes included more Whigs than Democrats, though well-known Democrats (Stephen Douglas, John C. Calhoun, Thomas Hart Benson, David Wilmot) outnumbered well-known Whigs (John Quincy Adams).

35. Hughes, "Christianity," 558 (text), 562 ("object," "consequences"), 566 ("authority"), ("peace and love"), 571 ("influence").

36. So excited was the abolitionist Wendell Phillips that he set aside his unusual scorn of Catholicism as a tyranny like slavery and read the pope's letter at an antislavery meeting in Boston's Faneuil Hall. The best short accounts on antebellum Catholics and the dilemmas of American slavery are John T. McGreevy, "Catholics and Abolition: A Historical and Theological Problem," in *Figures in the Carpet: Finding the Human Person in the American Past*, ed. Wilfred M. McClay (Grand Rapids, MI: Eerdmans, 2007), 405–28, and McGreevy, *Catholicism and American Freedom*, 43–76 (Wendell Phillips, 50). The best comprehensive account is Michael Hochgeschwender,

Wahrheit, Einheit, Ordnung: Die Skavenfrage und der amerikanische Katholizismus, 1835–1870 (Paderborn: Ferdinand Schöningh, 2006).

37. England, "Discourse," 184.

38. Pope Gregory XVI, *In Supremo Apostolatus: Condemning the Slave Trade*, 1839, Papal Encyclicals Online, https://www.papalencyclicals.net/greg16/g16sup.htm.

39. John England, "Letters to the Hon. John Forsyth, on the Subject of Domestic Slavery," in *Works*, 3:121–22 (Leviticus), 122 (Galatians). An American Jesuit had earlier enlisted these passages to justify American slavery, but in a private writing; see Hennesey, *American Catholics*, 143–44.

40. Hochgeschwender, *Wahrheit*, 150–51.

41. McGreevy, *Catholicism and American Freedom*, 51.

42. For Kendrick's career, see Shea, *Defenders of Our Faith*, 74–77; Sandra Yocum Mize, in *ANB*. Particularly helpful on Kenrick as biblical scholar is Gerald P. Fogarty, "The Quest for a Catholic Vernacular Bible in America," in Hatch and Noll, *BIBLE IN AMERICA*, 165–71; Gerald P. Fogarty, *American Catholic Biblical Scholarship: A History from the Early Republic to Vatican II* (San Francisco, CA: Harper & Row, 1989), 14–34; Gutjahr, *AMERICAN BIBLE*, 129, 134, 136.

43. First Baltimore Provincial Council (1829), quoted in Fogarty, "Vernacular Bible," 167–68.

44. Fogarty, *Catholic Bible Scholarship*, 21, 28.

45. Brownson review of Kenrick, *Brownson's Quarterly Review* (October 1859), quoted in Fogarty, *Catholic Bible Scholarship*, 22.

46. Francis Patrick Kenrick, "Introduction," in *The Pentateuch, Translated from the Vulgate, and Diligently Compared with the Original Text, Being a Revised Edition of the Douay Version, With Notes, Critical and Explanatory* (Baltimore, MD: Kelly, Heian & Piet, 1860), x.

47. Reasons for that failure are detailed in Fogarty, *Catholic Bible Scholarship*, 17–34.

48. McGreevy, *Catholicism and American Freedom*, 25–29.

49. Alessandro Gavazzi, "Lecture IX: The Inquisition and the Madiai," in *Father Gavazzi's Lectures in New York . . . Also, the Life of Father Gavazzi*, 3rd ed., trans. and ed. Julie de Marguerittes (New York: De Witt and Davenport, 1853), 258–59. On Gavazzi's violence-marred tour, see Billington, *Protestant Crusade*, 301–4.

50. *Chicago Tribune*, January 27, 1857, quoted in Richard Lougheed, *The Controversial Conversion of Charles Chiniquy* (Toronto: Clements Academic, 2008), 89.

51. Anon., "The Bible in Our Common Schools," *Common School Journal and Educational Reformer*, new ser., 4 (1852): 9.

52. Andrew Mach, "Free Speech or Violent Insurrection? Partisan and Rhetorical Reactions to the Cincinnati 'Bedini Affair' of 1853–54" (unpublished paper, University of Notre Dame, January 2015) and information from Linda Przybyszewski.

53. Cheever, quoted in McGreevy, "Catholicism and Abolition," 420.

54. John T. McGreevy, *American Jesuits and the World: How an Embattled Religious Order Made Modern Catholicism Global* (Princeton, NJ: Princeton University Press, 2016), 26–27, with 26–62 on the wider contexts for the story of Bapst, who nine years after being tarred and feathered in Maine became the first president of Boston College.

55. McGreevy, *Catholicism and American Freedom*, 7–14.

56. Edward Beecher, *The Papal Conspiracy Exposed, and Protestantism Defended, in the light of Reason, History, and Scripture* (Boston: Stearns, 1855), 13–14.

57. Richard Shaw, *Dagger John: The Unquiet Life and Times of Archbishop John Hughes of New York* (New York: Paulist, 1979), 273. This book provides a helpful general account of the bishop's public activities.

58. Orestes Brownson, "Presbyterian Confession of Faith," *Brownson's Quarterly Review* 8 (April 1846): 205–53; "Protestant Dissensions," *Brownson's Quarterly Review* 9 (April 1847): 163–90; "The Bible against Protestants," *Brownson's Quarterly Review* 22 (January 1860): 75–95; as precised in Patrick W. Carey, *Orestes A. Brownson: A Bibliography, 1826–1876* (Milwaukee, WI: Marquette University Press, 1996), 65, 67, 96. On Brownson's extensive engagement with many issues involving the Bible, essential guidance is provided by this bibliography as well as Patrick W. Carey, *Orestes A. Brownson: American Religious Weathervane* (Grand Rapids, MI: Eerdmans, 2004).

59. [Lawrence] Sheil, *The Bible Against Protestantism, and for Catholicity; Evinced in a conference between a Catholic, a Protestant (Episcopalian), and a Presbyterian*, 5th ed. (Boston: Patrick Donahoe, 1859), 9 ("conformable").

60. Papers of Francis Kenrick, Archdiocese of Baltimore, 31V10, MABA-19, with thanks to Margaret Abruzzo for this account.

61. John Gilmary Shea, *A Bibliographical Account of Catholic Bibles, Testaments, and Other Portions of Scripture Translated from the Latin Vulgate, and Published in the United States* (New York: Cromoisy, 1859), 4, 3.

62. Margaret Abruzzo, personal conversations; Patrick W. Carey, *Confession: Catholics, Repentance, and Forgiveness in America* (New York: Oxford University Press, 2018).

63. Pope Pius IX, "The Syllabus of Errors," 1864, Papal Encyclicals Online, https://www.papalencyclicals.net/pius09/p9syll.htm.

64. Lester J. Cappon, ed., *The Adams-Jefferson Letters* (Chapel Hill: University of North Carolina Press, 1959), Adams to Jefferson, February 3, 1821, 571.

65. Charles Lowell, quoted in McGreevy, *American Jesuits*, 42.

66. McGreevy, *Catholicism and American Freedom*, 28–32 (to many Protestants, "Catholic devotionalism seemed a distraction from real Christian work," 29).

Chapter 17

1. *HISTORICAL STATISTICS*, 57. "German speakers" is the accurate term since there was no "Germany" as such until 1871.

2. Jonathan D. Sarna, *American Judaism: A History* (New Haven: Yale University Press, 2004), 63.

3. *Newburyport (MA) Herald*, January 19, 1827, 1; Catherine A. Brekus, "Harriet Livermore, the Pilgrim Stranger: Female Preaching and Biblical Feminism in Early-Nineteenth-Century America," *Church History* 65 (September 1996): 389–404; on this sermon specifically, 389.

4. This section offers a much-simplified account of so-called American Lutheranism, which has been well treated by a number of historians; I have drawn especially on Theodore G. Tappert, ed., *Lutheran Confessional Theology in America, 1840–1880* (New York: Oxford University Press, 1972); David A. Gustafson, *Lutherans in Crisis: The Question of Identity in the American Republic* (Minneapolis, MN: Fortress, 1993); Paul A. Baglyos, "In This Land of Liberty: American Lutherans and the Young Republic, 1787–1837" (Ph.D. diss., University of Chicago, 1997); Steven M. Nolt, *Foreigners in Their Own Land: Pennsylvania Germans in the Early Republic* (University Park: Pennsylvania State University Press, 2002). The parallel story of the German Reformed "Mercersburg Theology" and its rejection of some "American" norms has been expertly recounted by many scholars, some of whom are referenced in my treatment of John W. Nevin and Philip Schaff in Noll, *AMERICA'S GOD*, 249–52, 323–24.

5. A. Gregg Roeber, "Readers and Writers of German," in *HISTORY OF THE BOOK*, 2:475. My printing history in this section relies especially on the excellent work of Roeber in this article (471–82); A. Gregg Roeber, "German and Dutch Books and Printing," in *HISTORY OF THE BOOK*, 1:298–313; Herman Wellenreuther, *Citizens in a Strange Land: A Study of German-American Broadsides and Their Meaning for Germans in North America, 1730–1830* (University Park: Pennsylvania State University Press, 2013).

6. On Philadelphia, see 317; Roeber, "Readers and Writers," 2:479.

7. For details of these Bible printings, see Gruber Rare Book Collection, Lutheran School of Theology Chicago, accessed April 1, 2020, https://gruber.lstc.edu/luthers_bible/following.php.

8. Roeber, "German and Dutch," 1:307.

9. Wellenreuther, *Citizens*, 15, 259–61.

10. Roeber, "Readers and Writers," 2:475–80.

11. *The National Union Catalogue, Pre-1956 Imprints*, vols. 53–54 (Chicago: American Library Association, 1980).

12. Samuel Seabury, *An Address to the Ministers and Congregations of the Presbyterian and Independent Persuasions* (New Haven, CT: Thomas and Samuel Green, 1790), 52.

13. J. H. C. Helmuth, *Betrachtung der Evangelischen Lehre von der Heiligen Schrift und Taufe* (Germantown, PA: Billmeyer, 1793), 67, with more on Helmuth in Noll, *AMERICA'S GOD*, 71, 117–18, 409–10, which draws from A. Gregg Roeber, "J. H. C. Helmuth, Evangelical Charity, and the Public Sphere in Pennsylvania, 1793–1800," *Pennsylvania Magazine of History and Biography* 121 (January–April 1997): 77–100.

14. Baglyos, "In This Land of Liberty," 239–42.

15. Schmucker's career has been the focus of much serious study; for one summary, see Gustafson, *Lutherans in Crisis*, 62–89 ("Samuel Schmucker: Leading Voice for American Lutherans").

16. S. S. Schmucker, *Elements of Popular Theology, with special reference to the Doctrines of the Reformation, as avowed before the Diet of Augsburg, MDXXX* (Andover, MA: Gould and Newman, 1834), 36–37; see Nolt, *Foreigners*, 113–15 on these translations and also Schmucker's advocacy of *sola scriptura*.

17. Gustafson, *Lutherans in Crisis*, 63–65.

18. Gustafson, *Lutherans in Crisis*, 126–27.

19. S. S. Schmucker, "The Doctrinal Basis and Ecclesiastical Position of the American Lutheran Church," in *The American Lutheran Church, Historically, Doctrinally, and Practically Delineated in Several Occasional Discourses* (Philadelphia, PA: E. W. Miller, 1852), 161–62.

20. The 1850 figure is from Edwin Scott Gaustad, *Historical Atlas of Religion in America*, 2nd ed. (New York: Harper & Row, 1976); for 1860, from Edwin Scott Gaustad and Philip Barlow, *New Historical Atlas of Religion in America*, 3rd ed. (New York: Oxford University Press, 2001).

21. E. Clifford Nelson, ed., *The Lutherans in North America* (Philadelphia, PA: Fortress, 1975), 175.

22. Charles P. Schaum, "From Martin Luther to C. F. W. Walther: A Timeline," in C. F. W. Walther, *Law and Gospel: How to Read and Apply the Bible*, ed. Charles P. Schaum (St. Louis, MO: Concordia, 2010), xliii.

23. D. Fürbringer, "Zur Lehre vom heiligen Predigtamt," *Lehre und Wehre* 1 (January 1833): 1–2. For Walther and his Missouri Synod Lutherans, the "symbols" included the Augsburg Confession along with Luther's *Small Catechism*, the 1577 Formula of Concord that reaffirmed the Augsburg Confession, and other statements.

24. "Wie werden wahrhaft lutherische Gemeinde gegründet und erzogen?," *Lehre und Wehre* 1 (June 1855): 161–75.

25. C. F. W. Walther, "Why Should Our Pastors, Teachers, and Professors Subscribe Unconditionally the Symbolical Writings of Our Church?," in Tappert, *Lutheran Confessional Theology*, 56.

26. Illuminating treatment of this general subject is found in Douglas A. Sweeney and Charles Hambrick-Stowe, eds., *Holding onto the Faith: Confessional Traditions in American Christianity* (Lanham, MD: University Press of America, 2008); and for the Dutch Reformed, James D. Bratt, *Dutch Calvinism in Modern America: A History of a Conservative Subculture* (Grand Rapids, MI: Eerdmans, 1984).

27. E. Clifford Nelson and Eugene L. Fevold, *The Lutheran Church among Norwegian Americans*, vol. 1: *1825–1890* (Minneapolis, MN: Augsburg, 1960), 180. My thanks to Louise Burton for this reference.

28. See, for instance, Lutheran Church–Missouri Synod, "The Lutheran Confessions," accessed October 8, 2021, https://www.lcms.org/about/beliefs/lutheran-confessions.

29. A good book on that development in a denomination that became part of the Evangelical Lutheran Church in America is Christa Klein, *Politics and Policy: The Genesis and Theology of Social Statements in the Lutheran Church in America* (Philadelphia, PA: Fortress, 1989).

30. For one attempt to assess this more recent history, see Mark A. Noll, "Ethnic, American, or Lutheran? Dilemmas for a Historic Confession in the New World," *Lutheran Theological Seminary Review*, Winter 1991, 17–38.

31. "Philadelphia Jews Appeal for Civil Rights—1783" and "'Sound the Great Horn for Our Freedom': A Shearith Israel Prayer—1784," in *Jews and the Founding of the Republic*, ed. Jonathan D. Sarna, Benny Kraut, and Samuel Joseph (New York: Markus Wiener, 1985), 95, 127.

32. For expert orientation, see Sarna, *American Judaism*, 62–111.

33. Sarna, *American Judaism*, 76–82.

34. Naomi W. Cohen, *Jews in Christian America: The Pursuit of Religious Equality* (New York: Oxford University Press, 1992), 5.

35. Sarna, *American Judaism*, 96–98.

36. Cohen, *Jews in Christian America*, 80.

37. For a fuller list, see Bertram Korn, "Isaac Leeser: Centennial Reflections," *American Jewish Archives* 19 (1967): 133.

38. See Sarna, *American Judaism*, 81–82; Lance J. Sussman, "Another Look at Isaac Leeser and the First Jewish Translation of the Bible in the United States," *Modern Judaism* 5 (May 1985): 159–90; and especially Jonathan D. Sarna and Nahum M. Sarna, "Jewish Bible Scholarship and Translations in the United States," in *The Bible and Bibles in America*, ed. Ernest S. Frerichs (Atlanta, GA: Scholars Press, 1988), 84–92 (entire chapter, 83–116).

39. Leeser, from the advertisement for English readers in *The Twenty-Four Books of the Holy Scriptures, carefully translated according to the Massoretic Text, after the best Jewish authorities, by Isaac Leeser*, 2nd ed. (Cincinnati, OH: Bloch, 1853), unnumbered prefatory advertisement.

40. *The Law of God, Volume First, containing The Book of Genesis, Edited, and with former translations diligently compared and revised, by Isaac Leeser* (Philadelphia, PA: C. Sherman, 5605 [1845]), vii.

41. *Twenty Four Books*, iv.

42. *Twenty Four Books*, iii–iv.

43. Jonathan D. Sarna, "Jewish-Christian Hostility in the United States: Perceptions from a Jewish Point of View," in *Uncivil Religion: Interreligious Hostility in America*, ed. Robert N. Bellah and Frederick E. Greenspahn (New York: Crossroad, 1987), 13.

44. Sussman, "Isaac Leeser," 173.

45. Short notice in *Biblical Repertory and Princeton Review* 26 (July 1854): 589–90.

46. On Raphall, see Sarna, *American Judaism*, 95, 112.

47. M. J. Raphall, "Bible View of Slavery," in *Fast Day Sermons: or, the Pulpit on the State of the* Country, ed. anon. (New York: Rudd and Carleton, 1860), 227–46.

48. Sarna, *American Judaism*, 81.

49. James Turner, *Philology: The Forgotten Origin of the Modern Humanities* (Princeton, NJ: Princeton University Press, 2014), 61. The following paragraphs are keyed to the fully contextual treatment of biblical higher criticism in Turner's book, though much other scholarship is pertinent, including especially Jerry Wayne Brown, *The Rise of Biblical Criticism in America, 1800–1870: The New England Scholars* (Middletown, CT: Wesleyan University Press, 1969); Jonathan Sheehan, *The Enlightenment Bible: Translation, Scholarship, Culture* (Princeton, NJ: Princeton University Press, 2005); Michael C. Legaspi, *The Death of Scripture and the Rise of Biblical Studies* (New York: Oxford University Press, 2010); Michael J. Lee, *The Erosion of Biblical Certainty: Battles over Authority and Interpretation in America* (New York: Palgrave Macmillan, 2016).

50. Turner, *Philology*, 145, 120.

51. Turner, *Philology*, 214.

52. Quoted in Brown, *Rise of Biblical Criticism*, 131.

53. Quoted in Brown, *Rise of Biblical Criticism*, 126.

54. Brown, *Rise of Biblical Criticism*, 180.

55. Turner, *Philology*, 224.

56. The following paragraphs are edited and abridged from Mark Noll, "Henry Hotze in Place: Religion, Science, Confederate Propaganda, and Race," in *Geographies of Knowledge: Science, Scale, and Spatiality in the Nineteenth Century*, ed. Robert J. Mayhew and Charles W. J. Withers (Baltimore, MD: Johns Hopkins University Press, 2020), 87–114. Indispensable are Robert E. Bonner, "Slavery, Confederate Diplomacy, and the Racialist Mission of Henry Hotze," *Civil War History* 51 (September 2005): 288–316 and Lonnie A. Burnett, ed., *Henry Hotze: Confederate Propagandist: Selected Writings on Revolution, Recognition, and Race* (Tuscaloosa: University of Alabama Press, 2008).

57. For a general account, see Reginald Horsman, *Josiah Nott of Mobile: Southerner, Physician, and Racial Theorist* (Baton Rouge: Louisiana State University Press, 1987), 171–205.

58. J. C. Nott and Geo. R. Gliddon, *Types of Mankind* (Philadelphia, PA: Lippincott, 1854), 56, 467, 260.

59. On the controversies, see David N. Livingstone, *Adam's Ancestors: Race, Religion, and the Politics of Human Origins* (Baltimore, MD: Johns Hopkins University Press, 2008), 174–86; William Stanton, *The Leopard's Spots: Scientific Attitudes toward Race in America, 1815–59* (Chicago: University of Chicago Press, 1960), 161–74; Adrian Desmond and James Moore, *Darwin's Sacred Cause: How a Hatred of Slavery Shaped Darwin's Views on Human Evolution* (Boston: Houghton Mifflin Harcourt, 2009), 262–66; Michael O'Brien, *Conjectures of Order: Intellectual Life and the American South, 1810–1860*, 2 vols. (Chapel Hill: University of North Carolina Press, 2004), 1:215–52; G. Blair Nelson, "'Men before Adam!' American Debates over the Unity and Antiquity of Humanity," in *When Science and Christianity Meet*, ed. David C. Lindberg and Ronald L. Numbers (Chicago: University of Chicago Press, 2003), 161–82, 304–7.

60. See Lester D. Stephens, *Science, Race, and Religion in the American South: John Bachman and the Christian Circle of Naturalists, 1815–1895* (Chapel Hill: University of North Carolina Press, 2000), 195–211.

61. Desmond and Moore, *Darwin's Sacred Cause*, 263–64.

62. O'Brien, *Conjectures of Order*, 1:248.

63. For helpful contexts, see Michael D. Biddis, *Father of Racist Ideology: The Social and Political Thought of Count Gobineau* (New York: Weybright and Telley, 1970) and Michael D. Biddis, ed., *Gobineau: Selected Political Writings* (New York: Harper & Row, 1970).

64. In a letter to Gobineau dated July 11, 1856, Hotze reported, "I am neither Unitarian [monogist] or Polygenist." Hotze said he did not care to dispute such points but was absolutely delighted that Gobineau had conclusively documented the

"original . . . diversity" of human racial types (Burnett, *Henry Hotze*, 187). Hotze quotations that follow come from this same letter.

65. Hotze, "Introduction," in Gobineau, *Moral and Intellectual Diversity of Races*, vii–viii.

66. Hotze, "Introduction," in Gobineau, *Moral and Intellectual Diversity of Races*, 15–16.

67. Gobineau, *Moral and Intellectual Diversity of Races*, 337.

68. Josiah Nott, Appendix C, "Biblical Connections on the Question of Unity or Plurality of Species," in Gobineau, *Moral and Intellectual Diversity of Races*, 506. See John William Draper, *History of the Conflict between Religion and Science* (New York: Appleton, 1875); A. D. White, *A History of the Warfare of Science and Theology in Christendom* (New York: Appleton, 1896).

69. On scientific racism, see George M. Fredrickson, *Racism: A Short History* (Princeton, NJ: Princeton University Press, 2002), 66–69, 79–82; Colin Kidd, *The Forging of Races: Race and Scripture in the Protestant Atlantic World* (New York: Cambridge University Press, 2006), 144–49.

70. Cocke in the *Southern Literary Messenger*, quoted in Horsman, *Josiah Nott*, 198.

71. Gobineau, *Moral and Intellectual Diversity of Races*, 338.

72. For a depiction of Gobineau in these terms, see Livingstone, *Adam's Ancestors*, 159.

73. On that development, see Kidd, *Forging of* Races, 149–52; and especially Eugene D. Genovese, *A Consuming Fire: The Fall of the Confederacy in the Mind of the White Christian South* (Athens: University of Georgia Press, 1998), 81–96.

74. Linford D. Fisher, "America's First Bible: Native Uses, Abuses, and Reuses of the Indian Bible of 1663," in *The Bible in American Life*, ed. Philip Goff, Arthur E. Farnsley II, and Peter J. Thuesen (New York: Oxford University Press, 2017), 35. For fuller context, see 35–47; Linford D. Fisher, *The Indian Great Awakening: Religion and the Shaping of Native Cultures in Early America* (New York: Oxford University Press, 2012), 24–29; Linford D. Fisher, "The Bible and Indigenous Language Translations in the Americas," in Gutjahr, *OXFORD HANDBOOK*, 39–59; and works cited in Noll, *IN THE BEGINNING*, 232–34.

75. *A Sermon at the Execution of Moses Paul, an Indian, who had been guilty of murder, preached at New Haven in America, by Samson Occom, a native American and missionary to the Indians . . . to which is added a short account of the late spread of the gospel among the Indians, Also observations on the language of the Muhhekaneew Indians . . . by Jonathan Edwards, D.D.* (1772; New Haven, CT: N.p., 1788).

76. Fisher, *Indian Great Awakening*, 66–67, 154–58; Bernd C. Peyer, *The Tutor'd Mind: Indian Missionary-Writers in Antebellum America* (Amherst: University of Massachusetts Press, 1997), 54–116.

77. See Peyer, *Tutor'd Mind*, 166–223; Theda Perdue, ed., *Cherokee Editor: The Writings of Elias Boudinot* (Knoxville: University of Tennessee Press, 1983); William G. McLoughlin, *Cherokee Renascence in the New Republic* (Princeton, NJ: Princeton University Press, 1986), 367–417, 450–51.

78. Elias Boudinot, *An Address to the Whites, Delivered in the First Presbyterian Church, on the 26th of May, 1826* (Philadelphia, PA: William Geddes, 1826), 3 (one blood), 7–10.

79. See Donald B. Smith on Copway in *The Dictionary of Canadian Biography*, accessed April 19, 2021, http://www.biographi.ca/en/bio/4517?revision_id=24935; Peyer,

Tutor'd Mind, 224–77; John Webster Grant, *Moon of Wintertime: Missionaries and the Indians of Canada in Encounter since 1534* (Toronto: University of Toronto Press, 1984), 91–93.

80. *The Life, History, and Travels, of Kah-ge-ga-gah-bowh (George Copway), a young Indian chief of the Ojebwa* [sic] *Nation, a convert to the Christian faith, and a missionary to his people for twelve years: with a sketch of the present state of the Ojebwa Nation, in regard to Christianity and their future prospects, Also an appeal* (Albany, NY: Weed and Parsons, 1847), 83.

81. Copway, *Life, History, and Travels*, 63.

82. Copway, *Life, History, and Travels*, 218–23.

83. Peyer, *Tutor'd Mind*, 277.

84. For Apess's challenge to the standard account of the United States' unique destiny, along with attention to the now considerable literature treating Apess, see Abram Van Engen, *City on a Hill: A History of American Exceptionalism* (New Haven, CT: Yale University Press, 2020), 141–47, 327–29. Excellent contextualization as well as accessible texts of Apess's publications are found in Barry O'Connell, ed., *On Our Own Ground: The Complete Writings of William Apess, a Pequot* (Amherst: University of Massachusetts Press, 1992). Also helpful on Apess is Peyer, *Tutor'd Mind*, 117–65.

85. William Apess, "A Son of the Forest" (1829), in O'Connell, *On Our Own Ground*, 10.

86. William Apess, "Indian Nullification of the Unconstitutional Laws of Massachusetts" (1835), in O'Connell, *On Our Own Ground*, 183.

87. William Apess, "Eulogy on King Philip" (1836), in O'Connell, *On Our Own Ground*, 304.

88. Copway, quoted in Smith, *Dictionary of Canadian Biography*.

Chapter 18

1. On the subjects of this chapter, my eyes were first opened by Catherine A. Brekus, *Strangers and Pilgrims: Female Preaching in America, 1740–1845* (Chapel Hill: University of North Carolina Press, 1998). The chapter is also especially indebted to Marion Ann Taylor and Agnes Choi, eds., *Handbook of Women Biblical Interpreters* (Grand Rapids, MI: Baker, 2012).

2. *Newburyport (MA) Herald*, January 8, 1827, 1.

3. Catherine A. Brekus, "Harriet Livermore, the Pilgrim Stranger: Female Preaching and Biblical Feminism in Early-Nineteenth-Century America," *Church History* 65 (September 1996): 396 ("literalist"), 401 (millennialism).

4. Henry D. Rack, *Reasonable Enthusiast: John Wesley and the Rise of Methodism*, 3rd ed. (London: Epworth, 2002), 244.

5. Brekus, *Strangers and Pilgrims*, 3, the total including a few from the late colonial period.

6. On women who published in earlier colonial history, see David D. Hall, "Readers and Writers in Early New England," in *HISTORY OF THE BOOK*, 1:148–50. For

the eighteenth century, see Catherine A. Brekus, *Sarah Osborn's World: The Rise of Evangelical Christianity in Early America* (New Haven, CT: Yale University Press, 2013) and Vincent Caretta, ed., *Phillis Wheatley: Complete Writings* (New York: Penguin, 2001).

7. Jonathan Elmer, "Warren, Mary Otis," in *ANB*.

8. [Judith Sargent Murray], *Some Deductions from the System Promulgated by the Page of Divine Revelation: Ranked in the order and form of a Catechism: Intended as an Assistant to the Christian Parent as Teacher* (Portsmouth, NH: Self-published, [1782]); quoted from Sheila L. Skemp, "A Unitarian Catechism," *Judith Sargent Murray: A Brief Biography with Documents* (Boston, MA: Bedford/St.Martin's, 1998), 129–30.

9. For helpful treatment of this work and Adams's entire career, see Thomas A. Tweed, "An American Pioneer in the Study of Religion: Hannah Adams (1755–1831) and her *Dictionary of All Religions*," *Journal of the American Academy of Religion* 60 (Fall 1992): 437–64.

10. Quoted in Sherri Trautwein, "Adams, Hannah," in *Handbook of Women Interpreters*, 31.

11. Hannah Adams, *A Dictionary of All Religions*, 4th ed. (New York: James Eastburn, Cummings and Hilliard, 1817), 371.

12. On these two works, see Trautwein, "Adams," 29–30, including the quotation from *Letters on the Gospels* (1824), iii.

13. See Bernon P. Lee, "Conversations on the Bible with a Lady of Philadelphia," in *Recovering Nineteenth-Century Women Interpreters of the Bible*, ed. Christiana de Groot and Marion Ann Taylor (Atlanta, GA: Society of Biblical Literature, 2007), 45–62.

14. Sarah Hall, *Selections from the Writings of Mrs. Sarah Hall, Author of Conversations on the Bible*, ed. Harrison Hall (Philadelphia, PA: Harrison Hall, 1833), 163.

15. Virginia Lieson Brereton, *From Sin to Salvation: Stories of Women's Conversions, 1800 to the Present* (Bloomington: University of Indiana Press, 1991), 17.

16. Harriet Livermore, *A Narration of Religious Experience* (1826), quoted in Brereton, *From Sin to Salvation*, 20–21.

17. Nancy Towle, *Vicissitudes Illustrated in the Experience of Nancy Towle, in Europe and America* (1832), 11, 227–28, quoted in Elizabeth Elkin Grammer, *Some Wild Visions: Autobiographies by Female Itinerant Evangelists in 19th-Century America* (New York: Oxford University Press, 2003), 114.

18. Zilpha Elaw, *Memoirs of the Life, Religious Experience, Ministerial Travels and Labors of Mrs. Zilpha Elaw, an American Female of Colour* (1846), 75, quoted in Grammer, *Wild Visions*, 20.

19. Renee Kwan Monkman, "Palmer, Phoebe," in *Handbook of Women Interpreters*, 391–92; and for excerpts from a number of Palmer's works on holiness, Thomas C. Oden, ed., *Phoebe Palmer: Selected Writings* (Mahwah, NJ: Paulist, 1988), 131–207.

20. Hannah More, quoted in Brereton, *From Sin to Salvation*, 25.

21. Harriet Beecher Stowe (1844), quoted in Marion Ann Taylor, "Harriet Beecher Stowe and the Mingling of Two Worlds: The Kitchen and the Study," in de Groot and Taylor, *Recovering Women Interpreters*, 102.

22. Grammer, *Wild Visions*, 105.

23. The conforming-subverting pattern is well described in Brereton, *From Sin to Salvation*, 28–29.

24. On how Stowe's use of the Bible in those works related to broader intellectual currents, see Noll, *AMERICA'S GOD*, 325–27 (*Minister's Wooing*), and Noll, *CIVIL WAR*, 42–44 (*Uncle Tom's Cabin*).

25. Sarah Moore Grimké, *Letters on the Equality of the Sexes, and the Condition of Women, Addressed to Mary S. Parker, President of the Boston Female Anti-Slavery Society* (Boston: Isaac Knapp, 1838), 4. These communications appeared first in *The Liberator* and the *New England Spectator*.

26. On her career as a biblical scholar, see Beverly Zink-Sawyer, "Blackwell, Antoinette Louisa Brown," in *Handbook of Women Interpreters*, 79–82.

27. For references to these biblical figures, see Brekus, *Strangers and Pilgrims*, 144, 217–20, 280; Grammer, *Wild Visions*, 52–53; *Handbook of Women Interpreters*, 186 (Zilpha Elaw), 239 (Sarah Hale), 241 (Sarah Hall), 509–10 (Sojourner Truth); Grimké, *Letters*, 101–8; Harriet Livermore, *Scriptural Evidence in Favour of Female Testimony, In meetings for Christian worship, in letters to a friend* (Portsmouth, NH: R. Foster, 1824), 27–28, 74–83; Phoebe Palmer, *The Promise of the Father: Or, A neglected Speciality of the Last Days, Addressed to the Clergy and Laity of all Christian Communities* (Boston: Degan and Foster and Palmer, 1859), chapter 12; cited from Craig L. Adams, *Commonplace Holiness* (blog), accessed April 3, 2020, https://www.craigladams.com/Palmer/Promise/index.html.

28. *Handbook of Women Interpreters*, 380 (Murray), 239 (Hale); Livermore, *Scriptural Evidence*, 22; Grimké, *Letters*, 4–5.

29. Grimké, *Letters*, 4.

30. Livermore, *Scriptural Evidence*, 97; Grammer, *Wild Visions*, 52 (Julia Foote); *Handbook of Women Interpreters*, 186 (Zilpha Elaw); Brekus, *Strangers and Pilgrims*, 219 (Jarena Lee and Rebecca Miller).

31. Grimke, *Letters*, 5, 23; also Livermore, *Scriptural Evidence*, 22.

32. *Handbook of Women Interpreters*, 285 (Rebecca Jackson). Full explanation of the difference between prediction and prescription is found in Grimké, *Letters*, 7–8, which she may have taken from a similar argument in Angelina Grimké's abolitionist *Appeal to Christian Women of the South* (New York: American Anti-Slavery Society, 1836), 3.

33. Grammer, *Wild Visions*, 52 (Nancy Towle), 108 (Zilpha Elaw); Livermore, *Scriptural Evidence*, 13; Grimké, *Letters*, 104; Palmer, *Promise of the Father*, chapters 4 and 12.

34. Grimké, *Letters*, 93.

35. Others are Col 3:18 and 1 Pet 3:2.

36. Antoinette L. Brown, "Exegesis of I Corinthians, XIV., 34, 35; and I Timothy, II, ll, 12," *Oberlin Quarterly Review* 4 (July 1849): 361–66 (entire article, 358–73).

37. Brown, "Exegesis," 372.

38. Brown, "Exegesis," 360, 366; Palmer, *Promise of the Father*, chapter 1. Hannah Adams specialized in interpreting world religions, as well as Christianity, by attending to the contexts of their development (*Handbook of Women Interpreters*, 29–30).

39. Livermore, *Scriptural Evidence*, 91, 99; Grammer, *Wild Visions*, 53 (Julia Foote).

40. Grimké, *Letters*, 114.

41. Livermore, *Scriptural Evidence*, 23 (and for opinions on these passages similar to Brown's, 91, 99).

42. Livermore, *Scriptural Evidence*, 120; Grammer, *Wild Visions*, 44 (Zilpha Elaw).

43. Grammer, *Wild Visions*, 45 (Jarena Lee), 48 (Julia Foote).

44. Grimké, *Letters*, 94–96 (quotation, 96).

45. Palmer, *Promise of the Father*, chapter 1; Brown, "Exegesis," 369. Grimké made the same point in *Letters*, 118.

46. Grimké, *Letters*, 97.

47. Livermore, *Scriptural* Evidence, 17; Grimke, *Letters*, 23–24; Grammer, *Wild Visions*, 17 (Amanda Berry Smith).

48. Palmer, *Promise of the Father*, title page. Many others cited the Joel and Acts passages, including Livermore, *Scriptural Evidence*, 6, 74; and several documented by Elizabeth Grammer, *Wild Visions*, 10, 51.

49. See especially the full documentation in Brekus, *Strangers and Pilgrims*, and Grammer, *Wild Visions*.

50. Livermore, *Scriptural Evidence*, 84, 108.

51. Brown, "Exegesis," 373.

52. Palmer, *Promise of the Father*, chapter 4.

53. Brekus, *Strangers and Pilgrims*, 281, 334.

54. Grimké, *Letters*, 123.

55. Livermore, *Scriptural Evidence*, 5, 8.

56. Grimké, *Letters*, 4.

57. Brekus, *Strangers and Pilgrims*, 307–9. Angelina Grimké, who remained more committed to the "Bible only" than did her sister Sarah, was also drawn to Millerite speculations in the early 1840s; see Anna M. Speicher, *The Religious World of Antislavery Women: Spirituality in the Lives of Five Abolitionist Lecturers* (Syracuse, NY: Syracuse University Press, 2000), 133–34.

58. The Grimké sisters are well positioned in the reforming currents of their times by Robert H. Abzug, *Cosmos Crumbling: American Reform and the Religious Imagination* (New York: Oxford University Press, 1994), 204–29; Speicher, *Religious World of Antislavery Women*, 3–4, 79–81, 90–92, 123–40.

59. Perceptive awareness of that connection is found in Margaret Bendroth, "The Disenchantment of Women: Gender and Religion at the Turn of the Century (1865–1930)," in *Figures in the Carpet: Finding the Human Person in the American Past*, ed. Wilfred M McClay (Grand Rapids, MI: Eerdmans, 2007), 146n3.

60. Helpful examples in an immense literature include Bertram Wyatt-Brown, *Lewis Tappan and the Evangelical War Against Slavery* (Cleveland, OH: Press of Case Western Reserve University, 1969); James Brewer Stewart, *Holy Warriors: The Abolitionists and American Slavery* (New York: Hill & Wang, 1976); Abzug, *Cosmos Crumbling*; Howe, *WHAT HATH GOD WROUGHT*, 164–202, 285–327; Walter A. MacDougall, *Throes of Democracy: The American Civil War Era, 1829–1977* (New York: Harper, 2008), 167–228.

61. Grimké, *Letters*, 51, 96, 123.

62. Grimké, *Appeal*, 2, 3.

63. Grimké, *Appeal*, 3, 22–23 (biblical women). The same connections between women's rights and abolition appeared in Sarah Grimké's *An Epistle to the clergy of the Southern States* (New York: N.p., 1836), esp. 1, 2, 17.

64. See Bruce M. Metzger, *The Canon of the New Testament: Its Origin, Development, and Significance* (New York: Oxford University Press, 1987).

65. On these opinions, see chapter 24.

66. See David Norton, *A History of the Bible as Literature*, 2 vols. (New York: Cambridge University Press, 1993), 1:217–18, 240–41.

67. See Shalom Goldman, *God's Sacred Tongue: Hebrew and the American Imagination* (Chapel Hill: University of North Carolina Press, 2004).

68. John Calvin, *Institutes of the Christian Religion* (1559), ed. John T. McNeill, trans. Ford Lewis Battles, 2 vols. (Philadelphia, PA: Westminster, 1950), 1:121 (I.xiii.1), 1:227 (I.xvii.13).

69. Particularly forceful among many studies on this subject is Brad S. Gregory, *The Unintended Reformation: How a Religious Revolution Secularized Society* (Cambridge, MA: Harvard University Press, 2012).

70. Murray, *Some Deductions*, passim.

71. Brown, "Exegesis," 358, 372.

72. Grimké, *Appeal*, 3, 2.

73. Grimké, *Letters*, 18, 80, 89, 117, 122.

74. Donna Grear Parker, "Wright, Frances," in *ANB*; Eric R. Schlereth, *An Age of Infidels: The Politics of Religious Controversy in the Early United States* (Philadelphia: University of Pennsylvania Press, 2013), 175, 194, 208. On perceived associations between the antireligious Wright and women preachers, see Brekus, *Strangers and Pilgrims*, 137, 278–81.

75. Nancy C. Unger, "Mott, Lucretia Coffin," in *ANB*; Speicher, *Religious World of Antislavery Women*, 29–34.

76. Lucretia Mott, "Abuses and Uses of the Bible," in *American Sermons: The Pilgrims to Martin Luther King Jr.*, ed. Michael Warner (New York: Library of America, 1999), 631, 635, 637, 638.

Chapter 19

1. For this chapter I have been most helped by Caroline L. Shanks, "The Biblical Anti-Slavery Argument of the Decade, 1830–1840," *Journal of Negro History* 16 (April 1931): 132–57; James Brewer Stewart, "Abolitionists, the Bible, and the Challenge of Slavery," in *The Bible and Social Reform*, ed. Ernest R. Sandeen (Philadelphia, PA: Fortress, 1982), 31–58; Robert Bruce Mullin, "Biblical Critics and the Battle over Slavery," *Journal of Presbyterian History* 61 (Summer 1983): 210–26; Larry E. Tise, *Proslavery: A History of the Defense of Slavery in America, 1701–1840* (Athens: University of Georgia Press, 1988); J. Albert Harrill, "The Use of the New

Testament in the American Slave Controversy: A Case History in the Hermeneutical Tensions between Biblical Criticism and Christian Moral Debate," *Religion and American Culture* 10 (Summer 2000): 149–86; Elizabeth Fox-Genovese and Eugene D. Genovese, *The Mind of the Master Class: History and Faith in the Southern Slaveholders' Worldview* (New York: Cambridge University Press, 2005), 409–648; Molly Oshatz, *Slavery and Sin: The Fight against Slavery and the Rise of Liberal Protestantism* (New York: Oxford University Press, 2012). But many other excellent works have also contributed, including those cited in chapter 9, notes 1 and 2, and chapter 10, note 1; as well as John R. McKivigan, *The War against Proslavery Religion: Abolitionism and the Northern Churches, 1830–1865* (Ithaca NY: Cornell University Press, 1984); Elizabeth Fox-Genovese and Eugene D. Genovese, "The Divine Sanction of the Social Order: Religious Foundations of the Southern Slaveholders' World View," *Journal of the American Academy of Religion* 55 (Summer 1987): 211–33; Mitchell Snay, *The Gospel of Disunion: Religion and Separatism in the Antebellum South* (New York: Cambridge University Press, 1993); Hugh Davis, *Leonard Bacon: New England Reformer and Antislavery Moderate* (Baton Rouge: Louisiana State University Press, 1998); John Patrick Daly, *When Slavery Was Called Freedom: Evangelicalism, Proslavery, and the Causes of the Civil War* (Lexington: University Press of Kentucky, 2002); Stephen R. Haynes, *Noah's Curse: The Biblical Justification of American Slavery* (New York: Oxford University Press, 2002); Holifield, *THEOLOGY IN AMERICA*, 494–504 ("The Dilemma of Slavery"); David Torbett, *Theology and Slavery: Charles Hodge and Horace Bushnell* (Macon, GA: Mercer University Press, 2006); David F. Holland, "Sovereign Silences and the Voice of War on the American Conflict over Slavery," *Law and History Review* 26 (Fall 2008): 571–94; Joseph A. Moore, *Founding Sins: How a Group of Antislavery Radicals Fought to Put Christ into the Constitution* (New York: Oxford University Press, 2016); Ryan C. McIlhenny, *To Preach Deliverance to the Captives: Freedom and Slavery in the Protestant Mind of George Bourne, 1780– 1845* (Baton Rouge: Louisiana State University Press, 2020); Jordan T. Watkins, *Slavery and Sacred Texts: The Bible, the Constituition, and Historical Consciousness in Antebellum America* (New York: Cambridge University Press, 2021).

2. The fifty-seven separate Bible defenses of slavery I examined included a few additions to the full list of titles found in Tise, *Proslavery*; thirty were published north of the Mason-Dixon line. Of these fifty-seven, only three came from periodicals where, as also in newspapers, many more appeared. Even from incomplete reading of available sources, documentation could be multiplied many times over for almost all of the chapter's assertions.

3. Thornton Stringfellow, *A Brief Examination of Scripture Testimony on the Institution of Slavery, in an Essay first published in the Religious Herald and republished by request: with Remarks on a Review of the Essay* (Richmond, VA: Religious Herald, 1841); this work was republished in 1850 (Washington, DC: Congressional Globe) and then included in E. N. Eliott, ed., *Cotton Is King, and Proslavery Arguments: comprising the writings of Hammond, Harper, Christy, Stringfellow, Hodge, Bledsoe, and Cartwright* (Augusta, GA: Pritchard, Abbott and Loomis, 1860). See also Stringfellow's more extensive works, *Scriptural and Statistical Views in Favor of Slavery* (Richmond, VA: J.

W. Randolph, 1856) and *Slavery: Its Origin, Nature and History. Its relations to society, to government, and to true religion, to human happiness and divine glory, Considered in the light of Bible teachings, moral justice, and political wisdom* (Alexandria: Virginia Sentinel, 1860).

4. Stringfellow, *Brief Examination*, 4, 5. Stringfellow mostly recapitulated the earlier interpretations explored in chapters 10 and 11.

5. Stringfellow, *Brief Examination*, 27–28; M. J. Raphall, "Bible View of Slavery," in *Fast Day Sermons: or, the Pulpit on the State of the Country*, ed. anon. (New York: Rudd and Carleton, 1861), 231–34 (quotation, 232); on Priest, see note 10; Robert L. Dabney, "Liberty and Slavery" (1856), in *Discussions of Robert L. Dabney*, 4 vols., ed. C. R. Vaughan (Richmond, VA: Whittet and Shepperson, 1892), 4:69. For the many proslavery authors who agreed with Dabney, see Fox-Genovese and Genovese, *Mind of the Master Class*, 523–24.

6. H[enry] R. Bascom, *Methodism and Slavery: with other matters in controversy between the North and the South, being a Review of the Manifesto of the Majority, in reply to the protest of the minority, of the late general conference of the Methodist E[piscopal] Church, in the case of Bishop Andrew* (Frankfort, KY: Hodges, Todd and Pruett, 1845).

7. N[athaniel] S. Wheaton, *A Discourse on St. Paul's Epistle to Philemon, exhibiting the duty of citizens of the northern states in regard to the Institution of Slavery* (Hartford, CT: Case, Tiffany, 1851), 27.

8. James Henley Thornwell, "Baptism of Servants," *Southern Presbyterian Review* 1 (June 1847): 63–102; James Henley Thornwell, "The Christian Doctrine of Slavery" (1850), in *The Collected Writings of James Henley Thornwell*, 4 vols., ed. John B. Adger and John L. Girardeau (Richmond, VA: Presbyterian Committee of Publication, 1873), 4:403, 411; James Henley Thornwell, "Duties of Masters," *Southern Presbyterian Review* 8 (October 1854): 272 (entire article, 266–83). For context, see James Oscar Farmer Jr., *The Metaphysical Confederacy: James Henley Thornwell and the Synthesis of Southern Values* (Macon, GA: Mercer University Press, 1986), 218–29. Another leading Presbyterian, Charles Colcock Jones, shared many of Thornwell's concerns; see chapter 9, 187.

9. Stringfellow, *Slavery: Its Origin, Nature and History*.

10. Josiah Priest, *Slavery, as it relates to the Negro, or African Race, examined in the light of circumstances, history and the Holy Scriptures; with an account of the Origin of the Black Man's Color, causes of his state of servitude and traces of his character as well in ancient as in modern times: with strictures on Abolitionism* (Albany, NY: C. Van Benthuysen, 1843), 65. Later editions appeared under some variation of the title *Bible defence of slavery: to which is added a faithful exposition of that system of pseudo philanthrophy* [sic]*, or fanaticism, yclept modern abolitionism, which threatens to dissolve the union . . .* , 6th stereotype ed. (Louisville, KY: Willis A. Bush, 1851) and further editions in 1859 and 1871. On Kames's theory, see David N. Livingstone, *Adam's Ancestors: Race, Religion and the Politics of Human Origins* (Baltimore, MD: Johns Hopkins University Press, 2008), 57–61.

11. Charles Hodge, "Slavery," *Princeton Review* 8 (1836), reprinted in Charles Hodge, *Essays and Reviews* (New York: Robert Carter and Brothers, 1857), 473–512; Moses

Stuart, *Conscience and the Constitution* (Boston: Crocker and Brewster, 1850). See also G. W. Blagdon, *The Principles on which a Preacher of the Gospel Should Condemn Sin* (Boston: Crocker and Brewster, 1837); G. W. Blagdon, *Remarks and a Discourse on Slavery* (Boston: Ticknor, Reed, and Fields, 1854); John C[hase] Lord, *"The Higher" Law in its application to the Fugitive Slave Bill: A Sermon on the duties men owe to God and to Governments* (Buffalo, NY: George Derby, 1851); Henry K. How, *Slaveholding Not Sinful: an answer . . . to John Van Dyke, Esq.'s Reply to the Argument of Rev. Dr. [Samuel Blanchard] Howe* (New Brunswick, NJ: Fredonian and Daily Office, 1856).

12. John Henry Hopkins, *Scriptural, Ecclesiastical, and Historical View of Slavery, from the days of the Patriarch Abraham, to the Nineteenth Century* (New York: W. I. Pooley, 1864), 6–7.

13. Simon Clough, *A Candid Appeal to the Citizens of the United States, proving that the doctrines advanced and the measures pursued by the Abolitionists, relative to the Subject of Emancipation, are inconsistent with the teachings and directions of the Bible, and that those Clergymen engaged in the dissemination of these principles should be immediately dismissed by their respective congregations, as False Teachers* (New York: A. K. Berton, 1834).

14. [George Patterson], *The Scripture Doctrine with Regard to Slavery* (Pottstown, PA: B. Bannan, 1854). Patterson is identified as the author in Larry E. Tise, "Patterson, George," *Dictionary of North Carolina Biography*, 1994, https://www.ncpedia.org/biography/patterson-george.

15. Joseph Tracy, *Natural Equality: a sermon before the Vermont Colonization Society* (Montpelier, VT: N.p., 1833), 11.

16. William G. Brownlow, *A Sermon on Slavery; A vindication of the Methodist Church, South* (Knoxville, TN: Kinsloe and Rice, 1857), 4.

17. Francis Patrick Kenrick, excerpt from *Theologia Moralis* (1843), in *American Catholics and Slavery, 1789–1866: An Anthology of Primary Documents*, ed. Kenneth J. Zanca (New York: University Press of America, 1994), 200. For insightful commentary on Kenrick's position and its later influence among Catholics, see Michael Hochgeschwender, *Wahrheit, Einheit, Ordnung: Die Sklavenfrage und der amerikanische Katholizismus* (Paderborn: Ferdinand Schöningh, 2006), 154–58.

18. Samuel Seabury, *American Slavery Distinguished from the Slavery of English Theorists, and Justified by the Law of Nature* (New York: Mason Brothers, 1861), 292–93.

19. For the very few proslavery voices who believed "the Bible sanctioned enslavement regardless of race," see Fox-Genovese and Genovese, *Mind of the Master Class*, 526; Elizabeth Fox-Genovese and Eugene D. Genovese, *Slavery in White and Black: Class and Race in the Southern Slaveholders' New World Order* (New York: Cambridge University Press, 2008), 212–14.

20. Stringfellow, *Slavery: Its Origin, Nature and History*, 3.

21. J. H. Thornwell, "Our National Sin," 49; B. M. Palmer, "Slavery a Divine Trust," 65; Henry J. Van Dyke, "The Character and Influence of Abolitionism," 152; William Adams, "Prayer for Rulers; Or Duty of Christian Patriots," 332, all in *Fast Day Sermons*.

22. Stringfellow, *Brief Examination*, 40; Hodge, "Slavery," in *Essays and Reviews*, 479.

23. Clough, *Candid Appeal*, 39.

24. Brownlow, *Sermon on Slavery*, 6; Thornwell, "Address to all Churches of Christ," in *Writings*, 4:446, 456.

25. Theron F. Schlabach, *The Mennonite Experience in America*, vol. 2: *Peace, Faith, Nation: Mennonites and Amish in Nineteenth-Century America* (Scottdale, PA: Herald, 1988), 173–200; James O. Lehman and Steven M. Nolte, *Mennonites, Amish, and the American Civil War* (Baltimore, MD: Johns Hopkins University Press, 2007).

26. Albert Barnes, *An Inquiry into the Scriptural View of Slavery* (Philadelphia, PA: Perkins and Purves, 1846), 65–67. See also Theodore Dwight Weld, *The Bible Against Slavery*, 4th ed. (New York: American Antislavery Society, 1838), 23–47.

27. See Stringfellow, *Brief Examination*, 6; and on the learned critique, Harrill, "Use of the New Testament," 151–52, 163–65.

28. Albert Taylor Bledsoe, *An Essay on Liberty and Slavery* (Philadelphia, PA: J. B. Lippincott, 1856), 66; Seabury, *American Slavery*, 291. This reading of the Golden Rule followed the interpretation given by William Graham in the immediate post-Revolutionary era; see chapter 10.

29. When Sarah Grimké incorporated the parallel between marriage and the master-slave relation into her appeal for women's rights, she argued that literal interpretation of other passages made wives equal in authority to husbands *and* entailed abolition, In response, anti-abolitionists crowed: the insanity of the one betrayed the anarchy of the other. See Sarah Moore Grimké, *Letters on the Equality of the Sexes, and the Condition of Women. Addressed to Mary S. Parker, President of the Boston Female Anti-Slavery Society* (Boston: Isaac Knapp, 1838), 15, 84, 96.

30. Stuart Robinson, *Slavery, as recognized in the Mosaic Civil Law, recognized also, and allowed in, the Abrahamic, Mosaic, and Christian Church* (Toronto: Rollo and Adam, 1865), 51n. For Robinson on slavery and his wide influence, see Luke E. Harlow, *Religion, Race, and the Making of Confederate Kentucky, 1830–1880* (New York: Cambridge University Press, 2014), 135–36, 155, 187–88.

31. Stringfellow, *Brief Examination*, 33 (misprint in original reads "no steal a man").

32. Frederick A. Ross, *Slavery Ordained of God* (Philadelphia, PA: J. P. Lippincott, 1857), 155–57. It was probably arguments in this work that Abraham Lincoln lampooned in October 1858 (as dated by Roy Basler), "Fragment on Pro-slavery Theology," in Lincoln, COLLECTED WORKS, 3:204–5.

33. Thornwell, "Our National Sin," 33; Francis Vinton, "Fanaticism Rebuked," in *Fast Day Sermons*, 255, 253.

34. Van Dyke, "The Character and Influence of Abolitionism," 152.

35. Palmer, "Slavery a Divine Trust," 57, 58, 66, 70 (mostly italicized).

36. Stringfellow, *Brief Examination*, 36; Ross, *Slavery Ordained of God*, 144; Robinson, *Slavery*, 74; Bledsoe, *Liberty and Slavery*, 223.

37. As for the earlier sections of this chapter, almost every assertion about biblical abolition, based on examining about forty antislavery works, could be illustrated with multiple examples.

38. Leonard Bacon, *Slavery Discussed in Occasional Essays, from 1833 to 1846* (New York: Baker and Scribner, 1846), 180.

39. Stuart, *Conscience and the Constitution*, 55. On Stuart's scholarly leadership, see John H. Giltner, *Moses Stuart: The Father of Biblical Science in America* (Atlanta, GA: Scholars Press, 1988).

40. Fox-Genovese and Genovese, *Mind of the Master Class*, 490, 527.

41. George Cheever, *The Guilt of Slavery and the Crime of Slaveholding, Demonstrated from the Hebrew and Greek Scriptures* (Boston: John P. Jewett, 1860), v, 464.

42. Harrill, "Use of the New Testament."

43. William Henry Brisbane, *Slaveholding Examined in the Light of the Holy Bible* (Philadelphia, PA: American and Foreign Anti-Slavery Society, 1847), vii–viii (index of Scripture texts). Although Theodore Dwight Weld was published by the American and Foreign Anti-Slavery Society, he and Sarah Grimké, who supported Garrison's more radical American Anti-Slavery Society, provided strong commendations for this work ("brevity, simplicity, clearness, compact logic, freedom from ambitious pretense of scholarship"; "bless the Lord for the Essay you have prepared . . . [may you] do yet greater things, to help forward the great work of regenerating the world," iii). I think Wallace Alcorn for alerting me to Brisbane's work.

44. A Citizen of Virginia [George Bourne], *A Condensed Anti-Slavery Bible Argument* (New York: S. W. Benedict, 1845), 9–12 (quotation, 9).

45. Cheever, *Guilt of Slavery*, xvi.

46. John G. Whittier, "Introduction" (1883), in *Letters of Lydia Maria Child* (New York: Negro Universities Press, 1969), xxiv. My thanks to Patti Mangis for pointing me to Whittier's words.

47. Lydia Maria Child, *An Appeal in Favor of that Class of Americans Called Africans* (Boston: Allen and Ticknor, 1833), 29.

48. *A Debate, Held. . . [in] October, 1845, between Rev. J. Blanchard . . . and N. L. Rice* (Cincinnati, OH: W. H. Moore, 1846), 44.

49. Henry Ward Beecher, "Peace Be Still," in *Fast Day Sermons*, 274–76 (Indians and Mexicans), 269 (Puritans), 290 (Spirit), 288 (quotation).

50. Absalom Jones, *A Thanksgiving Sermon, preached January 1, 1808, in St. Thomas's, or the African Episcopal Church, Philadelphia: On Account of the Abolition of the African slave trade, on that day, by the Congress of the United States* (Philadelphia, PA: Fry and Kammerer, 1808), 10–12.

51. Douglass's thorough immersion in Scripture is a main theme of David W. Blight, *Frederick Douglass, Prophet of Freedom* (New York: Simon and Schuster, 2018), esp. 228–51.

52. Eli Washington Caruthers, *American Slavery and the Immediate Duty of Southern Slaveholders*, ed. Jack R. Davidson (Eugene, OR: Pickwick, 2018), vii (prayer). The work challenged "the unjust, unchristian, and inhumane laws of the south, relating to slavery with the teachings of the Bible and the original instincts of our nature" (xi).

53. Jack R. Davidson, *Still Letting My People Go: An Analysis of Eli Washington Caruthers's Manuscript against American Slavery and Its Universal Application of Exodus 10:3* (Eugene, OR: Pickwick, 2018), 126–58.

54. James Patterson, *A Sermon on the Effects of the Hebrew Slavery as Connected with Slavery in this Country . . . July 4, 1825* (Philadelphia, PA: S. Probasco, 1825).

55. On the importance for Black Americans of Nimrod as a counter to the curse of Canaan, see Anthony B. Pinn and Allen Dwight Callahan, eds., *African American Religious Life and the Story of Nimrod* (New York: Palgrave Macmillan, 2008).

56. James W. C. Pennington, *A Text Book of the Origin and History, &c. &c. of the Colored People* (Hartford, CT: L. Skinner, 1841), 18, on Cain (5–7) and Canaan (7–18). Excellent on Pennington's conservative theology and his sophisticated abolitionism is Joel R. Iliff, "'Sustaining the Truth of the Bible': Black Evangelical Abolitionism and the Transatlantic Politics of Orthodoxy," *Journal of the Civil War Era* 11 (June 2021): 164–93.

57. Van Dyke, "Character and Influence of Abolitionism," 127–37.

58. Bourne, *Condensed Anti-Slavery Bible Argument*, 46–49 (quotation, 47).

59. Brisbane, *Slaveholding Examined*, iv, vi.

60. Cheever, *Guilt of Slavery*, ii, iii, iv.

61. Cheever, *Guilt of Slavery*, 466.

62. Excellent treatment of the widespread appeal to church history from all sides of the slavery debate is found in Paul Gutacker, "Seventeen Centuries of Sin: The Christian Past in Antebellum Slavery Debates," *Church History* 89 (June 2020): 307–32.

63. Tayler Lewis, "Patriarchal and Jewish Servitude No Argument for American Slavery," in *Fast Day Sermons*, 180 ("condition," "letter"), 181, 183–85, 187–88 (Jewish servitude), 182–85, 211–20 (Roman).

64. William E. Channing, *Slavery* (Boston: James Munroe, 1835), 109–11.

65. Francis Wayland and Richard Fuller, *Domestic Slavery Considered as a Scriptural Institution* (New York: Lewis Colby, 1845), 58.

66. Barnes, *Inquiry*, 203–28.

67. J. M. Pendleton, *Letters to Rev. W. C. Buck, in Review of His Articles on Slavery* (Louisville, KY: N.p., 1849), 3. For more on these arguments by Wayland, Pendleton, and Barnes, along with references to pertinent historical studies, see Noll, *CIVIL WAR*, 36–38, 46–47.

68. Channing, *Slavery*, 109. The rest of Channing's observation reflected a common attitude toward American Blacks that undercut the force of his critique: "not merely of barbarians but of Greeks, not merely of the ignored and debased, but the virtuous, educated, and refined."

69. Pendleton, *Letters*, 3.

70. John G. Fee, *The Sinfulness of Slaveholding Shown by Appeals to Reason and Scripture* (New York: John A. Gray, 1851), 29. On the local context for Pendleton and Fee, see Harlow, *Religion, Race, and the Making of Confederate Kentucky*, 86–100.

71. Lewis, "Patriarchal and Jewish Servitude," 181, 189, 190, 215, 217.

72. Daniel R. Goodwin, *Southern Slavery in its Present Aspects: Containing a Reply to a Late Work of the Bishop of Vermont on Slavery* (Philadelphia, PA: J. B. Lippincott, 1864), 116–17. In an 1859 speech, Abraham Lincoln spoke to Kentuckians who were "trying to establish the rightfulness of Slavery by reference to the Bible"; in response he too pointed out that "whenever you establish that slavery was right by the Bible, it

will occur that Slavery was the Slavery of the *white* man." "Speech at Cincinnati, Ohio" (September 17, 1859), in Lincoln, *COLLECTED WORKS*, 3:445.

73. Frederick Douglass, "The Pro-Slavery Mob and the Pro-Slavery Ministry," *Douglass' Monthly*, March 1861, 417–18.

74. Lewis, "Patriarchal and Jewish Servitude," 208.

75. Cortland Van Rensselaer, "Dr. Van Rensselaer's Reply to Dr. Armstrong, on Emancipation and the Church," *Presbyterian Magazine* 8 (February 1858), 77 (entire article, 70–85).

76. David Barrow, *Involuntary, Unmerited, Perpetual, Absolute, Hereditary Slavery, Examined; or the Principles of Nature, Reason, Justice, Policy, and Scripture* (Lexington, KY: D. and C. Bradford, 1808).

77. Albert Barnes, *The Church and Slavery*, 2nd ed. (Philadelphia, PA: Parry and McMillan, 1857), 27.

78. Cheever, *Guilt of Slavery*, 462.

79. Ronald G. Walters, *The Antislavery Appeal: American Abolitionism after 1830* (Baltimore, MD: Johns Hopkins University Press, 1976), 37.

80. Mitchell Snay, *Gospel of Disunion: Religion and Separatism in the Antebellum South* (New York: Cambridge University Press, 1993), 59.

81. William Ellery Channing, *Unitarian Christianity: A Discourse on Some of the Distinguishing Opinions of Unitarians* (1819; Boston: American Unitarian Association, 1919), 25.

82. Channing, *Unitarian Christianity*, 24–25.

83. Channing, *Slavery*, 2.

84. Goodwin, *Southern Slavery*, 114.

85. I am following the narrative outlined in James Brewer Stewart's superb essay "Abolitionists, the Bible, and the Challenge of Slavery," in *The Bible and Social Reform*, ed. Ernest R. Sandeen (Philadelphia, PA: Fortress, 1982), 31–57. Also insightful on the evolution of Garrison's views and those of others like him is Kathryn Gin Lum, *Damned Nation: Hell in America from the Revolution to Reconstruction* (New York: Oxford University Press, 2014), 186–98.

86. Ronald D. Graybill, "The Abolitionist-Millerite Connection," in *The Disappointed: Millerism and Millenarianism in the Nineteenth Century*, ed. Ronald L. Numbers and Jonathan M. Butler (Bloomington: Indiana University Press, 1987), 144–47.

87. On the significance of that break for Douglass's scriptural and constitutional views, see Daniel A. Morris, "Liberated from the Liberator: Frederick Douglass and Garrisonian Political Theology," *Political Theology* 18 (August 2017): 423–40; Jason Ross, "William Lloyd Garrison's Shattered Faith in Antislavery Constitutionalism: The Origins and Limits of the 'Garrisonian Critique,'" *American Political Thought* 9 (Spring 2020): 199–234.

88. William Lloyd Garrison, *Sonnets and Other Poems* (Boston: O. Johnson, 1843), 64.

89. Stewart, "Abolitionists," 39 (Garrison, *The Liberator*, July 26, 1836)

90. Stewart, "Abolitionists," 37 (Elizur Wight Jr., 1833).

91. Stewart, "Abolitionists," 45 (*The Liberator*, July 28, 1837).

92. William Lloyd Garrison, "Thomas Paine," *The Liberator*, November 21, 1845, 186.
93. Garrison, "Thomas Paine," 186.
94. Stewart, "Abolitionists," 49 (Henry C. Wright, *The Liberator*, May 11, 1848).
95. Barnes, *Church and Slavery*, 10–11.
96. Barnes, *Inquiry*, 57.

Chapter 20

1. Holifield, *THEOLOGY IN AMERICA*, 503.
2. For a helpful assessment of key works, including Walter Johnson, *River of Dark Dreams: Slavery and Empire in the Cotton Kingdom* (2013), Sven Beckert, *Empire of Cotton: A Global History* (2014), Edward E. Baptist, *The Half Has Never Been Told: Slavery and the Making of American Capitalism* (2014), and Sven Beckert and Seth Rockman, eds., *Slavery's Capitalism: A New History of American Economic Development* (2016), see Christopher Morris, "With 'the Economics-of-Slavery Culture Wars,' It's Déjà Vu All Over Again," *Journal of the Civil War Era* 10 (December 2020): 524–57.
3. See, as examples, Paul J. Polgar, *Standard-Bearers of Equality: America's First Abolition Movement* (Chapel Hill: University of North Carolina Press, 2019) and Andrew Delbanco, *The War before the War: Fugitive Slaves and the Struggle for America's Soul from the Revolution to the Civil War* (New York: Penguin, 2019).
4. See especially Michael O'Brien, *Conjectures of Order: Intellectual Life and the American South, 1810–1860*, 2 vols. (Chapel Hill: University of North Carolina Press, 2004) and Elizabeth Fox-Genovese and Eugene D. Genovese, *The Mind of the Master Class: History and Faith in the Southern Slaveholders' Worldview* (New York: Cambridge University Press, 2005).
5. Robert Alexander Young, *The Ethiopian Manifesto: Issued in Defence of the Black Man's Rights in the Scale of Universal Freedom* (New York: By the author, 1829).
6. See especially James Oakes, *Freedom National: The Destruction of Slavery in the United States, 1861–1865* (New York: Norton, 2013) and James Oakes, *The Scorpion's Sting: Antislavery and the Coming of the Civil War* (New York: Norton, 2014).
7. For my earlier conclusions, see Noll, *CIVIL WAR*, 40–45, 48–50.
8. Steven Keillor responding to my earlier judgment that, given antebellum intellectual conventions, the biblical proslavery position prevailed: "I think the Bible is quite clear that any economic system that destroys marriages, dehumanizes those that it exploits, includes prohibitions against training in Christianity, depends upon man-stealing (which Scripture explicitly prohibits), rests on the back of corrupt interpretations of Scripture (the 'curse of Ham'), and survives only by thoroughgoing violation of The Golden Rule is flat out sinful" (private communication, ca. 2011). For his own account, see Steven J. Keillor, *A Providential History of the United States*, vol. 3: *Raising a Great Power to a Global Mission: The Maturing Nation, 1862–1941* (St. Paul, MN: By the author, 2016), 1–132.

9. On the rejection of the biblical proslavery argument throughout the Christian world outside the United States, even by conservative Protestants and Catholics, see Noll, *CIVIL WAR*, 95–155.

10. "Elective affinity," in Oxford Reference online, accessed March 23, 2021, https://www-oxfordreference-com.proxy.library.nd.edu/search?q=elective+affinity&searchBtn=Search&isQuickSearch=true.

11. In Europe the reality of *eius regio, eius religio* preserved local Protestant cohesion: whoever controlled the region determined the religion, or in this case, *eius regio eia scriptura* (whoever controls the region can dictate a single meaning for the Bible). When Protestant regimes relaxed top-down control, as for the Netherlands in the seventeenth century, during the English Civil War at the middle of the same century, and for New England in the eighteenth, conflict arose immediately among Protestants all following *sola scriptura*. For New England, see Noll, *IN THE BEGINNING*, 98–124.

12. Alexander Campbell, quoted in Douglas A. Foster, *A Life of Alexander Campbell* (Grand Rapids, MI: Eerdmans, 2020), 140–41.

13. The nineteenth-century movement of American theology away from Calvinism may have contributed to the elision of biblical interpretation and providential interpretations of contemporary history since, at least in theory, Calvinists held that all human activities, including the ability to fathom Providence, were tainted by sin and limited by human finitude. Yet in practice, Congregational and Presbyterian "consistent Calvinists" could display as much self-confidence in their ability to discern the whys and wherefores of Providence as anyone else. For the theological history, see Holifield, *THEOLOGY IN AMERICA*, 341–94; Noll, *AMERICA'S GOD*, 269–329.

14. Oshatz, *Slavery and Sin*, 73–75.

15. Oshatz, *Slavery and Sin*, 75–80: Robert Bruce Mullin, "Biblical Critics and the Battle over Slavery," *Journal of Presbyterian History* 61 (Summer 1983): 210–26.

16. See Theodore Dwight Bozeman, *Protestants in an Age of Science: The Baconian Ideal and Antebellum Religious Thought* (Chapel Hill: University of North Carolina Press, 1979); Holifield, *THEOLOGY IN AMERICA*, 159–394; Noll, *AMERICA'S GOD*, 93–113, 233–38.

17. Moses Stuart, *A Commentary on the Epistle to the Romans* (Andover, MA: Flagg and Gould, 1835), 599, 610, 614, 615.

18. Moses Stuart, *Conscience and the Constitution* (Boston: Crocker and Brewster, 1850), 30–32, with fuller consideration of argumentation that was actually more complex than in this rendering: Noll, *CIVIL WAR*, 58–61.

19. Excellent is Bozeman, *Protestants in an Age of Science*.

20. Charles Hodge, *Systematic Theology*, 3 vols. (New York: Scribner's, 1871–72), 1:10–11. Hodge's programmatic statements have drawn as much attention as the theological expositions that followed in this large work, where Hodge only rarely came to theological conclusions by the strict Baconian reasoning he claimed to follow.

21. On that innovation, see Bruce Gordon and Euan Cameron, "Latin Bibles in the Early Modern Period," in *The New Cambridge History of the Bible*, vol. 3, *From 1450 to 1750*, ed. Euan Cameron (New York: Cambridge University Press, 2016), 213.

22. For Smith's statement of principle and the Campbell example, see Michael W. Casey, *The Battle over Hermeneutics in the Stone-Campbell Movement, 1800–1870* (Lewiston, NY: Edwin Mellen, 1998), 110–11.

23. David Norton, "English Bibles from c. 1520 to c. 1750," in Cameron, *Cambridge History of the Bible*, 317. The King James Version, which followed the Geneva Bible's versification, resulted in "an excellent study but a mediocre reading text" (332).

24. Gutjahr, *AMERICAN BIBLE*, 103; Paul Gutjahr, *The Book of Mormon: A Biography* (Princeton, NJ: Princeton University Press, 2012), 98. Soon, however, later editions appeared with the Book of Mormon text also divided into separate paragraph-verses.

25. Gerritt Smith, *Sermons and Speeches* (1861), 133, quoted in Oshatz, *Slavery and Sin*, 45.

26. In British usage, "Evangelical" (with a capital "E") first referred to the Church of England's revival-friendly party before broadening in the twentieth century to include non-Anglicans as well. See, on these figures, Roger Anstey, *The Atlantic Slave Trade and British Abolition, 1760–1810* (London: Macmillan, 1975), 186–89; Robert Pierce Forbes, "'A Man and a Brother': Racial Attitudes of the British Abolitionists" (unpublished paper, ca. 2005); Christopher Leslie Brown, *Moral Capital: Foundations of British Abolitionism* (Chapel Hill: University of North Carolina Press, 2006), 333–89; John M. G. Barclay, "'Am I Not a Man and a Brother'? The Bible and the British Anti-Slavery Campaign," *Expository Times* 119, no. 1 (2007): 3–14; John Coffey, "Evangelicals, Slavery and the Slave Trade: From Whitefield to Wilberforce," *Anvil* 24 (2007): 97–120; John Coffey, "'Tremble Britannia': Fear, Providence, and the Abolition of the Slave Trade, 1758–1807," *English Historical Review* 127 (2012): 844–81; and the many books of David Brion Davis.

27. Barclay, "'Am I Not a Man and a Brother?,'" 8, 14.

28. For "brother" or "brethren," see Frederick Douglass, "Slavery in the Pulpit of the Evangelical Alliance: An Address Delivered in London, England, on September 14, 1846," in *The Frederick Douglass Papers: Series One*, vol. 1, ed. John Blasingame et al. (New Haven, CT: Yale University Press, 1979), 407–16; Christopher L. Webber, *American to the Backbone: The Life of James W. C. Pennington, the Fugitive Slave Who Became One of the First Black Abolitionists* (New York: Pegasus, 2011), 154, 256; and for Thornwell, see chapter 19, note 8.

29. Tayler Lewis, "Patriarchal and Jewish Servitude No Argument for American Slavery," in *Fast Day Sermons*, ed. anon. (New York: Rudd and Carleton, 1861), 186, 187, 203, 206, 219–20.

30. See note 18.

31. Chapters 24 and 25 detail the broad history sketched in this paragraph.

Chapter 21

1. George C. Rable, *God's Almost Chosen People: A Religious History of the American Civil War* (Chapel Hill: University of North Carolina Press, 2010), 397.

2. Abraham Lincoln, "Speech at Edwardsville, Illinois" (May 18, 1858), 2:452; "'A House Divided Speech': Speech at Springfield, Illinois" (June 16, 1858), in Lincoln, *COLLECTED WORKS*, 2:461.

3. See on this speech, 462.

4. Outstanding on this song and its long afterlife is John Stauffer and Benjamin Soskis, *The Battle Hymn of the Republic: A Biography of the Song That Marches On* (New York: Oxford University Press, 2013): "[O]ne explanation for the apparent effortlessness with which the poem was written was Howe's intimate familiarity with the Bible. Starting as a child, she had read a passage from it daily" (75).

5. Rable, *God's Almost Chosen People*, 357.

6. J. T. Mills, "The Confederate Motto, No Compromise," *Army and Navy Messenger*, March 16, 1865, 2. Thanks to Kurt Berends for this quotation.

7. Serious treatment of religion in the Civil War remained remarkably underdeveloped into the 1980s, but has since become a major subgenre of impressive scholarship. A survey of important works published before 2006 is found in Noll, *CIVIL WAR*, 9–11, 163–65. The tide has continued to surge with works that include Harry S. Stout, *Upon the Altar of the Nation: A Moral History of the Civil War* (New York: Viking, 2006); Robert J. Miller, *Both Prayed to the Same God: Religion and Faith in the American Civil War* (Lanham, MD: Lexington, 2007); David Rolfs, *No Peace for the Wicked: Northern Protestant Soldiers and the American Civil War* (Knoxville: University of Tennessee Press, 2009); Rable, *God's Almost Chosen People*; David Goldfield, *America Aflame: How the Civil War Created a Nation* (New York: Bloomsbury, 2011); Sean A. Scott, *A Visitation of God: Northern Civilians Interpret the Civil War* (New York: Oxford University Press, 2011); Stauffer and Soskis, *Battle Hymn of the Republic*; Timothy L. Wesley, *The Politics of Faith during the Civil War* (Baton Rouge: Louisiana State University Press, 2013); T. Felder Dorn, *Challenges on the Emmaus Road: Episcopal Bishops Confront Slavery, Civil War, and Emancipation* (Columbia: University of South Carolina Press, 2013); Luke E. Harlow, *Religion, Race, and the Making of Confederate Kentucky, 1830–1880* (New York: Cambridge University Press, 2014); Robert R. Mathisen, ed., *The Routledge Sourcebook of Religion and the American Civil War: A History in Documents* (New York: Routledge, 2015); Max Longley, *For the Union and the Catholic Church: Four Converts in the Civil War* (Jefferson, NC: McFarland, 2015); William F. Quigley Jr., *Pure Heart: The Faith of a Father and Son in the War for a More Perfect Union* (Kent, OH: Kent State University Press, 2016); April E. Holm, *A Kingdom Divided: Evangelicals, Loyalty, and Sectionalism in the Civil War Era* (Baton Rouge: Louisiana State University Press, 2017); Lucas P. Volkman, *Houses Divided: Evangelical Schisms and the Crisis of the Union in Missouri* (New York: Oxford University Press, 2018); Benjamin L. Miller, *In God's Presence: Chaplains, Missionaries, and Religious Space during the American Civil War* (Lawrence: University Press of Kansas, 2019); Gracjan Kraszewski, *Catholic Confederates: Faith and Duty in the Civil War South* (Kent, OH: Kent State University Press, 2020); James P. Byrd, *A Holy Baptism of Fire and Blood: The Bible and the American Civil War* (New York: Oxford University Press, 2021). For a helpful survey,

see Chandra Manning, "Faith and Works: A Historiographical Review of Religion in the Civil War Era," *Journal of the Civil War Era* 10 (September 2020): 373–96.

8. Documentation for the northern revivals is found throughout Rolfs, *No Peace for the Wicked,* and Steven E. Woodworth, *While God Is Marching On: The Religious World of Civil War Soldiers* (Lawrence: University Press of Kansas, 2001).

9. Woodworth, *While God Is Marching On,* 56.

10. Rable, *God's Almost Chosen People,* 130; Henry Otis Dwight, *The Centennial History of the American Bible Society,* 2 vols. (New York: Macmillan, 1911), 2:577. ABS production doubled almost immediately after the start of the war, with over five and a half million total Bibles and testaments printed during the four years of the conflict.

11. Randall M. Miller, "Catholic Religion, Irish Ethnicity, and the Civil War," in *Religion and the American Civil War*, ed. Randall M. Miller, Harry S. Stout, and Charles Reagan Wilson (New York: Oxford University Press, 1998), 271.

12. Woodworth, *While God Is Marching On,* 166.

13. Rable, *God's Almost Chosen People,* 130; W. Harrison Daniel, "Bible Publication and Procurement in the Confederacy," *Journal of Southern History* 24 (1958): 191–201

14. Rable, *God's Almost Chosen People,* 130–31.

15. Rable, *God's Almost Chosen People,* 131.

16. Woodworth, *While God Is Marching On,* 71.

17. Both accounts, Rable, *God's Almost Chosen People,* 166.

18. Woodworth, *While God Is Marching On,* 72. For Mark Twain's spoofing of Bible-stopping-bullet stories, see Gutjahr, *AMERICAN BIBLE,* 113.

19. Both stories, Mathisen, *Routledge Sourcebook of Religion and the American Civil War,* 325.

20. Rable, *God's Almost Chosen People,* 166.

21. J. William Jones, *Christ in the Camp: Or, Religion in Lee's Army* (Richmond, VA: B. F. Johnson, 1887).

22. Mathisen, *Routledge Sourcebook of Religion and the American Civil War,* 131.

23. Rable, *God's Almost Chosen People,* 341.

24. Both April sermons, Woodworth, *While God Is Marching On,* 255.

25. Woodworth, *While God Is Marching On,* 210.

26. Rable, *God's Almost Chosen People,* 266.

27. For only a few of many others, see Rolfs, *No Peace for the Wicked,* 111, 193; Mathisen, *Routledge Sourcebook of Religion and the American Civil War* 146, 180; Woodworth, *While God Is Marching On,* 5, 51; Rable, *God's Almost Chosen People,* 366; Allen C. Guelzo, *Gettysburg: The Last Invasion* (New York: Knopf, 2013), 281.

28. Rolfs, *No Peace for the Wicked,* 123.

29. Woodworth, *While God Is Marching On,* 190–91.

30. Mathisen, *Routledge Sourcebook of Religion and the American Civil War,* 131–32.

31. Woodworth, *While God Is Marching On,* 69, 18.

32. Rable, *God's Almost Chosen People,* 161. See Kent T. Dollar, *Soldiers of the Cross: Confederate Soldier Christians and the Impact of War on Their Faith* (Macon, GA: Mercer University Press, 2005), for the nearly constant reference to Scripture by the three Methodists, two Episcopalians, two Presbyterians, and one Baptist profiled

by Dollar. (The one Catholic Dollar included expressed heightened spiritual concerns but not oriented to the Bible.)

33. Miller, *Both Prayed to the Same God*, 111.

34. Byrd, *Holy Baptism*, 303–7.

35. James P. Byrd, *Sacred Scripture, Sacred War: The Bible and the American Revolution* (New York: Oxford University Press, 2013), 170.

36. For examples, see Rable, *God's Almost Chosen People*, 315, 360, 364, 389; Dollar, *Soldiers of the Cross*, 89, 131, 159, 168, 197; Scott, *Visitation of God*, 76; Goldfield, *America Aflame*, 287.

37. Scott, *Visitation of God*, 76.

38. Rable, *God's Almost Chosen People*, 55.

39. Wesley, *Politics of Faith*, 74

40. Wesley, *Politics of Faith*, 74, 142; For more examples of Methodist political involvement, see 84; Rable, *God's Almost Chosen People*, 39, 63.

41. For such arguments, see Scott, *Visitation of God*, 169; Rable, *God's Almost Chosen People*, 224, 287.

42. Rable, *God's Almost Chosen People*, 20; Wesley, *Politics of Faith*, 184–85; Goldfield, *America Aflame*, 208, 267.

43. Scott, *Visitation of God*, 101; Noll, *CIVIL WAR*, 78.

44. Wesley, *Politics of Faith*, 133; Goldfield, *America Aflame*, 287.

45. For the earlier conflicts, see Noll, *IN THE BEGINNING*, 150–76, 271–324. The one exception was the Mexican War, which did not seem to elicit extensive biblical commentary; see John C. Pinheiro, *Missionaries of Republicanism: A Religious History of the Mexican-American War* (New York: Oxford University Press, 2014).

46. Rable, *God's Almost Chosen People*, 301; Scott, *Visitation of God*, 233–34; Rable, *God's Almost Chosen People*, 163.

47. Wesley, *Politics of Faith*, 39.

48. Rable, *God's Almost Chosen People*, 375.

49. Rable, *God's Almost Chosen People*, 77.

50. Scott, *Visitation of God*, 189.

51. Wesley, *Politics of Faith*, 47.

52. Scott, *Visitation of God*, 177; Rable, *God's Almost Chosen People*, 358.

53. Scott, *Visitation of God*, 110, 163–64.

54. For the Revolutionary period, see Noll, *IN THE BEGINNING*, 276–79.

55. Frank Moore, ed., *The Patriot Preachers of the American Revolution* (New York: N.p., 1860); John Wingate Thornton, ed., *The Pulpit of the American Revolution: Or, the Political Sermons of the Period of 1776* (Boston: Gould and Lincoln, 1860).

56. Examples in the next three paragraphs come from the superlative research in Rable's *God's Almost Chosen People*. Most of the other recent studies include many more such instances.

57. Rable, *God's Almost Chosen People*, 386. Joshua also served as a model for the ideal Confederate soldier (123).

58. Scott, *Visitation of God*, 31–32.

59. Wesley, *Politics of Faith*, 96, 100. Wesley's book explores debates over political preaching at length.

60. Wesley, *Politics of Faith*, 116.

61. Scott, *Visitation of God*, 126.

62. Rable, *God's Almost Chosen People*, 51.

63. Rable, *God's Almost Chosen People*, 44. On the importance of those special days, which represented the nationalization of an older Puritan tradition, see Harry S. Stout and Christopher Grasso, "Civil War, Religion, and Communications: The Case of Richmond," in Miller, Stout, and Wilson, *Religion and the American Civil War*, 313–59.

64. On the growing quantity of serious historical treatments of Catholics in the war years, see Mark A. Noll, "The Catholic Press, the Bible, and Protestant Responsibility for the Civil War," *Journal of the Civil War Era* 7 (September 2017): 371–72. Catholic responses are treated more extensively in this article (355–76).

65. On the foreign coverage, see Noll, *CIVIL WAR*, 139–55. The standard guide to the Catholic press is Eugene P. Willgang and Herta Hatzfeld, *Catholic Serials of the Nineteenth Century in the United States: A Descriptive Bibliography and Union List: Second Series*, 16 vols. (Washington, D.C.: Catholic University of American Press, 1959–67).

66. Mary Alphonsine Frawly, *Patrick Donahoe* (Washington, D.C.: Catholic University of America Press, 1946), esp. 34–84.

67. "The New York Times on Catholicity and Slavery, *Pilot*, June 8, 1861, 4.

68. "The Mormons and the Know-Nothings," *Pilot*, March 24, 1860, 4.

69. "Die Bibelschriften," *Der Wahrheits-Freund*, July 11, 1861, 558 ("Die Bibel wird nicht verstanden, wo sie gelesen wird, und nicht gelesen, wo sie verstanden werden könnte. . . . Um die Bibel wirklich zu verstehen, müsse man nicht nur den Wortsinn derselben, sondern auch eine den Text begleitende fortlaufende Erläuterung aller für Nichttheologen ohne Erklärung unverständlichen Worte etc. vor Augen haben.")

70. "Protestantism in Its Consequences," *New York Freeman's Journal*, March 9, 1861, 3.

71. "The Protestant Religion Not the Religion Established by Christ," *The Catholic* (Pittsburgh), July 21, 1866, 169.

72. "Religious Divisions and Political Union," *New York Tablet*, September 12, 1857, 8.

73. "Christian Patriotism," *New York Freeman's Journal*, July 6, 1861, 5.

74. "Who Are the Loyal Citizens?," *New York Tablet*, April 1, 1865, 8.

75. Lawrence B. Shell, *The Bible Against Protestantism and for Catholicity; Evinced in a Conference Between a Catholic, a Protestant Episcopalian, and a Presbyterian* (Boston: Patrick Donahoe, 1859). Donahoe advertised this volume in his paper as "A Book for the Times," *Pilot*, February 18, 1860, 4.

76. "The Sensation Preachers of the North and our National Crisis," *Pilot*, February 2, 1861, 4.

77. See in chapter 16, 350–51.

78. M. J. Spalding, *The History of the Protestant Reformation . . . in a Series of Essays*, 2 vols. (Louisville, KY: Webb & Levering, 1860), 1:288–314 ("Influence of the Reformation on the Bible, on Bible Reading, and Biblical Studies").

79. "The Bible in the Public Schools," *Pilot*, March 3, 1860, 8; "Bible Burning—A Misrepresentation," *Guardian* (Louisville, KY), February 2, 1861, 4–5; "The 'Carthage Republican' on Religious Slander," *Pilot*, April 13, 1861, 4.

80. "Bible History," *Pilot*, September 8, 1860, 1.

81. "La véracité de la Bible," *La Propagateur* (New Orleans), June 14, 1862, 1; two long articles on Colenso in *New York Tablet*, March 11, 1865, 12, and March 18, 1865, 5. The latter articles included considerable critique of Protestant "bibliolatry," but as a way of expounding Catholic teachings on biblical inspiration.

82. Alexis de Tocqueville, *Democracy in America*, ed. Eduardo Nolla, trans. James T. Schleifer, 4 vols. (Indianapolis, IN: Liberty Fund, 2010), 3:756.

83. "The Conversion of America, No. VIII," *Catholic Mirror* (Baltimore), March 10, 1860, 4.

84. In the ever-swelling tide of Lincoln scholarship, carefully nuanced accounts of his religion are found in Allen C. Guelzo, *Abraham Lincoln: Redeemer President* (Grand Rapids, MI: Eerdmans, 1999); Allen C. Guelzo, "God and Mr. Lincoln," *Lincoln Lore*, no. 1917 (Spring 2018): 15–21; Joseph R. Fornieri, *Abraham Lincoln's Political Faith* (DeKalb: Northern Illinois University Press, 2003); Stewart Winger, *Lincoln, Religion, and Romantic Cultural Politics* (DeKalb: Northern Illinois University Press, 2003); Richard J. Carwardine, *Lincoln: A Life of Purpose and Power* (New York: Knopf, 2006). My own efforts to address the subject include Noll, *AMERICA'S GOD*, 425–38.

85. Gordon Leidner, "How Many 'Lincoln Bibles,'" *Journal of the Abraham Lincoln Association* 41 (Winter 2020); 47–79.

86. Louis A. Warren, *Lincoln's Youth: Indiana Years, 1816–1830* (1959; Indianapolis: Indiana Historical Society, 1991), 30–32 and passim.

87. A. E. Elmore, *Lincoln's Gettysburg Address: Echoes of the Bible and Book of Common Prayer* (Carbondale: Southern Illinois University Press, 2009); Daniel L. Dreisbach, "Biblical Language and Themes in Lincoln's Gettysburg Address," *Perspectives on Political Science* 44 (2015): 34–39, doi:10.1080/10457097.2014.955447/.

88. On Lincoln's engagement with *The Christian's Defense* by Springfield Presbyterian minister James Smith, see Robert Bray, *Reading with Lincoln* (Carbondale: Southern Illinois University Press, 2010), 152–58.

89. Abraham Lincoln, "Reply to Loyal Colored People of Baltimore upon Presentation of a Bible" (September 7, 1864), in Lincoln, *COLLECTED WORKS*, 7:542.

90. Quotations in this paragraph are from Abraham Lincoln, "Second Inaugural Address" (March 4, 1865), in Lincoln, *COLLECTED WORKS*, 8:332–33.

91. Except where noted, the following paragraphs depend on Gary Phillip Zola, *We Called Him Father Abraham: Lincoln and American Jewry, a Documentary History* (Carbondale: Southern Illinois University Press, 2014) and Jonathan D. Sarna and Benjamin Shapell, *Lincoln and the Jews: A History* (New York: Thomas Dunne/ St. Martins, 2015). For an appreciation of these books, see Mark A. Noll, "Father Abraham," *Journal of the American Lincoln Association* 37 (Summer 2016): 68–76.

92. David Einhorn, "War With Amalek!" (March 19, 1864), in *American Sermons: The Pilgrims to Martin Luther King, Jr., ed.* Michael Warner (New York: Library of America, 1999), 665; and on Einhorn, Jonathan Sarna, *American Judaism: A History*

(New Haven, CT: Yale University Press, 2004), 98-99, 113. On Raphall's sermon, see in chapter 19, 401-2.

93. Goldfield, *America Aflame*, 299-300.

94. Sarna and Shapell, *Lincoln and the Jews*, 228-33.

95. Sarna and Shapell, *Lincoln and the Jews*, 118; Zola, *Father Abraham*, 100. See also Jonathan Sarna, *When General Grant Expelled the Jews* (New York: Schocken, 2012).

96. Sarna and Shapell, *Lincoln and the Jews*, 118.

97. Zola, *Father Abraham*, 1 (Dembitz), 226 (Wise). Emanuel Hertz included about thirty of those postassassination sermons in *Abraham Lincoln: The Tribute of the Synagogue* (New York: Bloch, 1927).

98. Bertram W. Korn, *American Jewry and the Civil War*, 2nd ed. (Philadelphia, PA: Jewish Publication Society of America, 1961), 214.

99. Abraham Lincoln, "First Inaugural Address" (March 4, 1861), in Lincoln, *COLLECTED WORKS*, 4:271.

100. Sarna and Shapell, *Lincoln and the Jews*, 112.

101. Sarna and Shapell, *Lincoln and the Jews*, 146; Zola, *Father Abraham*, 372.

102. Sarna and Shapell, *Lincoln and the Jews*, 140; Zola, *Father Abraham*, 40.

103. Colin Kidd, *The Forging of Races: Race and Scripture in the Protestant Atlantic World, 1600-2000* (New York: Cambridge University Press, 2006), 76.

104. Kidd, *Forging of Races*, 81.

105. Robert E. Bonner, "Slavery, Confederate Diplomacy, and the Racialist Mission of Henry Hotze," *Civil War History* 51 (September 2005): 290. For many more details on Hotze's London career, see Bonner's entire article (288-316) and Mark A. Noll, "Henry Hotze in Place: Religion, Science, Confederate Propaganda, and Race," in *Geographies of Knowledge: Science, Scale, and Spatiality*, ed. Robert J. Mayhew and Charles W. J. Withers (Baltimore, MD: Johns Hopkins University Press, 2020), 87-114.

106. "Address to Christians Throughout the World," *Index*, June 11, 1863, 108-10.

107. Scottish Ministers, "Reply to the Address of the Confederate Clergy," *Index*, November 5, 1863, 439.

108. [Hotze], "The Reply of the Scottish Clergy," *Index*, November 5, 1863, 441-42.

109. "Dr. Hunt on the Negro's Place in Nature," *Index*, November 26, 1863, 486-87, and December 3, 1863, 501-3.

110. On these societies, including much on their religious concerns, see David N. Livingstone, *Adam's Ancestors: Race, Religion and the Politics of Human Origins* (Baltimore, MD: Johns Hopkins University Press, 2008), 112-14, 170-73; Adrian Desmond and James Moore, *Darwin's Sacred Cause: How a Hatred of Slavery Shaped Darwin's Views on Human Evolution* (Boston: Houghton Mifflin Harcourt, 2009), 332-69; Timothy Larsen and Daniel J. King, "The Dependence of Sociocultural Anthropology on Theological Anthropology," in *Theologically Engaged Anthropology*, ed. J. Derrick Lemons (Oxford: Oxford University Press, 2018).

111. Hotze to Judah Benjamin, August 27, 1863, "C.S.A. Commercial Agency—London" (letter book), Henry Hotze Papers, 1861-1865 (MMC-0677), Library of Congress, Washington, D.C.

112. [Hotze], "The Negro's Place in Nature," *Index*, December 10, 1863, 523.

113. [Hotze], "The Negro Race in America," *Index*, August 12, 1865, 489.

Chapter 22

1. John Hope Franklin, *Reconstruction after the Civil War*, 2nd ed. (Chicago: University of Chicago Press, 1994), 185.

2. For an overview of recent historical writing, see Mark A. Noll, "The Future of Reconstruction Studies: Reconstructing Religion," *Journal of the Civil War Era* 7 (March 2017): 11 (precis); https://journalofthecivilwarera.org/forum-the-future-of-reconstruction-studies/reconstructing-religion/.

3. Sarah Berringer Gordon, *The Mormon Question: Polygamy and Constitutional Conflict in Nineteenth-Century America* (Chapel Hill: University of North Carolina Press, 2002).

4. Allen Guelzo, "Did Religion Make the American Civil War Worse?," *The Atlantic*, August 23. 2015, http://www.theatlantic.com/politics/archive/2015/08/did-relig ion-make-the-american-civil-war-worse/401633/.

5. I am following the helpful three-part emphases (African American, northern white, southern white) of Daniel W. Stowell, *Rebuilding Zion: The Religious Reconstruction of the South, 1863–1877* (New York: Oxford University Press, 1998).

6. Edward Blum, "'To Doubt This Would Be to Doubt God': Reconstruction and the Decline of Providential Confidence," in *Apocalypse and the Millennium in the Civil War Era*, ed. Ben Wright and Zachary W. Dresser (Baton Rouge: Louisiana State University Press, 2013), 246.

7. See especially Stowell, *Rebuilding Zion*, 65–99; Charles F. Irons, "'Two Divisions of the Same Great Army': Ecclesiastical Separation by Race and the Millennium," in Wright and Dresser, *Apocalypse and the Millennium*, 194–216; Dennis C. Dickerson, *The African Methodist Episcopal Church: A History* (New York: Cambridge University Press, 2020), 108–56.

8. Stowell, *Rebuilding Zion*, 73.

9. Stowell, *Rebuilding Zion*, 90, 96.

10. Matthew Harper, "Emancipation and African American Millennialism," in Wright and Dresser, *Apocalypse and the Millennium*, 165.

11. Leon F. Litwack, *Been in the Storm So Long: The Aftermath of Slavery* (New York: Knopf, 1981), 471; Eric Foner, *Reconstruction: America's Unfinished Revolution, 1863–1877* (1988), new ed. (New York: History Book Club, 2005), 88. For the leadership of Black ministers in Reconstruction political life, see Eric Foner, *Freedom's Lawmakers: A Directory of Black Officeholders during Reconstruction* (New York: Oxford University Press, 1993).

12. Clarence W. Walker, *A Rock in a Weary Land: The African Methodist Episcopal Church during the Civil War and Reconstruction* (Baton Rouge: Louisiana State University Press, 1982); William E. Montgomery, *Under Their Own Vine and Fig Tree: African*

American Churches in the South, 1865–1900 (Baton Rouge: Louisiana State University Press, 1993).

13. John Michael Giggie, *After Redemption: Jim Crow and the Transformation of African American Religion in the Delta, 1875–1915* (New York: Oxford University Press, 2008).

14. James B. Bennett, *Religion and the Rise of Jim Crow in New Orleans* (Princeton, NJ: Princeton University Press, 2005).

15. Curtis J. Evans, *The Burden of Black Religion* (New York: Oxford University Press, 2008).

16. Harper, "Emancipation," 160.

17. Excellent on their prehistory and history remain James Weldon Johnson, J. Rosamond Johnson, and Lawrence Brown, *The Book of American Negro Spirituals* (New York: Viking, 1925) and Dena J. Epstein, *Sinful Tunes and Spirituals: Black Folk Music to the Civil War* (Urbana: University of Illinois Press, 1977). Among the best works on the musical traditions that grew from the spirituals are James H. Cone, *The Spirituals and the Blues*, 2nd ed. (Maryknoll, NY: Orbis, 1991); Jon Michael Spencer, *Black Hymnody: A Hymnological History of the African-American Church* (Knoxville: University of Tennessee Press, 1992); Michael W. Harris, *The Rise of Gospel Blues: The Music of Thomas Andrew Dorsey in the Urban Church* (New York: Oxford University Press, 1992)

18. William Francis Allen, Charles Pickard Ware, and Lucy McKim Garrison, *Slave Songs of the United States* (New York: A. Simpson, 1867), ix.

19. Lydia Maria Child, "Charity Bowery," *Liberty Bell* 1 (1839): 42–43 (article, 26–43), http://womenwriters.digitalscholarship.emory.edu/content.php?level=div&id=child_charity_001&document=child_charity.

20. Toni P. Anderson, *"Tell Them We Are Singing for Jesus": The Original Fisk Jubilee Singers and Christian Reconstruction, 1871–1878* (Macon, GA: Mercer University Press, 2010), 104.

21. On the even higher proportion of former slaves in the Hampton Singers, see the informative article by Lori Shipley, "Music Education at Hampton Institute, 1868–1913," *Journal of History Research in Music Education* 32 (April 2011): 104–13 (entire article, 96–121).

22. On the early AMA, see Bertram Wyatt Brown, *Lewis Tappan and the Evangelical War against Slavery* (Cleveland, OH: Press of Case Western Reserve University, 1969), 287–300; Christopher L. Weber, *American to the Backbone: The Life of James W. C. Pennington* (New York: Pegasus, 2011), 239–42. Excellent on the music as well as the history of the Fisk singers is Anderson, *Fisk Jubilee Singers*.

23. On these approaches to biblical interpretation, see David C. Steinmetz, "The Superiority of Pre-Critical Exegesis," *Theology Today* 37 (April 1980): 27–38; T. M. Luhrmann, *When God Talks Back: Understanding the American Evangelical Relationship with God* (New York: Knopf, 2012), which includes discussion of the Jesuits' "Spiritual Exercises."

24. An intriguing parallel to African American spirituals has been documented by students of Native American Christianity where Bible-based songs also reflected hermeneutical approaches different from those in majority-white usage. As examples,

see Thomas McElwain, "'The Rainbow Will Carry Me': The Language of Seneca Iroquois Christianity as Reflected in Hymns," in *Religion in Native North America*, ed. Christopher Vecsey (Moscow: University of Idaho Press, 1990), 83–103; Michael David McNally, *Ojibwa Singers: Hymns, Grief, and a Native Culture in Motion* (St. Paul: Minnesota Historical Society, 2009).

25. Lewis O. Saum, *The Popular Mood of America, 1860–1890* (Lincoln: University of Nebraska Press, 1990), 79–83. For his earlier study, see chapter 8, 158.

26. Among many others on the strengthened concept of "spirituality," see George C. Rable, *God's Almost Chosen People: A Religious History of the American Civil War* (Chapel Hill: University of North Carolina Press, 2010), 394; Stowell, *Rebuilding Zion*, 147–48.

27. Beth Barton Schweiger, *The Gospel Working Up: Progress and the Pulpit in Nineteenth-Century Virginia* (New York: Oxford University Press, 2000), 125–27.

28. Andrew E. Murray, *Presbyterians and the Negro: A History* (Philadelphia, PA: Presbyterian Historical Society, 1966), 171.

29. Murray, *Presbyterians and the Negro*, 174.

30. Frances E. W. Harper, "Learning to Read," in Robert R. Mathisen, *Religion and the American Civil War: A History in Documents* (New York: Routledge, 2015), 189–90.

31. Edward J. Blum, *Reforging the White Republic: Race, Religion, and American Nationalism, 1875–1898* (Baton Rouge: Louisiana State University Press, 2005), 95.

32. W. Scott Poole, "Confederate Apocalypse: Theology and Violence in the White Reconstruction South," in *Vale of Tears: New Essays on Religion and Reconstruction*, ed. W. Scott Poole and Edward J. Blum (Macon, GA: Mercer University Press, 2005), 45.

33. Stephen V. Ash, *A Massacre in Memphis: The Race Riot That Shook the Nation One Year after the Civil War* (New York: Hill and Wang, 2013), 169–70.

34. Horace Bushnell, "Our Obligations to the Dead," in *Building Eras in Religion* (New York: Charles Scribner's Sons, 1881), 328–29.

35. Benjamin Morgan Palmer, "The Tribunal of History," *Southern Presbyterian Review* 23 (April 1872): 252, 260, 262 (article, 245–62). For Palmer's view of providence as a contemporary mystery, see Zachary W. Dresser, "Providence Revised: The Southern Presbyterian Old School in the Civil War and Reconstruction," in Wright and Dresser, *Apocalypse and the Millennium*, 132–39.

36. Donald G. Mathews, "Lynching Is Part of the Religion of Our People: Faith in the Christian South," in *Religion in the American South: Protestants and Others in History and Culture*, ed. Beth Barton Schweiger and Donald G. Mathews (Chapel Hill: University of North Carolina Press, 2004), 156.

37. Excellent treatment of this innovation, the works treated below, and many more details are found in Colin Kidd, *The Forging of Races: Race and Scripture in the Protestant Atlantic World, 1600–2000* (New York: Cambridge University Press, 2006), 147–51; David N. Livingstone, *Adam's Ancestors: Race, Religion and the Politics of Human Origins* (Baltimore, MD: Johns Hopkins University Press, 2008), 186–200. Two volumes in the collection by John David Smith, ed., *Anti-Black Thought, 1863–1925: "The Negro Problem," An Eleven-Volume Anthology of Racist Writings*

(New York: Garland, 1993) reprint eleven of the most important works sparked by Ariel: vol. 5, *The "Ariel" Controversy: Religion and "The Negro Problem," Part I*, and vol. 6, *The Biblical and "Scientific" Defense of Slavery: Religion and "The Negro Problem," Part II*.

38. A Minister [D. G. Philips], *Nachash: What Is It? or An Answer to the Question, "Who and What is the Negro?"* (Augusta, GA: James L. Gow, 1868), 32, 43.

39. M.S., *The Adamic Race: Reply to "Ariel" . . . "[The Negro] is Not a Beast; He is a Human Being"—"He has an Immortal Soul; But Not After the Image of God"—"And Every Attempt to Civilize Him, After Our Form, Has Resulted in His Speedy and Certain Destruction"* (New York: Russell Brothers, 1868).

40. A. Hoyle Lester, *The Pre-Adamite, or Who Tempted Eve? Scripture and Science in Union as Respects the Antiquity of Man* (Philadelphia: J. B. Lippincott, 1875).

41. Charles Carroll, *"The Negro a Beast" or "In the Image of God"* (St. Louis, MO: American Book and Bible, 1900); Charles Carroll, *The Tempter of Eve; or, The Criminality of Man's Social, Political, and Religious Equality with the Negro, and the Amalgamation to Which These Crimes Inevitably Lead, Discussed in the Light of the Scriptures, the Sciences, Profane History, Tradition, and the Testimony of the Monuments* (St. Louis, MO: Adamic, 1902), xiv. The quotation is from the second of these works. Further consideration of such developments for the period 1870–1900 are found in Paul Harvey, *Freedom's Coming: Religious Culture and the Shaping of the South from the Civil War through the Civil Rights Era* (Chapel Hill: University of North Carolina Press, 2005), 41–44.

42. Livingstone, *Adam's Ancestors*, 197. Livingstone also documents the wide circulation of Carroll's work and similar volumes among modern advocates of Christian Identity or Kingdom Identity (214–18), which Kidd describes as "Identity's anthropology of race hatred and separation" (*Forging of Races*, 218).

43. Kidd, *Forging of Races*, 142–67; George M. Fredrickson, *Racism: A Short History* (Princeton, NJ: Princeton University Press, 2002), 66–95.

44. On how Darwin's evolutionary theories made him an opponent of slavery (since he believed humanity constituted only a single species) but open to eugenics (since the human species included "weaker and inferior" elements), see Adrian Desmond and James Moore, *Darwin's Sacred Cause: How a Hatred of Slavery Shaped Darwin's Views of Human Evolution* (Boston: Houghton Mifflin Harcourt, 2009), 368.

45. See chapter 19, 402.

46. For excellent treatment of how "the curse of Canaan" became more important with figures like Palmer after the Civil War as an explanation for Black inferiority, see Stephen R. Haynes, *Noah's Curse: The Biblical Justification of American Slavery* (New York: Oxford University Press, 2002), 112–14. This book also documents (passim) the staying power of that interpretation into the present, as does Paul Harvey, "God and Negroes and Sin and Salvation: Racism, Racial Interchange and Interracialism in Southern Religious History," in Schweiger and Mathews, *Religion in the American South*, 287–89.

47. Luke E. Harlow, *Race, Religion, and the Making of Confederate Kentucky* (New York: Cambridge University Press, 2014), 196–221; Luke E. Harlow, "The Long

Life of Proslavery Religion," in *The World the Civil War Made*, ed. Gregory P. Downs and Kate Masur (Chapel Hill: University of North Carolina Press, 2015), 132–58.

48. *The Distinctive Principles of the Presbyterian Church in the United States . . . as Set Forth in the Formal Declarations, and Illustrated by Extracts from Proceedings of the General Assembly* (1871), quoted in Harlow, *Religion, Race, and Confederate Kentucky*, 207.

49. A fair-minded biography is Sean Michael Lewis, *Robert Lewis Dabney: A Southern Presbyterian Life* (Phillipsburg, NJ: P&R, 2005).

50. Robert Lewis Dabney, "The Negro and the Common School" (1876), in *Discussions of Robert L. Dabney*, vol. 4: *Secular*, ed. C. R. Vaughan (Mexico, MO: S. B. Ervin, 1897), 185–86.

51. Harlow, "The Long Life of Proslavery Religion," 151–52.

52. Excellent on this controversy and related legal issues are Steven K. Green, *The Bible, the School, and the Constitution: The Clash That Shaped Modern Church-State Doctrine* (New York: Oxford University Press, 2012), 96–117; Linda Przybyszewski, "Scarlet Fever, Stanley Matthews, and the Cincinnati Bible War," *Journal of Supreme Court History* 42 (November 2017): 256–74, https://doi.org/10.1111/jsch.12153.

53. *The Bible and the Public Schools: Arguments in . . . the Superior Court of Cincinnati, with the Opinions and Decisions of the Court* (Cincinnati, OH: Robert Clark, 1870), 9 (Northwest Ordinance), 158 (state court rulings), 32–33 (Calvin Stowe and Horace Mann), 39, 290–321 (1852 Constitution), 150 ("Bible"), 55 ("infidelity").

54. *The Bible and the Public Schools*, 147 (Jefferson), 63 (no religious test), 94 (Christianity), 64, 122, 132 (sectarianism).

55. *The Bible and the Public Schools*, 146.

56. Matthews would later play a key role in supporting his friend Rutherford B. Hayes in the contested 1876 presidential election and even later be appointed to the U.S. Supreme Court; see Przybyszewski, "Scarlet Fever."

57. Stanley Matthews for the board, in *The Bible and the Public Schools*, 207, 228.

58. Matthews, in *The Bible and the Public Schools*, 282.

59. Matthews, in *The Bible and the Public Schools*, 257.

60. Matthews, in *The Bible and the Public Schools*, 213 (supremacy), 224 (Catholics), 226 (Jews), 271 (Westminster Confession), 273 (Presbyterianism). For this American revision, which removed the original's affirmation of a role for government in the churches, see "The Westminster Confession of Faith, 1647," in *Creeds and Confessions of Faith in the Christian Tradition*, vol. 2: *Reformation Era*, ed. Jaroslav Pelikan and Valerie Hotchkiss (New Haven, CT: Yale University Press, 2003), 636.

61. *The Bible and the Public Schools*, 351.

62. Green, *The Bible, the School, and the Constitution*, 116.

63. For this decision, see Joan DelFattore, *The Fourth R: Conflicts over Religion in America's Public Schools* (New Haven, CT: Yale University Press, 2004), 56–57; for the *obiter dicta* echoing Matthews, see Przybyszewski, "Scarlet Fever."

64. John R. McKivigan and Mitchell Snay, "Introduction," in *Religion and the Antebellum Debate over Slavery*, ed. John R. McKivigan and Mitchell Snay (Athens: University of Georgia Press, 1998), 14.

65. Gaines M. Foster, *Moral Reconstruction: Christian Lobbyists and the Federal Legislation of Morality, 1865–1920* (Chapel Hill: University of North Carolina Press, 2002), 2. See also Gaines M. Foster, "The End of Slavery and the Origins of the Bible Belt," in Poole and Blum, *Vale of Tears*, 147–63.

66. For an authoritative synthesis of previous studies, including his own important work, see W. J. Rorabaugh, *Prohibition: A Concise History* (New York: Oxford University Press, 2018).

67. One especially energetic advocate for these causes was Sylvester Graham, who eventually made his mark through dietary reform. See Jonathan Riddle, "Prospering Body and Soul: Health Reform, Religion, and Capitalism in Antebellum America" (Ph.D. diss., University of Notre Dame, 2019).

68. See Robert C. Fuller, *Religion and Wine: A Cultural History of Wine Drinking in the United States* (Knoxville: University of Tennessee Press, 1996), 78–90 and especially Jennifer L. Woodruff Tait, *The Poisoned Chalice: Eucharistic Grapejuice and Common-Sense Realism in Victorian Methodism* (Tuscaloosa: University of Alabama Press, 2011).

69. John L. Merrill, "The Bible and the American Temperance Movement: Text, Context, and Pretext," *Harvard Theological Review* 81 (1988): 145–70.

70. Quoted in Merrill, "The Bible and Temperance," 168.

71. See Elizabeth B. Leonard on Annie Wittenmyer in *ANB* and Ruth Bordin, *Frances Willard: A Biography* (Chapel Hill: University of North Carolina Press, 1986).

72. Annie Wittenmyer, *History of the Women's Temperance Crusade: A Complete Official History of the Wonderful Uprising of the Christian Women of the United States against the Liquor Traffic, which Culminated in the Gospel Temperance Movement* (Philadelphia, PA: Office of the Christian Woman, 1878), 5.

73. Willard, in *History of the Women's Temperance Crusade*, 13–16.

74. Wittenmyer, *History of the Women's Temperance Crusade*, 31, 38–41.

75. For helpful context, see Paul C. Gutjahr, "Diversification in American Religious Publishing"; Candy Gunter Brown, "Religious Periodicals and Their Textual Communities"; and Louise Stevenson, "Homes, Books, and Reading," all in *HISTORY OF THE BOOK*, 3:194–203, 270–78, 319–331.

76. Henry Otis Dwight, *The Centennial History of the American Bible Society*, 2 vols. (New York: Macmillan, 1916), 2:576–77.

77. Information on Bible editions for this decade are again from the indispensable Margaret Hills, *ENGLISH BIBLE*, 266–87 (#1795–#1913); for the Holman Bible, 280 (#1874).

78. *WORLDCAT*: New York (eleven editions), Philadelphia (seven), Boston (three), Chicago (two), Cincinnati (two), New Haven (one).

79. Brown, "Religious Periodicals," 272.

80. Jeffrey D. Groves, "Periodicals and Serial Publication: Introduction," in *HISTORY OF THE BOOK*, 3:226–27.

81. Gutjahr, "Diversification," 200.

82. Gutjahr, "Diversification," 200.

83. Hills, *ENGLISH BIBLE*, 270 (#1817); see also Philip L. Barlow, *Mormons and the Bible: The Place of the Latter-day Saints in American Religion* (New York: Oxford University Press, 1991), 153–54.

Chapter 23

1. The Centennial is well positioned in the events of the year by Dee Brown, *The Year of the Century: 1876* (New York: Charles Scribner's Sons, 1966).

2. Excellent on the Blaine Amendment are Steven K. Green, *The Second Disestablishment: Church and State in Nineteenth-Century America* (New York: Oxford University Press, 2010), 289–311; Thomas C. Berg, "Disestablishment from Blaine to *Everson*: Federalism, School Wars, and the Emerging Modern State," in *No Establishment of Religion: America's Original Contribution to Religious Liberty*, ed. T. Jeremy Gunn and John Witte Jr. (New York: Oxford University Press, 2012), 312–28 (entire chapter, 307–40).

3. The complicated political maneuvering of the year is well treated in Roy Morris Jr., *Fraud of the Century: Rutherford B. Hayes, Samuel Tilden, and the Stolen Election of 1876* (New York: Simon & Schuster, 2003).

4. Robert T. Handy, *Undermined Establishment: Church-State Relations in America, 1880–1920* (Princeton, NJ: Princeton University Press, 1991), 4.

5. Quoted in Susan Jacoby, *The Great Agnostic: Robert Ingersoll and American Free Thought* (New Haven, CT: Yale University Press, 2013), 59

6. Quotations in Green, *Second Disestablishment*, 292 (Grant), 295 (the amendment).

7. Quoted in Berg, "Disestablishment," 315.

8. Quoted in Green, *Second Disestablishment*, 298.

9. Eric T. Brandt and Timothy Larsen, "The Old Atheism Revisited: Robert G. Ingersoll and the Bible," *Journal of the Historical Society* 11 (June 2011): 225. On Ingersoll's speeches before 1876, see Jacoby, *The Great Agnostic*, 57–58.

10. J. S. Ingram, *The Centennial Exposition, Described and Illustrated* (Philadelphia, PA: Hubbard Brothers, 1876), 86–87.

11. Ingram, *Centennial Exposition*, 80, 86.

12. Quoted in Brown, *Year of the Century*, 127 (113–33 has a lively description of events on opening day).

13. Brown, *Year of the Century*, 129.

14. Brown, *Year of the Century*, 141.

15. Ingram, *Centennial Exhibition*, 710.

16. "Search the Scriptures: for in them ye think ye have eternal life: John v-39. All Scripture is given by inspiration of God. I Timothy iii-16. The word of the Lord endureth for ever. I Peter i-25. Thy word is a lamp unto my feet, and a light unto my path. Psalm cxix-105." Free Library of Philadelphia Digital Collections, "A. J. Holman & Co.'s Exhibit: Main Building," accessed August 27, 2020, https://libwww.freelibrary.org/digital/item/1620.

17. For the edition displayed at the centennial, see Hills, *ENGLISH BIBLE*, 285 (#1902).

18. For events of the day, see Brown, *Year of the Centenary*, 165–66; Morris, *Fraud of the Century*, 126–27.

19. Brown, *Year of the Centenary*, 290.

20. Elizabeth Cady Stanton, Susan B. Anthony, and Matilda Joslyn Gage, eds., *History of Woman Suffrage*, vol. 1: *1848–1881* (New York: Fowler and Wells, 1881), 70–72.

21. Library of Congress, "Declaration of Rights of the Women of the United States by the National Woman Suffrage Association, July 4th, 1876," accessed January 11, 2021, https://www.loc.gov/resource/rbpe.16000300/.

22. More research would be welcome concerning religious commentary on the 1876 election. In a rapid perusal of the following I found fairly extensive reporting on the developing political story, but no discussion relating current events to biblical first principles: the weekly *Christian Union* out of New York City, edited by Lyman Abbott and Henry Ward Beecher; *The Christian Recorder* of the AME Church; and the *Methodist Quarterly Review*, which in each issue included an informative report on the contents of several other religious quarterlies.

23. Nicholas Lemann, *Redemption: The Last Battle of the Civil War* (New York: Farrar, Straus and Giroux, 2006).

24. Morris, *Fraud of the Century*, 227, 237.

25. David Hempton, *Evangelical Disenchantment: Nine Portraits of Faith and Doubt* (New Haven, CT: Yale University Press, 2008), 113.

26. Brown, *Year of the* Century, 143–44. Especially helpful on Julia Smith and her family are Susan J. Shaw, *A Religious History of Julia Evelina Smith's 1876 Translation of the Holy Bible* (Newburgh, IN: Multiple Ministries, 1993) and Emily Sampson, *With Her Own Eyes: The Story of Julia Smith, Her Life and Her Bible* (Knoxville: University of Tennessee Press, 2006).

27. Quoted in Sampson, *With Her Own Eyes*, 58.

28. Shaw, *Religious History*, 116.

29. The prices are specified in Elizabeth Cady Stanton, comp., *The Woman's Bible, Part I, Comments on Genesis, Exodus, Leviticus, Numbers, Deuteronomy* (New York: European Publishing, 1895), 151.

30. Julia Smith, trans., *The Holy Bible: Containing the Old and New Testaments; Translated Literally from the Original Tongues* (Hartford, CT: American Publishing, 1876), preface. For details, see Hills, *ENGLISH BIBLE*, 288–89 (#1918).

31. Frances Ellen Burr, quoted in Stanton, *The Woman's Bible, Part I*, 149.

32. On how that pamphlet illustrates the general irrelevance of straightforward biblical advocacy for the suffrage effort, see Kathi Kern, *Mrs. Stanton's Bible* (Ithaca, NY: Cornell University Press, 2001), 123.

33. Excellent on the person, the book, and its contexts is Kern, *Mrs. Stanton's Bible*. Also helpful for positioning Stanton for a history of the Bible is Priscilla Pope-Levison, "Stanton, Elizabeth Cady (1815–1902)," in *Handbook of Women Biblical Interpreters*, ed. Marion Ann Taylor and Agnes Choi (Grand Rapids, MI: Baker, 2012), 469–73.

34. Stanton's reliance on contemporary science (and contemporary scientific racism) helps explain her evolving attitudes toward African Americans. For her approval of

A. D. White's 1896 *History of the Warfare of Science and Theology* and its opinion that "the Bible . . . has been the great block in the way of civilization," see Elizabeth Cady Stanton, *The Woman's Bible, Part II, Comments on the Old and New Testament from Joshua to Revelation* (New York: European Publishing, 1898), 9. On her racial views, see Kern, *Mrs. Stanton's Bible*, 106–16.

35. For this prosopography, see James H. Smylie, "'The Woman's Bible' and the Spiritual Crisis," *Soundings* 59 (Fall 1976): 305–28.

36. Stanton, "Introduction," in *Woman's Bible*, 1:8–9.

37. Stanton, *Woman's Bible*, 1:14.

38. Stanton, "Preface," in *Woman's Bible*, 2:8.

39. Lucinda B. Chandlar, on 1 Tim 2:11, in Stanton, *Woman's Bible*, 2:162.

40. Stanton, *Woman's Bible*, 2:185.

41. On Stanton's motives and the great range of opinions her questions elicited, see Kern, *Mrs. Stanton's Bible*, 213–16.

42. Aileen S. Kraditor, *The Ideas of the Woman Suffrage Movement, 1890–1920* (New York: Columbia University Press, 1965), 77.

43. Stanton, *Woman's* Bible, 2:213 (Ingersoll), 2:212 (Blackwell), 2:199 (Livermore).

44. Stanton, *Woman's Bible*, 2:200–201.

45. Stanton, *Woman's* Bible, 2:215–17.

46. Helpful on Protestant women and religion in this era are Nancy Hardesty, Lucille Sider Dayton, and Donald W. Dayton, "Women in the Holiness Movement: Feminism in the Evangelical Tradition," in *Women of Spirit: Female Leadership in the Jewish and Christian Traditions*, ed. Rosemary Ruether and Eleanor McLaughlin (New York: Simon and Schuster, 1979), 225–54; Barbara Brown Zikmund, "Biblical Arguments and Women's Place in the Church," in *The Bible and Social Reform*, ed. Ernest R. Sandeen (Philadelphia, PA: Fortress, 1982), 85–104; Donna A. Behnke, *Religious Issues in Nineteenth-Century Feminism* (Troy, NY: Whiston, 1982), chapter 8 ("The Female Exegetes") and chapter 13 ("The Weight of Biblical Evidence"); Margaret Bendroth, "The Disenchantment of Women: Gender and Religion at the Turn of the Century (1865–1930)," in *Figures in the Carpet: Finding the Human Person in the American Past*, ed. Wilfred M. McClay (Grand Rapids, MI: Eerdmans, 2007), 162–84.

47. On Anthony, see Ann D. Gordon, in *ANB*.

48. Willard quoted in Kern, *Mrs. Stanton's Bible*, 120–21.

49. Anthony to Stanton, December 2, 1898, quoted in Kraditor, *Ideas of the Woman Suffrage Movement*, 78.

50. Carolyn Osiek, "The Feminist and the Bible: Hermeneutical Alternatives," in *Feminist Perspectives on Biblical Scholarship*, ed. Adela Yarbro Collins (Chico, CA: Scholar's Press, 1985), 93–106.

51. Helen H. Gardener, *Men, Women, and Gods, and Other Lectures*, 12th ed. (New York: Truth Seeker, 1885), 79. I thank Kimberly Hamlin for introducing me to Gardener.

52. Specifically on her engagement with Scripture, see Nancy A. Hardesty, "Willard, Frances Elizabeth (1839–98)," in Taylor and Choi, *Women Biblical Interpreters*, 533–37.

53. Frances Elizabeth Willard, *Women in the Pulpit* (Boston: D. Lothrop, 1888), 23–24, 31. Willard, however, weakened the force of her analogy (23) by asserting that a consensus now held that wine in the Bible had been "unfermented." This claim was doomed to the same fate as Theodore Dwight Weld's argument that the New Testament's *doulos* mean only "servant." As we have also seen, appeals to Onesimus and Canaan concerning Black people were by no means dead.

54. Agnes Choi, "Meyer, Lucy Rider (1849–1922)," in Taylor and Choi, *Women Biblical Interpreters*, 364–66.

55. Erin Vearncombe, "Phelps, Elizabeth Stuart (1844–1911)," in Taylor and Choi, *Women Biblical Interpreters*, 409 (entire article, 407–9).

56. Louise Seymour Houghton, *Hebrew Life and Thought: Being Interpretive Studies in the Literature of Israel* (Chicago: University of Chicago Press, 1906), 359–60, quoted in Gordon Oeste, "Houghton, Louise Seymour (1838–1920)," in Taylor and Choi, *Women Biblical Interpreters*, 267–68.

57. For the latter, see Margaret Lamberts Bendroth, *Fundamentalism and Gender, 1875 to the Present* (New Haven, CT: Yale University Press, 1994) and Betty A. DeBerg, *Ungodly Women: Gender and the First Wave of American Fundamentalism* (Minneapolis, MN: Fortress, 1990).

58. Quoted in Barbara Welter, "Something Remains to Dare: Introduction," in *The Original Feminist Attack on the Bible (The Woman's Bible)* (New York: Arno/New York Times, 1974), xv–xvi. For conservative use of the Bible against women's reforms, a good summary is found Behnke, *Religious Issues in Nineteenth-Century Feminism*, 221–44.

59. See Joy A. J. Howard, "Julia A. J. Foote (1823–1901)," *Legacy* 23 (2006): 86–93,

60. Julia A. J. Foote, *A Brand Plucked from the Fire: An Autobiographical Sketch by Mrs. Julia A. J. Foote (1886), in Spiritual Narratives*, ed. Sue E. Houchins (New York: Oxford University Press, 1988), 32 (Revelation), 46–47 (Ezekiel), 61 (Isaiah), 68 (the angel).

61. The career of Amanda Berry Smith followed Julia Foote with a complete immersion in Scripture, but with her memorable career extending beyond the United States to Britain, the Continent, India, and Liberia. See Amanda Smith, *An Autobiography: The Story of the Lord's Dealing with Mrs. Amanda Smith the Colored Evangelist* (1893), with a helpful introduction by Jualynne E. Dodson (New York: Oxford University Press, 1988) and Eric Brandt, "Smith, Amanda Berry (1837–1915)," in Taylor and Choi, *Women Biblical Interpreters*, 450–52.

62. John G. Stackhouse Jr., "Women in Public Ministry in Twentieth-Century Canadian and American Evangelicalism: Five Models," *Studies in Religion/Sciences Religieuses* 17 (Fall 1988): 471–85.

63. See Dana Lee Robert, *American Women in Mission: A Social History of Their Thought and Practice* (Macon, GA: Mercer University Press, 1996) and Karen E. Smith, "Beyond Public and Private Spheres: Another Look at Women in Baptist History and Historiography," *Baptist Quarterly* 34 (1991): 79–87.

64. See Virginia Lieson Brereton, *Training God's Army: The American Bible School, 1880–1940* (Bloomington: Indiana University Press, 1990) and Jeanette Hassey, *No Time for*

Silence: Evangelical Women in Public Ministry around the Turn of the Century (Grand Rapids, MI: Zondervan, 1986).

65. See Edith L. Blumhofer, ed., "Women and American Pentecostalism," *Pneuma* 17 (Spring 1995): 19–87; Grant Wacker, *Heaven Below: Early Pentecostals and American Culture* (Cambridge, MA: Harvard University Press, 2001), 103–4, 144; Cheryl Townsend Gilkes, "'Together and in Harness': Women's Traditions in the Sanctified Church," *Signs* 10 (Summer 1985): 678–99

66. Brown, *Year of the Century*, 171 (Custer), 54 (*Tom Sawyer*), 257 (Barnum), 188 (James), 193 (Lincoln), and 302 (the ALA).

Chapter 24

1. For positioning the latter decades of the nineteenth century I have benefited especially from Robert H. Wiebe, *The Search for Order, 1877–1920* (New York: Hill and Wang, 1967); William R. Hutchison, *The Modernist Impulse in American Protestantism* (Cambridge, MA: Harvard University Press, 1976); George M. Marsden, *Fundamentalism and American Culture: The Shaping of Twentieth-Century American Evangelicalism, 1875–1925* (New York: Oxford University Press, 1980); James Turner, *Without God, without Creed: The Origins of Unbelief in America* (Baltimore, MD: Johns Hopkins University Press, 1985); Martin E. Marty, *Modern American Religion*, vol. 1: *The Irony of It All, 1893–1919* (Chicago: University of Chicago Press, 1986); Robert T. Handy, *Undermined Establishment: Church-State Relations in America, 1880–1920* (Princeton, NJ: Princeton University Press, 1991); Gary Dorrien, *The Making of American Liberal Theology: Imagining Progressive Religion, 1805–1900* (Louisville, KY: Westminster/John Knox, 2001); Gary Dorrien, *The Making of American Liberal Theology: Idealism, Realism, and Modernity, 1900–1950* (Louisville, KY: Westminster/John Knox, 2003); James Turner, *Philology: The Forgotten Origins of the Modern Humanities* (Princeton, NJ: Princeton University Press, 2015).

2. An excellent survey is provided in Paul Harvey, *Freedom's Coming: Religious Culture and the Shaping of the South from the Civil War through the Civil Rights Era* (Chapel Hill: University of North Carolina Press, 2005).

3. That is, in South Carolina, North Carolina, Virginia, Florida, Tennessee, Texas, Kentucky. See Edwin Scott Gaustad and Philip L. Barlow, *New Historical Atlas of Religion in America* (New York: Oxford University Press, 2001), 376–81 (section C.17).

4. In 1920, the Republican Warren G. Harding eked out a narrow victory over the Democrat James Cox in Tennessee. See *PRESIDENTIAL ELECTIONS*, 136; and for broader treatment of these political-denominational affinities, Mark A. Noll, *God and Race in American Politics: A Short History* (Princeton, NJ: Princeton University Press, 2008).

5. For this distinction, I am indebted to Laura Rominger Porter, "From Sin to Crime: Evangelicals and the Public Moral Order in the Nineteenth-Century Upper South" (Ph.D. diss., University of Notre Dame, 2013).

6. Bill J. Leonard, *God's Last and Only Hope: The Fragmentation of the Southern Baptist Convention* (Grand Rapids, MI: Eerdmans, 1990), 15.

7. Paul Harvey, "'That Was about Equalization after Freedom': Southern Evangelicalism and the Politics of Reconstruction and Redemption, 1861–1900," in *Vale of Tears: New Essays on Religion and Reconstruction*, ed. Edward J. Blum and Scott Poole (Macon, GA: Mercer University Press, 2005), 76–77. On various uses of "redemption," all with Christian overtones, see also Daniel W. Stowell, *Rebuilding Zion: The Religious Reconstruction of the South, 1863–1877* (New York: Oxford University Press, 1998), 155; David W. Blight, *Race and Reunion: The Civil War in American Memory* (Cambridge, MA: Harvard University Press, 2001), 130, 358; Nicholas Lemann, *Redemption: The Last Battle of the Civil War* (New York: Farrar, Straus and Giroux, 2006).

8. Harvey, *Freedom's Coming*, 54.

9. See Frederick V. Mills, "Atticus G. Haygood (1839–1896)," in *New Georgia Encyclopedia*, accessed October 15, 2020, https://www.georgiaencyclopedia.org/articles/arts-culture/atticus-g-haygood-1839-1896; Elizabeth L. Jemison, *Christian Citizens: Reading the Bible in Black and White in the Postemancipation South* (Chapel Hill: University of North Carolina Press, 2020), 113–15, 128–29.

10. Atticus G. Haygood, *Our Brother in Black: His Freedom and His Future* (Nashville, TN: Southern Methodist Publishing House, 1881), 28–29 (wrath of men), 45 (truth makes free, Jn 8:32), 73 (Nehemiah), 195 (defraud, Lev 19:13).

11. From the *New Orleans Christian Advocate* (1882), quoted in Jemison, *Christian Citizens*, 114.

12. Quoted in Luke E. Harlow, *Religion, Race, and the Making of Confederate Kentucky, 1830–1880* (New York: Cambridge University Press, 2014), 222.

13. Insightful on this Methodist transition is Roger Robins, "Vernacular American Landscape: Methodists, Camp Meetings, and Social Respectability," *Religion and American Culture* 4 (Summer 1994): 165–91.

14. Quoted in Homer L. Calkin, "The Methodists and the Centennial of 1876," *Methodist History* 14 (June 1976): 101, 103.

15. W. J. Rorabaugh, *Prohibition: A Concise History* (New York: Oxford University Press, 2018), 28, 30, 39, 42, 63.

16. Handy, *Undermined Establishment*, 121–23.

17. See Jean Miller Schmidt, "Reexamining the Public/Private Split: Reforming the Continent and Spreading Scriptural Holiness," in *Perspectives on American Methodism: Interpretive Essays*, ed. Russell E. Richey, Kenneth E. Rowe, and Jean Miller Schmidt (Nashville, TN: Kingswood, 1993), 228–47.

18. See Gary Scott Smith, *Religion in the Oval Office: The Religious Lives of American Presidents* (New York: Oxford University Press, 2015), chapter 5 ("William McKinley: America as God's Instrument").

19. Sunday School lesson and Anon., "The Bible as a Text Book in Our Literary Institutions," *Sunday-School Journal*, new ser. 21 (October 27, 1889), 394–96.

20. Melvin E. Dieter, *The Holiness Revival of the Nineteenth Century*, 2nd ed. (Lanham, MD: Scarecrow, 1996).

21. For fuller consideration of this postbellum history, see Gary Scott Smith, *The Seeds of Secularization: Calvinism, Culture, and Pluralism in America, 1870–1915* (Grand Rapids, MI: Eerdmans, 1985) and Mark A. Noll, "Theology, Presbyterian History, and the Civil War," *Journal of Presbyterian History* 89 (Spring/Summer 2011): 5–16.

22. For excellent orientation, see James H. Moorhead, *American Apocalypse: Yankee Protestants and the Civil War, 1860–1869* (New Haven, CT: Yale University Press, 1978) and Lewis G. Vandervelde, *The Presbyterian Churches and the Federal Union, 1861–1869* (Cambridge, MA: Harvard University Press, 1932).

23. Luke E. Harlow, *Religion, Race, and Confederate Kentucky* (New York: Cambridge University Press, 2014), 201–5; Lucas P. Volkman, *House Divided: Evangelical Schisms and the Crisis of the Union in Missouri* (New York: Oxford University Press, 2018), 207–9.

24. For these changes, see *The Book of Confessions* (Louisville, KY: Office of the General Assembly, 2002), 160–64. The "missions" addition accompanied the expansion of American overseas missionary activity; the declaration on infants responded to the sentimentalization of death that the Civil War encouraged, as described in Drew Gilpin Faust, *The Republic of Suffering: Death and the American Civil War* (New York: Knopf, 2008).

25. R. V. Hunter, "The Church and the Masses," *Presbyterian and Reformed Review* 4 (1893): 78–93.

26. For illuminating context, see James D. Bratt, *Abraham Kuyper: Modern Calvinist, Christian Democrat* (Grand Rapids, MI: Eerdmans, 1998).

27. Quoted in Smith, *Seeds of Secularization*, 59. See also Gaines Foster, *Moral Reconstruction: Christian Lobbyists and the Federal Legislation of Morality, 1865–1920* (Chapel Hill: University of North Carolina Press, 2002). A fact worth noting is that the denominations promoting the National Reform Organization (Reformed Presbyterians, United Presbyterians, Wesleyan Methodists, Free Methodists, United Brethren) had, with Quakers, also been the most consistent opponents of slavery.

28. For example, David G. Wylie, "Three Views of the Public School Question," *Presbyterian and Reformed Review* 1 (1890): 465ff. For context, see Smith, *Seeds of Secularization*, 85–89.

29. As examples, see D. H. MacVicar, "Abjuration of Romanism," *Presbyterian and Reformed Review* 5 (1894): 303ff.; and against Mormons, William M. Sloane, "Christianity and Tolerance," *Presbyterian and Reformed Review* 2 (1891): 235ff.

30. Molly Oshatz, *Slavery and Sin: The Fight against Slavery and the Rise of Liberal Protestantism* (New York: Oxford University Press, 2012), 101. See Grant Wacker, "The Demise of Biblical Civilization," in Hatch and Noll, *BIBLE IN AMERICA*, 121–38. For a further examination of progressive moral sensibility, see Margaret Abruzzo, *Polemical Pain: Slavery, Cruelty, and the Rise of Humanitarianism* (Baltimore, MD: Johns Hopkins University Press, 2011).

31. Holifield, *THEOLOGY IN AMERICA*, 178–81; Noll, *AMERICA'S GOD*, 233–38.

32. Wacker, "Demise of Biblical Civilization," 124–26 (my emphasis on "wholly").

33. Dorrien, *American Liberal Theology, 1805–1900*, xvi.

34. Oshatz, *Slavery and Sin*, 4.

35. William E. Channing, "The Moral Argument against Calvinism," in *The Works of William E. Channing, D.D.*, 5 vols. (Boston: James Munroe, 1841), 1:218 (entire article 217–41). See Dorrien, *American Liberal Theology, 1805–1900*, 38.

36. Oshatz, *Slavery and Sin*, 100.

37. These articles appeared in *Bibliotheca Sacra* 29 (January 1872): 114–56 and 29 (October 1872): 602–22. See Oshatz, *Slavery and Sin*, 116–17, 171nn51–54.

38. In 1879 Theodore Munger, pastor of the Congregational Church in North Adams, Massachusetts, made about the same point in a celebratory memorial for William Lloyd Garrison. See Oshatz, *Slavery and* Sin, 120–21.

39. Newman Smyth, *Old Faiths in New Light* (New York: Charles Scribner's Sons, 1879), 105–8, 118 (progressive revelation), 116 (mystery). See Oshatz, *Slavery and Sin*, 127.

40. Charles Augustus Briggs, *Biblical Study, Its Principles, Methods, and History* (New York: Charles Scribner's Sons, 1883), 186; Oshatz, *Slavery and Sin*, 139.

41. Charles Jefferson, *Christianity and International Peace* (New York: Thomas Y. Crowell, 1915), 60–61, 68–69. I thank Raully Donahue for this citation.

42. William Newton Clarke, author in 1898 of "the first systematic theology from an American liberal perspective" (Dorrien, *American Liberal Theology, 1805–1900*, 406), cited "moral difficulties" from the Old Testament as supporting his conclusion that the New Testament "writers, instead of being final authorities concerning divine truth, were fellow interpreters of the gospel within himself and with all Christians." But he did not mention slavery specifically as one of those difficulties. William Newton Clarke, *Sixty Years with the Bible* (New York: Charles Scribner's Sons, 1909), 226, 91.

43. Lyman Abbott, *Reminiscences* (New York: Charles Scribner's Sons, 1909), 447–51, 461. For Abbott's deep investment in values keyed to American developments, see Benjamin J. Wetzel, *American Crusade: Christianity, Warfare, and National Identity, 1860–1920* (Ithaca, NY: Cornell University Press, 2022).

44. Channing, "Moral Argument against Calvinism," 240.

45. These nineteenth-century developments are detailed in Turner, *Without God*; Bruce Kuklick, *Churchmen and Philosophers: From Jonathan Edwards to John Dewey* (New Haven, CT: Yale University Press, 1985); George M. Marsden, "The Collapse of Evangelical Academia," in *Faith and Rationality: Reason and Belief in God*, ed. Alvin Plantinga and Nicholas Wolterstorff (Notre Dame, IN: University of Notre Dame Press, 1984), 219–64; Mark Noll, "The Rise and Long Life of the Protestant Enlightenment in America," in *Knowledge and Belief in America: Enlightenment Traditions and Modern Religious Thought*, ed. William M. Shea and Peter A. Huff (New York: Cambridge University Press, 1994), 88–124.

46. Louis Menand, *The Metaphysical Club* (New York: Farrar, Straus, and Giroux, 2001). See also George M. Fredrickson, *The Inner Civil War: Northern Intellectuals and the*

Crisis of the Union (New York: Harper & Row, 1965) and Anne C. Rose, *Victorian America and the Civil War* (New York: Cambridge University Press, 1992).

47. Higginson quoted in Turner, *Philology*, 370–17.

48. Toy, quoted in Mikeal C. Parsons, *Crawford Howell Toy: The Man, the Scholar, the Teacher* (Macon GA: Mercer University Press, 2019), 146–47.

49. Harper, quoted in Michael Lee, "Higher Criticism and Higher Education at the University of Chicago: William Rainey Harper's Vision of Religion in the Research University," *History of Education Quarterly* 48 (November 2008): 528–29 (entire article, 508–33). On the Harper-Moody friendship, see Lyle W. Dorsett, *A Passion for Souls: The Life of D. L. Moody* (Chicago: Moody, 1997), 366–67.

50. On Briggs's relative conservatism, see Dorrien, *American Liberal Theology, 1805–1900*, 369–70.

51. On Tholuck and his American influence, see Annette G. Aubert, *The German Roots of Nineteenth-Century American Theology* (New York: Oxford University Press, 2013) and Andrew Hansen, "Geschichte und Glaube: Protestant Theologians and the Problem of History" (Ph.D. diss, University of Notre Dame, 2013). On Dorner, see Dorrien, *American Liberal Theology, 1805–1900*, 284–90.

52. On that later influence from Ritschl, see Dorrien, *American Liberal Theology, 1805–1900*, 335–36.

53. See Richard A. Muller, "Henry Boynton Smith: Christocentric Theologian," *Journal of Presbyterian History* 61 (Winter 1983): 429–44; George M. Marsden on Smith, in *ANB*.

54. Of many useful studies, see Stephen R. Graham, *Cosmos in the Chaos: Philip Schaff's Interpretation of Nineteenth-Century American Religion* (Grand Rapids, MI: Eerdmans, 1995) and David R. Bains, "Philip Schaff and the Place of the Bible in the Organic Development of Protestantism," paper delivered at symposium "The Bible and the Reformation," Baylor University, October 2017.

55. Wacker, "Demise of Biblical Civilization," 133.

56. See Grant Wacker, *Augustus H. Strong and the Dilemma of Historical Consciousness* (Macon, GA: Mercer University Press, 1985) and William E. Ellis, *A Man of Books and a Man of the People: E. Y. Mullins and the Crisis of Moderate Southern Baptists Leadership* (Macon, GA: Mercer University Press, 1985).

57. Hodge quoted from 1872 in A. A. Hodge, *The Life of Charles Hodge* (New York: Charles Scribner's Sons, 1880), 521.

58. See especially Paul C. Gutjahr, *Charles Hodge: Guardian of American Orthodoxy* (New York: Oxford University Press, 2011) and Andrew Hoffecker, *Charles Hodge: The Pride of Princeton* (Phillipsburg, NJ: P&R, 2011).

59. See Gary L. W. Johnson, ed., *B. B. Warfield: Essays on His Life and Work* (Phillipsburg, NJ: P&R, 2007).

60. Benjamin Breckinridge Warfield, "A Calm View of the Freedman's Case," *Church at Home and Abroad*, January 1887, 62–65; and an essay including opposition to scientific or biblically grounded racism, "On the Antiquity and Unity of the Human Race," *Princeton Theological Review* 9 (1911): 1–25. See Bradley J. Gundlach, "'Wicked Caste': Warfield, Biblical Authority, and Jim Crow," in Johnson, *B. B. Warfield*, 136–69;

and, for comparison, Dorrien, *American Liberal Theology, 1805–1900*, 409 ("cultural racism captured all but a few Christian progressives").

61. For an example, see Warfield's critique of a book that followed the proof-text gathering procedure to explain Christian doctrine: review of R. A. Torrey's *What the Bible Teaches, Presbyterian and Reformed Review* 39 (1899): 562–64.

62. Geerhardus Vos, *Reformed Dogmatics*, 5 vols., trans. Richard B. Gaffin (Bellingham, WA: Lexham, 2013–16).

Chapter 25

1. On the New Year's Eve meetings, see Dee Brown, *The Year of the Century: 1876* (New York: Charles Scribner's Sons, 1966), 30–31. Solid biographies include James F. Findlay Jr., *Dwight L. Moody: American Evangelist, 1837–1899* (Chicago: University of Chicago Press, 1969) and Lyle W. Dorsett, *A Passion for Souls: The Life of D. L. Moody* (Chicago: Moody, 1997).

2. Washington Gladden, *Working People and Their Employers* (Boston: Lockwood, Brooks, 1876), 3.

3. "Obituary—John Hubbard," *Christian Cynosure*, February 24, 1876, quoted in Richard S. Taylor, "Beyond Immediate Emancipation: Jonathan Blanchard, Abolitionism, and the Emergence of American Fundamentalism," *Civil War History* 27 (1981): 270. Especially helpful for Blanchard are this article (260–74); Richard S. Taylor, "Seeking the Kingdom: A Study in the Career of Jonathan Blanchard, 1811–1892" (Ph.D. diss., Northern Illinois University, 1977); and George M. Marsden, *Fundamentalism and American Culture: The Shaping of Twentieth-Century Evangelicalism, 1870–1925* (New York: Oxford University Press, 1980), 27–32.

4. On this meeting, see Marsden, *Fundamentalism and American Culture*, 46; and for wider contexts, Ernest R. Sandeen, *The Roots of Fundamentalism: British and American Millenarianism, 1800–1930* (Chicago: University of Chicago Press, 1970) and C. Norman Kraus, *Dispensationalism in America* (Richmond, VA: John Knox, 1958).

5. Charles A. Briggs, *Address by Charles A. Briggs, D.D., on Occasion of his Inauguration* (New York: Brooks & Sherwood, 1876).

6. Asa Gray, *Darwiniana: Essays and Reviews Pertaining to Darwinism* (New York: D. Appleton, 1876).

7. Jonathan Blanchard, *A Perfect State of Society: Address before the "Society of Inquiry" in Oberlin Collegiate Institute* (Oberlin, OH: James Steele, 1839), quoted in Marsden, *Fundamentalism and American Culture*, 27.

8. *A Debate on Slavery, held on the First, Second, Third, and Sixth Days of October, 1845, in the City of Cincinnati, between Rev. J. Blanchard . . . and [Pastor] N. L. Rice* (Cincinnati, OH: W. H. Moore, 1846), 44.

9. Gladden, *Working People*, 31(Christ), 165 (strong drink), 43 (Golden Rule), 51 (power), 47–48 (affectioned).

10. See the section "Second Coming, Millennialism," in *The Cotton Mather Reader*, ed. Reiner Smolkinski and Kenneth P. Minkema (New Haven, CT: Yale University Press, 2022). For context in the second half of the nineteenth century, see James H. Morehead, *World without End: Mainstream American Protestant Visions of the Last Things, 1880–1925* (Bloomington: University of Indiana Press, 1999).

11. On Moody's focus on personal salvation, concern for social renewal flowing from personal regeneration, and silence on labor-industrial strife, see Findlay, *Moody*, 303–9; Dorsett, *Life of Moody*, 264–67; Heath W. Carter, *Union Made: Working People and the Rise of Social Christianity in Chicago* (New York: Oxford University Press, 2015), 81–82.

12. Dorsett, *Life of Moody*, 111, 126, 246.

13. On that late-life reversal, perhaps responding to direct criticism from Ida B. Wells, see Edward J. Blum, *Reforging the White Republic: Race, Religion, and American Nationalism, 1865–1898* (Baton Rouge: Louisiana State University Press, 2005), 143–44.

14. This paragraph depends on Randall J. Stephens, "From Abolitionists to Fundamentalists: The Transformation of the Wesleyan Methodists in the Nineteenth and Twentieth Centuries," *American Nineteenth Century History*, October 2015, 1–33, https://www.tandfonline.com/doi/full/10.1080/14664658.2015.1078141.

15. Taylor, "Beyond Immediate Emancipation," 270.

16. See Henry R. May, *Protestant Churches and Industrial America* (New York: Harper and Brothers, 1949); Howard Hopkins, *The Rise of the Social Gospel in American Protestantism, 1865–1915* (New Haven, CT: Yale University Press, 1940); Ronald C. White Jr., *Liberty and Justice for All: Racial Reform and the Social Gospel* (San Francisco, CA: Harper and Row, 1990); Gary Dorrien, *The Making of American Liberal Theology: Idealism, Realism, and Modernity, 1900–1950* (Louisville, KY: Westminster/John Knox, 2003), 73–150.

17. On that biblical grounding, see Christopher H. Evans, *The Kingdom Is Always but Coming: A Life of Walter Rauschenbusch* (Grand Rapids, MI: Eerdmans, 2004), 175–90, 276–83; Dorrien, *American Liberal Theology, 1900–1950*, 89–93, 98–105; Max Stackhouse, "Introduction," in *Walter Rauschenbusch: The Righteousness of the Kingdom* (Nashville, TN: Abingdon, 1968), 45–59.

18. See Jama Lazerow, *Religion and the Working Class in Antebellum America* (Washington, D.C.: Smithsonian Institute Press, 1995) and William R. Sutton, *Journeymen for Jesus: Evangelical Artisans Confront Capitalism in Jacksonian Baltimore* (University Park: Pennsylvania State University Press, 1998).

19. The next paragraphs depend especially on Carter, *Union Made*. But see also Ken Fones-Wolf, *Trade Union Gospel: Christianity and Labor in Industrial Philadelphia, 1865–1915* (Philadelphia, PA: Temple University Press, 1989) and William A. Mirola, *Redeeming Time: Protestantism and Chicago's Eight Hour Movement, 1866–1912* (Champaign: University of Illinois Press, 2015).

20. Cameron, quoted in Carter, *Union Made*, 40 (American republic), 47 (Psalms and Luke), 48 (against Gladden), 85 (Master).

21. McChesney, quoted in Carter, *Union Made*, 40.

22. August Spies, quoted in Carter, *Union Made*, 73.

23. Carter, *Union Made*, 120–24.

24. My thanks to Heath Carter for these references from the *Tribune*.

25. Quotations in Carter, *Union Made*, 39 (Rev. Wm. Patton), 86 (Albert Parsons).

26. For a fully contextualized account of this controversy, see James Turner, *Philology: The Forgotten Origins of the Modern Humanities* (Princeton, NJ: Princeton University Press, 2014), 364–68.

27. David N. Livingstone, "Finding Revelation in Anthropology: Alexander Winchell, William Robertson Smith, and the Heretical Imperative," *British Journal for the History of Science* 48 (September 2015): 435–54.

28. See Mikeal C. Parsons, *Crawford Howell Toy: The Man, the Scholar, the Teacher* (Macon, GA: Mercer University Press, 2019); and for context Turner, *Philology*, 217. This section has benefited especially from viewing American disputes over biblical higher criticism within the much broader intellectual history provided in Turner, *Philology*. Some of the excellent scholarship on these subjects is discussed in Mark A. Noll, *Between Faith and Criticism: Evangelicals, Scholarship, and the Bible in America*, 3rd ed. (Vancouver: Regent College, 2004).

29. For biography, Mark Stephen Massa, *Charles Augustus Briggs and the Crisis of Historical Criticism* (Minneapolis, MN: Fortress, 1990); and for positioning Briggs as a mediating figure between antebellum traditional Protestantism and twentieth-century theological modernism, Gary Dorrien, *American Liberal Theology: Imagining Progressive Religion, 1805–1900* (Louisville, KY: Westminster/John Knox, 1989), 337–70.

30. On the German influence, see chapter 24, 529–30.

31. On Dorner's influence on Briggs, see Dorrien, *American Liberal Theology, 1805–1900*, 338–43.

32. *HISTORICAL STATISTICS*, 212.

33. Briggs, *Address*, 6.

34. Briggs, *Address*, 14.

35. Briggs, *Address*, 15.

36. William Henry Green, "The Perpetual Authority of the Old Testament," *Presbyterian Quarterly and Princeton Review*, new series 22 (April 1877): 221 (entire article, 221–55).

37. For a blow-by-blow account, see Noll, *Between Faith and Criticism*, 15–22.

38. A. A. Hodge and B. B. Warfield, "Inspiration," *Presbyterian Review* 2 (April 1881): 237.

39. For more on this shift, see Noll, *Between Faith and Criticism*, 35–36.

40. Gerald Birney Smith, quoted in Lefferts A. Loetscher, "C. A. Briggs in the Retrospect of Half a Century," *Theology Today* 12 (April 1955): 41 (entire article, 27–42).

41. Quoted in Walter Unger, "'Earnestly Contending for the Faith': The Role of the Niagara Bible Conference in the Emergence of American Fundamentalism" (Ph.D. diss., Simon Fraser University, 1981), 332.

42. On that Anglo-Irish history, see especially Donald Harman Akenson, *Discovering the End of Time: Irish Evangelicals in the Age of Daniel O'Connell* (Montreal: McGill-Queen's University Press, 2016) and Donald Harman Akenson,

Exporting the Rapture: John Nelson Darby and the Victorian Conquest of North-American Evangelicalism (New York: Oxford University Press, 2018).

43. For expert treatments, see Kraus, *Dispensationalism in America*; Sandeen, *Roots of Fundamentalism*; Marsden, *Fundamentalism and American Culture*; Timothy P. Weber, "The Two-Edged Sword: The Fundamentalist Use of the Bible," in Hatch and Noll, *BIBLE IN AMERICA*, 101–20; Paul Boyer, *When Time Shall Be No More: Prophecy Belief in Modern American Culture* (Cambridge, MA: Harvard University Press, 1992); Brendan M. Pietsch, *Dispensational Modernism* (New York: Oxford University Press, 2015). For my own account, see *The Scandal of the Evangelical Mind* (Grand Rapids, MI: Eerdmans, 1989), 109–48.

44. They may also have been responding to the general loss of Protestant influence by defending approaches that prevailed when Protestant Bible believers dominated the culture; on that possibility, see Douglas W. Frank, *Less Than Conquerors: How Evangelicals Entered the Twentieth Century* (Grand Rapids, MI: Eerdmans, 1986).

45. Pietsch, *Dispensational Modernism*, 116.

46. James H. Brookes, *Present Truth: Being the Teaching of the Holy Ghost on the Second Coming of the Lord; the Deity of Christ; and the Personality of the Holy Ghost, with an Introduction to the Study of the Word* (Springfield, IL: Edmund A. Wilson, [1877]), 2 (first principle), 3 (second principle), 5 (fifth principle), 17–34 (first set of passages), 35–38 (second set).

47. On Moorhouse, see Akenson, *Exporting the Rapture*, 390; Pietsch, *Dispensational Modernism*, 102.

48. See Kathryn Teresa Long, *The Revival of 1857–58: Interpreting an American Religious Awakening* (New York: Oxford University Press, 1998), 84–85, 130–33; Akenson, *Exporting the Rapture*, 338, 435–37; and especially David Anthony Schmidt, "Scripture beyond Common Sense: Sentimental Bible Study and the Evangelical Practice of 'the Bible Reading,'" *Journal of Religious History*, May 2016, https://online library.wiley.com/doi/abs/10.1111/1467-9809.12366.

49. For a thorough study, see Todd Magnum and Mark Sweetnam, *The Scofield Bible: Its History and Impact on the Evangelical Church* (Colorado Springs, CO: Paternoster, 2009).

50. C. I. Scofield, *Rightly Dividing the Word of Truth (2 Tim ii.15): Being Ten Outline Studies of the Most Important Divisions of Scripture*, 11th ed. (New York: Fleming H. Revell, n.d.), 2.

51. *Scofield Reference Bible* (New York: Oxford University Press, 1909), [iv].

52. On the Oxford University Press connection, for which records seem to have disappeared, see Pietsch, *Dispensational Modernism*, 180–81; Magnum and Sweetnam, *Scofield Bible*, 7, 17, 169 (American sales topping 1 million by 1930, 2 million by 1946).

53. Information on these figures can be found in the books mentioned in note 4.

54. Marsden, *Fundamentalism and American Culture*, 51.

55. Pietsch, *Dispensational Modernism*, 184–85.

56. Especially insightful on this marriage of convenience is Sandeen, *Roots of Fundamentalism*.

57. Consideration of proprietary and sectarian traditions needs more nuance than I have provided here. As a prime example, the Salvation Army was a kind of sectarian movement arising from Methodism, yet it addressed the problems of urban America more effectively than any other Protestant organization.

58. For information on Brown's "Self-interpreting Bible," see Hills, *ENGLISH BIBLE*, 8–9 (#37). On this irony, see especially Weber, "The Two-Edged Sword."

59. This section is indebted especially to James R. Moore, *The Post-Darwinian Controversies: A Study of the Protestant Struggle to Come to Terms with Darwin in Great Britain and America, 1870–1900* (New York: Cambridge University Press, 1979); David N. Livingstone, *Darwin's Forgotten Defenders: The Encounter between Evangelical Theology and Evolutionary Thought* (Edinburgh: Scottish Academic Press, 1987); Ronald L. Numbers, *The Creationists: From Scientific Creationism to Intelligent Design*, expanded ed. (Cambridge, MA: Harvard University Press, 2006).

60. Huxley quoted in David N. Livingstone, *Dealing with Darwin: Place, Politics, and Rhetoric in Religious Engagements with Evolution* (Baltimore, MD: Johns Hopkins University Press, 2014), 60.

61. See Timothy Larsen, *A People of One Book: The Bible and the Victorians* (New York: Oxford University Press, 2011), 209–12.

62. Gray, *Darwiniana*, vi.

63. A. Hunter Dupree, *Asa Gray* (Cambridge, MA: Harvard University Press, 1959), 361.

64. For expert treatment of the Gray-Darwin relationship, see Dupree, *Asa Gray*, 233–305; Moore, *Post-Darwinian Controversies*, 269–80; Livingstone, *Darwin's Forgotten Defenders*, 60–64; Numbers, *The Creationists*, 34–38; Adrian Desmond and James Moore, *Darwin's Sacred Cause: How a Hatred of Slavery Shaped Darwin's Views of Human Evolution* (Boston: Houghton Mifflin, 2009), 248–50, 293–96, 322–31.

65. For this book, Gray's review, and additional material, see Mark A. Noll and David N. Livingstone, eds., *Charles Hodge, What Is Darwinism? And Other Writings on Science and Religion* (Grand Rapids, MI: Baker, 1994).

66. Gray, *Darwiniana*, 267 (First Cause), 270–71 (taint of atheism).

67. See A. A. Hodge, review of Asa Gray's *Natural Science and Religion*, *Presbyterian Review* 1 (1880): 586–89; and the thirty-nine essays and reviews reprinted in B. B. Warfield, *B. B. Warfield: Evolution, Science, and Scripture—Selected Writings*, ed. Mark A. Noll and David N. Livingstone (Grand Rapids, MI: Baker, 2000).

68. B. B. Warfield, "Creation, Evolution, and Mediate Creation," *Bible Student*, new series 1 (July 1901): 1–8.

69. George Frederick Wright, "The Passing of Evolution," in *The Fundamentals*, 4 vols., ed. R. A. Torrey and A. C. Dixon (Los Angeles: Bible Institute of Los Angeles, 1917), 4: 72–97. On Wright's transition, see Ronald L. Numbers, "George Frederick Wright: From Christian Darwinist to Fundamentalist," *Isis* 79 (1988): 624–45.

70. James Orr, "Science and Christian Faith," in Torrey and Dixon, *The Fundamentals*, 1:346.

71. For a definitive account, see Numbers, *The Creationists*, with 88–119 on the rise of militant anti-evolutionism in the 1920s.

72. Dupree, *Asa Gray*, 303. See also 278–79, 340 (Huxley), 364 (Fiske), and 301–3 (Spencer).

73. Lyman Abbott, *Reminiscences* (Boston: Houghton Mifflin, 1915), 456–57, with 453 on Briggs.

Chapter 26

1. *HISTORICAL STATISTICS,* 56–59; for the shift to urban areas, 9.

2. Jonathan D. Sarna, *American Judaism: A History* (New Haven, CT: Yale University Press, 2004), 153.

3. Austin Phelps, "Introduction," in Josiah Strong, *Our Country: Its Possible Future and Its Present Crisis* (New York: Baker & Taylor for the American Home Missionary Society, 1885), ii. After describing the various perils, Strong's penultimate chapter treated "the Anglo-Saxon and the world's future." Particularly insightful on this work is Robert T. Handy, *Undermined Establishment: Church-State Relations in America, 1880–1920* (Princeton, NJ: Princeton University Press, 1991), 17–18.

4. On the American Protective Association, see Handy, *Undermined Establishment,* 43–44; on European racial anti-Semitism, see Naomi W. Cohen, *Jews in Christian America: The Pursuit of Religious Equality* (New York: Oxford University Press, 1992), 89.

5. Representative Jewish expressions on the topic are found in Jonathan D. Sarna and David G. Dalin, *Religion and State in the American Jewish Experience* (Notre Dame, IN: University of Notre Dame Press, 1997), 181–226 ("Religion in the Public Schools").

6. Quoted in Cohen, *Jews in Christian America,* 83.

7. Jacob Rader Marcus, *United States Jewry, 1776–1985,* vol. 3 (Detroit, MI: Wayne State University Press, 1993), 186.

8. *The American Jewish Yearbook* 16 (5675 [1914]): 138; 17 (5676 [1915]): 203–4; 18 (5677 [1916]): 84–85.

9. On anti-Semitism in fiction, see Naomi A. Cohen, ed., *Essential Papers on Jewish-Christian Relations in the United States* (New York: New York University Press, 1990), 112–13; on Jewish perspectives of the Reform Association, see Howard M. Sachar, *A History of the Jews in America* (New York: Knopf, 1992), 81–82.

10. See Virginia L. Brereton, "The Public Schools Are Not Enough: The Bible and Private Schools," in *The Bible in American Education,* ed. David L. Barr and Nicholas Piediscalzi (Philadelphia, PA: Fortress, 1982), 43–45; Sarna, *American Judaism,* 80, 180–81, 186–87, 192.

11. Samuel T. Spear, "The Bible and the Public School," *Princeton Review* 54 (March 1877): 375. The next article in the same issue, however, repeated customary arguments for keeping the KJV in school: Lyman H. Atwater, "The State in Relation to Morality, Religion, and Education," *Princeton Review* 54 (March 1877): 395–422.

12. Anon., "Shall We Retain the Bible in Our Common Schools?," *Universalist Quarterly and General Review* 14 (April 1877): 200, 204.

13. Elizabeth Blanchard Cook, *The Nation's Book in the Nation's Schools* (Chicago: Chicago Woman's Educational Union, 1898), 159, 169–71 (Gibbons's extensive quotation). Thanks to Sarah Miglio for pointing me to the Cook book.

14. John O. Geiger, "The Edgerton Bible Case: Humphrey Desmond's Political Education of Wisconsin Catholics," *Journal of Church and State* 20 (Winter 1978): 13–28, quotations on 16, 19.

15. This paragraph depends on Madeleine Marie Klem, "The Most Sacred Rights of Parents: English-Speaking Catholics and Parental Rights in the Schools Question" (Ph.D. diss., University of Notre Dame, 2017).

16. Zachariah Montgomery, "The Bible in the Common Schools," *The Occidental*, November 26, 1864, quoted in Klem, "Most Sacred Rights of Parents," 35.

17. This paragraph depends on Philip Gleason, "The School Question: A Centennial Retrospect," in *Keeping the Faith: American Catholicism Past and Present* (Notre Dame, IN: University of Notre Dame Press, 1987), 115–35.

18. Gleason, "The School Question," 119.

19. Sarna, *American Judaism*, 132–207; and for a fuller account of how "Jews have creatively *adapted* their faith to their new [American] environment," see Jonathan D. Sarna, "American Judaism in Historical Perspective," *Historically Speaking*, May/June 2004, 11–15 (quotation, 13).

20. Sarna, *American Judaism*, 132.

21. Oscar Straus, *The Origin of Republican Form of Government in the United States* (1885), quoted in Jonathan D. Sarna, "The Cult of Synthesis in American Jewish Culture," *Jewish Social Studies*, new series 5 (Autumn 1998–Winter 1999): 55.

22. Emil G. Hirsch, "Abraham Lincoln," in *Abraham Lincoln: The Testimony of the Synagogue*, ed. Emanuel Hertz (New York: Bloch, 1927), 207

23. "Scriptures Held Guide for the Nation," *New York Times*, November 14, 1954. For a later similar assessment, see David Gelernter, "Americanism—and Its Enemies," *Commentary*, January 2005, 41–48.

24. For Schechter, see Sarna, *American Judaism*, 187–91 and passim; David B. Starr in *ANB*.

25. Solomon Schechter, "Abraham Lincoln" (lecture on February 11, 1909), in *Seminary Addresses and Other Papers* (1915; N.p.: Burning Bush Press, 1959), 156–57.

26. Solomon Schechter, "The Seminary as a Witness" (April 26, 1903), in *Seminary Addresses*, 48.

27. Quotations in this and the next paragraph are from Schechter, "The Seminary as a Witness," 48–50.

28. On that 1903 publication, see Hills, *ENGLISH BIBLE*, 338 (#2151). For the whole project, see Jonathan D. Sarna and Nahum M. Sarna, "Jewish Bible Scholarship and Translations in the United States," in *The Bible and Bibles in America* (Atlanta, GA: Scholars Press, 1988), 95–103; Jonathan D. Sarna, *JPS: The Americanization of Jewish Culture, 1888–1988* (Philadelphia, PA: Jewish Publication Society, 1989),

103–8 ("The Margolis Translation"), 108–16 ("The Compromise Translation"), 116–20 ("The Bible Commentary Project").

29. Solomon Schechter, "The Bible," *American Jewish Yearbook* 15 (5674 [1913]): 173, 174, 176–77.

30. See chapter 25, 549; and specifically for Jewish history, Yaakov Ariel, *On Behalf of Israel: American Fundamentalist Attitudes toward Jews, Judaism, and Zionism, 1865–1945* (Brooklyn, NY: Carlson, 1991); David A. Rausch, *Zionism within Early American Fundamentalism, 1878–1918* (New York: Edwin Mellen, 1979).

31. *The Holy Scriptures According to the Masoretic Text: A New Translation with the Aid of Previous Versions and with Constant Consultation of Jewish Authorities* (Philadelphia, PA: Jewish Publication Society of America, 1917), "Preface," iv, vii–viii. For details on its publication and later editions, see Hills, *ENGLISH BIBLE*, 356–57 (#2234).

32. See Sarna, *JPS*, 109–10, for an illuminating discussion of how this translation emerged from the Jewish Publication Society's translation committee.

33. Chiniquy's claim, which he made in his *Fifty Years in the Church of Rome* (1885), featured regularly in literature from the American Protective Association; see Paul Laverdure, "'The Jesuits Did It': Charles Chiniquy's Theory of Lincoln's Assassination," in *Historical Papers 2001: Canadian Society of Church History*, ed. Bruce L. Gunther (N.p.: Canadian Society of Church History, 2001), 125–40.

34. John T. McGreevy, *Catholicism and American Freedom: A History* (New York: Norton, 2003), 103, and with 91–126 especially helpful for this period.

35. Garfield, quoted in McGreevy, *Catholicism and American Freedom*, 93.

36. McNamara, quoted in Alexander E. Calloway, "Ex-Priests, Fenians, and the Independent Irish Catholic Church in New York City, 1878–1883," *New Hibernia Review* 24 (Spring 2020): 125 (this whole article is illuminating on McNamara, 117–36).

37. G. Dershon, "The Catholic Church and the Bible," *Catholic World* 7 (1871): 657.

38. Keane's and Hopkins's works are reprinted, along with a helpful introduction, in Joseph P. Chinnici, ed., *Devotion to the Holy Spirit in American Catholicism* (New York: Paulist, 1985).

39. *Baltimore Catechism #3, From the Third Plenary Council of Baltimore (1891 Version)*, questions 557–562, quoted here from Baltimore Catechism, accessed November 5, 2020, http://www.baltimore-catechism.com/index.htm.

40. For fuller consideration of this book and the responses it generated, see Mark A. Noll, "Bishop James Gibbons, the Bible, and Protestant America," *U.S. Catholic Historian* 31 (Summer 2013): 77–104.

41. John F. Hewitt, *The King's Highway; or, the Catholic Church the Way of Salvation as Revealed in the Holy Scriptures* (New York: Catholic Publication Society, 1874), iii–v.

42. Hewitt, *King's Highway*, 252.

43. It was reprinted three times, in 1870, 1893, and 1909 (*WORLDCAT*).

44. Edwin Scott Gaustad and Philip L. Barlow, *New Historical Atlas of Religion in America* (New York: Oxford University Press, 2001), 381, 400–401; John Tracy Ellis, *The Life of James Cardinal Gibbons: Archbishop of Baltimore, 1834–1921*, 2 vols. (Milwaukee, WI: Bruce, 1952), 1:73. Ellis's biography is a richly detailed account.

45. James Gibbons, *The Faith of Our Fathers: Being a Plain Exposition and Vindication of the Church Founded by Our Lord Jesus Christ* (1876), reprint ed. ([Rockford, IL]: TAN, 1980), "Preface" (dated November 21, 1876), ix. All later parenthetical page references are to this edition, which, with one exception noted, contains only superficial changes from the 1876 original. The TAN Books version reprints the "110th edition" by P. J. Kennedy & Sons, New York (n.d.).

46. Ellis, *Gibbons*, 1:146.

47. For an example of Catholic approval, see Anon. review of *Faith of Our Fathers*, *American Catholic Quarterly Review* 2 (April 1877): 382; and for appreciative Protestant comments, Charles G. Starbuck, "Richard Rothe," *Reformed Quarterly Review* 3 (July 1887): 399; "Inquiring Friends" (advice column), *Christian Union*, March 13, 1890, 375.

48. Eugene Exman, *The House of Harper* (1967; New York: Harper Perennial, 2010), 149–50 (on *Ben-Hur*); Amy Lifson, "Ben-Hur," *Humanities* 30, no. 6 (November–December 2009): 14–18.

49. Review of *The Faith of Our Fathers*, *Catholic Record* 12 (January 1877): 191. This same reviewer seconded other Catholic commendations by saying that the book "made a beginning toward the creating of a species of *American* Catholic literature" (192, my italics).

50. This quotation is from the 1877 John Murphy edition, p. 15; the TAN Books reprint of the 110th edition expands this passage slightly with an additional quotation from Psalm 25:8.

51. For the text and the incidence of this hymn's publication over time, see Frederick William Faber, "Faith of Our Fathers, Living Still" (1849), Hymnary, accessed August 23, 2013, http://www.hymnary.org/text/faith_of_our_fathers_living_still.

52. Edward J. Stearns, *Notes on Uncle Tom's Cabin: Being a Logical Answer to its Allegations and Inferences Against Slavery as an Institution* (Philadelphia, PA: Lippincott, Grambo, 1853). For controversy over Gibbons, see Edward J. Stearns, *The Faith of Our Forefathers: An Examination of Archbishop Gibbons's "Faith of Our Fathers,"* 6th ed. (New York: Thomas Whitaker, 1879), which generated two substantial Catholic responses: Anon., "Archbishop Gibbons and His Episcopalian Critic, Dr. Stearns," *American Catholic Quarterly Review* 5 (January 1880): 84–104; *The True Faith of Our Forefathers, by a Professor of Theology in Woodstock College, S. J., Maryland* (New York: American News Co., 1880), which in turn generated another book by Edward J. Stearns, *Archbishop's Champion Brought to Book: By the Author of "The Faith of Our Forefathers"* (New York: T. Whittaker, 1881).

53. Steven Green, *The Second Disestablishment: Church and State in Nineteenth-Century America* (New York: Oxford University Press, 2010), 298.

54. For orientation, see Gleason, "Keeping the Faith in America," in *Keeping the Faith*, 162–65; William Cossen, *Making Catholic America: Religious Nationalism in the Gilded and Progressive Era* (Ithaca, NY: Cornell University Press, 2021).

55. See John Farina, *An American Experience of God: The Spirituality of Isaac Hecker* (Mahwah, NJ: Paulist, 1982) and David J. O'Brien, *Isaac Hecker: An American Catholic* (Mahwah, NJ: Paulist, 1992).

56. Marvin O'Connell, *John Ireland and the American Catholic Church* (St. Paul: Minnesota Historical Society, 1988).

57. See especially R. Scott Appleby, *Church and Age Unite! The Modernist Impulse in American Catholicism* (Notre Dame, IN: University of Notre Dame Press, 1992).

58. For positive results from this encyclical that stimulated serious engagement with the theology of Thomas Aquinas, which Leo XIII had authorized, but also negative results from discouraging intellectual creativity and beneficial contact with broader intellectual currents, see Philip Gleason, *Contending with Modernity: Catholic Higher Education in the Twentieth Century* (New York: Oxford University Press, 1995).

59. Hugh Pope, O. P., *The Catholic Church and the Bible* (New York: Macmillan, 1928), 93, 8.

Chapter 27

1. William Vance Trollinger Jr., "An Outpouring of 'Faithful' Words: Protestant Publishing in the United States," in *HISTORY OF THE BOOK*, 4:375.

2. See the datasets (2016) in Lincoln Mullen, *America's Public Bible: Biblical Quotations in U.S. Newspapers*, accessed October 19, 2021, http://americaspublicbible.org.

3. Carl F. Kaestle and Janice A. Radway, "Prologue," in *HISTORY OF THE BOOK*, 4:3.

4. H. W. Brands, *American Colossus: The Triumph of Capitalism, 1865–1900* (New York: Anchor, 2010), 81.

5. Hills, *ENGLISH BIBLE*, 287–88 (#1913). It was published in New York, Chicago, and New Orleans.

6. Hills, *ENGLISH BIBLE*, 293–360 (#1948–#2251); some of the entries list multiple editions.

7. Indispensable is Hills, *ENGLISH BIBLE*, especially with an extensive note for the first Revised (or English Revised) Version publication, 295–96 (#1953). Outstanding on the ERV as a social-religious phenomenon are Kenneth Cmiel, *Democratic Eloquence: The Fight over Popular Speech in Nineteenth-Century America* (Berkeley: University of California Press, 1990), 206–23; Peter J. Thuesen, *In Discordance with the Scriptures: American Protestant Battles over Translating the Bible* (New York: Oxford University Press, 1999), 41–61. For an illuminating account of the ERV's English history, see David Daniell, *The Bible in English* (New Haven, CT: Yale University Press, 2003), 683–700.

8. As a comparison, in late 2020 and with an American population over six times as large, the first volume of Barack Obama's memoir covering his presidential years enjoyed a pre-order of "only" 850,000 copies. Jeffrey A. Trachtenberg, "Obama Memoir Sells More Than 887,000 Copies on First Day," *Wall Street Journal*, November 18, 2020, https://www.wsj.com/articles/barack-obama-memoir-sells-more-than-887-000-cop ies-on-first-day-11605743581.

9. Thuesen, *In Discordance*, 42.

10. Lloyd Wendt, *Chicago Tribune: The Rise of a Great American Newspaper* (Chicago: Rand McNally, 1979), 270.

11. Cmiel, *Democratic Eloquence*, 222.

12. Hills, *ENGLISH BIBLE*, 295–301 (#1953–#1980), with several separate editions listed at #1972 and #1977.

13. An example was *Where the Old and New Versions Differ: The Actual Changes in the Authorized and Revised New Testament, Printed in Parallel Columns* (New York: Anson D. F. Randolph, 1881).

14. James D. Hart, *The Popular Book: A History of America's Literary Tastes* (Westport, CT: Greenwood, 1950), 163–64.

15. Cmiel, *Democratic Eloquence*, 222.

16. Hills, *ENGLISH BIBLE*, 331–360. For the period 1901–20, Hills lists seventy-eight KJV editions, two for the ERV, and eighteen for the ASV, which was often printed in combination with the ERV or more commonly the KJV.

17. Daniell, *Bible in English*, 700.

18. Cmiel, *Democratic Eloquence*, 215.

19. The following examples are explored further in Cmiel, *Democratic Eloquence*, 215. It should be remembered, however, that it took more than a century before readers considered the KJV superior in its prose to the Geneva Bible.

20. Cmiel, *Democratic Eloquence*, 213.

21. For how those advances affected the work of the revisers, see Thuesen, *In Discordance*, 45–47.

22. Thuesen, *In Discordance*, 58–59; Cmiel, *Democratic Eloquence*, 208.

23. The exception was the ending of the Lord's Prayer that Scofield retained without a marginal note.

24. Cmiel, *Democratic Eloquence*, 106. The ABS's earlier work is detailed in David Norton, *A Textual History of the King James Bible* (New York: Cambridge University Press, 2005), 119–22.

25. Daniell, *Bible in English*, 699–700; Thuesen, *In Discordance*, 60–62.

26. Thuesen, *In Discordance*, 62–65.

27. Thuesen, *In Discordance*, 55, 49 (grannies), 54 (Talmage).

28. Hills, *ENGLISH BIBLE*, xxvi.

29. Peter J. Wosh, *Spreading the Word: The Bible Business in Nineteenth-Century America* (Ithaca, NY: Cornell University Press, 1994), 176.

30. Quoted in John Fea, *Bible Cause: A History of the American Bible Society* (New York: Oxford University Press, 2016), 96. On rising Methodist importance for the ABS, see Wosh, *Spreading the Word*, 185–88.

31. Particularly helpful on the importance of these family bibles is Liana Lupus, *The Book of Life: Family Bibles in America* (New York: MOBIA, 2011) and Colleen McDannell, *The Christian Home in Victorian America, 1840–1900* (Bloomington: University of Indiana Press, 1986).

32. Hills, *ENGLISH BIBLE*, 304 (#1993).

33. Hills, *ENGLISH BIBLE*, 287 (#1910).

34. R. Laurence Moore, *Selling God: American Religion in the Marketplace of Culture* (New York: Oxford University Press, 1994), 119, 94.

35. Totals in this and the next paragraph do not include editions published jointly with foreign firms, editions where the entire card in the National Union Catalogue was in a non-Roman script, or ABS editions published outside the United States. Enumerations are from *The National Union Catalogue, Pre-1956 Imprints* (Chicago: American Library Association, 1980), vols. 53 and 54.

36. Bibles in this period serving primarily non-Lutheran constituencies included thirty-five editions in Spanish, twelve in French, nine in Portuguese, six in Welsh, four in Polish, three in Czech, two each in Armenian, Dutch, Estonian, Gothic, and Russian, and one each in Bulgarian, Hungarian, Lithuanian, and Romanian.

37. James Kenneth Echols, "Charles Michael Jacobs, the Scriptures, and the Word of God: One Man's Struggle against Biblical Fundamentalism among American Lutherans" (Ph.D. diss., Yale University, 1989). For a work combining advocacy for biblical inerrancy as defined by American conservatives and for a Lutheran view of the Lord's Supper keyed to European authorities, see Johann Michael Reu, *Two Treatises on the Means of Grace* (Minneapolis, MN: Augsburg, 1952).

38. Information in this paragraph is from Hills, *ENGLISH BIBLE*, 252–367 (#1715–#2283).

39. This paragraph depends on Stephen John Lennox, "Biblical Interpretation in the American Holiness Movement, 1875–1920" (Ph.D. diss., Drew University, 1992).

40. Hills, *ENGLISH BIBLE*, 336 (#2142).

41. Hills, *ENGLISH BIBLE*, Thorn (257, #1749A), fonetik (264, #1786), Grant (314, #2044), Panin (353–54, #2220).

42. Hills, *ENGLISH BIBLE*, 365–66 (#2276).

43. Hills, *ENGLISH BIBLE*, Ballentine (327–28, #2102), Kent (339, #2158), Moffatt (357, #2235), Goodspeed (362, #2260). On the reception of the Goodspeed translation and a perceptive account of twentieth-century modern-language translations generally, see R. Bryan Bademan, "'Monkeying with the Bible': Edgar J. Goodspeed's *American Translation*," *Religion and American Culture* 16 (Winter 2006): 55–93.

44. Bertha M. H. Shambaugh, *Amana: The Community of True Inspiration* (Iowa City: State Historical Society of Iowa, 1908), 8, 23.

45. For orientation to her life, see Ronald L. Numbers, *Prophetess of Health: A Study of Ellen G. White*, 3rd ed. (Grand Rapids, MI: Eerdmans, 2008); and for Ellen White in the context of divine revelations in the nineteenth century, David F. Holland, *Sacred Borders: Continuing Revelation and Canonical Restraint in Early America* (New York: Oxford University Press, 2011), 161–68. The treatment here on Adventists and Scripture depends on Denis Kaiser, *Trust and Doubt: Perceptions of Divine Inspiration in Seventh-day Adventist History* (St. Peter am Hart, Austria: Seminar Schloss Bogenhofen, 2019) and Nicholas Miller, "The Bible and Seventh-day Adventists," in Gutjahr, *OXFORD HANDBOOK*, 627–44.

46. Miller, "Bible and Seventh-day Adventists," 627.

47. Kaiser, *Trust and Doubt*, 411.

48. White comments from the 1880s, quoted in Kaiser, *Trust and Doubt*, 182–83.

49. For positioning of Christian Science in its contemporary milieu, see Catherine L. Albanese, "Metaphysical Movements," in *The Cambridge History of Religions in America*, ed. Stephen J. Stein, 3 vols. (New York: Cambridge University Press, 2012), 2:435–56 (451–53 on Mary Baker Eddy).

50. Hills, *ENGLISH BIBLE*, 366–67 (#2280).

51. Mary Baker Eddy, *Science and Health with Key to the Scriptures* (1906; Boston: First Church of Christ Scientists, 1934), 479, 579.

52. Philip L. Barlow, *Mormons and the Bible: The Place of the Latter-day Saints in American Religion* (New York: Oxford University Press, 1991), 46–61 (Smith and Young), 81–84 (Orson Pratt), 103–47 (later leaders). Anthony A. Hutchinson expands on Barlow's categories in "LDS Approaches to the Holy Bible," *DIALOGUE: A Journal of Mormon Thought* 15 (Spring 1982): 99–125. For an insightful expansion, see David Holland, "The Bible and Mormonism," in Gutjahr, *OXFORD HANDBOOK*, 611–26.

53. Smith quoted in Robert Millet et al., *LDS Beliefs: A Doctrinal Reference* (Salt Lake City, UT: Deseret, 2011), 68–69.

54. Hills, *ENGLISH BIBLE*, 270 (#1817).

55. Holland, "Bible and Mormonism," 619.

56. For the full story, see Barlow, *Mormons and the Bible*, 148–81. This current LDS edition lists Joseph Smith's most substantial revisions of the text as an appendix.

57. Millett, *LDS Beliefs*, 68.

Chapter 28

1. Hills, *ENGLISH BIBLE*, 317 (#2056). In fact, during this period book publishing generally and Bible publishing in particular remained almost entirely northern enterprises.

2. William Vance Trollinger Jr., "An Outpouring of 'Faithful' Words: Protestant Publishing in the United States," in *HISTORY OF THE BOOK*, 4:371.

3. Hills, *ENGLISH BIBLE*, 356 (#2231). For Catholics, Cardinal James Gibbons introduced a "special edition for the Army and Navy" of the Douay-Rheims New Testament published by the Paulist Press (Hills, *ENGLISH BIBLE*, 358 [#2237]).

4. Hills, *ENGLISH BIBLE*, 363 (#2263).

5. John Fea, *The Bible Cause: A History of the American Bible Society* (New York: Oxford University Press, 2016), 98; personal visit to Ellis Island National Museum of Immigration, November 6, 2010.

6. Social Security Administration, "Popular Baby Names by Decade," accessed November 17, 2020, https://www.ssa.gov/oact/babynames/decades/.

7. Walter A. McDougall, *Throes of Democracy: The American Civil War Era, 1829–1877* (New York: Harper, 2008), 573; H. W. Brands, *American Colossus: The Triumph of Capitalism, 1865–1900* (New York: Anchor, 2010), 453.

8. *One Matters: Ministry Impact, Annual Report of 2017* (Nashville, TN: Gideons International, 2017).

9. White quoted in David C. Lindberg and Ronald L. Numbers, "Introduction," in *God and Nature: Historical Essays on the Encounter between Christianity and Science* (Berkeley: University of California Press, 1986), 2–3.

10. For outstanding studies that agree on what happened, but not on how to evaluate those changes, see Laurence R. Veysey, *The Emergence of the American University* (Chicago: University of Chicago Press, 1965) and George M. Marsden, *The Soul of the American University: From Protestant Establishment to Established Unbelief* (New York: Oxford University Press, 1994). On the persistence, see Conrad Cherry, Betty A. DeBerg, and Amanda Porterfield, *Religion on Campus* (Chapel Hill: University of North Carolina Press, 2001). On developments at Harvard, see Robert A. McCaughey, "The Transformation of American Academic Life: Harvard University, 1821–1892," *Perspectives in American History* 8 (1974): 239–332.

11. Ingersoll, quoted in Eric T. Brandt and Timothy Larsen, "The Old Atheism Revisited: Robert G. Ingersoll and the Bible," *Journal of the Historical Society* 11 (June 2011): 218; for "the evangelist of unbelief," see 238.

12. On Talmage and his philanthropies, see Heather Curtis, *Holy Humanitarians: American Evangelicals and Global Aid* (Cambridge, MA: Harvard University Press, 2018).

13. *The Ingersoll-Gladstone Controversy on Christianity: Two Articles from the North American Review* (New York: C. P. Farrell, 1898), 143. On Ingersoll's firm abolitionism and its relation to his skepticism, see Susan Jacoby, *The Great Agnostic: Robert Ingersoll and American Free Thought* (New Haven, CT: Yale University Press, 2013), 48–53.

14. Jacoby, *Great Agnostic*, 173–75.

15. Wallace quoted in Brandt and Larsen, "The Old Atheism," 224.

16. Review of *Ben-Hur*, *Baptist Review* 3 (April 1, 1881): 265. Similar judgments came from the *New York Tribune*, December 3, 1880; *Californian* 3 (April 1881): 377; *The Independent*, December 30, 1880.

17. E.H.L., Review of *Ben-Hur*, *American Church Review* 33 (January 1881): 253.

18. On the importance of Garfield's recommendation and general orientation to the *Ben-Hur* phenomenon, see Barbara Ryan and Milette Shamir, "Introduction," in *Bigger Than Ben-Hur: The Book, Its Adaptations, and Their Audiences*, ed. Barbara Ryan and Milette Shamir (Syracuse, NY: Syracuse University Press, 2016), 1–17 (Garfield, 8).

19. Review of *Ben-Hur Illustrated*, *Literary World* 22 (November 21, 1891): 428.

20. Jon Solomon, "A Timeline of Ben-Hur Companies, Brands, and Products," in Ryan and Shamir, *Bigger Than Ben-Hur*, 191–211, with scores more such items reaching into the twenty-first century.

21. Hilton Obenzinger, "Holy Lands, Restoration, and Zionism in Ben-Hur," in Ryan and Shamir, *Bigger Than Ben-Hur*, 87.

22. See chapter 7, 142.

23. Henry Ward Beecher, *The Life of Jesus, the Christ* (New York: J. P. Ford, 1871). On the European examples, see Daniel L. Pals, *Victorian Lives of Jesus* (San Antonio, TX: Trinity University Press, 1982).

24. Excellent on these books are Stephen Prothero, *American Jesus: How the Son of God Became a National Icon* (New York: Farrar, Straus and Giroux, 2003), 95–101; Richard

Wightman Fox, *Jesus in America: Personal Savior, Cultural Hero, National Obsessions* (San Francisco, CA: HarperSanFrancisco, 2004), 274–82.

25. William T. Stead, *If Christ Came to Chicago: A Plea for the Union of All Who Love in the Service of All Who Suffer* (Chicago: Laird and Lee, 1894).

26. See Amazon.com for the many editions of the book, WWJD bracelets, and much other related merchandise available today. For positioning the novel in Sheldon's liberal but securely middle-class context, see R. Laurence Moore, *Selling God: American Religion in the Marketplace of Culture* (New York: Oxford University Press, 1994), 209–10, 216–17. Authorial reliance on Jesus as the promoter of authors' own this-worldly causes continued in notable examples, like Upton Sinclair's *They Called Me Carpenter: A Tale of the Second Coming* (1922), with its denunciation of Hollywood's commercial decadence, and Bruce Barton's *The Man Nobody Knows* (1925), with its portrait of Jesus as the advertising whiz who pioneered modern business innovations.

27. WORLDCAT.

28. Harold Frederic, *The Damnation of Theron Ware* (New York: Stone and Kimball, 1896).

29. James P. Hart, *The Popular Book: A History of America's Literary Tastes* (Westport, CT: Greenwood, 1950), 168.

30. Prothero, *American Jesus*; Fox, *Jesus in America*; Stephen J. Nichols, *Jesus Made in America: A Cultural History from the Puritans to the Passion of the Christ* (Downers Grove, IL: InterVarsity Press, 2008). For the beginnings of this shift before the Civil War, see Eran Shalev, *American Zion: The Old Testament as a Political Text from the Revolution to the Civil War* (New Haven, CT: Yale University Press, 2013), 151–84.

31. Lincoln Mullen, *America's Public Bible: Biblical Quotations in U.S. Newspapers*, accessed November 24, 2020, http://americaspublicbible.org.

32. Lincoln Mullen, "Most Quoted Verses by Decade," accessed November 24, 2020, https://americaspublicbible.org/most-quoted-by-decade.html.

33. On the extensive newspaper treatment of Moody and his peers, see Josh McMullen, *Under the Big Top: Big Tent Revivalism and American Culture, 1885–1925* (New York: Oxford University Press, 2015), 140–46.

34. Next with about the same frequency of appearances came Exodus 20:13 ("Thou shalt not kill"); Proverbs 22:6 ("Train up a child in the way he should go: and when he is old, he will not depart from it"); Luke 2:4 ("Glory to God in the highest, and on earth peace, good will toward men"); Acts 20:35 (quoted earlier); and 1 Thessalonians 5:21 ("Prove all things; hold fast that which is good").

35. Stephen A. Marini, "A Ranked List of Most Frequently Printed Hymns, 1737–1960," in *Wonderful Words of Life: Hymns in American History and Theology*, ed. Richard J. Mouw and Mark A. Noll (Grand Rapids, MI: Eerdmans, 2004), 251–64. For Marini's own discerning analysis of the shift in hymn subject matter, see his "From Classical to Modern: Hymnody and the Development of American Evangelicalism, 1737–1970," in *Singing the Lord's Song in a Strange Land: Hymnody in the History of North American Protestantism*, ed. Edith L. Blumhofer and Mark A. Noll (Tuscaloosa: University of Alabama Press, 2004), 1–38.

36. Especially helpful on the author of these hymns is Edith L. Blumhofer, *Her Heart Can See: The Life and Hymns of Fanny J. Crosby* (Grand Rapids, MI: Eerdmans, 2005).

37. Richard J. Mouw, "'Some Poor Sailor, Tempest Tossed': Nautical Rescue Themes in Evangelical Hymnody," in Mouw and Noll, *Wonderful Words of Life*, 246. Mouw's essay (234–50) carries forward an analysis first developed in Sandra Sizer's perceptive *Gospel Hymns and Social Religion: The Rhetoric of 19th Century Revivalism* (Philadelphia, PA: Temple University Press, 1978).

38. Many such paintings, including several by Hicks, are reproduced with a helpful text in Anita Schorsch and Martin Grief, *The Morning Stars Sang: The Bible in Popular and Folk Art* (New York: University Books, 1978), 51, 89 (for Hicks).

39. See Paul C. Gutjahr on Ware in *ANB*; *Belshazzar's Feast* can be viewed at Detroit Institute of Arts, accessed November 10, 2020, https://www.dia.org/art/collection/object/belshazzars-feast-24436.

40. David Roberts, *The Holy Land: Syria, Iduema, Arabia, Egypt, and Nubia*, 3 vols. (London: F. G. Moon, 1842–50).

41. *New York Tribune*, April 10, 1898. Newspaper coverage is available through the Library of Congress's *Chronicling America*, the record of book publications from WORLDCAT. See *The Life of Our Saviour Jesus Christ: Three Hundred and Sixty-Five Compositions from the Four Gospels with Notes and Explanatory Drawings by J. James Tissot*, notes trans. Arthur Bell (New York: McClure-Tissot, 1899).

42. For illuminating discussion as well as images of the paintings, see Paul Staiti, "Ideology and Rhetoric in Erastus Salisbury Field's *The Historical Monument of the American Republic*," *Winterthur Portfolio* 27 (Spring 1992): 29–43 (quotation, 40); Anon., "The Historical Monument of the American Republic: Cotton Mather Meets the Millennium," University of Virginia, accessed November 10, 2020, https://xroads.virginia.edu/~CAP/FIELD/erastus.html. Field's painting *Death of the First Born* may be viewed at The Met, accessed November 10, 2020, https://www.metmuseum.org/art/collection/search/10878.

43. The material in this paragraph follows Dennis C. Dickerson, *The African Methodist Episcopal Church: A History* (Cambridge: Cambridge University Press, 2020), 175–76.

44. See for this image, Philadelphia Museum of Art, accessed January 19, 2020, https://philamuseum.org/collections/permanent/104384.html.

45. Brands, *American Colossus*, 238. For a copy of this image, see National Museum of American History, accessed November 11, 2020, https://americanhistory.si.edu/collections/search/object/nmah_1276028.

46. For this and Bellows's other images featuring Billy Sunday as well as his opinion of the preacher ("I believe Billy Sunday is the worst thing that ever happened to America. He is death to imagination, to spirituality, to art"), see Robert L. Gambone, *Art and Popular Religion in Evangelical America, 1915–1940* (Knoxville: University of Tennessee Press, 1989), 43–48.

47. Edgar Lee Masters, "The Wedding Feast," in *Starved Rock* (New York: Macmillan, 1919), 55–57. Bradford's "The Vanity of All Worldly Things," is one of the poems reprinted in an outstanding collection, Robert Atwan and Laurance Wieder, eds., *Chapters into Verse: Poetry in English Inspired by the Bible*, vol. 1: *Genesis to Malachi*; vol. 2: *Gospels to Revelation* (New York: Oxford University Press, 1993). See the *ANB*

for helpful biographical introductions on the poets mentioned in the following paragraphs.

48. Joel Barlow, "Along the Banks," in Atwan and Wieder, *Chapters into Verse*, 1:329.

49. Whittier, "Blind Bartimaeus," and Longfellow, "The Three Kings," in Atwan and Wieder, *Chapters into Verse*, 2:149–50; 2:40–42.

50. Whittier, "Ezekiel," in Atwan and Wieder, *Chapters into Verse*, 1:432.

51. Phillips Brooks, "O Little Town of Bethlehem" (1868), Hymnary, accessed March 26, 2021, https://hymnary.org/text/o_little_town_of_bethlehem.

52. Douglas Ullman Jr., "A Christmas Carol's Civil War Origins," American Battlefield Trust, accessed March 26, 2021, https://www.battlefields.org/learn/articles/christmas-bells.

53. John Greenleaf Whittier, "Ichabod!," in *Songs of Labor and Other Poems* (Boston: Ticknor, Reed, and Fields, 1850), 93–94. Longfellow, an equally ardent abolitionist, used the story of the eyeless Samson regaining his strength (Judges 16) in a poem titled "The Warning" (1841) to describe the ruin that could still result from what appeared at that date to the defeated slave power of the white South; (in Atwan and Wieder, *Chapters into Verse*, 1:190). For an indication of how concern about slavery could inspire poetic expression, see the substantial book edited by James G. Basker, *Amazing Grace: An Anthology of Poems about Slavery, 1660–1810* (New Haven, CT: Yale University Press, 2002).

54. Lindsay, "In Which Roosevelt is Compared to Saul," and "General William Booth Enters Heaven," in Atwan and Wieder, *Chapters into Verse*, 2:205; 2:343–44.

55. Whittier, "King Solomon and the Ant," in Atwan and Wieder, *Chapters into Verse*, 1:238.

56. Masters, "Oh ye Sabbatarians!," in *Starved Rock*, 88–89.

57. Roger Lundin, *Emily Dickinson and the Art of Belief* (Grand Rapids, MI: Eerdmans, 1998), 197–98.

58. Dickinson, "A little East of Jordan" and " 'Remember me' implored the thief," in Atwan and Wieder, *Chapters into Verse*, 1:95, 2:204.

59. Dickinson, "Abraham to kill him," "It always felt to me—a wrong," and "Sown in dishonor?," in Atwan and Wieder, *Chapters into Verse*, 1:78, 1:165, 2:285.

60. Dickinson, "I took my Power in my Hand," in Atwan and Wieder, *Chapters into Verse*, 1:199.

61. Dickinson "Eden is that old-fashioned House," "A Word made Flesh is seldom," and "Of Paul and Silas it is said," in Atwan and Wieder, *Chapters into Verse*, 1:43, 2:10–11, 2:256.

62. See especially Dorothy Huff Oberhaus, "'Tender Pioneer': Emily Dickinson's Poems on the Life of Christ," *American Literature* 59 (October 1987): 341–58.

63. Lundin, *Emily Dickinson*, 199–200.

64. *Church of the Holy Trinity v. United States*, 143 US (226) 1892, 471; David J. Brewer, *The United States a Christian Nation* (Philadelphia, PA: John C. Winston, 1905), 39. For a nuanced discussion of Brewer's stance, which included opposition to American imperial expansion and firm commitment to the separation of church and state,

see Steven K. Green, *The Second Disestablishment: Church and State in Nineteenth-Century America* (New York: Oxford University Press, 2010), 364–77.

65. Cases treating Bible reading in public schools would be the main exceptions; see chapter 14.

66. *Plessy v. Ferguson*, 163 U.S. 537 (1893), par. 48. For helpful context, see Linda Przybyszewski, *The Republic According to John Harlan* (Chapel Hill: University of North Carolina Press, 1999), 48 (Bible class), 90–99 (dissents).

67. Oliver Wendell Holmes Jr., *The Common Law* (Boston: Little, Brown, 1881), 1.

68. On Holmes's importance for these developments, see G. Edward White, *Law in American History*, vol. 2: *From Reconstruction through the 1920s* (New York: Oxford University Press, 2016), 226, 549–54.

69. In considering this case, I am following Sarah Barringer Gordon, *The Mormon Question: Polygamy and Constitutional Conflict in Nineteenth-Century America* (Chapel Hill: University of North Carolina Press, 2002), 114–44.

70. On this debate, see Philip L. Barlow, *Mormons and the Bible: The Place of the Latter-day Saints in American Religion* (New York: Oxford University Press 1991), 84–86.

71. *New York Times*, August 14, 1870, quoted in Barlow, *Mormons and the Bible*, 86.

72. Thomas M. Cooley, *A Treatise on the Constitutional Limitations Which Rest upon the Legislative Power of the States of the American Union* (1868), as discussed in Gordon, *Mormon Question*, 138.

73. Gordon, *Mormon Question*, 126, 128.

74. *Reynolds v. United States*, 98 U.S. 145 (1879), par. 115.

75. Gordon, *Mormon Question*, 122.

Chapter 29

1. A. N. Littlejohn (rector of Holy Trinity Church, Brooklyn), "Sermon VIII," in *Our Martyr President, Abraham Lincoln: Voices from the Pulpit of New York and Brooklyn* (New York: Tibbals and Whiting, 1865), 145–46.

2. Harry S. Stout, *Upon the Altar of the Nation: A Moral History of the Civil War* (New York: Viking, 2006), xviii; Robert N. Bellah, "Civil Religion in America," *Daedalus* 96 (Winter 1967): 12 (entire article, 1–21).

3. On all four occasions, a majority of published sermons came from urban presses in New England, the Mid-Atlantic, and the Midwest (for the last three), with Congregationalists, Presbyterians, and Episcopalians overrepresented (along with Methodists in 1881 and 1901).

4. Research on memorials for Washington and Lincoln, which was carried out from Readex microcards and by traveling to specialized libraries, supported conclusions in Mark Noll, "The Image of the United States as a Biblical Nation, 1776–1865," in Hatch and Noll, *BIBLE IN AMERICA*, 39–58. For Garfield and McKinley, separately published sermons were found through the Hathi Trust website and from newspapers in three searchable databases: America's Historical Newspapers, Proquest Historical

Newspapers, and Nineteenth-Century U.S. Newspapers. It indicates the character of national life in 1865 that President Johnson put off the originally designated day of mourning by a week when leaders of liturgical churches informed him that May 25 "was sacred to large numbers of Christians as one of rejoicing for the ascension of the Savior." Andrew Johnson, Proclamation 130, "Postponing the Day of Mourning for the Death of President Lincoln until June 1," April 29, 1865, American Presidency Project, https://www.presidency.ucsb.edu/documents/proclamation-130-postpon ing-the-day-mourning-for-the-death-president-lincoln-until-june-1.

5. Evan Shalev, *American Zion: The Old Testament as a Political Text from the Revolution to the Civil War* (New Haven, CT: Yale University Press, 2013), 2–3, 52–60.

6. Not included in the tabulated numbers are the seventeen texts from sixteen Jewish commemorative sermons preached in 1865 and published in Emanuel Hertz, ed., *Abraham Lincoln: The Tribute of the Synagogue* (New York: Bloch, 1927). Of those seventeen texts, three came from 2 Samuel 3 (David's lament for Abner) and three from Genesis chapters 12 and 15, using the biblical Abraham to honor the American Abraham.

7. In the sample of eighty-four separate texts, the only other four were Abel, David, Joseph, and Solomon.

8. Recitations of that episode included J. R. Day at Boston's First Methodist Episcopal Church, as reported in "In Memoriam: The Numerous Churches of the Hub and Vicinity Filled to Overflowing at the Special Sunday Services," *Boston Daily Globe*, September 26, 1881; John Chester, *A Sermon Preached on Sabbath, September 25, 1881, on the Lessons of the Life and Death of James Abram Garfield, Late President of the United States: in the Metropolitan Presbyterian Church, Washington, D.C.* (Washington, D.C.: Judd & Detweiler, 1881), 12.

9. See chapter 28, 607.

10. This sample of sermons from 2 Samuel 3:38 includes John Armstrong, *Sermon on the Death of General Washington Preached . . . at Pottstown* (Reading, PA: Jungmann & Bruckmann, 1800); Thomas Baldwin, *A Sermon, Delivered to the Second Baptist Society in Boston . . . December 29, 1799* (Boston: Manning & Loring, 1800); William Hague, "Sermon XII," in *Sermons Preached in Boston on the Death of Abraham Lincoln* (Boston: J. E. Tilton, 1865), 127–42; Littlejohn, "Sermon VIII"; P. G. Blight, "Sermon by Rev. P. G. Blight," in *Garfield Memorial Volume: Tribute from the Citizens of Jersey City to the Memory of James A. Garfield* (Jersey City, NJ: Davison, 1881), 27–36; T. K. Noble, sermon delivered to the Grand Army of the Republic in San Francisco, September 25, 1881, in *Gen. Garfield from the Log Cabin to the White House*, ed. J. B. McClure (Chicago: Rhodes & McClure, 1881), 169–75; Charles E. Benedict, the first sermon in *William McKinley: Character Sketches of America's Martyred Chieftain, Sermons and Addresses*, ed. Charles E. Benedict (New York: Blanchard, 1901), 12–21; E. P. Ingersoll, "A Lesson to Be Learned," in *The Pulpits of Brooklyn: Deliverances of Local Pastors on the Assassination and Eulogies on the Life and Character of William McKinley* (Brooklyn, NY: Brooklyn Daily Eagle, 1901), 19–20.

11. Armstrong, *Washington*, 39.

12. Hague, *Lincoln*, 140.

13. Blight, *Garfield*, 35.

14. Ingersoll, *McKinley*, 20.

15. Baldwin, *Washington*, 21.

16. Noble, *Garfield*, 173.

17. Among other noticeable changes, the later preachers referred more often to works of literature, as from Shakespeare, Carlyle, Longfellow, and others.

18. Ezra Stiles, *The United States Elevated to Glory and Honor* (New Haven, CT: Thomas & Samuel Green, 1783), 36.

19. Baldwin, *Washington*, 23.

20. Littlejohn, "Sermon VIII," 148.

21. Hague, *Lincoln*, both 132.

22. Noble, *Garfield*, 169, 170.

23. Ingersoll, *McKinley*, 19.

24. Armstrong, *Washington*, 36

25. On the decline of the jeremiad, the real change may have occurred right at the end of the Civil War, since Harry Stout and Christopher Grasso have shown that the jeremiad form continued vigorously in the North during the war and even flourished in the South, where it had not previously prevailed: Harry Stout and Christopher Grasso, "Civil War, Religion, and Communications: The Case of Richmond," in *Religion and the American Civil War*, ed. Randall M. Miller, Harry S. Stout, and Charles Reagan Wilson (New York: Oxford University Press, 1998), 313–59.

26. Hague, *Lincoln*, 139.

27. Noble, *Garfield*, 173, 174.

28. Ingersoll, *McKinley*, 20.

29. Garfield's diary included many references to personal Bible study and to how preachers handled Scripture in their sermons, though such commentary became less frequent during the Civil War years and as he took an active role in Washington as a congressman from Ohio; see Harry James Brown and Frederick D. Williams, eds., *The Diary of James A. Garfield*, 2 vols. (East Lansing: Michigan State University Press, 1967). Helpful context is provided by William C. Ringenberg, "The Religious Thought and Practice of James A. Garfield," in *The Stone-Campbell Movement*, ed. Michael W. Casey and Douglas A. Foster (Knoxville: University of Tennessee Press, 2002).

30. William McKinley, "Address of the President of the United States," in *Ecumenical Missionary Conference New York, 1900*, 2 vols. (New York: American Tract Society, 1900), 1:39. On the same day, April 21, 1900, former president Benjamin Harrison addressed the conference in even more directly Christian terms (26–29, 43–45), while comments by the sitting governor of New York, Theodore Roosevelt, reflected a vaguer theism (40–43).

31. Charles J. Guiteau, *The Truth: A Companion to the Bible* (Boston: D. Lathrop, 1879), 97.

32. Henry Bellows, "Sermon III," in *Our Martyr President*, 62. Bellows took his text from John 16:6–7 ("Sorrow hath filled your heart. . . . [I]f I go not away, the Comforter will not come unto you; but if I depart I will send him unto you.")

33. Queen Eliabeth II, "Christmas Broadcast," accessed November 11, 1021, https://www.royal.uk/christmas-broadcast-2010.

34. Verlyn Klinkenborg, "The King James Bible at 400," *New York Times*, January 8, 2011, www.nytimes.com/2011/01/09/opinion/09sun3.html.

35. The material that follows abridges a longer account: Mark Noll, "The King James Version at 300 in America: 'The Most Democratic Book in the World'," in *The King James Bible and the World It Made*, ed. David Lyle Jeffrey (Waco, TX: Baylor University Press, 2011), 71–98.

36. "Tercentenary of a Great Book," *The Youth's Companion*, February 9, 1911, 74; John F. Genug, "Why the Authorized Version Became an English Classic," *Biblical World* 37 (April 1911): 227; "Chicago Churchmen Prepare to Celebrate Tercentenary Anniversary of the King James Bible with Massmeeting and Special Exhibits," *Chicago Daily Tribune*, March 26, 1911. (In the notes that follow, full citations are repeated for articles that did not provide an author's name.)

37. Francis J. Grimké, *The Works of Francis J. Grimké*, ed. Carter G. Woodson, 4 vols. (Washington, D.C.: Associated Publishers, 1942), 1:473–89.

38. See Christopher H. Evans, *The Kingdom Is Always but Coming: A Life of Walter Rauschenbusch* (Grand Rapids, MI: Eerdmans, 2004), 175–202, 230–36.

39. Contents of the twelve pamphlets are found in the entry for *The Fundamentals* in WORLDCAT.

40. The year also witnessed a number of full-length books on the history of the Bible, mostly from Britain. Still useful is A. W. Pollard, *Records of the English Bible: The Documents Relating to the Translation and Publication of the Bible in English, 1525–1611* (London: Frowde, 1911).

41. That disruption provided the headline for one U.S. article, "Suffragette Stir at Bible Jubilee," *New York Times*, March 30, 1911. In Britain, the protest elicited biting criticism; see "Stray Thoughts," *Penny Illustrated Paper*, April 8, 1911, 482: "Had they got what they asked for these women would now be in a madhouse."

42. "Bible Anniversary in London: Premier Asquith and Ambassador Reid Speak at the Celebration," *New York Observer and Chronicle*, April 20, 1911, 496.

43. "Bible Memorial Here," *New York Times*, April 26, 1911.

44. "Honor 300 Years' Work of Bible," *Chicago Daily Tribune*, May 1, 1911.

45. "Defies Atheists to Equal Bible: W. J. Bryan Challenges Agnostics at King James Tercentenary Celebration," *Chicago Daily Tribune*, May 5, 1911.

46. Both statements are found in "Bible Memorial Here," *New York Times*, April 26, 1911.

47. "The American Tercentenary of the English Bible," *New York Times*, April 27, 1911.

48. "Honor 300 Years' Work of Bible," *Chicago Daily Tribune*, May 1, 1911.

49. Three of the longer lists are found in John Vaughan, "The Authorized Version of the Bible," *Living Age*, April 8, 1911, 82; Anon., "The Authorized Version," *Living Age*, April 15, 1911, 187; F. E. Tagg, *The Ter-Centenary of the Authorized Version of the English Bible, 1611–1911* (Baltimore, MD: Methodist Book Concern, 1911), 50.

50. "Chicago Churchmen Prepare to Celebrate Tercentenary Anniversary of the King James Bible with Massmeeting and Special Exhibits," *Chicago Daily Tribune*, March 26, 1911; J. Paterson Smyth, "Three Centuries of the English Bible: Social and Literary

Influence of the King James Version," *American Review of Reviews* 43 (May 1911): 571; Anon., "The Authorized Version," *Living Age*, April 15, 1911, 187; Genug, "Why the Authorized Version Became an English Classic," 228; John Fox, "The Influence of the English Bible on English Literature," *Princeton Theological Review* 9 (July 1911): 388.

51. Vaughan, "Authorized Version of the Bible," 78.

52. "The King James Bible and English Speech," *Macon Daily Telegraph*, April 2, 1911.

53. T. O. Crouse, "Introduction," in Tagg, *Ter-Centenary*, 4. For similar views, see Tagg in this same publication (51).

54. "Selling Bibles and Reading Them," *Colorado Springs Gazette*, April 6, 1911.

55. Edgar J. Goodspeed, "The New Testament of 1611, as a Translation," *Biblical World* 37 (April 2011): 271.

56. Walter R. Betteridge, "The Accuracy of the Authorized Version of the Old Testament," *Biblical World* 37 (April 2011): 264–65.

57. "Mr. Taft on the Bible," *Morning Oregonian*, April 2, 1911.

58. Quoted in Smyth, "Three Centuries of the English Bible," 575. The same quotation appears in Tagg, *Ter-Centenary*, 46; and, with variations, in many other sources.

59. Favorable comments mentioned the work of Richard Challoner in his eighteenth-century revisions of the Douay-Rheims version, as in E. Olive Dutcher, "The Douay Version," *Biblical World* 37 (April 1911): 243.

60. Tagg, *Ter-Centenary*, 36.

61. J.K., "The Tercentenary of the Authorized Version," *The Month* 117 (January–June 1911): 423.

62. "Pulpit, Press and Platform," *America*, April 29, 1911, 70–71. An American who introduced a polemical work by a British Catholic contended that "as the dust and darkness of the 'Reformation' fade away before the growing light of truth, people are coming to understand better . . . the partial Bible that was issued by the Reformers, as if it were the complete and genuine Word of God." M. M. Charleson, "Foreword," in Henry G. Graham, *Where We Got the Bible: Our Debt to the Catholic Church* (Pasadena, CA: N.p., 1911), 5.

63. Theodore Roosevelt, "The Bible and the Life of the People" (1911), in *Realizable Ideals* (Freeport, NY: Books for Libraries, 1969), 67, 69, 73, 74.

64. Roosevelt, "Bible," 74, 78, 83, 90.

65. Woodrow Wilson, *The Papers of Woodrow Wilson*, vol. 23: *1911–1912*, ed. Arthur S. Link (Princeton, NJ: Princeton University Press, 1977), Wilson to Mary Allen Hulbert Peck, 11.

66. Woodrow Wilson, "An Address in Denver on the Bible," in *Papers*, 23:13, 12–13.

67. Roosevelt, "Bible," 1–2.

68. Wilson, "An Address," 13, 18, 20.

69. Details of the event are from Bryan's weekly newspaper, *The Commoner*, May 12, 1911; the quotations that follow are from an eleven-page pamphlet, *Hon. William J. Bryan on the Bible: The Book of Supreme Influence* (New York: American Bible Society, 1911), the text of which is almost identical to what was printed in *The Commoner*.

70. For an interesting effort at responding to that question, to which Bryan did not reply, see a book published in that tricentennial year by a skeptic about biblical miracles,

M. M. Mangasarian, *The Bible Unveiled* (Chicago: Independent Religious Society, 1911), 28–34.

71. William Jennings Bryan, "Speech Concluding Debate on the Chicago Platform," in *The First Battle: The Story of the Campaign of 1896* (Chicago: W. B. Conkey, 1896), 206.

72. *Theodore Roosevelt's Confession of Faith before the Progressive Convention, August 6, 1912* (New York: Mail and Express, 1912), 32.

73. For a full account of Wilson's covenantal thinking, see John M. Mulder, *Woodrow Wilson: The Years of Preparation* (Princeton, NJ: Princeton University Press, 1978).

74. The judgments that follow depend on the work of Lawrence W. Levine, *Defender of the Faith: William Jennings Bryan, the Last Decade, 1915–1925* (New York: Oxford University Press, 1965); Arthur S. Link, "Woodrow Wilson and His Presbyterian Inheritance" and "The Higher Realism of Woodrow Wilson," in *The Higher Realism of Woodrow Wilson* (Nashville, TN: Vanderbilt University Press, 1971); John Milton Cooper, *The Warrior and the Priest: Woodrow Wilson and Theodore Roosevelt* (Cambridge, MA: Harvard University Press, 1983); Edward J. Larson, *Summer for the Gods: The Scopes Trial and America's Continuing Debate over Science and Religion* (New York: Basic Books, 1997); Richard M. Gamble, *The War for Righteousness: Progressive Christianity, the Great War, and the Rise of the Messianic Nation* (Wilmington, DE: ISI, 2003); Michael Kazin, *A Godly Hero: The Life of William Jennings Bryan* (New York: Knopf, 2006); Gary Scott Smith, *Faith and the Presidency: From George Washington to George W. Bush* (New York: Oxford University Press, 2006); Joshua David Hawley, *Theodore Roosevelt: Preacher of Righteousness* (New Haven, CT: Yale University Press, 2008); Cara Lea Burnidge, *A Peaceful Conquest: Woodrow Wilson, Religion, and the New World Order* (Chicago: University of Chicago Press, 2016); Barry Hankins, *Woodrow Wilson: Ruling Elder, Spiritual President* (New York: Oxford University Press, 2016); Benjamin J. Wetzel, *Theodore Roosevelt: Preaching from the Bully Pulpit* (New York: Oxford University Press, 2021).

75. Larson, *Summer for the Gods*, 103–4.

76. Burnidge, *A Peaceful Conquest*, 3.

77. Grimké, *Works*, 4:129 (letter of November 20, 1912).

78. Grimké, *Works*, 4:133–34 (letter of September 5, 1913).

79. Woodrow Wilson, *The Papers of Woodrow Wilson*, vol. 36: *January–May 1916*, ed. Arthur S. Link (Princeton, NJ: Princeton University Press, 1981), John Fox to Wilson, April 3, 1916, 481.

80. Wilson, "An Address," 23:15–26; Wilson, "Remarks Celebrating the Centennial of the American Bible Society," in *Papers*, 36:631.

81. For one version of this speech, see William Jennings Bryan, *William Jennings Bryan: Selections*, ed. Ray Ginger (Indianapolis, IN: Bobbs-Merrill, 1967), 135–50.

82. For support of this contention, though not with direct consideration of the Bible, see Levine, *Defender of the Faith*; Kazin, *Godly Hero*.

Chapter 30

1. Ida B. Wells, *Crusade for Justice: The Autobiography of Ida B. Wells*, 2nd ed., ed. Alfreda M. Duster and Eve L. Ewing (1970; Chicago: University of Chicago Press, 2020), 342–48 ("Arkansas Riot," quotations 345–46), 254 (Bible class).

2. Elizabeth McHenry on the activities encouraged by the National Association of Colored Women, in "Reading and Race Pride: The Literary Activism of Black Clubwoman," in *HISTORY OF THE BOOK*, 4:618n48, summarizing a main conclusion in Elizabeth Brooks Higginbotham, *Religious Discontent: The Women's Movement in the Black Baptist Church, 1880-1920* (Cambridge, MA: Harvard University Press, 1993).

3. Vincent L. Wimbush, ed., *African Americans and the Bible* (New York: Continuum, 2000).

4. James Abington, "Biblical Themes in the R. Nathaniel Dett Collection *Religious Folk-Songs of the Negro* (1927)," in Wimbush, *African Americans and the Bible*, 290. For further documentation from this same book on the complexities and often internal conflicts over Scripture in African American musical traditions, see Horace Clarence Boyer, "African American Gospel Music," 464–88; Keith D. Miller, "City Called Freedom: Biblical Metaphor in Spirits, Gospel Lyrics, and the Civil Rights Movement," 546–57; Mellonee Burnim, "Biblical Inspiration, Cultural Affirmation: The African American Gift of Song," 603–15; Cheryl Kirk-Duggan, "Hot Buttered Soulful Tunes and Cold Icy Passionate Truths: The Hermeneutics of Biblical Interpretation in R & B (Rhythm & Blues)," 782–803; and Charise Cheney, "Representin' God: Masculinity and the Use of the Bible in Rap Music," 804–816 (which records Black nationalist rejection of Scripture as well as affirmation).

5. Joel Barton Sutton, "Spirit and Polity in a Black Primitive Baptist Church" (Ph.D. diss., University of North Carolina, 1983), 172, quoted in Hans A. Baer, "The Role of the Bible and Other Sacred Texts in African American Denominations and Sects," in Wimbush, *African Americans and the Bible*, 98. On the importance of Scripture in all phases of the Migration, see Milton Sernett, "Re-Readings: The Great Migration and the Bible," in Wimbush, *African Americans and the Bible*, 448–63.

6. David W. Blight, *Frederick Douglass: Prophet of Freedom* (New York: Simon & Schuster, 2018), 677–78.

7. Blight, *Frederick Douglass*, 665.

8. Francis Grimké, *The Works of Francis Grimké*, 4 vols., ed. Carter G. Woodson (Washington, D.C.: Associated Publishers, 1942), 1:52–53.

9. H. Paul Thompson Jr., *A Most Stirring and Significant Episode: Religion and the Rise and Fall of Prohibition in Black Atlanta, 1865-1887* (Dekalb: Northern Illinois University Press, 2013), 126.

10. Thompson, *Stirring and Significant Episode*, 131. This book's helpful research extends well beyond Atlanta and treats African American temperance in the much larger framework of general social reform.

11. For basic biographical information, see the editorial apparatus in Wells, *Crusade for Justice* as well as Mia Bay's introduction to Ida B. Wells, *The Light of Truth: Writings of an Anti-Lynching Crusader* (New York: Penguin, 2014).

12. Norman B. Wood, *The White Side of a Black Subject . . . A Vindication of the Afro-American Race* (Chicago: American Publishing House, 1897), 11, 357, 381–82.

13. Wells, *A Red Record*, in *The Light of Truth*, 221, 311.

14. "The Bitter Cry of Black America: A New 'Uncle Tom's Cabin,'" *Westminster Gazette*, May 10, 1894, in Wells, *The Light of Truth*, 165.

15. Wells, *Crusade for Justice*, 131.

16. Wells, *Crusade for Justice*, 107–8.

17. *The Birth of a Nation*, which I viewed in the Motion Picture/TV Reading Room, Library of Congress, spring 2005.

18. For Wells's account of those efforts in Chicago and Philadelphia, see *Crusade for Justice*, 292–94.

19. *The Birth of Race*, Motion Picture/TV Reading Room, Library of Congress, spring 2005. For a particularly helpful account of this film, see Judith Weisenfeld, "'For the Cause of Mankind': The Bible, Racial Uplift, and Early Race Movies," in Wimbush, *African Americans and the Bible*, 732–35.

20. For a characteristic statement from Booker T. Washington, see his talk "The Place of the Bible in the Uplifting of the Human Race," referenced in *Booker T. Washington Papers*, vol. 5: *1899–1900*, ed. Louis R. Harlan, Raymond W. Smock, and Barbara S. Kraft (Champaign: University of Illinois Press, 1976), 543–44. Du Bois's complex religious beliefs are carefully explored in Edward J. Blum, *W. E. B. DuBois, American Prophet* (Philadelphia: University of Pennsylvania Press, 2007).

21. W. E. B. DuBois, *The Souls of Black Folk* (1903; Boston: Boston Globe, 2005), 42.

22. See especially Dennis C. Dickerson, *The African Methodist Episcopal Church: A History* (New York: Cambridge University Press, 2020), 108–236.

23. On Payne in the context of his times, see Dickerson, *African Methodist Episcopal Church*, 4–7, 74–77, 137–39, and passim; James T. Campbell, *Songs of Zion: The African Methodist Episcopal Church in the United States and South Africa* (1995; Chapel Hill: University of North Carolina Press, 1998), 38–43. Elizabeth Zoe Vicary provides a useful introduction in *ANB*.

24. *Sermons Delivered by Daniel A. Payne . . . before the General Conference of the A.M.E. Church, Indianapolis, In., May 1888*, ed. C. S. Smith (Nashville, TN: A.M.D. Sunday School Union, 1888), 5–41 ("The Quadrennial Sermon"), 43–64 ("The Ordination Sermon"). Payne's biblical frame of reference also informed his two-hundred-page exposition of Proverbs 22:6 ("Train up a child in the way he should go, and when he is old he will not depart from it"), *A Treatise on Domestic Education* (Cincinnati, OH: Cranston and Stowe, 1889).

25. Dennis C. Dickerson, "Homiletics and the Humble: Preaching in Georgia during the Turner Era, 1896–1908," in *African Methodism and Its Wesleyan Heritage: Reflections on AME History* (Nashville, TN: By the author, 2009), 113 (Georgia membership), 116–18.

26. On Du Bois's encomium, see Campbell, *Songs of Zion*, 269. On Crummell as missionary and Africanism, see 74–75; Andrew Walls, "Crummell, Alexander," in *Biographical Dictionary of Christian Missions*, ed. Gerald H. Anderson (New York: Macmillan, 1998), 161–62.

27. Alexander Crummell, "The Greatness of Christ" in *The Greatness of Christ and Other Sermons* (New York: Thomas Whitaker, 1882), 5 (from Matt 2:11); "Christ Receiving and Eating with Sinners," 188 (on Lk 15:2); "Joseph," 219, 231 (on Gen 49:22–24); Alexander Crummell, "Eulogium on Henry Highland Garnet," in *Africa and America: Addresses and Discourses* (Springfield, MA: Wiley, 1891), 271.

28. Edward Mikkelsen Jr., "Theophilus Gould Steward (1843–1924)," *Black Past*, January 22, 2007, https://www.blackpast.org/african-american-history/steward-theophilus-gould-1843-1925/.

29. T. G. Steward, *Genesis Re-Read; or the Latest Conclusions of Physical Science, Viewed in their Relation to the Mosaic Record* (Philadelphia, PA: A.M.E. Book Rooms, 1885), iii (Scripture), 201 (evangelical system), 212–14 (unity of the race), iii (credibility of the Bible). For setting this work in the context of AME theological development, see Dickerson, *African Methodist Episcopal Church*, 172–74.

30. James C. Embry, *Digest of Christian Theology, Designed for the Use of Beginners, in the Study of Theological Science* (Philadelphia, PA: A.M.E. Book Concern, 1890), iv, 67–69. For context, see Dickerson, *African Methodist Episcopal Church*, 172–74.

31. Charles Octavius Boothe, *Plain Theology for Plain People* (1890; Bellingham, WA: Lexham, 2017), with an informative introduction by Walter Strickland. See also David Roach, "Reprint of Ex-slave's Theology Book Opens 'Underexplored Vista,'" *Christianity Today*, February 27, 2018, http://www.christianitytoday.com/history/2018/february/reprint-of-ex-slave-theology-book-charles-octavius-boothe.html.

32. See Matthew Harper, "Emancipation and African American Millennialism," in *Apocalypse and the Millennium in the American Civil War Era* (Baton Rouge: Louisiana State University Press, 2013), 169, 173–74n43; Timothy Fulop, "The Future Golden Day of the Race: Millennialism and Black Americans in the Nadir, 1877–1901," *Harvard Theological Review* 84 (1991): 75–99.

33. T. G. Steward, *The End of the World: or, Clearing the Way for the Fullness of the Gentiles* (Philadelphia, PA: A.M.E. Church Book Room, 1888), 64 (course of empire), 69–75. In a sermon published with this work, the Rev. James Handy, head of the AME's missionary society, added an exposition of Psalm 68:31 ("Ethiopia shall soon stretch out her hands unto God") that predicted the Christianization of Africa that has actually happened in recent history (149–50). On Handy's missionary efforts, see Dickerson, *African Methodist Episcopal Church*, 146, 148.

34. "J. W. Hood, *The Plan of the Apocalypse* (York, PA: P. Anbstadt and Son, 1900); see also Documenting the American South, "Hood, J. W. (James Walker), 1831–1918," accessed August 5, 2020, https://docsouth.unc.edu/church/hood/bio.html.

35. Alexander Crummell, "Emigration: An Aid to the Evangelization of Africa," and "The Regeneration of Africa," in *Africa and America*, 405–429 (quotation, 429), 431–54.

36. Alexander Crummell, "The Destined Superiority of the Negro," in *Greatness of Christ*, 332–52 (quotation, 350–51).

37. Campbell, *Songs of Zion*, 81.
38. This paragraph depends on the illuminating article by Andre E. Johnson, "God Is a Negro: The (Rhetorical) Black Theology of Bishop Henry McNeal Turner," *Black Theology* 13 (April 2015): 29–40 (30, Turner at the Baptist convention and Morehouse's response; 36–37, Turner quoted from "God is a Negro," *Voice of Missions*, February 1898).
39. The novel includes the account of a conversion in which a female character "not only converted [the protagonist], but in placing the Scriptures before him in their true light, she redeemed those sacred writings from the charge of supporting the system of slavery." William Wells Brown, *Clotel; or, the President's Daughter: A Narrative of Slave Life* (London: Partridge and Oakey, 1853), 115.
40. William Wells Brown, *The Rising Sun; or, the Antecedents and Advancement of the Colored Race* (Boston: A. G. Brown, 1874), 46.
41. See especially Abraham Smith, "More Than a Mighty Hammer: George Washington Williams, Nineteenth-Century Racialized Discourse and the Reclamation of Nimrod," in *African American Religious Life and the Story of Nimrod*, ed. Anthony B. Pinn and Allen Dwight Callahan (New York: Palgrave Macmillan, 2008), 69–84; and for Williams in fuller context, Abraham Smith, "The Bible in African American Culture," in Gutjahr, *OXFORD HANDBOOK*, 202–3 (this article also documents the continuing use of the KJV in niche bibles published for present-day African American communities [198]).
42. George Washington Williams, *History of the Negro Race in America from 1619 to 1880: Negroes as slaves, as soldiers, and as citizens; together with a preliminary consideration of the unity of the human family, an historical sketch of Africa, and an account of the Negro governments of Sierra Leone and Liberia* (1882; New York: G. Putnam, 1885), 12, with most of this first chapter taken up with biblical exposition.
43. Indispensable is the splendid edition that Carter G. Woodson produced as one of the last efforts of this pioneering Black historian's pathbreaking career, *The Works of Francis J. Grimké*, vol. 1: *Addresses*, vol. 2: *Sermons*, vol. 3: *Stray Thoughts and Meditations*, vol. 4: *Letters* (Washington, D.C.: Associated Publishers, 1942). Woodson could be critical of some African American religious leaders, but he also defended the kind of "conservatism" he saw in figures like Grimké; see, for example, Carter G. Woodson, *The History of the Negro Church* (Washington, D.C.: Associated Publishers, 1921), 302–4 (Grimké, 303).
44. Grimké, quoted in Thabiti M. Anyabwile, ed., *The Faithful Preacher: Recapturing the Vision of Three Pioneering African-American Pastors* (Wheaton, IL: Crossway, 2007), 115.
45. See in this chapter, 644 (Douglass) and in chapter 29, 639 (letters to Woodrow Wilson). In 1884 the widowed Douglass asked Grimké to officiate at his marriage to Helen Pitts, who was white. For Grimké's response to criticism of the marriage from whites and Blacks, see his article "The Second Marriage of Frederick Douglass," *Journal of Negro History* 19 (July 1934): 324–29. Four of Grimké's sermons with a useful introduction are found in in Anyabwile, *Faithful Preacher*, 123–81. Several

helpful accounts illustrate the working of Grimké's spiritual-social holism: in his life as a Presbyterian, Henry Justin Ferry, "Racism and Reunion: A Black Protest by Francis James Grimke," *Journal of Presbyterian History* 50 (Summer 1972): 77–88; on his opposition to American participation in World War I, Louis B. Weeks III, "Racism, World War I and the Christian Life: Francis Grimké in the Nation's Capital," *Journal of Presbyterian History* 51 (Winter 1973): 471–88; and on his denunciation of lynching, Malcolm Foley, "'The Only Way to Stop a Mob': Francis Grimké's Biblical Case for Lynching Resistance," in *Every Leaf, Line, and Letter: Evangelicals and the Bible from the 1730s to the Present*, ed. Timothy Larsen (Downers Grove, IL: InterVarsity Press, 2021),

46. Woodson, introduction, in Grimké, *Works of Grimké*, 1:x (quoting letters of A. A. Hodge and McCosh from October 1879 and February 1881).

47. See his memorials for Bishop Payne at the latter's death in 1893 and for Crummell at his death in 1896: Grimké, *Works of Grimké*, 1:1–27 (Payne), 28–34 (Crummell).

48. Woodson, introduction, in Grimké, *Works of Grimké*, 1:xxii. See for Garrison (81–101), Whittier (101–22), Roosevelt (174–89).

49. Francis Grimké, "Temperance and the Negro Race," in *Works of Grimké*, 2:487.

50. Grimké, *Works of Grimké*, 3:465, 464 (this comment was made in late 1930).

51. See the three address on Douglass in Grimké, *Works of Grimké*, 1:34–54, 55–63, 63–71.

52. J. H. Thornwell, "Societies for Moral Reform," in *The Collected Writings of James Henley Thornwell*, ed. John B. Adger and John L. Girardeau, 4 vols. (Richmond, VA: Presbyterian Committee on Publication, 1873), 4:470.

53. Francis Grimké, "The Afro-American Pulpit in Relation to Race Elevation," *Works of Grimké*, 1:223–34.

54. Francis Grimké, "The Religious Aspect of Reconstruction," in Anyabwile, *Faithful Preacher*, 155.

55. Francis Grimké, "Christ's Program for the Saving of the World," in Anyabwile, *Faithful Preacher*, 173.

56. For the dating of this series, see Foley, "Only Way to Stop a Mob," 199–200; and on the outrage in North Carolina, David Zucchino, *Wilmington's Lie: The Murderous Coup of 1898 and the Rise of White Supremacy* (New York: Atlantic Monthly, 2020).

57. Francis Grimké, "Discouragements: Hostility of the Press, Silence and Cowardice of the Pulpit," *Works of Grimké*, 1: 234–36 (Elijah and Moses); "Sources from Which No Help May Be Expected," 253–54 (Brown), 256–57 (Douglass); "Signs of a Brighter Future," 267.

58. Francis Grimké, "God and Prayer as Factors in the Struggle," *Works of Grimké*, 1:274(Moses), 275 (Douglass), 286 (Pray for them).

59. Andrew E. Murray, *Presbyterians and the Negro: A History* (Philadelphia, PA: Presbyterian Historical Society, 1966), 182; Ferry, "Racism and Reunion," 81.

60. Grimké, *Works of Grimké*, G. F. McMiller to Grimké, November 4, 1914, 4:136; Grimké to Members of the Class of 1878, 216.

61. On those revisions, see chapter 24, 527.

62. Ferry, quoting from the pamphlet that Grimké printed of his speech, "Race and Reunion," 85.

63. Quoted in Ferry, "Racism and Reunion, 85.

64. On Warfield and race, see chapter 24, 536; B. B. Warfield, "The Proposed Union with the Cumberland Presbyterians," *Princeton Theological Review* 2 (1904): 294–316.

65. Ferry, "Racism and Reunion," 87; *Plessy v. Ferguson* 163 U.S. 537, par. 559. Excellent on the close, but somewhat ambivalent, connection between Grimké and Harlan is Linda Przybyszewski, *The Republic According to John Harlan* (Chapel Hill: University of North Carolina Press, 1999), 86–90, 109–15.

66. Dickerson, *African Methodist Episcopal Church*, 22, 46–55.

Epilogue

1. Especially interesting for comparative purposes are Preston Jones, *A Highly Favored Nation: The Bible and Canadian Meaning, 1860–1900* (Lanham, MD: University Press of America, 2008); Nick Spencer, *Freedom and Order: History, Politics and the English Bible* (London: Hodder and Stoughton, 2011); Meredith Lake, *The Bible in Australia: A Cultural History* (Sydney: New South, 2018).

2. C. S. Lewis, "Man or Rabbit?" (ca. 1946), in *God in the Dock: Essays on Theology and Ethics*, ed. Walter Hooper (Grand Rapids, MI: Eerdmans, 1970), 108–9.

3. The findings are detailed in Philip Goff, Arthur E. Farnsley II, and Peter J. Thuesen, "The Bible in American Life Today," in *The Bible in American Life*, ed. Philip Goff, Arthur E. Farnsley II, and Peter J. Thuesen (New York: Oxford University Press, 2017), 5–34. The findings are assessed in Mark A. Noll, "The Bible: Then and Now," in the same work (331–44).

4. The New International Version, which was sponsored by an interdenominational network of evangelical Protestants, was first published in 1973 (New Testament) and 1978 (complete). On the continued popularity of the KJV, see especially Paul C. Gutjahr, "From Monarchy to Democracy: The Dethroning of the King James Bible in the United States," in *The King James Bible after 400 Years*, ed. Hannibal Hamlin and Norman W. Jones (New York: Cambridge University Press, 2010), 146–63; but then as a kind of retraction, Paul C. Gutjahr, "Crowning the King: The Use of Production and Reception Studies to Determine the Most Popular English-Language Bible Translation in Contemporary America," in Goff, Farnsley, and Thuesen, *The Bible in American Life*, 283–91.

5. Noll, "The Bible," 339 (quoting the IUPUI research report).

6. See chapter 2, 45–48.

7. See chapter 21, 464.

8. See chapter 22, 487–88.

9. A. J. Maas, "The English Protestant Version of the Bible after Three Hundred Years," *Ecclesiastical Review: A Monthly Publication for the Clergy* 45 (November 1911): 613.

10. Frederick W. Loetscher, "The English Bible in the Spiritual Life of the English-Speaking People," *Princeton Theological Review* 9 (July 1911): 407.

11. Allen Dwight Callahan, *The Talking Book: African Americans and the Bible* (New Haven, CT: Yale University Press, 2006), 39.

12. Franklin D. Roosevelt, "Labor Day Radio Address," September 1, 1941, American Presidency Project, https://www.presidency.ucsb.edu/documents/labor-day-radio-address: "Preservation of these rights [of laboring men and women] is vitally important now, not only to us who enjoy them—but to the whole future of Christian civilization." Winston Churchill, "Their Finest Hour," June 18, 1940, International Churchill Society, https://winstonchurchill.org/resources/speeches/1940-the-finest-hour/their-finest-hour/: "The Battle for Britain is about to begin. Upon this battle depends the survival of Christian civilization."

13. The contribution of these churches is a prominent theme in Taylor Branch, *America in the King Years*, 3 vols. (New York: Simon and Schuster, 1988, 1998, 2006).

14. Quoted in Charles M. Payne, *I've Got the Light of Freedom: The Organizing Tradition and the Mississippi Freedom Struggle* (Berkeley: University of California Press, 1995), 309.

15. Dennis Dickerson, "African American Religious Intellectuals and the Theological Foundations of the Civil Rights Movement, 1930–55," *Church History* 74 (June 2005): 217–35. See also Clarence Taylor, *Black Religious Intellectuals: The Fight for Equality from Jim Crow to the Twenty-First Century* (New York: Routledge, 2002).

16. These categories are adapted from Joseph R. Fornieri, *Abraham Lincoln's Political Faith* (DeKalb: Northern Illinois University Press, 2003), 38–69.

17. Quotations here and in the following paragraphs are from the text on the website of the NAACP, accessed March 31, 2021, https://www.naacp.org/i-have-a-dream-speech-full-march-on-washington/.

18. David L. Chappell, *A Stone of Hope: Prophetic Religion and the Death of Jim Crow* (Chapel Hill: University of North Carolina Press, 2004).

19. Quotations that follow are from White House, "Remarks by the President in Eulogy for the Honorable Reverend Clementa Pinckney," June 26, 2015, https://obamawhitehouse.archives.gov/the-press-office/2015/06/26/remarks-president-eulogy-honorable-reverend-clementa-pinckney.

20. Bruce Metzger, "Preface," in *New Testament with Psalms and Proverbs: New Revised Standard Version* (Cambridge: Cambridge University Press, 1989), ix. For Schechter, see chapter 26, 569–70.

Permissions for work published earlier

Scripture Index

General Index